THE COLLINS
POCKET REFERENCE
ITALIAN
DICTIONARY

ITALIAN·ENGLISH   ENGLISH·ITALIAN

COLLINS
London and Glasgow

First published 1990

© William Collins Sons & Co. Ltd. 1990

First reprint 1990

ISBN 0 00 433256-3

Printed in Great Britain
Collins Clear-Type Press

INTRODUCTION

This dictionary of Italian and English is designed to provide the user with wide-ranging and up-to-date coverage of the two languages, and is ideal for both school and reference use.

A special feature of Collins dictionaries is the comprehensive 'sign-posting' of meanings on both sides of the dictionary, guiding the user to the most appropriate translation for a given context. We hope you will find this dictionary easy and pleasant to consult for all your study and reference needs.

ABBREVIAZIONI

ABBREVIATIONS

aggettivo	**a**	adjective
abbreviazione	**abbr**	abbreviation
avverbio	**ad**	adverb
amministrazione	**ADMIN**	administration
aeronautica, viaggi aerei	**AER**	flying, air travel
aggettivo	**ag**	adjective
agricoltura	**AGR**	agriculture
amministrazione	**AMM**	administration
anatomia	**ANAT**	anatomy
architettura	**ARCHIT**	architecture
astronomia, astrologia	**ASTR**	astronomy, astrology
l'automobile	**AUT**	the motor car and motoring
avverbio	**av**	adverb
aeronautica, viaggi aerei	**AVIAT**	flying, air travel
biologia	**BIOL**	biology
botanica	**BOT**	botany
inglese della Gran Bretagna	**Brit**	British English
consonante	**C**	consonant
chimica	**CHIM, CHEM**	chemistry
congiunzione	**cj**	conjunction
familiare (! da evitare)	**col(!)**	colloquial usage (! particularly offensive)
commercio, finanza, banca	**COMM**	commerce, finance, banking
informatica	**COMPUT**	computers
congiunzione	**cong**	conjunction
edilizia	**CONSTR**	building
sostantivo usato come aggettivo, non può essere usato né come attributo, né dopo il sostantivo qualificato	**cpd**	compound element: noun used as adjective and which cannot follow the noun it qualifies
cucina	**CUC, CULIN**	cookery
davanti a	**dav**	before
determinativo: articolo, aggettivo dimostrativo o indefinito etc	**det**	determiner: article, demonstrative etc
diritto	**DIR**	law
economia	**ECON**	economics
edilizia	**EDIL**	building
elettricità, elettronica	**ELETTR, ELEC**	electricity, electronics
esclamazione	**escl, excl**	exclamation
femminile	**f**	feminine
familiare (! da evitare)	**fam(!)**	colloquial usage (! particularly offensive)
ferrovia	**FERR**	railways
figurato	**fig**	figurative use
fisiologia	**FISIOL**	physiology
fotografia	**FOT**	photography
(verbo inglese) la cui particella è inseparabile dal verbo	**fus**	(phrasal verb) where the particle cannot be separated from main verb

nella maggior parte dei sensi; generalmente	gen	in most or all senses; generally
geografia, geologia	GEO	geography, geology
geometria	GEOM	geometry
impersonale	impers	impersonal
informatica	INFORM	computers
insegnamento, sistema scolastico e universitario	INS	schooling, schools and universities
invariabile	inv	invariable
irregolare	irg	irregular
grammatica, linguistica	LING	grammar, linguistics
maschile	m	masculine
matematica	MAT(H)	mathematics
termine medico, medicina	MED	medical term, medicine
il tempo, meteorologia	METEOR	the weather, meteorology
maschile o femminile, secondo il sesso	m/f	either masculine or feminine depending on sex
esercito, lingua militare	MIL	military matters
musica	MUS	music
sostantivo	n	noun
nautica	NAUT	sailing, navigation
numerale (aggettivo, sostantivo)	num	numeral adjective or noun
	o.s.	oneself
peggiorativo	peg, pej	derogatory, pejorative
fotografia	PHOT	photography
fisiologia	PHYSIOL	physiology
plurale	pl	plural
politica	POL	politics
participio passato	pp	past participle
preposizione	prep	preposition
psicologia, psichiatria	PSIC, PSYCH	psychology, psychiatry
tempo passato	pt	past tense
sostantivo che non si usa al plurale	q	uncountable noun: not used in the plural
qualcosa	qc	
qualcuno	qn	
religione, liturgia	REL	religions, church service
sostantivo	s	noun
	sb	somebody
insegnamento, sistema scolastico e universitario	SCOL	schooling, schools and universities
singolare	sg	singular
soggetto (grammaticale)	sog	(grammatical) subject
	sth	something
congiuntivo	sub	subjunctive
soggetto (grammaticale)	subj	(grammatical) subject
termine tecnico, tecnologia	TECN, TECH	technical term, technology
telecomunicazioni	TEL	telecommunications
tipografia	TIP	typography, printing

ABBREVIAZIONI		ABBREVIATIONS
televisione	**TV**	television
tipografia	**TYP**	typography, printing
inglese degli Stati Uniti	**US**	American English
vocale	**V**	vowel
verbo	**vb**	verb
verbo o gruppo verbale con funzione intransitiva	**vi**	verb or phrasal verb used intransitively
verbo riflessivo	**vr**	reflexive verb
verbo o gruppo verbale con funzione transitiva	**vt**	verb or phrasal verb used transitively
zoologia	**ZOOL**	zoology
marchio registrato	®	registered trademark
introduce un'equivalenza culturale	≈	introduces a cultural equivalent

TRASCRIZIONE FONETICA

PHONETIC TRANSCRIPTION

CONSONANTS CONSONANTI

VOWELS VOCALI

NB The pairing of some vowel sounds only indicates approximate equivalence/La messa in equivalenza di certi suoni indica solo una rassomiglianza approssimativa.

NB p, b, t, d, k, g are not aspirated in Italian/sono seguiti da un'aspirazione in inglese.

*pu*ppy	p	padre	
baby	b	bambino	
tent	t	tutto	
daddy	d	dado	
cork kiss chord	k	cane che	
gag guess	g	gola ghiro	
so rice kiss	s	sano	
cousin buzz	z	svago esame	
sheep sugar	ʃ	scena	
pleasure beige	ʒ		
church	tʃ	pece lanciare	
judge general	dʒ	giro gioco	
farm raffle	f	afa faro	
very rev	v	vero bravo	
thin maths	θ		
that other	ð		
little ball	l	letto ala	
	ʎ	gli	
rat brat	r	rete arco	
mummy comb	m	ramo madre	
no ran	n	no fumante	
	ɲ	gnomo	
singing bank	ŋ		
hat reheat	h		
yet	j	buio piacere	
wall bewail	w	uomo guaio	
loch	x		

heel bead	iː i	vino idea	
hit pity	ɪ		
	e	stella edera	
set tent	ɛ	epoca eccetto	
apple bat	æ a	mamma amore	
after car calm	ɑː		
fun cousin	ʌ		
over above	ə		
urn fern work	əː		
wash pot	ɔ	rosa occhio	
born cork	ɔː		
	o	ponte ognuno	
full soot	u	utile zucca	
boon lewd	uː		

DIPHTHONGS DITTONGHI

ɪə	beer tier	
ɛə	tear fair there	
eɪ	date plaice day	
aɪ	life buy cry	
au	owl foul now	
əu	low no	
ɔɪ	boil boy oily	
uə	poor tour	

MISCELLANEOUS

VARIE

* per l'inglese: la "r" finale viene pronunciata se seguita da una vocale.

' precedes the stressed syllable/precede la sillaba accentata.

ITALIAN PRONUNCIATION

VOWELS

Where the vowel **e** or the vowel **o** appears in a stressed syllable it can be either open [ɛ], [ɔ] or closed [e], [o]. As the open or closed pronunciation of these vowels is subject to regional variation, the distinction is of little importance to the user of this dictionary. Phonetic transcription for headwords containing these vowels will therefore only appear where other pronunciation difficulties are present.

CONSONANTS

c before "e" or "i" is pronounced *tch*.

ch is pronounced like the "k" in "kit".

g before "e" or "i" is pronounced like the "j" in "jet".

gh is pronounced like the "g" in "get".

gl before "e" or "i" is normally pronounced like the "lli" in "million", and in a few cases only like the "gl" in "glove".

gn is pronounced like the "ny" in "canyon".

sc before "e" or "i" is pronounced *sh*.

z is pronounced like the "ts" in "stetson", or like the "d's" in "bird's-eye".

Headwords containing the above consonants and consonantal groups have been given full phonetic transcription in this dictionary.

NB All double written consonants in Italian are fully sounded: eg. the *tt* in "tutto" is pronounced as in "ha*t t*rick".

ITALIANO - INGLESE
ITALIAN - ENGLISH

A

a *prep* (*a* + **il** = **al**, *a* + **lo** = **allo**, *a* + **l'** = **all'**, *a* + **la** = **alla**, *a* + **i** = **ai**, *a* + **gli** = **agli**, *a* + **le** = **alle**) **1** (*stato in luogo*) at; (: *in*) in; **essere alla stazione** to be at the station; **essere ~ casa/~ scuola/~ Roma** to be at home/at school/in Rome; **è ~ 10 km da qui** it's 10 km from here, it's 10 km away

2 (*moto a luogo*) to; **andare ~ casa/~ scuola** to go home/to school

3 (*tempo*) at; (*epoca, stagione*) in; **alle cinque** at five (o'clock); **~ mezzanotte/ Natale** at midnight/Christmas; **al mattino** in the morning; **~ maggio/ primavera** in May/spring; **~ cinquant'anni** at fifty (years of age); **~ domani!** see you tomorrow!

4 (*complemento di termine*) to; **dare qc ~ qn** to give sth to sb

5 (*mezzo, modo*) with, by; **~ piedi/ cavallo** on foot/horseback; **fatto ~ mano** made by hand, handmade; **una barca ~ motore** a motorboat; **~ uno ~ uno** one by one; **all'italiana** the Italian way, in the Italian fashion

6 (*rapporto*) a, per; (: *con prezzi*) at; **prendo 500.000 lire al mese** I get 500,000 lire *o* per-month; **pagato ~ ore** paid by the hour; **vendere qc ~ 500 lire il chilo** to sell sth at 500 lire *o* per kilo.

a'bate *sm* abbot.

abbacchi'ato, a [abbak'kjato] *ag* downhearted, in low spirits.

abbagli'ante [abbaʎ'ʎante] *ag* dazzling; **~i** *smpl* (AUT): **accendere gli ~i** to put one's headlights on full (*Brit*) *o* high (*US*) beam.

abbagli'are [abbaʎ'ʎare] *vt* to dazzle; (*illudere*) to delude; **ab'baglio** *sm* blunder; **prendere un abbaglio** to blunder, make a blunder.

abbai'are *vi* to bark.

abba'ino *sm* dormer window; (*soffitta*) attic room.

abbando'nare *vt* to leave, abandon, desert; (*trascurare*) to neglect; (*rinunciare a*) to abandon, give up; **~rsi** *vr* to let o.s. go; **~rsi a** (*ricordi, vizio*) to give o.s. up to; **abban'dono** *sm* abandoning; neglecting; (*stato*) abandonment; neglect; (*SPORT*) withdrawal; (*fig*) abandon; **in abbandono** (*edificio, giardino*) neglected.

abbas'sare *vt* to lower; (*radio*) to turn down; **~rsi** *vr* (*chinarsi*) to stoop; (*livello, sole*) to go down; (*fig:*

umiliarsi) to demean o.s.; **~ i fari** (AUT) to dip *o* dim (US) one's lights.

ab'basso *escl*: **~ il re!** down with the king!

abbas'tanza [abbas'tantsa] *av* (*a sufficienza*) enough; (*alquanto*) quite, rather, fairly; **non è ~ furbo** he's not shrewd enough; **un vino ~ dolce** quite a sweet wine, a fairly sweet wine; **averne ~ di qn/qc** to have had enough of sb/sth.

ab'battere *vt* (*muro, casa*) to pull down; (*ostacolo*) to knock down; (*albero*) to fell; (: *sog: vento*) to bring down; (*bestie da macello*) to slaughter; (*cane, cavallo*) to destroy, put down; (*selvaggina, aereo*) to shoot down; (*fig: sog: malattia, disgrazia*) to lay low; **~rsi** *vr* (*avvilirsi*) to lose heart; **averne ~ di** to lose heart; **abbat'tuto, a** *ag* (*fig*) despondent, depressed.

abba'zia [abbat'tsia] *sf* abbey.

abbece'dario [abbetʃe'darjo] *sm* primer.

abbel'lire *vt* to make beautiful; (*ornare*) to embellish.

abbeve'rare *vt* to water; **~rsi** *vr* to drink.

'abbi, 'abbia, abbi'amo, 'abbiano, abbi'ate *forme del vb* **avere**.

abbicci [abbit'tʃi] *sm inv* alphabet; (*sillabario*) primer; (*fig*) rudiments *pl*.

abbi'ente *ag* well-to-do, well-off.

abbi'etto, a *ag* = **abietto**.

abbiglia'mento [abbiʎʎa'mento] *sm* dress *q*; (*indumenti*) clothes *pl*; (*industria*) clothing industry.

abbigli'are [abbiʎ'ʎare] *vt* to dress up.

abbi'nare *vt*: **~ (a)** to combine (with).

abbindo'lare *vt* (*fig*) to cheat, trick.

abbocca'mento *sm* talks *pl*, meeting.

abboc'care *vt* (*tubi, canali*) to connect, join up // *vi* (*pesce*) to bite; (*tubi*) to join; **~ (all'amo)** (*fig*) to swallow the bait.

abboc'cato, a *ag* (*vino*) sweetish.

abbona'mento *sm* subscription; (*alle ferrovie etc*) season ticket; **fare l'~** to take out a subscription (*o* season ticket).

abbo'narsi *vr*: **~ a un giornale** to take out a subscription to a newspaper; **~ al teatro/alle ferrovie** to take out a season ticket for the theatre/the train; **abbo'nato, a** *sm/f* subscriber; season-ticket holder.

abbon'dante *ag* abundant, plentiful; (*giacca*) roomy.

abbon'danza [abbon'dantsa] *sf* abundance; plenty.

abbon'dare *vi* to abound, be plentiful; ~ in *o* di to be full of, abound in.

abbor'dabile *ag* (*persona*) approachable; (*prezzo*) reasonable.

abbor'dare *vt* (*nave*) to board; (*persona*) to approach; (*argomento*) to tackle; ~ una curva to take a bend.

abbotto'nare *vt* to button up, do up.

abboz'zare [abbot'tsare] *vt* to sketch, outline; (*SCULTURA*) to rough-hew; ~ un sorriso to give a hint of a smile; **ab'bozzo** *sm* sketch, outline; (*DIR*) draft.

abbracci'are [abbrat'tʃare] *vt* to embrace; (*persona*) to hug, embrace; (*professione*) to take up; (*contenere*) to include; ~rsi *vr* to hug *o* embrace (one another); **ab'braccio** *sm* hug, embrace.

abbreviazi'one [abbrevjat'tsjone] *sf* abbreviation.

abbron'zante [abbron'dzante] *ag* tanning, sun *cpd*.

abbron'zare [abbron'dzare] *vt* (*pelle*) to tan; (*metalli*) to bronze; ~rsi *vr* to tan, get a tan; **abbronza'tura** *sf* tan, suntan.

abbrusto'lire *vt* (*pane*) to toast; (*caffè*) to roast.

abbru'tire *vt* to exhaust; to degrade.

abbu'ono *sm* (*COMM*) allowance, discount; (*SPORT*) handicap.

abdi'care *vi* to abdicate; ~ a to give up, renounce.

aberrazi'one [aberrat'tsjone] *sf* aberration.

a'bete *sm* fir (tree); ~ rosso spruce.

abi'etto, a *ag* despicable, abject.

'abile *ag* (*idoneo*): ~ (a qc/a fare qc) fit (for sth/to do sth); (*capace*) able; (*astuto*) clever; (*accorto*) skilful; ~ al servizio militare fit for military service; **abilità** *sf inv* ability; cleverness; skill.

abili'tato, a *ag* qualified; (*TEL*) which has an outside line; **abilitazi'one** *sf* qualification.

a'bisso *sm* abyss, gulf.

abi'tacolo *sm* (*AER*) cockpit; (*AUT*) inside; (: *di camion*) cab.

abi'tante *sm/f* inhabitant.

abi'tare *vt* to live in, dwell in // *vi*: ~ in campagna/a Roma to live in the country/in Rome; **abi'tato, a** *ag* inhabited; lived in // *sm* (*anche*: centro abitato) built-up area; **abitazi'one** *sf* residence; house.

'abito *sm* dress *q*; (*da uomo*) suit; (*da donna*) dress; (*abitudine, disposizione, REL*) habit; ~i *smpl* clothes; in ~ da sera in evening dress.

abitu'ale *ag* usual, habitual; (*cliente*) regular.

abitu'are *vt*: ~ qn a to get sb used *o* accustomed to; ~rsi a to get used to, accustom o.s. to.

abitudi'nario, a *ag* of fixed habits //

sm/f regular customer.

abi'tudine *sf* habit; aver l'~ di fare qc to be in the habit of doing sth; d'~ usually; per ~ from *o* out of habit.

abo'lire *vt* to abolish; (*DIR*) to repeal.

abomi'nevole *ag* abominable.

abo'rigeno [abo'ridʒeno] *sm* aborigine.

abor'rire *vt* to abhor, detest.

abor'tire *vi* (*MED: accidentalmente*) to miscarry, have a miscarriage; (: *deliberatamente*) to have an abortion; (*fig*) to miscarry, fail; **a'borto** *sm* miscarriage; abortion; (*fig*) freak.

abrasi'one *sf* abrasion; **abra'sivo, a** *ag*, *sm* abrasive.

abro'gare *vt* to repeal, abrogate.

A'bruzzo *sm*: l'~, gli ~i the Abruzzi.

'abside *sf* apse.

a'bulico, a, ci, che *ag* lacking in will power.

abu'sare *vi*: ~ di to abuse, misuse; (*alcool*) to take to excess; (*approfittare, violare*) to take advantage of; **a'buso** *sm* abuse, misuse; excessive use.

a.C. *ad abbr* (= *avanti Cristo*) B.C.

'acca *sf* letter H; non capire un'~ not to understand a thing.

acca'demia *sf* (*società*) learned society; (*scuola: d'arte, militare*) academy; **acca'demico, a, ci, che** *ag* academic // *sm* academician.

acca'dere *vb impers* to happen, occur; **acca'duto** *sm*: raccontare l'accaduto to describe what has happened.

accalappi'are *vt* to catch; (*fig*) to trick, dupe.

accal'care *vt* to crowd, throng.

accal'darsi *vr* to grow hot.

accalo'rarsi *vr* (*fig*) to get excited.

accampa'mento *sm* camp.

accam'pare *vt* to encamp; (*fig*) to put forward, advance; ~rsi *vr* to camp.

accani'mento *sm* fury; (*tenacia*) tenacity, perseverance.

acca'nirsi *vr* (*infierire*) to rage; (*ostinarsi*) to persist; **acca'nito, a** *ag* (*odio, gelosia*) fierce, bitter; (*lavoratore*) assiduous, dogged; (*fumatore*) inveterate.

ac'canto *av* near, nearby; ~ a *prep* near, beside, close to.

accanto'nare *vt* (*problema*) to shelve; (*somma*) to set aside.

accapar'rare *vt* (*COMM*) to corner, buy up; (*versare una caparra*) to pay a deposit on; ~rsi qc (*fig: simpatia, voti*) to secure sth (for o.s.).

accapigli'arsi [akkapiʎ'ʎarsi] *vr* to come to blows; (*fig*) to quarrel.

accappa'toio *sm* bathrobe.

accappo'nare *vi*: far ~ la pelle a qn (*fig*) to bring sb out in goosepimples.

accarez'zare [akkaret'tsare] *vt* to caress, stroke, fondle; (*fig*) to toy with.

acca'sarsi *vr* to set up house; to get

married.

accasci'arsi [akkaʃ'ʃarsi] vr to collapse; (fig) to lose heart.

accat'tone, a smf beggar.

accaval'lare vt (gambe) to cross; **~rsi** vr (sovrapporsi) to overlap; (addensarsi) to gather.

acce'care [attʃe'kare] vt to blind // vi to go blind.

ac'cedere [at'tʃedere] vi: **~ a** to enter; (richiesta) to grant, accede to.

accele'rare [attʃele'rare] vt to speed up // vi (AUT) to accelerate; **~ il passo** to quicken one's pace; **accele'rato** sm (FERR) slow train; **accelera'tore** sm (AUT) accelerator; **accelerazi'one** sf acceleration.

ac'cendere [at'tʃendere] vt (fuoco, sigaretta) to light; (luce, televisione) to put o switch o turn on; (AUT: motore) to switch on; (COMM: conto) to open; (fig: suscitare) to inflame, stir up; **~rsi** vr (luce) to come o go on; (legna) to catch fire, ignite; **accen'dino** sm, **accendi'sigaro** sm (cigarette) lighter.

accen'nare [attʃen'nare] vt to indicate, point out; (MUS) to pick out the notes of; to hum // vi: **~ a** (fig: alludere a) to hint at; (: far atto di) to make as if; **~ un saluto** (con la mano) to make as if to wave; (col capo) to half nod; **accenna a piovere** it looks as if it's going to rain.

ac'cenno [at'tʃenno] sm (cenno) sign; nod; (allusione) hint.

accensi'one [attʃen'sjone] sf (vedi accendere) lighting; switching on; opening; (AUT) ignition.

accen'tare [attʃen'tare] vt (parlando) to stress; (scrivendo) to accent.

ac'cento [at'tʃento] sm accent; (FONETICA, fig) stress; (inflessione) tone (of voice).

accen'trare [attʃen'trare] vt to centralize.

accentu'are [attʃentu'are] vt to stress, emphasize; **~rsi** vr to become more noticeable.

accerchi'are [attʃer'kjare] vt to surround, encircle.

accerta'mento [attʃerta'mento] sm check; assessment.

accer'tare [attʃer'tare] vt to ascertain; (verificare) to check; (reddito) to assess; **~rsi** vr: **~rsi (di)** to make sure (of).

ac'ceso, a [at'tʃeso] pp di **accendere** // ag lit; on; open; (colore) bright.

acces'sibile [attʃes'sibile] ag (luogo) accessible; (persona) approachable; (prezzo) reasonable; (idea): **~ a qn** within the reach of sb.

ac'cesso [at'tʃesso] sm (anche INFORM) access; (MED) attack, fit; (impulso violento) fit, outburst.

acces'sorio, a [attʃes'sɔrjo] ag secondary, of secondary importance; **~i** smpl

accessories.

ac'cetta [at'tʃetta] sf hatchet.

accet'tabile [attʃet'tabile] ag acceptable.

accet'tare [attʃet'tare] vt to accept; **~ di fare qc** to agree to do sth; **accettazi'one** sf acceptance; (locale di servizio pubblico) reception; **accettazione bagagli** (AER) check-in (desk).

ac'cetto, a [at'tʃetto] ag: (ben) **~** welcome; (persona) well-liked.

accezi'one [attʃet'tsjone] sf meaning.

acchiap'pare [akkjap'pare] vt to catch.

acci'acco, chi [at'tʃakko] sm ailment.

acciaie'ria [attʃaje'ria] sf steelworks sg.

acci'aio [at'tʃajo] sm steel.

acciden'tale [attʃiden'tale] ag accidental.

acciden'tato, a [attʃiden'tato] ag (terreno etc) uneven.

acci'dente [attʃi'dente] sm (caso imprevisto) accident; (disgrazia) mishap; **non si capisce un ~** it's as clear as mud; **~i!** (fam: per rabbia) damn (it)!; (: per meraviglia) good heavens!

accigli'ato, a [attʃiʎ'ʎato] ag frowning.

ac'cingersi [at'tʃindʒersi] vr: **~ a fare** to be about to do.

acciuf'fare [attʃuf'fare] vt to seize, catch.

acci'uga, ghe [at'tʃuga] sf anchovy.

accla'mare vt (applaudire) to applaud; (eleggere) to acclaim; **acclamazi'one** sf applause; acclamation.

acclima'tare vt to acclimatize; **~rsi** vr to become acclimatized.

ac'cludere vt to enclose; **ac'cluso, a** pp di **accludere** // ag enclosed.

accocco'larsi vr to crouch.

accogli'ente [akkoʎ'ʎente] ag welcoming, friendly; **accogli'enza** sf reception; welcome.

ac'cogliere [ak'kɔʎʎere] vt (ricevere) to receive; (dare il benvenuto) to welcome; (approvare) to agree to, accept; (contenere) to hold, accommodate.

accol'lato, a ag (vestito) high-necked.

accoltel'lare vt to knife, stab.

ac'colto, a pp di **accogliere**.

accoman'dita sf (DIR) limited partnership.

accomia'tare vt to dismiss; **~rsi** vr: **~rsi (da)** to take one's leave (of).

accomoda'mento sm agreement, settlement.

accomo'dante ag accommodating.

accomo'dare vt (aggiustare) to repair, mend; (riordinare) to tidy; (conciliare) to settle; **~rsi** vr (sedersi) to sit down; **s'accomodi!** (venga avanti) come in!; (si sieda) take a seat!

accompagna'mento [akkompaɲɲa'mento] sm (MUS) accompaniment.

accompa'gnare [akkompaɲ'ɲare] vt to accompany, come o go with; (MUS) to accompany; (unire) to couple; **~ la porta** to close the door gently.

accomu'nare *vt* to pool, share; (*avvicinare*) to unite.

acconcia'tura [akkontʃa'tura] *sf* hair-style.

accondi'scendere [akkondiʃ'ʃendere] *vi*: ~ a to agree *o* consent to; **accondi'sceso, a** *pp di* **accondiscendere**.

acconsen'tire *vi*: ~ (a) to agree *o* consent (to).

acconten'tare *vt* to satisfy; ~rsi di to be satisfied with, content o.s. with.

ac'conto *sm* part payment; **pagare una somma in** ~ to pay a sum of money as a deposit.

accoppia'mento *sm* coupling, pairing off; mating; (*TECN*) coupling.

accoppi'are *vt* to couple, pair off; (*BIOL*) to mate; ~rsi *vr* to pair off; to mate.

accorci'are [akkor'tʃare] *vt* to shorten; ~rsi *vr* to become shorter.

accor'dare *vt* to reconcile; (*colori*) to match; (*MUS*) to tune; (*LING*): ~ qc con qc to make sth agree with sth; (*DIR*) to grant; ~rsi *vr* to agree, come to an agreement; (*colori*) to match.

ac'cordo *sm* agreement; (*armonia*) harmony; (*MUS*) chord; **essere d'~** to agree; **andare d'~** to get on well together; **d'~!** all right!, agreed!

ac'corgersi [ak'kordʒersi] *vr*: ~ di to notice; (*fig*) to realize; **accorgi'mento** *sm* shrewdness *q*; (*espediente*) trick, device.

ac'correre *vi* to run up.

ac'corto, a *pp di* **accorgersi** // *ag* shrewd; **stare** ~ to be on one's guard.

accos'tare *vt* (*avvicinare*): ~ qc a to bring sth near to, put sth near to; (*avvicinarsi a*) to approach; (*socchiudere: imposte*) to half-close; (: *porta*) to leave ajar // *vi* (*NAUT*) to come alongside; ~rsi a to draw near, approach; (*fig*) to support.

accovacci'arsi [akkovat'tʃarsi] *vr* to crouch.

accoz'zaglia [akkot'tsaʎʎa] *sf* (*peg: di idee, oggetti*) jumble, hotchpotch; (: *di persone*) odd assortment.

accredi'tare *vt* (*notizia*) to confirm the truth of; (*COMM*) to credit; (*diplomatico*) to accredit; ~rsi *vr* (*fig*) to gain credit.

ac'crescere [ak'kreʃʃere] *vt* to increase; ~rsi *vr* to increase, grow; **accresci'tivo, a** *ag, sm* (*LING*) augmentative; **accresci'uto, a** *pp di* **accrescere**.

accucci'arsi [akkut'tʃarsi] *vr* (*cane*) to lie down.

accu'dire *vt* (*anche*: *vi*: ~ a) to attend to.

accumu'lare *vt* to accumulate.

accura'tezza [akkura'tettsa] *sf* care; accuracy.

accu'rato, a *ag* (*diligente*) careful; (*preciso*) accurate.

ac'cusa *sf* accusation; (*DIR*) charge; **la pubblica** ~ the prosecution.

accu'sare *vt*: ~ qn di qc to accuse sb of sth; (*DIR*) to charge sb with sth; ~ **ricevuta di** (*COMM*) to acknowledge receipt of.

accu'sato, a *sm/f* accused; defendant.

accusa'tore, 'trice *sm/f* accuser // *sm* (*DIR*) prosecutor.

a'cerbo, a [a'tʃerbo] *ag* bitter; (*frutta*) sour, unripe; (*persona*) immature.

'acero ['atʃero] *sm* maple.

a'cerrimo, a [a'tʃerrimo] *ag* very fierce.

a'ceto [a'tʃeto] *sm* vinegar.

ace'tone [atʃe'tone] *sm* nail varnish remover.

A.C.I. ['atʃi] *sigla m* (= *Automobile Club d'Italia*) ≈ A.A.

'acido, a ['atʃido] *ag* (*sapore*) acid, sour; (*CHIM*) acid // *sm* (*CHIM*) acid.

'acino ['atʃino] *sm* berry; ~ **d'uva** grape.

'acne *sf* acne.

'acqua *sf* water; (*pioggia*) rain; ~**e** *sfpl* waters; **fare** ~ (*NAUT*) to leak, take in water; ~ **in bocca!** mum's the word!; ~ **corrente** running water; ~ **dolce** fresh water; ~ **minerale** mineral water; ~ **potabile** drinking water; ~ **salata** salt water; ~ **tonica** tonic water.

acqua'forte, pl acque'forti *sf* etching.

a'cquaio *sm* sink.

acqua'ragia [akkwa'radʒa] *sf* turpentine.

a'cquario *sm* aquarium; (*dello zodiaco*): A~ Aquarius.

acqua'santa *sf* holy water.

ac'quatico, a, ci, che *ag* aquatic; (*sport, sci*) water *cpd*.

acqua'vite *sf* brandy.

acquaz'zone [akkwat'tsone] *sm* cloudburst, heavy shower.

acque'dotto *sm* aqueduct; waterworks *pl*, water system.

'acqueo, a *ag*: **vapore** ~ water vapour.

acque'rello *sm* watercolour.

acquie'tare *vt* to appease; (*dolore*) to ease; ~rsi *vr* to calm down.

acqui'rente *sm/f* purchaser, buyer.

acqui'sire *vt* to acquire.

acquis'tare *vt* to purchase, buy; (*fig*) to gain; **a'cquisto** *sm* purchase; **fare acquisti** to go shopping.

acqui'trino *sm* bog, marsh.

acquo'lina *sf*: **far venire l'~ in bocca a qn** to make sb's mouth water.

a'cquoso, a *ag* watery.

'acre *ag* acrid, pungent; (*fig*) harsh, biting.

a'crobata, i, e *sm/f* acrobat.

acu'ire *vt* to sharpen.

a'culeo *sm* (*ZOOL*) sting; (*BOT*) prickle.

a'cume *sm* acumen, perspicacity.

a'custica *sf* (*scienza*) acoustics *sg*; (*di una sala*) acoustics *pl*.

a'cuto, a ag (appuntito) sharp, pointed; (suono, voce) shrill, piercing; (MAT, LING, MED) acute; (MUS) high-pitched; (fig: dolore, desiderio) intense; (: perspicace) acute, keen.

ad prep (dav V) = **a**.

adagi'are [ada'dʒarc] vt to lay o set down carefully; ~rsi vr to lie down, stretch out.

a'dagio [a'dadʒo] av slowly // sm (MUS) adagio; (proverbio) adage, saying.

adatta'mento sm adaptation.

adat'tare vt to adapt; (sistemare) to fit; ~rsi (a) (ambiente, tempi) to adapt (to); (essere adatto) to be suitable (for).

a'datto, a ag: ~ (a) suitable (for), right (for).

addebi'tare vt: ~ qc a qn to debit sb with sth; (fig: incolpare) to blame sb for sth.

ad'debito sm (COMM) debit.

adden'sare vt to thicken; ~rsi vr to thicken; (nuvole) to gather.

adden'tare vt to bite into.

adden'trarsi vr: ~ in to penetrate, go into.

ad'dentro av (fig): essere molto ~ in qc to be well-versed in sth.

addestra'mento sm training.

addes'trare vt, ~rsi vr to train; ~rsi in qc to practise (Brit) o practice (US) sth.

ad'detto, a ag: ~ a (persona) assigned to; (oggetto) intended for // sm employee; (funzionario) attaché; ~ commerciale/stampa commercial/press attaché; gli ~i ai lavori authorized personnel; (fig) those in the know.

addì av (AMM): ~ 3 luglio 1978 on the 3rd of July 1978 (Brit), on July 3rd 1978 (US).

addi'accio [ad'djattʃo] sm (MIL) bivouac; dormire all'~ to sleep in the open.

addi'etro av (indietro) behind; (nel passato, prima) before, ago.

ad'dio sm, escl goodbye, farewell.

addirit'tura av (veramente) really, absolutely; (perfino) even; (direttamente) directly, right away.

ad'dirsi vr: ~ a to suit, be suitable for.

addi'tare vt to point out; (fig) to expose.

addi'tivo, a sm additive.

addizio'nare [addittsjo'nare] vt (MAT) to add (up); **addizi'one** sf addition.

addob'bare vt to decorate; **ad'dobbo** sm decoration.

addol'cire [addol'tʃire] vt (caffè etc) to sweeten; (acqua, fig: carattere) to soften; ~rsi vr (fig) to mellow, soften.

addolo'rare vt to pain, grieve; ~rsi (per) to be distressed (by).

ad'dome sm abdomen.

addomesti'care vt to tame.

addormen'tare vt to put to sleep; ~rsi vr to fall asleep, go to sleep.

addos'sare vt (appoggiare): ~ qc a qc to lean sth against sth; (fig): ~ la colpa a qn to lay the blame on sb; ~rsi qc (responsabilità etc) to shoulder sth.

ad'dosso av (sulla persona) on; mettersi ~ il cappotto to put one's coat on; non ho soldi ~ I don't have any money on me; ~ a prep (sopra) on; (molto vicino) right next to; stare ~ a qn (fig) to breathe down sb's neck; dare ~ a qn (fig) to attack sb.

ad'durre vt (DIR) to produce; (citare) to cite.

adegu'are vt: ~ qc a to adjust o relate sth to; ~rsi vr to adapt; **adegu'ato, a** ag adequate; (conveniente) suitable; (equo) fair.

a'dempiere, adem'pire vt to fulfil, carry out.

ade'rente ag adhesive; (vestito) close-fitting // sm/f follower; **ade'renza** sf adhesion; **aderenze** sfpl (fig) connections, contacts.

ade'rire vi (stare attaccato) to adhere, stick; ~ a to adhere to, stick to; (fig: società, partito) to join; (: opinione) to support; (richiesta) to agree to.

ades'care vt to lure, entice.

adesi'one sf adhesion; (fig) agreement, acceptance; **ade'sivo, a** ag, sm adhesive.

a'desso av (ora) now; (or ora, poco fa) just now; (tra poco) any moment now.

adia'cente [adja'tʃente] ag adjacent.

adi'bire vt (usare): ~ qc a to turn sth into.

adi'rarsi vr: ~ (con o contro qn per qc) to get angry (with sb over sth).

a'dire vt (DIR): ~ le vie legali to take legal proceedings.

'adito sm: dare ~ a to give rise to.

adocchi'are [adok'kjare] vt (scorgere) to catch sight of; (occhieggiare) to eye.

adole'scente [adoleʃ'ʃente] ag, sm/f adolescent; **adole'scenza** sf adolescence.

adope'rare vt to use; ~rsi vr to strive; ~rsi per qn/qc to do one's best for sb/sth.

ado'rare vt to adore; (REL) to adore, worship.

adot'tare vt to adopt; (decisione, provvedimenti) to pass; **adot'tivo, a** ag (genitori) adoptive; (figlio, patria) adopted; **adozi'one** sf adoption.

adri'atico, a, ci, che ag Adriatic // sm: l'A~, il mare A~ the Adriatic, the Adriatic Sea.

adu'lare vt to adulate, flatter.

adulte'rare vt to adulterate.

adul'terio sm adultery.

a'dulto, a ag adult; (fig) mature // sm adult, grown-up.

adu'nanza [adu'nantsa] sf assembly, meeting.

adu'nare vt, ~rsi vr to assemble,

gather; **adu'nata** *sf* (*MIL*) parade, muster.

a'dunco, a, chi, che *ag* hooked.

a'ereo, a *ag* air *cpd*; (*radice*) aerial // *sm* aerial; (*aeroplano*) plane; ~ **a reazione** jet (plane); **ae'robica** *sf* aerobics *sg*; **aerodi'namico, a, ci, che** *ag* aerodynamic; (*affusolato*) streamlined // *sf* aerodynamics *sg*; **aero'nautica** *sf* (*scienza*) aeronautics *sg*; **aeronautica militare** air force; **aero'plano** *sm* (aero)plane (*Brit*), (air)plane (*US*); **aero'porto** *sm* airport; **aero'sol** *sm inv* aerosol.

'afa *sf* sultriness.

af'fabile *ag* affable.

affaccen'darsi [affattʃen'darsi] *vr*: ~ **intorno a qc** to busy o.s. with sth.

affacci'arsi [affat'tʃarsi] *vr*: ~ (a) to appear (at).

affa'mato, a *ag* starving; (*fig*): ~ (di) eager (for).

affan'nare *vt* to leave breathless; (*fig*) to worry; **~rsi** *vr*: **~rsi per qn/qc** to worry about sb/sth; **af'fanno** *sm* breathlessness; (*fig*) anxiety, worry; **affan'noso, a** *ag* (*respiro*) difficult; (*fig*) troubled, anxious.

af'fare *sm* (*faccenda*) matter, affair; (*COMM*) piece of business, (business) deal; (*occasione*) bargain; (*DIR*) case; (*fam: cosa*) thing; **~i** *smpl* (*COMM*) business *sg*; **ministro degli A~i esteri** Foreign Secretary (*Brit*), Secretary of State (*US*); **affa'rista, i** *sm* profiteer, unscrupulous businessman.

affasci'nante [affaʃʃi'nante] *ag* fascinating.

affasci'nare [affaʃʃi'nare] *vt* to bewitch; (*fig*) to charm, fascinate.

affati'care *vt* to tire; **~rsi** *vr* (*durar fatica*) to tire o.s. out.

af'fatto *av* completely; **non ... ~** not ... at all; **niente ~** not at all.

affer'mare *vt* (*dichiarare*) to maintain, affirm; **~rsi** *vr* to assert o.s., make one's name known; **affermazi'one** *sf* affirmation, assertion; (*successo*) achievement.

affer'rare *vt* to seize, grasp; (*fig: idea*) to grasp; **~rsi** *vr*: **~rsi a** to cling to.

affet'tare *vt* (*tagliare a fette*) to slice; (*ostentare*) to affect; **affet'tato, a** *ag* sliced; affected // *sm* sliced cold meat.

affet'tivo, a *ag* emotional, affective.

af'fetto *sm* affection; **affettu'oso, a** *ag* affectionate.

affezio'narsi [affettsjo'narsi] *vr*: ~ **a** to grow fond of.

affezi'one [affet'tsjone] *sf* (*affetto*) affection; (*MED*) ailment, disorder.

affian'care *vt* to place side by side; (*MIL*) to flank; (*fig*) to support; ~ **qc a** qc to place sth next to *o* beside sth; **~rsi a qn** to stand beside sb.

affia'tarsi *vr* to get on well together.

affibbi'are *vt* (*fig: dare*) to give.

affida'mento *sm* (*DIR: di bambino*) custody; (*fiducia*): **fare ~ su qn** to rely on sb; **non dà nessun ~** he's not to be trusted.

affi'dare *vt*: ~ **qc o qn a qn** to entrust sth *o* sb to sb; **~rsi** *vr*: **~rsi a** to place one's trust in.

affievo'lirsi *vr* to grow weak.

af'figgere [af'fiddʒere] *vt* to stick up, post up.

affi'lare *vt* to sharpen.

affili'are *vt* to affiliate; **~rsi** *vr*: **~rsi a** to become affiliated to.

affi'nare *vt* to sharpen.

affinché [affin'ke] *cong* in order that, so that.

af'fine *ag* similar; **affinità** *sf inv* affinity.

affio'rare *vi* to emerge.

affissi'one *sf* billposting.

af'fisso, a *pp di* **affiggere** // *sm* bill, poster; (*LING*) affix.

affit'tare *vt* (*dare in affitto*) to let, rent (out); (*prendere in affitto*) to rent; **af'fitto** *sm* rent; (*contratto*) lease.

af'fliggere [af'fliddʒere] *vt* to torment; **~rsi** *vr* to grieve; **af'flitto, a** *pp di* **affliggere**; **afflizi'one** *sf* distress, torment.

afflosci'arsi [affloʃ'ʃarsi] *vr* to go limp; (*frutta*) to go soft.

afflu'ente *sm* tributary; **afflu'enza** *sf* flow; (*di persone*) crowd.

afflu'ire *vi* to flow; (*fig: merci, persone*) to pour in; **af'flusso** *sm* influx.

affo'gare *vt, vi* to drown; **~rsi** *vr* to drown; (*deliberatamente*) to drown o.s.

affol'lare *vt, ~rsi* *vr* to crowd; **affol'lato, a** *ag* crowded.

affon'dare *vt* to sink.

affran'care *vt* to free, liberate; (*AMM*) to redeem; (*lettera*) to stamp; (: *meccanicamente*) to frank (*Brit*), meter (*US*); **~rsi** *vr* to free o.s.; **affranca'tura** *sf* (*di francobollo*) stamping; franking (*Brit*), metering (*US*); (*tassa di spedizione*) postage.

af'franto, a *ag* (*esausto*) worn out; (*abbattuto*) overcome.

af'fresco, schi *sm* fresco.

affret'tare *vt* to quicken, speed up; **~rsi** *vr* to hurry; **~rsi a fare qc** to hurry *o* hasten to do sth.

affron'tare *vt* (*pericolo etc*) to face; (*assalire: nemico*) to confront; **~rsi** *vr* (*reciproco*) to come to blows.

af'fronto *sm* affront, insult.

affumi'care *vt* to fill with smoke; to blacken with smoke; (*alimenti*) to smoke.

affuso'lato, a *ag* tapering.

a'foso, a *ag* sultry, close.

'Africa *sf*: l'~ Africa; **afri'cano, a** *ag*, *sm/f* African.

afrodi'siaco, a, ci, che *ag*, *sm* aphrodisiac.

a'genda [a'dʒɛnda] *sf* diary.

a'gente [a'dʒɛnte] *sm* agent; ~ **di cambio** stockbroker; ~ **di polizia** police officer; **agen'zia** *sf* agency; (*succursale*) branch; **agenzia di collocamento** employment agency; **agenzia immobiliare** estate agent's (office) (*Brit*), real estate office (*US*); **agenzia pubblicitaria/viaggi** advertising/travel agency.

agevo'lare [adʒevo'lare] *vt* to facilitate, make easy.

a'gevole [a'dʒevole] *ag* easy; (*strada*) smooth.

agganci'are [aggan'tʃare] *vt* to hook up; (*FERR*) to couple.

ag'geggio [ad'dʒeddʒo] *sm* gadget, contraption.

agget'tivo [addʒet'tivo] *sm* adjective.

agghiacci'ante [aggjat'tʃante] *ag* (*fig*) chilling.

agghin'darsi [aggin'darsi] *vr* to deck o.s. out.

aggior'nare [addʒor'nare] *vt* (*opera, manuale*) to bring up-to-date; (*seduta etc*) to postpone; ~**rsi** *vr* to bring (o keep) o.s. up-to-date; **aggior'nato, a** *ag* up-to-date.

aggi'rare [addʒi'rare] *vt* to go round; (*fig: ingannare*) to trick; ~**rsi** *vr* to wander about; **il prezzo s'aggira sul milione** the price is around the million mark.

aggiudi'care [addʒudi'kare] *vt* to award; (*all'asta*) to knock down; ~**rsi qc** to win sth.

ag'giungere [ad'dʒundʒere] *vt* to add; **aggi'unto, a** *pp* di **aggiungere** // *ag* assistant *cpd* // *sm* assistant // *sf* addition; **sindaco aggiunto** deputy mayor.

aggius'tare [addʒus'tare] *vt* (*accomodare*) to mend, repair; (*riassettare*) to adjust; (*fig: lite*) to settle; ~**rsi** *vr* (*arrangiarsi*) to make do; (*con senso reciproco*) to come to an agreement.

agglome'rato *sm* (*di rocce*) conglomerate; (*di legno*) chipboard; ~ **urbano** built-up area.

aggrap'parsi *vr*: ~ **a** to cling to.

aggra'vare *vt* (*aumentare*) to increase; (*appesantire: anche fig*) to weigh down, make heavy; (*fig: pena*) to make worse; ~**rsi** *vr* (*fig*) to worsen, become worse.

aggrazi'ato, a [aggrat'tsjato] *ag* graceful.

aggre'dire *vt* to attack, assault.

aggre'gare *vt*: ~ **qn a qc** to admit sb to sth; ~**rsi** *vr* to join; ~**rsi a** to join, become a member of; **aggre'gato, a** *ag* associated // *sm* aggregate; **aggregato urbano** built-up area.

aggressi'one *sf* aggression; (*atto*) attack, assault.

aggres'sivo, a *ag* aggressive.

aggrot'tare *vt*: ~ **le sopracciglia** to frown.

aggrovigli'are [aggroviʎ'ʎare] *vt* to tangle; ~**rsi** *vr* (*fig*) to become complicated.

agguan'tare *vt* to catch, seize.

aggu'ato *sm* trap; (*imboscata*) ambush; **tendere un ~ a qn** to set a trap for sb.

agguer'rito, a *ag* fierce.

agi'ato, a [a'dʒato] *ag* (*vita*) easy; (*persona*) well-off, well-to-do.

'agile ['adʒile] *ag* agile, nimble; **agilità** *sf* agility, nimbleness.

'agio ['adʒo] *sm* ease, comfort; ~**i** *smpl* comforts; **mettersi a proprio ~** to make o.s. at home *o* comfortable.

a'gire [a'dʒire] *vi* to act; (*esercitare un'azione*) to take effect; (*TECN*) to work, function; ~ **contro qn** (*DIR*) to take action against sb.

agi'tare [adʒi'tare] *vt* (*bottiglia*) to shake; (*mano, fazzoletto*) to wave; (*fig: turbare*) to disturb; (: *incitare*) to stir (up); (: *dibattere*) to discuss; ~**rsi** *vr* (*mare*) to be rough; (*malato, dormitore*) to toss and turn; (*bambino*) to fidget; (*emozionarsi*) to get upset; (*POL*) to agitate; **agi'tato, a** *ag* rough; restless; fidgety; upset, perturbed; **agitazi'one** *sf* agitation; (*POL*) unrest, agitation; **mettere in agitazione qn** to upset *o* distress sb.

'agli ['aʎʎi] *prep* + *det* vedi **a**.

'aglio ['aʎʎo] *sm* garlic.

a'gnello [aɲ'ɲɛllo] *sm* lamb.

'ago, *pl* aghi *sm* needle.

ago'nia *sf* agony.

ago'nistico, a, ci, che *ag* athletic; (*fig*) competitive.

agoniz'zare [agonid'dzare] *vi* to be dying.

agopun'tura *sf* acupuncture.

a'gosto *sm* August.

a'grario, a *ag* agrarian, agricultural; (*riforma*) land *cpd* // *sf* agriculture.

a'gricolo, a *ag* agricultural, farm *cpd*; **agricol'tore** *sm* farmer; **agricol'tura** *sf* agriculture, farming.

agri'foglio [agri'fɔʎʎo] *sm* holly.

agrimen'sore *sm* land surveyor.

agritu'rismo *sm* farm holidays *pl*.

'agro, a *ag* sour, sharp; ~**dolce** *ag* bittersweet; (*salsa*) sweet and sour.

a'grume *sm* (*spesso al pl: pianta*) citrus; (: *frutto*) citrus fruit.

aguz'zare [agut'tsare] *vt* to sharpen; ~ **gli orecchi** to prick up one's ears.

a'guzzo, a [a'guttso] *ag* sharp.

'ai *prep* + *det* vedi **a**.

'Aia *sf*: **l'~** the Hague.

'aia *sf* threshing-floor.

ai'rone *sm* heron.

aiu'ola *sf* flower bed.

aiu'tante *sm/f* assistant // *sm* (*MIL*) adjutant; (*NAUT*) master-at-arms; ~ **di campo** aide-de-camp.

aiu'tare *vt* to help; ~ **qn (a fare)** to help sb (to do).

ai'uto *sm* help, assistance, aid; (*aiutante*) assistant; **venire in ~ di qn** to come to sb's aid; ~ **chirurgo** assistant surgeon.

aiz'zare [aitˈtsare] *vt* to incite; ~ **i cani contro qn** to set the dogs on sb.

al *prep + det vedi* **a**.

'ala, *pl* **'ali** *sf* wing; **fare ~** to fall back, make way; ~ **destra/sinistra** (*SPORT*) right/left wing.

'alacre *ag* quick, brisk.

a'lano *sm* Great Dane.

a'lare *ag* wing *cpd*.

'alba *sf* dawn.

Alba'nia *sf*: **l'~** Albania.

'albatro *sm* albatross.

albeggi'are [albedˈdʒare] *vi*, *vb impers* to dawn.

albera'tura *sf* (*NAUT*) masts *pl*.

alberghi'ero, a [alberˈgjɛro] *ag* hotel *cpd*.

al'bergo, ghi *sm* hotel; ~ **della gioventù** youth hostel.

'albero *sm* tree; (*NAUT*) mast; (*TECN*) shaft; ~ **genealogico** family tree; ~ **a gomiti** crankshaft; ~ **di Natale** Christmas tree; ~ **maestro** mainmast; ~ **di trasmissione** transmission shaft.

albi'cocca, che *sf* apricot; **albi'cocco, chi** *sm* apricot tree.

'albo *sm* (*registro*) register, roll; (*AMM*) notice board.

'album *sm* album; ~ **da disegno** sketch book.

al'bume *sm* albumen.

'alce [ˈaltʃe] *sm* elk.

al'colico, a, ci, che *ag* alcoholic // *sm* alcoholic drink.

alcoliz'zato, a [alcolidˈdzato] *sm/f* alcoholic.

'alcool *sm* alcohol; **alco'olico** *etc vedi* **alcolico** *etc*.

al'cuno, a *det* (*dav sm*: **alcun** +*C*, *V*, **alcuno** + *s impura*, *gn*, *pn*, *ps*, *x*, *z*; *dav sf*: **alcuna** +*C*, **alcun'** +*V*) (*nessuno*): **non ... ~** no, not any; ~**i(e)** *det pl*, *pronome pl* some, a few; **non c'è ~a fretta** there's no hurry, there isn't any hurry; **senza alcun riguardo** without any consideration.

aldilà *sm*: **l'~** the after-life.

a'letta *sf* (*TECN*) fin; tab.

alfa'beto *sm* alphabet.

alfi'ere *sm* standard-bearer; (*MIL*) ensign; (*SCACCHI*) bishop.

al'fine *av* finally, in the end.

'alga, ghe *sf* seaweed *q*, alga.

'algebra [ˈaldʒebra] *sf* algebra.

Alge'ria [aldʒeˈria] *sf*: **l'~** Algeria.

ali'ante *sm* (*AER*) glider.

'alibi *sm inv* alibi.

a'lice [aˈlitʃe] *sf* anchovy.

alie'nare *vt* (*DIR*) to alienate, transfer; (*rendere ostile*) to alienate; ~**rsi qn** to alienate sb; **alie'nato, a** *ag* alienated; transferred; (*fuor di senno*) insane // *sm* lunatic, insane person; **alienazi'one** *sf* alienation; transfer; insanity.

ali'eno, a *ag* (*avverso*): ~ (**da**) opposed (to), averse (to) // *sm/f* alien.

alimen'tare *vt* to feed; (*TECN*) to feed; to supply; (*fig*) to sustain // *ag* food *cpd*; ~**i** *smpl* foodstuffs; (*anche*: **negozio di** ~**i**) grocer's shop; **alimentazi'one** *sf* feeding; supplying; (*gli alimenti*) diet.

ali'mento *sm* food; ~**i** *smpl* food *sg*; (*DIR*) alimony.

a'liquota *sf* share; (*d'imposta*) rate.

alis'cafo *sm* hydrofoil.

'alito *sm* breath.

all. *abbr* (= *allegato*) encl.

'alla *prep + det vedi* **a**.

allacci'are [allatˈtʃare] *vt* (*scarpe*) to tie, lace (up); (*cintura*) to do up, fasten; (*due località*) to link; (*luce*, *gas*) to connect; (*amicizia*) to form.

alla'gare *vt*, ~**rsi** *vr* to flood.

allar'gare *vt* to widen; (*vestito*) to let out; (*aprire*) to open; (*fig: dilatare*) to extend.

allar'mare *vt* to alarm.

al'larme *sm* alarm; ~ **aereo** air-raid warning.

allar'mismo *sm* scaremongering.

allat'tare *vt* to feed.

'alle *prep + det vedi* **a**.

alle'anza [alleˈantsa] *sf* alliance.

alle'arsi *vr* to form an alliance; **alle'ato, a** *ag* allied // *sm/f* ally.

alle'gare *vt* (*accludere*) to enclose; (*DIR: citare*) to cite, adduce; (*denti*) to set on edge; **alle'gato, a** *ag* enclosed // *sm* enclosure; **in allegato** enclosed.

allegge'rire [alleddʒeˈrire] *vt* to lighten, make lighter; (*fig: sofferenza*) to alleviate, lessen; (*: lavoro, tasse*) to reduce.

alle'gria *sf* gaiety, cheerfulness.

al'legro, a *ag* cheerful, merry; (*un po' brillo*) merry, tipsy; (*vivace: colore*) bright // *sm* (*MUS*) allegro.

allena'mento *sm* training.

alle'nare *vt*, ~**rsi** *vr* to train; **allena'tore** *sm* (*SPORT*) trainer, coach.

allen'tare *vt* to slacken; (*disciplina*) to relax; ~**rsi** *vr* to become slack; (*ingranaggio*) to work loose.

aller'gia, gie [allerˈdʒia] *sf* allergy; **al'lergico, a, ci, che** *ag* allergic.

alles'tire *vt* (*cena*) to prepare; (*esercito, nave*) to equip, fit out; (*spettacolo*) to stage.

allet'tare *vt* to lure, entice.

alleva'mento *sm* breeding, rearing;

(*luogo*) stock farm.

alle'vare *vt* (*animale*) to breed, rear; (*bambino*) to bring up.

allevi'are *vt* to alleviate.

alli'bire *vi* to be astounded.

allibra'tore *sm* bookmaker.

allie'tare *vt* to cheer up, gladden.

alli'evo *sm* pupil; (*apprendista*) apprentice; (*MIL*) cadet.

alliga'tore *sm* alligator.

alline'are *vt* (*persone, cose*) to line up; (*TIP*) to align; (*fig: economia, salari*) to adjust, align; ~**rsi** *vr* to line up; (*fig: a idee*): ~**rsi a** to come into line with.

'allo *prep* + *det vedi* **a**.

al'locco, a, chi, che *sm* tawny owl // *sm/f* oaf.

allocuzi'one [allokut'tsjone] *sf* address, solemn speech.

al'lodola *sf* (sky)lark.

alloggi'are [allod'dʒare] *vt* to accommodate // *vi* to live; **al'loggio** *sm* lodging, accommodation (*Brit*); accommodations (*US*); (*appartamento*) flat (*Brit*), apartment (*US*).

allontana'mento *sm* removal; dismissal.

allonta'nare *vt* to send away, send off; (*impiegato*) to dismiss; (*pericolo*) to avert, remove; (*estraniare*) to alienate; ~**rsi** *vr*: ~**rsi (da)** to go away (from); (*estraniarsi*) to become estranged (from).

al'lora *av* (*in quel momento*) then // *cong* (*in questo caso*) well then; (*dunque*) well then, so; **la gente d'~** people then *o* in those days; **da ~ in poi** from then on.

allor'ché [allor'ke] *cong* (*formale*) when, as soon as.

al'loro *sm* laurel.

'alluce ['allutʃe] *sm* big toe.

alluci'nante [allutʃi'nante] *ag* awful; (*fam*) amazing.

allucinazi'one [allutʃinat'tsjone] *sf* hallucination.

al'ludere *vi*: ~ **a** to allude to, hint at.

allu'minio *sm* aluminium (*Brit*), aluminum (*US*).

allun'gare *vt* to lengthen; (*distendere*) to prolong, extend; (*diluire*) to water down; ~**rsi** *vr* to lengthen; (*ragazzo*) to stretch, grow taller; (*sdraiarsi*) to lie down, stretch out.

allusi'one *sf* hint, allusion.

alluvi'one *sf* flood.

al'meno *av* at least // *cong*: (**se**) ~ if only; (**se**) ~ **piovesse!** if only it would rain!

a'lone *sm* halo.

'Alpi *sfpl*: **le** ~ the Alps.

alpi'nismo *sm* mountaineering, climbing; **alpi'nista, i, e** *sm/f* mountaineer, climber.

al'pino, a *ag* Alpine; mountain *cpd*.

al'quanto *av* rather, a little; ~, **a** *det* a

certain amount of, some // *pronome* a certain amount, some; ~**i(e)** *det pl*, *pronome pl* several, quite a few.

alt *escl* halt!, stop! // *sm*: **dare l'~** to call a halt.

alta'lena *sf* (*a funi*) swing; (*in bilico, anche fig*) seesaw.

al'tare *sm* altar.

alte'rare *vt* to alter, change; (*cibo*) to adulterate; (*registro*) to falsify; (*persona*) to irritate; ~**rsi** *vr* to alter; (*cibo*) to go bad; (*persona*) to lose one's temper.

al'terco, chi *sm* altercation, wrangle.

alter'nare *vt*, ~**rsi** *vr* to alternate; **alterna'tivo, a** *ag* alternative // *sf* alternative; **alter'nato, a** *ag* alternate; (*ELETTR*) alternating; **alterna'tore** *sm* alternator.

al'terno, a *ag* alternate; **a giorni ~i** on alternate days, every other day.

al'tezza [al'tettsa] *sf* height; width, breadth; depth; pitch; (*GEO*) latitude; (*titolo*) highness; (*fig: nobiltà*) greatness; **essere all'~ di** to be on a level with; (*fig*) to be up to *o* equal to; **altez'zoso, a** *ag* haughty.

al'ticcio, a, ci, ce [al'tittʃo] *ag* tipsy.

altipi'ano *sm* = **altopiano**.

alti'tudine *sf* altitude.

'alto, a *ag* high; (*persona*) tall; (*tessuto*) wide, broad; (*sonno, acque*) deep; (*suono*) high(-pitched); (*GEO*) upper; (: *settentrionale*) northern // *sm* top (part) // *av* high; (*parlare*) aloud, loudly; **il palazzo è ~ 20 metri** the building is 20 metres high; **il tessuto è ~ 70 cm** the material is 70 cm wide; **ad ~a voce** aloud; **a notte ~a** in the dead of night; **in ~** up, upwards; **at the top; dall'~ in o al basso** up and down; **degli ~i e bassi** (*fig*) ups and downs; ~**a fedeltà** high fidelity, hi-fi; ~**a moda** haute couture.

alto'forno *sm* blast furnace.

altolo'cato, a *ag* of high rank, highly placed.

altopar'lante *sm* loudspeaker.

altopi'ano *sm*, *pl* **altipiani** plateau, upland plain.

altret'tanto, a *ag*, *pronome* as much; (*pl*) as many // *av* equally; **tanti auguri!** — **grazie,** ~ all the best! — thank you, the same to you.

'altri *pronome inv* (*qualcuno*) somebody; (: *in espressioni negative*) anybody; (*un'altra persona*) another (person).

altri'menti *av* otherwise.

'altro, a ♦ *det* 1 (*diverso*) other, different; **questa è un'~a cosa** that's another *o* a different thing

2 (*supplementare*) other; **prendi un ~ cioccolatino** have another chocolate; **hai avuto ~e notizie?** have you had any more *o* any other news?

3 (*nel tempo*): **l'~ giorno** the other day;

l'altr'anno last year; l'~ ieri the day before yesterday; domani l'~ the day after tomorrow; quest'~ mese next month
4: d'~a parte on the other hand
◆ *pronome* 1 (*persona, cosa diversa o supplementare*): un ~, un'~a another (one); lo farà un ~ someone else will do it; ~i(e) others; gli ~i (*la gente*) others, other people; l'uno e l'~ both (of them); aiutarsi l'un l'~ to help one another; da un giorno all'~ from day to day; (*nel giro di 24 ore*) from one day to the next; (*da un momento all'altro*) any day now
2 (*sostantivato: solo maschile*) something else; (: *in espressioni interrogative*) anything else; non ho ~ da dire I have nothing else *o* I don't have anything else to say; più che ~ above all; se non ~ at least; tra l'~ among other things; ci mancherebbe ~! that's all we need!; non faccio ~ che lavorare I do nothing but work; contento? — ~ che! are you pleased? — and how!; *vedi* senza, noialtri, voialtri, tutto.

al'tronde *av*: d'~ on the other hand.

al'trove *av* elsewhere, somewhere else.

al'trui *ag inv* other people's // *sm*: l'~ other people's belongings *pl*.

altru'ista, i, e *ag* altruistic.

al'tura *sf* (*rialto*) height, high ground; (*alto mare*) open sea; pesca d'~ deep-sea fishing.

a'lunno, a *sm/f* pupil.

alve'are *sm* hive.

'alveo *sm* riverbed.

al'zare [al'tsare] *vt* to raise, lift; (*issare*) to hoist; (*costruire*) to build, erect; ~rsi *vr* to rise; (*dal letto*) to get up; (*crescere*) to grow tall (*o* taller); ~ le spalle to shrug one's shoulders; ~rsi in piedi to stand up, get to one's feet; al'zata *sf* lifting, raising; un'alzata di spalle a shrug.

a'mabile *ag* lovable; (*vino*) sweet.

a'maca, che *sf* hammock.

amalga'mare *vt*, ~rsi *vr* to amalgamate.

a'mante *ag*: ~ di (*musica etc*) fond of // *sm/f* lover/mistress.

a'mare *vt* to love; (*amico, musica, sport*) to like.

amareggi'ato, a [amared'dʒato] *ag* upset, saddened.

ama'rena *sf* sour black cherry.

ama'rezza [ama'rettsa] *sf* bitterness.

a'maro, a *ag* bitter // *sm* bitterness; (*liquore*) bitters *pl*.

ambasci'ata [ambaʃ'ʃata] *sf* embassy; (*messaggio*) message; ambascia'tore, 'trice *sm/f* ambassador/ambassadress.

ambe'due *ag inv*: ~ i ragazzi both boys // *pronome inv* both.

ambien'tare *vt* to acclimatize; (*romanzo, film*) to set; ~rsi *vr* to get used to one's surroundings.

ambi'ente *sm* environment; (*fig: insieme di persone*) milieu; (*stanza*) room.

am'biguo, a *ag* ambiguous; (*persona*) shady.

am'bire *vt* (*anche: vi*: ~ a) to aspire to.

'ambito *sm* sphere, field.

ambizi'one [ambit'tsjone] *sf* ambition; ambizi'oso, a *ag* ambitious.

'ambo *ag inv* both.

'ambra *sf* amber; ~ grigia ambergris.

ambu'lante *ag* travelling, itinerant.

ambu'lanza [ambu'lantsa] *sf* ambulance.

ambula'torio *sm* (*studio medico*) surgery.

amenità *sf inv* pleasantness *q*.

a'meno, a *ag* pleasant; (*strano*) funny, strange; (*spiritoso*) amusing.

A'merica *sf*: l'~ America; l'~ latina Latin America; ameri'cano, a *ag, sm/f* American.

a'mianto *sm* asbestos.

a'mica *sf vedi* amico.

ami'chevole [ami'kevole] *ag* friendly.

ami'cizia [ami'tʃittsja] *sf* friendship; ~e *sfpl* (*amici*) friends.

a'mico, a, ci, che *sm/f* friend; (*amante*) boyfriend/girlfriend; ~ del cuore *o* intimo bosom friend.

'amido *sm* starch.

ammac'care *vt* (*pentola*) to dent; (*persona*) to bruise; ~rsi *vr* to bruise.

ammaes'trare *vt* (*animale*) to train; (*persona*) to teach.

ammai'nare *vt* to lower, haul down.

amma'larsi *vr* to fall ill; amma'lato, a *ag* ill, sick // *sm/f* sick person; (*paziente*) patient.

ammali'are *vt* (*fig*) to enchant, charm.

am'manco, chi *sm* (ECON) deficit.

ammanet'tare *vt* to handcuff.

ammas'sare *vt* (*ammucchiare*) to amass; (*raccogliere*) to gather together; ~rsi *vr* to pile up; to gather; am'masso *sm* mass; (*mucchio*) pile, heap; (ECON) stockpile.

ammat'tire *vi* to go mad.

ammaz'zare [ammat'tsare] *vt* to kill; ~rsi *vr* (*uccidersi*) to kill o.s.; (*rimanere ucciso*) to be killed; ~rsi di lavoro to work o.s. to death.

am'menda *sf* amends *pl*; (DIR, SPORT) fine; fare ~ di qc to make amends for sth.

am'messo, a *pp di* ammettere // *cong*: ~ che supposing that.

am'mettere *vt* to admit; (*riconoscere: fatto*) to acknowledge, admit; (*permettere*) to allow, accept; (*supporre*) to suppose.

ammez'zato [ammed'dzato] *sm* (*anche*: piano ~) mezzanine, entresol.

ammic'care *vi*: ~ (a) to wink (at).

amminis'trare *vt* to run, manage;

(REL, DIR) to administer; **amministra'tivo, a** ag administrative; **amministra'tore** sm administrator; (di condominio) flats manager; **amministratore delegato** managing director; **amministrazi'one** sf management; administration.

ammiragli'ato [ammiraʎ'ʎato] sm admiralty.

ammi'raglio [ammi'raʎʎo] sm admiral.

ammi'rare vt to admire; **ammira'tore, 'trice** sm/f admirer; **ammirazi'one** sf admiration.

ammis'sibile ag admissible, acceptable.

ammissi'one sf admission; (approvazione) acknowledgment.

ammobili'are vt to furnish.

am'modo, a 'modo av properly // ag inv respectable, nice.

am'mollo sm: **lasciare in ~** to leave to soak.

ammo'niaca sf ammonia.

ammoni'mento sm warning; admonishment.

ammo'nire vt (avvertire) to warn; (rimproverare) to admonish; (DIR) to caution.

ammon'tare vi: **~ a** to amount to // sm (total) amount.

ammorbi'dente sm fabric conditioner.

ammorbi'dire vt to soften.

ammortiz'zare [ammortid'dzare] vt (ECON) to pay off, amortize; (: spese d'impianto) to write off; (AUT, TECN) to absorb, deaden; **ammortizza'tore** sm (AUT, TECN) shock-absorber.

ammucchi'are [ammuk'kjare] vt, **~rsi** vr to pile up, accumulate.

ammuf'fire vi to go mouldy (Brit) o moldy (US).

ammutina'mento sm mutiny.

ammuti'narsi vr to mutiny.

ammuto'lire vi to be struck dumb.

amnis'tia sf amnesty.

'amo sm (PESCA) hook; (fig) bait.

a'more sm love; **~i** smpl love affairs; **il tuo bambino è un ~** your baby's a darling; **fare l'~** o **all'~** to make love; **per ~** o **per forza** by hook or by crook; **amor proprio** self-esteem, pride; **amo'revole** ag loving, affectionate.

a'morfo, a ag amorphous; (fig: persona) lifeless.

amo'roso, a ag (affettuoso) loving, affectionate; (d'amore: sguardo) amorous; (: poesia, relazione) love cpd.

ampi'ezza [am'pjettsa] sf width, breadth; spaciousness; (fig: importanza) scale, size.

'ampio, a ag wide, broad; (spazioso) spacious; (abbondante: vestito) loose; (: gonna) full; (: spiegazione) ample, full.

am'plesso sm (eufemismo) embrace.

ampli'are vt (ingrandire) to enlarge; (allargare) to widen.

amplifi'care vt to amplify; (magnificare) to extol; **amplifica'tore** sm (TECN, MUS) amplifier.

am'polla sf (vasetto) cruet.

ampu'tare vt (MED) to amputate.

anabbagli'ante [anabbaʎ'ʎante] ag (AUT) dipped (Brit), dimmed (US); **~i** smpl dipped (Brit) o dimmed (US) headlights.

a'nagrafe sf (registro) register of births, marriages and deaths; (ufficio) registration office.

analfa'beta, i, e ag, sm/f illiterate.

anal'gesico, a, ci, che [anal'dʒɛziko] ag, sm analgesic.

a'nalisi sf inv analysis; (MED: esame) test; **~ grammaticale** parsing; **ana'lista, i, e** sm/f analyst; (PSIC) (psycho)analyst.

analiz'zare [analid'dzare] vt to analyse; (MED) to test.

analo'gia, 'gie [analo'dʒia] sf analogy.

a'nalogo, a, ghi, ghe ag analogous.

'ananas sm inv pineapple.

anar'chia [anar'kia] sf anarchy; **a'narchico, a, ci, che** ag anarchic(al) // sm/f anarchist.

'ANAS sigla f (= Azienda Nazionale Autonoma delle Strade) national roads department.

anato'mia sf anatomy; **ana'tomico, a, ci, che** ag anatomical; (sedile) contoured.

'anatra sf duck.

'anca, che sf (ANAT) hip; (ZOOL) haunch.

'anche cong (inoltre, pure) also, too; (perfino) even; **vengo anch'io** I'm coming too; **~ se** even if.

an'cora av still; (di nuovo) again; (di più) some more; (persino) **~ più forte** even stronger; **non ~** not yet; **~ una volta** once more, once again; **~ un po'** a little more; (di tempo) a little longer.

'ancora sf anchor; **gettare/levare l'~** to cast/weigh anchor; **anco'raggio** sm anchorage; **anco'rare** vt, **ancorarsi** vr to anchor.

anda'mento sm progress, movement; course; state.

an'dante ag (corrente) current; (di poco pregio) cheap, second-rate // sm (MUS) andante.

an'dare sm: **a lungo ~** in the long run // vi to go; (essere adatto): **~ a** to suit; (piacere): **il suo comportamento non mi va** I don't like the way he behaves; **ti va di andare al cinema?** do you feel like going to the cinema?; **andarsene** to go away; **questa camicia va lavata** this shirt needs a wash o should be washed; **~ a cavallo** to ride; **~ in macchina/aereo** to go by car/plane; **~ a fare qc** to go and do sth; **~ a pescare/sciare** to go fishing/skiing; **~ a male** to go bad; **come va?**

(*lavoro, progetto*) how are things?; **come va?** — **bene, grazie!** how are you? — fine, thanks!; **va fatto entro oggi** it's got to be done today; **ne va della nostra vita** our lives are at stake; **an'data** *sf* going; (*viaggio*) outward journey; **biglietto di sola andata** single (*Brit*) *o* one-way ticket; **biglietto di andata e ritorno** return (*Brit*) *o* round-trip (*US*) ticket; **anda'tura** *sf* (*modo di andare*) walk, gait; (*SPORT*) pace; (*NAUT*) tack.

an'dazzo [an'dattso] *sm* (*peg*): **prendere un brutto ~** to take a turn for the worse.

andirivi'eni *sm inv* coming and going.

'andito *sm* corridor, passage.

an'drone *sm* entrance hall.

a'neddoto *sm* anecdote.

ane'lare *vi*: **~ a** (*fig*) to long for, yearn for.

a'nelito *sm* (*fig*): **~ di** longing *o* yearning for.

a'nello *sm* ring; (*di catena*) link.

a'nemico, a, ci, che *ag* anaemic.

a'nemone *sm* anemone.

aneste'sia *sf* anaesthesia; **anes'tetico, a, ci, che** *ag, sm* anaesthetic.

anfite'atro *sm* amphitheatre.

an'fratto *sm* ravine.

an'gelico, a, ci, che [an'dʒɛliko] *ag* angelic(al).

'angelo ['andʒelo] *sm* angel; **~ custode** guardian angel.

anghe'ria [ange'ria] *sf* vexation.

an'gina [an'dʒina] *sf* tonsillitis; **~ pectoris** angina.

angli'cano, a *ag* Anglican.

angli'cismo [angli'tʃizmo] *sm* anglicism.

anglo'sassone *ag* Anglo-Saxon.

ango'lare *ag* angular.

angolazi'one [angolat'tsjone] *sf* (*FOT etc, fig*) angle.

'angolo *sm* corner; (*MAT*) angle.

an'goscia, sce [an'gɔʃʃa] *sf* deep anxiety, anguish *q*; **angosci'oso, a** *ag* (*d'angoscia*) anguished; (*che dà angoscia*) distressing, painful.

angu'illa *sf* eel.

an'guria *sf* watermelon.

an'gustia *sf* (*ansia*) anguish, distress; (*povertà*) poverty, want.

angusti'are *vt* to distress; **~rsi** *vr*: **~rsi (per)** to worry (about).

an'gusto, a *ag* (*stretto*) narrow; (*fig*) mean, petty.

'anice ['anitʃe] *sm* (*CUC*) aniseed; (*BOT*) anise.

a'nidride *sf* (*CHIM*): **~ carbonica/solforosa** carbon/sulphur dioxide.

'anima *sf* soul; (*abitante*) inhabitant; **non c'era ~ viva** there wasn't a living soul.

ani'male *sm, ag* animal.

ani'mare *vt* to give life to, liven up; (*incoraggiare*) to encourage; **~rsi** *vr* to become animated, come to life;

ani'mato, a *ag* animate; (*vivace*) lively, animated; (*: strada*) busy; **anima'tore, 'trice** *sm/f* guiding spirit; (*CINEMA*) animator; (*di festa*) life and soul; **animazi'one** *sf* liveliness; (*di strada*) bustle; (*CINEMA*) animation; **animazione teatrale** amateur dramatics.

'animo *sm* (*mente*) mind; (*cuore*) heart; (*coraggio*) courage; (*disposizione*) character, disposition; **avere in ~ di fare qc** to intend *o* have a mind to do sth; **perdersi d'~** to lose heart.

'anitra *sf* = **anatra**.

anna'cquare *vt* to water down, dilute.

annaffi'are *vt* to water; **annaffia'toio** *sm* watering can.

an'nali *smpl* annals.

annas'pare *vi* to flounder.

an'nata *sf* year; (*importo annuo*) annual amount; **vino d'~** vintage wine.

annebbi'are *vt* (*fig*) to cloud; **~rsi** *vr* to become foggy; (*vista*) to become dim.

annega'mento *sm* drowning.

anne'gare *vt, vi* to drown; **~rsi** *vr* (*accidentalmente*) to drown; (*deliberatamente*) to drown o.s.

anne'rire *vt* to blacken // *vi* to become black.

an'nesso, a *pp di* **annettere** // *ag* attached; (*POL*) annexed; **... e tutti gli ~i e connessi** ... and so on and so forth.

an'nettere *vt* (*POL*) to annex; (*accludere*) to attach.

annichi'lare, annichi'lire [anniki'lare, anniki'lire] *vt* to annihilate.

anni'darsi *vr* to nest.

annienta'mento *sm* annihilation, destruction.

annien'tare *vt* to annihilate, destroy.

anniver'sario *sm* anniversary.

'anno *sm* year.

anno'dare *vt* to knot, tie; (*fig: rapporto*) to form.

annoi'are *vt* to bore; (*seccare*) to annoy; **~rsi** *vr* to be bored; to be annoyed.

anno'tare *vt* (*registrare*) to note, note down; (*commentare*) to annotate; **annotazi'one** *sf* note; annotation.

annove'rare *vt* to number.

annu'ale *ag* annual.

annu'ario *sm* yearbook.

annu'ire *vi* to nod; (*acconsentire*) to agree.

annul'lare *vt* to annihilate, destroy; (*contratto, francobollo*) to cancel; (*matrimonio*) to annul; (*sentenza*) to quash; (*risultati*) to declare void.

annunci'are *vt* to announce; (*dar segni rivelatori*) to herald; **annuncia'tore, 'trice** *sm/f* (*RADIO, TV*) announcer; **l'Annunciazi'one** *sf* the Annunciation.

an'nuncio [an'nuntʃo] *sm* announcement; (*fig*) sign; **~ pubblicitario**

advertisement; **~i economici** classified advertisements, small ads.

'**annuo, a** *ag* annual, yearly.

annu'sare *vt* to sniff, smell; **~ tabacco** to take snuff.

'**ano** *sm* anus.

anoma'lia *sf* anomaly.

a'nomalo, a *ag* anomalous.

a'nonimo, a *ag* anonymous // *sm* (*autore*) anonymous writer (*o painter etc*); **società ~a** (*COMM*) joint stock company.

anor'male *ag* abnormal // *sm/f* subnormal person; (*eufemismo*) homosexual.

ANSA *sigla f* (= *Agenzia Nazionale Stampa Associata*) press agency.

'**ansa** *sf* (*manico*) handle; (*di fiume*) bend, loop.

'**ansia, ansietà** *sf* anxiety.

ansi'mare *vi* to pant.

ansi'oso, a *ag* anxious.

'**anta** *sf* (*di finestra*) shutter; (*di armadio*) door.

antago'nismo *sm* antagonism.

an'tartico, a, ci, che *ag* Antarctic // *sm*: **l'A~** the Antarctic.

antece'dente [antetʃe'dɛnte] *ag* preceding, previous.

ante'fatto *sm* previous events *pl*; previous history.

antegu'erra *sm* pre-war period.

ante'nato *sm* ancestor, forefather.

an'tenna *sf* (*RADIO, TV*) aerial; (*ZOOL*) antenna, feeler; (*NAUT*) yard.

ante'prima *sf* preview.

anteri'ore *ag* (*ruota, zampa*) front; (*fatti*) previous, preceding.

antia'ereo, a *ag* anti-aircraft.

antia'tomico, a, ci, che *ag* antinuclear; **rifugio ~** fallout shelter.

antibi'otico, a, ci, che *ag, sm* antibiotic.

anti'camera *sf* anteroom; **fare ~** to wait (for an audience).

antichità [antiki'ta] *sf inv* antiquity; (*oggetto*) antique.

antici'pare [antitʃi'pare] *vt* (*consegna, visita*) to bring forward, anticipate; (*somma di denaro*) to pay in advance; (*notizia*) to disclose // *vi* to be ahead of time; **anticipazi'one** *sf* anticipation; (*di notizia*) advance information; (*somma di denaro*) advance; **an'ticipo** *sm* anticipation; (*di denaro*) advance; **in anticipo** early, in advance.

an'tico, a, chi, che *ag* (*quadro, mobili*) antique; (*dell'antichità*) ancient; **all'~a** old-fashioned.

anticoncezio'nale [antikontʃettsjo'nale] *sm* contraceptive.

anticonfor'mista, i, e *ag, sm/f* nonconformist.

anti'corpo *sm* antibody.

anti'furto *sm* (*anche:* **sistema ~**) anti-

theft device.

An'tille *sfpl*: **le ~** the West Indies.

antin'cendio [antin'tʃendjo] *ag inv* fire *cpd*.

antio'rario [antio'rarjo] *ag*: **in senso ~** anticlockwise.

anti'pasto *sm* hors d'œuvre.

antipa'tia *sf* antipathy, dislike; **anti'patico, a, ci, che** *ag* unpleasant, disagreeable.

antiquari'ato *sm* antique trade; **un oggetto d'~** an antique.

anti'quario *sm* antique dealer.

anti'quato, a *ag* antiquated, old-fashioned.

antise'mita, i, e *ag* anti-Semitic.

anti'settico, a, ci, che *ag, sm* antiseptic.

antista'minico, a, ci, che *ag, sm* antihistamine.

antolo'gia, 'gie [antolo'dʒia] *sf* anthology.

anu'lare *ag* ring *cpd* // *sm* third finger.

'**anzi** ['antsi] *av* (*invece*) on the contrary; (*o meglio*) or rather, or better still.

anzianità [antsjani'ta] *sf* old age; (*AMM*) seniority.

anzi'ano, a [an'tsjano] *ag* old; (*AMM*) senior // *sm/f* old person; senior member.

anziché [antsi'ke] *cong* rather than.

anzi'tutto [antsi'tutto] *av* first of all.

apa'tia *sf* apathy, indifference.

'**ape** *sf* bee.

aperi'tivo *sm* aperitif.

a'perto, a *pp di* **aprire** // *ag* open; **all'~** in the open (air).

aper'tura *sf* opening; (*ampiezza*) width, spread; (*POL*) approach; (*FOT*) aperture; **~ alare** wing span.

'**apice** ['apitʃe] *sm* apex; (*fig*) height.

apicol'tore *sm* beekeeper.

ap'nea *sf*: **immergersi in ~** to dive without breathing apparatus.

a'polide *ag* stateless.

apoples'sia *sf* (*MED*) apoplexy.

a'postolo *sm* apostle.

a'postrofo *sm* apostrophe.

appa'gare *vt* to satisfy; **~rsi** *vr*: **~rsi di** to be satisfied with.

ap'palto *sm* (*COMM*) contract; **dare/prendere in ~ un lavoro** to let out/undertake a job on contract.

appan'nare *vt* (*vetro*) to mist; (*metallo*) to tarnish; (*vista*) to dim; **~rsi** *vr* to mist over; to tarnish; to grow dim.

appa'rato *sm* equipment, machinery; (*ANAT*) apparatus; **~ scenico** (*TEATRO*) props *pl*.

apparecchi'are [apparek'kjare] *vt* to prepare; (*tavola*) to set // *vi* to set the table; **apparecchia'tura** *sf* equipment; (*macchina*) machine, device.

appa'recchio [appa'rekkjo] *sm* piece of apparatus, device; (*aeroplano*) aircraft *inv*; ~ **televisivo/telefonico** television set/telephone.

appa'rente *ag* apparent; **appa'renza** *sf* appearance; in *o* **all'apparenza** apparently, to all appearances.

appa'rire *vi* to appear; *(sembrare)* to seem, appear; **appari'scente** *ag (colore)* garish, gaudy; *(bellezza)* striking.

apparta'mento *sm* flat *(Brit)*, apartment *(US)*.

appar'tarsi *vr* to withdraw; **appar'tato, a** *ag (luogo)* secluded.

apparte'nere *vi*: ~ **a** to belong to.

appassio'nare *vt* to thrill; *(commuovere)* to move; ~**rsi a qc** to take a great interest in sth; to be deeply moved by sth; **appassio'nato, a** *ag* passionate; *(entusiasta)*: **appassionato (di)** keen (on).

appas'sire *vi* to wither.

appel'larsi *vr (ricorrere)*: ~ **a** to appeal to; *(DIR)*: ~ **contro** to appeal against; **ap'pello** *sm* roll-call; *(implorazione, DIR)* appeal; **fare appello a** to appeal to.

ap'pena *av (a stento)* hardly, scarcely; *(solamente, da poco)* just // *cong* as soon as; *(non)* ~ **furono arrivati ...** as soon as they had arrived ...; ~ **... che** *o* **quando** no sooner ... than.

ap'pendere *vt* to hang (up).

appen'dice [appen'ditʃe] *sf* appendix; **romanzo d'~** popular serial.

appendi'cite [appendi'tʃite] *sf* appendicitis.

Appen'nini *smpl*: **gli** ~ the Apennines.

appesan'tire *vt* to make heavy; ~**rsi** *vr* to grow stout.

ap'peso, a *pp di* **appendere**.

appe'tito *sm* appetite; **appeti'toso, a** *ag* appetising; *(fig)* attractive, desirable.

appia'nare *vt* to level; *(fig)* to smooth away, iron out.

appiat'tire *vt* to flatten; ~**rsi** *vr* to become flatter; *(farsi piatto)* to flatten o.s.; ~**rsi al suolo** to lie flat on the ground.

appic'care *vt*: ~ **il fuoco a** to set fire to, set on fire.

appicci'care [appittʃi'kare] *vt* to stick; *(fig)*: ~ **qc a qn** to palm sth off on sb; ~**rsi** *vr* to stick; *(fig: persona)* to cling.

appi'eno *av* fully.

appigli'arsi [appiʎ'ʎarsi] *vr*: ~ **a** *(afferrarsi)* to take hold of; *(fig)* to cling to; **ap'piglio** *sm* hold; *(fig)* pretext.

appiso'larsi *vr* to doze off.

applau'dire *vt, vi* to applaud; **ap'plauso** *sm* applause.

appli'care *vt* to apply; *(regolamento)* to enforce; ~**rsi** *vr* to apply o.s.; **applicazi'one** *sf* application; enforcement.

appoggi'are [appod'dʒare] *vt (mettere contro)*: ~ **qc a qc** to lean *o* rest sth against sth; *(fig: sostenere)* to support;

~**rsi** *vr*: ~**rsi a** to lean against; *(fig)* to rely upon; **ap'poggio** *sm* support.

appollai'arsi *vr (anche fig)* to perch.

ap'porre *vt* to affix.

appor'tare *vt* to bring.

apposita'mente *av* specially; *(apposta)* on purpose.

ap'posito, a *ag* appropriate.

ap'posta *av* on purpose, deliberately.

appos'tare *vt* to lie in wait for; ~**rsi** *vr* to lie in wait.

ap'prendere *vt (imparare)* to learn; *(comprendere)* to grasp.

appren'dista, i, e *sm/f* apprentice.

apprensi'one *sf* apprehension; **appren'sivo, a** *ag* apprehensive.

ap'presso *av (accanto, vicino)* close by, near; *(dietro)* behind; *(dopo, più tardi)* after, later // *ag inv (dopo)*: **il giorno** ~ the next day; ~ **a** *prep (vicino a)* near, close to.

appres'tare *vt* to prepare, get ready; ~**rsi** *vr*: ~**rsi a fare qc** to prepare *o* get ready to do sth.

ap'pretto *sm* starch.

apprez'zabile [appret'tsabile] *ag* noteworthy, significant.

apprezza'mento [apprettsa'mento] *sm* appreciation; *(giudizio)* opinion.

apprez'zare [appret'tsare] *vt* to appreciate.

ap'proccio [ap'prɔttʃo] *sm* approach.

appro'dare *vi (NAUT)* to land; *(fig)*: **non** ~ **a nulla** to come to nothing; **ap'prodo** *sm* landing; *(luogo)* landing-place.

approfit'tare *vi*: ~ **di** to make the most of, profit by.

approfon'dire *vt* to deepen; *(fig)* to study in depth.

appropri'ato, a *ag* appropriate.

approssi'marsi *vr*: ~ **a** to approach.

approssima'tivo, a *ag* approximate, rough; *(impreciso)* inexact, imprecise.

appro'vare *vt (condotta, azione)* to approve of; *(candidato)* to pass; *(progetto di legge)* to approve; **approvazi'one** *sf* approval.

approvvigio'nare [approvvidʒo'nare] *vt* to supply; ~**rsi** *vr* to lay in provisions, stock up; ~ **qn di qc** to supply sb with sth.

appunta'mento *sm* appointment; *(amoroso)* date; **darsi** ~ to arrange to meet (one another).

appun'tato *sm (CARABINIERI)* corporal.

ap'punto *sm* note; *(rimprovero)* reproach // *av (proprio)* exactly, just; **per l'~!**, ~! exactly!

appu'rare *vt* to check, verify.

apribot'tiglie [apribot'tiʎʎe] *sm inv* bottleopener.

a'prile *sm* April.

a'prire *vt* to open; *(via, cadavere)* to open up; *(gas, luce, acqua)* to turn on // *vi* to open; ~**rsi** *vr* to open; ~**rsi a qn** to confide in sb, open one's heart to sb.

apris'catole *sm inv* tin (*Brit*) *o* can opener.

a'quario *sm* = **acquario**.

'aquila *sf* (*ZOOL*) eagle; (*fig*) genius.

aqui'lone *sm* (*giocattolo*) kite; (*vento*) North wind.

A'rabia 'Saudita *sf*: l'~ Saudi Arabia.

'arabo, a *ag*, *sm/f* Arab // *sm* (*LING*) Arabic.

a'rachide [a'rakide] *sf* peanut.

ara'gosta *sf* crayfish; lobster.

a'raldica *sf* heraldry.

a'rancia, ce [a'rantʃa] *sf* orange; **aranci'ata** *sf* orangeade; **a'rancio** *sm* (*BOT*) orange tree; (*colore*) orange // *ag inv* (*colore*) orange; **aranci'one** *ag inv*: (*color*) arancione bright orange.

a'rare *vt* to plough (*Brit*), plow (*US*).

a'ratro *sm* plough (*Brit*), plow (*US*).

a'razzo [a'rattso] *sm* tapestry.

arbi'trare *vt* (*SPORT*) to referee; to umpire; (*DIR*) to arbitrate.

arbi'trario, a *ag* arbitrary.

ar'bitrio *sm* will; (*abuso, sopruso*) arbitrary act.

'arbitro *sm* arbiter, judge; (*DIR*) arbitrator; (*SPORT*) referee; (: *TENNIS, CRICKET*) umpire.

ar'busto *sm* shrub.

'arca, che *sf* (*sarcofago*) sarcophagus; l'~ di Noè Noah's ark.

ar'cangelo [ar'kandʒelo] *sm* archangel.

ar'cano, a *ag* arcane, mysterious.

ar'cata *sf* (*ARCHIT, ANAT*) arch; (*ordine di archi*) arcade.

archeolo'gia [arkeolo'dʒia] *sf* arch(a)eology; **arche'ologo, a, gi, ghe** *sm/f* arch(a)eologist.

ar'chetto [ar'ketto] *sm* (*MUS*) bow.

archi'tetto [arki'tetto] *sm* architect; **archi'tettura** *sf* architecture.

ar'chivio [ar'kivjo] *sm* archives *pl*; (*INFORM*) file.

arci'ere [ar'tʃere] *sm* archer.

ar'cigno, a [ar'tʃiɲɲo] *ag* grim, severe.

arci'vescovo [artʃi'veskovo] *sm* archbishop.

'arco *sm* (*arma, MUS*) bow; (*ARCHIT*) arch; (*MAT*) arc.

arcoba'leno *sm* rainbow.

arcu'ato, a *ag* curved, bent; dalle gambe ~e bow-legged.

ar'dente *ag* burning; (*fig*) burning, ardent.

'ardere *vt, vi* to burn.

ar'desia *sf* slate.

ar'dire *vi* to dare // *sm* daring; **ar'dito, a** *ag* brave, daring, bold; (*sfacciato*) bold.

ar'dore *sm* blazing heat; (*fig*) ardour, fervour.

'arduo, a *ag* arduous, difficult.

'area *sf* area; (*EDIL*) land, ground.

a'rena *sf* arena; (*per corride*) bullring;

(*sabbia*) sand.

are'narsi *vr* to run aground.

areo'plano *sm* = **aeroplano**.

'argano *sm* winch.

argente'ria [ardʒente'ria] *sf* silverware, silver.

argenti'ere [ardʒen'tjere] *sm* silversmith.

Argen'tina [ardʒen'tina] *sf*: l'~ Argentina; **argen'tino, a** *ag*, *sm/f* Argentinian.

ar'gento [ar'dʒento] *sm* silver; ~ vivo quicksilver.

ar'gilla [ar'dʒilla] *sf* clay.

'argine ['ardʒine] *sm* embankment, bank; (*diga*) dyke, dike.

argomen'tare *vi* to argue.

argo'mento *sm* argument; (*motivo*) motive; (*materia, tema*) subject.

argu'ire *vt* to deduce.

ar'guto, a *ag* sharp, quick-witted; **ar'guzia** *sf* wit; (*battuta*) witty remark.

'aria *sf* air; (*espressione, aspetto*) air, look; (*MUS: melodia*) tune; (: *di opera*) aria; mandare all'~ qc to ruin *o* upset sth; all'~ aperta in the open (air).

'arido, a *ag* arid.

arieggi'are [arjed'dʒare] *vt* (*cambiare aria*) to air; (*imitare*) to imitate.

ari'ete *sm* ram; (*MIL*) battering ram; (*dello zodiaco*): A~ Aries.

a'ringa, ghe *sf* herring *inv*.

a'rista *sf* (*CUC*) chine of pork.

aristo'cratico, a, ci, che *ag* aristocratic.

arit'metica *sf* arithmetic.

arlec'chino [arlek'kino] *sm* harlequin.

'arma, i *sf* weapon, arm; (*parte dell'esercito*) arm; **chiamare alle ~i** to call up (*Brit*), draft (*US*); **sotto le ~i** in the army (*o* forces); **alle ~i!** to arms!; ~ **da fuoco** firearm.

ar'madio *sm* cupboard; (*per abiti*) wardrobe.

armamen'tario *sm* equipment, instruments *pl*.

arma'mento *sm* (*MIL*) armament; (: *materiale*) arms *pl*, weapons *pl*; (*NAUT*) fitting out; manning.

ar'mare *vt* to arm; (*arma da fuoco*) to cock; (*NAUT: nave*) to rig, fit out; to man; (*EDIL: volta, galleria*) to prop up, shore up; ~**rsi** *vr* to arm o.s.; (*MIL*) to take up arms; **arma'tura** *sf* (*struttura di sostegno*) framework; (*impalcatura*) scaffolding; (*STORIA*) armour *q*, suit of armour.

armeggi'are [armed'dʒare] *vi*: ~ (intorno a qc) to mess about (with sth).

armis'tizio [armis'tittsjo] *sm* armistice.

armo'nia *sf* harmony; **ar'monica, a, ci, che** *ag* harmonic; (*fig*) harmonious // *sf* (*MUS*) harmonica; **armoni'oso, a** *ag* harmonious.

armoniz'zare [armonid'dzare] *vt* to

harmonize; (*colori, abiti*) to match // *vi*
to be in harmony; to match.

ar'nese *sm* tool, implement; (*oggetto in-determinato*) thing, contraption; male in
~ (*malvestito*) badly dressed; (*di salute malferma*) in poor health; (*di condizioni economiche*) down-at heel.

'arnia *sf* hive.

a'roma, i *sm* aroma; fragrance; ~i *smpl* herbs and spices; aro'matico, a,
ci, che *ag* aromatic; (*cibo*) spicy.

'arpa *sf* (MUS) harp.

ar'peggio [ar'peddʒo] *sm* (MUS)
arpeggio.

ar'pia *sf* (*anche fig*) harpy.

arpi'one *sm* (*gancio*) hook; (*cardine*)
hinge; (PESCA) harpoon.

arrabat'tarsi *vr* to do all one can, strive.

arrabbi'are *vi* (*cane*) to be affected with
rabies; ~rsi *vr* (*essere preso dall'ira*) to
get angry, fly into a rage; arrabbi'ato,
a *ag* rabid, with rabies; furious, angry.

arraf'fare *vt* to snatch, seize; (*sottrarre*)
to pinch.

arrampi'carsi *vr* to climb (up).

arran'care *vi* to limp, hobble.

arran'giare [arran'dʒare] *vt* to arrange;
~rsi *vr* to manage, do the best one can.

arre'care *vt* to bring; (*causare*) to
cause.

arreda'mento *sm* (*studio*) interior
design; (*mobili etc*) furnishings *pl*.

arre'dare *vt* to furnish; arreda'tore,
'trice *sm/f* interior designer; ar'redo
sm fittings *pl*, furnishings *pl*.

ar'rendersi *vr* to surrender.

arres'tare *vt* (*fermare*) to stop, halt;
(*catturare*) to arrest; ~rsi *vr* (*fermarsi*)
to stop; ar'resto *sm* (*cessazione*) stop-ping; (*fermata*) stop; (*cattura*, MED)
arrest; subire un arresto to come to a
stop *o* standstill; mettere agli arresti to
place under arrest; arresti domiciliari
house arrest *sg*.

arre'trare *vt*, *vi* to withdraw; arre'trato,
a *ag* (*lavoro*) behind schedule; (*paese,
bambino*) backward; (*numero di
giornale*) back *cpd*; arretrati *smpl*
arrears.

arric'chire [arrik'kire] *vt* to enrich; ~rsi
vr to become rich.

arricci'are [arrit'tʃare] *vt* to curl; ~ il
naso to turn up one's nose.

ar'ringa, ghe *sf* harangue; (DIR)
address by counsel.

arrischi'are [arris'kjare] *vt* to risk; ~rsi
vr to venture, dare; arrischi'ato, a *ag*
risky; (*temerario*) reckless, rash.

arri'vare *vi* to arrive; (*accadere*) to
happen, occur; ~ a (*livello, grado etc*) to
reach; lui arriva a Roma alle 7 he gets
to *o* arrives at Rome at 7; non ci arrivo
I can't reach it; (*fig: non capisco*) I
can't understand it.

arrive'derci [arrive'dertʃi] *escl* goodbye!

arrive'derla *escl* (*forma di cortesia*)
goodbye!

arri'vista, i, e *sm/f* go-getter.

ar'rivo *sm* arrival; (SPORT) finish, finish-ing line.

arro'gante *ag* arrogant.

arro'lare *vb* = arruolare.

arros'sire *vi* (*per vergogna, timidezza*)
to blush, flush; (*per gioia, rabbia*) to
flush.

arros'tire *vt* to roast; (*pane*) to toast;
(*ai ferri*) to grill.

ar'rosto *sm*, *ag inv* roast.

arro'tare *vt* to sharpen; (*investire con
un veicolo*) to run over.

arroto'lare *vt* to roll up.

arroton'dare *vt* (*forma, oggetto*) to
round; (*stipendio*) to add to; (*somma*) to
round off.

arrovel'larsi *vr*: ~ (il cervello) to rack
one's brains.

arruf'fare *vt* to ruffle; (*fili*) to tangle;
(*fig: questione*) to confuse.

arruggi'nire [arruddʒi'nire] *vt* to rust;
~rsi *vr* to rust; (*fig*) to become rusty.

arruo'lare (MIL) *vt* to enlist; ~rsi *vr* to
enlist, join up.

arse'nale *sm* (MIL) arsenal; (*cantiere
navale*) dockyard.

'arso, a *pp di* ardere // *ag* (*bruciato*)
burnt; (*arido*) dry; ar'sura *sf* (*calore
opprimente*) burning heat; (*siccità*)
drought.

'arte *sf* art; (*abilità*) skill.

arte'fatto, a *ag* (*cibo*) adulterated; (*fig:
modi*) artificial.

ar'tefice [ar'tefitʃe] *sm/f* craftsman/
woman; (*autore*) author.

ar'teria *sf* artery.

'artico, a, ci, che *ag* Arctic.

artico'lare *ag* (ANAT) of the joints,
articular // *vt* to articulate;
(*suddividere*) to divide, split up;
articolazi'one *sf* articulation; (ANAT,
TECN) joint.

ar'ticolo *sm* article; ~ di fondo
(STAMPA) leader, leading article.

'Artide *sm*: l'~ the Arctic.

artifici'ale [artifi'tʃale] *ag* artificial.

arti'ficio [arti'fitʃo] *sm* (*espediente*) trick,
artifice; (*ricerca di effetto*) artificiality.

artigia'nato [artidʒa'nato] *sm* craftsman-ship; craftsmen *pl*.

artigi'ano, a [arti'dʒano] *sm/f* crafts-man/woman.

artiglie'ria [artiʎʎe'ria] *sf* artillery.

ar'tiglio [ar'tiʎʎo] *sm* claw; (*di rapaci*)
talon.

ar'tista, i, e *sm/f* artist; ar'tistico, a,
ci, che *ag* artistic.

'arto *sm* (ANAT) limb.

ar'trite *sf* (MED) arthritis.

ar'trosi *sf* osteoarthritis.

ar'zillo, a [ar'dzillo] *ag* lively, sprightly.

a'scella [aʃ'ʃella] *sf* (ANAT) armpit.

ascen'dente [aʃʃen'dɛnte] *sm* ancestor; (*fig*) ascendancy; (ASTR) ascendant.

ascensi'one [aʃʃen'sjone] *sf* (ALPINISMO) ascent; (REL): **l'A~** the Ascension.

ascen'sore [aʃʃen'sore] *sm* lift.

a'scesa [aʃ'ʃesa] *sf* ascent; (*al trono*) accession.

a'scesso [aʃ'ʃesso] *sm* (MED) abscess.

'ascia, *pl* **'asce** ['aʃʃa] *sf* axe.

asciugaca'pelli [aʃʃugaka'pelli] *sm* hairdrier.

asciuga'mano [aʃʃuga'mano] *sm* towel.

asciu'gare [aʃʃu'gare] *vt* to dry; **~rsi** *vr* to dry o.s.; (*diventare asciutto*) to dry.

asci'utto, a [aʃ'ʃutto] *ag* dry; (*fig: magro*) lean; (: *burbero*) curt; **restare a bocca ~a** (*fig*) to be disappointed.

ascol'tare *vt* to listen to; **ascolta'tore, 'trice** *sm/f* listener; **as'colto** *sm*: **essere o stare in ascolto** to be listening; **dare o prestare ascolto (a)** to pay attention (to).

as'falto *sm* asphalt.

asfissi'are *vt* to suffocate, asphyxiate; (*fig*) to bore to tears.

'Asia *sf*: **l'~** Asia; **asi'atico, a, ci, che** *ag*, *sm/f* Asiatic, Asian.

a'silo *sm* refuge, sanctuary; **~ (d'infanzia)** nursery(-school); **~ nido** crèche; **~ politico** political asylum.

'asino *sm* donkey, ass.

'asma *sf* asthma.

'asola *sf* buttonhole.

as'parago, gi *sm* asparagus *q*.

aspet'tare *vt* to wait for; (*anche* COMM) to await; (*aspettarsi*) to expect // *vi* to wait; **~rsi** *vr* to expect; **~ un bambino** to be expecting (a baby); **questo non me l'aspettavo** I wasn't expecting this; **aspetta'tiva** *sf* wait; expectation; **inferiore all'aspettativa** worse than expected; **essere in aspettativa** (AMM) to be on leave of absence.

as'petto *sm* (*apparenza*) aspect, appearance, look; (*punto di vista*) point of view; **di bell'~** good-looking.

aspi'rante *ag* (*attore etc*) aspiring // *sm/f* candidate, applicant.

aspira'polvere *sm inv* vacuum cleaner.

aspi'rare *vt* (*respirare*) to breathe in, inhale; (*sog: apparecchi*) to suck (up) // *vi*: **~ a** to aspire to; **aspira'tore** *sm* extractor fan.

aspi'rina *sf* aspirin.

aspor'tare *vt* (*anche* MED) to remove, take away.

'aspro, a *ag* (*sapore*) sour, tart; (*odore*) acrid, pungent; (*voce, clima, fig*) harsh; (*superficie*) rough; (*paesaggio*) rugged.

assaggi'are [assad'dʒare] *vt* to taste.

as'sai *av* (*molto*) a lot, much; (: *con ag*) very; (*a sufficienza*) enough // *ag inv* (*quantità*) a lot of, much; (*numero*) a lot of, many; **~ contento** very pleased.

assa'lire *vt* to attack, assail.

as'salto *sm* attack, assault.

assassi'nare *vt* to murder; to assassinate; (*fig*) to ruin; **assas'sinio** *sm* murder; assassination; **assas'sino, a** *ag* murderous // *sm/f* murderer; assassin.

'asse *sm* (TECN) axle; (MAT) axis // *sf* board; **~ f da stiro** ironing board.

assedi'are *vt* to besiege; **as'sedio** *sm* siege.

asse'gnare [assen'ɲare] *vt* to assign, allot; (*premio*) to award.

as'segno [as'seɲɲo] *sm* allowance; (*anche*: **~ bancario**) cheque (Brit), check (US); **contro ~** cash on delivery; **~ circolare** bank draft; **~ sbarrato** crossed cheque; **~ di viaggio** traveller's cheque; **~ a vuoto** dud cheque; **~i familiari** ≈ child benefit *q*.

assem'blea *sf* assembly.

assen'nato, a *ag* sensible.

as'senso *sm* assent, consent.

as'sente *ag* absent; (*fig*) faraway, vacant; **as'senza** *sf* absence.

asses'sore *sm* (POL) councillor.

assesta'mento *sm* (*sistemazione*) arrangement; (EDIL, GEOL) settlement.

asses'tare *vt* (*mettere in ordine*) to put in order, arrange; **~rsi** *vr* to settle in; **~ un colpo a qn** to deal sb a blow.

asse'tato, a *ag* thirsty, parched.

as'setto *sm* order, arrangement; (NAUT, AER) trim; **in ~ di guerra** on a war footing.

assicu'rare *vt* (*accertare*) to ensure; (*infondere certezza*) to assure; (*fermare, legare*) to make fast, secure; (*fare un contratto di assicurazione*) to insure; **~rsi** *vr* (*accertarsi*): **~rsi (di)** to make sure (of); (*contro il furto etc*): **~rsi (contro)** to insure o.s. (against); **assicu'rato, a** *ag* insured // *sf* (*anche*: **lettera assicurata**) registered letter; **assicurazi'one** *sf* assurance; insurance.

assidera'mento *sm* exposure.

assi'eme *av* (*insieme*) together; **~ a** *prep* (together) with.

assil'lare *vt* to pester, torment.

as'sillo *sm* (*fig*) worrying thought.

as'sise *sfpl* (DIR) assizes; **Corte f d'A~** Court of Assizes, ≈ Crown Court (Brit).

assis'tente *sm/f* assistant; **~ sociale** social worker; **~ di volo** (AER) steward/stewardess.

assis'tenza [assis'tɛntsa] *sf* assistance; **~ ospedaliera** free hospital treatment; **~ sanitaria** health service; **~ sociale** welfare services *pl*.

as'sistere *vt* (*aiutare*) to assist, help; (*curare*) to treat // *vi*: **~ (a qc)** (*essere presente*) to be present (at sth), to attend (sth).

'asso *sm* ace; **piantare qn in ~** to leave sb in the lurch.

associ'are [asso'tʃare] *vt* to associate; (*rendere partecipe*): ~ **qn a** (*affari*) to take sb into partnership in; (*partito*) to make sb a member of; ~**rsi** *vr* to enter into partnership; ~**rsi a** to become a member of, join; (*dolori, gioie*) to share in; ~ **qn alle carceri** to take sb to prison.

associazi'one [assotʃat'tsjone] *sf* association; (*COMM*) association, society; ~ **a o per delinquere** (*DIR*) criminal association.

asso'dato, a *ag* well-founded.

assogget'tare [assoddʒet'tare] *vt* to subject, subjugate.

asso'lato, a *ag* sunny.

assol'dare *vt* to recruit.

as'solto, a *pp di* **assolvere**.

assoluta'mente *av* absolutely.

asso'luto, a *ag* absolute.

assoluzi'one [assolut'tsjone] *sf* (*DIR*) acquittal; (*REL*) absolution.

as'solvere *vt* (*DIR*) to acquit; (*REL*) to absolve; (*adempiere*) to carry out, perform.

assomigli'are [assomiʎ'ʎare] *vi*: ~ **a** to resemble, look like.

asson'nato, a *ag* sleepy.

asso'pirsi *vr* to doze off.

assor'bente *ag* absorbent // *sm*: ~ **igienico** sanitary towel; ~ **interno** tampon.

assor'bire *vt* to absorb; (*fig: far proprio*) to assimilate.

assor'dare *vt* to deafen.

assorti'mento *sm* assortment.

assor'tito, a *ag* assorted; matched, matching.

as'sorto, a *ag* absorbed, engrossed.

assottigli'are [assottiʎ'ʎare] *vt* to make thin, to thin; (*aguzzare*) to sharpen; (*ridurre*) to reduce; ~**rsi** *vr* to grow thin; (*fig: ridursi*) to be reduced.

assue'fare *vt* to accustom; ~**rsi a** to get used to, accustom o.s. to.

as'sumere *vt* (*impiegato*) to take on, engage; (*responsabilità*) to assume, take upon o.s.; (*contegno, espressione*) to assume, put on; (*droga*) to consume; **as'sunto, a** *pp di* **assumere** // *sm* (*tesi*) proposition.

assurdità *sf inv* absurdity; **dire delle ~** to talk nonsense.

as'surdo, a *ag* absurd.

'asta *sf* pole; (*modo di vendita*) auction.

astante'ria *sf* casualty department.

aste'nersi *vr*: ~ (**da**) to abstain (from), refrain (from); (*POL*) to abstain (from).

aste'risco, schi *sm* asterisk.

astice ['astitʃe] *sm* lobster.

asti'nenza [asti'nɛntsa] *sf* abstinence; **essere in crisi di** ~ to suffer from withdrawal symptoms.

'astio *sm* rancour, resentment.

as'tratto, a *ag* abstract.

'astro *sm* star.

'astro... *prefisso*: **astrolo'gia** [astrolo'dʒia] *sf* astrology; **as'trologo, a, ghi, ghe** *sm/f* astrologer; **astro'nauta, i, e** *sm/f* astronaut; **astro'nave** *sf* space ship; **astrono'mia** *sf* astronomy; **astro'nomico, a, ci, che** *ag* astronomic(al).

as'tuccio [as'tuttʃo] *sm* case, box, holder.

as'tuto, a *ag* astute, cunning, shrewd; **as'tuzia** *sf* astuteness, shrewdness; (*azione*) trick.

A'tene *sf* Athens.

ate'neo *sm* university.

'ateo, a *ag, sm/f* atheist.

at'lante *sm* atlas.

at'lantico, a, ci, che *ag* Atlantic // *sm*: **l'A~, l'Oceano A~** the Atlantic, the Atlantic Ocean.

at'leta, i, e *sm/f* athlete; **at'letica** *sf* athletics *sg*; **atletica leggera** track and field events *pl*; **atletica pesante** weightlifting and wrestling.

atmos'fera *sf* atmosphere.

a'tomico, a, ci, che *ag* atomic; (*nucleare*) atomic, atom *cpd*, nuclear.

'atomo *sm* atom.

'atrio *sm* entrance hall, lobby.

a'troce [a'trotʃe] *ag* (*che provoca orrore*) dreadful; (*terribile*) atrocious.

attacca'mento *sm* (*fig*) attachment, affection.

attacca'panni *sm* hook, peg; (*mobile*) hall stand.

attac'care *vt* (*unire*) to attach; (*cucendo*) to sew on; (*far aderire*) to stick (on); (*appendere*) to hang (up); (*assalire: anche fig*) to attack; (*iniziare*) to begin, start; (*fig: contagiare*) to pass on // *vi* to stick, adhere; ~**rsi** *vr* to stick, adhere; (*trasmettersi per contagio*) to be contagious; (*afferrarsi*): ~**rsi (a)** to cling (to); (*fig: affezionarsi*): ~**rsi (a)** to become attached (to); ~ **discorso** to start a conversation; **at'tacco, chi** *sm* (*azione offensiva: anche fig*) attack; (*MED*) attack, fit; (*SCI*) binding; (*ELETTR*) socket.

atteggia'mento [atteddʒa'mento] *sm* attitude.

atteggi'arsi [atted'dʒarsi] *vr*: ~ **a** to pose as.

attem'pato, a *ag* elderly.

at'tendere *vt* to wait for, await // *vi*: ~ **a** to attend to.

atten'dibile *ag* (*storia*) credible; (*testimone*) reliable.

atte'nersi *vr*: ~ **a** to keep o stick to.

atten'tare *vi*: ~ **a** to make an attempt on; **atten'tato** *sm* attack; **attentato alla vita di qn** attempt on sb's life.

at'tento, a *ag* attentive; (*accurato*) careful, thorough; **stare** ~ **a qc** to pay attention to sth // *escl* be careful!

attenu'ante *sf* (*DIR*) extenuating

circumstance.

attenu'are *vt* to attenuate; (*dolore, rumore*) to lessen, deaden; (*pena, tasse*) to alleviate; ~**rsi** *vr* to ease, abate.

attenzi'one [atten'tsjone] *sf* attention // *escl* watch out!, be careful!

atter'raggio [atter'raddʒo] *sm* landing.

atter'rare *vt* to bring down // *vi* to land.

atter'rire *vt* to terrify.

at'teso, a *pp di* **attendere** // *sf* waiting; (*tempo trascorso aspettando*) wait; **essere in attesa di qc** to be waiting for sth.

attes'tato *sm* certificate.

'attico, ci *sm* attic.

at'tiguo, a *ag* adjacent, adjoining.

attil'lato, a *ag* (*vestito*) close-fitting, tight; (*persona*) dressed up.

'attimo *sm* moment; **in un ~** in a moment.

atti'nente *ag:* ~ **a** relating to, concerning.

atti'rare *vt* to attract.

atti'tudine *sf* (*disposizione*) aptitude; (*atteggiamento*) attitude.

atti'vare *vt* to activate; (*far funzionare*) to set going, start.

attività *sf inv* activity; (*COMM*) assets *pl*.

at'tivo, a *ag* active; (*COMM*) profit-making, credit *cpd* // *sm* (*COMM*) assets *pl*; **in ~** in credit.

attiz'zare [attit'tsare] *vt* (*fuoco*) to poke.

'atto *sm* act; (*azione, gesto*) action, act, deed; (*DIR: documento*) deed, document; ~**i** *smpl* (*di congressi etc*) proceedings; **mettere in ~** to put into action; **fare ~ di fare qc** to make as if to do sth.

at'tonito, a *ag* dumbfounded, astonished.

attorcigli'are [attortʃiʎ'ʎare] *vt,* ~**rsi** *vr* to twist.

at'tore, 'trice *smf* actor/actress.

at'torno *av,* ~ **a** *prep* round, around, about.

at'tracco, chi *sm* (*NAUT*) docking *q*; berth.

attra'ente *ag* attractive.

at'trarre *vt* to attract; **attrat'tiva** *sf* (*fig: fascino*) attraction, charm; **at'tratto, a** *pp di* **attrarre.**

attraversa'mento *sm:* ~ **pedonale** pedestrian crossing.

attraver'sare *vt* to cross; (*città, bosco, fig: periodo*) to go through; (*sog: fiume*) to run through.

attra'verso *prep* through; (*da una parte all'altra*) across.

attrazi'one [attrat'tsjone] *sf* attraction.

attrez'zare [attret'tsare] *vt* to equip; (*NAUT*) to rig; **attrezza'tura** *sf* equipment *q*; rigging; **at'trezzo** *sm* tool, instrument; (*SPORT*) piece of equipment.

attribu'ire *vt:* ~ **qc a qn** (*assegnare*) to

give *o* award sth to sb; (*quadro etc*) to attribute sth to sb; **attri'buto** *sm* attribute.

at'trice [at'tritʃe] *sf vedi* **attore.**

at'trito *sm* (*anche fig*) friction.

attu'ale *ag* (*presente*) present; (*di attualità*) topical; (*che è in atto*) actual; **attualità** *sf inv* topicality; (*avvenimento*) current event; **attual'mente** *av* at the moment, at present.

attu'are *vt* to carry out; ~**rsi** *vr* to be realized.

attu'tire *vt* to deaden, reduce.

au'dace [au'datʃe] *ag* audacious, daring, bold; (*provocante*) provocative; (*sfacciato*) impudent, bold; **au'dacia** *sf* audacity, daring; boldness; provocativeness; impudence.

audiovi'sivo, a *ag* audiovisual.

audizi'one [audit'tsjone] *sf* hearing; (*MUS*) audition.

'auge ['audʒe] *sf:* **in ~** popular.

augu'rare *vt* to wish; ~**rsi qc** to hope for sth.

au'gurio *sm* (*presagio*) omen; (*voto di benessere etc*) (good) wish; **essere di buon/cattivo ~** to be of good omen/be ominous; **fare gli ~i a qn** to give sb one's best wishes; **tanti ~i!** all the best!

'aula *sf* (*scolastica*) classroom; (*universitaria*) lecture theatre; (*di edificio pubblico*) hall.

aumen'tare *vt, vi* to increase; **au'mento** *sm* increase.

au'reola *sf* halo.

au'rora *sf* dawn.

ausili'are *ag, sm, smf* auxiliary.

aus'picio [aus'pitʃo] *sm* omen; (*protezione*) patronage; **sotto gli ~i di** under the auspices of.

aus'tero, a *ag* austere.

Aus'tralia *sf:* **l'~** Australia; **australi'ano, a** *ag, smf* Australian.

'Austria *sf:* **l'~** Austria; **aus'triaco, a, ci, che** *ag, smf* Austrian.

au'tentico, a, ci, che *ag* (*quadro, firma*) authentic, genuine; (*fatto*) true, genuine.

au'tista, i *sm* driver.

'auto *sf inv* car.

autoade'sivo, a *ag* self-adhesive // *sm* sticker.

autobiogra'fia *sf* autobiography.

auto'botte *sf* tanker.

'autobus *sm inv* bus.

auto'carro *sm* lorry (*Brit*), truck.

autocorri'era *sf* coach, bus.

au'tografo, a *ag, sm* autograph.

auto'linea *sf* bus company.

au'toma, i *sm* automaton.

auto'matico, a, ci, che *ag* automatic // *sm* (*bottone*) snap fastener; (*fucile*) automatic.

automazi'one [automat'tsjone] *sf* automation.

auto'mezzo [auto'mɛddzo] *sm* motor vehicle.

auto'mobile *sf* (motor) car.

autono'mia *sf* autonomy; (*di volo*) range.

au'tonomo, a *ag* autonomous, independent.

autop'sia *sf* post-mortem (examination), autopsy.

auto'radio *sf inv* (*apparecchio*) car radio; (*autoveicolo*) radio car.

au'tore, 'trice *sm/f* author; **l'~ del furto** the person who committed the robbery.

auto'revole *ag* authoritative; (*persona*) influential.

autori'messa *sf* garage.

autorità *sf inv* authority.

autoriz'zare [autorid'dzare] *vt* (*permettere*) to authorize; (*giustificare*) to allow, sanction; **autorizzazi'one** *sf* authorization.

autoscu'ola *sf* driving school.

autos'top *sm* hitchhiking; **autostop'pista, i, e** *sm/f* hitchhiker.

autos'trada *sf* motorway (*Brit*), highway (*US*).

auto'treno *sm* articulated lorry (*Brit*), semi (trailer) (*US*).

autove'icolo *sm* motor vehicle.

autovet'tura *sf* (motor) car.

au'tunno *sm* autumn.

avam'braccio, pl(f) cia [avam'brattʃo] *sm* forearm.

avangu'ardia *sf* vanguard.

a'vanti *av* (*stato in luogo*) in front; (*moto: andare, venire*) forward; (*tempo: prima*) before // *prep* (*luogo*): ~ **a** before, in front of; (*tempo*): ~ **Cristo** before Christ // *escl* (*entrate*) come (o go) in!; (*MIL*) forward!; (*coraggio*) come on! // *sm inv* (*SPORT*) forward; ~ **e indietro** backwards and forwards; **andare ~** to go forward; (*continuare*) to go on; (*precedere*) to go (on) ahead; (*orologio*) to be fast; **essere ~ negli studi** to be well advanced with one's studies.

avanza'mento [avantsa'mento] *sm* progress; promotion.

avan'zare [avan'tsare] *vt* (*spostare in avanti*) to move forward, advance; (*domanda*) to put forward; (*promuovere*) to promote; (*essere creditore*): ~ **qc da qn** to be owed sth by sb // *vi* (*andare avanti*) to move forward, advance; (*fig: progredire*) to make progress; (*essere d'avanzo*) to be left, remain; **avan'zata** *sf* (*MIL*) advance; **a'vanzo** *sm* (*residuo*) remains *pl*, leftovers *pl*; (*MAT*) remainder; (*COMM*) surplus; **averne d'avanzo di qc** to have more than enough of sth; **avanzo di galera** (*fig*) jailbird.

ava'ria *sf* (*guasto*) damage; (: *meccanico*) breakdown.

a'varo, a *ag* avaricious, miserly // *sm* miser.

a'vena *sf* oats *pl*.

a'vere ◆ *sm* (*COMM*) credit; **gli ~i** (*ricchezze*) wealth *sg*

◆ *vt* **1** (*possedere*) to have; **ha due bambini/una bella casa** she has (got) two children/a lovely house; **ha i capelli lunghi** he has (got) long hair; **non ho da mangiare/bere** I've (got) nothing to eat/ drink, I don't have anything to eat/drink

2 (*indossare*) to wear, have on; **aveva una maglietta rossa** he was wearing *o* he had on a red tee-shirt; **ha gli occhiali** he wears *o* has glasses

3 (*ricevere*) to get; **hai avuto l'assegno?** did you get *o* have you had the cheque?

4 (*età, dimensione*) to be; **ha 9 anni** he is 9 (years old); **la stanza ha 3 metri di lunghezza** the room is 3 metres in length; *vedi* **fame, paura** etc

5 (*tempo*): **quanti ne abbiamo oggi?** what's the date today?; **ne hai per molto?** will you be long?

6 (*fraseologia*): **avercela con qn** to be angry with sb; **cos'hai?** what's wrong *o* what's the matter (with you)?; **non ha niente a che vedere** *o* **fare con me** it's got nothing to do with me

◆ *vb ausiliare* **1** to have; **aver bevuto/ mangiato** to have drunk/eaten

2 (+ *da* + *infinito*): ~ **da fare qc** to have to do sth; **non hai che da chiederlo** you only have to ask him.

'avi *smpl* ancestors, forefathers.

avia'tore, 'trice *sm/f* aviator, pilot.

aviazi'one [avjat'tsjone] *sf* aviation; (*MIL*) air force.

avidità *sf* eagerness; greed.

'avido, a *ag* eager; (*peg*) greedy.

avo'cado *sm* avocado.

a'vorio *sm* ivory.

Avv. *abbr* = **avvocato**.

avvalla'mento *sm* sinking *q*; (*effetto*) depression.

avvalo'rare *vt* to confirm.

avvam'pare *vi* (*incendio*) to flare up.

avvantaggi'are [avvantad'dʒare] *vt* to favour; ~**rsi** *vr*: ~**rsi negli affari/sui concorrenti** to get ahead in business/of one's competitors.

avvele'nare *vt* to poison.

avve'nente *ag* attractive, charming.

avveni'mento *sm* event.

avve'nire *vi, vb impers* to happen, occur // *sm* future.

avven'tarsi *vr*: ~ **su** *o* **contro qn/qc** to hurl o.s. *o* rush at sb/sth.

avven'tato, a *ag* rash, reckless.

avven'tizio, a [avven'tittsjo] *ag* (*impiegato*) temporary; (*guadagno*) casual.

av'vento *sm* advent, coming; (*REL*): **l'A~** Advent.

avven'tore *sm* (regular) customer.

avven'tura *sf* adventure; *(amorosa)* affair.

avventu'rarsi *vr* to venture.

avventu'roso, a *ag* adventurous.

avve'rarsi *vr* to come true.

av'verbio *sm* adverb.

avver'sario, a *ag* opposing // *sm* opponent, adversary.

av'verso, a *ag (contrario)* contrary; *(sfavorevole)* unfavourable.

avver'tenza [avver'tɛntsa] *sf (ammonimento)* warning; *(cautela)* care; *(premessa)* foreword; ~e *sfpl (istruzioni per l'uso)* instructions.

avverti'mento *sm* warning.

avver'tire *vt (avvisare)* to warn; *(rendere consapevole)* to inform, notify; *(percepire)* to feel.

av'vezzo, a [av'vettso] *ag:* ~ a used to.

avvia'mento *sm (atto)* starting; *(effetto)* start; *(AUT)* starting; *(: dispositivo)* starter; *(COMM)* goodwill.

avvi'are *vt (mettere sul cammino)* to direct; *(impresa, trattativa)* to begin, start; *(motore)* to start; ~rsi *vr* to set off, set out.

avvicen'darsi [avvitʃen'darsi] *vr* to alternate.

avvici'nare [avvitʃi'nare] *vt* to bring near; *(trattare con: persona)* to approach; ~rsi *vr* ~rsi (a qn/qc) to approach (sb/sth), draw near to (sb/sth).

avvi'lire *vt (umiliare)* to humiliate; *(degradare)* to disgrace; *(scoraggiare)* to dishearten, discourage; ~rsi *vr (abbattersi)* to lose heart.

avvilup'pare *vt (avvolgere)* to wrap up; *(ingarbugliare)* to entangle.

avvinaz'zato, a [avvinat'tsato] *ag* drunk.

av'vincere [av'vintʃere] *vt* to charm, enthral.

avvinghi'are [avvin'gjare] *vt* to clasp; ~rsi *vr:* ~rsi a to cling to.

avvi'sare *vt (far sapere)* to inform; *(mettere in guardia)* to warn; **av'viso** *sm* warning; *(annuncio)* announcement; *(: affisso)* notice; *(inserzione pubblicitaria)* advertisement; a mio avviso in my opinion.

avvis'tare *vt* to sight.

avvi'tare *vt* to screw down *(o in)*.

avviz'zire [avvit'tsire] *vi* to wither.

avvo'cato, 'essa *sm/f (DIR)* barrister *(Brit)*, lawyer; *(fig)* defender, advocate.

av'volgere [av'vɔldʒere] *vt* to roll up; *(avviluppare)* to wrap up; ~rsi *vr (avvilupparsi)* to wrap o.s. up; **avvol'gibile** *sm* roller blind *(Brit)*, blind.

avvol'toio *sm* vulture.

azi'enda [ad'dzjɛnda] *sf* business, firm, concern; ~ agricola farm.

azio'nare [attsjo'nare] *vt* to activate.

azi'one [at'tsjone] *sf* action; *(COMM)* share; **azio'nista, i, e** *sm/f (COMM)* shareholder.

a'zoto [ad'dzɔto] *sm* nitrogen.

azzan'nare [attsan'nare] *vt* to sink one's teeth into.

azzar'darsi [addzar'darsi] *vr:* ~ a fare to dare (to) do; **azzar'dato, a** *ag (impresa)* risky; *(risposta)* rash.

az'zardo [ad'dzardo] *sm* risk.

azzec'care [attsek'kare] *vt (risposta etc)* to get right.

azzuf'farsi [attsuf'farsi] *vr* to come to blows.

az'zurro, a [ad'dzurro] *ag* blue // *sm (colore)* blue; **gli ~i** *(SPORT)* the Italian national team.

B

bab'beo *sm* simpleton.

'babbo *sm (fam)* dad, daddy; **B~ natale** Father Christmas.

bab'buccia, ce [bab'buttʃa] *sf* slipper; *(per neonati)* bootee.

ba'bordo *sm (NAUT)* port side.

ba'cato, a *ag* worm-eaten, rotten.

'bacca, che *sf* berry.

baccalà *sm* dried salted cod; *(fig peg)* dummy.

bac'cano *sm* din, clamour.

bac'cello [bat'tʃɛllo] *sm* pod.

bac'chetta [bak'ketta] *sf (verga)* stick, rod; *(di direttore d'orchestra)* baton; *(di tamburo)* drumstick; ~ **magica** magic wand.

baci'are [ba'tʃare] *vt* to kiss; ~rsi *vr* to kiss (one another).

baci'nella [batʃi'nɛlla] *sf* basin.

ba'cino [ba'tʃino] *sm* basin; *(MINERALOGIA)* field, bed; *(ANAT)* pelvis; *(NAUT)* dock.

'bacio ['batʃo] *sm* kiss.

'baco, chi *sm* worm; ~ da seta silkworm.

ba'dare *vi (fare attenzione)* to take care, be careful; *(occuparsi di):* ~ a to look after, take care of; *(dar ascolto):* ~ a to pay attention to; bada ai fatti tuoi! mind your own business!

ba'dia *sf* abbey.

ba'dile *sm* shovel.

'baffi *smpl* moustache *sg; (di animale)* whiskers; ridere sotto i ~ to laugh up one's sleeve; leccarsi i ~ to lick one's lips.

bagagli'aio [bagaʎ'ʎajo] *sm* luggage van *(Brit)* o car *(US)*; *(AUT)* boot *(Brit)*, trunk *(US)*.

ba'gagli [ba'gaʎʎi] *smpl* luggage *sg*.

bagli'ore [baʎ'ʎore] *sm* flash, dazzling light; un ~ di speranza a ray of hope.

ba'gnante [baɲ'ɲante] *smf* bather.

ba'gnare [baɲ'ɲare] *vt* to wet; *(inzuppare)* to soak; *(innaffiare)* to water; *(sog: fiume)* to flow through; *(: mare)* to wash, bathe; ~**rsi** *vr* (*al mare*) to go swimming *o* bathing; (*in vasca*) to have a bath.

ba'gnato, a [baɲ'ɲato] *ag* wet.

ba'gnino [baɲ'ɲino] *sm* lifeguard.

'bagno ['baɲɲo] *sm* bath; (*locale*) bathroom; (~**i** *smpl* (*stabilimento*) baths; **fare il** ~ to have a bath; (*nel mare*) to go swimming *o* bathing; **fare il** ~ **a qn** to give sb a bath; **mettere a** ~ to soak; ~ **schiuma** bubble bath.

bagnoma'ria [baɲɲoma'ria] *sm*: **cuocere a** ~ to cook in a double saucepan.

'baia *sf* bay.

baio'netta *sf* bayonet.

balaus'trata *sf* balustrade.

balbet'tare *vi* to stutter, stammer; (*bimbo*) to babble // *vt* to stammer out.

balbuzi'ente [balbut'tsjɛnte] *ag* stuttering, stammering.

bal'cone *sm* balcony.

baldac'chino [baldak'kino] *sm* canopy.

bal'danza [bal'dantsa] *sf* self-confidence, boldness.

'baldo, a *ag* bold, daring.

bal'doria *sf*: **fare** ~ to have a riotous time.

ba'lena *sf* whale.

baie'nare *vb impers*: **balena** there's lightning // *vi* to flash; **mi balenò un'idea** an idea flashed through my mind; **ba'leno** *sm* flash of lightning; **in un baleno** in a flash.

ba'lestra *sf* crossbow.

ba'lia *sf*: **in** ~ **di** at the mercy of.

'balla *sf* (*di merci*) bale; (*fandonia*) (tall) story.

bal'lare *vt, vi* to dance; **bal'lata** *sf* ballad.

balle'rina *sf* dancer; ballet dancer; (*scarpa*) ballet shoe.

balle'rino *sm* dancer; ballet dancer.

bal'letto *sm* ballet.

'ballo *sm* dance; (*azione*) dancing *q*; **essere in** ~ (*fig: persona*) to be involved; (*: cosa*) to be at stake.

ballot'taggio [ballot'taddʒo] *sm* (POL) second ballot.

balne'are *ag* seaside *cpd*; (*stagione*) bathing.

ba'locco, chi *sm* toy.

ba'lordo, a *ag* stupid, senseless.

'balsamo *sm* (*aroma*) balsam; (*lenimento*, *fig*) balm.

'Baltico *sm*: **il** (*mar*) ~ the Baltic (Sea).

balu'ardo *sm* bulwark.

'balza ['baltsa] *sf* (*dirupo*) crag; (*di stoffa*) frill.

bal'zare [bal'tsare] *vi* to bounce; (*lanciarsi*) to jump, leap; **'balzo** *sm* bounce; jump, leap; (*del terreno*) crag.

bam'bagia [bam'badʒa] *sf* (*ovatta*) cotton wool (*Brit*), absorbent cotton (*US*); (*cascame*) cotton waste.

bam'bina *ag, sf vedi* **bambino**.

bambi'naia *sf* nanny, nurse(maid).

bam'bino, a *sm/f* child.

bam'boccio [bam'bɔttʃo] *sm* plump child; (*pupazzo*) rag doll.

'bambola *sf* doll.

bambù *sm* bamboo.

ba'nale *ag* banal, commonplace.

ba'nana *sf* banana; **ba'nano** *sm* banana tree.

'banca, che *sf* bank; ~ **dei dati** data bank.

banca'rella *sf* stall.

ban'cario, a *ag* banking, bank *cpd* // *sm* bank clerk.

banca'rotta *sf* bankruptcy; **fare** ~ to go bankrupt.

ban'chetto [ban'ketto] *sm* banquet.

banchi'ere [ban'kjere] *sm* banker.

ban'china [ban'kina] *sf* (*di porto*) quay; (*per pedoni, ciclisti*) path; (*di stazione*) platform; ~ **cedevole** (AUT) soft verge (*Brit*) *o* shoulder (US).

'banco, chi *sm* bench; (*di negozio*) counter; (*di mercato*) stall; (*di officina*) (work-)bench; (GEO, *banca*) bank; ~ **di corallo** coral reef; ~ **degli imputati** dock; ~ **di prova** (*fig*) testing ground; ~ **dei testimoni** witness box.

'Bancomat *sm inv* ® automated banking; (*tessera*) cash card.

banco'nota *sf* banknote.

'banda *sf* band; (*di stoffa*) band, stripe; (*lato, parte*) side; ~ **perforata** punch tape.

banderu'ola *sf* (METEOR) weathercock, weathervane.

bandi'era *sf* flag, banner.

ban'dire *vt* to proclaim; (*esiliare*) to exile; (*fig*) to dispense with.

ban'dito *sm* outlaw, bandit.

bandi'tore *sm* (*di aste*) auctioneer.

'bando *sm* proclamation; (*esilio*) exile, banishment; ~ **alle chiacchiere!** that's enough talk!

'bandolo *sm*: **il** ~ **della matassa** (*fig*) the key to the problem.

bar *sm inv* bar.

'bara *sf* coffin.

ba'racca, che *sf* shed, hut; (*peg*) hovel; **mandare avanti la** ~ to keep things going.

bara'onda *sf* hubbub, bustle.

ba'rare *vi* to cheat.

'baratro *sm* abyss.

barat'tare *vt*: ~ **qc con** to barter sth for, swap sth for; **ba'ratto** *sm* barter.

ba'rattolo *sm* (*di latta*) tin; (*di vetro*) jar; (*di coccio*) pot.

'barba *sf* beard; **farsi la** ~ to shave; **farla in** ~ **a qn** (*fig*) to do sth to sb's face; **che** ~! what a bore!

barbabi'etola *sf* beetroot (*Brit*), beet (US); ~ **da zucchero** sugar beet.

bar'barico, a, ci, che *ag* barbarian; barbaric.

'barbaro, a *ag* barbarous; **~i** *smpl* barbarians.

barbi'ere *sm* barber.

bar'bone *sm* (*cane*) poodle; (*vagabondo*) tramp.

bar'buto, a *ag* bearded.

'barca, che *sf* boat; **~ a remi** rowing boat; **barcai'olo** *sm* boatman.

barcol'lare *vi* to stagger.

bar'cone *sm* (*per ponti di barche*) pontoon.

ba'rella *sf* (*lettiga*) stretcher.

ba'rile *sm* barrel, cask.

ba'rista, i, e *sm/f* barman/maid; bar owner.

ba'ritono *sm* baritone.

bar'lume *sm* glimmer, gleam.

ba'rocco, a, chi, che *ag, sm* baroque.

ba'rometro *sm* barometer.

ba'rone *sm* baron; **baro'nessa** *sf* baroness.

'barra *sf* bar; (*NAUT*) helm; (*linea grafica*) line, stroke.

barri'care *vt* to barricade; **barri'cata** *sf* barricade.

barri'era *sf* barrier; (*GEO*) reef.

ba'ruffa *sf* scuffle.

barzel'letta [bardzel'letta] *sf* joke, funny story.

ba'sare *vt* to base, found; **~rsi** *vr*: **~rsi su** (*sog: fatti, prove*) to be based *o* founded on; (*: persona*) to base one's arguments on.

'basco, a, schi, sche *ag* Basque // *sm* (*copricapo*) beret.

'base *sf* base; (*fig: fondamento*) basis; (*POL*) rank and file; **di ~** basic; **in ~ a** on the basis of, according to; **a ~ di caffè** coffee-based.

ba'setta *sf* sideburn.

ba'silica, che *sf* basilica.

ba'silico *sm* basil.

bassi'fondi *smpl* (*fig*) dregs.

'basso, a *ag* low; (*di statura*) short; (*meridionale*) southern // *sm* bottom, lower part; (*MUS*) bass; **la ~a Italia** southern Italy.

bassori'lievo *sm* bas-relief.

'basta *escl* (that's) enough!, that will do!

bas'tardo, a *ag* (*animale, pianta*) hybrid, crossbreed; (*persona*) illegitimate, bastard (*peg*) // *sm/f* illegitimate child, bastard (*peg*).

bas'tare *vi, vb impers* to be enough, be sufficient; **~ a qn** to be enough for sb; **basta chiedere** *o* **chieda a un vigile** you have only to *o* need only ask a policeman.

basti'mento *sm* ship, vessel.

basto'nare *vt* to beat, thrash.

baston'cino [baston'tʃino] *sm* (*SCI*) ski pole.

bas'tone *sm* stick; **~ da passeggio** walking stick.

bat'taglia [bat'taʎʎa] *sf* battle; fight.

bat'taglio [bat'taʎʎo] *sm* (*di campana*) clapper; (*di porta*) knocker.

battagli'one [battaʎ'ʎone] *sm* battalion.

bat'tello *sm* boat.

bat'tente *sm* (*imposta: di porta*) wing, flap; (*: di finestra*) shutter; (*batacchio: di porta*) knocker; (*: di orologio*) hammer; **chiudere i ~i** (*fig*) to shut up shop.

'battere *vt* to beat; (*grano*) to thresh; (*percorrere*) to scour // *vi* (*bussare*) to knock; (*urtare*): **~ contro** to hit *o* strike against; (*pioggia, sole*) to beat down; (*cuore*) to beat; (*TENNIS*) to serve; **~rsi** *vr* to fight; **~ le mani** to clap; **~ i piedi** to stamp one's feet; **~ le ore** to strike the hours; **~ su un argomento** to hammer home an argument; **~ a macchina** to type; **~ bandiera italiana** to fly the Italian flag; **~ in testa** (*AUT*) to knock; **in un batter d'occhio** in the twinkling of an eye.

bat'teri *smpl* bacteria.

batte'ria *sf* battery; (*MUS*) drums *pl*.

bat'tesimo *sm* baptism; christening.

battez'zare [batted'dzare] *vt* to baptize; to christen.

batticu'ore *sm* palpitations *pl*; **avere il ~** to be frightened to death.

batti'mano *sm* applause.

batti'panni *sm inv* carpet-beater.

battis'tero *sm* baptistry.

battis'trada *sm inv* (*di pneumatico*) tread; (*di gara*) pacemaker.

battitap'peto *sm* upright vacuum cleaner.

'battito *sm* beat, throb; **~ cardiaco** heartbeat; **~ della pioggia/dell'orologio** beating of the rain/ticking of the clock.

bat'tuta *sf* blow; (*di macchina da scrivere*) stroke; (*MUS*) bar; beat; (*TEATRO*) cue; (*frase spiritosa*) witty remark; (*di caccia*) beating; (*POLIZIA*) combing, scouring; (*TENNIS*) service.

ba'ule *sm* trunk; (*AUT*) boot (*Brit*), trunk (*US*).

'bava *sf* (*di animale*) slaver, slobber; (*di lumaca*) slime; (*di vento*) breath.

bava'glino [bavaʎ'ʎino] *sm* bib.

ba'vaglio [ba'vaʎʎo] *sm* gag.

'bavero *sm* collar.

ba'zar [bad'dzar] *sm inv* bazaar.

baz'zecola [bad'dzekola] *sf* trifle.

bazzi'care [battsi'kare] *vt* to frequent // *vi*: **~ in/con** to frequent.

be'ato, a *ag* blessed; (*fig*) happy; **~ te!** lucky you!

bec'caccia, ce [bek'kattʃa] *sf* woodcock.

bec'care *vt* to peck; (*fig: raffreddore*) to pick up, catch; **~rsi** *vr* (*fig*) to squabble.

beccheggi'are [bekked'dʒare] *vi* to pitch.

bec'chino [bek'kino] *sm* gravedigger.

'becco, chi *sm* beak, bill; (*di caffettiera etc*) spout; lip.

Be'fana *sf old woman who, according to legend, brings children their presents at the Epiphany; (Epifania) Epiphany; (donna brutta):* b~ hag, witch.

'beffa *sf* practical joke; farsi ~e di qn to make a fool of sb; **bef'fardo, a** *ag* scornful, mocking; **bef'fare** *vt (anche:* beffarsi di) to make a fool of, mock.

'bega, ghe *sf* quarrel.

'begli ['bελλi], **'bei, bel** *ag vedi* **bello.**

be'lare *vi* to bleat.

'belga, gi, ghe *ag, sm/f* Belgian.

'Belgio ['bεldʒo] *sm:* il ~ Belgium.

bel'lezza [bel'lettsa] *sf* beauty.

'bello, a *ag (dav sm* bel *+C,* bell' *+V,* bello *+ s impura, gn, pn, ps, x, z, pl* bei *+C,* begli *+ s impura etc o V)* beautiful, fine, lovely; *(uomo)* handsome // *sm (bellezza)* beauty; *(tempo)* fine weather // *sf (SPORT)* decider // *av:* fa ~ the weather is fine, it's fine; una ~a cifra a considerable sum of money; un bel niente absolutely nothing; è una truffa ~a e buona! it's a real fraud!; è bell'e finito it's already finished; adesso viene il ~ now comes the best bit; sul più ~ at the crucial point; cosa fai di ~? are you doing anything interesting?; belle arti fine arts.

'belva *sf* wild animal.

belve'dere *sm inv* panoramic viewpoint.

benché [ben'ke] *cong* although.

'benda *sf* bandage; *(per gli occhi)* blindfold; **ben'dare** *vt* to bandage; to blindfold.

'bene *av* well; *(completamente, affatto):* è ben difficile it's very difficult // *ag inv:* gente ~ well-to-do people // *sm* good; ~i *smpl (averi)* property *sg,* estate *sg;* io sto ~/poco ~ I'm well/not very well; va ~ all right; volere un ~ dell'anima a qn to love sb very much; un uomo per ~ a respectable man; fare ~ to do the right thing; fare ~ a *(salute)* to be good for; fare del ~ a qn to do sb a good turn; ~i di consumo consumer goods.

bene'detto, a *pp di* **benedire** // *ag* blessed, holy.

bene'dire *vt* to bless; to consecrate; **benedizi'one** *sf* blessing.

benedu'cato, a *ag* well-mannered.

benefi'cenza [benefi't∫entsa] *sf* charity.

bene'ficio [bene'fit∫o] *sm* benefit; con ~ d'inventario *(fig)* with reservations.

be'nefico, a, ci, che *ag* beneficial; charitable.

beneme'renza [beneme'rentsa] *sf* merit.

bene'merito, a *ag* meritorious.

be'nessere *sm* well-being.

benes'tante *ag* well-to-do.

benes'tare *sm* consent, approval.

be'nevolo, a *ag* benevolent.

be'nigno, a [be'niɲɲo] *ag* kind, kindly; *(critica etc)* favourable; *(MED)* benign.

benin'teso *av* of course.

bensì *cong* but (rather).

benve'nuto, a *ag, sm* welcome; dare il ~ a qn to welcome sb.

ben'zina [ben'dzina] *sf* petrol *(Brit),* gas *(US);* fare ~ to get petrol *(Brit)* o gas *(US);* **benzi'naio** *sm* petrol *(Brit)* o gas *(US)* pump attendant.

'bere *vt* to drink; darla a ~ a qn *(fig)* to fool sb.

ber'lina *sf (AUT)* saloon (car) *(Brit),* sedan *(US).*

Ber'lino *sf* Berlin.

ber'noccolo *sm* bump; *(inclinazione)* flair.

ber'retto *sm* cap.

bersagli'are [bersaλ'λare] *vt* to shoot at; *(colpire ripetutamente, fig)* to bombard; **bersagliato dalla sfortuna** dogged by ill fortune.

ber'saglio [ber'saλλo] *sm* target.

bes'temmia *sf* curse; *(REL)* blasphemy.

bestemmi'are *vi* to curse, swear; to blaspheme // *vt* to curse, swear at; to blaspheme.

'bestia *sf* animal; andare in ~ *(fig)* to fly into a rage; **besti'ale** *ag* beastly; animal *cpd; (fam):* fa un freddo bestiale it's bitterly cold; **besti'ame** *sm* livestock; *(bovino)* cattle *pl.*

'bettola *sf (peg)* dive.

be'tulla *sf* birch.

be'vanda *sf* drink, beverage.

bevi'tore, 'trice *sm/f* drinker.

be'vuto, a *pp di* **bere** // *sf* drink.

bi'ada *sf* fodder.

bianche'ria [bjanke'ria] *sf* linen; ~ intima underwear; ~ da donna ladies' underwear, lingerie.

bi'anco, a, chi, che *ag* white; *(non scritto)* blank // *sm* white; *(intonaco)* whitewash // *sm/f* white, white man/ woman; in ~ *(foglio, assegno)* blank; *(notte)* sleepless; in ~ e nero *(TV, FOT)* black and white; mangiare in ~ to follow a bland diet; pesce in ~ boiled fish; andare in ~ *(non riuscire)* to fail; ~ dell'uovo egg-white.

biasi'mare *vt* to disapprove of, censure; **bi'asimo** *sm* disapproval, censure.

'bibbia *sf* bible.

bibe'ron *sm inv* feeding bottle.

'bibita *sf* (soft) drink.

biblio'teca, che *sf* library; *(mobile)* bookcase; **bibliote'cario, a** *sm/f* librarian.

bicarbo'nato *sm:* ~ (di sodio) bicarbonate (of soda).

bicchi'ere [bik'kjere] *sm* glass.

bici'cletta [bit∫i'kletta] *sf* bicycle; andare in ~ to cycle.

bidé *sm inv* bidet.

bi'dello, a *sm/f (INS)* janitor.

bi'done *sm* drum, can; *(anche:* ~ dell'immondizia) (dust)bin; *(fam: truffa)* swindle; fare un ~ a qn *(fam)* to let sb down; to cheat sb.

bien'nale *ag* biennial.

bi'ennio *sm* period of two years.

bi'etola *sf* beet.

bifor'carsi *vr* to fork; **biforcazi'one** *sf* fork.

bighello'nare |bigello'nare| *vi* to loaf (about).

bigiotte'ria |bidʒotte'ria| *sf* costume jewellery; *(negozio)* jeweller's *(selling only costume jewellery)*.

bigli'ardo |biʎ'ʎardo| *sm* = **biliardo**.

bigliette'ria |biʎʎctte'ria| *sf (di stazione)* ticket office; booking office; *(di teatro)* box office.

bigli'etto |biʎ'ʎctto| *sm (per viaggi, spettacoli etc)* ticket; *(cartoncino)* card; *(anche: ~ di banca)* (bank)note; ~ **d'auguri/da visita** greetings/visiting card; ~ **d'andata e ritorno** return (ticket), round-trip ticket *(US)*.

bignè |biɲ'ɲe| *sm inv* cream puff.

bigo'dino *sm* roller, curler.

bi'gotto, a *ag* over-pious // *sm/f* church fiend.

bi'lancia, ce |bi'lantʃa| *sf (pesa)* scales *pl; (: di precisione)* balance; *(dello zodiaco)*: B~ Libra; ~ **commerciale/dei pagamenti** balance of trade/payments; **bilanci'are** *vt (pesare)* to weigh; *(: fig)* to weigh up; *(pareggiare)* to balance.

bi'lancio |bi'lantʃo| *sm (COMM)* balance(-sheet); *(statale)* budget; **fare il** ~ **di** *(fig)* to assess; ~ **consuntivo** (final) balance; ~ **preventivo** budget.

'bile *sf* bile; *(fig)* rage, anger.

bili'ardo *sm* billiards *sg*; billiard table.

'bilico, chi *sm*: **essere in** ~ to be balanced; *(fig)* to be undecided; **tenere qn in** ~ to keep sb in suspense.

bi'lingue *ag* bilingual.

bili'one *sm (mille milioni)* thousand million; *(milione di milioni)* billion *(Brit)*, trillion *(US)*.

'bimbo, a *sm/f* little boy/girl.

bimen'sile *ag* fortnightly.

bimes'trale *ag* two-monthly, bimonthly.

bi'nario, a *ag (sistema)* binary // *sm (railway)* track *o* line; *(piattaforma)* platform; ~ **morto** dead-end track.

bi'nocolo *sm* binoculars *pl*.

bio... *prefisso:* **bio'chimica** |bio'kimika| *sf* biochemistry; **biodegra'dabile** *ag* biodegradable; **biogra'fia** *sf* biography; **biolo'gia** *sf* biology; **bio'logico, a, ci, che** *ag* biological.

bi'ondo, a *ag* blond, fair.

bir'bante *sm* rogue, rascal.

biri'chino, a |biri'kino| *ag* mischievous // *sm/f* scamp, little rascal.

bi'rillo *sm* skittle *(Brit)*, pin *(US)*; ~i *smpl (gioco)* skittles *sg (Brit)*, bowling *(US)*.

'biro *sf inv* ® biro ®.

'birra *sf* beer; **a tutta** ~ *(fig)* at top speed; **birre'ria** *sf* ≈ bierkeller.

bis *escl, sm inv* encore.

bis'betico, a, ci, che *ag* ill-tempered, crabby.

bisbigli'are |bisbiʎ'ʎare| *vt, vi* to whisper.

'bisca, sche *sf* gambling-house.

'biscia, sce ['biʃʃa] *sf* snake; ~ **d'acqua** grass snake.

bis'cotto *sm* biscuit.

bises'tile *ag:* **anno** ~ leap year.

bis'lungo, a, ghi, ghe *ag* oblong.

bis'nonno, a *sm/f* great grandfather/grandmother.

biso'gnare |bizoɲ'ɲare| *vb impers:* **bisogna che tu parta/lo faccia** you'll have to go/do it; **bisogna parlargli** we'll *(o* I'll) have to talk to him.

bi'sogno |bi'zoɲɲo| *sm* need; ~i *smpl:* **fare i propri** ~i to relieve o.s.; **avere** ~ **di qc/di fare qc** to need sth/to do sth; **al** ~, **in caso di** ~ if need be; **biso'gnoso, a** *ag* needy, poor; **bisognoso di** in need of, needing.

bis'tecca, che *sf* steak, beefsteak.

bisticci'are |bistit'tʃare| *vi,* ~**rsi** *vr* to quarrel, bicker; **bis'ticcio** *sm* quarrel, squabble; *(gioco di parole)* pun.

'bisturi *sm* scalpel.

bi'sunto, a *ag* very greasy.

'bitter *sm inv* bitters *pl*.

bi'vacco, chi *sm* bivouac.

'bivio *sm* fork; *(fig)* dilemma.

'bizza ['biddza] *sf* tantrum; **fare le** ~**e** *(bambino)* to be naughty.

biz'zarro, a [bid'dzarro] *ag* bizarre, strange.

biz'zeffe [bid'dzɛffe]: **a** ~ *av* in plenty, galore.

blan'dire *vt* to soothe; to flatter.

'blando, a *ag* mild, gentle.

bla'sone *sm* coat of arms.

blate'rare *vi* to chatter, blether.

blin'dato, a *ag* armoured.

bloc'care *vt* to block; *(isolare)* to isolate, cut off; *(porto)* to blockade; *(prezzi, beni)* to freeze; *(meccanismo)* to jam; ~**rsi** *vr (motore)* to stall; *(freni, porta)* to jam, stick; *(ascensore)* to stop, get stuck.

'blocco, chi *sm* block; *(MIL)* blockade; *(dei fitti)* restriction; *(quadernetto)* pad; *(fig: unione)* coalition; *(il bloccare)* blocking; isolating; cutting-off; blockading; freezing; jamming; **in** ~ *(nell'insieme)* as a whole; *(COMM)* in bulk; ~ **cardiaco** cardiac arrest.

blu *ag inv, sm* dark blue.

'blusa *sf (camiciotto)* smock; *(camicetta)* blouse.

'boa *sm inv (ZOOL)* boa constrictor; *(sciarpa)* feather boa // *sf* buoy.

bo'ato *sm* rumble, roar.

bo'bina *sf* reel, spool; *(di pellicola)* spool; *(di film)* reel; *(ELETTR)* coil.

'bocca, che sf mouth; in ~ al lupo! good luck!

boc'caccia, ce [bok'kattʃa] sf (malalingua) gossip; **fare le ~ce** to pull faces.

boc'cale sm jug; ~ **da birra** tankard.

boc'cetta [bot'tʃetta] sf small bottle.

boccheggi'are [bokked'dʒare] vi to gasp.

boc'chino [bok'kino] sm (di sigaretta, sigaro: cannella) cigarette-holder; cigar-holder; (di pipa, strumenti musicali) mouthpiece.

'boccia, ce [bottʃa] sf bottle; (da vino) decanter, carafe; (palla) bowl; **gioco delle ~ce** bowls sg.

bocci'are [bot'tʃare] vt (proposta, progetto) to reject; (INS) to fail; (BOCCE) to hit; **boccia'tura** sf failure.

bocci'olo [bot'tʃɔlo] sm bud.

boc'cone sm mouthful, morsel.

boc'coni av face downwards.

'boia sm inv executioner; hangman.

boi'ata sf botch.

boicot'tare vt to boycott.

'bolide sm meteor; **come un** ~ like a flash, at top speed.

'bolla sf bubble; (MED) blister; ~ **papale** papal bull; ~ **di consegna** (COMM) delivery note.

bol'lare vt to stamp; (fig) to brand.

bol'lente ag boiling; boiling hot.

bol'letta sf bill; (ricevuta) receipt; **essere in** ~ to be hard up.

bollet'tino sm bulletin; (COMM) note; ~ **di spedizione** consignment note.

bol'lire vt, vi to boil; **bol'lito** sm (CUC) boiled meat.

bolli'tore sm (CUC) kettle; (per riscaldamento) boiler.

'bollo sm stamp.

'bomba sf bomb; **tornare a** ~ (fig) to get back to the point; ~ **atomica** atom bomb.

bombarda'mento sm bombardment; bombing.

bombar'dare vt to bombard; (da aereo) to bomb.

bombardi'ere sm bomber.

bom'betta sf bowler (hat).

'bombola sf cylinder.

bo'naccia, ce [bo'nattʃa] sf dead calm.

bo'nario, a ag good-natured, kind.

bo'nifica, che sf reclamation; reclaimed land.

bo'nifico, ci sm (riduzione, abbuono) discount; (versamento a terzi) credit transfer.

bontà sf goodness; (cortesia) kindness; **aver la** ~ **di fare qc** to be good o kind enough to do sth.

borbot'tare vi to mumble; (stomaco) to rumble.

'borchia ['borkja] sf stud.

borda'tura sf (SARTORIA) border, trim.

'bordo sm (NAUT) ship's side; (orlo) edge; (striscia di guarnizione) border, trim; **a** ~ **di** (nave, aereo) aboard, on board; (macchina) in.

bor'gata sf hamlet.

bor'ghese [bor'geze] ag (spesso peg) middle-class; bourgeois; **abito** ~ civilian dress; **borghe'sia** sf middle classes pl; bourgeoisie.

'borgo, ghi sm (paesino) village; (quartiere) district; (sobborgo) suburb.

'boria sf self-conceit, arrogance.

boro'talco sm talcum powder.

bor'raccia, ce [bor'rattʃa] sf canteen, water-bottle.

'borsa sf bag; (anche: ~ **da signora**) handbag; (ECON): **la B~** (valori) the Stock Exchange; ~ **nera** black market; ~ **della spesa** shopping bag; ~ **di studio** grant; **borsai'olo** sm pickpocket; **borsel'lino** sm purse; **bor'setta** sf handbag; **bor'sista, i, e** sm/f (ECON) speculator; (INS) grant-holder.

bos'caglia [bos'kaʎʎa] sf woodlands pl.

boscai'olo sm woodcutter; forester.

'bosco, schi sm wood; **bos'coso, a** ag wooded.

'bossolo sm cartridge-case.

bo'tanico, a, ci, che ag botanical // sm botanist // sf botany.

'botola sf trap door.

'botta sf blow; (rumore) bang.

'botte sf barrel, cask.

bot'tega, ghe sf shop; (officina) workshop; **botte'gaio, a** sm/f shopkeeper; **botte'ghino** sm ticket office; (del lotto) public lottery office.

bot'tiglia [bot'tiʎʎa] sf bottle; **bottiglie'ria** sf wine shop.

bot'tino sm (di guerra) booty; (di rapina, furto) loot.

'botto sm bang; crash; **di** ~ suddenly.

bot'tone sm button; **attaccare** ~ **a qn** (fig) to buttonhole sb.

bo'vino, a ag bovine; ~i smpl cattle.

boxe [bɔks] sf boxing.

'bozza ['bɔttsa] sf draft; sketch; (TIP) proof; **boz'zetto** sm sketch.

'bozzolo ['bɔttsolo] sm cocoon.

BR sigla fpl = **Brigate Rosse**.

brac'care vt to hunt.

brac'cetto [brat'tʃetto] sm: **a** ~ arm in arm.

bracci'ale [brat'tʃale] sm bracelet; (distintivo) armband; **braccia'letto** sm bracelet, bangle.

bracci'ante [brat'tʃante] sm (AGR) day labourer.

bracci'ata [brat'tʃata] sf (nel nuoto) stroke.

'braccio ['brattʃo] sm (pl(f) **braccia**: ANAT) arm; (pl(m) **bracci**: di gru, fiume) arm; (: di edificio) wing; ~ **di mare** sound; **bracci'olo** sm (appoggio) arm.

'bracco, chi sm hound.
bracconi'ere sm poacher.
'brace ['bratʃe] sf embers pl; **braci'ere** sm brazier.
braci'ola [bra'tʃɔla] sf (CUC) chop.
bra'mare vt: ~ qc/di fare to long for sth/to do.
'branca, che sf branch.
'branchia ['brankja] sf (ZOOL) gill.
'branco, chi sm (di cani, lupi) pack; (di uccelli, pecore) flock; (peg: di persone) gang, pack.
branco'lare vi to grope, feel one's way.
'branda sf camp bed.
bran'dello sm scrap, shred; a ~i in tatters, in rags.
bran'dire vt to brandish.
'brano sm piece; (di libro) passage.
bra'sato sm braised beef.
Bra'sile sm: il ~ Brazil; **brasili'ano, a** ag, sm/f Brazilian.
'bravo, a ag (abile) clever, capable, skilful; (buono) good, honest; (: bambino) good; (coraggioso) brave; ~! well done!; (al teatro) bravo!
bra'vura sf cleverness, skill.
'breccia, ce ['brettʃa] sf breach.
bre'tella sf (AUT) link; ~e sfpl braces.
'breve ag brief, short; in ~ in short.
brevet'tare vt to patent.
bre'vetto sm patent; ~ di pilotaggio pilot's licence (Brit) o license (US).
'brezza ['breddza] sf breeze.
'bricco, chi sm jug; ~ del caffè coffeepot.
bric'cone, a sm/f rogue, rascal.
'briciola ['britʃola] sf crumb.
'briciolo ['britʃolo] sm (specie fig) bit.
'briga, ghe sf (fastidio) trouble, bother; pigliarsi la ~ di fare qc to take the trouble to do sth.
brigadi'ere sm (dei carabinieri etc) ≈ sergeant.
bri'gante sm bandit.
bri'gata sf (MIL) brigade; (gruppo) group, party.
'briglia ['briʎʎa] sf rein; a ~ sciolta at full gallop; (fig) at full speed.
bril'lante ag bright; (anche fig) brilliant; (che luccica) shining // sm diamond.
bril'lare vi to shine; (mina) to blow up // vt (mina) to set off.
'brillo, a ag merry, tipsy.
'brina sf hoarfrost.
brin'dare vi: ~ a qn/qc to drink to o toast sb/sth.
'brindisi sm inv toast.
'brio sm liveliness, go; **bri'oso, a** ag lively.
bri'tannico, a, ci, che ag British.
'brivido sm shiver; (di ribrezzo) shudder; (fig) thrill.
brizzo'lato, a [brittso'lato] ag (persona) going grey; (barba, capelli) greying.

'brocca, che sf jug.
broc'cato sm brocade.
'broccolo sm broccoli sg.
'brodo sm broth; (per cucinare) stock; ~ ristretto consommé.
brogli'accio [broʎ'ʎattʃo] sm scribbling pad.
'broglio ['brɔʎʎo] sm: ~ elettorale gerrymandering.
bron'chite [bron'kite] sf (MED) bronchitis.
'broncio ['brontʃo] sm sulky expression; tenere il ~ to sulk.
'bronco, chi sm bronchial tube.
bronto'lare vi to grumble; (tuono, stomaco) to rumble.
'bronzo ['brondzo] sm bronze.
bru'care vt to browse on, nibble at.
brucia'pelo [brutʃa'pelo]: a ~ av point-blank.
bruci'are [bru'tʃare] vt to burn; (scottare) to scald // vi to burn; **brucia'tore** sm burner; **brucia'tura** sf (atto) burning q; (segno) burn; (scottatura) scald; **bruci'ore** sm burning o smarting sensation.
'bruco, chi sm caterpillar; grub.
brughi'era [bru'gjɛra] sf heath, moor.
bruli'care vi to swarm.
'brullo, a ag bare, bleak.
'bruma sf mist.
'bruno, a ag brown, dark; (persona) dark(-haired).
'brusco, a, schi, sche ag (sapore) sharp; (modi, persona) brusque, abrupt; (movimento) abrupt, sudden.
bru'sio sm buzz, buzzing.
bru'tale ag brutal.
'bruto, a ag (forza) brute cpd // sm brute.
brut'tezza [brut'tettsa] sf ugliness.
'brutto, a ag ugly; (cattivo) bad; (malattia, strada, affare) nasty, bad; ~ tempo bad weather; **brut'tura** sf (cosa brutta) ugly thing; (sudiciume) filth; (azione meschina) mean action.
Bru'xelles [bry'sɛl] sf Brussels.
'buca, che sf hole; (avvallamento) hollow; ~ delle lettere letterbox.
buca'neve sm inv snowdrop.
bu'care vt (forare) to make a hole (o holes) in; (pungere) to pierce; (biglietto) to punch; ~rsi vr (con eroina) to mainline; ~ una gomma to have a puncture.
bu'cato sm (operazione) washing; (panni) wash, washing.
'buccia, ce ['buttʃa] sf skin, peel; (corteccia) bark.
bucherel'lare [bukerel'lare] vt to riddle with holes.
'buco, chi sm hole.
bu'dello sm intestine; (fig: tubo) tube; (vicolo) alley; ~a sfpl bowels, guts.
bu'dino sm pudding.

'bue sm ox; (anche: carne di ~) beef.
'bufalo sm buffalo.
bu'fera sf storm.
'buffo, a ag funny; (TEATRO) comic.
bu'gia, 'gie [bu'dʒia] sf lie; (candeliere) candleholder; **bugi'ardo, a** ag lying, deceitful // sm/f liar.
bugi'gattolo [budʒi'gattolo] sm poky little room.
'buio, a ag dark // sm dark, darkness; fa ~ pesto it's pitch-dark.
'bulbo sm (BOT) bulb; ~ oculare eyeball.
Bulga'ria sf: la ~ Bulgaria.
bul'lone sm bolt.
buona'notte escl good night! // sf: dare la ~ a to say good night to.
buona'sera escl good evening!
buon gi'orno [bwon'dʒorno] escl good morning (o afternoon)!
buongus'taio, a sm/f gourmet.
buon'gusto sm good taste.
bu'ono, a ag (dav sm **buon** + C o V, **buono** + s impura, gn, pn, ps, x, z; dav sf **buon'** +V) good; (benevolo)= (con) good (to), kind (to); (adatto): ~ a/da fit for/to // sm good; (COMM) voucher, coupon; **alla buona** ag simple // av in a simple way, without any fuss; **buona fortuna** good luck; **buon compleanno** happy birthday; **buon divertimento** have a nice time; **a buon mercato** cheap; **di buon'ora** early; ~ **di cassa** cash voucher; ~ **di consegna** delivery note; ~ **fruttifero** bond bearing interest; ~ **a nulla** good-for-nothing; ~ **del tesoro** Treasury bill; **buon riposo** sleep well; **buon senso** common sense; **buon viaggio** bon voyage, have a good trip.
buontem'pone, a sm/f jovial person.
burat'tino sm puppet.
'burbero, a ag surly, gruff.
'burla sf prank, trick; **bur'lare** vt: burlare qc/qn, burlarsi di qc/qn to make fun of sth/sb.
burocra'zia [burokrat'tsia] sf bureaucracy.
bur'rasca, sche sf storm; **burras'coso, a** ag stormy.
'burro sm butter.
bur'rone sm ravine.
bus'care vt (anche: ~rsi: raffreddore) to get, catch; **buscarle** (fam) to get a hiding.
bus'sare vi to knock.
'bussola sf compass; **perdere la ~** (fig) to lose one's bearings.
'busta sf (da lettera) envelope; (astuccio) case; **in ~ aperta/chiusa** in an unsealed/sealed envelope; ~ **paga** pay packet.
busta'rella sf bribe, backhander.
'busto sm bust; (indumento) corset, girdle; **a mezzo ~** (foto) half-length.
but'tare vt to throw; (anche: ~ via) to

throw away; ~ **giù** (scritto) to scribble down, dash off; (cibo) to gulp down; (edificio) to pull down, demolish; (pasta, verdura) to put into boiling water; ~**rsi dalla finestra** to jump o throw o.s. out of the window.

C

ca'bina sf (di nave) cabin; (da spiaggia) beach hut; (di autocarro, treno) cab; (di aereo) cockpit; (di ascensore) cage; ~ **telefonica** call o (tele)phone box.
ca'cao sm cocoa.
'caccia ['kattʃa] sf hunting; (con fucile) shooting; (inseguimento) chase; (cacciagione) game // sm inv (aereo) fighter; (nave) destroyer; ~ **grossa** big-game hunting; ~ **all'uomo** manhunt.
cacciabombardi'ere [kattʃabombar'djɛre] sm fighter-bomber.
cacciagi'one [kattʃa'dʒone] sf game.
cacci'are [kat'tʃare] vt to hunt; (mandar via) to chase away; (ficcare) to shove, stick // vi to hunt; ~**rsi** vr (fam: mettersi): ~**rsi tra la folla** to plunge into the crowd; **dove s'è cacciata la mia borsa?** where has my bag got to?; ~**rsi nei guai** to get into trouble; ~ **fuori** qc to whip o pull sth out; ~ **un urlo** to let out a yell; **caccia'tore** sm hunter; **cacciatore di frodo** poacher.
caccia'vite [kattʃa'vite] sm inv screwdriver.
'cactus sm inv cactus.
ca'davere sm (dead) body, corpse.
ca'dente ag falling; (casa) tumbledown.
ca'denza [ka'dɛntsa] sf cadence; (andamento ritmico) rhythm; (MUS) cadenza.
ca'dere vi to fall; (denti, capelli) to fall out; (tetto) to fall in; **questa gonna cade bene** this skirt hangs well; **lasciar** ~ (anche fig) to drop; ~ **dal sonno** to be falling asleep on one's feet; ~ **dalle nuvole** (fig) to be taken aback.
ca'detto, a ag younger; (squadra) junior cpd // sm cadet.
ca'duta sf fall; **la ~ dei capelli** hair loss.
caffè sm inv coffee; (locale) café; ~ **macchiato** coffee with a dash of milk; ~ **macinato** ground coffee.
caffel'latte sm inv white coffee.
caffetti'era sf coffeepot.
cagio'nare [kadʒo'nare] vt to cause, be the cause of.
cagio'nevole [kadʒo'nevole] ag delicate, weak.
cagli'are [kaʎ'ʎare] vi to curdle.
'cagna ['kaɲɲa] sf (ZOOL, peg) bitch.
ca'gnesco, a, schi, sche ['kaɲ'nesko] ag (fig): **guardare qn in ~** to scowl at sb.
cala'brone sm hornet.

cala'maio sm inkpot; inkwell.

cala'maro sm squid.

cala'mita sf magnet.

calamità sf inv calamity, disaster.

ca'lare vt (far discendere) to lower; (MAGLIA) to decrease // vi (discendere) to go (o come) down; (tramontare) to set, go down; ~ **di peso** to lose weight.

'calca sf throng, press.

cal'cagno [kal'kaɲɲo] sm heel.

cal'care sm limestone // vt (premere coi piedi) to tread, press down; (premere con forza) to press down; (mettere in rilievo) to stress; ~ **la mano** to overdo it, exaggerate.

'calce ['kaltʃe] sm: **in ~** at the foot of the page // sf lime; ~ **viva** quicklime.

calces'truzzo [kaltʃes'truttso] sm concrete.

calci'are [kal'tʃare] vt, vi to kick; **calcia'tore** sm footballer.

cal'cina [kal'tʃina] sf (lime) mortar.

'calcio ['kaltʃo] sm (pedata) kick; (sport) football, soccer; (di pistola, fucile) butt; (CHIM) calcium; ~ **d'angolo** (SPORT) corner (kick); ~ **di punizione** (SPORT) free kick.

'calco, chi sm (ARTE) casting, moulding; cast, mould.

calco'lare vt to calculate, work out, reckon; (ponderare) to weigh (up); **calcola'tore, 'trice** ag calculating // sm calculator; (fig) calculating person // sf (anche: **macchina calcolatrice**) calculator; **calcolatore elettronico** computer.

'calcolo sm (anche MAT) calculation; (infinitesimale etc) calculus; (MED) stone; **fare i propri ~i** (fig) to weigh the pros and cons; **per ~** out of self-interest.

cal'daia sf boiler.

caldeggi'are [kalded'dʒare] vt to support.

'caldo, a ag warm; (molto ~) hot; (fig: appassionato) keen; hearty // sm heat; **ho ~** I'm warm; I'm hot; **fa ~** it's warm; it's hot.

calen'dario sm calendar.

'calibro sm (di arma) calibre, bore; (TECN) callipers pl; (fig) calibre; **di grosso ~** (fig) prominent.

'calice ['kalitʃe] sm goblet; (REL) chalice.

ca'ligine [ka'lidʒine] sf fog; (mista con fumo) smog.

'callo sm callus; (ai piedi) corn.

'calma sf calm.

cal'mante sm sedative, tranquillizer.

cal'mare vt to calm; (lenire) to soothe; ~**rsi** vr to grow calm, calm down; (vento) to abate; (dolori) to ease.

calmi'ere sm controlled price.

'calmo, a ag calm, quiet.

'calo sm (COMM: di prezzi) fall; (: di volume) shrinkage; (: di peso) loss.

ca'lore sm warmth; heat; **in ~** (ZOOL) on heat.

calo'ria sf calorie.

calo'roso, a ag warm.

calpes'tare vt to tread on, trample on; "**è vietato ~ l'erba**" "keep off the grass".

ca'lunnia sf slander; (scritta) libel.

cal'vario sm (fig) affliction, cross.

cal'vizie [kal'vittsje] sf baldness.

'calvo, a ag bald.

'calza ['kaltsa] sf (da donna) stocking; (da uomo) sock; **fare la ~** to knit; ~**e di nailon** nylons, (nylon) stockings.

cal'zare [kal'tsare] vt (scarpe, guanti: mettersi) to put on; (: portare) to wear // vi to fit; **calza'tura** sf footwear.

calzet'tone [kaltset'tone] sm heavy knee-length sock.

cal'zino [kal'tsino] sm sock.

calzo'laio [kaltso'lajo] sm shoemaker; (che ripara scarpe) cobbler; **calzole'ria** sf (negozio) shoe shop.

calzon'cini [kaltson'tʃini] smpl shorts.

cal'zone [kal'tsone] sm trouser leg; (CUC) savoury turnover made with pizza dough; ~**i** smpl trousers (Brit), pants (US).

cambi'ale sf bill (of exchange); (pagherò cambiario) promissory note.

cambia'mento sm change.

cambi'are vt to change; (modificare) to alter, change; (barattare): ~ (**qc con qn/qc**) to exchange (sth with sb/for sth) // vi to change, alter; ~**rsi** vr (variare abito) to change; ~ **casa** to move (house); ~ **idea** to change one's mind; ~ **treno** to change trains.

'cambio sm change; (modifica) alteration, change; (scambio, COMM) exchange; (corso dei cambi) rate (of exchange); (TECN, AUT) gears pl; **in ~ di** in exchange for; **dare il ~ a qn** to take over from sb.

'camera sf room; (anche: ~ **da letto**) bedroom; (POL) chamber, house; ~ **ardente** mortuary chapel; ~ **d'aria** inner tube; (di pallone) bladder; **C~ di Commercio** Chamber of Commerce; **C~ dei Deputati** Chamber of Deputies, ≈ House of Commons (Brit), ≈ House of Representatives (US); ~ **a gas** gas chamber; ~ **a un letto/a due letti/matrimoniale** single/twin-bedded/double room; ~ **oscura** (FOT) dark room.

came'rata, i, e sm/f companion, mate // sf dormitory.

cameri'era sf (domestica) maid; (che serve a tavola) waitress; (che fa le camere) chambermaid.

cameri'ere sm (man)servant; (di ristorante) waiter.

came'rino sm (TEATRO) dressing room.

'camice ['kamitʃe] sm (REL) alb; (per medici etc) white coat.

cami'cetta [kami'tʃetta] *sf* blouse.

ca'micia, cie [ka'mitʃa] *sf* (*da uomo*) shirt; (*da donna*) blouse; ~ **di forza** straitjacket; **camici'otto** *sm* casual shirt; (*per operai*) smock.

cami'netto *sm* hearth, fireplace.

ca'mino *sm* chimney; (*focolare*) fireplace, hearth.

'camion *sm inv* lorry (*Brit*), truck (*US*); **camion'cino** *sm* van.

cam'mello *sm* (*ZOOL*) camel; (*tessuto*) camel hair.

cammi'nare *vi* to walk; (*funzionare*) to work, go.

cam'mino *sm* walk; (*sentiero*) path; (*itinerario, direzione, tragitto*) way; **mettersi in** ~ to set o start off.

camo'milla *sf* camomile; (*infuso*) camomile tea.

ca'morra *sf* camorra; racket.

ca'moscio [ka'moʃʃo] *sm* chamois.

cam'pagna [kam'paɲɲa] *sf* country, countryside; (*POL, COMM, MIL*) campaign; **in** ~ in the country; **andare in** ~ to go to the country; **fare una** ~ to campaign; **campa'gnolo, a** *ag* country *cpd* // *sf* (*AUT*) cross-country vehicle.

cam'pale *ag* field *cpd*; (*fig*): **una giornata** ~ a hard day.

cam'pana *sf* bell; (*anche*: ~ **di vetro**) bell jar; **campa'nella** *sf* small bell; (*di tenda*) curtain ring; **campa'nello** *sm* (*all'uscio, da tavola*) bell.

campa'nile *sm* bell tower, belfry; **campani'lismo** *sm* parochialism.

cam'pare *vi* to live; (*tirare avanti*) to get by, manage.

cam'pato, a *ag*: ~ **in aria** unsound, unfounded.

campeggi'are [kamped'dʒare] *vi* to camp; (*risaltare*) to stand out; **campeggia'tore, 'trice** *sm/f* camper; **cam'peggio** *sm* camping; (*terreno*) camp site; **fare (del) campeggio** to go camping.

cam'pestre *ag* country *cpd*, rural.

campio'nario, a *ag*: **fiera** ~a trade fair // *sm* collection of samples.

campio'nato *sm* championship.

campi'one, 'essa *sm/f* (*SPORT*) champion // *sm* (*COMM*) sample.

'campo *sm* field; (*MIL*) field; (:*accampamento*) camp; (*spazio delimitato: sportivo etc*) ground; field; (*di quadro*) background; **i** ~**i** (*campagna*) the countryside; ~ **da aviazione** airfield; ~ **di concentramento** concentration camp; ~ **di golf** golf course; ~ **da tennis** tennis court; ~ **visivo** field of vision.

campo'santo, *pl* **campisanti** *sm* cemetery.

camuf'fare *vt* to disguise.

'Canada *sm*: **il** ~ Canada; **cana'dese** *ag, sm/f* Canadian // *sf* (*anche*: **tenda canadese**) ridge tent.

ca'naglia [ka'naʎʎa] *sf* rabble, mob; (*persona*) scoundrel, rogue.

ca'nale *sm* (*anche fig*) channel; (*artificiale*) canal.

'canapa *sf* hemp.

cana'rino *sm* canary.

cancel'lare [kantʃel'lare] *vt* (*con la gomma*) to rub out, erase; (*con la penna*) to strike out; (*annullare*) to annul, cancel; (*disdire*) to cancel.

cancelle'ria [kantʃelle'ria] *sf* chancery; (*quanto necessario per scrivere*) stationery.

cancelli'ere [kantʃel'ljere] *sm* chancellor; (*di tribunale*) clerk of the court.

can'cello [kan'tʃello] *sm* gate.

can'crena *sf* gangrene.

'cancro *sm* (*MED*) cancer; (*dello zodiaco*): **C**~ Cancer.

can'dela *sf* candle; ~ (**di accensione**) (*AUT*) spark(ing) plug.

cande'labro *sm* candelabra.

candeli'ere *sm* candlestick.

candi'dato, a *sm/f* candidate; (*aspirante a una carica*) applicant.

'candido, a *ag* white as snow; (*puro*) pure; (*sincero*) sincere, candid.

can'dito, a *ag* candied.

can'dore *sm* brilliant white; purity; sincerity, candour.

'cane *sm* dog; (*di pistola, fucile*) cock; **fa un freddo** ~ it's bitterly cold; **non c'era un** ~ there wasn't a soul; ~ **da caccia/guardia** hunting/guard dog; ~ **lupo** alsatian.

ca'nestro *sm* basket.

cangi'ante [kan'dʒante] *ag* iridescent.

can'guro *sm* kangaroo.

ca'nile *sm* kennel; (*di allevamento*) kennels *pl*; ~ **municipale** dog pound.

ca'nino, a *ag, sm* canine.

'canna *sf* (*pianta*) reed; (:*indica, da zucchero*) cane; (*bastone*) stick, cane; (*di fucile*) barrel; (*di organo*) pipe; ~ **fumaria** chimney flue; ~ **da pesca** (fishing) rod; ~ **da zucchero** sugar cane.

can'nella *sf* (*CUC*) cinnamon.

cannel'loni *smpl* pasta tubes stuffed with sauce and baked.

cannocchi'ale [kannok'kjale] *sm* telescope.

can'none *sm* (*MIL*) gun; (:*STORIA*) cannon; (*tubo*) pipe, tube; (*piega*) box pleat; (*fig*) ace.

can'nuccia, ce [kan'nuttʃa] *sf* (drinking) straw.

ca'noa *sf* canoe.

'canone *sm* canon, criterion; (*mensile, annuo*) rent; fee.

ca'nonico, ci *sm* (*REL*) canon.

ca'noro, a *ag* (*uccello*) singing, song *cpd*.

canot'taggio [kanot'taddʒo] *sm* rowing.

canotti'era sf vest.

ca'notto sm small boat, dinghy; canoe.

cano'vaccio [kano'vattʃo] sm (tela) canvas; (strofinaccio) duster; (trama) plot.

can'tante sm/f singer.

can'tare vt, vi to sing; **cantau'tore, 'trice** sm/f singer-composer.

canti'ere sm (EDIL) (building) site; (anche: ~ navale) shipyard.

canti'lena sf (filastrocca) lullaby; (fig) sing-song voice.

can'tina sf (locale) cellar; (bottega) wine shop.

'canto sm song; (arte) singing; (REL) chant; chanting; (poesia) poem, lyric; (parte di una poesia) canto; (parte, lato): **da un ~** on the one hand; **d'altro ~** on the other hand.

canto'nata sf corner; **prendere una ~** (fig) to blunder.

can'tone sm (in Svizzera) canton.

can'tuccio [kan'tuttʃo] sm corner, nook.

canzo'nare [kantso'nare] vt to tease.

can'zone [kan'tsone] sf song; (POESIA) canzone; **canzoni'ere** sm (MUS) songbook; (LETTERATURA) collection of poems.

'caos sm inv chaos; **ca'otico, a, ci, che** ag chaotic.

C.A.P. sigla m = **codice di avviamento postale**.

ca'pace [ka'patʃe] ag able, capable; (ampio, vasto) large, capacious; **sei ~ di farlo?** can you o are you able to do it?; **capacità** sf inv ability; (DIR, di recipiente) capacity; **capaci'tarsi** vr: **capacitarsi di** to make out, understand.

ca'panna sf hut.

capan'none sm (AGR) barn; (fabbricato industriale) (factory) shed.

ca'parbio, a ag stubborn.

ca'parra sf deposit, down payment.

ca'pello sm hair; **~i** smpl (capigliatura) hair sg.

capez'zale [kapet'tsale] sm bolster; (fig) bedside.

ca'pezzolo [ka'pettsolo] sm nipple.

capi'enza [ka'pjentsa] sf capacity.

capiglia'tura [kapiʎʎa'tura] sf hair.

ca'pire vt to understand.

capi'tale ag (mortale) capital; (fondamentale) main, chief // sf (città) capital // sm (ECON) capital; **capita'lismo** sm capitalism; **capita'lista, i, e** ag, sm/f capitalist.

capi'tano sm captain.

capi'tare vi (giungere casualmente) to happen to go, find o.s.; (accadere) to happen; (presentarsi: cosa) to turn up, present itself // vb impers to happen; **mi è capitato un guaio** I've had a spot of trouble.

capi'tello sm (ARCHIT) capital.

ca'pitolo sm chapter.

capi'tombolo sm headless fall, tumble.

'capo sm head; (persona) head, leader; (: in ufficio) head, boss; (: in tribù) chief; (di oggetti) head; top; end; (GEO) cape; **andare a ~** to start a new paragraph; **da ~** over again; **~ di bestiame** head inv of cattle; **~ di vestiario** item of clothing.

'capo... prefisso: **capocu'oco, chi** sm head cook; **Capo'danno** sm New Year; **capo'fitto: a capofitto** av headfirst, headlong; **capo'giro** sm dizziness q; **capola'voro, i** sm masterpiece; **capo'linea, pl capi'linea** sm terminus; **capo'lino** sm: **fare capolino** to peep out (o in etc); **capolu'ogo, pl ghi** o **capilu'oghi** sm chief town, administrative centre.

capo'rale sm (MIL) lance corporal (Brit), private first class (US).

'capo... prefisso: **capostazi'one, pl capistazi'one** sm station master; **capo'treno, pl capi'treno** o **capo'treni** sm guard.

capo'volgere [kapo'voldʒere] vt to overturn; (fig) to reverse; **~rsi** vr to overturn; (barca) to capsize; (fig) to be reversed; **capo'volto, a** pp di **capovolgere**.

'cappa sf (mantello) cape, cloak; (del camino) hood.

cap'pella sf (REL) chapel; **cappel'lano** sm chaplain.

cap'pello sm hat.

'cappero sm caper.

cap'pone sm capon.

cap'potto sm (over)coat.

cappuc'cino [kapput'tʃino] sm (frate) Capuchin monk; (bevanda) frothy white coffee.

cap'puccio [kap'puttʃo] sm (copricapo) hood; (della biro) cap.

'capra sf (she-)goat; **ca'pretto** sm kid.

ca'priccio [ka'prittʃo] sm caprice, whim; (bizza) tantrum; **fare i ~i** to be very naughty; **capricci'oso, a** ag capricious, whimsical; naughty.

Capri'corno sm Capricorn.

capri'ola sf somersault.

capri'olo sm roe deer.

'capro sm billy-goat; **~ espiatorio** (fig) scapegoat.

'capsula sf capsule; (di arma, per bottiglie) cap.

cap'tare vt (RADIO, TV) to pick up; (cattivarsi) to gain, win.

cara'bina sf rifle.

carabini'ere sm member of Italian military police force.

ca'raffa sf carafe.

cara'mella sf sweet.

ca'rattere sm character; (caratteristica) characteristic, trait; **avere un buon ~** to be good-natured; **caratte'ristico, a, ci, che** ag characteristic // sf characteristic, trait, peculiarity; **caratteriz'zare** *vt* to characterize, distinguish.

car'bone *sm* coal.

carbu'rante *sm* (motor) fuel.

carbura'tore *sm* carburettor.

car'cassa *sf* carcass; *(fig: peg: macchina etc)* (old) wreck.

carce'rato, a [kartʃe'rato] *sm/f* prisoner.

'carcere ['kartʃere] *sm* prison; *(pena)* imprisonment.

carci'ofo [kar'tʃɔfo] *sm* artichoke.

car'diaco, a, ci, che *ag* cardiac, heart *cpd.*

cardi'nale *ag*, *sm* cardinal.

'cardine *sm* hinge.

'cardo *sm* thistle.

ca'renza [ka'rɛntsa] *sf* lack, scarcity; *(vitaminica)* deficiency.

cares'tia *sf* famine; *(penuria)* scarcity, dearth.

ca'rezza [ka'rettsa] *sf* caress; **carez'zare** *vt* to caress, stroke, fondle.

'carica *sf vedi* **carico.**

cari'care *vt* to load; *(aggravare: anche fig)* to weigh down; *(orologio)* to wind up; *(batteria, MIL)* to charge.

'carico, a, chi, che *ag (che porta un peso)*: ~ **di** loaded *o* laden with; *(fucile)* loaded; *(orologio)* wound up; *(batteria)* charged; *(colore)* deep; *(caffè, tè)* strong // *sm (il caricare)* loading; *(ciò che si carica)* load; *(fig: peso)* burden, weight // *sf (mansione ufficiale)* office, position; *(MIL, TECN, ELETTR)* charge; **persona a** ~ dependent; **essere a** ~ **di qn** *(spese etc)* to be charged to sb; **ha una forte** ~**a di simpatia** he's very likeable.

carie *sf (dentaria)* decay.

ca'rino, a *ag* lovely, pretty, nice; *(simpatico)* nice.

carità *sf* charity; **per** ~! *(escl di rifiuto)* good heavens, no!

carnagi'one [karna'dʒone] *sf* complexion.

car'nale *ag (amore)* carnal; *(fratello)* blood *cpd.*

'carne *sf* flesh; *(bovina, ovina etc)* meat; ~ **di** manzo/maiale/pecora beef/pork/mutton; ~ **tritata** mince *(Brit)*, hamburger meat *(US)*, minced *(Brit)* o ground *(US)* meat.

car'nefice [kar'nefitʃe] *sm* executioner; hangman.

carne'vale *sm* carnival.

car'noso, a *ag* fleshy.

'caro, a *ag (amato)* dear; *(costoso)* dear, expensive.

ca'rogna [ka'roɲɲa] *sf* carrion; *(fig: fam)* swine.

caro'sello *sm* merry-go-round.

ca'rota *sf* carrot.

caro'vana *sf* caravan.

caro'vita *sm* high cost of living.

carpenti'ere *sm* carpenter.

car'pire *vt*: ~ **qc a qn** *(segreto etc)* to get sth out of sb.

car'poni *av* on all fours.

car'rabile *ag* suitable for vehicles; "**passo** ~" "keep clear".

car'raio, a *ag*: **passo** ~ vehicle entrance.

carreggi'ata [karred'dʒata] *sf* carriageway *(Brit)*, (road)way.

car'rello *sm* trolley; *(AER)* undercarriage; *(CINEMA)* dolly; *(di macchina da scrivere)* carriage.

carri'era *sf* career; **fare** ~ to get on; **a gran** ~ at full speed.

carri'ola *sf* wheelbarrow.

'carro *sm* cart, wagon; ~ **armato** tank.

car'rozza [kar'rɔttsa] *sf* carriage, coach.

carrozze'ria [karrottse'ria] *sf* body, coachwork *(Brit)*; *(officina)* coachbuilder's workshop *(Brit)*, body shop.

carroz'zina [karrot'tsina] *sf* pram *(Brit)*, baby carriage *(US)*.

'carta *sf* paper; *(al ristorante)* menu; *(GEO)* map; plan; *(documento, da gioco)* card; *(costituzione)* charter; ~**e** *sfpl (documenti)* papers, documents; **alla** ~ *(al ristorante)* à la carte; ~ **assegni** bank card; ~ **assorbente** blotting paper; ~ **bollata** *o* **da bollo** official stamped paper; ~ **di credito** credit card; ~ **(geografica)** map; ~ **d'identità** identity card; ~ **igienica** toilet paper; ~ **d'imbarco** *(AER, NAUT)* boarding card; ~ **da lettere** writing paper; ~ **libera** *(AMM)* unstamped paper; ~ **da parati** wallpaper; ~ **verde** *(AUT)* green card; ~ **vetrata** sandpaper; ~ **da visita** visiting card.

cartacar'bone, *pl* **cartecar'bone** *sf* carbon paper.

car'taccia, ce [kar'tattʃa] *sf* waste paper.

cartamo'neta *sf* paper money.

carta'pecora *sf* parchment.

carta'pesta *sf* papier-mâché.

car'teggio [kar'teddʒo] *sm* correspondence.

car'tella *sf (scheda)* card; *(custodia: di cartone)* folder; *(: di uomo d'affari etc)* briefcase; *(: di scolaro)* schoolbag, satchel; ~ **clinica** *(MED)* case sheet.

car'tello *sm* sign; *(pubblicitario)* poster; *(stradale)* sign, signpost; *(ECON)* cartel; *(in dimostrazioni)* placard; **cartel'lone** *sm (pubblicitario)* advertising poster; *(della tombola)* scoring frame; *(TEATRO)* playbill; **tenere il cartellone** *(spettacolo)* to have a long run.

carti'era *sf* paper mill.

car'tina *sf (AUT, GEO)* map.

car'toccio [kar'tɔttʃo] *sm* paper bag.

cartole'ria *sf* stationer's (shop).

carto'lina *sf* postcard.

car'tone *sm* cardboard; *(ARTE)* cartoon; ~**i animati** *smpl (CINEMA)* cartoons.

car'tuccia, ce [kar'tuttʃa] *sf* cartridge.

'casa *sf* house; *(specialmente la propria casa)* home; *(COMM)* firm, house; **essere**

a ~ to be at home; **vado a ~ mia/tua** I'm going home/to your house; ~ **di cura** nursing home; ~ **dello studente** student hostel; ~**e popolari** ≈ council houses (o flats) (*Brit*), ≈ public housing units (*US*).

ca'sacca, che *sf* military coat; (*di fantino*) blouse.

casalingo, a, ghi, ghe *ag* household, domestic; (*fatto a casa*) home-made; (*semplice*) homely; (*amante della casa*) home-loving // *sf* housewife; ~**ghi** *smpl* household articles; **cucina** ~**a** plain home cooking.

cas'care *vi* to fall; **cas'cata** *sf* fall; (*d'acqua*) cascade, waterfall.

'casco, schi *sm* helmet; (*del parrucchiere*) hair-drier; (*di banane*) bunch.

casei'ficio [kazei'fitʃo] *sm* creamery.

ca'sella *sf* pigeon-hole; ~ **postale** (C.P.) post office box (P.O. box).

casel'lario *sm* filing cabinet; ~ **giudiziale** court records *pl*.

ca'sello *sm* (*di autostrada*) toll-house.

ca'serma *sf* barracks *pl*.

ca'sino *sm* (*confusione*) row, racket; (*casa di prostituzione*) brothel.

casinò *sm inv* casino.

'caso *sm* chance; (*fatto, vicenda*) event, incident; (*possibilità*) possibility; (*MED, LING*) case; **a ~** at random; **per ~** by chance, by accident; **in ogni ~, in tutti i** ~**i** in any case, at any rate; **al ~** should the opportunity arise; **nel ~ che** in case; ~ **mai** if by chance; ~ **limite** borderline case.

'cassa *sf* case, crate, box; (*bara*) coffin; (*mobile*) chest; (*involucro: di orologio etc*) case; (*macchina*) cash register; (*luogo di pagamento*) checkout (counter); (*fondo*) fund; '(*istituto bancario*) bank; ~ **automatica prelievi** automatic telling machine, cash dispenser; ~ **continua** night safe; ~ **integrazione: mettere in** ~ **integrazione** ≈ to lay off; ~ **mutua** o **malattia** health insurance scheme; ~ **di risparmio** savings bank; ~ **toracica** (*ANAT*) chest.

cassa'forte, *pl* **casseforti** *sf* safe.

cassa'panca, *pl* **cassapanche** o **cassepanche** *sf* settle.

casseru'ola, casse'rola *sf* saucepan.

cas'setta *sf* box; (*per registratore*) cassette; (*CINEMA, TEATRO*) box-office takings *pl*; **film di** ~ box-office draw; ~ **di sicurezza** strongbox; ~ **delle lettere** letterbox.

cas'setto *sm* drawer; **casset'tone** *sm* chest of drawers.

cassi'ere, a *sm/f* cashier; (*di banca*) teller.

'casta *sf* caste.

cas'tagna [kas'taɲɲa] *sf* chestnut.

cas'tagno [kas'taɲɲo] *sm* chestnut

(tree).

cas'tano, a *ag* chestnut (brown).

cas'tello *sm* castle; (*TECN*) scaffolding.

casti'gare *vt* to punish; **cas'tigo, ghi** *sm* punishment.

castità *sf* chastity.

cas'toro *sm* beaver.

cas'trare *vt* to castrate; to geld; to doctor (*Brit*), fix (*US*).

casu'ale *ag* chance *cpd*.

cata'comba *sf* catacomb.

ca'talogo, ghi *sm* catalogue.

catarifran'gente [catarifran'dʒɛnte] *sm* (*AUT*) reflector.

ca'tarro *sm* catarrh.

ca'tasta *sf* stack, pile.

ca'tasto *sm* land register; land registry office.

ca'tastrofe *sf* catastrophe, disaster.

catego'ria *sf* category.

ca'tena *sf* chain; ~ **di montaggio** assembly line; ~**e da neve** (*AUT*) snow chains; **cate'naccio** *sm* bolt.

cate'ratta *sf* cataract; (*chiusa*) sluice-gate.

cati'nella *sf*: **piovere a** ~**e** to pour, rain cats and dogs.

ca'tino *sm* basin.

ca'trame *sm* tar.

'cattedra *sf* teacher's desk; (*di università*) chair.

catte'drale *sf* cathedral.

catti'veria *sf* malice, spite; naughtiness; (*atto*) spiteful act; (*parole*) malicious o spiteful remark.

cattività *sf* captivity.

cat'tivo, a *ag* bad; (*malvagio*) bad, wicked; (*turbolento: bambino*) bad, naughty; (: *mare*) rough; (*odore, sapore*) nasty, bad.

cat'tolico, a, ci, che *ag, sm/f* (Roman) Catholic.

cat'tura *sf* capture.

cattu'rare *vt* to capture.

cauccìù [kaut'tʃu] *sm* rubber.

'causa *sf* cause; (*DIR*) lawsuit, case, action; **a ~ di, per ~ di** because of; **fare** o **muovere ~ a qn** to take legal action against sb.

cau'sare *vt* to cause.

cau'tela *sf* caution, prudence.

caute'lare *vt* to protect; ~**rsi** *vr*: ~**rsi** (**da**) to take precautions (against).

'cauto, a *ag* cautious, prudent.

cauzi'one [kaut'tsjone] *sf* security; (*DIR*) bail.

cav. *abbr* = **cavaliere**.

'cava *sf* quarry.

caval'care *vt* (*cavallo*) to ride; (*muro*) to sit astride; (*sog: ponte*) to span; **caval'cata** *sf* ride; (*gruppo di persone*) riding party.

cavalca'via *sm inv* flyover.

cavalcioni [kaval'tʃoni]: **a ~ di** *prep* astride.

cavali'ere *sm* rider; (*feudale, titolo*) knight; (*soldato*) cavalryman; (*al ballo*) partner; **cavalle'resco, a, schi, sche** *ag* chivalrous; **cavalle'ria** *sf* chivalry; (*milizia a cavallo*) cavalry.

cavalle'rizzo, a [kavalle'rittso] *sm/f* riding instructor; circus rider.

caval'letta *sf* grasshopper.

caval'letto *sm* (*FOT*) tripod; (*da pittore*) easel.

ca'vallo *sm* horse; (*SCACCHI*) knight; (*AUT: anche: ~ vapore*) horsepower; (*dei pantaloni*) crotch; **a ~ on** horseback; **a ~ di** astride, straddling; **~ di battaglia** (*fig*) hobby-horse; **~ da corsa** racehorse.

ca'vare *vt* (*togliere*) to draw out, extract, take out; (*: giacca, scarpe*) to take off; (*: fame, sete, voglia*) to satisfy; **cavarsela** to get away with it; to manage, get on all right.

cava'tappi *sm inv* corkscrew.

ca'verna *sf* cave.

'cavia *sf* guinea pig.

cavi'ale *sm* caviar.

ca'viglia [ka'viʎʎa] *sf* ankle.

ca'villo *sm* quibble.

'cavo, a *ag* hollow // *sm* (*ANAT*) cavity; (*grossa corda*) rope, cable; (*ELETTR, TEL*) cable.

cavolfi'ore *sm* cauliflower.

'cavolo *sm* cabbage; (*fam*): **non m'importa un ~ I** don't give a damn; **~ di Bruxelles** Brussels sprout.

cazzu'ola [kat'tswɔla] *sf* trowel.

c/c *abbr* = **conto corrente.**

ce [tʃe] *pronome, av vedi* **ci.**

cece ['tʃetʃe] *sm* chickpea.

cecità [tʃetʃi'ta] *sf* blindness.

Cecoslo'vacchia [tʃekozlo'vakkja] *sf*: **la ~** Czechoslovakia; **cecoslo'vacco, a, chi, che** *ag, sm/f* Czechoslovakian.

'cedere ['tʃedere] *vt* (*concedere: posto*) to give up; (*DIR*) to transfer, make over // *vi* (*cadere*) to give way, subside; **~ (a)** to surrender (to), yield (to), give in (to); **ce'devole** *ag* (*terreno*) soft; (*fig*) yielding.

'cedola ['tʃedola] *sf* (*COMM*) coupon; voucher.

'cedro ['tʃedro] *sm* cedar; (*albero da frutto, frutto*) citron.

C.E.E. ['tʃe] *sigla f* = **Comunità Economica Europea.**

'ceffo ['tʃeffo] *sm* (*peg*) ugly mug.

cef'fone [tʃef'fone] *sm* slap, smack.

ce'larsi [tʃe'larsi] *vr* to hide.

cele'brare [tʃele'brare] *vt* to celebrate; **celebrazi'one** *sf* celebration.

'celebre ['tʃelebre] *ag* famous, celebrated; **celebrità** *sf inv* fame; (*persona*) celebrity.

'celere ['tʃelere] *ag* fast, swift; (*corso*) crash *cpd*.

ce'leste [tʃe'lɛste] *ag* celestial; heavenly; (*colore*) sky-blue.

'celibe ['tʃelibe] *ag* single, unmarried // *sm* bachelor.

'cella ['tʃella] *sf* cell.

'cellula ['tʃellula] *sf* (*BIOL, ELETTR, POL*) cell.

cemen'tare [tʃemen'tare] *vt* (*anche fig*) to cement.

ce'mento [tʃe'mento] *sm* cement; **~ armato** reinforced concrete.

'cena ['tʃena] *sf* dinner; (*leggera*) supper.

ce'nare [tʃe'nare] *vi* to dine, have dinner.

'cencio ['tʃentʃo] *sm* piece of cloth, rag; (*per spolverare*) duster.

'cenere ['tʃenere] *sf* ash.

'cenno ['tʃenno] *sm* (*segno*) sign, signal; (*gesto*) gesture; (*col capo*) nod; (*con la mano*), wave; (*allusione*) hint, mention; (*breve esposizione*) short account; **far ~ di sì/no** to nod (one's head)/shake one's head.

censi'mento [tʃensi'mento] *sm* census.

cen'sore [tʃen'sore] *sm* censor.

cen'sura [tʃen'sura] *sf* censorship; censor's office; (*fig*) censure.

cente'nario, a [tʃente'narjo] *ag* (*che ha cento anni*) hundred-year-old; (*che ricorre ogni cento anni*) centennial, centenary *cpd* // *sm/f* centenarian // *sm* centenary.

cen'tesimo, a [tʃen'tezimo] *ag, sm* hundredth.

cen'tigrado, a [tʃen'tigrado] *ag* centigrade; **20 gradi ~i** 20 degrees centigrade.

cen'timetro [tʃen'timetro] *sm* centimetre.

centi'naio, *pl(f)* **aia** [tʃenti'najo] *sm*: **un ~ (di)** a hundred; about a hundred.

'cento ['tʃento] *num* a hundred, one hundred.

cen'trale [tʃen'trale] *ag* central // *sf*: **~ telefonica** (telephone) exchange; **~ elettrica** electric power station; **centrali'nista** *sm/f* operator; **centra'lino** *sm* (telephone) exchange; (*di albergo etc*) switchboard.

cen'trare [tʃen'trare] *vt* to hit the centre of; (*TECN*) to centre.

cen'trifuga [tʃen'trifuga] *sf* spin-drier.

'centro ['tʃentro] *sm* centre; **~ commerciale** shopping centre; (*città*) commercial centre.

'ceppo ['tʃeppo] *sm* (*di albero*) stump; (*pezzo di legno*) log.

'cera ['tʃera] *sf* wax; (*aspetto*) appearance, look.

ce'ramica, che [tʃe'ramika] *sf* ceramic; (*ARTE*) ceramics *sg*.

cerbi'atto [tʃer'bjatto] *sm* (*ZOOL*) fawn.

'cerca ['tʃerka] *sf*: **in *o* alla ~ di** in search of.

cer'care [tʃer'kare] *vt* to look for, search for // *vi*: **~ di fare qc** to try to do sth.

'cerchia ['tʃerkja] sf circle.

'cerchio ['tʃerkjo] sm circle; (giocattolo, di botte) hoop.

cere'ale [tʃere'ale] sm cereal.

ceri'monia [tʃeri'mɔnja] sf ceremony; **cerimoni'oso, a** ag formal, ceremonious.

ce'rino [tʃe'rino] sm wax match.

'cernia ['tʃernja] sf (ZOOL) stone bass.

cerni'era [tʃer'njera] sf hinge; ~ lampo zip (fastener) (Brit), zipper (US).

'cernita ['tʃernita] sf selection.

'cero ['tʃero] sm (church) candle.

ce'rotto [tʃe'rɔtto] sm sticking plaster.

certa'mente [tʃerta'mente] av certainly, surely.

cer'tezza [tʃer'tettsa] sf certainty.

certifi'cato sm certificate; ~ **medico/di nascita** medical/birth certificate.

'certo, a ['tʃɛrto] ◆ ag (sicuro): ~ **(di/che)** certain o sure (of/that)
◆ det 1 (tale) certain; **un ~ signor** Smith a (certain) Mr Smith
2 (qualche; con valore intensivo) some; **dopo un ~ tempo** after some time; **un fatto di una ~a importanza** a matter of some importance; **di una ~a età** past one's prime, not so young
◆ pronome: ~i(e) pl some
◆ av (certamente) certainly; (senz'altro) of course; **di ~** certainly; **no (di) ~!**, **~ che no!** certainly not!; **sì ~,** yes indeed, certainly.

cer'tuni [tʃer'tuni] pronome pl some (people).

cer'vello, pl i (anche: pl(f) **a** o **e**) [tʃer'vello] sm brain.

'cervo, a ['tʃervo] sm/f stag/doe // sm deer; ~ **volante** stag beetle.

ce'sello [tʃe'zɛllo] sm chisel.

ce'soie [tʃe'zoje] sfpl shears.

ces'puglio [tʃes'puʎʎo] sm bush.

ces'sare [tʃes'sare] vi, vt to stop, cease; ~ **di fare qc** to stop doing sth; **cessate il fuoco** sm ceasefire.

'cesso ['tʃɛsso] sm (fam: gabinetto) bog.

'cesta ['tʃesta] sf (large) basket.

ces'tino [tʃes'tino] sm basket; (per la carta straccia) wastepaper basket; ~ **da viaggio** (FERR) packed lunch (o dinner).

'cesto ['tʃesto] sm basket.

'ceto ['tʃeto] sm (social) class.

cetrio'lino [tʃetrio'lino] sm gherkin.

cetri'olo [tʃetri'ɔlo] sm cucumber.

cfr. abbr (= confronta) cf.

CGIL sigla f (= Confederazione Generale Italiana del Lavoro) trades union organization.

che [ke] ◆ pronome 1 (relativo: persona: soggetto) who; (: oggetto) whom, that; (: cosa, animale) which, that; **il ragazzo ~ è venuto** the boy who came; **l'uomo ~ io vedo** the man (whom) I see; **il libro ~ è sul tavolo** the book which o that is on the table; **il libro ~ vedi** the book (which

o that) you see; **la sera ~ ti ho visto** the evening I saw you
2 (interrogativo, esclamativo) what; ~ **(cosa) fai?** what are you doing?; **a ~ (cosa) pensi?** what are you thinking about?; **non sa ~ (cosa) fare** he doesn't know what to do; **ma ~ dici!** what are you saying!
3 (indefinito): **quell'uomo ha un ~ di losco** there's something suspicious about that man; **un certo non so ~** an indefinable something
◆ det 1 (interrogativo: tra tanti) what; (: tra pochi) which; ~ **tipo di film preferisci?** what sort of film do you prefer?; ~ **vestito ti vuoi mettere?** what (o which) dress do you want to put on?
2 (esclamativo: seguito da aggettivo) how; (: seguito da sostantivo) what; ~ **buono!** how delicious!; ~ **bel vestito!** what a lovely dress!
◆ cong 1 (con proposizioni subordinate) that; **credo ~ verrà** I think he'll come; **voglio ~ tu studi** I want you to study; **so ~ tu c'eri** I know (that) you were there; **non ~: non ~ sia sbagliato, ma ...** not that it's wrong, but ...
2 (finale) so that; **vieni qua, ~ ti veda** come here, so (that) I can see you
3 (temporale): **arrivai ~ eri già partito** you had already left when I arrived; **sono anni ~ non lo vedo** I haven't seen him for years, it's years since I saw him
4 (in frasi imperative, concessive): ~ **venga pure!** let him come by all means!; ~ **tu sia benedetto!** may God bless you!
5 (comparativo: con più, meno) than; vedi anche **più, meno, così** etc.

cheti'chella [keti'kɛlla]: **alla ~** av stealthily, unobtrusively.

'cheto, a ['keto] ag quiet, silent.

chi [ki] pronome 1 (interrogativo: soggetto) who; (: oggetto) who, whom; ~ **è?** who is it?; **di ~ è questo libro?** whose book is this?, whose is this book?; **con ~ parli?** who are you talking to?; **a ~ pensi?** who are you thinking about?; ~ **di voi?** which of you?; **non so a ~ rivolgermi** I don't know who to ask
2 (relativo) whoever, anyone who; **dillo a ~ vuoi** tell whoever you like
3 (indefinito): ~ **... ~ ...** some ... others ...; ~ **dice una cosa, ~ dice un'altra** some say one thing, others say another.

chiacchie'rare [kjakkje'rare] vi to chat; (discorrere futilmente) to chatter; (far pettegolezzi) to gossip; **chiacchie'rata** sf chat; **chi'acchiere** sfpl: **fare due** o **quattro chiacchiere** to have a chat; **chiacchie'rone, a** ag talkative, chatty; gossipy // sm/f chatterbox; gossip.

chia'mare [kja'mare] vt to call; (rivolgersi a qn) to call (in), send for; ~**rsi** vr (aver nome) to be called; **mi**

chiamo Paolo my name is Paolo, I'm called Paolo; ~ **alle armi** to call up; ~ **in giudizio** to summon; **chia'mata** *sf* (*TEL*) call; (*MIL*) call-up.

chia'rezza [kja'rettsa] *sf* clearness; clarity.

chia'rire [kja'rire] *vt* to make clear; (*fig: spiegare*) to clear up, explain; ~**rsi** *vr* to become clear.

chi'aro, a ['kjaro] *ag* clear; (*luminoso*) clear, bright; (*colore*) pale, light.

chiaroveg'gente [kjaroved'dʒɛnte] *sm/f* clairvoyant.

chi'asso ['kjasso] *sm* uproar, row; **chias'soso, a** *ag* noisy, rowdy; (*vistoso*) showy, gaudy.

chi'ave ['kjave] *sf* key // *ag inv* key *cpd*; ~ **d'accensione** (*AUT*) ignition key; ~ **inglese** monkey wrench; ~ **di volta** (*anche fig*) keystone; **chiavis'tello** *sm* bolt.

chi'azza ['kjattsa] *sf* stain; splash.

'chicco, chi ['kikko] *sm* (*di cereale, riso*) grain; (*di caffè*) bean; ~ **d'uva** grape.

chi'edere ['kjɛdere] *vt* (*per sapere*) to ask; (*per avere*) to ask for // *vi*: ~ **di qn** to ask after sb; (*al telefono*) to ask for o want sb; ~ **qc a qn** to ask sb sth; to ask sb for sth.

chi'erico, ci ['kjɛriko] *sm* cleric; altar boy.

chi'esa ['kjɛza] *sf* church.

chi'esto, a *pp di* **chiedere.**

'chiglia ['kiʎʎa] *sf* keel.

'chilo ['kilo] *sm* kilo; **chilo'grammo** *sm* kilogram(me); **chi'lometro** *sm* kilometre.

'chimico, a, ci, che ['kimiko] *ag* chemical // *sm/f* chemist // *sf* chemistry.

'china ['kina] *sf* (*pendio*) slope, descent; (*BOT*) cinchona; (**inchiostro di**) ~ Indian ink.

chi'nare [ki'nare] *vt* to lower, bend; ~**rsi** *vr* to stoop, bend.

chi'nino [ki'nino] *sm* quinine.

chi'occia, ce ['kjɔttʃa] *sf* brooding hen.

chi'occiola ['kjɔttʃola] *sf* snail; **scala a** ~ spiral staircase.

chi'odo ['kjɔdo] *sm* nail; (*fig*) obsession.

chi'oma ['kjɔma] *sf* (*capelli*) head of hair; (*di albero*) foliage.

chi'osco, schi ['kjɔsko] *sm* kiosk, stall.

chi'ostro ['kjɔstro] *sm* cloister.

chiro'mante [kiro'mante] *sm/f* palmist.

chirur'gia [kirur'dʒia] *sf* surgery; **chi'rurgo, ghi** o **gi** *sm* surgeon.

chissà [kis'sa] *av* who knows, I wonder.

chi'tarra [ki'tarra] *sf* guitar.

chi'udere ['kjudere] *vt* to close, shut; (*luce, acqua*) to put off, turn off; (*definitivamente: fabbrica*) to close down, shut down; (*strada*) to close; (*recingere*) to enclose; (*porre termine*) to end // *vi* to close; to close down, shut down; to end; ~**rsi** *vr* to shut,

close; (*ritirarsi: anche fig*) to shut o.s. away; (*ferita*) to close up.

chi'unque [ki'unkwe] *pronome* (*relativo*) whoever; (*indefinito*) anyone, anybody; ~ **sia** whoever it is.

chi'uso, a ['kjuso] *pp di* **chiudere** // *sf* (*di corso d'acqua*) sluice, lock; (*recinto*) enclosure; (*di discorso etc*) conclusion, ending; **chiu'sura** *sf* closing; shutting; closing o shutting down; enclosing; putting o turning off; ending; (*dispositivo*) catch; fastening; fastener.

ci [tʃi] (*dav lo, la, li, le, ne diventa* **ce**) ◆ *pronome* **1** (*personale: complemento oggetto*) us; (*: a noi: complemento di termine*) (to) us; (*: riflessivo*) ourselves; (*: reciproco*) each other, one another; (*impersonale*): ~ **si veste** we get dressed; ~ **ha visti** he's seen us; **non** ~ **ha dato niente** he gave us nothing; ~ **vestiamo we get dressed**; ~ **amiamo** we love one another o each other

2 (*dimostrativo: di ciò, su ciò, in ciò etc*) about (o on o of) it; **non so cosa far**~ I don't know what to do about it; ~ **puoi contare** you can depend on it; **che c'entro io?** what have I got to do with it? ◆ *av* (*qui*) here; (*lì*) there; (*moto attraverso luogo*): ~ **passa sopra un ponte** a bridge passes over it; **non** ~ **passa più nessuno** nobody comes this way any more; **esser**~ *vedi* **essere.**

C.ia *abbr* (= *compagnia*) Co.

cia'batta [tʃa'batta] *sf* mule, slipper.

ci'alda ['tʃalda] *sf* (*CUC*) wafer.

ciam'bella [tʃam'bella] *sf* (*CUC*) ring-shaped cake; (*salvagente*) rubber ring.

ci'ao ['tʃao] *escl* (*all'arrivo*) hello!; (*alla partenza*) cheerio! (*Brit*), bye!

ciarla'tano [tʃarla'tano] *sm* charlatan.

cias'cuno, a [tʃas'kuno] (*dav sm:* **cia-scun** +*C, V,* **ciascuno** +*s impura, gn, pn, ps, x, z; dav sf:* **ciascuna** +*C,* **cia-scun'** +*V*) *det, pronome* each.

'cibo ['tʃibo] *sm* food.

ci'cala [tʃi'kala] *sf* cicada.

cica'trice [tʃika'tritʃe] *sf* scar.

'cicca ['tʃikka] *sf* cigarette end.

'ciccia ['tʃittʃa] *sf* (*fam: carne*) meat; (*: grasso umano*) fat, flesh.

cice'rone [tʃitʃe'rone] *sm* guide.

ci'clismo [tʃi'klizmo] *sm* cycling; **ci'clista, i, e** *sm/f* cyclist.

'ciclo ['tʃiklo] *sm* cycle; (*di malattia*) course.

ciclomo'tore [tʃiklomo'tore] *sm* moped.

ci'clone [tʃi'klone] *sm* cyclone.

ci'cogna [tʃi'koɲɲa] *sf* stork.

ci'coria [tʃi'kɔria] *sf* chicory.

ci'eco, a, chi, che ['tʃɛko] *ag* blind // *sm/f* blind man/woman.

ci'elo ['tʃɛlo] *sm* sky; (*REL*) heaven.

'cifra ['tʃifra] *sf* (*numero*) figure; numeral; (*somma di denaro*) sum, figure; (*monogramma*) monogram, initials *pl*;

(*codice*) code, cipher.

'ciglio ['tʃiʎʎo] *sm* (*margine*) edge, verge; (*pl(f)* **ciglia**: *delle palpebre*) (eye)lash; (eye)lid; (*sopracciglio*) eyebrow.

'cigno ['tʃiɲɲo] *sm* swan.

cigo'lare [tʃigo'lare] *vi* to squeak, creak.

'Cile ['tʃile] *sm*: il ~ Chile.

ci'lecca [tʃi'lekka] *sf*: far ~ to fail.

cili'egia, gie *o* **ge** [tʃi'ljedʒa] *sf* cherry; **cili'egio** *sm* cherry tree.

cilin'drata [tʃilin'drata] *sf* (AUT) (cubic) capacity; **una macchina di grossa** ~ a big-engined car.

ci'lindro [tʃi'lindro] *sm* cylinder; (*cappello*) top hat.

'cima ['tʃima] *sf* (*sommità*) top; (*di monte*) top, summit; (*estremità*) end; in ~ **a** at the top of; **da** ~ **a fondo** from top to bottom; (*fig*) from beginning to end.

'cimice ['tʃimitʃe] *sf* (ZOOL) bug; (*puntina*) drawing pin (*Brit*), thumbtack (US).

cimini'era [tʃimi'njɛra] *sf* chimney; (*di nave*) funnel.

cimi'tero [tʃimi'tɛro] *sm* cemetery.

ci'murro [tʃi'murro] *sm* (*di cani*) distemper.

'Cina ['tʃina] *sf*: la ~ China.

cin'cin, cin cin [tʃin'tʃin] *escl* cheers!

'cinema ['tʃinema] *sm inv* cinema; **cine'presa** *sf* cine-camera.

ci'nese [tʃi'nese] *ag*, *sm/f*, *sm* Chinese *inv*.

ci'netico, a, ci, che [tʃi'nɛtiko] *ag* kinetic.

'cingere ['tʃindʒere] *vt* (*attorniare*) to surround, encircle; ~ **la vita con una cintura** to put a belt round one's waist.

'cinghia ['tʃiŋgja] *sf* strap; (*cintura*, TECN) belt.

cinghi'ale [tʃin'gjale] *sm* wild boar.

cinguet'tare [tʃiŋgwet'tare] *vi* to twitter.

'cinico, a, ci, che ['tʃiniko] *ag* cynical // *sm/f* cynic; **ci'nismo** *sm* cynicism.

cin'quanta [tʃin'kwanta] *num* fifty; **cinquan'tesimo, a** *num* fiftieth.

cinquan'tina [tʃinkwan'tina] *sf* (*serie*): **una** ~ (**di**) about fifty; (*età*): **essere sulla** ~ to be about fifty.

'cinque ['tʃinkwe] *num* five; **avere** ~ **anni** to be five (years old); **il** ~ **dicembre 1988** the fifth of December 1988; **alle** ~ (*ora*) at five (o'clock).

cinque'cento [tʃinkwe'tʃento] *num* five hundred // *sm*: **il C~** the sixteenth century.

'cinto, a ['tʃinto] *pp di* **cingere**.

cin'tura [tʃin'tura] *sf* belt; ~ **di salvataggio** lifebelt (*Brit*), life preserver (US); ~ **di sicurezza** (AUT, AER) safety *o* seat belt.

ciò [tʃɔ] *pronome* this; that; ~ **che** what; ~ **nonostante** *o* **nondimeno** nevertheless, in spite of that.

ci'occa, che ['tʃɔkka] *sf* (*di capelli*) lock.

ciocco'lata [tʃokko'lata] *sf* chocolate; (*bevanda*) (hot) chocolate; **cioccola'tino** *sm* chocolate; **ciocco'lato** *sm* chocolate.

cioè [tʃo'ɛ] *av* that is (to say).

ciondo'lare [tʃondo'lare] *vi* to dangle; (*fig*) to loaf (about); **ci'ondolo** *sm* pendant.

ci'otola ['tʃɔtola] *sf* bowl.

ci'ottolo ['tʃɔttolo] *sm* pebble; (*di strada*) cobble(stone).

ci'polla [tʃi'polla] *sf* onion; (*di tulipano etc*) bulb.

ci'presso [tʃi'presso] *sm* cypress (tree).

'cipria ['tʃiprja] *sf* (face) powder.

'Cipro ['tʃipro] *sm* Cyprus.

'circa ['tʃirka] *av* about, roughly // *prep* about, concerning; **a mezzogiorno** ~ about midday.

'circo, chi ['tʃirko] *sm* circus.

circo'lare [tʃirko'lare] *vi* to circulate; (AUT) to drive (along), move (along) // *ag* circular // *sf* (AMM) circular; (*di autobus*) circle (line); **circolazi'one** *sf* circulation; (AUT): **la circolazione** (the) traffic.

'circolo ['tʃirkolo] *sm* circle.

circon'dare [tʃirkon'dare] *vt* to surround.

circonfe'renza [tʃirkonfe'rentsa] *sf* circumference.

circonvallazi'one [tʃirkonvallat'tsjone] *sf* ring road (*Brit*), beltway (US); (*per evitare una città*) by-pass.

circos'critto, a [tʃirkos'kritto] *pp di* **circoscrivere**.

circos'crivere [tʃirkos'krivere] *vt* to circumscribe; (*fig*) to limit, restrict; **circoscrizi'one** *sf* (AMM) district, area; **circoscrizione elettorale** constituency.

circos'petto, a [tʃirkos'petto] *ag* circumspect, cautious.

circos'tante [tʃirkos'tante] *ag* surrounding, neighbouring.

circos'tanza [tʃirkos'tantsa] *sf* circumstance; (*occasione*) occasion.

cir'cuito [tʃir'kuito] *sm* circuit.

CISL *sigla f* (= *Confederazione Italiana Sindacati Lavoratori*) *trades union organization*.

'ciste ['tʃiste] *sf* = **cisti**.

cis'terna [tʃis'tɛrna] *sf* tank, cistern.

'cisti ['tʃisti] *sf* cyst.

C.I.T. [tʃit] *sigla f* = *Compagnia Italiana Turismo*.

ci'tare [tʃi'tare] *vt* (DIR) to summon; (*autore*) to quote; (*a esempio, modello*) to cite; **citazi'one** *sf* summons *sg*; quotation; (*di persona*) mention.

ci'tofono [tʃi'tɔfono] *sm* entry phone; (*in uffici*) intercom.

città [tʃit'ta] *sf inv* town; (*importante*) city; ~ **universitaria** university campus.

cittadi'nanza [tʃittadi'nantsa] *sf* citizens

pl, inhabitants *pl* of a town (*o* city); (*DIR*) citizenship.

citta'dino, a [tʃitta'dino] *ag* town *cpd*; city *cpd* // *smf* (*di uno Stato*) citizen; (*abitante di città*) townsman, city dweller.

ci'uco, a, chi, che ['tʃuko] *sm/f* ass, donkey.

ci'uffo ['tʃuffo] *sm* tuft.

ci'vetta [tʃi'vetta] *sf* (*ZOOL*) owl; (*fig: donna*) coquette, flirt // *ag inv*: **auto/nave** ~ decoy car/ship.

'civico, a, ci, che ['tʃiviko] *ag* civic; (*museo*) municipal, town *cpd*; municipal, city *cpd*.

ci'vile [tʃi'vile] *ag* civil; (*non militare*) civilian; (*nazione*) civilized // *sm* civilian.

civilizzazi'one [tʃiviliddzat'tsjone] *sf* civilization.

civiltà [tʃivil'ta] *sf* civilization; (*cortesia*) civility.

'clacson *sm inv* (*AUT*) horn.

cla'more *sm* (*frastuono*) din, uproar, clamour; (*fig*) outcry; **clamo'roso, a** *ag* noisy; (*fig*) sensational.

clandes'tino, a *ag* clandestine; (*POL*) underground, clandestine // *sm/f* stowaway.

clari'netto *sm* clarinet.

'classe *sf* class; **di** ~ (*fig*) with class; of excellent quality.

'classico, a, ci, che *ag* classical; (*tradizionale: moda*) classic(al) // *sm* classic; classical author.

clas'sifica *sf* classification; (*SPORT*) placings *pl*.

classifi'care *vt* to classify; (*candidato, compito*) to grade; ~**rsi** *vr* to be placed.

'clausola *sf* (*DIR*) clause.

'clava *sf* club.

clavi'cembalo [klavi'tʃembalo] *sm* harpsichord.

cla'vicola *sf* (*ANAT*) collar bone.

cle'mente *ag* merciful; (*clima*) mild; **cle'menza** *sf* mercy, clemency; mildness.

'clero *sm* clergy.

cli'ente *sm/f* customer, client; **clien'tela** *sf* customers *pl*, clientèle.

'clima *sm* climate; **cli'matico, a, ci, che** *ag* climatic; **stazione climatica** health resort; **climatizzazi'one** *sf* (*TECN*) air conditioning.

'clinico, a, ci, che *ag* clinical // *sm* (*medico*) clinician // *sf* (*scienza*) clinical medicine; (*casa di cura*) clinic, nursing home; (*settore d'ospedale*) clinic.

clo'aca, che *sf* sewer.

'cloro *sm* chlorine.

cloro'formio *sm* chloroform.

club *sm inv* club.

c.m. *abbr* = **corrente mese**.

coabi'tare *vi* to live together, live under the same roof.

coagu'lare *vt* to coagulate // *vi*, ~**rsi** *vr* to coagulate; (*latte*) to curdle.

coalizi'one [koalit'tsjone] *sf* coalition.

co'atto, a *ag* (*DIR*) compulsory, forced.

'COBAS *sigla mpl* (= *Comitati di base*) independent trades unions.

coca'ina *sf* cocaine.

cocci'nella [kottʃi'nella] *sf* ladybird (*Brit*), ladybug (*US*).

'coccio ['kɔttʃo] *sm* earthenware; (*vaso*) earthenware pot; ~**i** *smpl* fragments (of pottery).

cocci'uto, a [kot'tʃuto] *ag* stubborn, pigheaded.

'cocco, chi *sm* (*pianta*) coconut palm; (*frutto*): **noce di** ~ coconut // *sm/f* (*fam*) darling.

cocco'drillo *sm* crocodile.

cocco'lare *vt* to cuddle, fondle.

co'cente [ko'tʃente] *ag* (*anche fig*) burning.

co'comero *sm* watermelon.

co'cuzzolo [ko'kuttsolo] *sm* top; (*di capo, cappello*) crown.

'coda *sf* tail; (*fila di persone, auto*) queue (*Brit*), line (*US*); (*di abiti*) train; **con la** ~ **dell'occhio** out of the corner of one's eye; **mettersi in** ~ to queue (up) (*Brit*), line up (*US*); to join the queue (*Brit*) *o* line (*US*); ~ **di cavallo** (*acconciatura*) ponytail.

co'dardo, a *ag* cowardly // *sm/f* coward.

'codice ['koditʃe] *sm* code; ~ **di avviamento postale (C.A.P.)** postcode (*Brit*), zip code (*US*); ~ **fiscale** tax code; ~ **della strada** highway code.

coe'rente *ag* coherent; **coe'renza** *sf* coherence.

coe'taneo, a *ag*, *sm/f* contemporary.

'cofano *sm* (*AUT*) bonnet (*Brit*), hood (*US*); (*forziere*) chest.

'cogli ['kɔʎʎi] *prep* + *det vedi* **con**.

'cogliere ['kɔʎʎere] *vt* (*fiore, frutto*) to pick, gather; (*sorprendere*) to catch, surprise; (*bersaglio*) to hit; (*fig: momento opportuno etc*) to grasp, seize, take; (*: capire*) to grasp; ~ **qn in flagrante** *o* **in fallo** to catch sb red-handed.

co'gnato, a [koɲ'ɲato] *sm/f* brother-/sister-in-law.

cognizi'one [koɲɲit'tsjone] *sf* knowledge.

co'gnome [koɲ'ɲome] *sm* surname.

'coi *prep* + *det vedi* **con**.

coinci'denza [kointʃi'dɛntsa] *sf* coincidence; (*FERR, AER, di autobus*) connection.

coin'cidere [koin'tʃidere] *vi* to coincide; **coin'ciso, a** *pp di* **coincidere**.

coin'volgere [koin'vɔldʒere] *vt*: ~ **in** to involve in; **coin'volto, a** *pp di* **coinvolgere**.

col *prep* + *det vedi* **con**.

cola'brodo *sm inv* strainer.

cola'pasta *sm inv* colander.

co'lare *vt* (*liquido*) to strain; (*pasta*) to drain; (*oro fuso*) to pour // *vi* (*sudore*) to drip; (*botte*) to leak; (*cera*) to melt; ~ a picco *vt*, *vi* (*nave*) to sink.

co'lata *sf* (*di lava*) flow; (*FONDERIA*) casting.

colazi'one [kolat'tsjone] *sf* (*anche*: prima ~) breakfast; (*anche*: seconda ~) lunch; fare ~ to have breakfast (*o* lunch).

co'lei *pronome vedi* colui.

co'lera *sm* (*MED*) cholera.

'colica *sf* (*MED*) colic.

'colla *prep + det vedi* con // *sf* glue; (*di farina*) paste.

collabo'rare *vi* to collaborate; ~ a to collaborate on; (*giornale*) to contribute to; **collabora'tore, 'trice** *sm/f* collaborator; contributor.

col'lana *sf* necklace; (*collezione*) collection, series.

col'lant [kɔ'lã] *sm inv* tights *pl*.

col'lare *sm* collar.

col'lasso *sm* (*MED*) collapse.

collau'dare *vt* to test, try out; **col'laudo** *sm* testing *q*; test.

'colle *sm* hill.

col'lega, ghi, ghe *sm/f* colleague.

còllega'mento *sm* connection; (*MIL*) liaison.

colle'gare *vt* to connect, join, link; ~rsi *vr* (*RADIO*, *TV*) to link up; ~rsi con (*TEL*) to get through to.

col'legio [kol'lɛdʒo] *sm* college; (*convitto*) boarding school; ~ elettorale (*POL*) constituency.

'collera *sf* anger.

col'lerico, a, ci, che *ag* quick-tempered, irascible.

col'letta *sf* collection.

collettività *sf* community.

collet'tivo, a *ag* collective; (*interesse*) general, everybody's; (*biglietto, visita etc*) group *cpd* // *sm* (*POL*) (political) group.

col'letto *sm* collar.

collezio'nare [kollettsjo'nare] *vt* to collect.

collezi'one [kollet'tsjone] *sf* collection.

colli'mare *vi* to correspond, coincide.

col'lina *sf* hill.

col'lirio *sm* eyewash.

collisi'one *sf* collision.

'collo *sm* neck; (*di abito*) neck, collar; (*pacco*) parcel; ~ del piede instep.

colloca'mento *sm* (*impiego*) employment; (*disposizione*) placing, arrangement.

collo'care *vt* (*libri, mobili*) to place; (*persona: trovare un lavoro per*) to find a job for, place; (*COMM: merce*) to find a market for.

col'loquio *sm* conversation, talk; (*ufficiale, per un lavoro*) interview; (*INS*) preliminary oral exam.

col'mare *vt*: ~ di (*anche fig*) to fill with; (*dare in abbondanza*) to load *o* overwhelm with; **'colmo, a** *ag*: colmo (di) full (of) // *sm* summit, top; (*fig*) height; al colmo della disperazione in the depths of despair; è il colmo! it's the last straw!

co'lombo, a *sm/f* dove; pigeon.

co'lonia *sf* colony; (*per bambini*) holiday camp; (*acqua*) ~ (eau de) cologne; **coloni'ale** *ag* colonial // *sm/f* colonist, settler.

co'lonna *sf* column; ~ vertebrale spine, spinal column.

colon'nello *sm* colonel.

co'lono *sm* (*coltivatore*) tenant farmer.

colo'rante *sm* colouring.

colo'rare *vt* to colour; (*disegno*) to colour in.

co'lore *sm* colour; a ~i in colour, colour *cpd*; farne di tutti i ~i to get up to all sorts of mischief.

colo'rito, a *ag* coloured; (*viso*) rosy, pink; (*linguaggio*) colourful // *sm* (*tinta*) colour; (*carnagione*) complexion.

co'loro *pronome pl vedi* colui.

co'losso *sm* colossus.

'colpa *sf* fault; (*biasimo*) blame; (*colpevolezza*) guilt; (*azione colpevole*) offence; (*peccato*) sin; di chi è la ~? whose fault is it?; è ~ sua it's his fault; per ~ di through, owing to; **col'pevole** *ag* guilty.

col'pire *vt* to hit, strike; (*fig*) to strike; rimanere colpito da qc to be amazed *o* struck by sth.

'colpo *sm* (*urto*) knock; (: *affettivo*) blow, shock; (: *aggressivo*) blow; (*di pistola*) shot; (*MED*) stroke; (*rapina*) raid; di ~ suddenly; fare ~ to make a strong impression; ~ di grazia coup de grâce; ~ di sole sunstroke; ~ di Stato coup d'état; ~ di telefono phone call; ~ di testa (sudden) impulse *o* whim; ~ di vento gust (of wind).

coltel'lata *sf* stab.

col'tello *sm* knife; ~ a serramanico clasp knife.

colti'vare *vt* to cultivate; (*verdura*) to grow, cultivate; **coltiva'tore** *sm* farmer; **coltivazi'one** *sf* cultivation; growing.

'colto, a *pp di* cogliere // *ag* (*istruito*) cultured, educated.

'coltre *sf* blanket.

col'tura *sf* cultivation.

co'lui, co'lei, pl co'loro *pronome* the one; ~ che parla the one *o* the man *o* the person who is speaking; colei che amo the one *o* the woman *o* the person (whom) I love.

'coma *sm inv* coma.

comanda'mento *sm* (*REL*) commandment.

coman'dante *sm* (*MIL*) commander,

commandant; (*di reggimento*) commanding officer; (*NAUT, AER*) captain.

coman'dare *vi* to be in command // *vt* to command; (*imporre*) to order, command; ~ **a qn di fare** to order sb to do; **co'mando** *sm* (*ingiunzione*) order, command; (*autorità*) command; (*TECN*) control.

co'mare *sf* (*madrina*) godmother.

combaci'are [komba'tʃare] *vi* to meet; (*fig: coincidere*) to coincide, correspond.

com'battere *vt* to fight; (*fig*) to combat, fight against // *vi* to fight; **combatti'mento** *sm* fight; fighting *q*; (*di pugilato*) match.

combi'nare *vt* to combine; (*organizzare*) to arrange; (*fam: fare*) to make, cause; **combinazi'one** *sf* combination; (*caso fortuito*) coincidence; **per combinazione** by chance.

combus'tibile *ag* combustible // *sm* fuel.

com'butta *sf* (*peg*): **in ~** in league.

'come ♦ *av* **1** (*alla maniera di*) like; **ti comporti ~ lui** you behave like him *o* like he does; **bianco ~ la neve** (as) white as snow; **~ se** as if, as though

2 (*in qualità di*) as a; **lavora ~ autista** he works as a driver

3 (*interrogativo*) how; **~ ti chiami?** what's your name?; **~ sta?** how are you?; **com'è il tuo amico?** what is your friend like?; **~?** (*prego?*) pardon?, sorry?; **~ mai?** how come?; **~ mai non ci hai avvertiti?** why on earth didn't you warn us?

4 (*esclamativo*): **~ sei bravo!** how clever you are!; **~ mi dispiace!** I'm terribly sorry!

♦ *cong* **1** (*in che modo*) how; **mi ha spiegato ~ l'ha conosciuto** he told me how he met him

2 (*correlativo*) as; (*con comparativi di maggioranza*) than; **non è bravo ~ pensavo** he isn't as clever as I thought; **è meglio di ~ pensassi** it's better than I thought

3 (*appena che, quando*) as soon as; **~ arrivò, iniziò a lavorare** as soon as he arrived, he set to work; *vedi* **così, tanto**.

'comico, a, ci, che *ag* (*TEATRO*) comic; (*buffo*) comical // *sm* (*attore*) comedian, comic actor; (*comicità*) comic spirit, comedy.

co'mignolo [ko'miɲɲolo] *sm* chimney top.

cominci'are [komin'tʃare] *vt, vi* to begin, start; **~ a fare/col fare** to begin to do/by doing.

comi'tato *sm* committee.

comi'tiva *sf* party, group.

co'mizio [ko'mittsjo] *sm* (*POL*) meeting, assembly.

com'mando *sm inv* commando (squad).

com'media *sf* comedy; (*opera teatrale*) play; (*: che fa ridere*) comedy; (*fig*) playacting *q*; **commedi'ante** *sm/f* (*peg*) third-rate actor/actress; (*: fig*) sham.

commemo'rare *vt* to commemorate.

commenda'tore *sm* official title awarded for services to one's country.

commen'tare *vt* to comment on; (*testo*) to annotate; (*RADIO, TV*) to give a commentary on; **commenta'tore, 'trice** *sm/f* commentator; **com'mento** *sm* comment; (*a un testo, RADIO, TV*) commentary.

commerci'ale [kommer'tʃale] *ag* commercial, trading; (*peg*) commercial.

commerci'ante [kommer'tʃante] *sm/f* trader, dealer; (*negoziante*) shopkeeper.

commerci'are [kommer'tʃare] *vt, vi*: **~ in** to deal *o* trade in.

com'mercio [kom'mertʃo] *sm* trade, commerce; **essere in ~** (*prodotto*) to be on the market *o* on sale; **essere nel ~** (*persona*) to be in business; **~ all'ingrosso/al minuto** wholesale/retail trade.

com'messo, a *pp di* **commettere** // *sm/f* shop assistant (*Brit*), sales clerk (*US*) // *sm* (*impiegato*) clerk // *sf* (*COMM*) order; **~ viaggiatore** commercial traveller.

commes'tibile *ag* edible; **~i** *smpl* foodstuffs.

com'mettere *vt* to commit.

com'miato *sm* leave-taking.

commi'nare *vt* (*DIR*) to threaten; to inflict.

commissari'ato *sm* (*AMM*) commissionership; (*: sede*) commissioner's office; (*: di polizia*) police station.

commis'sario *sm* commissioner; (*di pubblica sicurezza*) ≈ (police) superintendent (*Brit*), (police) captain (*US*); (*SPORT*) steward; (*membro di commissione*) member of a committee *o* board.

commissio'nario *sm* (*COMM*) agent, broker.

commissi'one *sf* (*incarico*) errand; (*comitato, percentuale*) commission; (*COMM: ordinazione*) order; **~i** *sfpl* (*acquisti*) shopping *sg*.

commit'tente *sm/f* (*COMM*) purchaser, customer.

com'mosso, a *pp di* **commuovere**.

commo'vente *ag* moving.

commozi'one [kommot'tsjone] *sf* emotion, deep feeling; **~ cerebrale** (*MED*) concussion.

commu'overe *vt* to move, affect; **~rsi** *vr* to be moved.

commu'tare *vt* (*pena*) to commute; (*ELETTR*) to change *o* switch over.

comò *sm inv* chest of drawers.

como'dino *sm* bedside table.

comodità *sf inv* comfort; convenience.

'comodo, a *ag* comfortable; *(facile)* easy; *(conveniente)* convenient; *(utile)* useful, handy // *sm* comfort; convenience; **con ~** at one's convenience *o* leisure; **fare il proprio ~** to do as one pleases; **far ~** to be useful *o* handy.

compae'sano, a *sm/f* fellow countryman; person from the same town.

com'pagine [kom'padʒine] *sf (squadra)* team.

compa'gnia [kompaɲ'nia] *sf* company; *(gruppo)* gathering.

com'pagno, a [kom'paɲɲo] *sm/f (di classe, gioco)* companion; *(POL)* comrade; **~ di lavoro** workmate.

compa'rare *vt* to compare.

compara'tivo, a *ag, sm* comparative.

compa'rire *vi* to appear; **com'parso, a** *pp di* **comparire** // *sf* appearance; *(TEATRO)* walk-on; *(CINEMA)* extra.

compartecipazi'one [kompartetʃipat'tsjone] *sf* sharing; *(quota)* share; **~ agli utili** profit-sharing.

comparti'mento *sm* compartment; *(AMM)* district.

compas'sato, a *ag (persona)* composed.

compassi'one *sf* compassion, pity; **avere ~ di qn** to feel sorry for sb, to pity sb.

com'passo *sm* (pair of) compasses *pl*; callipers *pl*.

compa'tibile *ag (scusabile)* excusable; *(conciliabile, INFORM)* compatible.

compa'tire *vt (aver compassione di)* to sympathize with, feel sorry for; *(scusare)* to make allowances for.

com'patto, a *ag* compact; *(roccia)* solid; *(folla)* dense; *(fig: gruppo, partito)* united, close-knit.

com'pendio *sm* summary; *(libro)* compendium.

compen'sare *vt (equilibrare)* to compensate for, make up for; **~ qn di** *(rimunerare)* to pay *o* remunerate sb for; *(risarcire)* to pay compensation to sb for; *(fig: fatiche, dolori)* to reward sb for; **com'penso** *sm* compensation; payment, remuneration; reward; **in compenso** *(d'altra parte)* on the other hand.

'compera *sf (acquisto)* purchase; **fare le ~e** to do the shopping.

compe'rare *vt* = **comprare**.

compe'tente *ag* competent; *(mancia)* apt, suitable; **compe'tenza** *sf* competence; **competenze** *sfpl (onorari)* fees.

com'petere *vi* to compete, vie; *(DIR: spettare)*: **~ a** to lie within the competence of; **competizi'one** *sf* competition.

compia'cente [kompja'tʃente] *ag* courteous, obliging; **compia'cenza** *sf* courtesy.

compia'cere [kompja'tʃere] *vi:* **~ a** to gratify, please // *vt* to please; **~rsi** *vr (provare soddisfazione)*: **~rsi di** *o* **per qc** to be delighted at sth; *(rallegrarsi)*: **~rsi con qn** to congratulate sb; *(degnarsi)*: **~rsi di fare** to be so good as to do; **compiaci'uto, a** *pp di* **compiacere**.

compi'angere [kom'pjandʒere] *vt* to sympathize with, feel sorry for; **compi'anto, a** *pp di* **compiangere**.

'compiere *vt (concludere)* to finish, complete; *(adempiere)* to carry out, fulfil; **~rsi** *vr (avverarsi)* to be fulfilled, come true; **~ gli anni** to have one's birthday.

com'pire *vt* = **compiere**.

compi'tare *vt* to spell out.

'compito *sm (incarico)* task, duty; *(dovere)* duty; *(INS)* exercise; *(: a casa)* piece of homework; **fare i ~i** to do one's homework.

com'pito, a *ag* well-mannered, polite.

comple'anno *sm* birthday.

complemen'tare *ag* complementary; *(INS: materia)* subsidiary.

comple'mento *sm* complement; *(MIL)* reserve (troops); **~ oggetto** *(LING)* direct object.

complessità *sf* complexity.

comples'sivo, a *ag (globale)* comprehensive, overall; *(totale: cifra)* total.

com'plesso, a *ag* complex // *sm (PSIC, EDIL)* complex; *(MUS: corale)* ensemble; *(: orchestrina)* band; *(: di musica pop)* group; **in** *o* **nel ~** on the whole.

comple'tare *vt* to complete.

com'pleto, a *ag* complete; *(teatro, autobus)* full // *sm* suit; **al ~** full; *(tutti presenti)* all present.

compli'care *vt* to complicate; **~rsi** *vr* to become complicated; **complicazi'one** *sf* complication.

'complice ['kɔmplitʃe] *sm/f* accomplice.

complimen'tarsi *vr:* **~ con** to congratulate.

compli'mento *sm* compliment; **~i** *smpl (cortesia eccessiva)* ceremony *sg*; *(ossequi)* regards, compliments; **~i!** congratulations!; **senza ~i!** don't stand on ceremony!; make yourself at home!; help yourself!

com'plotto *sm* plot, conspiracy.

compo'nente *sm/f* member // *sm* component.

componi'mento *sm (DIR)* settlement; *(INS)* composition; *(poetico, teatrale)* work.

com'porre *vt (musica, testo)* to compose; *(mettere in ordine)* to arrange; *(DIR: lite)* to settle; *(TIP)* to set; *(TEL)* to dial.

comporta'mento *sm* behaviour.
compor'tare *vt* (*implicare*) to involve; (*consentire*) to permit, allow (of); **~rsi** *vr* (*condursi*) to behave.
composi'tore, **'trice** *sm/f* composer; (*TIP*) compositor, typesetter.
composizi'one [kompozit'tsjone] *sf* composition; (*DIR*) settlement.
com'posta *sf vedi* **composto**.
compos'tezza [kompos'tettsa] *sf* composure; decorum.
com'posto, a *pp di* **comporre** // *ag* (*persona*) composed, self-possessed; (: *decoroso*) dignified; (*formato da più elementi*) compound *cpd* // *sm* compound // *sf* (*CUC*) stewed fruit *q*; (*AGR*) compost.
'compra *sf* = **compera**.
com'prare *vt* to buy; **compra'tore**, **'trice** *sm/f* buyer, purchaser.
com'prendere *vt* (*contenere*) to comprise, consist of; (*capire*) to understand.
comprensi'one *sf* understanding.
compren'sivo, a *ag* (*prezzo*): **~ di** inclusive of; (*indulgente*) understanding.
com'preso, a *pp di* **comprendere** // *ag* (*incluso*) included.
com'pressa *sf vedi* **compresso**.
compressi'one *sf* compression.
com'presso, a *pp di* **comprimere** // *ag* (*vedi comprimere*) pressed; compressed; repressed // *sf* (*MED: garza*) compress; (: *pastiglia*) tablet.
com'primere *vt* (*premere*) to press; (*FISICA*) to compress; (*fig*) to repress.
compro'messo, a *pp di* **compromettere** // *sm* compromise.
compro'mettere *vt* to compromise.
compro'vare *vt* to confirm.
com'punto, a *ag* contrite.
compu'tare *vt* to calculate; (*addebitare*): **~ qc a qn** to debit sb with sth.
com'puter *sm inv* computer.
computiste'ria *sf* accounting, bookkeeping.
'computo *sm* calculation.
comu'nale *ag* municipal, town *cpd*, ≈ borough *cpd*.
co'mune *ag* common; (*consueto*) common, everyday; (*di livello medio*) average; (*ordinario*) ordinary // *sm* (*AMM*) town council; (: *sede*) town hall // *sf* (*di persone*) commune; **fuori del ~** out of the ordinary; **avere in ~** to have in common, share; **mettere in ~** to share.
comuni'care *vt* (*notizia*) to pass on, convey; (*malattia*) to pass on; (*ansia etc*) to communicate; (*trasmettere: calore etc*) to transmit, communicate; (*REL*) to administer communion to // *vi* to communicate; **~rsi** *vr* (*propagarsi*): **~rsi a** to spread to; (*REL*) to receive communion.
comuni'cato *sm* communiqué; **~ stampa** press release.
comunicazi'one [komunikat'tsjone] *sf* communication; (*annuncio*) announcement; (*TEL*): **~ (telefonica)** (telephone) call; **dare la ~ a qn** to put sb through; **ottenere la ~** to get through.
comuni'one *sf* communion; **~ di beni** (*DIR*) joint ownership of property.
comu'nismo *sm* communism; **comu'nista, i, e** *ag, sm/f* communist.
comunità *sf inv* community; **C~ Economica Europea (C.E.E.)** European Economic Community (EEC).
co'munque *cong* however, no matter how // *av* (*in ogni modo*) in any case; (*tuttavia*) however, nevertheless.
con *prep* (*nei seguenti casi* **con** *può fondersi con l'articolo definito:* **con + il = col, con + gli = cogli, con + i = coi**) with; **partire col treno** to leave by train; **~ mio grande stupore** to my great astonishment; **~ tutto ciò** for all that.
co'nato *sm*: **~ di vomito** retching.
'conca, che *sf* (*GEO*) valley.
con'cedere [kon'tʃedere] *vt* (*accordare*) to grant; (*ammettere*) to admit, concede; **~rsi qc** to treat o.s. to sth, to allow o.s. sth.
concentra'mento [kontʃentra'mento] *sm* concentration.
concen'trare [kontʃen'trare] *vt*, **~rsi** *vr* to concentrate; **concentrazi'one** *sf* concentration.
conce'pire [kontʃe'pire] *vt* (*bambino*) to conceive; (*progetto, idea*) to conceive (of); (*metodo, piano*) to devise.
con'cernere [kon'tʃernere] *vt* to concern.
concer'tare [kontʃer'tare] *vt* (*MUS*) to harmonize; (*ordire*) to devise, plan; **~rsi** *vr* to agree.
con'certo [kon'tʃerto] *sm* (*MUS*) concert; (: *componimento*) concerto.
concessio'nario [kontʃessjo'narjo] *sm* (*COMM*) agent, dealer.
con'cesso, a [kon'tʃɛsso] *pp di* **concedere**.
con'cetto [kon'tʃetto] *sm* (*pensiero, idea*) concept; (*opinione*) opinion.
concezi'one [kontʃet'tsjone] *sf* conception.
con'chiglia [kon'kiʎʎa] *sf* shell.
'concia ['kɔntʃa] *sf* (*di pelle*) tanning; (*di tabacco*) curing; (*sostanza*) tannin.
conci'are [kon'tʃare] *vt* (*pelli*) to tan; (*tabacco*) to cure; (*fig: ridurre in cattivo stato*) to beat up; **~rsi** *vr* (*sporcarsi*) to get in a mess; (*vestirsi male*) to dress badly.
concili'are [kontʃi'ljare] *vt* to reconcile; (*contravvenzione*) to pay on the spot; (*favorire: sonno*) to be conducive to, induce; (*procurare: simpatia*) to gain; **~rsi qc** to gain *o* win sth (for o.s.); **~rsi**

qn to win sb over; ~rsi con to be reconciled with; **conciliazi'one** sf reconciliation; (DIR) settlement.

con'cilio [kon't∫iljo] sm (REL) council.

con'cime [kon't∫ime] sm manure; (chimico) fertilizer.

con'ciso, a [kon't∫izo] ag concise, succinct.

conci'tato, a [kont∫i'tato] ag excited, emotional.

concitta'dino, a [kont∫itta'dino] sm/f fellow citizen.

con'cludere vt to conclude; (portare a compimento) to conclude, finish, bring to an end; (operare positivamente) to achieve // vi (essere convincente) to be conclusive; ~rsi vr to come to an end, close; **conclusi'one** sf conclusion; (risultato) result; **conclu'sivo, a** ag conclusive; (finale) final; **con'cluso, a** pp di **concludere**.

concor'danza [konkor'dantsa] sf (anche LING) agreement.

concor'dare vt (tregua, prezzo) to agree on; (LING) to make agree // vi to agree; **concor'dato** sm agreement; (REL) concordat.

con'corde ag (d'accordo) in agreement; (simultaneo) simultaneous.

concor'rente sm/f competitor; (INS) candidate; **concor'renza** sf competition.

con'correre vi: ~ (in) (MAT) to converge o meet (in); ~ (a) (competere) to compete (for); (: INS: a una cattedra) to apply (for); (partecipare: a un'impresa) to take part (in), contribute (to); **con'corso, a** pp di **concorrere** // sm competition; (INS) competitive examination; **concorso di colpa** (DIR) contributory negligence.

con'creto, a ag concrete.

concussi'one sf (DIR) extortion.

con'danna sf sentence; conviction; condemnation.

condan'nare vt (DIR): ~ a to sentence to; ~ per to convict of; (disapprovare) to condemn; **condan'nato, a** sm/f convict.

conden'sare vt, ~rsi vr to condense; **condensazi'one** sf condensation.

condi'mento sm seasoning; dressing.

con'dire vt to season; (insalata) to dress.

condi'videre vt to share; **condi'viso, a** pp di **condividere**.

condizio'nale [kondittsjo'nale] ag conditional // sm (LING) conditional // sf (DIR) suspended sentence.

condizio'nare [kondittsjo'nare] vt to condition; **ad aria condizionata** air-conditioned.

condizi'one [kondit'tsjone] sf condition; ~i sfpl (di pagamento etc) terms, conditions; **a** ~ **che** on condition that, provided that.

condogli'anze [kondoʎ'ʎantse] sfpl condolences.

condo'minio sm joint ownership; (edificio) jointly-owned building.

condo'nare vt (DIR) to remit; **con'dono** sm remission; **condono fiscale** conditional amnesty for people evading tax.

con'dotta sf vedi **condotto.**

con'dotto, a pp di **condurre** // ag: **medico** ~ local authority doctor (in country district) // sm (canale, tubo) pipe, conduit; (ANAT) duct // sf (modo di comportarsi) conduct, behaviour; (di un affare etc) handling; (di acqua) piping; (incarico sanitario) country medical practice controlled by a local authority.

condu'cente [kondu't∫ente] sm driver.

con'durre vt to conduct; (azienda) to manage; (accompagnare: bambino) to take; (automobile) to drive; (trasportare: acqua, gas) to convey, conduct; (fig) to lead // vi to lead; **condursi** vr to behave, conduct o.s.

condut'tore ag: **filo** ~ (fig) thread // sm (di mezzi pubblici) driver; (FISICA) conductor.

con'farsi vr: ~ a to suit, agree with.

confederazi'one [konfederat'tsjone] sf confederation.

confe'renza [konfe'rentsa] sf (discorso) lecture; (riunione) conference; ~ **stampa** press conference; **conferenzi'ere, a** sm/f lecturer.

confe'rire vt: ~ qc a qn to give sth to sb, bestow sth on sb // vi to confer.

con'ferma sf confirmation.

confer'mare vt to confirm.

confes'sare vt, ~rsi vr to confess; **andare a** ~rsi (REL) to go to confession; **confessio'nale** ag, sm confessional; **confessi'one** sf confession; (setta religiosa) denomination; **confes'sore** sm confessor.

con'fetto sm sugared almond; (MED) pill.

confezio'nare [konfettsjo'nare] vt (vestito) to make (up); (merci, pacchi) to package.

confezi'one [konfet'tsjone] sf (di abiti: da uomo) tailoring; (: da donna) dressmaking; (imballaggio) packaging; ~i sfpl garments, clothes; ~ **regalo** gift pack.

confic'care vt: ~ qc in to hammer o drive sth into; ~rsi vr to stick.

confi'dare vi: ~ in to confide in, rely on // vt to confide; ~rsi con qn to confide in sb; **confi'dente** sm/f (persona amica) confidant/confidante; (informatore) informer; **confi'denza** sf (familiarità) intimacy, familiarity; (fiducia) trust, confidence; (rivelazione) confidence; **confidenzi'ale** ag familiar, friendly; (segreto) confidential.

configu'rarsi *vr*: ~ a to assume the shape *o* form of.

confi'nare *vi*: ~ con to border on // *vt* (*POL*) to intern; (*fig*) to confine; ~rsi *vr* (*isolarsi*): ~rsi in to shut o.s. up in.

Confin'dustria *sigla f* (= *Confederazione Generale dell'Industria Italiana*) *employers' association*, ≈ CBI (*Brit*).

con'fine *sm* boundary; (*di paese*) border, frontier.

con'fino *sm* internment.

confis'care *vt* to confiscate.

con'flitto *sm* conflict.

conflu'enza [konflu'ɛntsa] *sf* (*di fiumi*) confluence; (*di strade*) junction.

conflu'ire *vi* (*fiumi*) to flow into each other, meet; (*strade*) to meet.

con'fondere *vt* to mix up, confuse; (*imbarazzare*) to embarrass; ~rsi *vr* (*mescolarsi*) to mingle; (*turbarsi*) to be confused; (*sbagliare*) to get mixed up; ~ le idee a qn to mix sb up, confuse sb.

confor'mare *vt* (*adeguare*): ~ a to adapt *o* conform to; ~rsi *vr*: ~rsi (a) to conform (to).

conforme'mente *av* accordingly; ~ a in accordance with.

confor'tare *vt* to comfort, console; **confor'tevole** *ag* (*consolante*) comforting; (*comodo*) comfortable; **con'forto** *sm* comfort, consolation; comfort.

confron'tare *vt* to compare.

con'fronto *sm* comparison; in *o* a ~ di in comparison with, compared to; nei miei (*o* tuoi *etc*) ~i towards me (*o* you *etc*).

confusi'one *sf* confusion; (*chiasso*) racket, noise; (*imbarazzo*) embarrassment.

con'fuso, a *pp di* **confondere** // *ag* (*vedi confondere*) confused; embarrassed.

confu'tare *vt* to refute.

conge'dare [kondʒe'dare] *vt* to dismiss; (*MIL*) to demobilize; ~rsi *vr* to take one's leave; **con'gedo** *sm* (*anche MIL*) leave; prendere congedo da qn to take one's leave of sb; congedo assoluto (*MIL*) discharge.

conge'gnare [kondʒeɲ'ɲare] *vt* to construct, put together; **con'gegno** *sm* device, mechanism.

conge'lare [kondʒe'lare] *vt*, ~rsi *vr* to freeze; **congela'tore** *sm* freezer.

congestio'nare [kondʒestjo'nare] *vt* to congest.

congesti'one [kondʒes'tjone] *sf* congestion.

conget'tura [kondʒet'tura] *sf* conjecture, supposition.

con'giungere [kon'dʒundʒere] *vt*, ~rsi *vr* to join (together).

congiunti'vite [kondʒunti'vite] *sf* conjunctivitis.

congiun'tivo [kondʒun'tivo] *sm* (*LING*) subjunctive.

congi'unto, a [kon'dʒunto] *pp di* **congiungere** // *ag* (*unito*) joined // *sm/f* relative.

congiun'tura [kondʒun'tura] *sf* (*giuntura*) junction, join; (*ANAT*) joint; (*circostanza*) juncture; (*ECON*) economic situation.

congiunzi'one [kondʒun'tsjone] *sf* (*LING*) conjunction.

congi'ura [kon'dʒura] *sf* conspiracy; **congiu'rare** *vi* to conspire.

conglome'rato *sm* (*GEO*) conglomerate; (*fig*) conglomeration; (*EDIL*) concrete.

congratu'larsi *vr*: ~ con qn per qc to congratulate sb on sth.

congratulazi'oni [kongratulat'tsjoni] *sfpl* congratulations.

congrega, ghe *sf* band, bunch.

con'gresso *sm* congress.

congu'aglio [kon'gwaʎʎo] *sm* balancing, adjusting; (*somma di denaro*) balance.

coni'are *vt* to mint, coin; (*fig*) to coin.

co'niglio [ko'niʎʎo] *sm* rabbit.

coniu'gare *vt* (*LING*) to conjugate; ~rsi *vr* to get married; **coniu'gato, a** *ag* (*sposato*) married; **coniugazi'one** *sf* (*LING*) conjugation.

'coniuge ['kɔnjudʒe] *sm/f* spouse.

connazio'nale [konnattsjo'nale] *sm/f* fellow-countryman/woman.

connessi'one *sf* connection.

con'nesso, a *pp di* **connettere**.

con'nettere *vt* to connect, join // *vi* (*fig*) to think straight.

conni'vente *ag* conniving.

conno'tati *smpl* distinguishing marks.

'cono *sm* cone; ~ gelato ice-cream cone.

cono'scente [konoʃ'ʃente] *sm/f* acquaintance.

cono'scenza [konoʃ'ʃɛntsa] *sf* (*il sapere*) knowledge *q*; (*persona*) acquaintance; (*facoltà sensoriale*) consciousness *q*; perdere ~ to lose consciousness.

co'noscere [ko'noʃʃere] *vt* to know; ci siamo conosciuti a Firenze we (first) met in Florence; **conosci'tore, 'trice** *sm/f* connoisseur; **conosci'uto, a** *pp di* **conoscere** // *ag* well-known.

con'quista *sf* conquest.

conquis'tare *vt* to conquer; (*fig*) to gain, win.

consa'crare *vt* (*REL*) to consecrate; (*: sacerdote*) to ordain; (*dedicare*) to dedicate; (*fig: uso etc*) to sanction; ~rsi a to dedicate o.s. to.

consangu'ineo, a *sm/f* blood relation.

consa'pevole *ag*: ~ di aware *o* conscious of; **consapevo'lezza** *sf* awareness, consciousness.

'conscio, a, sci, sce ['kɔnʃo] *ag*: ~ di aware *o* conscious of.

consecu'tivo, a *ag* consecutive;

(*successivo: giorno*) following, next.

con'segna [kon'seɲɲa] *sf* delivery; (*merce consegnata*) consignment; (*custodia*) care, custody; (*MIL: ordine*) orders *pl*; (: *punizione*) confinement to barracks; **pagamento alla ~** cash on delivery; **dare qc in ~ a qn** to entrust sth to sb.

conse'gnare [konseɲ'ɲare] *vt* to deliver; (*affidare*) to entrust, hand over; (*MIL*) to confine to barracks.

consegu'enza [konse'gwɛntsa] *sf* consequence; **per o di ~** consequently.

consegu'ire *vt* to achieve // *vi* to follow, result.

con'senso *sm* approval, consent.

consen'tire *vi*: **~ a** to consent *o* agree to // *vt* to allow, permit.

con'serva *sf* (*CUC*) preserve; **~ di frutta** jam; **~ di pomodoro** tomato purée.

conser'vare *vt* (*CUC*) to preserve; (*custodire*) to keep; (: *dalla distruzione etc*) to preserve, conserve; **~rsi** *vr* to keep.

conserva'tore, 'trice *sm/f* (*POL*) conservative.

conservazi'one [konservat'tsjone] *sf* preservation; conservation.

conside'rare *vt* to consider; (*reputare*) to consider, regard; **~ molto qn** to think highly of sb; **considerazi'one** *sf* consideration; (*stima*) regard, esteem; **prendere in considerazione** to take into consideration; **conside'revole** *ag* considerable.

consigli'are [konsiʎ'ʎare] *vt* (*persona*) to advise; (*metodo, azione*) to recommend, advise, suggest; **~rsi** *vr*: **~rsi con qn** to ask sb for advice; **consigli'ere, a** *sm/f* adviser // *sm*: **consigliere d'amministrazione** board member; **consigliere comunale** town councillor; **con'siglio** *sm* (*suggerimento*) advice, piece of advice; (*assemblea*) council; **consiglio d'amministrazione** board; **il Consiglio dei Ministri** (*POL*) ≈ the Cabinet.

consis'tente *ag* thick; solid; (*fig*) sound, valid; **consis'tenza** *sf* consistency, thickness; solidity; validity.

con'sistere *vi*: **~ in** to consist of; **consis'tito, a** *pp* di **consistere**.

conso'lare *ag* consular // *vt* (*confortare*) to console, comfort; (*rallegrare*) to cheer up; **~rsi** *vr* to be comforted; cheer up.

conso'lato *sm* consulate.

consolazi'one [konsolat'tsjone] *sf* consolation, comfort.

'console *sm* consul // [kon'sɔl] *sf* (*quadro di comando*) console.

conso'nante *sf* consonant.

'consono, a *ag*: **~ a** consistent with, consonant with.

con'sorte *sm/f* consort.

con'sorzio [kon'sɔrtsjo] *sm* consortium.

con'stare *vi*: **~ di** to consist of // *vb impers*: **mi consta che** it has come to my knowledge that, it appears that.

consta'tare *vt* to establish, verify; **constatazi'one** *sf* observation; **constatazione amichevole** *jointly-agreed statement for insurance purposes*.

consu'eto, a *ag* habitual, usual; **consue'tudine** *sf* habit, custom; (*usanza*) custom.

consu'lente *sm/f* consultant; **consu'lenza** *sf* consultancy.

consul'tare *vt* to consult; **~rsi** *vr*: **~rsi con qn** to seek the advice of sb; **consultazi'one** *sf* consultation; **consultazioni** *sfpl* (*POL*) talks, consultations.

consu'mare *vt* (*logorare: abiti, scarpe*) to wear out; (*usare*) to consume, use up; (*mangiare, bere*) to consume; (*DIR*) to consummate; **~rsi** *vr* to wear out; to be used up; (*anche fig*) to be consumed; (*combustibile*) to burn out; **consuma'tore** *sm* consumer; **consumazi'one** *sf* (*bibita*) drink; (*spuntino*) snack; (*DIR*) consummation; wear; use.

consun'tivo *sm* (*ECON*) final balance.

con'tabile *ag* accounts *cpd*, accounting // *sm/f* accountant; **contabilità** *sf* (*attività, tecnica*) accounting, accountancy; (*insieme dei libri etc*) books *pl*, accounts *pl*; (*ufficio*) accounts department.

conta'dino, a *sm/f* countryman/woman; farm worker; (*peg*) peasant.

contagi'are [konta'dʒare] *vt* to infect.

con'tagio [kon'tadʒo] *sm* infection; (*per contatto diretto*) contagion; (*epidemia*) epidemic; **contagi'oso, a** *ag* infectious; contagious.

conta'gocce [konta'gottʃe] *sm inv* (*MED*) dropper.

contami'nare *vt* to contaminate.

con'tante *sm* cash; **pagare in ~i** to pay cash.

con'tare *vt* to count; (*considerare*) to consider // *vi* to count, be of importance; **~ su qn** to count *o* rely on sb; **~ di fare qc** to intend to do sth; **conta'tore** *sm* meter.

contat'tare *vt* to contact.

con'tatto *sm* contact.

'conte *sm* count.

conteggi'are [konted'dʒare] *vt* to charge, put on the bill; **con'teggio** *sm* calculation.

con'tegno [kon'teɲɲo] *sm* (*comportamento*) behaviour; (*atteggiamento*) attitude; **darsi un ~** to act nonchalant; to pull o.s. together.

contem'plare *vt* to contemplate, gaze at; (*DIR*) to make provision for.

contemporanea'mente *av* simultaneously; at the same time.

contempo'raneo, a *ag, sm/f* contemporary.

conten'dente *sm/f* opponent, adversary.

con'tendere *vi* (*competere*) to compete; (*litigare*) to quarrel // *vt*: ~ qc a qn to contend with *o* be in competition with sb for sth.

conte'nere *vt* to contain; **conteni'tore** *sm* container.

conten'tare *vt* to please, satisfy; ~rsi di to be satisfied with, content o.s. with.

conten'tezza [konten'tettsa] *sf* contentment.

con'tento, a *ag* pleased, glad; ~ di pleased with.

conte'nuto *sm* contents *pl*; (*argomento*) content.

con'teso, a *pp di* **contendere** // *sf* dispute, argument.

con'tessa *sf* countess.

contes'tare *vt* (*DIR*) to notify; (*fig*) to dispute; **contestazi'one** *sf* (*DIR*) notification; dispute; (*protesta*) protest.

con'testo *sm* context.

con'tiguo, a *ag*: ~ (a) adjacent (to).

continen'tale *ag, sm/f* continental.

conti'nente *ag* continent // *sm* (*GEO*) continent; (*: terra ferma*) mainland; **conti'nenza** *sf* continence.

contin'gente [kontin'dʒɛnte] *ag* contingent // *sm* (*COMM*) quota; (*MIL*) contingent; **contin'genza** *sf* circumstance; (*ECON*): (**indennità di**) **contingenza** cost-of-living allowance.

continu'are *vt* to continue (with), go on with // *vi* to continue, go on; ~ a fare qc to go on *o* continue doing sth; **continuazi'one** *sf* continuation.

con'tinuo, a *ag* (*numerazione*) continuous; (*pioggia*) continual, constant; (*ELETTR*): **corrente** ~a direct current; **di** ~ continually.

'conto *sm* (*calcolo*) calculation; (*COMM, ECON*) account; (*di ristorante, albergo*) bill; (*fig: stima*) consideration, esteem; **fare i** ~**i con qn** to settle one's account with sb; **fare** ~ **su qn/qc** to count *o* rely on sb; **rendere** ~ **a qn di qc** to be accountable to sb for sth; **tener** ~ **di qn/qc** to take sb/sth into account; **per** ~ **di** on behalf of; **per** ~ **mio** as far as I'm concerned; **a** ~**i fatti, in fin dei** ~**i** all things considered; ~ **corrente** current account; ~ **alla rovescia** countdown.

con'torcere [kon'tortʃere] *vt* to twist; (*panni*) to wring (out); ~rsi *vr* to twist, writhe.

contor'nare *vt* to surround.

con'torno *sm* (*linea*) outline, contour; (*ornamento*) border; (*CUC*) vegetables *pl*.

con'torto, a *pp di* **contorcere.**

contrabbandi'ere, a *sm/f* smuggler.

contrab'bando *sm* smuggling, contraband; **merce di** ~ contraband, smuggled goods *pl*.

contrab'basso *sm* (*MUS*) (double) bass.

contraccambi'are *vt* (*favore etc*) to return.

contraccet'tivo, a [kontrattʃet'tivo] *ag, sm* contraceptive.

contrac'colpo *sm* rebound; (*di arma da fuoco*) recoil; (*fig*) repercussion.

con'trada *sf* street; district.

contrad'detto, a *pp di* **contraddire.**

contrad'dire *vt* to contradict; **contraddit'torio, a** *ag* contradictory; (*sentimenti*) conflicting // *sm* (*DIR*) cross-examination; **contraddizi'one** *sf* contradiction.

contraf'fare *vt* (*persona*) to mimic; (*alterare: voce*) to disguise; (*firma*) to forge, counterfeit; **contraf'fatto, a** *pp di* **contraffare** // *ag* counterfeit; **contraffazi'one** *sf* mimicking *q*; disguising *q*; forging *q*; (*cosa contraffatta*) forgery.

contrap'peso *sm* counterbalance, counterweight.

contrap'porre *vt*: ~ qc a qc to counter sth with sth; (*paragonare*) to compare sth with sth; **contrap'posto, a** *pp di* **contrapporre.**

contraria'mente *av*: ~ a contrary to.

contrari'are *vt* (*contrastare*) to thwart, oppose; (*irritare*) to annoy, bother; ~rsi *vr* to get annoyed.

contrarietà *sf* adversity; (*fig*) aversion.

con'trario, a *ag* opposite; (*sfavorevole*) unfavourable // *sm* opposite; **essere** ~ **a qc** (*persona*) to be against sth; **in caso** ~ otherwise; **avere qc in** ~ to have some objection; **al** ~ on the contrary.

con'trarre *vt*, **contrarsi** *vr* to contract.

contrasse'gnare [kontrasse'ɲnare] *vt* to mark; **contras'segno** *sm* (*distintivo*) distinguishing mark; **spedire in contrassegno** to send C.O.D.

contras'tare *vt* (*avversare*) to oppose; (*impedire*) to bar; (*negare: diritto*) to contest, dispute // *vi*: ~ (**con**) (*essere in disaccordo*) to contrast (with); (*lottare*) to struggle (with); **con'trasto** *sm* contrast; (*conflitto*) conflict; (*litigio*) dispute.

contrat'tacco *sm* counterattack.

contrat'tare *vt, vi* to negotiate.

contrat'tempo *sm* hitch.

con'tratto, a *pp di* **contrarre** // *sm* contract; **contrattu'ale** *ag* contractual.

contravvenzi'one [kontravven'tsjone] *sf* contravention; (*ammenda*) fine.

contrazi'one [kontrat'tsjone] *sf* contraction; (*di prezzi etc*) reduction.

contribu'ente *sm/f* taxpayer; ratepayer (*Brit*), property tax payer (*US*).

contribu'ire *vi* to contribute; **contri'buto** *sm* contribution; (*tassa*) tax.

'contro *prep* against; ~ **di me/lui** against me/him; **pastiglie** ~ **la tosse** throat lozenges; ~ **pagamento** (*COMM*) on pay-

ment // *prefisso*: **contro'battere** *vt* (*fig:
a parole*) to answer back; (: *confutare*)
to refute; **controfi'gura** *sf* (*CINEMA*)
double; **controfir'mare** *vt* to countersign.

control'lare *vt* (*accertare*) to check;
(*sorvegliare*) to watch, control; (*tenere
nel proprio potere, fig: dominare*) to control; **con'trollo** *sm* check; watch; control; **controllo delle nascite** birth control;
control'lore *sm* (*FERR, AUTOBUS*) (ticket) inspector.

controprodu'cente [kontroprodu'tʃɛnte]
ag counterproductive.

contro'senso *sm* (*contraddizione*) contradiction in terms; (*assurdità*) nonsense.

controspio'naggio [kontrospio'naddʒo]
sm counterespionage.

contro'versia *sf* controversy; (*DIR*) dispute.

contro'verso, a *ag* controversial.

contro'voglia [kontro'vɔʎʎa] *av* unwillingly.

contu'macia [kontu'matʃa] *sf* (*DIR*)
default.

contur'bare *vt* to disturb, upset.

contusi'one *sf* (*MED*) bruise.

convale'scente [konvale'ʃɛnte] *ag*, *sm/f*
convalescent; **convale'scenza** *sf* con-
valescence.

convali'dare *vt* (*AMM*) to validate; (*fig:
sospetto, dubbio*) to confirm.

con'vegno [kon'veɲɲo] *sm* (*incontro*)
meeting; (*congresso*) convention, congress; (*luogo*) meeting place.

conve'nevoli *smpl* civilities.

conveni'ente *ag* suitable; (*vantaggioso*)
profitable; (: *prezzo*) cheap; **conveni'enza** *sf* suitability; advantage; cheap-
ness; **le convenienze** *sfpl* social conventions.

conve'nire *vi* (*riunirsi*) to gather,
assemble; (*concordare*) to agree;
(*tornare utile*) to be worthwhile // *vb
impers*: **conviene fare questo** it is advisable to do this; **conviene andarsene** we
should go; **ne convengo** I agree.

con'vento *sm* (*di frati*) monastery; (*di
suore*) convent.

convenzio'nale [konventsjo'nale] *ag* con-
ventional.

convenzi'one [konven'tsjone] *sf* (*DIR*)
agreement; (*nella società*) convention;
le ~i *sfpl* social conventions.

conver'sare *vi* to have a conversation,
converse.

conversazi'one [konversat'tsjone] *sf* conversation; **fare ~** to chat, have a chat.

conversi'one *sf* conversion; **~ ad U**
(*AUT*) U-turn.

conver'tire *vt* (*trasformare*) to change;
(*POL, REL*) to convert; **~rsi** *vr*: **~rsi (a)**
to be converted (to); **conver'tito, a**
sm/f convert.

con'vesso, a *ag* convex.

con'vincere [kon'vintʃere] *vt* to convince; **~ qn di qc** to convince sb of sth;
~ qn a fare qc to persuade sb to do sth;
con'vinto, a *pp di* **convincere**;
convinzi'one *sf* conviction, firm belief.

convis'suto, a *pp di* **convivere**.

con'vitto *sm* (*INS*) boarding school.

con'vivere *vi* to live together.

convo'care *vt* to call, convene; (*DIR*) to
summon; **convocazi'one** *sf* meeting;
summons *sg*.

convogli'are [konvoʎ'ʎare] *vt* to convey;
(*dirigere*) to direct, send; **con'voglio**
sm (*di veicoli*) convoy; (*FERR*) train.

coope'rare *vi*: **~ (a)** to cooperate (in);
coopera'tiva *sf* cooperative; **coopera-
zi'one** *sf* cooperation.

coordi'nare *vt* to coordinate; **coordi'nate** *sfpl* (*MAT, GEO*) coordi-
nates; **coordi'nati** *smpl* (*MODA*) coordi-
nates.

co'perchio [ko'perkjo] *sm* cover; (*di
pentola*) lid.

co'perta *sf* cover; (*di lana*) blanket; (*da
viaggio*) rug; (*NAUT*) deck.

coper'tina (*STAMPA*) cover, jacket.

co'perto, a *pp di* **coprire** // *ag* covered;
(*cielo*) overcast // *sm* place setting; (*posto a tavola*) place; (*al ristorante*) cover
charge; **~ di** covered in *o* with.

coper'tone *sm* (*telo impermeabile*)
tarpaulin; (*AUT*) rubber tyre.

coper'tura *sf* (*anche ECON, MIL*) cover;
(*di edificio*) roofing.

'copia *sf* copy; **brutta/bella ~** rough/final
copy.

copi'are *vt* to copy; **copia'trice** *sf*
copier, copying machine.

copi'one *sm* (*CINEMA, TEATRO*) script.

'coppa *sf* (*bicchiere*) goblet; (*per frutta,
gelato*) dish; (*trofeo*) cup, trophy; **~
dell'olio** (*Brit*) *o* pan (*US*).

'coppia *sf* (*di persone*) couple; (*di
animali, SPORT*) pair.

coprifu'oco, chi *sm* curfew.

copri'letto *sm* bedspread.

co'prire *vt* to cover; (*occupare: carica,
posto*) to hold; **~rsi** *vr* (*cielo*) to cloud
over; (*vestirsi*) to wrap up, cover up;
(*ECON*) to cover o.s.; **~rsi di** (*macchie,
muffa*) to become covered in.

co'raggio [ko'raddʒo] *sm* courage,
bravery; **~!** (*forza!*) come on!;
(*animo!*) cheer up!; **coraggi'oso, a** *ag*
courageous, brave.

co'rallo *sm* coral.

co'rano *sm* (*REL*) Koran.

co'razza [ko'rattsa] *sf* armour; (*di
animali*) carapace, shell; (*MIL*)
armour(-plating); **coraz'zata** *sf* battle-
ship.

corbelle'ria *sf* stupid remark; **~e** *sfpl*

nonsense *q.*

'**corda** *sf* cord; (*fune*) rope; (*spago, MUS*) string; **dare ~ a qn** to let sb have his (*o* her) way; **tenere sulla ~** qn to keep sb on tenterhooks; **tagliare la ~** to slip away, sneak off; **~e vocali** vocal cords.

cordi'ale *ag* cordial, warm // *sm* (*bevanda*) cordial.

cor'doglio [kor'dɔʎʎo] *sm* grief; (*lutto*) mourning.

cor'done *sm* cord, string; (*linea: di polizia*) cordon; **~ ombelicale** umbilical cord.

Co'rea *sf:* **la ~** Korea.

coreogra'fia *sf* choreography.

cori'andolo *sm* (*BOT*) coriander; **~i** *smpl* confetti *sg.*

cori'care *vt* to put to bed; **~rsi** *vr* to go to bed.

'**corna** *sfpl vedi* **corno.**

cor'nacchia [kor'nakkja] *sf* crow.

corna'musa *sf* bagpipes *pl.*

cor'netta *sf* (*MUS*) cornet; (*TEL*) receiver.

cor'netto *sm* (*CUC*) croissant; **~ acustico** ear trumpet.

cor'nice [kor'nitʃe] *sf* frame; (*fig*) setting, background.

'**corno** *sm* (*ZOOL: pl(f)* **~a**, *MUS*) horn; **fare le ~a a qn** to be unfaithful to sb; **cor'nuto, a** *ag* (*con corna*) horned; (*fam!: marito*) cuckolded // *sm* (*fam!*) cuckold; (*: insulto*) bastard (*!*).

Corno'vaglia [korno'vaʎʎa] *sf:* **la ~** Cornwall.

'**coro** *sm* chorus; (*REL*) choir.

co'rona *sf* crown; (*di fiori*) wreath; **coro'nare** *vt* to crown.

'**corpo** *sm* body; (*cadavere*) (dead) body; (*militare, diplomatico*) corps *inv*; (*di opere*) corpus; **prendere ~** to take shape; **a ~ a ~** hand-to-hand; **~ di ballo** corps de ballet; **~ di guardia** guardroom; **~ insegnante** teaching staff.

corpo'rale *ag* bodily; (*punizione*) corporal.

corpora'tura *sf* build, physique.

corporazi'one [korporat'tsjone] *sf* corporation.

corpu'lento, a *ag* stout.

corre'dare *vt:* **~ di** to provide *o* furnish with; **cor'redo** *sm* equipment; (*di sposa*) trousseau.

cor'reggere [kor'rɛddʒere] *vt* to correct; (*compiti*) to correct, mark.

cor'rente *ag* (*fiume*) flowing; (*acqua del rubinetto*) running; (*moneta, prezzo*) current; (*comune*) everyday // *sm:* **essere al ~ (di)** to be well-informed (about); **mettere al ~ (di)** to inform (of) // *sf* (*movimento di liquido*) current, stream; (*spiffero*) draught; (*ELETTR, METEOR*) current; (*fig*) trend, tendency; **la vostra lettera del 5 ~ mese** (*COMM*)

your letter of the 5th of this month; **corrente'mente** *av* commonly; **parlare una lingua correntemente** to speak a language fluently.

'**correre** *vi* to run; (*precipitarsi*) to rush; (*partecipare a una gara*) to race, run; (*fig: diffondersi*) to go round // *vt* (*SPORT: gara*) to compete in; (*rischio*) to run; (*pericolo*) to face; **~ dietro a qn** to run after sb; **corre voce che ...** it is rumoured that ....

cor'retto, a *pp di* **correggere** // *ag* (*comportamento*) correct, proper; **caffè ~ al cognac** coffee laced with brandy.

correzi'one [korret'tsjone] *sf* correction; marking; **~ di bozze** proofreading.

corri'doio *sm* corridor.

corri'dore *sm* (*SPORT*) runner; (*: su veicolo*) racer.

corri'era *sf* coach (*Brit*), bus.

corri'ere *sm* (*diplomatico, di guerra*) courier; (*posta*) mail, post; (*COMM*) carrier.

corrispet'tivo *sm* (*somma*) amount due.

corrispon'dente *ag* corresponding // *sm/f* correspondent.

corrispon'denza [korrispon'dɛntsa] *sf* correspondence.

corris'pondere *vi* (*equivalere*): **~ (a)** to correspond (to); (*per lettera*): **~ con** to correspond with // *vt* (*stipendio*) to pay; (*fig: amore*) to return; **corris'posto, a** *pp di* **corrispondere.**

corrobo'rare *vt* to strengthen, fortify; (*fig*) to corroborate, bear out.

cor'rodere *vt*, **~rsi** *vr* to corrode.

cor'rompere *vt* to corrupt; (*comprare*) to bribe.

corrosi'one *sf* corrosion.

cor'roso, a *pp di* **corrodere.**

cor'rotto, a *pp di* **corrompere** // *ag* corrupt.

corrucci'arsi [korrut'tʃarsi] *vr* to grow angry *o* vexed.

corru'gare *vt* to wrinkle; **~ la fronte** to knit one's brows.

corruzi'one [korrut'tsjone] *sf* corruption; bribery.

'**corsa** *sf* running *q*; (*gara*) race; (*di autobus, taxi*) journey, trip; **fare una ~** to run, dash; (*SPORT*) to run a race.

cor'sia *sf* (*AUT, SPORT*) lane; (*di ospedale*) ward.

cor'sivo *sm* cursive (writing); (*TIP*) italics *pl.*

'**corso, a** *pp di* **correre** // *sm* course; (*strada cittadina*) main street; (*di unità monetaria*) circulation; (*di titoli, valori*) rate, price; **dar libero ~ a** to give free expression to; **in ~** in progress, under way; (*annata*) current; **~ d'acqua** river, stream; (*artificiale*) waterway; **~ serale** evening class.

'**corte** *sf* (court)yard; (*DIR, regale*) court; **fare la ~ a qn** to court sb; **~**

marziale court-martial.

cor'teccia, ce [kor'tettʃa] *sf* bark.

corteggi'are [korted'dʒare] *vt* to court.

cor'teo *sm* procession.

cor'tese *ag* courteous; **corte'sia** *sf* courtesy; **per cortesia ... excuse me, please ....**

cortigi'ano, a [korti'dʒano] *sm/f* courtier // *sf* courtesan.

cor'tile *sm* (court)yard.

cor'tina *sf* curtain; (*anche fig*) screen.

'corto, a *ag* short; **essere a ~ di** qc to be short of sth; **~ circuito** short-circuit.

'corvo *sm* raven.

'cosa *sf* thing; (*faccenda*) affair, matter, business *q*; (**che**) **~?** what?; (**che**) **cos'è?** what is it?; **a ~ pensi?** what are you thinking about?; **a ~e fatte** when it's all over.

'coscia, sce ['kɔʃʃa] *sf* thigh; **~ di pollo** (*CUC*) chicken leg.

cosci'ente [koʃ'ʃɛnte] *ag* conscious; **~ di** conscious *o* aware of; **cosci'enza** *sf* conscience; (*consapevolezza*) consciousness; **coscienzi'oso, a** *ag* conscientious.

cosci'otto [koʃ'ʃɔtto] *sm* (*CUC*) leg.

cos'critto *sm* (*MIL*) conscript.

così ♦ *av* **1** (*in questo modo*) like this, (in) this way; (*in tal modo*) so; **le cose stanno ~** this is the way things stand; **non ho detto ~!** I didn't say that!; **come stai? — (e) ~ ~** how are you? — so-so; **e ~ via** and so on; **per ~ dire** so to speak **2** (*tanto*) so; **~ lontano** so far away; **un ragazzo ~ intelligente** such an intelligent boy ♦ *ag inv* (*tale*): **non ho mai visto un film ~** I've never seen such a film ♦ *cong* **1** (*perciò*) so, therefore **2: ~ ... come** as ... as; **non è ~ bravo come te** he's not as good as you; **~ ... che** so ... that.

cosid'detto, a *ag* so-called.

cos'metico, a, ci, che *ag*, *sm* cosmetic.

cos'pargere [kos'pardʒere] *vt*: **~ di** to sprinkle with; **cos'parso, a** *pp di* **cospargere.**

cos'petto *sm*: **al ~ di** in front of; in the presence of.

cos'picuo, a *ag* considerable, large.

cospi'rare *vi* to conspire; **cospirazi'one** *sf* conspiracy.

'costa *sf* (*tra terra e mare*) coast(line); (*litorale*) shore; (*ANAT*) rib; **la C~ Azzurra** the French Riviera.

costà *av* there.

cos'tante *ag* constant; (*persona*) steadfast // *sf* constant.

cos'tare *vi*, *vt* to cost; **~ caro** to be expensive, cost a lot.

cos'tata *sf* (*CUC*) large chop.

cos'tato *sm* (*ANAT*) ribs *pl*.

costeggi'are [kosted'dʒare] *vt* to be close to; to run alongside.

cos'tei *pronome vedi* **costui.**

costernazi'one [kosternat'tsjone] *sf* dismay, consternation.

costi'ero, a *ag* coastal, coast *cpd* // *sf* stretch of coast.

costitu'ire *vt* (*comitato, gruppo*) to set up, form; (*collezione*) to put together, build up; (*sog: elementi, parti: comporre*) to make up, constitute; (*rappresentare*) to constitute; (*DIR*) to appoint; **~rsi alla polizia** to give o.s. up to the police.

costituzio'nale [kostituttsjo'nale] *ag* constitutional.

costituzi'one [kostitut'tsjone] *sf* setting up; building up; constitution.

'costo *sm* cost; **a ogni** *o* **qualunque ~**, **a tutti i ~i** at all costs.

'costola *sf* (*ANAT*) rib.

costo'letta *sf* (*CUC*) cutlet.

cos'toro *pronome pl vedi* **costui.**

cos'toso, a *ag* expensive, costly.

cos'tretto, a *pp di* **costringere.**

cos'tringere [kos'trindʒere] *vt*: **~ qn a fare** qc to force sb to do sth; **cos'trizi'one** *sf* coercion.

costru'ire *vt* to construct, build; **cos'truzi'one** *sf* construction, building.

cos'tui, cos'tei, *pl* **cos'toro** *pronome* (*soggetto*) he/she; *pl* they; (*complemento*) him/her; *pl* them; **si può sapere chi è ~?** (*peg*) just who is that fellow?

cos'tume *sm* (*uso*) custom; (*foggia di vestire, indumento*) costume; **~i** *smpl* morals, morality *sg*; **il buon ~** public morality; **~ da bagno** bathing *o* swimming costume (*Brit*), swimsuit; (*da uomo*) bathing *o* swimming trunks *pl.*

co'tenna *sf* bacon rind.

co'togna [ko'toɲɲa] *sf* quince.

coto'letta *sf* (*di maiale, montone*) chop; (*di vitello, agnello*) cutlet.

co'tone *sm* cotton; **~ idrofilo** cotton wool (*Brit*), absorbent cotton (*US*).

'cotta *sf* (*fam: innamoramento*) crush.

'cottimo *sm*: **lavorare a ~** to do piecework.

'cotto, a *pp di* **cuocere** // *ag* cooked; (*fam: innamorato*) head-over-heels in love.

cot'tura *sf* cooking; (*in forno*) baking; (*in umido*) stewing.

co'vare *vt* to hatch; (*fig: malattia*) to be sickening for; (*: odio, rancore*) to nurse // *vi* (*fuoco, fig*) to smoulder.

'covo *sm* den.

co'vone *sm* sheaf.

'cozza ['kɔttsa] *sf* mussel.

coz'zare [kot'tsare] *vi*: **~ contro** to bang into, collide with.

C.P. *abbr* = **casella postale.**

'crampo *sm* cramp.

'cranio *sm* skull.

cra'vatta *sf* tie.

cre'anza [kre'antsa] *sf* manners *pl*.

cre'are *vt* to create; **cre'ato** *sm* creation; **crea'tore, 'trice** *ag* creative // *sm* creator; **crea'tura** *sf* creature; *(bimbo)* baby, infant; **creazi'one** *sf* creation; *(fondazione)* foundation, establishment.

cre'dente *sm/f* (REL) believer.

cre'denza [kre'dentsa] *sf* belief; *(armadio)* sideboard.

credenzi'ali [kreden'tsjali] *sfpl* credentials.

'credere *vt* to believe // *vi*: ~ **in**, ~ **a** to believe in; ~ **qn onesto** to believe sb (to be) honest; ~ **che** to believe *o* think that; ~**rsi furbo** to think one is clever.

'credito *sm* (anche COMM) credit; *(reputazione)* esteem, repute; **comprare a** ~ to buy on credit.

'credo *sm inv* creed.

'crema *sf* cream; *(con uova, zucchero etc)* custard; ~ **solare** sun cream.

cre'mare *vt* to cremate.

Crem'lino *sm*: **il** ~ the Kremlin.

'crepa *sf* crack.

cre paccio [kre'pattʃo] *sm* large crack, fissure; *(di ghiacciaio)* crevasse.

crepacu'ore *sm* broken heart.

cre'pare *vi* (fam: morire) to snuff it, kick the bucket; ~ **dalle risa** to split one's sides laughing.

crepi'tare *vi* (fuoco) to crackle; *(pioggia)* to patter.

cre'puscolo *sm* twilight, dusk.

'crescere ['kreʃʃere] *vi* to grow // *vt* (figli) to raise; **'crescita** *sf* growth; **cresci'uto, a** *pp di* **crescere**.

cresima *sf* (REL) confirmation.

'crespo, a *ag* (capelli) frizzy; *(tessuto)* puckered // *sm* crêpe.

'cresta *sf* crest; *(di polli, uccelli)* crest, comb.

'creta *sf* chalk; clay.

cre'tino, a *ag* stupid // *sm/f* idiot, fool.

cric *sm inv* (TECN) jack.

'cricca, che *sf* clique.

'cricco, chi *sm* = **cric**.

crimi'nale *ag*, *sm/f* criminal.

'crimine *sm* (DIR) crime.

'crine *sm* horsehair; **crini'era** *sf* mane.

crisan'temo *sm* chrysanthemum.

'crisi *sf inv* crisis; (MED) attack, fit; ~ **di nervi** attack *o* fit of nerves.

cristalliz'zare [kristalid'dzare] *vi*, ~**rsi** *vr* to crystallize; *(fig)* to become fossilized.

cris'tallo *sm* crystal.

cristia'nesimo *sm* Christianity.

cristi'ano, a *ag*, *sm/f* Christian.

'Cristo *sm* Christ.

cri'terio *sm* criterion; *(buon senso)* (common) sense.

'critica, che *sf vedi* **critico**.

criti'care *vt* to criticize.

'critico, a, ci, che *ag* critical // *sm* critic // *sf* criticism; **la** ~**a** (attività) criticism; *(persone)* the critics *pl*.

cri'vello *sm* riddle.

'croce ['krotʃe] *sf* cross; **in** ~ *(di traverso)* crosswise; *(fig)* on tenterhooks; **la C~ Rossa** the Red Cross.

croce'figgere [krotʃe'fiddʒere] *etc* = **crocifiggere** *etc*.

croce'via [krotʃe'via] *sm inv* crossroads *sg*.

croci'ata [kro'tʃata] *sf* crusade.

cro'cicchio [kro'tʃikkjo] *sm* crossroads *sg*.

croci'era [kro'tʃɛra] *sf* (viaggio) cruise; (ARCHIT) transept.

croci'figgere [krotʃi'fiddʒere] *vt* to crucify; **crocifissi'one** *sf* crucifixion; **croci'fisso, a** *pp di* **crocifiggere**.

crogi'olo, crogiu'olo [kro'dʒɔlo] *sm* (fig) melting pot.

crol'lare *vi* to collapse; **'crollo** *sm* collapse; *(di prezzi)* slump, sudden fall.

cro'mato, a *ag* chromium-plated.

'cromo *sm* chrome, chromium.

cromo'soma, i *sm* chromosome.

'cronaca, che *sf* chronicle; (STAMPA) news *sg*; (: rubrica) column; (TV, RADIO) commentary; **fatto** *o* **episodio di** ~ news item; ~ **nera** crime news *sg*; crime column.

'cronico, a, ci, che *ag* chronic.

cro'nista, i *sm* (STAMPA) reporter, columnist.

cronolo'gia [kronolo'dʒia] *sf* chronology.

cro'nometro *sm* chronometer; *(a scatto)* stopwatch.

'crosta *sf* crust.

cros'tacei [kros'tatʃei] *smpl* shellfish.

cros'tata *sf* (CUC) tart.

cros'tino *sm* (CUC) croûton; (: da antipasto) canapé.

'cruccio ['kruttʃo] *sm* worry, torment.

cruci'verba *sm inv* crossword (puzzle).

cru'dele *ag* cruel; **crudeltà** *sf* cruelty.

'crudo, a *ag* (non cotto) raw; *(aspro)* harsh, severe.

cru'miro *sm* (peg) blackleg (Brit), scab.

'crusca *sf* bran.

crus'cotto *sm* (AUT) dashboard.

'Cuba *sf* Cuba.

'cubico, a, ci, che *ag* cubic.

'cubo, a *ag* cubic // *sm* cube; **elevare al** ~ (MAT) to cube.

cuc'cagna [kuk'kaɲɲa] *sf*: **paese della** ~ land of plenty; **albero della** ~ greasy pole *(fig)*.

cuc'cetta [kut'tʃetta] *sf* (FERR) couchette; (NAUT) berth.

cucchiai'ata [kukja'jata] *sf* spoonful.

cucchia'ino [kukkja'ino] *sm* teaspoon; coffee spoon.

cucchi'aio [kuk'kjajo] *sm* spoon.

'cuccia, ce ['kuttʃa] *sf* dog's bed; **a** ~! down!

'cucciolo ['kuttʃolo] *sm* cub; *(di cane)* puppy.

cu'cina [ku'tʃina] *sf* (locale) kitchen;

(*arte culinaria*) cooking, cookery; (*le vivande*) food, cooking; (*apparecchio*) cooker; ~ **componibile** fitted kitchen; **cuci'nare** *vt* to cook.

cu'cire [ku'tʃire] *vt* to sew, stitch; **cuci'trice** *sf* stapler; **cuci'tura** *sf* sewing, stitching; (*costura*) seam.

cucù *sm inv*, **cu'culo** *sm* cuckoo.

'cuffia *sf* bonnet, cap; (*da infermiera*) cap; (*da bagno*) (bathing) cap; (*per ascoltare*) headphones *pl*, headset.

cu'gino, a [ku'dʒino] *sm/f* cousin.

'cui *pronome* **1** (*nei complementi indiretti: persona*) whom; (: *oggetto, animale*) which; **la persona/le persone a** ~ **accennavi** the person/people you were referring to o to whom you were referring; **i libri di** ~ **parlavo** the books I was talking about o about which I was talking; **il quartiere in** ~ **abito** the district where I live; **la ragione per** ~ the reason why **2** (*inserito tra articolo e sostantivo*) whose; **la donna i** ~ **figli sono scomparsi** the woman whose children have disappeared; **il signore, dal** ~ **figlio ho avuto il libro** the man from whose son I got the book.

culi'naria *sf* cookery.

'culla *sf* cradle.

cul'lare *vt* to rock.

culmi'nare *vi*: ~ **in** o **con** to culminate in.

'culmine *sm* top, summit.

'culo *sm* (*fam!*) arse (*Brit!*), ass (*US!*); (: *fig: fortuna*): **aver** ~ to have the luck of the devil.

'culto *sm* (*religione*) religion; (*adorazione*) worship, adoration; (*venerazione: anche fig*) cult.

cul'tura *sf* culture; education, learning; **cultu'rale** *ag* cultural.

cumula'tivo, a *ag* cumulative; (*prezzo*) inclusive; (*biglietto*) group *cpd*.

'cumulo *sm* (*mucchio*) pile, heap; (*METEOR*) cumulus.

'cuneo *sm* wedge.

cu'oca *sf vedi* **cuoco.**

cu'ocere ['kwɔtʃere] *vt* (*alimenti*) to cook; (*mattoni etc*) to fire // *vi* to cook; ~ **al forno** (*pane*) to bake; (*arrosto*) to roast; **cu'oco, a, chi, che** *sm/f* cook; (*di ristorante*) chef.

cu'oio *sm* leather; ~ **capelluto** scalp.

cu'ore *sm* heart; ~**i** *smpl* (*CARTE*) hearts; **avere buon** ~ to be kind-hearted; **stare a** ~ **a qn** to be important to sb.

cupi'digia [kupi'didʒa] *sf* greed, covetousness.

'cupo, a *ag* dark; (*suono*) dull; (*fig*) gloomy, dismal.

'cupola *sf* dome; cupola.

'cura *sf* care; (*MED: trattamento*) (course of) treatment; **aver** ~ **di** (*occuparsi di*) to look after; **a** ~ **di** (*li-**

bro*) edited by; ~ **dimagrante** diet.

cu'rare *vt* (*malato, malattia*) to treat; (: *guarire*) to cure; (*aver cura di*) to take care of; (*testo*) to edit; ~**rsi** *vr* to take care of o.s.; (*MED*) to follow a course of treatment; ~**rsi di** to pay attention to.

cu'rato *sm* parish priest; (*protestante*) vicar, minister.

cura'tore, 'trice *sm/f* (*DIR*) trustee; (*di antologia etc*) editor.

curio'sare *vi* to look round, wander round; (*tra libri*) to browse; ~ **nei negozi** to look o wander round the shops.

curiosità *sf inv* curiosity; (*cosa rara*) curio, curiosity.

curi'oso, a *ag* (*che vuol sapere*) curious, inquiring; (*ficcanaso*) curious, inquisitive; (*bizzarro*) strange, curious; **essere** ~ **di** to be curious about.

cur'sore *sm* (*INFORM*) cursor.

'curva *sf* curve; (*stradale*) bend, curve.

cur'vare *vt* to bend // *vi* (*veicolo*) to take a bend; (*strada*) to bend, curve; ~**rsi** *vr* to bend; (*legno*) to warp.

'curvo, a *ag* curved; (*piegato*) bent.

cusci'netto [kuʃʃi'netto] *sm* pad; (*TECN*) bearing // *ag inv*: **stato** ~ buffer state; ~ **a sfere** ball bearing.

cu'scino [kuʃ'ʃino] *sm* cushion; (*guanciale*) pillow.

'cuspide *sf* (*ARCHIT*) spire.

cus'tode *sm/f* keeper, custodian.

cus'todia *sf* care; (*DIR*) custody; (*astuccio*) case, holder.

custo'dire *vt* (*conservare*) to keep; (*assistere*) to look after, take care of; (*fare la guardia*) to guard.

'cute *sf* (*ANAT*) skin.

cu'ticola *sf* cuticle.

C.V. *abbr* (= *cavallo vapore*) h.p.

D

da *prep* (*da + il* = **dal**, *da + lo* = **dallo**, *da + l'* = **dall'**, *da + la* = **dalla**, *da + i* = **dai**, *da + gli* = **dagli**, *da + le* = **dalle**) **1** (*agente*) by; **dipinto** ~ **un grande artista** painted by a great artist **2** (*causa*) with; **tremare dalla paura** to tremble with fear **3** (*stato in luogo*) at; **abito** ~ **lui** I'm living at his house o with him; **sono dal giornalaio/**~ **Francesco** I'm at the newsagent's/Francesco's (house) **4** (*moto a luogo*) to; (*moto per luogo*) through; **vado** ~ **Pietro/dal giornalaio** I'm going to Pietro's (house)/to the newsagent's; **sono passati dalla finestra** they came in through the window **5** (*provenienza, allontanamento*) from; **arrivare/partire** ~ **Milano** to arrive/depart from Milan; **scendere dal treno/dalla macchina** to get off the train/out of the car; **si trova a 5 km** ~ **qui** it's 5 km from here

6 (*tempo: durata*) for; (: *a partire da: nel passato*) since; (: *nel futuro*) from; **vivo qui ~ un anno** I've been living here for a year; **è dalle 3 che ti aspetto** I've been waiting for you since 3 (o'clock); **~ oggi in poi** from today onwards; **~ bambino** as a child, when I (*o he etc*) was a child

7 (*modo, maniera*) like; **comportarsi ~ uomo** to behave like a man; **l'ho fatto ~ me** I did it (by) myself

8 (*descrittivo*): **una macchina ~ corsa** a racing car; **una ragazza dai capelli biondi** a girl with blonde hair; **un vestito ~ 100.000 lire** a 100,000 lire dress; **sordo ~ un orecchio** deaf in one ear.

dab'bene *ag inv* honest, decent.

dac'capo, da 'capo *av* (*di nuovo*) (once) again; (*dal principio*) all over again, from the beginning.

dacché [dak'ke] *cong* since.

'dado *sm* (*da gioco*) dice *o* die (*pl* dice); (*CUC*) stock (*Brit*) *o* bouillon (*US*) cube; (*TECN*) (screw)nut; **~i** *smpl* (game of) dice.

daf'fare, da 'fare *sm* work, toil.

'dagli [ˈdaʎʎi], **'dai** *prep* + *det vedi* **da**.

'daino *sm* (*fallow*) deer *inv*; (*pelle*) buckskin.

dal, dall', 'dalla, 'dalle, 'dallo *prep* + *det vedi* **da**.

dal'tonico, a, ci, che *ag* colour-blind.

'dama *sf* lady; (*nei balli*) partner; (*gioco*) draughts *sg* (*Brit*), checkers *sg* (*US*).

damigi'ana [damiˈdʒana] *sf* demijohn.

da'naro *sm* = **denaro**.

da'nese *ag* Danish // *sm/f* Dane // *sm* (*LING*) Danish.

Dani'marca *sf*: **la ~** Denmark.

dan'nare *vt* (*REL*) to damn; **~rsi** *vr* (*fig: tormentarsi*) to be worried to death; **far ~ qn** to drive sb mad; **dannazi'one** *sf* damnation.

danneggi'are [danneˈdʒare] *vt* to damage; (*rovinare*) to spoil; (*nuocere*) to harm.

'danno *sm* damage; (*a persona*) harm, injury; **~i** *smpl* (*DIR*) damages; **dan'noso, a** *ag*: **dannoso (a, per)** harmful (to), bad (for).

Da'nubio *sm*: **il ~** the Danube.

'danza [ˈdantsa] *sf*: **la ~** dancing; **una ~** a dance.

dan'zare [danˈtsare] *vt, vi* to dance.

dapper'tutto *av* everywhere.

dap'poco *ag inv* inept, worthless.

dap'prima *av* at first.

'dardo *sm* dart.

'dare *sm* (*COMM*) debit // *vt* to give; (*produrre: frutti, suono*) to produce // *vi* (*guardare*): **~ su** to look (out) onto; **~rsi** *vr*: **~rsi a** to dedicate o.s. to; **~rsi al commercio** to go into business; **~rsi al**

bere to take to drink; **~ da mangiare a qn** to give sb sth to eat; **~ per certo qc** to consider sth certain; **~ per morto qn** to give sb up for dead; **~rsi per vinto** to give in.

'darsena *sf* dock; dockyard.

'data *sf* date; **~ di nascita** date of birth.

da'tare *vt* to date // *vi*: **~ da** to date from.

'dato, a *ag* (*stabilito*) given // *sm* datum; **~i** *smpl* data *pl*; **~ che** given that; **un ~ di fatto** a fact.

'dattero *sm* date.

dattilogra'fare *vt* to type; **dattilogra'fia** *sf* typing; **datti'lografo, a** *sm/f* typist.

da'vanti *av* in front; (*dirimpetto*) opposite // *ag inv* front // *sm* front; **~ a** *prep* in front of; facing, opposite; (*in presenza di*) before, in front of.

davan'zale [davanˈtsale] *sm* windowsill.

da'vanzo, d'a'vanzo [daˈvantso] *av* more than enough.

dav'vero *av* really, indeed.

'dazio [ˈdattsjo] *sm* (*somma*) duty; (*luogo*) customs *pl*.

DC *sigla f* = **Democrazia Cristiana**.

d. C. *ad abbr* (= *dopo Cristo*) A.D.

'dea *sf* goddess.

'debito, a *ag* due, proper // *sm* debt; (*COMM: dare*) debit; **a tempo ~** at the right time; **debi'tore, 'trice** *sm/f* debtor.

'debole *ag* weak, feeble; (*suono*) faint; (*luce*) dim // *sm* weakness; **debo'lezza** *sf* weakness.

debut'tare *vi* to make one's début; **de'butto** *sm* début.

deca'denza [dekaˈdentsa] *sf* decline; (*DIR*) loss, forfeiture.

decaffei'nato, a *ag* decaffeinated.

decappot'tabile *ag*, *sf* convertible.

dece'duto, a [detʃeˈduto] *ag* deceased.

de'cennio [deˈtʃennjo] *sm* decade.

de'cente [deˈtʃente] *ag* decent, respectable, proper; (*accettabile*) satisfactory, decent.

de'cesso [deˈtʃesso] *sm* death; **atto di ~** death certificate.

de'cidere [deˈtʃidere] *vt*: **~ qc** to decide on sth; (*questione, lite*) to settle sth; **~ di fare/che** to decide to do/that; **~ di qc** (*sog: cosa*) to determine sth; **~rsi** (a fare) to decide (to do), make up one's mind (to do).

deci'frare [detʃiˈfrare] *vt* to decode; (*fig*) to decipher, make out.

deci'male [detʃiˈmale] *ag* decimal.

'decimo, a [ˈdetʃimo] *num* tenth.

de'cina [deˈtʃina] *sf* ten; (*circa dieci*): **una ~ (di)** about ten.

decisi'one [detʃiˈzjone] *sf* decision; **prendere una ~** to make a decision.

de'ciso, a [deˈtʃizo] *pp di* **decidere**.

declas'sare *vt* to downgrade; to lower in

status.

decli'nare *vi* (*pendio*) to slope down; (*fig: diminuire*) to decline; (*tramontare*) to set, go down // *vt* to decline; **declinazi'one** *sf* (*LING*) declension; **de'clino** *sm* decline.

decol'lare *vi* (*AER*) to take off; **de'collo** *sm* take-off.

decolo'rare *vt* to bleach.

decom'porre *vt*, **decomporsi** *vr* to decompose; **decom'posto, a** *pp di* **decomporre**.

deconge'lare [dekondʒe'lare] *vt* to defrost.

deco'rare *vt* to decorate; **decora'tore, 'trice** *sm/f* (*interior*) decorator; **decorazi'one** *sf* decoration.

de'coro *sm* decorum; **deco'roso, a** *ag* decorous, dignified.

de'correre *vi* to pass, elapse; (*avere effetto*) to run, have effect; **de'corso, a** *pp di* **decorrere** // *sm* (*evoluzione: anche MED*) course.

de'crescere [de'kreʃʃere] *vi* (*diminuire*) to decrease, diminish; (*acque*) to subside, go down; (*prezzi*) to go down; **decresci'uto, a** *pp di* **decrescere**.

de'creto *sm* decree; ~ **legge** *decree with the force of law.*

'dedalo *sm* maze, labyrinth.

'dedica, che *sf* dedication.

dedi'care *vt* to dedicate.

'dedito, a *ag*: ~ **a** (*studio etc*) dedicated *o* devoted to; (*vizio*) addicted to.

de'dotto, a *pp di* **dedurre**.

de'durre *vt* (*concludere*) to deduce; (*defalcare*) to deduct; **deduzi'one** *sf* deduction.

defal'care *vt* to deduct.

defe'rente *ag* respectful, deferential.

defe'rire *vt*: ~ **a** (*DIR*) to refer to.

defezi'one [defet'tsjone] *sf* defection, desertion.

defici'ente [defi'tʃɛnte] *ag* (*mancante*): ~ **di** deficient in; (*insufficiente*) insufficient // *sm/f* mental defective; (*peg: cretino*) idiot.

'deficit ['defitʃit] *sm inv* (*ECON*) deficit.

defi'nire *vt* to define; (*risolvere*) to settle; **defini'tivo, a** *ag* definitive, final; **definizi'one** *sf* definition; settlement.

deflet'tore *sm* (*AUT*) quarter-light.

de'flusso *sm* (*della marea*) ebb.

defor'mare *vt* (*alterare*) to put out of shape; (*corpo*) to deform; (*pensiero, fatto*) to distort; ~**rsi** *vr* to lose its shape.

de'forme *ag* deformed; disfigured; **deformità** *sf inv* deformity.

defrau'dare *vt*: ~ **qn di qc** to defraud sb of sth, cheat sb out of sth.

de'funto, a *ag* late *cpd* // *sm/f* deceased.

degene'rare [dedʒene'rare] *vi* to degenerate; **de'genere** *ag* degenerate.

de'gente [de'dʒɛnte] *sm/f* bedridden person; (*ricoverato in ospedale*) inpatient.

'degli ['deʎʎi] *prep* + *det vedi* **di**.

de'gnarsi [deɲ'ɲarsi] *vr*: ~ **di fare** to deign *o* condescend to do.

'degno, a *ag* dignified; ~ **di** worthy of; ~ **di lode** praiseworthy.

degra'dare *vt* (*MIL*) to demote; (*privare della dignità*) to degrade; ~**rsi** *vr* to demean o.s.

degustazi'one [degustat'tsjone] *sf* sampling, tasting.

'dei, del *prep* + *det vedi* **di**.

dela'tore, 'trice *sm/f* police informer.

'delega, ghe *sf* (*procura*) proxy.

dele'gare *vt* to delegate; **dele'gato** *sm* delegate.

del'fino *sm* (*ZOOL*) dolphin; (*STORIA*) dauphin; (*fig*) probable successor.

delibe'rare *vt* to come to a decision on // *vi* (*DIR*): ~ (**su qc**) to rule (on sth).

delica'tezza [delika'tettsa] *sf* (*anche CUC*) delicacy; frailty; thoughtfulness; tactfulness.

deli'cato, a *ag* delicate; (*salute*) delicate, frail; (*fig: gentile*) thoughtful, considerate; (*: che dimostra tatto*) tactful.

deline'are *vt* to outline; ~**rsi** *vr* to be outlined; (*fig*) to emerge.

delin'quente *sm/f* criminal, delinquent; **delin'quenza** *sf* criminality, delinquency; **delinquenza minorile** juvenile delinquency.

deli'rare *vi* to be delirious, rave; (*fig*) to rave.

de'lirio *sm* delirium; (*ragionamento insensato*) raving; (*fig*): **andare/mandare in** ~ to go/send into a frenzy.

de'litto *sm* crime.

de'lizia [de'littsja] *sf* delight; **delizi'oso, a** *ag* delightful; (*cibi*) delicious.

dell', 'della, 'delle, 'dello *prep* + *det vedi* **di**.

delta'plano *sm* hang-glider; **volo col** ~ hang-gliding.

de'ludere *vt* to disappoint; **delusi'one** *sf* disappointment; **de'luso, a** *pp di* **deludere**.

de'manio *sm* state property.

de'menza [de'mentsa] *sf* dementia; (*stupidità*) foolishness.

demo'cratico, a, ci, che *ag* democratic.

democra'zia [demokrat'tsia] *sf* democracy.

democristi'ano, a *ag, sm/f* Christian Democrat.

demo'lire *vt* to demolish.

'demone *sm* demon.

de'monio *sm* demon, devil; **il D**~ the Devil.

de'naro *sm* money.

denomi'nare *vt* to name; ~**rsi** *vr* to be named *o* called; **denominazi'one** *sf* name; denomination.

densità *sf inv* density.

'denso, a *ag* thick, dense.

den'tale *ag* dental.

'dente *sm* tooth; (*di forchetta*) prong; (*GEO: cima*) jagged peak; **al ~** (*CUC: pasta*) cooked so as to be firm when eaten; **~i del giudizio** wisdom teeth; **denti'era** *sf* (set of) false teeth *pl*.

denti'fricio [denti'fritʃo] *sm* toothpaste.

den'tista, i, e *sm/f* dentist.

'dentro *av* inside; (*in casa*) indoors; (*fig: nell'intimo*) inwardly // *prep*: **~ (a)** in; **piegato in ~** folded over; **qui/là ~** in here/there; **~ di sé** (*pensare, brontolare*) to oneself.

de'nuncia, ce *o* **cie** [de'nuntʃa], **de'nunzia** [de'nuntsja] *sf* denunciation; declaration; **~ dei redditi** (income) tax return.

denunci'are [denun'tʃare], **denunzi'are** [denun'tsjare] *vt* to denounce; (*dichiarare*) to declare.

denutrizi'one [denutrit'tsjone] *sf* malnutrition.

deodo'rante *sm* deodorant.

depe'rire *vi* to waste away.

depila'torio, a *ag* hair-removing *cpd*, depilatory.

dépli'ant [depli'ã] *sm inv* leaflet; (*opuscolo*) brochure.

deplo'revole *ag* deplorable.

de'porre *vt* (*depositare*) to put down; (*rimuovere: da una carica*) to remove; (*: re*) to depose; (*DIR*) to testify.

depor'tare *vt* to deport.

deposi'tare *vt* (*gen, GEO, ECON*) to deposit; (*lasciare*) to leave; (*merci*) to store.

de'posito *sm* deposit; (*luogo*) warehouse; depot; (*: MIL*) depot; **~ bagagli** left-luggage office.

deposizi'one [depozit'tsjone] *sf* deposition; (*da una carica*) removal.

de'posto, a *pp di* **deporre.**

depra'vato, a *ag* depraved // *sm/f* degenerate.

depre'dare *vt* to rob, plunder.

depressi'one *sf* depression.

de'presso, a *pp di* **deprimere** // *ag* depressed.

deprez'zare [depret'tsare] *vt* (*ECON*) to depreciate.

de'primere *vt* to depress.

depu'rare *vt* to purify.

depu'tato, a *o* **'essa** *sm/f* (*POL*) deputy, ≈ Member of Parliament (*Brit*), ≈ Member of Congress (*US*); **deputazi'one** *sf* deputation; (*POL*) position of deputy, ≈ parliamentary seat (*Brit*), ≈ seat in Congress (*US*).

deragli'are [deraʎ'ʎare] *vi* to be derailed; **far ~** to derail.

dere'litto, a *ag* derelict.

dere'tano *sm* (*fam*) bottom, buttocks *pl*.

de'ridere *vt* to mock, deride; **de'riso, a** *pp di* **deridere.**

de'riva *sf* (*NAUT, AER*) drift; **andare alla ~** (*anche fig*) to drift.

deri'vare *vi*: **~ da** to derive from // *vt* to derive; (*corso d'acqua*) to divert; **derivazi'one** *sf* derivation; diversion.

derma'tologo, a, gi, ghe *sm/f* dermatologist.

der'rate *sfpl* commodities; **~ alimentari** foodstuffs.

deru'bare *vt* to rob.

des'critto, a *pp di* **descrivere.**

des'crivere *vt* to describe; **descrizi'one** *sf* description.

de'serto, a *ag* deserted // *sm* (*GEO*) desert; **isola ~a** desert island.

deside'rare *vt* to want, wish for; (*sessualmente*) to desire; **~ fare/che qn faccia** to want *o* wish to do/sb to do; **desidera fare una passeggiata?** would you like to go for a walk?

desi'derio *sm* wish; (*più intenso, carnale*) desire.

deside'roso, a *ag*: **~ di** longing *o* eager for.

desi'nenza [dezi'nentsa] *sf* (*LING*) ending, inflexion.

de'sistere *vi*: **~ da** to give up, desist from; **desis'tito, a** *pp di* **desistere.**

deso'lato, a *ag* (*paesaggio*) desolate; (*persona: spiacente*) sorry.

des'tare *vt* to wake (up); (*fig*) to awaken, arouse; **~rsi** *vr* to wake (up).

desti'nare *vt* to destine; (*assegnare*) to appoint, assign; (*indirizzare*) to address; **~ qc a qn** to intend to give sth to sb, intend sb to have sth; **destina'tario, a** *sm/f* (*di lettera*) addressee.

destinazi'one [destinat'tsjone] *sf* destination; (*uso*) purpose.

des'tino *sm* destiny, fate.

destitu'ire *vt* to dismiss, remove.

'desto, a *ag* (wide) awake.

'destra *sf vedi* **destro.**

destreggi'arsi [destred'dʒarsi] *vr* to manoeuvre (*Brit*), maneuver (*US*).

des'trezza [des'trettsa] *sf* skill, dexterity.

'destro, a *ag* right, right-hand; (*abile*) skilful, adroit // *sf* (*mano*) right hand; (*parte*) right (side); (*POL*): **la ~a** the Right; **a ~a** (*essere*) on the right; (*andare*) to the right.

dete'nere *vt* (*incarico, primato*) to hold; (*proprietà*) to have, possess; (*in prigione*) to detain, hold; **dete'nuto, a** *sm/f* prisoner; **detenzi'one** *sf* holding; possession; detention.

deter'gente [deter'dʒente] *ag* detergent; (*crema, latte*) cleansing // *sm* detergent.

deterio'rare *vt* to damage; **~rsi** *vr* to deteriorate.

determi'nare *vt* to determine; **determinazi'one** *sf* determination; (*decisione*) decision.

deter'sivo *sm* detergent.
detes'tare *vt* to detest, hate.
de'trarre *vt*: ~ **(da)** to deduct (from), take away (from); **de'tratto, a** *pp di* **detrarre; detrazi'one** *sf* deduction; detrazione d'imposta tax allowance.
detri'mento *sm* detriment, harm; **a** ~ **di** to the detriment of.
de'trito *sm* (GEO) detritus.
dettagli'are [dettaġ'ġare] *vt* to detail, give full details of.
det'taglio [det'taʎʎo] *sm* detail; (COMM): **il** ~ retail; **al** ~ (COMM) retail; separately.
det'tare *vt* to dictate; ~ **legge** (*fig*) to lay down the law; **det'tato** *sm* dictation; **detta'tura** *sf* dictation.
'detto, a *pp di* **dire** // *ag* (*soprannominato*) called, known as; (*già nominato*) above-mentioned // *sm* saying; ~ **fatto** no sooner said than done.
detur'pare *vt* to disfigure; (*moralmente*) to sully.
devas'tare *vt* to devastate; (*fig*) to ravage.
devi'are *vi*: ~ **(da)** to turn off (from) // *vt* to divert; **deviazi'one** *sf* (*anche* AUT) diversion.
devo'luto, a *pp di* **devolvere.**
devoluzi'one [devolut'tsjone] *sf* (DIR) devolution, transfer.
de'volvere *vt* (DIR) to transfer, devolve.
de'voto, a *ag* (REL) devout, pious; (*affezionato*) devoted.
devozi'one [devot'tsjone] *sf* devoutness; (*anche* REL) devotion.
di *prep* (*di* + *il* = **del**, *di* + *lo* = **dello**, *di* + *l'* = **dell'**, *di* + *la* = **della**, *di* + *i* = **dei**, *di* + *gli* = **degli**, *di* + *le* = **delle**) 1 (*possesso, specificazione*) of; (*composto da, scritto da*) by; **la macchina** ~ **Paolo/mio fratello** Paolo's/my brother's car; **un amico** ~ **mio fratello** a friend of my brother's, one of my brother's friends; **un quadro** ~ **Botticelli** a painting by Botticelli
2 (*caratterizzazione, misura*) of; **una casa** ~ **mattoni** a brick house, a house made of bricks; **un orologio d'oro** a gold watch; **un bimbo** ~ **3 anni** a child of 3, a 3-year-old child
3 (*causa, mezzo, modo*) with; **tremare** ~ **paura** to tremble with fear; **morire** ~ **cancro** to die of cancer; **spalmare** ~ **burro** to spread with butter
4 (*argomento*) about, of; **discutere** ~ **sport** to talk about sport
5 (*luogo: provenienza*) from; out of; **essere** ~ **Roma** to be from Rome; **uscire** ~ **casa** to come out *o* leave the house
6 (*tempo*) in; **d'estate/d'inverno** in (the) summer/winter; ~ **notte** by night, at night; ~ **mattina/sera** in the morning/evening; ~ **domenica** on Sundays
◆ *det* (*una certa quantità di*) some; (:

negativo) any; (: *interrogativo*) any, some; **del pane** (some) bread; **delle caramelle** (some) sweets; **degli amici miei** some friends of mine; **vuoi del vino?** do you want some *o* any wine?
dia'bete *sm* diabetes *sg*.
di'acono *sm* (REL) deacon.
dia'dema, i *sm* diadem; (*di donna*) tiara.
dia'framma, i *sm* (*divisione*) screen; (ANAT, FOT, *contraccettivo*) diaphragm.
di'agnosi [di'aɲɲozi] *sf* diagnosis *sg*.
diago'nale *ag, sf* diagonal.
dia'gramma, i *sm* diagram.
dia'letto *sm* dialect.
di'alogo, ghi *sm* dialogue.
dia'mante *sm* diamond.
di'ametro *sm* diameter.
di'amine *escl*: **che** ~ **...?** what on earth ...?
diaposi'tiva *sf* transparency, slide.
di'ario *sm* diary; ~ **degli esami** (SCOL) exam timetable.
diar'rea *sf* diarrhoea.
di'avolo *sm* devil.
di'battere *vt* to debate, discuss; ~**rsi** *vr* to struggle; **di'battito** *sm* debate, discussion.
dicas'tero *sm* ministry.
di'cembre [di'tʃembre] *sm* December.
dice'ria [ditʃe'ria] *sf* rumour, piece of gossip.
dichia'rare [dikja'rare] *vt* to declare; **dichiarazi'one** *sf* declaration.
dician'nove [ditʃan'nɔve] *num* nineteen.
dicias'sette [ditʃas'sette] *num* seventeen.
dici'otto [ditʃɔtto] *num* eighteen.
dici'tura [ditʃi'tura] *sf* words *pl*, wording.
di'eci ['djɛtʃi] *num* ten; **die'cina** *sf* = **decina.**
'diesel ['dizəl] *sm inv* diesel engine.
di'eta *sf* diet; **essere a** ~ to be on a diet.
di'etro *av* behind; (*in fondo*) at the back // *prep* behind; (*tempo: dopo*) after // *sm* back, rear // *ag inv* back *cpd*; **le zampe di** ~ the hind legs; ~ **richiesta** on demand; (*scritta*) on application.
di'fatti *cong* in fact, as a matter of fact.
di'fendere *vt* to defend; **difen'sivo, a** *ag* defensive // *sf*: **stare sulla difensiva** (*anche fig*) to be on the defensive; **difen'sore, a** *sm/f* defender; **avvocato difensore** counsel for the defence; **di'feso, a** *pp di* **difendere** // *sf* defence.
difet'tare *vi* to be defective; ~ **di** to be lacking in, lack; **difet'tivo, a** *ag* defective.
di'fetto *sm* (*mancanza*): ~ **di** lack of; shortage of; (*di fabbricazione*) fault, flaw, defect; (*morale*) fault, failing, defect; (*fisico*) defect; **far** ~ to be lacking; **in** ~ **at** fault; in the wrong; **difet'toso, a** *ag* defective, faulty.
diffa'mare *vt* to slander; to libel.
diffe'rente *ag* different.

diffe'renza [diffe'rɛntsa] *sf* difference; a
~ di unlike.

differenzi'are [differen'tsjare] *vt* to
differentiate; ~rsi da to differentiate o.s.
from; to differ from.

diffe'rire *vt* to postpone, defer // *vi* to be
different.

dif'ficile [dif'fitʃile] *ag* difficult; (*persona*)
hard to please, difficult (to please);
(*poco probabile*): è ~ che sia libero it is
unlikely that he'll be free // *sm* difficult
part; difficulty; **difficoltà** *sf inv* difficulty.

dif'fida *sf* (*DIR*) warning, notice.

diffi'dare *vi*: ~ di to be suspicious *o* distrustful of // *vt* (*DIR*) to warn; ~ qn dal
fare qc to warn sb not to do sth, caution
sb against doing sth; **diffi'dente** *ag*
suspicious, distrustful; **diffi'denza** *sf*
suspicion, distrust.

dif'fondere *vt* (*luce, calore*) to diffuse;
(*notizie*) to spread, circulate; ~rsi *vr* to
spread; **diffusi'one** *sf* diffusion; spread;
(*anche di giornale*) circulation; (*FISICA*)
scattering; **dif'fuso, a** *pp di* **diffondere**
// *ag* (*malattia, fenomeno*) widespread.

difi'lato *av* (*direttamente*) straight, directly; (*subito*) straight away.

difte'rite *sf* (*MED*) diphtheria.

'**diga, ghe** *sf* dam; (*portuale*) breakwater.

dige'rente [didʒe'rɛnte] *ag* (*apparato*)
digestive.

dige'rire [didʒe'rire] *vt* to digest; **dige-
sti'one** *sf* digestion; **diges'tivo, a** *ag*
digestive // *sm* (after-dinner) liqueur.

digi'tale [didʒi'tale] *ag* digital; (*delle
dita*) finger *cpd*, digital // *sf* (*BOT*)
foxglove.

digi'tare [didʒi'tare] *vt, vi* (*INFORM*) to
key (in).

digiu'nare [didʒu'nare] *vi* to starve o.s.;
(*REL*) to fast; **digi'uno, a** *ag*: essere
digiuno not to have eaten // *sm* fast; a
digiuno on an empty stomach.

dignità [diɲɲi'ta] *sf inv* dignity; **di-
gni'toso, a** *ag* dignified.

'**DIGOS** [di'gos] *sigla f* (= *Divisione
Investigazioni Generali e Operazioni
Speciali*) *police department dealing with
political security.*

digri'gnare [digriɲ'ɲare] *vt*: ~ i denti to
grind one's teeth.

dila'gare *vi* to flood; (*fig*) to spread.

dilani'are *vt* (*preda*) to tear to pieces.

dilapi'dare *vt* to squander, waste.

dila'tare *vt* to dilate; (*gas*) to cause to
expand; (*passaggio, cavità*) to open
(up); ~rsi *vr* to dilate; (*FISICA*) to
expand.

dilazio'nare [dilattsjo'nare] *vt* to delay,
defer; **dilazi'one** *sf* delay; (*COMM: di
pagamento etc*) extension; (*rinvio*) postponement.

dileggi'are [diled'dʒare] *vt* to mock, de-

ride.

dilegu'are *vi*, ~rsi *vr* to vanish, disappear.

di'lemma, i *sm* dilemma.

dilet'tante *sm/f* dilettante; (*anche
SPORT*) amateur.

dilet'tare *vt* to give pleasure to, delight;
~rsi *vr*: ~rsi di to take pleasure in, enjoy.

di'letto, a *ag* dear, beloved // *sm*
pleasure, delight.

dili'gente [dili'dʒɛnte] *ag* (*scrupoloso*)
diligent; (*accurato*) careful, accurate;
dili'genza *sf* diligence; care; (*carrozza*)
stagecoach.

dilu'ire *vt* to dilute.

dilun'garsi *vr* (*fig*): ~ su to talk at
length on *o* about.

diluvi'are *vb impers* to pour (down).

di'luvio *sm* downpour; (*inondazione, fig*)
flood.

dima'grire *vi* to get thinner, lose weight.

dime'nare *vt* to wave, shake; ~rsi *vr* to
toss and turn; (*fig*) to struggle; ~ la
coda (*sog: cane*) to wag its tail.

dimensi'one *sf* dimension; (*grandezza*)
size.

dimenti'canza [dimenti'kantsa] *sf* for-
getfulness; (*errore*) oversight, slip; per
~ inadvertently.

dimenti'care *vt* to forget; ~rsi di qc to
forget sth.

di'messo, a *pp di* **dimettere** // *ag*
(*voce*) subdued; (*uomo, abito*) modest,
humble.

dimesti'chezza [dimesti'kettsa] *sf*
familiarity.

di'mettere *vt*: ~ qn da to dismiss sb
from; (*dall'ospedale*) to discharge sb
from; ~rsi (da) to resign (from).

dimez'zare [dimed'dzare] *vt* to halve.

diminu'ire *vt* to reduce, diminish; (*prezzi*) to bring down, reduce // *vi* to decrease, diminish; (*rumore*) to die down,
die away; (*prezzi*) to fall, go down;
diminuzi'one *sf* decreasing, dimin-
ishing.

dimissi'oni *sfpl* resignation *sg*; dare *o*
presentare le ~ to resign, hand in one's
resignation.

di'mora *sf* residence.

dimo'rare *vi* to reside.

dimos'trare *vt* to demonstrate, show;
(*provare*) to prove, demonstrate; ~rsi
vr: ~rsi molto abile to show o.s. *o* prove
to be very clever; **dimostra 30 anni** he
looks about 30 (years old); **dimo-
strazi'one** *sf* demonstration; proof.

di'namico, a, ci, che *ag* dynamic // *sf*
dynamics *sg*.

dina'mite *sf* dynamite.

'**dinamo** *sf inv* dynamo.

di'nanzi [di'nantsi]: ~ a *prep* in front of.

dini'ego, ghi *sm* refusal; denial.

dinocco'lato, a *ag* lanky; camminare ~

to walk with a slouch.

din'torno av round, (round) about; ~i smpl outskirts; **nei ~i di** in the vicinity o neighbourhood of.

'dio, pl **'dei** sm god; **D~** God; **gli dei** the gods; **D~ mio!** my goodness!, my God!

di'ocesi [di'ɔtʃezi] sf inv diocese.

dipa'nare vt (lana) to wind into a ball; (fig) to disentangle, sort out.

diparti'mento sm department.

dipen'dente ag dependent // smf employee; **dipen'denza** sf dependence; **essere alle dipendenze di qn** to be employed by sb o in sb's employ.

di'pendere vi: ~ **da** to depend on; (finanziariamente) to be dependent on; (derivare) to come from, be due to; **di'peso, a** pp di **dipendere**.

di'pingere [di'pindʒere] vt to paint; **di'pinto, a** pp di **dipingere** // sm painting.

di'ploma, i sm diploma.

diplo'mare vt to award a diploma to, graduate (US) // vi to obtain a diploma, graduate (US).

diplo'matico, a, ci, che ag diplomatic // sm diplomat.

diploma'zia [diplomat'tsia] sf diplomacy.

di'porto sm: **imbarcazione** f **da ~** pleasure craft.

dira'dare vt to thin (out); (visite) to reduce, make less frequent; **~rsi** vr to disperse; (nebbia) to clear (up).

dira'mare vt to issue // vi, **~rsi** vr (strade) to branch.

'dire vt to say; (segreto, fatto) to tell; ~ **qc a qn** to tell sb sth; ~ **a qn di fare qc** to tell sb to do sth; ~ **di sì/no** to say yes/ no; **si dice che ...** they say that ...; **si direbbe che ...** it looks (o sounds) as though ...; **dica, signora?** (in un negozio) yes, Madam, can I help you?

diret'tissimo sm (FERR) fast (through) train.

di'retto, a pp di **dirigere** // ag direct // sm (FERR) through train.

diret'tore, 'trice smf (di azienda) director; manager/ess; (di scuola elementare) head (teacher) (Brit), principal (US); ~ **d'orchestra** conductor.

direzi'one [diret'tsjone] sf board of directors; management; (senso di movimento) direction; **in ~ di** in the direction of, towards.

diri'gente [diri'dʒente] smf executive; (POL) leader // ag: **classe ~** ruling class.

di'rigere [di'ridʒere] vt to direct; (impresa) to run, manage; (MUS) to conduct; **~rsi** vr: **~rsi verso** o **a** to make o head for.

dirim'petto av opposite; ~ **a** prep opposite, facing.

di'ritto, a ag straight; (onesto) straight, upright // av straight, directly; **andare ~** to go straight on // sm right side;

(TENNIS) forehand; (MAGLIA) plain stitch; (prerogativa) right; (leggi, scienza): **il ~** law; **~i** smpl (tasse) duty sg; **stare ~** to stand up straight; **aver ~ a qc** to be entitled to sth; **~i d'autore** royalties.

dirit'tura sf (SPORT) straight; (fig) rectitude.

diroc'cato, a ag tumbledown, in ruins.

dirot'tare vt (nave, aereo) to change the course of; (aereo: sotto minaccia) to hijack; (traffico) to divert // vi (nave, aereo) to change course; **dirotta'tore, 'trice** smf hijacker.

di'rotto, a ag (pioggia) torrential; (pianto) unrestrained; **piovere a ~** to pour, rain cats and dogs; **piangere a ~** to cry one's heart out.

di'rupo sm crag, precipice.

disabi'tato, a ag uninhabited.

disabitu'arsi vr: ~ **a** to get out of the habit of.

disac'cordo sm disagreement.

disadat'tato, a ag (PSIC) maladjusted.

disa'dorno, a ag plain, unadorned.

disagi'ato, a [diza'dʒato] ag poor, needy; (vita) hard.

di'sagio [di'zadʒo] sm discomfort; (disturbo) inconvenience; (fig: imbarazzo) embarrassment; **~i** smpl hardship sg, poverty sg; **essere a ~** to be ill at ease.

disappro'vare vt to disapprove of; **disapprovazi'one** sf disapproval.

disap'punto sm disappointment.

disar'mare vt, vi to disarm; **di'sarmo** sm (MIL) disarmament.

di'sastro sm disaster.

disat'tento, a ag inattentive; **disattenzi'one** sf carelessness, lack of attention.

disa'vanzo [diza'vantso] sm (ECON) deficit.

disavven'tura sf misadventure, mishap.

dis'brigo, ghi sm (prompt) clearing up o settlement.

dis'capito sm: **a ~ di** to the detriment of.

dis'carica, che sf (di rifiuti) rubbish tip o dump.

discen'dente [diʃʃen'dɛnte] ag descending // smf descendant.

di'scendere [diʃ'ʃendere] vt to go (o come) down // vi to go (o come) down; (strada) to go down; (smontare) to get off; ~ **da** (famiglia) to be descended from; ~ **dalla macchina/dal treno** to get out of the car/out of o off the train; ~ **da cavallo** to dismount, get off one's horse.

di'scepolo, a [diʃ'ʃepolo] smf disciple.

di'scernere [diʃ'ʃernere] vt to discern.

di'sceso, a [diʃ'ʃeso] pp di **discendere** // sf descent; (pendio) slope; **in ~a** (strada) downhill cpd, sloping; **~a libera** (SCI) downhill (race).

disci'ogliere [diʃ'ʃɔʎʎere] vt, **~rsi** vr to

dissolve; *(fondere)* to melt; **disci'olto, a** *pp di* **disciogliere.**

disci'plina [diʃʃi'plina] *sf* discipline; **discipli'nare** *ag* disciplinary // *vt* to discipline.

'**disco, schi** *sm* disc; *(SPORT)* discus; *(fonografico)* record; *(INFORM)* disk; ~ **orario** *(AUT)* parking disc; ~ **rigido** *(INFORM)* hard disk; ~ **volante** flying saucer.

discol'pare *vt* to clear of blame.

disco'noscere [disko'noʃʃere] *vt (figlio)* to disown; *(meriti)* to ignore, disregard; **disconosci'uto, a** *pp di* **disconoscere.**

dis'corde *ag* conflicting, clashing; **dis'cordia** *sf* discord; *(dissidio)* disagreement, clash.

dis'correre *vi:* ~ **(di)** to talk (about).

dis'corso, a *pp di* **discorrere** // *sm* speech; *(conversazione)* conversation, talk.

dis'costo, a *ag* faraway, distant // *av* far away; ~ **da** *prep* far from.

disco'teca, che *sf (raccolta)* record library; *(luogo di ballo)* disco(thèque).

discre'panza [diskre'pantsa] *sf* disagreement.

dis'creto, a *ag* discreet; *(abbastanza buono)* reasonable, fair; **discrezi'one** *sf* discretion; *(giudizio)* judgment, discernment; **a discrezione di** at the discretion of.

discriminazi'one [diskriminat'tsjone] *sf* discrimination.

discussi'one *sf* discussion; *(litigio)* argument.

dis'cusso, a *pp di* **discutere.**

dis'cutere *vt* to discuss, debate; *(contestare)* to question // *vi (conversare):* ~ **(di)** to discuss; *(litigare)* to argue.

disde'gnare [disde'ɲare] *vt* to scorn.

dis'detto, a *pp di* **disdire** // *sf* cancellation; *(sfortuna)* bad luck.

dis'dire *vt (prenotazione)* to cancel; *(DIR):* ~ **un contratto d'affitto** to give notice (to quit).

dise'gnare [dise'ɲare] *vt* to draw; *(progettare)* to design; *(fig)* to outline; **disegna'tore, 'trice** *sm/f* designer.

di'segno [di'seɲɲo] *sm* drawing; design; outline.

diser'bante *sm* weed-killer.

diser'tare *vt, vi* to desert; **diser'tore** *sm (MIL)* deserter.

dis'fare *vt* to undo; *(valigie)* to unpack; *(meccanismo)* to take to pieces; *(lavoro, paese)* to destroy; *(neve)* to melt; ~**rsi** *vr* to come undone; *(neve)* to melt; ~ **il letto** to strip the bed; ~**rsi di qn** *(liberarsi)* to get rid of sb; **dis'fatto, a** *pp di* **disfare** // *sf (sconfitta)* rout.

dis'gelo [diz'dʒɛlo] *sm* thaw.

dis'grazia [diz'grattsja] *sf (sventura)* misfortune; *(incidente)* accident, mishap; **disgrazi'ato, a** *ag* unfortunate // *sm/f* wretch.

disgre'gare *vt,* ~**rsi** *vr* to break up.

disgu'ido *sm:* ~ **postale** error in postal delivery.

disgus'tare *vt* to disgust; ~**rsi** *vr:* ~**rsi di** to be disgusted by.

dis'gusto *sm* disgust; **disgus'toso, a** *ag* disgusting.

disidra'tare *vt* to dehydrate.

disil'ludere *vt* to disillusion, disenchant.

disimpa'rare *vt* to forget.

disimpe'gnare [dizimpe'ɲare] *vt (persona: da obblighi):* ~ **da** to release from; *(oggetto dato in pegno)* to redeem, get out of pawn; ~**rsi** *vr:* ~**rsi da** *(obblighi)* to release o.s. from, free o.s. from.

disinfet'tante *ag, sm* disinfectant.

disinfet'tare *vt* to disinfect.

disini'bito, a *ag* uninhibited.

disinte'grare *vt, vi* to disintegrate.

disinteres'sarsi *vr:* ~ **di** to take no interest in.

disinte'resse *sm* indifference; *(generosità)* unselfishness.

disintossi'care *vt (alcolizzato, drogato)* to treat for alcoholism (o drug addiction); ~ **l'organismo** to clear out one's system.

disin'volto, a *ag* casual, free and easy; **disinvol'tura** *sf* casualness, ease.

disles'sia *sf* dyslexia.

dislo'care *vt* to station, position.

dismi'sura *sf* excess; **a** ~ to excess, excessively.

disobbe'dire *etc* = **disubbidire** *etc.*

disoccu'pato, a *ag* unemployed // *sm/f* unemployed person; **disoccupazi'one** *sf* unemployment.

diso'nesto, a *ag* dishonest.

diso'nore *sm* dishonour, disgrace.

di'sopra *av (con contatto)* on top; *(senza contatto)* above; *(al piano superiore)* upstairs // *ag inv (superiore)* upper // *sm inv* top, upper part.

disordi'nato, a *ag* untidy; *(privo di misura)* irregular, wild.

di'sordine *sm (confusione)* disorder, confusion; *(sregolatezza)* debauchery.

disorien'tare *vt* to disorientate; ~**rsi** *vr (fig)* to get confused, lose one's bearings.

di'sotto *av* below, underneath; *(in fondo)* at the bottom; *(al piano inferiore)* downstairs // *ag inv (inferiore)* lower; bottom *cpd* // *sm inv (parte inferiore)* lower part; bottom.

dis'paccio [dis'pattʃo] *sm* dispatch.

'**dispari** *ag inv* odd, uneven.

dis'parte *in* ~ *av (da lato)* aside, apart; **tenersi** *o* **starsene in** ~ to keep to o.s., hold aloof.

dispendi'oso, a *ag* expensive.

dis'pensa *sf* pantry, larder; *(mobile)* sideboard; *(DIR)* exemption; *(REL)* dispensation; *(fascicolo)* number, issue.

dispen'sare vt (elemosine, favori) to distribute; (esonerare) to exempt.

dispe'rare vi: ~ (di) to despair (of); ~rsi vr to despair; **dispe'rato, a** ag (persona) in despair; (caso, tentativo) desperate; **disperazi'one** sf despair.

dis'perdere vt (disseminare) to disperse; (MIL) to scatter, rout; (fig: consumare) to waste, squander; ~rsi vr to disperse; to scatter; **dis'perso, a** pp di **disperdere** // sm/f missing person.

dis'petto sm spite q, spitefulness q; fare un ~ a qn to play a (nasty) trick on sb; a ~ di in spite of; **dispet'toso, a** ag spiteful.

dispia'cere [dispja'tʃere] sm (rammarico) regret, sorrow; (dolore) grief; ~i smpl troubles, worries // vi: ~ a to displease // vb impers: mi dispiace (che) I am sorry (that); se **non le dispiace**, me ne vado adesso if you don't mind, I'll go now; **dispiaci'uto, a** pp di **dispiacere** // ag sorry.

dispo'nibile ag available.

dis'porre vt (sistemare) to arrange; (preparare) to prepare; (DIR) to order; (persuadere): ~ qn a to incline o dispose sb towards // vi (decidere) to decide; (usufruire): ~ di to use, have at one's disposal; (essere dotato): ~ di to have; **disporsi** vr (ordinarsi) to place o.s., arrange o.s.; **disporsi a fare** to get ready to do.

disposi'tivo sm (meccanismo) device.

disposizi'one [dispozit'tsjone] sf arrangement, layout; (stato d'animo) mood; (tendenza) bent, inclination; (comando) order; (DIR) provision, regulation; a ~ di qn at sb's disposal.

dis'posto, a pp di **disporre**.

disprez'zare [dispret'tsare] vt to despise.

dis'prezzo [dis'prɛttso] sm contempt.

'disputa sf dispute, quarrel.

dispu'tare vt (contendere) to dispute, contest; (gara) to take part in // vi to quarrel; ~ di to discuss; ~rsi qc to fight for sth.

dissan'guare vt (fig: persona) to bleed white; (: patrimonio) to suck dry; ~rsi vr (MED) to lose blood; (fig: rovinarsi) to ruin o.s.

dissec'care vt, ~rsi vr to dry up.

dissemi'nare vt to scatter; (fig: notizie) to spread.

dis'senso sm dissent; (disapprovazione) disapproval.

dissente'ria sf dysentery.

dissen'tire vi: ~ (da) to disagree (with).

dissertazi'one [dissertat'tsjone] sf dissertation.

disser'vizio [disser'vittsjo] sm inefficiency.

disses'tare vt (ECON) to ruin; **dis'sesto** sm (financial) ruin.

disse'tante ag refreshing.

dis'sidio sm disagreement.

dis'simile ag different, dissimilar.

dissimu'lare vt (fingere) to dissemble; (nascondere) to conceal.

dissi'pare vt to dissipate; (scialacquare) to squander, waste.

dis'solto, a pp di **dissolvere**.

disso'lubile ag soluble.

disso'luto, a pp di **dissolvere** // ag dissolute, licentious.

dis'solvere vt to dissolve; (neve) to melt; (fumo) to disperse; ~rsi vr to dissolve; to melt; to disperse.

dissu'adere vt: ~ qn da to dissuade sb from; **dissu'aso, a** pp di **dissuadere**.

distac'care vt to detach, separate; (SPORT) to leave behind; ~rsi vr to be detached; (fig) to stand out; ~rsi da (fig: allontanarsi) to grow away from.

dis'tacco, chi sm (separazione) separation; (fig: indifferenza) detachment; (SPORT): vincere con un ~ di ... to win by a distance of ....

dis'tante av far away // ag: ~ (da) distant (from), far away (from).

dis'tanza [dis'tantsa] sf distance.

distanzi'are [distan'tsjare] vt to space out, place at intervals; (SPORT) to outdistance; (fig: superare) to outstrip, surpass.

dis'tare vi: distiamo pochi chilometri da Roma we are only a few kilometres (away) from Rome.

dis'tendere vt (coperta) to spread out; (gambe) to stretch (out); (mettere a giacere) to lay; (rilassare: muscoli, nervi) to relax; ~rsi vr (rilassarsi) to relax; (sdraiarsi) to lie down; **dis'tensi'one** sf stretching; relaxation; (POL) détente.

dis'teso, a pp di **distendere** // sf expanse, stretch.

distil'lare vt to distil.

distille'ria sf distillery.

dis'tinguere vt to distinguish.

dis'tinta sf (nota) note; (elenco) list.

distin'tivo, a ag distinctive; distinguishing // sm badge.

dis'tinto, a pp di **distinguere** // ag (dignitoso ed elegante) distinguished; ~i saluti (in lettera) yours faithfully.

distinzi'one [distin'tsjone] sf distinction.

dis'togliere [dis'tɔʎʎere] vt: ~ da to take away from; (fig) to dissuade from; **dis'tolto, a** pp di **distogliere**.

distorsi'one sf (MED) sprain; (FISICA, OTTICA) distortion.

dis'trarre vt to distract; (divertire) to entertain, amuse; **distrarsi** vr (non fare attenzione) to be distracted, let one's mind wander; (svagarsi) to amuse o enjoy o.s.; **dis'tratto, a** pp di **distrarre** // ag absent-minded; (disattento) inattentive; **distrazi'one** sf absent-mindedness;

inattention; (*svago*) distraction, entertainment.

dis'tretto *sm* district.

distribu'ire *vt* to distribute; (*CARTE*) to deal (out); (*consegnare: posta*) to deliver; (*lavoro*) to allocate, assign; (*ripartire*) to share out; **distribu'tore** *sm* (*di benzina*) petrol (*Brit*) *o* gas (*US*) pump; (*AUT, ELETTR*) distributor; (*automatico*) vending machine; **distribuzi'one** *sf* distribution; delivery.

distri'care *vt* to disentangle, unravel.

dis'truggere |dis'truddʒere| *vt* to destroy; **dis'trutto, a** *pp di* **distruggere**; **distruzi'one** *sf* destruction.

distur'bare *vt* to disturb, trouble; (*sonno, lezioni*) to disturb, interrupt; ~**rsi** *vr* to put o.s. out.

dis'turbo *sm* trouble, bother, inconvenience; (*indisposizione*) (slight) disorder, ailment; ~**i** *smpl* (*RADIO, TV*) static *sg*.

disubbidi'ente *ag* disobedient; **disubbidi'enza** *sf* disobedience.

disubbi'dire *vi*: ~ (**a qn**) to disobey (sb).

disugu'ale *ag* unequal; (*diverso*) different; (*irregolare*) uneven.

disu'mano, a *ag* inhuman.

di'suso *sm*: **andare** *o* **cadere in** ~ to fall into disuse.

'dita *fpl di* **dito**.

di'tale *sm* thimble.

'dito, *pl*(*f*) **'dita** *sm* finger; (*misura*) finger, finger's breadth; ~ (**del piede**) toe.

'ditta *sf* firm, business.

ditta'tore *sm* dictator.

ditta'tura *sf* dictatorship.

dit'tongo, ghi *sm* diphthong.

di'urno, a *ag* day *cpd*, daytime *cpd* // *sm* (*anche:* **albergo** ~) public toilets *with washing and shaving facilities etc*.

'diva *sf vedi* **divo**.

diva'gare *vi* to digress.

divam'pare *vi* to flare up, blaze up.

di'vano *sm* sofa; divan.

divari'care *vt* to open wide.

di'vario *sm* difference.

dive'nire *vi* = **diventare**; **dive'nuto, a** *pp di* **divenire**.

diven'tare *vi* to become; ~ **famoso/ professore** to become famous/a teacher.

di'verbio *sm* altercation.

di'vergere |di'verdʒere| *vi* to diverge.

diversifi'care *vt* to diversify, vary; to differentiate.

diversi'one *sf* diversion.

diversità *sf inv* difference, diversity; (*varietà*) variety.

diver'sivo *sm* diversion, distraction.

di'verso, a *ag* (*differente*): ~ (**da**) different (from); ~**i, e** *det pl* several, various; (*COMM*) sundry // *pronome pl* several (people), many (people).

diver'tente *ag* amusing.

diverti'mento *sm* amusement, pleasure; (*passatempo*) pastime, recreation.

diver'tire *vt* to amuse, entertain; ~**rsi** *vr* to amuse *o* enjoy o.s.

divi'dendo *sm* dividend.

di'videre *vt* (*anche MAT*) to divide; (*distribuire, ripartire*) to divide (up), split (up); ~**rsi** *vr* (*separarsi*) to separate; (*strade*) to fork.

divi'eto *sm* prohibition; "~ **di sosta**" (*AUT*) "no parking".

divinco'larsi *vr* to wriggle, writhe.

divinità *sf inv* divinity.

di'vino, a *ag* divine.

di'visa *sf* (*MIL etc*) uniform; (*COMM*) foreign currency.

divisi'one *sf* division.

di'viso, a *pp di* **dividere**.

'divo, a *sm/f* star.

divo'rare *vt* to devour.

divorzi'are |divor'tsjare| *vi*: ~ (**da qn**) to divorce (sb); **divorzi'ato, a** *sm/f* divorcee.

di'vorzio |di'vɔrtsjo| *sm* divorce.

divul'gare *vt* to divulge, disclose; (*rendere comprensibile*) to popularize; ~**rsi** *vr* to spread.

dizio'nario |ditsjo'narjo| *sm* dictionary.

dizi'one |dit'tsjone| *sf* diction; pronunciation.

do *sm* (*MUS*) C; (*: solfeggiando la scala*) do(h).

DOC |dɔk| *abbr* (= *denominazione di origine controllata*) label guaranteeing the quality of wine.

'doccia, ce |'dottʃa| *sf* (*bagno*) shower; (*condotto*) pipe; **fare la** ~ to have a shower.

do'cente |do'tʃɛnte| *ag* teaching // *sm/f* teacher; (*di università*) lecturer; **do'cenza** *sf* university teaching *o* lecturing.

'docile |'dɔtʃile| *ag* docile.

documen'tare *vt* to document; ~**rsi** *vr*: ~**rsi** (**su**) to gather information *o* material (about).

documen'tario *sm* documentary.

docu'mento *sm* document; ~**i** *smpl* (*d'identità etc*) papers.

'dodici |'doditʃi| *num* twelve.

do'gana *sf* (*ufficio*) customs *pl*; (*tassa*) (customs) duty; **passare la** ~ to go through customs; **doga'nale** *ag* customs *cpd*; **dogani'ere** *sm* customs officer.

'doglie |'dɔʎʎe| *sfpl* (*MED*) labour *sg*, labour pains.

'dolce |'doltʃe| *ag* sweet; (*colore*) soft; (*carattere, persona*) gentle, mild; (*fig: mite: clima*) mild; (*non ripido: pendio*) gentle // *sm* (*sapore dolce*) sweetness, sweet taste; (*CUC: portata*) sweet, dessert; (*: torta*) cake; **dol'cezza** *sf* sweetness; softness; mildness; gentleness; **dolci'umi** *smpl* sweets.

do'lente *ag* sorrowful, sad.

do'lere *vi* to be sore, hurt, ache; **~rsi** *vr* to complain; (*essere spiacente*): **~rsi di** to be sorry for; **mi duole la testa** my head aches, I've got a headache.

'dollaro *sm* dollar.

'dolo *sm* (*DIR*) malice.

Dolo'miti *sfpl*: **le ~** the Dolomites.

do'lore *sm* (*fisico*) pain; (*morale*) sorrow, grief; **dolo'roso, a** *ag* painful; sorrowful, sad.

do'loso, a *ag* (*DIR*) malicious.

do'manda *sf* (*interrogazione*) question; (*richiesta*) demand; (*: cortese*) request; (*DIR*: **richiesta scritta**) application; (*ECON*): **la ~** demand; **fare una ~ a qn** to ask sb a question; **fare ~** (**per un lavoro**) to apply (for a job).

doman'dare *vt* (*per avere*) to ask for; (*per sapere*) to ask; (*esigere*) to demand; **~rsi** *vr* to wonder; to ask o.s.; **~ qc a qn** to ask sb for sth; to ask sb sth.

do'mani *av* tomorrow // *sm*: **il ~** (*il futuro*) the future; (*il giorno successivo*) the next day; **~ l'altro** the day after tomorrow.

do'mare *vt* to tame.

domat'tina *av* tomorrow morning.

do'menica, che *sf* Sunday; **di** *o* **la ~** on Sundays; **domeni'cale** *ag* Sunday *cpd*.

do'mestica, che *sf vedi* **domestico**.

do'mestico, a, ci, che *ag* domestic // *sm/f* servant, domestic.

domi'cilio [domi'tʃiljo] *sm* (*DIR*) domicile, place of residence.

domi'nare *vt* to dominate; (*fig*: *sentimenti*) to control, master // *vi* to be in the dominant position; **~rsi** *vr* (*controllarsi*) to control o.s.; **~ su** (*fig*) to surpass, outclass; **dominazi'one** *sf* domination.

do'minio *sm* dominion; (*fig*: *campo*) field, domain.

do'nare *vt* to give, present; (*per beneficenza etc*) to donate // *vi* (*fig*): **~ a** to suit, become; **~ sangue** to give blood; **dona'tore, 'trice** *sm/f* donor; **donatore di sangue/di organi** blood/organ donor.

dondo'lare *vt* (*cullare*) to rock; **~rsi** *vr* to swing, sway; **'dondolo** *sm*: **sedia/ cavallo a dondolo** rocking chair/horse.

'donna *sf* woman; **~ di casa** housewife; home-loving woman; **~ di servizio** maid.

donnai'olo *sm* ladykiller.

don'nesco, a, schi, sche *ag* women's, woman's.

'donnola *sf* weasel.

'dono *sm* gift.

'dopo *av* (*tempo*) afterwards; (*: più tardi*) later; (*luogo*) after, next // *prep* after // *cong* (*temporale*): **~ aver studiato** after having studied; **~ mangiato va a dormire** after having

eaten *o* after a meal he goes for a sleep // *ag inv*: **il giorno ~** the following day; **un anno ~** a year later; **~ di me/lui** after me/him.

dopo'barba *sm inv* after-shave.

dopodo'mani *av* the day after tomorrow.

dopogu'erra *sm* postwar years *pl*.

dopo'pranzo [dopo'prandzo] *av* after lunch (*o* dinner).

doposcì [dopoʃ'ʃi] *sm inv* après-ski outfit.

doposcu'ola *sm inv* school club offering extra tuition and recreational facilities.

dopo'tutto *av* (*tutto considerato*) after all.

doppi'aggio [dop'pjaddʒo] *sm* (*CINEMA*) dubbing.

doppi'are *vt* (*NAUT*) to round; (*SPORT*) to lap; (*CINEMA*) to dub.

'doppio, a *ag* double; (*fig*: *falso*) double-dealing, deceitful // *sm* (*quantità*): **il ~ (di)** twice as much (*o* many), double the amount (*o* number) of; (*SPORT*) doubles *pl* // *av* double.

doppi'one *sm* duplicate (copy).

doppio'petto *sm* double-breasted jacket.

do'rare *vt* to gild; (*CUC*) to brown; **do'rato, a** *ag* golden; (*ricoperto d'oro*) gilt, gilded; **dora'tura** *sf* gilding.

dormicchi'are [dormik'kjare] *vi* to doze.

dormigli'one, a [dormiʎ'ʎone] *sm/f* sleepyhead.

dor'mire *vt, vi* to sleep; **dor'mita** *sf*: **farsi una dormita** to have a good sleep.

dormi'torio *sm* dormitory.

dormi'veglia [dormi'veʎʎa] *sm* drowsiness.

'dorso *sm* back; (*di montagna*) ridge, crest; (*di libro*) spine; **a ~ di cavallo** on horseback.

do'sare *vt* to measure out; (*MED*) to dose.

'dose *sf* quantity, amount; (*MED*) dose.

'dosso *sm* (*rilievo*) rise; (*di strada*) bump; (*dorso*): **levarsi di ~ i vestiti** to take one's clothes off.

do'tare *vt*: **~ di** to provide *o* supply with; (*fig*) to endow with; **dotazi'one** *sf* (*insieme di beni*) endowment; (*di macchine etc*) equipment.

'dote *sf* (*di sposa*) dowry; (*assegnata a un ente*) endowment; (*fig*) gift, talent.

Dott. *abbr* (= *dottore*) Dr.

'dotto, a *ag* (*colto*) learned // *sm* (*sapiente*) scholar; (*ANAT*) duct.

dotto'rato *sm* degree; **~ di ricerca** doctorate, doctor's degree.

dot'tore, essa *sm/f* doctor.

dot'trina *sf* doctrine.

Dott.ssa *abbr* (= *dottoressa*) Dr.

'dove ♦ *av* (*gen*) where; (*in cui*) where, in which; (*dovunque*) wherever; **~ sei?/ vai?** where are you?/are you going?;

dimmi dov'è tell me where it is; di ~ sei? where are you from?; per ~ si passa? which way should we go?; la città ~ abito the town where o in which I live; siediti ~ vuoi sit wherever you like ◆ *cong* (*mentre, laddove*) whereas.

do'vere *sm* (*obbligo*) duty // *vt* (*essere debitore*): ~ qc (a qn) to owe (sb) sth // *vi* (*seguito dall'infinito: obbligo*) to have to; rivolgersi a chi di ~ to apply to the appropriate authority o person; lui deve farlo he has to do it, he must do it; è dovuto partire he had to leave; ha dovuto pagare he had to pay; (: *intenzione*): devo partire domani I'm (due) to leave tomorrow; (: *probabilità*) dev'essere tardi it must be late; come si deve (*lavorare, comportarsi*) properly; una persona come si deve a respectable person.

dove'roso, a *ag* (right and) proper.

do'vunque *av* (*in qualunque luogo*) wherever; (*dappertutto*) everywhere; ~ io vada wherever I go.

do'vuto, a *ag* (*causato*): ~ a due to.

doz'zina [dod'dzina] *sf* dozen; una ~ di uova a dozen eggs.

dozzi'nale [doddzi'nale] *ag* cheap, second-rate.

dra'gare *vt* to dredge.

'drago, ghi *sm* dragon.

'dramma, i *sm* drama; dram'matico, a, ci, che *ag* dramatic; drammatiz'zare *vt* to dramatize; dramma'turgo, ghi *sm* playwright, dramatist.

drappeggi'are [draped'dʒare] *vt* to drape.

drap'pello *sm* (MIL) squad; (*gruppo*) band, group.

'drastico, a, ci, che *ag* drastic.

dre'naggio [dre'naddʒo] *sm* drainage.

dre'nare *vt* to drain.

'dritto, a *ag, av* = diritto.

driz'zare [drit'tsare] *vt* (*far tornare diritto*) to straighten; (*volgere: sguardo, occhi*) to turn, direct; (*innalzare: antenna, muro*) to erect; ~rsi *vr*: ~rsi (in piedi) to stand up; ~ le orecchie to prick up one's ears.

'droga, ghe *sf* (*sostanza aromatica*) spice; (*stupefacente*) drug; dro'gare *vt* to season, spice; to drug, dope; drogarsi *vr* to take drugs; dro'gato, a *sm/f* drug addict.

droghe'ria [droge'ria] *sf* grocer's shop (*Brit*), grocery (store) (*US*).

'dubbio, a *ag* (*incerto*) doubtful, dubious; (*ambiguo*) dubious // *sm* (*incertezza*) doubt; avere il ~ che to be afraid that, suspect that; mettere in ~ qc to question sth; dubbi'oso, a *ag* doubtful, dubious.

dubi'tare *vi*: ~ di to doubt; (*risultato*) to be doubtful of.

Dub'lino *sf* Dublin.

'duca, chi *sm* duke.

du'chessa [du'kessa] *sf* duchess.

'due *num* two.

due'cento [due'tʃɛnto] *num* two hundred // *sm*: il D~ the thirteenth century.

due'pezzi [due'pettsi] *sm* (*costume da bagno*) two-piece swimsuit; (*abito femminile*) two-piece suit.

du'etto *sm* duet.

'dunque *cong* (*perciò*) so, therefore; (*riprendendo il discorso*) well (then) // *inv*: venire al ~ to come to the point.

du'omo *sm* cathedral.

'duplex *sm inv* (TEL) party line.

dupli'cato *sm* duplicate.

'duplice ['dupliʃe] *ag* double, twofold; in ~ copia in duplicate.

du'rante *prep* during.

du'rare *vi* to last; ~ fatica a to have difficulty in; du'rata *sf* length (of time); duration; dura'turo, a *ag*, du'revole *ag* lasting.

du'rezza [du'rettsa] *sf* hardness; stubbornness; harshness; toughness.

'duro, a *ag* (*pietra, lavoro, materasso, problema*) hard; (*persona: ostinato*) stubborn, obstinate; (: *severo*) harsh, hard; (*voce*) harsh; (*carne*) tough // *sm* hardness; (*difficoltà*) hard part; (*persona*) tough guy; tener ~ to stand firm, hold out; ~ d'orecchi hard of hearing.

du'rone *sm* hard skin.

E

e, *dav V spesso* ed *cong* and; ~ lui? what about him?; ~ compralo! well buy it then!

E. *abbr* (= est) E.

è *vb vedi* essere.

'ebano *sm* ebony.

eb'bene *cong* well (then).

eb'brezza [eb'brettsa] *sf* intoxication.

'ebbro, a *ag* drunk; ~ di (*gioia etc*) beside o.s. o wild with.

'ebete *ag* stupid, idiotic.

ebollizi'one [ebollit'tsjone] *sf* boiling; punto di ~ boiling point.

e'braico, a, ci, che *ag* Hebrew, Hebraic // *sm* (LING) Hebrew.

e'breo, a *ag* Jewish // *sm/f* Jew/Jewess.

'Ebridi *sfpl*: le (isole) ~ the Hebrides.

ecc *av abbr* (= eccetera) etc.

ecce'denza [ettʃe'dɛntsa] *sf* excess, surplus.

ec'cedere [et'tʃɛdere] *vt* to exceed // *vi* to go too far; ~ nel bere/mangiare to indulge in drink/food to excess.

eccel'lente [ettʃel'lɛnte] *ag* excellent; eccel'lenza *sf* excellence; (*titolo*) Excellency.

ec'cellere [et'tʃɛllere] *vi*: ~ (in) to excel

(at); **ec'celso, a** *pp di* **eccellere.**

ec'centrico, a, ci, che [et'tʃentriko] *ag* eccentric.

ecces'sivo, a [ettʃes'sivo] *ag* excessive.

ec'cesso [et'tʃesso] *sm* excess; **all'~** (*gentile, generoso*) to excess, excessively; **~ di velocità** (*AUT*) speeding.

ec'cetera [et'tʃetera] *av* et cetera, and so on.

ec'cetto [et'tʃetto] *prep* except, with the exception of; **~ che** *cong* except, other than; **~ che (non)** unless.

eccettu'are [ettʃettu'are] *vt* to except.

eccezio'nale [ettʃetsjo'nale] *ag* exceptional.

eccezi'one [ettʃet'tsjone] *sf* exception; (*DIR*) objection; **a ~ di** with the exception of, except for; **d'~** exceptional.

ec'cidio [et'tʃidio] *sm* massacre.

ecci'tare [ettʃi'tare] *vt* (*curiosità, interesse*) to excite, arouse; (*folla*) to incite; **~rsi** *vr* to get excited; (*sessualmente*) to become aroused; **eccitazi'one** *sf* excitement.

'ecco *av* (*per dimostrare*): **~ il treno!** here's *o* here comes the train!; (*dav pronome*): **~mi!** here I am!; **~ne uno!** here's one (of them)!; (*dav pp*): **~ fatto!** there, that's it done!

echeggi'are [eked'dʒare] *vi* to echo.

e'clissi *sf* eclipse.

'eco, *pl(m)* **'echi** *sm o f* echo.

ecolo'gia [ekolo'dʒia] *sf* ecology.

econo'mia *sf* economy; (*scienza*) economics *sg*; (*risparmio: azione*) saving; **fare ~** to economize, make economies; **eco'nomico, a, ci, che** *ag* economic; (*poco costoso*) economical; **econo'mista, i** *sm* economist; **economiz'zare** *vt, vi* to save; **e'conomo, a** *ag* thrifty // *sm/f* (*INS*) bursar.

ed *cong vedi* **e.**

'edera *sf* ivy.

e'dicola *sf* newspaper kiosk *o* stand (*US*).

edifi'care *vt* to build; (*fig: teoria, azienda*) to establish; (*indurre al bene*) to edify.

edi'ficio [edi'fitʃo] *sm* building; (*fig*) structure.

e'dile *ag* building *cpd*; **edi'lizio, a** *ag* building *cpd* // *sf* building, building trade.

Edim'burgo *sf* Edinburgh.

edi'tore, 'trice *ag* publishing *cpd* // *sm/f* publisher; (*curatore*) editor; **edito'ria** *sf* publishing; **editori'ale** *ag* publishing *cpd* // *sm* editorial, leader.

edizi'one [edit'tsjone] *sf* edition; (*tiratura*) printing; (*di manifestazioni, feste etc*) production.

edu'care *vt* to educate; (*gusto, mente*) to train; **~ qn a fare** to train sb to do; **edu'cato, a** *ag* polite, well-mannered; **educazi'one** *sf* education; (*familiare*)

upbringing; (*comportamento*) (good) manners *pl*; **educazione fisica** (*INS*) physical training *o* education.

effemi'nato, a *ag* effeminate.

effet'tivo, a *ag* (*reale*) real, actual; (*impiegato, professore*) permanent; (*MIL*) regular // *sm* (*MIL*) strength; (*di patrimonio etc*) sum total.

ef'fetto *sm* effect; (*COMM: cambiale*) bill; (*fig: impressione*) impression; **in ~i** in fact, actually; **effettu'are** *vt* to effect, carry out.

effi'cace [effi'katʃe] *ag* effective.

effici'ente [effi'tʃente] *ag* efficient; **effici'enza** *sf* efficiency.

ef'fimero, a *ag* ephemeral.

E'geo [e'dʒɛo] *sm*: **l'~, il mare ~** the Aegean (Sea).

E'gitto [e'dʒitto] *sm*: **l'~** Egypt.

egizi'ano, a [edʒit'tsjano] *ag, sm/f* Egyptian.

'egli ['eʎʎi] *pronome* he; **~ stesso** he himself.

ego'ismo *sm* selfishness, egoism; **ego'ista, i, e** *ag* selfish, egoistic // *sm/f* egoist.

egr. *abbr* = **egregio.**

e'gregio, a, gi, gie [e'gredʒo] *ag* distinguished; (*nelle lettere*): **E~ Signore** Dear Sir.

eguagli'anza [egwaʎ'ʎantsa] *etc vedi* **uguaglianza** *etc*.

E.I. *abbr* = *Esercito Italiano*.

elabo'rare *vt* (*progetto*) to work out, elaborate; (*dati*) to process; (*digerire*) to digest; **elabora'tore** *sm* (*INFORM*): **elaboratore elettronico** computer; **elaborazi'one** *sf* elaboration; digestion; **elaborazione dei dati** data processing.

e'lastico, a, ci, che *ag* elastic; (*fig: andatura*) springy; (*: decisione, vedute*) flexible // *sm* (*gommino*) rubber band; (*per il cucito*) elastic *q*.

ele'fante *sm* elephant.

ele'gante *ag* elegant.

e'leggere [e'lɛddʒere] *vt* to elect.

elemen'tare *ag* elementary; **le (scuole) ~i** *sfpl* primary (*Brit*) *o* grade (*US*) school.

ele'mento *sm* element; (*parte componente*) element, component, part; **~i** *smpl* (*della scienza etc*) elements, rudiments.

ele'mosina *sf* charity, alms *pl*; **chiedere l'~** to beg.

elen'care *vt* to list.

e'lenco, chi *sm* list; **~ telefonico** telephone directory.

e'letto, a *pp di* **eleggere** // *sm/f* (*nominato*) elected member; **eletto'rale** *ag* electoral, election *cpd*; **eletto'rato** *sm* electorate; **elet'tore, 'trice** *sm/f* voter, elector.

elet'trauto *sm inv* workshop for car electrical repairs; (*tecnico*) car electrician.

elettri'cista, i [elettri'tʃista] *sm* electrician.

elettricità [elettritʃi'ta] *sf* electricity.

e'lettrico, a, ci, che *ag* electric(al).

elettriz'zare [elettrid'dzare] *vt* to electrify.

e'lettro... *prefisso:* **elettrocardio'gramma, i** *sm* electrocardiogram; **elettrodo'mestico, a, ci, che** *ag:* **apparecchi elettrodomestici** domestic (electrical) appliances; **elet'trone** *sm* electron; **elet'tronico, a, ci, che** *ag* electronic // *sf* electronics *sg*.

ele'vare *vt* to raise; (*edificio*) to erect; (*multa*) to impose.

elezi'one [elet'tsjone] *sf* election; ∼**i** *sfpl* (*POL*) election(s).

'elica, che *sf* propeller.

eli'cottero *sm* helicopter.

elimi'nare *vt* to eliminate; **elimina'toria** *sf* eliminating round.

'elio *sm* helium.

'ella *pronome* she; (*forma di cortesia*) you; ∼ **stessa** she herself; you yourself.

el'metto *sm* helmet.

e'logio [e'lɔdʒo] *sm* (*discorso, scritto*) eulogy; (*lode*) praise (*di solito q*).

elo'quente *ag* eloquent.

e'ludere *vt* to evade; **elu'sivo, a** *ag* evasive.

ema'nare *vt* to send out, give off; (*fig: leggi, decreti*) to issue // *vi:* ∼ **da** to come from.

emanci'pare [emant'ʃi'pare] *vt* to emancipate; ∼**rsi** *vr* (*fig*) to become liberated *o* emancipated.

embri'one *sm* embryo.

emenda'mento *sm* amendment.

emen'dare *vt* to amend.

emer'genza [emer'dʒentsa] *sf* emergency; **in caso di** ∼ in an emergency.

e'mergere [e'merdʒere] *vi* to emerge; (*sommergibile*) to surface; (*fig: distinguersi*) to stand out; **e'merso, a** *pp di* **emergere.**

e'messo, a *pp di* **emettere.**

e'mettere *vt* (*suono, luce*) to give out, emit; (*onde radio*) to send out; (*assegno, francobollo, ordine*) to issue; (*fig: giudizio*) to express, voice.

emi'crania *sf* migraine.

emi'grare *vi* to emigrate; **emigrazi'one** *sf* emigration.

emi'nente *ag* eminent, distinguished.

emis'fero *sm* hemisphere; ∼ **boreale/ australe** northern/southern hemisphere.

emissi'one *sf* (*vedi emettere*) emission; sending out; issue; (*RADIO*) broadcast.

emit'tente *ag* (*banca*) issuing; (*RADIO*) broadcasting, transmitting // *sf* (*RADIO*) transmitter.

emorra'gia, 'gie [emorra'dʒia] *sf* haemorrhage.

emo'tivo, a *ag* emotional.

emozio'nante [emottsjo'nante] *ag* exciting, thrilling.

emozio'nare [emottsjo'nare] *vt* (*appassionare*) to thrill, excite; (*commuovere*) to move; (*innervosire*) to upset; ∼**rsi** *vr* to be excited; to be moved; to be upset.

emozi'one [emot'tsjone] *sf* emotion; (*agitazione*) excitement.

'empio, a *ag* (*sacrilego*) impious; (*spietato*) cruel, pitiless; (*malvagio*) wicked, evil.

emulsi'one *sf* emulsion.

enciclope'dia [entʃiklope'dia] *sf* encyclopaedia.

endove'noso, a *ag* (*MED*) intravenous.

'ENEL ['enel] *sigla m* (= *Ente Nazionale per l'Energia Elettrica*) ≈ C.E.G.B. (= *Central Electricity Generating Board*).

ener'gia, 'gie [ener'dʒia] *sf* (*FISICA*) energy; (*fig*) energy, strength, vigour; **e'nergico, a, ci, che** *ag* energetic, vigorous.

'enfasi *sf* emphasis; (*peg*) bombast, pomposity; **en'fatico, a, ci, che** *ag* emphatic; pompous.

'ENIT ['enit] *sigla m* = *Ente Nazionale Italiano per il Turismo.*

en'nesimo, a *ag* (*MAT, fig*) nth; **per l'**∼**a volta** for the umpteenth time.

e'norme *ag* enormous, huge; **enormità** *sf inv* enormity, huge size; (*assurdità*) absurdity; **non dire enormità!** don't talk nonsense!

'ente *sm* (*istituzione*) body, board, corporation; (*FILOSOFIA*) being.

en'trambi, e *pronome pl* both (of them) // *ag pl:* ∼ **i ragazzi** both boys, both of the boys.

en'trare *vi* to enter, go (*o* come) in; ∼ **in** (*luogo*) to enter, go (*o* come) into; (*trovar posto, poter stare*) to fit into; (*essere ammesso a: club etc*) to join, become a member of; ∼ **in automobile** to get into the car; **far** ∼ **qn** (*visitatore etc*) to show sb in; **questo non c'entra** (*fig*) that's got nothing to do with it; **en'trata** *sf* entrance, entry; **entrate** *sfpl* (*COMM*) receipts, takings; (*ECON*) income *sg.*

'entro *prep* (*temporale*) within.

entusias'mare *vt* to excite, fill with enthusiasm; ∼**rsi** (**per qc/qn**) to become enthusiastic (about sth/sb); **entusi'asmo** *sm* enthusiasm; **entusi'asta, i, e** *ag* enthusiastic // *sm/f* enthusiast; **entusi'astico, a, ci, che** *ag* enthusiastic.

enunci'are [enun'tʃare] *vt* (*teoria*) to enunciate, set out.

'epico, a, ci, che *ag* epic.

epide'mia *sf* epidemic.

epi'dermide *sf* skin, epidermis.

Epifa'nia *sf* Epiphany.

epiles'sia *sf* epilepsy.

e'pilogo, ghi *sm* conclusion.

epi'sodio *sm* episode.

e'piteto *sm* epithet.

'epoca, che *sf* (*periodo storico*) age, era; (*tempo*) time; (*GEO*) age.

ep'pure *cong* and yet, nevertheless.

epu'rare *vt* (*POL*) to purge.

equa'tore *sm* equator.

equazi'one [ekwat'tsjone] *sf* (*MAT*) equation.

e'questre *ag* equestrian.

equi'latero, a *ag* equilateral.

equili'brare *vt* to balance; **equi'librio** *sm* balance, equilibrium; **perdere l'~** to lose one's balance.

e'quino, a *ag* horse *cpd*, equine.

equipaggi'are [ekwipad'dʒare] *vt* (*di persone*) to man; (*di mezzi*) to equip; **equi'paggio** *sm* crew.

equipa'rare *vt* to make equal.

equità *sf* equity, fairness.

equitazi'one [ekwitat'tsjone] *sf* (horse-) riding.

equiva'lente *ag, sm* equivalent; **equiva'lenza** *sf* equivalence.

equivo'care *vi* to misunderstand; **e'quivoco, a, ci, che** *ag* equivocal, ambiguous; (*sospetto*) dubious // *sm* misunderstanding; **a scanso di equivoci** to avoid any misunderstanding; **giocare sull'equivoco** to equivocate.

'equo, a *ag* fair, just.

'era *sf* era.

'erba *sf* grass; (*aromatica, medicinale*) herb; **in ~** (*fig*) budding; **er'baccia, ce** *sf* weed.

e'rede *sm/f* heir; **eredità** *sf* (*DIR*) inheritance; (*BIOL*) heredity; **lasciare qc in eredità a qn** to leave o bequeath sth to sb; **eredi'tare** *vt* to inherit; **eredi'tario, a** *ag* hereditary.

ere'mita, i *sm* hermit.

ere'sia *sf* heresy; **e'retico, a, ci, che** *ag* heretical // *sm/f* heretic.

e'retto, a *pp di* **erigere** // *ag* erect, upright; **erezi'one** *sf* (*FISIOL*) erection.

er'gastolo *sm* (*DIR*: *pena*) life imprisonment.

'erica *sf* heather.

e'rigere [e'ridʒere] *vt* to erect, raise; (*fig*: *fondare*) to found.

ermel'lino *sm* ermine.

er'metico, a, ci, che *ag* hermetic.

'ernia *sf* (*MED*) hernia.

e'roe *sm* hero.

ero'gare *vt* (*somme*) to distribute; (: *per beneficenza*) to donate; (*gas, servizi*) to supply.

e'roico, a, ci, che *ag* heroic.

ero'ina *sf* heroine; (*droga*) heroin.

ero'ismo *sm* heroism.

erosi'one *sf* erosion.

e'rotico, a, ci, che *ag* erotic.

er'rare *vi* (*vagare*) to wander, roam; (*sbagliare*) to be mistaken.

er'rore *sm* error, mistake; (*morale*) error; **per ~** by mistake.

'erta *sf* steep slope; **stare all'~** to be on the alert.

erut'tare *vt* (*sog: vulcano*) to throw out, belch.

eruzi'one [erut'tsjone] *sf* eruption.

esacer'bare [ezatʃer'bare] *vt* to exacerbate.

esage'rare [ezadʒe'rare] *vt* to exaggerate // *vi* to exaggerate; (*eccedere*) to go too far; **esagerazi'one** *sf* exaggeration.

e'sagono *sm* hexagon.

esal'tare *vt* to exalt; (*entusiasmare*) to excite, stir; **esal'tato, a** *sm/f* fanatic.

e'same *sm* examination; (*INS*) exam, examination; **fare** o **dare un ~** to sit o take an exam; **~ del sangue** blood test.

esami'nare *vt* to examine.

e'sanime *ag* lifeless.

esaspe'rare *vt* to exasperate; to exacerbate; **~rsi** *vr* to become annoyed o exasperated; **esasperazi'one** *sf* exasperation.

esatta'mente *av* exactly; accurately, precisely.

esat'tezza [ezat'tettsa] *sf* exactitude, accuracy, precision.

e'satto, a *pp di* **esigere** // *ag* (*calcolo, ora*) correct, right, exact; (*preciso*) accurate, precise; (*puntuale*) punctual.

esat'tore *sm* (*di imposte etc*) collector.

esau'dire *vt* to grant, fulfil.

esauri'ente *ag* exhaustive.

esauri'mento *sm* exhaustion; **~ nervoso** nervous breakdown.

esau'rire *vt* (*stancare*) to exhaust, wear out; (*provviste, miniera*) to exhaust; **~rsi** *vr* to exhaust o.s., wear o.s. out; (*provviste*) to run out; **esau'rito, a** *ag* exhausted; (*merci*) sold out; (*libri*) out of print; **registrare il tutto esaurito** (*TEATRO*) to have a full house; **e'sausto, a** *ag* exhausted.

'esca, pl esche *sf* bait.

escande'scenza [eskandeʃ'ʃentsa] *sf*: **dare in ~e** to lose one's temper, fly into a rage.

'esce, 'esci ['eʃe, 'eʃi] *vb vedi* **uscire**.

eschi'mese [eski'mese] *ag, sm/f* Eskimo.

escla'mare *vi* to exclaim, cry out; **esclamazi'one** *sf* exclamation.

es'cludere *vt* to exclude.

esclu'sivo, a *ag* exclusive // *sf* (*DIR, COMM*) exclusive o sole rights *pl*.

es'cluso, a *pp di* **escludere**.

'esco, 'escono *vb vedi* **uscire**.

escursi'one *sf* (*gita*) excursion, trip; (: *a piedi*) hike, walk; (*METEOR*) range.

ese'crare *vt* to loathe, abhor.

esecu'tivo, a *ag, sm* executive.

esecu'tore, 'trice *sm/f* (*MUS*) performer; (*DIR*) executor.

esecuzi'one [ezekut'tsjone] *sf* execution, carrying out; (*MUS*) performance; **~**

capitale execution.

esegu'ire vt to carry out, execute; (MUS) to perform, execute.

e'sempio sm example; **per ~** for example, for instance; **fare un ~** to give an example; **esem'plare** ag exemplary // sm example; (copia) copy; **esemplifi'care** vt to exemplify.

esen'tare vt: **~ qn/qc da** to exempt sb/ sth from.

e'sente ag: **~ da** (dispensato da) exempt from; (privo di) free from; **esenzi'one** sf exemption.

e'sequie sfpl funeral rites; funeral service sg.

eser'cente [ezer'tʃente] sm/f trader, dealer; shopkeeper.

eserci'tare [ezertʃi'tare] vt (professione) to practise (Brit), practice (US); (allenare: corpo, mente) to exercise, train; (diritto) to exercise; (influenza, pressione) to exert; **~rsi** vr to practise; **~rsi alla lotta** to practise fighting; **esercitazi'one** sf (scolastica, militare) exercise.

e'sercito [e'zertʃito] sm army.

eser'cizio [ezer'tʃittsjo] sm practice; exercising; (fisico, di matematica) exercise; (ECON) financial year; (azienda) business, concern; **in ~** (medico etc) practising.

esi'bire vt to exhibit, display; (documenti) to produce, present; **~rsi** vr (attore) to perform; (fig) to show off; **esibizi'one** sf exhibition; (di documento) presentation; (spettacolo) show, performance.

esi'gente [ezi'dʒente] ag demanding; **esi'genza** sf demand, requirement.

e'sigere [e'zidʒere] vt (pretendere) to demand; (richiedere) to demand, require; (imposte) to collect.

e'siguo, a ag small, slight.

'esile ag (persona) slender, slim; (stelo) thin; (voce) faint.

esili'are vt to exile; **e'silio** sm exile.

e'simere vt: **~ qn/qc da** to exempt sb/sth from; **~rsi** vr: **~rsi da** to get out of.

esis'tenza [ezis'tentsa] sf existence.

e'sistere vi to exist.

esis'tito, a pp di **esistere**.

esi'tare vi to hesitate; **esitazi'one** sf hesitation.

'esito sm result, outcome.

'esodo sm exodus.

esone'rare vt: **~ qn da** to exempt sb from.

e'sordio sm début.

esor'tare vt: **~ qn a fare** to urge sb to do.

e'sotico, a, ci, che ag exotic.

es'pandere vt to expand; (confini) to extend; (influenza) to extend, spread; **~rsi** vr to expand; **espansi'one** sf expansion; **espan'sivo, a** ag expansive,

communicative.

espatri'are vi to leave one's country.

espedi'ente sm expedient.

es'pellere vt to expel.

esperi'enza [espe'rjentsa] sf experience; (SCIENZA: prova) experiment.

esperi'mento sm experiment.

es'perto, a ag, sm expert.

espi'are vt to atone for.

espi'rare vt, vi to breathe out.

espli'care vt (attività) to carry out, perform.

es'plicito, a [es'plitʃito] ag explicit.

es'plodere vi (anche fig) to explode // vt to fire.

esplo'rare vt to explore; **esplora'tore** sm explorer; (anche: **giovane esploratore**) (boy) scout; (NAUT) scout (ship).

esplosi'one sf explosion; **esplo'sivo, a** ag, sm explosive; **es'ploso, a** pp di **esplodere**.

espo'nente sm/f (rappresentante) representative.

es'porre vt (merci) to display; (quadro) to exhibit, show; (fatti, idee) to explain, set out; (porre in pericolo, FOT) to expose.

espor'tare vt to export; **esportazi'one** sf exportation; export.

esposizi'one [espozit'tsjone] sf displaying; exhibiting; setting out; (anche FOT) exposure; (mostra) exhibition; (narrazione) explanation, exposition.

es'posto, a pp di **esporre** // ag: **~ a nord** facing north // sm (AMM) statement, account; (: petizione) petition.

espressi'one sf expression.

espres'sivo, a ag expressive.

es'presso, a pp di **esprimere** // ag express // sm (lettera) express letter; (anche: **treno ~**) express train; (anche: **caffè ~**) espresso.

es'primere vt to express; **~rsi** vr to express o.s.

espulsi'one sf expulsion; **es'pulso, a** pp di **espellere**.

'essa pronome f, **'esse** pronome fpl vedi **esso**.

es'senza [es'sentsa] sf essence; **essenzi'ale** ag essential; **l'essenziale** the main o most important thing.

'essere ◆ sm being; **~ umano** human being

◆ vb copulativo **1** (con attributo, sostantivo) to be; **sei giovane/simpatico** you are o you're young/nice; **è medico** he is o he's a doctor

2 (+ di: appartenere) to be; **di chi è la penna?** whose pen is it?; **è di Carla** it is o it's Carla's, it belongs to Carla

3 (+ di: provenire) to be; **è di Venezia** he is o he's from Venice

4 (data, ora): **è il 15 agosto/lunedì** it is o it's the 15th of August/Monday; **che ora è?, che ore sono?** what time is it?; **è**

l'una it is *o* it's one o'clock; **sono le due** it is *o* it's two o'clock

5 (*costare*): **quant'è?** how much is it?; **sono 20.000 lire** it's 20,000 lire

◆ *vb ausiliare* **1** (*attivo*): ~ **arrivato/venuto** to have arrived/come; **è già partita** she has already left

2 (*passivo*) to be; ~ **fatto da** to be made by; **è stata uccisa** she has been killed

3 (*riflessivo*): **si sono lavati** they washed, they got washed

4 (+ *da* + *infinito*): **è da farsi subito** it must be *o* is to be done immediately

◆ *vi* **1** (*esistere*, *trovarsi*) to be; **sono a casa** I'm at home; ~ **in piedi/seduto** to be standing/sitting

2: **esserci**: **c'è** there is; **ci sono** there are; **che c'è?** what's the matter?, what is it?; **ci sono!** (*fig*: *ho capito*) I get it!; *vedi anche* **ci**

◆ *vb impers*: **è tardi/Pasqua** it's late/Easter; **è possibile che venga** he may come; **è così** that's the way it is.

'esso, a *pronome* it; (*riferito a persona*: *soggetto*) he/she; (: *complemento*) him/her; **~i**, **e** *pronome pl* they; (*complemento*) them.

est *sm* east.

'estasi *sf* ecstasy.

es'tate *sf* summer.

es'tatico, a, ci, che *ag* ecstatic.

es'tendere *vt* to extend; **~rsi** *vr* (*diffondersi*) to spread; (*territorio*, *confini*) to extend; **estensi'one** *sf* extension; (*di superficie*) expanse; (*di voce*) range.

esteri'ore *ag* outward, external.

es'terno, a *ag* (*porta*, *muro*) outer, outside; (*scala*) outside; (*alunno*, *impressione*) external // *sm* outside, exterior // *sm/f* (*allievo*) day pupil; **per uso** ~ for external use only.

'estero, a *ag* foreign // *sm*: **all'~** abroad.

es'teso, a *pp di* **estendere** // *ag* extensive, large; **scrivere per** ~ to write in full.

es'tetico, a, ci, che *ag* aesthetic // *sf* (*disciplina*) aesthetics // *sf* (*bellezza*) attractiveness; **este'tista, i, e** *sm/f* beautician.

'estimo *sm* valuation; (*disciplina*) surveying.

es'tinguere *vt* to extinguish, put out; (*debito*) to pay off; **~rsi** *vr* to go out; (*specie*) to become extinct; **es'tinto, a** *pp di* **estinguere**; **estin'tore** *sm* (*fire*) extinguisher; **estinzi'one** *sf* putting out; (*di specie*) extinction.

estir'pare *vt* (*pianta*) to uproot, pull up; (*fig*: *vizio*) to eradicate.

es'tivo, a *ag* summer *cpd*.

es'torcere [es'tortʃere] *vt*: ~ **qc** (**a qn**) to extort sth (from sb); **es'torto, a** *pp di* **estorcere**.

estradizi'one [estradit'tsjone] *sf* extradition.

es'traneo, a *ag* foreign; (*discorso*) extraneous, unrelated // *sm/f* stranger; **rimanere** ~ **a qc** to take no part in sth.

es'trarre *vt* to extract; (*minerali*) to mine; (*sorteggiare*) to draw; **es'tratto, a** *pp di* **estrarre** // *sm* extract; (*di documento*) abstract; **estratto conto** statement of account; **estratto di nascita** birth certificate; **estrazi'one** *sf* extraction; mining; drawing *o*; draw.

estremità *sf inv* extremity, end // *sfpl* (*ANAT*) extremities.

es'tremo, a *ag* extreme; (*ultimo*: *ora*, *tentativo*) final, last // *sm* extreme; (*di pazienza*, *forze*) limit, end; **~i** *smpl* (*AMM*: *dati essenziali*) details, particulars; **l'~ Oriente** the Far East.

'estro *sm* (*capriccio*) whim, fancy; (*ispirazione creativa*) inspiration; **es'troso, a** *ag* whimsical, capricious; inspired.

estro'verso, a *ag*, *sm* extrovert.

'esule *sm/f* exile.

età *sf inv* age; **all'~ di 8 anni** at the age of 8, at 8 years of age; **ha la mia** ~ he (*o* she) is the same age as me *o* as I am; **raggiungere la maggiore** ~ to come of age; **essere in** ~ **minore** to be under age.

'etere *sm* ether; **e'tereo, a** *ag* ethereal.

eternità *sf* eternity.

e'terno, a *ag* eternal.

etero'geneo, a [etero'dʒɛneo] *ag* heterogeneous.

'etica *sf vedi* **etico**.

eti'chetta [eti'ketta] *sf* label; (*cerimoniale*): **l'~** etiquette.

'etico, a, ci, che *ag* ethical // *sf* ethics *sg*.

etimolo'gia, 'gie [etimolo'dʒia] *sf* etymology.

Eti'opia *sf*: **l'~** Ethiopia.

'Etna *sm*: **l'~** Etna.

'etnico, a, ci, che *ag* ethnic.

e'trusco, a, schi, sche *ag*, *sm/f* Etruscan.

'ettaro *sm* hectare (= *10,000 m²*).

'etto *sm abbr di* **ettogrammo**.

etto'grammo *sm* hectogram(me) (= *100 grams*).

Eucaris'tia *sf*: **l'~** the Eucharist.

Eu'ropa *sf*: **l'~** Europe; **euro'peo, a** *ag*, *sm/f* European.

evacu'are *vt* to evacuate.

e'vadere *vi* (*fuggire*): ~ **da** to escape from // *vt* (*sbrigare*) to deal with, dispatch; (*tasse*) to evade.

evan'gelico, a, ci, che [evan'dʒeliko] *ag* evangelical.

evapo'rare *vi* to evaporate; **evaporazi'one** *sf* evaporation.

evasi'one *sf* (*vedi evadere*) escape; dispatch; ~ **fiscale** tax evasion.

eva'sivo, a *ag* evasive.

e'vaso, a *pp di* **evadere** // *sm* escapee.

eveni'enza [eve'njɛntsa] *sf*: **pronto(a) per ogni ~** ready for any eventuality.

e'vento *sm* event.

eventu'ale *ag* possible.

evi'dente *ag* evident, obvious; **evi'denza** *sf* obviousness; **mettere in evidenza** to point out, highlight.

evi'tare *vt* to avoid; **~ di fare** to avoid doing; **~ qc a qn** to spare sb sth.

'evo *sm* age, epoch.

evo'care *vt* to evoke.

evo'luto, a *pp di* **evolvere** // *ag* (*civiltà*) (highly) developed, advanced; (*persona*) independent.

evoluzi'one [evolut'tsjone] *sf* evolution.

e'volversi *vr* to evolve.

ev'viva *escl* hurrah!; **~ il re!** long live the king!, hurrah for the king!

ex *prefisso* ex, former.

'extra *ag inv* first-rate; top-quality // *sm inv* extra; **extraconiu'gale** *ag* extra-marital.

F

fa *vb vedi* **fare** // *sm inv* (*MUS*) F; (: *solfeggiando la scala*) fa // *av*: **10 anni ~** 10 years ago.

fabbi'sogno [fabbi'zoɲɲo] *sm* needs *pl*, requirements *pl*.

'fabbrica *sf* factory; **fabbri'cante** *sm* manufacturer, maker; **fabbri'care** *vt* to build; (*produrre*) to manufacture, make; (*fig*) to fabricate, invent.

'fabbro *sm* (black)smith.

fac'cenda [fat'tʃɛnda] *sf* matter, affair; (*cosa da fare*) task, chore.

fac'chino [fak'kino] *sm* porter.

'faccia, ce [fattʃa] *sf* face; (*di moneta, medaglia*) side; **~ a ~** face to face.

facci'ata [fat'tʃata] *sf* façade; (*di pagina*) side.

'faccio [fattʃo] *vb vedi* **fare**.

fa'ceto, a [fa'tʃeto] *ag* witty, humorous.

'facile [fatʃile] *ag* easy; (*affabile*) easy-going; (*disposto*): **~ a** inclined to, prone to; (*probabile*): **è ~ che piova** it's likely to rain; **facilità** *sf* easiness; (*disposizione, dono*) aptitude; **facili'tare** *vt* to make easier.

facino'roso, a [fatʃino'roso] *ag* violent.

facoltà *sf inv* faculty; (*CHIMICA*) property; (*autorità*) power.

facolta'tivo, a *ag* optional; (*fermata d'autobus*) request *cpd*.

fac'simile *sm* facsimile.

'faggio [faddʒo] *sm* beech.

fagi'ano [fa'dʒano] *sm* pheasant.

fagio'lino [fadʒo'lino] *sm* French (*Brit*) *o* string bean.

fagi'olo [fa'dʒɔlo] *sm* bean.

fa'gotto *sm* bundle; (*MUS*) bassoon; **far ~** (*fig*) to pack up and go.

'fai *vb vedi* **fare**.

'falce [faltʃe] *sf* scythe; **fal'cetto** *sm* sickle; **falci'are** *vt* to cut; (*fig*) to mow down.

'falco, chi *sm* hawk.

fal'cone *sm* falcon.

'falda *sf* layer, stratum; (*di cappello*) brim; (*di cappotto*) tails *pl*; (*di monte*) lower slope; (*di tetto*) pitch; **nevica a larghe ~e** the snow is falling in large flakes; **abito a ~e** tails *pl*.

fale'gname [faleɲ'ɲame] *sm* joiner.

fal'lace [fal'latʃe] *ag* misleading, deceptive.

falli'mento *sm* failure; bankruptcy.

fal'lire *vi* (*non riuscire*): **~ (in)** to fail (in); (*DIR*) to go bankrupt // *vt* (*colpo, bersaglio*) to miss; **fal'lito, a** *ag* unsuccessful; bankrupt // *sm/f* bankrupt.

'fallo *sm* error, mistake; (*imperfezione*) defect, flaw; (*SPORT*) foul; fault; **senza ~** without fail.

falò *sm inv* bonfire.

fal'sare *vt* to distort, misrepresent; **fal'sario** *sm* forger; counterfeiter; **falsifi'care** *vt* to forge; (*monete*) to forge, counterfeit.

'falso, a *ag* false; (*errato*) wrong; (*falsificato*) forged; fake; (: *oro, gioielli*) imitation *cpd* // *sm* forgery; **giurare il ~** to commit perjury.

'fama *sf* fame; (*reputazione*) reputation, name.

'fame *sf* hunger; **aver ~** to be hungry; **fa'melico, a, ci, che** *ag* ravenous.

fa'miglia [fa'miʎʎa] *sf* family.

famili'are *ag* (*della famiglia*) family *cpd*; (*ben noto*) familiar; (*rapporti, atmosfera*) friendly; (*LING*) informal, colloquial // *sm/f* relative, relation; **familiarità** *sf* familiarity; friendliness; informality.

fa'moso, a *ag* famous, well-known.

fa'nale *sm* (*AUT*) light, lamp (*Brit*); (*luce stradale, NAUT*) light; (*di faro*) beacon.

fa'natico, a, ci, che *ag* fanatical; (*del teatro, calcio etc*): **~ di** *o* **per** mad *o* crazy about // *sm/f* fanatic; (*tifoso*) fan.

fanci'ullo, a [fan'tʃullo] *sm/f* child.

fan'donia *sf* tall story; **~e** *sfpl* nonsense *sg*.

fan'fara *sf* brass band; (*musica*) fanfare.

'fango, ghi *sm* mud; **fan'goso, a** *ag* muddy.

'fanno *vb vedi* **fare**.

fannul'lone *sm/f* idler, loafer.

fantasci'enza [fantaʃ'ʃɛntsa] *sf* science fiction.

fanta'sia *sf* fantasy, imagination; (*capriccio*) whim, caprice // *ag inv*: **vestito ~** patterned dress.

fan'tasma, i *sm* ghost, phantom.

fan'tastico, a, ci, che *ag* fantastic; (*potenza, ingegno*) imaginative.

'fante *sm* infantryman; (*CARTE*) jack,

knave (*Brit*); **fante'ria** *sf* infantry.
fan'toccio [fan'tɔttʃo] *sm* puppet.
fara'butto *sm* crook.
far'dello *sm* bundle; (*fig*) burden.
'fare ◆ *sm* 1 (*modo di fare*): con ~ di-stratto absent-mindedly; ha un ~ simpatico he has a pleasant manner
2: **sul far del giorno/della notte** at daybreak/nightfall
◆ *vt* 1 (*fabbricare, creare*) to make; (: *casa*) to build; (: *assegno*) to make out; ~ **un pasto/una promessa/un film** to make a meal/a promise/a film; ~ **rumore** to make a noise
2 (*effettuare: lavoro, attività, studi*) to do; (: *sport*) to play; **cosa fa?** (*adesso*) what are you doing?; (: *di professione*) what do you do?; ~ **psicologia/italiano** (*INS*) to do psychology/Italian; ~ **un viaggio** to go on a trip *o* journey; ~ **una passeggiata** to go for a walk; ~ **la spesa** to do the shopping
3 (*funzione*) to be; (*TEATRO*) to play, be; ~ **il medico** to be a doctor; ~ **il malato** (*fingere*) to act the invalid
4 (*suscitare: sentimenti*): ~ **paura a qn** to frighten sb; **mi fa rabbia** it makes me angry; (**non**) **fa niente** (*non importa*) it doesn't matter
5 (*ammontare*): **3 più 3 fa 6** 3 and 3 are *o* make 6; **fanno 6.000 lire** that's 6,000 lire; **Roma fa 2.000.000 di abitanti** Rome has 2,000,000 inhabitants; **che ora fai?** what time do you make it?
6 (+ *infinito*): **far ~ qc a qn** (*obbligare*) to make sb do sth; (*permettere*) to let sb do sth; **fammi vedere** let me see; **far partire il motore** to start (up) the engine; **far riparare la macchina/costruire una casa** to get *o* have the car repaired/a house built
7: ~**rsi**: ~**rsi una gonna** to make o.s. a skirt; ~**rsi un nome** to make a name for o.s.; ~**rsi la permanente** to get a perm; ~**rsi tagliare i capelli** to get one's hair cut; ~**rsi operare** to have an operation; **si è fatto lavare la macchina** he got somebody to wash the car
8 (*fraseologia*): **farcela** to succeed, manage; **non ce la faccio più** I can't go on; **ce la faremo** we'll make it; **me l'hanno fatta!** (*imbrogliare*) I've been done!; **lo facevo più giovane** I thought he was younger; **fare sì/no con la testa** to nod/shake one's head
◆ *vi* 1 (*agire*) to act, do; **fate come volete** do as you like; ~ **presto** to be quick; ~ **da** to act as; **non c'è niente da** ~ it's no use; **saperci** ~ **con qn/qc** to know how to deal with sb/sth; **faccia pure!** go ahead!
2 (*dire*) to say; "**davvero?**" **fece** "really?" he said
3: ~ **per** (*essere adatto*) to be suitable for; ~ **per** ~ **qc** to be about to do sth;

fece per andarsene he made as if to leave
4: ~**rsi: si fa così** you do it like this, this is the way it's done; **non si fa così!** (*rimprovero*) that's no way to behave!; **la festa non si fa** the party is off
5: ~ **a gara con qn** to compete *o* vie with sb; ~ **a pugni** to come to blows; ~ **in tempo a** ~ to be in time to do
◆ *vb impers*: **fa bel tempo** the weather is fine; **fa caldo/freddo** it's hot/cold; **fa notte** it's getting dark
◆ *vr*: ~**rsi** 1 (*diventare*) to become; ~**rsi prete** to become a priest; ~**rsi grande/vecchio** to grow tall/old
2 (*spostarsi*): ~**rsi avanti/indietro** to move forward/back
3 (*fam: drogarsi*) to be a junkie.
far'falla *sf* butterfly.
fa'rina *sf* flour.
farma'cia, 'cie [farma'tʃia] *sf* pharmacy; (*negozio*) chemist's (shop) (*Brit*), pharmacy; **farma'cista, i, e** *sm/f* chemist (*Brit*), pharmacist.
'farmaco, ci *o* **chi** *sm* drug, medicine.
'faro *sm* (*NAUT*) lighthouse; (*AER*) beacon; (*AUT*) headlight.
'farsa *sf* farce.
'fascia, sce ['faʃʃa] *sf* band, strip; (*MED*) bandage; (*di sindaco, ufficiale*) sash; (*parte di territorio*) strip, belt; (*di contribuenti etc*) group, band; **essere in** ~**sce** (*anche fig*) to be in one's infancy; ~ **oraria** time band.
fasci'are [faʃ'ʃare] *vt* to bind; (*MED*) to bandage; (*bambino*) to put a nappy (*Brit*) *o* diaper (*US*) on.
fa'scicolo [faʃ'ʃikolo] *sm* (*di documenti*) file, dossier; (*di rivista*) issue, number; (*opuscolo*) booklet, pamphlet.
'fascino ['faʃʃino] *sm* charm, fascination.
'fascio ['faʃʃo] *sm* bundle, sheaf; (*di fiori*) bunch; (*di luce*) beam; (*POL*): **il F~** the Fascist Party.
fa'scismo [faʃ'ʃizmo] *sm* fascism.
'fase *sf* phase; (*TECN*) stroke; **fuori** ~ (*motore*) rough.
fas'tidio *sm* bother, trouble; **dare** ~ **a qn** to bother *o* annoy sb; **sento** ~ **allo stomaco** my stomach's upset; **avere** ~**i con la polizia** to have trouble *o* bother with the police; **fastidi'oso, a** *ag* annoying, tiresome; (*schifiltoso*) fastidious.
'fasto *sm* pomp, splendour.
'fata *sf* fairy.
fa'tale *ag* fatal; (*inevitabile*) inevitable; (*fig*) irresistible; **fatalità** *sf inv* inevitability; (*avversità*) misfortune; (*fato*) fate, destiny.
fa'tica, che *sf* hard work, toil; (*sforzo*) effort; (*di metalli*) fatigue; **a** ~ with difficulty; **fare** ~ **a fare qc** to have a job doing sth; **fati'care** *vi* to toil; **faticare a fare qc** to have difficulty doing sth; **fati'coso, a** *ag* tiring, exhausting;

(*lavoro*) laborious.

'**fato** *sm* fate, destiny.

'**fatto, a** *pp di* **fare** // *ag*: **un uomo ~ a grown man; ~ a mano/in casa** hand-/home-made // *sm* fact; (*azione*) deed; (*avvenimento*) event, occurrence; (*di romanzo, film*) action, story; **cogliere qn sul ~** to catch sb red-handed; **il ~ sta o è che the fact remains o is that; in ~ di** as for, as far as ... is concerned.

fat'tore *sm* (*AGR*) farm manager; (*MAT, elemento costitutivo*) factor.

fatto'ria *sf* farm; farmhouse.

fatto'rino *sm* errand-boy; (*di ufficio*) office-boy; (*d'albergo*) porter.

fat'tura *sf* (*COMM*) invoice; (*di abito*) tailoring; (*malia*) spell.

fattu'rare *vt* (*COMM*) to invoice; (*prodotto*) to produce; (*vino*) to adulterate.

'**fatuo, a** *ag* vain, fatuous.

'**fauna** *sf* fauna.

fau'tore, trice *sm/f* advocate, supporter.

fa'vella *sf* speech.

fa'villa *sf* spark.

'**favola** *sf* (*fiaba*) fairy tale; (*d'intento morale*) fable; (*fandonia*) yarn; **favo'loso, a** *ag* fabulous; (*incredibile*) incredible.

fa'vore *sm* favour; **per ~** please; **fare un ~ a qn** to do sb a favour; **favo'revole** *ag* favourable.

favo'rire *vt* to favour; (*il commercio, l'industria, le arti*) to promote, encourage; **vuole ~?** won't you help yourself?; **favorisca in salotto** please come into the sitting room; **favo'rito, a** *ag*, *sm/f* favourite.

fazzo'letto [fatso'letto] *sm* handkerchief; (*per la testa*) (head)scarf.

feb'braio *sm* February.

'**febbre** *sf* fever; **aver la ~** to have a high temperature; **~ da fieno** hay fever; **feb'brile** *ag* (*anche fig*) feverish.

'**feccia, ce** ['fettʃa] *sf* dregs *pl*.

'**fecola** *sf* potato flour.

fecondazi'one [fekondat'tsjone] *sf* fertilization; **~ artificiale** artificial insemination.

fe'condo, a *ag* fertile.

'**fede** *sf* (*credenza*) belief, faith; (*REL*) faith; (*fiducia*) faith, trust; (*fedeltà*) loyalty; (*anello*) wedding ring; (*attestato*) certificate; **aver ~ in qn** to have faith in sb; **in buona/cattiva ~** in good/bad faith; "**in ~**" (*DIR*) "in witness whereof"; **fe'dele** *ag*: **fedele (a)** faithful (to) // *sm/f* follower; **i fedeli** (*REL*) the faithful; **fedeltà** *sf* faithfulness; (*coniugale*) fidelity; **alta fedeltà** (*RADIO*) high fidelity.

'**federa** *sf* pillowslip, pillowcase.

fede'rale *ag* federal.

'**fegato** *sm* liver; (*fig*) guts *pl*, nerve.

'**felce** ['feltʃe] *sf* fern.

fe'lice [fe'litʃe] *ag* happy; (*fortunato*) lucky; **felicità** *sf* happiness.

felici'tarsi [felitʃi'tarsi] *vr* (*congratularsi*): **~ con qn per qc** to congratulate sb on sth.

fe'lino, a *ag*, *sm* feline.

'**feltro** *sm* felt.

'**femmina** *sf* (*ZOOL, TECN*) female; (*figlia*) girl, daughter; (*spesso peg*) woman; **femmi'nile** *ag* feminine; (*sesso*) female; (*lavoro, giornale, moda*) woman's // *sm* (*LING*) feminine; **femmi'nismo** *sm* feminism.

'**fendere** *vt* to cut through; **fendi'nebbia** *sm inv* (*AUT*) fog lamp.

fe'nomeno *sm* phenomenon.

'**feretro** *sm* coffin.

feri'ale *ag* working *cpd*, work *cpd*, week *cpd*; **giorno ~** weekday.

'**ferie** *sfpl* holidays (*Brit*), vacation *sg* (*US*); **andare in ~** to go on holiday *o* vacation.

fe'rire *vt* to injure; (*deliberatamente*: *MIL etc*) to wound; (*colpire*) to hurt; **fe'rito, a** *sm/f* wounded *o* injured man/woman // *sf* injury; wound.

'**ferma** *sf* (*MIL*) (period of) service; (*CACCIA*): **cane da ~** pointer.

fer'maglio [fer'maʎʎo] *sm* clasp; (*gioiello*) brooch; (*per documenti*) clip.

fer'mare *vt* to stop, halt; (*POLIZIA*) to detain, hold; (*bottone etc*) to fasten, fix // *vi* to stop; **~rsi** *vr* to stop, halt; **~rsi a fare qc** to stop to do sth.

fer'mata *sf* stop; **~ dell'autobus** bus stop.

fer'mento *sm* (*anche fig*) ferment; (*lievito*) yeast.

fer'mezza [fer'mettsa] *sf* (*fig*) firmness, steadfastness.

'**fermo, a** *ag* still, motionless; (*veicolo*) stationary; (*orologio*) not working; (*saldo: anche fig*) firm; (*voce, mano*) steady // *escl* stop!; keep still! // *sm* (*chiusura*) catch, lock; (*DIR*): **~ di polizia** police detention.

'**fermo 'posta** *av*, *sm inv* poste restante (*Brit*), general delivery (*US*).

fe'roce [fe'rotʃe] *ag* (*animale*) wild, fierce, ferocious; (*persona*) cruel, fierce; (*fame, dolore*) raging.

ferra'gosto *sm* (*festa*) feast of the Assumption; (*periodo*) August holidays *pl*.

ferra'menta *sfpl* ironmongery *sg* (*Brit*), hardware *sg*; **negozio di ~** ironmonger's (*Brit*), hardware shop *o* store (*US*).

fer'rato, a *ag* (*FERR*): **strada ~a** railway (*Brit*) *o* railroad (*US*) line; (*fig*): **essere ~ in** to be well up in.

'**ferreo, a** *ag* iron *cpd*.

'**ferro** *sm* iron; **una bistecca ai ~i** a grilled steak; **~ battuto** wrought iron; **~ da calza** knitting needle; **~ di cavallo** horseshoe; **~ da stiro** iron.

ferro'via sf railway (Brit), railroad (US); **ferrovi'ario, a** ag railway cpd (Brit), railroad cpd (US); **ferrovi'ere** sm railwayman (Brit), railroad man (US).

'fertile ag fertile; **fertiliz'zante** sm fertilizer.

'fervido, a ag fervent.

fer'vore sm fervour, ardour; (punto culminante) height.

'fesso, a pp di **fendere** // ag (fam: sciocco) crazy, cracked.

fes'sura sf crack, split; (per gettone, moneta) slot.

'festa sf (religiosa) feast; (pubblica) holiday; (compleanno) birthday; (onomastico) name day; (ricevimento) celebration, party; **far ~** to have a holiday; to live it up; **far ~ a qn** to give sb a warm welcome.

festeggi'are [fested'dʒare] vt to celebrate; (persona) to have a celebration for.

fes'tino sm party; (con balli) ball.

fes'tivo, a ag (atmosfera) festive; **giorno ~** holiday.

fes'toso, a ag merry, joyful.

fe'ticcio [fe'tittʃo] sm fetish.

'feto sm foetus (Brit), fetus (US).

'fetta sf slice.

fettuc'cine [fettut'tʃine] sfpl (CUC) ribbon-shaped pasta.

FF.SS. abbr = Ferrovie dello Stato.

fi'aba sf fairy tale.

fi'acca sf weariness; (svogliatezza) listlessness.

fiac'care vt to weaken.

fi'acco, a, chi, che ag (stanco) tired, weary; (svogliato) listless; (debole) weak; (mercato) slack.

fi'accola sf torch.

fi'ala sf phial.

fi'amma sf flame.

fiam'mante ag (colore) flaming; **nuovo ~** brand new.

fiammeggi'are [fjammed'dʒare] vi to blaze.

fiam'mifero sm match.

fiam'mingo, a, ghi, ghe ag Flemish // sm/f Fleming // sm (LING) Flemish; (ZOOL) flamingo; **i F~ghi** the Flemish.

fiancheggi'are [fjanked'dʒare] vt to border; (fig) to support, back (up); (MIL) to flank.

fi'anco, chi sm side; (MIL) flank; **di ~** sideways, from the side; **a ~ a ~** side by side.

fi'asco, schi sm flask; (fig) fiasco; **fare ~** to be a fiasco.

fi'ato sm breath; (resistenza) stamina; **avere il ~ grosso** to be out of breath; **prendere ~** to catch one's breath; **~i** smpl (MUS) wind instruments; **strumento a ~** wind instrument.

'fibbia sf buckle.

'fibra sf fibre; (fig) constitution.

fic'care vt to push, thrust, drive; **~rsi** vr (andare a finire) to get to.

'fico, chi sm (pianta) fig tree; (frutto) fig; **~ d'India** prickly pear; **~ secco** dried fig.

fidanza'mento [fidantsa'mento] sm engagement.

fidan'zarsi [fidan'tsarsi] vr to get engaged; **fidan'zato, a** sm/f fiancé/fiancée.

fi'darsi vr: **~ di** to trust; **fi'dato, a** ag reliable, trustworthy.

'fido, a ag faithful, loyal // sm (COMM) credit.

fi'ducia [fi'dutʃa] sf confidence, trust; **incarico di ~** position of trust, responsible position; **persona di ~** reliable person.

fi'ele sm (MED) bile; (fig) bitterness.

fie'nile sm barn; hayloft.

fi'eno sm hay.

fi'era sf fair.

fie'rezza [fje'rettsa] sf pride.

fi'ero, a ag proud; (crudele) fierce, cruel; (audace) bold.

'fifa sf (fam): **aver ~** to have the jitters.

'figlia ['fiʎʎa] sf daughter.

figli'astro, a [fiʎ'ʎastro] sm/f stepson/daughter.

'figlio ['fiʎʎo] sm son; (senza distinzione di sesso) child; **~ di papà** spoilt, wealthy young man; **~ unico** only child; **figli'occio, a, ci, ce** sm/f godchild, godson/daughter.

fi'gura sf figure; (forma, aspetto esterno) form, shape; (illustrazione) picture, illustration; **far ~** to look smart; **fare una brutta ~** to make a bad impression.

figu'rare vi to appear // vt: **~rsi qc** to imagine sth; **~rsi** vr: **figurati!** imagine that!; **ti do noia? — ma figurati!** am I disturbing you? — not at all!

figura'tivo, a ag figurative.

figu'rina sf figurine; (cartoncino) picture card.

'fila sf row, line; (coda) queue; (serie) series, string; **di ~** in succession; **fare la ~** to queue; **in ~ indiana** in single file.

filantro'pia sf philanthropy.

fi'lare vt to spin // vi (baco, ragno) to spin; (formaggio fuso) to go stringy; (discorso) to hang together; (fam: amoreggiare) to go steady; (muoversi a forte velocità) to go at full speed; (: andarsene lestamente) to make o.s. scarce; **~ diritto** (fig) to toe the line.

filas'trocca, che sf nursery rhyme.

filate'lia sf philately, stamp collecting.

fi'lato, a ag spun // sm yarn; **3 giorni ~i** 3 days running o on end; **fila'tura** sf spinning; (luogo) spinning mill.

fi'letto sm (di vite) thread; (di carne) fillet.

fili'ale ag filial // sf (di impresa) branch.

fili'grana *sf* (*in oreficeria*) filigree; (*su carta*) watermark.

film *sm inv* film; **fil'mare** *vt* to film.

'filo *sm* (*anche fig*) thread; (*filato*) yarn; (*metallico*) wire; (*di lama, rasoio*) edge; per ~ e per segno in detail; ~ d'erba blade of grass; ~ di perle string of pearls; ~ spinato barbed wire; con un ~ di voce in a whisper.

'filobus *sm inv* trolley bus.

filon'cino [filon'tʃino] *sm* ≈ French stick.

fi'lone *sm* (*di minerali*) seam, vein; (*pane*) ≈ Vienna loaf; (*fig*) trend.

filoso'fia *sf* philosophy; **fi'losofo, a** *sm/f* philosopher.

fil'trare *vt, vi* to filter.

'filtro *sm* filter; ~ dell'olio (*AUT*) oil filter.

'filza ['filtsa] *sf* (*anche fig*) string.

fin *av, prep* = **fino**.

fi'nale *ag* final // *sm* (*di opera*) end, ending; (: *MUS*) finale // *sf* (*SPORT*) final; **finalità** *sf* (*scopo*) aim, purpose; **final'mente** *av* finally, at last.

fi'nanza [fi'nantsa] *sf* finance; ~e *sfpl* (*di individuo, Stato*) finances; **finanzi'ario, a** *ag* financial; **finanzi'ere** *sm* financier; (*guardia di finanza: doganale*) customs officer; (: *tributaria*) inland revenue official.

finché [fin'ke] *cong* (*per tutto il tempo che*) as long as; (*fino al momento in cui*) until; aspetta ~ io (non) sia ritornato wait until I get back.

'fine *ag* (*lamina, carta*) thin; (*capelli, polvere*) fine; (*vista, udito*) keen, sharp; (*persona*): **raffinata** refined, distinguished; (*osservazione*) subtle // *sf* end // *sm* aim, purpose; (*esito*) result, outcome; **secondo** ~ ulterior motive; in o alla ~ in the end, finally; ~ settimana *sm* o *f inv* weekend.

fi'nestra *sf* window; **fines'trino** *sm* (*di treno, auto*) window.

'fingere ['findʒere] *vt* to feign; (*supporre*) to imagine, suppose; ~rsi *vr*: ~rsi ubriaco/pazzo to pretend to be drunk/mad; ~ di fare to pretend to do.

fini'mondo *sm* pandemonium.

fi'nire *vt* to finish // *vi* to finish, end; ~ di fare (*compiere*) to finish doing; (*smettere*) to stop doing; ~ in galera to end up o finish up in prison; **fini'tura** *sf* finish.

finlan'dese *ag, sm* (*LING*) Finnish // *sm/f* Finn.

Fin'landia *sf*: la ~ Finland.

'fino, a *ag* (*capelli, seta*) fine; (*oro*) pure; (*fig: acuto*) shrewd // *av* (*spesso troncato in* fin: *pure, anche*) even // *prep* (*spesso troncato in* fin: *tempo*): fin quando? till when?; (: *luogo*): fin qui as far as here; ~ a (*tempo*) until, till; (*luogo*) as far as, (up) to; fin da domani from tomorrow onwards; fin da ieri since

yesterday; fin dalla nascita from o since birth.

fi'nocchio [fi'nɔkkjo] *sm* fennel; (*fam peg: pederasta*) queer.

fi'nora *av* up till now.

'finto, a *pp di* **fingere** // *ag* false; artificial // *sf* pretence, sham; (*SPORT*) feint; **far** ~a (*di fare*) to pretend (to do).

finzi'one [fin'tsjone] *sf* pretence, sham.

fi'occo, chi *sm* (*di nastro*) bow; (*di stoffa, lana*) flock; (*di neve*) flake; (*NAUT*) jib; **coi** ~**chi** (*fig*) first-rate; ~**chi di granoturco** cornflakes.

fi'ocina ['fjɔtʃina] *sf* harpoon.

fi'oco, a, chi, che *ag* faint, dim.

fi'onda *sf* catapult.

fio'raio, a *sm/f* florist.

fi'ore *sm* flower; ~i *smpl* (*CARTE*) clubs; a fior d'acqua on the surface of the water; avere i nervi a fior di pelle to be on edge.

fioren'tino, a *ag* Florentine.

fio'retto *sm* (*SCHERMA*) foil.

fio'rire *vi* (*rosa*) to flower; (*albero*) to blossom; (*fig*) to flourish.

Fi'renze [fi'rɛntse] *sf* Florence.

'firma *sf* signature; (*reputazione*) name.

fir'mare *vt* to sign.

fisar'monica, che *sf* accordion.

fis'cale *ag* fiscal, tax *cpd*; **medico** ~ doctor employed by Social Security to verify cases of sick leave.

fischi'are [fis'kjare] *vi* to whistle // *vt* to whistle; (*attore*) to boo, hiss.

'fischio ['fiskjo] *sm* whistle.

'fisco *sm* tax authorities *pl*, ≈ Inland Revenue (*Brit*), ≈ Internal Revenue Service (*US*).

'fisico, a, ci, che *ag* physical // *sm/f* physicist // *sm* physique // *sf* physics *sg*.

fisiolo'gia [fizjolo'dʒia] *sf* physiology.

fisiono'mia *sf* face, physiognomy.

fisiotera'pia *sf* physiotherapy.

fis'sare *vt* to fix, fasten; (*guardare intensamente*) to stare at; (*data, condizioni*) to fix, establish, set; (*prenotare*) to book; ~**rsi su** (*sog: sguardo, attenzione*) to focus on; (*fig: idea*) to become obsessed with; **fissazi'one** *sf* (*PSIC*) fixation.

'fisso, a *ag* fixed; (*stipendio, impiego*) regular // *av*: **guardare** ~ qc/qn to stare at sth/sb.

'fitta *sf vedi* **fitto**.

fit'tizio, a *ag* fictitious, imaginary.

'fitto, a *ag* thick, dense; (*pioggia*) heavy // *sm* depths *pl*, middle; (*affitto, pigione*) rent // *sf* sharp pain.

fi'ume *sm* river.

fiu'tare *vt* to smell, sniff; (*sog: animale*) to scent; (*fig: inganno*) to get wind of, smell; ~ tabacco/cocaina to take snuff/ cocaine; **fi'uto** *sm* (sense of) smell; (*fig*) nose.

fla'gello [fla'dʒɛllo] *sm* scourge.

fla'grante *ag* flagrant; **cogliere qn in ~** to catch sb red-handed.

fla'nella *sf* flannel.

flash [flaʃ] *sm inv* (FOT) flash; (*giornalistico*) newsflash.

'flauto *sm* flute.

'flebile *ag* faint, feeble.

'flemma *sf* (*calma*) coolness, phlegm; (MED) phlegm.

fles'sibile *ag* pliable; (*fig: che si adatta*) flexible.

'flesso, a *pp di* **flettere**.

flessu'oso, a *ag* supple, lithe; (*andatura*) flowing, graceful.

'flettere *vt* to bend.

F.lli *abbr* (= *fratelli*) Bros.

'flora *sf* flora.

'florido, a *ag* flourishing; (*fig*) glowing with health.

'floscio, a, sci, sce ['flɔʃʃo] *ag* (*cappello*) floppy, soft; (*muscoli*) flabby.

'flotta *sf* fleet.

'fluido, a *ag, sm* fluid.

flu'ire *vi* to flow.

fluo'oro *sm* fluorine.

fluo'ruro *sm* fluoride.

'flusso *sm* flow; (FISICA, MED) flux; **~ e riflusso** ebb and flow.

fluttu'are *vi* to rise and fall; (ECON) to fluctuate.

fluvi'ale *ag* river *cpd*, fluvial.

'foca, che *sf* (ZOOL) seal.

fo'caccia, ce [fo'kattʃa] *sf* kind of pizza; (*dolce*) bun.

'foce ['fotʃe] *sf* (GEO) mouth.

foco'laio *sm* (MED) centre of infection; (*fig*) hotbed.

foco'lare *sm* hearth, fireside; (TECN) furnace.

'fodera *sf* (*di vestito*) lining; (*di libro, poltrona*) cover; **fode'rare** *vt* to line; to cover.

'fodero *sm* (*di spada*) scabbard; (*di pugnale*) sheath; (*di pistola*) holster.

'foga *sf* enthusiasm, ardour.

'foggia, ge ['fɔddʒa] *sf* (*maniera*) style; (*aspetto*) form, shape; (*moda*) fashion, style.

'foglia ['fɔʎʎa] *sf* leaf; **~ d'argento/d'oro** silver/gold leaf; **fogli'ame** *sm* foliage, leaves *pl*.

'foglio ['fɔʎʎo] *sm* (*di carta*) sheet (of paper); (*di metallo*) sheet; (*documento*) document; (*banconota*) (bank)note; **~ rosa** (AUT) provisional licence; **~ di via** (DIR) expulsion order; **~ volante** pamphlet.

'fogna ['foɲɲa] *sf* drain, sewer; **fo-gna'tura** *sf* drainage, sewerage.

folgo'rare *vt* (*sog: fulmine*) to strike down; (: *alta tensione*) to electrocute.

'folla *sf* crowd, throng.

'folle *ag* mad, insane; (TECN) idle; **in ~** (AUT) in neutral.

fol'lia *sf* folly, foolishness; foolish act;

(*pazzia*) madness, lunacy.

'folto, a *ag* thick.

fomen'tare *vt* to stir up, foment.

fondamen'tale *ag* fundamental, basic.

fonda'mento *sm* foundation; **~a** *sfpl* (EDIL) foundations.

fon'dare *vt* to found; (*fig: dar base*): **~ qc su** to base sth on; **fondazi'one** *sf* foundation.

'fondere *vt* (*neve*) to melt; (*metallo*) to fuse, melt; (*colori*) to merge, blend; (: *imprese, gruppi*) to merge // *vi* to melt; **~rsi** *vr* to melt; (*fig: partiti, correnti*) to unite, merge; **fonde'ria** *sf* foundry.

'fondo, a *ag* deep // *sm* (*di recipiente, pozzo*) bottom; (*di stanza*) back; (*quantità di liquido che resta, deposito*) dregs *pl*; (*sfondo*) background; (*unità immobiliare*) property, estate; (*somma di denaro*) fund; (SPORT) long-distance race; **~i** *smpl* (*denaro*) funds; **a notte ~a** at dead of night; **in ~ a** at the bottom of; at the back of; (*strada*) at the end of; **andare a ~** (*nave*) to sink; **conoscere a ~** to know inside out; **dar ~ a** (*fig: provviste, soldi*) to use up; **in ~** (*fig*) after all, all things considered; **andare fino in ~ a** (*fig*) to examine thoroughly; **a ~ perduto** (COMM) without security; **~i di caffè** coffee grounds; **~i di magazzino** old o unsold stock *sg*.

fo'netica *sf* phonetics *sg*.

fon'tana *sf* fountain.

'fonte *sf* spring, source; (*fig*) source // *sm*: **~ battesimale** (REL) font.

fo'raggio [fo'raddʒo] *sm* fodder, forage.

fo'rare *vt* to pierce, make a hole in; (*pallone*) to burst; (*biglietto*) to punch; **~ una gomma** to burst a tyre (Brit) o tire (US).

'forbici ['fɔrbitʃi] *sfpl* scissors.

'forca, che *sf* (AGR) fork, pitchfork; (*patibolo*) gallows *sg*.

for'cella [for'tʃella] *sf* (TECN) fork; (*di monte*) pass.

for'chetta [for'ketta] *sf* fork.

for'cina [for'tʃina] *sf* hairpin.

'forcipe ['fɔrtʃipe] *sm* forceps *pl*.

fo'resta *sf* forest.

foresti'ero, a *ag* foreign // *sm/f* foreigner.

'forfora *sf* dandruff.

'forgia, ge ['fɔrdʒa] *sf* forge; **forgi'are** *vt* to forge.

'forma *sf* form; (*aspetto esteriore*) form, shape; (DIR: *procedura*) procedure; (*per calzature*) last; (*stampo da cucina*) mould; **~e** *sfpl* (*del corpo*) figure, shape; **le ~e** (*convenzioni*) appearances; **essere in ~** to be in good shape.

formag'gino [format'dʒino] *sm* processed cheese.

for'maggio [for'maddʒo] *sm* cheese.

for'male *ag* formal; **formalità** *sf inv*

formality.

for'mare vt to form, shape, make; (numero di telefono) to dial; (fig: carattere) to form, mould; ~rsi vr to form, take shape; **for'mato** sm format, size; **formazi'one** sf formation; (fig: educazione) training.

for'mica, che sf ant; **formi'caio** sm anthill.

formico'lare vi (gamba, braccio) to tingle; (brulicare: anche fig): ~ di to be swarming with; **mi formicola la gamba** I've got pins and needles in my leg, my leg's tingling; **formico'lio** sm pins and needles pl; swarming.

formi'dabile ag powerful, formidable; (straordinario) remarkable.

'formula sf formula; ~ di cortesia courtesy form.

formu'lare vt to formulate; to express.

for'nace [for'natʃe] sf (per laterizi etc) kiln; (per metalli) furnace.

for'naio sm baker.

for'nello sm (elettrico, a gas) ring; (di pipa) bowl.

for'nire vt: ~ qn di qc, ~ qc a qn to provide o supply sb with sth, to supply sth to sb.

'forno sm (di cucina) oven; (panetteria) bakery; (TECN: per calce etc) kiln; (: per metalli) furnace.

'foro sm (buco) hole; (STORIA) forum; (tribunale) (law) court.

'forse av perhaps, maybe; (circa) about; **essere in ~** to be in doubt.

forsen'nato, a ag mad, insane.

'forte ag strong; (suono) loud; (spesa) considerable, great; (passione, dolore) great, deep // av strongly; (velocemente) fast; (a voce alta) loud(ly); (violentemente) hard // sm (edificio) fort; (specialità) forte, strong point; **essere ~ in qc** to be good at sth.

for'tezza [for'tettsa] sf (morale) strength; (luogo fortificato) fortress.

for'tuito, a ag fortuitous, chance.

for'tuna sf (destino) fortune, luck; (buona sorte) success, fortune; (eredità, averi) fortune; **per ~** luckily, fortunately; **di ~** makeshift, improvised; **atterraggio di ~** emergency landing; **fortu'nato, a** ag lucky, fortunate; (coronato da successo) successful.

forvi'are vt, vi = **fuorviare**.

'forza ['fɔrtsa] sf strength; (potere) power; (FISICA) force; ~**e** sfpl (fisiche) strength ag; (MIL) forces // escl come on!; **per ~** against one's will; (naturalmente) of course; **a viva ~** by force; **a ~ di** by dint of; ~ **maggiore** circumstances beyond one's control; **la ~ pubblica** the police pl; **le ~e armate** the armed forces.

for'zare [for'tsare] vt to force; ~ **qn a fare** to force sb to do; **for'zato, a** ag

forced // sm (DIR) prisoner sentenced to hard labour.

fos'chia [fos'kia] sf mist, haze.

'fosco, a, schi, sche ag dark, gloomy.

'fosforo sm phosphorous.

'fossa sf pit; (di cimitero) grave; ~ **biologica** septic tank.

fos'sato sm ditch; (di fortezza) moat.

fos'setta sf dimple.

'fossile ag, sm fossil.

'fosso sm ditch; (MIL) trench.

'foto sf photo // prefisso: **foto'copia** sf photocopy; **fotocopi'are** vt to photocopy; **fotogra'fare** vt to photograph; **fotogra'fia** sf (procedimento) photography; (immagine) photograph; **fare una fotografia** to take a photograph; **una fotografia a colori/in bianco e nero** a colour/black and white photograph; **fo'tografo, a** sm/f photographer; **fotoro'manzo** sm romantic picture story.

fra prep = **tra**.

fracas'sare vt to shatter, smash; ~**rsi** vr to shatter, smash; (veicolo) to crash; **fra'casso** sm smash; crash; (baccano) din, racket.

'fradicio, a, ci, ce ['fraditʃo] ag (molto bagnato) soaking (wet); **ubriaco ~** blind drunk.

'fragile ['fradʒile] ag fragile; (fig: salute) delicate.

'fragola sf strawberry.

fra'gore sm roar; (di tuono) rumble.

frago'roso, a ag deafening.

fra'grante ag fragrant.

frain'tendere vt to misunderstand; **frain'teso, a** pp di **fraintendere**.

fram'mento sm fragment.

'frana sf landslide; (fig: persona): **essere una ~** to be useless; **fra'nare** vi to slip, slide down.

fran'cese [fran'tʃeze] ag French // sm/f Frenchman/woman // sm (LING) French; **i F~i** the French.

fran'chezza [fran'kettsa] sf frankness, openness.

'Francia ['frantʃa] sf: **la ~** France.

'franco, a, chi, che ag (COMM) free; (sincero) frank, open, sincere // sm (moneta) franc; **farla ~a** (fig) to get off scot-free; ~ **di dogana** duty-free; ~ **a domicilio** delivered free of charge; **prezzo ~ fabbrica** ex-works price; ~ **tiratore** sm sniper.

franco'bollo sm (postage) stamp.

fran'gente [fran'dʒɛnte] sm (onda) breaker; (scoglio emergente) reef; (circostanza) situation, circumstance.

'frangia, ge ['frandʒa] sf fringe.

frantu'mare vt, ~**rsi** vr to break into pieces, shatter.

frap'pé sm milk shake.

'frasca, sche sf (leafy) branch.

'frase sf (LING) sentence; (locuzione,

espressione, *MUS*) phrase; ~ **fatta** set phrase.

'frassino *sm* ash (tree).

frastagli'ato, a [frasta'ʎ'ʎato] *ag* (*costa*) indented, jagged.

frastor'nare *vt* to daze; to befuddle.

frastu'ono *sm* hubbub, din.

'frate *sm* friar, monk.

fratel'lanza [fratel'lantsa] *sf* brotherhood; (*associazione*) fraternity.

fratel'lastro *sm* stepbrother.

fra'tello *sm* brother; ~i *smpl* brothers; (*nel senso di fratelli e sorelle*) brothers and sisters.

fra'terno, a *ag* fraternal, brotherly.

frat'tanto *av* in the meantime, meanwhile.

frat'tempo *sm*: **nel** ~ in the meantime, meanwhile.

frat'tura *sf* fracture; (*fig*) split, break.

frazi'one [frat'tsjone] *sf* fraction; (*borgata*): ~ **di comune** hamlet.

'freccia, ce ['frettʃa] *sf* arrow; ~ **di direzione** (*AUT*) indicator.

fred'dare *vt* to shoot dead.

fred'dezza [fred'dettsa] *sf* coldness.

'freddo, a *ag, sm* cold; **fa** ~ it's cold; **aver** ~ to be cold; **a** ~ (*fig*) deliberately; **freddo'loso, a** *ag* sensitive to the cold.

fred'dura *sf* pun.

fre'gare *vt* to rub; (*fam: truffare*) to take in, cheat; (*: rubare*) to swipe, pinch; **fregarsene** (*fam!*): **chi se ne frega?** who gives a damn (about it)?

fre'gata *sf* rub; (*fam*) swindle; (*NAUT*) frigate.

'fregio ['fredʒo] *sm* (*ARCHIT*) frieze; (*ornamento*) decoration.

'fremere *vi*: ~ **di** to tremble *o* quiver with; **'fremito** *sm* tremor, quiver.

fre'nare *vt* (*veicolo*) to slow down; (*cavallo*) to rein in; (*lacrime*) to restrain, hold back // *vi* to brake; ~**rsi** *vr* (*fig*) to restrain o.s., control o.s.; **fre'nata** *sf*: **fare una frenata** to brake.

frene'sia *sf* frenzy.

'freno *sm* brake; (*morso*) bit; ~ **a disco** disc brake; ~ **a mano** handbrake; **tenere a** ~ to restrain.

frequen'tare *vt* (*scuola, corso*) to attend; (*locale, bar*) to go to, frequent; (*persone*) to see (often).

fre'quente *ag* frequent; **di** ~ frequently; **fre'quenza** *sf* frequency; (*INS*) attendance.

fres'chezza [fres'kettsa] *sf* freshness.

'fresco, a, schi, sche *ag* fresh; (*temperatura*) cool; (*notizia*) recent, fresh // *sm*: **godere il** ~ to enjoy the cool air; **stare** ~ (*fig*) to be in for it; **mettere al** ~ to put in a cool place.

'fretta *sf* hurry, haste; **in** ~ in a hurry; **in** ~ **e furia** in a mad rush; **aver** ~ to be in a hurry; **fretto'loso, a** *ag* (*persona*) in a hurry; (*lavoro etc*) hurried, rushed.

fri'abile *ag* (*terreno*) friable; (*pasta*) crumbly.

'friggere ['friddʒere] *vt* to fry // *vi* (*olio etc*) to sizzle.

'frigido, a ['fridʒido] *ag* (*MED*) frigid.

'frigo *sm* fridge.

frigo'rifero, a *ag* refrigerating // *sm* refrigerator.

fringu'ello *sm* chaffinch.

frit'tata *sf* omelette; **fare una** ~ (*fig*) to make a mess of things.

frit'tella *sf* (*CUC*) pancake; (*: ripiena*) fritter.

'fritto, a *pp di* **friggere** // *ag* fried // *sm* fried food; ~ **misto** mixed fry.

frit'tura *sf* (*CUC*): ~ **di pesce** mixed fried fish.

'frivolo, a *ag* frivolous.

frizi'one [frit'tsjone] *sf* friction; (*di pelle*) rub, rub-down; (*AUT*) clutch.

friz'zante [frid'dzante] *ag* (*anche fig*) sparkling.

'frizzo ['friddzo] *sm* witticism.

fro'dare *vt* to defraud, cheat.

'frode *sf* fraud; ~ **fiscale** tax evasion.

'frollo, a *ag* (*carne*) tender; (*: di selvaggina*) high; (*fig: persona*) soft; **pasta** ~**a** short(crust) pastry.

'fronda *sf* (*leafy*) branch; (*di partito politico*) internal opposition; ~**e** *sfpl* foliage *sg*.

fron'tale *ag* frontal; (*scontro*) head-on.

'fronte *sf* (*ANAT*) forehead; (*di edificio*) front, façade // *sm* (*MIL, POL, METEOR*) front; **a** ~, **di** ~ facing, opposite; **di** ~ **a** (*posizione*) opposite, facing, in front of; (*a paragone di*) compared with.

fronteggi'are [fronted'dʒare] *vt* (*avversari, difficoltà*) to face, stand up to; (*spese*) to cope with.

fronti'era *sf* border, frontier.

'fronzolo [frondzolo] *sm* frill.

'frottola *sf* fib; ~**e** *sfpl* nonsense *sg*.

fru'gare *vi* to rummage // *vt* to search.

frul'lare *vt* (*CUC*) to whisk // *vi* (*uccelli*) to flutter; **frul'lato** *sm* milk shake; fruit drink; **frulla'tore** *sm* electric mixer; **frul'lino** *sm* whisk.

fru'mento *sm* wheat.

fru'scio [fruʃ'ʃio] *sm* rustle; rustling; (*di acque*) murmur.

'frusta *sf* whip; (*CUC*) whisk.

frus'tare *vt* to whip.

frus'tino *sm* riding crop.

frus'trare *vt* to frustrate.

'frutta *sf* fruit; (*portata*) dessert; ~ **candita/secca** candied/dried fruit.

frut'tare *vi* to bear dividends, give a return.

frut'teto *sm* orchard.

frutti'vendolo, a *sm/f* greengrocer (*Brit*), produce dealer (*US*).

'frutto *sm* fruit; (*fig: risultato*) result(s); (*ECON: interesse*) interest; (*: reddito*) income; ~**i di mare** seafood *sg*.

FS *abbr* = Ferrovie dello Stato.

fu *vb vedi* **essere** // *ag inv*: il ~ Paolo Bianchi the late Paolo Bianchi.

fuci'lare [futʃi'lare] *vt* to shoot; **fuci'lata** *sf* rifle shot.

fu'cile [fu'tʃile] *sm* rifle, gun; *(da caccia)* shotgun, gun.

fu'cina [fu'tʃina] *sf* forge.

'fuga *sf* escape, flight; *(di gas, liquidi)* leak; *(MUS)* fugue; ~ **di cervelli** brain drain.

fu'gace [fu'gatʃe] *ag* fleeting, transient.

fug'gevole [fud'dʒevole] *ag* fleeting.

fuggi'asco, a, schi, sche [fud'dʒasko] *ag, sm/f* fugitive.

fuggi'fuggi [fuddʒi'fuddʒi] *sm* scramble, stampede.

fug'gire [fud'dʒire] *vi* to flee, run away; *(fig: passar veloce)* to fly // *vt* to avoid; **fuggi'tivo, a** *sm/f* fugitive, runaway.

ful'gore *sm* brilliance, splendour.

fu'liggine [fu'liddʒine] *sf* soot.

fulmi'nare *vt (sog: fulmine)* to strike; *(: elettricità)* to electrocute; *(con arma da fuoco)* to shoot dead; *(fig: con lo sguardo)* to look daggers at.

'fulmine *sm* thunderbolt; lightning *q.*

fumai'olo *sm (di nave)* funnel; *(di fabbrica)* chimney.

fu'mare *vi* to smoke; *(emettere vapore)* to steam // *vt* to smoke; **fu'mata** *sf (segnale)* smoke signal; **farsi una fumata** to have a smoke; **fuma'tore, 'trice** *sm/f* smoker.

fu'metto *sm* comic strip; ~**i** *smpl* comics.

'fumo *sm* smoke; *(vapore)* steam; *(il fumare tabacco)* smoking; ~**i** *smpl* fumes; **i** ~**i dell'alcool** the after-effects of drink; **vendere** ~ to deceive, cheat; **fu'moso, a** *ag* smoky; *(fig)* muddled.

fu'nambolo, a *sm/f* tightrope walker.

'fune *sf* rope, cord; *(più grossa)* cable.

'funebre *ag (rito)* funeral; *(aspetto)* gloomy, funereal.

fune'rale *sm* funeral.

'fungere ['fundʒere] *vi*: ~ **da** to act as.

'fungo, ghi *sm* fungus; *(commestibile)* mushroom; ~ **velenoso** toadstool.

funico'lare *sf* funicular railway.

funi'via *sf* cable railway.

funzio'nare [funtsjo'nare] *vi* to work, function; *(fungere)*: ~ **da** to act as.

funzio'nario [funtsjo'narjo] *sm* official.

funzi'one [fun'tsjone] *sf* function; *(carica)* post, position; *(REL)* service; **in** ~ *(meccanismo)* in operation; **in** ~ **di** *(come)* as; **fare la** ~ **di qn** *(farne le veci)* to take sb's place.

fu'oco, chi *sm* fire; *(fornello)* ring; *(FOT, FISICA)* focus; **dare** ~ **a qc** to set fire to sth; **far** ~ *(sparare)* to fire; ~ **d'artificio** firework.

fuorché [fwor'ke] *cong, prep* except.

fu'ori *av* outside; *(all'aperto)* outdoors, outside; *(fuori di casa, SPORT)* out; *(esclamativo)* get out! // *prep*: ~ **(di)** out of, outside // *sm* outside; **lasciar** ~ **qc/qn** to leave sth/sb out; **far** ~ **qn** *(fam)* to kill sb, do sb in; **essere** ~ **di sé** to be beside o.s.; ~ **luogo** *(inopportuno)* out of place, uncalled for; ~ **mano** out of the way, remote; ~ **pericolo** out of danger; ~ **uso** old-fashioned; obsolete.

fu'ori... *prefisso*: **fuori'bordo** *sm inv* speedboat (with outboard motor); outboard motor; **fuori'classe** *sm/f inv* (undisputed) champion; **fuorigi'oco** *sm* offside; **fuori'legge** *sm/f inv* outlaw; **fuori'serie** *ag inv (auto etc)* custom-built // *sf* custom-built car; **fuori'strada** *sm (AUT)* cross-country vehicle; **fuoru'scito, a, fuoriu'scito, a** *sm/f* exile; **fuorvi'are** *vt* to mislead; *(fig)* to lead astray // *vi* to go astray.

'furbo, a *ag* clever, smart; *(peg)* cunning.

fu'rente *ag*: ~ **(contro)** furious (with).

fur'fante *sm* rascal, scoundrel.

fur'gone *sm* van.

'furia *sf (ira)* fury, rage; *(fig: impeto)* fury, violence; *(fretta)* rush; **a** ~ **di** by dint of; **andare su tutte le** ~**e** to get into a towering rage; **furi'bondo, a** *ag* furious.

furi'oso, a *ag* furious; *(mare, vento)* raging.

fu'rore *sm* fury; *(esaltazione)* frenzy; **far** ~ to be all the rage.

fur'tivo, a *ag* furtive.

'furto *sm* theft; ~ **con scasso** burglary.

'fusa *sfpl*: **fare le** ~ to purr.

fu'sibile *sm (ELETTR)* fuse.

fusi'one *sf (di metalli)* fusion, melting; *(colata)* casting; *(COMM)* merger; *(fig)* merging.

'fuso, a *pp di* **fondere** // *sm (FILATURA)* spindle; ~ **orario** time zone.

fus'tagno [fus'taɲɲo] *sm* corduroy.

fus'tino *sm (di detersivo)*-tub.

'fusto *sm* stem; *(ANAT, di albero)* trunk; *(recipiente)* drum, can.

fu'turo, a *ag, sm* future.

G

gab'bare *vt* to take in, dupe; ~**rsi** *vr*: ~**rsi di qn** to make fun of sb.

'gabbia *sf* cage; *(DIR)* dock; *(da imballaggio)* crate; ~ **dell'ascensore** lift *(Brit)* o elevator *(US)* shaft; ~ **toracica** *(ANAT)* rib cage.

gabbi'ano *sm* (sea)gull.

gabi'netto *sm (MED etc)* consulting room; *(POL)* ministry; *(di decenza)* toilet, lavatory; *(INS: di fisica etc)* laboratory.

'gaffe [gaf] *sf inv* blunder.

gagli'ardo, a [gaʎ'ʎardo] *ag* strong,

vigorous.

'gaio, a *ag* cheerful, gay.

'gala *sf (sfarzo)* pomp; *(festa)* gala.

ga'lante *ag* gallant, courteous; *(avventura)* amorous; **galante'ria** *sf* gallantry.

galantu'omo, *pl* **galantu'omini** *sm* gentleman.

ga'lassia *sf* galaxy.

gala'teo *sm* (good) manners *pl.*

gale'otto *sm (rematore)* galley slave; *(carcerato)* convict.

ga'lera *sf (NAUT)* galley; *(prigione)* prison.

'galla *sf:* a ~ afloat; **venire a** ~ to surface, come to the surface; *(fig: verità)* to come out.

galleggi'ante [galled'dʒante] *ag* floating // *sm (natante)* barge; *(di pescatore, lenza, TECN)* float.

galleggi'are [galled'dʒare] *vi* to float.

galle'ria *sf (traforo)* tunnel; *(ARCHIT, d'arte)* gallery; *(TEATRO)* circle; *(strada coperta con negozi)* arcade.

'Galles *sm:* il ~ Wales; **gal'lese** *ag, sm (LING)* Welsh // *sm/f* Welshman/woman.

gal'letta *sf* cracker.

gal'lina *sf* hen.

'gallo *sm* cock.

gal'lone *sm* piece of braid; *(MIL)* stripe; *(unità di misura)* gallon.

galop'pare *vi* to gallop.

ga'loppo *sm* gallop; **al** *o* **di** ~ at a gallop.

'gamba *sf* leg; *(asta: di lettera)* stem; **in** ~ *(in buona salute)* well; *(bravo, sveglio)* bright, smart; **prendere qc sotto** ~ *(fig)* to treat sth too lightly.

gambe'retto *sm* shrimp.

'gambero *sm (di acqua dolce)* crayfish; *(di mare)* prawn.

'gambo *sm* stem; *(di frutta)* stalk.

'gamma *sf (MUS)* scale; *(di colori, fig)* range.

ga'nascia, sce [ga'naʃʃa] *sf* jaw; **~sce del freno** *(AUT)* brake shoes.

'gancio [ˈgantʃo] *sm* hook.

'gangheri [ˈgangeri] *smpl:* **uscire dai** ~ *(fig)* to fly into a temper.

'gara *sf* competition; *(SPORT)* competition; contest; match; (: *corsa)* race; **fare a** ~ to compete, vie.

ga'rage [ga'raʒ] *sm inv* garage.

garan'tire *vt* to guarantee; *(debito)* to stand surety for; *(dare per certo)* to assure.

garan'zia [garan'tsia] *sf* guarantee; *(pegno)* security.

gar'bato, a *ag* courteous, polite.

'garbo *sm (buone maniere)* politeness, courtesy; *(di vestito etc)* grace, style.

gareggi'are [gared'dʒare] *vi* to compete.

garga'rismo *sm* gargle; **fare i** ~i to gargle.

ga'rofano *sm* carnation; **chiodo di** ~

clove.

'garza [ˈgardza] *sf (per bende)* gauze.

gar'zone [gar'dzone] *sm (di negozio)* boy.

gas *sm inv* gas; **a tutto** ~ at full speed; **dare** ~ *(AUT)* to accelerate.

ga'solio *sm* diesel (oil).

ga's(s)ato, a *ag (bibita)* aerated, fizzy.

gas'soso, a *ag* gaseous; gassy // *sf* fizzy drink.

gastrono'mia *sf* gastronomy.

gat'tino *sm* kitten.

'gatto, a *sm/f* cat, tomcat/she-cat; ~ **sel-vatico** wildcat; ~ **delle nevi** *(AUT, SCI)* snowcat.

gatto'pardo *sm:* ~ **africano** serval; ~ **americano** ocelot.

'gaudio *sm* joy, happiness.

ga'vetta *sf (MIL)* mess tin; **venire dalla** ~ *(MIL, fig)* to rise from the ranks.

'gazza [ˈgaddza] *sf* magpie.

gaz'zella [gad'dzella] *sf* gazelle; *(dei carabinieri)* (high-speed) police car.

gaz'zetta [gad'dzetta] *sf* news sheet; **G~ Ufficiale** *official publication containing details of new laws.*

gel [dʒɛl] *sm inv* gel.

ge'lare [dʒe'lare] *vt, vi, vb impers* to freeze; **ge'lata** *sf* frost.

gelate'ria [dʒelate'ria] *sf* ice-cream shop.

gela'tina [dʒela'tina] *sf* gelatine; ~ **esplosiva** dynamite; ~ **di frutta** fruit jelly.

ge'lato, a [dʒe'lato] *ag* frozen // *sm* ice cream.

'gelido, a [ˈdʒɛlido] *ag* icy, ice-cold.

'gelo [ˈdʒɛlo] *sm (temperatura)* intense cold; *(brina)* frost; *(fig)* chill; **ge'lone** *sm* chilblain.

gelo'sia [dʒelo'sia] *sf* jealousy.

ge'loso, a [dʒe'loso] *ag* jealous.

'gelso [ˈdʒɛlso] *sm* mulberry (tree).

gelso'mino [dʒelso'mino] *sm* jasmine.

ge'mello, a [dʒe'mello] *ag, sm/f* twin; ~**i** *smpl (di camicia)* cufflinks; *(dello zodiaco)*: **G~i** Gemini *sg.*

'gemere [ˈdʒɛmere] *vi* to moan, groan; *(cigolare)* to creak; *(gocciolare)* to drip, ooze; **'gemito** *sm* moan, groan.

'gemma [ˈdʒɛmma] *sf (BOT)* bud; *(pietra preziosa)* gem.

gene'rale [dʒene'rale] *ag, sm* general; **in** ~ *(per sommi capi)* in general terms; *(di solito)* usually, in general; **a** ~ **richiesta** by popular request; **generalità** *sfpl (dati d'identità)* particulars; **generaliz'zare** *vt, vi* to generalize; **general'mente** *av* generally.

gene'rare [dʒene'rare] *vt (dar vita)* to give birth to; *(produrre)* to produce; *(causare)* to arouse; *(TECN)* to produce, generate; **genera'tore** *sm (TECN)* generator; **generazi'one** *sf* generation.

'genere [ˈdʒɛnere] *sm* kind, type, sort; *(BIOL)* genus; *(merce)* article, product; *(LING)* gender; *(ARTE, LETTERATURA)* genre; in ~ generally, as a rule; il ~ umano mankind; ~i alimentari foodstuffs.

ge'nerico, a, ci, che [dʒe'nɛriko] ag generic; (vago) vague, imprecise.

'genero ['dʒɛnero] sm son-in-law.

generosità [dʒenerosi'ta] sf generosity.

gene'roso, a [dʒene'roso] ag generous.

ge'netico, a, ci, che [dʒe'nɛtiko] ag genetic // sf genetics sg.

gen'giva [dʒen'dʒiva] sf (ANAT) gum.

geni'ale [dʒen'jale] ag (persona) of genius; (idea) ingenious, brilliant.

'genio ['dʒɛnjo] sm genius; andare a ~ a qn to be to sb's liking, appeal to sb.

geni'tale [dʒeni'tale] ag genital; ~i smpl genitals.

geni'tore [dʒeni'tore] sm parent, father o mother; ~i smpl parents.

gen'naio [dʒen'najo] sm January.

'Genova ['dʒɛnova] sf Genoa.

gen'taglia [dʒen'taʎʎa] sf (peg) rabble.

'gente ['dʒɛnte] sf people pl.

gen'tile [dʒen'tile] ag (persona, atto) kind; (: garbato) courteous, polite; (nelle lettere): G~ Signore Dear Sir; (: sulla busta): G~ Signor Fernando Villa Mr Fernando Villa; genti'lezza sf kindness; courtesy, politeness; per gentilezza (per favore) please.

gentilu'omo, pl gentilu'omini [dʒenti'lwɔmo] sm gentleman.

genu'ino, a [dʒenu'ino] ag (prodotto) natural; (persona, sentimento) genuine, sincere.

geogra'fia [dʒeogra'fia] sf geography.

geolo'gia [dʒeolo'dʒia] sf geology.

ge'ometra, i, e [dʒe'ɔmetra] sm/f (professionista) surveyor.

geome'tria [dʒeome'tria] sf geometry; geo'metrico, a, ci, che ag geometric(al).

ge'ranio [dʒe'ranjo] sm geranium.

gerar'chia [dʒerar'kia] sf hierarchy.

ge'rente [dʒe'rɛnte] sm/f manager/ manageress.

'gergo, ghi ['dʒɛrgo] sm jargon; slang.

geria'tria [dʒerja'tria] sf geriatrics sg.

Ger'mania [dʒer'manja] sf: la ~ Germany; la ~ occidentale/orientale West/East Germany.

'germe ['dʒɛrme] sm germ; (fig) seed.

germogli'are [dʒermoʎ'ʎare] vi to sprout; to germinate; ger'moglio sm shoot; bud.

gero'glifico, ci [dʒero'glifiko] sm hieroglyphic.

'gesso ['dʒɛsso] sm chalk; (SCULTURA, MED, EDIL) plaster; (statua) plaster figure; (minerale) gypsum.

gesti'one [dʒes'tjone] sf management.

ges'tire [dʒes'tire] vt to run, manage.

'gesto ['dʒɛsto] sm gesture.

ges'tore [dʒes'tore] sm manager.

Gesù [dʒe'zu] sm Jesus.

gesu'ita, i [dʒezu'ita] sm Jesuit.

get'tare [dʒet'tare] vt to throw; (anche: ~ via) to throw away o out; (SCULTURA) to cast; (EDIL) to lay; (acqua) to spout; (grido) to utter; ~rsi vr: ~rsi in (sog: fiume) to flow into; ~ uno sguardo su to take a quick look at; get'tata sf (di cemento, gesso, metalli) cast; (diga) jetty.

'getto ['dʒetto] sm (di gas, liquido, AER) jet; a ~ continuo uninterruptedly; di ~ (fig) straight off, in one go.

get'tone [dʒet'tone] sm token; (per giochi) counter; (: roulette etc) chip; ~ telefonico telephone token.

ghiacci'aio [gjat'tʃajo] sm glacier.

ghiacci'are [gjat'tʃare] vt to freeze; (fig): ~ qn to make sb's blood run cold // vi to freeze, ice over; ghiacci'ato, a ag frozen; (bevanda) ice-cold.

ghi'accio ['gjattʃo] sm ice.

ghiacci'olo [gjat'tʃɔlo] sm icicle; (tipo di gelato) ice lolly (Brit), popsicle (US).

ghi'aia ['gjaja] sf gravel.

ghi'anda ['gjanda] sf (BOT) acorn.

ghi'andola ['gjandola] sf gland.

ghigliot'tina [giʎʎot'tina] sf guillotine.

ghi'gnare [gin'nare] vi to sneer.

ghi'otto, a ['gjotto] ag greedy; (cibo) delicious, appetizing; ghiot'tone, a sm/f glutton.

ghiri'bizzo [giri'biddzo] sm whim.

ghiri'goro [giri'goro] sm scribble, squiggle.

ghir'landa [gir'landa] sf garland, wreath.

'ghiro ['giro] sm dormouse.

'ghisa ['giza] sf cast iron.

già [dʒa] av already; (ex, in precedenza) formerly // escl of course!, yes indeed!

gi'acca ['dʒakka] sf jacket; ~ a vento windcheater (Brit), windbreaker (US).

giacché [dʒak'ke] cong since, as.

giac'chetta [dʒak'ketta] sf (light) jacket.

gia'cenza [dʒa'tʃɛntsa] sf: merce in ~ goods in stock; capitale in ~ uninvested capital; ~e di magazzino unsold stock.

gia'cere [dʒa'tʃere] vi to lie; giaci'mento sm deposit.

gia'cinto [dʒa'tʃinto] sm hyacinth.

gi'ada ['dʒada] sf jade.

giagg'iolo [dʒadʒ'dʒɔlo] sm iris.

giagu'aro [dʒa'gwaro] sm jaguar.

gi'allo ['dʒallo] ag yellow; (carnagione) sallow // sm yellow; (anche: romanzo ~) detective novel; (anche: film ~) detective film; ~ dell'uovo yolk.

giam'mai [dʒam'mai] av never.

Giap'pone [dʒap'pone] sm Japan; giappo'nese ag, sm/f, sm Japanese inv.

gi'ara ['dʒara] sf jar.

giardi'naggio [dʒardi'naddʒo] sm gardening.

giardi'netta [dʒardi'netta] sf estate car (Brit), station wagon (US).

giardini'ere, a [dʒardi'njɛre] *sm/f* gardener // *sf* (*misto di sottaceti*) mixed pickles *pl*; (*automobile*) = **giardinetta**.

giar'dino [dʒar'dino] *sm* garden; ~ **d'infanzia** nursery school; ~ **pubblico** public gardens *pl*, (public) park; ~ **zoologico** zoo.

giarretti'era [dʒarret'tjɛra] *sf* garter.

giavel'lotto [dʒavel'lɔtto] *sm* javelin.

gi'gante, 'essa [dʒi'gante] *sm/f* giant // *ag* giant, gigantic; (*COMM*) giant-size; **gigan'tesco, a, schi, sche** *ag* gigantic.

'giglio [dʒiʎʎo] *sm* lily.

gilè [dʒi'lɛ] *sm inv* waistcoat.

gin [dʒin] *sm inv* gin.

gine'cologo, a, gi, ghe [dʒine'kɔlogo] *sm/f* gynaecologist.

gi'nepro [dʒi'nepro] *sm* juniper.

gi'nestra [dʒi'nɛstra] *sf* (*BOT*) broom.

Gi'nevra [dʒi'nevra] *sf* Geneva.

gingil'larsi [dʒindʒil'larsi] *vr* to fritter away one's time; (*giocare*): ~ **con** to fiddle with.

gin'gillo [dʒin'dʒillo] *sm* plaything.

gin'nasio [dʒin'nazjo] *sm the 4th and 5th year of secondary school in Italy.*

gin'nasta, i, e [dʒin'nasta] *sm/f* gymnast; **gin'nastica** *sf* gymnastics *sg*; (*esercizio fisico*) keep-fit exercises; (*INS*) physical education.

gi'nocchio [dʒi'nɔkkjo], *pl(m)* **gi'nocchi** *o pl(f)* **gi'nocchia** *sm* knee; **stare in** ~ to kneel, be on one's knees; **mettersi in** ~ to kneel (down); **ginocchi'oni** *av* on one's knees.

gio'care [dʒo'kare] *vt* to play; (*scommettere*) to stake, wager, bet; (*ingannare*) to take in // *vi* to play; (*a roulette etc*) to gamble; (*fig*) to play a part, be important; (*TECN: meccanismo*) to be loose; ~ **a** (*gioco, sport*) to play; (*cavalli*) to bet on; ~**rsi la carriera** to put one's career at risk; **gioca'tore, 'trice** *sm/f* player; gambler.

gio'cattolo [dʒo'kattolo] *sm* toy.

gio'chetto [dʒo'ketto] *sm* (*tranello*) trick; (*fig*): **è un** ~ it's child's play.

gi'oco, chi [dʒɔko] *sm* game; (*divertimento, TECN*) play; (*al casinò*) gambling; (*CARTE*) hand; (*insieme di pezzi etc necessari per un gioco*) set; **per** ~ for fun; **fare il doppio** ~ **con qn** to double-cross sb; ~ **d'azzardo** game of chance; ~ **della palla** football; ~ **degli scacchi** chess set; **i Giochi Olimpici** the Olympic Games.

giocoli'ere [dʒoko'ljɛre] *sm* juggler.

gio'coso, a [dʒo'koso] *ag* playful, jesting.

gi'ogo, ghi [dʒɔgo] *sm* yoke.

gi'oia [dʒɔja] *sf* joy, delight; (*pietra preziosa*) jewel, precious stone.

gioielle'ria [dʒojelle'ria] *sf* jeweller's craft; jeweller's (shop).

gioielli'ere, a [dʒojel'ljɛre] *sm/f* jeweller.

gioi'ello [dʒo'jɛllo] *sm* jewel, piece of jewellery; ~**i** *smpl* jewellery *sg*.

gioi'oso, a [dʒo'joso] *ag* joyful.

Gior'dania [dʒor'danja] *sf*: **la** ~ Jordan.

giorna'laio, a [dʒorna'lajo] *sm/f* newsagent (*Brit*), newsdealer (*US*).

gior'nale [dʒor'nale] *sm* (news)paper; (*diario*) journal, diary; (*COMM*) journal; ~ **di bordo** log; ~ **radio** radio news *sg*.

giornali'ero, a [dʒorna'ljero] *ag* daily; (*che varia: umore*) changeable // *sm* day labourer.

giorna'lismo [dʒorna'lizmo] *sm* journalism.

giorna'lista, i, e [dʒorna'lista] *sm/f* journalist.

gior'nata [dʒor'nata] *sf* day; ~ **lavorativa** working day.

gi'orno [dʒorno] *sm* day; (*opposto alla notte*) day, daytime; (*luce del* ~) daylight; **al** ~ per day; **di** ~ by day; **al** ~ **d'oggi** nowadays.

gi'ostra [dʒɔstra] *sf* (*per bimbi*) merry-go-round; (*torneo storico*) joust.

gi'ovane [dʒovane] *ag* young; (*aspetto*) youthful // *sm/f* youth/girl, young man/woman; **i** ~**i** young people; **giova'nile** *ag* youthful; (*scritti*) early; (*errore*) of youth; **giova'notto** *sm* young man.

gio'vare [dʒo'vare] *vi*: ~ **a** (*essere utile*) to be useful to; (*far bene*) to be good for // *vb impers* (*essere bene, utile*) to be useful; ~**rsi di qc** to make use of sth.

giovedì [dʒove'di] *sm inv* Thursday; **di** *o* **il** ~ on Thursdays.

gioventù [dʒoven'tu] *sf* (*periodo*) youth; (*i giovani*) young people *pl*, youth.

giovi'ale [dʒo'vjale] *ag* jovial, jolly.

giovi'nezza [dʒovi'nettsa] *sf* youth.

gira'dischi [dʒira'diski] *sm inv* record player.

gi'raffa [dʒi'raffa] *sf* giraffe.

gi'randola [dʒi'randola] *sf* (*fuoco d'artificio*) Catherine wheel; (*giocattolo*) toy windmill; (*banderuola*) weather vane, weathercock.

gi'rare [dʒi'rare] *vt* (*far ruotare*) to turn; (*percorrere, visitare*) to go round; (*CINEMA*) to shoot; to make; (*COMM*) to endorse // *vi* to turn; (*più veloce*) to spin; (*andare in giro*) to wander, go around; ~**rsi** *vr* to turn; ~ **attorno a** to go round; to revolve round; **far** ~ **la testa a qn** to make sb dizzy; (*fig*) to turn sb's head.

girar'rosto [dʒirar'rɔsto] *sm* (*CUC*) spit.

gira'sole [dʒira'sole] *sm* sunflower.

gi'rata [dʒi'rata] *sf* (*passeggiata*) stroll; (*con veicolo*) drive; (*COMM*) endorsement.

gira'volta [dʒira'vɔlta] *sf* twirl, turn; (*curva*) sharp bend; (*fig*) about-turn.

gi'revole [dʒi'revole] *ag* revolving, turning.

gi'rino [dʒi'rino] *sm* tadpole.

'giro ['dʒiro] *sm* (*circuito*, *cerchio*) circle; (*di chiave*, *manovella*) turn; (*viaggio*) tour, excursion; (*passeggiata*) stroll, walk; (*in macchina*) drive; (*in bicicletta*) ride; (SPORT: *della pista*) lap; (*di denaro*) circulation; (CARTE) hand; (TECN) revolution; **prendere in ~ qn** (*fig*) to pull sb's leg; **fare un ~** to go for a walk (*o* a drive *o* a ride); **andare in ~** to go about, walk around; **a stretto ~ di posta** by return of post; **nel ~ di un mese** in a month's time; **essere nel ~** (*fig*) to belong to a circle (of friends); **~ d'affari** (COMM) turnover; **~ di parole** circumlocution; **~ di prova** (AUT) test drive; **~ turistico** sightseeing tour; **giro-'collo** *sm*: **a girocollo** crew-neck *cpd*.

gironzo'lare [dʒirondzo'lare] *vi* to stroll about.

'gita ['dʒita] *sf* excursion, trip; **fare una ~** to go for a trip, go on an outing.

gi'tano, a [dʒi'tano] *sm/f* gipsy.

giù [dʒu] *av* down; (*dabbasso*) downstairs; **in ~** downwards, down; **~ di lì** (*pressappoco*) thereabouts; **bambini dai 6 anni in ~** children aged 6 and under; **~ per: cadere ~** per le scale to fall down the stairs; **essere ~** (*fig: di salute*) to be run down; (: *di spirito*) to be depressed.

giub'botto [dʒub'bɔtto] *sm* jerkin; **~ antiproiettile** bulletproof vest.

gi'ubilo ['dʒubilo] *sm* rejoicing.

giudi'care [dʒudi'kare] *vt* to judge; (*accusato*) to try; (*lite*) to arbitrate in; **~ qn/qc bello** to consider sb/sth (to be) beautiful.

gi'udice ['dʒuditʃe] *sm* judge; **~ conciliatore** justice of the peace; **~ popolare** member of a jury.

giu'dizio [dʒu'dittsjo] *sm* judgment; (*opinione*) opinion; (DIR) judgment, sentence; (: *processo*) trial; (: *verdetto*) verdict; **aver ~** to be wise *o* prudent; **citare in ~** to summons; **giudizi'oso, a** *ag* prudent, judicious.

gi'ugno ['dʒuɲɲo] *sm* June.

giul'lare [dʒul'lare] *sm* jester.

giu'menta [dʒu'menta] *sf* mare.

gi'unco, chi ['dʒunko] *sm* rush.

gi'ungere [dʒundʒere] *vi* to arrive // *vt* (*mani etc*) to join; **~ a** to arrive at, reach.

gi'ungla ['dʒungla] *sf* jungle.

gi'unto, a ['dʒunto] *pp di* **giungere** // *sm* (TECN) coupling, joint // *sf* addition; (*organo esecutivo*, *amministrativo*) council, board; **per ~a** into the bargain, in addition; **~a militare** military junta; **giun'tura** *sf* joint.

giuo'care [dʒwo'kare] *vt*, *vi* = **giocare**; **giuo'co** *sm* = **gioco**.

giura'mento [dʒura'mento] *sm* oath; **~ falso** perjury.

giu'rare [dʒu'rare] *vt* to swear // *vi* to swear, take an oath; **giu'rato, a** *ag*: **nemico giurato** sworn enemy // *sm/f* juror, juryman/woman.

giu'ria [dʒu'ria] *sf* jury.

giu'ridico, a, ci, che [dʒu'ridiko] *ag* legal.

giustifi'care [dʒustifi'kare] *vt* to justify; **giustificazi'one** *sf* justification; (INS) (note of) excuse.

gius'tizia [dʒus'tittsja] *sf* justice; **giu-stizi'are** *vt* to execute, put to death; **giustizi'ere** *sm* executioner.

gi'usto, a ['dʒusto] *ag* (*equo*) fair, just; (*vero*) true, correct; (*adatto*) right, suitable; (*preciso*) exact, correct // *av* (*esattamente*) exactly, precisely; (*per l'appunto*, *appena*) just; **arrivare ~** to arrive just in time; **ho ~ bisogno di te** you're just the person I need.

glaci'ale [gla'tʃale] *ag* glacial.

'glandola *sf* = **ghiandola**.

gli [ʎi] *det mpl* (*dav V, s impura, gn, pn, ps, x, z*) the // *pronome* (*a lui*) to him; (*a esso*) to it; (*in coppia con lo, la, li, le, ne: a lui, a lei, a loro etc*): **gliele do** I'm giving them to him (*o* her *o* them).

gli'ela ['ʎela] *etc vedi* **gli**.

glo'bale *ag* overall.

'globo *sm* globe.

'globulo *sm* (ANAT): **~ rosso/bianco** red/white corpuscle.

'gloria *sf* glory; **glori'oso, a** *ag* glorious.

glos'sario *sm* glossary.

'gnocchi ['ɲɔkki] *smpl* (CUC) small dumplings made of semolina pasta or potato.

'gobba *sf* (ANAT) hump; (*protuberanza*) bump.

'gobbo, a *ag* hunchbacked; (*ricurvo*) round-shouldered // *sm/f* hunchback.

'goccia, ce ['gottʃa] *sf* drop; **goccio'lare** *vi*, *vt* to drip.

go'dere *vi* (*compiacersi*): **~ (di)** to be delighted (at), rejoice (at); (*trarre vantaggio*): **~ di** to enjoy, benefit from // *vt* to enjoy; **~rsi la vita** to enjoy life; **~sela** to have a good time, enjoy o.s.; **godi'mento** *sm* enjoyment.

'goffo, a *ag* clumsy, awkward.

'gola *sf* (ANAT) throat; (*golosità*) gluttony, greed; (*di camino*) flue; (*di monte*) gorge; **fare ~** (*anche fig*) to tempt.

golf *sm inv* (SPORT) golf; (*maglia*) cardigan.

'golfo *sm* gulf.

go'loso, a *ag* greedy.

'gomito *sm* elbow; (*di strada etc*) sharp bend.

go'mitolo *sm* ball.

'gomma *sf* rubber; (*colla*) gum; (*per cancellare*) rubber, eraser; (*di veicolo*) tyre (Brit), tire (US); **~ a terra** flat tyre (Brit) *o* tire (US); **gommapi'uma** *sf* ®

foam rubber.

'gondola *sf* gondola; **gondoli'ere** *sm* gondolier.

gonfa'lone *sm* banner.

gonfi'are *vt* (*pallone*) to blow up, inflate; (*dilatare, ingrossare*) to swell; (*fig: notizia*) to exaggerate; **~rsi** *vr* to swell; (*fiume*) to rise; **'gonfio, a** *ag* swollen; (*stomaco*) bloated; (*vela*) full; **gonfi'ore** *sm* swelling.

gongo'lare *vi* to look pleased with o.s.; **~ di gioia** to be overjoyed.

'gonna *sf* skirt; **~ pantalone** culottes *pl*.

'gonzo ['gondzo] *sm* simpleton, fool.

gorgheggi'are [gorged'dʒare] *vi* to warble; to trill.

'gorgo, ghi *sm* whirlpool.

gorgogli'are [gorgoʎ'ʎare] *vi* to gurgle.

go'rilla *sm inv* gorilla; (*guardia del corpo*) bodyguard.

'gotta *sf* gout.

gover'nante *sm/f* ruler // *sf* (*di bambini*) governess; (*donna di servizio*) housekeeper.

gover'nare *vt* (*stato*) to govern, rule; (*pilotare, guidare*) to steer; (*bestiame*) to tend, look after; **governa'tivo, a** *ag* government *cpd*; **governa'tore** *sm* governor.

go'verno *sm* government.

gozzovigli'are [gottsoviʎ'ʎare] *vi* to make merry, carouse.

gracchi'are [grak'kjare] *vi* to caw.

graci'dare [gratʃi'dare] *vi* to croak.

'gracile ['gratʃile] *ag* frail, delicate.

gra'dasso *sm* boaster.

gradazi'one [gradat'tsjone] *sf* (*sfumatura*) gradation; **~ alcolica** alcoholic content, strength.

gra'devole *ag* pleasant, agreeable.

gradi'mento *sm* pleasure, satisfaction; **è di suo ~?** is it to your liking?

gradi'nata *sf* flight of steps; (*in teatro, stadio*) tiers *pl*.

gra'dino *sm* step; (*ALPINISMO*) foothold.

gra'dire *vt* (*accettare con piacere*) to accept; (*desiderare*) to wish, like; **gradisce una tazza di tè?** would you like a cup of tea?; **gra'dito, a** *ag* pleasing; welcome.

'grado *sm* (*MAT, FISICA etc*) degree; (*stadio*) degree, level; (*MIL, sociale*) rank; **essere in ~ di fare** to be in a position to do.

gradu'ale *ag* gradual.

gradu'are *vt* to grade; **gradu'ato, a** *ag* (*esercizi*) graded; (*scala, termometro*) graduated // *sm* (*MIL*) non-commissioned officer.

'graffa *sf* (*gancio*) clip; (*segno grafico*) brace.

graffi'are *vt* to scratch.

'graffio *sm* scratch.

gra'fia *sf* spelling; (*scrittura*) handwriting.

'grafico, a, ci, che *ag* graphic // *sm* graph; (*persona*) graphic designer // *sf* graphic arts *pl*.

gra'migna [gra'miɲɲa] *sf* weed; couch grass.

gram'matica, che *sf* grammar; **grammati'cale** *ag* grammatical.

'grammo *sm* gram(me).

gran *ag vedi* **grande**.

'grana *sf* (*granello, di minerali, corpi spezzati*) grain; (*fam: seccatura*) trouble; (: *soldi*) cash // *sm inv* Parmesan (cheese).

gra'naio *sm* granary, barn.

gra'nata *sf* (*frutto*) pomegranate; (*pietra preziosa*) garnet; (*proiettile*) grenade.

Gran Bre'tagna [granbre'taɲɲa] *sf*: **la ~** Great Britain.

'granchio ['grankjo] *sm* crab; (*fig*) blunder; **prendere un ~** (*fig*) to blunder.

grandango'lare *sm* wide-angle lens *sg*.

'grande, *qualche volta* **gran** +*C,* **grand'** +*V ag* (*grosso, largo, vasto*) big, large; (*alto*) tall; (*lungo*) long; (*in sensi astratti*) great // *sm/f* (*persona adulta*) adult, grown-up; (*chi ha ingegno e potenza*) great man/woman; **fare le cose in ~** to do things in style; **una gran bella donna** a very beautiful woman; **non è una gran cosa** *o* **un gran che** it's nothing special; **non ne so gran che** I don't know very much about it.

grandeggi'are [granded'dʒare] *vi* (*emergere per grandezza*): **~ su** to tower over; (*darsi arie*) to put on airs.

gran'dezza [gran'dettsa] *sf* (*dimensione*) size; magnitude; (*fig*) greatness; **in ~ naturale** lifesize.

grandi'nare *vb impers* to hail.

'grandine *sf* hail.

gran'duca, chi *sm* grand duke.

gra'nello *sm* (*di cereali, uva*) seed; (*di frutta*) pip; (*di sabbia, sale etc*) grain.

gra'nita *sf* kind of water ice.

gra'nito *sm* granite.

'grano *sm* (*in quasi tutti i sensi*) grain; (*frumento*) wheat; (*di rosario, collana*) bead; **~ di pepe** peppercorn.

gran'turco *sm* maize.

'granulo *sm* granule; (*MED*) pellet.

'grappa *sf* rough, strong brandy.

'grappolo *sm* bunch, cluster.

gras'setto *sm* (*TIP*) bold (type).

'grasso, a *ag* fat; (*cibo*) fatty; (*pelle*) greasy; (*terreno*) rich; (*fig: guadagno, annata*) plentiful; (: *volgare*) coarse, lewd // *sm* (*di persona, animale*) fat; (*sostanza che unge*) grease; **gras'-soccio, a, ci, ce** *ag* plump.

'grata *sf* grating.

gra'ticola *sf* grill.

gra'tifica, che *sf* bonus.

'gratis *av* free, for nothing.

grati'tudine *sf* gratitude.

'grato, a *ag* grateful; (*gradito*) pleasant, agreeable.

gratta'capo *sm* worry, headache.

grattaci'elo [gratta'tʃɛlo] *sm* skyscraper.

grat'tare *vt* (*pelle*) to scratch; (*raschiare*) to scrape; (*pane, formaggio, carote*) to grate; (*fam: rubare*) to pinch // *vi* (*stridere*) to grate; (*AUT*) to grind; ~**rsi** *vr* to scratch o.s.

grat'tugia, gie [grat'tudʒa] *sf* grater; **grattugi'are** *vt* to grate; **pane grattugiato** breadcrumbs *pl.*

gra'tuito, a *ag* free; (*fig*) gratuitous.

gra'vame *sm* tax; (*fig*) burden, weight.

gra'vare *vt* to burden // *vi*: ~ **su** to weigh on.

'grave *ag* (*danno, pericolo, peccato etc*) grave, serious; (*responsabilità*) heavy, grave; (*contegno*) grave, solemn; (*voce, suono*) deep, low-pitched; (*LING*): **accento** ~ grave accent; **un malato** ~ **a** person who is seriously ill.

gravi'danza [gravi'dantsa] *sf* pregnancy.

'gravido, a *ag* pregnant.

gravità *sf* seriousness; (*anche FISICA*) gravity.

gra'voso, a *ag* heavy, onerous.

'grazia ['grattsja] *sf* grace; (*favore*) favour; (*DIR*) pardon; **grazi'are** *vt* (*DIR*) to pardon.

'grazie ['grattsje] *escl* thank you!; ~ **mille!** *o* **tante!** *o* **infinite!** thank you very much!; ~ **a** thanks to.

grazi'oso, a [grat'tsjoso] *ag* charming, delightful; (*gentile*) gracious.

'Grecia ['grɛtʃa] *sf*: **la** ~ Greece; **'greco, a, ci, che** *ag, sm/f, sm* Greek.

'gregge, pl(f) **i** ['greddʒe] *sm* flock.

'greggio, a, gi, ge ['greddʒo] *ag* raw, unrefined; (*diamante*) rough, uncut; (*tessuto*) unbleached // *sm* (*anche:* petrolio ~) crude (oil).

grembi'ule *sm* apron; (*sopravveste*) overall.

'grembo *sm* lap; (*ventre della madre*) womb.

gre'mito, a *ag*: ~ (**di**) packed *o* crowded (with).

'gretto, a *ag* mean, stingy; (*fig*) narrow-minded.

'greve *ag* heavy.

'grezzo, a ['greddzo] *ag* = **greggio.**

gri'dare *vi* (*per chiamare*) to shout, cry (out); (*strillare*) to scream, yell // *vt* to shout (out), yell (out); ~ **aiuto** to cry *o* shout for help.

'grido, pl(m) **i** *o* **pl**(f) **a**, *sm* shout, cry; scream, yell; (*di animale*) cry; **di** ~ famous.

'grigio, a, gi, gie ['gridʒo] *ag, sm* grey.

'griglia ['griʎʎa] *sf* (*per arrostire*) grill; (*ELETTR*) grid; (*inferriata*) grating; **alla** ~ (*CUC*) grilled; **grigli'ata** *sf* (*CUC*) grill.

gril'letto *sm* trigger.

'grillo *sm* (*ZOOL*) cricket; (*fig*) whim.

grimal'dello *sm* picklock.

'grinta *sf* grim expression; (*SPORT*) fighting spirit.

'grinza ['grintsa] *sf* crease, wrinkle; (*ruga*) wrinkle; **non fare una** ~ (*fig: ragionamento*) to be faultless; **grin'zoso, a** *ag* creased; wrinkled.

grip'pare *vi* (*TECN*) to seize.

gris'sino *sm* bread-stick.

'gronda *sf* eaves *pl.*

gron'daia *sf* gutter.

gron'dare *vi* to pour; (*essere bagnato*): ~ **di** to be dripping with // *vt* to drip with.

'groppa *sf* (*di animale*) back, rump; (*fam: dell'uomo*) back, shoulders *pl.*

'groppo *sm* tangle; **avere un** ~ **alla gola** (*fig*) to have a lump in one's throat.

gros'sezza [gros'settsa] *sf* size; thickness.

gros'sista, i, e *sm/f* (*COMM*) wholesaler.

'grosso, a *ag* big, large; (*di spessore*) thick; (*grossolano: anche fig*) coarse; (*grave, insopportabile*) serious, great; (*tempo, mare*) rough // *sm*: **il** ~ **di** the bulk of; **un pezzo** ~ (*fig*) a VIP, a bigwig; **farla** ~**a** to do something very stupid; **dirle** ~**e** to tell tall stories; **sbagliarsi di** ~ to be completely wrong.

grosso'lano, a *ag* rough, coarse; (*fig*) coarse, crude; (*: errore*) stupid.

grosso'modo *av* roughly.

'grotta *sf* cave; grotto.

grot'tesco, a, schi, sche *ag* grotesque.

grovi'era *sm o f* gruyère (cheese).

gro'viglio [gro'viʎʎo] *sm* tangle; (*fig*) muddle.

gru *sf inv* crane.

'gruccia, ce ['gruttʃa] *sf* (*per camminare*) crutch; (*per abiti*) coathanger.

gru'gnire [gruɲ'ɲire] *vi* to grunt; **gru'gnito** *sm* grunt.

'grugno ['gruɲɲo] *sm* snout; (*fam: faccia*) mug.

'grullo, a *ag* silly, stupid.

'grumo *sm* (*di sangue*) clot; (*di farina etc*) lump.

'gruppo *sm* group; ~ **sanguigno** blood group.

gruvi'era *sm o f* = **groviera.**

guada'gnare [gwadaɲ'ɲare] *vt* (*ottenere*) to gain; (*soldi, stipendio*) to earn; (*vincere*) to win; (*raggiungere*) to reach.

gua'dagno [gwa'daɲɲo] *sm* earnings *pl*; (*COMM*) profit; (*vantaggio, utile*) advantage, gain; ~ **lordo/netto** gross/net earnings *pl.*

gu'ado *sm* ford; **passare a** ~ to ford.

gu'ai *escl*: ~ **a te** (*o* **lui** *etc*)! woe betide you (*o* him *etc*)!

gua'ina sf (*fodero*) sheath; (*indumento per donna*) girdle.

gu'aio sm trouble, mishap; (*inconveniente*) trouble, snag.

gua'ire vi to whine, yelp.

gu'ancia, ce ['gwantʃa] sf cheek.

guanci'ale [gwan'tʃale] sm pillow.

gu'anto sm glove.

gu'arda... prefisso: ~'**boschi** sm inv forester; ~'**caccia** sm inv gamekeeper; ~'**coste** sm inv coastguard; (*nave*) coastguard patrol vessel; ~'**linee** sm inv (SPORT) linesman.

guar'dare vt (*con lo sguardo: osservare*) to look at; (*film, televisione*) to watch; (*custodire*) to look after, take care of // vi to look; (*badare*): ~ a to pay attention to; (*luoghi: esser orientato*): ~ a to face; ~**rsi** vr to look at o.s.; ~**rsi da** (*astenersi*) to refrain from; (*stare in guardia*) to beware of; ~**rsi da fare** to take care not to do; **guarda di non sbagliare** try not to make a mistake; ~ **a vista qn** to keep a close watch on sb.

guarda'roba sm inv wardrobe; (*locale*) cloakroom; **guardarobi'ere, a** sm/f cloakroom attendant.

gu'ardia sf (*individuo, corpo*) guard; (*sorveglianza*) watch; **fare la** ~ **a qc/qn** to guard sth/sb; **stare in** ~ (*fig*) to be on one's guard; **di** ~ (*medico*) on call; ~ **carceraria** (*prison*) warder; ~ **del corpo** bodyguard; ~ **di finanza** (*corpo*) customs pl; (*persona*) customs officer; ~ **medica** emergency doctor service.

guardi'ano, a sm/f (*di carcere*) warder; (*di villa etc*) caretaker; (*di museo*) custodian; (*di zoo*) keeper; ~ **notturno** night watchman.

guar'dingo, a, ghi, ghe ag wary, cautious.

guardi'ola sf porter's lodge; (MIL) lookout tower.

guarigi'one [gwari'dʒone] sf recovery.

gua'rire vt (*persona, malattia*) to cure; (*ferita*) to heal // vi to recover, be cured; to heal (up).

guarnigi'one [gwarni'dʒone] sf garrison.

guar'nire vt (*ornare: abiti*) to trim; (CUC) to garnish; **guarnizi'one** sf trimming; garnish; (TECN) gasket.

guasta'feste sm/f inv spoilsport.

guas'tare vt to spoil, ruin; (*meccanismo*) to break; ~**rsi** vr (*cibo*) to go bad; (*meccanismo*) to break down; (*tempo*) to change for the worse; (*amici*) to quarrel, fall out.

gu'asto, a ag (*non funzionante*) broken; (: *telefono etc*) out of order; (*andato a male*) bad, rotten; (: *dente*) decayed, bad; (*fig: corrotto*) depraved // sm breakdown; (*avaria*) failure; ~ **al motore** engine failure.

guazza'buglio [gwattsa'buʎʎo] sm muddle.

gu'ercio, a, ci, ce ['gwertʃo] ag cross-eyed.

gu'erra sf war; (*tecnica: atomica, chimica etc*) warfare; **fare la** ~ (**a**) to wage war (against); ~ **mondiale** world war; **guerreggi'are** vi to wage war; **guerri'ero, a** ag warlike // sm warrior; **guer'riglia** sf guerrilla warfare; **guerrigli'ero** sm guerrilla.

'gufo sm owl.

gu'ida sf guide; (*comando, direzione*) guidance, direction; (AUT) driving; (: *sterzo*) steering; (*tappeto, di tenda, cassetto*) runner; ~ **a destra/sinistra** (AUT) right-/left-hand drive; ~ **telefonica** telephone directory.

gui'dare vt to guide; (*condurre a capo*) to lead; (*auto*) to drive; (*aereo, nave*) to pilot; **sai** ~? can you drive?; **guida'tore, trice** sm/f (*conducente*) driver.

guin'zaglio [gwin'tsaʎʎo] sm leash, lead.

gu'isa sf: **a** ~ **di** like, in the manner of.

guiz'zare [gwit'tsare] vi to dart; to flicker; to leap; ~ **via** (*fuggire*) to slip away.

'guscio ['guʃʃo] sm shell.

gus'tare vt (*cibi*) to taste; (: *assaporare con piacere*) to enjoy, savour; (*fig*) to enjoy, appreciate // vi: ~ **a** to please; **non mi gusta affatto** I don't like it at all.

'gusto sm taste; (*sapore*) flavour; (*godimento*) enjoyment; **al** ~ **di fragola** strawberry-flavoured; **mangiare di** ~ to eat heartily; **prenderci** ~: **ci ha preso** ~ he's acquired a taste for it, he's got to like it; **gus'toso, a** ag tasty; (*fig*) agreeable.

H

h abbr = **ora, altezza**.

ha, 'hai [a, ai] vb vedi **avere**.

hall [hɔl] sf inv hall, foyer.

'handicap ['handikap] sm inv handicap; **handicap'pato, a** ag handicapped // sm/f handicapped person, disabled person.

'hanno ['anno] vb vedi **avere**.

'hascisc ['haʃiʃ] sm hashish.

'herpes ['ɛrpes] sm (MED) herpes sg; ~ **zoster** shingles sg.

ho [ɔ] vb vedi **avere**.

'hobby ['hɔbi] sm inv hobby.

'hockey ['hɔki] sm hockey; ~ **su ghiaccio** ice hockey.

'hostess ['houstis] sf inv air hostess (Brit) o stewardess.

ho'tel sm inv hotel.

I

i det mpl the.

i'ato sm hiatus.

ibernazi'one [ibernat'tsjone] *sf* hibernation.

'ibrido, a *ag, sm* hybrid.

Id'dio *sm* God.

i'dea *sf* idea; (*opinione*) opinion, view; (*ideale*) ideal; **dare l'~ di** to seem, look like; **~ fissa** obsession; **neanche** *o* **neppure per ~!** certainly not!

ide'ale *ag, sm* ideal.

ide'are *vt* (*immaginare*) to think up, conceive; (*progettare*) to plan.

i'dentico, a, ci, che *ag* identical.

identifi'care *vt* to identify; **identificazi'one** *sf* identification.

identità *sf inv* identity.

idi'oma, i *sm* idiom, language; **idio'-matico, a, ci, che** *ag* idiomatic; **frase idiomatica** idiom.

idi'ota, i, e *ag* idiotic // *sm/f* idiot.

idola'trare *vt* to worship; (*fig*) to idolize.

'idolo *sm* idol.

idoneità *sf* suitability.

i'doneo, a *ag*: **~ a** a suitable for, fit for; (*MIL*) fit for; (*qualificato*) qualified for.

i'drante *sm* hydrant.

i'draulico, a, ci, che *ag* hydraulic // *sm* plumber // *sf* hydraulics *sg*.

idroe'lettrico, a, ci, che *ag* hydroelectric.

i'drofilo, a *ag vedi* **cotone**.

idrofo'bia *sf* rabies *sg*.

i'drogeno [i'drɔdʒeno] *sm* hydrogen.

idros'calo *sm* seaplane base.

idrovo'lante *sm* seaplane.

i'ena *sf* hyena.

i'eri *av, sm* yesterday; **il giornale di ~** yesterday's paper; **~ l'altro** the day before yesterday; **~ sera** yesterday evening.

igi'ene [i'dʒɛne] *sf* hygiene; **~ pubblica** public health; **igi'enico, a, ci, che** *ag* hygienic; (*salubre*) healthy.

i'gnaro, a [iɲ'ɲaro] *ag*: **~ di** unaware of, ignorant of.

i'gnobile [iɲ'ɲɔbile] *ag* despicable, vile.

igno'rante [iɲɲo'rante] *ag* ignorant.

igno'rare [iɲɲo'rare] *vt* (*non sapere, conoscere*) to be ignorant *o* unaware of, not to know; (*fingere di non vedere, sentire*) to ignore.

i'gnoto, a [iɲ'ɲɔto] *ag* unknown.

il *det m* (*pl* (*m*) **i**; *diventa* **lo** (*pl* **gli**) *davanti a s impura, gn, pn, ps, x, z; f* **la** (*pl* **le**) **1** the; **~ libro/lo studente/l'acqua** the book/the student/the water; **gli scolari** the pupils

2 (*astrazione*): **~ coraggio/l'amore/la giovinezza** courage/love/youth

3 (*tempo*): **~ mattino/la sera** in the morning/evening; **~ venerdì** *etc* (*abitualmente*) on Fridays *etc*; (*quel giorno*) on (the) Friday *etc*; **la settimana prossima** next week

4 (*distributivo*) a, an; **2.500 lire ~ chilo/paio** 2,500 lire a *o* per kilo/pair; **110 km**

l'ora 110 km an *o* per hour

5 (*partitivo*) some, any; **hai messo lo zucchero?** have you added sugar?; **hai comprato ~ latte?** did you buy (some *o* any) milk?

6 (*possesso*): **aprire gli occhi** to open one's eyes; **rompersi la gamba** to break one's leg; **avere i capelli neri/~ naso rosso** to have dark hair/a red nose; **mettiti le scarpe** put your shoes on

7 (*con nomi propri*): **~ Petrarca** Petrarch; **~ Presidente Reagan** President Reagan; **dov'è la Francesca?** where's Francesca?

8 (*con nomi geografici*): **~ Tevere** the Tiber; **l'Italia** Italy; **~ Regno Unito** the United Kingdom; **l'Everest** Everest; **le Alpi** the Alps.

'ilare *ag* cheerful; **ilarità** *sf* hilarity, mirth.

illangui'dire *vi* to grow weak *o* feeble.

illazi'one [illat'tsjone] *sf* inference, deduction.

ille'gale *ag* illegal.

illeg'gibile [illed'dʒibile] *ag* illegible.

ille'gittimo, a [ille'dʒittimo] *ag* illegitimate.

il'leso, a *ag* unhurt, unharmed.

illette'rato, a *ag* illiterate.

illi'bato, a *ag*: **donna ~a** virgin.

illimi'tato, a *ag* boundless; unlimited.

ill.mo *abbr* = **illustrissimo**.

il'ludere *vt* to deceive, delude; **~rsi** *vr* to deceive o.s., delude o.s.

illumi'nare *vt* to light up, illuminate; (*fig*) to enlighten; **~rsi** *vr* to light up; **~ a giorno** to floodlight; **illuminazi'one** *sf* lighting; illumination; floodlighting; (*fig*) flash of inspiration.

illusi'one *sf* illusion; **farsi delle ~i** to delude o.s.

illusio'nismo *sm* conjuring.

il'luso, a *pp di* **illudere**.

illus'trare *vt* to illustrate; **illustra'tivo, a** *ag* illustrative; **illustrazi'one** *sf* illustration.

il'lustre *ag* eminent, renowned; **illus'trissimo, a** *ag* (*negli indirizzi*) very revered.

imbacuc'care *vt, ~rsi vr* to wrap up.

imbal'laggio [imbal'laddʒo] *sm* packing *q*.

imbal'lare *vt* to pack; (*AUT*) to race; **~rsi** *vr* (*AUT*) to race.

imbalsa'mare *vt* to embalm.

imbambo'lato, a *ag* (*sguardo*) vacant, blank.

imban'dire *vt*: **~ un pranzo** to prepare a lavish meal.

imbaraz'zare [imbarat'tsare] *vt* (*mettere a disagio*) to embarrass; (*ostacolare: movimenti*) to hamper; (: *stomaco*) to lie heavily on.

imba'razzo [imba'rattso] *sm* (*disagio*) embarrassment; (*perplessità*) puzzlement, bewilderment; ~ **di stomaco** indigestion.

imbarca'dero sm landing stage.

imbar'care vt (passeggeri) to embark; (merci) to load; ~**rsi** vr: ~**rsi su** to board; ~**rsi per l'America** to sail for America; ~**rsi in** (fig: affare etc) to embark on.

imbarcazi'one [imbarkat'tsjone] sf (small) boat, (small) craft inv; ~ **di salvataggio** lifeboat.

im'barco, chi sm embarkation; loading; boarding; (banchina) landing stage.

imbas'tire vt (cucire) to tack; (fig: abbozzare) to sketch, outline.

im'battersi vr: ~ **in** (incontrare) to bump o run into.

imbat'tibile ag unbeatable, invincible.

imbavagli'are [imbavaʎ'ʎare] vt to gag.

imbec'cata sf (TEATRO) prompt.

imbe'cille [imbe'tʃille] ag idiotic // sm/f idiot; (MED) imbecile.

imbel'lire vt to adorn, embellish // vi to grow more beautiful.

im'berbe ag beardless.

im'bevere vt to soak; ~**rsi** vr: ~**rsi di** to soak up, absorb.

imbian'care vt to whiten; (muro) to whitewash // vi to become o turn white.

imbian'chino [imbjan'kino] sm (house) painter, painter and decorator.

imboc'care vt (bambino) to feed; (entrare: strada) to enter, turn into // vi: ~ **in** (sog: strada) to lead into; (: fiume) to flow into.

imbocca'tura sf mouth; (di strada, porto) entrance; (MUS, del morso) mouthpiece.

im'bocco, chi sm entrance.

imbos'care vt to hide; ~**rsi** vr (MIL) to evade military service.

imbos'cata sf ambush.

imbottigli'are [imbottiʎ'ʎare] vt to bottle; (NAUT) to blockade; (MIL) to hem in; ~**rsi** vr to be stuck in a traffic jam.

imbot'tire vt to stuff; (giacca) to pad; **imbot'tita** sf quilt; **imbotti'tura** sf stuffing; padding.

imbrat'tare vt to dirty, smear, daub.

imbrigli'are [imbriʎ'ʎare] vt to bridle.

imbroc'care vt (fig) to guess correctly.

imbrogli'are [imbroʎ'ʎare] vt to mix up; (fig: raggirare) to deceive, cheat; (: confondere) to confuse, mix up; ~**rsi** vr to get tangled; (fig) to become confused; **im'broglio** sm (groviglio) tangle; (situazione confusa) mess; (truffa) swindle, trick; **imbrogli'one, a** sm/f cheat, swindler.

imbronci'are [imbron'tʃare] vi (anche: ~**rsi**) to sulk; **imbronci'ato, a** ag sulky.

imbru'nire vi, vb impers to grow dark; **all'~** at dusk.

imbrut'tire vt to make ugly // vi to

become ugly.

imbu'care vt to post.

imbur'rare vt to butter.

im'buto sm funnel.

imi'tare vt to imitate; (riprodurre) to copy; (assomigliare) to look like; **imitazi'one** sf imitation.

immaco'lato, a ag spotless; immaculate.

immagazzi'nare [immagaddzi'nare] vt to store.

immagi'nare [immadʒi'nare] vt to imagine; (supporre) to suppose; (inventare) to invent; **s'immagini!** don't mention it!, not at all!; **immagi'nario, a** ag imaginary; **immaginazi'one** sf imagination; (cosa immaginata) fancy.

im'magine [im'madʒine] sf image; (rappresentazione grafica, mentale) picture.

imman'cabile ag certain; unfailing.

immangi'abile [imman'dʒabile] ag inedible.

immatrico'lare vt to register; ~**rsi** vr (INS) to matriculate, enrol; **immatricolazi'one** sf registration; matriculation, enrolment.

imma'turo, a ag (frutto) unripe; (persona) immature; (prematuro) premature.

immedesi'marsi vr: ~ **in** to identify with.

immediata'mente av immediately, at once.

immedi'ato, a ag immediate.

im'memore ag: ~ **di** forgetful of.

im'menso, a ag immense.

im'mergere [im'mɛrdʒere] vt to immerse, plunge; ~**rsi** vr to plunge; (sommergibile) to dive, submerge; (dedicarsi a): ~**rsi in** to immerse o.s. in.

immeri'tato, a ag undeserved.

immeri'tevole ag undeserving, unworthy.

immersi'one sf immersion; (di sommergibile) submersion, dive; (di palombaro) dive.

im'merso, a pp di **immergere**.

im'mettere vt: ~ (in) to introduce (into); ~ **dati in un computer** to enter data on a computer.

immi'grato, a sm/f immigrant; **immigrazi'one** sf immigration.

immi'nente ag imminent.

immischi'are [immis'kjare] vt: ~ **qn in** to involve sb in; ~**rsi in** to interfere o meddle in.

immissi'one sf (di aria, gas) intake; ~ **di dati** (INFORM) data entry.

im'mobile ag motionless, still; **(beni) ~i** smpl real estate sg; **immobili'are** ag (DIR) property cpd; **immobilità** sf stillness; immobility.

immo'desto, a ag immodest.

immo'lare vt to sacrifice, immolate.

immon'dizia [immon'dittsja] sf dirt,

filth; (*spesso al pl: spazzatura, rifiuti*) rubbish *q*, refuse *q*.

im'mondo, a *ag* filthy, foul.

immo'rale *ag* immoral.

immor'tale *ag* immortal.

im'mune *ag* (*esente*) exempt; (*MED, DIR*) immune; **immunità** *sf* immunity; **immunità parlamentare** parliamentary privilege.

immu'tabile *ag* immutable; unchanging.

impacchet'tare [impakket'tare] *vt* to pack up.

impacci'are [impat't∫are] *vt* to hinder, hamper; **impacci'ato, a** *ag* awkward, clumsy; (*imbarazzato*) embarrassed; **im'paccio** *sm* obstacle; (*imbarazzo*) embarrassment; (*situazione imbarazzante*) awkward situation.

im'pacco, chi *sm* (*MED*) compress.

impadro'nirsi *vr*: ~ di to seize, take possession of; (*fig: apprendere a fondo*) to master.

impa'gabile *ag* priceless.

impagi'nare [impadʒi'nare] *vt* (*TIP*) to paginate, page (up).

impagli'are [impaʎ'ʎare] *vt* to stuff (with straw).

impa'lato, a *ag* (*fig*) stiff as a board.

impalca'tura *sf* scaffolding.

impalli'dire *vi* to turn pale; (*fig*) to fade.

impa'nare *vt* (*CUC*) to dip in breadcrumbs.

impanta'narsi *vr* to sink (in the mud); (*fig*) to get bogged down.

impappi'narsi *vr* to stammer, falter.

impa'rare *vt* to learn.

impareggi'abile [impared'dʒabile] *ag* incomparable.

imparen'tarsi *vr*: ~ con to marry into.

'impari *ag inv* (*disuguale*) unequal; (*dispari*) odd.

impar'tire *vt* to bestow, give.

imparzi'ale [impar'tsjale] *ag* impartial, unbiased.

impas'sibile *ag* impassive.

impas'tare *vt* (*pasta*) to knead; (*colori*) to mix.

im'pasto *sm* (*l'impastare: di pane*) kneading; (: *di cemento*) mixing; (*pasta*) dough; (*anche fig*) mixture.

im'patto *sm* impact.

impau'rire *vt* to scare, frighten // *vi* (*anche*: ~rsi) to become scared o frightened.

impazi'ente [impat'tsjɛnte] *ag* impatient; **impazi'enza** *sf* impatience.

impaz'zata [impat'tsata] *sf*: all'~ (*precipitosamente*) at breakneck speed.

impaz'zire [impat'tsire] *vi* to go mad; ~ per qn/qc to be crazy about sb/sth.

impec'cabile *ag* impeccable.

impedi'mento *sm* obstacle, hindrance.

impe'dire *vt* (*vietare*): ~ a qn di fare to prevent sb from doing; (*ostruire*) to obstruct; (*impacciare*) to hamper, hinder.

impe'gnare [impeɲ'ɲare] *vt* (*dare in pegno*) to pawn; (*onore etc*) to pledge; (*prenotare*) to book, reserve; (*obbligare*) to oblige; (*occupare*) to keep busy; (*MIL: nemico*) to engage; ~rsi *vr* (*vincolarsi*): ~rsi a fare to undertake to do; (*mettersi risolutamente*): ~rsi in qc to devote o.s. to sth; ~rsi con qn (*accordarsi*) to come to an agreement with sb; **impegna'tivo, a** *ag* binding; (*lavoro*) demanding, exacting; **impe'gnato, a** *ag* (*occupato*) busy; (*fig: romanzo, autore*) committed, engagé.

im'pegno [im'peɲɲo] *sm* (*obbligo*) obligation; (*promessa*) promise, pledge; (*zelo*) diligence, zeal; (*compito, d'autore*) commitment.

impel'lente *ag* pressing, urgent.

impene'trabile *ag* impenetrable.

impen'narsi *vr* (*cavallo*) to rear up; (*AER*) to nose up; (*fig*) to bridle.

impen'sato, a *ag* unforeseen, unexpected.

impensie'rire *vt*, ~rsi *vr* to worry.

impe'rare *vi* (*anche fig*) to reign, rule.

impera'tivo, a *ag*, *sm* imperative.

impera'tore, 'trice *sm/f* emperor/empress.

imperdo'nabile *ag* unforgivable, unpardonable.

imper'fetto, a *ag* imperfect // *sm* (*LING*) imperfect (tense); **imperfezi'one** *sf* imperfection.

imperi'ale *ag* imperial.

imperi'oso, a *ag* (*persona*) imperious; (*motivo, esigenza*) urgent, pressing.

impe'rizia [impe'rittsja] *sf* lack of experience.

imperma'lirsi *vr* to take offence.

imperme'abile *ag* waterproof // *sm* raincoat.

imperni'are *vt*: ~ qc su to hinge sth on; (*fig*) to base sth on; ~rsi *vr* (*fig*): ~rsi su to be based on.

im'pero *sm* empire; (*forza, autorità*) rule, control.

imperscru'tabile *ag* inscrutable.

imperso'nale *ag* impersonal.

imperso'nare *vt* to personify; (*TEATRO*) to play, act (the part of).

imperter'rito, a *ag* fearless, undaunted; impassive.

imperti'nente *ag* impertinent.

imperver'sare *vi* to rage.

'impeto *sm* (*moto, forza*) force, impetus; (*assalto*) onslaught; (*fig: impulso*) impulse; (: *slancio*) transport; con ~ energetically; vehemently.

impet'tito, a *ag* stiff, erect.

impetu'oso, a *ag* (*vento*) strong, raging; (*persona*) impetuous.

impian'tare vt (motore) to install; (azienda, discussione) to establish, start.

impi'anto sm (installazione) installation; (apparecchiature) plant; (sistema) system; ~ **elettrico** wiring; ~ **sportivo** sports complex; ~**i di risalita** (SCI) ski lifts.

impias'trare, impiastricci'are [impjastrit'tʃare] vt to smear, dirty.

impi'astro sm poultice.

impic'care vt to hang; ~**rsi** vr to hang o.s.

impicci'are [impit'tʃare] vt to hinder, hamper; ~**rsi** vr to meddle, interfere; **im'piccio** sm (ostacolo) hindrance; (seccatura) trouble, bother; (affare imbrogliato) mess; **essere d'impiccio** to be in the way.

impie'gare vt (usare) to use, employ; (assumere) to employ, take on; (spendere: denaro, tempo) to spend; (investire) to invest; ~**rsi** vr to get a job, obtain employment; **impie'gato, a** sm/f employee.

im'piego, ghi sm (uso) use; (occupazione) employment; (posto di lavoro) (regular) job, post; (ECON) investment.

impieto'sire vt to move to pity; ~**rsi** vr to be moved to pity.

impie'trire vt (fig) to petrify.

impigli'are [impiʎ'ʎare] vt to catch, entangle; ~**rsi** vr to get caught up o entangled.

impi'grire vt to make lazy // vi (anche: ~**rsi**) to grow lazy.

impli'care vt to imply; (coinvolgere) to involve; ~**rsi** vr: ~**rsi (in)** to become involved (in); **implicazi'one** sf implication.

im'plicito, a [im'plitʃito] ag implicit.

impolve'rare vt to cover with dust; ~**rsi** vr to get dusty.

impo'nente ag imposing, impressive.

impo'nibile ag taxable // sm taxable income.

impopo'lare ag unpopular.

im'porre vt (imporre; (costringere) to force, make; (far valere) to impose, enforce; **imporsi** vr (persona) to assert o.s.; (cosa: rendersi necessario) to become necessary; (aver successo: moda, attore) to become popular; ~ **a qn di fare** to force sb to do, make sb do.

impor'tante ag important; **impor'tanza** sf importance; **dare importanza a qc** to attach importance to sth; **darsi importanza** to give o.s. airs.

impor'tare vt (introdurre dall'estero) to import // vi to matter, be important // vb impers (essere necessario) to be necessary; (interessare) to matter; **non importa!** it doesn't matter!; **non me ne importa!** I don't care!; **importazi'one** sf importation; (merci importate)

imports pl.

im'porto sm (total) amount.

importu'nare vt to bother.

impor'tuno, a ag irksome, annoying.

imposizi'one [impozit'tsjone] sf imposition; order, command; (onere, imposta) tax.

imposses'sarsi vr: ~ **di** to seize, take possession of.

impos'sibile ag impossible; **fare l'**~ to do one's utmost, do all one can; **impossibilità** sf impossibility; **essere nell'impossibilità di fare qc** to be unable to do sth.

im'posta sf (di finestra) shutter; (tassa) tax; ~ **sul reddito** income tax; ~ **sul valore aggiunto (I.V.A.)** value added tax (VAT) (Brit), sales tax (US).

impos'tare vt (imbucare) to post; (preparare) to plan, set out; (avviare) to begin, start off; (voce) to pitch.

im'posto, a pp di **imporre.**

impo'tente ag weak, powerless; (anche MED) impotent.

impove'rire vt to impoverish // vi (anche: ~**rsi**) to become poor.

imprati'cabile ag (strada) impassable; (campo da gioco) unplayable.

imprati'chire [imprati'kire] vt to train; ~**rsi in qc** to practise (Brit) o practice (US) sth.

impre'gnare [impreɲ'ɲare] vt: ~ **(di)** (imbevere) to soak o impregnate (with); (riempire: anche fig) to fill (with).

imprendi'tore sm (industriale) entrepreneur; (appaltatore) contractor; **piccolo** ~ small businessman.

im'presa sf (iniziativa) enterprise; (azione) exploit; (azienda) firm, concern.

impre'sario sm (TEATRO) manager, impresario; ~ **di pompe funebri** funeral director.

imprescin'dibile [impreʃʃin'dibile] ag not to be ignored.

impressio'nante ag impressive; upsetting.

impressio'nare vt to impress; (turbare) to upset; (FOT) to expose; ~**rsi** vr to be easily upset.

impressi'one sf impression; (fig: sensazione) sensation, feeling; (stampa) printing; **fare** ~ (colpire) to impress; (turbare) to frighten, upset; **fare buona/cattiva** ~ **a** to make a good/bad impression on.

im'presso, a pp di **imprimere.**

impres'tare vt: ~ **qc a qn** to lend sth to sb.

impreve'dibile ag unforeseeable; (persona) unpredictable.

imprevi'dente ag lacking in foresight.

impre'visto, a ag unexpected, unforeseen // sm unforeseen event; **salvo** ~**i** unless anything unexpected happens.

imprigio'nare [impridʒo'nare] *vt* to imprison.

im'primere *vt* (*anche fig*) to impress, stamp; (*comunicare: movimento*) to transmit, give.

impro'babile *ag* improbable, unlikely.

im'pronta *sf* imprint, impression, sign; (*di piede, mano*) print; (*fig*) mark, stamp; ~ **digitale** fingerprint.

impro'perio *sm* insult; ~**i** *smpl* abuse *sg*.

im'proprio, a *ag* improper; **arma** ~**a** offensive weapon.

improvvisa'mente *av* suddenly; unexpectedly.

improvvi'sare *vt* to improvise; ~**rsi** *vr*: ~**rsi cuoco** to (decide to) act as cook; **improvvi'sata** *sf* (pleasant) surprise.

improv'viso, a *ag* (*imprevisto*) unexpected; (*subitaneo*) sudden; **all'**~ unexpectedly; suddenly.

impru'dente *ag* unwise, rash.

impu'dente *ag* impudent.

impu'dico, a, chi, che *ag* immodest.

impu'gnare [impuɲ'ɲare] *vt* to grasp, grip; (*DIR*) to contest; **impugna'tura** *sf* grip, grasp; (*manico*) handle; (: *di spada*) hilt.

impul'sivo, a *ag* impulsive.

im'pulso *sm* impulse.

impun'tarsi *vr* to stop dead, refuse to budge; (*fig*) to be obstinate.

impu'tare *vt* (*ascrivere*): ~ **qc a** to attribute sth to; (*DIR: accusare*): ~ **qn di** to charge sb with, accuse sb of; **impu'tato, a** *sm/f* (*DIR*) accused, defendant; **imputazi'one** *sf* (*DIR*) charge.

imputri'dire *vi* to rot.

in (*in + il* = **nel**, *in + lo* = **nello**, *in + l'* = **nell'**, *in + la* = **nella**, *in + i* = **nei**, *in + gli* = **negli**, *in + le* = **nelle**) *prep* **1** (*stato in luogo*) in; **vivere** ~ **Italia/città** to live in Italy/town; **essere** ~ **casa/ufficio** to be at home/the office; **se fossi** ~ **te** if I were you
2 (*moto a luogo*) to; (: *dentro*) into; **andare** ~ **Germania/città** to go to Germany/town; **andare** ~ **ufficio** to go to the office; **entrare** ~ **macchina/casa** to get into the car/go into the house
3 (*tempo*) in; **nel 1989** in 1989; ~ **giugno/estate** in June/summer
4 (*modo, maniera*) in; ~ **silenzio** in silence; ~ **abito da sera** in evening dress; ~ **guerra** at war; ~ **vacanza** on holiday; **Maria Bianchi** ~ **Rossi** Maria Rossi née Bianchi
5 (*mezzo*) by; **viaggiare** ~ **autobus/treno** to travel by bus/train
6 (*materia*) made of; ~ **marmo** made of marble, marble *cpd*; **una collana** ~ **oro** a gold necklace
7 (*misura*) in; **siamo** ~ **quattro** there are four of us; ~ **tutto** in all

8 (*fine*): **dare** ~ **dono** to give as a gift; **spende tutto** ~ **alcool** he spends all his money on drink; ~ **onore di** in honour of.

i'nabile *ag*: ~ **a** incapable of; (*fisicamente, MIL*) unfit for; **inabilità** *sf* incapacity.

inabi'tabile *ag* uninhabitable.

inacces'sibile [inattʃes'sibile] *ag* (*luogo*) inaccessible; (*persona*) unapproachable; (*mistero*) unfathomable.

inaccet'tabile [inattʃet'tabile] *ag* unacceptable.

ina'datto, a *ag*: ~ (**a**) unsuitable *o* unfit (for).

inadegu'ato, a *ag* inadequate.

inadempi'enza [inadem'pjentsa] *sf*: ~ (**a**) non-fulfilment (of).

inaffer'rabile *ag* elusive; (*concetto, senso*) difficult to grasp.

ina'lare *vt* to inhale.

inalbe'rare *vt* (*NAUT*) to hoist, raise; ~**rsi** *vr* (*fig*) to flare up, fly off the handle.

inalte'rabile *ag* unchangeable; (*colore*) fast, permanent; (*affetto*) constant.

inalte'rato, a *ag* unchanged.

inami'dato, a *ag* starched.

inani'mato, a *ag* inanimate; (*senza vita: corpo*) lifeless.

inappa'gabile *ag* insatiable.

inappel'labile *ag* (*decisione*) final, irrevocable; (*DIR*) final, not open to appeal.

inappe'tenza [inappe'tɛntsa] *sf* (*MED*) lack of appetite.

inappun'tabile *ag* irreproachable, flawless.

inar'care *vt* (*schiena*) to arch; (*sopracciglia*) to raise; ~**rsi** *vr* to arch.

inari'dire *vt* to make arid, dry up // *vi* (*anche*: ~**rsi**) to dry up, become arid.

inaspet'tato, a *ag* unexpected.

inas'prire *vt* (*disciplina*) to tighten up, make harsher; (*carattere*) to embitter; ~**rsi** *vr* to become harsher; to become bitter; to become worse.

inattac'cabile *ag* (*anche fig*) unassailable; (*alibi*) cast-iron.

inatten'dibile *ag* unreliable.

inat'teso, a *ag* unexpected.

inattu'abile *ag* impracticable.

inau'dito, a *ag* unheard of.

inaugu'rare *vt* to inaugurate, open; (*monumento*) to unveil.

inavve'duto, a *ag* careless, inadvertent.

inavver'tenza [inavver'tɛntsa] *sf* carelessness, inadvertence.

incagli'are [inkaʎ'ʎare] *vi* (*NAUT: anche*: ~**rsi**) to run aground.

incal'lito, a *ag* calloused; (*fig*) hardened, inveterate; (: *insensibile*) hard.

incal'zare [inkal'tsare] *vt* to follow *o* pursue closely; (*fig*) to press // *vi* (*urgere*) to be pressing; (*essere imminente*) to be imminent.

incame'rare vt (DIR) to expropriate.

incammi'nare vt (fig: avviare) to start up; ~rsi vr to set off.

incande'scente [inkandeʃˈʃɛnte] ag incandescent, white-hot.

incan'tare vt to enchant, bewitch; ~rsi vr (rimanere intontito) to be spellbound; to be in a daze; (meccanismo: bloccarsi) to jam; **incanta'tore, 'trice** ag enchanting, bewitching // smf enchanter/ enchantress; **incan'tesimo** sm spell, charm; **incan'tevole** ag charming, enchanting.

in'canto sm spell, charm, enchantment; (asta) auction; **come per ~** as if by magic; **mettere all'~** to put up for auction.

incanu'tire vi to go white.

inca'pace [inkaˈpatʃe] ag incapable; **incapacità** sf inability; (DIR) incapacity.

incapo'nirsi vr to be stubborn, be determined.

incap'pare vi: ~ in qc/qn (anche fig) to run into sth/sb.

incapricci'arsi [inkaprittʃˈarsi] vr: ~ di to take a fancy to o for.

incapsu'lare vt (dente) to crown.

incarce'rare [inkartʃeˈrare] vt to imprison.

incari'care vt: ~ qn di fare to give sb the responsibility of doing; ~rsi di to take care o charge of; **incari'cato, a** ag: incaricato (di) in charge (of), responsible (for) // smf delegate, representative; **professore incaricato** teacher with a temporary appointment; **incaricato d'affari** (POL) chargé d'affaires.

in'carico, chi sm task, job.

incar'nare vt to embody; ~rsi vr to be embodied; (REL) to become incarnate.

incarta'mento sm dossier, file.

incar'tare vt to wrap (in paper).

incas'sare vt (merce) to pack (in cases); (gemma: incastonare) to set; (ECON: riscuotere) to collect; (PUGILATO: colpi) to take, stand up to; **in'casso** sm cashing, encashment; (introito) takings pl.

incasto'nare vt to set; **incastona'tura** sf setting.

incas'trare vt to fit in, insert; (fig: intrappolare) to catch; ~rsi vr (combaciare) to fit together; (restare bloccato) to become stuck; **in'castro** sm slot, groove; (punto di unione) joint.

incate'nare vt to chain up.

incatra'mare vt to tar.

incatti'vire vt to make wicked; ~rsi vr to turn nasty.

in'cauto, a ag imprudent, rash.

inca'vare vt to hollow out; **inca'vato, a** ag hollow; (occhi) sunken; **in'cavo** sm hollow; (solco) groove.

incendi'are [intʃenˈdjare] vt to set fire to; ~rsi vr to catch fire, burst into flames.

incendi'ario, a [intʃenˈdjarjo] ag incendiary // smf arsonist.

in'cendio [inˈtʃendjo] sm fire.

incene'rire [intʃeneˈrire] vt to burn to ashes, incinerate; (cadavere) to cremate; ~rsi vr to be burnt to ashes.

in'censo [inˈtʃenso] sm incense.

incensu'rato, a [intʃensuˈrato] ag (DIR): **essere ~** to have a clean record.

incen'tivo [intʃenˈtivo] sm incentive.

incep'pare vt to obstruct, hamper; ~rsi vr to jam.

ince'rata [intʃeˈrata] sf (tela) tarpaulin; (impermeabile) oilskins pl.

incer'tezza [intʃerˈtettsa] sf uncertainty.

in'certo, a [inˈtʃerto] ag uncertain; (irresoluto) undecided, hesitating // sm uncertainty.

in'cetta [inˈtʃetta] sf buying up; **fare ~ di qc** to buy up sth.

inchi'esta [inˈkjɛsta] sf investigation, inquiry.

inchi'nare [inkiˈnare] vt to bow; ~rsi vr to bend down; (per riverenza) to bow; (: donna) to curtsy; **in'chino** sm bow; curtsy.

inchio'dare [inkjoˈdare] vt to nail (down); ~ **la macchina** (AUT) to jam on the brakes.

inchi'ostro [inˈkjɔstro] sm ink; ~ **simpatico** invisible ink.

inciam'pare [intʃamˈpare] vi to trip, stumble.

inci'ampo [inˈtʃampo] sm obstacle; **essere d'~ a qn** (fig) to be in sb's way.

inciden'tale [intʃidenˈtale] ag incidental.

inci'dente [intʃiˈdente] sm accident; ~ **d'auto** car accident.

inci'denza [intʃiˈdentsa] sf incidence; **avere una forte ~ su qc** to affect sth greatly.

in'cidere [inˈtʃidere] vi: ~ **su** to bear upon, affect // vt (tagliare incavando) to cut into; (ARTE) to engrave; to etch; (canzone) to record.

in'cinta [inˈtʃinta] ag f pregnant.

incipri'are [intʃiˈprjare] vt to powder.

in'circa [inˈtʃirka] av: **all'~** more or less, very nearly.

incisi'one [intʃiˈzjone] sf cut; (disegno) engraving; etching; (registrazione) recording; (MED) incision.

in'ciso, a [inˈtʃizo] pp di **incidere** // sm: **per ~** incidentally, by the way.

inci'vile [intʃiˈvile] ag uncivilized; (villano) impolite.

incivi'lire [intʃiviˈlire] vt to civilize.

incl. abbr (= incluso) encl.

incli'nare vt to tilt // vi (fig): ~ **a qc/a fare** to incline towards sth/doing; to tend towards sth/to do; ~rsi vr (barca) to list; (aereo) to bank; **incli'nato, a** ag sloping; **inclinazi'one** sf slope; (fig) inclination, tendency; **in'cline** ag: incline a inclined to.

in'cludere vt to include; (accludere) to enclose; **inclu'sivo, a** ag: inclusivo di inclusive of; **in'cluso, a** pp di **includere** // ag included; enclosed.

incoe'rente ag incoherent; (contraddittorio) inconsistent.

in'cognito, a [in'kɔɲɲito] ag unknown // sm: in ~ incognito // sf (MAT, fig) unknown quantity.

incol'lare vt to glue, gum; (unire con colla) to stick together.

incolon'nare vt to draw up in columns.

inco'lore ag colourless.

incol'pare vt: ~ qn di to charge sb with.

in'colto, a ag (terreno) uncultivated; (trascurato: capelli) neglected; (persona) uneducated.

in'colume ag safe and sound, unhurt.

in'combere vi (sovrastare minacciando): ~ su to threaten, hang over.

incominci'are [inkomin'tʃare] vi, vt to begin, start.

in'comodo, a ag uncomfortable; (inopportuno) inconvenient // sm inconvenience, bother.

incompe'tente ag incompetent.

incompi'uto, a ag unfinished, incomplete.

incom'pleto, a ag incomplete.

incompren'sibile ag incomprehensible.

incom'preso, a ag not understood; misunderstood.

inconce'pibile [inkontʃe'pibile] ag inconceivable.

inconcili'abile [inkontʃi'ljabile] ag irreconcilable.

inconclu'dente ag inconclusive; (persona) ineffectual.

incondizio'nato, a [inkondittsjo'nato] ag unconditional.

inconfu'tabile ag irrefutable.

incongru'ente ag inconsistent.

in'congruo, a ag incongruous.

inconsa'pevole ag: ~ di unaware of, ignorant of.

in'conscio, a, sci, sce [in'kɔnʃo] ag unconscious // sm (PSIC): l'~ the unconscious.

inconsis'tente ag insubstantial; unfounded.

inconsu'eto, a ag unusual.

incon'sulto, a ag rash.

incon'trare vt to meet; (difficoltà) to meet with; ~rsi vr to meet.

incontras'tabile ag incontrovertible, indisputable.

in'contro av: ~ a (verso) towards // sm meeting; (SPORT) match; meeting; ~ di calcio football match.

inconveni'ente sm drawback, snag.

incoraggia'mento [inkoraddʒa'mento]

sm encouragement.

incoraggi'are [inkorad'dʒare] vt to encourage.

incornici'are [inkorni'tʃare] vt to frame.

incoro'nare vt to crown; **incoronazi'one** sf coronation.

incorpo'rare vt to incorporate; (fig: annettere) to annex.

in'correre vi: ~ in to meet with, run into.

incosci'ente [inkoʃ'ʃente] ag (inconscio) unconscious; (irresponsabile) reckless, thoughtless; **incosci'enza** sf unconsciousness; recklessness, thoughtlessness.

incre'dibile ag incredible, unbelievable.

in'credulo, a ag incredulous, disbelieving.

incremen'tare vt to increase; (dar sviluppo a) to promote.

incre'mento sm (sviluppo) development; (aumento numerico) increase, growth.

incres'parsi vr (acqua) to ripple; (capelli) to go frizzy; (pelle, tessuto) to wrinkle.

incrimi'nare vt (DIR) to charge.

incri'nare vt to crack; (fig: rapporti, amicizia) to cause to deteriorate; ~rsi vr to crack; to deteriora²e; **incrina'tura** sf crack; (fig) rift.

incroci'are [inkro'tʃare] vt to cross; (incontrare) to meet // vi (NAUT, AER) to cruise; ~rsi vr (strade) to cross, intersect; (persone, veicoli) to pass each other; ~ le braccia/le gambe to fold one's arms/cross one's legs; **incrocia'tore** sm cruiser.

in'crocio [in'krotʃo] sm (anche FERR) crossing; (di strade) crossroads.

incros'tare vt to encrust.

incuba'trice [inkuba'tritʃe] sf incubator.

'incubo sm nightmare.

in'cudine sf anvil.

incu'rante ag: ~ (di) heedless (of), careless (of).

incurio'sire vt to make curious; ~rsi vr to become curious.

incursi'one sf raid.

incur'vare vt, ~rsi vr to bend, curve.

in'cusso, a pp di **incutere**.

incusto'dito, a ag unguarded, unattended.

in'cutere vt to arouse; ~ timore/rispetto a qn to strike fear into sb/command sb's respect.

'indaco sm indigo.

indaffa'rato, a ag busy.

inda'gare vt to investigate.

in'dagine [in'dadʒine] sf investigation, inquiry; (ricerca) research, study.

indebi'tarsi vr to run o get into debt.

in'debito, a ag undue; undeserved.

indebo'lire vt, vi (anche: ~rsi) to weaken.

inde'cente [inde'tʃɛnte] *ag* indecent;
inde'cenza *sf* indecency.

inde'ciso, a [inde'tʃizo] *ag* indecisive;
(*irresoluto*) undecided.

inde'fesso, a *ag* untiring, indefatigable.

indefi'nito, a *ag* (*anche* LING) indefinite; (*impreciso, non determinato*)
undefined.

in'degno, a [in'deɲɲo] *ag* (*atto*) shameful; (*persona*) unworthy.

indelica'tezza [indelika'tettsa] *sf*
tactlessness.

indemoni'ato, a *ag* possessed (by the
devil).

in'denne *ag* unhurt, uninjured;
indennità *sf inv* (*rimborso: di spese*)
allowance; (: *di perdita*) compensation,
indemnity; **indennità di contingenza**
cost-of-living allowance; **indennità di tra-
sferta** travel expenses *pl*.

indenniz'zare [indennid'dzare] *vt* to
compensate; **inden'nizzo** *sm* (*somma*)
compensation, indemnity.

indero'gabile *ag* binding.

'India *sf*: l'~ India; **indi'ano, a** *ag* Indian // *sm/f* (*d'India*) Indian; (*d'America*) Red Indian.

indiavo'lato, a *ag* possessed (by the
devil); (*vivace, violento*) wild.

indi'care *vt* (*mostrare*) to show, indicate; (: *col dito*) to point to, point out;
(*consigliare*) to suggest, recommend;
indica'tivo, a *ag* indicative // *sm* (LING)
indicative (mood); **indica'tore** *sm*
(*elenco*) guide; directory; (TECN)
gauge; indicator; . **cartello indicatore**
sign; **indicatore di velocità** (AUT)
speedometer; **indicatore della benzina**
fuel gauge; **indicazi'one** *sf* indication;
(*informazione*) piece of information;
indicazioni per l'uso instructions for use.

'indice ['inditʃe] *sm* (ANAT: *dito*) index
finger, forefinger; (*lancetta*) needle,
pointer; (*fig: indizio*) sign; (TECN, MAT,
nei libri) index; ~ **di gradimento**
(RADIO, TV) popularity rating.

indi'cibile [indi'tʃibile] *ag* inexpressible.

indietreggi'are [indietred'dʒare] *vi* to
draw back, retreat.

indi'etro *av* back; (*guardare*) behind,
back; (*andare, cadere: anche*: **all'~**)
backwards; **rimanere ~** to be left
behind; **essere ~** (*col lavoro*) to be
behind; (*orologio*) to be slow; **rimandare
qc ~** to send sth back.

indi'feso, a *ag* (*città etc*) undefended;
(*persona*) defenceless.

indiffe'rente *ag* indifferent; **indiffe'-
renza** *sf* indifference.

in'digeno, a [in'didʒeno] *ag* indigenous,
native // *sm/f* native.

indi'gente [indi'dʒɛnte] *ag* poverty-
stricken, destitute; **indi'genza** *sf*
extreme poverty.

indigesti'one [indidʒes'tjone] *sf* indiges-

tion.

indi'gesto, a [indi'dʒɛsto] *ag* indigestible.

indi'gnare [indiɲ'ɲare] *vt* to fill with in-
dignation; **~rsi** *vr* to be (*o* get) indignant.

indimenti'cabile *ag* unforgettable.

indipen'dente *ag* independent;
indipen'denza *sf* independence.

in'dire *vt* (*concorso*) to announce;
(*elezioni*) to call.

indi'retto, a *ag* indirect.

indiriz'zare [indirit'tsare] *vt* (*dirigere*) to
direct; (*mandare*) to send; (*lettera*) to
address.

indi'rizzo [indi'rittso] *sm* address; (*direzione*) direction; (*avvio*) trend, course.

indis'creto, a *ag* indiscreet.

indis'cusso, a *ag* unquestioned.

indispen'sabile *ag* indispensable,
essential.

indispet'tire *vt* to irritate, annoy // *vi*
(*anche*: **~rsi**) to get irritated *o* annoyed.

in'divia *sf* endive.

individu'ale *ag* individual; **individualità** *sf* individuality.

individu'are *vt* (*dar forma distinta a*) to
characterize; (*determinare*) to locate;
(*riconoscere*) to single out.

indi'viduo *sm* individual.

indizi'are [indit'tsjare] *vt*: ~ **qn di qc** to
cast suspicion on sb for sth; **indizi'ato,
a** *ag* suspected // *sm/f* suspect.

in'dizio [in'dittsjo] *sm* (*segno*) sign, indication; (POLIZIA) clue; (DIR) piece of
evidence.

'indole *sf* nature, character.

indolen'zito, a [indolen'tsito] *ag* stiff,
aching; (*intorpidito*) numb.

indo'lore *ag* painless.

indo'mani *sm*: l'~ the next day, the
following day.

Indo'nesia *sf*: l'~ Indonesia.

indos'sare *vt* (*mettere indosso*) to put
on; (*avere indosso*) to have on;
indossa'tore, 'trice *sm/f* model.

in'dotto, a *pp di* **indurre**.

indottri'nare *vt* to indoctrinate.

indovi'nare *vt* (*scoprire*) to guess;
(*immaginare*) to imagine, guess; (*il
futuro*) to foretell; **indovi'nato, a** *ag*
successful; (*scelta*) inspired; **indovi'-
nello** *sm* riddle; **indo'vino, a** *sm/f* for-
tuneteller.

indubbia'mente *av* undoubtedly.

in'dubbio, a *ag* certain, undoubted.

indugi'are [indu'dʒare] *vi* to take one's
time, delay.

in'dugio [in'dudʒo] *sm* (*ritardo*) delay;
senza ~ without delay.

indul'gente [indul'dʒɛnte] *ag* indulgent;
(*giudice*) lenient; **indul'genza** *sf* in-
dulgence; leniency.

in'dulgere [in'duldʒere] *vi*: ~ **a**
(*accondiscendere*) to comply with;

(*abbandonarsi*) to indulge in; **in'dulto, a** *pp di* **indulgere** // *sm* (*DIR*) pardon.

indu'mento *sm* article of clothing, garment; ~**i** *smpl* clothes.

indu'rire *vt* to harden // *vi* (*anche:* ~**rsi**) to harden, become hard.

in'durre *vt*: ~ qn a fare qc to induce o persuade sb to do sth; ~ qn in errore to mislead sb.

in'dustria *sf* industry; **industri'ale** *ag* industrial // *sm* industrialist.

industri'arsi *vr* to do one's best, try hard.

industri'oso, a *ag* industrious, hardworking.

induzi'one [indut'tsjone] *sf* induction.

inebe'tito, a *ag* dazed, stunned.

inebri'are (*anche fig*) *vt* to intoxicate; ~**rsi** *vr* to become intoxicated.

inecce'pibile [inettʃe'pibile] *ag* unexceptionable.

i'nedia *sf* starvation.

i'nedito, a *ag* unpublished.

ineffi'cace [ineffi'katʃe] *ag* ineffective.

inneffici'ente [ineffi'tʃɛnte] *ag* inefficient.

inegu'ale *ag* unequal; (*irregolare*) uneven.

ine'rente *ag*: ~ a concerning, regarding.

i'nerme *ag* unarmed; defenceless.

inerpi'carsi *vr*: ~ (su) to clamber (up).

i'nerte *ag* inert; (*inattivo*) indolent, sluggish; **i'nerzia** *sf* inertia; indolence, sluggishness.

ine'satto, a *ag* (*impreciso*) inexact; (*erroneo*) incorrect; (*AMM: non riscosso*) uncollected.

inesis'tente *ag* non-existent.

inesperi'enza [inespe'rjɛntsa] *sf* inexperience.

ines'perto, a *ag* inexperienced.

i'netto, a *ag* (*incapace*) inept; (*che non ha attitudine*): ~ (a) unsuited (to).

ine'vaso, a *ag* (*ordine, corrispondenza*) outstanding.

inevi'tabile *ag* inevitable.

i'nezia [i'nɛttsja] *sf* trifle, thing of no importance.

infagot'tare *vt* to bundle up, wrap up; ~**rsi** *vr* to wrap up.

infal'libile *ag* infallible.

infa'mare *vt* to defame.

in'fame *ag* infamous; (*fig: cosa, compito*) awful, dreadful.

infan'tile *ag* child *cpd*; childlike; (*adulto, azione*) childish; **letteratura** ~ children's books *pl*.

in'fanzia [in'fantsja] *sf* childhood; (*bambini*) children *pl*; **prima** ~ babyhood, infancy.

infari'nare *vt* to cover with (o sprinkle with o dip in) flour; ~ **di zucchero** to sprinkle with sugar; **infarina'tura** *sf* (*fig*) smattering.

in'farto *sm* (*MED*): ~ (**cardiaco**) coronary.

infasti'dire *vt* to annoy, irritate; ~**rsi** *vr* to get annoyed o irritated.

infati'cabile *ag* tireless, untiring.

in'fatti *cong* as a matter of fact, in fact, actually.

infatu'arsi *vr*: ~ di o per to become infatuated with, fall for; **infatuazi'one** *sf* infatuation.

in'fausto, a *ag* unpropitious, unfavourable.

infe'condo, a *ag* infertile.

infe'dele *ag* unfaithful; **infedeltà** *sf* infidelity.

infe'lice [infe'litʃe] *ag* unhappy; (*sfortunato*) unlucky, unfortunate; (*inopportuno*) inopportune, ill-timed; (*mal riuscito: lavoro*) bad, poor; **infelicità** *sf* unhappiness.

inferi'ore *ag* lower; (*per intelligenza, qualità*) inferior // *sm/f* inferior; ~ a (*numero, quantità*) less o smaller than; (*meno buono*) inferior to; ~ **alla media** below average; **inferiorità** *sf* inferiority.

inferme'ria *sf* infirmary; (*di scuola, nave*) sick bay.

infermi'ere, a *sm/f* nurse.

infermità *sf inv* illness; infirmity.

in'fermo, a *ag* (*ammalato*) ill; (*debole*) infirm.

infer'nale *ag* infernal; (*proposito, complotto*) diabolical.

in'ferno *sm* hell.

inferri'ata *sf* grating.

infervo'rare *vt* to arouse enthusiasm in; ~**rsi** *vr* to get excited, get carried away.

infet'tare *vt* to infect; ~**rsi** *vr* to become infected; **infet'tivo, a** *ag* infectious; **in'fetto, a** *ag* infected; (*acque*) polluted, contaminated; **infezi'one** *sf* infection.

infiac'chire [infjak'kire] *vt* to weaken // *vi* (*anche:* ~**rsi**) to grow weak.

infiam'mabile *ag* inflammable.

infiam'mare *vt* to set alight; (*fig*, *MED*) to inflame; ~**rsi** *vr* to catch fire; (*MED*) to become inflamed; (*fig*): ~**rsi di** to be fired with; **infiammazi'one** *sf* (*MED*) inflammation.

in'fido, a *ag* unreliable, treacherous.

infie'rire *vi*: ~ **su** (*fisicamente*) to attack furiously; (*verbalmente*) to rage at; (*epidemia*) to rage over.

in'figgere [in'fiddʒere] *vt*: ~ qc in to thrust o drive sth into.

infi'lare *vt* (*ago*) to thread; (*mettere: chiave*) to insert; (: *anello, vestito*) to slip o put on; (*strada*) to turn into, take; ~**rsi** *vr*: ~**rsi in** to slip into; (*indossare*) to slip on; ~ **l'uscio** to slip in; to slip out.

infil'trarsi *vr* to penetrate, seep through; (*MIL*) to infiltrate; **infiltrazi'one** *sf* infiltration.

infil'zare [infil'tsare] *vt* (*infilare*) to string together; (*trafiggere*) to pierce.

'infimo, a *ag* lowest.

in'fine av finally; (insomma) in short.

infinità sf infinity; (in quantità): **un'~ di** an infinite number of.

infi'nito, a ag infinite; (LING) infinitive // sm infinity; (LING) infinitive; **all'~** (senza fine) endlessly.

infinocchi'are [infinok'kjare] vt (fam) to hoodwink.

infischi'arsi [infis'kjarsi] vr: **~ di** not to care about.

in'fisso, a pp di **infiggere** // sm fixture; (di porta, finestra) frame.

infit'tire vt, vi (anche: **~rsi**) to thicken.

inflazi'one [inflat'tsjone] sf inflation.

in'fliggere [in'fliddʒere] vt to inflict; **in'flitto, a** pp di **infliggere**.

influ'ente ag influential; **influ'enza** sf influence; (MED) influenza, flu.

influ'ire vi: **~ su** to influence.

in'flusso sm influence.

infol'tire vt, vi to thicken.

infon'dato, a ag unfounded, groundless.

in'fondere vt: **~ qc in qn** to instill sth in sb.

infor'care vt to fork (up); (bicicletta, cavallo) to get on; (occhiali) to put on.

infor'mare vt to inform, tell; **~rsi** vr: **~rsi (di o su)** to inquire (about).

infor'matica sf computer science.

informa'tivo, a ag informative.

informa'tore sm informer.

informazi'one [informat'tsjone] sf piece of information; **~i** sfpl information sg; **chiedere un'~** to ask for (some) information.

in'forme ag shapeless.

informico'larsi, informico'lirsi vr to have pins and needles.

infor'tunio sm accident; **~ sul lavoro** industrial accident, accident at work.

infos'sarsi vr (terreno) to sink; (guance) to become hollow; **infos'sato, a** ag hollow; (occhi) deep-set; (: per malattia) sunken.

in'frangere [in'frandʒere] vt to smash; (fig: legge, patti) to break; **~rsi** vr to smash, break; **infran'gibile** ag unbreakable; **in'franto, a** pp di **infrangere** // ag broken.

infrazi'one [infrat'tsjone] sf: **~ a** breaking of, violation of.

infredda'tura sf slight cold.

infreddo'lito, a ag cold, chilled.

infruttu'oso, a ag fruitless.

infu'ori av out; **all'~** outwards; **all'~ di** (eccetto) except, with the exception of.

infuri'are vi to rage; **~rsi** vr to fly into a rage.

infusi'one sf infusion.

in'fuso, a pp di **infondere** // sm infusion; **~ di camomilla** camomile tea.

Ing. abbr = **ingegnere**.

ingabbi'are vt to cage.

ingaggi'are [ingad'dʒare] vt (assumere con compenso) to take on, hire; (SPORT)

to sign on; (MIL) to engage; **in'gaggio** sm hiring; signing on.

ingan'nare vt to deceive; (coniuge) to be unfaithful to; (fisco) to cheat; (eludere) to dodge, elude; (fig: tempo) to while away // vi (apparenza) to be deceptive; **~rsi** vr to be mistaken, be wrong; **ingan'nevole** ag deceptive.

in'ganno sm deceit, deception; (azione) trick; (menzogna, frode) cheat, swindle; (illusione) illusion.

ingarbugli'are [ingarbuʎ'ʎare] vt to tangle; (fig) to confuse, muddle; **~rsi** vr to become confused o muddled.

inge'gnarsi [indʒen'narsi] vr to do one's best, try hard; **~ per vivere** to live by one's wits.

inge'gnere [indʒen'ɲere] sm engineer; **~ civile/navale** civil/naval engineer; **ingegne'ria** sf engineering.

in'gegno [in'dʒeɲɲo] sm (intelligenza) intelligence, brains pl; (capacità creativa) ingenuity; (disposizione) talent; **inge'gnoso, a** ag ingenious, clever.

ingelo'sire [indʒelo'zire] vt to make jealous // vi (anche: **~rsi**) to become jealous.

in'gente [in'dʒɛnte] ag huge, enormous.

ingenuità [indʒenui'ta] sf ingenuousness.

in'genuo, a [in'dʒɛnuo] ag ingenuous, naïve.

inges'sare [indʒes'sare] vt (MED) to put in plaster; **ingessa'tura** sf plaster.

Inghil'terra [ingil'tɛrra] sf: **l'~** England.

inghiot'tire [ingjot'tire] vt to swallow.

ingial'lire [indʒal'lire] vi to go yellow.

ingigan'tire [indʒigan'tire] vt to enlarge, magnify // vi to become gigantic o enormous.

inginocchi'arsi [indʒinok'kjarsi] vr to kneel (down).

ingiù [in'dʒu] av down, downwards.

ingi'uria [in'dʒurja] sf insult; (fig: danno) damage; **ingiuri'are** vt to insult, abuse; **ingiuri'oso, a** ag insulting, abusive.

ingius'tizia [indʒus'tittsja] sf injustice.

ingi'usto, a [in'dʒusto] ag unjust, unfair.

in'glese ag English // sm/f Englishman/ woman // sm (LING) English; **gli I~i** the English; **andarsene o filare all'~** to take French leave.

ingoi'are vt to gulp (down); (fig) to swallow (up).

ingol'fare vt, **~rsi** vr (motore) to flood.

ingom'brare vt (strada) to block; (stanza) to clutter up; **in'gombro, a** ag (strada, passaggio) blocked // sm obstacle; **essere d'ingombro** to be in the way.

in'gordo, a ag: **~ di** greedy for; (fig) greedy o avid for.

ingor'garsi vr to be blocked up, be choked up.

in'gorgo, ghi *sm* blockage, obstruction; *(anche:* ~ *stradale)* traffic jam.

ingoz'zare [ingot'tsare] *vt (animali)* to fatten; *(fig: persona)* to stuff; **~rsi** *vr:* **~rsi (di)** to stuff o.s. (with).

ingra'naggio [ingra'naddʒo] *sm (TECN)* gear; *(di orologio)* mechanism; **gli ~i della burocrazia** the bureaucratic machinery.

ingra'nare *vi* to mesh, engage // *vt* to engage; ~ **la marcia** to get into gear.

ingrandi'mento *sm* enlargement; extension.

ingran'dire *vt (anche FOT)* to enlarge; *(estendere)* to extend; *(OTTICA, fig)* to magnify // *vi (anche:* **~rsi)** to become larger o bigger; *(aumentare)* to grow, increase; *(espandersi)* to expand.

ingras'sare *vt* to make fat; *(animali)* to fatten; *(AGR: terreno)* to manure; *(lubrificare)* to oil, lubricate // *vi (anche:* **~rsi)** to get fat, put on weight.

in'grato, a *ag* ungrateful; *(lavoro)* thankless, unrewarding.

ingrazi'are [ingrat'tsjare] *vt:* **~rsi qn** to ingratiate o.s. with sb.

ingredi'ente *sm* ingredient.

in'gresso *sm (porta)* entrance; *(atrio)* hall; *(l'entrare)* entrance, entry; *(facoltà di entrare)* admission; **"~ libero"** "admission free".

ingros'sare *vt* to increase; *(folla, livello)* to swell // *vi (anche:* **~rsi)** to increase; to swell.

in'grosso *av:* **all'~** *(COMM)* wholesale; *(all'incirca)* roughly, about.

ingual'cibile [ingwal'tʃibile] *ag* crease-resistant.

ingua'ribile *ag* incurable.

'inguine *sm (ANAT)* groin.

ini'bire *vt* to forbid, prohibit; *(PSIC)* to inhibit; **inibizi'one** *sf* prohibition; inhibition.

iniet'tare *vt* to inject; **~rsi** *vr:* **~rsi di sangue** *(occhi)* to become bloodshot; **iniezi'one** *sf* injection.

inimi'carsi *vr:* ~ **con qn** to fall out with sb.

inimi'cizia [inimi'tʃittsja] *sf* animosity.

ininter'rotto, a *ag* unbroken; uninterrupted.

iniquità *sf inv* iniquity; *(atto)* wicked action.

inizi'ale [init'tsjale] *ag, sf* initial.

inizi'are [init'tsjare] *vi, vt* to begin, start; ~ **qn a** to initiate sb into; *(pittura etc)* to introduce sb to; ~ **a fare qc** to start doing sth.

inizia'tiva [inittsja'tiva] *sf* initiative; ~ **privata** private enterprise.

i'nizio [i'nittsjo] *sm* beginning; **all'~** at the beginning, at the start; **dare ~ a qc** to start sth, get sth going.

innaffi'are *etc* = **annaffiare** *etc*.

innal'zare [innal'tsare] *vt (sollevare,* *alzare)* to raise; *(rizzare)* to erect; **~rsi** *vr* to rise.

innamo'rare *vt* to enchant, charm; **~rsi** *vr:* **~rsi (di qn)** to fall in love (with sb); **innamo'rato, a** *ag (che nutre amore):* **innamorato (di)** in love (with); *(appassionato):* **innamorato di** very fond of // *sm/f* lover; sweetheart.

in'nanzi [in'nantsi] *av (stato in luogo)* in front, ahead; *(moto a luogo)* forward, on; *(tempo: prima)* before // *prep (prima)* before; ~ **a** in front of.

in'nato, a *ag* innate.

innatu'rale *ag* unnatural.

inne'gabile *ag* undeniable.

innervo'sire *vt* ~ **qn** to get on sb's nerves; **~rsi** *vr* to get irritated o upset.

innes'care *vt* to prime; **in'nesco, schi** *sm* primer.

innes'tare *vt (BOT, MED)* to graft; *(TECN)* to engage; *(inserire: presa)* to insert; **in'nesto** *sm* graft; grafting q; *(TECN)* clutch; *(ELETTR)* connection.

'inno *sm* hymn; ~ **nazionale** national anthem.

inno'cente [inno'tʃɛnte] *ag* innocent; **inno'cenza** *sf* innocence.

in'nocuo, a *ag* innocuous, harmless.

inno'vare *vt* to change, make innovations in.

innume'revole *ag* innumerable.

ino'doro, a *ag* odourless.

inol'trare *vt (AMM)* to pass on, forward; **~rsi** *vr (addentrarsi)* to advance, go forward.

i'noltre *av* besides, moreover.

inon'dare *vt* to flood; **inondazi'one** *sf* flooding q; flood.

inope'roso, a *ag* inactive, idle.

inoppor'tuno, a *ag* untimely, ill-timed; inappropriate; *(momento)* inopportune.

inorgo'glire [inorgoʎ'ʎire] *vt* to make proud // *vi (anche:* **~rsi)** to become proud; **~rsi di qc** to pride o.s. on sth.

inorri'dire *vt* to horrify // *vi* to be horrified.

inospi'tale *ag* inhospitable.

inosser'vato, a *ag (non notato)* unobserved; *(non rispettato)* not observed, not kept.

inossi'dabile *ag* stainless.

inqua'drare *vt (foto, immagine)* to frame; *(fig)* to situate, set.

inquie'tare *vt (turbare)* to disturb, worry; **~rsi** *vr* to worry, become anxious; *(impazientirsi)* to get upset.

inqui'eto, a *ag* restless; *(preoccupato)* worried, anxious; **inquie'tudine** *sf* anxiety, worry.

inqui'lino, a *sm/f* tenant.

inquina'mento *sm* pollution.

inqui'nare *vt* to pollute.

inqui'sire *vt, vi* to investigate; **inquisi'tore, 'trice** *ag (sguardo)* inquiring; **inquisizi'one** *sf (STORIA)* inquisition.

insabbi'are vt (fig: pratica) to shelve; ~**rsi** vr (arenarsi: barca) to run aground; (fig: pratica) to be shelved.

insac'cati smpl (CUC) sausages.

insa'lata sf salad; ~ **mista** mixed salad; **insalati'era** sf salad bowl.

insa'lubre ag unhealthy.

insa'nabile ag (piaga) which cannot be healed; (situazione) irremediable; (odio) implacable.

insangui'nare vt to stain with blood.

insa'puta sf: **all'**~ **di qn** without sb knowing.

insce'nare [inʃe'nare] vt (TEATRO) to stage, put on; (fig) to stage.

insedi'are vt to install; ~**rsi** vr to take up office; (popolo, colonia) to settle.

in'segna [in'seɲɲa] sf sign; (emblema) sign, emblem; (bandiera) flag, banner; ~**e** sfpl (decorazioni) insignia pl.

insegna'mento [inseɲɲa'mento] sm teaching.

inse'gnante [inseɲ'ɲante] ag teaching // smf teacher.

inse'gnare [inseɲ'ɲare] vt, vi to teach; ~ **a qn qc** to teach sb sth; ~ **a qn a fare qc** to teach sb (how) to do sth.

insegui'mento sm pursuit, chase.

insegui're vt to pursue, chase.

inselvati'chire [inselvati'kire] vi (anche: ~**rsi**) to grow wild.

insena'tura sf inlet, creek.

insen'sato, a ag senseless, stupid.

insen'sibile ag (nervo) insensible; (persona) indifferent.

inse'rire vt to insert; (ELETTR) to connect; (allegare) to enclose; (annuncio) to put in, place; ~**rsi** vr (fig): ~**rsi in** to become part of; **in'serto** sm (pubblicazione) insert.

inservi'ente smf attendant.

inserzi'one [inser'tsjone] sf insertion; (avviso) advertisement; **fare un'**~ **sul giornale** to put an advertisement in the paper.

insetti'cida, i [insetti'tʃida] sm insecticide.

in'setto sm insect.

in'sidia sf snare, trap; (pericolo) hidden danger; **insidi'are** vt: ~ **la vita di qn** to make an attempt on sb's life.

insi'eme av together // prep: ~ **a** o **con** together with // sm whole; (MAT, servizio, assortimento) set; (MODA) ensemble, outfit; **tutti** ~ **all** together; **tutto** ~ **all** together; (in una volta) at one go; **nell'**~ **on** the whole; **d'**~ (veduta etc) overall.

insignifi'cante [insiɲɲifi'kante] ag insignificant.

insi'gnire [insiɲ'ɲire] vt: ~ **qn di** to honour o decorate sb with.

insin'cero, a [insin'tʃero] ag insincere.

insinda'cabile ag unquestionable.

insinu'are vt (introdurre): ~ **qc in** to slip o slide sth into; (fig) to insinuate, imply; ~**rsi** vr: ~**rsi in** to seep into; (fig) to creep into; to worm one's way into.

insis'tente ag insistent; persistent.

in'sistere vi: ~ **su qc** to insist on sth; ~ **in qc/a fare** (perseverare) to persist in sth/in doing; **insis'tito, a** pp di **insistere**.

insoddis'fatto, a ag dissatisfied.

insoffe'rente ag intolerant.

insolazi'one [insolat'tsjone] sf (MED) sunstroke.

inso'lente ag insolent; **insolen'tire** vi to grow insolent // vt to insult, be rude to.

in'solito, a ag unusual, out of the ordinary.

inso'luto, a ag (non risolto) unsolved; (non pagato) unpaid, outstanding.

insol'vibile ag insolvent.

in'somma av (in breve, in conclusione) in short; (dunque) well // escl for heaven's sake!

in'sonne ag sleepless; **in'sonnia** sf insomnia, sleeplessness.

insonno'lito, a ag sleepy, drowsy.

insoppor'tabile ag unbearable.

in'sorgere [in'sordʒere] vi (ribellarsi) to rise up, rebel; (apparire) to come up, arise.

in'sorto, a pp di **insorgere** // smf rebel, insurgent.

insospet'tire vt to make suspicious // vi (anche: ~**rsi**) to become suspicious.

inspi'rare vt to breathe in, inhale.

in'stabile ag (carico, indole) unstable; (tempo) unsettled; (equilibrio) unsteady.

instal'lare vt to install; ~**rsi** vr (sistemarsi): ~**rsi in** to settle in; **installazi'one** sf installation.

instan'cabile ag untiring, indefatigable.

instau'rare vt to introduce, institute.

instra'dare vt: ~ (verso) to direct (towards).

insuc'cesso [insut'tʃesso] sm failure, flop.

insudici'are [insudi'tʃare] vt to dirty; ~**rsi** vr to get dirty.

insuffici'ente [insuffi'tʃɛnte] ag insufficient; (compito, allievo) inadequate; **insuffici'enza** sf insufficiency; inadequacy; (INS) fail.

insu'lare ag insular.

insu'lina sf insulin.

in'sulso, a ag (sciocco) inane, silly; (persona) dull, insipid.

insul'tare vt to insult, affront.

in'sulto sm insult, affront.

insussis'tente ag non-existent.

intac'care vt (fare tacche) to cut into; (corrodere) to corrode; (fig: cominciare ad usare: risparmi) to break into; (: ledere) to damage.

intagli'are [intaʎˈʎare] *vt* to carve; **in'taglio** *sm* carving.

intan'gibile [intanˈdʒibile] *ag* untouchable; inviolable.

in'tanto *av* (*nel frattempo*) meanwhile, in the meantime; (*per cominciare*) just to begin with; ~ **che** *cong* while.

in'tarsio *sm* inlaying *q*, marquetry *q*; inlay.

inta'sare *vt* to choke (up), block (up); (*AUT*) to obstruct, block; ~**rsi** *vr* to become choked *o* blocked.

intas'care *vt* to pocket.

in'tatto, a *ag* intact; (*puro*) unsullied.

intavo'lare *vt* to start, enter into.

inte'grale *ag* complete; (*pane, farina*) wholemeal (*Brit*), whole-wheat (*US*); (*MAT*): **calcolo** ~ integral calculus.

inte'grante *ag*: **parte** ~ integral part.

inte'grare *vt* to complete; (*MAT*) to integrate; ~**rsi** *vr* (*persona*) to become integrated.

integrità *sf* integrity.

'integro, a *ag* (*intatto, intero*) complete, whole; (*retto*) upright.

intelaia'tura *sf* frame; (*fig*) structure, framework.

intel'letto *sm* intellect; **intellettu'ale** *ag*, *sm/f* intellectual.

intelli'gente [intelliˈdʒɛnte] *ag* intelligent; **intelli'genza** *sf* intelligence.

intem'perie *sfpl* bad weather *sg*.

intempes'tivo, a *ag* untimely.

inten'dente *sm*: ~ **di Finanza** inland (*Brit*) *o* internal (*US*) revenue officer; **inten'denza** *sf*: intendenza di Finanza inland (*Brit*) *o* internal (*US*) revenue office.

in'tendere *vt* (*avere intenzione*): ~ **fare qc** to intend *o* mean to do sth; (*comprendere*) to understand; (*udire*) to hear; (*significare*) to mean; ~**rsi** *vr* (*conoscere*): ~**rsi di** to know a lot about, be a connoisseur of; (*accordarsi*) to get on (well); **intendersela con qn** (*avere una relazione amorosa*) to have an affair with sb; **intendi'mento** *sm* (*intelligenza*) understanding; (*proposito*) intention; **intendi'tore, 'trice** *sm/f* connoisseur, expert.

intene'rire *vt* (*fig*) to move (to pity); ~**rsi** *vr* (*fig*) to be moved.

inten'sivo, a *ag* intensive.

in'tenso, a *ag* intense.

in'tento, a *ag* (*teso, assorto*): ~ **(a)** intent (on), absorbed (in) // *sm* aim, purpose.

intenzio'nale [intentsjoˈnale] *ag* intentional.

intenzi'one [intenˈtsjone] *sf* intention; (*DIR*) intent; **avere** ~ **di fare qc** to intend to do sth, have the intention of doing sth.

interca'lare *sm* pet phrase, stock phrase // *vt* to insert.

interca'pedine *sf* gap, cavity.

intercet'tare [intertʃetˈtare] *vt* to intercept.

inter'detto, a *pp di* **interdire** // *ag* forbidden, prohibited; (*sconcertato*) dumbfounded // *sm* (*REL*) interdict.

inter'dire *vt* to forbid, prohibit, ban; (*REL*) to interdict; (*DIR*) to deprive of civil rights; **interdizi'one** *sf* prohibition, ban.

interessa'mento *sm* interest.

interes'sante *ag* interesting; **essere in stato** ~ to be expecting (a baby).

interes'sare *vt* to interest; (*concernere*) to concern, be of interest to; (*far intervenire*): ~ **qn a** to draw sb's attention to // *vi*: ~ **a** to interest, matter to; ~**rsi** *vr* (*mostrare interesse*): ~**rsi a** to take an interest in, be interested in; (*occuparsi*): ~**rsi di** to take care of.

inte'resse *sm* (*anche COMM*) interest.

inter'faccia, ce [interˈfattʃa] *sf* (*INFORM*) interface.

interfe'renza [interfeˈrentsa] *sf* interference.

interfe'rire *vi* to interfere.

interiezi'one [interjetˈtsjone] *sf* exclamation, interjection.

interi'ora *sfpl* entrails.

interi'ore *ag* interior, inner, inside, internal; (*fig*) inner.

inter'ludio *sm* (*MUS*) interlude.

inter'medio, a *ag* intermediate.

inter'mezzo [interˈmeddzo] *sm* (*intervallo*) interval; (*breve spettacolo*) intermezzo.

inter'nare *vt* (*arrestare*) to intern; (*MED*) to commit (to a mental institution).

internazio'nale [internattsjoˈnale] *ag* international.

in'terno, a *ag* (*di dentro*) internal, interior, inner; (*: mare*) inland; (*nazionale*) domestic; (*allievo*) boarding // *sm* inside, interior; (*di paese*) interior; (*fodera*) lining; (*di appartamento*) flat (number); (*TEL*) extension // *sm/f* (*INS*) boarder; ~**i** *smpl* (*CINEMA*) interior shots; **all'~** inside; **Ministero degli I~i** Ministry of the Interior, ≈ Home Office (*Brit*), Department of the Interior (*US*).

in'tero, a *ag* (*integro, intatto*) whole, entire; (*completo, totale*) complete; (*numero*) whole; (*non ridotto: biglietto*) full.

interpel'lare *vt* to consult.

inter'porre *vt* (*ostacolo*): ~ **qc a qc** to put sth in the way of sth; (*influenza*) to use; ~ **appello** (*DIR*) to appeal; **interporsi** *vr* to intervene; **interporsi fra** (*mettersi in mezzo*) to come between; **inter'posto, a** *pp di* **interporre**.

interpre'tare *vt* to interpret; **in'terprete** *sm/f* interpreter; (*TEATRO*) actor/actress, performer; (*MUS*) performer.

interro'gare vt to question; (INS) to test; **interroga'tivo, a** ag (occhi, sguardo) questioning, inquiring; (LING) interrogative // sm question; (fig) mystery; **interroga'torio, a** ag interrogatory, questioning // sm (DIR) questioning q; **interrogazi'one** sf questioning q; (INS) oral test.

inter'rompere vt to interrupt; (studi, trattative) to break off, interrupt; ~rsi vr to break off, stop; **inter'rotto, a** pp di **interrompere**.

interrut'tore sm switch.

interruzi'one [interrut'tsjone] sf interruption; break.

interse'care vt, ~rsi vr to intersect.

inter'stizio [inter'stittsjo] sm interstice, crack.

interur'bano, a ag inter-city; (TEL: chiamata) trunk cpd, long-distance; (: telefono) long-distance // sf trunk call, long-distance call.

inter'vallo sm interval; (spazio) space, gap.

interve'nire vi (partecipare): ~ a to take part in; (intromettersi: anche POL) to intervene; (MED: operare) to operate; **inter'vento** sm participation; (intromissione) intervention; (MED) operation; **fare un intervento nel corso di** (dibattito, programma) to take part in.

inter'vista sf interview; **intervis'tare** vt to interview.

in'teso, a pp di **intendere** // ag agreed // sf understanding; (accordo) agreement, understanding; **non darsi per ~ di qc** to take no notice of sth.

intes'tare vt (lettera) to address; (proprietà): ~ a to register in the name of; ~ **un assegno a qn** to make out a cheque to sb; **intestazi'one** sf heading; (su carta da lettere) letterhead; (registrazione) registration.

intes'tino, a ag (lotte) internal, civil // sm (ANAT) intestine.

inti'mare vt to order, command; **intimazi'one** sf order, command.

intimi'dire vt to intimidate // vi (anche: ~rsi) to grow shy.

intimità sf intimacy; privacy; (familiarità) familiarity.

'intimo, a ag intimate; (affetti, vita) private; (fig: profondo) inmost // sm (persona) intimate o close friend; (dell'animo) bottom, depths pl; **parti ~e** (ANAT) private parts.

intimo'rire vt to frighten; ~rsi vr to become frightened.

in'tingolo sm sauce; (pietanza) stew.

intiriz'zire [intirid'dzire] vt to numb // vi (anche: ~rsi) to go numb.

intito'lare vt to give a title to; (dedicare) to dedicate.

intolle'rabile ag intolerable.

intolle'rante ag intolerant.

in'tonaco, ci o **chi** sm plaster.

into'nare vt (canto) to start to sing; (armonizzare) to match; ~rsi vr (colori) to go together; ~rsi **a** (carnagione) to suit; (abito) to go with, match.

inton'tire vt to stun, daze // vi, ~rsi vr to be stunned o dazed.

in'toppo sm stumbling block, obstacle.

in'torno av around; ~ **a** prep (attorno a) around; (riguardo, circa) about.

intorpi'dire vt to numb; (fig) to make sluggish // vi (anche: ~rsi) to grow numb; (fig) to become sluggish.

intossi'care vt to poison; **intossicazi'one** sf poisoning.

intralci'are [intral'tʃare] vt to hamper, hold up.

intransi'tivo, a ag, sm intransitive.

intrapren'dente ag enterprising, go-ahead.

intra'prendere vt to undertake.

intrat'tabile ag intractable.

intratte'nere vt to entertain; to engage in conversation; ~rsi vr to linger; ~rsi **su qc** to dwell on sth.

intrave'dere vt to catch a glimpse of; (fig) to foresee.

intrecci'are [intret'tʃare] vt (capelli) to plait, braid; (intessere: anche fig) to weave, interweave, intertwine; ~rsi vr to intertwine, become interwoven; ~ **le mani** to clasp one's hands; **in'treccio** sm (fig: trama) plot, story.

intri'gare vi to manoeuvre (Brit), maneuver (US), scheme; **in'trigo, ghi** sm plot, intrigue.

in'trinseco, a, ci, che ag intrinsic.

in'triso, a ag: ~ **(di)** soaked (in).

intro'durre vt to introduce; (chiave etc): ~ **qc in** to insert sth into; (persone: far entrare) to show in; **introdursi** vr (moda, tecniche) to be introduced; **introdursi in** (persona: penetrare) to enter; (: entrare furtivamente) to steal o slip into; **introduzi'one** sf introduction.

in'troito sm income, revenue.

intro'mettersi vr to interfere, meddle; (interporsi) to intervene.

in'truglio [in'truʎʎo] sm concoction.

intrusi'one sf intrusion; interference.

in'truso, a sm/f intruder.

intu'ire vt to perceive by intuition; (rendersi conto) to realize; **in'tuito** sm intuition; (perspicacia) perspicacity; **intuizi'one** sf intuition.

inu'mano, a ag inhuman.

inumi'dire vt to dampen, moisten; ~rsi vr to become damp o wet.

i'nutile ag useless; (superfluo) pointless, unnecessary; **inutilità** sf uselessness; pointlessness.

inva'dente ag (fig) interfering, nosey.

in'vadere vt to invade; (affollare) to

swarm into, overrun; *(sog: acque)* to flood; **invadi'trice** *ag vedi* **invasore**.

inva'ghirsi [inva'girsi] *vr*: ~ **di** to take a fancy to.

invalidità *sf* infirmity; disability; *(DIR)* invalidity.

in'valido, a *ag (infermo)* infirm, invalid; *(al lavoro)* disabled; *(DIR: nullo)* invalid // *sm/f* invalid; disabled person.

in'vano *av* in vain.

invasi'one *sf* invasion.

in'vaso, a *pp di* **invadere**.

inva'sore, invadi'trice [invadi'tritʃe] *ag* invading // *sm* invader.

invecchi'are [invek'kjare] *vi (persona)* to grow old; *(vino, popolazione)* to age; *(moda)* to become dated // *vt* to age; *(far apparire più vecchio)* to make look older.

in'vece [in'vetʃe] *av* instead; *(al contrario)* on the contrary; ~ **di** *prep* instead of.

inve'ire *vi*: ~ **contro** to rail against.

inven'tare *vt* to invent; *(pericoli, pettegolezzi)* to make up, invent.

inven'tario *sm* inventory; *(COMM)* stocktaking *q*.

inven'tivo, a *ag* inventive // *sf* inventiveness.

inven'tore *sm* inventor.

invenzi'one [inven'tsjone] *sf* invention; *(bugia)* lie, story.

inver'nale *ag* winter *cpd*; *(simile all'inverno)* wintry.

in'verno *sm* winter.

invero'simile *ag* unlikely.

inversi'one *sf* inversion; reversal; "divieto d'~" *(AUT)* "no U-turns".

in'verso, a *ag* opposite; *(MAT)* inverse // *sm* contrary, opposite; **in senso** ~ in the opposite direction; **in ordine** ~ in reverse order.

inver'tire *vt* to invert, reverse; ~ **la marcia** *(AUT)* to do a U-turn; **inver'tito, a** *sm/f* homosexual.

investi'gare *vt, vi* to investigate; **investiga'tore, trice** *sm/f* investigator, detective; **investigazi'one** *sf* investigation, inquiry.

investi'mento *sm (ECON)* investment; *(scontro, urto)* crash, collision; *(incidente stradale)* road accident.

inves'tire *vt (denaro)* to invest; *(sog: veicolo: pedone)* to knock down; *(: altro veicolo)* to crash into; *(apostrofare)* to assail; *(incaricare)*: ~ **qn di** to invest sb with.

invi'are *vt* to send; **invi'ato, a** *sm/f* envoy; *(STAMPA)* correspondent.

in'vidia *sf* envy; **invidi'are** *vt*: ~ **qn (per qc)** to envy sb for sth; ~ **qc a qn** to envy sb sth; **invidi'oso, a** *ag* envious.

in'vio, 'vii *sm* sending; *(insieme di merci)* consignment.

invipe'rito, a *ag* furious.

invischi'are [invis'kjare] *vt (fig)*: ~ **qn in**

to involve sb in; ~rsi *vr*: ~rsi **(con qn/in qc)** to get mixed up *o* involved (with sb/in sth).

invi'sibile *ag* invisible.

invi'tare *vt* to invite; ~ **qn a fare** to invite sb to do; **invi'tato, a** *sm/f* guest; **in'vito** *sm* invitation.

invo'care *vt (chiedere: aiuto, pace)* to cry out for; *(appellarsi: la legge, Dio)* to appeal to, invoke.

invogli'are [invoʎ'ʎare] *vt*: ~ **qn a fare** to tempt sb to do, induce sb to do.

involon'tario, a *ag (errore)* unintentional; *(gesto)* involuntary.

invol'tino *sm (CUC)* roulade.

in'volto *sm (pacco)* parcel; *(fagotto)* bundle.

in'volucro *sm* cover, wrapping.

involuzi'one [involut'tsjone] *sf (di stile)* convolutedness; *(regresso)*: **subire un'~** to regress.

inzacche'rare [intsakke'rare] *vt* to spatter with mud.

inzup'pare [intsup'pare] *vt* to soak; ~rsi *vr* to get soaked.

'io *pronome* I // *sm inv*: **l'~** the ego, the self; ~ **stesso(a)** I myself.

i'odio *sm* iodine.

i'ogurt *sm inv* = **yoghurt**.

l'onio *sm*: **lo ~, il mar ~** the Ionian (Sea).

ipermer'cato *sm* hypermarket.

ipertensi'one *sf* high blood pressure, hypertension.

ip'nosi *sf* hypnosis; **ipno'tismo** *sm* hypnotism; **ipnotiz'zare** *vt* to hypnotize.

ipocri'sia *sf* hypocrisy.

i'pocrita, i, e *ag* hypocritical // *sm/f* hypocrite.

ipo'teca, che *sf* mortgage; **ipote'care** *vt* to mortgage.

i'potesi *sf inv* hypothesis; **ipo'tetico, a, ci, che** *ag* hypothetical.

'ippico, a, ci, che *ag* horse *cpd* // *sf* horseracing.

ippocas'tano *sm* horse chestnut.

ip'podromo *sm* racecourse.

ippo'potamo *sm* hippopotamus.

'ira *sf* anger, wrath.

l'ran *sm*: **l'~** Iran.

l'raq *sm*: **l'~** Iraq.

'iride *sf (arcobaleno)* rainbow; *(ANAT, BOT)* iris.

Ir'landa *sf*: **l'~** Ireland; **l'~ del Nord** Northern Ireland, Ulster; **la Repubblica d'~** Eire, the Republic of Ireland; **irlan'dese** *ag* Irish // *sm/f* Irishman/woman; **gli Irlandesi** the Irish.

iro'nia *sf* irony; **i'ronico, a, ci, che** *ag* ironic(al).

irradi'are *vt* to radiate; *(sog: raggi di luce: illuminare)* to shine on // *vi (diffondersi: anche)*: ~rsi to radiate; **irradiazi'one** *sf* radiation.

irragio'nevole [irradʒo'nevole] *ag* irrational; unreasonable.

irrazio'nale [irrattsjo'nale] *ag* irrational.

irre'ale *ag* unreal.

irrecupe'rabile *ag* irretrievable; (*fig: person*) irredeemable.

irrecu'sabile *ag* (*offerta*) not to be refused; (*prova*) irrefutable.

irrego'lare *ag* irregular; (*terreno*) uneven.

irremo'vibile *ag* (*fig*) unshakeable, unyielding.

irrepa'rabile *ag* irreparable; (*fig*) inevitable.

irrepe'ribile *ag* nowhere to be found.

irrequi'eto, a *ag* restless.

irresis'tibile *ag* irresistible.

irrespon'sabile *ag* irresponsible.

irridu'cibile [irridu'tʃibile] *ag* irreducible; (*fig*) indomitable.

irri'gare *vt* (*annaffiare*) to irrigate; (*sog: fiume etc*) to flow through; **irrigazi'one** *sf* irrigation.

irrigi'dire [irridʒi'dire] *vt*, ~**rsi** *vr* to stiffen.

irri'sorio, a *ag* derisory.

irri'tare *vt* (*mettere di malumore*) to irritate, annoy; (*MED*) to irritate; ~**rsi** *vr* (*stizzirsi*) to become irritated *o* annoyed; (*MED*) to become irritated; **irritazi'one** *sf* irritation; annoyance.

ir'rompere *vi*: ~ **in** to burst into.

irro'rare *vt* to sprinkle; (*AGR*) to spray.

irru'ente *ag* (*fig*) impetuous, violent.

irruzi'one [irrut'tsjone] *sf*: **fare ~ in** to burst into; (*sog: polizia*) to raid.

'irto, a *ag* bristly; ~ **di** bristling with.

is'critto, a *pp di* **iscrivere** // *sm/f* member; **per** *o* **in** ~ in writing.

is'crivere *vt* to register, enter; (*persona*): ~ **(a)** to register (in), enrol (in); ~**rsi** *vr*: ~**rsi (a)** (*club, partito*) to join; (*università*) to register *o* enrol (at); (*esame, concorso*) to register *o* enter (for); **iscrizi'one** *sf* (*epigrafe etc*) inscription; (*a scuola, società*) enrolment, registration; (*registrazione*) registration.

Is'lam *sm*: **l'~** Islam.

Is'landa *sf*: **l'~** Iceland.

'isola *sf* island; ~ **pedonale** (*AUT*) pedestrian precinct.

isola'mento *sm* isolation; (*TECN*) insulation.

iso'lante *ag* insulating // *sm* insulator.

iso'lare *vt* to isolate; (*TECN*) to insulate; (*: acusticamente*) to soundproof; **iso'lato, a** *ag* isolated; insulated // *sm* (*edificio*) block.

ispetto'rato *sm* inspectorate.

ispet'tore *sm* inspector.

ispezio'nare [ispettsjo'nare] *vt* to inspect.

ispezi'one [ispet'tsjone] *sf* inspection.

'ispido, a *ag* bristly, shaggy.

ispi'rare *vt* to inspire; ~**rsi** *vr*: ~**rsi a** to draw one's inspiration from.

Isra'ele *sm*: **l'~** Israel; **israeli'ano, a** *ag*, *sm/f* Israeli.

is'sare *vt* to hoist.

istan'taneo, a *ag* instantaneous // *sf* (*FOT*) snapshot.

is'tante *sm* instant, moment; **all'~**, **sull'~** instantly, immediately.

is'tanza [is'tantsa] *sf* petition, request.

is'terico, a, ci, che *ag* hysterical.

iste'rismo *sm* hysteria.

isti'gare *vt* to incite; **istigazi'one** *sf* incitement; **istigazione a delinquere** (*DIR*) incitement to crime.

is'tinto *sm* instinct.

istitu'ire *vt* (*fondare*) to institute, found; (*porre: confronto*) to establish; (*intraprendere: inchiesta*) to set up.

isti'tuto *sm* institute; (*di università*) department; (*ente, DIR*) institution; ~ **di bellezza** beauty salon.

istituzi'one [istitut'tsjone] *sf* institution.

'istmo *sm* (*GEO*) isthmus.

istra'dare *vt* = **instradare**.

'istrice ['istritʃe] *sm* porcupine.

istri'one *sm* (*peg*) ham actor.

istru'ire *vt* (*insegnare*) to teach; (*ammaestrare*) to train; (*informare*) to instruct, inform; (*DIR*) to prepare; **istrut'tore, 'trice** *sm/f* instructor // *ag*: **giudice istruttore** examining (*Brit*) *o* committing (*US*) magistrate; **istrut'toria** *sf* (*DIR*) (preliminary) investigation and hearing; **istruzi'one** *sf* education; training; (*direttiva*) instruction; (*DIR*) = **istruttoria**; **istruzioni per l'uso** instructions (for use).

I'talia *sf*: **l'~** Italy.

itali'ano, a *ag* Italian // *sm/f* Italian // *sm* (*LING*) Italian; **gli I~i** the Italians.

itine'rario *sm* itinerary.

itte'rizia [itte'rittsja] *sf* (*MED*) jaundice.

'ittico, a, ci, che *ag* fish *cpd*; fishing *cpd*.

Iugos'lavia *sf* = **Jugoslavia**.

iugos'lavo, a *ag*, *sm/f* = **jugoslavo, a**.

i'uta *sf* jute.

I.V.A. ['iva] *sigla f* = **imposta sul valore aggiunto**.

J

jazz [dʒaz] *sm* jazz.

jeans [dʒinz] *smpl* jeans.

Jugos'lavia [jugoz'lavja] *sf*: **la ~** Yugoslavia; **jugos'lavo, a** *ag*, *sm/f* Yugoslav(ian).

'juta ['juta] *sf* = **iuta**.

K

K *abbr* (*INFORM*) K.

k *abbr* (= *kilo*) k.

karatè *sm* karate.
Kg *abbr* (= *chilogrammo*) kg.
'killer *sm inv* gunman, hired gun.
km *abbr* (= *chilometro*) km.
'krapfen *sm inv* (*CUC*) doughnut.

L

l' *det vedi* **la, lo**).
la *det f* (*dav V* **l'**) the // *pronome* (*dav V* **l'**) (*oggetto: persona*) her; (: *cosa*) it; (: *forma di cortesia*) you // *sm inv* (*MUS*) A; (: *solfeggiando la scala*) la.
là *av* there; **di ~** (*da quel luogo*) from there; (*in quel luogo*) in there; (*dall'altra parte*) over there; **di ~ di** beyond; **per di ~** that way; **più in ~** (*spazio*) further on; (*tempo*) later on; **fatti in ~** move up; **~ dentro/sopra/sotto** in/up (*o* on)/under there; *vedi* **quello**.
'labbro *sm* (*pl(f)*: **labbra**: *solo nel senso ANAT*) lip.
labi'rinto *sm* labyrinth, maze.
labora'torio *sm* (*di ricerca*) laboratory; (*di arti, mestieri*) workshop; **~ linguistico** language laboratory.
labori'oso, a *ag* (*faticoso*) laborious; (*attivo*) hard-working.
labu'rista, i, e *ag* Labour (*Brit*) *cpd* // *sm/f* Labour Party member (*Brit*).
'lacca, che *sf* lacquer.
'laccio ['lattʃo] *sm* noose; (*legaccio, tirante*) lasso; (*di scarpa*) lace; **~ emostatico** tourniquet.
lace'rare [latʃe'rare] *vt* to tear to shreds, lacerate; **~rsi** *vr* to tear; **'lacero, a** *ag* (*logoro*) torn, tattered; (*MED*) lacerated.
'lacrima *sf* tear; **in ~e** in tears; **lacri'mare** *vi* to water; **lacri'mogeno, a** *ag*: **gas lacrimogeno** tear gas.
la'cuna *sf* (*fig*) gap.
'ladro *sm* thief; **ladro'cinio** *sm* theft, larceny.
laggiù [lad'dʒu] *av* down there; (*di là*) over there.
la'gnarsi [laɲ'narsi] *vr*: **~ (di)** to complain (about).
'lago, ghi *sm* lake.
'lagrima *etc* = **lacrima** *etc*.
la'guna *sf* lagoon.
'laico, a, ci, che *ag* (*apostolato*) lay; (*vita*) secular; (*scuola*) nondenominational // *sm/f* layman/woman // *sm* lay brother.
'lama *sf* blade // *sm inv* (*ZOOL*) llama; (*REL*) lama.
lambic'care *vt* to distil; **~rsi il cervello** to rack one's brains.
lam'bire *vt* to lick; to lap.
la'mella *sf* (*di metallo etc*) thin sheet, thin strip; (*di fungo*) gill.
lamen'tare *vt* to lament; **~rsi** *vr* (*emettere lamenti*) to moan, groan; (*rammaricarsi*): **~rsi (di)** to complain

(*about*); **lamen'tela** *sf* complaining *q*; **lamen'tevole** *ag* (*voce*) complaining, plaintive; (*destino*) pitiful; **la'mento** *sm* moan, groan; wail; **lamen'toso, a** *ag* plaintive.
la'metta *sf* razor blade.
lami'era *sf* sheet metal.
'lamina *sf* (*lastra sottile*) thin sheet (*o* layer *o* plate); **~ d'oro** gold leaf; gold foil; **lami'nare** *vt* to laminate; **lami'nato, a** *ag* laminated; (*tessuto*) lamé // *sm* laminate.
'lampada *sf* lamp; **~ a gas** gas lamp; **~ a spirito** blow lamp (*Brit*), blow torch (*US*); **~ da tavolo** table lamp.
lampa'dario *sm* chandelier.
lampa'dina *sf* light bulb; **~ tascabile** pocket torch (*Brit*) *o* flashlight (*US*).
lam'pante *ag* (*fig: evidente*) crystal clear, evident.
lampeggi'are [lamped'dʒare] *vi* (*luce, fari*) to flash // *vb impers*: **lampeggia** there's lightning; **lampeggia'tore** *sm* (*AUT*) indicator.
lampi'one *sm* street light *o* lamp (*Brit*).
'lampo *sm* (*METEOR*) flash of lightning; (*di luce, fig*) flash; **~i** *smpl* lightning *q* // *ag inv*: **cerniera ~** zip (fastener) (*Brit*), zipper (*US*); **guerra ~** blitzkrieg.
lam'pone *sm* raspberry.
'lana *sf* wool; **~ d'acciaio** steel wool; **pura ~ vergine** pure new wool; **~ di vetro** glass wool.
lan'cetta [lan'tʃetta] *sf* (*indice*) pointer, needle; (*di orologio*) hand.
'lancia ['lantʃa] *sf* (*arma*) lance; (: *picca*) spear; (*di pompa antincendio*) nozzle; (*imbarcazione*) launch.
lanciafi'amme [lantʃa'fjamme] *sm inv* flamethrower.
lanci'are [lan'tʃare] *vt* to throw, hurl, fling; (*SPORT*) to throw; (*far partire: automobile*) to get up to full speed; (*bombe*) to drop; (*razzo, prodotto, moda*) to launch; **~rsi** *vr*: **~rsi contro/su** to throw *o* hurl *o* fling o.s. against/on; **~rsi in** (*fig*) to embark on.
lanci'nante [lantʃi'nante] *ag* (*dolore*) shooting, throbbing; (*grido*) piercing.
'lancio ['lantʃo] *sm* throwing *q*; throw; dropping *q*; drop; launching *q*; launch; **~ del peso** putting the shot.
'landa *sf* (*GEO*) moor.
'languido, a *ag* (*fiacco*) languid, weak; (*tenero, malinconico*) languishing.
langu'ore *sm* weakness, languor.
lani'ficio [lani'fitʃo] *sm* woollen mill.
la'noso, a *ag* woolly.
lan'terna *sf* lantern; (*faro*) lighthouse.
la'nugine [la'nudʒine] *sf* down.
lapi'dare *vt* to stone.
lapi'dario, a *ag* (*fig*) terse.
'lapide *sf* (*di sepolcro*) tombstone; (*commemorativa*) plaque.
'lapis *sm inv* pencil.

Lap'ponia sf Lapland.

'lapsus sm inv slip.

'lardo sm bacon fat, lard.

lar'ghezza [lar'gettsa] sf width; breadth; looseness; generosity; ~ **di vedute** broad-mindedness.

'largo, a, ghi, ghe ag wide; broad; (maniche) wide; (abito: troppo ampio) loose; (fig) generous // sm width; breadth; (mare aperto): **il ~** the open sea // sf: **stare o tenersi alla ~a (da qn/qc)** to keep one's distance (from sb/sth), keep away (from sb/sth); ~ **due metri** two metres wide; ~ **di spalle** broad-shouldered; **di ~ghe vedute** broad-minded; **su ~a scala** on a large scale; **di manica ~a** generous, open-handed; **al ~ di Genova off** (the coast of) Genoa; **farsi ~ tra la folla** to push one's way through the crowd.

'larice ['larit∫e] sm (BOT) larch.

larin'gite [larin'dʒite] sf laryngitis.

'larva sf larva; (fig) shadow.

la'sagne [la'zaɲɲe] sfpl lasagna sg.

lasci'are [laʃ'ʃare] vt to leave; (abbandonare) to leave, abandon, give up; (cessare di tenere) to let go of // vb ausiliare: ~ **fare qn** to let sb do // vi: ~ **di fare** (smettere) to stop doing; **~rsi andare/truffare** to let o.s. go/be cheated; ~ **andare o correre o perdere** to let things go their own way; ~ **stare qc/qn** to leave sth/sb alone.

'lascito ['laʃʃito] sm (DIR) legacy.

laser ['lazer] ag, sm inv: **(raggio) ~** laser (beam).

lassa'tivo, a ag, sm laxative.

'lasso sm: ~ **di tempo** interval, lapse of time.

lassù av up there.

'lastra sf (di pietra) slab; (di metallo, FOT) plate; (di ghiaccio, vetro) sheet; (radiografica) X-ray (plate).

lastri'care vt to pave; **lastri'cato** sm, **'lastrico, ci o chi** sm paving.

late'rale ag lateral, side cpd; (uscita, ingresso etc) side cpd // sm (CALCIO) half-back.

late'rizio [late'rittsjo] sm (perforated) brick.

lati'fondo sm large estate.

la'tino, a ag, sm Latin; **~-ameri'cano a** ag Latin-American.

lati'tante sm/f fugitive (from justice).

lati'tudine sf latitude.

'lato, a ag (fig) wide, broad // sm side; (fig) aspect, point of view; **in senso ~** broadly speaking.

la'trare vi to bark.

latro'cinio [latro'tʃinjo] sm = **ladrocinio**.

'latta sf tin (plate); (recipiente) tin, can.

lat'taio, a sm/f milkman/woman; dairyman/woman.

lat'tante ag unweaned.

'latte sm milk; ~ **detergente** cleansing milk o lotion; ~ **secco o in polvere** dried o powdered milk; ~ **scremato** skimmed milk; **'latteo, a** ag milky; (dieta, prodotto) milk cpd; **latte'ria** sf dairy; **latti'cini** smpl dairy products.

lat'tina sf (di birra etc) can.

lat'tuga, ghe sf lettuce.

'laurea sf degree; **laure'ando, a** sm/f final-year student; **laure'are** vt to confer a degree on; **laurearsi** vr to graduate; **laure'ato, a** ag, sm/f graduate.

'lauro sm laurel.

'lauto, a ag (pranzo, mancia) lavish.

la'vabo sm washbasin.

la'vaggio [la'vaddʒo] sm washing q; ~ **del cervello** brainwashing q.

la'vagna [la'vaɲɲa] sf (GEO) slate; (di scuola) blackboard.

la'vanda sf (anche MED) wash; (BOT) lavender; **lavan'daia** sf washerwoman; **lavande'ria** sf laundry; **lavanderia automatica** launderette; **lavanderia a secco** dry-cleaner's; **lavan'dino** sm sink.

lavapi'atti sm/f dishwasher.

la'vare vt to wash; **~rsi** vr to wash, have a wash; ~ **a secco** to dry-clean; **~rsi le mani/i denti** to wash one's hands/clean one's teeth.

lava'secco sm o f inv drycleaner's.

lavasto'viglie [lavasto'viʎʎe] sm o f inv (macchina) dishwasher.

lava'toio sm (public) washhouse.

lava'trice [lava'tritʃe] sf washing machine.

lava'tura sf washing q; ~ **di piatti** dishwater.

lavo'rante sm/f worker.

lavo'rare vi to work; (fig: bar, studio etc) to do good business // vt to work; **~rsi qn** (persuaderlo) to work on sb; ~ **a** to work on; ~ **a maglia** to knit; **lavora'tivo, a** ag working; **lavora'tore, 'trice** sm/f worker // ag working; **lavorazi'one** sf (gen) working; (di legno, pietra) carving; (di film) making; (di prodotto) manufacture; (modo di esecuzione) workmanship; **lavo'rio** sm intense activity.

la'voro sm work; (occupazione) job, work q; (opera) piece of work, job; (ECON) labour; **~i forzati** hard labour sg; **~i pubblici** public works.

le det fpl the // pronome (oggetto) them; (: a lei, a essa) (to) her; (: forma di cortesia) (to) you.

le'ale ag loyal; (sincero) sincere; (onesto) fair; **lealtà** sf loyalty; sincerity; fairness.

'lebbra sf leprosy.

'lecca 'lecca sm inv lollipop.

leccapi'edi sm/f inv (peg) toady, bootlicker.

lec'care vt to lick; (sog: gatto: latte etc) to lick o lap up; (fig) to flatter; **~rsi i baffi** to lick one's lips; **lec'cata** sf lick.

'leccio ['lɛttʃo] sm holm oak, ilex.

leccor'nia sf titbit, delicacy.

'lecito, a ['lɛtʃito] ag permitted, allowed.

'ledere vt to damage, injure.

'lega, ghe sf league; (di metalli) alloy.

le'gaccio [le'gattʃo] sm string, lace.

le'gale ag legal // sm lawyer; **legaliz'zare** vt to authenticate; (regolarizzare) to legalize.

le'game sm (corda, fig: affettivo) tie, bond; (nesso logico) link, connection.

le'gare vt (prigioniero, capelli, cane) to tie (up); (libro) to bind; (CHIM) to alloy; (fig: collegare) to bind, join // vi (far lega) to unite; (fig) to get on well.

lega'tario, a sm/f (DIR) legatee.

le'gato sm (REL) legate; (DIR) legacy, bequest.

lega'tura sf (di libro) binding; (MUS) ligature.

le'genda [le'dʒɛnda] sf (di carta geografica etc) = **leggenda**.

'legge ['lɛddʒe] sf law.

leg'genda [led'dʒɛnda] sf (narrazione) legend; (di carta geografica etc) key, legend.

'leggere ['lɛddʒere] vt, vi to read.

legge'rezza [ledd'ʒe'rettsa] sf lightness; thoughtlessness; fickleness.

leg'gero, a [led'dʒero] ag light; (agile, snello) nimble, agile, light; (tè, caffè) weak; (fig: non grave, piccolo) slight; (: spensierato) thoughtless; (: incostante) fickle; free and easy; **alla ~a** thoughtlessly.

leggi'adro, a [led'dʒadro] ag pretty, lovely; (movimenti) graceful.

leg'gio, 'gii [led'dʒio] sm lectern; (MUS) music stand.

legisla'tura [ledʒizla'tura] sf legislature.

legislazi'one [ledʒizlat'tsjone] sf legislation.

le'gittimo, a [le'dʒittimo] ag legitimate; (fig: giustificato, lecito) justified, legitimate; **~a difesa** (DIR) self-defence.

'legna ['leɲɲa] sf firewood; **le'gname** sm wood, timber.

'legno ['leɲɲo] sm wood; (pezzo di ~) piece of wood; **di ~** wooden; **~ compensato** plywood; **le'gnoso, a** ag wooden; woody; (carne) tough.

le'gumi smpl (BOT) pulses.

'lei pronome (soggetto) she; (oggetto: per dare rilievo, con preposizione) her; (forma di cortesia: anche: **L~**) you // sm: **dare del ~ a qn** to address sb as "lei"; **~ stessa** she herself; you yourself.

'lembo sm (di abito, strada) edge; (striscia sottile: di terra) strip.

'lemma, i sm headword.

'lemme 'lemme av (very) very slowly.

'lena sf (fig) energy, stamina.

le'nire vt to soothe.

'lente sf (OTTICA) lens sg; **~ d'ingrandimento** magnifying glass; **~i a contatto** o **corneali** contact lenses.

len'tezza [len'tettsa] sf slowness.

len'ticchia [len'tikkja] sf lentil.

len'tiggine [len'tiddʒine] sf freckle.

'lento, a ag slow; (molle: fune) slack; (non stretto: vite, abito) loose // sm (ballo) slow dance.

'lenza ['lɛntsa] sf fishing-line.

lenzu'olo [len'tswɔlo] sm sheet; **~a** sfpl pair of sheets.

le'one sm lion; (dello zodiaco): **L~** Leo.

lepo'rino, a ag: **labbro ~** harelip.

'lepre sf hare.

'lercio, a, ci, cie ['lɛrtʃo] ag filthy.

'lesbica, che sf lesbian.

lesi'nare vt to be stingy with // vi: **~ (su)** to skimp (on), be stingy (with).

lesi'one sf (MED) lesion; (DIR) injury, damage; (EDIL) crack.

'leso, a pp di **ledere** // ag (offeso) injured; **parte ~a** (DIR) injured party.

les'sare vt (CUC) to boil.

'lessico, ci sm vocabulary; lexicon.

'lesso, a ag boiled // sm boiled meat.

'lesto, a ag quick; (agile) nimble; **~ di mano** (per rubare) light-fingered; (per picchiare) free with one's fists.

le'tale ag lethal; fatal.

leta'maio sm dunghill.

le'tame sm manure, dung.

le'targo, ghi sm lethargy; (ZOOL) hibernation.

le'tizia [le'tittsja] sf joy, happiness.

'lettera sf letter; **~e** sfpl (letteratura) literature sg; (studi umanistici) arts (subjects); **alla ~** literally; **in ~e** in words, in full; **lette'rale** ag literal.

lette'rario, a ag literary.

lette'rato, a ag well-read, scholarly.

lettera'tura sf literature.

let'tiga, ghe sf (portantina) litter; (barella) stretcher.

let'tino sm cot (Brit), crib (US).

'letto, a pp di **leggere** // sm bed; **andare a ~** to go to bed; **~ a castello** bunk beds pl; **~ a una piazza/a due piazze** o **matrimoniale** single/double bed.

let'tore, 'trice sm/f reader; (INS) (foreign language) assistant (Brit), (foreign) teaching assistant (US) // sm (TECN): **~ ottico** optical character reader.

let'tura sf reading.

leuce'mia [leutʃe'mia] sf leukaemia.

'leva sf lever; (MIL) conscription; **far ~ su qn** to work on sb; **~ del cambio** (AUT) gear lever.

le'vante sm east; (vento) East wind; **il L~** the Levant.

le'vare vt (occhi, braccio) to raise; (sollevare, togliere: tassa, divieto) to lift; (indumenti) to take off, remove;

(*rimuovere*) to take away; (: *dal di sopra*) to take off; (: *dal di dentro*) to take out; ~**rsi** *vr* to get up; (*sole*) to rise; **le'vata** *sf* (*di posta*) collection.

leva'toio, a *ag*: **ponte ~** drawbridge.

leva'tura *sf* intelligence, mental capacity.

levi'gare *vt* to smooth; (*con carta vetrata*) to sand.

levri'ere *sm* greyhound.

lezi'one [let'tsjone] *sf* lesson; (*all'università, sgridata*) lecture; **fare ~** to teach; to lecture.

lezi'oso, a [let'tsjoso] *ag* affected; simpering.

'**lezzo** ['leddzo] *sm* stench, stink.

li *pronome pl* (*oggetto*) them.

lì *av* there; **di** *o* **da ~** from there; **per di ~ that** way; **di ~ a pochi giorni** a few days later; ~ **per ~** there and then; at first; **essere ~** (**~**) **per fare** to be on the point of doing, be about to do; ~ **dentro** in there; ~ **sotto** under there; ~ **sopra** on there; up there; *vedi* **quello**.

liba'nese *ag, sm/f* Lebanese *inv*.

Li'bano *sm*: **il ~** the Lebanon.

'**libbra** *sf* (*peso*) pound.

li'beccio [li'bettʃo] *sm* south-west wind.

li'bello *sm* libel.

li'bellula *sf* dragonfly.

libe'rale *ag, sm/f* liberal.

liberaliz'zare [liberalid'dzare] *vt* to liberalize.

libe'rare *vt* (*rendere libero: prigioniero*) to release; (: *popolo*) to free, liberate; (*sgombrare: passaggio*) to clear; (: *stanza*) to vacate; (*produrre: energia*) to release; ~**rsi** *vr*: ~**rsi di qc/qn** to get rid of sth/sb; **libera'tore, 'trice** *ag* liberating // *sm/f* liberator; **liberazi'one** *sf* liberation, freeing; release; rescuing.

'**libero, a** *ag* free; (*strada*) clear; (*non occupato: posto etc*) vacant; not taken; empty; not engaged; ~ **di fare qc** free to do sth; ~ **da** free from; ~ **arbitrio** free will; ~ **professionista** self-employed professional person; ~ **scambio** free trade; **libertà** *sf inv* freedom; (*tempo disponibile*) free time // *sfpl* (*licenza*) liberties; **in libertà provvisoria/vigilata** released without bail/on probation; **libertà di riunione** right to hold meetings.

'**Libia** *sf*: **la ~** Libya; '**libico, a, ci, che** *ag, sm/f* Libyan.

li'bidine *sf* lust.

li'braio *sm* bookseller.

li'brario, a *ag* book *cpd*.

li'brarsi *vr* to hover.

libre'ria *sf* (*bottega*) bookshop; (*stanza*) library; (*mobile*) bookcase.

li'bretto *sm* booklet; (*taccuino*) notebook; (*MUS*) libretto; ~ **degli assegni** cheque book; ~ **di circolazione** (*AUT*) logbook; ~ **di risparmio** (savings) bank-book, passbook; ~ **universitario** student's report book.

'**libro** *sm* book; ~ **bianco** (*POL*) white paper; ~ **di cassa** cash book; ~ **mastro** ledger; ~ **paga** payroll.

li'cenza [li'tʃɛntsa] *sf* (*permesso*) permission, leave; (*di pesca, caccia, circolazione*) permit, licence; (*MIL*) leave; (*INS*) school leaving certificate; (*libertà*) liberty; licence; licentiousness; **andare in ~** (*MIL*) to go on leave.

licenzia'mento [litʃentsja'mento] *sm* dismissal.

licenzi'are [litʃen'tsjare] *vt* (*impiegato*) to dismiss; (*INS*) to award a certificate to; ~**rsi** *vr* (*impiegato*) to resign, hand in one's notice; (*INS*) to obtain one's school-leaving certificate.

li'ceo [li'tʃɛo] *sm* (*INS*) secondary (*Brit*) *o* high (*US*) school (*for 14- to 19-year-olds*).

'**lido** *sm* beach, shore.

li'eto, a *ag* happy, glad; "**molto ~**" (*nelle presentazioni*) "pleased to meet you".

li'eve *ag* light; (*di poco conto*) slight; (*sommesso: voce*) faint, soft.

lievi'tare *vi* (*anche fig*) to rise // *vt* to leaven.

li'evito *sm* yeast; ~ **di birra** brewer's yeast.

'**ligio, a, gi, gie** ['lidʒo] *ag* faithful, loyal.

'**lilla, lillà** *sm inv* lilac.

'**lima** *sf* file.

limacci'oso, a [limat'tʃoso] *ag* slimy; muddy.

li'mare *vt* to file (down); (*fig*) to polish.

'**limbo** *sm* (*REL*) limbo.

li'metta *sf* nail file.

limi'tare *vt* to limit, restrict; (*circoscrivere*) to bound, surround; **limita'tivo, a** *ag* limiting, restricting; **limita'to, a** *ag* limited, restricted.

'**limite** *sm* limit; (*confine*) border, boundary; ~ **di velocità** speed limit.

li'mitrofo, a *ag* neighbouring.

limo'nata *sf* lemonade (*Brit*), (lemon) soda (*US*); lemon squash (*Brit*), lemonade (*US*).

li'mone *sm* (*pianta*) lemon tree; (*frutto*) lemon.

'**limpido, a** *ag* clear; (*acqua*) limpid, clear.

'**lince** ['lintʃe] *sf* lynx.

linci'are *vt* to lynch.

'**lindo, a** *ag* tidy, spick and span; (*biancheria*) clean.

'**linea** *sf* line; (*di mezzi pubblici di trasporto: itinerario*) route; (: *servizio*) service; **a grandi ~e** in outline; **mantenere la ~** to look after one's figure; **di ~**: **aereo di ~** airliner; **nave di ~** liner; **volo di ~** scheduled flight; ~ **aerea** airline; ~ **di partenza/d'arrivo**

(*SPORT*) starting/finishing line; ~ **di tiro** line of fire.

linea'menti *smpl* features; (*fig*) outlines.

line'are *ag* linear; (*fig*) coherent, logical.

line'etta *sf* (*trattino*) dash; (*d'unione*) hyphen.

lin'gotto *sm* ingot, bar.

'lingua *sf* (*ANAT, CUC*) tongue; (*idioma*) language; **mostrare la ~** to stick out one's tongue; **di ~ italiana** Italian-speaking; ~ **madre** mother tongue; **una ~ di terra** a spit of land.

lingu'aggio [lin'gwaddʒo] *sm* language.

lingu'etta *sf* (*di strumento*) reed; (*di scarpa, TECN*) tongue; (*di busta*) flap.

lingu'istica *sf* linguistics *sg*.

'lino *sm* (*pianta*) flax; (*tessuto*) linen.

li'noleum *sm inv* linoleum, lino.

lique'fare *vt* (*render liquido*) to liquefy; (*fondere*) to melt; **~rsi** *vr* to liquefy; to melt.

liqui'dare *vt* (*società, beni; persona: uccidere*) to liquidate; (*persona: sbarazzarsene*) to get rid of; (*conto, problema*) to settle; (*COMM: merce*) to sell off, clear; **liquidazi'one** *sf* liquidation; settlement; clearance sale.

liquidità *sf* liquidity.

'liquido, a *ag, sm* liquid; ~ **per freni** brake fluid.

liqui'rizia [likwi'rittsja] *sf* liquorice.

li'quore *sm* liqueur.

'lira *sf* (*unità monetaria*) lira; (*MUS*) lyre; ~ **sterlina** pound sterling.

'lirico, a, ci, che *ag* lyric(al); (*MUS*) lyric // *sf* (*poesia*) lyric poetry; (*componimento poetico*) lyric; (*MUS*) opera; **cantante/teatro ~** opera singer/house.

'lisca, sche *sf* (*di pesce*) fishbone.

lisci'are [liʃ'ʃare] *vt* to smooth; (*fig*) to flatter.

'liscio, a, sci, sce ['liʃʃo] *ag* smooth; (*capelli*) straight; (*mobile*) plain; (*bevanda alcolica*) neat; (*fig*) straightforward, simple // *av*: **andare ~** to go smoothly; **passarla ~a** to get away with it.

'liso, a *ag* worn out, threadbare.

'lista *sf* (*striscia*) strip; (*elenco*) list; ~ **elettorale** electoral roll; ~ **delle vivande** menu.

lis'tino *sm* list; ~ **dei cambi** (foreign) exchange rate; ~ **dei prezzi** price list.

'lite *sf* quarrel, argument; (*DIR*) lawsuit.

liti'gare *vi* to quarrel; (*DIR*) to litigate.

li'tigio [li'tidʒo] *sm* quarrel; **litigi'oso, a** *ag* quarrelsome; (*DIR*) litigious.

litogra'fia *sf* (*sistema*) lithography; (*stampa*) lithograph.

lito'rale *ag* coastal, coast *cpd* // *sm* coast.

'litro *sm* litre.

livel'lare *vt* to level, make level; **~rsi** *vr*

to become level; (*fig*) to level out, balance out.

li'vello *sm* level; (*fig*) level, standard; **ad alto ~** (*fig*) high-level; ~ **del mare** sea level.

'livido, a *ag* livid; (*per percosse*) bruised, black and blue; (*cielo*) leaden // *sm* bruise.

li'vore *sm* malice, spite.

Li'vorno *sf* Livorno, Leghorn.

li'vrea *sf* livery.

'lizza ['littsa] *sf* lists *pl*; **scendere in ~** (*anche fig*) to enter the lists.

lo *det m* (*dav s impura, gn, pn, ps, x, z; dav V* **l'**) the // *pronome* (*dav V* **l'**) (*oggetto: persona*) him; (: *cosa*) it; ~ **sapevo I knew it; ~ so I know; sii buono, anche se lui non ~** è be good, even if he isn't.

lo'cale *ag* local // *sm* room; (*luogo pubblico*) premises *pl*; ~ **notturno** nightclub; **località** *sf inv* locality; **localiz'zare** *vt* (*circoscrivere*) to confine, localize; (*accertare*) to locate, place.

lo'canda *sf* inn; **locandi'ere, a** *sm/f* innkeeper.

loca'tario, a *sm/f* tenant.

loca'tore, 'trice *sm/f* landlord/lady.

locazi'one [lokat'tsjone] *sf* (*da parte del locatario*) renting *q*; (*da parte del locatore*) renting out *q*, letting *q*; (*contratto di*) ~ **lease**; (*canone di*) ~ **rent**; **dare in ~** to rent out, let.

locomo'tiva *sf* locomotive.

locomo'tore *sm* electric locomotive.

locomozi'one [lokomot'tsjone] *sf* locomotion; **mezzi di ~** vehicles, means of transport.

lo'custa *sf* locust.

locuzi'one [lokut'tsjone] *sf* phrase, expression.

lo'dare *vt* to praise.

'lode *sf* praise; (*INS*): **laurearsi con 110 e ~** ≈ to graduate with a first-class honours degree (*Brit*), graduate summa cum laude (*US*).

'loden *sm inv* (*stoffa*) loden; (*cappotto*) loden overcoat.

lo'devole *ag* praiseworthy.

loga'ritmo *sm* logarithm.

'loggia, ge ['lɔddʒa] *sf* (*ARCHIT*) loggia; (*circolo massonico*) lodge; **loggi'one** *sm* (*di teatro*): **il loggione the Gods** *sg*.

'logico, a, ci, che ['lɔdʒiko] *ag* logical // *sf* logic.

logo'rare *vt* to wear out; (*sciupare*) to waste; **~rsi** *vr* to wear out; (*fig*) to wear o.s. out.

logo'rio *sm* wear and tear; (*fig*) strain.

'logoro, a *ag* (*stoffa*) worn out, threadbare; (*persona*) worn out.

lom'baggine [lom'baddʒine] *sf* lumbago.

Lombar'dia *sf*: **la ~** Lombardy.

lom'bata *sf* (*taglio di carne*) loin.

'lombo *sm* (*ANAT*) loin.

lom'brico, chi *sm* earthworm.
londi'nese *ag* London *cpd* // *sm/f* Londoner.
'Londra *sf* London.
lon'gevo, a [lon'dʒɛvo] *ag* long-lived.
longi'tudine [londʒi'tudine] *sf* longitude.
lonta'nanza [lonta'nantsa] *sf* distance; absence.
lon'tano, a *ag* (*distante*) distant, far-away; (*assente*) absent; (*vago: sospetto*) slight, remote; (*tempo: remoto*) far-off, distant; (*parente*) distant, remote // *av* far; **è ~a la casa?** is it far to the house?, is the house far from here?; **è ~ un chilometro** it's a kilometre away *o* a kilometre from here; **più ~** farther; **da *o* di ~** from a distance; **~ da** a long way from; **alla ~a** slightly, vaguely.
'lontra *sf* otter.
lo'quace [lo'kwatʃe] *ag* talkative, loquacious; (*fig: gesto etc*) eloquent.
'lordo, a *ag* (*distante*) dirty, filthy; (*peso, stipendio*) gross.
'loro *pronome pl* (*oggetto, con preposizione*) them; (*complemento di termine*) to them; (*soggetto*) they; (*forma di cortesia: anche: **L~***) you; to you; **il(la) ~, i(le) ~** *det* their; (*forma di cortesia: anche: **L~***) your // *pronome* theirs; (*forma di cortesia: anche: **L~***) yours; **~ stessi(e)** they themselves; you yourselves.
'losco, a, schi, sche *ag* (*fig*) shady, suspicious.
'lotta *sf* struggle, fight; (*SPORT*) wrestling; **~ libera** all-in wrestling; **lot'tare** *vi* to fight, struggle; to wrestle; **lotta'tore, trice** *sm/f* wrestler.
lotte'ria *sf* lottery; (*di gara ippica*) sweepstake.
'lotto *sm* (*gioco*) (state) lottery; (*parte*) lot; (*EDIL*) site.
lozi'one [lot'tsjone] *sf* lotion.
lubrifi'cante *sm* lubricant.
lubrifi'care *vt* to lubricate.
luc'chetto [luk'ketto] *sm* padlock.
lucci'care [luttʃi'kare] *vi* to sparkle, glitter, twinkle.
'luccio ['luttʃo] *sm* (*ZOOL*) pike.
'lucciola ['luttʃola] *sf* (*ZOOL*) firefly; glowworm.
'luce [lutʃe] *sf* light; (*finestra*) window; **alla ~ di** by the light of; **fare ~ su qc** (*fig*) to shed *o* throw light on sth; **~ del sole/della luna** sun/moonlight; **lu'cente** *ag* shining.
lu'cerna [lu'tʃɛrna] *sf* oil-lamp.
lucer'nario [lutʃer'narjo] *sm* skylight.
lu'certola [lu'tʃɛrtola] *sf* lizard.
luci'dare [lutʃi'dare] *vt* to polish; (*ricalcare*) to trace.
lucida'trice [lutʃida'tritʃe] *sf* floor polisher.
'lucido, a ['lutʃido] *ag* shining, bright;

(*lucidato*) polished; (*fig*) lucid // *sm* shine, lustre; (*per scarpe etc*) polish; (*disegno*) tracing.
'lucro *sm* profit, gain; **lu'croso, a** *ag* lucrative, profitable.
lu'dibrio *sm* mockery *q*; (*oggetto di scherno*) laughing-stock.
'luglio ['luʎʎo] *sm* July.
'lugubre *ag* gloomy.
'lui *pronome* (*soggetto*) he; (*oggetto: per dare rilievo, con preposizione*) him; **~ stesso** he himself.
lu'maca, che *sf* slug; (*chiocciola*) snail.
'lume *sm* light; (*lampada*) lamp; (*fig*): **chiedere ~i a qn** to ask sb for advice; **a ~ di naso** (*fig*) by rule of thumb.
lumi'naria *sf* (*per feste*) illuminations *pl*.
lumi'noso, a *ag* (*che emette luce*) luminous; (*cielo, colore, stanza*) bright; (*sorgente*) of light, light *cpd*; (*fig: sorriso*) bright, radiant.
'luna *sf* moon; **~ nuova/piena** new/full moon; **~ di miele** honeymoon.
'luna park *sm inv* amusement park, funfair.
lu'nare *ag* lunar, moon *cpd*.
lu'nario *sm* almanac; **sbarcare il ~** to make ends meet.
lu'natico, a, ci, che *ag* whimsical, temperamental.
lunedì *sm inv* Monday; **di *o* il ~** on Mondays.
lun'gaggine [lun'gaddʒine] *sf* slowness; **~i della burocrazia** red tape.
lun'ghezza [lun'gettsa] *sf* length; **~ d'onda** (*FISICA*) wavelength.
'lungi ['lundʒi]: **~ da** *prep* far from.
'lungo, a, ghi, ghe *ag* long; (*lento: persona*) slow; (*diluito: caffè, brodo*) weak, watery, thin // *sm* length // *prep* along; **~ 3 metri** 3 metres long; **a ~** for a long time; **a ~ andare** in the long run; **di gran ~a** (*molto*) by far; **andare in ~** *o* **per le lunghe** to drag on; **saperla ~a** to know what's what; **in ~ e in largo** far and wide, all over; **~ il corso dei secoli** throughout the centuries.
lungo'mare *sm* promenade.
lu'notto *sm* (*AUT*) rear *o* back window.
lu'ogo, ghi *sm* place; (*posto: di incidente etc*) scene, site; (*punto, passo di libro*) passage; **in ~ di** instead of; **in primo ~** in the first place; **aver ~** to take place; **dar ~ a** to give rise to; **~ comune** commonplace; **~ di nascita** birthplace; (*AMM*) place of birth; **~ di provenienza** place of origin.
luogote'nente *sm* (*MIL*) lieutenant.
lu'para *sf* sawn-off shotgun.
'lupo, a *sm/f* wolf.
'luppolo *sm* (*BOT*) hop.
'lurido, a *ag* filthy.
lu'singa, ghe *sf* (*spesso al pl*) flattery *q*.

lusin'gare *vt* to flatter; **lusinghi'ero, a** *ag* flattering, gratifying.

lus'sare *vt* (*MED*) to dislocate.

Lussem'burgo *sm* (*stato*): il ~ Luxembourg // *sf* (*città*) Luxembourg.

'lusso *sm* luxury; di ~ luxury *cpd*; **lussu'oso, a** *ag* luxurious.

lussureggi'are [lussured'dʒare] *vi* to be luxuriant.

lus'suria *sf* lust.

lus'trare *vt* to polish, shine.

lustras'carpe *sm/f inv* shoeshine.

lus'trino *sm* sequin.

'lustro, a *ag* shiny; (*pelliccia*) glossy // *sm* shine, gloss; (*fig*) prestige, glory; (*quinquennio*) five-year period.

'lutto *sm* mourning; essere in/portare il ~ to be in/wear mourning; **luttu'oso, a** *ag* mournful, sad.

M

ma *cong* but; ~ insomma! for goodness sake!; ~ no! of course not!

'macabro, a *ag* gruesome, macabre.

macché [mak'ke] *escl* not at all!, certainly not!

macche'roni [makke'roni] *smpl* macaroni *sg*.

'macchia ['makkja] *sf* stain, spot; (*chiazza di diverso colore*) spot; splash, patch; (*tipo di boscaglia*) scrub; alla ~ (*fig*) in hiding; **macchi'are** *vt* (*sporcare*) to stain, mark; **macchiarsi** *vr* (*persona*) to get o.s. dirty; (*stoffa*) to stain; to get stained *o* marked.

'macchina ['makkina] *sf* machine; (*motore, locomotiva*) engine; (*automobile*) car; (*fig*: *meccanismo*) machinery; **andare in** ~ (*AUT*) to go by car; (*STAMPA*) to go to press; ~ da cucire sewing machine; ~ fotografica camera; ~ da presa cine *o* movie camera; ~ da scrivere typewriter; ~ a vapore steam engine.

macchi'nare [makki'nare] *vt* to plot.

macchi'nario [makki'narjo] *sm* machinery.

macchi'netta [makki'netta] *sf* (*fam*: *caffettiera*) percolator; (: *accendino*) lighter.

macchi'nista, i [makki'nista] *sm* (*di treno*) engine-driver; (*di nave*) engineer; (*TEATRO, TV*) stagehand.

macchi'noso, a [makki'noso] *ag* complex, complicated.

mace'donia [matʃe'dɔnja] *sf* fruit salad.

macel'laio [matʃel'lajo] *sm* butcher.

macel'lare [matʃel'lare] *vt* to slaughter, butcher; **macelle'ria** *sf* butcher's (shop); **ma'cello** *sm* (*mattatoio*) slaughterhouse, abattoir (*Brit*); (*fig*) slaughter, massacre; (: *disastro*) shambles *sg*.

mace'rare [matʃe'rare] *vt* to macerate; (*CUC*) to marinate; ~rsi *vr* (*fig*): ~rsi in to be consumed with.

ma'cerie [ma'tʃɛrje] *sfpl* rubble *sg*, debris *sg*.

ma'cigno [ma'tʃiɲɲo] *sm* (*masso*) rock, boulder.

maci'lento, a [matʃi'lɛnto] *ag* emaciated.

'macina ['matʃina] *sf* (*pietra*) millstone; (*macchina*) grinder; **macina'caffè** *sm inv* coffee grinder; **macina'pepe** *sm inv* peppermill.

maci'nare [matʃi'nare] *vt* to grind; (*carne*) to mince (*Brit*), grind (*US*); **maci'nato** *sm* meal, flour; (*carne*) minced (*Brit*) *o* ground (*US*) meat.

maci'nino [matʃi'nino] *sm* coffee grinder; peppermill.

'madido, a *ag*: ~ (di) wet *o* moist (with).

Ma'donna *sf* (*REL*) Our Lady.

mador'nale *ag* enormous, huge.

'madre *sf* mother; (*matrice di bolletta*) counterfoil // *ag inv* mother *cpd*; ragazza ~ unmarried mother; scena ~ (*TEATRO*) principal scene; (*fig*) terrible scene.

madre'lingua *sf* mother tongue, native language.

madre'perla *sf* mother-of-pearl.

ma'drina *sf* godmother.

maestà *sf inv* majesty; **maes'toso, a** *ag* majestic.

ma'estra *sf vedi* **maestro**.

maes'trale *sm* north-west wind, mistral.

maes'tranze [maes'trantse] *sfpl* workforce *sg*.

maes'tria *sf* mastery, skill.

ma'estro, a *sm/f* (*INS*: anche: ~ di scuola *o* elementare) primary (*Brit*) *o* grade school (*US*) teacher; (*esperto*) expert // *sm* (*artigiano, fig*: *guida*) master; (*MUS*) maestro // *ag* (*principale*) main; (*di grande abilità*) masterly, skilful; ~a d'asilo nursery teacher; ~ di cerimonie master of ceremonies.

'mafia *sf* Mafia; **mafi'oso** *sm* member of the Mafia.

'maga *sf* sorceress.

ma'gagna [ma'gaɲɲa] *sf* defect, flaw, blemish; (*noia, guaio*) problem.

ma'gari *escl* (*esprime desiderio*): ~ fosse vero! if only it were true!; ti piacerebbe andare in Scozia? — ~! would you like to go to Scotland? — and how! // *av* (*anche*) even; (*forse*) perhaps.

magaz'zino [magad'dzino] *sm* warehouse; grande ~ department store.

'maggio ['maddʒo] *sm* May.

maggio'rana [maddʒo'rana] *sf* (*BOT*) (sweet) marjoram.

maggio'ranza [maddʒo'rantsa] *sf* majority.

maggio'rare [maddʒo'rare] *vt* to increase, raise.

maggior'domo [maddʒor'dɔmo] *sm* butler.

maggi'ore [mad'dʒore] *ag (comparativo: più grande)* bigger, larger; taller; greater; (: *più vecchio: sorella, fratello*) older, elder; (: *di grado superiore*) senior; (: *più importante, MIL, MUS*) major; *(superlativo)* biggest, largest; tallest; greatest; oldest, eldest // *sm/f (di grado)* superior; *(di età)* elder; *(MIL)* major; (: *AER*) squadron leader; **la maggior parte** the majority; **andare per la ~** *(cantante etc)* to be very popular; **maggio'renne** *ag* of age // *sm/f* person who has come of age; **maggior'mente** *av* much more; *(con senso superlativo)* most.

ma'gia [ma'dʒia] *sf* magic; **'magico, a, ci, che** *ag* magic; *(fig)* fascinating, charming, magical.

'magio ['madʒo] *sm (REL)*: **i re Magi** the Magi, the Three Wise Men.

magis'tero [madʒis'tero] *sm* teaching; *(fig: maestria)* skill; *(INS)*: **facoltà di M~** ≈ teachers' training college; **magis'trale** *ag* primary *(Brit) o* grade school *(US)* teachers', primary *(Brit) o* grade school *(US)* teaching *cpd*; skilful.

magis'trato [madʒis'trato] *sm* magistrate; **magistra'tura** *sf* magistrature; *(magistrati)*: **la magistratura** the Bench.

'maglia ['maʎʎa] *sf* stitch; *(lavoro ai ferri)* knitting *q*; *(tessuto, SPORT)* jersey; *(maglione)* jersey, sweater; *(di catena)* link; *(di rete)* mesh; **~ diritta/rovescia** plain/purl; **maglie'ria** *sf* knitwear; *(negozio)* knitwear shop; **magli'etta** *sf (canottiera)* vest; *(tipo camicia)* T-shirt; **magli'ficio** *sm* knitwear factory.

'maglio ['maʎʎo] *sm (martello)* mallet; *(macchina)* power hammer.

ma'gnete [maɲ'nete] *sm* magnet; **ma'gnetico, a, ci, che** *ag* magnetic.

magne'tofono [maɲne'tɔfono] *sm* tape recorder.

ma'gnifico, a, ci, che [maɲ'nifiko] *ag* magnificent, splendid; *(ospite)* generous.

'magno, a ['maɲno] *ag*: **aula ~a** main hall.

ma'gnolia [maɲ'nɔlja] *sf* magnolia.

'mago, ghi *sm (stregone)* magician, wizard; *(illusionista)* magician.

ma'grezza [ma'grettsa] *sf* thinness.

'magro, a *ag (very)* thin, skinny; *(carne)* lean; *(formaggio)* low-fat; *(fig: scarso, misero)* meagre, poor; (: *meschino: scusa*) poor, lame; **mangiare di ~** not to eat meat.

'mai *av (nessuna volta)* never; *(talvolta)* ever; **non ... ~** never; **~ più** never again; **come ~?** why *(o* how) on earth?; **chi/dove/quando ~?** whoever/wherever/ whenever?

mai'ale *sm (ZOOL)* pig; *(carne)* pork.

maio'nese *sf* mayonnaise.

'mais *sm inv* maize.

mai'uscolo, a *ag (lettera)* capital; *(fig)* enormous, huge // *sf* capital letter.

mal *av, sm vedi* **male**.

malac'corto, a *ag* rash, careless.

mala'fede *sf* bad faith.

mala'mente *av* badly; dangerously.

malan'dato, a *ag (persona: di salute)* in poor health; (: *di condizioni finanziarie*) badly off; *(trascurato)* shabby.

ma'lanno *sm (disgrazia)* misfortune; *(malattia)* ailment.

mala'pena *sf*: **a ~** hardly, scarcely.

ma'laria *sf (MED)* malaria.

mala'sorte *sf* bad luck.

mala'ticcio, a [mala'tittʃo] *ag* sickly.

ma'lato, a *ag* ill, sick; *(gamba)* bad; *(pianta)* diseased // *sm/f* sick person; *(in ospedale)* patient; **malat'tia** *sf (infettiva etc)* illness, disease; *(cattiva salute)* illness, sickness; *(di pianta)* disease.

malau'gurio *sm* bad *o* ill omen.

mala'vita *sf* underworld.

mala'voglia [mala'vɔʎʎa] *sf*: **di ~** unwillingly, reluctantly.

mal'concio, a, ci, ce [mal'kontʃo] *ag* in a sorry state.

malcon'tento *sm* discontent.

malcos'tume *sm* immorality.

mal'destro, a *ag (inabile)* inexpert, inexperienced; *(goffo)* awkward.

maldi'cenza [maldi'tʃɛntsa] *sf* malicious gossip.

maldis'posto, a *ag*: **~ (verso)** ill-disposed (towards).

'male *av* badly // *sm (ciò che è ingiusto, disonesto)* evil; *(danno, svantaggio)* harm; *(sventura)* misfortune; *(dolore fisico, morale)* pain, ache; **di ~ in peggio** from bad to worse; **sentirsi ~** to feel ill; **far ~** *(dolere)* to hurt; **far ~ alla salute** to be bad for one's health; **far del ~ a qn** to hurt *o* harm sb; **restare *o* rimanere ~** to be sorry; to be disappointed; to be hurt; **andare a ~** to go bad; **come va? — non c'è ~** how are you? — not bad; **mal di mare** seasickness; **avere mal di gola/ testa** to have a sore throat/a headache; **aver ~ ai piedi** to have sore feet.

male'detto, a *pp di* **maledire** // *ag* cursed, damned; *(fig: fam)* damned, blasted.

male'dire *vt* to curse; **maledizi'one** *sf* curse; **maledizione!** damn it!

maledu'cato, a *ag* rude, ill-mannered.

male'fatta *sf* misdeed.

male'ficio [male'fitʃo] *sm* witchcraft.

ma'lefico, a, ci, che *ag (aria, cibo)* harmful, bad; *(influsso, azione)* evil.

ma'lessere *sm* indisposition, slight illness; *(fig)* uneasiness.

ma'levolo, a *ag* malevolent.

malfa'mato, a *ag* notorious.

mal'fatto, a *ag* (*persona*) deformed; (*oggetto*) badly made; (*lavoro*) badly done.

malfat'tore, 'trice *sm/f* wrongdoer.

mal'fermo, a *ag* unsteady, shaky; (*salute*) poor, delicate.

malformazi'one [malformat'tsjone] *sf* malformation.

malgo'verno *sm* maladministration.

mal'grado *prep* in spite of, despite // *cong* although; **mio** (*o* **tuo** *etc*) ~ against my (*o* your *etc*) will.

ma'lia *sf* spell; (*fig*: *fascino*) charm.

mali'gnare [malin'nare] *vi*: ~ **su** to malign, speak ill of.

ma'ligno, a [ma'linno] *ag* (*malvagio*) malicious, malignant; (*MED*) malignant.

malinco'nia *sf* melancholy, gloom; **malin'conico, a, ci, che** *ag* melancholy.

malincu'ore: a ~ *av* reluctantly, unwillingly.

malintenzio'nato, a [malintentsjo'nato] *ag* ill-intentioned.

malin'teso, a *ag* misunderstood; (*riguardo, senso del dovere*) mistaken, wrong // *sm* misunderstanding.

ma'lizia [ma'littsja] *sf* (*malignità*) malice; (*furbizia*) cunning; (*espediente*) trick; **mali'zioso, a** *ag* malicious, cunning; (*vivace, birichino*) mischievous.

malme'nare *vt* to beat up; (*fig*) to ill-treat.

mal'messo, a *ag* shabby.

malnu'trito, a *ag* undernourished; **malnutrizi'one** *sf* malnutrition.

ma'locchio [ma'lɔkkjo] *sm* evil eye.

ma'lora *sf*: **andare in** ~ to go to the dogs.

ma'lore *sm* (sudden) illness.

mal'sano, a *ag* unhealthy.

malsi'curo, a *ag* unsafe.

'Malta *sf*: **la** ~ Malta.

'malta *sf* (*EDIL*) mortar.

mal'tempo *sm* bad weather.

'malto *sm* malt.

maltrat'tare *vt* to ill-treat.

malu'more *sm* bad mood; (*irritabilità*) bad temper; (*discordia*) ill feeling; **di** ~ in a bad mood.

mal'vagio, a, gi, gie [mal'vadʒo] *ag* wicked, evil.

malversazi'one [malversat'tsjone] *sf* (*DIR*) embezzlement.

mal'visto, a *ag*: ~ (**da**) disliked (by), unpopular (with).

malvi'vente *sm* criminal.

malvolenti'eri *av* unwillingly, reluctantly.

'mamma *sf* mummy, mum; ~ **mia!** my goodness!

mam'mella *sf* (*ANAT*) breast; (*di vacca, capra etc*) udder.

mam'mifero *sm* mammal.

'mammola *sf* (*BOT*) violet.

ma'nata *sf* (*colpo*) slap; (*quantità*) handful.

'manca *sf* left (hand); **a destra e a** ~ left, right and centre, on all sides.

man'canza [man'kantsa] *sf* lack; (*carenza*) shortage, scarcity; (*fallo*) fault; (*imperfezione*) failing, shortcoming; **per** ~ **di tempo** through lack of time; **in** ~ **di meglio** for lack of anything better.

man'care *vi* (*essere insufficiente*) to be lacking; (*venir meno*) to fail; (*sbagliare*) to be wrong, make a mistake; (*non esserci*) to be missing, not to be there; (*essere lontano*): ~ (**da**) to be away (from) // *vt* to miss; ~ **di** to lack; ~ **a** (*promessa*) to fail to keep; **tu mi manchi** I miss you; **mancò poco che morisse** he very nearly died; **mancano ancora 10 sterline** we're still £10 short; **manca un quarto alle 6** it's a quarter to 6; **man'cato, a** *ag* (*tentativo*) unsuccessful; (*artista*) failed.

'mancia, ce ['mantʃa] *sf* tip; ~ **competente** reward.

manci'ata [man'tʃata] *sf* handful.

man'cino, a [man'tʃino] *ag* (*braccio*) left; (*persona*) left-handed; (*fig*) underhand.

'manco *av* (*nemmeno*): ~ **per sogno** *o* **per idea!** not on your life!

man'dare *vt* to send; (*far funzionare: macchina*) to drive; (*emettere*) to send out; (: *grido*) to give, utter, let out; ~ **a chiamare qn** to send for sb; ~ **avanti** (*fig*: *famiglia*) to provide for; (: *fabbrica*) to run, look after; ~ **giù** to send down; (*anche fig*) to swallow; ~ **via** to send away; (*licenziare*) to fire.

manda'rino *sm* mandarin (orange); (*cinese*) mandarin.

man'data *sf* (*quantità*) lot, batch; (*di chiave*) turn; **chiudere a doppia** ~ to double-lock.

manda'tario *sm* (*DIR*) representative, agent.

man'dato *sm* (*incarico*) commission; (*DIR: provvedimento*) warrant; (*di deputato etc*) mandate; (*ordine di pagamento*) postal *o* money order; ~ **d'arresto** warrant for arrest.

man'dibola *sf* mandible, jaw.

'mandorla *sf* almond; **'mandorlo** *sm* almond tree.

'mandria *sf* herd.

maneggi'are [maned'dʒare] *vt* (*creta, cera*) to mould, work, fashion; (*arnesi, utensili*) to handle; (: *adoperare*) to use; (*fig: persone, denaro*) to handle, deal with; **ma'neggio** *sm* moulding; handling; use; (*intrigo*) plot, scheme; (*per cavalli*) riding school.

ma'nesco, a, schi, sche *ag* free with one's fists.

ma'nette *sfpl* handcuffs.

manga'nello *sm* club.

manga'nese *sm* manganese.

mange'reccio, a, ci, ce [mandʒe'rettʃo] *ag* edible.

mangia'dischi [mandʒa'diski] *sm inv* record player.

mangi'are [man'dʒare] *vt* to eat; (*intaccare*) to eat into o away; (*CARTE, SCACCHI etc*) to take // *vi* to eat // *sm* eating; (*cibo*) food; (*cucina*) cooking; ~**rsi le parole** to mumble; ~**rsi le unghie** to bite one's nails; **mangia'toia** *sf* feeding-trough.

man'gime [man'dʒime] *sm* fodder.

'mango, ghi *sm* mango.

ma'nia *sf* (*PSIC*) mania; (*fig*) obsession, craze; **ma'niaco, a, ci, che** *ag* suffering from a mania; **maniaco (di)** obsessed (by), crazy (about).

'manica *sf* sleeve; (*fig: gruppo*) gang, bunch; (*GEO*): **la M~**, **il Canale della M~** the (English) Channel; **essere di ~ larga/stretta** to be easy-going/strict; ~ **a vento** (*AER*) wind sock.

mani'chino [mani'kino] *sm* (*di sarto, vetrina*) dummy.

'manico, ci *sm* handle; (*MUS*) neck.

mani'comio *sm* mental hospital; (*fig*) madhouse.

mani'cotto *sm* muff; (*TECN*) coupling; sleeve.

mani'cure *sm o f inv* manicure // *sf inv* manicurist.

mani'era *sf* way, manner; (*stile*) style, manner; ~**e** *sfpl* manners; **in ~ che** so that; **in ~ da** so as to; **in tutte le ~e** at all costs.

manie'rato, a *ag* affected.

manifat'tura *sf* (*lavorazione*) manufacture; (*stabilimento*) factory.

manifes'tare *vt* to show, display; (*esprimere*) to express; (*rivelare*) to reveal, disclose // *vi* to demonstrate; ~**rsi** *vr* to show o.s.; ~**rsi amico** to prove o.s. (to be) a friend; **manifestazi'one** *sf* show, display; expression; (*sintomo*) sign, symptom; (*dimostrazione pubblica*) demonstration; (*cerimonia*) event.

mani'festo, a *ag* obvious, evident // *sm* poster, bill; (*scritto ideologico*) manifesto.

ma'niglia [ma'niʎʎa] *sf* handle; (*sostegno: negli autobus etc*) strap.

manipo'lare *vt* to manipulate; (*alterare: vino*) to adulterate; **manipolazi'one** *sf* manipulation; adulteration.

manis'calco, chi *sm* blacksmith.

'manna *sf* (*REL*) manna.

man'naia *sf* (*del boia*) (executioner's) axe; (*per carni*) cleaver.

man'naro: **lupo ~** *sm* werewolf.

'mano, i *sf* hand; (*strato: di vernice etc*) coat; **di prima ~** (*notizia*) first-hand; **di seconda ~** second-hand; **man ~** little by little, gradually; **man ~ che** as; **darsi o stringersi la ~** to shake hands; **mettere le ~i avanti** (*fig*) to safeguard o.s.; **restare a ~i vuote** to be left empty-handed; **venire alle ~i** to come to blows; **a ~** by hand; ~**i in alto!** hands up!

mano'dopera *sf* labour.

mano'messo, a *pp di* **manomettere**.

ma'nometro *sm* gauge, manometer.

mano'mettere *vt* (*alterare*) to tamper with; (*aprire indebitamente*) to break open illegally.

ma'nopola *sf* (*dell'armatura*) gauntlet; (*guanto*) mitt; (*di impugnatura*) handgrip; (*pomello*) knob.

manos'critto, a *ag* handwritten // *sm* manuscript.

mano'vale *sm* labourer.

mano'vella *sf* handle; (*TECN*) crank.

ma'novra *sf* manoeuvre (*Brit*), maneuver (*US*); (*FERR*) shunting; **mano'vrare** *vt* (*veicolo*) to manoeuvre (*Brit*), maneuver (*US*); (*macchina, congegno*) to operate; (*fig: persona*) to manipulate // *vi* to manoeuvre.

manro'vescio [manro'veʃʃo] *sm* slap (*with back of hand*).

man'sarda *sf* attic.

mansi'one *sf* task, duty, job.

mansu'eto, a *ag* gentle, docile.

man'tello *sm* cloak; (*fig: di neve etc*) blanket, mantle; (*TECN: involucro*) casing, shell; (*ZOOL*) coat.

mante'nere *vt* to maintain; (*adempiere: promesse*) to keep, abide by; (*provvedere a*) to support, maintain; ~**rsi** *vr*: ~**rsi calmo/giovane** to stay calm/young; **manteni'mento** *sm* maintenance.

'mantice ['mantitʃe] *sm* bellows *pl*; (*di carrozza, automobile*) hood.

'manto *sm* cloak; ~ **stradale** road surface.

manu'ale *ag* manual // *sm* (*testo*) manual, handbook.

ma'nubrio *sm* handle; (*di bicicletta etc*) handlebars *pl*; (*SPORT*) dumbbell.

manu'fatto *sm* manufactured article.

manutenzi'one [manuten'tsjone] *sf* maintenance, upkeep; (*d'impianti*) maintenance, servicing.

'manzo ['mandzo] *sm* (*ZOOL*) steer; (*carne*) beef.

'mappa *sf* (*GEO*) map; **mappa'mondo** *sm* map of the world; (*globo girevole*) globe.

ma'rasma, i *sm* (*fig*) decay, decline.

mara'tona *sf* marathon.

'marca, che *sf* mark; (*bollo*) stamp; (*COMM: di prodotti*) brand; (*contrassegno, scontrino*) ticket, check; **prodotto di ~** (*di buona qualità*) high-class product; ~ **da bollo** official stamp.

mar'care *vt* (*munire di contrassegno*) to

mark; (*a fuoco*) to brand; (*SPORT*: *gol*) to score; (: *avversario*) to mark; (*accentuare*) to stress; ~ **visita** (*MIL*) to report sick.

'**Marche** ['marke] *sfpl*: **le ~ the Marches** (*region of central Italy*).

mar'**chese, a** [mar'keze] *sm/f* marquis *o* marquess/marchioness.

marchi'**are** [mar'kjare] *vt* to brand; '**marchio** *sm* (*di bestiame, COMM, fig*) brand; **marchio depositato** registered trademark; **marchio di fabbrica** trademark.

'**marcia, ce** ['martʃa] *sf* (*anche MUS, MIL*) march; (*funzionamento*) running; (*il camminare*) walking; (*AUT*) gear; **mettere in ~** to start; **mettersi in ~** to get moving; **far ~ indietro** (*AUT*) to reverse; (*fig*) to back-pedal.

marciapi'**ede** [martʃa'pjɛde] *sm* (*di strada*) pavement (*Brit*), sidewalk (*US*); (*FERR*) platform.

marci'**are** [mar'tʃare] *vi* to march; (*andare*: *treno, macchina*) to go; (*funzionare*) to run, work.

'**marcio, a, ci, ce** ['martʃo] *ag* (*frutta, legno*) rotten, bad; (*MED*) festering; (*fig*) corrupt, rotten.

mar'**cire** [mar'tʃire] *vi* (*andare a male*) to go bad, rot; (*suppurare*) to fester; (*fig*) to rot, waste away.

'**marco, chi** *sm* (*unità monetaria*) mark.

'**mare** *sm* sea; **in ~** at sea; **andare al ~** (*in vacanza etc*) to go to the seaside; **il M~ del Nord** the North Sea.

ma'**rea** *sf* tide; **alta/bassa ~** high/low tide.

mareggi'**ata** [mared'dʒata] *sf* heavy sea.

ma'**remma** *sf* (*GEO*) maremma, swampy coastal area.

mare'**moto** *sm* seaquake.

maresci'**allo** [mareʃ'ʃallo] *sm* (*MIL*) marshal; (: *sottufficiale*) warrant officer.

marga'**rina** *sf* margarine.

marghe'**rita** [marge'rita] *sf* (*ox-eye*) daisy, marguerite; (*di stampante*) daisy wheel; **margheri'tina** *sf* daisy.

'**margine** ['mardʒine] *sm* margin; (*di bosco, via*) edge, border.

ma'**rina** *sf* navy; (*costa*) coast; (*quadro*) seascape; **~ militare/mercantile** navy/merchant navy (*Brit*) *o* marine (*US*).

mari'**naio** *sm* sailor.

mari'**nare** *vt* (*CUC*) to marinate; **~ la scuola** to play truant; **mari'nata** *sf* marinade.

ma'**rino, a** *ag* sea *cpd*, marine.

mario'**netta** *sf* puppet.

mari'**tare** *vt* to marry; **~rsi** *vr*: **~rsi a** *o* **con qn** to marry sb, get married to sb.

ma'**rito** *sm* husband.

ma'**rittimo, a** *ag* maritime, sea *cpd*.

mar'**maglia** [mar'maʎʎa] *sf* mob, riffraff.

marmel'**lata** *sf* jam; (*di agrumi*) marmalade.

mar'**mitta** *sf* (*recipiente*) pot; (*AUT*) silencer.

'**marmo** *sm* marble.

mar'**mocchio** [mar'mɔkkjo] *sm* (*fam*) tot, kid.

mar'**motta** *sf* (*ZOOL*) marmot.

Ma'**rocco** *sm*: **il ~** Morocco.

ma'**roso** *sm* breaker.

mar'**rone** *ag inv* brown // *sm* (*BOT*) chestnut.

mar'**sala** *sm inv* (*vino*) Marsala.

mar'**sina** *sf* tails *pl*, tail coat.

marte'**dì** *sm inv* Tuesday; **di** *o* **il ~ on Tuesdays; ~ grasso** Shrove Tuesday.

martel'**lare** *vt* to hammer // *vi* (*pulsare*) to throb; (: *cuore*) to thump.

mar'**tello** *sm* hammer; (*di uscio*) knocker.

mar'**tire** *sm/f* martyr; **mar'tirio** *sm* martyrdom; (*fig*) agony, torture.

'**martora** *sf* marten.

martori'**are** *vt* to torment, torture.

mar'**xista, i, e** *ag, sm/f* Marxist.

marza'**pane** [martsa'pane] *sm* marzipan.

'**marzo** ['martso] *sm* March.

mascal'**zone** [maskal'tsone] *sm* rascal, scoundrel.

ma'**scella** [maʃ'ʃella] *sf* (*ANAT*) jaw.

'**maschera** ['maskera] *sf* mask; (*travestimento*) disguise; (: *per un ballo etc*) fancy dress; (*TEATRO, CINEMA*) usher/usherette; (*personaggio del teatro*) stock character; **masche'rare** *vt* to mask; (*travestire*) to disguise; to dress up; (*fig: celare*) to hide, conceal; (*MIL*) to camouflage; **~rsi da** to disguise o.s. as; to dress up as; (*fig*) to masquerade as.

mas'**chile** [mas'kile] *ag* masculine; (*sesso, popolazione*) male; (*abiti*) men's; (*per ragazzi: scuola*) boys'.

'**maschio, a** ['maskjo] *ag* (*BIOL*) male; (*virile*) manly // *sm* (*anche ZOOL, TECN*) male; (*uomo*) man; (*ragazzo*) boy; (*figlio*) son.

masco'**lino, a** *ag* masculine.

'**massa** *sf* mass; (*di errori etc*): **una ~ di** heaps of, masses of; (*di gente*) mass, multitude; (*ELETTR*) earth; **in ~** (*COMM*) in bulk; (*tutti insieme*) en masse; **adunata in ~** mass meeting; **di ~** (*cultura, manifestazione*) mass *cpd*; **la ~ del popolo** the masses *pl*.

mas'**sacro** *sm* massacre, slaughter; (*fig*) mess, disaster.

mas'**saggio** [mas'saddʒo] *sm* massage.

mas'**saia** *sf* housewife.

masse'**rizie** [masse'rittsje] *sfpl* (household) furnishings.

mas'**siccio, a, ci, ce** [mas'sittʃo] *ag* (*oro, legno*) solid; (*palazzo*) massive; (*corporatura*) stout // *sm* (*GEO*) massif.

'massima *sf vedi* **massimo.**

massi'male *sm* maximum.

'massimo, a *ag, sm* maximum // *sf* (*sentenza, regola*) maxim; (*METEOR*) maximum temperature; **al ~** at (the) most; **in linea di ~a** generally speaking.

'masso *sm* rock, boulder.

mas'sone *sm* freemason; **massone'ria** *sf* freemasonry.

masti'care *vt* to chew.

'mastice ['mastitʃe] *sm* mastic; (*per vetri*) putty.

mas'tino *sm* mastiff.

ma'tassa *sf* skein.

mate'matico, a, ci, che *ag* mathematical // *sm/f* mathematician // *sf* mathematics *sg*.

mate'rasso *sm* mattress; **~ a molle** spring *o* interior-sprung mattress.

ma'teria *sf* (*FISICA*) matter; (*TECN, COMM*) material, matter *q*; (*disciplina*) subject; (*argomento*) subject matter, material; **~e prime** raw materials; **in ~ di** (*per quanto concerne*) on the subject of; **materi'ale** *ag* material; (*fig: grossolano*) rough, rude // *sm* material; (*insieme di strumenti etc*) equipment *q*, materials *pl*.

maternità *sf* motherhood, maternity; (*clinica*) maternity hospital.

ma'terno, a *ag* (*amore, cura etc*) maternal, motherly; (*nonno*) maternal; (*lingua, terra*) mother *cpd*.

ma'tita *sf* pencil.

ma'trice [ma'tritʃe] *sf* matrix; (*COMM*) counterfoil; (*fig: origine*) background.

ma'tricola *sf* (*registro*) register; (*numero*) registration number; (*nell'università*) freshman, fresher.

ma'trigna [ma'triɲɲa] *sf* stepmother.

matrimoni'ale *ag* matrimonial, marriage *cpd*.

matri'monio *sm* marriage, matrimony; (*durata*) marriage, married life; (*cerimonia*) wedding.

ma'trona *sf* (*fig*) matronly woman.

mat'tina *sf* morning; **matti'nata** *sf* morning; (*spettacolo*) matinée, afternoon performance; **mattini'ero, a** *ag*: **essere mattiniero** to be an early riser; **mat'tino** *sm* morning.

'matto, a *ag* mad, crazy; (*fig: falso*) false, imitation; (: *opaco*) matt, dull // *sm/f* madman/woman; **avere una voglia ~a di qc** to be dying for sth.

mat'tone *sm* brick; (*fig*): **questo libro/film è un ~** this book/film is heavy going.

matto'nella *sf* tile.

matu'rare *vi* (*anche*: **~rsi**) (*frutta, grano*) to ripen; (*ascesso*) to come to a head; (*fig: persona, idea, ECON*) to mature // *vt* to ripen; to (make) mature.

maturità *sf* maturity; (*di frutta*) ripeness, maturity; (*INS*) school-leaving examination, ≈ GCE A-levels (*Brit*).

ma'turo, a *ag* mature; (*frutto*) ripe, mature.

'mazza ['mattsa] *sf* (*bastone*) club; (*martello*) sledge-hammer; (*SPORT: da golf*) club; (: *da baseball, cricket*) bat.

maz'zata [mat'tsata] *sf* (*anche fig*) heavy blow.

'mazzo ['mattso] *sm* (*di fiori, chiavi etc*) bunch; (*di carte da gioco*) pack.

me *pronome* me; **~ stesso(a)** myself; **sei bravo quanto ~** you are as clever as I (am) *o* as me.

me'andro *sm* meander.

M.E.C. [mɛk] *sigla m* (= *Mercato Comune Europeo*) EEC.

mec'canico, a, ci, che *ag* mechanical // *sm* mechanic // *sf* mechanics *sg*; (*attività tecnologica*) mechanical engineering; (*meccanismo*) mechanism.

mecca'nismo *sm* mechanism.

me'daglia [me'daʎʎa] *sf* medal; **medagli'one** *sm* (*ARCHIT*) medallion; (*gioiello*) locket.

me'desimo, a *ag* same; (*in persona*): **io ~** I myself.

'media *sf vedi* **medio.**

medi'ano, a *ag* median; (*valore*) mean // *sm* (*CALCIO*) half-back.

medi'ante *prep* by means of.

medi'are *vt* (*fare da mediatore*) to act as mediator in; (*MAT*) to average.

media'tore, 'trice *sm/f* mediator; (*COMM*) middle man, agent.

medica'mento *sm* medicine, drug.

medi'care *vt* to treat; (*ferita*) to dress; **medicazi'one** *sf* treatment, medication; dressing.

medi'cina [medi'tʃina] *sf* medicine; **~ legale** forensic medicine; **medici'nale** *ag* medicinal // *sm* drug, medicine.

'medico, a, ci, che *ag* medical // *sm* doctor; **~ generico** general practitioner, GP.

medie'vale *ag* medieval.

'medio, a *ag* average; (*punto, ceto*) middle; (*altezza, statura*) medium // *sm* (*dito*) middle finger // *sf* average; (*MAT*) mean; (*INS: voto*) end-of-term average; **in ~a** on average; **licenza ~a** *leaving certificate awarded at the end of 3 years of secondary education*; **scuola ~a** *first 3 years of secondary school.*

medi'ocre *ag* mediocre, poor.

medioe'vale *ag* = **medievale.**

medio'evo *sm* Middle Ages *pl.*

medi'tare *vt* to ponder over, meditate on; (*progettare*) to plan, think out // *vi* to meditate.

mediter'raneo, a *ag* Mediterranean; **il** (*mare*) **M~** the Mediterranean (Sea).

me'dusa *sf* (*ZOOL*) jellyfish.

me'gafono *sm* megaphone.

'meglio ['mɛʎʎo] *av, ag inv* better; (*con senso superlativo*) best // *sm* (*la cosa migliore*): **il ~** the best (thing); **faresti**

~ ad andartene you had better leave; alla ~ as best one can; andar di bene in ~ to get better and better; fare del proprio ~ to do one's best; per il ~ for the best; aver la ~ su qn to get the better of sb.

'mela sf apple; ~ cotogna quince.

mela'grana sf pomegranate.

melan'zana [melan'dzana] sf aubergine (Brit), eggplant (US).

me'lassa sf molasses sg, treacle.

me'lenso, a ag dull, stupid.

mel'lifluo, a ag (peg) sugary, honeyed.

'melma sf mud, mire.

'melo sm apple tree.

melo'dia sf melody.

me'lone sm (musk)melon.

'membra sfpl vedi membro.

'membro sm member; (pl(f) ~a: arto) limb.

memo'randum sm inv memorandum.

me'moria sf memory; ~e sfpl (opera autobiografica) memoirs; a ~ (imparare, sapere) by heart; a ~ d'uomo within living memory; memori'ale sm (raccolta di memorie) memoirs pl; (DIR) memorial.

mena'dito: a ~ av perfectly, thoroughly; sapere qc a ~ to have sth at one's fingertips.

me'nare vt to lead; (picchiare) to hit, beat; (dare: colpi) to deal; ~ la coda (cane) to wag its tail.

mendi'cante smf beggar.

mendi'care vt to beg for // vi to beg.

'meno ◆ av 1 (in minore misura) less; dovresti mangiare ~ you should eat less, you shouldn't eat so much

2 (comparativo): ~ ... di not as ... as, less ... than; sono ~ alto di te I'm not as tall as you (are), I'm less tall than you (are); ~ ... che not as ... as, less ... than; ~ che mai less than ever; è ~ intelligente che ricco he's more rich than intelligent; ~ fumo più mangio the less I smoke the more I eat

3 (superlativo) least; il ~ dotato degli studenti the least gifted of the students; è quello che compro ~ spesso it's the one I buy least often

4 (MAT) minus; 8 ~ 5 8 minus 5, 8 take away 5; sono le 8 ~ un quarto it's a quarter to 8; ~ 5 gradi 5 degrees below zero, minus 5 degrees; mille lire in ~ a thousand lire less

5 (fraseologia): quanto ~ poteva telefonare he could at least have phoned; non so se accettare o ~ I don't know whether to accept or not; fare a ~ di qc/ qn to do without sth/sb; non potevo fare a ~ di ridere I couldn't help laughing; ~ male! thank goodness!; ~ male che sei arrivato it's a good job that you've come

◆ ag inv (tempo, denaro) less; (errori, persone) fewer; ha fatto ~ errori di tutti

he made fewer mistakes than anyone, he made the fewest mistakes of all

◆ sm inv 1: il ~ (il minimo) the least; parlare del più e del ~ to talk about this and that

2 (MAT) minus

◆ prep (eccetto) except (for), apart from; a ~ che, a ~ di unless; a ~ che non piova unless it rains; non posso, a ~ di prendere ferie I can't, unless I take some leave.

meno'mare vt (danneggiare) to maim, disable.

meno'pausa sf menopause.

'mensa sf (locale) canteen; (: MIL) mess; (: nelle università) refectory.

men'sile ag monthly // sm (periodico) monthly (magazine); (stipendio) monthly salary.

'mensola sf bracket; (ripiano) shelf; (ARCHIT) corbel.

'menta sf mint; (anche: ~ piperita) peppermint; (bibita) peppermint cordial; (caramella) mint, peppermint.

men'tale ag mental; mentalità sf inv mentality.

'mente sf mind; imparare/sapere qc a ~ to learn/know sth by heart; avere in ~ qc to have sth in mind; passare di ~ a qn to slip sb's mind.

men'tire vi to lie.

'mento sm chin.

men'tolo sm menthol.

'mentre cong (temporale) while; (avversativo) whereas.

menzio'nare [mentsjo'nare] vt to mention.

menzi'one [men'tsjone] sf mention; fare ~ di to mention.

men'zogna [men'tsɔɲɲa] sf lie.

mera'viglia [mera'viʎʎa] sf amazement, wonder; (persona, cosa) marvel, wonder; a ~ perfectly, wonderfully; meravigli'are vt to amaze, astonish; meravigliarsi (di) to marvel (at); (stupirsi) to be amazed (at), be astonished (at); meravigli'oso, a ag wonderful, marvellous.

mer'cante sm merchant; ~ d'arte art dealer; ~ di cavalli horse dealer; mercanteggi'are vt (onore, voto) to sell // vi to bargain, haggle; mercan'tile ag commercial, mercantile; (nave, marina) merchant cpd // sm (nave) merchantman; mercan'zia sf merchandise, goods pl.

mer'cato sm market; ~ dei cambi exchange market; M~ Comune (Europeo) (European) Common Market; ~ nero black market.

'merce ['mertʃe] sf goods pl, merchandise; ~ deperibile perishable goods pl.

mercé [mer'tʃe] sf mercy.

merce'nario, a [mertʃe'narjo] ag, sm

mercenary.

merce'ria [mertʃe'ria] *sf* (*articoli*) haberdashery (*Brit*), notions *pl* (*US*); (*bottega*) haberdasher's shop (*Brit*), notions store (*US*).

mercoledì *sm inv* Wednesday; **di** *o* **il** ~ on Wednesdays; ~ **delle Ceneri** Ash Wednesday.

mer'curio *sm* mercury.

'merda *sf* (*fam!*) shit (!).

me'renda *sf* afternoon snack.

meridi'ano, a *ag* meridian; **midday** *cpd*, **noonday** // *sm* meridian // *sf* (*orologio*) sundial.

meridio'nale *ag* southern // *sm/f* southerner.

meridi'one *sm* south.

me'ringa, ghe *sf* (*CUC*) meringue.

meri'tare *vt* to deserve, merit // *vb impers*: **merita andare** it's worth going.

meri'tevole *ag* worthy.

'merito *sm* merit; (*valore*) worth; **in** ~ **a** as regards, with regard to; **dare** ~ **a qn di** to give sb credit for; **finire a pari** ~ to finish joint first (*o* second *etc*); **to tie**; **meri'torio, a** *ag* praiseworthy.

mer'letto *sm* lace.

'merlo *sm* (*ZOOL*) blackbird; (*ARCHIT*) battlement.

mer'luzzo [mer'luttso] *sm* (*ZOOL*) cod.

mes'chino, a [mes'kino] *ag* wretched; (*scarso*) scanty, poor; (*persona: gretta*) mean; (: *limitata*) narrow-minded, petty.

mesco'lanza [mesko'lantsa] *sf* mixture.

mesco'lare *vt* to mix; (*vini, colori*) to blend; (*mettere in disordine*) to mix up, muddle up; (*carte*) to shuffle; ~**rsi** *vr* to mix; to blend; to get mixed up; (*fig*): ~**rsi** in to get mixed up in, meddle in.

'mese *sm* month.

'messa *sf* (*REL*) mass; (*il mettere*): ~ **in moto** starting; ~ **in piega** set; ~ **a punto** (*TECN*) adjustment; (*AUT*) tuning; (*fig*) clarification; ~ **in scena** = **messinscena**.

messag'gero [messad'dʒero] *sm* messenger.

mes'saggio [mes'saddʒo] *sm* message.

mes'sale *sm* (*REL*) missal.

'messe *sf* harvest.

Mes'sia *sm inv* (*REL*): **il** ~ the Messiah.

'Messico *sm*: **il** ~ Mexico.

messin'scena [messin'ʃɛna] *sf* (*TEATRO*) production.

'messo, a *pp di* **mettere** // *sm* messenger.

mesti'ere *sm* (*professione*) job; (: *manuale*) trade; (: *artigianale*) craft; (*fig: abilità nel lavoro*) skill, technique; **essere del** ~ to know the tricks of the trade.

'mesto, a *ag* sad, melancholy.

'mestola *sf* (*CUC*) ladle; (*EDIL*) trowel.

'mestolo *sm* (*CUC*) ladle.

mestruazi'one [mestruat'tsjone] *sf* menstruation.

'meta *sf* destination; (*fig*) aim, goal.

metà *sf inv* half; (*punto di mezzo*) middle; **dividere qc a** *o* **per** ~ to divide sth in half, halve sth; **fare a** ~ (**di qc con qn**) to go halves (with sb in sth); **a** ~ **prezzo** at half price; **a** ~ **strada** halfway.

me'tafora *sf* metaphor.

me'tallico, a, ci, che *ag* (*di metallo*) metal *cpd*; (*splendore, rumore etc*) metallic.

me'tallo *sm* metal.

metalmec'canico, a, ci, che *ag* engineering *cpd* // *sm* engineering worker.

me'tano *sm* methane.

meteorolo'gia [meteorolo'dʒia] *sf* meteorology; **meteoro'logico, a, ci, che** *ag* meteorological, weather *cpd*.

me'ticcio, a, ci, ce [me'tittʃo] *sm/f* half-caste, half-breed.

me'todico, a, ci, che *ag* methodical.

'metodo *sm* method; (*manuale*) tutor (*Brit*), manual.

'metrico, a, ci, che *ag* metric; (*POESIA*) metrical // *sf* metrics *sg*.

'metro *sm* metre; (*nastro*) tape measure; (*asta*) (metre) rule.

metropoli'tano, a *ag* metropolitan // *sf* underground, subway.

'mettere *vt* to put; (*abito*) to put on; (: *portare*) to wear; (*installare: telefono*) to put in; (*fig: provocare*): ~ **fame/ allegria a qn** to make sb hungry/happy; (*supporre*): **mettiamo che ...** let's suppose *o* say that ... ; ~**rsi** *vr* (*persona*) to put o.s.; (*oggetto*) to go; (*disporsi: faccenda*) to turn out; ~**rsi a sedere** to sit down; ~**rsi a letto** to get into bed; (*per malattia*) to take to one's bed; ~**rsi il cappello** to put on one's hat; ~**rsi a** (*cominciare*) to begin to, start to; ~**rsi al lavoro** to set to work; ~**rsi con qn** (*in società*) to team up with sb; (*in coppia*) to start going out with sb; ~**rci**: ~**rci molta cura/molto tempo** to take a lot of care/a lot of time; **ci ho messo 3 ore** per **venire** it's taken me 3 hours to get here; ~**rcela tutta** to do one's best; ~ **a tacere qn/qc** to keep sb/sth quiet; ~ **su casa** to set up house; ~ **su un negozio** to start a shop; ~ **via** to put away.

mez'zadro [med'dzadro] *sm* (*AGR*) sharecropper.

mezza'luna [meddza'luna] *sf* half-moon; (*dell'islamismo*) crescent; (*coltello*) (semicircular) chopping knife.

mezza'nino [meddza'nino] *sm* mezzanine (floor).

mez'zano, a [med'dzano] *ag* (*medio*) average, medium; (*figlio*) middle *cpd* // *sm/f* (*intermediario*) go-between; (*ruffiano*) pimp.

mezza'notte [meddza'nɔtte] *sf* midnight.

'mezzo, a ['mɛddzo] *ag* half; **un ~ litro/panino** half a litre/roll // *av* half-; **~ morto** half-dead // *sm* (*metà*) half; (*parte centrale: di strada etc*) middle; (*per raggiungere un fine*) means *sg*; (*veicolo*) vehicle; (*nell'indicare l'ora*): **le nove e ~** half past nine; **mezzogiorno e ~** half past twelve // *sf*: **la ~a** half-past twelve (*in the afternoon*); **~i** *smpl* (*possibilità economiche*) means; **di ~a età** middle-aged; **un soprabito di ~a stagione** a spring (*o* autumn) coat; **di ~** middle, in the middle; **andarci di ~** (*patir danno*) to suffer; **levarsi** *o* **togliersi di ~** to get out of the way; **in ~ a** in the middle of; **per** *o* **a ~ di** by means of; **~i di comunicazione di massa** mass media *pl*; **~i pubblici** public transport *sg*; **~i di trasporto** means of transport.

mezzogi'orno [meddzo'dʒorno] *sm* midday, noon; (*GEO*) south; **a ~** at 12 (o'clock) *o* midday *o* noon; **il ~ d'Italia** southern Italy.

mez'z'ora, mez'zora [med'dzora] *sf* half-hour, half an hour.

mi *pronome* (*dav lo, la, li, le, ne diventa* **me**) (*oggetto*) me; (*complemento di termine*) to me; (*riflessivo*) myself // *sm* (*MUS*) E; (: *solfeggiando la scala*) mi.

'mia *vedi* **mio.**

miago'lare *vi* to miaow, mew.

'mica *sf* (*CHIM*) mica // *av* (*fam*): **non ... ~** not ... at all; **non sono ~ stanco** I'm not a bit tired; **non sarà ~ partito?** he wouldn't have left, would he?; **~ male** not bad.

'miccia, ce ['mittʃa] *sf* fuse.

micidi'ale [mitʃi'djale] *ag* fatal; (*dannosissimo*) deadly.

mi'crofono *sm* microphone.

micros'copio *sm* microscope.

mi'dollo, *pl(f)* **~a** *sm* (*ANAT*) marrow.

'mie, mi'ei *vedi* **mio.**

mi'ele *sm* honey.

mi'etere *vt* (*AGR*) to reap, harvest; (*fig: vite*) to take, claim.

migli'aio [miʎ'ʎajo], *pl(f)* **~a** *sm* thousand; **un ~** (di) about a thousand; **a ~a** by the thousand, in thousands.

'miglio ['miʎʎo] *sm* (*BOT*) millet; (*pl(f)* **~a:** *unità di misura*) mile; **~ marino** *o* **nautico** nautical mile.

migliora'mento [miʎʎora'mento] *sm* improvement.

miglio'rare [miʎʎo'rare] *vt*, *vi* to improve.

migli'ore [miʎ'ʎore] *ag* (*comparativo*) better; (*superlativo*) best // *sm*: **il ~** the best (*thing*) // *sm/f*: **il(la) ~** the best (*person*); **il miglior vino di questa regione** the best wine in this area.

'mignolo ['miɲɲolo] *sm* (*ANAT*) little finger, pinkie; (: *dito del piede*) little toe.

mi'grare *vi* to migrate.

'mila *pl di* **mille.**

Mi'lano *sf* Milan.

miliar'dario, a *sm/f* millionaire.

mili'ardo *sm* thousand million, billion (*US*).

mili'are *ag*: **pietra ~** milestone.

mili'one *sm* million; **un ~ di lire** a million lire.

mili'tante *ag*, *sm/f* militant.

mili'tare *vi* (*MIL*) to be a soldier, serve; (*fig: in un partito*) to be a militant // *ag* military // *sm* serviceman; **fare il ~** to do one's military service.

'milite *sm* soldier.

millan'tatore, 'trice *sm/f* boaster.

'mille *num* (*pl* **mila**) *a o* one thousand; **dieci mila** ten thousand.

mille'foglie [mille'fɔʎʎe] *sm inv* (*CUC*) cream *o* vanilla slice.

mil'lennio *sm* millennium.

millepi'edi *sm inv* centipede.

mil'lesimo, a *ag*, *sm* thousandth.

milli'grammo *sm* milligram(me).

mil'limetro *sm* millimetre.

'milza ['miltsa] *sf* (*ANAT*) spleen.

mimetiz'zare [mimetid'dzare] *vt* to camouflage; **~rsi** *vr* to camouflage o.s.

'mimica *sf* (*arte*) mime.

'mimo *sm* (*attore, componimento*) mime.

mi'mosa *sf* mimosa.

'mina *sf* (*esplosiva*) mine; (*di matita*) lead.

mi'naccia, ce [mi'nattʃa] *sf* threat; **minacci'are** *vt* to threaten; **minacciare qn di morte** to threaten to kill sb; **minacciare di fare qc** to threaten to do sth; **minacci'oso, a** *ag* threatening.

mi'nare *vt* (*MIL*) to mine; (*fig*) to undermine.

mina'tore *sm* miner.

mina'torio, a *ag* threatening.

mine'rale *ag*, *sm* mineral.

mine'rario, a *ag* (*delle miniere*) mining; (*dei minerali*) ore *cpd*.

mi'nestra *sf* soup; **~ in brodo/di verdure** noodle/vegetable soup; **mines'trone** *sm* thick vegetable and pasta soup.

mingher'lino, a [minger'lino] *ag* thin, slender.

'mini *ag inv* mini // *sf inv* miniskirt.

minia'tura *sf* miniature.

mini'era *sf* mine.

mini'gonna *sf* miniskirt.

'minimo, a *ag* minimum, least, slightest; (*piccolissimo*) very small, slight; (*il più basso*) lowest, minimum // *sm* minimum; **al ~** at least; **girare al ~** (*AUT*) to idle.

minis'tero *sm* (*POL, REL*) ministry; (*governo*) government; **~ delle Finanze** Ministry of Finance, ≈ Treasury.

mi'nistro *sm* (*POL, REL*) minister; **~ delle Finanze** Minister of Finance, ≈ Chancellor of the Exchequer.

mino'ranza [mino'rantsa] *sf* minority.
mino'rato, a *ag* handicapped // *smf* physically (o mentally) handicapped person.
mi'nore *ag* (*comparativo*) less; (*più piccolo*) smaller; (*numero*) lower; (*inferiore*) lower, inferior; (*meno importante*) minor; (*più giovane*) younger; (*superlativo*) least; smallest; lowest; youngest // *smf* (*minorenne*) minor, person under age.
mino'renne *ag* under age // *smf* minor, person under age.
mi'nuscolo, a *ag* (*scrittura, carattere*) small; (*piccolissimo*) tiny // *sf* small letter.
mi'nuta *sf* rough copy, draft.
mi'nuto, a *ag* tiny, minute; (*pioggia*) fine; (*corporatura*) delicate, fine; (*lavoro*) detailed // *sm* (*unità di misura*) minute; **al ~** (*COMM*) retail.
'mio, 'mia, mi'ei, 'mie *det*: **il ~, la mia** *etc* my // *pronome*: **il ~, la mia** *etc* mine; **i miei** my family; **un ~ amico** a friend of mine.
'miope *ag* short-sighted.
'mira *sf* (*anche fig*) aim; **prendere la ~** to take aim; **prendere di ~ qn** (*fig*) to pick on sb.
mi'rabile *ag* admirable, wonderful.
mi'racolo *sm* miracle.
mi'raggio [mi'raddʒo] *sm* mirage.
mi'rare *vi*: **~ a** to aim at.
mi'rino *sm* (*TECN*) sight; (*FOT*) viewer, viewfinder.
mir'tillo *sm* bilberry (*Brit*), blueberry (*US*), whortleberry.
mi'scela [miʃ'ʃela] *sf* mixture; (*di caffè*) blend.
miscel'lanea [miʃʃel'lanea] *sf* miscellany.
'mischia ['miskja] *sf* scuffle; (*RUGBY*) scrum, scrummage.
mischi'are [mis'kjare] *vt*, **~rsi** *vr* to mix, blend.
mis'cuglio [mis'kuʎʎo] *sm* mixture, hotchpotch, jumble.
mise'rabile *ag* (*infelice*) miserable, wretched; (*povero*) poverty-stricken; (*di scarso valore*) miserable.
mi'seria *sf* extreme poverty; (*infelicità*) misery; **~e** *sfpl* (*del mondo etc*) misfortunes, troubles; **porca ~!** (*fam*) blast!, damn!
miseri'cordia *sf* mercy, pity.
'misero, a *ag* miserable, wretched; (*povero*) poverty-stricken; (*insufficiente*) miserable.
mis'fatto *sm* misdeed, crime.
mi'sogino [mi'zɔdʒino] *sm* misogynist.
'missile *sm* missile.
missio'nario, a *ag*, *smf* missionary.
missi'one *sf* mission.
misteri'oso, a *ag* mysterious.
mis'tero *sm* mystery.

mistifi'care *vt* to fool, bamboozle.
'misto, a *ag* mixed; (*scuola*) mixed, coeducational // *sm* mixture.
mis'tura *sf* mixture.
mi'sura *sf* measure; (*misurazione, dimensione*) measurement; (*taglia*) size; (*provvedimento*) measure, step; (*moderazione*) moderation; (*MUS*) time; (: *divisione*) bar; (*fig: limite*) bounds *pl*, limit; **nella ~ in cui** inasmuch as, insofar as; **su ~** made to measure.
misu'rare *vt* (*ambiente, stoffa*) to measure; (*terreno*) to survey; (*abito*) to try on; (*pesare*) to weigh; (*fig: parole etc*) to weigh up; (: *spese, cibo*) to limit // *vi* to measure; **~rsi** *vr*: **~rsi con qn** to have a confrontation with sb; to compete with sb; **misu'rato, a** *ag* (*ponderato*) measured; (*prudente*) cautious; (*moderato*) moderate.
'mite *ag* mild; (*prezzo*) moderate, reasonable.
miti'gare *vt* to mitigate, lessen; (*lenire*) to soothe, relieve; **~rsi** *vr* (*odio*) to subside; (*tempo*) to become milder.
'mito *sm* myth; **mitolo'gia, 'gie** *sf* mythology.
'mitra *sf* (*REL*) mitre // *sm inv* (*arma*) sub-machine gun.
mitraglia'trice [mitraʎʎa'tritʃe] *sf* machine gun.
mit'tente *smf* sender.
'mobile *ag* mobile; (*parte di macchina*) moving; (*DIR: bene*) movable, personal // *sm* (*arredamento*) piece of furniture; **~i** *smpl* furniture *sg*.
mo'bilia *sf* furniture.
mobili'are *ag* (*DIR*) personal, movable.
mo'bilio *sm* = **mobilia**.
mobili'tare *vt* to mobilize.
mocas'sino *sm* moccasin.
'moccolo *sm* (*di candela*) candle-end; (*fam: bestemmia*) oath; (: *moccio*) snot; **reggere il ~** to play gooseberry (*Brit*), act as chaperon.
'moda *sf* fashion; **alla ~, di ~** fashionable, in fashion.
modalità *sf inv* formality.
mo'della *sf* model.
model'lare *vt* (*creta*) to model, shape; **~rsi** *vr*: **~rsi su** to model o.s. on.
mo'dello *sm* model; (*stampo*) mould // *ag inv* model *cpd*.
'modem *sm inv* modem.
mode'rare *vt* to moderate; **~rsi** *vr* to restrain o.s.; **mode'rato, a** *ag* moderate.
modera'tore, 'trice *smf* moderator.
mo'derno, a *ag* modern.
mo'destia *sf* modesty.
mo'desto, a *ag* modest.
'modico, a, ci, che *ag* reasonable, moderate.
mo'difica, che *sf* modification.
modifi'care *vt* to modify, alter; **~rsi** *vr*

to alter, change.

mo'dista sf milliner.

'modo sm way, manner; (mezzo) means, way; (occasione) opportunity; (LING) mood; (MUS) mode; ~i smpl manners; a suo ~, a ~ suo in his own way; ad o in ogni ~ anyway; di o in ~ che so that; in ~ da so as to; in tutti i ~i at all costs; (comunque sia) anyway; (in ogni caso) in any case; in qualche ~ somehow or other; ~ di dire turn of phrase; per ~ di dire so to speak.

modu'lare vt to modulate; **modulazi'one** sf modulation; **modulazione di frequenza** frequency modulation.

'modulo sm (modello) form; (ARCHIT, lunare, di comando) module.

'mogano sm mahogany.

'mogio, a, gi, gie ['mɔdʒo] ag down in the dumps, dejected.

'moglie ['moʎʎe] sf wife.

mo'ine sfpl cajolery sg; (leziosità) affectation sg.

'mola sf millstone; (utensile abrasivo) grindstone.

mo'lare sm (dente) molar.

'mole sf mass; (dimensioni) size; (edificio grandioso) massive structure.

moles'tare vt to bother, annoy; **mo'lestia** sf annoyance, bother; **recar molestia a qn** to bother sb; **mo'lesto, a** ag annoying.

'molla sf spring; ~e sfpl tongs.

mol'lare vt to release, let go; (NAUT) to ease; (fig: ceffone) to give // vi (cedere) to give in.

'molle ag soft; (muscoli) flabby; (fig: debole) weak, feeble.

mol'letta sf (per capelli) hairgrip; (per panni stesi) clothes peg; ~e sfpl (per zucchero) tongs.

'mollica, che sf crumb, soft part.

mol'lusco, schi sm mollusc.

'molo sm mole, breakwater; jetty.

mol'teplice [mol'teplitʃe] ag (formato di più elementi) complex; ~i pl (svariati: interessi, attività) numerous, various.

moltipli'care vt to multiply; ~rsi vr to multiply; to increase in number; **molti-plicazi'one** sf multiplication.

'molto, a ◆ det (quantità) a lot of, much; (numero) a lot of, many; ~ pane/carbone a lot of bread/coal; ~a gente a lot of people, many people; ~i libri a lot of books, many books; non ho ~ tempo I haven't got much time; per ~ (tempo) for a long time

◆ av 1 a lot, (very) much; viaggia ~ he travels a lot; non viaggia ~ he doesn't travel much o a lot

2 (intensivo: con aggettivi, avverbi) very; (: con participio passato) (very) much; ~ buono very good; ~ migliore, ~ meglio much o a lot better

◆ pronome much, a lot; ~i(e) pronome pl many, a lot; ~i pensano che ... many (people) think ....

momen'taneo, a ag momentary, fleeting.

mo'mento sm moment; da un ~ all'altro at any moment; (all'improvviso) suddenly; al ~ di fare just as I was (o you were o he was etc) doing; per il ~ for the time being; dal ~ che ever since; (dato che) since; a ~i (da un ~ all'altro) any time o moment now; (quasi) nearly.

'monaca, che sf nun.

'Monaco sf Monaco; ~ (di Baviera) Munich.

'monaco, ci sm monk.

mo'narca, chi sm monarch; **monar'chia** sf monarchy.

monas'tero sm (di monaci) monastery; (di monache) convent; **mo'nastico, a, ci, che** ag monastic.

'monco, a, chi, che ag maimed; (fig) incomplete; ~ d'un braccio one-armed.

mon'dana sf prostitute.

mon'dano, a ag (anche fig) worldly; (dell'alta società) society cpd; fashionable.

mon'dare vt (frutta, patate) to peel; (piselli) to shell; (pulire) to clean.

mondi'ale ag (campionato, popolazione) world cpd; (influenza) world-wide.

'mondo sm world; (grande quantità): un ~ di lots of, a host of; il bel ~ high society.

mo'nello, a sm/f street urchin; (ragazzo vivace) scamp, imp.

mo'neta sf coin; (ECON: valuta) currency; (denaro spicciolo) (small) change; ~ estera foreign currency; ~ legale legal tender; **mone'tario, a** ag monetary.

mongo'loide ag, sm/f (MED) mongol.

'monito sm warning.

'monitor sm inv (TECN, TV) monitor.

monoco'lore ag (POL): governo ~ one-party government.

mono'polio sm monopoly.

mo'notono, a ag monotonous.

monsi'gnore [monsiɲ'ɲore] sm (REL: titolo) Your (o His) Grace.

mon'sone sm monsoon.

monta'carichi [monta'kariki] sm inv hoist, goods lift.

mon'taggio [mon'taddʒo] sm (TECN) assembly; (CINEMA) editing.

mon'tagna [mon'taɲɲa] sf mountain; (zona montuosa): la ~ the mountains pl; andare in ~ to go to the mountains; ~e russe roller coaster sg, big dipper sg (Brit); **monta'gnoso, a** ag mountainous.

monta'naro, a ag mountain cpd // sm/f mountain dweller.

mon'tano, a ag mountain cpd; alpine.

mon'tare vt to go (o come) up; (cavallo) to ride; (apparecchiatura) to set up, assemble; (CUC) to whip; (ZOOL) to cover; (incastonare) to mount, set; (CINEMA) to edit; (FOT) to mount // vi to go (o come) up; (a cavallo): ~ bene/male to ride well/badly; (aumentare di livello, volume) to rise; ~rsi vr to become big-headed; ~ qc to exaggerate sth; ~ qn o la testa a qn to turn sb's head; ~ in bicicletta/macchina/treno to get on a bicycle/into a car/on a train; ~ a cavallo to get on o mount a horse.

monta'tura sf assembling q; (di occhiali) frames pl; (di gioiello) mounting, setting; (fig): ~ pubblicitaria publicity stunt.

'monte sm mountain; a ~ upstream; mandare a ~ qc to upset sth, cause sth to fail; il M~ Bianco Mont Blanc; ~ di pietà pawnshop.

mon'tone sm (ZOOL) ram; carne di ~ mutton.

montu'oso, a ag mountainous.

monu'mento sm monument.

'mora sf (del rovo) blackberry; (del gelso) mulberry; (DIR) delay; (: somma) arrears pl.

mo'rale ag moral // sf (scienza) ethics sg, moral philosophy; (complesso di norme) moral standards pl, morality; (condotta) morals pl; (insegnamento morale) moral // sm morale; essere giù di ~ to be feeling down; **moralità** sf morality; (condotta) morals pl.

'morbido, a ag soft; (pelle) soft, smooth.

mor'billo sm (MED) measles sg.

'morbo sm disease.

mor'boso, a ag (fig) morbid.

mor'dace [mor'datʃe] ag biting, cutting.

mor'dente sm (fig: di satira, critica) bite; (: di persona) drive.

'mordere vt to bite; (addentare) to bite into; (corrodere) to eat into.

mori'bondo, a ag dying, moribund.

morige'rato, a [moridʒe'rato] ag of good morals.

mo'rire vi to die; (abitudine, civiltà) to die out; ~ di fame to die of hunger; (fig) to be starving; ~ di noia/paura to be bored/scared to death; fa un caldo da ~ it's terribly hot.

mormo'rare vi to murmur; (brontolare) to grumble.

'moro, a ag dark(-haired); dark(-complexioned); i M~i smpl (STORIA) the Moors.

mo'roso, a ag in arrears // sm/f (fam: innamorato) sweetheart.

'morsa sf (TECN) vice; (fig: stretta) grip.

morsi'care vt to nibble (at), gnaw (at); (sog: insetto) to bite.

'morso, a pp di mordere // sm bite; (di insetto) sting; (parte della briglia) bit; ~i della fame pangs of hunger.

mor'taio sm mortar.

mor'tale ag, sm mortal; **mortalità** sf mortality, death rate.

'morte sf death.

mortifi'care vt to mortify.

'morto, a pp di morire // ag dead // sm/f dead man/woman; i ~i the dead; fare il ~ (nell'acqua) to float on one's back; il Mar M~ the Dead Sea.

mor'torio sm (anche fig) funeral.

mo'saico, ci sm mosaic.

'mosca, sche sf fly; ~ cieca blindman's-buff.

'Mosca sf Moscow.

mos'cato sm muscatel (wine).

mosce'rino [moʃʃe'rino] sm midge, gnat.

mos'chea [mos'kɛa] sf mosque.

mos'chetto [mos'ketto] sm musket.

'moscio, a, sci, sce ['moʃʃo] ag (fig) lifeless.

mos'cone sm (ZOOL) bluebottle; (barca) pedalo; (: a remi) kind of pedalo with oars.

'mossa sf movement; (nel gioco) move.

'mosso, a pp di muovere // ag (mare) rough; (capelli) wavy; (FOT) blurred; (ritmo, prosa) animated.

mos'tarda sf mustard.

'mostra sf exhibition, show; (ostentazione) show; in ~ on show; far ~ di (fingere) to pretend; far ~ di sé to show off.

mos'trare vt to show // vi: ~ di fare to pretend to do; ~rsi vr to appear.

'mostro sm monster; **mostru'oso, a** ag monstrous.

mo'tel sm inv motel.

moti'vare vt (causare) to cause; (giustificare) to justify, account for; **motivazi'one** sf justification; motive; (PSIC) motivation.

mo'tivo sm (causa) reason, cause; (movente) motive; (letterario) (central) theme; (disegno) motif, design, pattern; (MUS) motif; per quale ~? why?, for what reason?

'moto sm (anche FISICA) motion; (movimento, gesto) movement; (esercizio fisico) exercise; (sommossa) rising, revolt; (commozione) feeling, impulse // sf inv (motocicletta) motorbike; mettere in ~ to set in motion; (AUT) to start up.

motoci'cletta [mototʃi'kletta] sf motorcycle; **motoci'clismo** sm motorcycling, motorcycle racing; **motoci'clista, i, e** sm/f motorcyclist.

mo'tore, 'trice ag motor; (TECN) driving // sm engine, motor; a ~ motor cpd, power-driven; ~ a combustione interna/a reazione internal combustion/jet engine;

moto'rino *sm* moped; **motorino di avviamento** (*AUT*) starter; **motoriz'zato, a** *ag* (*truppe*) motorized; (*persona*) having a car *o* transport.

motos'cafo *sm* motorboat.

mot'teggio [mot'teddʒo] *sm* banter.

'motto *sm* (*battuta scherzosa*) witty remark; (*frase emblematica*) motto, maxim.

mo'vente *sm* motive.

movimen'tare *vt* to liven up.

movi'mento *sm* movement; (*fig*) activity, hustle and bustle; (*MUS*) tempo, movement.

mozi'one [mot'tsjone] *sf* (*POL*) motion.

moz'zare [mot'tsare] *vt* to cut off; (*coda*) to dock; ~ **il fiato** *o* **il respiro a qn** (*fig*) to take sb's breath away.

mozza'rella [mottsa'rɛlla] *sf* mozzarella (*a moist Neapolitan curd cheese*).

mozzi'cone [mottsi'kone] *sm* stub, butt, end; (*anche:* ~ **di sigaretta**) cigarette end.

'mozzo *sm* ['mɔddzo] (*MECCANICA*) hub; ['mottso] (*NAUT*) ship's boy; ~ **di stalla** stable boy.

'mucca, che *sf* cow.

'mucchio ['mukkjo] *sm* pile, heap; (*fig*): **un** ~ **di** lots of, heaps of.

'muco, chi *sm* mucus.

'muffa *sf* mould, mildew.

mug'gire [mud'dʒire] *vi* (*vacca*) to low, moo; (*toro*) to bellow; (*fig*) to roar; **mug'gito** *sm* low, moo; bellow; roar.

mu'ghetto [mu'getto] *sm* lily of the valley.

mu'gnaio, a [muɲ'ɲajo] *sm/f* miller.

mugo'lare *vi* (*cane*) to whimper, whine; (*fig: persona*) to moan.

muli'nare *vi* to whirl, spin (round and round).

muli'nello *sm* (*moto vorticoso*) eddy, whirl; (*di canna da pesca*) reel; (*NAUT*) windlass.

mu'lino *sm* mill; ~ **a vento** windmill.

'mulo *sm* mule.

'multa *sf* fine; **mul'tare** *vt* to fine.

'multiplo, a *ag, sm* multiple.

'mummia *sf* mummy.

'mungere ['mundʒere] *vt* (*anche fig*) to milk.

munici'pale [munitʃi'pale] *ag* municipal; town *cpd*.

muni'cipio [muni'tʃipjo] *sm* town council, corporation; (*edificio*) town hall.

mu'nire *vt*: ~ **qc/qn di** to equip sth/sb with.

munizi'oni [munit'tsjoni] *sfpl* (*MIL*) ammunition *sg*.

'munto, a *pp di* **mungere**.

mu'overe *vt* to move; (*ruota, macchina*) to drive; (*sollevare: questione, obiezione*) to raise, bring up; (: *accusa*) to make, bring forward; ~**rsi** *vr* to move; **muoviti!** hurry up!, get a move

on!

'mura *sfpl vedi* **muro.**

mu'raglia [mu'raʎʎa] *sf* (high) wall.

mu'rale *ag* wall *cpd*; mural.

mu'rare *vt* (*persona, porta*) to wall up.

mura'tore *sm* mason; bricklayer.

'muro *sm* wall; ~**a** *sfpl* (*cinta cittadina*) walls; **a** ~ wall *cpd*; (*armadio etc*) built-in; ~ **del suono** sound barrier; **mettere al** ~ (*fucilare*) to shoot *o* execute (by firing squad).

'muschio ['muskjo] *sm* (*ZOOL*) musk; (*BOT*) moss.

musco'lare *ag* muscular, muscle *cpd*.

'muscolo *sm* (*ANAT*) muscle.

mu'seo *sm* museum.

museru'ola *sf* muzzle.

'musica *sf* music; ~ **da ballo/camera** dance/chamber music; **musi'cale** *ag* musical; **musi'cista, i, e** *sm/f* musician.

'muso *sm* muzzle; (*di auto, aereo*) nose; **tenere il** ~ to sulk; **mu'sone, a** *sm/f* sulky person.

'mussola *sf* muslin.

'muta *sf* (*di animali*) moulting; (*di serpenti*) sloughing; (*per immersioni subacquee*) diving suit; (*gruppo di cani*) pack.

muta'mento *sm* change.

mu'tande *sfpl* (*da uomo*) (under)pants; **mutan'dine** *sfpl* (*da donna, bambino*) pants (*Brit*), briefs; **mutandine di plastica** plastic pants.

mu'tare *vt, vi* to change, alter; **mutazi'one** *sf* change, alteration; (*BIOL*) mutation; **mu'tevole** *ag* changeable.

muti'lare *vt* to mutilate, maim; (*fig*) to mutilate, deface; **muti'lato, a** *sm/f* disabled person (*through loss of limbs*).

mu'tismo *sm* (*MED*) mutism; (*atteggiamento*) (stubborn) silence.

'muto, a *ag* (*MED*) dumb; (*emozione, dolore, CINEMA*) silent; (*LING*) silent, mute; (*carta geografica*) blank; ~ **per lo stupore** *etc* speechless with amazement *etc*.

'mutua *sf* (*anche:* **cassa** ~) health insurance scheme.

mutu'are *vt* (*fig*) to borrow.

mutu'ato, a *sm/f* member of a health insurance scheme.

'mutuo, a *ag* (*reciproco*) mutual // *sm* (*ECON*) (long-term) loan.

N

N. *abbr* (= *nord*) N.

'nacchere ['nakkere] *sfpl* castanets.

'nafta *sf* naphtha; (*per motori diesel*) diesel oil.

nafta'lina *sf* (*CHIM*) naphthalene; (*tarmicida*) mothballs *pl*.

'naia *sf* (*ZOOL*) cobra; (*MIL*) slang term

for national service.

'**nailon** *sm* nylon.

'**nanna** *sf* (*linguaggio infantile*): **andare a** ~ to go to beddy-byes.

'**nano, a** *ag, sm/f* dwarf.

napole'tano, a *ag, sm/f* Neapolitan.

'**Napoli** *sf* Naples.

'**nappa** *sf* tassel.

nar'ciso [nar'tʃizo] *sm* narcissus.

nar'cosi *sf* narcosis.

nar'cotico, ci *sm* narcotic.

na'rice [na'ritʃe] *sf* nostril.

nar'rare *vt* to tell the story of, recount; **narra'tivo, a** *ag* narrative // *sf* (*branca letteraria*) fiction; **narra'tore, 'trice** *sm/f* narrator; **narrazi'one** *sf* narration; (*racconto*) story, tale.

na'sale *ag* nasal.

'**nascere** ['naʃʃere] *vi* (*bambino*) to be born; (*pianta*) to come *o* spring up; (*fiume*) to rise, have its source; (*sole*) to rise; (*dente*) to come through; (*fig: derivare, conseguire*): ~ **da** to arise from, be born out of; **è nata nel 1952** she was born in 1952; '**nascita** *sf* birth.

nas'condere *vt* to hide, conceal; ~**rsi** *vr* tc hide; **nascon'diglio** *sm* hiding place; **nascon'dino** *sm* (*gioco*) hide-and-seek; **nas'costo, a** *pp di* **nascondere** // *ag* hidden; **di nascosto** secretly.

na'sello *sm* (ZOOL) hake.

'**naso** *sm* nose.

'**nastro** *sm* ribbon; (*magnetico, isolante, SPORT*) tape; ~ **adesivo** adhesive tape; ~ **trasportatore** conveyor belt.

nas'turzio [nas'turtsjo] *sm* nasturtium.

na'tale *ag* of one's birth // *sm* (REL): **N~** Christmas; (*giorno della nascita*) birth-day; (*del Natale*) Christmas *cpd*.

na'tante *sm* craft *inv*, boat.

'**natica, che** *sf* (ANAT) buttock.

na'tio, a, 'tii, 'tie *ag* native.

Natività *sf* (REL) Nativity.

na'tivo, a *ag, sm/f* native.

'**nato, a** *pp di* **nascere** // *ag*: **un attore** ~ a born actor; ~**a** Pieri née Pieri.

na'tura *sf* nature; **pagare in** ~ to pay in kind; ~ **morta** still life.

natu'rale *ag* natural; **natura'lezza** *sf* naturalness; **natura'lista, i, e** *sm/f* naturalist.

naturaliz'zare [naturalid'dzare] *vt* to naturalize.

natural'mente *av* naturally; (*certamente, sì*) of course.

naufra'gare *vi* (*nave*) to be wrecked; (*persona*) to be shipwrecked; (*fig*) to fall through; **nau'fragio** *sm* shipwreck; (*fig*) ruin, failure; '**naufrago, ghi** *sm* cast-away, shipwreck victim.

'**nausea** *sf* nausea; **nausea'bondo, a** *ag* nauseating, sickening; **nause'are** *vt* to nauseate, make (feel) sick.

'**nautico, a, ci, che** *ag* nautical // *sf*

(*art of*) navigation.

na'vale *ag* naval.

na'vata *sf* (*anche:* ~ **centrale**) nave; (*anche:* ~ **laterale**) aisle.

'**nave** *sf* ship, vessel; ~ **cisterna** tanker; ~ **da guerra** warship; ~ **passeggeri** passenger ship; ~ **spaziale** spaceship.

na'vetta *sf* shuttle; (*servizio di collegamento*) shuttle (service).

navi'cella [navi'tʃella] *sf* (*di aerostato*) gondola.

navi'gabile *ag* navigable.

navi'gare *vi* to sail; **navigazi'one** *sf* navigation.

na'viglio [na'viʎʎo] *sm* fleet, ships *pl*; (*canale artificiale*) canal; ~ **da pesca** fishing fleet.

nazio'nale [nattsjo'nale] *ag* national // *sf* (SPORT) national team; **naziona'lismo** *sm* nationalism; **nazionalità** *sf inv* nationality.

nazi'one [nat'tsjone] *sf* nation.

ne ◆ *pronome* **1** (*di lui, lei, loro*) of him/her/them; about him/her/them; ~ **riconosco la voce** I recognize his (*o* her) voice **2** (*di questa, quella cosa*) of it; about it; ~ **voglio ancora** I want some more (of it *o* them); **non parliamone più!** let's not talk about it any more!

3 (*con valore partitivo*): **hai dei libri?** — **sì,** ~ **ho** have you any books? — yes, I have (some); **hai del pane?** — **no, non** ~ **ho** have you any bread? — no, I haven't any; **quanti anni hai?** — ~ **ho 17** how old are you? — I'm 17

◆ *av* (*moto da luogo: da lì*) from there; ~ **vengo ora** I've just come from there.

né *cong*: ~ ... ~ neither ... nor; ~ **l'uno** ~ **l'altro lo vuole** neither of them wants it; **non parla** ~ **l'italiano** ~ **il tedesco** he speaks neither Italian nor German, he doesn't speak either Italian or German; **non piove** ~ **nevica** it isn't raining or snowing.

ne'anche [ne'anke] *av, cong* not even; **non ...** ~ not even; ~ **se volesse potrebbe venire** he couldn't come even if he wanted to; **non l'ho visto** — ~ **io** I didn't see him — neither did I *o* I didn't either; ~ **per idea** *o* **sogno!** not on your life!

'**nebbia** *sf* fog; (*foschia*) mist; **nebbi'oso, a** *ag* foggy; misty.

nebu'loso, a *ag* (*atmosfera*) hazy; (*fig*) hazy, vague.

necessaria'mente [netʃessarja'mɛnte] *av* necessarily.

neces'sario, a [netʃes'sarjo] *ag* necessary.

necessità [netʃessi'ta] *sf inv* necessity; (*povertà*) need, poverty; **necessi'tare** *vt* to require // *vi* (*aver bisogno*): **necessitare di** to need.

necro'logio [nekro'lɔdʒo] *sm* obituary notice; (*registro*) register of deaths.

ne'fando, a *ag* infamous, wicked.

ne'fasto, a *ag* inauspicious, ill-omened.

ne'gare *vt* to deny; (*rifiutare*) to deny, refuse; ~ **di aver fatto/che** to deny having done/that; **nega'tivo, a** *ag, sf, sm* negative; **negazi'one** *sf* negation.

ne'gletto, a [ne'glɛtto] *ag* (*trascurato*) neglected.

'negli ['neʎʎi] *prep* + *det vedi* **in**.

negli'gente [negli'dʒɛnte] *ag* negligent, careless; **negli'genza** *sf* negligence, carelessness.

negozi'ante [negot'tsjante] *sm/f* trader, dealer; (*bottegaio*) shopkeeper (*Brit*), storekeeper (*US*).

negozi'are [negot'tsjare] *vt* to negotiate // *vi*: ~ **in** to trade *o* deal in; **negozi'ato** *sm* negotiation.

ne'gozio [ne'gɔttsjo] *sm* (*locale*) shop (*Brit*), store (*US*); (*affare*) (piece of) business *q*.

'negro, a *ag, sm/f* Negro.

'nei, nel, nell', 'nella, 'nelle, 'nello *prep* + *det vedi* **in**.

'nembo *sm* (*METEOR*) nimbus.

ne'mico, a, ci, che *ag* hostile; (*MIL*) enemy *cpd* // *sm/f* enemy; **essere** ~ **di** to be strongly averse *o* opposed to.

nem'meno *av, cong* = **neanche**.

'nenia *sf* dirge; (*motivo monotono*) monotonous tune.

'neo *sm* mole; (*fig*) (slight) flaw.

**'neo... *prefisso* neo... .

'neon *sm* (*CHIM*) neon.

neo'nato, a *ag* newborn // *sm/f* newborn baby.

neozelan'dese [neoddzelan'dese] *ag* New Zealand *cpd* // *sm/f* New Zealander.

nep'pure *av, cong* = **neanche**.

'nerbo *sm* lash; (*fig*) strength, backbone; **nerbo'ruto, a** *ag* muscular; robust.

ne'retto *sm* (*TIP*) bold type.

'nero, a *ag* black; (*scuro*) dark // *sm* black; **il Mar N~** the Black Sea.

nerva'tura *sf* (*ANAT*) nervous system; (*BOT*) veining; (*ARCHIT, TECN*) rib.

'nervo *sm* (*ANAT*) nerve; (*BOT*) vein; **avere i ~i** to be on edge; **dare sui ~i a qn** to get on sb's nerves; **ner'voso, a** *ag* nervous; (*irritabile*) irritable // *sm* (*fam*): **far venire il nervoso a qn** to get on sb's nerves.

'nespola *sf* (*BOT*) medlar; (*fig*) blow, punch; **'nespolo** *sm* medlar tree.

'nesso *sm* connection, link.

nes'suno, a *det* (*dav sm* **nessun** + *C, V*, **nessuno** + *s impura, gn, pn, ps, x, z*; *dav sf* **nessuna** + *C*, **nessun'** + *V*) (*non uno*) no, *espressione negativa* + any; (*qualche*) any // *pronome* (*non uno*) no one, nobody, *espressione negativa* + any(one); (: *cosa*) none, *espressione negativa* + any; (*qualcuno*) anyone, anybody; (*qualcosa*) anything; **non c'è nessun libro** there isn't any book, there is no book; **hai ~a obiezione?** do you have any objections?; ~ **è venuto, non è venuto** ~ nobody came; **nessun altro** no one else, nobody else; **nessun'altra cosa** nothing else; **in nessun luogo** nowhere.

net'tare *vt* to clean // *sm* ['nɛttare] nectar.

net'tezza [net'tettsa] *sf* cleanness, cleanliness; ~ **urbana** cleansing department.

'netto, a *ag* (*pulito*) clean; (*chiaro*) clear, clear-cut; (*deciso*) definite; (*ECON*) net.

nettur'bino *sm* dustman (*Brit*), garbage collector (*US*).

neu'rosi *sf* = **nevrosi**.

neu'trale *ag* neutral; **neutralità** *sf* neutrality; **neutraliz'zare** *vt* to neutralize.

'neutro, a *ag* neutral; (*LING*) neuter // *sm* (*LING*) neuter.

ne'vaio *sm* snowfield.

'neve *sf* snow; **nevi'care** *vb impers* to snow; **nevi'cata** *sf* snowfall.

ne'vischio [ne'viskjo] *sm* sleet.

ne'voso, a *ag* snowy; snow-covered.

nevral'gia [nevral'dʒia] *sf* neuralgia.

nevras'tenico, a, ci, che *ag* (*MED*) neurasthenic; (*fig*) hot-tempered.

ne'vrosi *sf* neurosis.

'nibbio *sm* (*ZOOL*) kite.

'nicchia ['nikkja] *sf* niche; (*naturale*) cavity, hollow.

nicchi'are [nik'kjare] *vi* to shilly-shally, hesitate.

'nichel ['nikel] *sm* nickel.

nico'tina *sf* nicotine.

'nido *sm* nest; **a** ~ **d'ape** (*tessuto etc*) honeycomb *cpd*.

ni'ente ◆ *pronome* **1** (*nessuna cosa*) nothing; ~ **può fermarlo** nothing can stop him; ~ **di** ~ absolutely nothing; **nient'altro** nothing else; **nient'altro che** nothing but, just, only; ~ **affatto** not at all, not in the least; **come se** ~ **fosse** as if nothing had happened; **cose da** ~ trivial matters; **per** ~ (*gratis, invano*) for nothing

2 (*qualcosa*): **hai bisogno di** ~? do you need anything?

3: **non ...** ~ nothing, *espressione negativa* + anything; **non ho visto** ~ **I** saw nothing, I didn't see anything; **non ho** ~ **da dire** I have nothing *o* haven't anything to say

◆ *sm* nothing; **un bel** ~ absolutely nothing; **basta un** ~ **per farla piangere** the slightest thing is enough to make her cry

◆ *av* (*in nessuna misura*): **non ...** ~ not ... at all; **non è (per)** ~ **buono** it isn't good at all.

nientedi'meno, niente'meno *av* actually, even // *escl* really!, I say!

'Nilo *sm*: **il** ~ the Nile.

'ninfa *sf* nymph.

nin'fea *sf* water lily.

ninna-'nanna *sf* lullaby.

'ninnolo *sm* (*balocco*) plaything; (*gingillo*) knick-knack.

ni'pote *sm/f* (*di zii*) nephew/niece; (*di nonni*) grandson/daughter, grandchild.

'nitido, a *ag* clear; (*specchio*) bright.

ni'trato *sm* nitrate.

'nitrico, a, ci, che *ag* nitric.

ni'trire *vi* to neigh.

ni'trito *sm* (*di cavallo*) neighing *q*; neigh; (*CHIM*) nitrite.

nitroglice'rina [nitroglitʃe'rina] *sf* nitroglycerine.

'niveo, a *ag* snow-white.

no *av* (*risposta*) no; **vieni o ~?** are you coming or not?; **perché ~?** why not?; **lo conosciamo?** — **tu ~ ma io sì do** we know him? — you don't but I do; **verrai, ~?** you'll come, won't you?

'nobile *ag* noble // *sm/f* noble, nobleman/ woman; **nobili'are** *ag* noble; **nobiltà** *sf* nobility; (*di azione etc*) nobleness.

'nocca, che *sf* (*ANAT*) knuckle.

nocci'ola [not'tʃɔla] *ag inv* (*colore*) hazel, light brown // *sf* hazelnut.

'nocciolo ['nɔttʃolo] *sm* (*di frutto*) stone; (*fig*) heart, core; [not'tʃɔlo] (*albero*) hazel.

'noce ['notʃe] *sm* (*albero*) walnut tree // *sf* (*frutto*) walnut; **~ moscata** nutmeg.

no'civo, a [no'tʃivo] *ag* harmful, noxious.

'nodo *sm* (*di cravatta, legname, NAUT*) knot; (*AUT, FERR*) junction; (*MED, ASTR, BOT*) node; (*fig: legame*) bond, tie; (*: punto centrale*) heart, crux; **avere un ~ alla gola** to have a lump in one's throat; **no'doso, a** *ag* (*tronco*) gnarled.

'noi *pronome* (*soggetto*) we; (*oggetto: per dare rilievo, con preposizione*) us; **~ stessi(e)** we ourselves; (*oggetto*) ourselves.

'noia *sf* boredom; (*disturbo, impaccio*) bother *q*, trouble *q*; **avere qn/qc a ~** not to like sb/sth; **mi è venuto a ~** I'm tired of it; **dare ~ a** to annoy; **avere delle ~e con qn** to have trouble with sb.

noi'altri *pronome* we.

noi'oso, a *ag* boring; (*fastidioso*) annoying, troublesome.

noleggi'are [noled'dʒare] *vt* (*prendere a noleggio*) to hire (*Brit*), rent; (*dare a noleggio*) to hire out (*Brit*), rent (out); (*aereo, nave*) to charter; **no'leggio** *sm* hire (*Brit*), rental; charter.

'nolo *sm* hire (*Brit*), rental; charter; (*per trasporto merci*) freight; **prendere/ dare a ~** qc to hire/hire out sth.

'nomade *ag* nomadic // *sm/f* nomad.

'nome *sm* name; (*LING*) noun; **in/a ~ di** in the name of; **di ~** per **~** (*chiamato*) called, named; **conoscere qn di ~** to know sb by name; **~ d'arte** stage name; **~ di battesimo** Christian name; **~ depositato** trade name; **~ di famiglia** surname.

no'mea *sf* notoriety.

no'mignolo [no'miɲɲolo] *sm* nickname.

'nomina *sf* appointment.

nomi'nale *ag* nominal; (*LING*) noun *cpd*.

nomi'nare *vt* to name; (*eleggere*) to appoint; (*citare*) to mention.

nomina'tivo, a *ag* (*LING*) nominative; (*ECON*) registered // *sm* (*LING: anche: caso ~*) nominative (case); (*AMM*) name.

non *av* not // *prefisso* non-; *vedi* **affatto, appena** *etc*.

nonché [non'ke] *cong* (*tanto più, tanto meno*) let alone; (*e inoltre*) as well as.

noncu'rante *ag:* **~** (*di*) careless (of), indifferent (to); **noncu'ranza** *sf* carelessness, indifference.

nondi'meno *cong* (*tuttavia*) however; (*nonostante*) nevertheless.

'nonno, a *sm/f* grandfather/mother; (*in senso più familiare*) grandma/grandpa; **~i** *smpl* grandparents.

non'nulla *sm inv:* **un ~** nothing, a trifle.

'nono, a *ag, sm* ninth.

nonos'tante *prep* in spite of, notwithstanding // *cong* although, even though.

nontiscordardimé *sm inv* (*BOT*) forget-me-not.

nord *sm* North // *ag inv* north; northern; **il Mare del N~** the North Sea; **nor'dest** *sm* north-east; **'nordico, a, ci, che** *ag* nordic, northern European; **nor'dovest** *sm* north-west.

'norma *sf* (*principio*) norm; (*regola*) regulation, rule; (*consuetudine*) custom, rule; **a ~ di legge** according to law, as laid down by law.

nor'male *ag* normal; standard *cpd*; **normalità** *sf* normality; **normaliz'zare** *vt* to normalize, bring back to normal.

normal'mente *av* normally.

norve'gese [norve'dʒese] *ag, sm/f, sm* Norwegian.

Nor'vegia [nor'vedʒa] *sf:* **la ~** Norway.

nostal'gia [nostal'dʒia] *sf* (*di casa, paese*) homesickness; (*del passato*) nostalgia; **nos'talgico, a, ci, che** *ag* homesick; nostalgic.

nos'trano, a *ag* local; national; home-produced.

'nostro, a *det:* **il(la) ~(a)** *etc* our // *pronome:* **il(la) ~(a)** *etc* ours // *sm:* **il ~** our money; our belongings; **i ~i** our family; our own people; **è dei ~i** he's one of us.

'nota *sf* (*segno*) mark; (*comunicazione scritta, MUS*) note; (*fattura*) bill; (*elenco*) list; **degno di ~** noteworthy, worthy of note.

no'tabile *ag* notable; (*persona*) important // *sm* prominent citizen.

no'taio *sm* notary.

no'tare *vt* (*segnare: errori*) to mark;

(*registrare*) to note (down), write down; (*rilevare, osservare*) to note, notice; **farsi** ~ to get o.s. noticed.

notazi'one [notat'tsjone] *sf* (*MUS*) notation.

no'tevole *ag* (*talento*) notable, remarkable; (*peso*) considerable.

no'tifica, che *sf* notification.

notifi'care *vt* (*DIR*): ~ qc a qn to notify sb of sth, give sb notice of sth.

no'tizia [no'tittsja] *sf* (*piece of*) news *sg*; (*informazione*) piece of information; ~e *sfpl* news *sg*; information *sg*; **notizi'ario** *sm* (*RADIO, TV, STAMPA*) news *sg*.

'noto, a *ag* (well-)known.

notorietà *sf* fame; notoriety.

no'torio, a *ag* well-known; (*peg*) notorious.

not'tambulo, a *sm/f* night-bird (*fig*).

not'tata *sf* night.

'notte *sf* night; **di** ~ at night; (*durante la notte*) in the night, during the night; **peggio che andar di** ~ worse than ever; ~ **bianca** sleepless night; **notte'tempo** *av* at night; during the night.

not'turno, a *ag* nocturnal; (*servizio, guardiano*) night *cpd*.

no'vanta *num* ninety; **novan'tesimo, a** *num* ninetieth; **novan'tina** *sf*: **una novantina (di)** about ninety.

'nove *num* nine.

nove'cento [nove'tʃɛnto] *num* nine hundred // *sm*: **il N~** the twentieth century.

no'vella *sf* (*LETTERATURA*) short story.

novel'lino, a *ag* (*pivello*) green, inexperienced.

no'vello, a *ag* (*piante, patate*) new; (*insalata, verdura*) early; (*sposo*) newly-married.

no'vembre *sm* November.

novi'lunio *sm* (*ASTR*) new moon.

novità *sf inv* novelty; (*innovazione*) innovation; (*cosa originale, insolita*) something new; (*notizia*) (*piece of*) news *sg*; **le ~ della moda** the latest fashions.

novizi'ato [novit'tsjato] *sm* (*REL*) novitiate; (*tirocinio*) apprenticeship.

no'vizio, a [no'vittsjo] *sm/f* (*REL*) novice; (*tirocinante*) beginner, apprentice.

nozi'one [not'tsjone] *sf* notion, idea; ~i *sfpl* basic knowledge *sg*, rudiments.

'nozze ['nɔttse] *sfpl* wedding *sg*, marriage *sg*; ~ **d'argento/d'oro** silver/golden wedding *sg*.

ns. *abbr* (*COMM*) = **nostro**.

'nube *sf* cloud; **nubi'fragio** *sm* cloudburst.

'nubile *ag* (*donna*) unmarried, single.

'nuca *sf* nape of the neck.

nucle'are *ag* nuclear.

'nucleo *sm* nucleus; (*gruppo*) team, unit, group; (*MIL, POLIZIA*) squad; **il ~ familiare** the family unit.

nu'dista, i, e *sm/f* nudist.

'nudo, a *ag* (*persona*) bare, naked, nude; (*membra*) bare, naked; (*montagna*) bare // *sm* (*ARTE*) nude.

'nugolo *sm*: **un ~ di** a whole host of.

'nulla *pronome, av* = **niente** // *sm*: **il ~** nothing.

nulla'osta *sm inv* authorization.

nullità *sf inv* nullity; (*persona*) nonentity.

'nullo, a *ag* useless, worthless; (*DIR*) null (and void); (*SPORT*): **incontro ~** draw.

nume'rale *ag, sm* numeral.

nume'rare *vt* to number; **numerazi'one** *sf* numbering; (*araba, decimale*) notation.

nu'merico, a, ci, che *ag* numerical.

'numero *sm* number; (*romano, arabo*) numeral; (*di spettacolo*) act, turn; ~ **civico** house number; **nume'roso, a** *ag* numerous, many; (*con sostantivo sg: adunanza etc*) large.

'nunzio ['nuntsjo] *sm* (*REL*) nuncio.

nu'ocere ['nwɔtʃere] *vi*: ~ **a** to harm, damage; **nuoci'uto, a** *pp di* **nuocere**.

nu'ora *sf* daughter-in-law.

nuo'tare *vi* to swim; (*galleggiare: oggetti*) to float; **nuota'tore, 'trice** *sm/f* swimmer; **nu'oto** *sm* swimming.

nu'ova *sf vedi* **nuovo**.

nuova'mente *av* again.

Nu'ova Ze'landa [-dze'landa] *sf*: **la ~** New Zealand.

nu'ovo, a *ag* new // *sf* (*notizia*) (*piece of*) news *sg*; **di** ~ again; ~ **fiammante** *o* **di zecca** brand-new.

nutri'ente *ag* nutritious, nourishing.

nutri'mento *sm* food, nourishment.

nu'trire *vt* to feed; (*fig: sentimenti*) to harbour, nurse; **nutri'tivo, a** *ag* nutritional; (*alimento*) nutritious; **nutrizi'one** *sf* nutrition.

'nuvola *sf* cloud; **'nuvolo, a** *ag*, **nuvo'loso, a** *ag* cloudy.

nuzi'ale [nut'tsjale] *ag* nuptial; wedding *cpd*.

O

o *cong* (*dav V spesso* **od**) or; ~ ... ~ either ... or; ~ **l'uno** ~ **l'altro** either (of them).

O. *abbr* (= **ovest**) W.

'oasi *sf inv* oasis.

obbedi'ente *etc vedi* **ubbidiente** *etc*.

obbli'gare *vt* (*costringere*): ~ **qn a fare** to force o oblige sb to do; (*DIR*) to bind; ~**rsi** *vr*: ~**rsi a fare** to undertake to do; **obbli'gato, a** *ag* (*costretto, grato*) obliged; (*percorso, tappa*) set, fixed; **obbli'gatorio, a** *ag* compulsory, obligatory; **obbligazi'one** *sf* obligation; (*COMM*) bond, debenture; **'obbligo, ghi**

sm obligation; (*dovere*) duty; **avere l'obbligo di fare, essere nell'obbligo di fare** to be obliged to do; **essere d'obbligo** (*discorso, applauso*) to be called for.

ob'brobrio *sm* disgrace; (*fig*) mess, eyesore.

o'beso, a *ag* obese.

obiet'tare *vt*: ~ **che** to object that; ~ **su qc** to object to sth, raise objections concerning sth.

obiet'tivo, a *ag* objective // *sm* (*OTTICA, FOT*) lens *sg*, objective; (*MIL, fig*) objective.

obiet'tore *sm* objector; ~ **di coscienza** conscientious objector.

obiezi'one [objet'tsjone] *sf* objection.

obi'torio *sm* morgue, mortuary.

o'bliquo, a *ag* oblique; (*inclinato*) slanting; (*fig*) devious, underhand; **sguardo** ~ sidelong glance.

oblò *sm inv* porthole.

o'blungo, a, ghi, ghe *ag* oblong.

'oboe *sm* (*MUS*) oboe.

obsole'scenza [obsoleʃ'ʃɛntsa] *sf* (*ECON*) obsolescence.

'oca, pl 'oche *sf* goose.

occasi'one *sf* (*caso favorevole*) opportunity; (*causa, motivo, circostanza*) occasion; (*COMM*) bargain; **d'~** (*a buon prezzo*) bargain *cpd*; (*usato*) secondhand.

occhi'aia [ok'kjaja] *sf* eye socket; ~**e** *sfpl* shadows (under the eyes).

occhi'ali [ok'kjali] *smpl* glasses, spectacles; ~ **da sole** sunglasses.

occhi'ata [ok'kjata] *sf* look, glance; **dare un'~ a** to have a look at.

occhieggi'are [okkjed'dʒare] *vi* (*apparire qua e là*) to peep (out).

occhi'ello [ok'kjɛllo] *sm* buttonhole; (*asola*) eyelet.

'occhio [ˈɔkkjo] *sm* eye; ~**! careful!,** watch out!; **a** ~ **nudo** with the naked eye; **a quattr'~i** privately, tête-à-tête; **dare all'~ o nell'~ a qn** to catch sb's eye; **fare l'~ a qc** to get used to sth; **tenere d'~ qn** to keep an eye on sb; **vedere di buon/mal ~ qc** to look favourably/unfavourably on sth.

occhio'lino [okkjo'lino] *sm*: **fare l'~ a qn** to wink at sb.

occiden'tale [ottʃiden'tale] *ag* western // *sm/f* Westerner.

occi'dente [ottʃi'dɛnte] *sm* west; (*POL*): **l'O~** the West; **a ~** in the west.

oc'cipite [ot'tʃipite] *sm* back of the head, occiput.

oc'cludere *vt* to block; **occlusi'one** *sf* blockage, obstruction; **oc'cluso, a** *pp di* **occludere**.

occor'rente *ag* necessary // *sm* all that is necessary.

occor'renza [okkor'rɛntsa] *sf* necessity, need; **all'~** in case of need.

oc'correre *vi* to be needed, be required //

vb impers: **occorre farlo** it must be done; **occorre che tu parta** you must leave, you'll have to leave; **mi occorrono i soldi** I need the money; **oc'corso, a** *pp di* **occorrere**.

occul'tare *vt* to hide, conceal.

oc'culto, a *ag* hidden, concealed; (*scienze, forze*) occult.

occu'pare *vt* to occupy; (*manodopera*) to employ; (*ingombrare*) to occupy, take up; ~**rsi** *vr* to occupy o.s., keep o.s. busy; (*impiegarsi*) to get a job; ~**rsi di** (*interessarsi*) to take an interest in; (*prendersi cura di*) to look after, take care of; **occu'pato, a** *ag* (*MIL, POL*) occupied; (*persona: affaccendato*) busy; (*posto, sedia*) taken; (*toilette, TEL*) engaged; **occupazi'one** *sf* occupation; (*impiego, lavoro*) job; (*ECON*) employment.

o'ceano [o'tʃeano] *sm* ocean.

'ocra *sf* ochre.

ocu'lare *ag* ocular, eye *cpd*; **testimone** ~ eye witness.

ocu'lato, a *ag* (*attento*) cautious, prudent; (*accorto*) shrewd.

ocu'lista, i, e *sm/f* eye specialist, oculist.

'ode *sf* ode.

odi'are *vt* to hate, detest.

odi'erno, a *ag* today's, of today; (*attuale*) present.

'odio *sm* hatred; **avere in ~ qc/qn** to hate *o* detest sth/sb; **odi'oso, a** *ag* hateful, odious.

odo'rare *vt* (*annusare*) to smell; (*profumare*) to perfume, scent // *vi*: ~ (**di**) to smell (of); **odo'rato** *sm* sense of smell.

o'dore *sm* smell; **gli ~i** *smpl* (*CUC*) (aromatic) herbs; **odo'roso, a** *ag* sweet-smelling.

of'fendere *vt* to offend; (*violare*) to break, violate; (*insultare*) to insult; (*ferire*) to hurt; ~**rsi** *vr* (*con senso reciproco*) to insult one another; (*risentirsi*): ~**rsi (di)** to take offence (at), be offended (by); **offen'sivo, a** *ag*, *sf* offensive.

offe'rente *sm* (*in aste*): **al maggior ~** to the highest bidder.

of'ferto, a *pp di* **offrire** // *sf* offer; (*donazione, anche REL*) offering; (*in gara d'appalto*) tender; (*in aste*) bid; (*ECON*) supply; "~**e d'impiego**" "situations vacant"; **fare un'~a** to make an offer; **to tender; to bid.**

of'feso, a *pp di* **offendere** // *ag* offended; (*fisicamente*) hurt, injured // *sm/f* offended party // *sf* insult, affront; (*MIL*) attack; (*DIR*) offence; **essere ~ con qn** to be annoyed with sb; **parte ~a** (*DIR*) plaintiff.

offi'cina [offi'tʃina] *sf* workshop.

of'frire *vt* to offer; ~**rsi** *vr* (*proporsi*) to

offer (o.s.), volunteer; (*occasione*) to present itself; (*esporsi*): ~**rsi a** to expose o.s. to; **ti offro da bere** I'll buy you a drink.

offus'care *vt* to obscure, darken; (*fig: intelletto*) to dim, cloud; (: *fama*) to obscure, overshadow; ~**rsi** *vr* to grow dark; to cloud, grow dim; to be obscured.

of'talmico, a, ci, che *ag* ophthalmic.

oggettività [oddʒettiviˈta] *sf* objectivity.

ogget'tivo, a [oddʒetˈtivo] *ag* objective.

og'getto [odˈdʒɛtto] *sm* object; (*materia, argomento*) subject (matter); ~**i smarriti** lost property *sg*.

'oggi [ˈɔddʒi] *av, sm* today; ~ **a otto a** week today; **oggigi'orno** *av* nowadays.

o'giva [oˈdʒiva] *sf* ogive, pointed arch.

'ogni [ˈoɲɲi] *det* every, each; (*tutti*) all; (*con valore distributivo*) every; ~ **uomo è mortale** all men are mortal; **viene ~ due giorni** he comes every two days; ~ **cosa** everything; **ad ~ costo** at all costs, at any price; **in ~ luogo** everywhere; ~ **tanto** every so often; ~ **volta che** every time that.

Ognis'santi [oɲɲisˈsanti] *sm* All Saints' Day.

o'gnuno [oɲˈɲuno] *pronome* everyone, everybody.

'ohi *escl* oh!; (*esprimente dolore*) ow!

ohimè *escl* oh dear!

O'landa *sf*: **l'~** Holland; **olan'dese** *ag* Dutch // *sm* (*LING*) Dutch // *sm/f* Dutchman/woman; **gli Olandesi** the Dutch.

oleo'dotto *sm* oil pipeline.

ole'oso, a *ag* oily; (*che contiene olio*) oil-yielding.

ol'fatto *sm* sense of smell.

oli'are *vt* to oil.

oli'era *sf* oil cruet.

olim'piadi *sfpl* Olympic games; **o'limpico, a, ci, che** *ag* Olympic.

'olio *sm* oil; **sott'~** (*CUC*) in oil; ~ **di fegato di merluzzo** cod liver oil; ~ **d'oliva** olive oil; ~ **di semi** vegetable oil.

o'liva *sf* olive; **oli'vastro, a** *ag* olive(-coloured); (*carnagione*) sallow; **oli'veto** *sm* olive grove; **o'livo** *sm* olive tree.

'olmo *sm* elm.

oltraggi'are [oltradˈdʒare] *vt* to outrage; to offend gravely.

ol'traggio [olˈtraddʒo] *sm* outrage; offence, insult; ~ **a pubblico ufficiale** (*DIR*) insulting a public official; ~ **al pudore** (*DIR*) indecent behaviour; **oltraggi'oso, a** *ag* offensive.

ol'tralpe *av* beyond the Alps.

ol'tranza [olˈtrantsa] *sf*: **a ~** to the last, to the bitter end.

'oltre *av* (*più in là*) further; (*di più: aspettare*) longer, more // *prep* (*di là da*) beyond, over, on the other side of; (*più di*) more than, over; (*in aggiunta a*)

besides; (*eccetto*): ~ **a** except, apart from; **oltre'mare** *av* overseas; **oltrepas'sare** *vt* to go beyond, exceed.

o'maggio [oˈmaddʒo] *sm* (*dono*) gift; (*segno di rispetto*) homage, tribute; ~**i** *smpl* (*complimenti*) respects; **rendere ~ a** to pay homage *o* tribute to; **in ~** (*copia, biglietto*) complimentary.

ombeli'cale *ag* umbilical.

ombe'lico, chi *sm* navel.

'ombra *sf* (*zona non assolata, fantasma*) shade; (*sagoma scura*) shadow; **sedere all'~** to sit in the shade; **restare nell'~** (*fig*) to remain in obscurity.

ombreggi'are [ombredˈdʒare] *vt* to shade.

om'brello *sm* umbrella; **ombrel'lone** *sm* beach umbrella.

om'bretto *sm* eyeshadow.

om'broso, a *ag* shady, shaded; (*cavallo*) nervous, skittish; (*persona*) touchy, easily offended.

ome'lia *sf* (*REL*) homily, sermon.

omeopa'tia *sf* homoeopathy.

omertà *sf* conspiracy of silence.

o'messo, a *pp di* **omettere**.

o'mettere *vt* to omit, leave out; ~ **di fare** to omit *o* fail to do.

omi'cida, i, e [omiˈtʃida] *ag* homicidal, murderous // *sm/f* murderer/eress.

omi'cidio [omiˈtʃidjo] *sm* murder; ~ **colposo** culpable homicide.

omissi'one *sf* omission; ~ **di soccorso** (*DIR*) failure to stop and give assistance.

omogeneiz'zato [omodʒeneidˈdzato] *sm* baby food.

omo'geneo, a [omoˈdʒɛneo] *ag* homogeneous.

omolo'gare *vt* to approve, recognize; to ratify.

o'monimo, a *sm/f* namesake // *sm* (*LING*) homonym.

omosessu'ale *ag, sm/f* homosexual.

'oncia, ce [ˈontʃa] *sf* ounce.

'onda *sf* wave; **mettere** *o* **mandare in ~** (*RADIO, TV*) to broadcast; **andare in ~** (*RADIO, TV*) to go on the air; ~**e corte/medie/lunghe** short/medium/long wave; **on'data** *sf* wave, billow; (*fig*) wave, surge; **a ondate** in waves; **ondata di caldo** heatwave.

'onde *cong* (*affinché: con il congiuntivo*) so that, in order that; (: *con l'infinito*) so as to, in order to.

ondeggi'are [ondedˈdʒare] *vi* (*acqua*) to ripple; (*muoversi sulle onde: barca*) to rock, roll; (*fig: muoversi come le onde, barcollare*) to sway; (: *essere incerto*) to waver.

ondula'torio, a *ag* undulating; (*FISICA*) undulatory, wave *cpd*.

ondulazi'one [ondulatˈtsjone] *sf* undulation; (*acconciatura*) wave.

'onere *sm* burden; ~**i fiscali** taxes; **one'roso, a** *ag* (*fig*) heavy, onerous.

onestà *sf* honesty.

o'nesto, a *ag* (*probo, retto*) honest; (*giusto*) fair; (*casto*) chaste, virtuous.

'onice [ˈɔnitʃe] *sf* onyx.

onnipo'tente *ag* omnipotent.

onnisci'ente [ɔnniʃˈʃɛnte] *ag* omniscient.

onniveg'gente [ɔnnivedˈdʒɛnte] *ag* all-seeing.

ono'mastico, ci *sm* name-day.

ono'ranze [onoˈrantse] *sfpl* honours.

ono'rare *vt* to honour; (*far onore a*) to do credit to; **~rsi** *vr*: **~rsi di** to feel honoured at, be proud of.

ono'rario, a *ag* honorary // *sm* fee.

o'nore *sm* honour; **in ~ di** in honour of; **fare gli ~i di casa** to play host (*o* hostess); **fare ~ a** to honour; (*pranzo*) to do justice to; (*famiglia*) to be a credit to; **farsi ~** to distinguish o.s.; **ono'revole** *ag* honourable // *smf* (*POL*) ≈ Member of Parliament (*Brit*), ≈ Congressman/woman (*US*); **onorifi'cenza** *sf* honour; decoration; **ono'rifico, a, ci, che** *ag* honorary.

'onta *sf* shame, disgrace.

'O.N.U. [ˈɔnu] *sigla f* (= *Organizzazione delle Nazioni Unite*) UN, UNO.

o'paco, a, chi, che *ag* (*vetro*) opaque; (*metallo*) dull, matt.

o'pale *sm o f* opal.

'opera *sf* work; (*azione rilevante*) action, deed, work; (*MUS*) work; opus; (: *melodramma*) opera; (: *teatro*) opera house; (*ente*) institution, organization; **~ d'arte** work of art; **~ lirica** (grand) opera; **~e pubbliche** public works.

ope'raio, a *ag* working-class; workers' // *smf* worker; **classe ~a** working class.

ope'rare *vt* to carry out, make; (*MED*) to operate on // *vi* to operate, work; (*rimedio*) to act, work; (*MED*) to operate; **~rsi** *vr* to occur, take place; (*MED*) to have an operation; **~rsi d'appendicite** to have one's appendix out; **opera'tivo, a** *ag* operative, operating; **opera'tore, 'trice** *smf* operator; (*TV, CINEMA*) cameraman; **operatore economico** agent, broker; **operatore turistico** tour operator; **opera'torio, a** *ag* (*MED*) operating; **operazi'one** *sf* operation.

ope'retta *sf* (*MUS*) operetta, light opera.

ope'roso, a *ag* busy, active, hardworking.

opi'ficio [opiˈfitʃo] *sm* factory, works *pl*.

opini'one *sf* opinion.

'oppio *sm* opium.

oppo'nente *ag* opposing // *smf* opponent.

op'porre *vt* to oppose; **opporsi** *vr*: **opporsi (a qc)** to oppose (sth); to object (to sth); **~ resistenza/un rifiuto** to offer resistance/refuse.

opportu'nista, i, e *smf* opportunist.

opportunità *sf inv* opportunity; (*convenienza*) opportuneness, timeliness.

oppor'tuno, a *ag* timely, opportune.

opposi'tore, 'trice *smf* opposer, opponent.

opposizi'one [oppozitˈtsjone] *sf* opposition; (*DIR*) objection.

op'posto, a *pp di* **opporre** // *ag* opposite; (*opinioni*) conflicting // *sm* opposite, contrary; **all'~** on the contrary.

oppressi'one *sf* oppression.

oppres'sivo, a *ag* oppressive.

op'presso, a *pp di* **opprimere**.

oppres'sore *sm* oppressor.

op'primere *vt* (*premere, gravare*) to weigh down; (*estenuare*: *sog*: *caldo*) to suffocate, oppress; (*tiranneggiare*: *popolo*) to oppress.

oppu'gnare [oppunˈɲare] *vt* (*fig*) to refute.

op'pure *cong* or (else).

op'tare *vi*: **~ per** to opt for.

o'puscolo *sm* booklet, pamphlet.

opzi'one [opˈtsjone] *sf* option.

'ora *sf* (*60 minuti*) hour; (*momento*) time; **che ~ è?, che ~e sono?** what time is it?; **non veder l'~ di fare** to long to do, look forward to doing; **di buon'~** early; **alla buon'~!** at last!; **~ legale** *o* **estiva** summer time (*Brit*), daylight saving time (*US*); **~ locale** local time; **~ di punta** (*AUT*) rush hour // *av* (*adesso*) now; (*poco fa*): **è uscito proprio ~** he's just gone out; (*tra poco*) presently, in a minute; (*correlativo*): **~ ... ~** now ... now; **d'~ in avanti** *o* **poi** from now on; **or ~** just now, a moment ago; **5 anni ~ sono** 5 years ago; **~ come ~** right now, at present.

o'racolo *sm* oracle.

'orafo *sm* goldsmith.

o'rale *ag, sm* oral.

ora'mai *av* = **ormai**.

o'rario, a *ag* hourly; (*fuso, segnale*) time *cpd*; (*velocità*) per hour // *sm* timetable, schedule; (*di ufficio, visite etc*) hours *pl*, time(s *pl*).

ora'tore, 'trice *smf* speaker; orator.

ora'torio, a *ag* oratorical // *sm* (*REL*) oratory; (*MUS*) oratorio // *sf* (*arte*) oratory.

ora'zione [oratˈtsjone] *sf* (*REL*) prayer; (*discorso*) speech, oration.

or'bene *cong* so, well (then).

'orbita *sf* (*ASTR, FISICA*) orbit; (*ANAT*) (eye-)socket.

or'chestra [orˈkɛstra] *sf* orchestra; **orches'trale** *ag* orchestral // *smf* orchestra player; **orches'trare** *vt* to orchestrate; (*fig*) to mount, stage-manage.

orchi'dea [orkiˈdɛa] *sf* orchid.

'orco, chi *sm* ogre.

'orda *sf* horde.

or'digno [orˈdiɲɲo] *sm* (*esplosivo*) explosive device.

ordi'nale *ag, sm* ordinal.

ordina'mento sm order, arrangement; (regolamento) regulations pl, rules pl; ~ scolastico/giuridico education/legal system.

ordi'nanza [ordi'nantsa] sf (DIR, MIL) order; (persona: MIL) orderly, batman; d'~ (MIL) regulation cpd.

ordi'nare vt (mettere in ordine) to arrange, organize; (COMM) to order; (prescrivere: medicina) to prescribe; (comandare): ~ a qn di fare qc to order o command sb to do sth; (REL) to ordain.

ordi'nario, a ag (comune) ordinary; everyday; standard; (grossolano) coarse, common // sm ordinary; (INS: di università) full professor.

ordi'nato, a ag tidy, orderly.

ordinazi'one [ordinat'tsjone] sf (COMM) order; (REL) ordination; eseguire qc su ~ to make sth to order.

'ordine sm order; (carattere): d'~ pratico of a practical nature; all'~ (COMM: assegno) to order; di prim'~ first-class; fino a nuovo ~ until further notice; essere in ~ (documenti) to be in order; (stanza, persona) to be tidy; mettere in ~ to put in order, tidy (up); ~ del giorno (di seduta) agenda; (MIL) order of the day; ~ di pagamento (COMM) order for payment; l'~ pubblico law and order; i ~i (sacri) (REL) holy orders.

or'dire vt (fig) to plot, scheme; **or'dito** sm (di tessuto) warp.

orec'chino [orek'kino] sm earring.

o'recchio [o'rekkjo], pl(f) **o'recchie** sm (ANAT) ear.

orecchi'oni [orek'kjoni] smpl (MED) mumps sg.

o'refice [o'refitʃe] sm goldsmith; jeweller; **orefice'ria** sf (arte) goldsmith's art; (negozio) jeweller's (shop).

'orfano, a ag orphan(ed) // sm/f orphan; ~ di padre/madre fatherless/motherless; **orfano'trofio** sm orphanage.

orga'netto sm barrel organ; (fam: armonica a bocca) mouth organ; (: fisarmonica) accordion.

or'ganico, a, ci, che ag organic // sm personnel, staff.

organi'gramma, i sm organization chart.

orga'nismo sm (BIOL) organism; (corpo umano) body; (AMM) body, organism.

organiz'zare [organid'dzare] vt to organize; ~rsi vr to get organized; **organizza'tore, 'trice** ag organizing // sm/f organizer; **organizzazi'one** sf organization.

'organo sm organ; (di congegno) part; (portavoce) spokesman, mouthpiece.

or'gasmo sm (FISIOL) orgasm; (fig) agitation, anxiety.

'orgia, ge ['ordʒa] sf orgy.

or'goglio [or'goʎʎo] sm pride; **orgogli'oso, a** ag proud.

orien'tale ag oriental; eastern; east.

orienta'mento sm positioning; orientation; direction; senso di ~ sense of direction; perdere l'~ to lose one's bearings; ~ professionale careers guidance.

orien'tare vt (situare) to position; (fig) to direct, orientate; ~rsi vr to find one's bearings; (fig: tendere) to tend, lean; (: indirizzarsi): ~rsi verso to take up, go in for.

ori'ente sm east; l'O~ the East, the Orient; a ~ in the east.

o'rigano sm oregano.

origi'nale [oridʒi'nale] ag original; (bizzarro) eccentric // sm original; **originalità** sf originality; eccentricity.

origi'nare [oridʒi'nare] vt to bring about, produce // vi: ~ da to arise o spring from.

origi'nario, a [oridʒi'narjo] ag original; essere ~ di to be a native of; (provenire da) to originate from; to be native to.

o'rigine [o'ridʒine] sf origin; all'~ originally; d'~ inglese of English origin; dare ~ a to give rise to.

origli'are [oriʎ'ʎare] vi: ~ (a) to eavesdrop (on).

o'rina sf urine; **ori'nale** sm chamberpot.

ori'nare vi to urinate // vt to pass; **orina'toio** sm (public) urinal.

ori'undo, a ag: essere ~ di Milano etc to be of Milanese etc extraction o origin // sm/f person of foreign extraction o origin.

orizzon'tale [oriddzon'tale] ag horizontal.

oriz'zonte [orid'dzonte] sm horizon.

or'lare vt to hem.

'orlo sm edge, border; (di recipiente) rim, brim; (di vestito etc) hem.

'orma sf (di persona) footprint; (di animale) track; (impronta, traccia) mark, trace.

or'mai av by now, by this time; (adesso) now; (quasi) almost, nearly.

ormeggi'are [ormed'dʒare] vt (NAUT) to moor; **or'meggio** sm (atto) mooring q; (luogo) moorings pl.

or'mone sm hormone.

ornamen'tale ag ornamental, decorative.

orna'mento sm ornament, decoration.

or'nare vt to adorn, decorate; ~rsi vr: ~rsi (di) to deck o.s. (out) (with); **or'nato, a** ag ornate.

ornitolo'gia [ornitolo'dʒia] sf ornithology.

'oro sm gold; d'~, in ~ gold cpd; d'~ (colore, occasione) golden; (persona) marvellous.

orologe'ria [orolodʒe'ria] sf watchmaking q; watchmaker's (shop); clock-

maker's (shop); **bomba a ~** time bomb.
orologi'aio [orolo'dʒajo] *sm* watchmaker; clockmaker.
oro'logio [oro'lɔdʒo] *sm* clock; (*da tasca, da polso*) watch; **~ da polso** wristwatch; **~ al quarzo** quartz watch; **~ a sveglia** alarm clock.
o'roscopo *sm* horoscope.
or'rendo, a *ag* (*spaventoso*) horrible, awful; (*bruttissimo*) hideous.
or'ribile *ag* horrible.
'orrido, a *ag* fearful, horrid.
orripi'lante *ag* hair-raising, horrifying.
or'rore *sm* horror; **avere in ~ qn/qc** to loathe *o* detest sb/sth; **mi fanno ~** I loathe *o* detest them.
orsacchi'otto [orsak'kjɔtto] *sm* teddy bear.
'orso *sm* bear; **~ bruno/bianco** brown/polar bear.
or'taggio [or'taddʒo] *sm* vegetable.
or'tica, che *sf* (stinging) nettle.
orti'caria *sf* nettle rash.
orticol'tura *sf* horticulture.
'orto *sm* vegetable garden, kitchen garden; (*AGR*) market garden (*Brit*), truck farm (*US*).
orto'dosso, a *ag* orthodox.
ortogra'fia *sf* spelling.
orto'lano, a *sm/f* (*venditore*) greengrocer (*Brit*), produce dealer (*US*).
ortope'dia *sf* orthopaedics *sg*; **orto'pedico, a, ci, che** *ag* orthopaedic // *sm* orthopaedic specialist.
orzai'olo [ordza'jɔlo] *sm* (*MED*) stye.
or'zata [or'dzata] *sf* barley water.
'orzo [ordzo] *sm* barley.
o'sare *vt, vi* to dare; **~ fare** to dare (to) do.
oscenità [oʃʃeni'ta] *sf inv* obscenity.
o'sceno, a [oʃ'ʃeno] *ag* obscene; (*ripugnante*) ghastly.
oscil'lare [oʃʃil'lare] *vi* (*pendolo*) to swing; (*dondolare: al vento etc*) to rock; (*variare*) to fluctuate; (*TECN*) to oscillate; (*fig*): **~ fra** to waver *o* hesitate between; **oscillazi'one** *sf* oscillation; (*di prezzi, temperatura*) fluctuation.
oscura'mento *sm* darkening; obscuring; (*in tempo di guerra*) blackout.
oscu'rare *vt* to darken, obscure; (*fig*) to obscure; **~rsi** *vr* (*cielo*) to darken, cloud over; (*persona*): **si oscurò in volto** his face clouded over.
os'curo, a *ag* dark; (*fig*) obscure; humble, lowly // *sm*: **all'~** in the dark; **tenere qn all'~ di qc** to keep sb in the dark about sth.
ospe'dale *sm* hospital; **ospedali'ero, a** *ag* hospital *cpd*.
ospi'tale *ag* hospitable; **ospitalità** *sf* hospitality.
ospi'tare *vt* to give hospitality to; (*sog: albergo*) to accommodate.
'ospite *sm/f* (*persona che ospita*) host/

hostess; (*persona ospitata*) guest.
os'pizio [os'pittsjo] *sm* (*per vecchi etc*) home.
'ossa *sfpl vedi* **osso**.
ossa'tura *sf* (*ANAT*) skeletal structure, frame; (*TECN, fig*) framework.
'osseo, a *ag* bony; (*tessuto etc*) bone *cpd*.
os'sequio *sm* deference, respect; **~i** *smpl* (*saluto*) respects, regards; **ossequi'oso, a** *ag* obsequious.
osser'vanza [osser'vantsa] *sf* observance.
osser'vare *vt* to observe, watch; (*esaminare*) to examine; (*notare, rilevare*) to notice, observe; (*DIR: la legge*) to observe, respect; (*mantenere: silenzio*) to keep, observe; **far ~ qc a qn** to point sth out to sb; **osserva'tore, 'trice** *ag* observant, perceptive // *sm/f* observer; **osserva'torio** *sm* (*ASTR*) observatory; (*MIL*) observation post; **osservazi'one** *sf* observation; (*di legge etc*) observance; (*considerazione critica*) observation, remark; (*rimprovero*) reproof; **in osservazione** under observation.
ossessio'nare *vt* to obsess, haunt; (*tormentare*) to torment, harass.
ossessi'one *sf* obsession.
os'sesso, a *ag* (*spiritato*) possessed.
os'sia *cong* that is, to be precise.
ossi'dare *vt*, **~rsi** *vr* to oxidize.
'ossido *sm* oxide; **~ di carbonio** carbon monoxide.
ossige'nare [ossidʒe'nare] *vt* to oxygenate; (*decolorare*) to bleach; **acqua ossigenata** hydrogen peroxide.
os'sigeno *sm* oxygen.
'osso *sm* (*pl(f)* **ossa** *nel senso ANAT*) bone; **d'~** (*bottone etc*) of bone, bone *cpd*.
osso'buco, *pl* **ossi'buchi** *sm* (*CUC*) marrowbone; (: *piatto*) stew made with knuckle of veal in tomato sauce.
os'suto, a *ag* bony.
ostaco'lare *vt* to block, obstruct.
os'tacolo *sm* obstacle; (*EQUITAZIONE*) hurdle, jump.
os'taggio [os'taddʒo] *sm* hostage.
'oste, os'tessa *sm/f* innkeeper.
osteggi'are [osted'dʒare] *vt* to oppose, be opposed to.
os'tello *sm*: **~ della gioventù** youth hostel.
osten'tare *vt* to make a show of, flaunt; **ostentazi'one** *sf* ostentation, show.
oste'ria *sf* inn.
os'tessa *sf vedi* **oste**.
os'tetrico, a, ci, che *ag* obstetric // *sm* obstetrician // *sf* midwife.
'ostia *sf* (*REL*) host; (*per medicinali*) wafer.
'ostico, a, ci, che *ag* (*fig*) harsh; hard, difficult; unpleasant.
os'tile *ag* hostile; **ostilità** *sf inv* hostility // *sfpl* (*MIL*) hostilities.

osti'narsi vr to insist, dig one's heels in; ~ a fare to persist (obstinately) in doing; **osti'nato, a** ag (caparbio) obstinate; (tenace) persistent, determined; **ostinazi'one** sf obstinacy; persistence.

ostra'cismo [ostra'tʃizmo] sm ostracism.

'ostrica, che sf oyster.

ostru'ire vt to obstruct, block; **ostruzi'one** sf obstruction, blockage.

'otre sm (recipiente) goatskin.

ottago'nale ag octagonal.

ot'tagono sm octagon.

ot'tanta num eighty; **ottan'tesimo, a** num eightieth; **ottan'tina** sf: una ottantina (di) about eighty.

ot'tavo, a num eighth // sf octave.

ottempe'rare vi: ~ a to comply with, obey.

ottene'brare vt to darken; (fig) to cloud.

otte'nere vt to obtain, get; (risultato) to achieve, obtain.

'ottico, a, ci, che ag (della vista: nervo) optic; (dell'ottica) optical // sm optician // sf (scienza) optics sg; (FOT: lenti, prismi etc) optics pl.

ottima'mente av excellently, very well.

otti'mismo sm optimism; **otti'mista, i, e** sm/f optimist.

'ottimo, a ag excellent, very good.

'otto num eight.

ot'tobre sm October.

otto'cento [otto'tʃɛnto] num eight hundred // sm: **l'O~** the nineteenth century.

ot'tone sm brass; **gli ~i** (MUS) the brass.

ot'tundere vt (fig) to dull.

ottu'rare vt to close (up); (dente) to fill; **ottura'tore** sm (FOT) shutter; (nelle armi) breechblock; **otturazi'one** sf closing (up); (dentaria) filling.

ot'tuso, a pp di **ottundere** // ag (MAT, fig) obtuse; (suono) dull.

o'vaia sf, **o'vaio** sm (ANAT) ovary.

o'vale ag, sm oval.

o'vatta sf cotton wool; (per imbottire) padding, wadding; **ovat'tare** vt (fig: smorzare) to muffle.

ovazi'one [ovat'tsjone] sf ovation.

'ovest sm west.

o'vile sm pen, enclosure.

o'vino, a ag sheep cpd, ovine.

ovulazi'one [ovulat'tsjone] sf ovulation.

'ovulo sm (FISIOL) ovum.

o'vunque av = **dovunque**.

ov'vero cong (ossia) that is, to be precise; (oppure) or (else).

ovvi'are vi: ~ a to obviate.

'ovvio, a ag obvious.

ozi'are [ot'tsjare] vi to laze, idle.

'ozio ['ottsjo] sm idleness; (tempo libero) leisure; ore d'~ leisure time; stare in ~ to be idle; **ozi'oso, a** ag idle.

o'zono [o'dzɔno] sm ozone.

P

pa'cato, a ag quiet, calm.

pac'chetto [pak'ketto] sm packet; ~ azionario (COMM) shareholding.

'pacco, chi sm parcel; (involto) bundle.

'pace ['patʃe] sf peace; darsi ~ to resign o.s.

pacifi'care [patʃifi'kare] vt (riconciliare) to reconcile, make peace between; (mettere in pace) to pacify.

pa'cifico, a, ci, che [pa'tʃi:fiko] ag (persona) peaceable; (vita) peaceful; (fig: indiscusso) indisputable; (: ovvio) obvious, clear // sm: il P~, l'Oceano P~ the Pacific (Ocean).

paci'fista, i, e [patʃi'fista] sm/f pacifist.

pa'della sf frying pan; (per infermi) bedpan.

padigli'one [padiʎ'ʎone] sm pavilion; (AUT) roof.

'Padova sf Padua.

'padre sm father; **~i** smpl (antenati) forefathers; **pa'drino** sm godfather.

padro'nanza [padro'nantsa] sf command, mastery.

pa'drone, a sm/f master/mistress; (proprietario) owner; (datore di lavoro) employer; essere ~ di sé to be in control of o.s.; ~ di casa master/mistress of the house; (per gli inquilini) landlord/lady; **padroneggi'are** vt (fig: sentimenti) to master, control; (: materia) to master, know thoroughly; **padroneggiarsi** vr to control o.s.

pae'saggio [pae'zaddʒo] sm landscape.

pae'sano, a ag country cpd // sm/f villager; countryman/woman.

pa'ese sm (nazione) country, nation; (terra) country, land; (villaggio) village; ~ di provenienza country of origin; i P~i Bassi the Netherlands.

paf'futo, a ag chubby, plump.

'paga, ghe sf pay, wages pl.

paga'mento sm payment.

pa'gano, a ag, sm/f pagan.

pa'gare vt to pay; (acquisto, fig: colpa) to pay for; (contraccambiare) to repay, pay back // vi to pay; quanto l'hai pagato? how much did you pay for it?; ~ con carta di credito to pay by credit card; ~ in contanti to pay cash.

pa'gella [pa'dʒella] sf (INS) report card.

'paggio ['paddʒo] sm page(boy).

paghe'rò [page'rɔ] sm inv acknowledgement of a debt, IOU.

'pagina ['padʒina] sf page.

'paglia ['paʎʎa] sf straw.

pagliac'cetto [paʎʎat'tʃetto] sm (per bambini) rompers pl.

pagli'accio [paʎ'ʎattʃo] sm clown.

pagli'etta [paʎ'ʎetta] sf (cappello per

uomo) (straw) boater; (*per tegami etc*) steel wool.

pa'gnotta [paɲ'nɔtta] *sf* round loaf.

'paio, *pl(f)* **'paia** *sm* pair; **un ~ di** (*alcuni*) a couple of.

pai'olo, paiu'olo *sm* (copper) pot.

'pala *sf* shovel; (*di remo, ventilatore, elica*) blade; (*di ruota*) paddle.

pa'lato *sm* palate.

pa'lazzo [pa'lattso] *sm* (*reggia*) palace; (*edificio*) building; **~ di giustizia** courthouse; **~ dello sport** sports stadium.

pal'chetto [pal'ketto] *sm* shelf.

'palco, chi *sm* (*TEATRO*) box; (*tavolato*) platform, stand; (*ripiano*) layer.

palco'scenico, ci [palkoʃ'ʃɛniko] *sm* (*TEATRO*) stage.

pale'sare *vt* to reveal, disclose; **~rsi** *vr* to reveal *o* show o.s.

pa'lese *ag* clear, evident.

Pales'tina *sf*: **la ~** Palestine.

pa'lestra *sf* gymnasium; (*esercizio atletico*) exercise, training; (*fig*) training ground, school.

pa'letta *sf* spade; (*per il focolare*) shovel; (*del capostazione*) signalling disc.

pa'letto *sm* stake, peg; (*spranga*) bolt.

'palio *sm* (*gara*): **il P~** horserace run at Siena; **mettere qc in ~** to offer sth as a prize.

'palla *sf* ball; (*pallottola*) bullet; **~ canestro** *sm* basketball; **~ nuoto** *sm* water polo; **~ volo** *sm* volleyball.

palleggi'are [palled'dʒare] *vi* (*CALCIO*) to practise with the ball; (*TENNIS*) to knock up.

pallia'tivo *sm* palliative; (*fig*) stopgap measure.

'pallido, a *ag* pale.

pal'lina *sf* (*bilia*) marble.

pallon'cino [pallon'tʃino] *sm* balloon; (*lampioncino*) Chinese lantern.

pal'lone *sm* (*palla*) ball; (*CALCIO*) football; (*aerostato*) balloon; **gioco del ~** football.

pal'lore *sm* pallor, paleness.

pal'lottola *sf* pèllet; (*proiettile*) bullet.

'palma *sf* (*ANAT*) = **palmo**; (*BOT, simbolo*) palm; **~ da datteri** date palm.

'palmo *sm* (*ANAT*) palm; **restare con un ~ di naso** to be badly disappointed.

'palo *sm* (*legno appuntito*) stake; (*sostegno*) pole; **fare da** *o* **il ~** (*fig*) to act as look-out.

palom'baro *sm* diver.

pa'lombo *sm* (*pesce*) dogfish.

pal'pare *vt* to feel, finger.

'palpebra *sf* eyelid.

palpi'tare *vi* (*cuore, polso*) to beat; (: *più forte*) to pound, throb; (*fremere*) to quiver; **'palpito** *sm* (*del cuore*) beat; (*fig: d'amore etc*) throb.

paltò *sm inv* overcoat.

pa'lude *sf* marsh, swamp; **palu'doso, a**

ag marshy, swampy.

pa'lustre *ag* marsh *cpd*, swamp *cpd*.

'pampino *sm* vine leaf.

'panca, che *sf* bench.

pan'cetta [pan'tʃetta] *sf* (*CUC*) bacon.

pan'chetto [pan'ketto] *sm* stool; footstool.

pan'china [pan'kina] *sf* garden seat; (*di giardino pubblico*) (park) bench.

'pancia, ce ['pantʃa] *sf* belly, stomach; **mettere** *o* **fare ~** to be getting a paunch; **avere mal di ~** to have stomach ache *o* a sore stomach.

panci'otto [pan'tʃotto] *sm* waistcoat.

'pancreas *sm inv* pancreas.

'panda *sm inv* panda.

pande'monio *sm* pandemonium.

'pane *sm* bread; (*pagnotta*) loaf (of bread); (*forma*): **un ~ di burro/cera etc** a pat of butter/bar of wax *etc*; **guadagnarsi il ~** to earn one's living; **~ a cassetta** sliced bread; **~ integrale** wholemeal bread; **~ tostato** toast.

panette'ria *sf* (*forno*) bakery; (*negozio*) baker's (shop), bakery.

panetti'ere, a *smf* baker.

panet'tone *sm* a kind of spiced brioche with sultanas, eaten at Christmas.

pangrat'tato *sm* breadcrumbs *pl*.

'panico, a, ci, che *ag, sm* panic.

pani'ere *sm* basket.

pani'ficio [pani'fitʃo] *sm* (*forno*) bakery; (*negozio*) baker's (shop), bakery.

pa'nino *sm* roll; **~ imbottito** filled roll; sandwich; **panino'teca** *sf* sandwich bar.

'panna *sf* (*CUC*) cream; (*TECN*) = **panne**; **~ da cucina** cooking cream; **~ montata** whipped cream.

'panne *sf inv*: **essere in ~** (*AUT*) to have broken down.

pan'nello *sm* panel.

'panno *sm* cloth; **~i** *smpl* (*abiti*) clothes; **mettiti nei miei ~i** (*fig*) put yourself in my shoes.

pan'nocchia [pan'nɔkkja] *sf* (*di mais etc*) ear.

panno'lino *sm* (*per bambini*) nappy (*Brit*), diaper (*US*).

pano'rama, i *sm* panorama; **pano'ramico, a, ci, che** *ag* panoramic; **strada panoramica** scenic route.

panta'loni *smpl* trousers (*Brit*), pants (*US*), **pair** *sg* of trousers *o* pants.

pan'tano *sm* bog.

pan'tera *sf* panther.

pan'tofola *sf* slipper.

panto'mima *sf* pantomime.

pan'zana [pan'tsana] *sf* fib, tall story.

pao'nazzo, a [pao'nattso] *ag* purple.

'papa, i *sm* pope.

papà *sm inv* dad(dy).

pa'pale *ag* papal.

pa'pato *sm* papacy.

pa'pavero *sm* poppy.

'papero, a *smf* (*ZOOL*) gosling // *sf* (*fig*)

slip of the tongue, blunder.
pa'piro sm papyrus.
'**pappa** sf baby cereal.
pappa'gallo sm parrot; (fig: uomo)
Romeo, wolf.
pappa'gorgia, ge [pappa'gɔrdʒa] sf
double chin.
pap'pare vt (fam: anche: ~rsi) to
gobble up.
'**para** sf: suole di ~ crepe soles.
pa'rabola sf (MAT) parabola; (REL)
parable.
para'brezza [para'breddza] sm inv (AUT)
windscreen (Brit), windshield (US).
paraca'dute sm inv parachute.
para'carro sm kerbstone (Brit), curb-
stone (US).
para'diso sm paradise.
parados'sale ag paradoxical.
para'dosso sm paradox.
para'fango, ghi sm mudguard.
paraf'fina sf paraffin, paraffin wax.
para'fulmine sm lightning conductor.
pa'raggi [pa'raddʒi] smpl: nei ~ in the
vicinity, in the neighbourhood.
parago'nare vt: ~ con/a to compare
with/to.
para'gone sm comparison; (esempio
analogo) analogy, parallel; **reggere al ~**
to stand comparison.
pa'ragrafo sm paragraph.
pa'ralisi sf paralysis; **para'litico, a, ci,
che** ag, sm/f paralytic.
paraliz'zare [paralid'dzare] vt to
paralyze.
paral'lelo, a ag parallel // sm (GEO)
parallel; (comparazione): fare un ~ tra
to draw a parallel between // sf parallel
(line); ~e sfpl (attrezzo ginnico) parallel
bars.
para'lume sm lampshade.
pa'rametro sm parameter.
para'noia sf paranoia; **para'noico, a,
ci, che** ag, sm/f paranoid.
para'occhi [para'ɔkki] smpl blinkers.
para'piglia [para'piʎʎa] sm commotion,
uproar.
pa'rare vt (addobbare) to adorn, deck;
(proteggere) to shield, protect;
(scansare: colpo) to parry; (CALCIO) to
save // vi: dove vuole andare a ~? what
are you driving at?; ~rsi vr (presentarsi) to appear, present o.s.
para'sole sm inv parasol, sunshade.
paras'sita, i sm parasite.
pa'rata sf (SPORT) save; (MIL) review,
parade.
para'tia sf (di nave) bulkhead.
para'urti sm inv (AUT) bumper.
para'vento sm folding screen; fare da ~
a qn (fig) to shield sb.
par'cella [par'tʃɛlla] sf account, fee (of
lawyer etc).
parcheggi'are [parked'dʒare] vt to park;
par'cheggio sm parking q; (luogo) car

park; (singolo posto) parking space.
par'chimetro [par'kimetro] sm parking
meter.
'**parco, chi** sm park; (spazio per
deposito) depot; (complesso di veicoli)
fleet.
'**parco, a, chi, che** ag: ~ (in) (sobrio)
moderate (in); (avaro) sparing (with).
pa'recchio [pa'rekkjo] det quite a lot
of; (tempo) quite a lot of, a long; ~i(e)
det pl quite a lot of, several // pronome
quite a lot, quite a bit; (tempo) quite a
while, a long time; ~i(e) pronome pl
quite a lot, several // av (con ag) quite,
rather; (con vb) quite a lot, quite a bit.
pareggi'are [pared'dʒare] vt to make
equal; (terreno) to level, make level;
(bilancio, conti) to balance // vi (SPORT)
to draw; **pa'reggio** sm (ECON) balance;
(SPORT) draw.
paren'tado sm relatives pl, relations pl.
pa'rente sm/f relative, relation.
paren'tela sf (vincolo di sangue, fig) relationship; (insieme dei parenti) relations pl, relatives pl.
pa'rentesi sf (segno grafico) bracket,
parenthesis; (frase incisa) parenthesis;
(digressione) parenthesis, digression.
pa'rere sm (opinione) opinion; (consiglio) advice, opinion; **a mio ~** in my
opinion // vi to seem, appear // vb
impers: **pare che** it seems o appears
that, they say that; **mi pare che** it seems
to me that; **mi pare di sì** I think so; **fai
come ti pare** do as you like; **che ti pare
del mio libro?** what do you think of my
book?
pa'rete sf wall.
'**pari** ag inv (uguale) equal, same; (in
giochi) equal; drawn, tied; (MAT) even //
sm inv (POL: di Gran Bretagna) peer //
sm/f inv peer, equal; **copiato ~ ~** copied
word for word; **alla ~** on the same level;
ragazza alla ~ au pair girl; **mettersi alla
~ con** to place o.s. on the same level as;
mettersi in ~ con to catch up with;
andare di ~ passo con qn to keep pace
with sb.
Pa'rigi [pa'ridʒi] sf Paris.
pa'riglia [pa'riʎʎa] sf pair; **rendere la ~**
to give tit for tat.
parità sf parity, equality; (SPORT) draw,
tie.
parlamen'tare ag parliamentary // sm/f
≈ Member of Parliament (Brit), ≈
Congressman/woman (US) // vi to
negotiate, parley.
parla'mento sm parliament.
parlan'tina sf (fam) talkativeness;
avere una buona ~ to have the gift of the
gab.
par'lare vi to speak, talk; (confidare
cose segrete) to talk // vt to speak; ~ (a
qn) di to speak o talk (to sb) about;
parla'torio sm (di carcere etc) visiting

room; (REL) parlour.

parmigi'ano [parmi'dʒano] sm (grana) Parmesan (cheese).

paro'dia sf parody.

pa'rola sf word; (facoltà) speech; ~e sfpl (chiacchiere) talk sg; **chiedere la ~** to ask permission to speak; **prendere la ~** to take the floor; ~ **d'onore** word of honour; ~ **d'ordine** (MIL) password; ~e **incrociate** crossword (puzzle) sg; **paro'laccia, ce** sf bad word, swearword.

par'rocchia [par'rɔkkja] sf parish; parish church.

'parroco, ci sm parish priest.

par'rucca, che sf wig.

parrucchi'ere, a [parruk'kjɛre] sm/f hairdresser // sm barber.

parsi'monia sf frugality, thrift.

'parso, a pp di parere.

'parte sf part; (lato) side; (quota spettante a ciascuno) share; (direzione) direction; (POL) party; faction; (DIR) party; **a ~** ag separate // av separately; **scherzi a ~** joking aside; **a ~ ciò** apart from that; **da ~** (in disparte) to one side, aside; **d'altra ~** on the other hand; **da ~ di** (per conto di) on behalf of; **da ~ mia** as far as I'm concerned, as for me; **da ~ a ~** right through; **da ogni ~** on all sides, everywhere; (moto da luogo) from all sides; **da nessuna ~** nowhere; **da questa ~** (in questa direzione) this way; **prendere ~ a qc** to take part in sth; **mettere da ~** to put aside; **mettere qn a ~ di qc** to inform sb of sth.

parteci'pare [partetʃi'pare] vi: ~ **a** to take part in, participate in; (utili etc) to share in; (spese etc) to contribute to; (dolore, successo di qn) to share (in); **partecipazi'one** sf participation; sharing; (ECON) interest; **partecipazione agli utili** profit-sharing; **partecipazioni di nozze** wedding announcement card; **par'tecipe** ag participating; **essere partecipe di** to take part in, participate in; to share (in); (consapevole) to be aware of.

parteggi'are [parted'dʒare] vi: ~ **per** to side with, be on the side of.

par'tenza [par'tɛntsa] sf departure; (SPORT) start; **essere in ~** to be about to leave, be leaving.

parti'cella [parti'tʃɛlla] sf particle.

parti'cipio [parti'tʃipjo] sm participle.

partico'lare ag (specifico) particular; (proprio) personal, private; (speciale) special, particular; (caratteristico) distinctive, characteristic; (fuori dal comune) peculiar // sm detail, particular; **in ~** in particular, particularly; **particolarità** sf inv particularity; detail; characteristic, feature.

partigi'ano, a [parti'dʒano] ag partisan // sm (fautore) supporter, champion;

(MIL) partisan.

par'tire vi to go, leave; (allontanarsi) to go (o drive etc) away o off; (petardo, colpo) to go off; (fig: avere inizio, SPORT) to start; **sono partita da Roma alle 7** I left Rome at 7; **il volo parte da Ciampino** the flight leaves from Ciampino; **a ~ da** from.

par'tita sf (COMM) lot, consignment; (ECON: registrazione) entry, item; (CARTE, SPORT: gioco) game; (: competizione) match, game; ~ **di caccia** hunting party; ~ **IVA** VAT registration number.

par'tito sm (POL) party; (decisione) decision, resolution; (persona da maritare) match.

parti'tura sf (MUS) score.

'parto sm (MED) delivery, (child)birth; labour; **parto'rire** vt to give birth to; (fig) to produce.

parzi'ale [par'tsjale] ag (limitato) partial; (non obiettivo) biased, partial.

'pascere ['paʃʃere] vi to graze // vt (brucare) to graze on; (far pascolare) to graze, pasture; **pasci'uto, a** pp di **pascere**.

pasco'lare vt, vi to graze.

'pascolo sm pasture.

'Pasqua sf Easter; **pas'quale** ag Easter cpd.

pas'sabile ag fairly good, passable.

pas'saggio [pas'saddʒo] sm passing q, passage; (traversata) crossing q, passage; (luogo, prezzo della traversata, brano di libro etc) passage; (su veicolo altrui) lift (Brit), ride; (SPORT) pass; **di ~** (persona) passing through; ~ **pedonale/a livello** pedestrian/level (Brit) o grade (US) crossing.

pas'sante sm/f passer-by // sm loop.

passa'porto sm passport.

pas'sare vi (andare) to go; (veicolo, pedone) to pass (by), go by; (fare una breve sosta: postino etc) to come, call; (: amico: per fare una visita) to call o drop in; (sole, aria, luce) to get through; (trascorrere: giorni, tempo) to pass, go by; (fig: proposta di legge) to be passed; (: dolore) to pass, go away; (CARTE) to pass // vt (attraversare) to cross; (trasmettere: messaggio): ~ **qc a qn** to pass sth on to sb; (dare): ~ **qc a qn** to pass sth to sb, give sb sth; (trascorrere: tempo) to spend; (superare: esame) to pass; (triturare: verdura) to strain; (approvare) to pass, approve; (oltrepassare, sorpassare: anche fig) to go beyond, pass; (fig: subire) to go through; ~ **da ... a** to pass from ... to; ~ **di padre in figlio** to be handed down o to pass from father to son; ~ **per** (anche fig) to go through; ~ **per stupido/un genio** to be taken for a fool/a genius; ~ **sopra** (anche fig) to pass over; ~ **at-**

traverso (*anche fig*) to go through; ~ **alla storia** to pass into history; ~ **a un esame** to go up (to the next class) after an exam; ~ **inosservato** to go unnoticed; ~ **di moda** to go out of fashion; **le passo il Signor X** (*al telefono*) here is Mr X; I'm putting you through to Mr X; **lasciar** ~ **qn/qc** to let sb/sth through; **passarsela: come te la passi?** how are you getting on *o* along?

pas'sata *sf*: **dare una** ~ **di vernice a qc** to give sth a coat of paint; **dare una** ~ **al giornale** to have a look at the paper, skim through the paper.

passa'tempo *sm* pastime, hobby.

pas'sato, a *ag* past; (*sfiorito*) faded // *sm* past; (*LING*) past (tense); ~ **prossimo** (*LING*) present perfect; ~ **remoto** (*LING*) past historic; ~ **di verdura** (*CUC*) vegetable purée.

passaver'dura *sm inv* vegetable mill.

passeg'gero, a [passed'dʒero] *ag* passing // *sm/f* passenger.

passeggi'are [passed'dʒare] *vi* to go for a walk; (*in veicolo*) to go for a drive; **passeggi'ata** *sf* walk; drive; (*luogo*) promenade; **fare una passeggiata** to go for a walk (*o* drive); **passeg'gino** *sm* pushchair (*Brit*), stroller (*US*); **pas'seggio** *sm* walk, stroll; (*luogo*) promenade.

passe'rella *sf* footbridge; (*di nave, aereo*) gangway; (*pedana*) catwalk.

'passero *sm* sparrow.

pas'sibile *ag*: ~ **di** liable to.

passi'one *sf* passion.

pas'sivo, a *ag* passive // *sm* (*LING*) passive; (*ECON*) debit; (: *complesso dei debiti*) liabilities *pl*.

'passo *sm* step; (*andatura*) pace; (*rumore*) (foot)step; (*orma*) footprint; (*passaggio, fig: brano*) passage; (*valico*) pass; **a** ~ **d'uomo** at walking pace; ~ **(a)** ~ step by step; **fare due** *o* **quattro** ~**i** to go for a walk *o* a stroll; **di questo** ~ at this rate; "~ **carraio**" "vehicle entrance — keep clear".

'pasta *sf* (*CUC*) dough; (: *impasto per dolce*) pastry; (: *anche*: ~ **alimentare**) pasta; (*massa molle di materia*) paste; (*fig: indole*) nature; ~**e** *sfpl* (*pasticcini*) pastries; ~ **in brodo** noodle soup.

pastasci'utta [pastaʃ'ʃutta] *sf* pasta.

pas'tella *sf* batter.

pas'tello *sm* pastel.

pas'tetta *sf* (*CUC*) = **pastella**.

pas'ticca, che *sf* = **pastiglia**.

pasticce'ria [pastittʃe'ria] *sf* (*pasticcini*) pastries *pl*, cakes *pl*; (*negozio*) cake shop; (*arte*) confectionery.

pasticci'are [pastit'tʃare] *vt* to mess up, make a mess of // *vi* to make a mess.

pasticci'ere, a [pastit'tʃere] *sm/f* pastrycook; confectioner.

pas'ticcio [pas'tittʃo] *sm* (*CUC*) pie;

(*lavoro disordinato, imbroglio*) mess; **trovarsi nei** ~**i** to get into trouble.

pasti'ficio [pasti'fitʃo] *sm* pasta factory.

pas'tiglia [pas'tiʎʎa] *sf* pastille, lozenge.

pas'tina *sf* small pasta shapes used in soup.

pasti'naca, che *sf* parsnip.

'pasto *sm* meal.

pas'tore *sm* shepherd; (*REL*) pastor, minister; (*anche*: **cane** ~) sheepdog.

pastoriz'zare [pastorid'dzare] *vt* to pasteurize.

pas'toso, a *ag* doughy; pasty; (*fig: voce, colore*) mellow, soft.

pas'trano *sm* greatcoat.

pas'tura *sf* pasture.

pa'tata *sf* potato; ~**e fritte** chips (*Brit*), French fries; **pata'tine** *sfpl* (*potato*) crisps.

pata'trac *sm* (*crollo: anche fig*) crash.

pa'tella *sf* (*ZOOL*) limpet.

pa'tema, i *sm* anxiety, worry.

pa'tente *sf* licence; (*anche*: ~ **di guida**) driving licence (*Brit*), driver's license (*US*).

paternità *sf* paternity, fatherhood.

pa'terno, a *ag* (*affetto, consigli*) fatherly; (*casa, autorità*) paternal.

pa'tetico, a, ci, che *ag* pathetic; (*commovente*) moving, touching.

pa'tibolo *sm* gallows *sg*, scaffold.

'patina *sf* (*su rame etc*) patina; (*sulla lingua*) fur, coating.

pa'tire *vt, vi* to suffer.

pa'tito, a *sm/f* enthusiast, fan, lover.

patolo'gia [patolo'dʒia] *sf* pathology; **pato'logico, a, ci, che** *ag* pathological.

'patria *sf* homeland.

patri'arca, chi *sm* patriarch.

pa'trigno [pa'triɲo] *sm* stepfather.

patri'monio *sm* estate, property; (*fig*) heritage.

patri'ota, i, e *sm/f* patriot; **patri'ottico, a, ci, che** *ag* patriotic; **patriot'tismo** *sm* patriotism.

patroci'nare [patrotʃi'nare] *vt* (*DIR: difendere*) to defend; (*sostenere*) to sponsor, support; **patro'cinio** *sm* defence; support, sponsorship.

patro'nato *sm* patronage; (*istituzione benefica*) charitable institution *o* society.

pa'trono *sm* (*REL*) patron saint; (*socio di patronato*) patron; (*DIR*) counsel.

'patta *sf* flap; (*dei pantaloni*) fly.

patteggi'are [patted'dʒare] *vt, vi* to negotiate.

patti'naggio [patti'naddʒo] *sm* skating.

patti'nare *vi* to skate; ~ **sul ghiaccio** to ice-skate; **pattina'tore, 'trice** *sm/f* skater; **'pattino** *sm* skate; (*di slitta*) runner; (*AER*) skid; (*TECN*) sliding block; **pattini** (*da ghiaccio*) (ice) skates; **pattini a rotelle** roller skates; [pat'tino] (*barca*) kind of pedalo with oars.

'patto *sm* (*accordo*) pact, agreement;

(*condizione*) term, condition; a ~ che on condition that.

pat'tuglia [pat'tuʎʎa] *sf* (*MIL*) patrol.

pattu'ire *vt* to reach an agreement on.

pattumi'era *sf* (dust)bin (*Brit*), ashcan (*US*).

pa'ura *sf* fear; aver ~ di/di fare/che to be frightened *o* afraid of/of doing/that; far ~ a to frighten; **per ~ di/che** for fear of/that; **pau'roso, a** *ag* (*che fa paura*) frightening; (*che ha paura*) fearful, timorous.

'pausa *sf* (*sosta*) break; (*nel parlare, MUS*) pause.

pavi'mento *sm* floor.

pa'vone *sm* peacock; **pavoneggi'arsi** *vr* to strut about, show off.

pazien'tare [pattsjen'tare] *vi* to be patient.

pazi'ente [pat'tsjente] *ag*, *sm/f* patient; **pazi'enza** *sf* patience.

paz'zesco, a, schi, sche [pat'tsesko] *ag* mad, crazy.

paz'zia [pat'tsia] *sf* (*MED*) madness, insanity; (*azione*) folly; (*di azione, decisione*) madness, folly.

'pazzo, a ['pattso] *ag* (*MED*) mad, insane; (*strano*) wild, mad // *sm/f* madman/woman; ~ **di** (*gioia, amore etc*) mad *o* crazy with; ~ **per qc/qn** mad *o* crazy about sth/sb.

PCI *sigla m* = *Partito Comunista Italiano*.

'pecca, che *sf* defect, flaw, fault.

peccami'noso, a *ag* sinful.

pec'care *vi* to sin; (*fig*) to err.

pec'cato *sm* sin; **è un ~ che** it's a pity that; **che ~!** what a shame *o* pity!

pecca'tore, 'trice *sm/f* sinner.

pece ['petʃe] *sf* pitch.

Pe'chino [pe'kino] *sf* Peking.

'pecora *sf* sheep; **peco'raio** *sm* shepherd; **peco'rino** *sm* sheep's milk cheese.

peculi'are *ag*: ~ **di** peculiar to.

pe'daggio [pe'daddʒo] *sm* toll.

pedago'gia [pedago'dʒia] *sf* pedagogy, educational methods *pl*.

peda'lare *vi* to pedal; (*andare in bicicletta*) to cycle.

pe'dale *sm* pedal.

pe'dana *sf* footboard; (*SPORT: nel salto*) springboard; (: *nella scherma*) piste.

pe'dante *ag* pedantic // *sm/f* pedant.

pe'data *sf* (*impronta*) footprint; (*colpo*) kick; **prendere a ~e qn/qc** to kick sb/sth.

pede'rasta, i *sm* pederast; homosexual.

pedi'atra, i, e *sm/f* paediatrician; **pedia'tria** *sf* paediatrics *sg*.

pedi'cure *sm/f inv* chiropodist.

pe'dina *sf* (*della dama*) draughtsman (*Brit*), draftsman (*US*); (*fig*) pawn.

pedi'nare *vt* to shadow, tail.

pedo'nale *ag* pedestrian.

pe'done, a *sm/f* pedestrian // *sm*

(*SCACCHI*) pawn.

'peggio ['peddʒo] *av*, *ag inv* worse // *sm o f*: **il** *o* **la ~** the worst; **alla ~** at worst, if the worst comes to the worst; **peggiora'mento** *sm* worsening; **peggio'rare** *vt* to make worse, worsen // *vi* to grow worse, worsen; **peggiora'tivo, a** *ag* pejorative; **peggi'ore** *ag* (*comparativo*) worse; (*superlativo*) worst // *sm/f*: **il(la) peggiore** the worst (person).

'pegno ['peɲɲo] *sm* (*DIR*) security, pledge; (*nei giochi di società*) forfeit; (*fig*) pledge, token; **dare in ~ qc** to pawn sth.

pe'lame *sm* (*di animale*) coat, fur.

pe'lare *vt* (*spennare*) to pluck; (*spellare*) to skin; (*sbucciare*) to peel; (*fig*) to make pay through the nose; ~**rsi** *vr* to go bald.

pel'lame *sm* skins *pl*, hides *pl*.

'pelle *sf* skin; (*di animale*) skin, hide; (*cuoio*) leather; **avere la ~ d'oca** to have goose pimples *o* goose flesh.

pellegri'naggio [pellegri'naddʒo] *sm* pilgrimage.

pelle'grino, a *sm/f* pilgrim.

pelle'rossa, pelli'rossa, pl pelli'rosse *sm/f* Red Indian.

pellette'ria *sf* leather goods *pl*; (*negozio*) leather goods shop.

pelli'cano *sm* pelican.

pellicce'ria [pellittʃe'ria] *sf* (*negozio*) furrier's (shop); (*quantità di pellicce*) furs *pl*.

pel'liccia, ce [pel'littʃa] *sf* (*mantello di animale*) coat, fur; (*indumento*) fur coat.

pel'licola *sf* (*membrana sottile*) film, layer; (*FOT, CINEMA*) film.

'pelo *sm* hair; (*pelame*) coat, hair; (*pelliccia*) fur; (*di tappeto*) pile; (*di liquido*) surface; **per un ~**: **per un ~ non ho perduto il treno** I very nearly missed the train; **c'è mancato un ~ che** affogasse he escaped drowning by the skin of his teeth; **pe'loso, a** *ag* hairy.

'peltro *sm* pewter.

pe'luria *sf* down.

'pena *sf* (*DIR*) sentence; (*punizione*) punishment; (*sofferenza*) sadness *q*, sorrow; (*fatica*) trouble *q*, effort; (*difficoltà*) difficulty; **far ~** to be pitiful; **mi fai ~** I feel sorry for you; **prendersi** *o* **darsi la ~ di fare** to go to the trouble of doing; ~ **di morte** death sentence; ~ **pecuniaria** fine; **pe'nale** *ag* penal; **penalità** *sf inv* penalty; **penaliz'zare** *vt* (*SPORT*) to penalize.

pe'nare *vi* (*patire*) to suffer; (*faticare*) to struggle.

pen'dente *ag* hanging; leaning // *sm* (*ciondolo*) pendant; (*orecchino*) drop earring; **pen'denza** *sf* slope, slant; (*grado d'inclinazione*) gradient; (*ECON*) outstanding account.

'pendere *vi* (*essere appeso*): ~ **da** to hang from; (*essere inclinato*) to lean; (*fig: incombere*): ~ **su** to hang over.

pen'dio, 'dii *sm* slope, slant; (*luogo in pendenza*) slope.

'pendola *sf* pendulum clock.

pendo'lare *sm/f* commuter.

'pendolo *sm* (*peso*) pendulum; (*anche: orologio a* ~) pendulum clock.

'pene *sm* penis.

pene'trante *ag* piercing, penetrating.

pene'trare *vi* to come *o* get in // *vt* to penetrate; ~ **in** to enter; (*sog: proiettile*) to penetrate; (: *acqua, aria*) to go *o* come into.

penicil'lina [penitʃil'lina] *sf* penicillin.

pe'nisola *sf* peninsula.

peni'tenza [peni'tɛntsa] *sf* penitence; (*punizione*) penance.

penitenzi'ario [peniten'tsjarjo] *sm* prison.

'penna *sf* (*di uccello*) feather; (*per scrivere*) pen; ~e *sfpl* (*CUC*) quills (*type of pasta*); ~ **a feltro/ stilografica/a sfera** felt-tip/fountain/ballpoint pen.

penna'rello *sm* felt(-tip) pen.

pennel'lare *vi* to paint.

pen'nello *sm* brush; (*per dipingere*) (paint)brush; **a** ~ (*perfettamente*) to perfection, perfectly; ~ **per la barba** shaving brush.

pen'nino *sm* nib.

pen'none *sm* (*NAUT*) yard; (*stendardo*) banner, standard.

pe'nombra *sf* half-light, dim light.

pe'noso, a *ag* painful, distressing; (*faticoso*) tiring, laborious.

pen'sare *vi* to think // *vt* to think; (*inventare, escogitare*) to think out; ~ **a** to think of; (*amico, vacanze*) to think of *o* about; (*problema*) to think about; ~ **di fare qc** to think of doing sth; **ci penso io** I'll see to *o* take care of it.

pensi'ero *sm* thought; (*modo di pensare, dottrina*) thinking *q*; (*preoccupazione*) worry, care, trouble; **stare in** ~ **per qn** to be worried about sb; **pensie'roso, a** *ag* thoughtful.

'pensile *ag* hanging.

pensio'nante *sm/f* (*presso una famiglia*) lodger; (*di albergo*) guest.

pensio'nato, a *sm/f* pensioner.

pensi'one *sf* (*al prestatore di lavoro*) pension; (*vitto e alloggio*) board and lodging; (*albergo*) boarding house; **andare in** ~ to retire; **mezza** ~ half board; ~ **completa** full board.

pen'soso, a *ag* thoughtful, pensive, lost in thought.

pentapar'tito *sm* five-party government.

Pente'coste *sf* Pentecost, Whit Sunday (*Brit*).

penti'mento *sm* repentance, contrition.

pen'tirsi *vr*: ~ **di** to repent of; (*rammaricarsi*) to regret, be sorry for.

'pentola *sf* pot; ~ **a pressione** pressure cooker.

pe'nultimo, a *ag* last but one (*Brit*), next to last, penultimate.

pe'nuria *sf* shortage.

penzo'lare [pendzo'lare] *vi* to dangle, hang loosely; **penzo'loni** *av* dangling, hanging down; **stare penzoloni** to dangle, hang down.

'pepe *sm* pepper; ~ **macinato/in grani** ground/whole pepper.

pepe'rone *sm* pepper, capsicum; (*piccante*) chili.

pe'pita *sf* nugget.

per *prep* **1** (*moto attraverso luogo*) through; **i ladri sono passati** ~ **la finestra** the thieves got in (*o* out) through the window; **l'ho cercato** ~ **tutta la casa** I've searched the whole house *o* all over the house for it

2 (*moto a luogo*) for, to; **partire** ~ **la Germania/il mare** to leave for Germany/ the sea; **il treno** ~ **Roma** the Rome train, the train for *o* to Rome

3 (*stato in luogo*): **seduto/sdraiato** ~ **terra** sitting/lying on the ground

4 (*tempo*) for; ~ **anni/lungo tempo** for years/a long time; ~ **tutta l'estate** throughout the summer, all summer long; **lo rividi** ~ **Natale** I saw him again at Christmas; **lo faccio** ~ **lunedì** I'll do it for Monday

5 (*mezzo, maniera*) by; ~ **lettera/via aerea/ferrovia** by letter/airmail/rail; **prendere qn** ~ **un braccio** to take sb by the arm

6 (*causa, scopo*) for; **assente** ~ **malattia** absent because of *o* through *o* owing to illness; **ottimo** ~ **il mal di gola** excellent for sore throats

7 (*limitazione*) for; **è troppo difficile** ~ **lui** it's too difficult for him; ~ **quel che mi riguarda** as far as I'm concerned; ~ **poco che sia** however little it may be; ~ **questa volta ti perdono** I'll forgive you this time

8 (*prezzo, misura*) for; (*distributivo*) a, per; **venduto** ~ **3 milioni** sold for 3 million; **1000 lire** ~ **persona** 1000 lire a *o* per person; **uno** ~ **volta** one at a time; **uno** ~ **uno** one by one; **5** ~ **cento** 5 per cent; **3** ~ **4 fa 12** 3 times 4 equals 12; **dividere/moltiplicare 12** ~ **4** to divide/ multiply 12 by 4

9 (*in qualità di*) as; (*al posto di*) for; **avere qn** ~ **professore** to have sb as a teacher; **ti ho preso** ~ **Mario** I mistook you for Mario, I though you were Mario; **dare** ~ **morto qn** to give sb up for dead

10 (*seguito da vb: finale*): ~ **fare qc** (so as) to do sth, in order to do sth; (: *causale*): ~ **aver fatto qc** for having done sth; (: *consecutivo*): **è abbastanza**

grande ~ **andarci da solo** he's big enough to go on his own.

'pera sf pear.

pe'raltro av moreover, what's more.

per'bene ag inv respectable, decent // av (con cura) properly, well.

percentu'ale [pertʃentu'ale] sf percentage.

perce'pire [pertʃe'pire] vt (sentire) to perceive; (ricevere) to receive; **percezi'one** sf perception.

perché [per'ke] ♦ av why; ~ **no?** why not?; ~ **non vuoi andarci?** why don't you want to go?; **spiegami** ~ **l'hai fatto** tell me why you did it
♦ cong **1** (causale) because; **non posso uscire** ~ **ho da fare** I can't go out because o as I've a lot to do
2 (finale) in order that, so that; **te lo do** ~ **tu lo legga** I'm giving it to you so (that) you can read it
3 (consecutivo): **è troppo forte** ~ **si possa batterlo** he's too strong to be beaten
♦ sm inv reason; **il** ~ **di** the reason for.

perció [per'tʃɔ] cong so, for this (o that) reason.

per'correre vt (luogo) to go all over; (: paese) to travel up and down, go all over; (distanza) to cover.

per'corso, a pp di **percorrere** // sm (tragitto) journey; (tratto) route.

per'cosso, a pp di **percuotere** // sf blow.

percu'otere vt to hit, strike.

percussi'one sf percussion; **strumenti a** ~ (MUS) percussion instruments.

'perdere vt to lose; (lasciarsi sfuggire) to miss; (sprecare: tempo, denaro) to waste; (mandare in rovina: persona) to ruin // vi to lose; (serbatoio etc) to leak; ~**rsi** vr (smarrirsi) to get lost; (svanire) to disappear, vanish; **saper** ~ to be a good loser; **lascia** ~! forget it!, never mind!

perdigi'orno [perdi'dʒorno] sm/f inv idler, waster.

'perdita sf loss; (spreco) waste; (fuoriuscita) leak; **siamo in** ~ (COMM) we are running at a loss; **a** ~ **d'occhio** as far as the eye can see.

perdi'tempo sm/f inv waster, idler.

perdo'nare vt to pardon, forgive; (scusare) to excuse, pardon.

per'dono sm forgiveness; (DIR) pardon.

perdu'rare vi to go on, last; (perseverare) to persist.

perduta'mente av desperately, passionately.

per'duto, a pp di **perdere**.

peregri'nare vi to wander, roam.

pe'renne ag eternal, perpetual, perennial; (BOT) perennial.

peren'torio, a ag peremptory; (definitivo) final.

per'fetto, a ag perfect // sm (LING) perfect (tense).

perfezio'nare [perfettsjo'nare] vt to improve, perfect; ~**rsi** vr to improve.

perfezi'one [perfet'tsjone] sf perfection.

'perfido, a ag perfidious, treacherous.

per'fino av even.

perfo'rare vt to perforate; to punch a hole (o holes) in; (banda, schede) to punch; (trivellare) to drill; **perfora'tore, 'trice** sm/f punch-card operator // sm (utensile) punch; (INFORM): **perforatore di schede** card punch // sf (TECN) boring o drilling machine; (INFORM) card punch; **perforazi'one** sf perforation; punching; drilling; (INFORM) punch; (MED) perforation.

perga'mena sf parchment.

peri'colante ag precarious.

pe'ricolo sm danger; **mettere in** ~ to endanger, put in danger; **perico'loso, a** ag dangerous.

perife'ria sf periphery; (di città) outskirts pl.

pe'rifrasi sf circumlocution.

pe'rimetro sm perimeter.

peri'odico, a, ci, che ag periodic(al); (MAT) recurring // sm periodical.

pe'riodo sm period.

peripe'zie [peripet'tsie] sfpl ups and downs, vicissitudes.

pe'rire vi to perish, die.

pe'rito, a ag expert, skilled // sm/f expert; (agronomo, navale) surveyor; **un** ~ **chimico** a qualified chemist.

pe'rizia [pe'rittsja] sf (abilità) ability; (giudizio tecnico) expert opinion; expert's report.

'perla sf pearl; **per'lina** sf bead.

perlus'trare vt to patrol.

perma'loso, a ag touchy.

perma'nente ag permanent // sf permanent wave, perm; **perma'nenza** sf permanence; (soggiorno) stay.

perma'nere vi to remain.

perme'are vt to permeate.

per'messo, a pp di **permettere** // sm (autorizzazione) permission, leave; (dato a militare, impiegato) leave; (licenza) licence, permit; (MIL: foglio) pass; ~**?**, **è** ~? (posso entrare?) may I come in?; (posso passare?) excuse me; ~ **di** lavoro/pesca work/fishing permit.

per'mettere vt to allow, permit; ~ **a qn** qc/di fare to allow sb sth/to do; ~**rsi** qc/ di fare to allow o.s. sth/to do; (avere la possibilità) to afford sth/to do.

per'nacchia [per'nakkja] sf (fam): **fare una** ~ to blow a raspberry.

per'nice [per'nitʃe] sf partridge.

'perno sm pivot.

pernot'tare vi to spend the night, stay overnight.

'pero sm pear tree.

però cong (ma) but; (tuttavia) however,

nevertheless.

pero'rare *vt* (*DIR*, *fig*): ~ la causa di qn to plead sb's case.

perpendico'lare *ag*, *sf* perpendicular.

perpe'trare *vt* to perpetrate.

perpetu'are *vt* to perpetuate.

per'petuo, a *ag* perpetual.

per'plesso, a *ag* perplexed; uncertain, undecided.

perqui'sire *vt* to search; **perquisizi'one** *sf* (police) search.

persecu'tore *sm* persecutor.

persecuzi'one [persekut'tsjone] *sf* persecution.

persegu'ire *vt* to pursue.

persegui'tare *vt* to persecute.

perseve'rante *ag* persevering.

perseve'rare *vi* to persevere.

'Persia *sf*: la ~ Persia.

persi'ano, a *ag*, *sm/f* Persian // *sf* shutter; ~a avvolgibile Venetian blind.

'persico, a, ci, che *ag*: il golfo P~ the Persian Gulf.

per'sino *av* = **perfino**.

persis'tente *ag* persistent.

per'sistere *vi* to persist; ~ a fare to persist in doing; **persis'tito, a** *pp di* **persistere**.

'perso, a *pp di* **perdere**.

per'sona *sf* person; (*qualcuno*): una ~ someone, somebody, *espressione interrogativa* + anyone *o* anybody; ~e *sfpl* people; **non c'è ~ che ...** there's nobody who ..., there isn't anybody who ....

perso'naggio [perso'nadd3o] *sm* (*persona ragguardevole*) personality, figure; (*tipo*) character, individual; (*LETTERATURA*) character.

perso'nale *ag* personal // *sm* staff; personnel; (*figura fisica*) build.

personalità *sf inv* personality.

personifi'care *vt* to personify; to embody.

perspi'cace [perspi'katfe] *ag* shrewd, discerning.

persu'adere *vt*: ~ qn (di qc/a fare) to persuade sb (of sth/to do); **persuasi'one** *sf* persuasion; **persua'sivo, a** *ag* persuasive; **persu'aso, a** *pp di* **persuadere**.

per'tanto *cong* (*quindi*) so, therefore.

'pertica, che *sf* pole.

perti'nente *ag*: ~ (a) relevant (to), pertinent (to).

per'tosse *sf* whooping cough.

per'tugio [per'tud3o] *sm* hole, opening.

pertur'bare *vt* to disturb; (*persona*) to disturb, perturb; **perturbazi'one** *sf* disruption; perturbation; **perturbazione atmosferica** atmospheric disturbance.

per'vadere *vt* to pervade; **per'vaso, a** *pp di* **pervadere**.

perve'nire *vi*: ~ a to reach, arrive at, come to; (*venire in possesso*): gli

pervenne una fortuna he inherited a fortune; far ~ qc a to have sth sent to; **perve'nuto, a** *pp di* **pervenire**.

per'verso, a *ag* depraved; perverse.

perver'tire *vt* to pervert.

p. es. *abbr* (= *per esempio*) e.g.

'pesa *sf* weighing *q*; weighbridge.

pe'sante *ag* heavy; (*fig*: *noioso*) dull, boring.

pe'sare *vt* to weigh // *vi* (*avere un peso*) to weigh; (*essere pesante*) to be heavy; (*fig*) to carry weight; ~ su (*fig*) to lie heavy on; to influence; to hang over; mi pesa sgridarlo I find it hard to scold him.

'pesca *sf* (*pl* **pesche**: *frutto*) peach; (*il pescare*) fishing; andare a ~ to go fishing; ~ **di beneficenza** (*lotteria*) lucky dip; ~ **con la lenza** angling.

pes'care *vt* (*pesce*) to fish for; to catch; (*qc nell'acqua*) to fish out; (*fig*: *trovare*) to get hold of, find.

pesca'tore *sm* fisherman; angler.

'pesce ['peffe] *sm* fish *gen inv*; P~i (*dello zodiaco*) Pisces; ~ **d'aprile!** April Fool!; ~ **spada** swordfish; **pesce'cane** *sm* shark.

pesche'reccio [peske'rettfo] *sm* fishing boat.

pesche'ria [peske'ria] *sf* fishmonger's (shop) (*Brit*), fish store (*US*).

peschi'era [pes'kjɛra] *sf* fishpond.

pesci'vendolo, a [peffi'vendolo] *sm/f* fishmonger (*Brit*), fish merchant (*US*).

'pesco, schi *sm* peach tree.

pes'coso, a *ag* abounding in fish.

'peso *sm* weight; (*SPORT*) shot; rubare sul ~ to give short weight; essere di ~ a qn (*fig*) to be a burden to sb; ~ **lordo/netto** gross/net weight; ~ **piuma/mosca/gallo/medio/massimo** (*PUGILATO*) feather-/fly-/bantam-/middle-/heavyweight.

pessi'mismo *sm* pessimism; **pessi'mista, i, e** *ag* pessimistic // *sm/f* pessimist.

'pessimo, a *ag* very bad, awful.

pes'tare *vt* to tread on, trample on; (*sale*, *pepe*) to grind; (*uva*, *aglio*) to crush; (*fig*: *picchiare*): ~ qn to beat sb up.

'peste *sf* plague; (*persona*) nuisance, pest.

pes'tello *sm* pestle.

pesti'lenza [pesti'lentsa] *sf* pestilence; (*fetore*) stench.

'pesto, a *ag*: c'è buio ~ it's pitch-dark; occhio ~ black eye // *sm* (*CUC*) sauce made with basil, garlic, cheese and oil.

'petalo *sm* (*BOT*) petal.

pe'tardo *sm* firecracker, banger (*Brit*).

petizi'one [petit'tsjone] *sf* petition.

'peto *sm* (*fam*!) fart (!).

petrol'chimica [petrol'kimika] *sf* petrochemical industry.

petroli'era *sf* (*nave*) oil tanker.

petro'lifero, a *ag* oil-bearing; oil *cpd*.

pe'trolio sm oil, petroleum; (per lampada, fornello) paraffin.

pettego'lare vi to gossip.

pettego'lezzo [pettego'leddzo] sm gossip q; **fare ~i** to gossip.

pet'tegolo, a ag gossipy // sm/f gossip.

petti'nare vt to comb (the hair of); **~rsi** vr to comb one's hair; **pettina'tura** sf (acconciatura) hairstyle.

'pettine sm comb; (ZOOL) scallop.

petti'rosso sm robin.

'petto sm chest; (seno) breast, bust; (CUC: di carne bovina) brisket; (: di pollo etc) breast; **a doppio ~** (abito) double-breasted; **petto'ruto, a** ag broad-chested; full-breasted.

petu'lante ag insolent.

'pezza ['pɛttsa] sf piece of cloth; (toppa) patch; (cencio) rag, cloth.

pez'zato, a [pet'tsato] ag piebald.

pez'zente [pet'tsɛnte] sm/f beggar.

'pezzo ['pɛttso] sm (gen) piece; (brandello, frammento) piece, bit; (di macchina, arnese etc) part; (STAMPA) article; (di tempo): **aspettare un ~** to wait quite a while o some time; **in o a ~i** in pieces; **andare in ~i** to break into pieces; **un bel ~ d'uomo** a fine figure of a man; **abito a due ~i** two-piece suit; **~ di cronaca** (STAMPA) report; **~ grosso** (fig) bigwig; **~ di ricambio** spare part.

pia'cente [pja'tʃɛnte] ag attractive, pleasant.

pia'cere [pja'tʃere] vi to please; **una ragazza che piace** a likeable girl; an attractive girl; **~ a: mi piace** I like it; **quei ragazzi non mi piacciono** I don't like those boys; **gli piacerebbe andare al cinema** he would like to go to the cinema // sm pleasure; (favore) favour; **"~!"** (nelle presentazioni) "pleased to meet you!"; **con ~** certainly, with pleasure; **per ~!** please; **fare un ~ a qn** to do sb a favour; **pia'cevole** ag pleasant, agreeable; **piaci'uto, a** pp di **piacere**.

pi'aga, ghe sf (lesione) sore; (ferita: anche fig) wound; (fig: flagello) scourge, curse; (: persona) pest, nuisance.

piagnis'teo [pjaɲɲis'tɛo] sm whining, whimpering.

piagnuco'lare [pjaɲɲuko'lare] vi to whimper.

pi'alla sf (arnese) plane; **pial'lare** vt to plane.

pi'ana sf stretch of level ground; (più esteso) plain.

pianeggi'ante [pjaned'dʒante] ag flat, level.

piane'rottolo sm landing.

pia'neta sm (ASTR) planet.

pi'angere ['pjandʒere] vi to cry, weep; (occhi) to water // vt to cry, weep; (lamentare) to bewail, lament; **~ la morte di qn** to mourn sb's death.

pianifi'care vt to plan; **pianificazi'one** sf planning.

pia'nista, i, e sm/f pianist.

pi'ano, a ag (piatto) flat, level; (MAT) plane; (facile) straightforward, simple; (chiaro) clear, plain // av (adagio) slowly; (a bassa voce) softly; (con cautela) slowly, carefully // sm (MAT) plane; (GEO) plain; (livello) level, plane; (di edificio) floor; (programma) plan; (MUS) piano; **pian ~** very slowly; (poco a poco) little by little; **in primo/secondo ~** in the foreground/background; **di primo ~** (fig) prominent, high-ranking.

piano'forte sm piano, pianoforte.

pi'anta sf (BOT) plant; (ANAT: anche: **~ del piede**) sole (of the foot); (grafico) plan; (topografica) map; **in ~ stabile** on the permanent staff; **piantagi'one** sf plantation; **pian'tare** vt to plant; (conficcare) to drive o hammer in; (tenda) to put up, pitch; (fig: lasciare) to leave, desert; **~rsi** vr: **~rsi davanti a qn** to plant o.s. in front of sb; **piantala!** (fam) cut it out!

pianter'reno sm ground floor.

pi'anto, a pp di **piangere** // sm tears pl, crying.

pian'tone sm (vigilante) sentry, guard; (soldato) orderly; (AUT) steering column.

pia'nura sf plain.

pi'astra sf plate; (di pietra) slab; (di fornello) hotplate; **~ di registrazione** tape deck; **panino alla ~** ≈ toasted sandwich.

pias'trella sf tile.

pias'trina sf (MIL) identity disc.

piatta'forma sf (anche fig) platform.

piat'tino sm saucer.

pi'atto, a ag flat; (fig: scialbo) dull // sm (recipiente, vivanda) dish; (portata) course; (parte piana) flat (part); **~i** smpl (MUS) cymbals; **~ fondo** soup dish; **~ forte** main course; **~ del giorno** dish of the day, plat du jour; **~ del giradischi** turntable; **~i già pronti** (CULIN) ready-cooked dishes.

pi'azza ['pjattsa] sf square; (COMM) market; **far ~ pulita** to make a clean sweep; **~ d'armi** (MIL) parade ground; **piaz'zale** sm (large) square.

piaz'zare [pjat'tsare] vt to place; (COMM) to market, sell; **~rsi** vr (SPORT) to be placed.

piaz'zista, i [pjat'tsista] sm (COMM) commercial traveller.

piaz'zola [pjat'tsɔla] sf (AUT) lay-by.

'picca, che sf pike; **~che** sfpl (CARTE) spades.

pic'cante ag hot, pungent; (fig) racy; biting.

pic'carsi vr: **~ di fare** to pride o.s. on one's ability to do; **~ per qc** to take offence at sth.

pic'chetto [pik'ketto] *sm* (*MIL, di scioperanti*) picket.

picchi'are [pik'kjare] *vt* (*persona: colpire*) to hit, strike; (: *prendere a botte*) to beat (up); (*battere*) to beat; (*sbattere*) to bang // *vi* (*bussare*) to knock; (: *con forza*) to bang; (*colpire*) to hit, strike; (*sole*) to beat down; **picchi'ata** *sf* (*percosse*) beating, thrashing; (*AER*) dive.

picchiet'tare [pikkjet'tare] *vt* (*punteggiare*) to spot, dot; (*colpire*) to tap.

'picchio ['pikkjo] *sm* woodpecker.

pic'cino, a [pit'tʃino] *ag* tiny, very small.

piccio'naia [pittʃo'naja] *sf* pigeon-loft; (*TEATRO*): **la ~** the gods *sg*.

picci'one [pit'tʃone] *sm* pigeon.

'picco, chi *sm* peak; **a ~** vertically.

'piccolo, a *ag* small; (*oggetto, mano, di età: bambino*) small, little (*dav sostantivo*); (*di breve durata: viaggio*) short; (*fig*) mean, petty // *sm/f* child, little one; **~i** *smpl* (*di animale*) young *pl*; **in ~** in miniature.

pic'cone *sm* pick(-axe).

pic'cozza [pik'kottsa] *sf* ice-axe.

pic'nic *sm inv* picnic.

pi'docchio [pi'dokkjo] *sm* louse.

pi'ede *sm* foot; (*di mobile*) leg; **in ~i** standing; **a ~i** on foot; **a ~i nudi** barefoot; **su due ~i** (*fig*) at once; **prendere ~** (*fig*) to gain ground, catch on; **sul ~ di guerra** (*MIL*) ready for action; **~ di porco** crowbar.

piedis'tallo, piedes'tallo *sm* pedestal.

pi'ega, ghe *sf* (*piegatura, GEO*) fold; (*di gonna*) pleat; (*di pantaloni*) crease; (*grinza*) wrinkle, crease; **prendere una brutta ~** (*avvenimento*) to take a turn for the worse.

pie'gare *vt* to fold; (*braccia, gambe, testa*) to bend // *vi* to bend; **~rsi** *vr* to bend; (*fig*): **~rsi (a)** to yield (to), submit (to); **pieghet'tare** *vt* to pleat; **pie'ghevole** *ag* pliable, flexible; (*porta*) folding; (*fig*) yielding, docile.

Pie'monte *sm*: **il ~** Piedmont.

pi'ena *sf vedi* **pieno**.

pi'eno, a *ag* full; (*muro, mattone*) solid // *sm* (*colmo*) height, peak; (*carico*) full load // *sf* (*di fiume*) flood, spate; (*gran folla*) crowd, throng; **~ di** full of; **in ~ giorno** in broad daylight; **fare il ~** (*di benzina*) to fill up (with petrol).

pietà *sf* pity; (*REL*) piety; **senza ~** pitiless, merciless; **avere ~ di** (*compassione*) to pity, feel sorry for; (*misericordia*) to have pity o mercy on.

pie'tanza [pje'tantsa] *sf* dish; (*main*) course.

pie'toso, a *ag* (*compassionevole*) pitying, compassionate; (*che desta pietà*) pitiful.

pi'etra *sf* stone; **~ preziosa** precious stone, gem; **pie'traia** *sf* (*terreno*) stony ground; **pietrifi'care** *vt* to petrify; (*fig*) to transfix, paralyze.

'piffero *sm* (*MUS*) pipe.

pigi'ama, i [pi'dʒama] *sm* pyjamas *pl*.

'pigia 'pigia ['pidʒa'pidʒa] *sm* crowd, press.

pigi'are [pi'dʒare] *vt* to press.

pigi'one [pi'dʒone] *sf* rent.

pigli'are [piʎ'ʎare] *vt* to take, grab; (*afferrare*) to catch.

'piglio ['piʎʎo] *sm* look, expression.

pig'meo, a *sm/f* pygmy.

'pigna ['pinɲa] *sf* pine cone.

pi'gnolo, a [pin'ɲɔlo] *ag* pernickety.

pigo'lare *vi* to cheep, chirp.

pi'grizia [pi'grittsja] *sf* laziness.

'pigro, a *ag* lazy.

'pila *sf* (*catasta, di ponte*) pile; (*ELETTR*) battery; (*fam: torcia*) torch (*Brit*), flashlight.

pi'lastro *sm* pillar.

'pillola *sf* pill; **prendere la ~** to be on the pill.

pi'lone *sm* (*di ponte*) pier; (*di linea elettrica*) pylon.

pi'lota, i, e *sm/f* pilot; (*AUT*) driver // *ag inv* pilot *cpd*; **~ automatico** automatic pilot; **pilo'tare** *vt* to pilot; to drive.

pi'mento *sm* pimento, allspice.

pinaco'teca, che *sf* art gallery.

pi'neta *sf* pinewood.

ping-'pong [piŋ'pɔŋ] *sm* table tennis.

'pingue *ag* fat, corpulent.

pingu'ino *sm* (*ZOOL*) penguin.

'pinna *sf* fin; (*di pinguino, spatola di gomma*) flipper.

'pino *sm* pine (tree); **pi'nolo** *sm* pine kernel.

'pinza ['pintsa] *sf* pliers *pl*; (*MED*) forceps *pl*; (*ZOOL*) pincer.

pin'zette [pin'tsette] *sfpl* tweezers.

'pio, a, 'pii, 'pie *ag* pious; (*opere, istituzione*) charitable, charity *cpd*.

pi'oggia, ge ['pjɔddʒa] *sf* rain; **~ acida** acid rain.

pi'olo *sm* peg; (*di scala*) rung.

piom'bare *vi* to fall heavily; (*gettarsi con impeto*): **~ su** to fall upon, assail // *vt* (*dente*) to fill; **piomba'tura** *sf* (*di dente*) filling.

piom'bino *sm* (*sigillo*) (lead) seal; (*del filo a piombo*) plummet; (*PESCA*) sinker.

pi'ombo *sm* (*CHIM*) lead; (*sigillo*) (lead) seal; (*proiettile*) (lead) shot; **a ~** (*cadere*) straight down.

pioni'ere *sm/f* pioneer.

pi'oppo *sm* poplar.

pi'overe *vb impers* to rain // *vi* (*fig: scendere dall'alto*) to rain down; (: *affluire in gran numero*): **~ in** to pour into; **piovigi'nare** *vb impers* to drizzle; **pio'voso, a** *ag* rainy.

pi'ovra *sf* octopus.

'pipa *sf* pipe.

pipì *sf* (*fam*): fare ~ to have a wee (wee).

pipis'trello *sm* (*ZOOL*) bat.

pi'ramide *sf* pyramid.

pi'rata, i *sm* pirate; ~ della strada hit-and-run driver.

Pire'nei *smpl*: i ~ the Pyrenees.

'pirico, a, ci, che *ag*: polvere ~a gunpowder.

pi'rite *sf* pyrite.

pi'rofilo, a *ag* heat-resistant.

pi'roga, ghe *sf* dug-out canoe.

pi'romane *sm/f* pyromaniac; arsonist.

pi'roscafo *sm* steamer, steamship.

pisci'are [piʃ'ʃare] *vi* (*fam!*) to piss (!), pee (!).

pi'scina [piʃ'ʃina] *sf* (swimming) pool; (*stabilimento*) (swimming) baths *pl*.

pi'sello *sm* pea.

piso'lino *sm* nap.

'pista *sf* (*traccia*) track, trail; (*di stadio*) track; (*di pattinaggio*) rink; (*da sci*) run; (*AER*) runway; (*di circo*) ring; ~ da ballo dance floor.

pis'tacchio [pis'takkjo] *sm* pistachio (tree); pistachio (nut).

pis'tola *sf* pistol, gun.

pis'tone *sm* piston.

pi'tone *sm* python.

pit'tore, 'trice *sm/f* painter; **pitto'resco, a, schi, sche** *ag* picturesque.

pit'tura *sf* painting; **pittu'rare** *vt* to paint.

più ◆ *av* 1 (*in maggiore quantità*) more; ~ del solito more than usual; in ~, di ~ more; ne voglio di ~ I want some more; ci sono 3 persone in o di ~ there are 3 more o extra people; ~ o meno more or less; per di ~ (*inoltre*) what's more, moreover

2 (*comparativo*) more, aggettivo corto + ...er; ~ ... di/che more ... than; lavoro ~ di te/Paola I work harder than you/Paola; è ~ intelligente che ricco he's more intelligent than rich

3 (*superlativo*) most, aggettivo corto + ...est; il ~ grande/intelligente the biggest/most intelligent; è quello che compro ~ spesso that's the one I buy most often; al ~ presto as soon as possible; al ~ tardi at the latest

4 (*negazione*): non ... ~ no more, no longer; non ho ~ soldi I've got no more money, I don't have any more money; non lavoro ~ I'm no longer working, I don't work any more; a ~ non posso (*gridare*) at the top of one's voice; (*correre*) as fast as one can

5 (*MAT*) plus; 4 ~ 5 fa 9 4 plus 5 equals 9; ~ 5 gradi 5 degrees above freezing, plus 5

◆ *prep* plus

◆ *ag inv* 1: ~ ... (di) more ... (than); ~ denaro/tempo more money/time; ~

persone di quante ci aspettassimo more people than we expected

2 (*numerosi, diversi*) several; l'aspettai per ~ giorni I waited for it for several days

◆ *sm* 1 (*la maggior parte*): il ~ è fatto most of it is done

2 (*MAT*) plus (sign)

3: i ~ the majority.

piucchepper'fetto [pjukkepper'fɛtto] *sm* (*LING*) pluperfect, past perfect.

pi'uma *sf* feather; ~e *sfpl* down *sg*; (*piumaggio*) plumage *sg*, feathers; **piu'maggio** *sm* plumage, feathers *pl*; **piu'mino** *sm* (eider)down; (*per letto*) eiderdown; (: *tipo danese*) duvet, continental quilt; (*giacca*) quilted jacket (*with goose-feather padding*); (*per cipria*) powder puff; (*per spolverare*) feather duster.

piut'tosto *av* rather; ~ che (*anziché*) rather than.

pi'vello, a *sm/f* greenhorn.

'pizza ['pittsa] *sf* pizza; **pizze'ria** *sf* place where pizzas are made, sold or eaten.

pizzi'cagnolo, a [pittsi'kaɲɲolo] *sm/f* specialist grocer.

pizzi'care [pittsi'kare] *vt* (*stringere*) to nip, pinch; (*pungere*) to sting; to bite; (*MUS*) to pluck // *vi* (*prudere*) to itch, be itchy; (*cibo*) to be hot o spicy.

pizziche'ria [pittsike'ria] *sf* delicatessen (shop).

'pizzico, chi ['pittsiko] *sm* (*pizzicotto*) pinch, nip; (*piccola quantità*) pinch, dash; (*d'insetto*) sting; bite.

pizzi'cotto [pittsi'kɔtto] *sm* pinch, nip.

'pizzo ['pittso] *sm* (*merletto*) lace; (*barbetta*) goatee beard.

pla'care *vt* to placate, soothe; ~rsi *vr* to calm down.

'placca, che *sf* plate; (*con iscrizione*) plaque; (*anche*: ~ dentaria) (dental) plaque; **plac'care** *vt* to plate; **placcato** in oro/argento gold-/silver-plated.

'placido, a ['platʃido] *ag* placid, calm.

plagi'are [pla'dʒare] *vt* (*copiare*) to plagiarize; **'plagio** *sm* plagiarism.

pla'nare *vi* (*AER*) to glide.

'plancia, ce ['plantʃa] *sf* (*NAUT*) bridge.

plane'tario, a *ag* planetary // *sm* (*locale*) planetarium.

'plasma *sm* plasma.

plas'mare *vt* to mould, shape.

'plastico, a, ci, che *ag* plastic // *sm* (*rappresentazione*) relief model; (*esplosivo*): bomba al ~ plastic bomb // *sf* (*arte*) plastic arts *pl*; (*MED*) plastic surgery; (*sostanza*) plastic.

plasti'lina *sf* ® plasticine ®.

'platano *sm* plane tree.

pla'tea *sf* (*TEATRO*) stalls *pl*.

'platino *sm* platinum.

pla'tonico, a, ci, che *ag* platonic.

plau'sibile *ag* plausible.

'**plauso** sm (fig) approval.
ple'baglia |ple'baʎʎa| sf (peg) rabble, mob.
'**plebe** sf common people; **ple'beo, a** ag plebeian; (volgare) coarse, common.
ple'nario, a ag plenary.
pleni'lunio sm full moon.
'**plettro** sm plectrum.
pleu'rite sf pleurisy.
'**plico, chi** sm (pacco) parcel; **in ~ a parte** (COMM) under separate cover.
plo'tone sm (MIL) platoon; **~ d'esecuzione** firing squad.
'**plumbeo, a** ag leaden.
plu'rale ag, sm plural; **pluralità** sf plurality; (maggioranza) majority.
plusva'lore sm (ECON) surplus.
pneu'matico, a, ci, che ag inflatable; pneumatic // sm (AUT) tyre (Brit), tire (US).
po' av, sm vedi **poco**.
'**poco, a, chi, che ◆** ag 1 (quantità) little, not much; (numero) few, not many; **~ pane/denaro/spazio** little o not much bread/money/space; **~che persone/idee** few o not many people/ideas; **ci vediamo tra ~** (sottinteso: tempo) see you soon
◆ av 1 (in piccola quantità) little, not much; (numero limitato) few, not many; **guadagna ~** he doesn't earn much, he earns little
2 (con ag, av) (a) little, not very; **sta ~ bene** he isn't very well; **è ~ più vecchia di lui** she's a little o slightly older than him
3 (tempo): **~ dopo/prima** shortly afterwards/before; **il film dura ~** the film doesn't last very long; **ci vediamo molto ~** we don't see each other very often, we hardly ever see each other
4: un po' a little, a bit; **è un po' corto** it's a little o a bit short; **arriverà fra un po'** he'll arrive shortly o in a little while
5: a dir ~ to say the least; **a ~ a ~** a little by little; **per ~ non cadevo** I nearly fell; **è una cosa da ~** it's nothing, it's of no importance; **una persona da ~** a worthless person
◆ pronome (a) little; **~chi(che)** pronome pl (persone) few (people); (cose) few
◆ sm 1 little; **vive del ~ che ha** he lives on the little he has
2: un po' a little; **un po' di zucchero** a little sugar; **un bel po' di denaro** quite a lot of money; **un po' per ciascuno** a bit each.
po'dere sm (AGR) farm.
pode'roso, a ag powerful.
podestà sm inv (nel fascismo) podesta, mayor.
'**podio** sm dais, platform; (MUS) podium.
po'dismo sm (SPORT) track events pl.
po'ema, i sm poem.

poe'sia sf (arte) poetry; (componimento) poem.
po'eta, 'essa sm/f poet/poetess; **po'etico, a, ci, che** ag poetic(al).
poggi'are |pod'dʒare| vt to lean, rest; (posare) to lay, place; **poggia'testa** sm inv (AUT) headrest.
'**poggio** |'pɔddʒo| sm hillock, knoll.
'**poi** av then; (alla fine) finally, at last; **e ~** (inoltre) and besides; **questa ~ (è bella)!** (ironico) that's a good one!
poiché |poi'ke| cong since, as.
'**poker** sm poker.
po'lacco, a, chi, che ag Polish // sm/f Pole.
po'lare ag polar.
po'lemico, a, ci, che ag polemic(al), controversial // sf controversy.
po'lenta sf (CUC) sort of thick porridge made with maize flour.
poli'clinico, ci sm general hospital, polyclinic.
poli'estere sm polyester.
polio(mie'lite) sf polio(myelitis).
'**polipo** sm polyp.
polisti'rolo sm polystyrene.
poli'tecnico, ci sm postgraduate technical college.
politiciz'zare |politid'dzare| vt to politicize.
po'litico, a, ci, che ag political // sm/f politician // sf politics sg; (linea di condotta) policy.
poli'zia |polit'tsia| sf police; **~ giudiziaria** ≈ Criminal Investigation Department (CID) (Brit), ≈ Federal Bureau of Investigation (FBI) (US); **~ stradale** traffic police; **polizi'esco, a, schi, sche** ag police cpd; (film, romanzo) detective cpd; **polizi'otto** sm policeman; **cane poliziotto** police dog; **donna poliziotto** policewoman.
'**polizza** |'pɔlittsa| sf (COMM) bill; **~ di assicurazione** insurance policy; **~ di carico** bill of-lading.
pol'laio sm henhouse.
pol'lame sm poultry.
pol'lastro sm (ZOOL) cockerel.
'**pollice** |'pɔllitʃe| sm thumb.
'**polline** sm pollen.
'**pollo** sm chicken.
pol'mone sm lung; **polmo'nite** sf pneumonia.
'**polo** sm (GEO, FISICA) pole; (gioco) polo; **il ~ sud/nord** the South/North Pole.
Po'lonia sf: **la ~** Poland.
'**polpa** sf flesh, pulp; (carne) lean meat.
pol'paccio |pol'pattʃo| sm (ANAT) calf.
pol'petta sf (CUC) meatball; **polpet'tone** sm (CUC) meatloaf.
'**polpo** sm octopus.
pol'poso, a ag fleshy.
pol'sino sm cuff.
'**polso** sm (ANAT) wrist; (pulsazione) pulse; (fig: forza) drive, vigour.

pol'tiglia [pol'tiʎʎa] *sf* (*composto*) mash, mush; (*di fango e neve*) slush.

pol'trire *vi* to laze about.

pol'trona *sf* armchair; (*TEATRO: posto*) seat in the front stalls (*Brit*) o orchestra (*US*).

pol'trone *ag* lazy, slothful.

'polvere *sf* dust; (*anche:* ~ **da sparo**) (gun)powder; (*sostanza ridotta minutissima*) powder, dust; **latte in** ~ dried o powdered milk; **caffè in** ~ instant coffee; **sapone in** ~ soap powder; **polveri'era** *sf* powder magazine; **polveriz'zare** *vt* to pulverize; (*nebulizzare*) to atomize; (*fig*) to crush, pulverize; to smash; **polve'rone** *sm* thick cloud of dust; **polve'roso, a** *ag* dusty.

po'mata *sf* ointment, cream.

po'mello *sm* knob.

pomeridi'ano, a *ag* afternoon *cpd*; **nelle ore** ~**e** in the afternoon.

pome'riggio [pome'riddʒo] *sm* afternoon.

'pomice ['pɔmitʃe] *sf* pumice.

'pomo *sm* (*mela*) apple; (*ornamentale*) knob; (*di sella*) pommel; ~ **d'Adamo** (*ANAT*) Adam's apple.

pomo'doro *sm* tomato.

'pompa *sf* pump; (*sfarzo*) pomp (and ceremony); ~**e funebri** funeral parlour *sg* (*Brit*), undertaker's *sg*; **pom'pare** *vt* to pump; (*trarre*) to pump out; (*gonfiare d'aria*) to pump up.

pom'pelmo *sm* grapefruit.

pompi'ere *sm* fireman.

pom'poso, a *ag* pompous.

ponde'rare *vt* to ponder over, consider carefully.

ponde'roso, a *ag* (*anche fig*) weighty.

po'nente *sm* west.

'ponte *sm* bridge; (*di nave*) deck; (*: anche:* ~ **di comando**) bridge; (*impalcatura*) scaffold; **fare il** ~ (*fig*) to take the extra day off (*between 2 public holidays*); **governo** ~ interim government; ~ **aereo** airlift; ~ **sospeso** suspension bridge.

pon'tefice [pon'tefitʃe] *sm* (*REL*) pontiff.

pontifi'care *vi* (*anche fig*) to pontificate.

ponti'ficio, a, ci, cie [ponti'fitʃo] *ag* papal.

popo'lano, a *ag* popular, of the people.

popo'lare *ag* popular; (*quartiere, clientela*) working-class // *vt* (*rendere abitato*) to populate; ~**rsi** *vr* to fill with people, get crowded; **popolarità** *sf* popularity; **popolazi'one** *sf* population.

'popolo *sm* people; **popo'loso, a** *ag* densely populated.

po'pone *sm* melon.

'poppa *sf* (*di nave*) stern; (*mammella*) breast.

pop'pare *vt* to suck.

poppa'toio *sm* (feeding) bottle.

porcel'lana [portʃel'lana] *sf* porcelain, china; piece of china.

porcel'lino, a [portʃel'lino] *sm/f* piglet.

porche'ria [porke'ria] *sf* filth, muck; (*fig: oscenità*) obscenity; (*: azione disonesta*) dirty trick; (*: cosa mal fatta*) rubbish.

por'cile [por'tʃile] *sm* pigsty.

por'cino, a [por'tʃino] *ag* of pigs, pork *cpd* // *sm* (*fungo*) type of edible mushroom.

'porco, ci *sm* pig; (*carne*) pork.

porcos'pino *sm* porcupine.

'porgere ['pɔrdʒere] *vt* to hand, give; (*tendere*) to hold out.

pornogra'fia *sf* pornography; **porno'grafico, a, ci, che** *ag* pornographic.

'poro *sm* pore; **po'roso, a** *ag* porous.

'porpora *sf* purple.

'porre *vt* (*mettere*) to put; (*collocare*) to place; (*posare*) to lay (down), put (down); (*fig: supporre*): **poniamo (il caso) che** ... let's suppose that ...; **porsi** *vr* (*mettersi*): **porsi a sedere/in cammino** to sit down/set off; ~ **una domanda a qn** to ask sb a question, put a question to sb.

'porro *sm* (*BOT*) leek; (*MED*) wart.

'porta *sf* door; (*SPORT*) goal; ~**e sfpl** (*di città*) gates; **a** ~**e chiuse** (*DIR*) in camera.

'porta... *prefisso*: **porta'bagagli** *sm inv* (*facchino*) porter; (*AUT, FERR*) luggage rack; **portabandi'era** *sm inv* standard bearer; **porta'cenere** *sm inv* ashtray; **portachi'avi** *sm inv* keyring; **porta'cipria** *sm inv* powder compact; **porta'erei** *sm inv* (*nave*) aircraft carrier // *sm inv* (*aereo*) aircraft transporter; **portafi'nestra, pl portefi'nestre** *sf* French window; **porta'foglio** *sm* (*busta*) wallet; (*cartella*) briefcase; (*POL, BORSA*) portfolio; **portafor'tuna** *sm inv* lucky charm; mascot; **portagi'oie** *sm inv*, **portagioi'elli** *sm inv* jewellery box.

porta'lettere *sm/f inv* postman/woman (*Brit*), mailman/woman (*US*).

porta'mento *sm* carriage, bearing.

portamo'nete *sm inv* purse.

por'tante *ag* (*muro etc*) supporting, load-bearing.

portan'tina *sf* sedan chair; (*per ammalati*) stretcher.

por'tare *vt* (*sostenere, sorreggere: peso, bambino, pacco*) to carry; (*indossare: abito, occhiali*) to wear; (*: capelli lunghi*) to have; (*avere: nome, titolo*) to have, bear; (*recare*): ~ **qc a qn** to take (o bring) sth to sb; (*fig: sentimenti*) to bear; ~**rsi** *vr* (*recarsi*) to go; ~ **avanti** (*discorso, idea*) to pursue; ~ **via** to take away; (*rubare*) to take; ~ **i bambini a spasso** to take the children for a walk; ~

fortuna to bring good luck.

portasiga'rette *sm inv* cigarette case.

por'tata *sf* (*vivanda*) course; (*AUT*) carrying (*o* loading) capacity; (*di arma*) range; (*volume d'acqua*) (rate of) flow; (*fig: limite*) scope, capability; (*: importanza*) impact, import; **alla ~ di tutti** (*conoscenza*) within everybody's capabilities; (*prezzo*) within everybody's means; **a/fuori ~** (di) within/out of reach (of); **a ~ di mano** within (arm's) reach.

por'tatile *ag* portable.

por'tato, a *ag* (*incline*): **~ a** inclined *o* apt to.

porta'tore, 'trice *sm/f* (*anche COMM*) bearer; (*MED*) carrier.

portau'ovo *sm inv* eggcup.

porta'voce [porta'votʃe] *sm/f inv* spokesman/woman.

por'tento *sm* wonder, marvel.

'portico, ci *sm* portico.

porti'era *sf* (*AUT*) door.

porti'ere *sm* (*portinaio*) concierge, caretaker; (*di hotel*) porter; (*nel calcio*) goalkeeper.

porti'naio, a *sm/f* concierge, caretaker.

portine'ria *sf* caretaker's lodge.

'porto, a *pp di* **porgere** // *sm* (*NAUT*) harbour, port; (*spesa di trasporto*) carriage // *sm inv* port (wine); **~ d'armi** (*documento*) gun licence.

Porto'gallo *sm*: **il ~** Portugal; **porto'ghese** *ag*, *sm/f*, *sm* Portuguese *inv*.

por'tone *sm* main entrance, main door.

portu'ale *ag* harbour *cpd*, port *cpd* // *sm* dock worker.

porzi'one [por'tsjone] *sf* portion, share; (*di cibo*) portion, helping.

'posa *sf* (*FOT*) exposure; (*atteggiamento, di modello*) pose.

po'sare *vt* to put (down), lay (down) // *vi* (*ponte, edificio, teoria*): **~ su** to rest on; (*FOT, atteggiarsi*) to pose; **~rsi** *vr* (*aereo*) to land; (*uccello*) to alight; (*sguardo*) to settle.

po'sata *sf* piece of cutlery; **~e** *sfpl* cutlery *sg*.

po'sato, a *ag* serious.

pos'critto *sm* postscript.

posi'tivo, a *ag* positive.

posizi'one [pozit'tsjone] *sf* position; **prendere ~** (*fig*) to take a stand; **luci di ~** (*AUT*) sidelights.

posolo'gia, 'gie [pozolo'dʒia] *sf* dosage, directions *pl* for use.

pos'porre *vt* to place after; (*differire*) to postpone, defer; **pos'posto, a** *pp di* **posporre**.

posse'dere *vt* to own, possess; (*qualità, virtù*) to have, possess; (*conoscere a fondo: lingua etc*) to have a thorough knowledge of; (*sog: ira etc*) to possess; **possedi'mento** *sm* possession.

posses'sivo, a *ag* possessive.

pos'sesso *sm* ownership *q*; possession.

posses'sore *sm* owner.

pos'sibile *ag* possible // *sm*: **fare tutto il ~ to** do everything possible; **nei limiti del ~** as far as possible; **al più tardi ~** as late as possible; **possibilità** *sf inv* possibility // *sfpl* (*mezzi*) means; **aver la possibilità di fare** to be in a position to do; to have the opportunity to do.

possi'dente *sm/f* landowner.

'posta *sf* (*servizio*) post, postal service; (*corrispondenza*) post, mail; (*ufficio postale*) post office; (*nei giochi d'azzardo*) stake; **~e** *sfpl* (*amministrazione*) post office; **~ aerea** airmail; **ministro delle P~e e Telecomunicazioni** Postmaster General; **posta'giro** *sm* post office cheque, postal giro (*Brit*); **pos'tale** *ag* postal, post office *cpd*.

post'bellico, a, ci, che *ag* postwar.

posteggi'are [posted'dʒare] *vt, vi* to park; **pos'teggio** *sm* car park (*Brit*), parking lot (*US*); (*di taxi*) rank (*Brit*), stand (*US*).

postelegra'fonico, a, ci, che *ag* postal and telecommunications *cpd*.

posteri'ore *ag* (*dietro*) back; (*dopo*) later // *sm* (*fam: sedere*) behind.

pos'ticcio, a, ci, ce [pos'tittʃo] *ag* false // *sm* hairpiece.

postici'pare [postitʃi'pare] *vt* to defer, postpone.

pos'tilla *sf* marginal note.

pos'tino *sm* postman (*Brit*), mailman (*US*).

'posto, a *pp di* **porre** // *sm* (*sito, posizione*) place; (*impiego*) job; (*spazio libero*) room, space; (*di parcheggio*) space; (*sedile: al teatro, in treno etc*) seat; (*MIL*) post; **a ~** (*in ordine*) in place, tidy; (*: persona*) reliable; **al ~ di** in place of; **sul ~** on the spot; **mettere a ~** to tidy (up), put in order; (*faccende*) to straighten out; **~ di blocco** roadblock; **~ di polizia** police station.

pos'tribolo *sm* brothel.

'postumo, a *ag* posthumous; (*tardivo*) belated; **~i** *smpl* (*conseguenze*) after-effects, consequences.

po'tabile *ag* drinkable; **acqua ~** drinking water.

po'tare *vt* to prune.

po'tassio *sm* potassium.

po'tente *ag* (*nazione*) strong, powerful; (*veleno, farmaco*) potent, strong; **po'tenza** *sf* power; (*forza*) strength.

potenzi'ale [poten'tsjale] *ag*, *sm* potential.

po'tere ♦ *sm* power; **al ~** (*partito etc*) in power; **~ d'acquisto** purchasing power ♦ *vb ausiliare* **1** (*essere in grado di*) can, be able to; **non ha potuto ripararlo** he couldn't *o* he wasn't able to repair it;

non è potuto venire he couldn't o he wasn't able to come; **spiacente di non poter aiutare** sorry not to be able to help **2** (avere il permesso) can, may, be allowed to; **posso entrare?** can o may I come in?; **si può sapere dove sei stato?** where on earth have you been? **3** (eventualità) may, might, could; **potrebbe essere vero** it might o could be true; **può aver avuto un incidente** he may o might o could have had an accident; **può darsi** perhaps; **può darsi** o **essere che non venga** he may o might not come **4** (augurio): **potessi almeno parlargli!** if only I could speak to him! **5** (suggerimento): **potresti almeno scusarti!** you could at least apologize! ♦ vt can, be able to; **può molto per noi** he can do a lot for us; **non ne posso più** (per stanchezza) I'm exhausted; (per rabbia) I can't take any more.

potestà sf (potere) power; (DIR) authority.

'povero, a ag poor; (disadorno) plain, bare // sm/f poor man/woman; **i ~i** the poor; **~ di** lacking in, having little; **povertà** sf poverty.

'pozza ['pottsa] sf pool.

poz'zanghera [pot'tsangera] sf puddle.

'pozzo ['pottso] sm well; (cava: di carbone) pit; (di miniera) shaft; **~ petrolifero** oil well.

pran'zare [pran'dzare] vi to dine, have dinner; to lunch, have lunch.

'pranzo ['prandzo] sm dinner; (a mezzogiorno) lunch.

'prassi sf usual procedure.

'pratica, che sf practice; (esperienza) experience; (conoscenza) knowledge, familiarity; (tirocinio) training, practice; (AMM: affare) matter, case; (: incartamento) file, dossier; **in ~** (praticamente) in practice; **mettere in ~** to put into practice.

prati'cabile ag (progetto) practicable, feasible; (luogo) passable, practicable.

prati'cante sm/f apprentice, trainee; (REL) (regular) churchgoer.

prati'care vt to practise; (SPORT: tennis etc) to play; (: nuoto, scherma etc) to go in for; (eseguire: apertura, buco) to make; **~ uno sconto** to give a discount.

'pratico, a, ci, che ag practical; **~ di** (esperto) experienced o skilled in; (familiare) familiar with.

'prato sm meadow; (di giardino) lawn.

preav'viso sm notice; **telefonata con ~** personal o person to person call.

pre'cario, a ag precarious; (INS) temporary.

precauzi'one [prekaut'tsjone] sf caution, care; (misura) precaution.

prece'dente [pretʃe'dɛnte] ag previous // sm precedent; **il discorso/film ~** the previous o preceding speech/film; **senza ~i** unprecedented; **~i penali** criminal record sg; **prece'denza** sf priority, precedence; (AUT) right of way.

pre'cedere [pre'tʃedere] vt to precede, go (o come) before.

pre'cetto [pre'tʃetto] sm precept; (MIL) call-up notice.

precet'tore [pretʃet'tore] sm (private) tutor.

precipi'tare [pretʃipi'tare] vi (cadere) to fall headlong; (fig: situazione) to get out of control // vt (gettare dall'alto in basso) to hurl, fling; (fig: affrettare) to rush; **~rsi** vr (gettarsi) to hurl o fling o.s.; (affrettarsi) to rush; **precipitazi'one** sf (METEOR) precipitation; (fig) haste; **precipi'toso, a** ag (caduta, fuga) headlong; (fig: avventato) rash, reckless; (: affrettato) hasty, rushed.

preci'pizio [pretʃi'pittsjo] sm precipice; **a ~** (fig: correre) headlong.

preci'sare [pretʃi'zare] vt to state, specify; (spiegare) to explain (in detail).

precisi'one [pretʃi'zjone] sf precision; accuracy.

pre'ciso, a [pre'tʃizo] ag (esatto) precise; (accurato) accurate, precise; (deciso: idee) precise, definite; (uguale): **2 vestiti ~i** 2 dresses exactly the same; **sono le 9 ~e** it's exactly 9 o'clock.

pre'cludere vt to block, obstruct; **pre'cluso, a** pp di **precludere**.

pre'coce [pre'kɔtʃe] ag early; (bambino) precocious; (vecchiaia) premature.

precon'cetto [prekon'tʃetto] sm preconceived idea, prejudice.

precur'sore sm forerunner, precursor.

'preda sf (bottino) booty; (animale, fig) prey; **essere ~ di** to fall prey to; **essere in ~ a** to be prey to; **preda'tore** sm predator.

predeces'sore, a [predetʃes'sore] sm/f predecessor.

predesti'nare vt to predestine.

pre'detto, a pp di **predire**.

'predica, che sf sermon; (fig) lecture, talking-to.

predi'care vt, vi to preach.

predi'cato sm (LING) predicate.

predi'letto, a pp di **prediligere** // ag, sm/f favourite.

predilezi'one [predilet'tsjone] sf fondness, partiality; **avere una ~ per qc/qn** to be partial to sth/fond of sb.

predi'ligere [predi'lidʒere] vt to prefer, have a preference for.

pre'dire vt to foretell, predict.

predis'porre vt to get ready, prepare; **~ qn a qc** to predispose sb to sth; **predis'posto, a** pp di **predisporre**.

predizi'one [predit'tsjone] sf prediction.

predomi'nare *vi* to predominate; **predo'minio** *sm* predominance; supremacy.

prefabbri'cato, a *ag* (EDIL) prefabricated.

prefazi'one [prefat'tsjone] *sf* preface, foreword.

prefe'renza [prefe'rɛntsa] *sf* preference; **preferenzi'ale** *ag* preferential; **corsia ~** bus and taxi lane.

prefe'rire *vt* to prefer, like better; **~ il caffè al tè** to prefer coffee to tea, like coffee better than tea.

pre'fetto *sm* prefect; **prefet'tura** *sf* prefecture.

pre'figgersi [pre'fiddʒersi] *vr*: **~rsi uno scopo** to set o.s. a goal.

pre'fisso, a *pp di* **prefiggere** // *sm* (LING) prefix; (TEL) dialling (Brit) o dial (US) code.

pre'gare *vi* to pray // *vt* (REL) to pray to; (implorare) to beg; (chiedere): **~ qn di fare** to ask sb to do; **farsi ~** to need coaxing o persuading.

pre'gevole [pre'dʒevole] *ag* valuable.

preghi'era [pre'gjɛra] *sf* (REL) prayer; (domanda) request.

pregi'ato, a [pre'dʒato] *ag* (di valore) valuable; **vino ~** vintage wine.

'pregio ['prɛdʒo] *sm* (stima) esteem, regard; (qualità) (good) quality, merit; (valore) value, worth.

pregiudi'care [predʒudi'kare] *vt* to prejudice, harm, be detrimental to; **pregiudi'cato, a** *sm/f* (DIR) previous offender.

pregiu'dizio [predʒu'dittsjo] *sm* (idea errata) prejudice; (danno) harm q.

'pregno, a ['preɲɲo] *ag* (gravido) pregnant; (saturo): **~ di** full of, saturated with.

'prego *escl* (a chi ringrazia) don't mention it!; (invitando qn ad accomodarsi) please sit down!; (invitando qn ad andare prima) after you!

pregus'tare *vt* to look forward to.

preis'torico, a, ci, che *ag* prehistoric.

pre'lato *sm* prelate.

prele'vare *vt* (denaro) to withdraw; (campione) to take; (sog: polizia) to take, capture.

preli'evo *sm* (MED): **fare un ~ (di)** to take a sample (of).

prelimi'nare *ag* preliminary; **~i** *smpl* preliminary talks; preliminaries.

pre'ludio *sm* prelude.

pré-ma'man [prema'mã] *sm inv* maternity dress.

prema'turo, a *ag* premature.

premeditazi'one [premeditat'tsjone] *sf* (DIR) premeditation; **con ~** *ag* premeditated // **with intent.**

'premere *vt* to press // *vi*: **~ su** to press down on; (fig) to put pressure on; **~ a** (fig: importare) to matter to.

pre'messo, a *pp di* **premettere** // *sf* introductory statement, introduction.

pre'mettere *vt* to put before; (dire prima) to start by saying, state first.

premi'are *vt* to give a prize to; (fig: merito, onestà) to reward.

'premio *sm* prize; (ricompensa) reward; (COMM) premium; (AMM: indennità) bonus.

premu'nirsi *vr*: **~ di** to provide o.s. with; **~ contro** to protect o.s. from, guard o.s. against.

pre'mura *sf* (fretta) haste, hurry; (riguardo) attention, care; **premu'roso, a** *ag* thoughtful, considerate.

prena'tale *ag* antenatal.

'prendere *vt* to take; (andare a prendere) to get, fetch; (ottenere) to get; (guadagnare) to get, earn; (catturare: ladro, pesce) to catch; (collaboratore, dipendente) to take on; (passeggero) to pick up; (chiedere: somma, prezzo) to charge, ask; (trattare: persona) to handle // *vi* (colla, cemento) to set; (pianta) to take; (fuoco: nel camino) to catch; (voltare): **~ a destra** to turn to (the) right; **~rsi** *vr* (azzuffarsi): **~rsi a pugni** to come to blows; **prendi qualcosa?** (da bere, da mangiare) would you like something to eat (o drink)?; **prendo un caffè** I'll have a coffee; **~ a fare qc** to start doing sth; **~ qn/qc per** (scambiare) to take sb/sth for; **~ fuoco** to catch fire; **~ parte a** to take part in; **~rsi cura di qn/qc** to look after sb/sth; **prendersela** (adirarsi) to get annoyed; (preoccuparsi) to get upset, worry.

prendi'sole *sm inv* sundress.

preno'tare *vt* to book, reserve; **prenotazi'one** *sf* booking, reservation.

preoccu'pare *vt* to worry; to preoccupy; **~rsi** *vr*: **~rsi di qn/qc** to worry about sb/sth; **~rsi per qn** to be anxious for sb; **preoccupazi'one** *sf* worry, anxiety.

prepa'rare *vt* to prepare; (esame, concorso) to prepare for; **~rsi** *vr* (vestirsi) to get ready; **~rsi a qc/a fare** to get ready o prepare (o.s.) for sth/to do; **~ da mangiare** to prepare a meal; **prepara'tivi** *smpl* preparations; **prepa'rato** *sm* (prodotto) preparation; **preparazi'one** *sf* preparation.

preposizi'one [prepozit'tsjone] *sf* (LING) preposition.

prepo'tente *ag* (persona) domineering, arrogant; (bisogno, desiderio) overwhelming, pressing // *sm/f* bully; **prepo'tenza** *sf* arrogance; arrogant behaviour.

'presa *sf* taking q; catching q; (di città) capture; (indurimento: di cemento) setting; (appiglio, SPORT) hold; (di acqua, gas) (supply) point; (ELETTR): **~ (di corrente)** socket; (: al muro) point;

(*piccola quantità*: *di sale etc*) pinch; (CARTE) trick; **far ~** (*colla*) to set; **far ~ sul pubblico** to catch the public's imagination; **~ d'aria** air inlet; **essere alle ~e con qc** (*fig*) to be struggling with sth.

pre'sagio |pre'zadʒo| *sm* omen.

presa'gire |preza'dʒire| *vt* to foresee.

'presbite *ag* long-sighted.

presbi'terio *sm* presbytery.

pre'scindere |preʃ'ʃindere| *vi*: **~ da** to leave out of consideration; **a ~ da** apart from.

pres'critto, a *pp di* **prescrivere**.

pres'crivere *vt* to prescribe; **pre-scrizi'one** *sf* (MED, DIR) prescription; (*norma*) rule, regulation.

presen'tare *vt* to present; (*far co-noscere*): **~ qn (a)** to introduce sb (to); (AMM: *inoltrare*) to submit; **~rsi** *vr* (*re-carsi, farsi vedere*) to present o.s., appear; (*farsi conoscere*) to introduce o.s.; (*occasione*) to arise; **~rsi come candidato** (POL) to stand as a candidate; **~rsi bene/male** to have a good/poor appearance; **presentazi'one** *sf* pres-entation; introduction.

pre'sente *ag* present; (*questo*) this // *sm* present; **i ~i** those present; **aver ~ qc/qn** to remember sth/sb.

presenti'mento *sm* premonition.

pre'senza |pre'zɛntsa| *sf* presence; (*aspetto esteriore*) appearance; **~ di spirito** presence of mind.

pre'sepio, pre'sepe *sm* crib.

preser'vare *vt* to protect; to save; **preserva'tivo** *sm* sheath, condom.

'preside *smf* (INS) head (teacher) (*Brit*), principal (*US*); (*di facoltà uni-versitaria*) dean.

presi'dente *sm* (POL) president; (*di assemblea, COMM*) chairman; **~ del consiglio** prime minister; **presi-den'tessa** *sf* president; president's wife; chairwoman; **presi'denza** *sf* presi-dency; office of president; chairman-ship.

presidi'are *vt* to garrison; **pre'sidio** *sm* garrison.

presi'edere *vt* to preside over // *vi*: **~ a** to direct, be in charge of.

'preso, a *pp di* **prendere**.

'pressa *sf* (TECN) press.

pressap'poco *av* about, roughly.

pres'sare *vt* to press.

pressi'one *sf* pressure; **far ~ su qn** to put pressure on sb; **~ sanguigna** blood pressure.

'presso *av* (*vicino*) nearby, close at hand // *prep* (*vicino a*) near; (*accanto a*) beside, next to; (*in casa di*): **~ qn** at sb's home; (*nelle lettere*) care of (*abbr* c/o); (*alle dipendenze di*): **lavora ~ di noi** he works for *o* with us // *smpl*: **nei ~i di** near, in the vicinity of.

pressuriz'zare |pressurid'dzare| *vt* to pressurize.

presta'nome *sm/f inv* (*peg*) figurehead.

pres'tante *ag* good-looking.

pres'tare *vt*: **~ (qc a qn)** to lend (sb sth *o* sth to sb); **~rsi** *vr* (*offrirsi*): **~rsi a fare** to offer to do; (*essere adatto*): **~rsi a** to lend itself to, be suitable for; **~ aiuto** to lend a hand; **~ attenzione** to pay attention; **~ fede a qc/qn** to give credence to sth/sb; **~ orecchio** to listen; **prestazi'one** *sf* (TECN, SPORT) performance; **prestazioni** *sfpl* (*di persona: servizi*) services.

prestigia'tore, 'trice |prestidʒa'tore| *sm/f* conjurer.

pres'tigio |pres'tidʒo| *sm* (*potere*) prestige; (*illusione*): **gioco di ~** conjur-ing trick.

'prestito *sm* lending *q*; loan; **dar in ~ to** lend; **prendere in ~** to borrow.

'presto *av* (*tra poco*) soon; (*in fretta*) quickly; (*di buon'ora*) early; **a ~** see you soon; **fare ~ a fare qc** to hurry up and do sth; (*non costare fatica*) to have no trouble doing sth; **si fa ~ a criticare** it's easy to criticize.

pre'sumere *vt* to presume, assume; **pre'sunto, a** *pp di* **presumere**.

presuntu'oso, a *ag* presumptuous.

presunzi'one |prezun'tsjone| *sf* presump-tion.

presup'porre *vt* to suppose; to pre-suppose.

'prete *sm* priest.

preten'dente *smf* pretender // *sm* (*corteggiatore*) suitor.

pre'tendere *vt* (*esigere*) to demand, re-quire; (*sostenere*): **~ che** to claim that; **pretende di aver sempre ragione** he thinks he's always right.

pretenzi'oso, a |preten'tsjoso| *ag* pre-tentious.

pre'teso, a *pp di* **pretendere** // *sf* (*esigenza*) claim, demand; (*presunzione, sfarzo*) pretentiousness; **senza ~e** un-pretentious.

pre'testo *sm* pretext, excuse.

pre'tore *sm* magistrate.

preva'lente *ag* prevailing; **preva'lenza** *sf* predominance.

preva'lere *vi* to prevail; **pre'valso, a** *pp di* **prevalere**.

preve'dere *vt* (*indovinare*) to foresee; (*presagire*) to foretell; (*considerare*) to make provision for.

preve'nire *vt* (*anticipare*) to forestall; to anticipate; (*evitare*) to avoid, prevent; (*avvertire*): **~ qn (di)** to warn sb (of); to inform sb (of).

preven'tivo, a *ag* preventive // *sm* (COMM) estimate.

prevenzi'one |preven'tsjone| *sf* preven-tion; (*preconcetto*) prejudice.

previ'dente *ag* showing foresight;

prudent; **previ'denza** sf foresight;
istituto di previdenza provident institution; **previdenza sociale** social security
(Brit), welfare (US).

previsi'one sf forecast, prediction; ~i
meteorologiche o del tempo weather
forecast sg.

pre'visto, a pp di **prevedere** // sm:
più/meno del ~ more/less than expected.

prezi'oso, a [pret'tsjoso] ag precious; invaluable // sm jewel; valuable.

prez'zemolo [pret'tsemolo] sm parsley.

'prezzo ['prettso] sm price; ~
d'acquisto/di vendita buying/selling
price.

prigi'one [pri'dʒone] sf prison;
prigio'nia sf imprisonment;
prigioni'ero, a ag captive // sm/f
prisoner.

pri'mario, a ag primary; (principale)
chief, leading, primary // sm (MED)
chief physician.

pri'mate sm (REL, ZOOL) primate.

pri'mato sm supremacy; (SPORT) record.

prima'vera sf spring; **primave'rile** ag
spring cpd.

primeggi'are [primed'dʒare] vi to excel,
be one of the best.

primi'tivo, a ag primitive; original.

pri'mizie [pri'mittsje] sfpl early produce
sg.

'primo, a ag first; (fig) initial; basic;
prime // sm/f first (one) // sm (CUC) first
course; (in data): il ~ luglio the first of
July // sf (TEATRO) first night; (CINEMA)
première; (AUT) first (gear); le ~e ore
del mattino the early hours of the morning; ai ~i di maggio at the beginning of
May; viaggiare in ~a to travel first-
class; in ~ luogo first of all, in the first
place; di prim'ordine o ~a qùalità first-
class, first-rate; in un ~ tempo at first;
~a donna leading lady; (di opera lirica)
prima donna.

primo'genito, a [primo'dʒɛnito] ag, sm/
f firstborn.

primordi'ale ag primordial.

'primula sf primrose.

princi'pale [printʃi'pale] ag main,
principal // sm manager, boss.

princi'pato [printʃi'pato] sm principality.

'principe ['printʃipe] sm prince; ~
ereditario crown prince; **princi'pessa** sf
princess.

principi'ante [printʃi'pjante] sm/f
beginner.

prin'cipio [prin'tʃipjo] sm (inizio) begin-

ning, start; (origine) origin, cause;
(concetto, norma) principle; al o in ~ at
first; per ~ on principle.

pri'ore sm (REL) prior.

priorità sf priority.

'prisma, i sm prism.

pri'vare vt: ~ qn di to deprive sb of;
~rsi di to go o do without.

priva'tiva sf (ECON) monopoly.

pri'vato, a ag private // sm/f private
citizen; in ~ in private.

privazi'one [privat'tsjone] sf privation,
hardship.

privilegi'are [privile'dʒare] vt to grant a
privilege to.

privi'legio [privi'lɛdʒo] sm privilege.

'privo, a ag: ~ di without, lacking.

pro prep for, on behalf of // sm inv
(utilità) advantage, benefit; a che ~?
what's the use?; il ~ e il contro the pros
and cons.

pro'babile ag probable, likely;
probabilità sf inv probability.

pro'blema, i sm problem.

pro'boscide [pro'bɔʃʃide] sf (di elefante)
trunk.

procacci'are [prokat'tʃare] vt to get,
obtain.

pro'cedere [pro'tʃedere] vi to proceed;
(comportarsi) to behave; (iniziare): ~ a
to start; ~ contro (DIR) to start legal
proceedings against; **procedi'mento**
sm (modo di condurre) procedure; (di
avvenimenti) course; (TECN) process;
procedimento penale (DIR) criminal
proceedings; **proce'dura** sf (DIR)
procedure.

proces'sare [protʃes'sare] vt (DIR) to
try.

processi'one [protʃes'sjone] sf procession.

pro'cesso [pro'tʃesso] sm (DIR) trial;
proceedings pl; (metodo) process.

pro'cinto [pro'tʃinto] sm: in ~ di fare
about to do, on the point of doing.

pro'clama, i sm proclamation.

procla'mare vt to proclaim.

procre'are vt to procreate.

pro'cura sf (DIR) proxy; power of
attorney; (ufficio) attorney's office.

procu'rare vt: ~ qc a qn (fornire) to get
o obtain sth for sb; (causare: noie etc)
to bring o give sb sth.

procura'tore, 'trice sm/f (DIR) ≈
solicitor; (: chi ha la procura) attorney;
proxy; ~ generale (in corte d'appello)
public prosecutor; (in corte di
cassazione) Attorney General; ~ della
Repubblica (in corte d'assise, tribunale)
public prosecutor.

prodi'gare vt to be lavish with; ~rsi per
qn to do all one can for sb.

pro'digio [pro'didʒo] sm marvel, wonder; (persona) prodigy; **prodigi'oso, a**
ag prodigious; phenomenal.

'prodigo, a, ghi, ghe *ag* lavish, extravagant.

pro'dotto, a *pp di* **produrre** // *sm* product; ~i agricoli farm produce *sg.*

pro'durre *vt* to produce; **produttività** *sf* productivity; **produt'tivo, a** *ag* productive; **produt'tore, 'trice** *sm/f* producer; **produzi'one** *sf* production; *(rendimento)* output.

pro'emio *sm* introduction, preface.

Prof. *abbr* (= *professore*) Prof.

profa'nare *vt* to desecrate.

pro'fano, a *ag* *(mondano)* secular; profane; *(sacrilego)* profane.

profe'rire *vt* to utter.

profes'sare *vt* to profess; *(medicina etc)* to practise.

professio'nale *ag* professional.

professi'one *sf* profession; **professio'nista, i, e** *sm/f* professional.

profes'sore, 'essa *sm/f* (*INS*) teacher; (: *di università*) lecturer; (: *titolare di cattedra*) professor.

pro'feta, i *sm* prophet; **profe'zia** *sf* prophecy.

pro'ficuo, a *ag* useful, profitable.

profi'lare *vt* to outline; *(ornare: vestito)* to edge; ~**rsi** *vr* to stand out, be silhouetted; to loom up.

pro'filo *sm* profile; *(breve descrizione)* sketch, outline; **di** ~ in profile.

profit'tare *vi*: ~ **di** *(trarre profitto)* to profit by; *(approfittare)* to take advantage of.

pro'fitto *sm* advantage, profit, benefit; *(fig: progresso)* progress; *(COMM)* profit.

profondità *sf inv* depth.

pro'fondo, a *ag* deep; *(rancore, meditazione)* profound // *sm* depth(s *pl*), bottom; ~ **8 metri** 8 metres deep.

'profugo, a, ghi, ghe *sm/f* refugee.

profu'mare *vt* to perfume // *vi* to be fragrant; ~**rsi** *vr* to put on perfume *o* scent.

profume'ria *sf* perfumery; *(negozio)* perfume shop.

pro'fumo *sm* *(prodotto)* perfume, scent; *(fragranza)* scent, fragrance.

profusi'one *sf* profusion; **a** ~ in plenty.

proget'tare *vt* [prodʒet'tare] *vt* to plan; *(TECN: edificio)* to plan, design; **pro'getto** *sm* plan; *(idea)* plan, project; **progetto di legge** bill.

pro'gramma, i *sm* programme; *(TV, RADIO)* programmes *pl*; *(INS)* syllabus, curriculum; *(INFORM)* program; **program'mare** *vt* *(TV, RADIO)* to put on; *(INFORM)* to program; *(ECON)* to plan; **programma'tore, 'trice** *sm/f* (*INFORM*) computer programmer.

progre'dire *vi* to progress, make progress.

progres'sivo, a *ag* progressive.

pro'gresso *sm* progress *q*; fare ~i to make progress.

proi'bire *vt* to forbid, prohibit; **proibi'tivo, a** *ag* prohibitive; **proibizi'one** *sf* prohibition.

proiet'tare *vt* *(gen, GEOM, CINEMA)* to project; (: *presentare*) to show, screen; *(luce, ombra)* to throw, cast, project; **proi'ettile** *sm* projectile, bullet *(o shell etc)*; **proiet'tore** *sm* (*CINEMA*) projector; *(AUT)* headlamp; *(MIL)* searchlight; **proiezi'one** *sf* (*CINEMA*) projection; showing.

'prole *sf* children *pl*, offspring.

prole'tario, a *ag, sm* proletarian.

prolife'rare *vi* *(fig)* to proliferate.

pro'lisso, a *ag* verbose.

'prologo, ghi *sm* prologue.

pro'lunga, ghe *sf* *(di cavo elettrico etc)* extension.

prolun'gare *vt* *(discorso, attesa)* to prolong; *(linea, termine)* to extend.

prome'moria *sm inv* memorandum.

pro'messa *sf* promise.

pro'messo, a *pp di* **promettere.**

pro'mettere *vt* to promise // *vi* to be *o* look promising; ~ **a qn di fare** to promise sb that one will do.

promi'nente *ag* prominent.

promiscuità *sf* promiscuousness.

promon'torio *sm* promontory, headland.

pro'mosso, a *pp di* **promuovere.**

promo'tore, 'trice *sm/f* promoter, organizer.

promozi'one [promot'tsjone] *sf* promotion.

promul'gare *vt* to promulgate.

promu'overe *vt* to promote.

proni'pote *sm/f* *(di nonni)* great-grandchild, great-grandson/grand-daughter; *(di zii)* great-nephew/niece; ~**i** *smpl (discendenti)* descendants.

pro'nome *sm* (*LING*) pronoun.

pron'tezza [pron'tettsa] *sf* readiness; quickness, promptness.

'pronto, a *ag* ready; *(rapido)* fast, quick, prompt; ~! (*TEL*) hello!; ~ **all'ira** quick-tempered; ~ **soccorso** first aid.

prontu'ario *sm* manual, handbook.

pro'nuncia [pro'nuntʃa] *etc* = **pronunzia** *etc.*

pro'nunzia [pro'nuntsja] *sf* pronunciation; **pronunzi'are** *vt* *(parola, sentenza)* to pronounce; *(dire)* to utter; *(discorso)* to deliver; **pronunziarsi** *vr* to declare one's opinion; **pronunzi'ato, a** *ag* *(spiccato)* pronounced, marked; *(sporgente)* prominent.

propa'ganda *sf* propaganda.

propa'gare *vt* *(notizia, malattia)* to spread; *(REL, BIOL)* to propagate; ~**rsi** *vr* to spread; *(BIOL)* to propagate; *(FISICA)* to be propagated.

pro'pendere *vi*: ~ **per** to favour, lean towards; **propensi'one** *sf* inclination, propensity; **pro'penso, a** *pp di*

propendere.

propi'nare *vt* to administer.

pro'pizio, a [pro'pittsjo] *ag* favourable.

pro'porre *vt* (*suggerire*): ~ qc (a qn) to suggest sth (to sb); (*candidato*) to put forward; (*legge, brindisi*) to propose; ~ di fare to suggest *o* propose doing; **proporsi di fare** to propose *o* intend to do; **proporsi una meta** to set o.s. a goal.

proporzio'nale [proportsjo'nale] *ag* proportional.

proporzio'nare [proportsjo'nare] *vt*: ~ qc a to proportion *o* adjust sth to.

proporzi'one [proportsjo'ne] *sf* proportion; **in ~ a** in proportion to.

pro'posito *sm* (*intenzione*) intention, aim; (*argomento*) subject, matter; a ~ di regarding, with regard to; di ~ (*apposta*) deliberately, on purpose; a ~ by the way; **capitare a** ~ (*cosa, persona*) to turn up at the right time.

proposizi'one [propozit'tsjone] *sf* (*LING*) clause; (: *periodo*) sentence.

pro'posto, a *pp di* **proporre** // *sf* proposal; (*suggerimento*) suggestion; ~a **di legge** bill.

proprietà *sf inv* (*ciò che si possiede*) property *gen* q, estate; (*caratteristica*) property; (*correttezza*) correctness; **proprie'tario, a** *smf* owner; (*di albergo etc*) proprietor, owner; (*per l'inquilino*) landlord/lady.

'proprio, a *ag* (*possessivo*) own; (: *impersonale*) one's; (*esatto*) exact, correct, proper; (*senso, significato*) literal; (*LING: nome*) proper; (*particolare*): ~ di characteristic of, peculiar to // *av* (*precisamente*) just, exactly; (*davvero*) really; (*affatto*): **non** ... ~ not ... at all; **l'ha visto con i** (**suoi**) ~i **occhi** he saw it with his own eyes.

'prora *sf* (*NAUT*) bow('s pl), prow.

'proroga, ghe *sf* extension; postponement; **proro'gare** *vt* to extend; (*differire*) to postpone, defer.

pro'rompere *vi* to burst out; **pro'rotto, a** *pp di* **prorompere**.

'prosa *sf* prose; **pro'saico, a, ci, che** *ag* (*fig*) prosaic, mundane.

pro'sciogliere [proʃ'ʃɔʎʎere] *vt* to release; (*DIR*) to acquit; **prosci'olto, a** *pp di* **prosciogliere**.

prosciu'gare [proʃʃu'gare] *vt* (*terreni*) to drain, reclaim; ~**rsi** *vr* to dry up.

prosci'utto [proʃ'ʃutto] *sm* ham.

prosegui'mento *sm* continuation; **buon** ~! all the best!; (*a chi viaggia*) enjoy the rest of your journey!

prosegu'ire *vt* to carry on with, continue // *vi* to carry on, go on.

prospe'rare *vi* to thrive; **prosperità** *sf* prosperity; **'prospero, a** *ag* (*fiorente*) flourishing, thriving, prosperous; **pro-spe'roso, a** *ag* (*robusto*) hale and hearty; (: *ragazza*) buxom.

prospet'tare *vt* (*esporre*) to point out, show; ~**rsi** *vr* to look, appear.

prospet'tiva *sf* (*ARTE*) perspective; (*veduta*) view; (*fig: previsione, possibilità*) prospect.

pros'petto *sm* (*DISEGNO*) elevation; (*veduta*) view, prospect; (*facciata*) façade, front; (*tabella*) table; (*sommario*) summary.

prospici'ente [prospi'tʃente] *ag*: ~ qc facing *o* overlooking sth.

prossimità *sf* nearness, proximity; **in ~ di** near (to), close to.

'prossimo, a *ag* (*vicino*): ~ a near (to), close to; (*che viene subito dopo*) next; (*parente*) close // *sm* neighbour, fellow man.

prosti'tuta *sf* prostitute; **prostituzi'one** *sf* prostitution.

pros'trare *vt* (*fig*) to exhaust, wear out; ~**rsi** *vr* (*fig*) to humble o.s.

protago'nista, i, e *smf* protagonist.

pro'teggere [pro'tɛddʒere] *vt* to protect.

prote'ina *sf* protein.

pro'tendere *vt* to stretch out; **pro'teso, a** *pp di* **protendere**.

pro'testa *sf* protest.

protes'tante *ag, smf* Protestant.

protes'tare *vt, vi* to protest; ~**rsi** *vr*: ~**rsi innocente** *etc* to protest one's innocence *o* that one is innocent *etc*.

protet'tivo, a *ag* protective.

pro'tetto, a *pp di* **proteggere**.

protet'tore, 'trice *smf* protector; (*sostenitore*) patron.

protezi'one [protet'tsjone] *sf* protection; (*patrocinio*) patronage.

protocol'lare *vt* to register // *ag* formal; of protocol.

proto'collo *sm* protocol; (*registro*) register of documents.

pro'totipo *sm* prototype.

pro'trarre *vt* (*prolungare*) to prolong; **pro'tratto, a** *pp di* **protrarre**.

protube'ranza [protube'rantsa] *sf* protuberance, bulge.

'prova *sf* (*esperimento, cimento*) test, trial; (*tentativo*) attempt, try; (*MAT, testimonianza, documento etc*) proof; (*DIR*) evidence *q*, proof; (*INS*) exam, test; (*TEATRO*) rehearsal; (*di abito*) fitting; **a ~ di** (*in testimonianza di*) as proof of; **a ~ di fuoco** fireproof; **fino a ~ contraria** until it is proved otherwise; **mettere alla ~** to put to the test; **giro di ~** test *o* trial run; ~ **generale** (*TEATRO*) dress rehearsal.

pro'vare *vt* (*sperimentare*) to test; (*tentare*) to try, attempt; (*assaggiare*) to try, taste; (*sperimentare in sé*) to experience; (*sentire*) to feel; (*cimentare*) to put to the test; (*dimostrare*) to prove; (*abito*) to try on; ~**rsi** *vr*: ~**rsi (a fare)** to try *o* attempt (to do); ~ **a fare** to try *o* attempt to do.

proveni'enza [prove'njɛntsa] *sf* origin, source.

prove'nire *vi*: ~ **da** to come from.

pro'venti *smpl* revenue *sg*.

prove'nuto, a *pp di* **provenire**.

pro'verbio *sm* proverb.

pro'vetta *sf* test tube; **bambino in ~** test-tube baby.

pro'vetto, a *ag* skilled, experienced.

pro'vincia, ce *o* **cie** [pro'vintʃa] *sf* province; **provinci'ale** *ag* provincial; **(strada) provinciale** main road (*Brit*), highway (*US*).

pro'vino *sm* (*CINEMA*) screen test; (*campione*) specimen.

provo'cante *ag* (*attraente*) provocative.

provo'care *vt* (*causare*) to cause, bring about; (*eccitare: riso, pietà*) to arouse; (*irritare, sfidare*) to provoke; **provoca'torio, a** *ag* provocative; **provocazi'one** *sf* provocation.

provve'dere *vi* (*disporre*): ~ **(a)** to provide (for); (*prendere un provvedimento*) to take steps, act // *vt*: ~ **qc a** qn to supply sth to sb; ~**rsi** *vr*: ~**rsi di** to provide o.s. with; **provvedi'mento** *sm* measure; (*di previdenza*) precaution.

provvi'denza [provvi'dɛntsa] *sf*: **la ~** providence; **provvidenzi'ale** *ag* providential.

provvigi'one [provvi'dʒone] *sf* (*COMM*) commission.

provvi'sorio, a *ag* temporary.

prov'vista *sf* provision, supply.

'prua *sf* (*NAUT*) = **prora**.

pru'dente *ag* cautious, prudent; (*assennato*) sensible, wise; **pru'denza** *sf* prudence, caution; wisdom.

'prudere *vi* to itch, be itchy.

'prugna ['pruɲɲa] *sf* plum; ~ **secca** prune.

prurigi'noso, a [pruridʒi'noso] *ag* itchy.

pru'rito *sm* itchiness *q*; itch.

P.S. *abbr* (= *postscriptum*) P.S.; (*POLIZIA*) = **Pubblica Sicurezza**.

pseu'donimo *sm* pseudonym.

PSI *sigla m* = *Partito Socialista Italiano*.

psicana'lista, i, e *sm/f* psychoanalyst.

'psiche ['psike] *sf* (*PSIC*) psyche.

psichi'atra, i, e [psi'kjatra] *sm/f* psychiatrist; **psichi'atrico, a, ci, che** *ag* psychiatric.

'psichico, a, ci, che ['psikiko] *ag* psychological.

psicolo'gia [psikolo'dʒia] *sf* psychology; **psico'logico, a, ci, che** *ag* psychological; **psi'cologo, a, gi, ghe** *sm/f* psychologist.

psico'patico, a, ci, che *ag* psychopathic // *sm/f* psychopath.

P.T. *abbr* = *Posta e Telegrafi*.

pubbli'care *vt* to publish.

pubblicazi'one [pubblikat'tsjone] *sf* publication; ~**i (matrimoniali)** *sfpl* (marriage) banns.

pubbli'cista, i, e [pubbli'tʃista] *sm/f* (*STAMPA*) occasional contributor.

pubblicità [pubbliʧi'ta] *sf* (*diffusione*) publicity; (*attività*) advertising; (*annunci nei giornali*) advertisements *pl*; **pubblici'tario, a** *ag* advertising *cpd*; (*trovata, film*) publicity *cpd*.

'pubblico, a, ci, che *ag* public; (*statale: scuola etc*) state *cpd* // *sm* public; (*spettatori*) audience; **in ~** in public; ~ **funzionario** civil servant; **P~ Ministero** Public Prosecutor's Office; **la P~a Sicurezza** the police.

'pube *sm* (*ANAT*) pubis.

pubertà *sf* puberty.

'pudico, a, ci, che *ag* modest.

pu'dore *sm* modesty.

puericul'tura *sf* paediatric nursing; infant care.

pue'rile *ag* childish.

pugi'lato [pudʒi'lato] *sm* boxing.

'pugile ['pudʒile] *sm* boxer.

pugna'lare [puɲɲa'lare] *vt* to stab.

pu'gnale [puɲ'ɲale] *sm* dagger.

'pugno ['puɲɲo] *sm* fist; (*colpo*) punch; (*quantità*) fistful.

'pulce ['pultʃe] *sf* flea.

pul'cino [pul'tʃino] *sm* chick.

pu'ledro, a *sm/f* colt/filly.

pu'leggia, ge [pu'leddʒa] *sf* pulley.

pu'lire *vt* to clean; (*lucidare*) to polish; **pu'lito, a** *ag* (*anche fig*) clean; (*ordinato*) neat, tidy // *sf* quick clean; **puli'tura** *sf* cleaning; **pulitura a secco** dry cleaning; **puli'zia** *sf* cleaning; cleanness; **fare le pulizie** to do the cleaning, do the housework.

'pullman *sm inv* coach.

pul'lover *sm inv* pullover, jumper.

pullu'lare *vi* to swarm, teem.

pul'mino *sm* minibus.

'pulpito *sm* pulpit.

pul'sante *sm* (push-)button.

pul'sare *vi* to pulsate, beat; **pulsazi'one** *sf* beat.

pul'viscolo *sm* fine dust.

'puma *sm inv* puma.

pun'gente [pun'dʒɛnte] *ag* prickly; stinging; (*anche fig*) biting.

'pungere ['pundʒere] *vt* to prick; (*sog: insetto, ortica*) to sting; (: *freddo*) to bite.

pungigli'one [pundʒiʎ'ʎone] *sm* sting.

pu'nire *vt* to punish; **punizi'one** *sf* punishment; (*SPORT*) penalty.

'punta *sf* point; (*parte terminale*) tip, end; (*di monte*) peak; (*di costa*) promontory; (*minima parte*) touch, trace; **in ~ di piedi** on tip-toe; **ore di ~** peak hours; **uomo di ~** front-rank *o* leading man.

pun'tare *vt* (*piedi a terra, gomiti sul tavolo*) to plant; (*dirigere: pistola*) to point; (*scommettere*) to bet // *vi* (*mi-*

rare): ~ **a** to aim at; (*avviarsi*): ~ **su** to head o make for; (*fig: contare*): ~ **su** to count o rely on.

pun'tata *sf* (*gita*) short trip; (*scommessa*) bet; (*parte di opera*) instalment; **romanzo a ~e** serial.

punteggia'tura [puntedd‿ʒa'tura] *sf* (*LING*) punctuation.

pun'teggio [pun'tedd‿ʒo] *sm* score.

puntel'lare *vt* to support.

pun'tello *sm* prop, support.

puntigli'oso, a [puntiʎ'ʎoso] *ag* punctilious.

pun'tina *sf*: ~ **da disegno** drawing pin.

pun'tino *sm* dot; **fare qc a ~** to do sth properly.

'punto, a *pp di* **pungere** // *sm* (*segno, macchiolina*) dot; (*LING*) full stop; (*MAT, momento, di punteggio, fig: argomento*) point; (*posto*) spot; (*a scuola*) mark; (*nel cucire, nella maglia, MED*) stitch // *av*: **non ... ~** not at all; **due ~i** *sm* (*LING*) colon; **sul ~ di fare** (just) about to do; **fare il ~** (*NAUT*) to take a bearing; (*fig*): **fare il ~ della situazione** to take stock of the situation; to sum up the situation; **alle 6 in ~** at 6 o'clock sharp o on the dot; **essere a buon ~** to have reached a satisfactory stage; **mettere a ~** to adjust; (*motore*) to tune; (*cannocchiale*) to focus; (*fig*) to settle; **di ~ in bianco** point-blank; **~ cardinale** point of the compass, cardinal point; **~ debole** weak point; **~ esclamativo/ interrogativo** exclamation/question mark; **~ di riferimento** landmark; (*fig*) point of reference; **~ di vendita** retail outlet; **~ e virgola** semicolon; **~ di vista** (*fig*) point of view; **~i di sospensione** suspension points.

puntu'ale *ag* punctual; **puntualità** *sf* punctuality.

pun'tura *sf* (*di ago*) prick; (*di insetto*) sting, bite; (*MED*) puncture; (: *iniezione*) injection; (*dolore*) sharp pain.

punzecchi'are [puntsek'kjare] *vt* to prick; (*fig*) to tease.

pun'zone [pun'tsone] *sm* (*per metalli*) stamp, die.

'pupa *sf* doll.

pu'pazzo [pu'pattso] *sm* puppet.

pu'pillo, a *sm/f* (*DIR*) ward; (*prediletto*) favourite, pet // *sf* (*ANAT*) pupil.

purché [pur'ke] *cong* provided that, on condition that.

'pure *cong* (*tuttavia*) and yet, nevertheless; (*anche se*) even if // *av* (*anche*) too, also; **pur di** (*al fine di*) just to; **faccia ~!** go ahead!, please do!

purè *sm*, **pu'rea** *sf* (*CUC*) purée; (: *di patate*) mashed potatoes.

pu'rezza [pu'rettsa] *sf* purity.

'purga, ghe *sf* (*MED*) purging q; purge; (*POL*) purge.

pur'gante *sm* (*MED*) purgative, purge.

pur'gare *vt* (*MED, POL*) to purge; (*pulire*) to clean.

purga'torio *sm* purgatory.

purifi'care *vt* to purify; (*metallo*) to refine.

puri'tano, a *ag, sm/f* puritan.

'puro, a *ag* pure; (*acqua*) clear, limpid; (*vino*) undiluted; **puro'sangue** *sm/f inv* thoroughbred.

pur'troppo *av* unfortunately.

'pustola *sf* pimple.

puti'ferio *sm* rumpus, row.

putre'fare *vi* to putrefy, rot; **putre'fatto, a** *pp di* **putrefare**.

'putrido, a *ag* putrid, rotten.

put'tana *sf* (*fam!*) whore (!).

'puzza ['puttsa] *sf* = **puzzo**.

puz'zare [put'tsare] *vi* to stink.

'puzzo ['puttso] *sm* stink, foul smell.

'puzzola ['puttsola] *sf* polecat.

puzzo'lente [puttso'lɛnte] *ag* stinking.

Q

qua *av* here; **in ~** (*verso questa parte*) this way; **da un anno in ~** for a year now; **da quando in ~?** since when?; **per di ~** (*passare*) this way; **al di ~ di** (*fiume, strada*) on this side of; **~ dentro/fuori** *etc* in/out here *etc*; **vedi questo**.

qua'derno *sm* notebook; (*per scuola*) exercise book.

qua'drante *sm* quadrant; (*di orologio*) face.

qua'drare *vi* (*bilancio*) to balance, tally; (*descrizione*) to correspond; (*fig*): **~ a** to please, be to one's liking // *vt* (*MAT*) to square; **non mi quadra** I don't like it; **qua'drato, a** *ag* square; (*fig: equilibrato*) level-headed, sensible; (: *peg*) square // *sm* (*MAT*) square; (*PUGILATO*) ring; **5 al quadrato** 5 squared.

qua'dretto *sm*: **a ~i** (*tessuto*) checked; (*foglio*) squared.

quadri'foglio [kwadri'fɔʎʎo] *sm* four-leaf clover.

'quadro *sm* (*pittura*) painting, picture; (*quadrato*) square; (*tabella*) table, chart; (*TECN*) board, panel; (*TEATRO*) scene; (*fig: scena, spettacolo*) sight; (: *descrizione*) outline, description; **~i** *smpl* (*POL*) party organizers; (*MIL*) cadres; (*COMM*) managerial staff; (*CARTE*) diamonds.

'quadruplo, a *ag, sm* quadruple.

quaggiù [kwad'dʒu] *av* down here.

'quaglia ['kwaʎʎa] *sf* quail.

'qualche ['kwalke] *det* **1** some, a few; (*in interrogative*) any; **ho comprato ~ libro** I've bought some o a few books; **~ volta** sometimes; **hai ~ sigaretta?** have you any cigarettes?

2 (*uno*): **c'è ~ medico?** is there a

doctor?; in ~ modo somehow
3 (*un certo, parecchio*) some; **un personaggio di ~ rilievo** a figure of some importance
4: ~ **cosa** = qualcosa.
qualche'duno [kwalke'duno] *pronome* = qualcuno.
qual'cosa *pronome* something; (*in espressioni interrogative*) anything; **qualcos'altro** something else; anything else; ~ **di nuovo** something new; anything new; ~ **da mangiare** something to eat; anything to eat; **c'è ~ che non va?** is there something *o* anything wrong?
qual'cuno *pronome* (*persona*) someone, somebody; (: *in espressioni interrogative*) anyone, anybody; (*alcuni*) some; ~ **è favorevole a noi** some are on our side; **qualcun altro** someone *o* somebody else; anyone *o* anybody else.
'quale (*spesso troncato in* qual) ◆ *det* **1** (*interrogativo*) what; (: *scegliendo tra due o più cose o persone*) which; ~ **uomo/denaro?** what man/money?; which man/money?; ~**i sono i tuoi programmi?** what are your plans?; ~ **stanza preferisci?** which room do you prefer?
2 (*relativo: come*): **il risultato fu ~ ci si aspettava** the result was as expected
3 (*esclamativo*) what; ~ **disgrazia!** what bad luck!
◆ *pronome* **1** (*interrogativo*) which; ~ **dei due scegli?** which of the two do you want?
2 (*relativo*): **il(la) ~** (*persona: soggetto*) who; (: *oggetto, con preposizione*) whom; (*cosa*) which; (*possessivo*) whose; **suo padre, il ~ è avvocato, ...** his father, who is a lawyer, ...; **il signore con il ~ parlavo** the gentleman to whom I was speaking; **l'albergo al ~ ci siamo fermati** the hotel where we stayed *o* which we stayed at; **la signora della ~ ammiriamo la bellezza** the lady whose beauty we admire
3 (*relativo: in elenchi*) such as, like; **piante ~i l'edera** plants like *o* such as ivy; ~ **sindaco di questa città** as mayor of this town.
qua'lifica, che *sf* qualification; (*titolo*) title.
qualifi'care *vt* to qualify; (*definire*): ~ **qn/qc come** to describe sb/sth as; ~**rsi** *vr* (*anche* SPORT) to qualify; **qualifica'tivo, a** *ag* qualifying; **qualificazi'one** *sf* qualification; **gara di qualificazione** (SPORT) qualifying event.
qualità *sf inv* quality; **in ~ di** in one's capacity as.
qua'lora *cong* in case, if.
qual'siasi, qua'lunque *det inv* any; (*quale che sia*) whatever; (*discriminativo*) whichever; (*posposto: mediocre*) poor, indifferent; ordinary; **mettiti un vestito ~** put on any old

dress; ~ **cosa** anything; ~ **cosa accada** whatever happens; **a ~ costo** at any cost, whatever the cost; **l'uomo ~** the man in the street; ~ **persona** anyone, anybody.
'quando *cong, av* when; ~ **sarò ricco** when I'm rich; **da ~** (*dacché*) since; (*interrogativo*): **da ~ sei qui?** how long have you been here?; **quand'anche** even if.
quantità *sf inv* quantity; (*gran numero*): **una ~ di** a great deal of; a lot of; **in grande ~** in large quantities; **quantita'tivo** *sm* (COMM) amount, quantity.
'quanto, a ◆ *det* **1** (*interrogativo: quantità*) how much; (: *numero*) how many; ~ **pane/denaro?** how much bread/money?; ~**i libri/ragazzi?** how many books/boys?; ~ **tempo** how long?; ~**i anni hai?** how old are you?
2 (*esclamativo*): ~**e storie!** what a lot of nonsense!; ~ **tempo sprecato!** what a waste of time!
3 (*relativo: quantità*) as much ... as; (: *numero*) as many ... as; **ho ~ denaro mi occorre** I have as much money as I need; **prendi ~i libri vuoi** take as many books as you like
◆ *pronome* **1** (*interrogativo: quantità*) how much; (: *numero*) how many; (: *tempo*) how long; ~ **mi dai?** how much will you give me?; ~**i me ne hai portati?** how many did you bring me?; **da ~ sei qui?** how long have you been here?; ~**i ne abbiamo oggi?** what's the date today?
2 (*relativo: quantità*) as much as; (: *numero*) as many as; **farò ~ posso** I'll do as much as I can; **possono venire ~i sono stati invitati** all those who have been invited can come
◆ *av* **1** (*interrogativo: con ag, av*) how; (: *con vb*) how much; ~ **stanco ti sembrava?** how tired did he seem to you?; ~ **corre la tua moto?** how fast can your motorbike go?; ~ **costa?** how much does it cost?; **quant'è?** how much is it?
2 (*esclamativo: con ag, av*) how; (: *con vb*) how much; ~ **sono felice!** how happy I am!; **sapessi ~ abbiamo camminato!** if you knew how far we've walked!; **studierò ~ posso** I'll study as much as *o* all I can; ~ **prima** as soon as possible
3: **in ~** (*in qualità di*) as; (*perché, per il fatto che*) as, since; (**in**) **~ a** (*per ciò che riguarda*) as regards
4: **per ~** (*nonostante, anche se*) however; **per ~ si sforzi, non ce la farà** try as he may, he won't manage it; **per ~ sia brava, fa degli errori** however good she may be, she makes mistakes; **per ~ io sappia** as far as I know.
quan'tunque *cong* although, though.
qua'ranta *num* forty.
quaran'tena *sf* quarantine.

quaran'tesimo, a *num* fortieth.

quaran'tina *sf:* una ~ **(di)** about forty.

qua'resima *sf:* la ~ Lent.

'quarta *sf vedi* **quarto.**

quar'tetto *sm* quartet(te).

quarti'ere *sm* district, area; *(MIL)* quarters *pl;* ~ **generale** headquarters *pl,* HQ.

'quarto, a *ag* fourth // *sm* fourth; *(quarta parte)* quarter // *sf (AUT)* fourth (gear); **le 6 e un** ~ a quarter past six; ~ **d'ora** quarter of an hour; ~**i di finale** quarter final.

'quarzo ['kwartso] *sm* quartz.

'quasi *av* almost, nearly // *cong (anche:* ~ **che)** as if; **(non)** ... ~ **mai** hardly ever; ~ ~ **me ne andrei** I've half a mind to leave.

quassù *av* up here.

'quatto, a *ag* crouched, squatting; *(silenzioso)* silent; ~ ~ very quietly; stealthily.

quat'tordici [kwat'torditʃi] *num* fourteen.

quat'trini *smpl* money *sg,* cash *sg.*

'quattro *num* four; **in** ~ **e quattr'otto** in less than no time; **quattro'cento** *num* four hundred // *sm:* **il Quattrocento** the fifteenth century; **quattro'mila** *num* four thousand.

'quello, a ◆ *det (dav sm* **quel** + *C,* **quell'** + *V,* **quello** + *s impura, gn, pn, ps, x, z; pl* **quei** + *C,* **quegli** + *V o s impura, gn, pn, ps, x, z; dav sf* **quella** + *C,* **quell'** + *V; pl* **quelle)** that; those *pl;* ~**a casa** that house; **quegli uomini** those men; **voglio** ~**a camicia** (lì *o* là) I want that shirt

◆ *pronome* **1** *(dimostrativo)* that (one); those (ones) *pl; (ciò)* that; **conosci** ~**a?** do you know that woman?; **prendo** ~ **bianco** I'll take the white one; **chi è** ~**?** who's that?; **prendiamo** ~ (lì *o* là) let's take that one (there)

2 *(relativo):* ~**(a) che** *(persona)* the one (who); *(cosa)* the one (which), the one (that);* ~**i(e) che** *(persone)* those who; *(cose)* those which; **è lui** ~ **che non voleva venire** he's the one who didn't want to come; **ho fatto** ~ **che potevo** I did what I could.

'quercia, ce ['kwertʃa] *sf* oak (tree); *(legno)* oak.

que'rela *sf (DIR)* (legal) action; **quere'lare** *vt* to bring an action against.

que'sito *sm* question, query; problem.

questio'nare *vi:* ~ **di/su qc** to argue about/over sth.

questio'nario *sm* questionnaire.

questi'one *sf* problem, question; *(controversia)* issue; *(litigio)* quarrel; **in** ~ in question; **fuor di** ~ out of the question; **è** ~ **di tempo** it's a matter *o* question of time.

'questo, a ◆ *det* **1** *(dimostrativo)* this; these *pl;* ~ **libro** (qui *o* qua) this book;

io prendo ~ **cappotto, tu quello** I'll take this coat, you take that one; **quest'oggi** today; ~**a sera** this evening

2 *(enfatico):* **non fatemi più prendere di** ~**e paure** don't frighten me like that again

◆ *pronome (dimostrativo)* this (one); these (ones) *pl; (ciò)* this; **prendo** ~ (qui *o* qua) I'll take this one; **preferisci** ~**i o quelli?** do you prefer these (ones) or those (ones)?; ~ **intendevo io** this is what I meant; **vengono Paolo e Luca:** ~ **da Roma, quello da Palermo** Paolo and Luca are coming: the former from Palermo, the latter from Rome.

ques'tore *sm* ≈ chief constable *(Brit),* ≈ police commissioner *(US).*

'questua *sf* collection (of alms).

ques'tura *sf* police headquarters *pl.*

qui *av* here; **da** *o* **di** ~ from here; **di** ~ **in avanti** from now on; **di** ~ **a poco/una settimana** in a little while/a week's time; ~ **dentro/sopra/vicino** in/up/near here; *vedi* **questo.**

quie'tanza [kwje'tantsa] *sf* receipt.

quie'tare *vt* to calm, soothe.

qui'ete *sf* quiet, quietness; calmness; stillness; peace.

qui'eto, a *ag* quiet; *(notte)* calm, still; *(mare)* calm.

'quindi *av* then // *cong* therefore, so.

'quindici ['kwinditʃi] *num* fifteen; ~ **giorni** a fortnight *(Brit),* two weeks.

quindi'cina [kwindi'tʃina] *sf (serie):* una ~ **(di)** about fifteen; **fra una** ~ **di giorni** in a fortnight.

quin'quennio *sm* period of five years.

quin'tale *sm* quintal *(100 kg).*

'quinte *sfpl (TEATRO)* wings.

'quinto, a *num* fifth.

'quota *sf (parte)* quota, share; *(altezza)* height, altitude; *(IPPICA)* odds *pl;* **prendere/perdere** ~ *(AER)* to gain/lose height *o* altitude; ~ **d'iscrizione** enrolment fee; *(ad un club)* membership fee.

quo'tare *vt (BORSA)* to quote; **quotazi'one** *sf* quotation.

quotidi'ano, a *ag* daily; *(banale)* everyday // *sm (giornale)* daily (paper).

quozi'ente [kwot'tsjɛnte] *sm (MAT)* quotient; ~ **d'intelligenza** intelligence quotient, IQ.

R

ra'barbaro *sm* rhubarb.

'rabbia *sf (ira)* anger, rage; *(accanimento, furia)* fury; *(MED: idrofobia)* rabies *sg.*

rab'bino *sm* rabbi.

rabbi'oso, a *ag* angry, furious; *(facile all'ira)* quick-tempered; *(forze, acqua etc)* furious, raging; *(MED)* rabid, mad.

rabbo'nire *vt,* ~**rsi** *vr* to calm down.

rabbrivi'dire *vi* to shudder, shiver.

rabbui'arsi *vr* to grow dark.

raccapez'zarsi [rakkapet'tsarsi] *vr:* **non ~** to be at a loss.

raccapricci'ante [rakkaprit'tʃante] *ag* horrifying.

raccatta'palle *sm inv* (SPORT) ballboy.

raccat'tare *vt* to pick up.

rac'chetta [rak'ketta] *sf* (*per tennis*) racket; (*per ping-pong*) bat; **~ da neve** snowshoe; **~ da sci** ski stick.

racchi'udere [rak'kjudere] *vt* to contain; **racchi'uso, a** *pp di* **racchiudere.**

rac'cogliere [rak'kɔʎʎere] *vt* to collect; (*raccattare*) to pick up; (*frutti, fiori*) to pick, pluck; (AGR) to harvest; (*approvazione, voti*) to win; (*profughi*) to take in; **~rsi** *vr* to gather; (*fig*) to gather one's thoughts; to meditate; **raccogli'mento** *sm* meditation; **raccogli'tore** *sm* (*cartella*) folder, binder; **raccoglitore a fogli mobili** loose-leaf binder.

rac'colto, a *pp di* **raccogliere** // *ag* (*persona: pensoso*) thoughtful; (*luogo: appartato*) secluded, quiet // *sm* (AGR) crop, harvest // *sf* collecting *q*; collection; (AGR) harvesting *q*, gathering *q*; harvest, crop; (*adunata*) gathering.

raccoman'dare *vt* to recommend; (*affidare*) to entrust; (*esortare*): **~ a qn di non fare** to tell *o* warn sb not to do; **~rsi** *vr:* **~rsi a qn** to commend o.s. to sb; **mi raccomando!** don't forget!; **raccoman'data** *sf* (*anche:* **lettera raccomandata**) recorded-delivery letter; **raccomandazi'one** *sf* recommendation.

raccon'tare *vt:* **~ (a qn)** (*dire*) to tell (sb); (*narrare*) to relate (to sb), tell (sb) about; **rac'conto** *sm* telling *q*, relating *q*; (*fatto raccontato*) story, tale.

raccorci'are [rakkor'tʃare] *vt* to shorten.

rac'cordo *sm* (TECN: *giunzione*) connection, joint; (AUT: *di autostrada*) slip road (*Brit*), entrance (*o* exit) ramp (US); **~ anulare** (AUT) ring road (*Brit*), beltway (US).

ra'chitico, a, ci, che [ra'kitiko] *ag* suffering from rickets; (*fig*) scraggy, scrawny.

racimo'lare [ratʃimo'lare] *vt* (*fig*) to scrape together, glean.

'rada *sf* (*natural*) harbour.

'radar *sm* radar.

raddol'cire [raddol'tʃire] *vt* (*persona, carattere*) to soften; **~rsi** *vr* (*tempo*) to grow milder; (*persona*) to soften, mellow.

raddoppi'are *vt, vi* to double.

raddriz'zare [raddrit'tsare] *vt* to straighten; (*fig: correggere*) to put straight, correct.

'radere *vt* (*barba*) to shave off; (*mento*) to shave; (*fig: rasentare*) to graze; to skim; **~rsi** *vr* to shave (o.s.); **~ al suolo** to raze to the ground.

radi'ale *ag* radial.

radi'are *vt* to strike off.

radia'tore *sm* radiator.

radiazi'one [radjat'tsjone] *sf* (FISICA) radiation; (*cancellazione*) striking off.

radi'cale *ag* radical // *sm* (LING) root.

ra'dicchio [ra'dikkjo] *sm* chicory.

ra'dice [ra'ditʃe] *sf* root.

'radio *sf inv* radio // *sm* (CHIM) radium; **radioat'tivo, a** *ag* radioactive; **radiodiffusi'one** *sf* (*radio*) broadcasting; **radiogra'fare** *vt* to X-ray; **radiogra'fia** *sf* radiography; (*foto*) X-ray photograph.

radi'oso, a *ag* radiant.

radiostazi'one [radjostat'tsjone] *sf* radio station.

radiotera'pia *sf* radiotherapy.

'rado, a *ag* (*capelli*) sparse, thin; (*visite*) infrequent; **di ~** rarely.

radu'nare *vt,* **~rsi** *vr* to gather, assemble.

ra'dura *sf* clearing.

'rafano *sm* horseradish.

raffazzo'nare [raffattso'nare] *vt* to patch up.

raf'fermo, a *ag* stale.

'raffica, che *sf* (METEOR) gust (of wind); (*di colpi: scarica*) burst of gunfire.

raffigu'rare *vt* to represent.

raffi'nare *vt* to refine; **raffina'tezza** *sf* refinement; **raffi'nato, a** *ag* refined; **raffine'ria** *sf* refinery.

raffor'zare [raffor'tsare] *vt* to reinforce.

raffredda'mento *sm* cooling.

raffred'dare *vt* to cool; (*fig*) to dampen, have a cooling effect on; **~rsi** *vr* to grow cool *o* cold; (*prendere un raffreddore*) to catch a cold; (*fig*) to cool (off).

raffred'dato, a *ag* (MED): **essere ~** to have a cold.

raffred'dore *sm* (MED) cold.

raf'fronto *sm* comparison.

'rafia *sf* (*fibra*) raffia.

ra'gazzo, a [ra'gattso] *sm/f* boy/girl; (*fam: fidanzato*) boyfriend/girlfriend.

raggi'ante [rad'dʒante] *ag* radiant, shining.

'raggio ['raddʒo] *sm* (*di sole etc*) ray; (MAT, *distanza*) radius; (*di ruota etc*) spoke; **~ d'azione** range; **~i X** X-rays.

raggi'rare [raddʒi'rare] *vt* to take in, trick; **rag'giro** *sm* trick.

raggi'ungere [rad'dʒundʒere] *vt* to reach; (*persona: riprendere*) to catch up (with); (*bersaglio*) to hit; (*fig: meta*) to achieve; **raggi'unto, a** *pp di* **raggiungere.**

raggomito'larsi *vr* to curl up.

raggranel'lare *vt* to scrape together.

raggrin'zare [raggrin'tsare] *vt, vi* (*anche:* **~rsi**) to wrinkle.

raggrup'pare *vt* to group (together).

raggu'aglio [rag'gwaʎʎo] *sm* comparison; *(informazione, relazione)* piece of information.

ragguar'devole *ag (degno di riguardo)* distinguished, notable; *(notevole: somma)* considerable.

ragiona'mento [radʒona'mento] *sm* reasoning *q*; arguing *q*; argument.

ragio'nare [radʒo'nare] *vi (usare la ragione)* to reason; *(discorrere)*: ~ (di) to argue (about).

ragi'one [ra'dʒone] *sf* reason; *(dimostrazione, prova)* argument, reason; *(diritto)* right; **aver** ~ to be right; **aver** ~ **di qn** to get the better of sb; **dare** ~ **a qn** to agree with sb; to prove sb right; **perdere la** ~ to become insane; *(fig)* to take leave of one's senses; **in** ~ **di** at the rate of; to the amount of; according to; **a** *o* **con** ~ rightly, justly; ~ **sociale** *(COMM)* corporate name; **a ragion veduta** after due consideration.

ragione'ria [radʒone'ria] *sf* accountancy; accounts department.

ragio'nevole [radʒo'nevole] *ag* reasonable.

ragioni'ere, a [radʒo'njɛre] *sm/f* accountant.

ragli'are [raʎ'ʎare] *vi* to bray.

ragna'tela [raɲɲa'tela] *sf* cobweb, spider's web.

'ragno ['raɲɲo] *sm* spider.

ragù *sm inv (CUC)* meat sauce; stew.

RAI-TV [raiti'vu] *sigla f* = *Radio televisione italiana.*

rallegra'menti *smpl* congratulations.

ralle'grare *vt* to cheer up; ~**rsi** *vr* to cheer up; *(provare allegrezza)* to rejoice; ~**rsi con qn** to congratulate sb.

rallen'tare *vt* to slow down; *(fig)* to lessen, slacken // *vi* to slow down.

raman'zina [raman'dzina] *sf* lecture, telling-off.

'rame *sm (CHIM)* copper.

rammari'carsi *vr*: ~ (di) *(rincrescersi)* to be sorry (about), regret; *(lamentarsi)* to complain (about); **ram'marico, chi** *sm* regret.

rammen'dare *vt* to mend; *(calza)* to darn; **ram'mendo** *sm* mending *q*; darning *q*; mend; darn.

rammen'tare *vt* to remember, recall; *(richiamare alla memoria)*: ~ **qc a qn** to remind sb of sth; ~**rsi** *vr*: ~**rsi (di qc)** to remember (sth).

rammol'lire *vt* to soften // *vi (anche:* ~**rsi)** to go soft.

'ramo *sm* branch.

ramo'scello [ramoʃ'ʃɛllo] *sm* twig.

'rampa *sf* flight (of stairs); ~ **di lancio** launching pad.

rampi'cante *ag (BOT)* climbing.

ram'pone *sm* harpoon; *(ALPINISMO)* crampon.

'rana *sf* frog.

'rancido, a ['rantʃido] *ag* rancid.

ran'core *sm* rancour, resentment.

ran'dagio, a, gi, gie *o* **ge** [ran'dadʒo] *ag (gatto, cane)* stray.

ran'dello *sm* club, cudgel.

'rango, ghi *sm (condizione sociale, MIL: riga)* rank.

rannicchi'arsi [rannik'kjarsi] *vr* to crouch, huddle.

rannuvo'larsi *vr* to cloud over, become overcast.

ra'nocchio [ra'nɔkkjo] *sm* (edible) frog.

'rantolo *sm* wheeze; *(di agonizzanti)* death rattle.

'rapa *sf (BOT)* turnip.

ra'pace [ra'patʃe] *ag (animale)* predatory; *(fig)* rapacious, grasping // *sm* bird of prey.

ra'pare *vt (capelli)* to crop, cut very short.

'rapida *sf vedi* **rapido.**

rapida'mente *av* quickly, rapidly.

rapidità *sf* speed.

'rapido, a *ag* fast; *(esame, occhiata)* quick, rapid // *sm (FERR)* express (train) // *sf (di fiume)* rapid.

rapi'mento *sm* kidnapping; *(fig)* rapture.

ra'pina *sf* robbery; ~ **a mano armata** armed robbery; **rapi'nare** *vt* to rob; **rapina'tore, 'trice** *sm/f* robber.

ra'pire *vt (cose)* to steal; *(persone)* to kidnap; *(fig)* to enrapture, delight; **rapi'tore, 'trice** *sm/f* kidnapper.

rappor'tare *vt (confrontare)* to compare; *(riprodurre)* to reproduce.

rap'porto *sm (resoconto)* report; *(legame)* relationship; *(MAT, TECN)* ratio; ~**i** *smpl (fra persone, paesi)* relations; ~**i sessuali** sexual intercourse *sg.*

rap'prendersi *vr* to coagulate, clot; *(latte)* to curdle.

rappre'saglia [rappre'saʎʎa] *sf* reprisal, retaliation.

rappresen'tante *sm/f* representative; **rappresen'tanza** *sf* delegation, deputation; *(COMM: ufficio, sede)* agency.

rappresen'tare *vt* to represent; *(TEATRO)* to perform; **rappresenta'tivo, a** *ag* representative; **rappresentazi'one** *sf* representation; performing *q*; *(spettacolo)* performance.

rap'preso, a *pp di* **rapprendere.**

rapso'dia *sf* rhapsody.

rara'mente *av* seldom, rarely.

rare'fatto, a *ag* rarefied.

'raro, a *ag* rare.

ra'sare *vt (barba etc)* to shave off; *(siepi, erba)* to trim, cut; ~**rsi** *vr* to shave (o.s.).

raschi'are [ras'kjare] *vt* to scrape; *(macchia, fango)* to scrape off // *vi* to clear one's throat.

rasen'tare *vt (andar rasente)* to keep

close to; (*sfiorare*) to skim along (*o* over); (*fig*) to border on.

ra'sente *prep*: ~ **(a)** close to, very near.

'raso, a *pp di* **radere** // *ag* (*barba*) shaved; (*capelli*) cropped; (*con misure di capacità*) level; (*pieno: bicchiere*) full to the brim // *sm* (*tessuto*) satin; ~ **terra** close to the ground; **un cucchiaio** ~ **a** level spoonful.

ra'soio *sm* razor; ~ **elettrico** electric shaver *o* razor.

ras'segna [ras'seɲɲa] *sf* (*MIL*) inspection, review; (*esame*) inspection; (*resoconto*) review, survey; (*pubblicazione letteraria etc*) review; (*mostra*) exhibition, show; **passare in** ~ (*MIL, fig*) to review.

rasse'gnare [rasseɲ'ɲare] *vt*: ~ **le dimissioni** to resign, hand in one's resignation; **~rsi** *vr* (*accettare*): **~rsi a qc/a fare**) to resign o.s. (to sth/to doing); **rassegnazi'one** *sf* resignation.

rassere'narsi *vr* (*tempo*) to clear up.

rasset'tare *vt* to tidy, put in order; (*aggiustare*) to repair, mend.

rassicu'rare *vt* to reassure.

rasso'dare *vt* to harden, stiffen.

rassomigli'anza [rassomiʎ'ʎantsa] *sf* resemblance.

rassomigli'are [rassomiʎ'ʎare] *vi*: ~ **a** to resemble, look like.

rastrel'lare *vt* to rake; (*fig: perlustrare*) to comb.

rastrelli'era *sf* rack; (*per piatti*) dish rack.

ras'trello *sm* rake.

'rata *sf* (*quota*) instalment; **pagare a** ~**e** to pay by instalments *o* on hire purchase (*Brit*).

ratifi'care *vt* (*DIR*) to ratify.

'ratto *sm* (*DIR*) abduction; (*ZOOL*) rat.

rattop'pare *vt* to patch; **rat'toppo** *sm* patching *q*; patch.

rattrap'pire *vt* to make stiff; **~rsi** *vr* to be stiff.

rattris'tare *vt* to sadden; **~rsi** *vr* to become sad.

'rauco, a, chi, che *ag* hoarse.

rava'nello *sm* radish.

ravi'oli *smpl* ravioli *sg*.

ravve'dersi *vr* to mend one's ways.

ravvici'nare [ravvitʃi'nare] *vt* (*avvicinare*): ~ **qc a** to bring sth nearer to; (*: due tubi*) to bring closer together; (*riconciliare*) to reconcile, bring together.

ravvi'sare *vt* to recognize.

ravvi'vare *vt* to revive; (*fig*) to brighten up, enliven; **~rsi** *vr* to revive; to brighten up.

razio'cinio [ratsjo'tʃinjo] *sm* reasoning *q*; reason; (*buon senso*) common sense.

razio'nale [rattsjo'nale] *ag* rational.

razio'nare [rattsjo'nare] *vt* to ration.

razi'one [rat'tsjone] *sf* ration; (*porzione*)

portion, share.

'razza ['rattsa] *sf* race; (*ZOOL*) breed; (*discendenza, stirpe*) stock, race; (*sorta*) sort, kind.

raz'zia [rat'tsia] *sf* raid, foray.

razzi'ale [rat'tsjale] *ag* racial.

raz'zismo [rat'tsizmo] *sm* racism, racialism.

raz'zista, i, e [rat'tsista] *ag, sm/f* racist, racialist.

'razzo ['raddzo] *sm* rocket.

razzo'lare [rattso'lare] *vi* (*galline*) to scratch about.

re *sm inv* king; (*MUS*) D; (*: solfeggiando la scala*) re.

rea'gire [rea'dʒire] *vi* to react.

re'ale *ag* real; (*di, da re*) royal // *sm*: **il** ~ **reality; rea'lismo** *sm* realism; **rea'lista, i, e** *sm/f* realist; (*POL*) royalist.

realiz'zare [realid'dzare] *vt* (*progetto etc*) to realize, carry out; (*sogno, desiderio*) to realize, fulfil; (*scopo*) to achieve; (*COMM: titoli etc*) to realize; (*CALCIO etc*) to score; **~rsi** *vr* to be realized; **realizzazi'one** *sf* realization; fulfilment; achievement.

real'mente *av* really, actually.

realtà *sf inv* reality.

re'ato *sm* offence.

reat'tore *sm* (*FISICA*) reactor; (*AER: aereo*) jet; (*: motore*) jet engine.

reazio'nario, a [reattsjo'narjo] *ag* (*POL*) reactionary.

reazi'one [reat'tsjone] *sf* reaction.

'rebbio *sm* prong.

recapi'tare *vt* to deliver.

re'capito *sm* (*indirizzo*) address; (*consegna*) delivery.

re'care *vt* (*portare*) to bring; (*avere su di sé*) to carry, bear; (*cagionare*) to cause, bring; **~rsi** *vr* to go.

re'cedere [re'tʃedere] *vi* to withdraw.

recensi'one [retʃen'sjone] *sf* review; **recen'sire** *vt* to review.

re'cente [re'tʃente] *ag* recent; **di** ~ recently; **recente'mente** *av* recently.

recessi'one [retʃes'sjone] *sf* (*ECON*) recession.

re'cidere [re'tʃidere] *vt* to cut off, chop off.

reci'divo, a [retʃi'divo] *sm/f* (*DIR*) second (*o* habitual) offender, recidivist.

re'cinto [re'tʃinto] *sm* enclosure; (*ciò che recinge*) fence; surrounding wall.

recipi'ente [retʃi'pjente] *sm* container.

re'ciproco, a, ci, che [re'tʃiproko] *ag* reciprocal.

re'ciso, a [re'tʃizo] *pp di* **recidere**.

'recita ['rɛtʃita] *sf* performance.

reci'tare [retʃi'tare] *vt* (*poesia, lezione*) to recite; (*dramma*) to perform; (*ruolo*) to play *o* act (the part of); **recitazi'one** *sf* recitation; (*di attore*) acting.

recla'mare *vi* to complain // *vt*

(richiedere) to demand.

ré'clame [re'klam] *sf inv* advertising *q*; advertisement, advert *(Brit)*, ad *(fam)*.

re'clamo *sm* complaint.

reclusi'one *sf (DIR)* imprisonment.

'recluta *sf* recruit; **reclu'tare** *vt* to recruit.

re'condito, a *ag* secluded; *(fig)* secret, hidden.

recriminazi'one [rekriminat'tsjone] *sf* recrimination.

recrude'scenza [rekrudeʃ'ʃɛntsa] *sf* fresh outbreak.

recupe'rare *vt* = **ricuperare**.

redargu'ire *vt* to rebuke.

re'datto, a *pp di* **redigere; redat'tore, 'trice** *sm/f (STAMPA)* editor; *(: di articolo)* writer; *(di dizionario etc)* compiler; **redattore capo** chief editor; **redazi'one** *sf* editing; writing; *(sede)* editorial office(s); *(personale)* editorial staff; *(versione)* version.

reddi'tizio, a [reddi'tittsjo] *ag* profitable.

'reddito *sm* income; *(dello Stato)* revenue; *(di un capitale)* yield.

re'dento, a *pp di* **redimere**.

redenzi'one [reden'tsjone] *sf* redemption.

re'digere [re'didʒere] *vt* to write; *(contratto)* to draw up.

re'dimere *vt* to deliver; *(REL)* to redeem.

'redini *sfpl* reins.

'reduce ['redutʃe] *ag*: ~ **da** returning from, back from // *sm/f* survivor.

refe'rendum *sm inv* referendum.

refe'renza [refe'rɛntsa] *sf* reference.

re'ferto *sm* medical report.

refet'torio *sm* refectory.

refrat'tario, a *ag* refractory.

refrige'rare [refridʒe'rare] *vt* to refrigerate; *(rinfrescare)* to cool, refresh.

rega'lare *vt* to give (as a present), make a present of.

re'gale *ag* regal.

re'galo *sm* gift, present.

re'gata *sf* regatta.

reg'gente [red'dʒɛnte] *sm/f* regent.

'reggere ['reddʒere] *vt (tenere)* to hold; *(sostenere)* to support, bear, hold up; *(portare)* to carry, bear; *(resistere)* to withstand; *(dirigere: impresa)* to manage, run; *(governare)* to rule, govern; *(LING)* to take, be followed by // *vi (resistere)*: ~ **a** to stand up to, hold out against; *(sopportare)*: ~ **a** to stand; *(durare)* to last; *(fig: teoria etc)* to hold water; ~**rsi** *vr (stare ritto)* to stand; *(fig: dominarsi)* to control o.s.; ~**rsi sulle gambe** *o* **in piedi** to stand up.

'reggia, ge ['reddʒa] *sf* royal palace.

reggi'calze [reddʒi'kaltse] *sm inv* suspender belt.

reggi'mento [reddʒi'mento] *sm (MIL)* regiment.

reggi'petto [reddʒi'pɛtto] *sm*, **reggi'seno** [reddʒi'seno] *sm* bra.

re'gia, 'gie [re'dʒia] *sf (TV, CINEMA etc)* direction.

re'gime [re'dʒime] *sm (POL)* regime; *(DIR: aureo, patrimoniale etc)* system; *(MED)* diet; *(TECN)* (engine) speed.

re'gina [re'dʒina] *sf* queen.

'regio, a, gi, gie ['rɛdʒo] *ag* royal.

regio'nale [redʒo'nale] *ag* regional.

regi'one [re'dʒone] *sf* region; *(territorio)* region, district, area.

re'gista, i, e [re'dʒista] *sm/f (TV, CINEMA etc)* director.

regis'trare [redʒis'trare] *vt (AMM)* to register; *(COMM)* to enter; *(notare)* to note, take note of; *(canzone, conversazione, sog: strumento di misura)* to record; *(mettere a punto)* to adjust, regulate; *(bagagli)* to check in; **registra'tore** *sm (strumento)* recorder, register; *(magnetofono)* tape recorder; **registratore di cassa** cash register; **regis'trazi'one** *sf* recording; *(AMM)* registration; *(COMM)* entry; *(di bagagli)* check-in.

re'gistro [re'dʒistro] *sm (libro)* register; ledger; logbook; *(DIR)* registry; *(MUS, TECN)* register.

re'gnare [reɲ'ɲare] *vi* to reign, rule; *(fig)* to reign.

'regno ['reɲɲo] *sm* kingdom; *(periodo)* reign; *(fig)* realm; **il** ~ **animale/vegetale** the animal/vegetable kingdom; **il R**~ **Unito** the United Kingdom.

'regola *sf* rule; **a** ~ **d'arte** duly; perfectly; **in** ~ in order.

regola'mento *sm (complesso di norme)* regulations *pl*; *(di debito)* settlement; ~ **di conti** *(fig)* settling of scores.

rego'lare *ag* regular; *(in regola: domanda)* in order, lawful // *vt* to regulate, control; *(apparecchio)* to adjust, regulate; *(questione, conto, debito)* to settle; ~**rsi** *vr (moderarsi)*: ~**rsi nel bere/nello spendere** to control one's drinking/spending; *(comportarsi)* to behave, act; **regolarità** *sf inv* regularity.

'regolo *sm* ruler; ~ **calcolatore** slide rule.

reinte'grare *vt (energie)* to recover; *(in una carica)* to reinstate.

rela'tivo, a *ag* relative.

relazi'one [relat'tsjone] *sf (fra cose, persone)* relation(ship); *(resoconto)* report, account; ~**i** *sfpl (conoscenze)* connections.

rele'gare *vt* to banish; *(fig)* to relegate.

religi'one [reli'dʒone] *sf* religion; **religi'oso, a** *ag* religious // *sm/f* monk/nun.

re'liquia *sf* relic.

re'litto *sm* wreck; *(fig)* down-and-out.

re'mare *vi* to row.

remini'scenze [reminiʃ'ʃɛntse] *sfpl* reminiscences.

remissi'one *sf* remission.

remis'sivo, a *ag* submissive, compliant.

'remo *sm* oar.

re'moto, a *ag* remote.

'rendere *vt* (*ridare*) to return, give back; (: *saluto etc*) to return; (*produrre*) to yield, bring in; (*esprimere, tradurre*) to render; (*far diventare*): ~ **qc possibile** to make sth possible; ~ **grazie a qn** to thank sb; ~**rsi utile** to make o.s. useful; ~**rsi conto di qc** to realize sth.

rendi'conto *sm* (*rapporto*) report, account; (*AMM, COMM*) statement of account.

rendi'mento *sm* (*reddito*) yield; (*di manodopera, TECN*) efficiency; (*capacità di produrre*) output; (*di studenti*) performance.

'rendita *sf* (*di individuo*) private *o* unearned income; (*COMM*) revenue; ~ **annua** annuity.

'rene *sm* kidney.

'reni *sfpl* back *sg*.

reni'tente *ag* reluctant, unwilling; ~ **ai consigli di qn** unwilling to follow sb's advice; **essere** ~ **alla leva** (*MIL*) to fail to report for military service.

'renna *sf* reindeer *inv*.

'Reno *sm*: **il** ~ **the** Rhine.

'reo, a *sm/f* (*DIR*) offender.

re'parto *sm* department, section; (*MIL*) detachment.

repel'lente *ag* repulsive.

repen'taglio [repen'taʎʎo] *sm*: **mettere a** ~ to jeopardize, risk.

repen'tino, a *ag* sudden, unexpected.

repe'rire *vt* to find, trace.

re'perto *sm* (*ARCHEOLOGIA*) find; (*MED*) report; (*DIR*: *anche*: ~ **giudiziario**) exhibit.

reper'torio *sm* (*TEATRO*) repertory; (*elenco*) index, (alphabetical) list.

'replica, che *sf* repetition; reply, answer; (*obiezione*) objection; (*TEATRO, CINEMA*) repeat performance; (*copia*) replica.

repli'care *vt* (*ripetere*) to repeat; (*rispondere*) to answer, reply.

repressi'one *sf* repression.

re'presso, a *pp di* **reprimere.**

re'primere *vt* to suppress, repress.

re'pubblica, che *sf* republic; **repub-bli'cano, a** *ag, sm/f* republican.

repu'tare *vt* to consider, judge.

reputazi'one [reputat'tsjone] *sf* reputation.

'requie *sf*: **senza** ~ unceasingly.

requi'sire *vt* to requisition.

requi'sito *sm* requirement.

requisizi'one [rekwizit'tsjone] *sf* requisition.

'resa *sf* (*l'arrendersi*) surrender; (*re-stituzione, rendimento*) return; ~ **dei conti** rendering of accounts; (*fig*) day of reckoning.

resi'dente *ag* resident; **resi'denza** *sf* residence; **residenzi'ale** *ag* residential.

re'siduo, a *ag* residual, remaining // *sm* remainder; (*CHIM*) residue.

'resina *sf* resin.

resis'tente *ag* (*che resiste*): ~ **a** resistant to; (*forte*) strong; (*duraturo*) long-lasting, durable; ~ **al caldo** heat-resistant; **resis'tenza** *sf* resistance; (*di persona: fisica*) stamina, endurance; (: *mentale*) endurance, resistance.

re'sistere *vi* to resist; ~ **a** (*assalto, tentazioni*) to resist; (*dolore, sog: pianta*) to withstand; (*non patir danno*) to be resistant to; **resis'tito, a** *pp di* **resistere.**

'reso, a *pp di* **rendere.**

reso'conto *sm* report, account.

res'pingere [res'pindʒere] *vt* to drive back, repel; (*rifiutare*) to reject; (*INS: bocciare*) to fail; **res'pinto, a** *pp di* **respingere.**

respi'rare *vi* to breathe; (*fig*) to get one's breath; to breathe again // *vt* to breathe (in), inhale; **respira'tore** *sm* respirator; **respirazi'one** *sf* breathing; **respirazione artificiale** artificial respiration; **res'piro** *sm* breathing *q*; (*singolo atto*) breath; (*fig*) respite, rest; **mandare un respiro di sollievo** to give a sigh of relief.

respon'sabile *ag* responsible // *sm/f* person responsible; (*capo*) person in charge; ~ **di** responsible for; (*DIR*) liable for; **responsabilità** *sf inv* responsibility; (*legale*) liability.

res'ponso *sm* answer.

'ressa *sf* crowd, throng.

res'tare *vi* (*rimanere*) to remain, stay; (*diventare*): ~ **orfano/cieco** to become *o* be left an orphan/become blind; (*trovarsi*): ~ **sorpreso** to be surprised; (*avanzare*) to be left, remain; ~ **d'accordo** to agree; **non resta più niente** there's nothing left; **restano pochi giorni** there are only a few days left.

restau'rare *vt* to restore; **re-staurazi'one** *sf* (*POL*) restoration; **res'tauro** *sm* (*di edifici etc*) restoration.

res'tio, a, 'tii, 'tie *ag* restive; (*persona*): ~ **a** reluctant to.

restitu'ire *vt* to return, give back; (*energie, forze*) to restore.

'resto *sm* remainder, rest; (*denaro*) change; (*MAT*) remainder; ~**i** *smpl* leftovers; (*di città*) remains; **del** ~ moreover, besides; ~**i mortali** (mortal) remains.

res'tringere [res'trindʒere] *vt* to reduce; (*vestito*) to take in; (*stoffa*) to shrink; (*fig*) to restrict, limit; ~**rsi** *vr* (*strada*) to narrow; (*stoffa*) to shrink; **re-**

strizi'one sf restriction.

'**rete** sf net; (fig) trap, snare; (di recinzione) wire netting; (AUT, FERR, di spionaggio etc) network; **segnare una ~** (CALCIO) to score a goal; **~ del letto** (sprung) bed base.

reti'cente [reti'tʃɛnte] ag reticent.

retico'lato sm grid; (rete metallica) wire netting; (di filo spinato) barbed wire (fence).

'**retina** sf (ANAT) retina.

re'torico, a, ci, che ag rhetorical // sf rhetoric.

retribu'ire vt to pay; (premiare) to reward; **retribuzi'one** sf payment; reward.

'**retro** sm inv back // av (dietro): **vedi ~** see over(leaf).

retro'cedere [retro'tʃɛdere] vi to withdraw // vt (CALCIO) to relegate; (MIL) to degrade.

re'trogrado, a ag (fig) reactionary, backward-looking.

retro'marcia [retro'martʃa] sf (AUT) reverse; (: dispositivo) reverse gear.

retrospet'tivo, a ag retrospective.

retrovi'sore sm (AUT) (rear-view) mirror.

'**retta** sf (MAT) straight line; (di convitto) charge for bed and board; (fig: ascolto): **dar ~ a** to listen to, pay attention to.

rettango'lare ag rectangular.

ret'tangolo, a ag right-angled // sm rectangle.

ret'tifica, che sf rectification, correction.

rettifi'care vt (curva) to straighten; (fig) to rectify, correct.

'**rettile** sm reptile.

retti'lineo, a ag rectilinear.

retti'tudine sf rectitude, uprightness.

'**retto, a** pp di **reggere** // ag straight; (MAT): **angolo ~** right angle; (onesto) honest, upright; (giusto, esatto) correct, proper, right.

ret'tore sm (REL) rector; (di università) ≈ chancellor.

reuma'tismo sm rheumatism.

reve'rendo, a ag: **il ~ padre Belli** the Reverend Father Belli.

rever'sibile ag reversible.

revisio'nare vt (conti) to audit; (TECN) to overhaul, service; (DIR: processo) to review; (componimento) to revise.

revisi'one sf auditing q; audit; servicing q; overhaul; review; revision.

revi'sore sm: **~ di conti/bozze** auditor/proofreader.

'**revoca** sf revocation.

revo'care vt to revoke.

re'volver sm inv revolver.

riabili'tare vt to rehabilitate; (fig) to restore to favour.

rial'zare vt to raise, lift;

(alzare di più) to heighten, raise; (aumentare: prezzi) to increase, raise // vi (prezzi) to rise, increase; **ri'alzo** sm (di prezzi) increase, rise; (sporgenza) rise.

rianimazi'one [rianimat'tsjone] sf (MED) resuscitation; **centro di ~** intensive care unit.

riap'pendere vt to rehang; (TEL) to hang up.

ria'prire vt, **~rsi** vr to reopen, open again.

ri'armo sm (MIL) rearmament.

rias'setto sm (di stanza etc) rearrangement; (ordinamento) reorganization.

rias'sumere vt (riprendere) to resume; (impiegare di nuovo) to re-employ; (sintetizzare) to summarize; **rias'sunto, a** pp di **riassumere** // sm summary.

ria'vere vt to have again; (avere indietro) to get back; (riacquistare) to recover; **~rsi** vr to recover.

riba'dire vt (fig) to confirm.

ri'balta sf flap; (TEATRO: proscenio) front of the stage; (: apparecchio d'illuminazione) footlights pl; (fig) limelight.

ribal'tabile ag (sedile) tip-up.

ribal'tare vt, vi (anche: **~rsi**) to turn over, tip over.

ribas'sare vt to lower, bring down // vi to come down, fall; **ri'basso** sm reduction, fall.

ri'battere vt to return, hit back; (confutare) to refute; **~ che** to retort that.

ribel'larsi vr: **~ (a)** to rebel (against); **ri'belle** ag (soldati) rebel; (ragazzo) rebellious // sm/f rebel; **ribelli'one** sf rebellion.

'**ribes** sm inv currant; **~ nero** blackcurrant; **~ rosso** redcurrant.

ribol'lire vi (fermentare) to ferment; (fare bolle) to bubble, boil; (fig) to seethe.

ri'brezzo [ri'breddzo] sm disgust, loathing; **far ~ a** to disgust.

ribut'tante ag disgusting, revolting.

rica'dere vi to fall again; (scendere a terra, fig: nel peccato etc) to fall back; (vestiti, capelli etc) to hang (down); (riversarsi: fatiche, colpe): **~ su** to fall on; **rica'duta** sf (MED) relapse.

rical'care vt (disegni) to trace; (fig) to follow faithfully.

rica'mare vt to embroider.

ricambi'are vt to change again; (contraccambiare) to repay, return; **ri'cambio** sm exchange, return; (FISIOL) metabolism; **ricambi** smpl, **pezzi di ricambio** spare parts.

ri'camo sm embroidery.

ricapito'lare vt to recapitulate, sum up.

ricari'care vt (arma, macchina fotografica) to reload; (pipa) to refill; (orologio) to rewind; (batteria) to recharge.

ricat'tare vt to blackmail; **ricatta'tore, 'trice** sm/f blackmailer; **ri'catto** sm blackmail.

rica'vare vt (estrarre) to draw out, extract; (ottenere) to obtain, gain; **ri'cavo** sm proceeds pl.

ric'chezza [rik'kettsa] sf wealth; (fig) richness; **~e** sfpl (beni) wealth sg, riches.

'riccio, a ['rittʃo] ag curly // sm (ZOOL) hedgehog; (: anche: ~ di mare) sea urchin; **'ricciolo** sm curl; **ricci'uto, a** ag curly.

'ricco, a, chi, che ag rich; (persona, paese) rich, wealthy // sm/f rich man/ woman; i **~chi** the rich; **~ di** full of; rich in.

ri'cerca, che [ri'tʃerka] sf search; (indagine) investigation, inquiry; (studio): **la ~** research; **una ~** piece of research.

ricer'care [ritʃer'kare] vt (motivi, cause) to look for, try to determine; (successo, piacere) to pursue; (onore, gloria) to seek; **ricer'cato, a** ag (apprezzato) much sought-after; (affettato) studied, affected // sm/f (POLIZIA) wanted man/ woman.

ri'cetta [ri'tʃetta] sf (MED) prescription; (CUC) recipe.

ricettazi'one [ritʃettat'tsjone] sf (DIR) receiving (stolen goods).

ri'cevere [ri'tʃevere] vt to receive; (stipendio, lettera) to get, receive; (accogliere: ospite) to welcome; (vedere: cliente, rappresentante etc) to see; **ricevi'mento** sm receiving q; (trattenimento) reception; **ricevi'tore** sm (TECN) receiver; **ricevitore delle imposte** tax collector; **rice'vuta** sf receipt; **ricevuta fiscale** receipt for tax purposes; **ricezi'one** sf (RADIO, TV) reception.

richia'mare [rikja'mare] vt (chiamare indietro, ritelefonare) to call back; (ambasciatore, truppe) to recall; (rimproverare) to reprimand; (attirare) to attract, draw; **~rsi a** (riferirsi a) to refer to; **richi'amo** sm call; recall; reprimand; attraction.

richi'edere [ri'kjedere] vt to ask again for; (chiedere indietro): **~ qc** to ask for sth back; (chiedere: per sapere) to ask; (: per avere) to ask for; (AMM: documenti) to apply for; (esigere) to need, require; **richi'esto, a** pp di **richiedere** // sf (domanda) request; (AMM) application, request; (esigenza) demand, request; **a richiesta** on request.

'ricino ['ritʃino] sm: **olio di ~** castor oil.

ricogni'zione [rikoɲɲit'tsjone] sf (MIL) reconnaissance; (DIR) recognition, acknowledgement.

ricominci'are [rikomin'tʃare] vt, vi to start again, begin again.

ricom'pensa sf reward.

ricompen'sare vt to reward.

riconcili'are [rikontʃi'ljare] vt to reconcile; **~rsi** vr to be reconciled; **riconciliazi'one** sf reconciliation.

ricono'scente [rikonoʃ'ʃente] ag grateful; **ricono'scenza** sf gratitude.

rico'noscere [riko'noʃʃere] vt to recognize; (DIR: figlio, debito) to acknowledge; (ammettere: errore) to admit, acknowledge; **riconosci'mento** sm recognition; acknowledgement; (identificazione) identification; **riconosci'uto, a** pp di **riconoscere**.

rico'prire vt (coprire) to cover; (occupare: carica) to hold.

ricor'dare vt to remember, recall; (richiamare alla memoria): **~ qc a qn** to remind sb of sth; **~rsi** vr: **~rsi (di)** to remember; **~rsi di qc/di** aver fatto to remember sth/having done.

ri'cordo sm memory; (regalo) keepsake, souvenir; (di viaggio) souvenir; **~i** smpl (memorie) memoirs.

ricor'rente ag recurrent, recurring; **ricor'renza** sf recurrence; (festività) anniversary.

ri'correre vi (ripetersi) to recur; **~ a** (rivolgersi) to turn to; (: DIR) to appeal to; (servirsi di) to have recourse to; **ri'corso, a** pp di **ricorrere** // sm recurrence; (DIR) appeal; **far ricorso a =** ricorrere a.

ricostru'ire vt (casa) to rebuild; (fatti) to reconstruct; **ricostruzi'one** sf rebuilding q; reconstruction.

ri'cotta sf soft white unsalted cheese made from sheep's milk.

ricove'rare vt to give shelter to; **~ qn in ospedale** to admit sb to hospital.

ri'covero sm shelter, refuge; (MIL) shelter; (MED) admission (to hospital).

ricre'are vt to recreate; (rinvigorire) to restore; (fig: distrarre) to amuse.

ricreazi'one [rikreat'tsjone] sf recreation, entertainment; (INS) break.

ri'credersi vr to change one's mind.

ricupe'rare vt (rientrare in possesso di) to recover, get back; (tempo perduto) to make up for; (NAUT) to salvage; (: naufraghi) to rescue; (delinquente) to rehabilitate; **~ lo svantaggio** (SPORT) to close the gap.

ridacchi'are [ridak'kjare] vi to snigger.

ri'dare vt to return, give back.

'ridere vi to laugh; (deridere, beffare): **~ di** to laugh at, make fun of.

ri'detto, a pp di **ridire**.

ri'dicolo, a ag ridiculous, absurd.

ridimensio'nare vt to reorganize; (fig) to see things in the right perspective.

ri'dire vt to repeat; (criticare) to find fault with; to object to; **trova sempre qualcosa da ~** he always manages to find fault.

ridon'dante ag redundant.

ri'dotto, a *pp di* **ridurre**.

ri'durre *vt* (*anche* CHIM, MAT) to reduce; (*prezzo, spese*) to cut, reduce; (*accorciare: opera letteraria*) to abridge; (: RADIO, TV) to adapt; **ridursi** *vr* (*diminuirsi*) to be reduced, shrink; **ridursi a** to be reduced to; **ridursi pelle e ossa** to be reduced to skin and bone; **riduzi'one** *sf* reduction; abridgement; adaptation.

riem'pire *vt* to fill (up); (*modulo*) to fill in *o* out; **~rsi** *vr* to fill (up); (*mangiare troppo*) to stuff o.s.; **~ qc di** to fill sth (up) with.

rien'tranza [rien'trantsa] *sf* recess; indentation.

rien'trare *vi* (*entrare di nuovo*) to go (*o* come) back in; (*tornare*) to return; (*fare una rientranza*) to go in, curve inwards; to be indented; (*riguardare*): **~ in** to be included among, form part of; **ri'entro** *sm* (*ritorno*) return; (*di astronave*) re-entry.

riepilo'gare *vt* to summarize // *vi* to recapitulate.

ri'fare *vt* to do again; (*ricostruire*) to make again; (*nodo*) to tie again, do up again; (*imitare*) to imitate, copy; **~rsi** *vr* (*risarcirsi*): **~rsi di** to make up for; (*vendicarsi*): **~rsi di qc su qn** to get one's own back on sb for sth; (*riferirsi*): **~rsi a** to go back to; to follow; **~ il letto** to make the bed; **~rsi una vita** to make a new life for o.s.; **ri'fatto, a** *pp di* **rifare**.

riferi'mento *sm* reference; **in** *o* **con ~ a** with reference to.

rife'rire *vt* (*riportare*) to report; (*ascrivere*): **~ qc a** to attribute sth to // *vi* to do a report; **~rsi** *vr*: **~rsi a** to refer to.

rifi'nire *vt* to finish off, put the finishing touches to; **rifini'tura** *sf* finishing touch; **rifiniture** *sfpl* (*di mobile, auto*) finish *sg*.

rifiu'tare *vt* to refuse; **~ di fare** to refuse to do; **rifi'uto** *sm* refusal; **rifiuti** *smpl* (*spazzatura*) rubbish *sg*, refuse *sg*.

riflessi'one *sf* (FISICA, *meditazione*) reflection; (*il pensare*) thought, reflection; (*osservazione*) remark.

rifles'sivo, a *ag* (*persona*) thoughtful, reflective; (LING) reflexive.

ri'flesso, a *pp di* **riflettere** // *sm* (*di luce, rispecchiamento*) reflection; (FISIOL) reflex; **di** *o* **per ~** indirectly.

ri'flettere *vt* to reflect // *vi* to think; **~rsi** *vr* to be reflected; **~ su** to think over.

riflet'tore *sm* reflector; (*proiettore*) floodlight; searchlight.

ri'flusso *sm* flowing back; (*della marea*) ebb; **un'epoca di ~** an era of nostalgia.

ri'fondere *vt* (*rimborsare*) to refund, repay.

ri'forma *sf* reform; **la R~** (REL) the Reformation.

rifor'mare *vt* to re-form; (*cambiare, innovare*) to reform; (MIL: *recluta*) to declare unfit for service; (: *soldato*) to invalid out, discharge; **riforma'torio** *sm* (DIR) community home (*Brit*), reformatory (US).

riforni'mento *sm* supplying; providing; restocking; **~i** *smpl* supplies, provisions.

rifor'nire *vt* (*provvedere*): **~ di** to supply *o* provide with; (*fornire di nuovo: casa etc*) to restock.

ri'frangere [ri'frandʒere] *vt* to refract; **ri'fratto, a** *pp di* **rifrangere**; **ri'frazi'one** *sf* refraction.

rifug'gire [rifud'dʒire] *vi* to escape again; (*fig*): **~ da** to shun.

rifugi'arsi [rifu'dʒarsi] *vr* to take refuge; **rifugi'ato, a** *sm/f* refugee.

ri'fugio [ri'fudʒo] *sm* refuge, shelter; (*in montagna*) shelter; **~ antiaereo** air-raid shelter.

'riga, ghe *sf* line; (*striscia*) stripe; (*di persone, cose*) line, row; (*regolo*) ruler; (*scriminatura*) parting; **mettersi in ~** to line up; **a ~ghe** (*foglio*) lined; (*vestito*) striped.

ri'gagnolo [ri'gaɲɲolo] *sm* rivulet.

ri'gare *vt* (*foglio*) to rule // *vi*: **~ diritto** (*fig*) to toe the line.

rigatti'ere *sm* junk dealer.

riget'tare [ridʒet'tare] *vt* (*gettare indietro*) to throw back; (*fig: respingere*) to reject; (*vomitare*) to bring *o* throw up; **ri'getto** *sm* (*anche* MED) rejection.

rigidità [ridʒidi'ta] *sf* rigidity; stiffness; severity, rigours *pl*; strictness.

'rigido, a ['ridʒido] *ag* rigid, stiff; (*membra etc: indurite*) stiff; (METEOR) harsh, severe; (*fig*) strict.

rigi'rare [ridʒi'rare] *vt* to turn; **~rsi** *vr* to turn round; (*nel letto*) to turn over; **~ qc tra le mani** to turn sth over in one's hands; **~ il discorso** to change the subject.

'rigo, ghi *sm* line; (MUS) staff, stave.

rigogli'oso, a [rigoʎ'ʎoso] *ag* (*pianta*) luxuriant; (*fig: commercio, sviluppo*) thriving.

ri'gonfio, a *ag* swollen.

ri'gore *sm* (METEOR) harshness, rigours *pl*; (*fig*) severity, strictness; (*anche: calcio di ~*) penalty; **di ~** compulsory; **a rigor di termini** strictly speaking; **rigo'roso, a** *ag* (*severo: persona, ordine*) strict; (*preciso*) rigorous.

rigover'nare *vt* to wash (up).

riguar'dare *vt* to look at again; (*considerare*) to regard, consider; (*concernere*) to regard, concern; **~rsi** *vr* (*aver cura di sé*) to look after o.s.

rigu'ardo *sm* (*attenzione*) care; (*considerazione*) regard, respect; **~ a** concerning, with regard to; **non aver ~i nell'agire/nel parlare** to act/speak freely.

rilasci'are [rilaʃ'ʃare] *vt* (*rimettere in*

libertà) to release; (*AMM: documenti*) to issue; **ri'lascio** *sm* release; issue.

rilas'sare *vt* to relax; **~rsi** *vr* to relax; (*fig: disciplina*) to become slack.

rile'gare *vt* (*libro*) to bind; **rilega'tura** *sf* binding.

ri'leggere [ri'lɛddʒere] *vt* to reread, read again; (*rivedere*) to read over.

ri'lento: a ~ *av* slowly.

rileva'mento *sm* (*topografico, statistico*) survey; (*NAUT*) bearing.

rile'vante *ag* considerable; important.

rile'vare *vt* (*ricavare*) to find; (*notare*) to notice; (*mettere in evidenza*) to point out; (*venire a conoscere: notizia*) to learn; (*raccogliere: dati*) to gather, collect; (*TOPOGRAFIA*) to survey; (*MIL*) to relieve; (*COMM*) to take over.

rili'evo *sm* (*ARTE, GEO*) relief; (*fig: rilevanza*) importance; (*osservazione*) point, remark; (*TOPOGRAFIA*) survey; **dar ~ a** o **mettere in ~ qc** (*fig*) to bring sth out, highlight sth.

rilut'tante *ag* reluctant; **rilut'tanza** *sf* reluctance.

'rima *sf* rhyme; (*verso*) verse.

riman'dare *vt* to send again; (*restituire, rinviare*) to send back, return; (*differire*): **~ qc** (a) to postpone sth o put sth off (till); (*fare riferimento*): **~ qn a** to refer sb to; **essere rimandato** (*INS*) to have to repeat one's exams; **ri'mando** *sm* (*rinvio*) return; (*dilazione*) postponement; (*riferimento*) cross-reference.

rima'nente *ag* remaining // *sm* rest, remainder; **i ~i** (*persone*) the rest of them, the others; **rima'nenza** *sf* rest, remainder; **rimanenze** *sfpl* (*COMM*) unsold stock *sg*.

rima'nere *vi* (*restare*) to remain, stay; (*avanzare*) to be left, remain; (*restare stupito*): **~** to be amazed; (*restare, mancare*): **rimangono poche settimane a Pasqua** there are only a few weeks left till Easter; **rimane da vedere se it** remains to be seen whether; (*diventare*): **~ vedovo** to be left a widower; (*trovarsi*): **~ confuso/sorpreso** to be confused/surprised.

ri'mare *vt*, *vi* to rhyme.

rimargi'nare [rimardʒi'nare] *vt*, *vi* (*anche*: **~rsi**) to heal.

ri'masto, a *pp di* **rimanere**.

rima'sugli [rima'suʎʎi] *smpl* leftovers.

rimbal'zare [rimbal'tsare] *vi* to bounce back, rebound; (*proiettile*) to ricochet; **rim'balzo** *sm* rebound; ricochet.

rimbam'bito, a *ag* senile, in one's dotage.

rimboc'care *vt* (*orlo*) to turn up; (*coperta*) to tuck in; (*maniche, pantaloni*) to turn o roll up.

rimbom'bare *vi* to resound.

rimbor'sare *vt* to pay back, repay; **rim'borso** *sm* repayment.

rimedi'are *vi*: **~ a** to remedy // *vt* (*fam: procurarsi*) to get o scrape together.

ri'medio *sm* (*medicina*) medicine; (*cura, fig*) remedy, cure.

rimesco'lare *vt* to mix well, stir well; (*carte*) to shuffle; **sentirsi ~ il sangue** (*per paura*) to feel one's blood run cold; (*per rabbia*) to feel one's blood boil.

ri'messa *sf* (*locale: per veicoli*) garage; (: *per aerei*) hangar; (*COMM: di merce*) consignment; (: *di denaro*) remittance; (*TENNIS*) return; (*CALCIO: anche*: **~ in gioco**) throw-in.

ri'messo, a *pp di* **rimettere**.

ri'mettere *vt* (*mettere di nuovo*) to put back; (*indossare di nuovo*): **~ qc** to put sth back on, put sth on again; (*restituire*) to return, give back; (*affidare*) to entrust; (: *decisione*) to refer; (*condonare*) to remit; (*COMM: merci*) to deliver; (: *denaro*) to remit; (*vomitare*) to bring up; (*perdere: anche*: **rimetterci**) to lose; **~rsi al bello** (*tempo*) to clear up; **~rsi in salute** to get better, recover one's health.

'rimmel *sm inv* ® mascara.

rimoder'nare *vt* to modernize.

rimon'tare *vt* (*meccanismo*) to reassemble; (: *tenda*) to put up again // *vi* (*salire di nuovo*): **~ in** (*macchina, treno*) to get back into; (*SPORT*) to close the gap.

rimorchi'are [rimor'kjare] *vt* to tow; (*fig: ragazza*) to pick up; **rimorchia'tore** *sm* (*NAUT*) tug(boat).

ri'morchio [ri'mɔrkjo] *sm* tow; (*veicolo*) trailer.

ri'morso *sm* remorse.

rimozi'one [rimot'tsjone] *sf* removal; (*da un impiego*) dismissal; (*PSIC*) repression.

rim'pasto *sm* (*POL*) reshuffle.

rimpatri'are *vi* to return home // *vt* to repatriate; **rim'patrio** *sm* repatriation.

rimpi'angere [rim'pjandʒere] *vt* to regret; (*persona*) to miss; **rimpi'anto, a** *pp di* **rimpiangere** // *sm* regret.

rimpiat'tino *sm* hide-and-seek.

rimpiaz'zare [rimpjat'tsare] *vt* to replace.

rimpiccio'lire [rimpittʃo'lire] *vt* to make smaller // *vi* (*anche*: **~rsi**) to become smaller.

rimpin'zare [rimpin'tsare] *vt*: **~ di** to cram o stuff with.

rimprove'rare *vt* to rebuke, reprimand; **rim'provero** *sm* rebuke, reprimand.

rimugi'nare [rimudʒi'nare] *vt* (*fig*) to turn over in one's mind.

rimunerazi'one [rimunerat'tsjone] *sf* remuneration; (*premio*) reward.

rimu'overe *vt* to remove; (*destituire*) to dismiss.

Rinasci'mento [rinaʃʃi'mento] *sm*: **il ~** the Renaissance.

ri'nascita [ri'naʃʃita] *sf* rebirth, revival.

rincal'zare [rinkal'tsare] *vt* (*palo, albero*) to support, prop up; (*lenzuola*) to tuck in.

rinca'rare *vt* to increase the price of // *vi* to go up, become more expensive.

rinca'sare *vi* to go home.

rinchi'udere [rin'kjudere] *vt* to shut (*o* lock) up; ~rsi *vr*: ~rsi in to shut o.s. up in; ~rsi in se stesso to withdraw into o.s.; **rinchi'uso, a** *pp di* **rinchiudere**.

rin'correre *vt* to chase, run after; **rin'corso, a** *pp di* **rincorrere** // *sf* short run.

rin'crescere [rin'kreʃʃere] *vb impers*: mi rincresce che/di non poter fare I'm sorry that/I can't do, I regret that/being unable to do; **rincresci'mento** *sm* regret; **rincresci'uto, a** *pp di* **rincrescere**.

rincu'lare *vi* to draw back; (*arma*) to recoil.

rinfacci'are [rinfat'tʃare] *vt* (*fig*): ~ qc a qn to throw sth in sb's face.

rinfor'zare [rinfor'tsare] *vt* to reinforce, strengthen // *vi* (*anche*: ~rsi) to grow stronger; **rin'forzo** *sm*: mettere un rinforzo a to strengthen; di rinforzo (*asse, sbarra*) strengthening; (*esercito*) supporting; (*personale*) extra, additional; rinforzi *smpl* (*MIL*) reinforcements.

rinfran'care *vt* to encourage, reassure.

rinfres'care *vt* (*atmosfera, temperatura*) to cool (down); (*abito, pareti*) to freshen up // *vi* (*tempo*) to grow cooler; ~rsi *vr* (*ristorarsi*) to refresh o.s.; (*lavarsi*) to freshen up; **rin'fresco, schi** *sm* (*festa*) party; rinfreschi *smpl* refreshments.

rin'fusa *sf*: alla ~ in confusion, higgledy-piggledy.

ringhi'are [rin'gjare] *vi* to growl, snarl.

ringhi'era [rin'gjera] *sf* railing; (*delle scale*) banister(s *pl*).

ringiova'nire [rindʒova'nire] *vt* (*sog*: *vestito, acconciatura etc*): ~ qn to make sb look younger; (: *vacanze etc*) to rejuvenate // *vi* (*anche*: ~rsi) to become (*o* look) younger.

ringrazia'mento [ringrattsja'mento] *sm* thanks *pl*.

ringrazi'are [ringrat'tsjare] *vt* to thank; ~ qn di qc to thank sb for sth.

rinne'gare *vt* (*fede*) to renounce; (*figlio*) to disown, repudiate; **rinne'gato, a** *sm/f* renegade.

rinnova'mento *sm* renewal; (*economico*) revival.

rinno'vare *vt* to renew; (*ripetere*) to repeat, renew; ~rsi *vr* (*fenomeno*) to be repeated, recur; **rin'novo** *sm* (*di contratto*) renewal; "chiuso per rinnovo dei locali" "closed for alterations".

rinoce'ronte [rinotʃe'ronte] *sm* rhinoceros.

rino'mato, a *ag* renowned, celebrated.

rinsal'dare *vt* to strengthen.

rintoc'care *vi* (*campana*) to toll; (*orologio*) to strike.

rintracci'are [rintrat'tʃare] *vt* to track down.

rintro'nare *vi* to boom, roar // *vt* (*assordare*) to deafen; (*stordire*) to stun.

ri'nuncia [ri'nuntʃa] *etc* = **rinunzia** *etc*.

ri'nunzia [ri'nuntsja] *sf* renunciation.

rinunzi'are [rinun'tsjare] *vi*: ~ a to give up, renounce.

rinve'nire *vt* to find, recover; (*scoprire*) to discover, find out // *vi* (*riprendere i sensi*) to come round; (*riprendere l'aspetto naturale*) to revive.

rinvi'are *vt* (*rimandare indietro*) to send back, return; (*differire*): ~ qc (a) to postpone sth *o* put sth off (till); to adjourn sth (till); (*fare un rimando*): ~ qn a to refer sb to.

rinvigo'rire *vt* to strengthen.

rin'vio, 'vii *sm* (*rimando*) return; (*differimento*) postponement; (: *di seduta*) adjournment; (*in un testo*) cross-reference.

ri'one *sm* district, quarter.

riordi'nare *vt* (*rimettere in ordine*) to tidy; (*riorganizzare*) to reorganize.

riorganiz'zare [riorganid'dzare] *vt* to re-organize.

ripa'gare *vt* to repay.

ripa'rare *vt* (*proteggere*) to protect, defend; (*correggere*: *male, torto*) to make up for; (: *errore*) to put right; (*aggiustare*) to repair // *vi* (*mettere rimedio*): ~ a to make up for; ~rsi *vr* (*rifugiarsi*) to take refuge *o* shelter; **riparazi'one** *sf* (*di un torto*) reparation; (*di guasto, scarpe*) repairing *q*; repair; (*risarcimento*) compensation.

ri'paro *sm* (*protezione*) shelter, protection; (*rimedio*) remedy.

ripar'tire *vt* (*dividere*) to divide up; (*distribuire*) to share out // *vi* to set off again; to leave again.

ripas'sare *vi* to come (*o* go) back // *vt* (*scritto, lezione*) to go over (again).

ripen'sare *vi* to think; (*cambiare pensiero*) to change one's mind; (*tornare col pensiero*): ~ a to recall.

ripercu'otersi *vr*: ~ su (*fig*) to have repercussions on.

ripercussi'one *sf* (*fig*): avere una ~ *o* delle ~i su to have repercussions on.

ripes'care *vt* (*pesce*) to catch again; (*persona, cosa*) to fish out; (*fig*: *ritrovare*) to dig out.

ri'petere *vt* to repeat; (*ripassare*) to go over; **ripetizi'one** *sf* repetition; (*di lezione*) revision; ripetizioni *sfpl* (*INS*) private tutoring *o* coaching *sg*.

ripi'ano *sm* (*GEO*) terrace; (*di mobile*) shelf.

ri'picca *sf*: per ~ out of spite.

'ripido, a *ag* steep.

ripie'gare vt to refold; (piegare più volte) to fold (up) // vi (MIL) to retreat, fall back; (fig: accontentarsi): ~ su to make do with; ~rsi vr to bend; **ripi'ego, ghi** sm expedient.

ripi'eno, a ag full; (CUC) stuffed; (: panino) filled // sm (CUC) stuffing.

ri'porre vt (porre al suo posto) to put back, replace; (mettere via) to put away; (fiducia, speranza): ~ qc in qn to place o put sth in sb.

ripor'tare vt (portare indietro) to bring (o take) back; (riferire) to report; (citare) to quote; (ricevere) to receive, get; (vittoria) to gain; (successo) to have; (MAT) to carry; ~rsi a (anche fig) to go back to; (riferirsi a) to refer to; ~ danni to suffer damage.

ripo'sare vt (bicchiere, valigia) to put down; (dare sollievo) to rest // vi to rest; ~rsi vr to rest; **ri'poso** sm rest; (MIL): riposo! at ease!; a riposo (in pensione) retired; giorno di riposo day off.

ripos'tiglio [ripos'tiλλo] sm lumber-room.

ri'posto, a pp di riporre.

ri'prendere vt (prigioniero, fortezza) to recapture; (prendere indietro) to take back; (ricominciare: lavoro) to resume; (andare a prendere) to fetch, come back for; (assumere di nuovo: impiegati) to take on again, re-employ; (rimproverare) to tell off; (restringere: abito) to take in; (CINEMA) to shoot; ~rsi vr to recover; (correggersi) to correct o.s.; **ri'preso, a** pp di riprendere // sf recapture; resumption; (economica, da malattia, emozione) recovery; (AUT) acceleration q; (TEATRO, CINEMA) rerun; (CINEMA: presa) shooting q; shot; (SPORT) second half; (: PUGILATO) round; a più riprese on several occasions, several times.

ripristi'nare vt to restore.

ripro'durre vt to reproduce; **riprodursi** vr (BIOL) to reproduce; (riformarsi) to form again; **riprodut'tivo, a** ag reproductive; **riproduzi'one** sf reproduction; **riproduzione vietata** all rights reserved.

ripudi'are vt to repudiate, disown.

ripu'gnante [ripuɲ'ɲante] ag disgusting, repulsive.

ripu'gnare [ripuɲ'ɲare] vi: ~ a qn to repel o disgust sb.

ripu'lire vt to clean up; (sog: ladri) to clean out; (perfezionare) to polish, refine.

ri'quadro sm square; (ARCHIT) panel.

ri'saia sf paddy field.

risa'lire vi (ritornare in su) to go back up; ~ a (ritornare con la mente) to go back to; (datare da) to date back to, go back to.

risal'tare vi (fig: distinguersi) to stand out; (ARCHIT) to project, jut out; **ri'salto** sm prominence; (sporgenza) projection; **mettere** o **porre in risalto** qc to make sth stand out.

risa'nare vt (guarire) to heal, cure; (palude) to reclaim; (economia) to improve; (bilancio) to reorganize.

risa'puto, a ag: è ~ che ... everyone knows that ..., it is common knowledge that ....

risarci'mento [risartʃi'mento] sm: ~ (di) compensation (for).

risar'cire [risar'tʃire] vt (cose) to pay compensation for; (persona): ~ qn di qc to compensate sb for sth.

ri'sata sf laugh.

riscalda'mento sm heating; ~ centrale central heating.

riscal'dare vt (scaldare) to heat; (: mani, persona) to warm; (minestra) to reheat; ~rsi vr to warm up.

riscat'tare vt (prigioniero) to ransom, pay a ransom for; (DIR) to redeem; ~rsi vr (da disonore) to redeem o.s.; **ris'catto** sm ransom; redemption.

rischia'rare [riskja'rare] vt (illuminare) to light up; (colore) to make lighter; ~rsi vr (tempo) to clear up; (cielo) to clear; (fig: volto) to brighten up; ~rsi la voce to clear one's throat.

rischi'are [ris'kjare] vt to risk // vi: ~ di fare qc to risk o run the risk of doing sth.

'rischio ['riskjo] sm risk; **rischi'oso, a** ag risky, dangerous.

riscia'cquare [riʃʃa'kware] vt to rinse.

riscon'trare vt (confrontare: due cose) to compare; (esaminare) to check, verify; (rilevare) to find; **ris'contro** sm comparison; check, verification; (AMM: lettera di risposta) reply.

riscossi'one sf collection.

ris'cosso, a pp di riscuotere // sf (riconquista) recovery, reconquest.

ris'cuotere vt (ritirare una somma dovuta) to collect; (: stipendio) to draw, collect; (assegno) to cash; (fig: successo etc) to win, earn; ~rsi vr: ~rsi (da) to shake o.s. (out of), rouse o.s. (from).

risenti'mento sm resentment.

risen'tire vt to hear again; (provare) to feel // vi: ~ di to feel (o show) the effects of; ~rsi vr: ~rsi di o per to take offence at, resent; **risen'tito, a** ag resentful.

ri'serbo sm reserve.

ri'serva sf reserve; (di caccia, pesca) preserve; (restrizione, di indigeni) reservation; di ~ (provviste etc) in reserve.

riser'vare vt (tenere in serbo) to keep, put aside; (prenotare) to book, reserve; ~rsi vr: ~rsi di fare qc to intend to do sth; **riser'vato, a** ag (prenotato, fig: persona) reserved; (confidenziale) con-

fidential; **riserva'tezza** sf reserve.
risi'edere vi: ~ a o in to reside in.
'risma sf (di carta) ream; (fig) kind,
sort.
'riso, a pp di ridere // sm (pl(f) ~a: il
ridere): un ~ a laugh; il ~ laughter;
(pianta) rice.
riso'lino sm snigger.
ri'solto, a pp di **risolvere**.
risolu'tezza [risolu'tettsa] sf determination.
riso'luto, a ag determined, resolute.
risoluzi'one [risolut'tsjone] sf solving q;
(MAT) solution; (decisione, di immagine)
resolution.
ri'solvere vt (difficoltà, controversia) to
resolve; (problema) to solve;
(decidere): ~ di fare to resolve to do;
~rsi vr (decidersi): ~rsi a fare to make
up one's mind to do; (andare a finire):
~rsi in to end up, turn out; ~rsi in nulla
to come to nothing.
riso'nanza [riso'nantsa] sf resonance;
aver vasta ~ (fig: fatto etc) to be known
far and wide.
riso'nare vt, vi = **risuonare**.
ri'sorgere [ri'sordʒere] vi to rise again;
risorgi'mento sm revival; il
Risorgimento (STORIA) the Risorgimento.
ri'sorsa sf expedient, resort; ~e sfpl
(naturali, finanziarie etc) resources;
persona piena di ~e resourceful person.
ri'sorto, a pp di **risorgere**.
ri'sotto sm (CUC) risotto.
risparmi'are vt to save; (non uccidere)
to spare // vi to save; ~ qc a qn to spare
sb sth.
ris'parmio sm saving q; (denaro) savings pl.
rispec'chiare [rispek'kjare] vt to reflect.
rispet'tabile ag respectable.
rispet'tare vt to respect; farsi ~ to
command respect.
rispet'tivo, a ag respective.
ris'petto sm respect; ~i smpl (saluti)
respects, regards; ~ a (in paragone a)
compared to; (in relazione a) as regards, as for; **rispet'toso, a** ag respectful.
ris'plendere vi to shine.
ris'pondere vi to answer, reply; (freni)
to respond; ~ a (domanda) to answer,
reply to; (persona) to answer; (invito)
to reply to; (provocazione, sog: veicolo,
apparecchio) to respond to; (corrispondere) to correspond to; (: speranze,
bisogno) to answer; ~ di to answer for;
ris'posto, a pp di **rispondere** // sf
answer, reply; in risposta in a reply to.
'rissa sf brawl.
ristabi'lire vt to re-establish, restore;
(persona: sog: riposo etc) to restore to
health; ~rsi vr to recover.
rista'gnare [ristaɲ'ɲare] vi (acqua) to

become stagnant; (sangue) to cease
flowing; (fig: industria) to stagnate;
ris'tagno sm stagnation.
ris'tampa sf reprinting q; reprint.
risto'rante sm restaurant.
risto'rarsi vr to have something to eat
and drink; (riposarsi) to rest, have a
rest; **ris'toro** sm (bevanda, cibo) re-
freshment; servizio di ristoro (FERR) refreshments pl.
ristret'tezza [ristret'tettsa] sf (strettezza)
narrowness; (fig: scarsezza) scarcity,
lack; (: meschinità) meanness; ~e sfpl
(povertà) financial straits.
ris'tretto, a pp di **restringere** // ag
(racchiuso) enclosed, hemmed in;
(angusto) narrow; (limitato): ~ (a) restricted o limited (to); (CUC: brodo)
thick; (: caffè) extra strong.
risucchi'are [risuk'kjare] vt to suck in.
risul'tare vi (dimostrarsi) to prove (to
be), turn out (to be); (riuscire): ~
vincitore to emerge as the winner; ~ da
(provenire) to result from, be the result
of; mi risulta che ... I understand that
...; non mi risulta not as far as I know;
risul'tato sm result.
risuo'nare vi (rimbombare) to resound.
risurrezi'one [risurret'tsjone] sf (REL)
resurrection.
risusci'tare [risuʃʃi'tare] vt to resuscitate, restore to life; (fig) to revive,
bring back // vi to rise (from the dead).
ris'veglio [riz'veʎʎo] sm waking up; (fig)
revival.
ris'volto sm (di giacca) lapel; (di
pantaloni) turn-up; (di manica) cuff; (di
tasca) flap; (di libro) inside flap; (fig)
implication.
ritagli'are [ritaʎ'ʎare] vt (tagliar via) to
cut out; **ri'taglio** sm (di giornale)
cutting, clipping; (di stoffa etc) scrap;
nei ritagli di tempo in one's spare time.
ritar'dare vi (persona, treno) to be late;
(orologio) to be slow // vt (rallentare) to
slow down; (impedire) to delay, hold up;
(differire) to postpone, delay; **ritar-
da'tario, a** sm/f latecomer.
ri'tardo sm delay; (di persona aspettata)
lateness q; (fig: mentale) backward-
ness; in ~ late.
ri'tegno [ri'teɲɲo] sm restraint.
rite'nere vt (trattenere) to hold back; (:
somma) to deduct; (giudicare) to consider, believe; **rite'nuta** sf (sul salario)
deduction.
riti'rare vt to withdraw; (POL:
richiamare) to recall; (andare a prendere: pacco etc) to collect, pick up; ~rsi
vr to withdraw; (da un'attività) to retire; (stoffa) to shrink; (marea) to recede; **riti'rata** sf (MIL) retreat; (latrina)
lavatory; **ri'tiro** sm withdrawal; recall;
collection; (luogo appartato) retreat.
'ritmo sm rhythm; (fig) rate; (: della

vita) pace, tempo.

'rito *sm* rite; **di** ~ usual, customary.

ritoc'care *vt* (*disegno, fotografia*) to touch up; (*testo*) to alter; **ri'tocco, chi** *sm* touching up *q*; alteration.

ritor'nare *vi* to return, go (*o come*) back; (*ripresentarsi*) to recur; (*ridiventare*): ~ **ricco** to become rich again // *vt* (*restituire*) to return, give back.

ritor'nello *sm* refrain.

ri'torno *sm* return; **essere di** ~ to be back; **avere un** ~ **di fiamma** (*AUT*) to backfire; (*fig: persona*) to be back in love again.

ri'trarre *vt* (*trarre indietro, via*) to withdraw; (*distogliere: sguardo*) to turn away; (*rappresentare*) to portray, depict; (*ricavare*) to get, obtain.

ritrat'tare *vt* (*disdire*) to retract, take back; (*trattare nuovamente*) to deal with again.

ri'tratto, a *pp di* **ritrarre** // *sm* portrait.

ri'troso, a *ag* (*restio*): ~ **(a)** reluctant (to); (*schivo*) shy; **andare a** ~ to go backwards.

ritro'vare *vt* to find; (*salute*) to regain; (*persona*) to find; to meet again; **~rsi** *vr* (*essere, capitare*) to find o.s.; (*raccapezzarsi*) to find one's way; (*con senso reciproco*) to meet (again); **ri'trovo** *sm* meeting place; **ritrovo notturno** night club.

'ritto, a *ag* (*in piedi*) standing, on one's feet; (*levato in alto*) erect, raised; (*: capelli*) standing on end; (*posto verticalmente*) upright.

ritu'ale *ag, sm* ritual.

riuni'one *sf* (*adunanza*) meeting; (*riconciliazione*) reunion.

riu'nire *vt* (*ricongiungere*) to join (together); (*riconciliare*) to reunite, bring together (again); **~rsi** *vr* (*adunarsi*) to meet; (*tornare a stare insieme*) to be reunited.

riu'scire [riuʃ'ʃire] *vi* (*uscire di nuovo*) to go out again, go back out; (*aver esito: fatti, azioni*) to go, turn out; (*aver successo*) to succeed, be successful; (*essere, apparire*) to be, prove; (*raggiungere il fine*) to manage, succeed; ~ **a fare qc** to manage to do *o* succeed in doing *o* be able to do sth; **questo mi riesce nuovo** this is new to me; **riu'scita** *sf* (*esito*) result, outcome; (*buon esito*) success.

'riva *sf* (*di fiume*) bank; (*di lago, mare*) shore.

ri'vale *sm/f* rival; **rivalità** *sf* rivalry.

ri'valsa *sf* (*rivincita*) revenge; (*risarcimento*) compensation.

rivalu'tare *vt* (*ECON*) to revalue.

rivan'gare *vt* (*ricordi etc*) to dig up (again).

rive'dere *vt* to see again; (*ripassare*) to

revise; (*verificare*) to check.

rive'lare *vt* to reveal; (*divulgare*) to reveal, disclose; (*dare indizio*) to reveal, show; **~rsi** *vr* (*manifestarsi*) to be revealed; **~rsi onesto** *etc* to prove to be honest *etc*; **rivela'tore** *sm* (*TECN*) detector; (*FOT*) developer; **rivelazi'one** *sf* revelation.

rivendi'care *vt* to claim, demand.

ri'vendita *sf* (*bottega*) retailer's (shop).

rivendi'tore, 'trice *sm/f* retailer; ~ **autorizzato** (*COMM*) authorized dealer.

ri'verbero *sm* (*di luce, calore*) reflection; (*di suono*) reverberation.

rive'renza [rive'rentsa] *sf* reverence; (*inchino*) bow; curtsey.

rive'rire *vt* (*rispettare*) to revere; (*salutare*) to pay one's respects to.

river'sare *vt* (*anche fig*) to pour; **~rsi** *vr* (*fig: persone*) to pour out.

rivesti'mento *sm* covering; coating.

rives'tire *vt* to dress again; (*ricoprire*) to cover; to coat; (*fig: carica*) to hold; **~rsi** *vr* to get dressed again; to change (one's clothes).

rivi'era *sf* coast; **la** ~ **italiana** the Italian Riviera.

ri'vincita [ri'vintʃita] *sf* (*SPORT*) return match; (*fig*) revenge.

rivis'suto, a *pp di* **rivivere**.

ri'vista *sf* review; (*periodico*) magazine, review; (*TEATRO*) revue; variety show.

ri'vivere *vi* (*riacquistare forza*) to come alive again; (*tornare in uso*) to be revived // *vt* to relive.

ri'volgere [ri'voldʒere] *vt* (*attenzione, sguardo*) to turn, direct; (*parole*) to address; **~rsi** *vr* to turn round; (*fig: dirigersi per informazioni*): **~rsi a** to go and see, go and speak to; (*: ufficio*) to enquire at.

ri'volta *sf* revolt, rebellion.

rivol'tare *vt* to turn over; (*con l'interno all'esterno*) to turn inside out; (*disgustare: stomaco*) to upset, turn; **~rsi** *vr* (*ribellarsi*): **~rsi (a)** to rebel (against).

rivol'tella *sf* revolver.

ri'volto, a *pp di* **rivolgere**.

rivoluzio'nare [rivoluttsjo'nare] *vt* to revolutionize.

rivoluzio'nario, a [rivoluttsjo'narjo] *ag, sm/f* revolutionary.

rivoluzi'one [rivolut'tsjone] *sf* revolution.

riz'zare [rit'tsare] *vt* to raise, erect; **~rsi** *vr* to stand up; (*capelli*) to stand on end.

'roba *sf* stuff, things *pl*; (*possessi, beni*) belongings *pl*, things *pl*, possessions *pl*; ~ **da mangiare** things *pl* to eat, food; ~ **da matti** sheer madness *o* lunacy.

'robot *sm inv* robot.

ro'busto, a *ag* robust, sturdy; (*solido: catena*) strong.

'rocca, che *sf* fortress.

rocca'forte *sf* stronghold.

roc'chetto [rok'ketto] *sm* reel, spool.

'roccia, ce ['rɔttʃa] *sf* rock; **fare ~** (*SPORT*) to go rock climbing; **roc'cioso, a** *ag* rocky.

ro'daggio [ro'daddʒo] *sm* running (*Brit*) *o* breaking (*US*) in; **in ~** running (*Brit*) *o* breaking (*US*) in.

'Rodano *sm*: **il ~** the Rhone.

'rodere *vt* to gnaw (at); (*distruggere poco a poco*) to eat into.

rodi'tore *sm* (*ZOOL*) rodent.

rodo'dendro *sm* rhododendron.

'rogna ['rɔɲɲa] *sf* (*MED*) scabies *sg*; (*fig*) bother, nuisance.

ro'gnone [roɲ'ɲone] *sm* (*CUC*) kidney.

'rogo, ghi *sm* (*per cadaveri*) (funeral) pyre; (*supplizio*): **il ~** the stake.

rol'lio *sm* roll(ing).

'Roma *sf* Rome.

Roma'nia *sf*: **la ~** Romania.

ro'manico, a, ci, che *ag* Romanesque.

ro'mano, a *ag, sm/f* Roman.

romanti'cismo /romanti'tʃizmo] *sm* romanticism.

ro'mantico, a, ci, che *ag* romantic.

ro'manza [ro'mandza] *sf* (*MUS, LETTE-RATURA*) romance.

roman'zesco, a, schi, sche [roman'dzesko] *ag* (*stile, personaggi*) fictional; (*fig*) storybook *cpd*.

romanzi'ere [roman'dzjɛre] *sm* novelist.

ro'manzo, a [ro'mandzo] *ag* (*LING*) romance *cpd* // *sm* (*medievale*) romance; (*moderno*) novel; **~ d'appendice** serial (story).

rom'bare *vi* to rumble, thunder, roar.

'rombo *sm* rumble, thunder, roar; (*MAT*) rhombus; (*ZOOL*) turbot; brill.

ro'meno, a *ag, sm/f, sm* = **rumeno, a.**

'rompere *vt* to break; (*conversazione, fidanzamento*) to break off // *vi* to break; **~rsi** *vr* to break; **mi rompe le scatole** (*fam*) he (*o* she) is a pain in the neck; **~rsi un braccio** to break an arm; **rompi'capo** *sm* worry, headache; (*indovinello*) puzzle; (*in enigmistica*) brainteaser; **rompighi'accio** *sm* (*NAUT*) icebreaker; **rompis'catole** *sm/f inv* (*fam*) pest, pain in the neck.

'ronda *sf* (*MIL*) rounds *pl*, patrol.

ron'della *sf* (*TECN*) washer.

'rondine *sf* (*ZOOL*) swallow.

ron'done *sm* (*ZOOL*) swift.

ron'zare [ron'dzare] *vi* to buzz, hum.

ron'zino [ron'dzino] *sm* (*peg: cavallo*) nag.

'rosa *sf* rose // *ag inv, sm* pink; **ro'saio** *sm* (*pianta*) rosebush, rose tree; (*giardino*) rose garden; **ro'sario** *sm* (*REL*) rosary; **ro'sato, a** *ag* pink, rosy // *sm* (*vino*) rosé (wine); **ro'seo, a** *ag* (*anche fig*) rosy.

rosicchi'are [rosik'kjare] *vt* to gnaw (at); (*mangiucchiare*) to nibble (at).

rosma'rino *sm* rosemary.

'roso, a *pp di* **rodere.**

roso'lare *vt* (*CUC*) to brown.

roso'lia *sf* (*MED*) German measles *sg*, rubella.

ro'sone *sm* rosette; (*vetrata*) rose window.

'rospo *sm* (*ZOOL*) toad.

ros'setto *sm* (*per labbra*) lipstick; (*per guance*) rouge.

'rosso, a *ag, sm, sm/f* red; **il mar R~** the Red Sea; **~ d'uovo** egg yolk; **ros'sore** *sm* flush, blush.

rosticce'ria [rostittʃe'ria] *sf* shop selling roast meat and other cooked food.

'rostro *sm* rostrum; (*becco*) beak.

ro'tabile *ag* (*percorribile*): **strada ~** roadway; (*FERR*): **materiale *m* ~** rolling stock.

ro'taia *sf* rut, track; (*FERR*) rail.

ro'tare *vt, vi* to rotate; **rotazi'one** *sf* rotation.

rote'are *vt, vi* to whirl; **~ gli occhi** to roll one's eyes.

ro'tella *sf* small wheel; (*di mobile*) castor.

roto'lare *vt, vi* to roll; **~rsi** *vr* to roll (about).

'rotolo *sm* roll; **andare a ~i** (*fig*) to go to rack and ruin.

ro'tondo, a *ag* round // *sf* rotunda.

ro'tore *sm* rotor.

'rotta *sf* (*AER, NAUT*) course, route; (*MIL*) rout; **a ~ di collo** at breakneck speed; **essere in ~ con qn** to be on bad terms with sb.

rot'tame *sm* fragment, scrap, broken bit; **~i** *smpl* (*di nave, aereo etc*) wreckage *sg*; **~i di ferro** scrap iron *sg*.

'rotto, a *pp di* **rompere** // *ag* broken; (*calzoni*) torn, split; (*persona: pratico, resistente*): **~ a** accustomed *o* inured to; **per il ~ della cuffia** by the skin of one's teeth.

rot'tura *sf* breaking *q*; break; breaking off; (*MED*) fracture, break.

rou'lotte [ru'lɔt] *sf* caravan.

ro'vente *ag* red-hot.

'rovere *sm* oak.

rovesci'are [rovef'ʃare] *vt* (*versare in giù*) to pour; (: *accidentalmente*) to spill; (*capovolgere*) to turn upside down; (*gettare a terra*) to knock down; (: *fig: governo*) to overthrow; (*piegare all'indietro: testa*) to throw back; **~rsi** *vr* (*sedia, macchina*) to overturn; (*barca*) to capsize; (*liquido*) to spill; (*fig: situazione*) to be reversed.

ro'vescio, sci [ro'vɛʃʃo] *sm* other side, wrong side; (*della mano*) back; (*di moneta*) reverse; (*pioggia*) sudden downpour; (*fig*) setback; (*MAGLIA: anche: punto ~*) purl (stitch); (*TENNIS*) backhand (stroke); **a ~** upside-down; inside-out; **capire qc a ~** to misunderstand sth.

ro'vina *sf* ruin; **~e** *sfpl* ruins; **andare in ~** (*andare a pezzi*) to collapse; (*fig*) to go to rack and ruin.

rovi'nare *vi* to collapse, fall down // *vt* (*far cadere giù: casa*) to demolish; (*danneggiare, fig*) to ruin; **rovi'noso, a** *ag* disastrous; damaging; violent.

rovis'tare *vt* (*casa*) to ransack; (*tasche*) to rummage in (*o* through).

'rovo *sm* (*BOT*) blackberry bush, bramble bush.

'rozzo, a ['roddzo] *ag* rough, coarse.

'ruba *sf*: andare a ~ to sell like hot cakes.

ru'bare *vt* to steal; ~ qc a qn to steal sth from sb.

rubi'netto *sm* tap, faucet (*US*).

ru'bino *sm* ruby.

ru'brica, che *sf* (*STAMPA*) column; (*quadernetto*) index book; address book.

'rude *ag* tough, rough.

'rudere *sm* (*rovina*) ruins *pl.*

rudimen'tale *ag* rudimentary, basic.

rudi'menti *smpl* rudiments; basic principles; basic knowledge *sg.*

ruffi'ano *sm* pimp.

'ruga, ghe *sf* wrinkle.

'ruggine ['ruddʒine] *sf* rust.

rug'gire [rud'dʒire] *vi* to roar.

rugi'ada [ru'dʒada] *sf* dew.

ru'goso, a *ag* wrinkled.

rul'lare *vi* (*tamburo, nave*) to roll; (*aereo*) to taxi.

'rullo *sm* (*di tamburi*) roll; (*arnese cilindrico, TIP*) roller; ~ compressore steam roller; ~ di pellicola roll of film.

rum *sm* rum.

ru'meno, a *ag, sm/f, sm* Romanian.

rumi'nare *vt* (*ZOOL*) to ruminate.

ru'more *sm*: un ~ a noise, a sound; (*fig*) a rumour; il ~ noise; **rumo'roso, a** *ag* noisy.

ru'olo *sm* (*TEATRO, fig*) role, part; (*elenco*) roll, register, list; di ~ permanent, on the permanent staff.

ru'ota *sf* wheel; a ~ (*forma*) circular; ~ anteriore/posteriore front/back wheel; ~ di scorta spare wheel.

ruo'tare *vt, vi* = **rotare**.

'rupe *sf* cliff.

ru'rale *ag* rural, country *cpd.*

ru'scello [ruʃ'ʃello] *sm* stream.

'ruspa *sf* excavator.

rus'sare *vi* to snore.

'Russia *sf*: la ~ Russia; **'russo, a** *ag, sm/f, sm* Russian.

'rustico, a, ci, che *ag* rustic; (*fig*) rough, unrefined.

rut'tare *vi* to belch; **'rutto** *sm* belch.

'ruvido, a *ag* rough, coarse.

ruzzo'lare [ruttso'lare] *vi* to tumble down; **ruzzo'loni** *av*: cadere ruzzoloni to tumble down; fare le scale ruzzoloni to tumble down the stairs.

S

S. *abbr* (= *sud*) S.

sa *vb vedi* **sapere**.

'sabato *sm* Saturday; di *o* il ~ on Saturdays.

'sabbia *sf* sand; ~e mobili quicksand(s); **sabbi'oso, a** *ag* sandy.

sabo'taggio [sabo'taddʒo] *sm* sabotage.

sabo'tare *vt* to sabotage.

'sacca, che *sf* bag; (*bisaccia*) haversack; (*insenatura*) inlet; ~ da viaggio travelling bag.

sacca'rina *sf* saccharin(e).

sac'cente [sat'tʃente] *sm/f* know-all (*Brit*), know-it-all (*US*).

saccheggi'are [sakked'dʒare] *vt* to sack, plunder; **sac'cheggio** *sm* sack(ing).

sac'chetto [sak'ketto] *sm* (small) bag; (small) sack.

'sacco, chi *sm* bag; (*per carbone etc*) sack; (*ANAT, BIOL*) sac; (*tela*) sacking; (*saccheggio*) sack(ing); (*fig: grande quantità*): un ~ di lots of, heaps of; ~ a pelo sleeping bag; ~ per i rifiuti bin bag.

sacer'dote [satʃer'dote] *sm* priest; **sacer'dozio** *sm* priesthood.

sacra'mento *sm* sacrament.

sacrifi'care *vt* to sacrifice; ~rsi *vr* to sacrifice o.s.; (*privarsi di qc*) to make sacrifices.

sacri'ficio [sakri'fitʃo] *sm* sacrifice.

sacri'legio [sakri'ledʒo] *sm* sacrilege.

'sacro, a *ag* sacred.

'sadico, a, ci, che *ag* sadistic // *sm/f* sadist.

sa'etta *sf* arrow; (*fulmine: anche fig*) thunderbolt; flash of lightning.

sa'fari *sm inv* safari.

sa'gace [sa'gatʃe] *ag* shrewd, sagacious.

sag'gezza [sad'dʒettsa] *sf* wisdom.

saggi'are [sad'dʒare] *vt* (*metalli*) to assay; (*fig*) to test.

'saggio, a, gi, ge ['saddʒo] *ag* wise // *sm* (*persona*) sage; (*operazione sperimentale*) test; (: *dell'oro*) assay; (*fig: prova*) proof; (*campione indicativo*) sample; (*ricerca, esame critico*) essay.

Sagit'tario [sadʒit'tarjo] *sm* Sagittarius.

'sagoma *sf* (*profilo*) outline, profile; (*forma*) form, shape; (*TECN*) template; (*bersaglio*) target; (*fig: persona*) character.

'sagra *sf* festival.

sagres'tano *sm* sacristan; sexton.

sagres'tia *sf* sacristy; (*culto protestante*) vestry.

Sa'hara [sa'ara] *sm*: il (deserto del) ~ the Sahara (Desert).

'sai *vb vedi* **sapere**.

'sala *sf* hall; (*stanza*) room; ~ d'aspetto waiting room; ~ da ballo ballroom; ~ per concerti concert hall; ~ da gioco gaming room; ~ **operatoria** operating theatre; ~ **da pranzo** dining room.

sa'lame sm salami q, salami sausage.

sala'moia sf (CUC) brine.

sa'lare vt to salt.

salari'ato, a sm/f wage-earner.

sa'lario sm pay, wages pl.

sa'lato, a ag (sapore) salty; (CUC) salted, salt cpd; (fig: discorso etc) biting, sharp; (: prezzi) steep, stiff.

sal'dare vt (congiungere) to join, bind; (parti metalliche) to solder; (: con saldatura autogena) to weld; (conto) to settle, pay; **salda'tura** sf soldering; welding; (punto saldato) soldered joint; weld.

sal'dezza [sal'dettsa] sf firmness; strength.

'saldo, a ag (resistente, forte) strong, firm; (fermo) firm, steady, stable; (fig) firm, steadfast // sm (svendita) sale; (di conto) settlement; (ECON) balance.

'sale sm salt; (fig): **ha poco ~ in zucca** he doesn't have much sense; ~ **fino/grosso** table/cooking salt.

'salice ['salitʃe] sm willow; ~ **piangente** weeping willow.

sali'ente ag (fig) salient, main.

sali'era sf salt cellar.

sa'lino, a ag saline // sf saltworks sg.

sa'lire vi to go (o come) up; (aereo etc) to climb, go up; (passeggero) to get on; (sentiero, prezzi, livello) to go up, rise // vt (scale, gradini) to go (o come) up; ~ **su** to climb (up); ~ **sul treno/sull'autobus** to board the train/the bus; ~ **in macchina** to get into the car; **sa'lita** sf climb, ascent; (erta) hill, slope; **in salita** ag, av uphill.

sa'liva sf saliva.

'salma sf corpse.

'salmo sm psalm.

sal'mone sm salmon.

sa'lone sm (stanza) sitting room, lounge; (in albergo) lounge; (su nave) lounge, saloon; (mostra) show, exhibition; ~ **di bellezza** beauty salon.

sa'lotto sm lounge, sitting room; (mobilio) lounge suite.

sal'pare vi (NAUT) to set sail; (anche: ~ l'ancora) to weigh anchor.

'salsa sf (CUC) sauce; ~ **di pomodoro** tomato sauce.

sal'siccia, ce [sal'sittʃa] sf pork sausage.

sal'tare vi to jump, leap; (esplodere) to blow up, explode; (: valvola) to blow; (venir via) to pop off; (non aver luogo: corso etc) to be cancelled // vt to jump (over), leap (over); (fig: pranzo, capitolo) to skip, miss (out); (CUC) to sauté; **far ~** to blow up; to burst open; ~ **fuori** (fig: apparire all'improvviso) to turn up.

saltel'lare vi to skip; to hop.

saltim'banco sm acrobat.

'salto sm jump; (SPORT) jumping; **fare un ~** to jump, leap; **fare un ~ da qn** to pop over to sb's (place); ~ **in alto/lungo** high/long jump; ~ **con l'asta** pole vaulting; ~ **mortale** somersault.

saltu'ario, a ag occasional, irregular.

sa'lubre ag healthy, salubrious.

salume'ria sf delicatessen.

sa'lumi smpl salted pork meats.

salu'tare ag healthy; (fig) salutary, beneficial // vt (per dire buon giorno, fig) to greet; (per dire addio) to say goodbye to; (MIL) to salute.

sa'lute sf health; ~**!** (a chi starnutisce) bless you!; (nei brindisi) cheers!; **bere alla ~ di qn** to drink (to) sb's health.

sa'luto sm (gesto) wave; (parola) greeting; (MIL) salute; ~**i** smpl greetings; **cari ~i** best regards; **vogliate gradire i nostri più distinti ~i** Yours faithfully.

salvacon'dotto sm (MIL) safe-conduct.

salva'gente [salva'dʒɛnte] sm (NAUT) lifebuoy; (stradale) traffic island; ~ **a ciambella** life belt; ~ **a giubbotto** life-jacket.

salvaguar'dare vt to safeguard.

sal'vare vt to save; (trarre da un pericolo) to rescue; (proteggere) to protect; ~**rsi** vr to save o.s.; to escape; **salva'taggio** sm rescue; **salva'tore, 'trice** sm/f saviour.

'salve escl (fam) hi!

sal'vezza [sal'vettsa] sf salvation; (sicurezza) safety.

'salvia sf (BOT) sage.

'salvo, a ag safe, unhurt, unharmed; (fuori pericolo) safe, out of danger // sm: **in ~** safe // prep (eccetto) except; **mettere qc in ~** to put sth in a safe place; ~ **che** cong (a meno che) unless; (eccetto che) except (that); ~ **imprevisti** barring accidents.

sam'buco sm elder (tree).

sa'nare vt to heal, cure; (economia) to put right.

san'cire [san'tʃire] vt to sanction.

'sandalo sm (BOT) sandalwood; (calzatura) sandal.

'sangue sm blood; **farsi cattivo ~** to fret, get in a state; ~ **freddo** (fig) sangfroid, calm; **a ~ freddo** in cold blood; **sangu'igno, a** ag blood cpd; (colore) blood-red; **sangui'nare** vi to bleed; **sangui'noso, a** ag bloody; **sangui'suga** sf leech.

sani'tà sf health; (salubrità) healthiness; **Ministero della S~** Department of Health; ~ **mentale** sanity.

sani'tario, a ag health cpd; (condizioni) sanitary // sm (AMM) doctor; (impianti) ~**i** smpl bathroom o sanitary fittings.

'sanno vb vedi **sapere**.

'sano, a ag healthy; (denti, costituzione) healthy, sound; (integro) whole, unbroken; (fig: politica, consigli) sound; ~

di mente sane; di ~a pianta completely, entirely; ~ e salvo safe and sound.

santifi'care *vt* to sanctify; (*feste*) to observe.

santità *sf* sanctity; holiness; Sua/Vostra ~ (*titolo di Papa*) His/Your Holiness.

'santo, a *ag* holy; (*fig*) saintly; (*seguito da nome proprio: dav sm* **san** + *C*, **sant'** + *V*, **santo** + *s impura, gn, pn, ps, x, z; dav sf* **santa** + *C*, **sant'** + *V*) saint // *sm/f* saint; **la S~a Sede** the Holy See.

santu'ario *sm* sanctuary.

sanzio'nare [santsjo'nare] *vt* to sanction.

sanzi'one [san'tsjone] *sf* sanction; (*penale, civile*) sanction, penalty.

sa'pere *vt* to know; (*essere capace di*): **so nuotare** I know how to swim, I can swim // *vi*: ~ **di** (*aver sapore*) to taste of; (*aver odore*) to smell of // *sm* knowledge; **far ~ qc a qn** to inform sb about sth, let sb know sth; **mi sa che non sia vero** I don't think that's true.

sapi'enza [sa'pjentsa] *sf* wisdom.

sa'pone *sm* soap; ~ **da bucato** washing soap; **sapo'netta** *sf* cake o bar o tablet of soap.

sa'pore *sm* taste, flavour; **sapo'rito, a** *ag* tasty.

sappi'amo *vb vedi* **sapere**.

saraci'nesca [saratʃi'neska] *sf* (*serranda*) rolling shutter.

sar'casmo *sm* sarcasm *q*; sarcastic remark.

Sar'degna [sar'deɲɲa] *sf*: **la ~** Sardinia.

sar'dina *sf* sardine.

'sardo, a *ag, sm/f* Sardinian.

'sarto, a *sm/f* tailor/dressmaker; **sarto'ria** *sf* tailor's (shop); dressmaker's (shop); (*casa di moda*) fashion house; (*arte*) couture.

'sasso *sm* stone; (*ciottolo*) pebble; (*masso*) rock.

sas'sofono *sm* saxophone.

sas'soso, a *ag* stony; pebbly.

'Satana *sm* Satan; **sa'tanico, a, ci, che** *ag* satanic, fiendish.

sa'tellite *sm, ag* satellite.

'satira *sf* satire.

'saturo, a *ag* saturated; (*fig*): ~ **di** full of.

S.A.U.B. ['saub] *sigla f* (= *Struttura Amministrativa Unificata di Base*) *state welfare system*.

'sauna *sf* sauna.

Sa'voia *sf*: **la ~** Savoy.

savoi'ardo, a *ag* of Savoy, Savoyard // *sm* (*biscotto*) sponge finger.

sazi'are [sat'tsjare] *vt* to satisfy, satiate; ~**rsi** *vr* (*riempirsi di cibo*): ~**rsi (di)** to eat one's fill (of); (*fig*): ~**rsi di** to grow tired o weary of.

'sazio, a ['sattsjo] *ag*: ~ **(di)** sated (with), full (of); (*fig: stufo*) fed up (with), sick (of).

sba'dato, a *ag* careless, inattentive.

sbadigli'are [zbadiʎ'ʎare] *vi* to yawn; **sba'diglio** *sm* yawn.

sbagli'are [zbaʎ'ʎare] *vt* to make a mistake in, get wrong // *vi* to make a mistake, be mistaken, be wrong; (*operare in modo non giusto*) to err; ~**rsi** *vr* to make a mistake, be mistaken, be wrong; ~ **la mira/strada** to miss one's aim/take the wrong road; **'sbaglio** *sm* mistake, error; (*morale*) error; **fare uno sbaglio** to make a mistake.

sbal'lare *vt* (*merce*) to unpack // *vi* (*nel fare un conto*) to overestimate; (*fam*: *gergo della droga*) to get high.

sballot'tare *vt* to toss (about).

sbalor'dire *vt* to stun, amaze // *vi* to be stunned, be amazed; **sbalordi'tivo, a** *ag* amazing; (*prezzo*) incredible, absurd.

sbal'zare [zbal'tsare] *vt* to throw, hurl // *vi* (*balzare*) to bounce; (*saltare*) to leap, bound; **'sbalzo** *sm* (*spostamento improvviso*) jolt, jerk; **a sbalzi** jerkily; (*fig*) in fits and starts; **uno sbalzo di temperatura** a sudden change in temperature.

sban'dare *vi* (*NAUT*) to list; (*AER*) to bank; (*AUT*) to skid; ~**rsi** *vr* (*folla*) to disperse; (*fig: famiglia*) to break up.

sbandie'rare *vt* (*bandiera*) to wave; (*fig*) to parade, show off.

sbaragli'are [zbaraʎ'ʎare] *vt* (*MIL*) to rout; (*in gare sportive etc*) to beat, defeat.

sba'raglio [zba'raʎʎo] *sm* rout; defeat; **gettarsi allo ~** to risk everything.

sbaraz'zarsi [zbarat'tsarsi] *vr*: ~ **di** to get rid of, rid o.s. of.

sbar'care *vt* (*passeggeri*) to disembark; (*merci*) to unload // *vi* to disembark; **'sbarco** *sm* disembarkation; unloading; (*MIL*) landing.

'sbarra *sf* bar; (*di passaggio a livello*) barrier; (*DIR*): **presentarsi alla ~** to appear before the court.

sbarra'mento *sm* (*stradale*) barrier; (*diga*) dam, barrage; (*MIL*) barrage.

sbar'rare *vt* (*strada etc*) to block, bar; (*assegno*) to cross; ~ **il passo** to bar the way; ~ **gli occhi** to open one's eyes wide.

'sbattere *vt* (*porta*) to slam, bang; (*tappeti, ali, CUC*) to beat; (*urtare*) to knock, hit // *vi* (*porta, finestra*) to bang; (*agitarsi: ali, vele etc*) to flap; **me ne sbatto!** (*fam*) I don't give a damn!; **sbat'tuto, a** *ag* (*viso, aria*) dejected, worn out; (*uovo*) beaten.

sba'vare *vi* to dribble; (*colore*) to smear, smudge.

sbia'dire *vi* (*anche*: ~**rsi**), *vt* to fade; **sbia'dito, a** *ag* faded; (*fig*) colourless, dull.

sbian'care *vt* to whiten; (*tessuto*) to bleach // *vi* (*impallidire*) to grow pale o white.

sbi'eco, a, chi, che *ag* (*storto*) squint, askew; di ~: **guardare qn di ~** (*fig*) to look askance at sb; **tagliare una stoffa di ~** to cut a material on the bias.

sbigot'tire *vt* to dismay, stun // *vi* (*anche:* ~**rsi**) to be dismayed.

sbilanci'are [zbilan'tʃare] *vt* to throw off balance; ~**rsi** *vr* (*perdere l'equilibrio*) to overbalance, lose one's balance; (*fig: compromettersi*) to compromise o.s.

sbirci'are [zbir'tʃare] *vt* to cast sidelong glances at, eye.

'sbirro *sm* (*peg*) cop.

sbizzar'rirsi [zbiddzar'rirsi] *vr* to indulge one's whims.

sbloc'care *vt* to unblock, free; (*freno*) to release; (*prezzi, affitti*) to decontrol.

sboc'care *vi*: ~ **in** (*fiume*) to flow into; (*strada*) to lead into; (*persona*) to come (out) into; (*fig: concludersi*) to end (up) in.

sboc'cato, a *ag* (*persona*) foul-mouthed; (*linguaggio*) foul.

sbocci'are [zbot'tʃare] *vi* (*fiore*) to bloom, open (out).

'sbocco, chi *sm* (*di fiume*) mouth; (*di strada*) end; (*di tubazione, COMM*) outlet; (*uscita: anche fig*) way out; **siamo in una situazione senza ~chi** there's no way out of this for us.

sbol'lire *vi* (*fig*) to cool down, calm down.

'sbornia *sf* (*fam*): **prendersi una ~** to get plastered.

sbor'sare *vt* (*denaro*) to pay out.

sbot'tare *vi*: ~ **in una risata/per la collera** to burst out laughing/explode with anger.

sbotto'nare *vt* to unbutton, undo.

sbracci'ato, a [zbrat'tʃato] *ag* (*camicia*) sleeveless; (*persona*) bare-armed.

sbrai'tare *vi* to yell, bawl.

sbra'nare *vt* to tear to pieces.

sbricio'lare [zbritʃo'lare] *vt*, ~**rsi** *vr* to crumble.

sbri'gare *vt* to deal with, get through; (*cliente*) to attend to, deal with; ~**rsi** *vr* to hurry (up); **sbriga'tivo, a** *ag* (*persona, modo*) quick, expeditious; (*giudizio*) hasty.

sbrindel'lato, a *ag* tattered, in tatters.

sbrodo'lare *vt* to stain, dirty.

'sbronzo, a ['zbrontso] *ag* (*fam: ubriaco*) tight // *sf*: **prendersi una ~a** to get tight *o* plastered.

sbu'care *vi* to come out, emerge; (*apparire improvvisamente*) to pop out (*o* up).

sbucci'are [zbut'tʃare] *vt* (*arancia, patata*) to peel; (*piselli*) to shell; ~**rsi un ginocchio** to graze one's knee.

sbudel'larsi *vr*: ~ **dalle risa** to split one's sides laughing.

sbuf'fare *vi* (*persona, cavallo*) to snort; (*: ansimare*) to puff, pant; (*treno*) to

puff; **'sbuffo** *sm* (*di aria, fumo, vapore*) puff; **maniche a sbuffo** puff(ed) sleeves.

'scabbia *sf* (*MED*) scabies *sg*.

sca'broso, a *ag* (*fig: difficile*) difficult, thorny; (*: imbarazzante*) embarrassing; (*: sconcio*) indecent.

scacchi'era [skak'kjɛra] *sf* chessboard.

scacci'are [skat'tʃare] *vt* to chase away *o* out, drive away *o* out.

'scacco, chi *sm* (*pezzo del gioco*) chessman; (*quadretto di scacchiera*) square; (*fig*) setback, reverse; ~**chi** *smpl* (*gioco*) chess *sg*; **a ~chi** (*tessuto*) check(ed); **scacco'matto** *sm* checkmate.

sca'dente *ag* shoddy, of poor quality.

sca'denza [ska'dɛntsa] *sf* (*di cambiale, contratto*) maturity; (*di passaporto*) expiry date; **a breve/lunga ~** short-/long-term; **data di ~** expiry date.

sca'dere *vi* (*contratto etc*) to expire; (*debito*) to fall due; (*valore, forze, peso*) to decline, go down.

sca'fandro *sm* (*di palombaro*) diving suit; (*di astronauta*) space-suit.

scaf'fale *sm* shelf; (*mobile*) set of shelves.

'scafo *sm* (*NAUT, AER*) hull.

scagio'nare [skadʒo'nare] *vt* to exonerate, free from blame.

'scaglia ['skaʎʎa] *sf* (*ZOOL*) scale; (*scheggia*) chip, flake.

scagli'are [skaʎ'ʎare] *vt* (*lanciare: anche fig*) to hurl, fling; ~**rsi** *vr*: ~**rsi su** *o* **contro** to hurl *o* fling o.s. at; (*fig*) to rail at.

scaglio'nare [skaʎʎo'nare] *vt* (*pagamenti*) to space out, spread out; (*MIL*) to echelon; **scagli'one** *sm* echelon; (*GEO*) terrace; **a scaglioni in groups.**

'scala *sf* (*a gradini etc*) staircase, stairs *pl*; (*a pioli, di corda*) ladder; (*MUS, GEO, di colori, valori, fig*) scale; ~ *sfpl* (*scalinata*) stairs; **su vasta ~/~ ridotta** on a large/small scale; ~ **a libretto** stepladder; ~ **mobile** escalator; (*ECON*) ~ **mobile** (**dei salari**) index-linked pay scale.

sca'lare *vt* (*ALPINISMO, muro*) to climb, scale; (*debito*) to scale down, reduce; **sca'lata** *sf* scaling *q*, climbing *q*; (*arrampicata, fig*) climb; **scala'tore, 'trice** *sm/f* climber.

scalda'bagno [skalda'baɲɲo] *sm* water-heater.

scal'dare *vt* to heat; ~**rsi** *vr* to warm up, heat up; (*al fuoco, al sole*) to warm o.s.; (*fig*) to get excited.

scal'fire *vt* to scratch.

scali'nata *sf* staircase.

sca'lino *sm* (*anche fig*) step; (*di scala a pioli*) rung.

'scalo *sm* (*NAUT*) slipway; (*: porto d'approdo*) port of call; (*AER*) stopover; **fare ~ (a)** (*NAUT*) to call (at), put in (at); (*AER*) to land (at), make a stop (at); ~ **merci** (FERR) goods (Brit) o freight yard.

scalop'pina sf (CUC) escalope.

scal'pello sm chisel.

scal'pore sm noise, row; **far** ~ (notizia) to cause a sensation o a stir.

'**scaltro, a** ag cunning, shrewd.

scal'zare [skal'tsare] vt (albero) to bare the roots of; (muro, fig: autorità) to undermine.

'**scalzo, a** ['skaltso] ag barefoot.

scambi'are vt to exchange; (confondere): ~ qn/qc per to take o mistake sb/sth for; **mi hanno scambiato il cappello** they've given me the wrong hat.

scambi'evole ag mutual, reciprocal.

'**scambio** sm exchange; (FERR) points pl; **fare (uno)** ~ to make a swap.

scampa'gnata [skampaɲ'ɲata] sf trip to the country.

scampa'nare vi to peal.

scam'pare vt (salvare) to rescue, save; (evitare: morte, prigione) to escape // vi: ~ (a qc) to survive (sth), escape (sth); **scamparla bella** to have a narrow escape.

'**scampo** sm (salvezza) escape; (ZOOL) prawn; **cercare** ~ **nella fuga** to seek safety in flight.

'**scampolo** sm remnant.

scanala'tura sf (incavo) channel, groove.

scandagli'are [skandaʎ'ʎare] vt (NAUT) to sound; (fig) to sound out; to probe.

scandaliz'zare [skandalid'dzare] vt to shock, scandalize; ~**rsi** vr to be shocked.

'**scandalo** sm scandal.

Scandi'navia sf: **la** ~ Scandinavia; **scandi'navo, a** ag, sm/f Scandinavian.

scan'dire vt (versi) to scan; (parole) to articulate, pronounce distinctly; ~ **il tempo** (MUS) to beat time.

scan'nare vt (animale) to butcher, slaughter; (persona) to cut o slit the throat of.

'**scanno** sm seat, bench.

scansafa'tiche [skansafa'tike] sm/f inv idler, loafer.

scan'sare vt (rimuovere) to move (aside), shift; (schivare: schiaffo) to dodge; (sfuggire) to avoid; ~**rsi** vr to move aside.

scan'sia sf shelves pl; (per libri) bookcase.

'**scanso** sm: **a** ~ **di** in order to avoid, as a precaution against.

scanti'nato sm basement.

scanto'nare vi to turn the corner; (svignarsela) to sneak off.

scapes'trato, a ag dissolute.

'**scapito** sm (perdita) loss; (danno) damage, detriment; **a** ~ **di** to the detriment of.

'**scapola** sf shoulder blade.

'**scapolo** sm bachelor.

scappa'mento sm (AUT) exhaust.

scap'pare vi (fuggire) to escape; (andare via in fretta) to rush off; **lasciarsi** ~ **un'occasione** to let an opportunity go by; ~ **di prigione** to escape from prison; ~ **di mano** (oggetto) to slip out of one's hands; ~ **di mente a qn** to slip sb's mind; **mi scappò detto I** let it slip; **scap'pata** sf quick visit o call; **scappa'tella** sf escapade; **scappa'toia** sf way out.

scara'beo sm beetle.

scarabocchi'are [skarabok'kjare] vt to scribble, scrawl; **scara'bocchio** sm scribble, scrawl.

scara'faggio [skara'faddʒo] sm cockroach.

scaraven'tare vt to fling, hurl.

scarce'rare [skartʃe'rare] vt to release (from prison).

'**scarica, che** sf (di più armi) volley of shots; (di sassi, pugni) hail, shower; (ELETTR) discharge; ~ **di mitra** burst of machine-gun fire.

scari'care vt (merci, camion etc) to unload; (passeggeri) to set down, put off; (arma) to unload; (: sparare, ELETTR) to discharge; (sog: corso d'acqua) to empty, pour; (fig: liberare da un peso) to unburden, relieve; ~**rsi** vr (orologio) to run o wind down; (batteria, accumulatore) to go flat o dead; (fig: rilassarsi) to unwind; (: sfogarsi) to let off steam; **il fulmine si scaricò su un albero** the lightning struck a tree; **scarica'tore** sm loader; (di porto) docker.

'**scarico, a, chi, che** ag unloaded; (orologio) run down; (accumulatore) dead, flat // sm (di merci, materiali) unloading; (di immondizie) dumping, tipping (Brit); (: luogo) rubbish dump; (TECN: deflusso) draining; (: dispositivo) drain; (AUT) exhaust.

scar'latto, a ag scarlet.

'**scarno, a** ag thin, bony.

'**scarpa** sf shoe; ~**e da ginnastica/tennis** gym/tennis shoes.

scar'pata sf escarpment.

scarseggi'are [skarsed'dʒare] vi to be scarce; ~ **di** to be short of, lack.

scar'sezza [skar'settsa] sf scarcity, lack.

'**scarso, a** ag (insufficiente) insufficient, meagre; (povero: annata) poor, lean; (INS: voto) poor; ~ **di** lacking in; **3 chili** ~**i** just under 3 kilos, barely 3 kilos.

scarta'mento sm (FERR) gauge; ~ **normale/ridotto** standard/narrow gauge.

scar'tare vt (pacco) to unwrap; (idea) to reject; (MIL) to declare unfit for military service; (carte da gioco) to discard; (CALCIO) to dodge (past) // vi to swerve.

'**scarto** sm (cosa scartata, anche COMM) reject; (di veicolo) swerve; (differenza) gap, difference.

scassi'nare vt to break, force.

'scasso sm vedi **furto**.

scate'nare vt (fig) to incite, stir up; ~**rsi** vr (temporale) to break; (rivolta) to break out; (persona: infuriarsi) to rage.

'scatola sf box; (di latta) tin (Brit), can; **cibi in** ~ tinned (Brit) o canned foods; ~ **cranica** cranium.

scat'tare vt (fotografia) to take // vi (congegno, molla etc) to be released; (balzare) to spring up; (SPORT) to put on a spurt; (fig: per l'ira) to fly into a rage; ~ **in piedi** to spring to one's feet.

'scatto sm (dispositivo) release; (: di arma da fuoco) trigger mechanism; (rumore) click; (balzo) jump, start; (SPORT) spurt; (fig: di ira etc) fit; (: di stipendio) increment; **di** ~ suddenly.

scatu'rire vi to gush, spring.

scaval'care vt (ostacolo) to pass (o climb) over; (fig) to get ahead of, overtake.

sca'vare vt (terreno) to dig; (legno) to hollow out; (pozzo, galleria) to bore; (città sepolta etc) to excavate.

'scavo sm excavating q; excavation.

'scegliere ['ʃeʎʎere] vt to choose, select.

sce'icco, chi [ʃe'ikko] sm sheik.

scelle'rato, a [ʃelle'rato] ag wicked, evil.

scel'lino [ʃel'lino] sm shilling.

'scelto, a ['ʃelto] pp di **scegliere** // ag (gruppo) carefully selected; (frutta, verdura) choice, top quality; (MIL: specializzato) crack cpd, highly skilled // sf choice; selection; **di prima** ~**a** top grade o quality; **frutta o formaggi a** ~**a** choice of fruit or cheese.

sce'mare [ʃe'mare] vt, vi to diminish.

'scemo, a ['ʃemo] ag stupid, silly.

'scempio ['ʃempjo] sm slaughter, massacre; (fig) ruin; **far** ~ **di** (fig) to play havoc with, ruin.

'scena ['ʃena] sf (gen) scene; (palcoscenico) stage; **le** ~**e** (fig: teatro) the stage; **fare una** ~ to make a scene; **andare in** ~ to be staged o put on o performed; **mettere in** ~ to stage.

sce'nario [ʃe'narjo] sm scenery; (di film) scenario.

sce'nata [ʃe'nata] sf row, scene.

'scendere ['ʃendere] vi to go (o come) down; (strada, sole) to go down; (notte) to fall; (passeggero: fermarsi) to get out, alight; (fig: temperatura, prezzi) to go o come down, fall, drop // vi (scale, pendio) to go (o come) down; ~ **dalle scale** to go (o come) down the stairs; ~ **dal treno** to get off o out of the train; ~ **dalla macchina** to get out of the car; ~ **da cavallo** to dismount, get off one's horse.

'scenico, a, ci, che ['ʃeniko] ag stage cpd, scenic.

scervel'lato, a [ʃervel'lato] ag feather-brained, scatterbrained.

'sceso, a ['ʃeso] pp di **scendere**.

'scettico, a, ci, che ['ʃettiko] ag sceptical.

'scettro ['ʃettro] sm sceptre.

'scheda ['skeda] sf (index) card; ~ **elettorale** ballot paper; ~ **perforata** punch card; **sche'dare** vt (dati) to file; (libri) to catalogue; (registrare: anche POLIZIA) to put on one's files; **sche'dario** sm file; (mobile) filing cabinet.

'scheggia, ge ['skeddʒa] sf splinter, sliver.

'scheletro ['skeletro] sm skeleton.

'schema, i ['skema] sm (diagramma) diagram, sketch; (progetto, abbozzo) outline, plan.

'scherma ['skerma] sf fencing.

scher'maglia [sker'maʎʎa] sf (fig) skirmish.

'schermo ['skermo] sm shield, screen; (CINEMA, TV) screen.

scher'nire [sker'nire] vt to mock, sneer at; **'scherno** sm mockery, derision.

scher'zare [sker'tsare] vi to joke.

'scherzo ['skertso] sm joke; (tiro) trick; (MUS) scherzo; **è uno** ~! (una cosa facile) it's child's play!, it's easy!; **per** ~ in jest; for a joke o a laugh; **fare un brutto** ~ **a qn** to play a nasty trick on sb; **scher'zoso, a** ag (tono, gesto) playful; (osservazione) facetious; **è un tipo scherzoso** he likes a joke.

schiaccia'noci [skjattʃa'notʃi] sm inv nutcracker.

schiacci'are [skjat'tʃare] vt (dito) to crush; (noci) to crack; ~ **un pisolino** to have a nap.

schiaffeggi'are [skjaffed'dʒare] vt to slap.

schi'affo ['skjaffo] sm slap.

schiamaz'zare [skjamat'tsare] vi to squawk, cackle.

schian'tare [skjan'tare] vt to break, tear apart; ~**rsi** vr to break (up), shatter; **schi'anto** sm (rumore) crash; tearing sound; **è uno schianto!** (fam) it's (o he's o she's) terrific!; **di schianto** all of a sudden.

schia'rire [skja'rire] vt to lighten, make lighter // vi (anche: ~**rsi**) to grow lighter; (tornar sereno) to clear, brighten up; ~**rsi la voce** to clear one's throat.

schiavitù [skjavi'tu] sf slavery.

schi'avo, a [skja'vo] sm/f slave.

schi'ena ['skjena] sf (ANAT) back; **schie'nale** sm (di sedia) back.

schi'era [skjera] sf (MIL) rank; (gruppo) group, band.

schiera'mento [skjera'mento] sm (MIL, SPORT) formation; (fig) alliance.

schie'rare [skje'rare] vt (esercito) to line up, draw up, marshal; ~**rsi** vr to line up; (fig): ~**rsi con** o **dalla parte di/**

contro qn to side with/oppose sb.
schi'etto, a ['skjɛtto] *ag* (*puro*) pure;
(*fig*) frank, straightforward; sincere.

'schifo ['skifo] *sm* disgust; **fare ~** (*essere fatto male, dare pessimi risultati*) to be awful; **mi fa ~** it makes me sick, it's disgusting; **quel libro è uno ~** that book's rotten; **schi'foso, a** *ag* disgusting, revolting; (*molto scadente*) rotten, lousy.

schioc'care [skjɔk'kare] *vt* (*frusta*) to crack; (*dita*) to snap; (*lingua*) to click; **~ le labbra** to smack one's lips.

schi'udere ['skjudere] *vt*, **~rsi** *vr* to open.

schi'uma ['skjuma] *sf* foam; (*di sapone*) lather; (*di latte*) froth; (*fig: feccia*) scum; **schiu'mare** *vt* to skim // *vi* to foam.

schi'uso, a ['skjuso] *pp di* **schiudere**.

schi'vare [ski'vare] *vt* to dodge, avoid.

'schivo, a ['skivo] *ag* (*ritroso*) stand-offish, reserved; (*timido*) shy.

schiz'zare [skit'tsare] *vt* (*spruzzare*) to spurt, squirt; (*sporcare*) to splash, spatter; (*fig: abbozzare*) to sketch // *vi* to spurt, squirt; (*saltar fuori*) to dart up (*o off etc*).

schizzi'noso, a [skittsi'noso] *ag* fussy, finicky.

'schizzo ['skittso] *sm* ·(*di liquido*) spurt; splash, spatter; (*abbozzo*) sketch.

sci [ʃi] *sm* (*attrezzo*) ski; (*attività*) skiing; **~ nautico** water-skiing.

'scia, *pl* **'scie** ['ʃia] *sf* (*di imbarcazione*) wake; (*di profumo*) trail.

scià [ʃa] *sm inv* shah.

sci'abola ['ʃabola] *sf* sabre.

scia'callo [ʃa'kallo] *sm* jackal.

sciac'quare [ʃak'kware] *vt* to rinse.

scia'gura [ʃa'gura] *sf* disaster, calamity; misfortune; **sciagu'rato, a** *ag* unfortunate; (*malvagio*) wicked.

scialac'quare [ʃalak'kware] *vt* to squander.

scia'lare [ʃa'lare] *vi* to lead a life of luxury.

sci'albo, a ['ʃalbo] *ag* pale, dull; (*fig*) dull, colourless.

sci'alle ['ʃalle] *sm* shawl.

scia'luppa [ʃa'luppa] *sf* (*NAUT*) sloop; (*anche: ~ di salvataggio*) lifeboat.

sci'ame ['ʃame] *sm* swarm.

scian'cato, a [ʃan'kato] *ag* lame; (*mobile*) rickety.

sci'are [ʃi'are] *vi* to ski.

sci'arpa ['ʃarpa] *sf* scarf; (*fascia*) sash.

scia'tore, 'trice [ʃia'tore] *sm/f* skier.

sci'atto, a ['ʃatto] *ag* (*persona: nell'aspetto*) slovenly, unkempt; (: *nel lavoro*) sloppy, careless.

scien'tifico, a, ci, che [ʃen'tifiko] *ag* scientific.

sci'enza ['ʃɛntsa] *sf* science; (*sapere*) knowledge; **~e** *sfpl* (*INS*) science *sg*; **~e**

naturali natural sciences; **scienzi'ato, a** *sm/f* scientist.

'scimmia ['ʃimmja] *sf* monkey; **scimmiot'tare** *vt* to ape, mimic.

scimpanzé [ʃimpan'tse] *sm inv* chimpanzee.

scimu'nito, a [ʃimu'nito] *ag* silly, idiotic.

'scindere ['ʃindere] *vt*, **~rsi** *vr* to split (up).

scin'tilla [ʃin'tilla] *sf* spark; **scintil'lare** *vi* to spark; (*acqua, occhi*) to sparkle.

scioc'chezza [ʃok'kettsa] *sf* stupidity *q*; stupid *o* foolish thing; **dire ~e** to talk nonsense.

sci'occo, a, chi, che ['ʃɔkko] *ag* stupid, foolish.

sci'ogliere ['ʃɔʎʎere] *vt* (*nodo*) to untie; (*capelli*) to loosen; (*persona, animale*) to untie, release; (*fig: persona*): **~ da** to release from; (*neve*) to melt; (*nell'acqua: zucchero etc*) to dissolve; (*fig: mistero*) to solve; (*porre fine a: contratto*) to cancel; (: *società, matrimonio*) to dissolve; (: *riunione*) to bring to an end; **~rsi** *vr* to loosen, come untied; to melt; to dissolve; (*assemblea etc*) to break up; **~ i muscoli** to limber up.

sciol'tezza [ʃol'tettsa] *sf* agility; suppleness; ease.

sci'olto, a ['ʃɔlto] *pp di* **sciogliere** // *ag* loose; (*agile*) agile, nimble; supple; (*disinvolto*) free and easy; **versi ~i** (*POESIA*) blank verse.

sciope'rante [ʃope'rante] *sm/f* striker.

sciope'rare [ʃope'rare] *vi* to strike, go on strike.

sci'opero ['ʃopero] *sm* strike; **fare ~** to strike; **~ bianco** work-to-rule (*Brit*); **slowdown** (*US*); **~ selvaggio** wildcat strike; **~ a singhiozzo** on-off strike.

sci'rocco [ʃi'rokko] *sm* sirocco.

sci'roppo [ʃi'roppo] *sm* syrup.

'scisma, i ['ʃizma] *sm* (*REL*) schism.

scissi'one [ʃis'sjone] *sf* (*anche fig*) split, division; (*FISICA*) fission.

'scisso, a ['ʃisso] *pp di* **scindere**.

sciu'pare [ʃu'pare] *vt* (*abito, libro, appetito*) to spoil, ruin; (*tempo, denaro*) to waste; **~rsi** *vr* to get spoilt *o* ruined; (*rovinarsi la salute*) to ruin one's health.

scivo'lare [ʃivo'lare] *vi* to slide *o* glide along; (*involontariamente*) to slip, slide; **'scivolo** *sm* slide; (*TECN*) chute.

scle'rosi *sf* sclerosis.

scoc'care *vt* (*freccia*) to shoot // *vi* (*guizzare*) to shoot up; (*battere: ora*) to strike.

scocci'are [skot'tʃare] (*fam*) *vt* to bother, annoy; **~rsi** *vr* to be bothered *o* annoyed.

sco'della *sf* bowl.

scodinzo'lare [skodintso'lare] *vi* to wag its tail.

scogli'era [skoʎ'ʎɛra] *sf* reef; cliff.

'scoglio ['skɔʎʎo] *sm* (*al mare*) rock.

scoi'attolo *sm* squirrel.

sco'lare *ag*: età ~ school age // *vt* to drain // *vi* to drip.

scola'resca *sf* schoolchildren *pl*, pupils *pl*.

sco'laro, a *sm/f* pupil, schoolboy/girl.

sco'lastico, a, ci, che *ag* school *cpd*; scholastic.

scol'lare *vt* (*staccare*) to unstick; ~**rsi** *vr* to come unstuck.

scolla'tura *sf* neckline.

'scolo *sm* drainage.

scolo'rire *vt* to fade; to discolour // *vi* (*anche:* ~**rsi**) to fade; to become discoloured; (*impallidire*) to turn pale.

scol'pire *vt* to carve, sculpt.

scombi'nare *vt* to mess up, upset.

scombusso'lare *vt* to upset.

scom'messo, a *pp di* **scommettere** // *sf* bet, wager.

scom'mettere *vt, vi* to bet.

scomo'dare *vt* to trouble, bother; to disturb; ~**rsi** *vr* to put o.s. out; ~**rsi a fare** to go to the bother *o* trouble of doing.

'scomodo, a *ag* uncomfortable; (*sistemazione, posto*) awkward, inconvenient.

scompa'rire *vi* (*sparire*) to disappear, vanish; (*fig*) to be insignificant; **scom'parso, a** *pp di* **scomparire** // *sf* disappearance.

scomparti'mento *sm* (*FERR*) compartment.

scom'parto *sm* compartment, division.

scompigli'are [skompiʎ'ʎare] *vt* (*cassetto, capelli*) to mess up, disarrange; (*fig: piani*) to upset; **scom'piglio** *sm* mess, confusion.

scom'porre *vt* (*parola, numero*) to break up; (*CHIM*) to decompose; **scomporsi** *vr* (*fig*) to get upset, lose one's composure; **scom'posto, a** *pp di* **scomporre** // *ag* (*gesto*) unseemly; (*capelli*) ruffled, dishevelled.

sco'munica *sf* excommunication.

scomuni'care *vt* to excommunicate.

sconcer'tare [skontʃer'tare] *vt* to disconcert, bewilder.

'sconcio, a, ci, ce ['skontʃo] *ag* (*osceno*) indecent, obscene // *sm* (*cosa riprovevole, mal fatta*) disgrace.

sconfes'sare *vt* to renounce, disavow; to repudiate.

scon'figgere [skon'fiddʒere] *vt* to defeat, overcome.

sconfi'nare *vi* to cross the border; (*in proprietà privata*) to trespass; (*fig*): ~ **da** to stray *o* digress from; **sconfi'nato, a** *ag* boundless, unlimited.

scon'fitto, a *pp di* **sconfiggere** // *sf* defeat.

scon'forto *sm* despondency.

scongiu'rare [skondʒu'rare] *vt* (*implorare*) to entreat, beseech, implore; (*eludere: pericolo*) to ward off, avert; **scongi'uro** *sm* entreaty; (*esorcismo*) exorcism; **fare gli scongiuri** to touch wood (*Brit*), knock on wood (*US*).

scon'nesso, a *ag* (*fig: discorso*) incoherent, rambling.

sconosci'uto, a [skonof'ʃuto] *ag* unknown; new, strange // *sm/f* stranger; unknown person.

sconquas'sare *vt* to shatter, smash.

sconside'rato, a *ag* thoughtless, rash.

sconsigli'are [skonsiʎ'ʎare] *vt*: ~ **qc a qn** to advise sb against sth; ~ **qn dal fare qc** to advise sb not to do *o* against doing sth.

sconso'lato, a *ag* inconsolable; desolate.

scon'tare *vt* (*COMM: detrarre*) to deduct; (*: debito*) to pay off; (*: cambiale*) to discount; (*pena*) to serve; (*colpa, errori*) to pay for, suffer for.

scon'tato, a *ag* (*previsto*) foreseen, taken for granted; **dare per** ~ **che** to take it for granted that.

scon'tento, a *ag*: ~ (**di**) discontented *o* dissatisfied (with) // *sm* discontent, dissatisfaction.

'sconto *sm* discount; **fare uno** ~ to give a discount.

scon'trarsi *vr* (*treni etc*) to crash, collide; (*venire ad uno scontro, fig*) to clash; ~ **con** to crash into, collide with.

scon'trino *sm* ticket.

'scontro *sm* clash, encounter; crash, collision.

scon'troso, a *ag* sullen, surly; (*permaloso*) touchy.

sconveni'ente *ag* unseemly, improper.

scon'volgere [skon'vɔldʒere] *vt* to throw into confusion, upset; (*turbare*) to shake, disturb, upset; **scon'volto, a** *pp di* **sconvolgere**.

'scopa *sf* broom; (*CARTE*) Italian card game; **sco'pare** *vt* to sweep.

sco'perto, a *pp di* **scoprire** // *ag* uncovered; (*capo*) uncovered, bare; (*macchina*) open; (*MIL*) exposed, without cover; (*conto*) overdrawn // *sf* discovery.

'scopo *sm* aim, purpose; **a che** ~? what for?

scoppi'are *vi* (*spaccarsi*) to burst; (*esplodere*) to explode; (*fig*) to break out; ~ **in pianto** *o* **a piangere** to burst out crying; ~ **dalle risa** *o* **dal ridere** to split one's sides laughing.

scoppiet'tare *vi* to crackle.

'scoppio *sm* explosion; (*di tuono, arma etc*) crash, bang; (*fig: di risa, ira*) fit, outburst; (*: di guerra*) outbreak; **a** ~ **ritardato** delayed-action.

sco'prire *vt* to discover; (*liberare da ciò che copre*) to uncover; (*: monumento*) to unveil; ~**rsi** *vr* to put on lighter clothes; (*fig*) to give o.s. away.

scoraggi'are [skorad'dʒare] *vt* to discourage; **~rsi** *vr* to become discouraged, lose heart.

scorcia'toia [skortʃa'toja] *sf* short cut.

'scorcio ['skortʃo] *sm* (ARTE) foreshortening; (*di secolo, periodo*) end, close.

scor'dare *vt* to forget; **~rsi** *vr:* **~rsi di qc/di fare** to forget sth/to do.

'scorgere ['skordʒere] *vt* to make out, distinguish, see.

sco'ria *sf* (*di metalli*) slag; (*vulcanica*) scoria; **~e radioattive** (FISICA) radioactive waste *sg*.

'scorno *sm* ignominy, disgrace.

scorpacci'ata [skorpat'tʃata] *sf:* **fare una ~ (di)** to stuff o.s. (with), eat one's fill (of).

scorpi'one *sm* scorpion; (*dello zodiaco*): **S~** Scorpio.

scorraz'zare [skorrat'tsare] *vi* to run about.

'scorrere *vt* (*giornale, lettera*) to run *o* skim through // *vi* (*liquido, fiume*) to run, flow; (*fune*) to run; (*cassetto, porta*) to slide easily; (*tempo*) to pass (by).

scor'retto, a *ag* incorrect; (*sgarbato*) impolite; (*sconveniente*) improper.

scor'revole *ag* (*porta*) sliding; (*fig: stile*) fluent, flowing.

scorri'banda *sf* (MIL) raid; (*escursione*) trip, excursion.

'scorso, a *pp di* **scorrere** // *ag* last // *sf* quick look, glance.

scor'soio, a *ag:* **nodo ~** noose.

'scorta *sf* (*di personalità, convoglio*) escort; (*provvista*) supply, stock; **scor'tare** *vt* to escort.

scor'tese *ag* discourteous, rude; **scorte'sia** *sf* discourtesy, rudeness; (*azione*) discourtesy.

scorti'care *vt* to skin.

'scorto, a *pp di* **scorgere**.

'scorza ['skordza] *sf* (*di albero*) bark; (*di agrumi*) peel, skin.

sco'sceso, a [skoʃ'ʃeso] *ag* steep.

'scosso, a *pp di* **scuotere** // *ag* (*turbato*) shaken, upset // *sf* jerk, jolt, shake; (ELETTR, *fig*) shock.

scos'tante *ag* (*fig*) off-putting (*Brit*), unpleasant.

scos'tare *vt* to move (away), shift; **~rsi** *vr* to move away.

scostu'mato, a *ag* immoral, dissolute.

scot'tare *vt* (*ustionare*) to burn; (: *con liquido bollente*) to scald // *vi* to burn; (*caffè*) to be too hot; **scotta'tura** *sf* burn; scald.

'scotto, a *ag* overcooked // *sm* (*fig*): **pagare lo ~ (di)** to pay the penalty (for).

sco'vare *vt* to drive out, flush out; (*fig*) to discover.

'Scozia ['skɔttsja] *sf:* **la ~** Scotland; **scoz'zese** *ag* Scottish // *sm/f* Scot.

scredi'tare *vt* to discredit.

screpo'lare *vt*, **~rsi** *vr* to crack; **screpola'tura** *sf* cracking *q*; crack.

screzi'ato, a [skret'tsjato] *ag* streaked.

'screzio ['skrɛttsjo] *sm* disagreement.

scricchio'lare [skrikkjo'lare] *vi* to creak, squeak.

'scricciolo ['skrittʃolo] *sm* wren.

'scrigno ['skriɲɲo] *sm* casket.

scrimina'tura *sf* parting.

'scritto, a *pp di* **scrivere** // *ag* written // *sm* writing; (*lettera*) letter, note // *sf* inscription; **~i** *smpl* (*letterari etc*) writing *sg*; **per o in ~** in writing.

scrit'toio *sm* writing desk.

scrit'tore, 'trice *sm/f* writer.

scrit'tura *sf* writing; (COMM) entry; (*contratto*) contract; (REL): **la Sacra S~** the Scriptures *pl*; **~e** *sfpl* (COMM) accounts, books.

scrittu'rare *vt* (TEATRO, CINEMA) to sign up, engage; (COMM) to enter.

scriva'nia *sf* desk.

scri'vente *sm/f* writer.

'scrivere *vt* to write; **come si scrive?** how is it spelt?, how do you write it?

scroc'cone, a *sm/f* scrounger.

'scrofa *sf* (ZOOL) sow.

scrol'lare *vt* to shake; **~rsi** *vr* (*anche fig*) to give o.s. a shake; **~ le spalle/il capo** to shrug one's shoulders/shake one's head.

scrosci'are [skroʃ'ʃare] *vi* (*pioggia*) to pour down, pelt down; (*torrente, fig: applausi*) to thunder, roar; **'scroscio** *sm* pelting; thunder, roar; (*di applausi*) burst.

scros'tare *vt* (*intonaco*) to scrape off, strip; **~rsi** *vr* to peel off, flake off.

'scrupolo *sm* scruple; (*meticolosità*) care, conscientiousness.

scru'tare *vt* to scrutinize; (*intenzioni, causa*) to examine, scrutinize.

scruti'nare *vt* (*voti*) to count; **scru'tinio** *sm* (*votazione*) ballot; (*insieme delle operazioni*) poll; (INS) (*meeting for*) assignment of marks at end of a term or year.

scu'cire [sku'tʃire] *vt* (*orlo etc*) to unpick, undo.

scude'ria *sf* stable.

scu'detto *sm* (SPORT) (championship) shield; (*distintivo*) badge.

'scudo *sm* shield.

scul'tore, 'trice *sm/f* sculptor.

scul'tura *sf* sculpture.

scu'ola *sf* school; **~ elementare/materna/media** primary (*Brit*) *o* grade (*US*)/nursery/secondary (*Brit*) *o* high (*US*) school; **~ guida** driving school; **~ dell'obbligo** compulsory education; **~e serali** evening classes, night school *sg*; **~ tecnica** technical college.

scu'otere *vt* to shake; **~rsi** *vr* to jump, be startled; (*fig: muoversi*) to rouse o.s., stir o.s.; (: *turbarsi*) to be shaken.

'**scure** *sf* axe.

'**scuro, a** *ag* dark; (*fig: espressione*) grim // *sm* darkness; dark colour; (*imposta*) (window) shutter; **verde/rosso** *etc* ~ dark green/red *etc*.

scur'rile *ag* scurrilous.

'**scusa** *sf* excuse; ~**e** *sfpl* apology *sg*, apologies; **chiedere** ~ **a qn (per)** to apologize to sb (for); **chiedo** ~ I'm sorry; (*disturbando etc*) excuse me.

scu'sare *vt* to excuse; ~**rsi** *vr*: ~**rsi (di)** to apologize (for); (**mi**) **scusi** I'm sorry; (*per richiamare l'attenzione*) excuse me.

sde'gnato, a [zdeɲ'ɲato] *ag* indignant, angry.

'**sdegno** ['zdeɲɲo] *sm* scorn, disdain; **sde'gnoso, a** *ag* scornful, disdainful.

sdoga'nare *vt* (*merci*) to clear through customs.

sdolci'nato, a [zdoltʃi'nato] *ag* mawkish, oversentimental.

sdoppi'are *vt* (*dividere*) to divide *o* split in two.

sdrai'arsi *vr* to stretch out, lie down.

'**sdraio** *sm*: **sedia a** ~ deck chair.

sdruccio'levole [zdruttʃo'levole] *ag* slippery.

se ◆ *pronome vedi* **si**

◆ *cong* **1** (*condizionale, ipotetica*) if; ~ **nevica non vengo** I won't come if it snows; **sarei rimasto** ~ **me l'avessero chiesto** I would have stayed if they'd asked me; **non puoi fare altro** ~ **non telefonare** all you can do is phone; ~ **mai if, if ever**; **siamo noi** ~ **mai che le siamo grati it is we who should be grateful to you**; ~ **no** (*altrimenti*) or (else), otherwise **2** (*in frasi dubitative, interrogative indirette*) if, whether; **non so** ~ **scrivere o telefonare** I don't know whether *o* if I should write or phone.

sé *pronome* (*gen*) oneself; (*esso, essa, lui, lei, loro*) itself; himself; herself; themselves; ~ **stesso(a)** *pronome* oneself; itself; himself; herself; ~ **stessi(e)** *pronome pl* themselves.

seb'bene *cong* although, though.

sec. *abbr* (= *secolo*) c.

'**secca** *sf vedi* **secco**.

sec'care *vt* to dry; (*prosciugare*) to dry up; (*fig: importunare*) to annoy, bother // *vi* to dry; to dry up; ~**rsi** *vr* to dry; to dry up; (*fig*) to grow annoyed; **secca'tura** *sf* (*fig*) bother *q*, trouble *q*.

'**secchia** ['sekkja] *sf* bucket, pail.

'**secco, a, chi, che** *ag* dry; (*fichi, pesce*) dried; (*foglie, ramo*) withered; (*magro: persona*) thin, skinny; (*fig: risposta, modo di fare*) curt, abrupt; (: *colpo*) clean, sharp // *sm* (*siccità*) drought // *sf* (*del mare*) shallows *pl*; **restarci** ~ (*fig: morire sul colpo*) to drop dead; **mettere in** ~ (*barca*) to beach;

rimanere in *o* **a** ~ (*NAUT*) to run aground; (*fig*) to be left in the lurch.

seco'lare *ag* age-old, centuries-old; (*laico, mondano*) secular.

'**secolo** *sm* century; (*epoca*) age.

se'conda *sf vedi* **secondo**.

secon'dario, a *ag* secondary.

se'condo, a *ag* second // *sm* second; (*di pranzo*) main course // *sf* (*AUT*) second (gear) // *prep* according to; (*nel modo prescritto*) in accordance with; ~ **me** in my opinion, to my mind; **di** ~**a classe** second-class; **di** ~**a mano** second-hand; **viaggiare in** ~**a** to travel second-class; **a** ~**a di** *prep* according to; in accordance with.

'**sedano** *sm* celery.

seda'tivo, a *ag, sm* sedative.

'**sede** *sf* seat; (*di ditta*) head office; (*di organizzazione*) headquarters *pl*; **in** ~ **di** (*in occasione di*) during; ~ **sociale** registered office.

seden'tario, a *ag* sedentary.

se'dere *vi* to sit, be seated; ~**rsi** *vr* to sit down // *sm* (*deretano*) behind, bottom.

'**sedia** *sf* chair.

sedi'cente [sedi'tʃente] *ag* self-styled.

'**sedici** ['seditʃi] *num* sixteen.

se'dile *sm* seat; (*panchina*) bench.

sedizi'one [sedit'tsjone] *sf* revolt, rebellion.

se'dotto, a *pp di* **sedurre**.

sedu'cente [sedu'tʃente] *ag* seductive; (*proposta*) very attractive.

se'durre *vt* to seduce.

se'duta *sf* session, sitting; (*riunione*) meeting; ~ **spiritica** séance; ~ **stante** (*fig*) immediately.

seduzi'one [sedut'tsjone] *sf* seduction; (*fascino*) charm, appeal.

'**sega, ghe** *sf* saw.

'**segale** *sf* rye.

se'gare *vt* to saw; (*recidere*) to saw off; **sega'tura** *sf* (*residuo*) sawdust.

'**seggio** ['seddʒo] *sm* seat; ~ **elettorale** polling station.

'**seggiola** ['seddʒola] *sf* chair; **seggio'lino** *sm* seat; (*per bambini*) child's chair; **seggio'lone** *sm* (*per bambini*) highchair.

seggio'via [seddʒo'via] *sf* chairlift.

seghe'ria [sege'ria] *sf* sawmill.

segna'lare [seɲɲa'lare] *vt* (*manovra etc*) to signal; to indicate; (*annunciare*) to announce; to report; (*fig: far conoscere*) to point out; (: *persona*) to single out; ~**rsi** *vr* (*distinguersi*) to distinguish o.s.

se'gnale [seɲ'ɲale] *sm* signal; (*cartello*): ~ **stradale** road sign; ~ **d'allarme** alarm; (*FERR*) communication cord; ~ **orario** (*RADIO*) time signal; **segna'letica** (*RADIO*) signalling, signposting; segnaletica stradale road signs *pl*.

se'gnare [seɲ'ɲare] *vt* to mark; (*prendere nota*) to note; (*indicare*) to indicate, mark; (*SPORT: goal*) to score; ~**rsi** *vr* (*REL*) to make the sign of the cross, cross o.s.

'**segno** ['seɲɲo] *sm* sign; (*impronta, contrassegno*) mark; (*limite*) limit, bounds *pl*; (*bersaglio*) target; **fare** ~ **di sì/no** to nod (one's head)/shake one's head; **fare** ~ **a qn di fermarsi** to motion (to) sb to stop; **cogliere** *o* **colpire nel** ~ (*fig*) to hit the mark.

segre'gare *vt* to segregate, isolate; **segregazi'one** *sf* segregation.

segre'tario, a *sm/f* secretary; ~ **comunale** town clerk; ~ **di Stato** Secretary of State.

segre'teria *sf* (*di ditta, scuola*) (secretary's) office; (*d'organizzazione internazionale*) secretariat; (*POL etc: carica*) office of Secretary; ~ **telefonica** answering service.

segre'tezza [segre'tettsa] *sf* secrecy.

se'greto, a *ag* secret // *sm* secret; **secrecy** *q*; **in** ~ in secret, secretly.

segu'ace [se'gwatʃe] *sm/f* follower, disciple.

segu'ente *ag* following, next.

segu'ire *vt* to follow; (*frequentare: corso*) to attend // *vi* to follow; (*continuare: testo*) to continue.

segui'tare *vt* to continue, carry on with // *vi* to continue, carry on.

'**seguito** *sm* (*scorta*) suite, retinue; (*discepoli*) followers *pl*; (*favore*) following; (*serie*) sequence, series *sg*; (*continuazione*) continuation; (*consequenza*) result; **di** ~ **a** at a stretch, on end; **in** ~ later on; **in** ~ **a**, **a** ~ **di** following; (*a causa di*) as a result of, owing to.

'**sei** *vb vedi* **essere** // *num* six.

sei'cento [sei'tʃɛnto] *num* six hundred // *sm*: **il S**~ the seventeenth century.

selci'ato [sel'tʃato] *sm* cobbled surface.

selezio'nare [selettsjo'nare] *vt* to select.

selezi'one [selet'tsjone] *sf* selection.

'**sella** *sf* saddle; **sel'lare** *vt* to saddle.

selvag'gina [selvad'dʒina] *sf* (*animali*) game.

sel'vaggio, a, gi, ge [sel'vaddʒo] *ag* wild; (*tribù*) savage, uncivilized; (*fig*) savage, brutal // *sm/f* savage.

sel'vatico, a, ci, che *ag* wild.

se'maforo *sm* (*AUT*) traffic lights *pl*.

sem'brare *vi* to seem // *vb impers*: **sembra che** it seems that; **mi sembra che** it seems to me that; **I think (that)**; ~ **di essere** to seem to be.

'**seme** *sm* seed; (*sperma*) semen; (*CARTE*) suit.

se'mestre *sm* half-year, six-month period.

'**semi...** *prefisso* semi...; **semi'cerchio** *sm* semicircle; **semifi'nale** *sf* semifinal; **semi'freddo, a** *ag* (*CUC*) chilled // *sm* ice-cream cake.

'**semina** *sf* (*AGR*) sowing.

semi'nare *vt* to sow.

semi'nario *sm* seminar; (*REL*) seminary.

seminter'rato *sm* basement; (*appartamento*) basement flat.

se'mitico, a, ci, che *ag* semitic.

sem'mai = se mai; *vedi* se.

'semola *sf* bran; ~ **di grano duro** durum wheat.

semo'lino *sm* semolina.

'semplice ['semplitʃe] *ag* simple; (*di un solo elemento*) single; **semplice'mente** *av* simply; **semplicità** *sf* simplicity.

'sempre *av* always; (*ancora*) still; **posso** ~ **tentare** I can always *o* still try; **da** ~ always; **per** ~ forever; **una volta per** ~ once and for all; ~ **che** *cong* provided (that); ~ **più** more and more; ~ **meno** less and less.

sempre'verde *ag, sm o f* (*BOT*) evergreen.

'senape *sf* (*CUC*) mustard.

se'nato *sm* senate; **sena'tore, 'trice** *sm/f* senator.

'senno *sm* judgment, (common) sense; **col** ~ **di poi** with hindsight.

sennò *av* = se no; *vedi* se.

'seno *sm* (*ANAT: petto, mammella*) breast; (: *grembo, fig*) womb; (: *cavità*) sinus; (*GEO*) inlet, creek; (*MAT*) sine.

sen'sato, a *ag* sensible.

sensazio'nale [sensattsjo'nale] *ag* sensational.

sensazi'one [sensat'tsjone] *sf* feeling, sensation; **avere la** ~ **che** to have a feeling that; **fare** ~ to cause a sensation, create a stir.

sen'sibile *ag* sensitive; (*ai sensi*) perceptible; (*rilevante, notevole*) appreciable, noticeable; ~ **a** sensitive to; **sensibilità** *sf* sensitivity.

'senso *sm* (*FISIOL, istinto*) sense; (*impressione, sensazione*) feeling, sensation; (*significato*) meaning, sense; (*direzione*) direction; ~**i** *smpl* (*coscienza*) consciousness *sg*; (*sensualità*) senses; **ciò non ha** ~ that doesn't make sense; **fare** ~ **a** (*ripugnare*) to disgust, repel; ~ **comune** common sense; **in** ~ **orario/antiorario** clockwise/anticlockwise; **a** ~ **unico** (*strada*) one-way; "~ **vietato**" (*AUT*) "no entry".

sensu'ale *ag* sensual; sensuous; **sensualità** *sf* sensuality; sensuousness.

sen'tenza [sen'tɛntsa] *sf* (*DIR*) sentence; (*massima*) maxim; **sentenzi'are** *vi* (*DIR*) to pass judgment.

senti'ero *sm* path.

sentimen'tale *ag* sentimental; (*vita, avventura*) love *cpd*.

senti'mento *sm* feeling.

senti'nella *sf* sentry.

sen'tire *vt* (*percepire al tatto, fig*) to feel; (*udire*) to hear; (*ascoltare*) to listen to; (*odore*) to smell; (*avvertire con il gusto, assaggiare*) to taste // *vi:* ~ **di** (*avere sapore*) to taste of; (*avere odore*) to smell of; ~**rsi** *vr* (*uso reciproco*) to be in touch; ~**rsi bene/male** to feel well/unwell *o* ill; ~**rsi di fare qc** (*essere disposto*) to feel like doing sth.

sen'tito, a *ag* (*sincero*) sincere, warm; **per** ~ **dire** by hearsay.

'senza ['sɛntsa] *prep, cong* without; ~ **dir nulla** without saying a word; **fare** ~ **qc** to do without sth; ~ **di me** without me; ~ **che io lo sapessi** without me *o* my knowing; **senz'altro** of course, certainly; ~ **dubbio** no doubt; ~ **scrupoli** unscrupulous; ~ **amici** friendless.

sepa'rare *vt* to separate; (*dividere*) to divide; (*tenere distinto*) to distinguish; ~**rsi** *vr* (*coniugi*) to separate, part; (*amici*) to part, leave each other; ~**rsi da** (*coniuge*) to separate *o* part from; (*amico, socio*) to part company with; (*oggetto*) to part with; **sepa'rato, a** *ag* (*letti, conto etc*) separate; (*coniugi*) separated; **separazi'one** *sf* separation.

se'polcro *sm* sepulchre.

se'polto, a *pp di* **seppellire**.

seppel'lire *vt* to bury.

'seppia *sf* cuttlefish // *ag inv* sepia.

se'quenza [se'kwentsa] *sf* sequence.

seques'trare *vt* (*DIR*) to impound; (*rapire*) to kidnap; (*costringere in un luogo*) to keep, confine; **se'questro** *sm* (*DIR*) impoundment; **sequestro di persona** kidnapping.

'sera *sf* evening; **di** ~ in the evening; **domani** ~ tomorrow evening, tomorrow night; **se'rale** *ag* evening *cpd*; **se'rata** *sf* evening; (*ricevimento*) party.

ser'bare *vt* to keep; (*mettere da parte*) to put aside; ~ **rancore/odio verso qn** to bear sb a grudge/hate sb.

serba'toio *sm* tank; (*cisterna*) cistern.

'serbo *sm:* **mettere/tenere** *o* **avere in** ~ **qc** to put/keep sth aside.

se'reno, a *ag* (*tempo, cielo*) clear; (*fig*) serene, calm.

ser'gente [ser'dʒɛnte] *sm* (*MIL*) sergeant.

'serie *sf inv* (*successione*) series *inv*; (*gruppo, collezione: di chiavi etc*) set; (*SPORT*) division; league; (*COMM*): **modello di** ~/**fuori** ~ standard/custom-built model; **in** ~ in quick succession; (*COMM*) mass *cpd*.

serietà *sf* seriousness; reliability.

'serio, a *ag* serious; (*impiegato*) responsible, reliable; (*ditta, cliente*) reliable, dependable; **sul** ~ (*davvero*) really, truly; (*seriamente*) seriously, in earnest.

ser'mone *sm* sermon.

serpeggi'are [serped'dʒare] *vi* to wind; (*fig*) to spread.

ser'pente *sm* snake; ~ **a sonagli** rattlesnake.

'serra *sf* greenhouse; hothouse.

ser'randa *sf* roller shutter.

ser'rare *vt* to close, shut; (*a chiave*) to lock; (*stringere*) to tighten; (*premere: nemico*) to close in on; ~ **i pugni/i denti** to clench one's fists/teeth; ~ **le file** to close ranks.

serra'tura *sf* lock.

'serva *sf vedi* **servo**.

ser'vire *vt* to serve; (*clienti: al ristorante*) to wait on; (: *al negozio*) to serve, attend to; (*fig: giovare*) to aid, help; (*CARTE*) to deal // *vi* (*TENNIS*) to serve; (*essere utile*): ~ **a qn** to be of use to sb; ~ **a qc/a fare** (*utensile etc*) to be used for sth/for doing; ~ **(a qn) da** to serve as (for sb); ~**rsi** *vr* (*usare*): ~**rsi di** to use; (*prendere: cibo*): ~**rsi (di)** to help o.s. (to); (*essere cliente abituale*): ~**rsi da** to be a regular customer at, go to.

servitù *sf* servitude; slavery; (*personale di servizio*) servants *pl*, domestic staff.

servizi'evole [servit'tsjevole] *ag* obliging, willing to help.

ser'vizio [ser'vittsjo] *sm* service; (*al ristorante: sul conto*) service (charge); (*STAMPA, TV, RADIO*) report; (*da tè, caffè etc*) set, service; ~**i** *smpl* (*di casa*) kitchen and bathroom; (*ECON*) services; **essere di** ~ to be on duty; **fuori** ~ (*telefono etc*) out of order; ~ **compreso** service included; ~ **militare** military service; ~**i segreti** secret service *sg*.

'servo, a *sm/f* servant.

ses'santa *num* sixty; **sessan'tesimo, a** *num* sixtieth.

sessan'tina *sf:* **una** ~ **(di)** about sixty.

sessi'one *sf* session.

'sesso *sm* sex; **sessu'ale** *ag* sexual, sex *cpd*.

ses'tante *sm* sextant.

'sesto, a *ag, sm* sixth.

'seta *sf* silk.

'sete *sf* thirst; **avere** ~ to be thirsty.

'setola *sf* bristle.

'setta *sf* sect.

set'tanta *num* seventy; **settan'tesimo, a** *num* seventieth.

settan'tina *sf:* **una** ~ **(di)** about seventy.

'sette *num* seven.

sette'cento [sette'tʃɛnto] *num* seven hundred // *sm:* **il S**~ the eighteenth century.

set'tembre *sm* September.

settentri'onale *ag* northern.

settentri'one *sm* north.

'settico, a, ci, che *ag* (*MED*) septic.

setti'mana *sf* week; **settima'nale** *ag, sm* weekly.

'settimo, a *ag, sm* seventh.

set'tore *sm* sector.

severità *sf* severity.

se'vero, a *ag* severe.

se'vizie [se'vittsje] *sfpl* torture *sg*;

sevizi'are vt to torture.

sezio'nare [settsjo'nare] vt to divide into sections; (MED) to dissect.

sezi'one [set'tsjone] sf section; (MED) dissection.

sfaccen'dato, a [sfattʃen'dato] ag idle.

sfacci'ato, a [sfat'tʃato] ag (maleducato) cheeky, impudent; (vistoso) gaudy.

sfa'celo [sfa'tʃɛlo] sm (fig) ruin, collapse.

sfal'darsi vr to flake (off).

'sfarzo ['sfartso] sm pomp, splendour.

sfasci'are [sfaʃ'ʃare] vt (ferita) to unbandage; (distruggere: porta) to smash, shatter; ~rsi vr (rompersi) to smash, shatter.

sfa'tare vt (leggenda) to explode.

sfavil'lare vi to spark, send out sparks; (risplendere) to sparkle.

sfavo'revole ag unfavourable.

'sfera sf sphere; **'sferico, a, ci, che** ag spherical.

sfer'rare vt (fig: colpo) to land, deal; (: attacco) to launch.

sfer'zare [sfer'tsare] vt to whip; (fig) to lash out at.

sfi'brare vt (indebolire) to exhaust, enervate.

'sfida sf challenge; **sfi'dare** vt to challenge; (fig) to defy, brave.

sfi'ducia [sfi'dutʃa] sf distrust, mistrust.

sfigu'rare vt (persona) to disfigure; (quadro, statua) to deface // vi (far cattiva figura) to make a bad impression.

sfi'lare vt (ago) to unthread; (abito, scarpe) to slip off // vi (truppe) to march past; (atleti) to parade; ~rsi vr (perle etc) to come unstrung; (orlo, tessuto) to fray; (calza) to run, ladder; **sfi'lata** sf march past; parade; sfilata di moda fashion show.

'sfinge ['sfindʒe] sf sphinx.

sfi'nito, a ag exhausted.

sfio'rare vt to brush (against); (argomento) to touch upon.

sfio'rire vi to wither, fade.

sfo'cato, a ag (FOT) out of focus.

sfoci'are [sfo'tʃare] vi: ~ in to flow into; (fig: malcontento) to develop into.

sfo'gare vt to vent, pour out; ~rsi vr (sfogare la propria rabbia) to give vent to one's anger; (confidarsi): ~rsi (con) to pour out one's feelings (to); non sfogarti su di me! don't take your bad temper out on me!

sfoggi'are [sfod'dʒare] vt, vi to show off.

'sfoglia ['sfoʎʎa] sf sheet of pasta dough; pasta ~ (CUC) puff pastry.

sfogli'are [sfoʎ'ʎare] vt (libro) to leaf through.

'sfogo, ghi sm outlet; (eruzione cutanea) rash; (fig) outburst; dare ~ a (fig) to give vent to.

sfolgo'rante ag (luce) blazing; (fig: vittoria) brilliant.

sfol'lare vt to empty, clear // vi to disperse; ~ da (città) to evacuate.

sfon'dare vt (porta) to break down; (scarpe) to wear a hole in; (cesto, scatola) to burst, knock the bottom out of; (MIL) to break through // vi (riuscire) to make a name for o.s.

'sfondo sm background.

sfor'mato sm (CUC) type of soufflé.

sfor'nito, a ag: ~ di lacking in, without; (negozio) out of.

sfor'tuna sf misfortune, ill luck q; avere ~ to be unlucky; **sfortu'nato, a** ag unlucky; (impresa, film) unsuccessful.

sfor'zare [sfor'tsare] vt to force; (voce, occhi) to strain; ~rsi vr: ~rsi di o a o per fare to try hard to do.

'sforzo ['sfortso] sm effort; (tensione eccessiva, TECN) strain; fare uno ~ to make an effort.

sfrat'tare vt to evict; **'sfratto** sm eviction.

sfrecci'are [sfret'tʃare] vi to shoot o flash past.

sfregi'are [sfre'dʒare] vt to slash, gash; (persona) to disfigure; (quadro) to deface; **'sfregio** sm gash; scar; (fig) insult.

sfre'nato, a ag (fig) unrestrained, unbridled.

sfron'tato, a ag shameless.

sfrutta'mento sm exploitation.

sfrut'tare vt (terreno) to overwork, exhaust; (miniera) to exploit, work; (fig: operai, occasione, potere) to exploit.

sfug'gire [sfud'dʒire] vi to escape; ~ a (custode) to escape (from); (morte) to escape; ~ a qn (dettaglio, nome) to escape sb; ~ di mano a qn to slip out of sb's hand (o hands); **sfug'gita:** di sfuggita ad (rapidamente, in fretta) in passing.

sfu'mare vt (colori, contorni) to soften, shade off // vi to shade (off), fade; (fig: svanire) to vanish, disappear; (: speranze) to come to nothing; **sfuma'tura** sf shading off q; (tonalità) shade, tone; (fig) touch, hint.

sfuri'ata sf (scatto di collera) fit of anger; (rimprovero) sharp rebuke.

sga'bello sm stool.

sgabuz'zino [zgabud'dzino] sm lumber room.

sgambet'tare vi to kick one's legs about.

sgam'betto sm: far lo ~ a qn to trip sb up; (fig) to oust sb.

sganasci'arsi [zganaʃ'ʃarsi] vr: ~ dalle risa to roar with laughter.

sganci'are [zgan'tʃare] vt to unhook; (FERR) to uncouple; (bombe: da aereo) to release, drop; (fig: fam: soldi) to fork out; ~rsi vr (fig): ~rsi (da) to get away (from).

sganghe'rato, a [zgange'rato] *ag*
(*porta*) off its hinges; (*auto*) ramshackle; (*risata*) wild, boisterous.

sgar'bato, a *ag* rude, impolite.

'sgarbo *sm*: fare uno ~ a qn to be rude
to sb.

sgattaio'lare *vi* to sneak away *o* off.

sge'lare [zdʒe'lare] *vi*, *vt* to thaw.

'sghembo, a ['zgembo] *ag* (*obliquo*)
slanting; (*storto*) crooked.

sghignaz'zare [zgiɲɲat'tsare] *vi* to laugh
scornfully.

sgob'bare *vi* (*fam: scolaro*) to swot; (:
operaio) to slog.

sgoccio'lare [zgottʃo'lare] *vt* (*vuotare*)
to drain (to the last drop) // *vi* (*acqua*)
to drip; (*recipiente*) to drain.

sgo'larsi *vr* to talk (*o* shout *o* sing) o.s.
hoarse.

sgomb(e)'rare *vt* to clear; (*andarsene
da: stanza*) to vacate; (*evacuare*) to
evacuate.

'sgombro, a *ag*: ~ (**di**) clear (of), free
(from) // *sm* (ZOOL) mackerel; (*anche:
sgombero*) clearing; vacating; evacua-
tion; (: *trasloco*) removal.

sgomen'tare *vt* to dismay; **~rsi** *vr* to
be dismayed; **sgo'mento, a** *ag* dismayed // *sm* dismay, consternation.

sgonfi'are *vt* to let down, deflate; **~rsi**
vr to go down.

'sgorbio *sm* blot; scribble.

sgor'gare *vi* to gush (out).

sgoz'zare [zgot'tsare] *vt* to cut the throat
of.

sgra'devole *ag* unpleasant, disagreeable.

sgra'dito, a *ag* unpleasant, unwelcome.

sgra'nare *vt* (*piselli*) to shell; ~ gli occhi to open one's eyes wide.

sgran'chirsi [zgran'kirsi] *vr* to stretch; ~
le gambe to stretch one's legs.

sgranocchi'are [zgranok'kjare] *vt* to
munch.

'sgravio *sm*: ~ fiscale tax relief.

sgrazi'ato, a [zgrat'tsjato] *ag* clumsy,
ungainly.

sgreto'lare *vt* to cause to crumble; **~rsi**
vr to crumble.

sgri'dare *vt* to scold; **sgri'data** *sf* scold-
ing.

sguai'ato, a *ag* coarse, vulgar.

sgual'cire [zgwal'tʃire] *vt* to crumple
(up), crease.

sgual'drina *sf* (*peg*) slut.

sgu'ardo *sm* (*occhiata*) look, glance;
(*espressione*) look (in one's eye).

sguaz'zare [zgwat'tsare] *vi* (*nell'acqua*)
to splash about; (*nella melma*) to
wallow; ~ **nell'oro** to be rolling in
money.

sguinzagli'are [zgwintsaʎ'ʎare] *vt* to let
off the leash; (*fig: persona*): ~ qn dietro
a qn to set sb on sb.

sgusci'are [zguʃ'ʃare] *vt* to shell // *vi*

(*sfuggire di mano*) to slip; ~ **via** to slip
o slink away.

'shampoo ['ʃampo] *sm inv* shampoo.

shock [ʃɔk] *sm inv* shock.

si ◆ *sm* (MUS) B; (*solfeggiando la scala*)
ti

◆ *pronome* (*dav lo, la, li, le, ne diventa*
se) **1** (*riflessivo: maschile*) himself; (:
femminile) herself; (: *neutro*) itself; (:
impersonale) oneself; (: *pl*) themselves;
lavarsi to wash (oneself); ~ **è tagliato** he
has cut himself; ~ **credono importanti**
they think a lot of themselves

2 (*riflessivo: con complemento oggetto*):
lavarsi le mani to wash one's hands; ~
sta lavando i capelli he (*o* she) is washing his (*o* her) hair

3 (*reciproco*) one another, each other; **si
amano** they love one another *o* each
other

4 (*passivo*): ~ **ripara facilmente** it is
easily repaired

5 (*impersonale*): ~ **dice che ...** they *o*
people say that ...; ~ **vede che è vecchio**
one *o* you can see that it's old

6 (*noi*) we; **tra poco** ~ **parte** we're leaving soon.

sì *av* yes; **un giorno** ~ **e uno no** every
other day.

'sia *cong*: ~ ... ~ (*o ... o*): ~ **che lavori**,
~ **che non lavori** whether he works or
not; (*tanto ... quanto*): **verranno** ~ **Luigi**
~ **suo fratello** both Luigi and his brother
will be coming.

si'amo *vb vedi* **essere**.

sibi'lare *vi* to hiss; (*fischiare*) to whistle;
'sibilo *sm* hiss; whistle.

si'cario *sm* hired killer.

sicché [sik'ke] *cong* (*perciò*) so (that),
therefore; (*e quindi*) (and) so.

siccità [sittʃi'ta] *sf* drought.

sic'come *cong* since, as.

Si'cilia [si'tʃilja] *sf*: **la** ~ Sicily;
sicili'ano, a *ag, sm/f* Sicilian.

sicu'rezza [siku'rettsa] *sf* safety;
security; (*fiducia*) confidence; (*certezza*)
certainty; **di** ~ safety *cpd*; **la** ~ **stradale**
road safety.

si'curo, a *ag* safe; (*ben difeso*) secure;
(*fiducioso*) confident; (*certo*) sure,
certain; (*notizia, amico*) reliable;
(*esperto*) skilled (*av* (*anche*: **di** ~)
certainly; **essere/mettere al** ~ **to be**
safe/put in a safe place; ~ **di sé** self-
confident, sure of o.s.; **sentirsi** ~ to feel
safe *o* secure.

siderur'gia [siderur'dʒia] *sf* iron and
steel industry.

'sidro *sm* cider.

si'epe *sf* hedge.

si'ero *sm* (MED) serum.

si'esta *sf* siesta, (afternoon) nap.

si'ete *vb vedi* **essere**.

si'filide *sf* syphilis.

si'fone *sm* siphon.

Sig. *abbr* (= *signore*) Mr.
siga'retta *sf* cigarette.
'sigaro *sm* cigar.
Sigg. *abbr* (= *signori*) Messrs.
sigil'lare [sidʒil'lare] *vt* to seal.
si'gillo [si'dʒillo] *sm* seal.
'sigla *sf* initials *pl*; acronym, abbreviation; ~ **automobilistica** *abbreviation of province on vehicle number plate*; ~ **musicale** signature tune.
si'glare *vt* to initial.
Sig.na *abbr* (= *signorina*) Miss.
signifi'care [siɲɲifi'kare] *vt* to mean; **significa'tivo, a** *ag* significant; **signi'ficato** *sm* meaning.
si'gnora [siɲ'ɲora] *sf* lady; **la ~ X** Mrs ['mɪsɪz] X; **buon giorno S~/Signore/Signorina** good morning; (*deferente*) good morning Madam/Sir/Madam; (*quando si conosce il nome*) good morning Mrs/Mr/Miss X; **Gentile S~/Signore/Signorina** (*in una lettera*) Dear Madam/Sir/Madam; **il signor Rossi e ~** Mr Rossi and his wife; **~e e signori** ladies and gentlemen.
si'gnore [siɲ'ɲore] *sm* gentleman; (*padrone*) lord, master; (*REL*): **il S~** the Lord; **il signor X** Mr ['mɪstə*] X; **i ~i Bianchi** (*coniugi*) Mr and Mrs Bianchi; *vedi anche* **signora**.
signo'rile [siɲɲo'rile] *ag* refined.
signo'rina [siɲɲo'rina] *sf* young lady; **la ~ X** Miss X; *vedi anche* **signora**.
Sig.ra *abbr* (= *signora*) Mrs.
silenzia'tore [silentsja'tore] *sm* silencer.
si'lenzio [si'lentsjo] *sm* silence; **fare ~** to be quiet, stop talking; **silenzi'oso, a** *ag* silent, quiet.
si'licio [si'litʃo] *sm* silicon; **piastrina di ~** silicon chip.
'sillaba *sf* syllable.
silu'rare *vt* to torpedo; (*fig: privare del comando*) to oust.
si'luro *sm* torpedo.
simboleggi'are [simboled'dʒare] *vt* to symbolize.
'simbolo *sm* symbol.
'simile *ag* (*analogo*) similar; (*di questo tipo*): **un uomo ~** such a man, a man like this; **libri ~i** such books; **~ a** similar to; **i suoi ~i** one's fellow men; one's peers.
simme'tria *sf* symmetry.
simpa'tia *sf* (*qualità*) pleasantness; (*inclinazione*) liking; **avere ~ per qn** to like sb, have a liking for sb; **sim'patico, a, ci, che** *ag* (*persona*) nice, pleasant, likeable; (*casa, albergo etc*) nice, pleasant.
simpatiz'zare [simpatid'dzare] *vi:* ~ **con** to take a liking to.
sim'posio *sm* symposium.
simu'lare *vt* to sham, simulate; (*TECN*) to simulate; **simulazi'one** *sf* shamming; simulation.
simul'taneo, a *ag* simultaneous.

sina'goga, ghe *sf* synagogue.
sincerità [sintʃeri'ta] *sf* sincerity.
sin'cero, a [sin'tʃero] *ag* sincere; genuine; heartfelt.
'sincope *sf* syncopation; (*MED*) blackout.
sinda'cale *ag* (trade-)union *cpd*; **sindaca'lista, i, e** *sm/f* trade unionist.
sinda'cato *sm* (*di lavoratori*) (trade) union; (*AMM, ECON, DIR*) syndicate, trust, pool; ~ **dei datori di lavoro** employers' association, employers' federation.
'sindaco, ci *sm* mayor.
sinfo'nia *sf* (*MUS*) symphony.
singhioz'zare [singjot'tsare] *vi* to sob; to hiccup.
singhi'ozzo [sin'gjottso] *sm* sob; (*MED*) hiccup; **avere il ~** to have the hiccups; **a ~** (*fig*) by fits and starts.
singo'lare *ag* (*insolito*) remarkable, singular; (*LING*) singular // *sm* (*LING*) singular; (*TENNIS*): ~ **maschile/femminile** men's/women's singles.
'singolo, a *ag* single, individual // *sm* (*persona*) individual; (*TENNIS*) = **singolare**.
si'nistro, a *ag* left, left-hand; (*fig*) sinister // *sm* (*incidente*) accident // *sf* (*POL*) left (wing); **a ~a** on the left; (*direzione*) to the left.
'sino *prep* = **fino**.
si'nonimo, a *ag* synonymous // *sm* synonym; ~ **di** synonymous with.
sin'tassi *sf* syntax.
'sintesi *sf* synthesis; (*riassunto*) summary, résumé.
sin'tetico, a, ci, che *ag* synthetic.
sintetiz'zare [sintetid'dzare] *vt* to synthesize; (*riassumere*) to summarize.
sinto'matico, a, ci, che *ag* symptomatic.
'sintomo *sm* symptom.
sinu'oso, a *ag* (*strada*) winding.
S.I.P. *sigla f* (= *Società italiana per l'esercizio telefonico*) Italian telephone company.
si'pario *sm* (*TEATRO*) curtain.
si'rena *sf* (*apparecchio*) siren; (*nella mitologia, fig*) siren, mermaid.
'Siria *sf:* **la ~** Syria.
si'ringa, ghe *sf* syringe.
'sismico, a, ci, che *ag* seismic.
sis'mografo *sm* seismograph.
sis'tema, i *sm* system; method, way; ~ **di vita** way of life.
siste'mare *vt* (*mettere a posto*) to tidy, put in order; (*risolvere: questione*) to sort out, settle; (*procurare un lavoro a*) to find a job for; (*dare un alloggio a*) to settle, find accommodation for; **~rsi** *vr* (*problema*) to be settled; (*persona: trovare alloggio*) to find accommodation (*Brit*) *o* accommodations (*US*); (*: trovarsi un lavoro*) to get fixed up with a

job; ti sistemo io! I'll soon sort you out!

siste'matico, a, ci, che *ag* systematic.

sistemazi'one [sistemat'tsjone] *sf*
arrangement, order; settlement; employment; accommodation (*Brit*), accommodations (*US*).

'sito *sm* (*letterario*) place.

situ'are *vt* to site, situate; **situ'ato, a**
ag: situato a/su situated at/on.

situazi'one [situat'tsjone] *sf* situation.

slacci'are [zlat'tʃare] *vt* to undo, unfasten.

slanci'arsi [zlan'tʃarsi] *vr* to dash, fling
o.s.; **slanci'ato, a** *ag* slender; **'slancio**
sm dash, leap; (*fig*) surge; di slancio
impetuously.

sla'vato, a *ag* faded, washed out; (*fig:
viso, occhi*) pale, colourless.

'slavo, a *ag* Slav(onic), Slavic.

sle'ale *ag* disloyal; (*concorrenza etc*) unfair.

sle'gare *vt* to untie.

'slitta *sf* sledge; (*trainata*) sleigh.

slit'tare *vi* to slip, slide; (*AUT*) to skid.

slo'gare *vt* (*MED*) to dislocate.

sloggi'are [zlod'dʒare] *vt* (*inquilino*) to
turn out; (*nemico*) to drive out, dislodge
// *vi* to move out.

smacchi'are [zmak'kjare] *vt* to remove
stains from.

'smacco, chi *sm* humiliating defeat.

smagli'ante [zmaʎ'ʎante] *ag* brilliant,
dazzling.

smaglia'tura [zmaʎʎa'tura] *sf* (*su maglia, calza*) ladder; (*della pelle*) stretch
mark.

smalizi'ato, a [smalit'tsjato] *ag* shrewd,
cunning.

smal'tare *vt* to enamel; (*ceramica*) to
glaze; (*unghie*) to varnish.

smal'tire *vt* (*merce*) to sell off; (*rifiuti*)
to dispose of; (*cibo*) to digest; (*peso*) to
lose; (*rabbia*) to get over; ~ la sbornia
to sober up.

'smalto *sm* (*anche: di denti*) enamel;
(*per ceramica*) glaze; ~ per unghie nail
varnish.

'smania *sf* agitation, restlessness; (*fig*):
~ di thirst for, craving for; avere la ~
addosso to have the fidgets; avere la ~
di fare to be desperate to do.

smantel'lare *vt* to dismantle.

smarri'mento *sm* loss; (*fig*) bewilderment; dismay.

smar'rire *vt* to lose; (*non riuscire a
trovare*) to mislay; ~rsi *vr* (*perdersi*) to
lose one's way, get lost; (*: oggetto*) to go
astray; **smar'rito, a** *ag* (*sbigottito*)
bewildered.

smasche'rare [zmaske'rare] *vt* to unmask.

smemo'rato, a *ag* forgetful.

smen'tire *vt* (*negare*) to deny;
(*testimonianza*) to refute; (*reputazione*)
to give the lie to; ~rsi *vr* to be in-

consistent; **smen'tita** *sf* denial; retraction.

sme'raldo *sm* emerald.

smerci'are [zmer'tʃare] *vt* (*COMM*) to
sell; (*: svendere*) to sell off.

sme'riglio [zme'riʎʎo] *sm* emery.

'smesso, a *pp di* **smettere**.

'smettere *vt* to stop; (*vestiti*) to stop
wearing // *vi* to stop, cease; ~ di fare to
stop doing.

'smilzo, a ['zmiltso] *ag* thin, lean.

sminu'ire *vt* to diminish, lessen; (*fig*) to
belittle.

sminuz'zare [zminut'tsare] *vt* to break
into small pieces; to crumble.

smis'tare *vt* (*pacchi etc*) to sort; (*FERR*)
to shunt.

smisu'rato, a *ag* boundless, immeasurable; (*grandissimo*) immense, enormous.

smobili'tare *vt* to demobilize.

smo'dato, a *ag* immoderate.

smoking ['smɔukiŋ] *sm inv* dinner jacket.

smon'tare *vt* (*mobile, macchina etc*) to
take to pieces, dismantle; (*fig: scoraggiare*) to dishearten // *vi* (*scendere:
da cavallo*) to dismount; (*: da treno*) to
get off; (*terminare il lavoro*) to stop
(work); ~rsi *vr* to lose heart; to lose
one's enthusiasm.

'smorfia *sf* grimace; (*atteggiamento
lezioso*) simpering; fare ~e to make
faces; to simper; **smorfi'oso, a** *ag*
simpering.

'smorto, a *ag* (*viso*) pale, wan; (*colore*)
dull.

smor'zare [zmor'tsare] *vt* (*suoni*) to
deaden; (*colori*) to tone down; (*luce*) to
dim; (*sete*) to quench; (*entusiasmo*) to
dampen; ~rsi *vr* (*suono, luce*) to fade;
(*entusiasmo*) to dampen.

'smosso, a *pp di* **smuovere**.

smotta'mento *sm* landslide.

'smunto, a *ag* haggard, pinched.

smu'overe *vt* to move, shift; (*fig:
commuovere*) to move; (*: dall'inerzia*)
to rouse, stir; ~rsi *vr* to move, shift.

smus'sare *vt* (*angolo*) to round off,
smooth; (*lama etc*) to blunt; ~rsi *vr* to
become blunt.

snatu'rato, a *ag* inhuman, heartless.

'snello, a *ag* (*agile*) agile; (*svelto*)
slender, slim.

sner'vare *vt* to enervate, wear out; ~rsi
vr to become enervated.

sni'dare *vt* to drive out, flush out.

snob'bare *vt* to snub.

sno'bismo *sm* snobbery.

snoccio'lare [znottʃo'lare] *vt* (*frutta*) to
stone; (*fig: orazioni*) to rattle off; (*: verità*) to blab.

sno'dare *vt* (*rendere agile, mobile*) to
loosen; ~rsi *vr* to come loose;
(*articolarsi*) to bend; (*strada, fiume*) to
wind.

so *vb vedi* **sapere**.

so'ave *ag* sweet, gentle, soft.

sobbal'zare [sobbal'tsare] *vi* to jolt, jerk; (*trasalire*) to jump, start; **sob'balzo** *sm* jerk, jolt; jump, start.

sobbar'carsi *vr*: ~ **a** to take on, undertake.

sob'borgo, ghi *sm* suburb.

sobil'lare *vt* to stir up, incite.

'sobrio, a *ag* sober.

socchi'udere [sok'kjudere] *vt* (*porta*) to leave ajar; (*occhi*) to half-close; **socchi'uso, a** *pp di* **socchiudere**.

soc'correre *vt* to help, assist; **soc'corso, a** *pp di* **soccorrere** // *sm* help, aid, assistance; **soccorsi** *smpl* relief *sg*, aid *sg*; **soccorso stradale** breakdown service.

socialdemo'cratico, à, ci, che [sotʃaldemo'kratiko] *sm/f* Social Democrat.

soci'ale [so'tʃale] *ag* social; (*di associazione*) club *cpd*, association *cpd*.

socia'lismo [sotʃa'lizmo] *sm* socialism; **socia'lista, i, e** *ag, sm/f* socialist.

società [sotʃe'ta] *sf inv* society; (*sportiva*) club; (*COMM*) company; ~ **per azioni** (**S.p.A.**) limited (*Brit*) *o* incorporated (*US*) company; ~ **a responsabilità limitata** (**S.r.l.**) *type of limited liability company*.

soci'evole [so'tʃevole] *ag* sociable.

'socio ['sɔtʃo] *sm* (*DIR, COMM*) partner; (*membro di associazione*) member.

'soda *sf* (*CHIM*) soda; (*acqua gassata*) soda (water).

soda'lizio [soda'littsjo] *sm* association, society.

soddisfa'cente [soddisfa'tʃɛnte] *ag* satisfactory.

soddis'fare *vt, vi*: ~ **a** to satisfy; (*impegno*) to fulfil; (*debito*) to pay off; (*richiesta*) to meet, comply with; (*offesa*) to make amends for; **soddis'fatto, a** *pp di* **soddisfare** // *ag* satisfied; **soddisfatto di** happy *o* satisfied with; pleased with; **soddisfazi'one** *sf* satisfaction.

'sodo, a *ag* firm, hard // *av* (*picchiare, lavorare*) hard; **dormire** ~ to sleep soundly.

sofà *sm inv* sofa.

soffe'renza [soffe'rɛntsa] *sf* suffering.

sof'ferto, a *pp di* **soffrire**.

soffi'are *vt* to blow; (*notizia, segreto*) to whisper // *vi* to blow; (*sbuffare*) to puff (and blow); ~**rsi il naso** to blow one's nose; ~ **qc/qn a qn** (*fig*) to pinch *o* steal sth/sb from sb; ~ **via qc** to blow sth away.

'soffice ['sɔffitʃe] *ag* soft.

'soffio *sm* (*di vento*) breath; (*di fumo*) puff; (*MED*) murmur.

sof'fitta *sf* attic.

sof'fitto *sm* ceiling.

soffo'care *vi* (*anche*: ~**rsi**) to suffocate, choke // *vt* to suffocate, choke; (*fig*) to stifle, suppress.

sof'friggere [sof'friddʒere] *vt* to fry lightly.

sof'frire *vt* to suffer, endure; (*sopportare*) to bear, stand // *vi* to suffer; to be in pain; ~ (**di**) **qc** (*MED*) to suffer from sth.

sof'fritto, a *pp di* **soffriggere** // *sm* (*CUC*) fried mixture of herbs, bacon and onions.

sofisti'cato, a *ag* sophisticated; (*vino*) adulterated.

sogget'tivo, a [soddʒet'tivo] *ag* subjective.

sog'getto, a [sod'dʒɛtto] *ag*: ~ **a** (*sottomesso*) subject to; (*esposto: a variazioni, danni etc*) subject *o* liable to // *sm* subject.

soggezi'one [soddʒet'tsjone] *sf* subjection; (*timidezza*) awe; **avere** ~ **di qn** to stand in awe of sb; to be ill at ease in sb's presence.

sogghi'gnare [soggin'nare] *vi* to sneer.

soggior'nare [soddʒor'nare] *vi* to stay; **soggi'orno** *sm* (*invernale, marino*) stay; (*stanza*) living room.

sog'giungere [sod'dʒundʒere] *vt* to add.

'soglia ['sɔʎʎa] *sf* doorstep; (*anche fig*) threshold.

sogli'ola ['sɔʎʎola] *sf* (*ZOOL*) sole.

so'gnare [son'nare] *vt, vi* to dream; ~ **a occhi aperti** to daydream; **sogna'tore, 'trice** *sm/f* dreamer.

'sogno ['sonno] *sm* dream.

'soia *sf* (*BOT*) soya.

sol *sm* (*MUS*) G; (: *solfeggiando la scala*) so(h).

so'laio *sm* (*soffitta*) attic.

sola'mente *av* only, just.

so'lare *ag* solar, sun *cpd*.

'solco, chi *sm* (*scavo, fig: ruga*) furrow; (*incavo*) rut, track; (*di disco*) groove; (*scia*) wake.

sol'dato *sm* soldier; ~ **semplice** private.

'soldo *sm* (*fig*): **non avere un** ~ to be penniless; **non vale un** ~ it's not worth a penny; ~**i** *smpl* (*denaro*) money *sg*.

'sole *sm* sun; (*luce*) sun(light); (*tempo assolato*) sun(shine); **prendere il** ~ to sunbathe.

soleggi'ato, a [soled'dʒato] *ag* sunny.

so'lenne *ag* solemn; **solennità** *sf* solemnity; (*festività*) holiday, feast day.

sol'fato *sm* (*CHIM*) sulphate.

soli'dale *ag*: **essere** ~ (**con**) to be in agreement (with).

solidarietà *sf* solidarity.

'solido, a *ag* solid; (*forte, robusto*) sturdy, solid; (*fig: ditta*) sound, solid // *sm* (*MAT*) solid.

soli'loquio *sm* soliloquy.

so'lista, i, e *ag* solo // *sm/f* soloist.

solita'mente *av* usually, as a rule.

soli'tario, a *ag* (*senza compagnia*) solitary, lonely; (*solo, isolato*) solitary, lone; (*deserto*) lonely // *sm* (*gioiello, gioco*) solitaire.

'solito, a *ag* usual; **essere ~ fare** to be in the habit of doing; **di ~** usually; **più tardi del ~** later than usual; **come al ~** as usual.

soli'tudine *sf* solitude.

solleci'tare [solletʃi'tare] *vt* (*lavoro*) to speed up; (*persona*) to urge on; (*chiedere con insistenza*) to press for, request urgently; (*stimolare*): **~ qn a fare** to urge sb to do; (*TECN*) to stress; **solle-citazi'one** *sf* entreaty, request; (*fig*) incentive; (*TECN*) stress.

sol'lecito, a [sol'letʃito] *ag* prompt, quick // *sm* (*lettera*) reminder; **solleci'tudine** *sf* promptness, speed.

solleti'care *vt* to tickle.

sol'letico *sm* tickling; **soffrire il ~** to be ticklish.

solleva'mento *sm* raising; lifting; revolt; **~ pesi** (*SPORT*) weight-lifting.

solle'vare *vt* to lift, raise; (*fig: persona: alleggerire*): **~ (da)** to relieve (of); (: *dar conforto*) to comfort, relieve; (: *questione*) to raise; (: *far insorgere*) to stir (to revolt); **~rsi** *vr* to rise; (*fig: riprendersi*) to recover; (: *ribellarsi*) to rise up.

solli'evo *sm* relief; (*conforto*) comfort.

'solo, a *ag* alone; (*in senso spirituale: isolato*) lonely; (*unico*): **un ~ libro** only one book, a single book; (*con ag numerale*): **veniamo noi tre ~i** just *o* only the three of us are coming // *av* (*soltanto*) only, just; **non ~ ... ma anche** not only ... but also; **fare qc da ~** to do sth (all) by oneself; **da me ~** single-handed, on my own.

sol'tanto *av* only.

so'lubile *ag* (*sostanza*) soluble.

soluzi'one [solut'tsjone] *sf* solution.

sol'vente *ag, sm* solvent.

'soma *sf*: **bestia da ~** beast of burden.

so'maro *sm* ass, donkey.

somigli'anza [somiʎ'ʎantsa] *sf* resemblance.

somigli'are [somiʎ'ʎare] *vi*: **~ a** to be like, resemble; (*nell'aspetto fisico*) to look like; **~rsi** *vr* to be (*o* look) alike.

'somma *sf* (*MAT*) sum; (*di denaro*) sum (of money); (*complesso di varie cose*) whole amount, sum total.

som'mare *vt* to add up; (*aggiungere*) to add; **tutto sommato** all things considered.

som'mario, a *ag* (*racconto, indagine*) brief; (*giustizia*) summary // *sm* summary.

som'mergere [som'mɛrdʒere] *vt* to submerge.

sommer'gibile [sommer'dʒibile] *sm* submarine.

som'merso, a *pp di* **sommergere**.

som'messo, a *ag* (*voce*) soft, subdued.

somminis'trare *vt* to give, administer.

sommità *sf inv* summit, top; (*fig*) height.

'sommo, a *ag* highest; (*rispetto etc*) highest, greatest; (*poeta, artista*) great, outstanding // *sm* (*fig*) height; **per ~i capi** briefly, covering the main points.

som'mossa *sf* uprising.

so'nare *etc* = **suonare** *etc*.

son'daggio [son'daddʒo] *sm* sounding; probe; boring, drilling; (*indagine*) survey; **~ d'opinioni** opinion poll.

son'dare *vt* (*NAUT*) to sound; (*atmosfera, piaga*) to probe; (*MINERALOGIA*) to bore, drill; (*fig: opinione etc*) to survey, poll.

so'netto *sm* sonnet.

son'nambulo, a *sm/f* sleepwalker.

sonnecchi'are [sonnek'kjare] *vi* to doze, nod.

son'nifero *sm* sleeping drug (*o* pill).

'sonno *sm* sleep; **prendere ~** to fall asleep; **aver ~** to be sleepy.

'sono *vb vedi* **essere**.

so'noro, a *ag* (*ambiente*) resonant; (*voce*) sonorous, ringing; (*onde, film*) sound *cpd*.

sontu'oso, a *ag* sumptuous; lavish.

sopo'rifero, a *ag* soporific.

soppe'sare *vt* to weigh in one's hand(s), feel the weight of; (*fig*) to weigh up.

soppi'atto: di ~ *av* secretly; furtively.

soppor'tare *vt* (*reggere*) to support; (*subire: perdita, spese*) to bear, sustain; (*soffrire: dolore*) to bear, endure; (*sog: cosa: freddo*) to withstand; (*sog: persona: freddo, vino*) to take; (*tollerare*) to put up with, tolerate.

sop'presso, a *pp di* **sopprimere**.

sop'primere *vt* (*carica, privilegi, testimone*) to do away with; (*pubblicazione*) to suppress; (*parola, frase*) to delete.

'sopra *prep* (*gen*) on; (*al di sopra di, più in alto di*) above; over; (*riguardo a*) on, about // *av* on top; (*attaccato, scritto*) on it; (*al di sopra*) above; (*al piano superiore*) upstairs; **donne ~ 30** women over 30 (years of age); **abito di ~** I live upstairs; **dormirci ~** (*fig*) to sleep on it.

so'prabito *sm* overcoat.

soprac'ciglio [soprat'tʃiʎʎo], *pl(f)* **soprac'ciglia** *sm* eyebrow.

sopracco'perta *sf* (*di letto*) bedspread; (*di libro*) jacket.

soprad'detto, a *ag* aforesaid.

sopraf'fare *vt* to overcome, overwhelm; **sopraf'fatto, a** *pp di* **sopraffare**.

sopraf'fino, a *ag* (*pranzo, vino*) excellent.

sopraggi'ungere [soprad'dʒundʒere] *vi* (*giungere all'improvviso*) to arrive (unexpectedly); (*accadere*) to occur (unexpectedly).

sopral'luogo, ghi sm (di esperti) inspection; (di polizia) on-the-spot investigation.

sopram'mobile sm ornament.

soprannatu'rale ag supernatural.

sopran'nome sm nickname.

so'prano, a sm/f (persona) soprano // sm (voce) soprano.

soprappensi'ero av lost in thought.

sopras'salto sm: di ~ with a start; suddenly.

soprasse'dere vi: ~ a to delay, put off.

soprat'tutto av (anzitutto) above all; (specialmente) especially.

soprav'vento sm: avere/prendere il ~ su to have/get the upper hand over.

sopravvis'suto, a pp di **sopravvivere.**

soprav'vivere vi to survive; (continuare a vivere): ~ (in) to live on (in); ~ a (incidente etc) to survive; (persona) to outlive.

soprinten'dente sm/f supervisor; (statale: di belle arti etc) keeper; **soprinten'denza** sf supervision; (ente): **soprintendenza alle Belle Arti** government department responsible for monuments and artistic treasures.

so'pruso sm abuse of power; **subire un ~** to be abused.

soq'quadro sm: **mettere a ~** to turn upside-down.

sor'betto sm sorbet, water ice.

sor'bire vt to sip; (fig) to put up with.

'sorcio, ci ['sortʃo] sm mouse.

'sordido, a ag sordid; (fig: gretto) stingy.

sor'dina sf: **in ~** softly; (fig) on the sly.

sordità sf deafness.

'sordo, a ag deaf; (rumore) muffled; (dolore) dull; (odio, rancore) veiled // sm/f deaf person; **sordo'muto, a** ag deaf-and-dumb // sm/f deaf-mute.

so'rella sf sister; **sorel'lastra** sf stepsister.

sor'gente [sor'dʒɛnte] sf (acqua che sgorga) spring; (di fiume, FISICA, fig) source.

'sorgere ['sordʒere] vi to rise; (scaturire) to spring, rise; (fig: difficoltà) to arise.

sormon'tare vt (fig) to overcome, surmount.

sorni'one, a ag sly.

sorpas'sare vt (AUT) to overtake; (fig) to surpass; (: eccedere) to exceed, go beyond; ~ **in altezza** to be higher than; (persona) to be taller than.

sorpren'dente ag surprising.

sor'prendere vt (cogliere: in flagrante etc) to catch; (stupire) to surprise; ~**rsi** vr: ~**rsi (di)** to be surprised (at); **sor'preso, a** pp di **sorprendere** // sf surprise; **fare una sorpresa a qn** to give sb a surprise.

sor'reggere [sor'rɛddʒere] vt to support, hold up; (fig) to sustain; **sor'retto, a** pp di **sorreggere.**

sor'ridere vi to smile; **sor'riso, a** pp di **sorridere** // sm smile.

'sorso sm sip.

'sorta sf sort, kind; **di ~** whatever, of any kind, at all.

'sorte sf (fato) fate, destiny; (evento fortuito) chance; **tirare a ~** to draw lots.

sor'teggio [sor'teddʒo] sm draw.

sorti'legio [sorti'lɛdʒo] sm witchcraft q; (incantesimo) spell; **fare un ~ a qn** to cast a spell on sb.

sor'tita sf (MIL) sortie.

'sorto, a pp di **sorgere.**

sorvegli'anza [sorveʎ'ʎantsa] sf watch; supervision; (POLIZIA, MIL) surveillance.

sorvegli'are [sorveʎ'ʎare] vt (bambino, bagagli, prigioniero) to watch, keep an eye on; (malato) to watch over; (territorio, casa) to watch o keep watch over; (lavori) to supervise.

sorvo'lare vt (territorio) to fly over // vi: ~ **su** (fig) to skim over.

'sosia sm inv double.

sos'pendere vt (appendere) to hang (up); (interrompere, privare di una carica) to suspend; (rimandare) to defer; ~ **un quadro al muro/un lampadario al soffitto** to hang a picture on the wall/a chandelier from the ceiling; **sospensi'one** sf (anche CHIM, AUT) suspension; deferment; **sos'peso, a** pp di **sospendere** q (appeso): sospeso a hanging on (o from); (treno, autobus) cancelled; **in sospeso** in abeyance; (conto) outstanding; **tenere in sospeso** (fig) to keep in suspense.

sospet'tare vt to suspect // vi: ~ **di** to suspect; (diffidare) to be suspicious of.

sos'petto, a ag suspicious // sm suspicion; **sospet'toso, a** ag suspicious.

sos'pingere [sos'pindʒere] vt to drive, push; **sos'pinto, a** pp di **sospingere.**

sospi'rare vi to sigh // vt to long for, yearn for; **sos'piro** sm sigh.

'sosta sf (fermata) stop, halt; (pausa) pause, break; **senza ~** non-stop, without a break.

sostan'tivo sm noun, substantive.

sos'tanza [sos'tantsa] sf substance; ~**e** sfpl (ricchezze) wealth sg, possessions; **in ~** in short, to sum up; **sostanzi'oso, a** ag (cibo) nourishing, substantial.

sos'tare vi (fermarsi) to stop (for a while), stay; (fare una pausa) to take a break.

sos'tegno [sos'teɲɲo] sm support.

soste'nere vt to support; (prendere su di sé) to take on, bear; (resistere) to withstand, stand up to; (affermare): ~ **che** to maintain that; ~**rsi** vr to hold o.s. up, support o.s.; (fig) to keep up one's strength; ~ gli esami to sit exams; **sosteni'tore, 'trice** *sm/f* supporter.

sostenta'mento *sm* maintenance, support.

soste'nuto, a *ag* (*stile*) elevated; (*velocità, ritmo*) sustained; (*prezzo*) high // *sm/f*: **fare il(la) ~(a)** to be standoffish, keep one's distance.

sostitu'ire *vt* (*mettere al posto di*): ~ **qn/qc a** to substitute sb/sth for; (*prendere il posto di: persona*) to substitute for; (: *cosa*) to take the place of.

sosti'tuto, a *sm/f* substitute.

sostituzi'one [sostitut'tsjone] *sf* substitution; **in ~ di** as a substitute for, in place of.

sotta'ceti [sotta'tʃeti] *smpl* pickles.

sot'tana *sf* (*sottoveste*) underskirt; (*gonna*) skirt; (REL) soutane, cassock.

sotter'fugio [sotter'fudʒo] *sm* subterfuge.

sotter'raneo, a *ag* underground // *sm* cellar.

sotter'rare *vt* to bury.

sottigli'ezza [sottiʎ'ʎettsa] *sf* thinness; slimness; (*fig*: *acutezza*) subtlety; shrewdness; **~e** *sfpl* (*pedanteria*) quibbles.

sot'tile *ag* thin; (*figura, caviglia*) thin, slim, slender; (*fine*: *polvere, capelli*) fine; (*fig*: *leggero*) light; (: *vista*) sharp, keen; (: *olfatto*) fine, discriminating; (: *mente*) subtle; shrewd // *sm*: **non andare per il ~** not to mince matters.

sottin'tendere *vt* (*intendere qc non espresso*) to understand; (*implicare*) to imply; **sottin'teso, a** *pp di* **sottintendere** // *sm* allusion; **parlare senza sottintesi** to speak plainly.

'**sotto** *prep* (*gen*) under; (*più in basso di*) below // *av* underneath, beneath; below; (*al piano inferiore*): (**al piano**) **di ~** downstairs; ~ **forma di** in the form of; ~ **il monte** at the foot of the mountain; **siamo ~ Natale** it's nearly Christmas; ~ **la pioggia/il sole** in the rain/sun(shine); ~ **terra** underground; ~ **voce** in a low voice; **chiuso ~ vuoto** vacuum-packed.

sottoline'are *vt* to underline; (*fig*) to emphasize, stress.

sottoma'rino, a *ag* (*flora*) submarine; (*cavo, navigazione*) underwater // *sm* (NAUT) submarine.

sotto'messo, a *pp di* **sottomettere**.

sotto'mettere *vt* to subdue, subjugate; ~**rsi** *vr* to submit.

sottopas'saggio [sottopas'saddʒo] *sm* (AUT) underpass; (*pedonale*) subway, underpass.

sotto'porre *vt* (*costringere*) to subject; (*fig*: *presentare*) to submit; **sottoporsi** *vr* to submit; **sottoporsi a** (*subire*) to undergo; **sotto'posto, a** *pp di* **sottoporre**.

sottos'critto, a *pp di* **sottoscrivere**.

sottos'crivere *vt* to sign // *vi*: ~ **a** to

subscribe to; **sottoscrizi'one** *sf* signing; subscription.

sottosegre'tario *sm*: ~ **di Stato** Under-Secretary of State (*Brit*), Assistant Secretary of State (*US*).

sotto'sopra *av* upside-down.

sotto'terra *av* underground.

sotto'titolo *sm* subtitle.

sotto'veste *sf* underskirt.

sotto'voce [sotto'votʃe] *av* in a low voice.

sot'trarre *vt* (MAT) to subtract, take away; ~ **qn/qc a** (*togliere*) to remove sb/sth from; (*salvare*) to save *o* rescue sb/sth from; ~ **qc a qn** (*rubare*) to steal sth from sb; **sottrarsi** *vr*: **sottrarsi a** (*sfuggire*) to escape; (*evitare*) to avoid; **sot'tratto, a** *pp di* **sottrarre**; **sottrazi'one** *sf* subtraction; removal.

sovi'etico, a, ci, che *ag* Soviet // *sm/f* Soviet citizen.

sovraccari'care *vt* to overload.

sovrannatu'rale *ag* = **soprannaturale.**

so'vrano, a *ag* sovereign; (*fig*: *sommo*) supreme // *sm/f* sovereign, monarch.

sovrap'porre *vt* to place on top of, put on top of.

sovras'tare *vi*: ~ **a**, *vt* (*vallata, fiume*) to overhang; (*fig*) to hang over, threaten.

sovrinten'dente *sm/f* = **soprinten-dente; sovrinten'denza** *sf* = **soprin-tendenza.**

sovru'mano, a *ag* superhuman.

sovvenzi'one [sovven'tsjone] *sf* subsidy, grant.

sovver'sivo, a *ag* subversive.

'**sozzo, a** [ˈsottso] *ag* filthy, dirty.

S.p.A. *abbr* = **società per azioni.**

spac'care *vt* to split, break; (*legna*) to chop; ~**rsi** *vr* to split, break; **spacca'tura** *sf* split.

spacci'are [spat'tʃare] *vt* (*vendere*) to sell (off); (*mettere in circolazione*) to circulate; (*droga*) to peddle, push; ~**rsi** *vr*: ~**rsi per** (*farsi credere*) to pass o.s. off as, pretend to be; **spaccia'tore, 'trice** *sm/f* (*di droga*) pusher; (*di denaro falso*) dealer; '**spaccio** *sm* (*di merce rubata, droga*): **spaccio (di)** trafficking (in); (*in denaro falso*): **spaccio (di)** passing (of); (*vendita*) sale; (*bottega*) shop.

'**spacco, chi** *sm* (*fenditura*) split, crack; (*strappo*) tear; (*di gonna*) slit.

spac'cone *sm/f* boaster, braggart.

'**spada** *sf* sword.

spae'sato, a *ag* disorientated, lost.

spa'ghetti [spa'getti] *smpl* (CUC) spaghetti *sg*.

'**Spagna** [ˈspaɲɲa] *sf*: **la ~** Spain; **spa'gnolo, a** *ag* Spanish // *sm/f* Spaniard // *sm* (LING) Spanish; **gli Spagnoli** the Spanish.

'spago, ghi sm string, twine.
spai'ato, a ag (calza, guanto) odd.
spalan'care vt, ~rsi vr to open wide.
spa'lare vt to shovel.
'spalla sf shoulder; (fig: TEATRO) stooge; ~**e** sfpl (dorso) back; **spalleggi'are** vt to back up, support.
spal'letta sf (parapetto) parapet.
spalli'era sf (di sedia etc) back; (di letto: da capo) head(board); (: da piedi) foot(board); (GINNASTICA) wall bars pl.
spal'mare vt to spread.
'spalti smpl (di stadio) terracing.
'spandere vt to spread; (versare) to pour (out); ~rsi vr to spread; **'spanto, a** pp di **spandere**.
spa'rare vt to fire // vi (far fuoco) to fire; (tirare) to shoot; **spara'tore** sm gunman; **spara'toria** sf exchange of shots.
sparecchi'are [sparek'kjare] vt: ~ (la tavola) to clear the table.
spa'reggio [spa'reddʒo] sm (SPORT) play-off.
'spargere ['spardʒere] vt (sparpagliare) to scatter; (versare: vino) to spill; (: lacrime, sangue) to shed; (diffondere) to spread; (emanare) to give off (o out); ~rsi vr to spread; **spargi'mento** sm scattering, strewing; spilling; shedding; spargimento di sangue bloodshed.
spa'rire vi to disappear, vanish.
spar'lare vi: ~ di to run down, speak ill of.
'sparo sm shot.
sparpagli'are [sparpaʎ'ʎare] vt, ~rsi vr to scatter.
'sparso, a pp di **spargere** // ag scattered; (sciolto) loose.
spar'tire vt (eredità, bottino) to share out; (avversari) to separate.
sparti'traffico sm inv (AUT) central reservation (Brit), median (strip) (US).
spa'ruto, a ag (viso etc) haggard.
sparvi'ero sm (ZOOL) sparrowhawk.
spasi'mare vi to be in agony; ~ di fare (fig) to yearn to do; ~ per qn to be madly in love with sb.
'spasimo sm pang; **'spasmo** sm (MED) spasm; **spas'modico, a, ci, che** ag (angoscioso) agonizing; (MED) spasmodic.
spassio'nato, a ag dispassionate, impartial.
'spasso sm (divertimento) amusement, enjoyment; andare a ~ to go out for a walk; essere a ~ (fig) to be out of work; mandare qn a ~ (fig) to give sb the sack.
spau'racchio [spau'rakkjo] sm scarecrow.
spau'rire vt to frighten, terrify.
spa'valdo, a ag arrogant, bold.
spaventa'passeri sm inv scarecrow.
spaven'tare vt to frighten, scare; ~rsi

vr to be frightened, be scared; to get a fright; **spa'vento** sm fear, fright; far spavento a qn to give sb a fright; **spaven'toso, a** ag frightening, terrible; (fig: fam) tremendous, fantastic.
spazien'tire [spattsjen'tire] vi (anche: ~rsi) to lose one's patience.
'spazio ['spattsjo] sm space; ~ **aereo** airspace; **spazi'oso, a** ag spacious.
spazzaca'mino [spattsaka'mino] sm chimney sweep.
spaz'zare [spat'tsare] vt to sweep; (foglie etc) to sweep up; (cacciare) to sweep away; **spazza'tura** sf sweepings pl; (immondizia) rubbish; **spaz'zino** sm street sweeper.
'spazzola ['spattsola] sf brush; ~ **per abiti** clothesbrush; ~ **da capelli** hairbrush; **spazzo'lare** vt to brush; **spazzo'lino** sm (small) brush; spazzolino da denti toothbrush.
specchi'arsi [spek'kjarsi] vr to look at o.s. in a mirror; (riflettersi) to be mirrored, be reflected.
'specchio ['spekkjo] sm mirror.
speci'ale [spe'tʃale] ag special; **specia'lista, i, e** sm/f specialist; **specialità** sf inv speciality; (branca di studio) special field, speciality; **specializ'zarsi** vr: specializzarsi (in) to specialize (in); **special'mente** av especially, particularly.
'specie ['spetʃe] sf inv (BIOL, BOT, ZOOL) species inv; (tipo) kind, sort // av especially, particularly; una ~ di a kind of; fare ~ a qn to surprise sb; la ~ umana mankind.
specifi'care [spetʃifi'kare] vt to specify, state.
spe'cifico, a, ci, che [spe'tʃifiko] ag specific.
specu'lare vi: ~ su (COMM) to speculate in; (sfruttare) to exploit; (meditare) to speculate on; **speculazi'one** sf speculation.
spe'dire vt to send; **spedizi'one** sf sending; (collo) consignment; (scientifica etc) expedition.
'spegnere ['spεɲɲere] vt (fuoco, sigaretta) to put out, extinguish; (apparecchio elettrico) to turn o switch off; (gas) to turn off; (fig: suoni, passioni) to stifle; (debito) to extinguish; ~rsi vr to go out; to go off; (morire) to pass away.
spel'lare vt (scuoiare) to skin; (scorticare) to graze; ~rsi vr to peel.
'spendere vt to spend.
spen'nare vt to pluck.
spensie'rato, a ag carefree.
'spento, a pp di **spegnere** // ag (suono) muffled; (colore) dull; (sigaretta) out; (civiltà, vulcano) extinct.
spe'ranza [spe'rantsa] sf hope.
spe'rare vt to hope for // vi: ~ **in** to trust in; ~ **che/di fare** to hope that/to do; lo

spero, spero di sì I hope so.

sper'duto, a *ag* (*isolato*) out-of-the-way; (*persona*: *smarrita, a disagio*) lost.

spergi'uro, a [sper'dʒuro] *sm/f* perjurer // *sm* perjury.

sperimen'tale *ag* experimental.

sperimen'tare *vt* to experiment with, test; (*fig*) to test, put to the test.

'sperma, i *sm* (*BIOL*) sperm.

spe'rone *sm* spur.

sperpe'rare *vt* to squander.

'spesa *sf* (*somma di denaro*) expense; (*costo*) cost; (*acquisto*) purchase; (*fam*: *acquisto del cibo quotidiano*) shopping; ~**e** *sfpl* expenses; (*COMM*) costs; charges; fare la ~ to do the shopping; a ~**e di** (*a carico di*) at the expense of; ~**e generali** overheads; ~**e postali** postage *sg*; ~**e di viaggio** travelling expenses.

'speso, a *pp di* **spendere**.

'spesso, a *ag* (*fitto*) thick; (*frequente*) frequent // *av* often; ~**e volte** frequently, often.

spes'sore *sm* thickness.

spet'tabile *ag* (*abbr*: Spett.: *in lettere*): ~ **ditta X** Messrs X and Co.

spet'tacolo *sm* (*rappresentazione*) performance, show; (*vista, scena*) sight; **dare** ~ **di sé** to make an exhibition *o* a spectacle of o.s.; **spettaco'loso, a** *ag* spectacular.

spet'tare *vi*: ~ **a** (*decisione*) to be up to; (*stipendio*) to be due to; **spetta a te decidere** it's up to you to decide.

spetta'tore, 'trice *sm/f* (*CINEMA, TEATRO*) member of the audience; (*di avvenimento*) onlooker, witness.

spetti'nare *vt*: ~ **qn** to ruffle sb's hair; ~**rsi** *vr* to get one's hair in a mess.

'spettro *sm* (*fantasma*) spectre; (*FISICA*) spectrum.

'spezie [spɛttsje] *sfpl* (*CUC*) spices.

spez'zare [spet'tsare] *vt* (*rompere*) to break; (*fig*: *interrompere*) to break up; ~**rsi** *vr* to break.

spezza'tino [spettsa'tino] *sm* (*CUC*) stew.

spezzet'tare [spettset'tare] *vt* to break up (*o* chop) into small pieces.

'spia *sf* spy; (*confidente della polizia*) informer; (*ELETTR*) indicating light; warning light; (*fessura*) peep-hole; (*fig*: *sintomo*) sign, indication.

spia'cente [spja'tʃɛnte] *ag* sorry; **essere** ~ **di qc/di fare qc** to be sorry about sth/ for doing sth.

spia'cevole [spja'tʃevole] *ag* unpleasant, disagreeable.

spi'aggia, ge ['spjaddʒa] *sf* beach.

spia'nare *vt* (*terreno*) to level, make level; (*edificio*) to raze to the ground; (*pasta*) to roll out; (*rendere liscio*) to smooth (out).

spi'ano *sm*: **a tutto** ~ (*lavorare*) nonstop, without a break; (*spendere*) lavishly.

spian'tato, a *ag* penniless, ruined.

spi'are *vt* to spy on; (*occasione etc*) to watch *o* wait for.

spi'azzo ['spjattso] *sm* open space; (*radura*) clearing.

spic'care *vt* (*assegno, mandato di cattura*) to issue // *vi* (*risaltare*) to stand out; ~ **il volo** to fly off; (*fig*) to spread one's wings; ~ **un balzo** to leap; **spic'cato, a** *ag* (*marcato*) marked, strong; (*notevole*) remarkable.

'spicchio ['spikkjo] *sm* (*di agrumi*) segment; (*di aglio*) clove; (*parte*) piece, slice.

spicci'arsi [spit'tʃarsi] *vr* to hurry up.

'spicciolo, a ['spittʃolo] *ag*: **moneta** ~**a**, ~**i** *smpl* (small) change.

'spicco, chi *sm*: **di** ~ outstanding; (*tema*) main, principal; **fare** ~ to stand out.

spi'edo *sm* (*CUC*) spit.

spie'gare *vt* (*far capire*) to explain; (*tovaglia*) to unfold; (*vele*) to unfurl; ~**rsi** *vr* to explain o.s., make o.s. clear; ~ **qc a qn** to explain sth to sb; **il problema si spiega** one can understand the problem; **spiegazi'one** *sf* explanation.

spiegaz'zare [spjegat'tsare] *vt* to crease, crumple.

spie'tato, a *ag* ruthless, pitiless.

spiffe'rare *vt* (*fam*) to blurt out, blab.

'spiga, ghe *sf* (*BOT*) ear.

spigli'ato, a [spiʎ'ʎato] *ag* self-possessed, self-confident.

'spigolo *sm* corner; (*MAT*) edge.

'spilla *sf* brooch; (*da cravatta, cappello*) pin.

spil'lare *vt* (*vino, fig*) to tap; ~ **denaro/ notizie a qn** to tap sb for money/ information.

'spillo *sm* pin; (*spilla*) brooch; ~ **di sicurezza** *o* **da balia** safety pin; ~ **di sicurezza** (*MIL*) (safety) pin.

spi'lorcio, a, ci, ce [spi'lortʃo] *ag* mean, stingy.

'spina *sf* (*BOT*) thorn; (*ZOOL*) spine, prickle; (*di pesce*) bone; (*ELETTR*) plug; (*di botte*) bunghole; **birra alla** ~ draught beer; ~ **dorsale** (*ANAT*) backbone.

spi'nacio [spi'natʃo] *sm* spinach; (*CUC*): ~**i** spinach *sg*.

spi'nale *ag* (*ANAT*) spinal.

'spingere ['spindʒere] *vt* to push; (*condurre*: *anche fig*) to drive; (*stimolare*): ~ **qn a fare** to urge *o* press sb to do; ~**rsi** *vr* (*inoltrarsi*) to push on, carry on; ~**rsi troppo lontano** (*anche fig*) to go too far.

spi'noso, a *ag* thorny, prickly.

'spinto, a *pp di* **spingere** // *sf* (*urto*) push; (*FISICA*) thrust; (*fig*: *stimolo*) incentive, spur; (: *appoggio*) string-pulling *q*; **dare una** ~**a a qn** (*fig*) to pull strings for sb.

spio'naggio [spio'naddʒo] *sm* espionage,

spying.

spi'overe *vi* (*scorrere*) to flow down; (*ricadere*) to hang down, fall.

'spira *sf* coil.

spi'raglio [spi'raλλo] *sm* (*fessura*) chink, narrow opening; (*raggio di luce, fig*) glimmer, gleam.

spi'rale *sf* spiral; (*contraccettivo*) coil; a ~ spiral(-shaped).

spi'rare *vi* (*vento*) to blow; (*morire*) to expire, pass away.

spiri'tato, a *ag* possessed; (*fig: persona, espressione*) wild.

spiri'tismo *sm* spiritualism.

'spirito *sm* (*REL, CHIM, disposizione d'animo, di legge etc, fantasma*) spirit; (*pensieri, intelletto*) mind; (*arguzia*) wit; (*umorismo*) humour, wit; lo S~ Santo the Holy Spirit o Ghost.

spirito'saggine [spirito'saddʒine] *sf* witticism; (*peg*) wisecrack.

spiri'toso, a *ag* witty.

spiritu'ale *ag* spiritual.

'splendere *vi* to shine.

'splendido, a *ag* splendid; (*splendente*) shining; (*sfarzoso*) magnificent, splendid.

splen'dore *sm* splendour; (*luce intensa*) brilliance, brightness.

spodes'tare *vt* to deprive of power; (*sovrano*) to depose.

'spoglia ['spɔλλa] *sf vedi* spoglio.

spogli'are [spoλ'λare] *vt* (*svestire*) to undress; (*privare, fig: depredare*): ~ qn di qc to deprive sb of sth; (*togliere ornamenti: anche fig*): ~ qn/qc di to strip sb/sth of; ~rsi *vr* to undress, strip; ~rsi di (*ricchezze etc*) to deprive o.s. of, give up; (*pregiudizi*) to rid o.s. of; **spoglia'toio** *sm* dressing room; (*di scuola etc*) cloakroom; (*SPORT*) changing room; **'spoglio, a** *ag* (*pianta, terreno*) bare; (*privo*): spoglio di stripped of; lacking in, without // *sm* (*di voti*) counting // *sf* (*ZOOL*) skin, hide; (: *di rettile*) slough; **'spoglie** *sfpl* (*salma*) remains; (*preda*) spoils, booty *sg*.

'spola *sf* shuttle; (*bobina di filo*) cop; fare la ~ (*fra*) to go to and fro o shuttle (between).

spol'pare *vt* to strip the flesh off.

spolve'rare *vt* (*anche CUC*) to dust; (*con spazzola*) to brush; (*con battipanni*) to beat; (*fig*) to polish off // *vi* to dust.

'sponda *sf* (*di fiume*) bank; (*di mare, lago*) shore; (*bordo*) edge.

spon'taneo, a *ag* spontaneous; (*persona*) unaffected, natural.

spopo'lare *vt* to depopulate // *vi* (*attirare folla*) to draw the crowds; ~rsi *vr* to become depopulated.

spor'care *vt* to dirty, make dirty; (*fig*) to sully, soil; ~rsi *vr* to get dirty.

spor'cizia [spor'tʃittsja] *sf* (*stato*) dirtiness; (*sudiciume*) dirt, filth; (*cosa sporca*) dirt q, something dirty; (*fig: cosa oscena*) obscenity.

'sporco, a, chi, che *ag* dirty, filthy.

spor'genza [spor'dʒentsa] *sf* projection.

'sporgere ['spɔrdʒere] *vt* to put out, stretch out // *vi* (*venire in fuori*) to stick out; ~rsi *vr* to lean out; ~ querela contro qn (*DIR*) to take legal action against sb.

sport *sm inv* sport.

'sporta *sf* shopping bag.

spor'tello *sm* (*di treno, auto etc*) door; (*di banca, ufficio*) window, counter; ~ automatico (*BANCA*) cash dispenser, automated telling machine.

spor'tivo, a *ag* (*gara, giornale*) sports cpd; (*persona*) sporty; (*abito*) casual; (*spirito, atteggiamento*) sporting.

'sporto, a *pp di* sporgere.

'sposa *sf* bride; (*moglie*) wife.

sposa'lizio [spoza'littsjo] *sm* wedding.

spo'sare *vt* to marry; (*fig: idea, fede*) to espouse; ~rsi *vr* to get married, marry; ~rsi con qn to marry sb, get married to sb; **spo'sato, a** *ag* married.

'sposo *sm* (*bride*)groom; (*marito*) husband; gli ~i *smpl* the newlyweds.

spos'sato, a *ag* exhausted, weary.

spos'tare *vt* to move, shift; (*cambiare: orario*) to change; ~rsi *vr* to move.

'spranga, ghe *sf* (*sbarra*) bar.

'sprazzo ['sprattso] *sm* (*di sole etc*) flash; (*fig: di gioia etc*) burst.

spre'care *vt* to waste; ~rsi *vr* (*persona*) to waste one's energy; **'spreco** *sm* waste.

spre'gevole [spre'dʒevole] *ag* contemptible, despicable.

spregiudi'cato, a [spredʒudi'kato] *ag* unprejudiced, unbiased; (*peg*) unscrupulous.

'spremere *vt* to squeeze.

spre'muta *sf* fresh juice; ~ d'arancia fresh orange juice.

sprez'zante [spret'tsante] *ag* scornful, contemptuous.

sprigio'nare [spridʒo'nare] *vt* to give off, emit; ~rsi *vr* to emanate; (*uscire con impeto*) to burst out.

spriz'zare [sprit'tsare] *vt, vi* to spurt; ~ gioia/salute to be bursting with joy/health.

sprofon'dare *vi* to sink; (*casa*) to collapse; (*suolo*) to give way, subside; ~rsi *vr*: ~rsi in (*poltrona*) to sink into; (*fig*) to become immersed o absorbed in.

spro'nare *vt* to spur (on).

'sprone *sm* (*sperone, fig*) spur.

spropor'zionato, a [sproportsjo'nato] *ag* disproportionate, out of all proportion.

sproporzi'one [spropor'tsjone] *sf* disproportion.

sproposi'tato, a *ag* (*lettera, discorso*) full of mistakes; (*fig: costo*) excessive, enormous.

spro'posito _sm_ blunder; **a ~ at the wrong time**; (_rispondere, parlare_) irrelevantly.

sprovve'duto, a _ag_ inexperienced, naïve.

sprov'visto, a _ag_ (_mancante_): **~ di** lacking in, without; **alla ~a** unawares.

spruz'zare [sprut'tsare] _vt_ (_a nebulizzazione_) to spray; (_aspergere_) to sprinkle; (_inzaccherare_) to splash; **'spruzzo** _sm_ spray; splash.

'spugna ['spuɲɲa] _sf_ (ZOOL) sponge; (_tessuto_) towelling; **spu'gnoso, a** _ag_ spongy.

'spuma _sf_ (_schiuma_) foam; (_bibita_) mineral water.

spu'mante _sm_ sparkling wine.

spumeggi'ante [spumed'dʒante] _ag_ (_birra_) foaming; (_vino, fig_) sparkling.

spu'mone _sm_ (CUC) mousse.

spun'tare _vt_ (_coltello_) to break the point of; (_capelli_) to trim // _vi_ (_uscire: germogli_) to sprout; (: _capelli_) to begin to grow; (: _denti_) to come through; (_apparire_) to appear (suddenly); **~rsi** _vr_ to become blunt, lose its point; **spuntarla** (_fig_) to make it, win through.

spun'tino _sm_ snack.

'spunto _sm_ (TEATRO, MUS) cue; (_fig_) starting point; **dare lo ~ a** (_fig_) to give rise to.

spur'gare _vt_ (_fogna_) to clean, clear; **~rsi** _vr_ (MED) to expectorate.

spu'tare _vt_ to spit out; (_fig_) to belch (out) // _vi_ to spit; **'sputo** _sm_ spittle _q_, spit _q_.

'squadra _sf_ (_strumento_) (set) square; (_gruppo_) team, squad; (_di operai_) gang, squad; (MIL) squad; (: AER, NAUT) squadron; (SPORT) team; **lavoro a ~e** teamwork.

squa'drare _vt_ to square, make square; (_osservare_) to look at closely.

squa'driglia [skwa'driʎʎa] _sf_ (AER) flight; (NAUT) squadron.

squa'drone _sm_ squadron.

squagli'arsi [skwaʎ'ʎarsi] _vr_ to melt; (_fig_) to sneak off.

squa'lifica _sf_ disqualification.

squalifi'care _vt_ to disqualify.

'squallido, a _ag_ wretched, bleak.

squal'lore _sm_ wretchedness, bleakness.

'squalo _sm_ shark.

'squama _sf_ scale; **squa'mare** _vt_ to scale; **squamarsi** _vr_ to flake _o_ peel (off).

squarcia'gola [skwartʃa'gola]: **a ~** _av_ at the top of one's voice.

squar'tare _vt_ to quarter, cut up.

squattri'nato, a _ag_ penniless.

squili'brare _vt_ to unbalance; **squili'brato, a** _ag_ (PSIC) unbalanced; **squi'librio** _sm_ (_differenza, sbilancio_) imbalance; (PSIC) unbalance.

squil'lante _ag_ shrill, sharp.

squil'lare _vi_ (_campanello, telefono_) to

ring (out); (_tromba_) to blare; **'squillo** _sm_ ring, ringing _q_; blare; **ragazza** _f_ **squillo** _inv_ call girl.

squi'sito, a _ag_ exquisite; (_cibo_) delicious; (_persona_) delightful.

squit'tire _vi_ (_uccello_) to squawk; (_topo_) to squeak.

sradi'care _vt_ to uproot; (_fig_) to eradicate.

sragio'nare [zradʒo'nare] _vi_ to talk nonsense, rave.

srego'lato, a _ag_ (_senza ordine: vita_) disorderly; (_smodato_) immoderate; (_dissoluto_) dissolute.

S.r.l. _abbr_ = **società a responsabilità limitata.**

'stabile _ag_ stable, steady; (_tempo: non variabile_) settled; (TEATRO: _compagnia_) resident // _sm_ (_edificio_) building.

stabili'mento _sm_ (_edificio_) establishment; (_fabbrica_) plant, factory.

stabi'lire _vt_ to establish; (_fissare: prezzi, data_) to fix; (_decidere_) to decide; **~rsi** _vr_ (_prendere dimora_) to settle.

stac'care _vt_ (_levare_) to detach, remove; (_separare: anche fig_) to separate, divide; (_strappare_) to tear off (_o_ out); (_scandire: parole_) to pronounce clearly; (SPORT) to leave behind; **~rsi** _vr_ (_bottone etc_) to come off; (_scostarsi_): **~rsi (da)** to move away (from); (_fig: separarsi_): **~rsi da** to leave; **non ~ gli occhi da qn** not to take one's eyes off sb.

'stadio _sm_ (SPORT) stadium; (_periodo, fase_) phase, stage.

'staffa _sf_ (_di sella_, TECN) stirrup; **perdere le ~e** (_fig_) to fly off the handle.

staf'fetta _sf_ (_messo_) dispatch rider; (SPORT) relay race.

stagio'nale [stadʒo'nale] _ag_ seasonal.

stagio'nare [stadʒo'nare] _vt_ (_legno_) to season; (_formaggi, vino_) to mature.

stagi'one [sta'dʒone] _sf_ season; **alta/bassa ~** high/low season.

stagli'arsi [staʎ'ʎarsi] _vr_ to stand out, be silhouetted.

sta'gnare [staɲ'ɲare] _vt_ (_vaso, tegame_) to tin-plate; (_barca, botte_) to make watertight; (_sangue_) to stop // _vi_ to stagnate.

'stagno, a ['staɲɲo] _ag_ watertight; (_a tenuta d'aria_) airtight // _sm_ (_acquitrino_) pond; (CHIM) tin.

sta'gnola [staɲ'ɲola] _sf_ tinfoil.

'stalla _sf_ (_per bovini_) cowshed; (_per cavalli_) stable.

stal'lone _sm_ stallion.

sta'mani, stamat'tina _av_ this morning.

'stampa _sf_ (TIP, FOT: _tecnica_) printing; (_impressione, copia fotografica_) print; (_insieme di quotidiani, giornalisti etc_) press; **~e** _sfpl_ printed matter.

stam'pante _sf_ (INFORM) printer.

stam'pare _vt_ to print; (_pubblicare_) to

publish; (*coniare*) to strike, coin; (*imprimere*: *anche fig*) to impress.

stampa'tello *sm* block letters *pl*.

stam'pella *sf* crutch.

'stampo *sm* mould; (*fig*: *indole*) type, kind, sort.

sta'nare *vt* to drive out.

stan'care *vt* to tire, make tired; (*annoiare*) to bore; (*infastidire*) to annoy; ~rsi *vr* to get tired, tire o.s. out; ~rsi (di) to grow weary (of), grow tired (of).

stan'chezza [stan'kettsa] *sf* tiredness, fatigue.

'stanco, a, chi, che *ag* tired; ~ di tired of, fed up with.

'stanga, ghe *sm* bar; (*di carro*) shaft.

stan'gata *sf* (*colpo*: *anche fig*) blow; (*cattivo risultato*) poor result; (*CALCIO*) shot.

sta'notte *av* tonight; (*notte passata*) last night.

'stante *prep*: a sé ~ (*appartamento*, *casa*) independent, separate.

stan'tio, a, 'tii, 'tie *ag* stale; (*burro*) rancid; (*fig*) old.

stan'tuffo *sm* piston.

'stanza ['stantsa] *sf* room; (*POESIA*) stanza; ~ da letto bedroom.

stanzi'are [stan'tsjare] *vt* to allocate.

stap'pare *vt* to uncork; to uncap.

'stare *vi* (*restare in un luogo*) to stay, remain; (*abitare*) to stay, live; (*essere situato*) to be, be situated; (*anche*: ~ in **piedi**) to be, stand; (*essere*, *trovarsi*) to be; (*dipendere*): se stesse in me if it were up to me, if it depended on me; (*seguito da gerundio*): sta studiando he's studying; starci (*esserci spazio*): nel baule non ci sta più niente there's no more room in the boot; (*accettare*) to accept; ci stai? is that okay with you?; ~ a (*attenersi a*) to follow, stick to; (*seguito dall'infinito*): stiamo a discutere we're talking; (*toccare a*): sta a te giocare it's your turn to play; ~ per fare qc to be about to do sth; come sta? how are you?; io sto bene/male I'm very well/not very well; ~ a qn (*abiti etc*) to fit sb; queste scarpe mi stanno strette these shoes are tight for me; il rosso ti sta bene red suits you.

starnu'tire *vi* to sneeze; **star'nuto** *sm* sneeze.

sta'sera *av* this evening, tonight.

sta'tale *ag* state *cpd* // *sm/f* state employee, local authority employee; (*nell'amministrazione*) ≈ civil servant.

sta'tista, i *sm* statesman.

sta'tistica *sf* statistics *sg*.

'stato, a *pp di* essere, stare // *sm* (*condizione*) state, condition; (*POL*) state; (*DIR*) status; essere in ~ d'accusa (*DIR*) to be committed for trial; ~ d'assedio/

d'emergenza state of siege/emergency; ~ **civile** (*AMM*) marital status; ~ **maggiore** (*MIL*) staff; gli S~i Uniti (d'America) the United States (of America).

'statua *sf* statue.

statuni'tense *ag* United States *cpd*, of the United States.

sta'tura *sf* (*ANAT*) height, stature; (*fig*) stature.

sta'tuto *sm* (*DIR*) statute; constitution.

sta'volta *av* this time.

stazio'nario, a [stattsjo'narjo] *ag* stationary; (*fig*) unchanged.

stazi'one [stat'tsjone] *sf* station; (*balneare*, *termale*) resort; ~ **degli autobus** bus station; ~ **balneare** seaside resort; ~ **ferroviaria** railway (*Brit*) o railroad (*US*) station; ~ **invernale** winter sports resort; ~ **di polizia** police station (*in small town*); ~ **di servizio** service o petrol (*Brit*) o filling station.

'stecca, che *sf* stick; (*di ombrello*) rib; (*di sigarette*) carton; (*MED*) splint; (*stonatura*): fare una ~ to sing (o play) a wrong note.

stec'cato *sm* fence.

stec'chito, a [stek'kito] *ag* dried up; (*persona*) skinny; lasciar ~ qn (*fig*) to leave sb flabbergasted; morto ~ stone dead.

'stella *sf* star; ~ **alpina** (*BOT*) edelweiss; ~ **di mare** (*ZOOL*) starfish.

'stelo *sm* stem; (*asta*) rod; lampada a ~ standard lamp.

'stemma, i *sm* coat of arms.

stempe'rare *vt* to dilute; to dissolve; (*colori*) to mix.

sten'dardo *sm* standard.

'stendere *vt* (*braccia*, *gambe*) to stretch (out); (*tovaglia*) to spread (out); (*bucato*) to hang out; (*mettere a giacere*) to lay (down); (*spalmare*: *colore*) to spread; (*mettere per iscritto*) to draw up; ~rsi *vr* (*coricarsi*) to stretch out, lie down; (*estendersi*) to extend, stretch.

stenodatti'lografo, a *sm/f* shorthand typist (*Brit*), stenographer (*US*).

stenogra'fare *vt* to take down in shorthand; **stenogra'fia** *sf* shorthand.

sten'tare *vi*: ~ a fare to find it hard to do, have difficulty doing.

'stento *sm* (*fatica*) difficulty; ~i *smpl* (*privazioni*) hardship *sg*, privation *sg*; a ~ *av* with difficulty, barely.

'sterco *sm* dung.

'stereo('fonico, a, ci, che) *ag* stereo(phonic).

'sterile *ag* sterile; (*terra*) barren; (*fig*) futile, fruitless; **sterilità** *sf* sterility.

sterili'zzare [sterilid'dzare] *vt* to sterilize; **sterilizzazi'one** *sf* sterilization.

ster'lina *sf* pound (sterling).

stermi'nare *vt* to exterminate, wipe out.

stermi'nato, a *ag* immense; endless.

ster'minio *sm* extermination, destruction.

'sterno *sm* (ANAT) breastbone.

ster'zare [ster'tsare] *vt, vi* (AUT) to steer; **'sterzo** *sm* steering; (*volante*) steering wheel.

'steso, a *pp di* **stendere.**

'stesso, a *ag* same; (*rafforzativo: in persona, proprio*): **il re ~** the king himself *o* in person *o* **pronome: lo(la) ~(a)** the same (one); **i suoi ~i avversari lo ammirano** even his enemies admire him; **fa lo ~** it doesn't matter; **per me è lo ~** it's all the same to me, it doesn't matter to me; *vedi* **io, tu** *etc.*

ste'sura *sf* drafting *q*, drawing up *q*; draft.

'stigma, i *sm* stigma.

'stigmate *sfpl* (REL) stigmata.

sti'lare *vt* to draw up, draft.

'stile *sm* style; **sti'lista, i** *sm* designer.

stil'lare *vi* (*trasudare*) to ooze; (*gocciolare*) to drip; **stilli'cidio** *sm* (*fig*) continual pestering (*o* moaning *etc*).

stilo'grafica, che *sf* (*anche:* **penna ~**) fountain pen.

'stima *sf* esteem; valuation; assessment, estimate.

sti'mare *vt* (*persona*) to esteem, hold in high regard; (*terreno, casa etc*) to value; (*stabilire in misura approssimativa*) to estimate, assess; (*ritenere*): **~ che** to consider that; **~rsi fortunato** to consider o.s. (to be) lucky.

stimo'lare *vt* to stimulate; (*incitare*): **~ qn (a fare)** to spur sb on (to do).

'stimolo *sm* (*anche fig*) stimulus.

'stinco, chi *sm* shin; shinbone.

'stingere ['stindʒere] *vt, vi* (*anche:* **~rsi**) to fade; **'stinto, a** *pp di* **stingere.**

sti'pare *vt* to cram, pack; **~rsi** *vr* (*accalcarsi*) to crowd, throng.

sti'pendio *sm* salary.

'stipite *sm* (*di porta, finestra*) jamb.

stipu'lare *vt* (*redigere*) to draw up.

sti'rare *vt* (*abito*) to iron; (*distendere*) to stretch; (*strappare: muscolo*) to strain; **~rsi** *vr* to stretch (o.s.); **stira'tura** *sf* ironing.

'stirpe *sf* birth, stock; descendants *pl.*

stiti'chezza [stiti'kettsa] *sf* constipation.

'stitico, a, ci, che *ag* constipated.

'stiva *sf* (*di nave*) hold.

sti'vale *sm* boot.

'stizza ['stittsa] *sf* anger, vexation; **stiz'zirsi** *vr* to lose one's temper; **stiz'zoso, a** *ag* (*persona*) quick-tempered, irascible; (*risposta*) angry.

stocca'fisso *sm* stockfish, dried cod.

stoc'cata *sf* (*colpo*) stab, thrust; (*fig*) gibe, cutting remark.

'stoffa *sf* material, fabric; (*fig*): **aver la ~ di** to have the makings of.

'stola *sf* stole.

'stolto, a *ag* stupid, foolish.

'stomaco, chi *sm* stomach; **dare di ~** to vomit, be sick.

sto'nare *vt* to sing (*o* play) out of tune // *vi* to be out of tune, sing (*o* play) out of tune; (*fig*) to be out of place, jar; (: *colori*) to clash; **stona'tura** *sf* (*suono*) false note.

stop *sm inv* (TEL) stop; (AUT: *cartello*) stop sign; (: *fanalino d'arresto*) brakelight.

'stoppa *sf* tow.

'stoppia *sf* (AGR) stubble.

stop'pino *sm* wick; (*miccia*) fuse.

'storcere ['stortʃere] *vt* to twist; **~rsi** *vr* to writhe, twist; **~ il naso** (*fig*) to turn up one's nose; **~rsi la caviglia** to twist one's ankle.

stor'dire *vt* (*intontire*) to stun, daze; **~rsi** *vr*: **~rsi col bere** to dull one's senses with drink; **stor'dito, a** *ag* stunned; (*sventato*) scatterbrained, heedless.

'storia *sf* (*scienza, avvenimenti*) history; (*racconto, bugia*) story; (*faccenda, questione*) business *q*; (*pretesto*) excuse, pretext; **~e** *sfpl* (*smancerie*) fuss *sg*; **'storico, a, ci, che** *ag* historic(al) // *sm* historian.

stori'one *sm* (ZOOL) sturgeon.

stor'mire *vi* to rustle.

'stormo *sm* (*di uccelli*) flock.

stor'nare *vt* (COMM) to transfer.

'storno *sm* starling.

storpi'are *vt* to cripple, maim; (*fig: parole*) to mangle; (: *significato*) to twist.

'storpio, a *ag* crippled, maimed.

'storto, a *pp di* **storcere** // *ag* (*chiodo*) twisted, bent; (*gamba, quadro*) crooked; (*fig: ragionamento*) false, wrong // *sf* (*distorsione*) sprain, twist; (*recipiente*) retort.

sto'viglie [sto'viʎʎe] *sfpl* dishes *pl*, crockery.

'strabico, a, ci, che *ag* squint-eyed; (*occhi*) squint.

stra'bismo *sm* squinting.

stra'carico, a, chi, che *ag* overloaded.

stracci'are [strat'tʃare] *vt* to tear.

'straccio, a, ci, ce ['strattʃo] *ag*: **carta ~a** waste paper // *sm* rag; (*per pulire*) cloth, duster; **stracci'vendolo** *sm* ragman.

stra'cotto, a *ag* overcooked // *sm* (CUC) beef stew.

'strada *sf* road; (*di città*) street; (*cammino, via, fig*) way; **farsi ~** (*fig*) to do well for o.s.; **essere fuori ~** (*fig*) to be on the wrong track; **~ facendo** on the way; **~ senza uscita** dead end; **stra'dale** *ag* road *cpd.*

strafalci'one [strafal'tʃone] *sm* blunder, howler.

stra'fare *vi* to overdo it; **stra'fatto, a** *pp di* **strafare.**

strafot'tente *ag*: **è ~** he doesn't give a

damn, he couldn't care less.

'**strage** ['stradʒe] sf massacre, slaughter.

stralu'nato, a ag (occhi) rolling; (persona) beside o.s., very upset.

stramaz'zare [stramat'tsare] vi to fall heavily.

'**strambo, a** ag strange, queer.

strampa'lato, a ag odd, eccentric.

stra'nezza [stra'nettsa] sf strangeness.

strango'lare vt to strangle; ~rsi vr to choke.

strani'ero, a ag foreign // sm/f foreigner.

'**strano, a** ag strange, odd.

straordi'nario, a ag extraordinary; (treno etc) special // sm (lavoro) overtime.

strapaz'zare [strapat'tsare] vt to ill-treat; ~rsi vr to tire o.s. out, overdo things; **stra'pazzo** sm strain, fatigue; **da strapazzo** (fig) third-rate.

strapi'ombo sm overhanging rock; **a** ~ overhanging.

strapo'tere sm excessive power.

strap'pare vt (gen) to tear, rip; (pagina etc) to tear off, tear out; (sradicare) to pull up; (togliere): ~ **qc a qn** to snatch sth from sb; (fig) to wrest sth from sb; ~rsi vr (lacerarsi) to rip, tear; (rompersi) to break; ~rsi **un muscolo** to tear a muscle; '**strappo** sm pull, tug; tear, rip; **fare uno strappo alla regola** to make an exception to the rule; **strappo muscolare** torn muscle.

strapun'tino sm jump o foldaway seat.

strari'pare vi to overflow.

strasci'care [straʃʃi'kare] vt to trail; (piedi) to drag; ~ **le parole** to drawl.

'**strascico, chi** ['straʃʃiko] sm (di abito) train; (conseguenza) after-effect.

strata'gemma, i [strata'dʒemma] sm stratagem.

strate'gia, 'gie [strate'dʒia] sf strategy; **stra'tegico, a, ci, che** ag strategic.

'**strato** sm layer; (rivestimento) coat, coating; (GEO, fig) stratum; (METEOR) stratus.

stratos'fera sf stratosphere.

strava'gante ag odd, eccentric; **strava'ganza** sf eccentricity.

stra'vecchio, a [stra'vekkjo] ag very old.

stra'vizio [stra'vittsjo] sm excess.

stra'volgere [stra'vɔldʒere] vt (volto) to contort; (fig: animo) to trouble deeply; (: verità) to twist, distort; **stra'volto, a** pp di **stravolgere**.

strazi'are [strat'tsjare] vt to torture, torment; '**strazio** sm torture; (fig: cosa fatta male): **essere uno** ~ to be appalling.

'**strega, ghe** sf witch.

stre'gare vt to bewitch.

stre'gone sm (mago) wizard; (di tribù) witch doctor.

'**stregua** sf: **alla** ~ **di** by the same

standard as.

stre'mare vt to exhaust.

'**stremo** sm very end; **essere allo** ~ to be at the end of one's tether.

'**strenna** sf Christmas present.

'**strenuo, a** ag brave, courageous.

strepi'toso, a ag clamorous, deafening; (fig: successo) resounding.

stres'sante ag stressful.

'**stretta** sf vedi **stretto**.

stretta'mente av tightly; (rigorosamente) strictly.

stret'tezza [stret'tettsa] sf narrowness; ~e sfpl poverty sg, straitened circumstances.

'**stretto, a** pp di **stringere** // ag (corridoio, limiti) narrow; (gonna, scarpe, nodo, curva) tight; (intimo: parente, amico) close; (rigoroso: osservanza) strict; (preciso: significato) precise, exact // sm (braccio di mare) strait // sf (di mano) grasp; (finanziaria) squeeze; (fig: dolore, turbamento) pang; **a denti** ~i with clenched teeth; **lo** ~ **necessario** the bare minimum; **una** ~a **di mano** a handshake; **essere alle** ~e **to have one's back to the wall; **stret'toia** sf bottleneck; (fig) tricky situation.

stri'ato, a ag streaked.

'**stridere** vi (porta) to squeak; (animale) to screech, shriek; (colori) to clash; '**strido, **pl(f)** **strida** sm screech, shriek; **stri'dore** sm screeching, shrieking; '**stridulo, a** ag shrill.

stril'lare vt, vi to scream, shriek; '**strillo** sm scream, shriek.

stril'lone sm newspaper seller.

strimin'zito, a [strimin'tsito] ag (misero) shabby; (molto magro) skinny.

strimpel'lare vt (MUS) to strum.

'**stringa, ghe** sf lace.

strin'gato, a ag (fig) concise.

'**stringere** ['strindʒere] vt (avvicinare due cose) to press (together), squeeze (together); (tenere stretto) to hold tight, clasp, clutch; (pugno, mascella, denti) to clench; (labbra) to compress; (avvitare) to tighten; (abito) to take in; (sog: scarpe) to pinch, be tight for; (fig: concludere: patto) to make; (: accelerare: passo, tempo) to quicken // vi (essere stretto) to be tight; (tempo: incalzare) to be pressing; ~rsi vr (accostarsi): ~rsi **a** to press o.s. up against; ~ **la mano a qn** to shake sb's hand; ~ **gli occhi** to screw up one's eyes.

'**striscia, sce** ['striʃʃa] sf (di carta, tessuto etc) strip; (riga) stripe; ~sce (pedonali) zebra crossing sg.

strisci'are [striʃ'ʃare] vt (piedi) to drag; (muro, macchina) to graze // vi to crawl, creep.

'**striscio** ['striʃʃo] sm graze; (MED) smear; **colpire di** ~ to graze.

strito'lare vt to grind.

striz'zare [strit'tsare] vt (arancia) to squeeze; (panni) to wring (out); ~ l'occhio to wink.

'strofa sf, **'strofe** sf inv strophe.

strofi'naccio [strofi'nattʃo] sm duster, cloth; (per piatti) dishcloth; (per pavimenti) floorcloth.

strofi'nare vt to rub.

stron'care vt to break off; (fig: ribellione) to suppress, put down; (: film, libro) to tear to pieces.

stropicci'are [stropit'tʃare] vt to rub.

stroz'zare [strot'tsare] vt (soffocare) to choke, strangle; ~rsi vr to choke; **strozza'tura** sf (restringimento) narrowing; (di strada etc) bottleneck.

'struggere [strudd'ʒere] vt (fig) to consume; ~rsi vr (fig): ~rsi di to be consumed with.

strumen'tale ag (MUS) instrumental.

strumentaliz'zare [strumentalid'dzare] vt to exploit, use to one's own ends.

stru'mento sm (arnese, fig) instrument, tool; (MUS) instrument; ~ a corda o ad arco/a fiato stringed/wind instrument.

'strutto sm lard.

strut'tura sf structure; **struttu'rare** vt to structure.

'struzzo ['struttso] sm ostrich.

stuc'care vt (muro) to plaster; (vetro) to putty; (decorare con stucchi) to stucco.

stuc'chevole [stuk'kevole] ag nauseating; (fig) tedious, boring.

'stucco, chi sm plaster; (da vetri) putty; (ornamentale) stucco; **rimanere di ~** (fig) to be dumbfounded.

stu'dente, 'essa sm/f student; (scolaro) pupil, schoolboy/girl; **studen'tesco, a, schi, sche** ag student cpd; school cpd.

studi'are vt to study.

'studio sm studying; (ricerca, saggio, stanza) study; (di professionista) office; (di artista, CINEMA, TV, RADIO) studio; ~i smpl (INS) studies; ~ medico doctor's surgery (Brit) o office (US).

studi'oso, a ag studious, hard- working // sm/f scholar.

'stufa sf stove; ~ **elettrica** electric fire o heater.

stu'fare vt (CUC) to stew; (fig: fam) to bore; **stu'fato** sm (CUC) stew; **'stufo, a** ag (fam): **essere stufo di** to be fed up with, be sick and tired of.

stu'oia sf mat.

stupefa'cente [stupefa'tʃente] ag stunning, astounding // sm drug, narcotic.

stu'pendo, a ag marvellous, wonderful.

stupi'daggine [stupi'daddʒine] sf stupid thing (to do o say).

stupidità sf stupidity.

'stupido, a ag stupid.

stu'pire vt to amaze, stun // vi (anche: ~rsi): ~ (di) to be amazed (at), be stunned (by).

stu'pore sm amazement, astonishment.

'stupro sm rape.

stu'rare vt (lavandino) to clear.

stuzzica'denti [stuttsika'dɛnti] sm toothpick.

stuzzi'care [stuttsi'kare] vt (ferita etc) to poke (at), prod (at); (fig) to tease; (: appetito) to whet; (: curiosità) to stimulate; ~ **i denti** to pick one's teeth.

su ◆ prep (su + il = **sul**, su + lo = **sullo**, su + l' = **sull'**, su + la = **sulla**, su + i = **sui**, su + gli = **sugli**, su + le = **sulle**) **1** (gen) on; (moto) on(to); (in cima a) on (top of); **mettilo sul tavolo** put it on the table; **un paesino sul mare** a village by the sea

2 (argomento) about, on; **un libro ~ Cesare** a book on o about Caesar

3 (circa) about; **costerà sui 3 milioni** it will cost about 3 million; **una ragazza sui 17 anni** a girl of about 17 (years of age)

4: ~ **misura** made to measure; ~ **richiesta** on request; **3 casi ~ dieci** 3 cases out of 10

◆ av **1** (in alto, verso l'alto) up; **vieni ~** come on up; **guarda ~** look up; ~ **le mani!** hands up!; **in ~** (verso l'alto) up(wards); (in poi) onwards; **dai 20 anni in ~** from the age of 20 onwards

2 (addosso) on; **cos'hai ~?** what have you got on?

◆ escl come on!; ~ **coraggio!** come on, cheer up!

'sua vedi **suo**.

su'bacqueo, a ag underwater // sm skindiver.

sub'buglio [sub'buʎʎo] sm confusion, turmoil.

subcosci'ente [subkoʃ'ʃɛnte] ag, sm subconscious.

'subdolo, a ag underhand, sneaky.

suben'trare vi: ~ **a qn in qc** to take over sth from sb.

su'bire vt to suffer, endure.

subis'sare vt (fig): ~ **di** to overwhelm with, load with.

subi'taneo, a ag sudden.

'subito av immediately, at once, straight away.

subodo'rare vt (insidia etc) to smell, suspect.

subordi'nato, a ag subordinate; (dipendente): ~ **a** dependent on, subject to.

subur'bano, a ag suburban.

succe'daneo [suttʃe'daneo] sm substitute.

suc'cedere [sut'tʃedere] vi (prendere il posto di qn): ~ **a** to succeed; (venire dopo): ~ **a** to follow; (accadere) to happen; ~rsi vr to follow each other; ~ **al trono** to succeed to the throne; **successi'one** sf succession; **succes'sivo, a** ag successive; **suc'cesso, a** pp di **succedere** // sm (esito) outcome;

(*buona riuscita*) success; **di successo** (*libro, personaggio*) successful.

succhi'are [suk'kjare] *vt* to suck (up). /

suc'cinto, a [sut'tʃinto] *ag* (*discorso*) succinct; (*abito*) brief.

'succo, chi *sm* juice; (*fig*) essence, gist; ~ **di frutta** fruit juice; **suc'coso, a** *ag* juicy; (*fig*) pithy.

succur'sale *sf* branch (office).

sud *sm* south // *ag inv* south; (*lato*) south, southern.

Su'dafrica *sm*: il ~ South Africa; **suda-fri'cano, a** *ag, sm/f* South African.

Suda'merica *sm*: il ~ South America; **sudameri'cano, a** *ag, sm/f* South American.

su'dare *vi* to perspire, sweat; ~ **freddo** to come out in a cold sweat; **su'data** *sf* sweat; **ho fatto una bella sudata per finirlo in tempo** it was a real sweat to get it finished in time.

sud'detto, a *ag* above-mentioned.

sud'dito, a *sm/f* subject.

suddi'videre *vt* to subdivide.

su'dest *sm* south-east.

'sudicio, a, ci, ce ['suditʃo] *ag* dirty, filthy; **sudici'ume** *sm* dirt, filth.

su'dore *sm* perspiration, sweat.

su'dovest *sm* south-west.

'sue *vedi* suo.

suffici'ente [suffi'tʃente] *ag* enough, sufficient; (*borioso*) self-important; (*INS*) satisfactory; **suffici'enza** *sf* self-importance; pass mark; **a sufficienza** *av* enough; **ne ho avuto a sufficienza!** I've had enough of this!

suf'fisso *sm* (*LING*) suffix.

suf'fragio [suf'fradʒo] *sm* (*voto*) vote; ~ **universale** universal suffrage.

suggel'lare [suddʒel'lare] *vt* (*fig*) to seal.

suggeri'mento [suddʒeri'mento] *sm* suggestion; (*consiglio*) piece of advice, advice *q*.

sugge'rire [suddʒe'rire] *vt* (*risposta*) to tell; (*consigliare*) to advise; (*proporre*) to suggest; (*TEATRO*) to prompt; **suggeri'tore, 'trice** *sm/f* (*TEATRO*) prompter.

suggestio'nare [suddʒestjo'nare] *vt* to influence.

suggesti'one [suddʒes'tjone] *sf* (*PSIC*) suggestion; (*istigazione*) instigation.

sugges'tivo, a [suddʒes'tivo] *ag* (*paesaggio*) evocative; (*teoria*) interesting, attractive.

'sughero ['sugero] *sm* cork.

'sugli ['suʎʎi] *prep* + *det vedi* su.

'sugo, ghi *sm* (*succo*) juice; (*di carne*) gravy; (*condimento*) sauce; (*fig*) gist, essence.

'sui *prep* + *det vedi* su.

sui'cida, i, e [sui'tʃida] *ag* suicidal // *sm/f* suicide.

suici'darsi [suitʃi'darsi] *vr* to commit suicide.

sui'cidio [sui'tʃidjo] *sm* suicide.

su'ino, a *ag*: **carne** ~**a** pork // *sm* pig; ~**i** *smpl* swine *pl*.

sul, sull', 'sulla, 'sulle, 'sullo *prep* + *det vedi* su.

sulta'nina *ag f*: (uva) ~ sultana.

sul'tano, a *sm/f* sultan/sultana.

'sunto *sm* summary.

'suo, 'sua, 'sue, su'oi *det*: il ~, la sua *etc* (*di lui*) his; (*di lei*) her; (*di esso*) its; (*con valore indefinito*) one's, his/her; (*forma di cortesia: anche*: S~) your // *pronome*: il ~, la sua *etc* his; hers; yours; i suoi (*parenti*) his (*o* her *o* one's *o* your) family.

su'ocero, a ['swɔtʃero] *sm/f* father/mother-in-law; i ~**i** *smpl* father-and mother-in-law.

su'oi *vedi* suo.

su'ola *sf* (*di scarpa*) sole.

su'olo *sm* (*terreno*) ground; (*terra*) soil.

suo'nare *vt* (*MUS*) to play; (*campana*) to ring; (*ore*) to strike; (*clacson, allarme*) to sound // *vi* to play; (*telefono, campana*) to ring; (*ore*) to strike; (*clacson, fig: parole*) to sound.

su'ono *sm* sound.

su'ora *sf* (*REL*) sister.

'super *sf* (*anche*: benzina ~) ≈ four-star (petrol) (*Brit*), premium (*US*).

supe'rare *vt* (*oltrepassare: limite*) to exceed, surpass; (*percorrere*) to cover; (*attraversare: fiume*) to cross; (*sorpassare: veicolo*) to overtake; (*fig: essere più bravo di*) to surpass, outdo; (*: difficoltà*) to overcome; (*: esame*) to get through; ~ **qn in altezza/peso** to be taller/heavier than sb; **ha superato la cinquantina** he's over fifty (years of age).

su'perbia *sf* pride.

su'perbo, a *ag* proud; (*fig*) magnificent, superb.

superfici'ale [superfi'tʃale] *ag* superficial.

super'ficie, ci [super'fitʃe] *sf* surface.

su'perfluo, a *ag* superfluous.

superi'ore *ag* (*piano, arto, classi*) upper; (*più elevato: temperatura, livello*): ~ (a) higher (than); (*migliore*): ~ (a) superior (to); ~, a *sm/f* (*anche REL*) superior; **superiorità** *sf* superiority.

superla'tivo, a *ag, sm* superlative.

supermer'cato *sm* supermarket.

su'perstite *ag* surviving // *sm/f* survivor.

superstizi'one [superstit'tsjone] *sf* superstition; **superstizi'oso, a** *ag* superstitious.

su'pino, a *ag* supine.

suppel'lettile *sf* furnishings *pl*.

suppergiù [supper'dʒu] *av* more or less, roughly.

supplemen'tare *ag* extra; (*treno*) relief *cpd*; (*entrate*) additional.

supple'mento *sm* supplement.

sup'plente *ag* temporary; (*insegnante*) supply *cpd* (*Brit*), substitute *cpd* (*US*) // *smf* temporary member of staff; supply (o substitute) teacher.

'supplica, che *sf* (*preghiera*) plea; (*domanda scritta*) petition, request.

suppli'care *vt* to implore, beseech.

sup'plire *vi*: ~ **a** to make up for, compensate for.

sup'plizio [sup'plittsjo] *sm* torture.

sup'porre *vt* to suppose.

sup'porto *sm* (*sostegno*) support.

sup'posta *sf* (*MED*) suppository.

sup'posto, a *pp di* **supporre**.

su'premo, a *ag* supreme.

surge'lare [surdʒe'lare] *vt* to (deep-) freeze; **surge'lati** *smpl* frozen food *sg*.

sur'plus *sm inv* (*ECON*) surplus.

surriscal'dare *vt* to overheat.

surro'gato *sm* substitute.

suscet'tibile [suʃʃet'tibile] *ag* (*sensibile*) touchy, sensitive; (*soggetto*): ~ **di** miglioramento that can be improved, open to improvement.

susci'tare [suʃʃi'tare] *vt* to provoke, arouse.

su'sina *sf* plum; **su'sino** *sm* plum (tree).

sussegu'ire *vt* to follow; ~**rsi** *vr* to follow one another.

sussidi'ario, a *ag* subsidiary; auxiliary.

sus'sidio *sm* subsidy.

sussis'tenza [sussis'tɛntsa] *sf* subsistence.

sus'sistere *vi* to exist; (*essere fondato*) to be valid *o* sound.

sussul'tare *vi* to shudder.

sussur'rare *vt*, *vi* to whisper, murmur; **sus'surro** *sm* whisper, murmur.

sutu'rare *vt* (*MED*) to stitch up, suture.

sva'gare *vt* (*distrarre*) to distract; (*divertire*) to amuse; ~**rsi** *vr* to amuse o.s.; to enjoy o.s.

'svago, ghi *sm* (*riposo*) relaxation; (*ricreazione*) amusement; (*passatempo*) pastime.

svaligi'are [zvali'dʒare] *vt* to rob, burgle (*Brit*), burglarize (*US*).

svalu'tare *vt* (*ECON*) to devalue; (*fig*) to belittle; ~**rsi** *vr* (*ECON*) to be devalued; **svalutazi'one** *sf* devaluation.

sva'nire *vi* to disappear, vanish.

svan'taggio [zvan'taddʒo] *sm* disadvantage; (*inconveniente*) drawback, disadvantage.

svapo'rare *vi* to evaporate.

svari'ato, a *ag* varied; various.

'svastica *sf* swastika.

sve'dese *ag* Swedish // *smf* Swede // *sm* (*LING*) Swedish.

'sveglia ['zveʎʎa] *sf* waking up; (*orologio*) alarm (clock); **suonare la ~** (*MIL*) to sound the reveille.

svegli'are [zveʎ'ʎare] *vt* to wake up; (*fig*) to awaken, arouse; ~**rsi** *vr* to wake

up; (*fig*) to be revived, reawaken.

'sveglio, a ['zveʎʎo] *ag* awake; (*fig*) quick-witted.

sve'lare *vt* to reveal.

'svelto, a *ag* (*passo*) quick; (*mente*) quick, alert; (*linea*) slim, slender; **alla ~a** *av* quickly.

'svendita *sf* (*COMM*) (clearance) sale.

sveni'mento *sm* fainting fit, faint.

sve'nire *vi* to faint.

sven'tare *vt* to foil, thwart.

sven'tato, a *ag* (*distratto*) scatterbrained; (*imprudente*) rash.

svento'lare *vt*, *vi* to wave, flutter.

sven'trare *vt* to disembowel.

sven'tura *sf* misfortune; **sventu'rato, a** *ag* unlucky, unfortunate.

sve'nuto, a *pp di* **svenire**.

svergo'gnato, a [zvergoɲ'ɲato] *ag* shameless.

sver'nare *vi* to spend the winter.

sves'tire *vt* to undress; ~**rsi** *vr* to get undressed.

'Svezia ['zvɛttsja] *sf*: **la ~** Sweden.

svez'zare [zvet'tsare] *vt* to wean.

svi'are *vt* to divert; (*fig*) to lead astray; ~**rsi** *vr* to go astray.

svi'gnarsela [zviɲ'ɲarsela] *vr* to slip away, sneak off.

svilup'pare *vt*, ~**rsi** *vr* to develop.

svi'luppo *sm* development.

'svincolo *sm* (*COMM*) clearance; (*stradale*) motorway (*Brit*) *o* expressway (*US*) intersection.

svisce'rare [zviʃʃe'rare] *vt* (*fig*: *argomento*) to examine in depth; **svisce'rato, a** *ag* (*amore*) passionate; (*lodi*) obsequious.

'svista *sf* oversight.

svi'tare *vt* to unscrew.

'Svizzera ['zvittsera] *sf*: **la ~** Switzerland.

'svizzero, a ['zvittsero] *ag*, *smf* Swiss.

svogli'ato, a [zvoʎ'ʎato] *ag* listless; (*pigro*) lazy.

svolaz'zare [zvolat'tsare] *vi* to flutter.

'svolgere ['zvɔldʒere] *vt* to unwind; (*srotolare*) to unroll; (*fig*: *argomento*) to develop; (: *piano, programma*) to carry out; ~**rsi** *vr* to unwind; to unroll; (*fig*: *aver luogo*) to take place; (: *procedere*) to go on; **svolgi'mento** *sm* development; carrying out; (*andamento*) course.

'svolta *sf* (*atto*) turning *q*; (*curva*) turn, bend; (*fig*) turning-point.

svol'tare *vi* to turn.

'svolto, a *pp di* **svolgere**.

svuo'tare *vt* to empty (out).

T

tabac'caio, a *smf* tobacconist.

tabacche'ria [tabakke'ria] *sf* tobacconist's (shop).

ta'bacco, chi *sm* tobacco.

ta'bella *sf* (*tavola*) table; (*elenco*) list.

taber'nacolo *sm* tabernacle.

tabu'lato *sm* (*INFORM*) printout.

'tacca, che *sf* notch, nick; **di mezza ~** (*fig*) mediocre.

tac'cagno, a [tak'kaɲɲo] *ag* mean, stingy.

tac'cheggio [tak'keddʒo] *sm* shoplifting.

tac'chino [tak'kino] *sm* turkey.

tacci'are [tat'tʃare] *vt*: **~ qn di** to accuse sb of.

'tacco, chi *sm* heel.

taccu'ino *sm* notebook.

ta'cere [ta'tʃere] *vi* to be silent *o* quiet; (*smettere di parlare*) to fall silent // *vt* to keep to oneself, say nothing about; **far ~ qn** to make sb be quiet; (*fig*) to silence sb.

ta'chimetro [ta'kimetro] *sm* speedometer.

'tacito, a ['tatʃito] *ag* silent; (*sottinteso*) tacit, unspoken.

ta'fano *sm* horsefly.

taffe'ruglio [taffe'ruʎʎo] *sm* brawl, scuffle.

taffettà *sm* taffeta.

'taglia ['taʎʎa] *sf* (*statura*) height; (*misura*) size; (*riscatto*) ransom; (*ricompensa*) reward.

taglia'carte [taʎʎa'karte] *sm inv* paper-knife.

tagli'ando [taʎ'ʎando] *sm* coupon.

tagli'are [taʎ'ʎare] *vt* to cut; (*recidere, interrompere*) to cut off; (*intersecare*) to cut across, intersect; (*carne*) to carve; (*vini*) to blend // *vi* to cut; (*prendere una scorciatoia*) to take a short-cut; **~ corto** (*fig*) to cut short.

taglia'telle [taʎʎa'tɛlle] *sfpl* tagliatelle *pl*.

tagli'ente [taʎ'ʎɛnte] *ag* sharp.

'taglio ['taʎʎo] *sm* cutting *q*; cut; (*parte tagliente*) cutting edge; (*di abito*) cut, style; (*di stoffa: lunghezza*) length; (*di vini*) blending; **di ~** on edge, edgeways; **banconote di piccolo/grosso ~** notes of small/large denomination.

tagli'ola [taʎ'ʎola] *sf* trap, snare.

tagliuz'zare [taʎʎut'tsare] *vt* to cut into small pieces.

'talco *sm* talcum powder.

'tale ♦ *det* 1 (*simile, così grande*) such; **un(a) ~ ... such** (a) ...; **non accetto ~i discorsi** I won't allow such talk; **è di una ~ arroganza** he is so arrogant; **fa una ~ confusione!** he makes such a mess!

2 (*persona o cosa indeterminata*) such-and-such; **il giorno ~ all'ora ~** on such-and-such a day at such-and-such a time; **la tal persona** that person; **ha telefonato una ~ Giovanna** somebody called Giovanna phoned

3 (*nelle similitudini*): **~ ... ~** like ...

like; **~ padre ~ figlio** like father, like son; **hai il vestito ~ quale il mio** your dress is just *o* exactly like mine

♦ *pronome* (*indefinito: persona*): **un(a) ~** someone; **quel** (*o* **quella**) **~** that person, that man (*o* woman); **il tal dei ~i** what's-his-name.

ta'lento *sm* talent.

talis'mano *sm* talisman.

tallon'cino [tallon'tʃino] *sm* counterfoil.

tal'lone *sm* heel.

tal'mente *av* so.

ta'lora *av* = **talvolta**.

'talpa *sf* (*ZOOL*) mole.

tal'volta *av* sometimes, at times.

tambu'rello *sm* tambourine.

tam'buro *sm* drum.

Ta'migi [ta'midʒi] *sm*: **il ~** the Thames.

tampo'nare *vt* (*otturare*) to plug; (*urtare: macchina*) to crash *o* ram into.

tam'pone *sm* (*MED*) wad, pad; (*per timbri*) ink-pad; (*respingente*) buffer; **~ assorbente** tampon.

'tana *sf* lair, den.

'tanfo *sm* stench; musty smell.

tan'gente [tan'dʒɛnte] *ag* (*MAT*): **~ a** tangential to // *sf* tangent; (*quota*) share.

tan'tino: un ~ *av* a little, a bit.

'tanto, a ♦ *det* 1 (*molto: quantità*) a lot of, much; (: *numero*) a lot of, many; (*così ~: quantità*) so much, such a lot of; (: *numero*) so many, such a lot of; **~e volte** so many times, so often; **~i auguri!** all the best!; **~e grazie** many thanks; **~ tempo** so long, such a long time; **ogni ~i chilometri** every so many kilometres

2: **~ ... quanto** (*quantità*) as much ... as; (*numero*) as many ... as; **ho ~a pazienza quanta ne hai tu** I have as much patience as you have *o* as you; **ha ~i amici quanti nemici** he has as many friends as he has enemies

3 (*rafforzativo*) such; **ho aspettato per ~ tempo** I waited so long *o* for such a long time

♦ *pronome* 1 (*molto*) much, a lot; (*così ~*) so much, such a lot; **~i(e)** many, a lot; so many, such a lot; **credevo ce ne fosse ~** I thought there was (such) a lot, I thought there was plenty

2: **~ quanto** (*denaro*) as much as; (*cioccolatini*) as many as; **ne ho ~ quanto basta** I have as much as I need; **due volte ~** twice as much

3 (*indeterminato*) so much; **~ per l'affitto, ~ per il gas** so much for the rent, so much for the gas; **costa un ~ al metro** it costs so much per metre; **di in ~, ogni ~** every so often; **~ vale che ... I** (*o* **we** *etc*) may as well ...; **~ meglio!** so much the better!; **~ peggio per lui!** so much the worse for him!

♦ *av* 1 (*molto*) very; **vengo ~ volentieri** I'd be very glad to come; **non ci vuole ~**

a capirlo it doesn't take much to understand it

2 (*così* ~: *con ag, av*) so; (: *con vb*) so much, such a lot; è ~ **bella!** she's so beautiful!; **non urlare** ~ don't shout so much; **sto** ~ **meglio adesso** I'm so much better now; ~ ... **che** so ... (that); ~ ... **da** so ... as

3: ~ ... **quanto** as ... as; **conosco** ~ **Carlo quanto suo padre** I know both Carlo and his father; **non è poi** ~ **complicato quanto sembri** it's not as difficult as it seems; ~ **più insisti,** ~ **più non mollerà** the more you insist, the more stubborn he'll be; **quanto più ...** ~ **meno** the more ... the less

4 (*solamente*) just; ~ **per cambiare/ scherzare** just for a change/a joke; **una volta** ~ for once

5 (*a lungo*) (for) long

♦ *cong* after all.

'tappa *sf* (*luogo di sosta, fermata*) stop, halt; (*parte di un percorso*) stage, leg; (*SPORT*) lap; **a** ~**e** in stages.

tap'pare *vt* to plug, stop up; (*bottiglia*) to cork.

tap'peto *sm* carpet; (*anche:* tappetino) rug; (*di tavolo*) cloth; (*SPORT*) mat; **andare al** ~ to go down for the count; **mettere sul** ~ (*fig*) to bring up for discussion.

tappez'zare [tappet'tsare] *vt* (*con carta*) to paper; (*rivestire*): ~ **qc (di)** to cover sth (with); **tappezze'ria** *sf* (*tessuto*) tapestry; (*carta da parato*) wallpaper; (*arte*) upholstery; **far da tappezzeria** (*fig*) to be a wallflower; **tappezzi'ere** *sm* upholsterer.

'tappo *sm* stopper; (*in sughero*) cork.

tarchi'ato, a [tar'kjato] *ag* stocky, thickset.

tar'dare *vi* to be late // *vt* to delay; ~ **a fare** to delay doing.

'tardi *av* late; **più** ~ later (on); **al più** ~ at the latest; **sul** ~ (*verso sera*) late in the day; **far** ~ to be late; (*restare alzato*) to stay up late.

tar'divo, a *ag* (*primavera*) late; (*rimedio*) belated, tardy; (*fig: bambino*) retarded.

'tardo, a *ag* (*lento, fig: ottuso*) slow; (*tempo: avanzato*) late.

'targa, ghe *sf* plate; (*AUT*) number (*Brit*) o license (*US*) plate.

ta'riffa *sf* (*gen*) rate, tariff; (*di trasporti*) fare; (*elenco*) price list; tariff.

'tarlo *sm* woodworm.

'tarma *sf* moth.

ta'rocco, chi *sm* tarot card; ~**chi** *smpl* (*gioco*) tarot *sg*.

tartagli'are [tartaʎ'ʎare] *vi* to stutter, stammer.

'tartaro, a *ag, sm* (*in tutti i sensi*) tartar.

tarta'ruga, ghe *sf* tortoise; (*di mare*) turtle; (*materiale*) tortoiseshell.

tar'tina *sf* canapé.

tar'tufo *sm* (*BOT*) truffle.

'tasca, sche *sf* pocket; **tas'cabile** *ag* (*libro*) pocket *cpd*; **tasca'pane** *sm* haversack; **tas'chino** *sm* breast pocket.

'tassa *sf* (*imposta*) tax; (*doganale*) duty; (*per iscrizione: a scuola etc*) fee; ~ **di circolazione/di soggiorno** road/tourist tax.

tas'sametro *sm* taximeter.

tas'sare *vt* to tax; to levy a duty on.

tassa'tivo, a *ag* peremptory.

tassazi'one [tassat'tsjone] *sf* taxation.

tas'sello *sm* plug; wedge.

tassì *sm inv* = **taxi**; **tas'sista, i, e** *sm/f* taxi driver.

'tasso *sm* (*di natalità, d'interesse etc*) rate; (*BOT*) yew; (*ZOOL*) badger; ~ **di cambio/d'interesse** rate of exchange/ interest.

tas'tare *vt* to feel; ~ **il terreno** (*fig*) to see how the land lies.

tasti'era *sf* keyboard.

'tasto *sm* key; (*tatto*) touch, feel.

tas'toni *av*: **procedere (a)** ~ to grope one's way forward.

'tattico, a, ci, che *ag* tactical // *sf* tactics *pl*.

'tatto *sm* (*senso*) touch; (*fig*) tact; **duro al** ~ hard to the touch; **aver** ~ to be tactful, have tact.

tatu'aggio [tatu'addʒo] *sm* tattooing; (*disegno*) tattoo.

tatu'are *vt* to tattoo.

'tavola *sf* table; (*asse*) plank, board; (*lastra*) tablet; (*quadro*) panel (painting); (*illustrazione*) plate; ~ **calda** snack bar; ~ **pieghevole** folding table.

tavo'lato *sm* boarding; (*pavimento*) wooden floor.

tavo'letta *sf* tablet, bar; **a** ~ (*AUT*) flat out.

tavo'lino *sm* small table; (*scrivania*) desk.

'tavolo *sm* table.

tavo'lozza [tavo'lɔttsa] *sf* (*ARTE*) palette.

'taxi *sm inv* taxi.

'tazza ['tattsa] *sf* cup; ~ **da caffè/tè** coffee/tea cup; **una** ~ **di caffè/tè** a cup of coffee/tea.

te *pronome* (*soggetto: in forme comparative, oggetto*) you.

tè *sm inv* tea; (*trattenimento*) tea party.

tea'trale *ag* theatrical.

te'atro *sm* theatre.

'tecnico, a, ci, che *ag* technical // *sm/f* technician // *sf* technique; (*tecnologia*) technology.

tecnolo'gia [teknolo'dʒia] *sf* technology.

te'desco, a, schi, sche *ag, sm/f, sm* German.

'tedio *sm* tedium, boredom.

te'game *sm* (*CUC*) pan.

'tegola *sf* tile.

tei'era *sf* teapot.

'tela *sf* (*tessuto*) cloth; (*per vele, quadri*)

canvas; (*dipinto*) canvas, painting; **di ~** (*calzoni*) (heavy) cotton *cpd*; (*scarpe, borsa*) canvas *cpd*; **~ cerata** oilcloth; (*copertone*) tarpaulin.

te'laio *sm* (*apparecchio*) loom; (*struttura*) frame.

tele'camera *sf* television camera.

tele'cronaca *sf* television report.

tele'ferica, che *sf* cableway.

telefo'nare *vi* to telephone, ring; to make a phone call // *vt* to telephone; **~ a** to phone up, ring up, call up.

telefo'nata *sf* (*telephone*) call; **~ a carico del destinatario** reverse charge (*Brit*) *o* collect (*US*) call.

tele'fonico, a, ci, che *ag* (tele)phone *cpd*.

telefo'nista, i, e *sm/f* telephonist; (*d'impresa*) switchboard operator.

te'lefono *sm* telephone; **~ a gettoni** ≈ pay phone.

telegior'nale [teledʒor'nale] *sm* television news (programme).

te'legrafo *sm* telegraph; (*ufficio*) telegraph office.

tele'gramma, i *sm* telegram.

tele'matica *sf* data transmission; telematics *sg*.

telepa'tia *sf* telepathy.

teles'copio *sm* telescope.

teleselezi'one [teleselet'tsjone] *sf* direct dialling.

telespetta'tore, 'trice *sm/f* (television) viewer.

televisi'one *sf* television.

televi'sore *sm* television set.

'telex *sm inv* telex.

'tema, i *sm* theme; (*INS*) essay, composition.

teme'rario, a *ag* rash, reckless.

te'mere *vt* to fear, be afraid of; (*essere sensibile a: freddo, calore*) to be sensitive to // *vi* to be afraid; (*essere preoccupato*): **~ per** to worry about, fear for; **~ di/che** to be afraid of/that.

temperama'tite *sm inv* pencil sharpener.

tempera'mento *sm* temperament.

tempe'rare *vt* (*aguzzare*) to sharpen; (*fig*) to moderate, control, temper.

tempe'rato, a *ag* moderate, temperate; (*clima*) temperate.

tempera'tura *sf* temperature.

tempe'rino *sm* penknife.

tem'pesta *sf* storm; **~ di sabbia/neve** sand/snowstorm.

tempes'tare *vt*: **~ qn di domande** to bombard sb with questions; **~ qn di colpi** to rain blows on sb.

tempes'tivo, a *ag* timely.

tempes'toso, a *ag* stormy.

'tempia *sf* (*ANAT*) temple.

'tempio *sm* (*edificio*) temple.

'tempo *sm* (*METEOR*) weather; (*cronologico*) time; (*epoca*) time, times

pl; (*di film, gioco: parte*) part; (*MUS*) time; (: *battuta*) beat; (*LING*) tense; **un ~** once; **~ fa** some time ago; **al ~ stesso** *o* **a un ~** at the same time; **per ~** early; **aver fatto il suo ~** to have had its (*o his etc*) day; **primo/secondo ~** (*TEATRO*) first/second part; (*SPORT*) first/second half; **in ~ utile** in due time *o* course.

tempo'rale *ag* temporal // *sm* (*METEOR*) (thunder)storm.

tempo'raneo, a *ag* temporary.

temporeggi'are [tempored'dʒare] *vi* to play for time, temporize.

tem'prare *vt* to temper.

te'nace [te'natʃe] *ag* strong, tough; (*fig*) tenacious; **te'nacia** *sf* tenacity.

te'naglie [te'naʎʎe] *sfpl* pincers *pl*.

'tenda *sf* (*riparo*) awning; (*di finestra*) curtain; (*per campeggio etc*) tent.

ten'denza [ten'dentsa] *sf* tendency; (*orientamento*) trend; **avere ~ a** *o* **per qc** to have a bent for sth.

'tendere *vt* (*allungare al massimo*) to stretch, draw tight; (*porgere: mano*) to hold out; (*fig: trappola*) to lay, set // *vi*: **~ a qc/a fare** to tend towards sth/to do; **~ l'orecchio** to prick up one's ears; **il tempo tende al caldo** the weather is getting hot; **un blu che tende al verde** a greenish blue.

ten'dina *sf* curtain.

'tendine *sm* tendon, sinew.

ten'done *sm* (*da circo*) tent.

'tenebre *sfpl* darkness *sg*; **tene'broso, a** *ag* dark, gloomy.

te'nente *sm* lieutenant.

te'nere *vt* to hold; (*conservare, mantenere*) to keep; (*ritenere, considerare*) to consider; (*spazio: occupare*) to take up, occupy; (*seguire: strada*) to keep to // *vi* to hold; (*colori*) to be fast; (*dare importanza*): **~ a** to care about; **~ a fare** to want to do, be keen to do; **~rsi** *vr* (*stare in una determinata posizione*) to stand; (*stimarsi*) to consider o.s.; (*aggrapparsi*): **~rsi a** to hold on to; (*attenersi*): **~rsi a** to stick to; **~ una conferenza** to give a lecture; **~ conto di qc** to take sth into consideration; **~ presente qc** to bear sth in mind.

'tenero, a *ag* tender; (*pietra, cera, colore*) soft; (*fig*) tender, loving.

'tenia *sf* tapeworm.

'tennis *sm* tennis.

te'nore *sm* (*tono*) tone; (*MUS*) tenor; **~ di vita** way of life; (*livello*) standard of living.

tensi'one *sf* tension.

ten'tare *vt* (*indurre*) to tempt; (*provare*): **~ qc/di fare** to attempt *o* try sth/to do; **tenta'tivo** *sm* attempt; **tentazi'one** *sf* temptation.

tenten'nare *vi* to shake, be unsteady; (*fig*) to hesitate, waver // *vt*: **~ il capo** to shake one's head.

ten'toni *av*: andare a ~ (*anche fig*) to grope one's way.

'tenue *ag* (*sottile*) fine; (*colore*) soft; (*fig*) slender, slight.

te'nuta *sf* (*capacità*) capacity; (*divisa*) uniform; (*abito*) dress; (*AGR*) estate; a ~ d'aria airtight; ~ di strada roadholding power.

teo'logia [teolo'dʒia] *sf* theology; **te'ologo, gi** *sm* theologian.

teo'rema, i *sm* theorem.

teo'ria *sf* theory; **te'orico, a, ci, che** *ag* theoretic (al).

'tepido, a *ag* = tiepido.

te'pore *sm* warmth.

'teppa *sf* mob, hooligans *pl*; **tep'pismo** *sm* hooliganism; **tep'pista, i** *sm* hooligan.

tera'pia *sf* therapy.

tergicris'tallo [terdʒikris'tallo] *sm* windscreen (*Brit*) *o* windshield (*US*) wiper.

tergiver'sare [terdʒiver'sare] *vi* to shilly-shally.

'tergo *sm*: a ~ behind; vedi a ~ please turn over.

ter'male *ag* thermal; stazione *f* ~ spa.

'terme *sfpl* thermal baths.

'termico, a, ci, che *ag* thermic; (*unità*) thermal.

termi'nale *ag, sm* terminal.

termi'nare *vt* to end; (*lavoro*) to finish // *vi* to end.

'termine *sm* term; (*fine, estremità*) end; (*di territorio*) boundary, limit; contratto a ~ (*COMM*) forward contract; a breve/lungo ~ short-/long-term; parlare senza mezzi ~i to talk frankly, not to mince one's words.

ter'mometro *sm* thermometer.

termonucle'are *ag* thermonuclear.

'termos *sm inv* = thermos.

termosi'fone *sm* radiator; (*riscaldamento a*) ~ central heating.

ter'mostato *sm* thermostat.

'terra *sf* (*gen, ELETTR*) earth; (*sostanza*) soil, earth; (*opposto al mare*) land *q*; (*regione, paese*) land; (*argilla*) clay; ~e *sfpl* (*possedimento*) lands, land *sg*; a *o* per ~ (*stato*) on the ground (*o floor*); (*moto*) to the ground, down; mettere a ~ (*ELETTR*) to earth.

terra'cotta *sf* terracotta; vasellame *m* di ~ earthenware.

terra'ferma *sf* dry land, terra firma; (*continente*) mainland.

terrapi'eno *sm* embankment, bank.

ter'razza [ter'rattsa] *sf*, **ter'razzo** [ter'rattso] *sm* terrace.

terre'moto *sm* earthquake.

ter'reno, a *ag* (*vita, beni*) earthly // *sm* (*suolo, fig*) ground; (*COMM*) land *q*, plot (of land); site; (*SPORT, MIL*) field.

ter'restre *ag* (*superficie*) of the earth, earth's; (*di terra: battaglia, animale*) land *cpd*; (*REL*) earthly, worldly.

ter'ribile *ag* terrible, dreadful.

terrifi'cante *ag* terrifying.

territori'ale *ag* territorial.

terri'torio *sm* territory.

ter'rore *sm* terror; **terro'rismo** *sm* terrorism; **terro'rista, i, e** *sm/f* terrorist.

'terso, a *ag* clear.

'terzo, a ['tɛrtso] *ag* third // *sm* (*frazione*) third; (*DIR*) third party; ~i *smpl* (*altri*) others, other people; la ~a pagina (*STAMPA*) the Arts page.

'tesa *sf* brim.

'teschio ['tɛskjo] *sm* skull.

'tesi *sf* thesis.

'teso, a *pp di* tendere // *ag* (*tirato*) taut, tight; (*fig*) tense.

teso'reria *sf* treasury.

tesori'ere *sm* treasurer.

te'soro *sm* treasure; il Ministero del T~ the Treasury.

'tessera *sf* (*documento*) card.

'tessere *vt* to weave; **'tessile** *ag, sm* textile; **tessi'tore, 'trice** *sm/f* weaver; **tessi'tura** *sf* weaving.

tes'suto *sm* fabric, material; (*BIOL*) tissue; (*fig*) web.

'testa *sf* head; (*di cose: estremità, parte anteriore*) head, front; di ~ *ag* (*vettura etc*) front; tenere ~ a qn (*nemico etc*) to stand up to sb; fare di ~ propria to go one's own way; in ~ (*SPORT*) in the lead; ~ o croce? heads or tails?; avere la ~ dura to be stubborn; ~ di serie (*TENNIS*) seed, seeded player.

testa'mento *sm* (*atto*) will; l'Antico/il Nuovo T~ (*REL*) the Old/New Testament.

tes'tardo, a *ag* stubborn, pig-headed.

tes'tata *sf* (*parte anteriore*) head; (*intestazione*) heading.

'teste *sm/f* witness.

tes'ticolo *sm* testicle.

testi'mone *sm/f* (*DIR*) witness.

testimoni'anza [testimo'njantsa] *sf* testimony.

testimoni'are *vt* to testify; (*fig*) to bear witness to, testify to // *vi* to give evidence, testify.

'testo *sm* text; fare ~ (*opera, autore*) to be authoritative; questo libro non fa ~ this book is not essential reading; **te-stu'ale** *ag* textual; literal, word for word.

tes'tuggine [tes'tuddʒine] *sf* tortoise; (*di mare*) turtle.

'tetano *sm* (*MED*) tetanus.

'tetro, a *ag* gloomy.

'tetto *sm* roof; **tet'toia** *sf* roofing; canopy.

'Tevere *sm*: il ~ the Tiber.

Tg. *abbr* = telegiornale.

'thermos ® ['tɛrmos] *sm inv* vacuum *o* Thermos ® flask.

ti *pronome* (*dav lo, la, li, le, ne diventa* te) (*oggetto*) you; (*complemento di* *termine*) (to) you; (*riflessivo*) yourself.

ti'ara *sf* (REL) tiara.

'tibia *sf* tibia, shinbone.

tic *sm inv* tic, (nervous) twitch; (*fig*) mannerism.

ticchet'tio [tikket'tio] *sm* (*di macchina da scrivere*) clatter; (*di orologio*) ticking; (*della pioggia*) patter.

'ticchio ['tikkjo] *sm* (*ghiribizzo*) whim; (*tic*) tic, (nervous) twitch.

ti'epido, a *ag* lukewarm, tepid.

ti'fare *vi*: ~ **per** to be a fan of; (*parteggiare*) to side with.

'tifo *sm* (MED) typhus; (*fig*): **fare il** ~ **per** to be a fan of.

tifoi'dea *sf* typhoid.

ti'fone *sm* typhoon.

ti'foso, a *sm/f* (SPORT etc) fan.

'tiglio ['tiʎʎo] *sm* lime (tree), linden (tree).

'tigre *sf* tiger.

tim'ballo *sm* (*strumento*) kettledrum; (CUC) timbale.

'timbro *sm* stamp; (MUS) timbre, tone.

'timido, a *ag* shy; timid.

'timo *sm* thyme.

ti'mone *sm* (NAUT) rudder; **timoni'ere** *sm* helmsman.

ti'more *sm* (*paura*) fear; (*rispetto*) awe; **timo'roso, a** *ag* timid, timorous.

'timpano *sm* (ANAT) eardrum; (MUS): ~**i** *smpl* kettledrums, timpani.

'tingere ['tindʒere] *vt* to dye.

'tino *sm* vat.

ti'nozza [ti'nɔttsa] *sf* tub.

'tinta *sf* (*materia colorante*) dye; (*colore*) colour, shade; **tinta'rella** *sf* (*fam*) (sun)tan.

tintin'nare *vi* to tinkle.

'tinto, a *pp di* **tingere**.

tinto'ria *sf* (*officina*) dyeworks *sg*; (*lavasecco*) dry cleaner's (shop).

tin'tura *sf* (*operazione*) dyeing; (*colorante*) dye; ~ **di iodio** tincture of iodine.

'tipico, a, ci, che *ag* typical.

'tipo *sm* type; (*genere*) kind, type; (*fam*) chap, fellow.

tipogra'fia *sf* typography; (*procedimento*) letterpress (printing); (*officina*) printing house; **tipo'grafico, a, ci, che** *ag* typographic(al); letterpress *cpd*; **ti'pografo** *sm* typographer.

ti'ranno, a *ag* tyrannical // *sm* tyrant.

ti'rante *sm* (*per tenda*) guy.

ti'rare *vt* (*gen*) to pull; (*estrarre*): ~ **qc da** to take o pull sth out of; to get sth out of; to extract sth from; (*chiudere: tenda etc*) to draw, pull; (*tracciare, disegnare*) to draw, trace; (*lanciare: sasso, palla*) to throw; (*stampare*) to print; (*pistola, freccia*) to fire // *vi* (*pipa, camino*) to draw; (*vento*) to blow; (*abito*) to be tight; (*fare fuoco*) to fire; (*fare del tiro, CALCIO*) to shoot; ~ **avanti** *vi* to struggle on // *vt* to keep going; ~ **fuori** *vt*

(*estrarre*) to take out, pull out; ~ **giù** *vt* (*abbassare*) to bring down; ~ **su** *vt* to pull up; (*capelli*) to put up; (*fig: bambino*) to bring up; ~**rsi indietro** to move back.

tira'tore *sm* gunman; **un buon** ~ a good shot; ~ **scelto** marksman.

tira'tura *sf* (*azione*) printing; (*di libro*) (print) run; (*di giornale*) circulation.

'tirchio, a ['tirkjo] *ag* mean, stingy.

'tiro *sm* shooting *q*, firing *q*; (*colpo, sparo*) shot; (*di palla: lancio*) throwing *q*; throw; (*fig*) trick; **cavallo da** ~ draught (*Brit*) o draft (*US*) horse; ~ **a segno** target shooting; (*luogo*) shooting range.

tiro'cinio [tiro'tʃinjo] *sm* apprenticeship; (*professionale*) training.

ti'roide *sf* thyroid (gland).

Tir'reno *sm*: **il (mar)** ~ the Tyrrhenian Sea.

ti'sana *sf* herb tea.

tito'lare *ag* appointed; (*sovrano*) titular // *sm/f* incumbent; (*proprietario*) owner; (CALCIO) regular player.

'titolo *sm* title; (*di giornale*) headline; (*diploma*) qualification; (COMM) security; (*: azione*) share; **a che** ~? for what reason?; **a** ~ **di amicizia** out of friendship; **a** ~ **di premio** as a prize; ~ **di credito** share; ~ **di proprietà** title deed.

titu'bante *ag* hesitant, irresolute.

'tizio, a ['tittsjo] *sm/f* fellow, chap.

tiz'zone [tit'tsone] *sm* brand.

toc'cante *ag* touching.

toc'care *vt* to touch; (*tastare*) to feel; (*fig: riguardare*) to concern; (*: commuovere*) to touch, move; (*: pungere*) to hurt, wound; (*: far cenno a: argomento*) to touch on, mention // *vi*: ~ **a** (*accadere*) to happen to; (*spettare*) to be up to; ~ (**il fondo**) (*in acqua*) to touch the bottom; **tocca a te difenderci** it's up to you to defend us; **a chi tocca?** whose turn is it?; **mi toccò pagare** I had to pay.

'tocco, chi *sm* touch; (ARTE) stroke, touch.

'toga, ghe *sf* toga; (*di magistrato, professore*) gown.

'togliere ['tɔʎʎere] *vt* (*rimuovere*) to take away (o off), remove; (*riprendere, non concedere più*) to take away, remove; (MAT) to take away, subtract; (*liberare*) to free; ~ **qc a qn** to take sth (away) from sb; **ciò non toglie che** nevertheless, be that as it may; ~**rsi il cappello** to take off one's hat.

toi'lette [twa'lɛt] *sf inv*, **to'letta** *sf* toilet; (*mobile*) dressing table.

tolle'ranza [tolle'rantsa] *sf* tolerance.

tolle'rare *vt* to tolerate.

'tolto, a *pp di* **togliere**.

to'maia *sf* (*di scarpa*) upper.

'tomba *sf* tomb.

tom'bino *sm* manhole cover.

'tombola *sf* (*gioco*) tombola; (*ruzzolone*) tumble.

'tomo *sm* volume.

'tonaca, che *sf* (*REL*) habit.

to'nare *vi* = **tuonare**.

'tondo, a *ag* round.

'tonfo *sm* splash; (*rumore sordo*) thud; (*caduta*): **fare un ~** to take a tumble.

'tonico, a, ci, che *ag, sm* tonic.

tonifi'care *vt* (*muscoli, pelle*) to tone up; (*irrobustire*) to invigorate, brace.

tonnel'laggio [tonnel'laddʒo] *sm* (*NAUT*) tonnage.

tonnel'lata *sf* ton.

'tonno *sm* tuna (fish).

'tono *sm* (*gen*) tone; (*MUS*: *di pezzo*) key; (*di colore*) shade, tone.

ton'silla *sf* tonsil; **tonsil'lite** *sf* tonsillitis.

'tonto, a *ag* dull, stupid.

to'pazio [to'pattsjo] *sm* topaz.

'topo *sm* mouse.

topogra'fia *sf* topography.

'toppa *sf* (*serratura*) keyhole; (*pezza*) patch.

to'race [to'ratʃe] *sm* chest.

'torba *sf* peat.

'torbido, a *ag* (*liquido*) cloudy; (: *fiume*) muddy; (*fig*) dark; troubled // *sm*: **pescare nel ~** (*fig*) to fish in troubled water.

'torcere ['tortʃere] *vt* to twist; (*biancheria*) to wring (out); **~rsi** *vr* to twist, writhe.

torchi'are [tor'kjare] *vt* to press; **'torchio** *sm* press; **torchio tipografico** printing press.

'torcia, ce ['tortʃa] *sf* torch; **~ elettrica** torch (*Brit*), flashlight (*US*).

torci'collo [tortʃi'kɔllo] *sm* stiff neck.

'tordo *sm* thrush.

To'rino *sf* Turin.

tor'menta *sf* snowstorm.

tormen'tare *vt* to torment; **~rsi** *vr* to fret, worry o.s.; **tor'mento** *sm* torment.

torna'conto *sm* advantage, benefit.

tor'nado *sm* tornado.

tor'nante *sm* hairpin bend.

tor'nare *vi* to return, go (*o* come) back; (*ridiventare: anche fig*) to become (again); (*riuscire giusto, esatto: conto*) to work out; (*risultare*) to turn out (to be), prove (to be); **~ utile** to prove *o* turn out (to be) useful; **~ a casa** to go (*o* come) home.

torna'sole *sm inv* litmus.

tor'neo *sm* tournament.

'tornio *sm* lathe.

'toro *sm* bull; (*dello zodiaco*): **T~** Taurus.

tor'pedine *sf* torpedo; **torpedini'era** *sf* torpedo boat.

'torre *sf* tower; (*SCACCHI*) rook, castle;

~ di controllo (*AER*) control tower.

torrefazi'one [torrefat'tsjone] *sf* roasting.

tor'rente *sm* torrent.

tor'retta *sf* turret.

torri'one *sm* keep.

tor'rone *sm* nougat.

torsi'one *sf* twisting; torsion.

'torso *sm* torso, trunk; (*ARTE*) torso.

'torsolo *sm* (*di cavolo etc*) stump; (*di frutta*) core.

'torta *sf* cake.

'torto, a *pp di* **torcere** // *ag* (*ritorto*) twisted; (*storto*) twisted, crooked // *sm* (*ingiustizia*) wrong; (*colpa*) fault; **a ~** wrongly; **aver ~** to be wrong.

'tortora *sf* turtle dove.

tortu'oso, a *ag* (*strada*) twisting; (*fig*) tortuous.

tor'tura *sf* torture; **tortu'rare** *vt* to torture.

'torvo, a *ag* menacing, grim.

tosa'erba *sm o f inv* (lawn)mower.

to'sare *vt* (*pecora*) to shear; (*siepe*) to clip, trim.

Tos'cana *sf*: **la ~** Tuscany; **tos'cano, a** *ag, sm/f* Tuscan // *sm* (*sigaro*) strong Italian cigar.

'tosse *sf* cough.

'tossico, a, ci, che *ag* toxic.

tossicodipen'dente, tossi'comane *sm/f* drug addict.

tos'sire *vi* to cough.

tosta'pane *sm inv* toaster.

tos'tare *vt* to toast; (*caffè*) to roast.

'tosto, a *ag*: **faccia ~a** cheek.

to'tale *ag, sm* total; **totalità** *sf*: **la totalità di** all of, the total amount (*o* number) of; **the whole + sg;** **totaliz'zare** *vt* to total; (*SPORT*: *punti*) to score.

toto'calcio [toto'kaltʃo] *sm gambling pool betting on football results*, ≈ (football) pools *pl* (*Brit*).

to'vaglia [to'vaʎʎa] *sf* tablecloth; **tovagli'olo** *sm* napkin.

'tozzo, a ['tottso] *ag* squat // *sm*: **~ di pane** crust of bread.

tra *prep* (*di due persone, cose*) between; (*di più persone, cose*) among(st); (*tempo: entro*) within, in; **~ 5 giorni** in 5 days' time; **sia detto ~ noi ...** between you and me ...; **litigano ~ (di) loro** they're fighting amongst themselves; **~ breve** soon; **~ sé e sé** (*parlare etc*) to oneself.

trabal'lare *vi* to stagger, totter.

traboc'care *vi* to overflow.

traboc'chetto [trabok'ketto] *sm* (*fig*) trap.

tracan'nare *vt* to gulp down.

'traccia, ce ['trattʃa] *sf* (*segno, striscia*) trail, track; (*orma*) tracks *pl*; (*residuo, testimonianza*) trace, sign; (*abbozzo*) outline.

tracci'are [trat'tʃare] *vt* to trace, mark

(out); (*disegnare*) to draw; (*fig:*
abbozzare) to outline; **tracci'ato** *sm*
(*grafico*) layout, plan.

tra'chea [tra'kɛa] *sf* windpipe, trachea.

tra'colla *sf* shoulder strap; **borsa a ~**
shoulder bag.

tra'collo *sm* (*fig*) collapse, crash.

traco'tante *ag* overbearing, arrogant.

tradi'mento *sm* betrayal; (*DIR, MIL*)
treason.

tra'dire *vt* to betray; (*coniuge*) to be unfaithful to; (*doveri: mancare*) to fail in;
(*rivelare*) to give away, reveal;
tradi'tore, 'trice *sm/f* traitor.

tradizio'nale [tradittsjo'nale] *ag* tradi-
tional.

tradizi'one [tradit'tsjone] *sf* tradition.

tra'dotto, a *pp di* **tradurre**.

tra'durre *vt* to translate; (*spiegare*) to
render, convey; **tradut'tore, 'trice** *sm/f*
translator; **traduzi'one** *sf* translation.

tra'ente *sm/f* (*ECON*) drawer.

trafe'lato, a *ag* out of breath.

traffi'cante *sm/f* dealer; (*peg*) traffick-
er.

traffi'care *vi* (*commerciare*): ~ (**in**) to
trade (in), deal (in); (*affaccendarsi*) to
busy o.s. // *vt* (*peg*) to traffic in.

'traffico, ci *sm* traffic; (*commercio*)
trade, traffic.

tra'figgere [tra'fiddʒere] *vt* to run
through, stab; (*fig*) to pierce; **tra'fitto,**
a *pp di* **trafiggere**.

trafo'rare *vt* to bore, drill; **tra'foro** *sm*
(*azione*) boring, drilling; (*galleria*)
tunnel.

tra'gedia [tra'dʒedja] *sf* tragedy.

tra'ghetto [tra'getto] *sm* crossing;
(*barca*) ferry(boat).

'tragico, a, ci, che ['tradʒiko] *ag* tragic.

tra'gitto [tra'dʒitto] *sm* (*passaggio*)
crossing; (*viaggio*) journey.

tragu'ardo *sm* (*SPORT*) finishing line;
(*fig*) goal, aim.

traiet'toria *sf* trajectory.

trai'nare *vt* to drag, haul; (*rimorchiare*)
to tow; **'traino** *sm* (*carro*) wagon;
(*slitta*) sledge; (*carico*) load.

tralasci'are [tralaʃ'ʃare] *vt* (*studi*) to
neglect; (*dettagli*) to leave out, omit.

'tralcio ['traltʃo] *sm* (*BOT*) shoot.

tra'liccio [tra'littʃo] *sm* (*tela*) ticking;
(*struttura*) trellis; (*ELETTR*) pylon.

tram *sm inv* tram.

'trama *sf* (*filo*) weft, woof; (*fig:*
argomento, maneggio) plot.

traman'dare *vt* to pass on, hand down.

tra'mare *vt* (*fig*) to scheme, plot.

tram'busto *sm* turmoil.

trames'tio *sm* bustle.

tramez'zino [tramed'dzino] *sm* sandwich.

tra'mezzo [tra'mɛddzo] *sm* (*EDIL*) partition.

'tramite *prep* through.

tramon'tare *vi* to set, go down;
tra'monto *sm* setting; (*del sole*) sunset.

tramor'tire *vi* to faint // *vt* to stun.

trampo'lino *sm* (*per tuffi*) springboard,
diving board; (*per lo sci*) ski-jump.

'trampolo *sm* stilt.

tramu'tare *vt*: ~ **in** to change into, turn
into.

tra'nello *sm* trap.

trangugi'are [trangu'dʒare] *vt* to gulp
down.

'tranne *prep* except (for), but (for); ~
che *cong* unless.

tranquil'lante *sm* (*MED*) tranquillizer.

tranquillità *sf* calm, stillness; quietness;
peace of mind.

tranquilliz'zare [trankwillid'dzare] *vt* to
reassure.

tran'quillo, a *ag* calm, quiet; (*bambino,*
scolaro) quiet; (*sereno*) with one's mind
at rest; **sta'** ~ don't worry.

transat'lantico, a, ci, che *ag*
transatlantic // *sm* transatlantic liner.

tran'satto, a *pp di* **transigere**.

transazi'one [transat'tsjone] *sf* compromise; (*DIR*) settlement; (*COMM*) transaction, deal.

tran'senna *sf* barrier.

tran'sigere [tran'sidʒere] *vi* (*DIR*) to
reach a settlement; (*venire a patti*) to
compromise, come to an agreement.

tran'sistor *sm*, **transis'tore** *sm*
transistor.

transi'tabile *ag* passable.

transi'tare *vi* to pass.

transi'tivo, a *ag* transitive.

'transito *sm* transit; **di ~** (*merci*) in
transit; (*stazione*) transit *cpd*; "**divieto**
di ~" "no entry".

transi'torio, a *ag* transitory, transient;
(*provvisorio*) provisional.

tran'via *sf* tramway (*Brit*), streetcar line
(*US*).

'trapano *sm* (*utensile*) drill; (: *MED*)
trepan.

trapas'sare *vt* to pierce.

tra'passo *sm* passage.

trape'lare *vi* to leak, drip; (*fig*) to leak
out.

tra'pezio [tra'pɛttsjo] *sm* (*MAT*)
trapezium; (*attrezzo ginnico*) trapeze.

trapian'tare *vt* to transplant;
trapi'anto *sm* transplanting; (*MED*)
transplant.

'trappola *sf* trap.

tra'punta *sf* quilt.

'trarre *vt* to draw, pull; (*portare*) to
take; (*prendere, tirare fuori*) to take
(out), draw; (*derivare*) to obtain; ~
origine da qc to have its origins *o*
originate in sth.

trasa'lire *vi* to start, jump.

trasan'dato, a *ag* shabby.

trasbor'dare *vt* to transfer; (*NAUT*) to
tran(s)ship // *vi* (*NAUT*) to change ship;

(AER) to change plane; (FERR) to change (trains).

trasci'nare [traʃʃi'nare] vt to drag; ~rsi vr to drag o.s. along; (fig) to drag on.

tras'correre vt (tempo) to spend, pass // vi to pass; **tras'corso, a** pp di trascorrere.

tras'critto, a pp di trascrivere.

tras'crivere vt to transcribe.

trascu'rare vt to neglect; (non considerare) to disregard; **trascura'tezza** sf carelessness, negligence; **trascu'rato, a** ag (casa) neglected; (persona) careless, negligent.

traseco'lato, a ag astounded, amazed.

trasferi'mento sm transfer; (trasloco) removal, move.

trasfe'rire vt to transfer; ~rsi vr to move; **tras'ferta** sf transfer; (indennità) travelling expenses pl; (SPORT) away game.

trasfigu'rare vt to transfigure.

trasfor'mare vt to transform, change.

trasfusi'one sf (MED) transfusion.

trasgre'dire vt to disobey, contravene.

tras'lato, a ag metaphorical, figurative.

traslo'care vt to move, transfer; ~rsi vr to move; **tras'loco, chi** sm removal.

tras'messo, a pp di trasmettere.

tras'mettere vt (passare): ~ qc a qn to pass sth on to sb; (mandare) to send; (TECN, TEL, MED) to transmit; (TV, RADIO) to broadcast; **trasmetti'tore** sm transmitter; **trasmissi'one** sf (gen, FISICA, TECN) transmission; (passaggio) transmission, passing on; (TV, RADIO) broadcast; **trasmit'tente** sf transmitting o broadcasting station.

traso'gnato, a [trasoɲ'ɲato] ag dreamy.

traspa'rente ag transparent.

traspa'rire vi to show (through).

traspi'rare vi to perspire; (fig) to come to light, leak out; **traspirazi'one** sf perspiration.

traspor'tare vt to carry, move; (merce) to transport, convey; **lasciarsi ~** (da qc) (fig) to let o.s. be carried away (by sth); **tras'porto** sm transport.

trastul'lare vt to amuse; ~rsi vr to amuse o.s.

trasu'dare vi (filtrare) to ooze; (sudare) to sweat // vt to ooze with.

trasver'sale ag transverse, cross(-); running at right angles.

trasvo'lare vt to fly over.

'tratta sf (ECON) draft; (di persone): la ~ delle bianche the white slave trade.

tratta'mento sm treatment; (servizio) service.

trat'tare vt (gen) to treat; (commerciare) to deal in; (svolgere: argomento) to discuss, deal with; (negoziare) to negotiate // vi: ~ di to deal with; ~ con (persona) to deal with; **si tratta di ...** it's about ...; **tratta'tive**

sfpl negotiations; **trat'tato** sm (testo) treatise; (accordo) treaty; **trattazi'one** sf treatment.

tratteggi'are [tratted'dʒare] vt (disegnare: a tratti) to sketch, outline; (: col tratteggio) to hatch.

tratte'nere vt (far rimanere: persona) to detain; (intrattenere: ospiti) to entertain; (tenere, frenare, reprimere) to hold back, keep back; (astenersi dal consegnare) to hold, keep; (detrarre: somma) to deduct; ~rsi vr (astenersi) to restrain o.s., stop o.s.; (soffermarsi) to stay, remain.

tratteni'mento sm entertainment; (festa) party.

tratte'nuta sf deduction.

trat'tino sm dash; (in parole composte) hyphen.

'tratto, a pp di trarre // sm (di penna, matita) stroke; (parte) part, piece; (di strada) stretch; (di mare, cielo) expanse; (di tempo) period (of time); ~i smpl (caratteristiche) features; (modo di fare) ways, manners; **a un ~, d'un ~** suddenly.

trat'tore sm tractor.

tratto'ria sf restaurant.

'trauma, i sm trauma; **trau'matico, a, ci, che** ag traumatic.

tra'vaglio [tra'vaʎʎo] sm (angoscia) pain, suffering; (MED) pains pl; ~ **di parto** labour pains.

trava'sare vt to decant.

'trave sf beam.

tra'versa sf (trave) crosspiece; (via) sidestreet; (FERR) sleeper (Brit), (railroad) tie (US); (CALCIO) crossbar.

traver'sare vt to cross; **traver'sata** sf crossing; (AER) flight, trip.

traver'sie sfpl mishaps, misfortunes.

traver'sina sf (FERR) sleeper (Brit), (railroad) tie (US).

tra'verso, a ag oblique; **di ~** ag askew // av sideways; **andare di ~** (cibo) to go down the wrong way; **guardare di ~** to look askance at.

travesti'mento sm disguise.

traves'tire vt to disguise; ~rsi vr to disguise o.s.

travi'are vt (fig) to lead astray.

travi'sare vt (fig) to distort, misrepresent.

tra'volgere [tra'vɔldʒere] vt to sweep away, carry away; (fig) to overwhelm; **tra'volto, a** pp di travolgere.

tre num three.

trebbi'are vt to thresh.

'treccia, ce ['trettʃa] sf plait, braid.

tre'cento [tre'tʃento] num three hundred // sm: **il T~** the fourteenth century.

'tredici ['treditʃi] num thirteen.

'tregua sf truce; (fig) respite.

tre'mare vi: ~ **di** (freddo etc) to shiver o tremble with; (paura, rabbia) to shake *o* tremble with.

tre'mendo, a *ag* terrible, awful.

tre'mila *num* three thousand.

'tremito *sm* trembling *q*; shaking *q*; shivering *q*.

tremo'lare *vi* to tremble; (*luce*) to flicker; (*foglie*) to quiver.

tre'more *sm* tremor.

'treno *sm* train; ~ **di gomme** set of tyres (*Brit*) *o* tires (*US*); ~ **merci** goods (*Brit*) *o* freight train; ~ **viaggiatori** passenger train.

'trenta *num* thirty; **tren'tesimo, a** *num* thirtieth; **tren'tina** *sf:* **una trentina (di)** thirty or so, about thirty.

'trepido, a *ag* anxious.

treppi'ede *sm* tripod; (*CUC*) trivet.

'tresca, sche *sf* (*fig*) intrigue; (*: relazione amorosa*) affair.

'trespolo *sm* trestle.

tri'angolo *sm* triangle.

tribù *sf inv* tribe.

tri'buna *sf* (*podio*) platform; (*in aule etc*) gallery; (*di stadio*) stand.

tribu'nale *sm* court.

tribu'tare *vt* to bestow.

tri'buto *sm* tax; (*fig*) tribute.

tri'checo, chi [tri'kɛko] *sm* (*ZOOL*) walrus.

tri'ciclo [tri'tʃiklo] *sm* tricycle.

trico'lore *ag* three-coloured // *sm* tricolour; (*bandiera italiana*) Italian flag.

tri'dente *sm* trident.

tri'foglio [tri'fɔʎʎo] *sm* clover.

'triglia [triʎʎa] *sf* red mullet.

tril'lare *vi* (*MUS*) to trill.

tri'mestre *sm* period of three months; (*INS*) term, quarter (*US*); (*COMM*) quarter.

'trina *sf* lace.

trin'cea [trin'tʃea] *sf* trench; **trince'rare** *vt* to entrench.

trinci'are [trin'tʃare] *vt* to cut up.

trion'fare *vi* to triumph, win; ~ **su** to triumph over, overcome; **tri'onfo** *sm* triumph.

tripli'care *vt* to triple.

'triplice ['triplitʃe] *ag* triple; **in ~ copia** in triplicate.

'triplo, a *ag* triple; treble // *sm:* **il ~ (di)** three times as much (as); **la spesa è ~a** it costs three times as much.

'tripode *sm* tripod.

'trippa *sf* (*CUC*) tripe.

'triste *ag* sad; (*luogo*) dreary, gloomy; **tris'tezza** *sf* sadness; gloominess.

trita'carne *sm inv* mincer, grinder (*US*).

tri'tare *vt* to mince, grind (*US*).

'trito, a *ag* (*tritato*) minced, ground (*US*); ~ **e ritrito** (*fig*) trite, hackneyed.

'trittico, ci *sm* (*ARTE*) triptych.

trivel'lare *vt* to drill.

trivi'ale *ag* vulgar, low.

tro'feo *sm* trophy.

'trogolo *sm* (*per maiali*) trough.

'tromba *sf* (*MUS*) trumpet; (*AUT*) horn; ~ **d'aria** whirlwind; ~ **delle scale** stairwell.

trom'bone *sm* trombone.

trom'bosi *sf* thrombosis.

tron'care *vt* to cut off; (*spezzare*) to break off.

'tronco, a, chi, che *ag* cut off; broken off; (*LING*) truncated; (*fig*) cut short // *sm* (*BOT, ANAT*) trunk; (*fig: tratto*) section; (*: pezzo: di lancia*) stump; **licenziare qn in ~** to fire sb on the spot.

troneggi'are [troned'dʒare] *vi:* ~ **(su)** to tower (over).

tronfio, a *ag* conceited.

'trono *sm* throne.

tropi'cale *ag* tropical.

'tropico, ci *sm* tropic; **~ci** *smpl* tropics.

'troppo, a ◆ *det* (*in eccesso: quantità*) too much; (*: numero*) too many; **c'era ~a gente** there were too many people; **fa ~ caldo** it's too hot

◆ *pronome* (*in eccesso: quantità*) too much; (*: numero*) too many; **ne hai messo ~** you've put in too much; **meglio ~i che pochi** better too many than too few

◆ *av* (*eccessivamente: con ag, av*) too; (*: con vb*) too much; ~ **amaro/tardi** bitter/late; **lavora ~** he works too much; **di ~** too much; too many; **qualche tazza di ~** a few cups too many; **3000 lire di ~** 3000 lire too much; **essere di ~** to be in the way.

'trota *sf* trout.

trot'tare *vi* to trot; **trotterel'lare** *vi* to trot along; (*bambino*) to toddle; **'trotto** *sm* trot.

'trottola *sf* spinning top.

tro'vare *vt* to find; (*giudicare*): **trovo che I find** *o* think that; **~rsi** *vr* (*reciproco: incontrarsi*) to meet; (*essere, stare*) to be; (*arrivare, capitare*) to find o.s.; **andare a ~ qn** to go and see sb; ~ **qn colpevole** to find sb guilty; **~rsi bene** (*in un luogo, con qn*) to get on well; **tro'vata** *sf* good idea.

truc'care *vt* (*falsare*) to fake; (*attore etc*) to make up; (*travestire*) to disguise; (*SPORT*) to fix; (*AUT*) to soup up; **~rsi** *vr* to make up (one's face); **trucca'tore, 'trice** *sm/f* (*CINEMA, TEATRO*) make-up artist.

'trucco, chi *sm* trick; (*cosmesi*) make-up.

'truce ['trutʃe] *ag* fierce.

truci'dare [trutʃi'dare] *vt* to slaughter.

'truciolo ['trutʃolo] *sm* shaving.

'truffa *sf* fraud, swindle; **truf'fare** *vt* to swindle, cheat.

'truppa *sf* troop.

tu *pronome* you; ~ **stesso(a)** you yourself; **dare del ~ a qn** to address sb as "tu".

'tua *vedi* **tuo.**

'tuba *sf* (MUS) tuba; (*cappello*) top hat.

tu'bare *vi* to coo.

tuba'tura *sf*, **tubazi'one** [tubat'tsjone] *sf* piping *q*, pipes *pl*.

tu'betto *sm* tube.

'tubo *sm* tube; pipe; ~ **digerente** (ANAT) alimentary canal, digestive tract; ~ **di scappamento** (AUT) exhaust pipe.

'tue *vedi* **tuo.**

tuf'fare *vt* to plunge, dip; ~**rsi** *vr* to plunge, dive; **'tuffo** *sm* dive; (*breve bagno*) dip.

tu'gurio *sm* hovel.

tuli'pano *sm* tulip.

tume'farsi *vr* (MED) to swell.

'tumido, a *ag* swollen.

tu'more *sm* (MED) tumour.

tu'multo *sm* uproar, commotion; (*sommossa*) riot; (*fig*) turmoil; **tumul-tu'oso, a** *ag* rowdy, unruly; (*fig*) turbulent, stormy.

'tunica, che *sf* tunic.

Tuni'sia *sf*: **la** ~ Tunisia.

'tuo, 'tua, 'tuoi, 'tue *det*: **il** ~, **la tua** *etc* your // *pronome*: **il** ~, **la tua** *etc* yours.

tuo'nare *vi* to thunder; **tuona** it is thundering, there's some thunder.

tu'ono *sm* thunder.

tu'orlo *sm* yolk.

tu'racciolo [tu'rattʃolo] *sm* cap, top; (*di sughero*) cork.

tu'rare *vt* to stop, plug; (*con sughero*) to cork; ~**rsi il naso** to hold one's nose.

turba'mento *sm* disturbance; (*di animo*) anxiety, agitation.

tur'bante *sm* turban.

tur'bare *vt* to disturb, trouble.

turbi'nare *vi* to whirl.

'turbine *sm* whirlwind; ~ **di neve** swirl of snow; ~ **di polvere/sabbia** dust/sandstorm.

turbo'lento, a *ag* turbulent; (*ragazzo*) boisterous, unruly.

turbo'lenza [turbo'lɛntsa] *sf* turbulence.

tur'chese [tur'kese] *sf* turquoise.

Tur'chia [tur'kia] *sf*: **la** ~ Turkey.

tur'chino, a [tur'kino] *ag* deep blue.

'turco, a, chi, che *ag* Turkish // *sm/f* Turk/Turkish woman // *sm* (LING) Turkish; **parlare** ~ (*fig*) to talk double-dutch.

tu'rismo *sm* tourism; tourist industry; **tu'rista, i, e** *sm/f* tourist; **tu'ristico, a, ci, che** *ag* tourist *cpd*.

'turno *sm* turn; (*di lavoro*) shift; **di** ~ (*soldato, medico, custode*) on duty; **a** ~ (*rispondere*) in turn; (*lavorare*) in shifts; **fare a** ~ **a fare qc** to take turns to do sth; **è il suo** ~ it's your (*o his etc*) turn.

'turpe *ag* filthy, vile; **turpi'loquio** *sm* obscene language.

'tuta *sf* overalls *pl*; (SPORT) tracksuit.

tu'tela *sf* (DIR: *di minore*) guardianship; (: *protezione*) protection; (*difesa*) defence; **tute'lare** *vt* to protect, defend.

tu'tore, 'trice *sm/f* (DIR) guardian.

tutta'via *cong* nevertheless, yet.

'tutto, a ◆ *det* **1** (*intero*) all; ~ **il latte** all the milk; ~**a la notte** all night, the whole night; ~ **il libro** the whole book; ~**a una bottiglia** a whole bottle

2 (*pl, collettivo*) all; every; ~**i i libri** all the books; ~**e le notti** every night; ~**i i venerdì** every Friday; ~**i gli uomini** all the men; (*collettivo*) all men; ~**i e due** both *o* each of us (*o them o you*); ~**i e cinque** all five of us (*o them o you*)

3 (*completamente*): **era** ~**a sporca** she was all dirty; **tremava** ~ he was trembling all over; **è** ~**a sua madre** she's just *o* exactly like her mother

4: **a tutt'oggi** so far, up till now; **a** ~**a velocità** at full *o* top speed

◆ *pronome* **1** (*ogni cosa*) everything, all; (*qualsiasi cosa*) anything; **ha mangiato** ~ he's eaten everything; ~ **considerato** all things considered; **in** ~: **10,000 lire in** ~ 10,000 lire in all; **in** ~ **eravamo 50** there were 50 of us in all

2: ~**i(e)** (*ognuno*) all, everybody; **vengono** ~**i** they are all coming, everybody's coming; ~**i quanti** all and sundry

◆ *av* (*completamente*) entirely, quite; **è** ~ **il contrario** it's quite *o* exactly the opposite; **tutt'al più**: **saranno stati tutt'al più una cinquantina** there were about fifty of them at (the very) most; **tutt'al più possiamo prendere un treno** if the worst comes to the worst we can take a train; **tutt'altro** on the contrary; **è tutt'altro che felice** he's anything but happy; **tutt'a un tratto** suddenly

◆ *sm*: **il** ~ the whole lot, all of it.

tutto'fare *ag inv*: **domestica** ~ general maid; **ragazzo** ~ office boy // *sm/f inv* handyman/woman.

tut'tora *av* still.

U

ubbidi'ente *ag* obedient; **ubbidi'enza** *sf* obedience.

ubbi'dire *vi* to obey; ~ **a** to obey; (*sog: veicolo, macchina*) to respond to.

ubiquità *sf*: **non ho il dono dell'**~ I can't be everywhere at once.

ubria'care *vt*: ~ **qn** to get sb drunk; (*sog: alcool*) to make sb drunk; (*fig*) to make sb's head spin *o* reel; ~**rsi** *vr* to get drunk; ~**rsi di** (*fig*) to become intoxicated with.

ubri'aco, a, chi, che *ag, sm/f* drunk.

uccelli'era [uttʃel'ljɛra] *sf* aviary.

uccel'lino [uttʃel'lino] *sm* baby bird, chick.

uc'cello [ut'tʃɛllo] *sm* bird.

uc'cidere [ut'tʃidere] *vt* to kill; ~**rsi** *vr*

(*suicidarsi*) to kill o.s.; (*perdere la vita*) to be killed; **uccisi'one** *sf* killing; **uc'ciso, a** *pp di* **uccidere; ucci'sore, uccidi'trice** *smlf* killer.

udi'enza [u'djɛntsa] *sf* audience; (*DIR*) hearing; **dare ~ (a)** to grant an audience (to).

u'dire *vt* to hear; **udi'tivo, a** *ag* auditory; **u'dito** *sm* (sense of) hearing; **udi'tore, 'trice** *smlf* listener; (*INS*) unregistered student (*attending lectures*); **udi'torio** *sm* (*persone*) audience.

uffa *escl* tut!

uffici'ale [uffi'tʃale] *ag* official // *sm* (*AMM*) official, officer; (*MIL*) officer; ~ **di stato civile** registrar.

uf'ficio [uf'fitʃo] *sm* (*gen*) office; (*dovere*) duty; (*mansione*) task, function, job; (*agenzia*) agency, bureau; (*REL*) service; **d'~** *ag* office *cpd*; official // *av* officially; ~ **di collocamento** employment office; ~ **informazioni** information bureau; ~ **oggetti smarriti** lost property office (*Brit*), lost and found (*US*); ~ **postale** post office.

uffici'oso, a [uffi'tʃoso] *ag* unofficial.

'ufo: a ~ *av* free, for nothing.

uggi'oso, a [ud'dʒoso] *ag* tiresome; (*tempo*) dull.

uguagli'anza [ugwaʎ'ʎantsa] *sf* equality.

uguagli'are [ugwaʎ'ʎare] *vt* to make equal; (*essere uguale*) to equal, be equal to; (*livellare*) to level; ~**rsi a** *o* **con qn** (*paragonarsi*) to compare o.s. to sb.

ugu'ale *ag* equal; (*identico*) identical, the same; (*uniforme*) level, even // *av*: **costano** ~ they cost the same; **sono bravi** ~ they're equally good; **ugual'mente** *av* equally; (*lo stesso*) all the same.

'ulcera ['ultʃera] *sf* ulcer.

u'liva *etc* = **oliva** *etc*.

ulteri'ore *ag* further.

ulti'mare *vt* to finish, complete.

'ultimo, a *ag* (*finale*) last; (*estremo*) farthest, utmost; (*recente: notizia, moda*) latest; (*fig: sommo, fondamentale*) ultimate // *smlf* last (one); **fino all'~** to the last, until the end; **da ~, in ~** in the end; **abitare all'~ piano** to live on the top floor; **per** ~ (*entrare, arrivare*) last.

ulu'lare *vi* to howl; **ulu'lato** *sm* howling *q*; howl.

umanità *sf* humanity; **umani'tario, a** *ag* humanitarian.

u'mano, a *ag* human; (*comprensivo*) humane.

umbi'lico *sm* = **ombelico**.

umet'tare *vt* to dampen, moisten.

umidità *sf* dampness; humidity.

'umido, a *ag* damp; (*mano, occhi*) moist; (*clima*) humid // *sm* dampness, damp; **carne in** ~ stew.

'umile *ag* humble.

umili'are *vt* to humiliate; ~**rsi** *vr* to

humble o.s.; **umiliazi'one** *sf* humiliation.

umiltà *sf* humility, humbleness.

u'more *sm* (*disposizione d'animo*) mood; (*carattere*) temper; **di buon/cattivo** ~ in a good/bad mood.

umo'rismo *sm* humour; **avere il senso dell'**~ to have a sense of humour; **umo'rista, i, e** *smlf* humorist; **umo'ristico, a, ci, che** *ag* humorous, funny.

un, un', una *vedi* **uno**.

u'nanime *ag* unanimous; **unanimità** *sf* unanimity; **all'unanimità** unanimously.

unci'netto [untʃi'netto] *sm* crochet hook.

un'cino [un'tʃino] *sm* hook.

'undici ['unditʃi] *num* eleven.

'ungere ['undʒere] *vt* to grease, oil; (*REL*) to anoint; (*fig*) to flatter, butter up; ~**rsi** *vr* (*sporcarsi*) to get covered in grease; ~**rsi con la crema** to put on cream.

unghe'rese [unge'rese] *ag, smlf, sm* Hungarian.

Unghe'ria [unge'ria] *sf:* **l'**~ Hungary.

'unghia ['ungja] *sf* (*ANAT*) nail; (*di animale*) claw; (*di rapace*) talon; (*di cavallo*) hoof; **unghi'ata** *sf* (*graffio*) scratch.

ungu'ento *sm* ointment.

'unico, a, ci, che *ag* (*solo*) only; (*ineguagliabile*) unique; (*singolo: binario*) single; **figlio(a)** ~**(a)** only son/daughter, only child.

unifi'care *vt* to unite, unify; (*sistemi*) to standardize; **unificazi'one** *sf* uniting; unification; standardization.

uni'forme *ag* uniform; (*superficie*) even // *sf* (*divisa*) uniform.

unilate'rale *ag* one-sided; (*DIR*) unilateral.

uni'one *sf* union; (*fig: concordia*) unity, harmony; **l'U~ Sovietica** the Soviet Union.

u'nire *vt* to unite; (*congiungere*) to join, connect; (*: ingredienti, colori*) to combine; (*in matrimonio*) to unite, join together; ~**rsi** *vr* to unite; (*in matrimonio*) to be joined together; ~ **qc a** to unite sth with; to join *o* connect sth with; to combine sth with; ~**rsi a** (*gruppo, società*) to join.

unità *sf inv* (*unione, concordia*) unity; (*MAT, MIL, COMM, di misura*) unit; **uni'tario, a** *ag* unitary; **prezzo unitario** price per unit.

u'nito, a *ag* (*paese*) united; (*amici, famiglia*) close; **in tinta** ~**a** plain, self-coloured.

univer'sale *ag* universal; general.

università *sf inv* university; **universi'tario, a** *ag* university *cpd* // *smlf* (*studente*) university student; (*insegnante*) academic, university lecturer.

uni'verso *sm* universe.

'uno, a (*dav sm* un + *C*, *V*, uno + *s impura, gn, pn, ps, x, z; dav sf* un' + *V*, una + *C*) ◆ *articolo indefinito* **1** a; (*dav vocale*) an; **un bambino** a child; **~a strada** a street; **~ zingaro** a gypsy **2** (*intensivo*): **ho avuto ~a paura!** I got such a fright!
◆ *pronome* **1** one; **prendine ~** take one (of them); **l'~ o l'altro** either (of them); **l'~ e l'altro** both (of them); **aiutarsi l'un l'altro** to help one another *o* each other; **sono entrati l'~ dopo l'altro** they came in one after the other
2 (*un tale*) someone, somebody
3 (*con valore impersonale*) one, you; **se ~ vuole** if one wants, if you want
◆ *num one*; **~a mela e due pere** one apple and two pears; **~ più ~ fa due** one plus one equals two, one and one are two
◆ *sf*: **è l'~a** it's one (o'clock).

'unto, a *pp di* **ungere** // *ag* greasy, oily // *sm* grease; **untu'oso, a** *ag* greasy, oily.

u'omo, *pl* **u'omini** *sm* man; **da ~** (*abito, scarpe*) men's, for men; **~ d'affari** businessman; **~ di paglia** stooge; **~ rana** frogman.

u'opo *sm*: **all'~** if necessary.

u'ovo, *pl(f)* **u'ova** *sm* egg; **~ affogato** poached egg; **~ bazzotto/sodo** soft-/hard-boiled egg; **~ alla coque** boiled egg; **~ di Pasqua** Easter egg; **uova strapazzate** scrambled eggs.

ura'gano *sm* hurricane.

urba'nistica *sf* town planning.

ur'bano, a *ag* urban, city *cpd*, town *cpd*; (*TEL: chiamata*) local; (*fig*) urbane.

ur'gente [ur'dʒɛnte] *ag* urgent; **ur'genza** *sf* urgency; **in caso d'urgenza** in (case of) an emergency; **d'urgenza** *ag* emergency // *av* urgently, as a matter of urgency.

'urgere ['urdʒere] *vi* to be urgent; to be needed urgently.

u'rina *sf* = **orina**.

ur'lare *vi* (*persona*) to scream, yell; (*animale, vento*) to howl // *vt* to scream, yell.

'urlo, *pl(m)* **'urli**, *pl(f)* **'urla** *sm* scream, yell; howl.

'urna *sf* urn; (*elettorale*) ballot-box; **andare alle ~e** to go to the polls.

urrà *escl* hurrah!

U.R.S.S. *abbr f*: **l'~** the USSR.

ur'tare *vt* to bump into, knock against; (*fig: irritare*) to annoy // *vi*: **~ contro** *o* **in** to bump into, knock against, crash into; (*fig: imbattersi*) to come up against; **~rsi** *vr* (*reciproco: scontrarsi*) to collide; (: *fig*) to clash; (*irritarsi*) to get annoyed; **'urto** *sm* (*colpo*) knock, bump; (*scontro*) crash, collision; (*fig*) clash.

U.S.A. ['uza] *smpl*: **gli ~** the USA.

u'sanza [u'zantsa] *sf* custom; (*moda*) fashion.

u'sare *vt* to use, employ // *vi* (*servirsi*): **~ di** to use; (: *diritto*) to exercise; (*essere di moda*) to be fashionable; (*essere solito*): **~ fare** to be in the habit of doing, be accustomed to doing // *vb impersonale*: **qui usa così** it's the custom round here; **u'sato, a** *ag* (*consumato*) worn; (*di seconda mano*) used, second-hand // *sm* second-hand goods *pl*.

usci'ere [uʃ'ʃɛre] *sm* usher.

'uscio ['uʃʃo] *sm* door.

u'scire [uʃ'ʃire] *vi* (*gen*) to come out; (*partire, andare a passeggio, a uno spettacolo etc*) to go out; (*essere sorteggiato: numero*) to come up; **~ da** (*gen*) to leave; (*posto*) to go (*o* come) out of, leave; (*solco, vasca etc*) to come out of; (*muro*) to stick out of; (*competenza etc*) to be outside; (*infanzia, adolescenza*) to leave behind; (*famiglia nobile etc*) to come from; **~ da** *o* **di casa** to go out; (*fig*) to leave home; **~ in automobile** to go out in the car, go for a drive; **~ di strada** (*AUT*) to go off *o* leave the road.

u'scita [uʃ'ʃita] *sf* (*passaggio, varco*) exit, way out; (*per divertimento*) outing; (*ECON: somma*) expenditure; (*TEATRO*) entrance; (*fig: battuta*) witty remark; **~ di sicurezza** emergency exit.

usi'gnolo [uziɲ'nɔlo] *sm* nightingale.

U.S.L. [uzl] *sigla f* (= *unità sanitaria locale*) local health centre.

'uso *sm* (*utilizzazione*) use; (*esercizio*) practice; (*abitudine*) custom; **a ~ di** for (the use of); **d'~** (*corrente*) in use; **fuori ~** out of use.

usti'one *sf* burn.

usu'ale *ag* common, everyday.

u'sura *sf* usury; (*logoramento*) wear (and tear).

uten'sile *sm* tool, implement; **~i da cucina** kitchen utensils.

u'tente *sm/f* user.

'utero *sm* uterus.

'utile *ag* useful // *sm* (*vantaggio*) advantage, benefit; (*ECON: profitto*) profit; **utilità** *sf* usefulness *q*; use; (*vantaggio*) benefit; **utili'tario, a** *ag* utilitarian // *sf* (*AUT*) economy car.

utiliz'zare [utilid'dzare] *vt* to use, make use of, utilize.

'uva *sf* grapes *pl*; **~ passa** raisins *pl*; **~ spina** gooseberry.

V

v. *abbr* (= *vedi*) v.

va *vb vedi* **andare**.

va'cante *ag* vacant.

va'canza [va'kantsa] *sf* (*l'essere vacante*) vacancy; (*riposo, ferie*) holiday(s *pl*)

(*Brit*), vacation (*US*); (*giorno di permesso*) day off, holiday; ~e *sfpl* (*periodo di ferie*) holidays (*Brit*), vacation *sg* (*US*); essere/andare in ~ to be/go on holiday o vacation; ~e estive summer holiday(s) o vacation.

'**vacca, che** *sf* cow.

vacci'nare [vattʃi'nare] *vt* to vaccinate.

vacil'lare [vatʃil'lare] *vi* to sway, wobble; (*luce*) to flicker; (*fig: memoria, coraggio*) to be failing, falter.

'**vacuo, a** *ag* (*fig*) empty, vacuous // *sm* vacuum.

'**vado** *vb vedi* **andare**.

vaga'bondo, a *sm/f* tramp, vagrant; (*fannullone*) idler, loafer.

va'gare *vi* to wander.

vagheggi'are [vaged'dʒare] *vt* to long for, dream of.

va'gina [va'dʒina] *sf* vagina.

va'gire [va'dʒire] *vi* to whimper.

'**vaglia** ['vaʎʎa] *sm inv* money order; ~ postale postal order.

vagli'are [vaʎ'ʎare] *vt* to sift; (*fig*) to weigh up; '**vaglio** *sm* sieve.

'**vago, a, ghi, ghe** *ag* vague.

va'gone *sm* (*FERR: per passeggeri*) coach; (: *per merci*) truck, wagon; ~ letto sleeper, sleeping car; ~ ristorante dining o restaurant car.

'**vai** *vb vedi* **andare**.

vai'olo *sm* smallpox.

va'langa, ghe *sf* avalanche.

va'lente *ag* able, talented.

va'lere *vi* (*avere forza, potenza*) to have influence; (*essere valido*) to be valid; (*avere vigore, autorità*) to hold, apply; (*essere capace: poeta, studente*) to be good, be able // *vt* (*prezzo, sforzo*) to be worth; (*corrispondere*) to correspond to; (*procurare*): ~ qc a qn to earn sb sth; ~rsi di to make use of, take advantage of; far ~ (*autorità etc*) to assert; vale a dire that is to say; ~ la pena to be worth the effort o worth it.

va'levole *ag* valid.

vali'care *vt* to cross.

'**valico, chi** *sm* (*passo*) pass.

'**valido, a** *ag* valid; (*rimedio*) effective; (*aiuto*) real; (*persona*) worthwhile.

valige'ria [validʒe'ria] *sf* leather goods *pl*; leather goods factory; leather goods shop.

va'ligia, gie *o* **ge** [va'lidʒa] *sf* (*suit*)case; fare le ~gie to pack (up); ~ diplomatica diplomatic bag.

val'lata *sf* valley.

'**valle** *sf* valley; a ~ (*di fiume*) downstream; scendere a ~ to go downhill.

val'letto *sm* valet.

va'lore *sm* (*gen*) value; (*merito*) merit, worth; (*coraggio*) valour, courage; (*COMM: titolo*) security; ~i *smpl* (*oggetti preziosi*) valuables.

valoriz'zare [valorid'dzare] *vt* (*terreno*)

to develop; (*fig*) to make the most of.

'**valso, a** *pp di* **valere**.

va'luta *sf* currency, money; (*BANCA*): ~ 15 gennaio interest to run from January 15th.

valu'tare *vt* (*casa, gioiello, fig*) to value; (*stabilire: peso, entrate, fig*) to estimate; **valutazi'one** *sf* valuation; estimate.

'**valvola** *sf* (*TECN, ANAT*) valve; (*ELETTR*) fuse.

'**valzer** ['valtser] *sm inv* waltz.

vam'pata *sf* (*di fiamma*) blaze; (*di calore*) blast; (: *al viso*) flush.

vam'piro *sm* vampire.

vanda'lismo *sm* vandalism.

'**vandalo** *sm* vandal.

vaneggi'are [vaned'dʒare] *vi* to rave.

'**vanga, ghe** *sf* spade; **van'gare** *vt* to dig.

van'gelo [van'dʒɛlo] *sm* gospel.

va'niglia [va'niʎʎa] *sf* vanilla.

vanità *sf* vanity; (*di promessa*) emptiness; (*di sforzo*) futility; **vani'toso, a** *ag* vain, conceited.

'**vanno** *vb vedi* **andare**.

'**vano, a** *ag* vain // *sm* (*spazio*) space; (*apertura*) opening; (*stanza*) room.

van'taggio [van'taddʒo] *sm* advantage; essere/portarsi in ~ (*SPORT*) to be in/take the lead; **vantaggi'oso, a** *ag* advantageous; favourable.

van'tare *vt* to praise, speak highly of; ~rsi *vr*: ~rsi (di/di aver fatto) to boast o brag (about/about having done); **vante'ria** *sf* boasting; '**vanto** *sm* boasting; (*merito*) virtue, merit; (*gloria*) pride.

'**vanvera** *sf*: a ~ haphazardly; parlare a ~ to talk nonsense.

va'pore *sm* vapour; (*anche*: ~ acqueo) steam; (*nave*) steamer; a ~ (*turbina etc*) steam *cpd*; al ~ (*CUC*) steamed; **vapo'retto** *sm* steamer; **vapori'era** *sf* (*FERR*) steam engine; **vaporiz'zare** *vt* to vaporize; **vapo'roso, a** *ag* (*tessuto*) filmy; (*capelli*) soft and full.

va'rare *vt* (*NAUT, fig*) to launch; (*DIR*) to pass.

var'care *vt* to cross.

'**varco, chi** *sm* passage; aprirsi un ~ tra la folla to push one's way through the crowd.

vari'abile *ag* variable; (*tempo, umore*) changeable, variable // *sf* (*MAT*) variable.

vari'are *vt, vi* to vary; ~ di opinione to change one's mind; **variazi'one** *sf* variation; change.

va'rice [va'ritʃe] *sf* varicose vein.

vari'cella [vari'tʃɛlla] *sf* chickenpox.

vari'coso, a *ag* varicose.

varie'gato, a *ag* variegated.

varietà *sf inv* variety // *sm inv* variety show.

'**vario, a** *ag* varied; (*parecchi: col so-*

stantivo al pl) various; (*mutevole: umore*) changeable; **vario'pinto, a** *ag* multicoloured.

'varo *sm* (NAUT, *fig*) launch; (*di leggi*) passing.

va'saio *sm* potter.

'vasca, sche *sf* basin; (*anche:* ~ *da bagno*) bathtub, bath.

va'scello [vaʃˈʃɛllo] *sm* (NAUT) vessel, ship.

vase'lina *sf* vaseline.

vasel'lame *sm* (*stoviglie*) crockery; (: *di porcellana*) china; ~ **d'oro/d'argento** gold/silver plate.

'vaso *sm* (*recipiente*) pot; (: *barattolo*) jar; (: *decorativo*) vase; (ANAT) vessel; ~ **da fiori** vase; (*per piante*) flowerpot.

vas'soio *sm* tray.

'vasto, a *ag* vast, immense.

Vati'cano *sm*: **il** ~ **the Vatican**.

ve *pronome, av vedi* **vi**.

vecchi'aia [vekˈkjaja] *sf* old age.

'vecchio, a [ˈvɛkkjo] *ag* old // *sm/f* old man/woman; **i** ~**i** the old.

'vece [ˈvetʃe] *sf*: **in** ~ **di** in the place of, for; **fare le** ~**i di** **qn** to take sb's place.

ve'dere *vt, vi* to see; ~**rsi** *vr* to meet, see one another; **avere a che** ~ **con** to have something to do with; **far** ~ **qc a qn** to show sb sth; **farsi** ~ to show o.s.; (*farsi vivo*) to show one's face; **vedi di non farlo** make sure *o* see you don't do it; **non (ci) si vede** (*è buio etc*) you can't see a thing; **non lo posso** ~ (*fig*) I can't stand him.

ve'detta *sf* (*sentinella, posto*) look-out; (NAUT) patrol boat.

'vedovo, a *sm/f* widower/widow.

ve'duta *sf* view.

vee'mente *ag* vehement; violent.

vege'tale [vedʒeˈtale] *ag, sm* vegetable.

vegetari'ano, a [vedʒetaˈrjano] *ag, sm/f* vegetarian.

'vegeto, a [ˈvɛdʒeto] *ag* (*pianta*) thriving; (*persona*) strong, vigorous.

'veglia [ˈveʎʎa] *sf* wakefulness; (*sorveglianza*) watch; (*trattenimento*) evening gathering; **fare la** ~ **a un malato** to watch over a sick person.

vegli'are [veʎˈʎare] *vi* to be awake; to stay *o* sit up; (*stare vigile*) to watch; to keep watch // *vt* (*malato, morto*) to watch over, sit up with.

ve'icolo *sm* vehicle; ~ **spaziale** spacecraft *inv*.

'vela *sf* (NAUT: *tela*) sail; (*sport*) sailing.

ve'lare *vt* to veil; ~**rsi** *vr* (*occhi, luna*) to mist over; (*voce*) to become husky; ~**rsi il viso** to cover one's face (with a veil); **ve'lato, a** *ag* veiled.

veleggi'are [veledˈdʒare] *vi* to sail; (AER) to glide.

ve'leno *sm* poison; **vele'noso, a** *ag* poisonous.

veli'ero *sm* sailing ship.

ve'lina *sf* (*anche:* **carta** ~: *per imballare*) tissue paper; (: *per copie*) flimsy paper; (*copia*) carbon copy.

ve'livolo *sm* aircraft.

velleità *sf inv* vain ambition, vain desire.

'vello *sm* fleece.

vel'luto *sm* velvet; ~ **a coste** cord.

'velo *sm* veil; (*tessuto*) voile.

ve'loce [veˈlotʃe] *ag* fast, quick // *av* fast, quickly; **velo'cista, i, e** *sm/f* (SPORT) sprinter; **velocità** *sf* speed; **a forte velocità** at high speed; **velocità di crociera** cruising speed.

ve'lodromo *sm* velodrome.

'vena *sf* (*gen*) vein; (*filone*) vein, seam; (*fig: ispirazione*) inspiration; (: *umore*) mood; **essere in** ~ **di qc** to be in the mood for sth.

ve'nale *ag* (*prezzo, valore*) market *cpd*; (*fig*) venal; mercenary.

ven'demmia *sf* (*raccolta*) grape harvest; (*quantità d'uva*) grape crop, grapes *pl*; (*vino ottenuto*) vintage; **vendemmi'are** *vt* to harvest // *vi* to harvest the grapes.

'vendere *vt* to sell; "**vendesi**" "for sale".

ven'detta *sf* revenge.

vendi'care *vt* to avenge; ~**rsi** *vr*: ~**rsi (di)** to avenge o.s. (for); (*per rancore*) to take one's revenge (for); ~**rsi su qn** to revenge o.s. on sb; **vendica'tivo, a** *ag* vindictive.

'vendita *sf* sale; **la** ~ (*attività*) selling; (*smercio*) sales *pl*; **in** ~ on sale; ~ **all'asta** sale by auction; **vendi'tore** *sm* seller, vendor; (*gestore di negozio*) trader, dealer.

ve'nefico, a, ci, che *ag* poisonous.

vene'rabile *ag*, **vene'rando, a** *ag* venerable.

vene'rare *vt* to venerate.

venerdì *sm inv* Friday; **di** *o* **il** ~ on Fridays; **V**~ **Santo** Good Friday.

ve'nereo, a *ag* venereal.

'veneto, a *ag, sm/f* Venetian.

Ve'nezia [veˈnɛttsja] *sf* Venice; **venezi'ano, a** *ag, sm/f* Venetian.

veni'ale *ag* venial.

ve'nire *vi* to come; (*riuscire: dolce, fotografia*) to turn out; (*come ausiliare: essere*): **viene ammirato da tutti** he is admired by everyone; ~ **da** to come from; **quanto viene?** how much does it cost?; **far** ~ (*mandare a chiamare*) to send for; ~ **giù** to come down; ~ **meno** (*svenire*) to faint; ~ **meno a qc** not to fulfil sth; ~ **su** to come up; ~ **a trovare qn** to come and see sb; ~ **via** to come away.

ven'taglio [venˈtaʎʎo] *sm* fan.

ven'tata *sf* gust (of wind).

ven'tenne *ag*: **una ragazza** ~ a twenty-year-old girl, a girl of twenty.

ven'tesimo, a *num* twentieth.

'venti num twenty.

venti'lare vt (stanza) to air, ventilate; (fig: idea, proposta) to air; **ventila'tore** sm ventilator, fan.

ven'tina sf: una ~ (di) around twenty, twenty or so.

venti'sette num twenty-seven; il ~ (giorno di paga) (monthly) pay day.

'vento sm wind.

'ventola sf (AUT, TECN) fan.

ven'tosa sf (ZOOL) sucker; (di gomma) suction pad.

ven'toso, a ag windy.

'ventre sm stomach.

ven'tura sf: andare alla ~ to trust to luck; soldato di ~ mercenary.

ven'turo, a ag next, coming.

ve'nuto, a pp di **venire** // sf coming, arrival.

vera'mente av really.

ver'bale ag verbal // sm (di riunione) minutes pl.

'verbo sm (LING) verb; (parola) word; (REL): il V~ the Word.

'verde ag, sm green; essere al ~ to be broke; ~ **bottiglia/oliva** ag inv bottle/ olive green.

verde'rame sm verdigris.

ver'detto sm verdict.

ver'dura sf vegetables pl.

vere'condo, a ag modest.

'verga, ghe sf rod.

ver'gato a ag (foglio) ruled.

'vergine ['vɛrdʒine] sf virgin; (dello zodiaco): V~ Virgo // ag virgin; (ragazza): essere ~ to be a virgin.

ver'gogna [ver'goɲɲa] sf shame; (timidezza) shyness, embarrassment; **vergo'gnarsi** vr: vergognarsi (di) to be o feel ashamed (of); to be shy (about), be embarrassed (about); **vergo'gnoso, a** ag ashamed; (timido) shy, embarrassed; (causa di vergogna: azione) shameful.

ve'rifica, che sf checking q, check.

verifi'care vt (controllare) to check; (confermare) to confirm, bear out.

verità sf inv truth.

veriti'ero, a ag (che dice la verità) truthful; (conforme a verità) true.

'verme sm worm.

vermi'celli [vermi'tʃelli] smpl vermicelli sg.

ver'miglio [ver'miʎʎo] sm vermilion, scarlet.

'vermut sm inv vermouth.

ver'nice [ver'nitʃe] sf (colorazione) paint; (trasparente) varnish; (pelle) patent leather; "~ **fresca**" "wet paint"; **vernici'are** vt to paint; to varnish.

'vero, a ag (veridico: fatti, testimonianza) true; (autentico) real // sm (verità) truth; (realtà) (real) life; un ~ e proprio delinquente a real criminal, an out and out criminal.

vero'simile ag likely, probable.

ver'ruca, che sf wart.

versa'mento sm (pagamento) payment; (deposito di denaro) deposit.

ver'sante sm slopes pl, side.

ver'sare vt (fare uscire: vino, farina) to pour (out); (spargere: lacrime, sangue) to shed; (rovesciare) to spill; (ECON) to pay; (: depositare) to deposit, pay in; **~rsi** vr (rovesciarsi) to spill; (fiume, folla): **~rsi (in)** to pour (into).

versa'tile ag versatile.

ver'setto sm (REL) verse.

versi'one sf version; (traduzione) translation.

'verso sm (di poesia) verse, line; (di animale, uccello, venditore ambulante) cry; (direzione) direction; (modo) way; (di foglio di carta) verso; (di moneta) reverse; **~i** smpl (poesia) verse sg; **non c'è ~ di persuaderlo** there's no way of persuading him, he can't be persuaded // prep (in direzione di) toward(s); (nei pressi di) near, around (about); (in senso temporale) about, around; (nei confronti di) for; ~ **di me** towards me; ~ **sera** towards evening.

verti'cale ag, sf vertical.

'vertice ['vɛrtitʃe] sm summit, top; (MAT) vertex; **conferenza al** ~ (POL) summit conference.

ver'tigine [ver'tidʒine] sf dizziness q; dizzy spell; (MED) vertigo; **avere le ~i** to feel dizzy; **vertigi'noso, a** ag (altezza) dizzy; (fig) breathtakingly high (o deep etc).

ve'scica, che [veʃ'ʃika] sf (ANAT) bladder; (MED) blister.

'vescovo sm bishop.

'vespa sf wasp.

'vespro sm (REL) vespers pl.

ves'sillo sm standard; (bandiera) flag.

ves'taglia [ves'taʎʎa] sf dressing gown.

'veste sf garment; (rivestimento) covering; (qualità, facoltà) capacity; **~i** sfpl clothes, clothing sg; **in ~ ufficiale** (fig) in an official capacity; **in ~ di** in the guise of, as; **vesti'ario** sm wardrobe, clothes pl.

ves'tibolo sm (entrance) hall.

ves'tire vt (bambino, malato) to dress; (avere indosso) to have on, wear; **~rsi** vr to dress, get dressed; **ves'tito, a** ag dressed // sm garment; (da donna) dress; (da uomo) suit; **vestiti** smpl clothes; **vestito di bianco** dressed in white.

Ve'suvio sm: il ~ Vesuvius.

vete'rano, a ag, sm/f veteran.

veteri'nario, a ag veterinary // sm veterinary surgeon (Brit), veterinarian (US), vet // sf veterinary medicine.

'veto sm inv veto.

ve'traio sm glassmaker; glazier.

ve'trato, a ag (porta, finestra) glazed;

(*che contiene vetro*) glass *cpd* // *sf* glass door (*o* window); (*di chiesa*) stained glass window.

vetre'ria *sf* (*stabilimento*) glassworks *sg*; (*oggetti di vetro*) glassware.

ve'trina *sf* (*di negozio*) (shop) window; (*armadio*) display cabinet; **vetri'nista, i, e** *sm/f* window dresser.

vetri'olo *sm* vitriol.

'vetro *sm* glass; (*per finestra, porta*) pane (of glass).

'vetta *sf* peak, summit, top.

vet'tore *sm* (*MAT, FISICA*) vector; (*chi trasporta*) carrier.

vetto'vaglie [vetto'vaʎʎe] *sfpl* supplies.

vet'tura *sf* (*carrozza*) carriage; (*FERR*) carriage (*Brit*), car (*US*); (*auto*) car (*Brit*), automobile (*US*).

vezzeggi'are [vettsed'dʒare] *vt* to fondle, caress; **vezzeggia'tivo** *sm* (*LING*) term of endearment.

'vezzo ['vettso] *sm* habit; **~i** *smpl* (*smancerie*) affected ways; (*leggiadria*) charms; **vez'zoso, a** *ag* (*grazioso*) charming, pretty; (*lezioso*) affected.

vi, *dav* **lo, la, li, le, ne diventa ve** *pronome* (*oggetto*) you; (*complemento di termine*) (to) you; (*riflessivo*) yourselves; (*reciproco*) each other // *av* (*lì*) there; (*qui*) here; (*per questo/quel luogo*) through here/there; **~ è/sono** there is/are.

'via *sf* (*gen*) way; (*strada*) street; (*sentiero, pista*) path, track; (*AMM: procedimento*) channels *pl* // *prep* (*passando per*) via, by way of // *av* away // *escl* go away!; (*suvvia*) come on!; (*SPORT*) go! // *sm* (*SPORT*) starting signal; **in ~ di guarigione** on the road to recovery; **per ~ di** (*a causa di*) because of, on account of; **in o per ~** on the way; **per ~ aerea** by air; (*lettere*) by airmail; **andare/essere ~** to go/be away; **~ ~ che** (*a mano a mano*) as; **dare il ~** (*SPORT*) to give the starting signal; **dare il ~ a** (*fig*) to start; **V~ lattea** (*ASTR*) Milky Way; **~ di mezzo** middle course; **in ~ provvisoria** provisionally.

viabilità *sf* (*di strada*) practicability; (*rete stradale*) roads *pl*, road network.

via'dotto *sm* viaduct.

viaggi'are [viad'dʒare] *vi* to travel; **viaggia'tore, 'trice** *ag* travelling // *sm* traveller; (*passeggero*) passenger.

vi'aggio ['vjaddʒo] *sm* travel(ling); (*tragitto*) journey, trip; **buon ~!** have a good trip!; **~ di nozze** honeymoon.

vi'ale *sm* avenue.

via'vai *sm* coming and going, bustle.

vi'brare *vi* to vibrate; (*agitarsi*): **~ (di)** to quiver (with).

vi'cario *sm* (*apostolico etc*) vicar.

'vice ['vitʃe] *sm/f* deputy // *prefisso*: **~'console** *sm* vice-consul; **~diret'tore** *sm* assistant manager.

vi'cenda [vi'tʃɛnda] *sf* event; **a ~ in** turn; **vicen'devole** *ag* mutual, reciprocal.

vice'versa [vitʃe'vɛrsa] *av* vice versa; **da Roma a Pisa e ~** from Rome to Pisa and back.

vici'nanza [vitʃi'nantsa] *sf* nearness, closeness; **~e** *sfpl* neighbourhood, vicinity.

vici'nato [vitʃi'nato] *sm* neighbourhood; (*vicini*) neighbours *pl*.

vi'cino, a [vi'tʃino] *ag* (*gen*) near; (*nello spazio*) near, nearby; (*accanto*) next; (*nel tempo*) near, close at hand // *sm/f* neighbour // *av* near, close; **da ~** (*guardare*) close up; (*esaminare, seguire*) closely; (*conoscere*) well, intimately; **~ a** *prep* near (to), close to; (*accanto a*) beside; **~ di casa** neighbour.

'vicolo *sm* alley; **~ cieco** blind alley.

'video *sm inv* (*TV: schermo*) screen; **~cas'setta** *sf* videocassette; **~regi-stra'tore** *sm* video (recorder).

vie'tare *vt* to forbid; (*AMM*) to prohibit; **~ a qn di fare** to forbid sb to do; to prohibit sb from doing; **"vietato fumare/l'ingresso"** "no smoking/admittance".

Viet'nam *sm*: **il ~** Vietnam; **vietna'mita, i, e** *ag, sm/f, sm* Vietnamese *inv*.

vi'gente [vi'dʒɛnte] *ag* in force.

vigi'lante [vidʒi'lante] *ag* vigilant, watchful.

vigi'lare [vidʒi'lare] *vt* to watch over, keep an eye on; **~ che** to make sure that, see to it that.

'vigile ['vidʒile] *ag* watchful // *sm* (*anche*: **~ urbano**) policeman (*in towns*); **~ del fuoco** fireman.

vi'gilia [vi'dʒilja] *sf* (*giorno antecedente*) eve; **la ~ di Natale** Christmas Eve.

vigli'acco, a, chi, che [viʎ'ʎakko] *ag* cowardly // *sm/f* coward.

'vigna ['viɲɲa] *sf*, **vi'gneto** [viɲ'ɲeto] *sm* vineyard.

vi'gnetta [viɲ'ɲetta] *sf* cartoon.

vi'gore *sm* vigour; (*DIR*): **essere/entrare in ~** to be in/come into force; **vigo'roso, a** *ag* vigorous.

'vile *ag* (*spregevole*) low, mean, base; (*codardo*) cowardly.

vili'pendio *sm* contempt, scorn; public insult.

'villa *sf* villa.

vil'laggio [vil'laddʒo] *sm* village.

villa'nia *sf* rudeness, lack of manners; **fare** (*o* **dire**) **una ~ a qn** to be rude to sb.

vil'lano, a *ag* rude, ill-mannered // *sm* boor.

villeggia'tura [villeddʒa'tura] *sf* holiday(s *pl*) (*Brit*), vacation (*US*).

vil'lino *sm* small house (with a garden), cottage.

vil'loso, a *ag* hairy.

viltà sf cowardice q; cowardly act.

'vimine sm wicker; **mobili di ~i** wicker furniture sg.

'vincere ['vintʃere] vt (in guerra, al gioco, a una gara) to defeat, beat; (premio, guerra, partita) to win; (fig) to overcome, conquer // vi to win; **~ qn in bellezza** to be better-looking than sb; **'vincita** sf win; (denaro vinto) winnings pl; **vinci'tore** sm winner; (MIL) victor.

vinco'lare vt to bind; (COMM: denaro) to tie up; **'vincolo** sm (fig) bond, tie; (DIR: servitù) obligation.

vi'nicolo, a ag wine cpd.

'vino sm wine; **~ bianco/rosso** white/red wine.

'vinto, a pp di **vincere**.

vi'ola sf (BOT) violet; (MUS) viola // ag, sm inv (colore) purple.

vio'lare vt (chiesa) to desecrate, violate; (giuramento, legge) to violate.

violen'tare vt to use violence on; (donna) to rape.

vio'lento, a ag violent; **vio'lenza** sf violence; **violenza carnale** rape.

vio'letto, a ag, sm (colore) violet // sf (BOT) violet.

violi'nista, i, e sm/f violinist.

vio'lino sm violin.

violon'cello [violon'tʃɛllo] sm cello.

vi'ottolo sm path, track.

'vipera sf viper, adder.

vi'raggio [vi'raddʒo] sm (NAUT, AER) turn; (FOT) toning.

vi'rare vt (NAUT) to haul (in), heave (in) // vi (NAUT, AER) to turn; (FOT) to tone; **~ di bordo** (NAUT) to tack.

'virgola sf (LING) comma; (MAT) point; **virgo'lette** sfpl inverted commas, quotation marks.

vi'rile ag (proprio dell'uomo) masculine; (non puerile, da uomo) manly, virile.

virtù sf inv virtue; **in o per ~ di** by virtue of, by.

virtu'ale ag virtual.

virtu'oso, a ag virtuous // sm/f (MUS etc) virtuoso.

'virus sm inv virus.

'viscere ['viʃʃere] sm (ANAT) internal organ // sfpl (di animale) entrails pl; (fig) bowels pl.

'vischio ['viskjo] sm (BOT) mistletoe; (pania) birdlime; **vischi'oso, a** ag sticky.

'viscido, a ['viʃʃido] ag slimy.

vi'sibile ag visible.

visi'bilio sm: **andare in ~** to go into raptures.

visibilità sf visibility.

visi'era sf (di elmo) visor; (di berretto) peak.

visi'one sf vision; **prendere ~ di qc** to examine sth, look sth over; **prima/seconda ~** (CINEMA) first/second showing.

'visita sf visit; (MED) visit, call; (: esame) examination; **visi'tare** vt to visit; (MED) to visit, call on; (: esaminare) to examine; **visita'tore, 'trice** sm/f visitor.

vi'sivo, a ag visual.

'viso sm face.

vi'sone sm mink.

'vispo, a ag quick, lively.

vis'suto, a pp di **vivere** // ag (aria, modo di fare) experienced.

'vista sf (facoltà) (eye)sight; (fatto di vedere): **la ~ di** the sight of; (veduta) view; **sparare a ~** to shoot on sight; **in ~** in sight; **perdere qn di ~** to lose sight of sb; (fig) to lose touch with sb; **a ~ d'occhio** as far as the eye can see; (fig) before one's very eyes; **far ~ di fare** to pretend to do.

'visto, a pp di **vedere** // sm visa; **~ che** cong seeing (that).

vis'toso, a ag gaudy, garish; (ingente) considerable.

visu'ale ag visual; **visualizza'tore** sm (INFORM) visual display unit, VDU.

'vita sf life; (ANAT) waist; **a ~** for life.

vita'mina sf vitamin.

'vite sf (BOT) vine; (TECN) screw.

vi'tello sm (ZOOL) calf; (carne) veal; (pelle) calfskin.

vi'ticcio [vi'tittʃo] sm (BOT) tendril.

viticol'tore sm wine grower; **viticol'tura** sf wine growing.

'vitreo, a ag vitreous; (occhio, sguardo) glassy.

'vittima sf victim.

'vitto sm food; (in un albergo etc) board; **~ e alloggio** board and lodging.

vit'toria sf victory.

'viva escl: **~ il re!** long live the king!

vi'vace [vi'vatʃe] ag (vivo, animato) lively; (: mente) lively, sharp; (colore) bright; **vivacità** sf vivacity; liveliness; brightness.

vi'vaio sm (di pesci) hatchery; (AGR) nursery.

vi'vanda sf food; (piatto) dish.

vi'vente ag living, alive; **i ~i** the living.

'vivere vi to live // vt to live; (passare: brutto momento) to live through, go through; (sentire: gioie, pene di qn) to share // sm life; (anche: modo di ~) way of life; **~i** smpl food sg, provisions; **~ di** to live on.

'vivido, a ag (colore) vivid, bright.

'vivo, a ag (vivente) alive, living; (: animale) lively; (fig) lively; (: colore) bright, brilliant; **i ~i** the living; **~ e vegeto** hale and hearty; **farsi ~** to show one's face; **to be heard from**; **ritrarre dal ~** to paint from life; **pungere qn nel ~** (fig) to cut sb to the quick.

vizi'are [vit'tsjare] vt (bambino) to spoil;

(*corrompere moralmente*) to corrupt; **vizi'ato, a** *ag* spoilt; (*aria, acqua*) polluted.

'vizio ['vittsjo] *sm* (*morale*) vice; (*cattiva abitudine*) bad habit; (*imperfezione*) flaw, defect; (*errore*) fault, mistake; **vizi'oso, a** *ag* depraved; defective; (*inesatto*) incorrect, wrong.

vocabo'lario *sm* (*dizionario*) dictionary; (*lessico*) vocabulary.

vo'cabolo *sm* word.

vo'cale *ag* vocal // *sf* vowel.

vocazi'one [vokat'tsjone] *sf* vocation; (*fig*) natural bent.

'voce ['votʃe] *sf* voice; (*diceria*) rumour; (*di un elenco, in bilancio*) item; **aver ~ in capitolo** (*fig*) to have a say in the matter.

voci'are [vo'tʃare] *vi* to shout, yell.

'voga *sf* (*NAUT*) rowing; (*usanza*): **essere in ~** to be in fashion *o* in vogue.

vo'gare *vi* to row.

'voglia ['vɔʎʎa] *sf* desire, wish; (*macchia*) birthmark; **aver ~ di qc/di fare** to feel like sth/like doing; (*più forte*) to want sth/to do.

'voi *pronome* you; **voi'altri** *pronome* you.

vo'lano *sm* (*SPORT*) shuttlecock; (*TECN*) flywheel.

vo'lante *ag* flying // *sm* (steering) wheel.

volan'tino *sm* leaflet.

vo'lare *vi* (*uccello, aereo, fig*) to fly; (*cappello*) to blow away *o* off, fly away *o* off; **~ via** to fly away *o* off.

vo'latile *ag* (*CHIM*) volatile // *sm* (*ZOOL*) bird.

volente'roso, a *ag* willing.

volenti'eri *av* willingly; "**~**" "with pleasure", "I'd be glad to".

vo'lere ♦ *sm* will, wish(es); **contro il ~ di** against the wishes of; **per ~ di qn** in obedience to sb's will *o* wishes
♦ *vt* 1 (*esigere, desiderare*) to want; **voler fare/che qn faccia** to want to do/sb to do; **volete del caffè?** would you like *o* do you want some coffee?; **vorrei questo/fare** I would *o* I'd like this/to do; **come vuoi** as you like; **senza ~** (*inavvertitamente*) without meaning *o*, unintentionally
2 (*consentire*): **vogliate attendere, per piacere** please wait; **vogliamo andare?** shall we go?; **vuole essere così gentile da ...?** would you be so kind as to ...?; **non ha voluto ricevermi** he wouldn't see me
3: **volerci** (*essere necessario: materiale, attenzione*) to need; (: *tempo*) to take; **quanta farina ci vuole per questa torta?** how much flour do you need for this cake?; **ci vuole un'ora per arrivare a Venezia** it takes an hour to get to Venice
4: **voler bene a qn** (*amore*) to love sb; (*affetto*) to be fond of sb, like sb very much; **voler male a qn** to dislike sb;

volerne a qn to bear sb a grudge; **voler dire** to mean.

vol'gare *ag* vulgar; **volgariz'zare** *vt* to popularize.

'volgere ['vɔldʒere] *vt* to turn // *vi* to turn; (*tendere*): **~ a**: **il tempo volge al brutto** the weather is breaking; **un rosso che volge al viola** a red verging on purple; **~rsi** *vr* to turn; **~ al peggio** to take a turn for the worse; **~ al termine** to draw to an end.

'volgo *sm* common people.

voli'era *sf* aviary.

voli'tivo, a *ag* strong-willed.

'volo *sm* flight; **al ~**: **colpire qc al ~** to hit sth as it flies past; **capire al ~** to understand straight away.

volontà *sf* will; **a ~** (*mangiare, bere*) as much as one likes; **buona/cattiva ~** goodwill/lack of goodwill.

volon'tario, a *ag* voluntary // *sm* (*MIL*) volunteer.

'volpe *sf* fox.

'volta *sf* (*momento, circostanza*) time; (*turno, giro*) turn; (*curva*) turn, bend; (*ARCHIT*) vault; (*direzione*): **partire alla ~ di** to set off for; **a mia** (*o tua etc*) **~** in turn; **una ~** once; **una ~ sola** only once; **due ~e** twice; **una cosa per ~** one thing at a time; **una ~ per tutte** once and for all; **a ~e** at times, sometimes; **una ~ che** (*temporale*) once; (*causale*) since; **3 ~e 4** 3 times 4.

volta'faccia [volta'fattʃa] *sm inv* (*fig*) volte-face.

vol'taggio [vol'taddʒo] *sm* (*ELETTR*) voltage.

vol'tare *vt* to turn; (*girare: moneta*) to turn over; (*rigirare*) to turn round // *vi* to turn; **~rsi** *vr* to turn; to turn over; to turn round.

volteggi'are [volted'dʒare] *vi* (*volare*) to circle; (*in equitazione*) to do trick riding; (*in ginnastica*) to vault; to perform acrobatics.

'volto, a *pp di* **volgere** // *sm* face.

vo'lubile *ag* changeable, fickle.

vo'lume *sm* volume; **volumi'noso, a** *ag* voluminous, bulky.

voluttà *sf* sensual pleasure *o* delight; **voluttu'oso, a** *ag* voluptuous.

vomi'tare *vt, vi* to vomit; **'vomito** *sm* vomiting *q*; vomit.

'vongola *sf* clam.

vo'race [vo'ratʃe] *ag* voracious, greedy.

vo'ragine [vo'radʒine] *sf* abyss, chasm.

'vortice ['vɔrtitʃe] *sm* whirlwind; whirlpool; (*fig*) whirl.

'vostro, a *det*: **il(la) ~(a)** *etc* your // *pronome*: **il(la) ~(a)** *etc* yours.

vo'tante *sm/f* voter.

vo'tare *vi* to vote // *vt* (*sottoporre a votazione*) to take a vote on; (*approvare*) to vote for; (*REL*): **~ qc a** to dedicate sth to; **votazi'one** *sf* vote, voting; **votazioni** *sfpl* (*POL*) votes; (*INS*) marks.

'voto *sm* (*POL*) vote; (*INS*) mark; (*REL*) vow; (: *offerta*) votive offering; **aver ~i belli/brutti** (*INS*) to get good/bad marks.

vs. *abbr* (*COMM*) = **vostro.**

vul'cano *sm* volcano.

vulne'rabile *ag* vulnerable.

vuo'tare *vt*, **~rsi** *vr* to empty.

vu'oto, a *ag* empty; (*fig: privo*): **~ di** (*senso etc*) devoid of // *sm* empty space, gap; (*spazio in bianco*) blank; (*FISICA*) vacuum; (*fig: mancanza*) gap, void; **a mani ~e** empty-handed; **~ d'aria** air pocket; **~ a rendere** returnable bottle.

W X Y

watt [vat] *sm inv* watt.

'weekend ['wi:kend] *sm inv* weekend.

'whisky ['wiski] *sm inv* whisky.

'xeres ['ksɛres] *sm inv* sherry.

xero'copia [ksero'kɔpja] *sf* xerox ®, photocopy.

xi'lofono [ksi'lɔfono] *sm* xylophone.

yacht [jɔt] *sm inv* yacht.

'yoghurt ['jɔgurt] *sm inv* yoghourt.

Z

zabai'one [dzaba'jone] *sm dessert made of egg yolks, sugar and marsala.*

zaf'fata [tsaf'fata] *sf* (*tanfo*) stench.

zaffe'rano [dzaffe'rano] *sm* saffron.

zaf'firo [dzaf'firo] *sm* sapphire.

'zaino ['dzaino] *sm* rucksack.

'zampa ['tsampa] *sf* (*di animale: gamba*) leg; (: *piede*) paw; **a quattro ~e** on all fours.

zampil'lare [tsampil'lare] *vi* to gush, spurt; **zam'pillo** *sm* gush, spurt.

zam'pogna [tsam'poɲɲa] *sf instrument similar to bagpipes.*

'zanna ['tsanna] *sf* (*di elefante*) tusk; (*di carnivori*) fang.

zan'zara [dzan'dzara] *sf* mosquito; **zanzari'era** *sf* mosquito net.

'zappa ['tsappa] *sf* hoe; **zap'pare** *vt* to hoe.

zar, za'rina [tsar, tsa'rina] *sm/f* tsar/ tsarina.

'zattera ['dzattera] *sf* raft.

za'vorra [dza'vorra] *sf* ballast.

'zazzera ['tsattsera] *sf* shock of hair.

'zebra ['dzɛbra] *sf* zebra; **~e** *sfpl* (*AUT*) zebra crossing *sg* (*Brit*), crosswalk *sg* (*US*).

zecca, che ['tsekka] *sf* (*ZOOL*) tick; (*officina di monete*) mint.

'zelo ['dzɛlo] *sm* zeal.

'zenit ['dzɛnit] *sm* zenith.

'zenzero ['dzendzero] *sm* ginger.

'zeppa ['tseppa] *sf* wedge.

'zeppo, a ['tseppo] *ag*: **~ di** crammed *o* packed with.

zer'bino [dzer'bino] *sm* doormat.

'zero ['dzɛro] *sm* zero, nought; **vincere per tre a ~** (*SPORT*) to win three-nil.

'zeta ['dzɛta] *sm o f* zed, (the letter) z.

'zia ['tsia] *sf* aunt.

zibel'lino [dzibel'lino] *sm* sable.

'zigomo ['dzigomo] *sm* cheekbone.

zig'zag [dzig'dzag] *sm inv* zigzag; **andare a ~** to zigzag.

zim'bello [dzim'bɛllo] *sm* (*oggetto di burle*) laughing-stock.

'zinco ['dzinko] *sm* zinc.

'zingaro, a ['dzingaro] *sm/f* gipsy.

'zio ['tsio], *pl* **'zii** *sm* uncle; **zii** *smpl* (*zio e zia*) uncle and aunt.

zi'tella [dzi'tɛlla] *sf* spinster; (*peg*) old maid.

'zitto, a ['tsitto] *ag* quiet, silent; **sta' ~!** be quiet!

ziz'zania [dzid'dzanja] *sf* (*fig*): **gettare** *o* **seminare ~** to sow discord.

'zoccolo ['tsɔkkolo] *sm* (*calzatura*) clog; (*di cavallo etc*) hoof; (*basamento*) base; plinth.

zo'diaco [dzo'diako] *sm* zodiac.

'zolfo ['tsolfo] *sm* sulphur.

'zolla ['dzɔlla] *sf* clod (of earth).

zol'letta [dzol'letta] *sf* sugar lump.

'zona ['dzɔna] *sf* zone, area; **~ di depressione** (*METEOR*) trough of low pressure; **~ pedonale** pedestrian precinct; **~ verde** (*di abitato*) green area.

'zonzo ['dzondzo]: **a ~** *av*: **andare a ~** to wander about, stroll about.

zoo ['dzɔo] *sm inv* zoo.

zoolo'gia [dzoolo'dʒia] *sf* zoology.

zoppi'care [tsoppi'kare] *vi* to limp; to be shaky, rickety.

'zoppo, a ['tsɔppo] *ag* lame; (*fig: mobile*) shaky, rickety.

zoti'cone [dzoti'kone] *sm* lout.

'zucca, che ['tsukka] *sf* (*BOT*) marrow; pumpkin.

zucche'rare [tsukke'rare] *vt* to put sugar in; **zucche'rato, a** *ag* sweet, sweetened.

zuccheri'era [tsukke'rjɛra] *sf* sugar bowl.

zuccheri'ficio [tsukkeri'fitʃo] *sm* sugar refinery.

zucche'rino, a [tsukke'rino] *ag* sugary, sweet.

'zucchero ['tsukkero] *sm* sugar.

zuc'china [tsuk'kina] *sf*, **zuc'chino** [tsuk'kino] *sm* courgette (*Brit*), zucchini (*US*).

'zuffa ['tsuffa] *sf* brawl.

'zuppa ['tsuppa] *sf* soup; (*fig*) mixture, muddle; **~ inglese** (*CUC*) dessert made with sponge cake, custard and chocolate, ≈ trifle (*Brit*); **zuppi'era** *sf* soup tureen.

'zuppo, a ['tsuppo] *ag*: **~ (di)** drenched (with), soaked (with).

ENGLISH - ITALIAN
INGLESE - ITALIANO

A

A [eɪ] n (MUS) la m; (AUT): ~ road ≈ strada statale.

a indefinite article (before vowel or silent h: an) [eɪ, ə, æn, ən, n] **1** un (uno + s impure, gn, pn, ps, x, z), f una (un' + vowel); ~ book un libro; ~ mirror uno specchio; **an apple** una mela; **she's ~ doctor** è medico
2 (instead of the number 'one') un(o), f una; ~ **year ago** un anno fa; ~ **hundred/thousand** etc **pounds** cento/mille etc sterline
3 (in expressing ratios, prices etc) a, per; **3 ~ day/week** 3 al giorno/alla settimana; **10 km an hour** 10 km all'ora; **£5 ~ person** 5 sterline a persona or per persona.

A.A. n abbr (= Alcoholics Anonymous) AA; (Brit: = Automobile Association) ≈ A.C.I. m.

A.A.A. n abbr (US: = American Automobile Association) ≈ A.C.I. m.

aback [ə'bæk] ad: **to be taken ~** essere sbalordito(a).

abandon [ə'bændən] vt abbandonare // n abbandono; **with ~** sfrenatamente, spensieratamente.

abashed [ə'bæʃt] a imbarazzato(a).

abate [ə'beɪt] vi calmarsi.

abattoir ['æbətwɑː*] n (Brit) mattatoio.

abbey ['æbɪ] n abbazia, badia.

abbot ['æbət] n abate m.

abbreviation [əbriːvɪ'eɪʃən] n abbreviazione f.

abdicate ['æbdɪkeɪt] vt abdicare a // vi abdicare.

abdomen ['æbdəmən] n addome m.

abduct [æb'dʌkt] vt rapire.

aberration [æbə'reɪʃən] n aberrazione f.

abet [ə'bet] vt see **aid**.

abeyance [ə'beɪəns] n: **in ~** (law) in disuso; (matter) in sospeso.

abide [ə'baɪd] vt: **I can't ~ it/him** non lo posso soffrire or sopportare; **to ~ by** vt fus conformarsi a.

ability [ə'bɪlɪtɪ] n abilità f inv.

abject ['æbdʒekt] a (poverty) abietto(a); (apology) umiliante.

ablaze [ə'bleɪz] a in fiamme.

able ['eɪbl] a capace; **to be ~ to do sth** essere capace di fare qc, poter fare qc; **ably** ad abilmente.

abnormal [æb'nɔːməl] a anormale.

aboard [ə'bɔːd] ad a bordo // prep a bordo di.

abode [ə'bəud] n: **of no fixed ~** senza fissa dimora.

abolish [ə'bɔlɪʃ] vt abolire.

abominable [ə'bɔmɪnəbl] a abominevole.

aborigine [æbə'rɪdʒɪnɪ] n aborigeno/ a.

abort [ə'bɔːt] vt abortire; **~ion** [ə'bɔːʃən] n aborto; **to have an ~ion** abortire; **~ive** a abortivo(a).

abound [ə'baund] vi abbondare; **to ~ in** abbondare di.

about [ə'baut] ◆ ad **1** (approximately) circa, quasi; ~ **a hundred/thousand** etc un centinaio/migliaio etc, circa cento/ mille etc; **it takes ~ 10 hours** ci vogliono circa 10 ore; **at ~ 2 o'clock** verso le 2; **I've just ~ finished** ho quasi finito
2 (referring to place) qua e là, in giro; **to leave things lying ~** lasciare delle cose in giro; **to run ~** correre qua e là; **to walk ~** camminare
3: to be ~ to do sth stare per fare qc
◆ prep **1** (relating to) su, di; **a book ~ London** un libro su Londra; **what is it ~?** di che si tratta?; (book, film etc) di cosa tratta?; **we talked ~ it** ne abbiamo parlato; **what or how ~ doing this?** che ne dici di fare questo?
2 (referring to place): **to walk ~ the town** camminare per la città; **her clothes were scattered ~ the room** i suoi vestiti erano sparsi or in giro per tutta la stanza.

about-face [ə'baut'feɪs] n, **about-turn** [ə'baut'təːn] n dietro front m inv.

above [ə'bʌv] ad, prep sopra; **mentioned ~** suddetto; ~ **all** soprattutto; **~board** a aperto(a); onesto(a).

abrasive [ə'breɪzɪv] a abrasivo(a); (fig) caustico(a).

abreast [ə'brest] ad di fianco; **to keep ~ of** tenersi aggiornato su.

abridge [ə'brɪdʒ] vt ridurre.

abroad [ə'brɔːd] ad all'estero.

abrupt [ə'brʌpt] a (steep) erto(a); (sudden) improvviso(a); (gruff, blunt) brusco(a).

abscess ['æbsɪs] n ascesso.

abscond [əb'skɔnd] vi scappare.

absence ['æbsəns] n assenza.

absent ['æbsənt] a assente; **~ee** [-'tiː] n assente m/f; **~-minded** a distratto(a).

absolute ['æbsəluːt] a assoluto(a); **~ly** [-'luːtlɪ] ad assolutamente.

absolve [əb'zɔlv] vt: **to ~ sb (from)** (sin) assolvere qn (da); (oath) sciogliere qn (da).

absorb [əb'zɔːb] vt assorbire; **to be ~ed**

in a book essere immerso in un libro; **~ent cotton** n (US) cotone m idrofilo.

absorption [əb'sɔːpʃən] n assorbimento.

abstain [əb'steɪn] vi: **to ~ (from)** astenersi (da).

abstemious [əb'stiːmɪəs] a astemio(a).

abstract ['æbstrækt] a astratto(a).

absurd [əb'sɔːd] a assurdo(a).

abuse n [ə'bjuːs] abuso; (insults) ingiurie fpl // vt [ə'bjuːz] abusare di; **abusive** a ingiurioso(a).

abysmal [ə'bɪzməl] a spaventoso(a).

abyss [ə'bɪs] n abisso.

AC abbr (= alternating current) c.a.

academic [ækə'dɛmɪk] a accademico(a); (pej: issue) puramente formale // n universitario/a.

academy [ə'kædəmɪ] n (learned body) accademia; (school) scuola privata; **~ of music** conservatorio.

accelerate [æk'sɛləreɪt] vt, vi accelerare; **accelerator** n acceleratore m.

accent ['æksɛnt] n accento.

accept [ək'sɛpt] vt accettare; **~able** a accettabile; **~ance** n accettazione f.

access ['æksɛs] n accesso; **~ible** [æk'sɛsəbl] a accessibile.

accessory [æk'sɛsərɪ] n accessorio; **toilet accessories** npl articoli mpl da toilette.

accident ['æksɪdənt] n incidente m; (chance) caso; **by ~** per caso; **~al** [-'dɛntl] a accidentale; **~ally** [-'dɛntəlɪ] ad per caso; **~-prone** a: he's very **~-prone** è un vero passaguai.

acclaim [ə'kleɪm] vt acclamare // n acclamazione f.

accommodate [ə'kɒmədeɪt] vt alloggiare; (oblige, help) favorire.

accommodating [ə'kɒmədeɪtɪŋ] a compiacente.

accommodation [əkɒmə'deɪʃən] n (US: ~s) alloggio.

accompany [ə'kʌmpənɪ] vt accompagnare.

accomplice [ə'kʌmplɪs] n complice m/f.

accomplish [ə'kʌmplɪʃ] vt compiere; **~ed** a (person) esperto(a); **~ment** n compimento; realizzazione f; **~ments** npl doti fpl.

accord [ə'kɔːd] n accordo // vt accordare; **of his own ~** di propria iniziativa; **~ance** n: **in ~ance with** in conformità con; **~ing to** prep secondo; **~ingly** ad in conformità.

accordion [ə'kɔːdɪən] n fisarmonica.

accost [ə'kɒst] vt avvicinare.

account [ə'kaʊnt] n (COMM) conto; (report) descrizione f; **~s** npl (COMM) conti mpl; **of little ~** di poca importanza; **on ~** in acconto; **on no ~** per nessun motivo; **on ~ of** a causa di; **to take into ~**, **take ~ of** tener conto di; **to ~ for** spiegare; giustificare; **~able** a responsabile.

accountancy [ə'kaʊntənsɪ] n ragioneria.

accountant [ə'kaʊntənt] n ragioniere/a.

account number n numero di conto.

accumulate [ə'kjuːmjuleɪt] vt accumulare // vi accumularsi.

accuracy ['ækjurəsɪ] n precisione f.

accurate ['ækjurɪt] a preciso(a); **~ly** ad precisamente.

accusation [ækju'zeɪʃən] n accusa.

accuse [ə'kjuːz] vt accusare; **~d** n accusato/a.

accustom [ə'kʌstəm] vt abituare; **~ed** a (usual) abituale; **~ed to** abituato(a) a.

ace [eɪs] n asso.

ache [eɪk] n male m, dolore m // vi (be sore) far male, dolere; **my head ~s** mi fa male la testa.

achieve [ə'tʃiːv] vt (aim) raggiungere; (victory, success) ottenere; (task) compiere; **~ment** n compimento; successo.

acid ['æsɪd] a acido(a) // n acido; **~ rain** n pioggia acida.

acknowledge [ək'nɒlɪdʒ] vt (letter: also: **~ receipt of**) confermare la ricevuta di; (fact) riconoscere; **~ment** n conferma; riconoscimento.

acne ['æknɪ] n acne f.

acorn ['eɪkɔːn] n ghianda.

acoustic [ə'kuːstɪk] a acustico(a); **~s** n, npl acustica.

acquaint [ə'kweɪnt] vt: **to ~ sb with sth** far sapere qc a qn; **to be ~ed with** (person) conoscere; **~ance** n conoscenza; (person) conoscente m/f.

acquiesce [ækwɪ'ɛs] vi: **to ~ (in)** acconsentire (a).

acquire [ə'kwaɪə*] vt acquistare.

acquisition [ækwɪ'zɪʃən] n acquisto.

acquit [ə'kwɪt] vt assolvere; **to ~ o.s. well** comportarsi bene; **~tal** n assoluzione f.

acre ['eɪkə*] n acro (= 4047 m²).

acrid ['ækrɪd] a acre; pungente.

acrimonious [ækrɪ'məʊnɪəs] a astioso(a).

acrobat ['ækrəbæt] n acrobata m/f.

across [ə'krɒs] prep (on the other side) dall'altra parte di; (crosswise) attraverso // ad dall'altra parte; in larghezza; **to walk ~ (the road)** attraversare (la strada); **~ from** di fronte a.

acrylic [ə'krɪlɪk] a acrilico(a) // n acrilico.

act [ækt] n atto; (in music-hall etc) numero; (LAW) decreto // vi agire; (THEATRE) recitare; (pretend) fingere // vt (part) recitare; **to ~ as** agire da; **~ing** a che fa le funzioni di // n (of actor) recitazione f; (activity): **to do some ~ing** fare del teatro (or del cinema).

action ['ækʃən] n azione f; (MIL) combattimento; (LAW) processo; **out of ~** fuori combattimento; fuori servizio; **to take ~** agire; **~ replay** n (TV) replay m *inv.*

activate ['æktɪveɪt] *vt* (*mechanism*) fare funzionare; (*CHEM, PHYSICS*) rendere attivo(a).

active ['æktɪv] *a* attivo(a); **~ly** *ad* (*participate*) attivamente; (*discourage, dislike*) vivamente.

activity [æk'tɪvɪtɪ] *n* attività *f inv*.

actor ['æktə*] *n* attore *m*.

actress ['æktrɪs] *n* attrice *f*.

actual ['æktjuəl] *a* reale, vero(a); **~ly** *ad* veramente; (*even*) addirittura.

acumen ['ækjumən] *n* acume *m*.

acute [ə'kju:t] *a* acuto(a); (*mind, person*) perspicace.

ad [æd] *n abbr* = **advertisement**.

A.D. *ad abbr* (= *Anno Domini*) d.C.

adamant ['ædəmənt] *a* irremovibile.

adapt [ə'dæpt] *vt* adattare // *vi*: to ~ (to) adattarsi (a); **~able** *a* (*device*) adattabile; (*person*) che sa adattarsi; **~er** *or* **~or** *n* (*ELEC*) adattatore *m*.

add [æd] *vt* aggiungere; (*figures: also*: to ~ up) addizionare // *vi*: to ~ to (*increase*) aumentare; it doesn't ~ up (*fig*) non quadra, non ha senso.

adder ['ædə*] *n* vipera.

addict ['ædɪkt] *n* tossicomane *m/f*; (*fig*) fanatico/a; **~ed** [ə'dɪktɪd] *a*: to be **~ed** to (*drink etc*) essere dedito a; (*fig: football etc*) essere tifoso di; **~ion** [ə'dɪkʃən] *n* (*MED*) tossicomania; **~ive** [ə'dɪktɪv] *a* che dà assuefazione.

addition [ə'dɪʃən] *n* addizione *f*; in ~ inoltre; in ~ to oltre; **~al** *a* supplementare.

additive ['ædɪtɪv] *n* additivo.

address [ə'drɛs] *n* indirizzo; (*talk*) discorso // *vt* indirizzare; (*speak to*) fare un discorso a.

adept ['ædɛpt] *a*: ~ at esperto(a) in.

adequate ['ædɪkwɪt] *a* adeguato(a); sufficiente.

adhere [əd'hɪə*] *vi*: to ~ to aderire a; (*fig: rule, decision*) seguire.

adhesion [əd'hi:ʒən] *n* adesione *f*.

adhesive [əd'hi:zɪv] *a* adesivo(a) // *n* adesivo; **~ tape** *n* (*Brit: for parcels etc*) nastro adesivo; (*US: MED*) cerotto adesivo.

adjective ['ædʒɛktɪv] *n* aggettivo.

adjoining [ə'dʒɔɪnɪŋ] *a* accanto *inv*, adiacente.

adjourn [ə'dʒə:n] *vt* rimandare // *vi* essere aggiornato(a); (*go*) spostarsi.

adjudicate [ə'dʒu:dɪkeɪt] *vt* (*contest*) giudicare; (*claim*) decidere su.

adjust [ə'dʒʌst] *vt* aggiustare; (*COMM*) rettificare // *vi*: to ~ (to) adattarsi (a); **~able** *a* regolabile.

ad-lib [æd'lɪb] *vt, vi* improvvisare // *ad*: ad lib a piacere, a volontà.

administer [əd'mɪnɪstə*] *vt* amministrare; (*justice*) somministrare.

administration [ədmɪnɪs'treɪʃən] *n*

amministrazione *f*.

administrative [əd'mɪnɪstrətɪv] *a* amministrativo(a).

admiral ['ædmərəl] *n* ammiraglio; **A~ty** *n* (*Brit: also*: **A~ty Board**) Ministero della Marina.

admiration [ædmə'reɪʃən] *n* ammirazione *f*.

admire [əd'maɪə*] *vt* ammirare.

admission [əd'mɪʃən] *n* ammissione *f*; (*to exhibition, night club etc*) ingresso; (*confession*) confessione *f*.

admit [əd'mɪt] *vt* ammettere; far entrare; (*agree*) riconoscere; to ~ to riconoscere; **~tance** *n* ingresso; **~tedly** *ad* bisogna pur riconoscere (che).

admonish [əd'mɔnɪʃ] *vt* ammonire.

ad nauseam [æd'nɔ:sɪæm] *ad* fino alla nausea, a non finire.

ado [ə'du:] *n*: without (any) more ~ senza più indugi.

adolescence [ædəu'lɛsns] *n* adolescenza.

adolescent [ædəu'lɛsnt] *a, n* adolescente (*m/f*).

adopt [ə'dɔpt] *vt* adottare; **~ed** *a* adottivo(a); **~ion** [ə'dɔpʃən] *n* adozione *f*.

adore [ə'dɔ:*] *vt* adorare.

Adriatic (Sea) [eɪdrɪ'ætɪk('si:)] *n* Adriatico.

adrift [ə'drɪft] *ad* alla deriva.

adroit [ə'drɔɪt] *a* abile, destro(a).

adult ['ædʌlt] *n* adulto/a.

adultery [ə'dʌltərɪ] *n* adulterio.

advance [əd'vɑ:ns] *n* avanzamento; (*money*) anticipo // *vt* avanzare; (*date, money*) anticipare // *vi* avanzare; in ~ in anticipo; **~d** *a* avanzato(a); (*SCOL: studies*) superiore.

advantage [əd'vɑ:ntɪdʒ] *n* (*also TENNIS*) vantaggio; to take ~ of approfittarsi di.

advent ['ædvənt] *n* avvento; **A~** Avvento.

adventure [əd'vɛntʃə*] *n* avventura.

adverb ['ædvə:b] *n* avverbio.

adverse ['ædvə:s] *a* avverso(a); ~ to contrario(a) a.

advert ['ædvə:t] *n abbr* (*Brit*) = **advertisement**.

advertise ['ædvətaɪz] *vi* (*vt*) fare pubblicità *or* réclame (a); fare un'inserzione (per vendere); to ~ for (*staff*) mettere un annuncio sul giornale per trovare.

advertisement [əd'və:tɪsmənt] *n* (*COMM*) réclame *f inv*, pubblicità *f inv*; (*in classified ads*) inserzione *f*.

advertiser ['ædvətaɪzə*] *n* (*in newspaper etc*) inserzionista *m/f*.

advertising ['ædvətaɪzɪŋ] *n* pubblicità.

advice [əd'vaɪs] *n* consigli *mpl*; (*notification*) avviso; piece of ~ consiglio; to take legal ~ consultare un avvocato.

advisable [əd'vaɪzəbl] *a* consigliabile.

advise [əd'vaɪz] *vt* consigliare; to ~ sb of sth informare qn di qc; to ~ sb against sth/doing sth sconsigliare qc a qn/a qn di fare qc; **~dly** [-ədlɪ] ad (*deliberately*) di proposito; **~r** n consigliere/a; **advisory** [-ərɪ] a consultivo/a.

advocate n ['ædvəkɪt] (*upholder*) sostenitore/trice; (*LAW*) avvocato (difensore) // vt ['ædvəkeɪt] propugnare; to be an ~ of essere a favore di.

aerial ['ɛərɪəl] n antenna // a aereo(a).

aerobics [ɛə'rəubɪks] n aerobica.

aeroplane ['ɛərəpleɪn] n (*Brit*) aeroplano.

aerosol ['ɛərəsɔl] n (*Brit*) aerosol m inv.

aesthetic [ɪs'θetɪk] a estetico/a.

afar [ə'fɑː°] ad: from ~ da lontano.

affair [ə'fɛə°] n affare m; (*also*: love ~) relazione f amorosa.

affect [ə'fɛkt] vt toccare; (*feign*) fingere; **~ed** a affettato(a).

affection [ə'fɛkʃən] n affezione f; **~ate** a affettuoso(a).

affirmation [æfə'meɪʃən] n affermazione f.

affix [ə'fɪks] vt apporre; attaccare.

afflict [ə'flɪkt] vt affliggere.

affluence ['æfluəns] n abbondanza, opulenza.

affluent ['æfluənt] a abbondante; opulente; (*person*) ricco(a).

afford [ə'fɔːd] vt permettersi; (*provide*) fornire.

afield [ə'fiːld] ad: far ~ lontano.

afloat [ə'fləut] a, ad a galla.

afoot [ə'fut] ad: there is something ~ si sta preparando qualcosa.

afraid [ə'freɪd] a impaurito(a); to be ~ of or to a aver paura di; I am ~ that I'll be late mi dispiace, ma farò tardi.

afresh [ə'frɛʃ] ad di nuovo.

Africa ['æfrɪkə] n Africa; **~n** a, n africano(a).

aft [ɑːft] ad a poppa, verso poppa.

after ['ɑːftə°] prep, ad dopo // cj dopo che; what/who are you ~? che/chi cerca?; ~ he left/having done dopo che se ne fu andato/dopo aver fatto; ~ all dopo tutto; ~ you! dopo di lei!; **~effects** npl conseguenze fpl; (*of illness*) postumi mpl; **~life** n vita dell'al di là; **~math** n conseguenze fpl; in the ~math of nel periodo dopo; **~noon** n pomeriggio; **~s** n (*col*: *dessert*) dessert m inv; **~sales service** n (*Brit*) servizio assistenza clienti; **~shave (lotion)** n dopobarba m inv; **~thought** n: as an ~thought come aggiunta; **~wards** ad dopo.

again [ə'gɛn] ad di nuovo; to begin/ see ~ ricominciare/rivedere; not ... ~ non ... più; ~ and ~ ripetutamente.

against [ə'genst] prep contro; ~ a blue background su uno sfondo azzurro.

age [eɪdʒ] n età f inv // vt, vi invecchiare; it's been ~s since sono secoli che; he is 20 years of ~ ha 20 anni; to

come of ~ diventare maggiorenne; **~d 10** di 10 anni; the **~d** ['eɪdʒɪd] gli anziani; ~ **group** n generazione f; ~ **limit** n limite m d'età.

agency ['eɪdʒənsɪ] n agenzia; through or by the ~ of grazie a.

agenda [ə'dʒɛndə] n ordine m del giorno.

agent ['eɪdʒənt] n agente m.

aggregate ['ægrɪgeɪt] n aggregato.

aggressive [ə'grɛsɪv] a aggressivo(a).

aggrieved [ə'griːvd] a addolorato(a).

aghast [ə'gɑːst] a sbigottito(a).

agitate ['ædʒɪteɪt] vt turbare; agitare; to ~ for agitarsi per.

ago [ə'gəu] ad: 2 days ~ 2 giorni fa; not long ~ poco tempo fa; how long ~? quanto tempo fa?

agog [ə'gɔg] a ansioso(a), emozionato(a).

agonizing ['ægənaɪzɪŋ] a straziante.

agony ['ægənɪ] n agonia.

agree [ə'griː] vt (*price*) pattuire // vi: to ~ (with) essere d'accordo (con); (*LING*) concordare (con); to ~ to sth/to do sth accettare qc/di fare qc; to ~ that (*admit*) ammettere che; to ~ on sth accordarsi su qc; garlic doesn't ~ with me l'aglio non mi va; **~able** a gradevole; (*willing*) disposto(a); are you ~able to this? è d'accordo con questo?; **~d** a (*time, place*) stabilito(a); **~ment** n accordo; in ~ment d'accordo.

agricultural [ægrɪ'kʌltʃərəl] a agricolo(a).

agriculture ['ægrɪkʌltʃə°] n agricoltura.

aground [ə'graund] ad: to run ~ arenarsi.

ahead [ə'hɛd] ad avanti; davanti; ~ of davanti a; (*fig*: *schedule etc*) in anticipo su; ~ of time in anticipo; go right or straight ~ tiri diritto; they were (right) ~ of us erano (proprio) davanti a noi.

aid [eɪd] n aiuto // vt aiutare; in ~ of a favore di; to ~ and abet (*LAW*) essere complice di.

aide [eɪd] n (*person*) aiutante m.

AIDS [eɪdz] n abbr (= acquired immune deficiency syndrome) AIDS m.

ailing ['eɪlɪŋ] a sofferente.

ailment ['eɪlmənt] n indisposizione f.

aim [eɪm] vt: to ~ sth at (*such as gun*) mirare a, puntare qc a; (*camera, remark*) rivolgere qc a; (*missile*) lanciare qc contro; (*blow etc*) tirare qc a // vi (*also*: to take ~) prendere la mira // n mira; to ~ at mirare a; to ~ to do aver l'intenzione di fare; **~less** a senza scopo.

ain't [eɪnt] (*col*) = **am not**; **aren't**; **isn't**.

air [ɛə°] n aria // vt aerare; (*grievances, ideas*) esprimere pubblicamente // cpd (*currents*) d'aria; (*attack*) aereo(a); to throw sth into the ~ lanciare qc in aria; by ~ (*travel*) in aereo; on the ~ (*RADIO, TV*) in onda; **~bed** n (*Brit*) materassino; **~borne** *a* in volo; aerotrasportato(a); ~ **conditioning** *n* condizionamento d'aria; **~craft** *n* (*pl inv*) apparecchio; **~craft carrier** *n* portaerei *f inv*; **~field** *n* campo d'aviazione; **A~ Force** *n* aviazione *f* militare; ~ **freshener** *n* deodorante *m* per ambienti; **~gun** *n* fucile *m* ad aria compressa; **~ hostess** *n* (*Brit*) hostess *f inv*; ~ **letter** *n* (*Brit*) aerogramma *m*; **~lift** *n* ponte *m* aereo; **~line** *n* linea aerea; **~liner** *n* aereo di linea; **~lock** *n* cassa d'aria; **~mail** *n*: by **~mail** per via aerea; ~ **mattress** *n* materassino; **~plane** *n* (*US*) aeroplano; **~port** *n* aeroporto; ~ **raid** *n* incursione *f* aerea; **~sick** *a* che ha il mal d'aereo; **~space** *n* spazio aereo; **~strip** *n* pista d'atterraggio; ~ **terminal** *n* air-terminal *m inv*; **~tight** *a* ermetico(a); ~ **traffic controller** *n* controllore *m* del traffico aereo; **~y** *a* arioso(a); (*manners*) noncurante.

aisle [aɪl] *n* (*of church*) navata laterale; navata centrale; (*of plane*) corridoio.

ajar [ə'dʒɑː*] *a* socchiuso(a).

akin [ə'kɪn] *a*: ~ **to** simile a.

alacrity [ə'lækrɪtɪ] *n*: **with** ~ con prontezza.

alarm [ə'lɑːm] *n* allarme *m* // *vt* allarmare; ~ **clock** *n* sveglia.

alas [ə'læs] *excl* ohimè!, ahimè!

albeit [ɔːl'biːɪt] *cj* sebbene+ *sub*, benché + *sub*.

album [ˈælbəm] *n* album *m inv*; (*L.P.*) 33 giri *m inv*, L.P. *m inv*.

alcohol [ˈælkəhɔl] *n* alcool *m*; **~ic** [-'hɔlɪk] *a* alcolico(a) // *n* alcolizzato/a.

alderman [ˈɔːldəmən] *n* consigliere *m* comunale.

ale [eɪl] *n* birra.

alert [ə'ləːt] *a* vivo(a); (*watchful*) vigile // *n* allarme *m* // *vt* avvertire; mettere in guardia; **on the ~** all'erta.

algebra [ˈældʒɪbrə] *n* algebra.

alias [ˈeɪlɪəs] *ad* alias // *n* pseudonimo, falso nome *m*.

alibi [ˈælɪbaɪ] *n* alibi *m inv*.

alien [ˈeɪlɪən] *n* straniero/a // *a*: ~ (**to**) estraneo(a) (a); **~ate** *vt* alienare.

alight [ə'laɪt] *a* acceso(a) // *vi* scendere; (*bird*) posarsi.

align [ə'laɪn] *vt* allineare.

alike [ə'laɪk] *a* simile // *ad* sia ... sia; **to look ~** assomigliarsi.

alimony [ˈælɪmənɪ] *n* (*payment*) alimenti *mpl*.

alive [ə'laɪv] *a* vivo(a); (*active*) attivo(a).

all [ɔːl] ◆ *a* tutto(a); ~ **day** tutto il giorno; ~ **night** tutta la notte; ~ **men** tutti gli uomini; ~ **five came** sono venuti tutti e cinque; ~ **the books** tutti i libri; ~ **the food** tutto il cibo; ~ **the time** sempre; tutto il tempo; ~ **his life** tutta la vita

◆ *pronoun* **1** tutto(a); **I ate it ~, I ate ~ of it** l'ho mangiato tutto; ~ **of us went** tutti noi siamo andati; ~ **of the boys went** tutti i ragazzi sono andati

2 (*in phrases*): **above ~** soprattutto; **after ~** dopotutto; **at ~**: **not at ~** (*in answer to question*) niente affatto; (*in answer to thanks*) prego!, di niente!, s'immagini!; **I'm not at ~ tired** non sono affatto stanco(a); **anything at ~ will do** andrà bene qualsiasi cosa; ~ **in ~** tutto sommato

◆ *ad*: ~ **alone** tutto(a) solo(a); **it's not as hard as ~ that** non è poi così difficile; ~ **the more/the better** tanto più/meglio; ~ **but** quasi; **the score is two ~** il punteggio è di due a due.

allay [ə'leɪ] *vt* (*fears*) dissipare.

all clear *n* (*also fig*) segnale *m* di cessato allarme.

allegation [ælɪˈɡeɪʃən] *n* asserzione *f*.

allege [ə'lɛdʒ] *vt* asserire; **~dly** [ə'lɛdʒɪdlɪ] *ad* secondo quanto si asserisce.

allegiance [ə'liːdʒəns] *n* fedeltà.

allergic [ə'ləːdʒɪk] *a*: ~ **to** allergico(a) a.

allergy [ˈælədʒɪ] *n* allergia.

alleviate [ə'liːvɪeɪt] *vt* sollevare.

alley [ˈælɪ] *n* vicolo; (*in garden*) vialetto.

alliance [ə'laɪəns] *n* alleanza.

allied [ˈælaɪd] *a* alleato(a).

all-in [ˈɔːlɪn] *a* (*Brit*: *also ad*: **charge**) tutto compreso; ~ **wrestling** *n* lotta americana.

all-night [ˈɔːlˈnaɪt] *a* aperto(a) (*or* che dura) tutta la notte.

allocate [ˈæləkeɪt] *vt* (*share out*) distribuire; (*duties, sum, time*): **to ~ sth to** assegnare qc a; **to ~ sth for** stanziare qc per.

allot [ə'lɔt] *vt* (*share out*) spartire; **to ~ sth to** (*time*) dare qc a; (*duties*) assegnare qc a; **~ment** *n* (*share*) spartizione *f*; (*garden*) lotto di terra.

all-out [ˈɔːlaʊt] *a* (*effort etc*) totale // *ad*: **to go all out for** mettercela tutta per.

allow [ə'laʊ] *vt* (*practice, behaviour*) permettere; (*sum to spend etc*) accordare; (*sum, time estimated*) dare; (*concede*): **to ~ that** ammettere che; **to ~ sb to do** permettere a qn di fare; **he is ~ed to do** lo può fare; **to ~ for** *vt fus* tener conto di; **~ance** *n* (*money received*) assegno; indennità *f inv*; (*TAX*) detrazione *f* di imposta; **to make ~ances for** tener conto di.

alloy [ˈælɔɪ] *n* lega.

all right *ad* (*feel, work*) bene; (*as answer*) va bene.

all-round [ˈɔːlˈraʊnd] *a* completo(a).

all-time [ˈɔːlˈtaɪm] *a* (*record*) assoluto(a).

allude [ə'luːd] *vi*: **to ~ to** alludere a.

alluring [ə'ljʊərɪŋ] *a* seducente.

ally ['ælaɪ] *n* alleato.
almighty [ɔ:l'maɪtɪ] *a* onnipotente.
almond ['ɑ:mənd] *n* mandorla.
almost ['ɔ:lməust] *ad* quasi.
alms [ɑ:mz] *npl* elemosina *sg*.
aloft [ə'lɔft] *ad* in alto; (NAUT) sull'alberatura.
alone [ə'ləun] *a, ad* solo(a); **to leave sb ~** lasciare qn in pace; **to leave sth ~** lasciare stare qc; **let ~** ... figuriamoci poi ..., tanto meno ... .
along [ə'lɔŋ] *prep* lungo // *ad*: **is he coming ~?** viene con noi?; **he was hopping/limping ~** veniva saltellando/zoppicando; **~ with** insieme con; **all ~** (all the time) sempre, fin dall'inizio; **~side** *prep* accanto a; lungo // *ad* accanto.
aloof [ə'lu:f] *a* distaccato(a) // *ad*: **to stand ~** tenersi a distanza *or* in disparte.
aloud [ə'laud] *ad* ad alta voce.
alphabet ['ælfəbet] *n* alfabeto.
alpine ['ælpaɪn] *a* alpino(a).
Alps [ælps] *npl*: **the ~** le Alpi.
already [ɔ:l'redɪ] *ad* già.
alright ['ɔ:l'raɪt] *ad* (Brit) = **all right**.
Alsatian [æl'seɪʃən] *n* (Brit: dog) pastore *m* tedesco, (cane *m*) lupo.
also ['ɔ:lsəu] *ad* anche.
altar ['ɔltə*] *n* altare *m*.
alter ['ɔltə*] *vt, vi* alterare.
alternate [ɔl'tə:nɪt] alterno(a) // *vb* ['ɔltə:neɪt] *vi*: **to ~ (with)** alternarsi (a) // *vt* alternare; **on ~ days** ogni due giorni; **alternating** *a* (current) alternato(a).
alternative [ɔl'tə:nətɪv] *a* (solutions) alternativo(a); (solution) altro(a) // *n* (choice) alternativa; (other possibility) altra possibilità; **~ly** *ad* alternativamente.
alternator ['ɔltə:neɪtə*] *n* (AUT) alternatore *m*.
although [ɔ:l'ðəu] *cj* benché + sub, sebbene + sub.
altitude ['æltɪtju:d] *n* altitudine *f*.
alto ['æltəu] *n* contralto; (male) contraltino.
altogether [ɔ:ltə'gɛðə*] *ad* del tutto, completamente; (on the whole) tutto considerato; (in all) in tutto.
aluminium [ælju'mɪnɪəm], (US) **aluminum** [ə'lu:mɪnəm] *n* alluminio.
always ['ɔ:lweɪz] *ad* sempre.
am [æm] *vb* see **be**.
a.m. *ad abbr* (= ante meridiem) della mattina.
amalgamate [ə'mælgəmeɪt] *vt* amalgamare // *vi* amalgamarsi.
amateur ['æmətə*] *n* dilettante *m/f* // *a* (SPORT) dilettante; **~ish** *a* (pej) da dilettante.
amaze [ə'meɪz] *vt* stupire; **to be ~d (at)** essere sbalordito (da); **~ment** *n* stupore *m*; **amazing** *a* sorprendente, sbalorditivo(a); (bargain) sensazionale.

ambassador [æm'bæsədə*] *n* ambasciatore/trice.
amber ['æmbə*] *n* ambra; **at ~** (Brit AUT) giallo.
ambiguous [æm'bɪgjuəs] *a* ambiguo(a).
ambition [æm'bɪʃən] *n* ambizione *f*.
ambitious [æm'bɪʃəs] *a* ambizioso(a).
amble ['æmbl] *vi* (gen: to ~ along) camminare tranquillamente.
ambulance ['æmbjuləns] *n* ambulanza.
ambush ['æmbuʃ] *n* imboscata // *vt* fare un'imboscata a.
amenable [ə'mi:nəbl] *a*: **~ to** (advice etc) ben disposto(a) a.
amend [ə'mɛnd] *vt* (law) emendare; (text) correggere // *vi* emendarsi; **to make ~s** fare ammenda.
amenities [ə'mi:nɪtɪz] *npl* attrezzature *fpl* ricreative e culturali.
America [ə'mɛrɪkə] *n* America; **~n** *a, n* americano(a).
amiable ['eɪmɪəbl] *a* amabile, gentile.
amicable ['æmɪkəbl] *a* amichevole.
amid(st) [ə'mɪd(st)] *prep* fra, tra, in mezzo a.
amiss [ə'mɪs] *a, ad*: **there's something ~** c'è qualcosa che non va bene; **don't take it ~** non prendertela a male.
ammonia [ə'məunɪə] *n* ammoniaca.
ammunition [æmju'nɪʃən] *n* munizioni *fpl*.
amok [ə'mɔk] *ad*: **to run ~** diventare pazzo(a) furioso(a).
among(st) [ə'mʌŋ(st)] *prep* fra, tra, in mezzo a.
amorous ['æmərəs] *a* amoroso(a).
amount [ə'maunt] *n* somma; ammontare *m*; quantità *f inv* // *vi*: **to ~ to** (total) ammontare a; (be same as) essere come.
amp(ère) ['æmp(ɛə*)] *n* ampère *m inv*.
ample ['æmpl] *a* ampio(a); spazioso(a); (enough): **this is ~** questo è più che sufficiente; **to have ~ time/room** avere assai tempo/posto.
amplifier ['æmplɪfaɪə*] *n* amplificatore *m*.
amuck [ə'mʌk] *ad* = **amok**.
amuse [ə'mju:z] *vt* divertire; **~ment** *n* divertimento; **~ment arcade** *n* sala giochi.
an [æn, ən, n] *indefinite article see* **a**.
anaemic [ə'ni:mɪk] *a* anemico(a).
anaesthetic [ænɪs'θɛtɪk] *a* anestetico(a) // *n* anestetico.
analog(ue) ['ænəlɔg] *a* (watch, computer) analogico(a).
analyse ['ænəlaɪz] *vt* (Brit) analizzare.
analysis, *pl* **analyses** [ə'næləsɪs, -sɪ:z] *n* analisi *f inv*.
analyst ['ænəlɪst] *n* (POL etc) analista *m/f*; (US) (psic)analista *m/f*.
analyze ['ænəlaɪz] *vt* (US) = **analyse**.
anarchist ['ænəkɪst] *a, n* anarchico(a).
anarchy ['ænəkɪ] *n* anarchia.

anathema [ə'næθɪmə] *n*: that is ~ to him non vuole nemmeno sentirne parlare.

anatomy [ə'nætəmɪ] *n* anatomia.

ancestor ['ænsɪstə*] *n* antenato/a.

ancestral [æn'sestrəl] *a* avito(a).

anchor ['æŋkə*] *n* ancora // *vi* (*also*: to drop ~) gettare l'ancora // *vt* ancorare; to weigh ~ salpare *or* levare l'ancora.

anchovy ['æntʃəvɪ] *n* acciuga.

ancient ['eɪnʃənt] *a* antico(a); (*fig*) anziano(a).

ancillary [æn'sɪlərɪ] *a* ausiliario(a).

and [ænd] *cj* e (*often* ed *before vowel*); ~ so on e così via; try ~ come cerca di venire; he talked ~ talked non la finiva di parlare; better ~ better sempre meglio.

anew [ə'nju:] *ad* di nuovo.

angel ['eɪndʒəl] *n* angelo.

anger ['æŋgə*] *n* rabbia // *vt* arrabbiare.

angina [æn'dʒaɪnə] *n* angina pectoris.

angle ['æŋgl] *n* angolo; **from their ~** dal loro punto di vista; **~r** *n* pescatore *m* con la lenza.

Anglican ['æŋglɪkən] *a*, *n* anglicano(a).

angling ['æŋglɪŋ] *n* pesca con la lenza.

Anglo- ['æŋgləu] *prefix* anglo....

angry ['æŋgrɪ] *a* arrabbiato(a), furioso(a); **to be ~ with sb/at sth** essere in collera con qn/per qc; **to get ~** arrabbiarsi; **to make sb ~** fare arrabbiare qn.

anguish ['æŋgwɪʃ] *n* angoscia.

animal ['ænɪməl] *a*, *n* animale (*m*).

animate *vt* ['ænɪmeɪt] animare // *a* ['ænɪmɪt] animato(a); **~d** *a* animato(a).

aniseed ['ænɪsi:d] *n* semi *mpl* di anice.

ankle ['æŋkl] *n* caviglia; **~ sock** *n* calzino.

annex *n* ['æneks] (*also: Brit*: **annexe**) edificio annesso // *vt* [ə'neks] annettere.

annihilate [ə'naɪəleɪt] *vt* annientare.

anniversary [ænɪ'və:sərɪ] *n* anniversario.

announce [ə'nauns] *vt* annunciare; **~ment** *n* annuncio; (*letter, card*) partecipazione *f*; **~r** *n* (RADIO, TV: *between programmes*) annunciatore/trice; (: *in a programme*) presentatore/trice.

annoy [ə'nɔɪ] *vt* dare fastidio a; **don't get ~ed!** non irritarti!; **~ance** *n* fastidio; (*cause of ~ance*) noia; **~ing** *a* noioso(a).

annual ['ænjuəl] *a* annuale // *n* (BOT) pianta annua; (*book*) annuario.

annul [ə'nʌl] *vt* annullare; (*law*) rescindere.

annum ['ænəm] *n see* **per**.

anonymous [ə'nɒnɪməs] *a* anonimo(a).

anorak ['ænəræk] *n* giacca a vento.

another [ə'nʌðə*] *a*: ~ book (*one more*) un altro libro, ancora un libro; (*a different one*) un altro libro // *pronoun* un altro(un'altra), ancora uno(a); *see also* **one**.

answer ['ɑ:nsə*] *n* risposta; soluzione *f* // *vi* rispondere // *vt* (*reply to*) rispondere a; (*problem*) risolvere; (*prayer*) esaudire; **to ~ the phone** rispondere (al telefono); **in ~ to your letter** in risposta alla sua lettera; **to ~ the bell** rispondere al campanello; **to ~ the door** aprire la porta; **to ~ back** *vi* ribattere; **to ~ for** *vt fus* essere responsabile di; **to ~ to** *vt fus* (*description*) corrispondere a; **~able** *a*: **~able (to sb/for sth)** responsabile (verso qn/di qc); **~ing machine** *n* segreteria (telefonica) automatica.

ant [ænt] *n* formica.

antagonism [æn'tægənɪzəm] *n* antagonismo.

antagonize [æn'tægənaɪz] *vt* provocare l'ostilità di.

Antarctic [ænt'ɑ:ktɪk] *n*: **the ~** l'Antartide *f* // *a* antartico(a).

antenatal ['æntɪ'neɪtl] *a* prenatale; **~ clinic** *n* assistenza medica preparto.

anthem ['ænθəm] *n* antifona; **national ~** inno nazionale.

anthology [æn'θɒlədʒɪ] *n* antologia.

antibiotic ['æntɪbaɪ'ɒtɪk] *a* antibiotico(a) // *n* antibiotico.

antibody ['æntɪbɒdɪ] *n* anticorpo.

anticipate [æn'tɪsɪpeɪt] *vt* prevedere; pregustare; (*wishes, request*) prevenire.

anticipation [æntɪsɪ'peɪʃən] *n* anticipazione *f*; (*expectation*) aspettative *fpl*.

anticlimax ['æntɪ'klaɪmæks] *n*: **it was an ~** fu una completa delusione.

anticlockwise ['æntɪ'klɒkwaɪz] *a*, *ad* in senso antiorario.

antics ['æntɪks] *npl* buffonerie *fpl*.

antifreeze ['æntɪ'fri:z] *n* anticongelante *m*.

antihistamine [æntɪ'hɪstəmɪn] *n* antistaminico.

antiquated ['æntɪkweɪtɪd] *a* antiquato(a).

antique [æn'ti:k] *n* antichità *f inv* // *a* antico(a); **~ shop** *n* negozio d'antichità.

antiquity [æn'tɪkwɪtɪ] *n* antichità *f inv*.

anti-Semitism ['æntɪ'semɪtɪzəm] *n* antisemitismo.

antiseptic [æntɪ'septɪk] *a* antisettico(a) // *n* antisettico.

antisocial ['æntɪ'səuʃəl] *a* asociale; (*against society*) antisociale.

antlers ['æntləz] *npl* palchi *mpl*.

anvil ['ænvɪl] *n* incudine *f*.

anxiety [æŋ'zaɪətɪ] *n* ansia; (*keenness*): ~ **to do** smania di fare.

anxious ['æŋkʃəs] *a* ansioso(a), inquieto(a); (*keen*): ~ **to do/that** impaziente di fare/che + *sub*.

any ['enɪ] ♦ *a* **1** (*in questions etc*): **have you ~ butter?** hai del burro?, hai un po' di burro?; **have you ~ children?** hai bambini?; **if there are ~ tickets left** se ci sono ancora (dei) biglietti, se c'è ancora

qualche biglietto
2 (with negative): I haven't ~ money/
books non ho soldi/libri
3 (no matter which) qualsiasi,
qualunque; **choose** ~ **book you like** scegli
un libro qualsiasi
4 (in phrases): **in** ~ **case** in ogni caso;
~ **day now** da un giorno all'altro; **at** ~
moment in qualsiasi momento, da un
momento all'altro; **at** ~ **rate** ad ogni
modo
◆ pronoun **1** (in questions, with
negative): **have you got** ~? ne hai?; **can**
~ **of you sing?** qualcuno di voi sa
cantare?; **I haven't** ~ (of them) non ne
ho
2 (no matter which one(s)): **take** ~ **of**
those books (you like) prendi uno
qualsiasi di quei libri
◆ ad **1** (in questions etc): **do you want**
~ **more soup/sandwiches?** vuoi ancora un
po' di minestra/degli altri panini?; **are**
you feeling ~ **better?** ti senti meglio?
2 (with negative): **I can't hear him** ~
more non lo sento più; **don't wait** ~ **long-**
er non aspettare più.
anybody ['ɛnɪbɔdɪ] pronoun (in questions
etc) qualcuno, nessuno; (with negative)
nessuno; (no matter who) chiunque; **can**
you see ~? vedi qualcuno or nessuno?; **if**
~ **should phone ...** se telefona qualcuno
...; **I can't see** ~ non vedo nessuno; ~
could do it chiunque potrebbe farlo.
anyhow ['ɛnɪhau] ad (at any rate) ad
ogni modo, comunque; (haphazard): **do**
it ~ **you like** fallo come ti pare; **I shall**
go ~ ci andrò lo stesso or comunque; **she**
leaves things just ~ lascia tutto come
capita.
anyone ['ɛnɪwʌn] pronoun = **anybody**.
anything ['ɛnɪθɪŋ] pronoun (in question
etc) qualcosa, qualche; (with negative)
niente; (no matter what): **you can say** ~
you like puoi dire quello che ti pare; **can**
you see ~? vedi niente or qualcosa?; **if**
~ **happens he ...** se mi dovesse
succedere qualcosa ...; **I can't see** ~ non
vedo niente; ~ **will do** va bene qualsiasi
cosa or tutto.
anyway ['ɛnɪweɪ] ad (at any rate) ad
ogni modo, comunque; (besides) ad ogni
modo.
anywhere ['ɛnɪwɛə*] ad (in questions
etc) da qualche parte; (with negative)
da nessuna parte; (no matter where) da
qualsiasi or qualunque parte, dovunque;
can you see him ~? lo vedi da qualche
parte?; **I can't see him** ~ non lo vedo da
nessuna parte; ~ **in the world** dovunque
nel mondo.
apart [ə'pɑːt] ad (to one side) a parte;
(separately) separatamente; **with one's**
legs ~ con le gambe divaricate; **10 miles**
~ a 10 miglia di distanza (l'uno dall'altro); **to take** ~ smontare; ~ **from** prep a

parte, eccetto.
apartheid [ə'pɑːteɪt] n apartheid f.
apartment [ə'pɑːtmənt] n (US)
appartamento; ~ **building** n (US)
stabile m, caseggiato.
apathetic [æpə'θetɪk] a apatico(a).
ape [eɪp] n scimmia // vt scimmiottare.
aperture ['æpətʃuə*] n apertura.
apex ['eɪpɛks] n apice m.
apiece [ə'piːs] ad ciascuno(a).
apologetic [əpɔlə'dʒetɪk] a (tone, letter)
di scusa.
apologize [ə'pɔlədʒaɪz] vi: **to** ~ (for sth
to sb) scusarsi (di qc a qn), chiedere
scusa (a qn per qc).
apology [ə'pɔlədʒɪ] n scuse fpl.
apostle [ə'pɔsl] n apostolo.
apostrophe [ə'pɔstrəfɪ] n (sign) apo-
strofo.
appalling [ə'pɔːlɪŋ] a spaventoso(a).
apparatus [æpə'reɪtəs] n apparato; (in
gymnasium) attrezzatura.
apparel [ə'pærl] n (US) abbigliamento,
confezioni fpl.
apparent [ə'pærənt] a evidente; ~**ly** ad
evidentemente.
apparition [æpə'rɪʃən] n apparizione f.
appeal [ə'piːl] vi (LAW) appellarsi alla
legge // n (LAW) appello; (request) richiesta; (charm) attrattiva; **to** ~ **for**
chiedere (con insistenza); **to** ~ **to** (subj:
person) appellarsi a; (subj: thing)
piacere a; **to** ~ **to sb for mercy** chiedere
pietà a qn; **it doesn't** ~ **to me** mi dice
poco; ~**ing** a (nice) attraente; (touching) commovente.
appear [ə'pɪə*] vi apparire; (LAW)
comparire; (publication) essere pub-
blicato(a); (seem) sembrare; **it would** ~
that sembra che; **to** ~ **in Hamlet**
recitare nell'Amleto; **to** ~ **on TV**
presentarsi in televisione; ~**ance** n
apparizione f; apparenza; (look, aspect)
aspetto.
appease [ə'piːz] vt calmare, appagare.
appendage [ə'pendɪdʒ] n aggiunta.
appendicitis [əpendɪ'saɪtɪs] n appendicite
f.
appendix, pl **appendices** [ə'pendɪks,
-siːz] n appendice f.
appetite ['æpɪtaɪt] n appetito.
appetizer ['æpɪtaɪzə*] n stuzzichino.
applaud [ə'plɔːd] vt, vi applaudire.
applause [ə'plɔːz] n applauso.
apple ['æpl] n mela; ~ **tree** n melo.
appliance [ə'plaɪəns] n apparecchio.
applicant ['æplɪkənt] n candidato/a.
application [æplɪ'keɪʃən] n applicazione
f; (for a job, a grant etc) domanda; ~
form n modulo per la domanda.
applied [ə'plaɪd] a applicato(a).
apply [ə'plaɪ] vt: **to** ~ (to) (paint,
ointment) dare (a); (theory, technique)
applicare (a) // vi: **to** ~ **to** (ask)
rivolgersi a; (be suitable for, relevant

_to_) riguardare, riferirsi a; **to ~ (for)** (_permit, grant, job_) fare domanda (per); **to ~ the brakes** frenare; **to ~ o.s. to** dedicarsi a.

appoint [ə'pɔɪnt] _vt_ nominare; **~ment** _n_ nomina; (_arrangement to meet_) appuntamento; **to make an ~ment** (_with_) prendere un appuntamento (con).

appraisal [ə'preɪzl] _n_ valutazione _f_.

appreciate [ə'pri:ʃɪeɪt] _vt_ (_like_) apprezzare; (_be grateful for_) essere riconoscente di; (_be aware of_) rendersi conto di // _vi_ (_FINANCE_) aumentare.

appreciation [əpri:ʃɪ'eɪʃən] _n_ apprezzamento; (_FINANCE_) aumento del valore.

appreciative [ə'pri:ʃɪətɪv] _a_ (_person_) sensibile; (_comment_) elogiativo(a).

apprehend [æprɪ'hend] _vt_ (_arrest_) arrestare.

apprehension [æprɪ'henʃən] _n_ (_fear_) inquietudine _f_.

apprehensive [æprɪ'hensɪv] _a_ apprensivo(a).

apprentice [ə'prentɪs] _n_ apprendista _m/f_; **~ship** _n_ apprendistato.

approach [ə'prəʊtʃ] _vi_ avvicinarsi // _vt_ (_come near_) avvicinarsi a; (_ask, apply to_) rivolgersi a; (_subject, passer-by_) avvicinare // _n_ approccio; accesso; (_to problem_) modo di affrontare; **~able** _a_ accessibile.

appropriate _a_ [ə'prəʊprɪɪt] appropriato(a); adatto(a) // _vt_ [ə'prəʊprɪeɪt] (_take_) appropriarsi.

approval [ə'pru:vəl] _n_ approvazione _f_; **on ~** (_COMM_) in prova, in esame.

approve [ə'pru:v] _vt, vi_ approvare; **to ~ of** _vt fus_ approvare; **~d school** _n_ (_Brit_) riformatorio.

approximate _a_ [ə'prɒksɪmɪt] approssimativo(a); **~ly** _ad_ circa.

apricot ['eɪprɪkɒt] _n_ albicocca.

April ['eɪprəl] _n_ aprile _m_; **~ fool!** pesce d'aprile!

apron ['eɪprən] _n_ grembiule _m_.

apt [æpt] _a_ (_suitable_) adatto(a); (_able_) capace; (_likely_): **to be ~ to do** avere tendenza a fare.

aptitude ['æptɪtju:d] _n_ abilità _f inv_.

aqualung ['ækwəlʌŋ] _n_ autorespiratore _m_.

aquarium [ə'kwɛərɪəm] _n_ acquario.

Aquarius [ə'kwɛərɪəs] _n_ Acquario.

Arab ['ærəb] _n_ arabo/a.

Arabian [ə'reɪbɪən] _a_ arabo(a).

Arabic ['ærəbɪk] _a_ arabico(a) // _n_ arabo; **~ numerals** numeri _mpl_ arabi, numerazione _f_ araba.

arbitrary ['ɑ:bɪtrərɪ] _a_ arbitrario(a).

arbitration [ɑ:bɪ'treɪʃən] _n_ (_LAW_) arbitrato; (_INDUSTRY_) arbitraggio.

arcade [ɑ:'keɪd] _n_ portico; (_passage with shops_) galleria.

arch [ɑ:tʃ] _n_ arco; (_of foot_) arco plantare

// _vt_ inarcare // _a_ malizioso(a).

archaeologist [ɑ:kɪ'ɒlədʒɪst] _n_ archeologo/a.

archaeology [ɑ:kɪ'ɒlədʒɪ] _n_ archeologia.

archbishop [ɑ:tʃ'bɪʃəp] _n_ arcivescovo.

arch-enemy ['ɑ:tʃ'enəmɪ] _n_ arcinemico/a.

archeology [ɑ:kɪ'ɒlədʒɪ] _etc_ = **archaeology** _etc_.

archer ['ɑ:tʃə*] _n_ arciere _m_; **~y** _n_ tiro all'arco.

architect ['ɑ:kɪtekt] _n_ architetto; **~ure** ['ɑ:kɪtektʃə*] _n_ architettura.

archives ['ɑ:kaɪvz] _npl_ archivi _mpl_.

archway ['ɑ:tʃweɪ] _n_ arco.

Arctic ['ɑ:ktɪk] _a_ artico(a) // _n_: **the ~** l'Artico.

ardent ['ɑ:dənt] _a_ ardente.

are [ɑ:*] _vb_ see **be**.

area ['ɛərɪə] _n_ (_GEOM_) area; (_zone_) zona; (: _smaller_) settore _m_.

aren't [ɑ:nt] = **are not**.

Argentina [ɑ:dʒən'ti:nə] _n_ Argentina; **Argentinian** [-'tɪnɪən] _a, n_ argentino(a).

arguably ['ɑ:gjʊəblɪ] _ad_: **it is ~ ...** si può sostenere che sia ....

argue ['ɑ:gju:] _vi_ (_quarrel_) litigare; (_reason_) ragionare; **to ~ that** sostenere che.

argument ['ɑ:gjumənt] _n_ (_reasons_) argomento; (_quarrel_) lite _f_; (_debate_) discussione _f_; **~ative** [ɑ:gju'mentətɪv] _a_ litigioso(a).

Aries ['ɛərɪz] _n_ Ariete _m_.

arise, _pt_ **arose**, _pp_ **arisen** [ə'raɪz, -'rəʊz, -'rɪzn] _vi_ alzarsi; (_opportunity, problem_) presentarsi; **to ~ from** risultare da.

aristocrat ['ærɪstəkræt] _n_ aristocratico/a.

arithmetic [ə'rɪθmətɪk] _n_ aritmetica.

ark [ɑ:k] _n_: **Noah's A~** l'arca di Noè.

arm [ɑ:m] _n_ braccio // _vt_ armare; **~s** _npl_ (_weapons_) armi _fpl_; **~ in ~** a braccetto.

armaments ['ɑ:məmənts] _npl_ armamenti _mpl_.

arm: **~chair** _n_ poltrona; **~ed** _a_ armato(a); **~ed robbery** _n_ rapina a mano armata.

armour, (_US_) **armor** ['ɑ:mə*] _n_ armatura; (_also:_ **~-plating**) corazza, blindatura; (_MIL: tanks_) mezzi _mpl_ blindati; **~ed car** _n_ autoblinda _f inv_; **~y** _n_ arsenale _m_.

armpit ['ɑ:mpɪt] _n_ ascella.

armrest ['ɑ:mrest] _n_ bracciolo.

army ['ɑ:mɪ] _n_ esercito.

aroma [ə'rəʊmə] _n_ aroma.

arose [ə'rəʊz] _pt of_ **arise**.

around [ə'raʊnd] _ad_ attorno, intorno // _prep_ intorno a; (_fig: about_): **~ £5/3 o'clock** circa 5 sterline/le 3; **is he ~?** è in giro?

arouse [ə'raʊz] _vt_ (_sleeper_) svegliare; (_curiosity, passions_) suscitare.

arrange [ə'reɪndʒ] _vt_ sistemare; (_programme_) preparare; **to ~ to do sth**

mettersi d'accordo per fare qc; **~ment** n sistemazione f; (plans etc): **~ments** progetti mpl, piani mpl.

array [ə'reɪ] n: **~ of** fila di.

arrears [ə'rɪəz] npl arretrati mpl; **to be in ~ with** one's rent essere in arretrato con l'affitto.

arrest [ə'rɛst] vt arrestare; (sb's attention) attirare // n arresto; **under ~** in arresto.

arrival [ə'raɪvəl] n arrivo; (person) arrivato/a; **a new ~** un nuovo venuto; (baby) un neonato.

arrive [ə'raɪv] vi arrivare; **to ~ at** vt fus (fig) raggiungere.

arrogant ['ærəgənt] a arrogante.

arrow ['ærəu] n freccia.

arse [ɑːs] n (col!) culo (!).

arson ['ɑːsn] n incendio doloso.

art [ɑːt] n arte f; (craft) mestiere m; **A~s** npl (SCOL) Lettere fpl.

artefact ['ɑːtɪfækt] n manufatto.

artery ['ɑːtərɪ] n arteria.

art gallery n galleria d'arte.

arthritis [ɑː'θraɪtɪs] n artrite f.

artichoke ['ɑːtɪtʃəuk] n carciofo; **Jerusalem ~** topinambur m inv.

article ['ɑːtɪkl] n articolo; (Brit LAW: training): **~s** npl contratto di tirocinio; **~ of clothing** capo di vestiario.

articulate a [ɑː'tɪkjulɪt] (person) che si esprime forbitamente; (speech) articolato(a) // vi [ɑː'tɪkjuleɪt] articolare; **~d lorry** n (Brit) autotreno.

artificial [ɑːtɪ'fɪʃəl] a artificiale; **~ respiration** n respirazione f artificiale.

artillery [ɑː'tɪlərɪ] n artiglieria.

artisan ['ɑːtɪzæn] n artigiano/a.

artist ['ɑːtɪst] n artista m/f; **~ic** [ɑː'tɪstɪk] a artistico(a); **~ry** n arte f.

artless ['ɑːtlɪs] a semplice, ingenuo(a).

art school n scuola d'arte.

as [æz] ♦ cj **1** (referring to time) mentre; **~ the years went by** col passare degli anni; **he came in ~** I was leaving arrivò mentre stavo uscendo; **~ from tomorrow** da domani

2 (in comparisons): **~ big ~** grande come; **twice ~ big ~** due volte più grande di; **~ much/many ~** tanto quanto/tanti quanti; **~ soon ~ possible** prima possibile

3 (since, because) dal momento che, siccome

4 (referring to manner, way) come; **do ~ you wish** fa' come vuoi; **~ she said** come ha detto lei

5 (concerning): **~ for or to that** per quanto riguarda or quanto a quello

6: **~ if or though** come se; **he looked ~ if he was ill** sembrava stare male; see also **long, such, well**

♦ prep: **he works ~ a driver** fa l'autista; **~ chairman of the company, he ...** come presidente della compagnia, lui ...;

he gave me it **~ a present** me lo ha regalato.

a.s.a.p. abbr (= as soon as possible) prima possibile.

ascend [ə'sɛnd] vt salire.

ascent [ə'sɛnt] n salita.

ascertain [æsə'teɪn] vt accertare.

ash [æʃ] n (dust) cenere f; (also: **~ tree**) frassino.

ashamed [ə'ʃeɪmd] a vergognoso(a); **to be ~ of** vergognarsi di.

ashen ['æʃn] a (pale) livido(a).

ashore [ə'ʃɔː*] ad a terra.

ashtray ['æʃtreɪ] n portacenere m.

Ash Wednesday n mercoledì m inv delle Ceneri.

Asia ['eɪʃə] n Asia; **~n** a, n asiatico(a).

aside [ə'saɪd] ad da parte // n a parte m.

ask [ɑːsk] vt (request) chiedere; (question) domandare; (invite) invitare; **to ~ sb sth/sb to do sth** chiedere qc a qn/a qn di fare qc; **to ~ sb about sth** chiedere a qn di qc; **to ~ (sb) a question** fare una domanda (a qn); **to ~ sb out to dinner** invitare qn a mangiare fuori; **to ~ after** vt fus chiedere di; **to ~ for** vt fus chiedere.

askance [ə'skɑːns] ad: **to look ~ at sb** guardare qn di traverso.

askew [ə'skjuː] ad di traverso, storto.

asleep [ə'sliːp] a addormentato(a); **to be ~** dormire; **to fall ~** addormentarsi.

asparagus [əs'pærəgəs] n asparagi mpl.

aspect ['æspɛkt] n aspetto.

aspersions [əs'pɔːʃənz] npl: **to cast ~ on** diffamare.

asphyxiation [æsfɪksɪ'eɪʃən] n asfissia.

aspire [əs'paɪə*] vi: **to ~ to** aspirare a.

aspirin ['æsprɪn] n aspirina.

ass [æs] n asino; (col) scemo/a; (US col!) culo (!).

assailant [ə'seɪlənt] n assalitore m.

assassinate [ə'sæsɪneɪt] vt assassinare; **assassination** [əsæsɪ'neɪʃən] n assassinio.

assault [ə'sɔːlt] n (MIL) assalto; (gen: attack) aggressione f // vt assaltare; aggredire; (sexually) violentare.

assemble [ə'sɛmbl] vt riunire; (TECH) montare // vi riunirsi.

assembly [ə'sɛmblɪ] n (meeting) assemblea; (construction) montaggio; **~ line** n catena di montaggio.

assent [ə'sɛnt] n assenso, consenso.

assert [ə'sɔːt] vt asserire; (insist on) far valere.

assess [ə'sɛs] vt valutare; **~ment** n valutazione f.

asset ['æsɛt] n vantaggio; **~s** npl beni mpl; disponibilità fpl; attivo.

assign [ə'saɪn] vt: **to ~ (to)** (task) assegnare (a); (resources) riservare (a); (cause, meaning) attribuire (a); **to ~ a date to sth** fissare la data di qc; **~ment** n compito.

assist [ə'sɪst] *vt* assistere, aiutare; **~ance** *n* assistenza, aiuto; **~ant** *n* assistente *m/f*; (*Brit: also*: **shop ~ant**) commesso/a.

associate [ə'səuʃɪɪt] *a* associato(a); (*member*) aggiunto(a) // *n* collega *m/f*; (*in business*) socio/a // *vb* [ə'səuʃɪeɪt] *vt* associare // *vi*: **to ~ with sb** frequentare qn.

association [əsəusɪ'eɪʃən] *n* associazione *f*.

assorted [ə'sɔ:tɪd] *a* assortito(a).

assortment [ə'sɔ:tmənt] *n* assortimento.

assume [ə'sju:m] *vt* supporre; (*responsibilities etc*) assumere; (*attitude, name*) prendere; **~d name** *n* nome *m* falso.

assumption [ə'sʌmpʃən] *n* supposizione *f*, ipotesi *f inv*.

assurance [ə'ʃuərəns] *n* assicurazione *f*; (*self-confidence*) fiducia in se stesso.

assure [ə'ʃuə*] *vt* assicurare.

astern [ə'stə:n] *ad* a poppa.

asthma ['æsmə] *n* asma.

astonish [ə'stɔnɪʃ] *vt* stupire; **~ment** *n* stupore *m*.

astound [ə'staund] *vt* sbalordire.

astray [ə'streɪ] *ad*: **to go ~** smarrirsi; (*fig*) traviarsi.

astride [ə'straɪd] *prep* a cavalcioni di.

astrology [əs'trɔlədʒɪ] *n* astrologia.

astronaut ['æstrənɔ:t] *n* astronauta *m/f*.

astronomy [əs'trɔnəmɪ] *n* astronomia.

astute [əs'tju:t] *a* astuto(a).

asylum [ə'saɪləm] *n* asilo; (*building*) manicomio.

at [æt] *prep* **1** (*referring to position, direction*) a; **~ the top** in cima; **~ the desk** al banco, alla scrivania; **~ home/school** a casa/scuola; **~ the baker's** dal panettiere; **to look ~ sth** guardare qc; **to throw sth ~ sb** lanciare qc a qn
2 (*referring to time*) a; **~ 4 o'clock** alle 4; **~ night** di notte; **~ Christmas** a Natale; **~ times** a volte
3 (*referring to rates, speed etc*) a; **~ £1 a kilo** a 1 sterlina al chilo; **two ~ a time** due alla volta, due per volta; **~ 50 km/h** a 50 km/h
4 (*referring to manner*): **~ a stroke** d'un solo colpo; **~ peace** in pace
5 (*referring to activity*): **to be ~ work** essere al lavoro; **to play ~ cowboys** giocare ai cowboy; **to be good ~ sth/doing sth** essere bravo in qc/a fare qc
6 (*referring to cause*): **shocked/surprised/annoyed ~ sth** colpito da/sorpreso da/arrabbiato per qc; **I went ~ his suggestion** ci sono andato dietro suo consiglio.

ate [eɪt] *pt of* **eat**.

atheist ['eɪθɪɪst] *n* ateo/a.

Athens ['æθɪnz] *n* Atene *f*.

athlete ['æθli:t] *n* atleta *m/f*.

athletic [æθ'lɛtɪk] *a* atletico(a); **~s** *n*

atletica.

Atlantic [ət'læntɪk] *a* atlantico(a) // *n*: **the ~ (Ocean)** l'Atlantico, l'Oceano Atlantico.

atlas ['ætləs] *n* atlante *m*.

atmosphere ['ætməsfɪə*] *n* atmosfera.

atom ['ætəm] *n* atomo; **~ic** [ə'tɔmɪk] *a* atomico(a); **~(ic) bomb** *n* bomba atomica; **~izer** ['ætəmaɪzə*] *n* atomizzatore *m*.

atone [ə'təun] *vi*: **to ~ for** espiare.

atrocious [ə'trəuʃəs] *a* pessimo(a), atroce.

attach [ə'tætʃ] *vt* attaccare; (*document, letter*) allegare; (*MIL: troops*) assegnare; **to be ~ed to sb/ sth** (*to like*) essere affezionato(a) a qn/qc.

attaché case [ə'tæʃeɪ-] *n* valigetta per documenti.

attachment [ə'tætʃmənt] *n* (*tool*) accessorio; (*love*): **~ (to)** affetto (per).

attack [ə'tæk] *vt* attaccare; (*task etc*) iniziare; (*problem*) affrontare // *n* attacco; (*also*: **heart ~**) infarto.

attain [ə'teɪn] *vt* (*also*: **to ~ to**) arrivare a, raggiungere; **~ments** *npl* cognizioni *fpl*.

attempt [ə'tɛmpt] *n* tentativo // *vt* tentare; **to make an ~ on sb's life** attentare alla vita di qn.

attend [ə'tɛnd] *vt* frequentare; (*meeting, talk*) andare a; (*patient*) assistere; **to ~ to** *vt fus* (*needs, affairs etc*) prendersi cura di; (*customer*) occuparsi di; **~ance** *n* (*being present*) presenza; (*people present*) gente *f* presente; **~ant** *n* custode *m/f*; persona di servizio // *a* concomitante.

attention [ə'tɛnʃən] *n* attenzione *f*; **~!** (*MIL*) attenti!; **for the ~ of** (*ADMIN*) per l'attenzione di.

attentive [ə'tɛntɪv] *a* attento(a); (*kind*) premuroso(a).

attic ['ætɪk] *n* soffitta.

attitude ['ætɪtju:d] *n* atteggiamento; posa.

attorney [ə'tə:nɪ] *n* (*lawyer*) avvocato; (*having proxy*) mandatario; **A~ General** *n* (*Brit*) Procuratore *m* Generale; (*US*) Ministro della Giustizia.

attract [ə'trækt] *vt* attirare; **~ion** [ə'trækʃən] *n* (*gen pl*: *pleasant things*) attrattiva; (*PHYSICS, fig*: *towards sth*) attrazione *f*; **~ive** *a* attraente.

attribute *n* ['ætrɪbju:t] attributo // *vt* [ə'trɪbju:t]: **to ~ sth to** attribuire qc a.

attrition [ə'trɪʃən] *n*: **war of ~** guerra di logoramento.

aubergine ['əubəʒi:n] *n* melanzana.

auburn ['ɔ:bən] *a* tizianesco(a).

auction ['ɔ:kʃən] *n* (*also*: **sale by ~**) asta // *vt* (*also*: **to sell by ~**) vendere all'asta; (*also*: **to put up for ~**) mettere all'asta; **~eer** [-'nɪə*] *n* banditore *m*.

audible ['ɔ:dɪbl] *a* udibile.

audience ['ɔːdɪəns] n (people) pubblico; spettatori mpl; ascoltatori mpl; (interview) udienza.

audio-typist ['ɔːdɪəʊ'taɪpɪst] n dattilografo/a che trascrive da nastro.

audio-visual [ɔːdɪəʊ'vɪzjʊəl] a audiovisivo(a); ~ **aid** n sussidio audiovisivo.

audit [ɔːdɪt] vt rivedere, verificare.

audition [ɔː'dɪʃən] n audizione f.

auditor ['ɔːdɪtə*] n revisore m.

augment [ɔːg'mɛnt] vt, vi aumentare.

augur ['ɔːgə*] vi: it ~s well promette bene.

August ['ɔːgəst] n agosto.

aunt [ɑːnt] n zia; ~**ie**, ~**y** n zietta.

au pair ['əʊ'pɛə*] n (also: ~ **girl**) (ragazza f) alla pari inv.

aura ['ɔːrə] n aura.

auspicious [ɔːs'pɪʃəs] a propizio(a).

austerity [ɔs'tɛrɪtɪ] n austerità.

Australia [ɔs'treɪlɪə] n Australia; ~**n** a, n australiano(a).

Austria ['ɔstrɪə] n Austria; ~**n** a, n austriaco(a).

authentic [ɔː'θɛntɪk] a autentico(a).

author ['ɔːθə*] n autore/trice.

authoritarian [ɔːθɔrɪ'tɛərɪən] a autoritario(a).

authoritative [ɔː'θɔrɪtətɪv] a (account etc) autorevole; (manner) autoritario(a).

authority [ɔː'θɔrɪtɪ] n autorità f inv; (permission) autorizzazione f; the authorities npl le autorità.

authorize ['ɔːθəraɪz] vt autorizzare.

auto ['ɔːtəʊ] n (US) auto f inv.

autobiography [ɔːtəbaɪ'ɔgrəfɪ] n autobiografia.

autograph ['ɔːtəgrɑːf] n autografo // vt firmare.

automatic [ɔːtə'mætɪk] a automatico(a) // n (gun) arma automatica; (Brit AUT) automobile f con cambio automatico; ~**ally** ad automaticamente.

automation [ɔːtə'meɪʃən] n automazione f.

automaton, pl **automata** [ɔː'tɔmətən, -tə] n automa m.

automobile ['ɔːtəməbiːl] n (US) automobile f.

autonomy [ɔː'tɔnəmɪ] n autonomia.

autumn ['ɔːtəm] n autunno.

auxiliary [ɔːg'zɪlɪərɪ] n ausiliario(a) // n ausiliare m/f.

Av. abbr = **avenue.**

avail [ə'veɪl] vt: to ~ o.s. of servirsi di; approfittarsi di // n: to no ~ inutilmente.

available [ə'veɪləbl] a disponibile.

avalanche ['ævəlɑːnʃ] n valanga.

avant-garde ['ævãŋ'gɑːd] a d'avanguardia.

Ave. abbr = **avenue.**

avenge [ə'vɛndʒ] vt vendicare.

avenue ['ævənjuː] n viale m.

average ['ævərɪdʒ] n media // a medio(a) // vt (a certain figure) fare di or in media; on ~ in media; **to ~ out** vi: to ~ out at aggirarsi in media su, essere in media di.

averse [ə'vɜːs] a: to be ~ to sth/doing essere contrario a qc/a fare.

avert [ə'vɜːt] vt evitare, prevenire; (one's eyes) distogliere.

aviary ['eɪvɪərɪ] n voliera, uccelliera.

avocado [ævə'kɑːdəʊ] n (also: Brit: ~ **pear**) avocado m inv.

avoid [ə'vɔɪd] vt evitare.

await [ə'weɪt] vt aspettare.

awake [ə'weɪk] a sveglio(a) // vb (pt awoke, pp awoken, awaked) vt svegliare // vi svegliarsi; ~**ning** [ə'weɪknɪŋ] n risveglio.

award [ə'wɔːd] n premio; (LAW) decreto // vt assegnare; (LAW: damages) decretare.

aware [ə'wɛə*] a: ~ of (conscious) conscio(a) di; (informed) informato(a) di; to become ~ of accorgersi di; ~**ness** n consapevolezza.

awash [ə'wɔʃ] a: ~ (with) inondato(a) (da).

away [ə'weɪ] a, ad via; lontano(a); two kilometres ~ a due chilometri di distanza; two hours ~ by car a due ore di distanza in macchina; the holiday was two weeks ~ mancavano due settimane alle vacanze; ~ from lontano da; he's ~ for a week è andato via per una settimana; he was working/pedalling etc ~ la particella indica la continuità e l'energia dell'azione: lavorava/pedalava etc più che poteva; to fade/wither etc ~ la particella rinforza l'idea della diminuzione; ~ game n (SPORT) partita fuori casa.

awe [ɔː] n timore m; ~-**inspiring,** ~**some** a imponente.

awful ['ɔːfəl] a terribile; ~**ly** ad (very) terribilmente.

awhile [ə'waɪl] ad (per) un po'.

awkward ['ɔːkwəd] a (clumsy) goffo(a); (inconvenient) scomodo(a); (embarrassing) imbarazzante.

awning ['ɔːnɪŋ] n (of shop, hotel etc) tenda.

awoke, awoken [ə'wəʊk, -kən] pt, pp of **awake.**

awry [ə'raɪ] ad di traverso // a storto(a); to go ~ andare a monte.

axe, (US) **ax** [æks] n scure f // vt (project etc) abolire; (jobs) sopprimere.

axis, pl **axes** ['æksɪs, -siːz] n asse m.

axle ['æksl] n (also: ~-**tree**) asse m.

ay(e) [aɪ] excl (yes) sì.

B

B [bi:] n (MUS) si m.

B.A. n abbr = **Bachelor of Arts**.

baby ['beɪbɪ] n bambino/a; **~ carriage** n (US) carrozzina; **~-sit** vi fare il (or la) babysitter; **~-sitter** n baby-sitter m/f inv.

bachelor ['bætʃələ*] n scapolo; **B~ of Arts/Science** (**B.A./B.Sc.**) ≈ laureato/a in lettere/scienze.

back [bæk] n (of person, horse) dorso, schiena; (of hand) dorso; (of house, car) didietro; (of train) coda; (of chair) schienale m; (of page) rovescio; (FOOTBALL) difensore m // vt (candidate: also: **~ up**) appoggiare; (horse: at races) puntare su; (car) guidare a marcia indietro // vi indietreggiare; (car etc) fare marcia indietro // a (in compounds) posteriore, di dietro; **~ seats/wheels** (AUT) sedili mpl/ruote fpl posteriori; **~ payments** arretrati mpl // ad (not forward) indietro; (returned): he's ~ è tornato; he ran ~ tornò indietro di corsa; (restitution): throw the ball ~ ritira la palla; can I have it ~? posso riaverlo?; (again): he called ~ ha richiamato; to **~ down** vi fare marcia indietro; to **~ out** vi (of promise) tirarsi indietro; to **~ up** vt (support) appoggiare, sostenere; (COMPUT) fare una copia di riserva di; **~bencher** n (Brit) membro del Parlamento senza potere amministrativo; **~bone** n spina dorsale; **~cloth** n scena di sfondo; **~date** vt (letter) retrodatare; **~dated pay rise** aumento retroattivo; **~drop** n = **~cloth**; **~fire** vi (AUT) dar ritorni di fiamma; (plans) fallire; **~ground** n sfondo; (of events) background m inv; (basic knowledge) base f; (experience) esperienza; **family ~ground** ambiente m familiare; **~hand** n (TENNIS: also: **~hand stroke**) rovescio; **~handed** a (fig) ambiguo(a); **~hander** n (Brit: bribe) bustarella; **~ing** n (fig) appoggio; **~lash** n contraccolpo, ripercussione f; **~log** n: **~log of work** lavoro arretrato; **~ number** n (of magazine etc) numero arretrato; **~pack** n zaino; **~ pay** n arretrato di paga; **~side** n (col) sedere m; **~stage** ad nel retroscena; **~stroke** n nuoto sul dorso; **~up** a (train, plane) supplementare; (COMPUT) di riserva // n (support) appoggio, sostegno; (also: **~up file**) file m inv di riserva; **~ward** a (movement) indietro inv; (person) tardivo(a); (country) arretrato(a); **~wards** ad indietro; (fall, walk) all'indietro; **~water** n (fig) posto morto; **~yard** n cortile m dietro la casa.

bacon ['beɪkən] n pancetta.

bad [bæd] a cattivo(a); (child) cattivello(a); (meat, food) andato(a) a male; his ~ leg la sua gamba malata; to go ~ andare a male.

bade [bæd] pt of **bid**.

badge [bædʒ] n insegna; (of policeman) stemma m.

badger ['bædʒə*] n tasso.

badly ['bædlɪ] ad (work, dress etc) male; ~ **wounded** gravemente ferito; he needs it ~ ne ha gran bisogno; ~ **off** a povero(a).

badminton ['bædmɪntən] n badminton m.

bad-tempered ['bæd'tempəd] a irritabile; di malumore.

baffle ['bæfl] vt (puzzle) confondere.

bag [bæg] n sacco; (handbag etc) borsa; (of hunter) carniere m; bottino // vt (col: take) mettersi in tasca; prendersi; **~s of** (col: lots of) un sacco di; **~gage** n bagagli mpl; **~gy** a largo(a), sformato(a); **~pipes** npl cornamusa.

bail [beɪl] n cauzione f // vt (prisoner: also: **grant ~ to**) concedere la libertà provvisoria su cauzione a; (boat: also: **~ out**) aggottare; **on ~** (accused person) in libertà provvisoria su cauzione; to **~ out** vt (prisoner) ottenere la libertà provvisoria su cauzione di; see also **bale**.

bailiff ['beɪlɪf] n usciere m; fattore m.

bait [beɪt] n esca // vt (fig) tormentare.

bake [beɪk] vt cuocere al forno // vi cuocersi al forno; **~d beans** npl fagioli mpl all'uccelletto; **~r** n fornaio/a, panettiere/a; **~ry** n panetteria; **baking** n cottura (al forno).

balance ['bæləns] n equilibrio; (COMM: sum) bilancio; (scales) bilancia // vt tenere in equilibrio; (pros and cons) soppesare; (budget) far quadrare; (account) pareggiare; (compensate) contrappesare; **~ of trade/payments** bilancia commerciale/dei pagamenti; **~d** a (personality, diet) equilibrato(a); **~ sheet** n bilancio.

balcony ['bælkənɪ] n balcone m.

bald [bɔ:ld] a calvo(a).

bale [beɪl] n balla; to **~ out** vi (of a plane) gettarsi col paracadute.

baleful ['beɪlful] a funesto(a).

ball [bɔ:l] n palla; (football) pallone m; (for golf) pallina; (dance) ballo.

ballast ['bæləst] n zavorra.

ball bearings npl cuscinetti a sfere.

ballerina [bælə'ri:nə] n ballerina.

ballet ['bæleɪ] n balletto; (art) danza classica.

balloon [bə'lu:n] n pallone m; (in comic strip) fumetto.

ballot ['bælət] n scrutinio.

ball-point pen ['bɔ:lpɔɪnt-] n penna a sfera.

ballroom ['bɔːlrum] *n* sala da ballo.
balm [bɑːm] *n* balsamo.
ban [bæn] *n* interdizione *f* // *vt* interdire.
banana [bə'nɑːnə] *n* banana.
band [bænd] *n* banda; (*at a dance*) orchestra; (*MIL*) fanfara; **to ~ together** *vi* collegarsi.
bandage ['bændɪdʒ] *n* benda.
bandaid ['bændeɪd] *n* (*US*) cerotto.
bandwagon ['bændwægən] *n*: **to jump on the ~** (*fig*) seguire la corrente.
bandy ['bændɪ] *vt* (*jokes, insults*) scambiare.
bandy-legged ['bændɪ'lɛgɪd] *a* dalle gambe storte.
bang [bæŋ] *n* botta; (*of door*) lo sbattere; (*blow*) colpo // *vt* battere (violentemente); (*door*) sbattere // *vi* scoppiare; sbattere.
bangle ['bæŋgl] *n* braccialetto.
bangs [bæŋz] *npl* (*US: fringe*) frangia, frangetta.
banish ['bænɪʃ] *vt* bandire.
banister(s) ['bænɪstə(z)] *n(pl)* ringhiera.
bank [bæŋk] *n* banca, banco; (*of river, lake*) riva, sponda; (*of earth*) banco // *vi* (*AVIAT*) inclinarsi in virata; **to ~ on** *vt fus* contare su; **~ account** *n* conto in banca; **~ card** *n* carta assegni; **~er** *n* banchiere *m*; **~er's card** *n* (*Brit*) = **~ card**; **B~ holiday** *n* (*Brit*) giorno di festa (*in cui le banche sono chiuse*); **~ing** *n* attività bancaria; professione *f* di banchiere; **~note** *n* banconota; **~ rate** *n* tasso bancario.
bankrupt ['bæŋkrʌpt] *a* fallito(a); **to go ~ fallire**; **~cy** *n* fallimento.
bank statement *n* estratto conto.
banner ['bænə*] *n* bandiera.
banns [bænz] *npl* pubblicazioni *fpl* di matrimonio.
baptism ['bæptɪzəm] *n* battesimo.
bar [bɑː*] *n* barra; (*of window etc*) sbarra; (*of chocolate*) tavoletta; (*fig*) ostacolo; restrizione *f*; (*pub*) bar *m inv*; (*counter: in pub*) banco; (*MUS*) battuta // *vt* (*road, window*) sbarrare; (*person*) escludere; (*activity*) interdire; **~ of soap** saponetta; **the B~** (*LAW*) l'Ordine *m* degli avvocati; **behind ~s** (*prisoner*) dietro le sbarre; **~ none** senza eccezione.
barbaric [bɑː'bærɪk] *a* barbarico(a).
barbecue ['bɑːbɪkjuː] *n* barbecue *m inv*.
barbed wire ['bɑːbd-] *n* filo spinato.
barber ['bɑːbə*] *n* barbiere *m*.
bar code *n* (*on goods*) codice *m* a barre.
bare [bɛə*] *a* nudo(a) // *vt* scoprire, denudare; (*teeth*) mostrare; **~back** *ad* senza sella; **~faced** *a* sfacciato(a); **~foot** *a*, *ad* scalzo(a); **~ly** *ad* appena.
bargain ['bɑːgɪn] *n* (*transaction*) contratto; (*good buy*) affare *m* // *vi* trattare; **into the ~** per giunta; **to ~ for** *vt fus*: he got more than he ~ed for gli è andata peggio di quel che si aspettasse

or che avesse calcolato.
barge [bɑːdʒ] *n* chiatta; **to ~ in** *vi* (*walk in*) piombare dentro; (*interrupt talk*) intromettersi a sproposito; **to ~ into** *vt fus* urtare contro.
bark [bɑːk] *n* (*of tree*) corteccia; (*of dog*) abbaio // *vi* abbaiare.
barley ['bɑːlɪ] *n* orzo.
barmaid ['bɑːmeɪd] *n* cameriera al banco.
barman ['bɑːmən] *n* barista *m*.
barn [bɑːn] *n* granaio.
barometer [bə'rɒmɪtə*] *n* barometro.
baron ['bærən] *n* barone *m*; **~ess** *n* baronessa.
barracks ['bærəks] *npl* caserma.
barrage ['bærɑːʒ] *n* (*MIL, dam*) sbarramento; (*fig*) fiume *m*.
barrel ['bærəl] *n* barile *m*; (*of gun*) canna.
barren ['bærən] *a* sterile; (*soil*) arido(a).
barricade [bærɪ'keɪd] *n* barricata.
barrier ['bærɪə*] *n* barriera.
barring ['bɑːrɪŋ] *prep* salvo.
barrister ['bærɪstə*] *n* (*Brit*) avvocato/essa (*con diritto di parlare davanti a tutte le corti*).
barrow ['bærəu] *n* (*cart*) carriola.
bartender ['bɑːtɛndə*] *n* (*US*) barista *m*.
barter ['bɑːtə*] *n* baratto // *vt*: **to ~ sth for** barattare qc con.
base [beɪs] *n* base *f* // *vt*: **to ~ sth on** basare qc su // *a* vile.
baseball ['beɪsbɔːl] *n* baseball *m*.
basement ['beɪsmənt] *n* seminterrato; (*of shop*) interrato.
bases ['beɪsiːz] *npl of* **basis**; ['beɪsɪz] *npl of* **base**.
bash [bæʃ] *vt* (*col*) picchiare.
bashful ['bæʃful] *a* timido(a).
basic ['beɪsɪk] *a* rudimentale; essenziale; **~ally** [-lɪ] *ad* fondamentalmente; sostanzialmente.
basil ['bæzl] *n* basilico.
basin ['beɪsn] *n* (*vessel, also GEO*) bacino; (*also:* **wash~**) lavabo.
basis, *pl* **bases** ['beɪsɪs, -siːz] *n* base *f*.
bask [bɑːsk] *vi*: **to ~ in the sun** crogiolarsi al sole.
basket ['bɑːskɪt] *n* cesta; (*smaller*) cestino; (*with handle*) paniere *m*; **~ball** *n* pallacanestro *f*.
bass [beɪs] *n* (*MUS*) basso.
bassoon [bə'suːn] *n* fagotto.
bastard ['bɑːstəd] *n* bastardo/a; (*col!*) stronzo (*!*).
bat [bæt] *n* pipistrello; (*for baseball etc*) mazza; (*Brit: for table tennis*) racchetta // *vt*: he didn't ~ an eyelid non batté ciglio.
batch [bætʃ] *n* (*of bread*) infornata; (*of papers*) cumulo.
bated ['beɪtɪd] *a*: with ~ breath col fiato sospeso.
bath [bɑːθ, *pl* bɑːðz] *n* (*see also* **baths**)

bagno; (*bathtub*) vasca da bagno // *vt* far fare il bagno a; **to have a ~** fare un bagno.

bathe [beɪð] *vi* fare il bagno // *vt* bagnare.

bathing ['beɪðɪŋ] *n* bagni *mpl*; **~ cap** *n* cuffia da bagno; **~ costume**, (*US*) **~ suit** *n* costume *m* da bagno.

bath: **~robe** *n* accappatoio; **~room** *n* stanza da bagno.

baths [bɑːðz] *npl* bagni *mpl* pubblici.

bath towel *n* asciugamano da bagno.

baton ['bætən] *n* (*MUS*) bacchetta; (*club*) manganello.

batter ['bætə*] *vt* battere // *n* pastetta; **~ed** *a* (*hat*) sformato(a); (*pan*) ammaccato(a).

battery ['bætərɪ] *n* batteria; (*of torch*) pila.

battle ['bætl] *n* battaglia // *vi* battagliare, lottare; **~field** *n* campo di battaglia; **~ship** *n* nave *f* da guerra.

bawdy ['bɔːdɪ] *a* piccante.

bawl [bɔːl] *vi* urlare.

bay [beɪ] *n* (*of sea*) baia; **to hold sb at ~** tenere qn a bada.

bay window *n* bovindo.

bazaar [bəˈzɑː*] *n* bazar *m inv*; vendita di beneficenza.

b. & b., **B. & B.** *abbr* = **bed and breakfast.**

BBC *n abbr* (= *British Broadcasting Corporation*) rete nazionale di radio-televisione in Gran Bretagna.

B.C. *ad abbr* (= *before Christ*) a.C.

be [biː], *pt* **was, were**, *pp* **been** ◆ *auxiliary vb* **1** (*with present participle*): *forming continuous tenses*): **what are you doing?** che fa?, che sta facendo?; **they're coming tomorrow** vengono domani; **I've been waiting for her for hours** sono ore che l'aspetto

2 (*with pp: forming passives*) essere; **to ~ killed** essere *or* venire ucciso(a); **the box had been opened** la scatola era stata aperta; **the thief was nowhere to ~ seen** il ladro non si trovava da nessuna parte

3 (*in tag questions*): **it was fun, wasn't it?** è stato divertente, no?; **he's good-looking, isn't he?** è un bell'uomo, vero?; **she's back, is she?** così è tornata, eh?

4 (+ *to* + *infinitive*): **the house is to ~ sold** abbiamo (*or* hanno *etc*) intenzione di vendere casa; **you're to ~ congratulated for all your work** dovremo farvi i complimenti per tutto il vostro lavoro; **he's not to open it** non deve aprirlo

◆ *vb* + *complement* **1** (*gen*) essere; **I'm English** sono inglese; **I'm tired** sono stanco(a); **I'm hot/cold** ho caldo/freddo; **he's a doctor** è medico; **2 and 2 are 4** 2 più 2 fa 4; **~ careful!** sta attento(a)!; **~ good** sii buono(a)

2 (*of health*) stare; **how are you?** come

sta?; **he's very ill** sta molto male

3 (*of age*): **how old are you?** quanti anni hai?; **I'm sixteen (years old)** ho sedici anni

4 (*cost*) costare; **how much was the meal?** quant'era *or* quanto costava il pranzo?; **that'll ~ £5, please** (fa) 5 sterline, per favore

◆ *vi* **1** (*exist, occur etc*) essere, esistere; **the best singer that ever was** il migliore cantante mai esistito *or* di tutti tempi; **~ that as it may** comunque sia, sia come sia; **so ~ it** sia pure, e sia

2 (*referring to place*) essere, trovarsi; **I won't ~ here tomorrow** non ci sarò domani; **Edinburgh is in Scotland** Edimburgo si trova in Scozia

3 (*referring to movement*): **where have you been?** dov'è stato?; **I've been to China** sono stato in Cina

◆ *impersonal vb* **1** (*referring to time, distance*) essere; **it's 5 o'clock** sono le 5; **it's the 28th of April** è il 28 aprile; **it's 10 km to the village** di qui al paese sono 10 km

2 (*referring to the weather*) fare; **it's too hot/cold** fa troppo caldo/freddo; **it's windy** c'è vento

3 (*emphatic*): **it's me** sono io; **it was Maria who paid the bill** è stata Maria che ha pagato il conto.

beach [biːtʃ] *n* spiaggia // *vt* tirare in secco.

beacon ['biːkən] *n* (*lighthouse*) faro; (*marker*) segnale *m*.

bead [biːd] *n* perlina.

beak [biːk] *n* becco.

beaker ['biːkə*] *n* coppa.

beam [biːm] *n* trave *f*; (*of light*) raggio // *vi* brillare.

bean [biːn] *n* fagiolo; (*of coffee*) chicco; **runner ~** fagiolino; **broad ~** fava; **~sprouts** *npl* germogli *mpl* di soia.

bear [bɛə*] *n* orso // *vb* (*pt* **bore**, *pp* **borne**) *vt* portare; (*endure*) sopportare // *vi*: **to ~ right/left** piegare a destra/sinistra; **to ~ out** *vt* (*suspicions*) confermare, convalidare; (*person*) dare il proprio appoggio a; **to ~ up** *vi* (*person*) fare buon viso a cattiva sorte.

beard [bɪəd] *n* barba.

bearer ['bɛərə*] *n* portatore *m*.

bearing ['bɛərɪŋ] *n* portamento; (*connection*) rapporto; **~s** *npl* (*also*: **ball ~s**) cuscinetti *mpl* a sfere; **to take a ~** fare un rilevamento; **to find one's ~s** orientarsi.

beast [biːst] *n* bestia; **~ly** *a* meschino(a); (*weather*) da cani.

beat [biːt] *n* colpo; (*of heart*) battito; (*MUS*) tempo; (*of policeman*) giro // *vt* (*pt* **beat**, *pp* **beaten**) battere; **off the ~en track** fuori mano; **to ~ time** battere il tempo; **~ it!** (*col*) fila!, fuori dai piedi!; **to ~ off** *vt* respingere; **to ~**

up *vt* (*col: person*) picchiare; (*eggs*) sbattere; ~**ing** *n* bastonata.

beautiful ['bju:tɪful] *a* bello(a); ~**ly** *ad* splendidamente.

beauty ['bju:tɪ] *n* bellezza; ~ **salon** *n* istituto di bellezza; ~ **spot** *n* neo; (*Brit: TOURISM*) luogo pittoresco.

beaver ['bi:və*] *n* castoro.

became [bɪ'keɪm] *pt of* **become**.

because [bɪ'kɔz] *cj* perché; ~ **of** *prep* a causa di.

beck [bɛk] *n*: to be at sb's ~ and call essere a completa disposizione di qn.

beckon ['bɛkən] *vt* (*also:* ~ to) chiamare con un cenno.

become [bɪ'kʌm] *vt* (*irg: like* come) diventare; to ~ fat/thin ingrassarsi/ dimagrire; what has ~ of him? che gli è successo?

becoming [bɪ'kʌmɪŋ] *a* (*behaviour*) che si conviene; (*clothes*) grazioso(a).

bed [bɛd] *n* letto; (*of flowers*) aiuola; (*of coal, clay*) strato; **single/double** ~ letto a una piazza/a due piazze *or* matrimoniale; ~ **and breakfast** (**b. & b.**) *n* (*place*) ≈ pensione *f* familiare; (*terms*) camera con colazione; ~**clothes** *npl* biancheria e coperte *fpl* da letto; ~**ding** *n* coperte e lenzuola *fpl*.

bedlam ['bɛdləm] *n* baraonda.

bedraggled [bɪ'drægld] *a* fradicio(a).

bed: ~**ridden** *a* costretto(a) a letto; ~**room** *n* camera da letto; ~**side** *n*: at sb's ~side al capezzale di qn; ~**sit(ter)** *n* (*Brit*) monolocale *m*; ~**spread** *n* copriletto; ~**time** *n*: it's ~time è ora di andare a letto.

bee [bi:] *n* ape *f*.

beech [bi:tʃ] *n* faggio.

beef [bi:f] *n* manzo; **roast** ~ arrosto di manzo; ~**burger** *n* hamburger *m inv*; ~**eater** *n* guardia della Torre di Londra.

beehive ['bi:haɪv] *n* alveare *m*.

beeline ['bi:laɪn] *n*: to make a ~ for buttarsi a capo fitto verso.

been [bi:n] *pp of* **be**.

beer [bɪə*] *n* birra.

beetle ['bi:tl] *n* scarafaggio; coleottero.

beetroot ['bi:tru:t] *n* (*Brit*) barbabietola.

before [bɪ'fɔ:*] *prep* (*in time*) prima di; (*in space*) davanti a // *cj* prima che + *sub*; prima di // *ad* prima; ~ **going** prima di andare; ~ **she goes** prima che vada; **the week** ~ la settimana prima; I've seen it ~ l'ho già visto; I've never seen it ~ è la prima volta che lo vedo; ~**hand** *ad* in anticipo.

beg [bɛg] *vi* chiedere l'elemosina // *vt* chiedere in elemosina; (*favour*) chiedere; (*entreat*) pregare.

began [bɪ'gæn] *pt of* **begin**.

beggar ['bɛgə*] *n* mendicante *m/f*.

begin [bɪ'gɪn], *pt* **began**, *pp* **begun** *vt*, *vi* cominciare; to ~ **doing** *or* to do sth incominciare *or* iniziare a fare qc; ~**ner**

n principiante *m/f*; ~**ning** *n* inizio, principio.

begun [bɪ'gʌn] *pp of* **begin**.

behalf [bɪ'ha:f] *n*: on ~ of per conto di; a nome di.

behave [bɪ'heɪv] *vi* comportarsi; (*well: also:* ~ o.s.) comportarsi bene.

behaviour, (*US*) **behavior** [bɪ'heɪvjə*] *n* comportamento, condotta.

behead [bɪ'hɛd] *vt* decapitare.

beheld [bɪ'hɛld] *pt, pp of* **behold**.

behind [bɪ'haɪnd] *prep* dietro; (*followed by pronoun*) dietro di; (*time*) in ritardo con // *ad* dietro; in ritardo // *n* didietro; to be ~ (*schedule*) essere in ritardo rispetto al programma; ~ **the scenes** (*fig*) dietro le quinte.

behold [bɪ'həʊld] *vt* (*irg: like* hold) vedere, scorgere.

beige [beɪʒ] *a* beige *inv*.

being ['bi:ɪŋ] *n* essere *m*; to come into ~ cominciare ad esistere.

belated [bɪ'leɪtɪd] *a* tardo(a).

belch [bɛltʃ] *vi* ruttare // *vt* (*gen:* ~ out: *smoke etc*) eruttare.

belfry ['bɛlfrɪ] *n* campanile *m*.

Belgian ['bɛldʒən] *a, n* belga (*m/f*).

Belgium ['bɛldʒəm] *n* Belgio.

belie [bɪ'laɪ] *vt* smentire.

belief [bɪ'li:f] *n* (*opinion*) opinione *f*, convinzione *f*; (*trust, faith*) fede *f*; (*acceptance as true*) credenza.

believe [bɪ'li:v] *vt, vi* credere; to ~ in (*God*) credere in; (*ghosts*) credere a; (*method*) avere fiducia in; ~**r** *n* (*REL*) credente *m/f*; (*in idea, activity*): to be a ~r in credere in.

belittle [bɪ'lɪtl] *vt* sminuire.

bell [bɛl] *n* campana; (*small, on door, electric*) campanello.

bellow ['bɛləʊ] *vi* muggire.

bellows ['bɛləʊz] *npl* soffietto.

belly ['bɛlɪ] *n* pancia.

belong [bɪ'lɒŋ] *vi*: to ~ to appartenere a; (*club etc*) essere socio di; **this book** ~**s here** questo libro va qui; ~**ings** *npl* cose *fpl*, roba.

beloved [bɪ'lʌvɪd] *a* adorato(a).

below [bɪ'ləʊ] *prep* sotto, al di sotto di // *ad* sotto, di sotto; giù; **see** ~ vedi sotto *or* oltre.

belt [bɛlt] *n* cintura; (*TECH*) cinghia // *vt* (*thrash*) picchiare // *vi* (*col*) filarsela; ~**way** *n* (*US AUT*: ring road) circonvallazione *f*; (: *motorway*) autostrada.

bemused [bɪ'mju:zd] *a* perplesso(a), stupito(a).

bench [bɛntʃ] *n* panca; (*in workshop*) banco; **the B~** (*LAW*) la Corte.

bend [bɛnd] *vb* (*pt, pp* **bent**) *vt* curvare; (*leg, arm*) piegare // *vi* curvarsi; piegarsi // *n* (*Brit: in road*) curva; (*in pipe, river*) gomito; **to** ~ **down** *vi* chinarsi; **to** ~ **over** *vi* piegarsi.

beneath [bɪ'ni:θ] *prep* sotto, al di sotto di; (*unworthy of*) indegno(a) di // *ad* sotto, di sotto.

benefactor ['bɛnɪfæktə*] *n* benefattore *m*.

beneficial [bɛnɪ'fɪʃəl] *a* che fa bene; vantaggioso(a).

benefit ['bɛnɪfɪt] *n* beneficio, vantaggio; (*allowance of money*) indennità *f inv* // *vt* far bene a // *vi*: he'll ~ from it ne trarrà beneficio *or* profitto.

benevolent [bɪ'nɛvələnt] *a* benevolo(a).

benign [bɪ'naɪn] *a* (*person, smile*) benevolo(a); (*MED*) benigno(a).

bent [bɛnt] *pt, pp of* **bend** // *n* inclinazione *f* // *a* (*col: dishonest*) losco(a); to be ~ on essere deciso(a) a.

bequest [bɪ'kwɛst] *n* lascito.

bereaved [bɪ'ri:vd] *n*: the ~ i familiari in lutto.

beret ['bɛreɪ] *n* berretto.

berm [bə:m] *n* (*US AUT*) corsia d'emergenza.

berry ['bɛrɪ] *n* bacca.

berserk [bə'sə:k] *a*: to go ~ montare su tutte le furie.

berth [bə:θ] *n* (*bed*) cuccetta; (*for ship*) ormeggio // *vi* (*in harbour*) entrare in porto; (*at anchor*) gettare l'ancora.

beseech [bɪ'si:tʃ], *pt, pp* **besought** *vt* implorare.

beset, *pt, pp* **beset** [bɪ'sɛt] *vt* assalire.

beside [bɪ'saɪd] *prep* accanto a; to be ~ o.s. (*with anger*) essere fuori di sé; that's ~ the point non c'entra.

besides [bɪ'saɪdz] *ad* inoltre, per di più // *prep* oltre a; a parte.

besiege [bɪ'si:dʒ] *vt* (*town*) assediare; (*fig*) tempestare.

besought [bɪ'sɔːt] *pt, pp of* **beseech**.

best [bɛst] *a* migliore // *ad* meglio; the ~ part of (*quantity*) la maggior parte di; at ~ tutt'al più; to make the ~ of sth cavare il meglio possibile da qc; to do one's ~ fare del proprio meglio; to the ~ of my knowledge per quel che ne so; to the ~ of my ability al massimo delle mie capacità; ~ **man** *n* testimone *m* dello sposo.

bestow [bɪ'stəu] *vt* accordare; (*title*) conferire.

bet [bɛt] *n* scommessa // *vt, vi* (*pt, pp* **bet** *or* **betted**) scommettere.

betray [bɪ'treɪ] *vt* tradire; ~**al** *n* tradimento.

better ['bɛtə*] *a* migliore // *ad* meglio // *vt* migliorare // *n*: to get the ~ of avere la meglio su; you had ~ do it è meglio che lo faccia; he thought ~ of it cambiò idea; to get ~ migliorare; ~ **off** *a* più ricco(a); (*fig*): you'd be ~ off this way starebbe meglio così.

betting ['bɛtɪŋ] *n* scommesse *fpl*; ~ **shop** *n* (*Brit*) ufficio dell'allibratore.

between [bɪ'twi:n] *prep* tra // *ad* in mezzo, nel mezzo.

beverage ['bɛvərɪdʒ] *n* bevanda.

bevy ['bɛvɪ] *n* banda.

beware [bɪ'wɛə*] *vt, vi*: to ~ (of) stare attento(a) (a).

bewildered [bɪ'wɪldəd] *a* sconcertato(a), confuso(a).

bewitching [bɪ'wɪtʃɪŋ] *a* affascinante.

beyond [bɪ'jɔnd] *prep* (*in space*) oltre; (*exceeding*) al di sopra di // *ad* di là; ~ doubt senza dubbio.

bias ['baɪəs] *n* (*prejudice*) pregiudizio; (*preference*) preferenza; ~**(s)ed** *a* parziale.

bib [bɪb] *n* bavaglino.

Bible ['baɪbl] *n* Bibbia.

bicarbonate of soda [baɪ'kɑːbənɪt-] *n* bicarbonato (di sodio).

bicker ['bɪkə*] *vi* bisticciare.

bicycle ['baɪsɪkl] *n* bicicletta.

bid [bɪd] *n* offerta; (*attempt*) tentativo // *vb* (*pt* **bade** [bæd] *or* **bid**, *pp* **bidden** ['bɪdn] *or* **bid**) *vi* fare un'offerta // *vt* fare un'offerta di; to ~ sb good day dire buon giorno a qn; ~**der** *n*: the highest ~**der** il maggior offerente; ~**ding** *n* offerte *fpl*.

bide [baɪd] *vt*: to ~ one's time aspettare il momento giusto.

bier [bɪə*] *n* bara.

bifocals [baɪ'fəuklz] *npl* occhiali *mpl* bifocali.

big [bɪg] *a* grande; grosso(a).

big dipper [-'dɪpə*] *n* montagne *fpl* russe, otto *m inv* volante.

bigheaded ['bɪg'hɛdɪd] *a* presuntuoso(a).

bigot ['bɪgət] *n* persona gretta; ~**ed** *a* gretto(a); ~**ry** *n* grettezza.

big top *n* tendone *m* del circo.

bike [baɪk] *n* bici *f inv*.

bikini [bɪ'ki:nɪ] *n* bikini *m inv*.

bilingual [baɪ'lɪŋgwəl] *a* bilingue.

bill [bɪl] *n* conto; (*POL*) atto; (*US: banknote*) banconota; (*of bird*) becco; "post no ~s" "divieto di affissione"; to fit *or* fill the ~ (*fig*) fare al caso; ~**board** *n* tabellone *m*.

billet ['bɪlɪt] *n* alloggio.

billfold ['bɪlfəuld] *n* (*US*) portafoglio.

billiards ['bɪljədz] *n* biliardo.

billion ['bɪljən] *n* (*Brit*) bilione *m*; (*US*) miliardo.

bin [bɪn] *n* (*for coal, rubbish*) bidone *m*; (*for bread*) cassetta; (*dust*~) pattumiera; (*litter* ~) cestino.

bind [baɪnd], *pt, pp* **bound** *vt* legare; (*oblige*) obbligare; ~**ing** *n* (*of book*) legatura // *a* (*contract*) vincolante.

binge [bɪndʒ] *n* (*col*): to go on a ~ fare baldoria.

bingo ['bɪŋgəu] *n* gioco simile alla tombola.

binoculars [bɪ'nɔkjuləz] *npl* binocolo.

bio... [baɪə'...] *prefix*: ~**chemistry** *n* biochimica; ~**graphy** [baɪ'ɔgrəfɪ] *n* bio-

grafia; **~logical** a biologico(a); **~logy**
[baɪˈɔlɔdʒɪ] n biologia.

birch [bəːtʃ] n betulla.

bird [bəːd] n uccello; (Brit: col: girl)
bambola; **~'s eye view** n vista
panoramica; **~ watcher** n ornitologo/a
dilettante.

Biro [ˈbaɪrəu] ® biro f inv ®.

birth [bəːθ] n nascita; **~ certificate** n
certificato di nascita; **~ control** n controllo delle nascite; contraccezione f;
~day n compleanno; **~ rate** n indice m
di natalità.

biscuit [ˈbɪskɪt] n (Brit) biscotto.

bisect [baɪˈsɛkt] vt tagliare in due
(parti).

bishop [ˈbɪʃəp] n vescovo.

bit [bɪt] pt of **bite** // n pezzo; (of tool)
punta; (COMPUT) bit m inv; (of horse)
morso; a **~ of** un po' di; a **~ mad** un po'
matto; **~ by** ~ a poco a poco.

bitch [bɪtʃ] n (dog) cagna; (col!) vacca.

bite [baɪt] vt, vi (pt bit [bɪt], pp bitten
[ˈbɪtn] mordere // n morso; (insect ~)
puntura; (mouthful) boccone m; let's
have a ~ (to eat) mangiamo un
boccone; to ~ one's nails mangiarsi le
unghie.

bitter [ˈbɪtə*] a amaro(a); (wind,
criticism) pungente // n (Brit: beer)
birra amara; **~ness** n amarezza; gusto
amaro.

blab [blæb] vi parlare troppo.

black [blæk] a nero(a) // n nero;
(person): B~ negro/a // vt (Brit IN-
DUSTRY) boicottare; to give sb a ~ eye
fare un occhio nero a qn; in the ~ (bank
account) in attivo; ~ **and blue** a
tutto(a) pesto(a); **~berry** n mora;
~bird n merlo; **~board** n lavagna;
~currant n ribes m inv; **~en** vt
annerire; ~ **ice** n strato trasparente di
ghiaccio; **~leg** n (Brit) crumiro; **~list**
n lista nera; **~mail** n ricatto // vt
ricattare; ~ **market** n mercato nero;
~out n oscuramento; (fainting)
svenimento; the **B~ Sea** n il Mar
Nero; ~ **sheep** n pecora nera; **~smith**
n fabbro ferraio; ~ **spot** n (AUT) luogo
famigerato per gli incidenti; (for unemployment etc) zona critica.

bladder [ˈblædə*] n vescica.

blade [bleɪd] n lama; (of oar) pala; ~ of
grass filo d'erba.

blame [bleɪm] n colpa // vt: to ~ sb/sth
for sth dare la colpa di qc a qn/qc; who's
to ~? chi è colpevole?

bland [blænd] a mite; (taste) blando(a).

blank [blæŋk] a bianco(a); (look) di-
stratto(a) // n spazio vuoto; (cartridge)
cartuccia a salve; ~ **cheque** n assegno
in bianco.

blanket [ˈblæŋkɪt] n coperta.

blare [blɛə*] vi strombettare.

blasphemy [ˈblæsfɪmɪ] n bestemmia.

blast [blɑːst] n raffica di vento;
esplosione f // vt far saltare; **~-off** n
(SPACE) lancio.

blatant [ˈbleɪtənt] a flagrante.

blaze [bleɪz] n (fire) incendio; (fig)
vampata // vi (fire) ardere,
fiammeggiare; (fig) infiammarsi // vt: to
~ a trail (fig) tracciare una via nuova.

blazer [ˈbleɪzə*] n blazer m inv.

bleach [bliːtʃ] n (also: household ~)
varechina // vt (material) candeggiare;
~ed a (hair) decolorato(a); **~ers** npl
(US SPORT) posti mpl di gradinata.

bleak [bliːk] a tetro(a).

bleary-eyed [ˈblɪərɪˈaɪd] a dagli occhi
offuscati.

bleat [bliːt] vi belare.

bleed, pt, pp bled [bliːd, blɛd] vt
dissanguare // vi sanguinare; my nose is
~ing mi viene fuori sangue dal naso.

bleeper [ˈbliːpə*] n (device) cicalino.

blemish [ˈblɛmɪʃ] n macchia.

blend [blɛnd] n miscela // vt mescolare //
vi (colours etc) armonizzare.

bless, pt, pp blessed or blest [blɛs,
blɛst] vt benedire; **~ing** n benedizione f;
fortuna.

blew [bluː] pt of blow.

blight [blaɪt] n (of plants) golpe f // vt
(hopes etc) deludere; (life) rovinare.

blimey [ˈblaɪmɪ] excl (Brit col) accidenti!

blind [blaɪnd] a cieco(a) // n (for window)
avvolgibile m; (Venetian ~) veneziana //
vt accecare; ~ **alley** n vicolo cieco; ~
corner n (Brit) svolta cieca; **~fold** n
benda // a, ad bendato(a) // vt bendare
gli occhi a; **~ly** ad ciecamente; **~ness**
n cecità; ~ **spot** n (AUT etc) punto
cieco; (fig) punto debole.

blink [blɪŋk] vi battere gli occhi; (light)
lampeggiare; **~ers** npl paraocchi mpl.

bliss [blɪs] n estasi f.

blister [ˈblɪstə*] n (on skin) vescica; (on
paintwork) bolla // vi (paint) coprirsi di
bolle.

blithely [ˈblaɪðlɪ] ad allegramente.

blizzard [ˈblɪzəd] n bufera di neve.

bloated [ˈbləutɪd] a gonfio(a).

blob [blɔb] n (drop) goccia; (stain, spot)
macchia.

bloc [blɔk] n (POL) blocco.

block [blɔk] n blocco; (in pipes) ingombro; (toy) cubo; (of buildings) isolato //
vt bloccare; **~ade** [-ˈkeɪd] n blocco // vt
assediare; **~age** n ostacolo; **~buster** n
(film, book) grande successo; ~ **of flats**
n (Brit) caseggiato; ~ **letters** npl stampatello.

bloke [bləuk] n (Brit col) tizio.

blonde [blɔnd] a, n biondo(a).

blood [blʌd] n sangue m; ~ **donor** n
donatore/trice di sangue; ~ **group** n
gruppo sanguigno; **~hound** n segugio;
~ **poisoning** n setticemia; ~ **pressure**
n pressione f sanguigna; **~shed** n

spargimento di sangue; ~**shot** *a*: ~**shot eyes** occhi iniettati di sangue; ~**stream** *n* flusso del sangue; ~ **test** *n* analisi *f* *inv* del sangue; ~**thirsty** *a* assetato(a) di sangue; ~**y** *a* sanguinoso(a); (*Brit* *col!*): **this** ~**y** ... questo maledetto ...; ~**y awful/good** (*col!*) veramente terribile/ forte; ~**y-minded** *a* (*Brit col*) indisponente.

bloom [blu:m] *n* fiore *m* // *vi* essere in fiore.

blossom ['blɔsəm] *n* fiore *m*; (*with pl sense*) fiori *mpl* // *vi* essere in fiore.

blot [blɔt] *n* macchia // *vt* macchiare; **to ~ out** *vt* (*memories*) cancellare; (*view*) nascondere; (*nation, city*) annientare.

blotchy ['blɔtʃɪ] *a* (*complexion*) coperto(a) di macchie.

blotting paper ['blɔtɪŋ-] *n* carta assorbente.

blouse [blauz] *n* (*feminine garment*) camicetta.

blow [bləʊ] *n* colpo // *vb* (*pt* **blew**, *pp* **blown** [blu:, bləʊn]) *vi* soffiare // *vt* (*fuse*) far saltare; **to ~ one's nose** soffiarsi il naso; **to ~ a whistle** fischiare; **to ~ away** *vt* portare via; **to ~ down** *vt* abbattere; **to ~ off** *vt* far volare via; **to ~ out** *vi* scoppiare; **to ~ over** *vi* calmarsi; **to ~ up** *vi* saltare in aria // *vt* far saltare in aria; (*tyre*) gonfiare; (*PHOT*) ingrandire; ~**dry** *n* messa in piega a fôhn; ~**lamp** *n* (*Brit*) lampada a benzina per saldare; ~**out** *n* (*of tyre*) scoppio; ~**torch** *n* = ~**lamp**.

blue [blu:] *a* azzurro(a); ~ **film/barzelletta** pornografico(a); **out of the ~** (*fig*) all'improvviso; **to have the** ~**s** essere depresso(a); ~**bottle** *n* moscone *m*; ~ **jeans** *npl* blue-jeans *mpl*; ~**print** *n* (*fig*): ~**print** (**for**) formula (di).

bluff [blʌf] *vi* bluffare // *n* bluff *m inv* // *a* (*person*) brusco(a); **to call sb's ~** mettere alla prova il bluff di qn.

blunder ['blʌndə*] *n* abbaglio // *vi* prendere un abbaglio.

blunt [blʌnt] *a* smussato(a); spuntato(a); (*person*) brusco(a) // *vt* smussare; spuntare.

blur [blə:*] *n* cosa offuscata // *vt* offuscare.

blurb [blə:b] *n* trafiletto pubblicitario.

blurt [blə:t]: **to ~ out** *vt* lasciarsi sfuggire.

blush [blʌʃ] *vi* arrossire // *n* rossore *m*.

blustery ['blʌstərɪ] *a* (*weather*) burrascoso(a).

boar [bɔ:*] *n* cinghiale *m*.

board [bɔ:d] *n* tavola; (*on wall*) tabellone *m*; (*committee*) consiglio, comitato; (*in firm*) consiglio d'amministrazione // *vt* (*ship*) salire a bordo di; (*train*) salire su; (*NAUT, AVIAT*): **on ~ a** bordo; **full ~** (*Brit*) pensione completa;

half ~ (*Brit*) mezza pensione; ~ **and lodging** vitto e alloggio; **which goes by the ~** (*fig*) che viene abbandonato; **to ~ up** *vt* (*door*) chiudere con assi; ~**er** *n* pensionante *m/f*; (*SCOL*) convittore/trice; ~**ing card** *n* (*AVIAT, NAUT*) carta d'imbarco; ~**ing house** *n* pensione *f*; ~**ing school** *n* collegio; ~ **room** *n* sala del consiglio.

boast [bəʊst] *vi*: **to ~ (about *or* of)** vantarsi (di) // *vt* vantare // *n* vanteria; vanto.

boat [bəʊt] *n* nave *f*; (*small*) barca; ~**er** *n* (*hat*) paglietta; ~**swain** ['bəʊsn] *n* nostromo.

bob [bɔb] *vi* (*boat, cork on water: also:* ~ **up and down**) andare su e giù // *n* (*Brit col*) = **shilling**; **to ~ up** *vi* saltare fuori.

bobby ['bɔbɪ] *n* (*Brit col*) poliziotto.

bobsleigh ['bɔbsleɪ] *n* bob *m inv*.

bode [bəʊd] *vi*: **to ~ well/ill (for)** essere di buon/cattivo auspicio (per).

bodily ['bɔdɪlɪ] *a* fisico(a), corporale // *ad* corporalmente; interamente; in persona.

body ['bɔdɪ] *n* corpo; (*of car*) carrozzeria; (*of plane*) fusoliera; (*fig: quantity*) quantità *f inv*; **a wine with** ~ un vino corposo; ~**-building** *n* culturismo; ~**guard** *n* guardia del corpo; ~**work** *n* carrozzeria.

bog [bɔg] *n* palude *f* // *vt*: **to get ~ged down** (*fig*) impantanarsi.

boggle ['bɔgl] *vi*: **the mind ~s** è incredibile.

bogus ['bəʊgəs] *a* falso(a); finto(a).

boil [bɔɪl] *vt*, *vi* bollire // *n* (*MED*) foruncolo; **to come to the** (*Brit*) *or* a (*US*) ~ raggiungere l'ebollizione; **to ~ down** *vi* (*fig*): **to ~ down to** ridursi a; **to ~ over** *vi* traboccare (bollendo); ~**ed egg** *n* uovo alla coque; ~**ed potatoes** *npl* patate *fpl* bollite *or* lesse; ~**er** *n* caldaia; ~**er suit** *n* (*Brit*) tuta; ~**ing point** *n* punto di ebollizione.

boisterous ['bɔɪstərəs] *a* chiassoso(a).

bold [bəʊld] *a* audace; (*child*) impudente; (*outline*) chiaro(a); (*colour*) deciso(a).

bollard ['bɔləd] *n* (*Brit AUT*) colonnina luminosa.

bolster ['bəʊlstə*] *n* capezzale *m*; **to ~ up** *vt* sostenere.

bolt [bəʊlt] *n* chiavistello; (*with nut*) bullone *m* // *ad*: ~ **upright** diritto(a) come un fuso // *vt* serrare; (*food*) mangiare in fretta // *vi* scappare via.

bomb [bɔm] *n* bomba // *vt* bombardare; ~ **disposal unit** *n* corpo degli artificieri; ~**er** *n* (*AVIAT*) bombardiere *m*; ~**shell** *n* (*fig*) notizia bomba.

bona fide ['bəʊnə'faɪdɪ] *a* sincero(a); (*offer*) onesto(a).

bond [bɔnd] *n* legame *m*; (*binding*

promise, FINANCE) obbligazione *f;* (COMM): in ~ in attesa di sdoganamento.

bondage ['bɔndɪdʒ] *n* schiavitù *f.*

bone [bəun] *n* osso; (*of fish*) spina, lisca // *vt* disossare; togliere le spine a; ~ **idle,** ~ **lazy** *a* pigrissimo(a).

bonfire ['bɔnfaɪə*] *n* falò *m inv.*

bonnet ['bɔnɪt] *n* cuffia; (*Brit: of car*) cofano.

bonus ['bəunəs] *n* premio.

bony ['bəunɪ] *a* (*arm, face,* MED: *tissue*) osseo(a); (*meat*) pieno(a) di ossi; (*fish*) pieno(a) di spine.

boo [bu:] *excl* ba! // *vt* fischiare // *n* fischio.

booby trap ['bu:bɪ-] *n* trappola.

book [buk] *n* libro; (*of stamps etc*) blocchetto // *vt* (*ticket, seat, room*) prenotare; (*driver*) multare; (*football player*) ammonire; ~**s** *npl* (COMM) conti *mpl*; ~**case** *n* scaffale *m*; ~**ing office** *n* (*Brit* RAIL) biglietteria; (: THEATRE) botteghino; ~-**keeping** *n* contabilità; ~**let** *n* libricino; ~**maker** *n* allibratore *m*; ~**seller** *n* libraio; ~**shop,** ~ **store** *n* libreria.

boom [bu:m] *n* (*noise*) rimbombo; (*busy period*) boom *m inv* // *vi* rimbombare; andare a gonfie vele.

boon [bu:n] *n* vantaggio.

boost [bu:st] *n* spinta // *vt* spingere; ~**er** *n* (MED) richiamo.

boot [bu:t] *n* stivale *m*; (*for hiking*) scarpone *m* da montagna; (*for football etc*) scarpa; (*Brit: of car*) portabagagli *m inv* // *vt* (COMPUT) inizializzare; to ~ (*in addition*) per giunta, in più.

booth [bu:ð] *n* (*at fair*) baraccone *m*; (*of cinema, telephone, voting* ~) cabina.

booty ['bu:tɪ] *n* bottino.

booze [bu:z] *n* (*col*) alcool *m.*

border ['bɔ:də*] *n* orlo; margine *m*; (*of a country*) frontiera; the B~**s** la zona di confine tra l'Inghilterra e la Scozia; to ~ **on** *vt fus* confinare con; ~**line** *n* (*fig*) linea di demarcazione; ~**line case** *n* caso limite.

bore [bɔ:*] *pt of* **bear** // *vt* (*hole*) perforare; (*person*) annoiare // *n* (*person*) seccatore/trice; (*of gun*) calibro; to be ~**d** annoiarsi; ~**dom** *n* noia; **boring** *a* noioso(a).

born [bɔ:n] *a*: to be ~ nascere; I was ~ in 1960 sono nato nel 1960.

borne [bɔ:n] *pp of* **bear.**

borough ['bʌrə] *n* comune *m.*

borrow ['bɔrəu] *vt*: to ~ **sth** (**from sb**) prendere in prestito qc (da qn).

bosom ['buzəm] *n* petto; (*fig*) seno.

boss [bɔs] *n* capo // *vt* comandare; ~**y** *a* prepotente.

bosun ['bəusn] *n* nostromo.

botany ['bɔtənɪ] *n* botanica.

botch [bɔtʃ] *vt* (*also:* ~ **up**) fare un pa-

sticcio di.

both [bəuθ] *a* entrambi(e), tutt'e due // *pronoun*: ~ (**of them**) entrambi(e); ~ **of us went,** we ~ went ci siamo andati tutt'e due // *ad*: they sell ~ **meat and poultry** vendono insieme la carne ed il pollame.

bother ['bɔðə*] *vt* (*worry*) preoccupare; (*annoy*) infastidire // *vi* (*gen*: ~ o.s.) preoccuparsi // *n*: it is a ~ to have to do è una seccatura dover fare; it was no ~ non c'era problema; to ~ **doing sth** darsi la pena di fare qc.

bottle ['bɔtl] *n* bottiglia; (*baby's*) biberon *m inv* // *vt* imbottigliare; **to** ~ **up** *vt* contenere; ~**neck** *n* ingorgo; ~-**opener** *n* apribottiglie *m inv.*

bottom ['bɔtəm] *n* fondo; (*buttocks*) sedere *m* // *a* più basso(a); ultimo(a); **at the** ~ **of** in fondo a.

bough [bau] *n* ramo.

bought [bɔ:t] *pt, pp of* **buy.**

boulder ['bəuldə*] *n* masso (tondeggiante).

bounce [bauns] *vi* (*ball*) rimbalzare; (*cheque*) essere restituito(a) // *vt* far rimbalzare // *n* (*rebound*) rimbalzo; ~**r** *n* (*col*) buttafuori *m inv.*

bound [baund] *pt, pp of* **bind** // *n* (*gen pl*) limite *m*; (*leap*) salto // *vt* (*leap*) saltare; (*limit*) delimitare // *a*: to be ~ to do sth (*obliged*) essere costretto(a) a fare qc; he's ~ to fail (*likely*) è certo di fallire; ~ **for** diretto(a) a; **out of** ~**s** il cui accesso è vietato.

boundary ['baundrɪ] *n* confine *m.*

bourgeois ['buəʒwɑ:] *a, n* borghese (*m/f*).

bout [baut] *n* periodo; (*of malaria etc*) attacco; (BOXING *etc*) incontro.

bow *n* [bəu] nodo; (*weapon*) arco; (MUS) archetto; [bau] (*with body*) inchino; (NAUT: *also:* ~**s**) prua // *vi* [bau] inchinarsi; (*yield*): to ~ to *or* before sottomettersi a.

bowels ['bauəlz] *npl* intestini *mpl*; (*fig*) viscere *fpl.*

bowl [bəul] *n* (*for eating*) scodella; (*for washing*) bacino; (*ball*) boccia; (*of pipe*) fornello // *vi* (CRICKET) servire (la palla); ~**s** *n* gioco delle bocce.

bow-legged ['bəu'lɛgɪd] *a* dalle gambe storte.

bowler ['bəulə*] *n* giocatore *m* di bocce; (CRICKET) giocatore che serve la palla; (*Brit: also:* ~ **hat**) bombetta.

bowling ['bəulɪŋ] *n* (*game*) gioco delle bocce; ~ **alley** *n* pista da bowling; ~ **green** *n* campo di bocce.

bow tie *n* cravatta a farfalla.

box [bɔks] *n* scatola; (*also:* **cardboard** ~) cartone *m*; (THEATRE) palco // *vi* fare del pugilato; ~**er** *n* (*person*) pugile *m*; ~**ing** *n* (SPORT) pugilato; **B~ing Day** *n* (*Brit*) Santo Stefano; ~**ing gloves** *npl* guantoni *mpl* da pugile; **~ing ring** *n* ring *m inv*; **~ office** *n* biglietteria; **~ room** *n* ripostiglio.

boy [bɔɪ] *n* ragazzo.

boycott ['bɔɪkɔt] *n* boicottaggio // *vt* boicottare.

boyfriend ['bɔɪfrɛnd] *n* ragazzo.

B.R. *abbr* = **British Rail**.

bra [brɑ:] *n* reggipetto, reggiseno.

brace [breɪs] *n* sostegno; (*on teeth*) apparecchio correttore; (*tool*) trapano // *vt* rinforzare, sostenere; **~s** *npl* (*Brit*) bretelle *fpl*; **to ~ o.s.** (*fig*) farsi coraggio.

bracelet ['breɪslɪt] *n* braccialetto.

bracing ['breɪsɪŋ] *a* invigorante.

bracken ['brækən] *n* felce *f*.

bracket ['brækɪt] *n* (*TECH*) mensola; (*group*) gruppo; (*TYP*) parentesi *f inv* // *vt* mettere fra parentesi.

brag [bræg] *vi* vantarsi.

braid [breɪd] *n* (*trimming*) passamano; (*of hair*) treccia.

brain [breɪn] *n* cervello; **~s** *npl* cervella *fpl*; **he's got ~s** è intelligente; **~child** *n* creatura, creazione *f*; **~wash** *vt* fare un lavaggio di cervello a; **~wave** *n* lampo di genio; **~y** *a* intelligente.

braise [breɪz] *vt* brasare.

brake [breɪk] *n* (*on vehicle*) freno // *vt, vi* frenare; **~ fluid** *n* liquido dei freni; **~ light** *n* (fanalino dello) stop *m inv*.

bramble ['bræmbl] *n* rovo.

bran [bræn] *n* crusca.

branch [brɑ:ntʃ] *n* ramo; (*COMM*) succursale *f* // *vi* diramarsi.

brand [brænd] *n* marca // *vt* (*cattle*) marcare (a ferro rovente).

brand-new ['brænd'nju:] *a* nuovo(a) di zecca.

brandy ['brændɪ] *n* brandy *m inv*.

brash [bræʃ] *a* sfacciato(a).

brass [brɑ:s] *n* ottone *m*; **the ~** (*MUS*) gli ottoni; **~ band** *n* fanfara.

brassière ['bræsɪə*] *n* reggipetto, reggiseno.

brat [bræt] *n* (*pej*) marmocchio, monello/a.

bravado [brə'vɑ:dəu] *n* spavalderia.

brave [breɪv] *a* coraggioso(a) // *n* guerriero *m* pelle rossa *inv* // *vt* affrontare; **~ry** *n* coraggio.

brawl [brɔ:l] *n* rissa.

brawn [brɔ:n] *n* muscolo; (*meat*) carne *f* di testa di maiale.

bray [breɪ] *vi* ragliare.

brazen ['breɪzn] *a* svergognato(a) // *vt*: **to ~ it out** fare lo sfacciato.

brazier ['breɪzɪə*] *n* braciere *m*.

Brazil [brə'zɪl] *n* Brasile *m*.

breach [bri:tʃ] *vt* aprire una breccia in // *n* (*gap*) breccia, varco; (*breaking*): **~ of contract** rottura di contratto; **~ of the peace** violazione *f* dell'ordine pubblico.

bread [brɛd] *n* pane *m*; **~ and butter** *n* pane e burro; (*fig*) mezzi *mpl* di sussi-

stenza; **~bin**, (*US*) **~box** *n* cassetta *f* portapane *inv*; **~crumbs** *npl* briciole *fpl*; (*CULIN*) pangrattato; **~line** *n*: **to be on the ~line** avere appena denaro per vivere.

breadth [brɛtθ] *n* larghezza.

breadwinner ['brɛdwɪnə*] *n* chi guadagna il pane per tutta la famiglia.

break [breɪk] *vb* (*pt* **broke** [brəuk], *pp* **broken** ['brəukən]) *vt* rompere; (*law*) violare // *vi* rompersi; (*weather*) cambiare // *n* (*gap*) breccia; (*fracture*) rottura; (*rest, also SCOL*) intervallo; (: *short*) pausa; (*chance*) possibilità *f inv*; **to ~ one's leg etc** rompersi la gamba *etc*; **to ~ a record** battere un primato; **to ~ the news to sb** comunicare per prima la notizia a qn; **to ~ down** *vt* (*figures, data*) analizzare // *vi* crollare; (*MED*) avere un esaurimento (nervoso); (*AUT*) guastarsi; **to ~ even** *vi* coprire le spese; **to ~ free** *or* **loose** *vi* spezzare i legami; **to ~ in** *vt* (*horse etc*) domare // *vi* (*burglar*) fare irruzione; **to ~ into** *vt fus* (*house*) fare irruzione in; **to ~ off** *vi* (*speaker*) interrompersi; (*branch*) troncarsi; **to ~ open** *vt* (*door etc*) sfondare; **to ~ out** *vi* evadere; **to ~ out in spots** coprirsi di macchie; **to ~ up** *vi* (*partnership*) sciogliersi; (*friends*) separarsi // *vt* fare in pezzi, spaccare; (*fight etc*) interrompere, far cessare; **~age** *n* rottura; **~down** *n* (*AUT*) guasto; (*in communications*) interruzione *f*; (*MED*): *also*: **nervous ~down**) esaurimento nervoso; **~down van** *n* (*Brit*) carro *m* attrezzi *inv*; **~er** *n* frangente *m*.

breakfast ['brɛkfəst] *n* colazione *f*.

break: **~-in** *n* irruzione *f*; **~ing and entering** *n* (*LAW*) violazione *f* di domicilio con scasso; **~through** *n* (*MIL*) breccia; (*fig*) passo avanti; **~water** *n* frangiflutti *m inv*.

breast [brɛst] *n* (*of woman*) seno; (*chest*) petto; **~-feed** *vt, vi* (*irg: like* **feed**) allattare (al seno); **~-stroke** *n* nuoto a rana.

breath [brɛθ] *n* fiato; **out of ~** senza fiato.

Breathalyser ['brɛθəlaɪzə*] *n* ® (*Brit*) alcoltest *m inv*.

breathe [bri:ð] *vt, vi* respirare; **to ~ in** *vt* respirare // *vi* inspirare; **to ~ out** *vt, vi* espirare; **~r** *n* attimo di respiro; **breathing** *n* respiro, respirazione *f*.

breathless ['brɛθlɪs] *a* senza fiato.

breath-taking ['brɛθteɪkɪŋ] *a* sbalorditivo(a).

breed [bri:d] *vb* (*pt, pp* **bred** [brɛd]) *vt* allevare // *vi* riprodursi // *n* razza, varietà *f inv*; **~ing** *n* riproduzione *f*; allevamento; (*upbringing*) educazione *f*.

breeze [bri:z] *n* brezza.

breezy ['bri:zɪ] *a* arioso(a); allegro(a).

brew [bru:] vt (tea) fare un infuso di; (beer) fare; (plot) tramare // vi (tea) essere in infusione; (beer) essere in fermentazione; (fig) bollire in pentola; ~er n birraio; ~ery n fabbrica di birra.

bribe [braɪb] n bustarella // vt comprare; ~ry n corruzione f.

brick [brɪk] n mattone m; ~layer n muratore m.

bridal ['braɪdl] a nuziale.

bride [braɪd] n sposa; ~groom n sposo; ~smaid n damigella d'onore.

bridge [brɪdʒ] n ponte m; (NAUT) ponte di comando; (of nose) dorso; (CARDS, DENTISTRY) bridge m inv // vt (river) fare un ponte sopra; (gap) colmare.

bridle ['braɪdl] n briglia // vt tenere a freno; (horse) mettere la briglia a; ~ path n sentiero (per cavalli).

brief [bri:f] a breve // n (LAW) comparsa // vt dare istruzioni a; ~s npl mutande fpl; ~case n cartella; ~ing n istruzioni fpl; ~ly ad (glance) di sfuggita; (explain, say) brevemente.

bright [braɪt] a luminoso(a); (person) sveglio(a); (colour) vivace; ~en (also: ~en up) vt (room) rendere luminoso(a); ornare // vi schiarirsi; (person) rallegrarsi.

brilliance ['brɪljəns] n splendore m.

brilliant ['brɪljənt] a splendente.

brim [brɪm] n orlo.

brine [braɪn] n acqua salmastra; (CULIN) salamoia.

bring [brɪŋ], pt, pp brought vt portare; to ~ about vt causare; to ~ back vt riportare; to ~ down vt portare giù; abbattere; to ~ forward vt portare avanti; (in time) anticipare; to ~ off vt (task, plan) portare a compimento; to ~ out vt (meaning) mettere in evidenza; to ~ round vt (unconscious person) far rinvenire; to ~ up vt allevare; (question) introdurre; (food: vomit) rimettere, rigurgitare.

brink [brɪŋk] n orlo.

brisk [brɪsk] a vivace.

bristle ['brɪsl] n setola // vi rizzarsi; bristling with irto(a) di.

Britain ['brɪtən] n (also: Great ~) Gran Bretagna.

British ['brɪtɪʃ] a britannico(a); the ~ npl i Britannici; the ~ Isles npl le Isole Britanniche; ~ Rail (B.R.) n compagnia ferroviaria britannica, ≈ Ferrovie fpl dello Stato (F.S.).

Briton ['brɪtən] n britannico/a.

brittle ['brɪtl] a fragile.

broach [brəutʃ] vt (subject) affrontare.

broad [brɔ:d] a largo(a); (distinction) generale; (accent) spiccato(a); in ~ daylight in pieno giorno; ~cast n trasmissione f // vb (pt, pp ~cast) vt trasmettere per radio (or per televisione) // vi fare una trasmissione; ~en vt allargare // vi allargarsi; ~ly ad (fig) in generale; ~-minded a di mente aperta.

broccoli ['brɔkəlɪ] n broccoli mpl.

brochure ['brəuʃjuə*] n dépliant m inv.

broil [brɔɪl] vt cuocere a fuoco vivo.

broke [brəuk] pt of break // a (col) squattrinato(a).

broken ['brəukn] pp of break // a: ~ leg etc gamba etc rotta; in ~ English in un inglese stentato; ~-hearted a: to be ~ hearted avere il cuore spezzato.

broker ['brəukə*] n agente m.

brolly ['brɔlɪ] n (Brit col) ombrello.

bronchitis [brɔŋ'kaɪtɪs] n bronchite f.

bronze [brɔnz] n bronzo.

brooch [brəutʃ] n spilla.

brood [bru:d] n covata // vi (hen) covare; (person) rimuginare.

brook [bruk] n ruscello.

broom [brum] n scopa; ~stick n manico di scopa.

Bros. abbr (= Brothers) F.lli.

broth [brɔθ] n brodo.

brothel ['brɔθl] n bordello.

brother ['brʌðə*] n fratello; ~-in-law n cognato.

brought [brɔ:t] pt, pp of bring.

brow [brau] n fronte f; (rare, gen: eye~) sopracciglio; (of hill) cima.

brown [braun] a bruno(a), marrone // n (colour) bruno or marrone // vt (CULIN) rosolare; ~ bread n pane m integrale, pane nero.

brownie ['braunɪ] n giovane esploratrice f.

brown paper n carta da pacchi or da imballaggio.

brown sugar n zucchero greggio.

browse [brauz] vi (among books) curiosare fra i libri.

bruise [bru:z] n ammaccatura // vt ammaccare.

brunette [bru:'net] n bruna.

brunt [brʌnt] n: the ~ of (attack, criticism etc) il peso maggiore di.

brush [brʌʃ] n spazzola; (quarrel) schermaglia // vt spazzolare; (gen: ~ past, ~ against) sfiorare; to ~ aside vt scostare; to ~ up vt (knowledge) rinfrescare; ~wood n macchia.

Brussels ['brʌslz] n Bruxelles f; ~ sprout n cavolo di Bruxelles.

brutal ['bru:tl] a brutale.

brute [bru:t] n bestia // a: by ~ force con la forza, a viva forza.

B.Sc. n abbr = Bachelor of Science.

bubble ['bʌbl] n bolla // vi ribollire; (sparkle, fig) essere effervescente; ~ bath n bagnoschiuma m inv.

buck [bʌk] n maschio (di camoscio, caprone, coniglio etc); (US col) dollaro // vi sgroppare; to pass the ~ (to sb) scaricare (su di qn) la propria responsabilità; to ~ up vi (cheer up) rianimarsi.

bucket ['bʌkɪt] n secchio.
buckle ['bʌkl] n fibbia // vt affibbiare; (warp) deformare.
bud [bʌd] n gemma; (of flower) boccio // vi germogliare; (flower) sbocciare.
Buddhism ['budɪzəm] n buddismo.
budding ['bʌdɪŋ] a (poet etc) in erba.
buddy ['bʌdɪ] n (US) compagno.
budge [bʌdʒ] vt scostare // vi spostarsi.
budgerigar ['bʌdʒərɪgɑ:*] n pappagallino.
budget ['bʌdʒɪt] n bilancio preventivo // vi: to ~ for sth fare il bilancio per qc.
budgie ['bʌdʒɪ] n = budgerigar.
buff [bʌf] a color camoscio // n (enthusiast) appassionato/a.
buffalo, pl ~ or ~es ['bʌfələu] n bufalo; (US) bisonte m.
buffer ['bʌfə*] n respingente m; (COMPUT) memoria tampone, buffer m inv.
buffet n ['bufeɪ] (food, Brit: bar) buffet m inv // vt ['bʌfɪt] schiaffeggiare; scuotere; urtare; ~ car n (Brit RAIL) ≈ servizio ristoro.
bug [bʌg] n (insect) cimice f; (: gen) insetto; (fig: germ) virus m inv; (spy device) microfono spia // vt mettere sotto controllo; ~bear n spauracchio.
bugle ['bju:gl] n tromba.
build [bɪld] n (of person) corporatura // vt (pt, pp built) costruire; to ~ up vt accumulare; aumentare; ~er n costruttore m; ~ing n costruzione f; edificio; (also: ~ing trade) edilizia; ~ing society n (Brit) società f inv immobiliare.
built [bɪlt] pt, pp of build; ~-in a (cupboard) a muro; (device) incorporato(a); ~-up area n abitato.
bulb [bʌlb] n (BOT) bulbo; (ELEC) lampadina.
bulge [bʌldʒ] n rigonfiamento // vi essere protuberante or rigonfio(a); to be bulging with essere pieno(a) or zeppo(a) di.
bulk [bʌlk] n massa, volume m; in ~ a pacchi (or cassette etc); (COMM) all'ingrosso; the ~ of il grosso di; ~y a grosso(a); voluminoso(a).
bull [bul] n toro; ~dog n bulldog m inv.
bulldozer ['buldəuzə*] n bulldozer m inv.
bullet ['bulɪt] n pallottola.
bulletin ['bulɪtɪn] n bollettino.
bulletproof ['bulɪtpru:f] a (car) blindato(a); (vest etc) antiproiettile inv.
bullfight ['bulfaɪt] n corrida; ~er n torero; ~ing n tauromachia.
bullion ['buljən] n oro or argento in lingotti.
bullock ['bulək] n giovenco.
bullring ['bulrɪŋ] n arena (per corride).
bull's-eye ['bulzaɪ] n centro del bersaglio.
bully ['bulɪ] n prepotente m // vt angariare; (frighten) intimidire.

bum [bʌm] n (col: backside) culo; (tramp) vagabondo/a.
bumblebee ['bʌmblbi:] n bombo.
bump [bʌmp] n (blow) colpo; (jolt) scossa; (on road etc) protuberanza; (on head) bernoccolo // vt battere; to ~ into vt fus scontrarsi con; ~er n paraurti m inv // a: ~er harvest raccolto eccezionale.
bumptious ['bʌmpʃəs] a presuntuoso(a).
bumpy ['bʌmpɪ] a (road) dissestato(a).
bun [bʌn] n focaccia; (of hair) crocchia.
bunch [bʌntʃ] n (of flowers, keys) mazzo; (of bananas) ciuffo; (of people) gruppo; ~ of grapes grappolo d'uva.
bundle ['bʌndl] n fascio // vt (also: ~ up) legare in un fascio; (put): to ~ sth/sb into spingere qc/qn in.
bungalow ['bʌngələu] n bungalow m inv.
bungle ['bʌŋgl] vt abborracciare.
bunion ['bʌnjən] n callo (al piede).
bunk [bʌŋk] n cuccetta; ~ beds npl letti mpl a castello.
bunker ['bʌŋkə*] n (coal store) ripostiglio per il carbone; (MIL, GOLF) bunker m inv.
bunny ['bʌnɪ] n (also: ~ rabbit) coniglietto.
bunting ['bʌntɪŋ] n pavesi mpl, bandierine fpl.
buoy [bɔɪ] n boa; to ~ up vt tenere a galla; (fig) sostenere; ~ant a galleggiante; (fig) vivace.
burden ['bə:dn] n carico, fardello // vt caricare; (oppress) opprimere.
bureau, pl ~x [bjuə'rəu, -z] n (Brit: writing desk) scrivania; (US: chest of drawers) cassettone m; (office) ufficio, agenzia.
bureaucracy [bjuə'rɒkrəsɪ] n burocrazia.
burglar ['bə:glə*] n scassinatore m; ~ alarm n campanello antifurto; ~y n furto con scasso.
burial ['berɪəl] n sepoltura.
burly ['bə:lɪ] a robusto(a).
Burma ['bə:mə] n Birmania.
burn [bə:n] vt, vi (pt, pp burned or burnt) bruciare // n bruciatura, scottatura; to ~ down vt distruggere col fuoco; ~er n (on cooker) fornello; (TECH) bruciatore m, becco (a gas).
burnt [bə:nt] pt, pp of burn.
burrow ['bʌrəu] n tana // vt scavare.
bursar ['bə:sə*] n economo/a; (Brit: student) borsista m/f; ~y n (Brit) borsa di studio.
burst [bə:st] vb (pt, pp burst) vt far scoppiare (or esplodere) // vi esplodere; (tyre) scoppiare // n scoppio; (also: ~ pipe) rottura nel tubo, perdita; to ~ into flames/tears scoppiare in fiamme/lacrime; to ~ out laughing scoppiare a ridere; to be ~ing with essere pronto a scoppiare di; to ~ into vt fus (room etc) irrompere in; to ~ open vi aprirsi

improvvisamente; (*door*) spalancarsi.

bury ['bɛrɪ] *vt* seppellire.

bus, ~es [bʌs, 'bʌsɪz] *n* autobus *m inv.*

bush [buʃ] *n* cespuglio; (*scrub land*) macchia; **to beat about the ~** menare il cane per l'aia.

bushy ['buʃɪ] *a* cespuglioso(a).

busily ['bɪzɪlɪ] *ad* con impegno, alacremente.

business ['bɪznɪs] *n* (*matter*) affare *m*; (*trading*) affari *mpl*; (*firm*) azienda; (*job, duty*) lavoro; **to be away on ~** essere andato via per affari; **it's none of my ~** questo non mi riguarda; **he means ~** non scherza; **~like** *a* serio(a); efficiente; **~man/woman** *n* uomo/donna d'affari; **~ trip** *n* viaggio d'affari.

busker ['bʌskə*] *n* (*Brit*) suonatore/trice ambulante.

bus-stop ['bʌsstɔp] *n* fermata d'autobus.

bust [bʌst] *n* busto; (*ANAT*) seno // *a* (*col: broken*) rotto(a); **to go ~** fallire.

bustle ['bʌsl] *n* movimento, attività // *vi* darsi da fare; **bustling** *a* (*person*) indaffarato(a); (*town*) animato(a).

busy ['bɪzɪ] *a* occupato(a); (*shop, street*) molto frequentato(a) // *vt*: **to ~ o.s. with** darsi da fare; **~body** *n* ficcanaso; **~ signal** *n* (*US TEL*) segnale *m* di occupato.

but [bʌt] ♦ *cj* ma; **I'd love to come, ~ I'm busy** vorrei tanto venire, ma ho da fare

♦ *prep* (*apart from, except*) eccetto, tranne, meno; **he was nothing ~ trouble** non dava altro che guai; **no-one ~ him can do it** nessuno può farlo tranne lui; **~ for you/your help** se non fosse per te/per il tuo aiuto; **anything ~ that** tutto ma non questo

♦ *ad* (*just, only*) solo, soltanto; **she's ~ a child** è solo una bambina; **had I ~ known** se solo avessi saputo; **I can ~ try** tentar non nuoce; **all ~ finished** quasi finito.

butcher ['butʃə*] *n* macellaio // *vt* macellare.

butler ['bʌtlə*] *n* maggiordomo.

butt [bʌt] *n* (*cask*) grossa botte *f*; (*thick end*) estremità *f inv* più grossa; (*of gun*) calcio; (*of cigarette*) mozzicone *m*; (*Brit fig: target*) oggetto // *vt* cozzare; **to ~ in** *vi* (*interrupt*) interrompere.

butter ['bʌtə*] *n* burro // *vt* imburrare; **~cup** *n* ranuncolo.

butterfly ['bʌtəflaɪ] *n* farfalla; (*SWIMMING*: *also*: **~ stroke**) (nuoto a) farfalla.

buttocks ['bʌtəks] *npl* natiche *fpl.*

button ['bʌtn] *n* bottone *m* // *vt* (*also*: **~ up**) abbottonare // *vi* abbottonarsi.

buttress ['bʌtrɪs] *n* contrafforte *f.*

buxom ['bʌksəm] *a* formoso(a).

buy [baɪ], *pt, pp* **bought** *vt* comprare; **to ~ sb sth/sth from sb** comprare qc per

qn/qc da qn; **to ~ sb a drink** offrire da bere a qn; **~er** *n* compratore/trice.

buzz [bʌz] *n* ronzio; (*col: phone call*) colpo di telefono // *vi* ronzare.

buzzer ['bʌzə*] *n* cicalino.

buzz word *n* (*col*) termine *m* di gran moda.

by [baɪ] ♦ *prep* 1 (*referring to cause, agent*) da; **killed ~ lightning** ucciso da un fulmine; **surrounded ~ a fence** circondato da uno steccato; **a painting ~ Picasso** un quadro di Picasso

2 (*referring to method, manner, means*): **~ bus/car/train** in autobus/ macchina/treno, con l'autobus/la macchina/il treno; **to pay ~ cheque** pagare con (un) assegno; **~ moonlight** al chiaro di luna; **~ saving hard, he ...** risparmiando molto, lui ...

3 (*via, through*) per; **we came ~ Dover** siamo venuti via Dover

4 (*close to, past*) accanto a; **the house ~ the river** la casa sul fiume; **a holiday ~ the sea** una vacanza al mare; **she sat ~ his bed** si sedette accanto al suo letto; **she rushed ~ me** mi è passata accanto correndo; **I go ~ the post office every day** passo davanti all'ufficio postale ogni giorno

5 (*not later than*) per, entro; **~ 4 o'clock** per or entro le 4; **~ this time tomorrow** domani a quest'ora; **~ the time I got here it was too late** quando sono arrivato era ormai troppo tardi

6 (*during*): **~ day/night** di giorno/notte

7 (*amount*) a; **~ the kilo/metre** a chili/ metri; **paid ~ the hour** pagato all'ora; **one ~ one** uno per uno; **little ~ little** a poco a poco

8 (*MATH, measure*): **to divide/multiply ~ 3** dividere/moltiplicare per 3; **it's broader ~ a metre** è più largo di un metro, è più largo di un metro

9 (*according to*) per; **to play ~ the rules** attenersi alle regole; **it's all right ~ me** per me va bene

10: (**all**) **~ oneself** *etc* (tutto(a)) solo(a); **he did it (all) ~ himself** lo ha fatto (tutto) da solo

11: **~ the way** a proposito; **this wasn't my idea ~ the way** l'altro l'idea non è stata mia

♦ *ad* 1 *see* **go, pass** *etc*

2: **~ and ~** (*in past*) poco dopo; (*in future*) fra breve; **~ and large** nel complesso.

bye(-bye) ['baɪ('baɪ)] *excl* ciao!, arrivederci!

by(e)-law ['baɪlɔ:] *n* legge *f* locale.

by-election ['baɪɪlɛkʃən] *n* (*Brit*) elezione *f* straordinaria.

bygone ['baɪgɔn] *a* passato(a) // *n*: **let ~s be ~s** mettiamoci una pietra sopra.

bypass ['baɪpɑ:s] *n* circonvallazione *f*; (*MED*) by-pass *m inv* // *vt* fare una deviazione intorno a.

by-product ['baɪprɔdʌkt] n sottoprodotto; (fig) conseguenza secondaria.

bystander ['baɪstændə*] n spettatore/trice.

byte [baɪt] n (COMPUT) byte m inv, bicarattere m.

byword ['baɪwə:d] n: to be a ~ for essere sinonimo di.

by-your-leave ['baɪjɔ:'li:v] n: without so much as a ~ senza nemmeno chiedere il permesso.

C

C [si:] n (MUS) do.

C.A. n abbr = **chartered accountant**.

cab [kæb] n taxi m inv; (of train, truck) cabina; (horse-drawn) carrozza.

cabaret ['kæbəreɪ] n cabaret m inv.

cabbage ['kæbɪdʒ] n cavolo.

cabin ['kæbɪn] n capanna; (on ship) cabina.

cabinet ['kæbɪnɪt] n (POL) consiglio dei ministri; (furniture) armadietto; (also: display ~) vetrinetta; ~-maker n stipettaio.

cable ['keɪbl] n cavo; fune f; (TEL) cablogramma m // vt telegrafare; ~-car n funivia; ~ television n televisione f via cavo.

cache [kæʃ] n: a ~ of food etc un deposito segreto di viveri etc.

cackle ['kækl] vi schiamazzare.

cactus, pl **cacti** ['kæktəs, -taɪ] n cactus m inv.

cadet [kə'dɛt] n (MIL) cadetto.

cadge [kædʒ] vt (col) scroccare.

café ['kæfeɪ] n caffè m inv.

cafeteria [kæfɪ'tɪərɪə] n self-service m inv.

cage [keɪdʒ] n gabbia.

cagey ['keɪdʒɪ] a (col) chiuso(a); guardingo(a).

cagoule [kə'gu:l] n K-way m inv ®.

cajole [kə'dʒəul] vt allettare.

cake [keɪk] n torta; ~ of soap saponetta; ~d a: ~d with incrostato(a) di.

calculate ['kælkjuleɪt] vt· calcolare; **calculation** [-'leɪʃən] n calcolo; **calculator** n calcolatrice f.

calendar ['kæləndə*] n calendario; ~ year n anno civile.

calf [ka:f], pl **calves** n (of cow) vitello; (of other animals) piccolo; (also: ~skin) (pelle f di) vitello; (ANAT) polpaccio.

calibre, (US) caliber ['kælɪbə*] n calibro.

call [kɔ:l] vt (gen, also TEL) chiamare // vi chiamare; (visit: also: ~ in, ~ round): to ~ (for) passare (a prendere) // n (shout) grido, urlo; (visit) visita; (also: telephone ~) telefonata; to be ~ed (person, object) chiamarsi; to be on ~

essere a disposizione; **to ~ back** vi (return) ritornare; (TEL) ritelefonare, richiamare; **to ~ for** vt fus richiedere; **to ~ off** vt disdire; **to ~ on** vt fus (visit) passare da; (request): to ~ on sb to do chiedere a qn di fare; **to ~ out** vi (in pain) urlare; (to person) chiamare; **to ~ up** vt (MIL) richiamare; ~box n (Brit) cabina telefonica; ~er n persona che chiama; visitatore/trice; ~ girl n ragazza f squillo inv; ~-in n (US: phone-in) trasmissione f a filo diretto con gli ascoltatori; ~ing n vocazione f; ~ing card n (US) biglietto da visita.

callous ['kæləs] a indurito(a), insensibile.

calm [ka:m] a calmo(a) // n calma // vt calmare; **to ~ down** vi calmarsi // vt calmare.

Calor gas ['kælə*-] n ® butano.

calorie ['kælərɪ] n caloria.

calves [ka:vz] npl of **calf**.

camber ['kæmbə*] n (of road) bombatura.

Cambodia [kæm'bəudjə] n Cambogia.

came [keɪm] pt of **come**.

camel ['kæməl] n cammello.

camera ['kæmərə] n macchina fotografica; (also: cine-~, movie ~) cinepresa; in ~ a porte chiuse; ~man n cameraman m inv.

camouflage ['kæməfla:ʒ] n camuffamento; (MIL) mimetizzazione f // vt camuffare; mimetizzare.

camp [kæmp] n campeggio; (MIL) campo // vi campeggiare; accamparsi.

campaign [kæm'peɪn] n (MIL, POL etc) campagna // vi (also fig) fare una campagna.

campbed ['kæmp'bɛd] n (Brit) brandina.

camper ['kæmpə*] n campeggiatore/trice.

camping ['kæmpɪŋ] n campeggio; to go ~ andare in campeggio.

campsite ['kæmpsaɪt] n campeggio.

campus ['kæmpəs] n campus m inv.

can [kæn] auxiliary vb see next headword // n (of milk) scatola; (of oil) bidone m; (of water) tanica; (tin) scatola // vt mettere in scatola.

can [kæn] ◆ n, vt see previous headword
◆ auxiliary vb (negative **cannot**, **can't**; conditional and pt **could**) **1** (be able to) potere; **I ~'t go any further** non posso andare oltre; **you ~ do it if you try** sei in grado di farlo — basta provarci; **I'll help you all I ~** ti aiuterò come potrò; **I ~'t see you** non ti vedo
2 (know how to) sapere, essere capace di; **I ~ swim** so nuotare; **~ you speak French?** parla francese?
3 (may) potere; **could I have a word with you?** posso parlarle un momento?
4 (expressing disbelief, puzzlement etc): **it ~'t be true!** non può essere vero!; **what CAN he want?** cosa può mai volere?

5 (expressing possibility, suggestion etc): he could be in the library può darsi che sia in biblioteca; she could have been delayed può aver avuto un contrattempo.

Canada ['kænədə] n Canada m.

Canadian [kə'neɪdɪən] a, n canadese (m/f).

canal [kə'næl] n canale m.

canary [kə'neərɪ] n canarino.

cancel ['kænsəl] vt annullare; (train) sopprimere; (cross out) cancellare; ~lation [-'leɪʃən] n annullamento; soppressione f; cancellazione f; (TOURISM) prenotazione f annullata.

cancer ['kænsə*] n cancro; C~ (sign) Cancro.

candid ['kændɪd] a onesto(a).

candidate ['kændɪdeɪt] n candidato/a.

candle ['kændl] n candela; (in church) cero; by ~light a lume di candela; ~stick n (also: ~ holder) bugia; (bigger, ornate) candeliere m.

candour, (US) **candor** ['kændə*] n sincerità.

candy ['kændɪ] n zucchero candito; (US) caramella; caramelle fpl; ~-floss n (Brit) zucchero filato.

cane [keɪn] n canna; (SCOL) verga // vt (Brit SCOL) punire a colpi di verga.

canister ['kænɪstə*] n scatola metallica.

cannabis ['kænəbɪs] n canapa indiana.

canned ['kænd] a (food) in scatola.

cannon, pl ~ or ~s ['kænən] n (gun) cannone m.

cannot ['kænɔt] = can not.

canny ['kænɪ] a furbo(a).

canoe [kə'nu:] n canoa; (SPORT) canotto.

canon ['kænən] n (clergyman) canonico; (standard) canone m.

can opener [-'əʊpnə*] n apriscatole m inv.

canopy ['kænəpɪ] n baldacchino.

can't [kænt] = can not.

cantankerous [kæn'tæŋkərəs] a stizzoso(a).

canteen [kæn'ti:n] n mensa; (Brit: of cutlery) portaposate m inv.

canter ['kæntə*] n piccolo galoppo.

canvas ['kænvəs] n tela.

canvassing ['kænvəsɪŋ] n (POL) sollecitazione f; (COMM) indagine f di mercato.

canyon ['kænjən] n canyon m inv.

cap [kæp] n (also Brit FOOTBALL) berretto; (of pen) coperchio; (of bottle) tappo // vt tappare; (outdo) superare.

capability [keɪpə'bɪlɪtɪ] n capacità f inv, abilità f inv.

capable ['keɪpəbl] a capace.

capacity [kə'pæsɪtɪ] n capacità f inv; (of lift etc) capienza.

cape [keɪp] n (garment) cappa; (GEO) capo.

capital ['kæpɪtl] n (also: ~ city) capitale

f; (money) capitale m; (also: ~ letter) (lettera) maiuscola; ~ gains tax n imposta sulla plusvalenza; ~ism n capitalismo; ~ist a, n capitalista (m/f); ~ize: to ~ize on vt fus trarre vantaggio da; ~ punishment n pena capitale.

Capricorn ['kæprɪkɔ:n] n Capricorno.

capsize [kæp'saɪz] vt capovolgere // vi capovolgersi.

capsule ['kæpsju:l] n capsula.

captain ['kæptɪn] n capitano.

caption ['kæpʃən] n leggenda.

captivate ['kæptɪveɪt] vt avvincere.

captive ['kæptɪv] a, n prigioniero(a).

captivity [kæp'tɪvɪtɪ] n prigionia; in ~ (animal) in cattività.

capture ['kæptʃə*] vt catturare, prendere; (attention) attirare // n cattura; (data ~) registrazione f or rilevazione f di dati.

car [kɑ:*] n macchina, automobile f.

carafe [kə'ræf] n caraffa.

caramel ['kærəməl] n caramello.

caravan ['kærəvæn] n (Brit) roulotte f inv; (of camels) carovana; ~ site n (Brit) campeggio per roulotte.

carbohydrates [kɑ:bəʊ'haɪdreɪts] npl (foods) carboidrati mpl.

carbon ['kɑ:bən] n carbonio; ~ paper n carta carbone.

carburettor, (US) **carburetor** [kɑ:bju'retə*] n carburatore m.

card [kɑ:d] n carta; (visiting ~ etc) biglietto; (Christmas ~ etc) cartolina; ~board n cartone m; ~ game n gioco di carte.

cardiac ['kɑ:dɪæk] a cardiaco(a).

cardigan ['kɑ:dɪgən] n cardigan m inv.

cardinal ['kɑ:dɪnl] a, n cardinale (m).

card index n schedario.

care [kɛə*] n cura, attenzione f; (worry) preoccupazione f // vi: to ~ about interessarsi di; ~ of (c/o) presso (c/o); in sb's ~ alle cure di qn; to take ~ (to do) fare attenzione (a fare); to take ~ of curarsi di; I don't ~ non me ne importa; to ~ for vt fus aver cura di; (like) volere bene a.

career [kə'rɪə*] n carriera // vi (also: ~ along) andare di (gran) carriera.

carefree ['kɛəfri:] a sgombro(a) di preoccupazioni.

careful ['kɛəful] a attento(a); (cautious) cauto(a); (be) ~! attenzione!; ~ly ad con cura; cautamente.

careless ['kɛəlɪs] a negligente; (heedless) spensierato(a).

caress [kə'rɛs] n carezza // vt accarezzare.

caretaker ['kɛəteɪkə*] n custode m.

car-ferry ['kɑ:fɛrɪ] n traghetto.

cargo, pl ~es ['kɑ:gəʊ] n carico.

car hire n autonoleggio.

Caribbean [kærɪ'bi:ən] a: the ~ (Sea) il Mar dei Caraibi.

caring [ˈkeərɪŋ] a (person) premuroso(a); (society, organization) umanitario(a).

carnage [ˈkaːnɪdʒ] n carneficina.

carnation [kaːˈneɪʃən] n garofano.

carnival [ˈkaːnɪvəl] n (public celebration) carnevale m; (US: funfair) luna park m inv.

carol [ˈkærəl] n: (Christmas) ~ canto di Natale.

carp [kaːp] n (fish) carpa; **to** ~ **at** vt fus trovare a ridire su.

car park n (Brit) parcheggio.

carpenter [ˈkaːpɪntə*] n carpentiere m.

carpentry [ˈkaːpɪntrɪ] n carpenteria.

carpet [ˈkaːpɪt] n tappeto // vt coprire con tappeto; ~ **slippers** npl pantofole fpl; ~ **sweeper** n scopatappeti m inv.

carriage [ˈkærɪdʒ] n vettura; (of goods) trasporto; (of typewriter) carrello; (bearing) portamento; ~ **return** n (on typewriter etc) leva (or tasto) del ritorno a capo; ~**way** n (Brit: part of road) carreggiata.

carrier [ˈkærɪə*] n (of disease) portatore/trice; (COMM) impresa di trasporti; (NAUT) portaerei f inv; (on car, bicycle) portabagagli m inv; ~ **bag** n (Brit) sacchetto.

carrot [ˈkærət] n carota.

carry [ˈkærɪ] vt (subj: person) portare; (: vehicle) trasportare; (a motion, bill) far passare; (involve: responsibilities etc) comportare // vi (sound) farsi sentire; **to be** or **get carried away** (fig) entusiasmarsi; **to** ~ **on** vi: **to** ~ **on with** sth/doing continuare qc/a fare // vt mandare avanti; **to** ~ **out** vt (orders) eseguire; (investigation) svolgere; ~**cot** n culla portabile; ~**-on** n (col: fuss) casino, confusione f.

cart [kaːt] n carro // vt (col) trascinare.

carton [ˈkaːtən] n (box) scatola di cartone; (of yogurt) cartone m; (of cigarettes) stecca.

cartoon [kaːˈtuːn] n (PRESS) disegno umoristico; (satirical) caricatura; (comic strip) fumetto; (CINEMA) disegno animato.

cartridge [ˈkaːtrɪdʒ] n (for gun, pen) cartuccia; (for camera) caricatore m; (music tape) cassetta.

carve [kaːv] vt (meat) trinciare; (wood, stone) intagliare; **to** ~ **up** vt (meat) tagliare; (fig: country) suddividere; **carving** n (in wood etc) scultura; **carving knife** n trinciante m.

car wash n lavaggio auto.

case [keɪs] n caso; (LAW) causa, processo; (box) scatola; (Brit: also: suit~) valigia; **he hasn't put forward his** ~ **very well** non ha dimostrato bene il suo caso; **in** ~ **of** in caso di; **in** ~ **he** caso mai lui; **just in** ~ in caso di bisogno.

cash [kæʃ] n denaro; (coins, notes) denaro liquido // vt incassare; **to pay** (in) ~ pagare in contanti; ~ **on delivery** (C.O.D.) (COMM) pagamento alla consegna; ~**book** n giornale m di cassa; ~ **card** n tesserino di prelievo; ~ **desk** n (Brit) cassa; ~ **dispenser** n sportello automatico.

cashew [kæˈʃuː] n (also: ~ **nut**) anacardio.

cashier [kæˈʃɪə*] n cassiere/a.

cashmere [ˈkæʃmɪə*] n cachemire m.

cash register n registratore m di cassa.

casing [ˈkeɪsɪŋ] n rivestimento.

casino [kəˈsiːnəu] n casinò m inv.

cask [kaːsk] n botte f.

casket [ˈkaːskɪt] n cofanetto; (US: coffin) bara.

casserole [ˈkæsərəul] n casseruola; (food): **chicken** ~ pollo in casseruola.

cassette [kæˈset] n cassetta; ~ **player** n riproduttore m a cassette; ~ **recorder** n registratore m a cassette.

cast [kaːst] vt (pt, pp **cast**) (throw) gettare; (shed) perdere; spogliarsi di; (metal) gettare, fondere; (THEATRE): **to** ~ **sb as Hamlet** scegliere qn per la parte di Amleto // n (THEATRE) complesso di attori; (mould) forma; (also: plaster ~) ingessatura; **to** ~ **one's vote** votare, dare il voto; **to** ~ **off** vi (NAUT) salpare.

castaway [ˈkaːstəwəɪ] n naufrago/a.

caster sugar [ˈkaːstə*-] n (Brit) zucchero semolato.

casting [ˈkaːstɪŋ] a: ~ **vote** (Brit) voto decisivo.

cast iron n ghisa.

castle [ˈkaːsl] n castello; (fortified) rocca.

castor [ˈkaːstə*] n (wheel) rotella; ~ **oil** n olio di ricino.

castrate [kæsˈtreɪt] vt castrare.

casual [ˈkæʒjul] a (by chance) casuale, fortuito(a); (irregular: work etc) avventizio(a); (unconcerned) noncurante, indifferente; ~ **wear** casual m; ~**ly** ad con disinvoltura; casualmente.

casualty [ˈkæʒjultɪ] n ferito/a; (dead) morto/a, vittima.

cat [kæt] n gatto.

catalogue, (US) **catalog** [ˈkætələg] n catalogo // vt catalogare.

catalyst [ˈkætəlɪst] n catalizzatore m.

catapult [ˈkætəpʌlt] n catapulta; fionda.

cataract [ˈkætərækt] n (also MED) cateratta.

catarrh [kəˈtaː*] n catarro.

catastrophe [kəˈtæstrəfɪ] n catastrofe f.

catch [kætʃ] vb (pt, pp **caught**) vt (train, thief, cold) acchiappare; (ball) afferrare; (person: by surprise) sorprendere; (understand) comprendere; (get entangled) impigliare // vi (fire) prendere // n (fish etc caught) retata, presa; (*trick*) inganno; (*TECH*) gancio; to ~ sb's attention *or* eye attirare l'attenzione di qn; to ~ fire prendere fuoco; to ~ sight of scorgere; **to ~ on** *vi* capire; (*become popular*) affermarsi, far presa; **to ~ up** *vi* mettersi in pari // *vt* (*also*: ~ up with) raggiungere.

catching ['kætʃɪŋ] *a* (*MED*) contagioso(a).

catchment area ['kætʃmənt-] *n* (*Brit SCOL*) circoscrizione *f* scolare; (*GEO*) bacino pluviale.

catch phrase *n* slogan *m inv*; frase *f* fatta.

catchy ['kætʃɪ] *a* orecchiabile.

category ['kætɪɡərɪ] *n* categoria.

cater ['keɪtə*] *vi* (*gen*: ~ for) provvedere da mangiare (per); **to ~ for** *vt fus* (*Brit*: *needs*) provvedere a; (: *readers, consumers*) incontrare i gusti di; **~er** *n* fornitore *m*; **~ing** *n* approvvigionamento.

caterpillar ['kætəpɪlə*] *n* bruco; ~ **track** *n* catena a cingoli.

cathedral [kə'θi:drəl] *n* cattedrale *f*, duomo.

catholic ['kæθəlɪk] *a* universale; aperto(a); eclettico(a); **C~** *a*, *n* (*REL*) cattolico(a).

cat's-eye [kæts'aɪ] *n* (*Brit AUT*) catarifrangente *m*.

cattle ['kætl] *npl* bestiame *m*, bestie *fpl*.

catty ['kætɪ] *a* maligno(a), dispettoso(a).

caucus ['kɔ:kəs] *n* (*POL*: *group*) comitato di dirigenti; (: *US*) (riunione *f* del) comitato elettorale.

caught [kɔ:t] *pt*, *pp* of **catch**.

cauliflower ['kɔlɪflauə*] *n* cavolfiore *m*.

cause [kɔ:z] *n* causa // *vt* causare.

caution ['kɔ:ʃən] *n* prudenza; (*warning*) avvertimento // *vt* avvertire; ammonire.

cautious ['kɔ:ʃəs] *a* cauto(a), prudente.

cavalry ['kævəlrɪ] *n* cavalleria.

cave [keɪv] *n* caverna, grotta; **to ~ in** *vi* (*roof etc*) crollare; **~man** *n* uomo delle caverne.

caviar(e) ['kævɪɑ:*] *n* caviale *m*.

cavort [kə'vɔ:t] *vi* far capriole.

CB *n abbr* (= *Citizens' Band* (*Radio*)): ~ **radio** (**set**) baracchino.

CBI *n abbr* (= *Confederation of British Industries*) ≈ Confindustria.

cc *abbr* = *cubic centimetres*; *carbon copy*.

cease [si:s] *vt*, *vi* cessare; **~fire** *n* cessate il fuoco *m inv*; **~less** *a* incessante, continuo(a).

cedar ['si:də*] *n* cedro.

ceiling ['si:lɪŋ] *n* soffitto.

celebrate ['sɛlɪbreɪt] *vt*, *vi* celebrare; **~d** *a* celebre; **celebration** [-'breɪʃən] *n* celebrazione *f*.

celery ['sɛlərɪ] *n* sedano.

cell [sɛl] *n* cella; (*BIOL*) cellula; (*ELEC*) elemento (di batteria).

cellar ['sɛlə*] *n* sottosuolo, cantina.

'cello ['tʃɛləu] *n* violoncello.

Celt [kɛlt, sɛlt] *n* celta *m/f*.

Celtic ['kɛltɪk, 'sɛltɪk] *a* celtico(a).

cement [sə'mɛnt] *n* cemento // *vt* cementare; ~ **mixer** *n* betoniera.

cemetery ['sɛmɪtrɪ] *n* cimitero.

censor ['sɛnsə*] *n* censore *m* // *vt* censurare; **~ship** *n* censura.

censure ['sɛnʃə*] *vt* riprovare, censurare.

census ['sɛnsəs] *n* censimento.

cent [sɛnt] *n* (*US*: *coin*) centesimo (= *1:100 di un dollaro*); *see also* **per**.

centenary [sɛn'ti:nərɪ] *n* centenario.

center ['sɛntə*] *n*, *vt* (*US*) = **centre**.

centi... ['sɛntɪ] *prefix*: **~grade** *a* centigrado(a); **~metre**, (*US*) **~meter** *n* centimetro.

centipede ['sɛntɪpi:d] *n* centopiedi *m inv*.

central ['sɛntrəl] *a* centrale; **C~ America** *n* America centrale; ~ **heating** *n* riscaldamento centrale; **~ize** *vt* accentrare.

centre, (*US*) **center** ['sɛntə*] *n* centro // *vt* centrare; **~-forward** *n* (*SPORT*) centroavanti *m inv*; **~-half** *n* (*SPORT*) centromediano.

century ['sɛntjurɪ] *n* secolo; **20th** ~ ventesimo secolo.

ceramic [sɪ'ræmɪk] *a* ceramico(a); **~s** *npl* ceramica.

cereal ['si:rɪəl] *n* cereale *m*.

ceremony ['sɛrɪmənɪ] *n* cerimonia; **to stand on** ~ fare complimenti.

certain ['sə:tən] *a* certo(a); **to make** ~ **of** assicurarsi di; **for** ~ per certo, di sicuro; **~ly** *ad* certamente, certo; **~ty** *n* certezza.

certificate [sə'tɪfɪkɪt] *n* certificato; diploma *m*.

certified ['sə:tɪfaɪd]: ~ **mail** *n* (*US*) posta raccomandata con ricevuta di ritorno; ~ **public accountant** (**CPA**) *n* (*US*) = commercialista *m/f*.

cervical ['sə:vɪkl] *a*: ~ **cancer** cancro della cervice; ~ **smear** Pap-test *m inv*.

cervix ['sə:vɪks] *n* cervice *f*.

cesspit ['sɛspɪt], **cesspool** ['sɛspu:l] *n* pozzo nero.

cf. *abbr* (= *compare*) cfr.

ch. *abbr* (= *chapter*) cap.

chafe [tʃeɪf] *vt* fregare, irritare.

chaffinch ['tʃæfɪntʃ] *n* fringuello.

chain [tʃeɪn] *n* catena // *vt* (*also*: ~ up) incatenare; ~ **reaction** *n* reazione *f* a catena; ~ **smoke** *vi* fumare una sigaretta dopo l'altra; ~ **store** *n* negozio a catena.

chair [tʃeə*] *n* sedia; (*armchair*) poltrona; (*of university*) cattedra // *vt* (*meeting*) presiedere; **~lift** *n* seggiovia; **~man** *n* presidente *m*.

chalice ['tʃælɪs] *n* calice *m*.

chalk [tʃɔ:k] *n* gesso.

challenge ['tʃælɪndʒ] n sfida // vt sfidare; (statement, right) mettere in dubbio; to ~ sb to do sfidare qn a fare; **challenging** a sfidante; provocatorio(a).

chamber ['tʃeɪmbə*] n camera; ~ of **commerce** n camera di commercio; ~**maid** n cameriera; ~ **music** n musica da camera.

chamois [ʃæmwɑ:] n camoscio; ~ **leather** ['ʃæmɪ-] n pelle f di camoscio.

champagne [ʃæm'peɪn] n champagne m inv.

champion ['tʃæmpɪən] n campione/essa; ~**ship** n campionato.

chance [tʃɑ:ns] n caso; (opportunity) occasione f; (likelihood) possibilità f inv // vt: to ~ it rischiare, provarci // a fortuito(a); to take a ~ rischiarlo; by ~ per caso.

chancellor ['tʃɑ:nsələ*] n cancelliere m; C~ **of the Exchequer** n (Brit) Cancelliere dello Scacchiere.

chandelier [ʃændə'lɪə*] n lampadario.

change [tʃeɪndʒ] vt cambiare; (transform): to ~ sb into trasformare qn in // vi cambiarsi; (be transformed): to ~ into trasformarsi in // n cambiamento; (money) resto; to ~ one's mind cambiare idea; a ~ of clothes un cambio (di vestiti); for a ~ tanto per cambiare; small ~ spiccioli mpl, moneta; ~**able** a (weather) variabile; ~ **machine** n distributore automatico di monete; ~**over** n cambiamento, passaggio.

changing ['tʃeɪndʒɪŋ] a che cambia; (colours) cangiante; ~ **room** n (Brit: in shop) camerino; (: SPORT) spogliatoio.

channel ['tʃænl] n canale m; (of river, sea) alveo // vt canalizzare; **through** the usual ~s per le solite vie; the (English) C~ la Manica; the C~ **Islands** npl le Isole Normanne.

chant [tʃɑ:nt] n canto; salmodia // vt cantare; salmodiare.

chaos ['keɪɔs] n caos m.

chaotic [keɪ'ɔtɪk] a caotico(a).

chap [tʃæp] n (Brit col: man) tipo.

chapel ['tʃæpəl] n cappella.

chaperon ['ʃæpərəʊn] n accompagnatrice f // vt accompagnare.

chaplain ['tʃæplɪn] n cappellano.

chapped [tʃæpt] a (skin, lips) screpolato(a).

chapter ['tʃæptə*] n capitolo.

char [tʃɑ:*] vt (burn) carbonizzare // n (Brit) = **charlady**.

character ['kærɪktə*] n carattere m; (in novel, film) personaggio; (eccentric) originale m // vt; ~**istic** ['-rɪstɪk] a caratteristico(a) // n caratteristica.

charade [ʃə'rɑ:d] n sciarada.

charcoal ['tʃɑ:kəʊl] n carbone m di legna.

charge [tʃɑ:dʒ] n accusa; (cost) prezzo; (of gun, battery, MIL: attack) carica // vt

(gun, battery, MIL: enemy) caricare; (customer) fare pagare a; (sum) fare pagare; (LAW): to ~ sb (with) accusare qn (di) // vi (gen with: up, along etc) lanciarsi; ~s npl: bank ~s commissioni fpl bancarie; is there a ~? c'è da pagare?; to reverse the ~s (TEL) fare una telefonata a carico del destinatario; to take ~ of incaricarsi di; to be in ~ of essere responsabile per; to ~ an expense (up) to sb addebitare una spesa a qn; ~ **card** n carta f clienti inv.

chariot ['tʃærɪət] n carro.

charitable ['tʃærɪtəbl] a caritatevole.

charity ['tʃærɪtɪ] n carità; (organization) opera pia.

charlady ['tʃɑ:leɪdɪ] n (Brit) domestica a ore.

charlatan ['ʃɑ:lətən] n ciarlatano.

charm [tʃɑ:m] n fascino; (on bracelet) ciondolo // vt affascinare, incantare; ~**ing** a affascinante.

chart [tʃɑ:t] n tabella; grafico; (map) carta nautica // vt fare una carta nautica di.

charter ['tʃɑ:tə*] vt (plane) noleggiare // n (document) carta; ~**ed accountant** (C.A.) n (Brit) ragioniere/a professionista; ~ **flight** n volo m charter inv.

chase [tʃeɪs] vt inseguire; (away) cacciare // n caccia.

chasm ['kæzəm] n abisso.

chassis ['ʃæsɪ] n telaio.

chastity ['tʃæstɪtɪ] n castità.

chat [tʃæt] vi (also: have a ~) chiacchierare // n chiacchierata; ~ **show** n (Brit) talk show m inv.

chatter ['tʃætə*] vi (person) ciarlare // n ciarle fpl; her teeth were ~ing batteva i denti; ~**box** n chiacchierone/a.

chatty ['tʃætɪ] a (style) familiare; (person) chiacchierino(a).

chauffeur ['ʃəʊfə*] n autista m.

chauvinist ['ʃəʊvɪnɪst] n (male ~) maschilista m; (nationalist) sciovinista m/f.

cheap [tʃi:p] a a buon mercato; (joke) grossolano(a); (poor quality) di cattiva qualità // ad a buon mercato; ~**en** vt ribassare; (fig) avvilire; ~**er** a meno caro(a); ~**ly** ad a buon prezzo, a buon mercato.

cheat [tʃi:t] vi imbrogliare; (at school) copiare // vt ingannare; (rob) defraudare // n imbroglione m; copione m; (trick) inganno.

check [tʃek] vt verificare; (passport, ticket) controllare; (halt) fermare; (restrain) contenere // n verifica; controllo; (curb) freno; (bill) conto; (pattern: gen pl) quadretti mpl; (US) = **cheque** // a (also: ~ed: pattern, cloth) a quadretti; to ~ in vi (in hotel) registrare; (at airport) presentarsi all'accettazione // vt (luggage) depositare; to ~ out vi (in hotel) saldare il conto // vt (luggage) ritirare; **to ~ up** *vi*: to ~ up (on sth) investigare (qc); **to ~ up on sb** informarsi sul conto di qn; **~ered** *a* (US) = **chequered**; **~ers** *n* (US) dama; **~-in (desk)** *n* check-in *m inv*, accettazione *f* (bagagli *inv*); **~ing account** *n* (US) conto corrente; **~mate** *n* scaccomatto; **~out** *n* (in supermarket) cassa; **~point** *n* posto di blocco; **~room** *n* (US) deposito *m* bagagli *inv*; **~up** *n* (MED) controllo medico.

cheek [tʃiːk] *n* guancia; (impudence) faccia tosta; **~bone** *n* zigomo; **~y** *a* sfacciato(a).

cheep [tʃiːp] *vi* pigolare.

cheer [tʃɪə*] *vt* applaudire; (gladden) rallegrare // *vi* applaudire // *n* (gen pl) applausi *mpl*; evviva *mpl*; **~s!** salute!; **to ~ up** *vi* rallegrarsi, farsi animo // *vt* rallegrare; **~ful** *a* allegro(a).

cheerio ['tʃɪərɪ'əu] *excl* (Brit) ciao!

cheese [tʃiːz] *n* formaggio; **~board** *n* piatto del (or per il) formaggio.

cheetah ['tʃiːtə] *n* ghepardo.

chef [ʃɛf] *n* capocuoco.

chemical ['kemɪkəl] *a* chimico(a) // *n* prodotto chimico.

chemist ['kemɪst] *n* (Brit: pharmacist) farmacista *m/f*; (scientist) chimico/a; **~ry** *n* chimica; **~'s (shop)** *n* (Brit) farmacia.

cheque [tʃek] *n* (Brit) assegno; **~book** *n* libretto degli assegni; **~ card** *n* carta *f* assegni *inv*.

chequered ['tʃekəd] *a* (fig) movimentato(a).

cherish ['tʃerɪʃ] *vt* aver caro; (hope etc) nutrire.

cherry ['tʃerɪ] *n* ciliegia.

chess [tʃes] *n* scacchi *mpl*; **~board** *n* scacchiera; **~man** *n* pezzo degli scacchi.

chest [tʃest] *n* petto; (box) cassa; **~ of drawers** *n* cassettone *m*.

chestnut ['tʃesnʌt] *n* castagna; (also: ~ tree) castagno.

chew [tʃuː] *vt* masticare; **~ing gum** *n* chewing gum *m*.

chic [ʃiːk] *a* elegante.

chick [tʃɪk] *n* pulcino; (US col) pollastrella.

chicken ['tʃɪkɪn] *n* pollo; **to ~ out** *vi* (col) avere fifa; **~pox** *n* varicella.

chicory ['tʃɪkərɪ] *n* cicoria.

chief [tʃiːf] *n* capo // *a* principale; **~ constable** *n* (Brit) = questore *m*; **~ executive** *n* direttore *m* generale; **~ly** *ad* per lo più, soprattutto.

chilblain ['tʃɪlbleɪn] *n* gelone *m*.

child, *pl* **~ren** [tʃaɪld, 'tʃɪldrən] *n* bambino/a; **~birth** *n* parto; **~hood** *n* infanzia; **~ish** *a* puerile; **~like** *a* fanciullesco(a); **~ minder** *n* (Brit) bambinaia.

Chile ['tʃɪlɪ] *n* Cile *m*.

chill [tʃɪl] *n* freddo; (MED) infreddatura // *a* freddo(a), gelido(a) // *vt* raffreddare.

chil(l)i ['tʃɪlɪ] *n* peperoncino.

chilly ['tʃɪlɪ] *a* freddo(a), fresco(a); to feel ~ sentirsi infreddolito(a).

chime [tʃaɪm] *n* carillon *m inv* // *vi* suonare, scampanare.

chimney ['tʃɪmnɪ] *n* camino; **~ sweep** *n* spazzacamino.

chimpanzee [tʃɪmpæn'ziː] *n* scimpanzé *m inv*.

chin [tʃɪn] *n* mento.

China ['tʃaɪnə] *n* Cina.

china ['tʃaɪnə] *n* porcellana.

Chinese [tʃaɪ'niːz] *a* cinese // *n* (pl inv) cinese *m/f*; (LING) cinese *m*.

chink [tʃɪŋk] *n* (opening) fessura; (noise) tintinnio.

chip [tʃɪp] *n* (gen pl: CULIN) patatina fritta; (: US: also: potato ~) patatina; (of wood, glass, stone) scheggia; (also: micro~) chip *m inv* // *vt* (cup, plate) scheggiare; **to ~ in** *vi* (col: contribute) contribuire; (: interrupt) intromettersi.

chiropodist [kɪ'rɔpədɪst] *n* (Brit) pedicure *m/f inv*.

chirp [tʃəːp] *vi* cinguettare.

chisel ['tʃɪzl] *n* cesello.

chit [tʃɪt] *n* biglietto.

chivalry ['ʃɪvəlrɪ] *n* cavalleria; cortesia.

chives [tʃaɪvz] *npl* erba cipollina.

chock [tʃɔk] *n* zeppa; **~-a-block**, **~-full** *a* pieno(a) zeppo(a).

chocolate ['tʃɔklɪt] *n* (substance) cioccolato, cioccolata; (drink) cioccolata; (a sweet) cioccolatino.

choice [tʃɔɪs] *n* scelta // *a* scelto(a).

choir ['kwaɪə*] *n* coro; **~boy** *n* corista *m* fanciullo.

choke [tʃəuk] *vi* soffocare // *vt* soffocare; (block) ingombrare // *n* (AUT) valvola dell'aria.

cholera ['kɔlərə] *n* colera *m*.

cholesterol [kə'lestərɔl] *n* colesterolo.

choose [tʃuːz], *pt* **chose**, *pp* **chosen** *vt* scegliere; **to ~ to do** decidere di fare; preferire fare.

choosy ['tʃuːzɪ] *a* schizzinoso(a).

chop [tʃɔp] *vt* (wood) spaccare; (CULIN: also: ~ up) tritare // *n* colpo netto; (CULIN) costoletta; **~s** *npl* (jaws) mascelle *fpl*.

chopper ['tʃɔpə*] *n* (helicopter) elicottero.

choppy ['tʃɔpɪ] *a* (sea) mosso(a).

chopsticks ['tʃɔpstɪks] *npl* bastoncini *mpl* cinesi.

choral ['kɔːrəl] *a* corale.

chord [kɔːd] *n* (MUS) accordo.

chore [tʃɔː*] *n* faccenda; **household ~s** faccende *fpl* domestiche.

choreographer [kɔrɪ'ɔgrəfə*] *n* coreografo/a.

chorister ['kɔrɪstə*] *n* corista *m/f*.

chortle ['tʃɔːtl] *vi* ridacchiare.

chorus ['kɔːrəs] *n* coro; *(repeated part of song, also fig)* ritornello.

chose [tʃəuz] *pt of* **choose.**

chosen ['tʃəuzn] *pp of* **choose.**

Christ [kraɪst] *n* Cristo.

christen ['krɪsn] *vt* battezzare.

Christian ['krɪstɪən] *a, n* cristiano(a); **~ity** [-'ænɪtɪ] *n* cristianesimo; **~ name** *n* nome *m* (di battesimo).

Christmas ['krɪsməs] *n* Natale *m*; **Merry ~!** Buon Natale!; **~ card** *n* cartolina di Natale; **~ Day** *n* il giorno di Natale; **~ Eve** *n* la vigilia di Natale; **~ tree** *n* albero di Natale.

chrome [krəum], **chromium** ['krəumɪəm] *n* cromo.

chronic ['krɔnɪk] *a* cronico(a).

chronicle ['krɔnɪkl] *n* cronaca.

chronological [krɔnə'lɔdʒɪkəl] *a* cronologico(a).

chrysanthemum [krɪ'sænθəməm] *n* crisantemo.

chubby ['tʃʌbɪ] *a* paffuto(a).

chuck [tʃʌk] *vt* buttare, gettare; **to ~ out** *vt* buttar fuori; **to ~ (up)** *vt (Brit)* piantare.

chuckle ['tʃʌkl] *vi* ridere sommessamente.

chug [tʃʌg] *vi* fare ciuf ciuf.

chum [tʃʌm] *n* compagno/a.

chunk [tʃʌŋk] *n* pezzo; *(of bread)* tocco.

church [tʃəːtʃ] *n* chiesa; **~yard** *n* sagrato.

churlish ['tʃəːlɪʃ] *a* rozzo(a), sgarbato(a).

churn [tʃəːn] *n (for butter)* zangola; *(for transport: also:* milk **~)** bidone *m*; **to ~ out** *vt* sfornare.

chute [ʃuːt] *n* cascata; *(also:* rubbish **~)** canale *m* di scarico; *(Brit: children's slide)* scivolo.

chutney ['tʃʌtnɪ] *n* salsa piccante *(di frutta, zucchero e spezie).*

CIA *n abbr (US:* = *Central Intelligence Agency)* CIA *f.*

CID *n abbr (Brit:* = *Criminal Investigation Department)* ≈ polizia giudiziaria.

cider ['saɪdə*] *n* sidro.

cigar [sɪ'gɑː*] *n* sigaro.

cigarette [sɪgə'rɛt] *n* sigaretta; **~ case** *n* portasigarette *m inv*; **~ end** *n* mozzicone *m.*

cinder ['sɪndə*] *n* cenere *f.*

Cinderella [sɪndə'rɛlə] *n* Cenerentola.

cine ['sɪnɪ]: **~-camera** *n (Brit)* cinepresa; **~-film** *n (Brit)* pellicola.

cinema ['sɪnəmə] *n* cinema *m inv.*

cinnamon ['sɪnəmən] *n* cannella.

cipher ['saɪfə*] *n* cifra; *(fig: faceless employee etc)* persona di nessun conto.

circle ['səːkl] *n* cerchio; *(of friends etc)* circolo; *(in cinema)* galleria // *vi* girare in circolo // *vt (surround)* circondare; *(move round)* girare intorno a.

circuit ['səːkɪt] *n* circuito; **~ous** [səː'kjuɪtəs] *a* indiretto(a).

circular ['səːkjulə*] *a, n* circolare *(f).*

circulate ['səːkjuleɪt] *vi* circolare // *vt* far circolare; **circulation** [-'leɪʃən] *n* circolazione *f; (of newspaper)* tiratura.

circumstances ['səːkəmstənsɪz] *npl* circostanze *fpl; (financial condition)* condizioni *fpl* finanziarie.

circumvent [səːkəm'vɛnt] *vt* aggirare.

circus ['səːkəs] *n* circo.

cistern ['sɪstən] *n* cisterna; *(in toilet)* serbatoio d'acqua.

citizen ['sɪtɪzn] *n (POL)* cittadino/a; *(resident)*: the **~s** of this town gli abitanti di questa città; **~ship** *n* cittadinanza.

citrus fruit ['sɪtrəs-] *n* agrume *m.*

city ['sɪtɪ] *n* città *f inv;* the **C~** la Città di Londra *(centro commerciale).*

civic ['sɪvɪk] *a* civico(a); **~ centre** *n (Brit)* centro civico.

civil ['sɪvɪl] *a* civile; **~ engineer** *n* ingegnere *m* civile; **~ian** [sɪ'vɪlɪən] *a, n* borghese *(m/f).*

civilization [sɪvɪlaɪ'zeɪʃən] *n* civiltà *f inv.*

civilized ['sɪvɪlaɪzd] *a* civilizzato(a); *(fig)* cortese.

civil: **~ law** *n* codice *m* civile; *(study)* diritto civile; **~ servant** *n* impiegato/a statale; **C~ Service** *n* amministrazione *f* statale; **~ war** *n* guerra civile.

clad [klæd] *a:* **~ (in)** vestito(a) (di).

claim [kleɪm] *vt* rivendicare; sostenere, pretendere; *(damages)* richiedere // *vi (for insurance)* fare una domanda d'indennizzo // *n* rivendicazione *f;* pretesa; *(right)* diritto; *(insurance)* **~** domanda d'indennizzo; **~ant** *n (ADMIN, LAW)* richiedente *m/f.*

clairvoyant [klɛə'vɔɪənt] *n* chiaroveggente *m/f.*

clam [klæm] *n* vongola.

clamber ['klæmbə*] *vi* arrampicarsi.

clammy ['klæmɪ] *a (weather)* caldo(a) umido(a); *(hands)* viscido(a).

clamour, *(US)* **clamor** ['klæmə*] *vi:* to **~ for** chiedere a gran voce.

clamp [klæmp] *n* pinza; morsa // *vt* ammorsare; **to ~ down on** *vt fus* dare un giro di vite a.

clan [klæn] *n* clan *m inv.*

clang [klæŋ] *n* fragore *m*, suono metallico.

clap [klæp] *vi* applaudire; **~ping** *n* applausi *mpl.*

claret ['klærət] *n* vino di Bordeaux.

clarify ['klærɪfaɪ] *vt* chiarificare, chiarire.

clarinet [klærɪ'nɛt] *n* clarinetto.

clarity ['klærɪtɪ] *n* chiarità.

clash [klæʃ] *n* frastuono; *(fig)* scontro // *vi* scontrarsi; cozzare.

clasp [klɑːsp] *n* fermaglio, fibbia // *vt* stringere.

class [klɑːs] *n* classe *f* // *vt* classificare.

classic ['klæsɪk] *a* classico(a) // *n* classico; **~al** *a* classico(a).

classified ['klæsɪfaɪd] *a* (*information*) segreto(a), riservato(a); **~ advertisement**, **~ ad** *n* annuncio economico.

classmate ['klɑ:smeɪt] *n* compagno/a di classe.

classroom ['klɑ:srum] *n* aula.

clatter ['klætə*] *n* acciottolio; scalpitio // *vi* acciottolare; scalpitare.

clause [klɔ:z] *n* clausola; (*LING*) proposizione *f*.

claw [klɔ:] *n* tenaglia; (*of bird of prey*) artiglio; (*of lobster*) pinza // *vt* (*also: ~ at*) graffiare; afferrare.

clay [kleɪ] *n* argilla.

clean [kli:n] *a* pulito(a); (*clear, smooth*) liscio(a) // *vt* pulire; **to ~ out** *vt* ripulire; **to ~ up** *vi* far pulizia // *vt* (*also fig*) ripulire; **~er** *n* (*person*) donna delle pulizie; (*also: dry ~er*) tintore/a; (*product*) smacchiatore *m*; **~ing** *n* pulizia; **~liness** ['klɛnlɪnɪs] *n* pulizia.

cleanse [klɛnz] *vt* pulire; purificare; **~r** *n* detergente *m*.

clean-shaven ['kli:n'ʃeɪvn] *a* sbarbato(a).

cleansing department ['klɛnzɪŋ-] *n* (*Brit*) nettezza urbana.

clear [klɪə*] *a* chiaro(a); (*road, way*) libero(a) // *vt* sgombrare; liberare; (*table*) sparecchiare; (*COMM: goods*) liquidare; (: *debt*) liquidare, saldare; (: *cheque*) fare la compensazione di; (*LAW: suspect*) discolpare; (*obstacle*) superare // *vi* (*weather*) rasserenarsi; (*fog*) andarsene // *ad:* **~ of** distante da; **to ~ up** *vi* schiarirsi // *vt* mettere in ordine; (*mystery*) risolvere; **~ance** *n* (*removal*) sgombro; (*free space*) spazio; (*permission*) autorizzazione *f*, permesso; **~-cut** *a* ben delineato, distinto(a); **~ing** *n* radura; **~ing bank** *n* (*Brit*) banca (che fa uso della camera di compensazione); **~ly** *ad* chiaramente; **~way** *n* (*Brit*) strada con divieto di sosta.

cleaver ['kli:və*] *n* mannaia.

clef [klɛf] *n* (*MUS*) chiave *f*.

cleft [klɛft] *n* (*in rock*) crepa, fenditura.

clench [klɛntʃ] *vt* stringere.

clergy ['klə:dʒɪ] *n* clero; **~man** *n* ecclesiastico.

clerical ['klɛrɪkəl] *a* d'impiegato; (*REL*) cericale.

clerk [klɑ:k, (*US*) klə:rk] *n* impiegato/a; (*US: sales person*) commesso/a.

clever ['klɛvə*] *a* (*mentally*) intelligente; (*deft, skilful*) abile; (*device, arrangement*) ingegnoso(a).

click [klɪk] *vi* scattare // *vt* (*heels etc*) battere; (*tongue*) far schioccare.

client ['klaɪənt] *n* cliente *m/f*.

cliff [klɪf] *n* scogliera scoscesa, rupe *f*.

climate ['klaɪmɪt] *n* clima *m*.

climax ['klaɪmæks] *n* culmine *m*.

climb [klaɪm] *vi* salire; (*clamber*) arrampicarsi // *vt* salire; (*CLIMBING*) scalare // *n* salita; arrampicata; scalata; **~-down** *n* marcia indietro; **~er** *n* (*also: rock ~er*) rocciatore/trice; alpinista *m/f*; **~ing** *n* (*also: rock ~ing*) alpinismo.

clinch [klɪntʃ] *vt* (*deal*) concludere.

cling [klɪŋ], *pt, pp* **clung** *vi:* **to ~ (to)** tenersi stretto(a) (a); (*of clothes*) aderire strettamente (a).

clinic ['klɪnɪk] *n* clinica.

clink [klɪŋk] *vi* tintinnare.

clip [klɪp] *n* (*for hair*) forcina; (*also: paper ~*) graffetta; (*holding hose etc*) anello d'attacco // *vt* (*also: ~ together*: *papers*) attaccare insieme; (*hair, nails*) tagliare; (*hedge*) tosare; **~pers** *npl* macchinetta per capelli; (*also: nail ~pers*) forbicine *fpl* per le unghie; **~ping** *n* (*from newspaper*) ritaglio.

clique [kli:k] *n* cricca.

cloak [kləuk] *n* mantello // *vt* avvolgere; **~room** *n* (*for coats etc*) guardaroba *m inv*; (*Brit: W.C.*) gabinetti *mpl*.

clock [klɔk] *n* orologio; **to ~ in** *or* **on** *vi* timbrare il cartellino (all'entrata); **to ~ off** *or* **out** *vi* timbrare il cartellino (all'uscita); **~wise** *ad* in senso orario; **~work** *n* movimento *or* meccanismo a orologeria // *a* a molla.

clog [klɔg] *n* zoccolo // *vt* intasare // *vi* intasarsi, bloccarsi.

cloister ['klɔɪstə*] *n* chiostro.

clone [kləun] *n* clone *m*.

close *a, ad and derivatives* [kləus] *a:* **~ (to)** vicino(a) (a); (*writing, texture*) fitto(a); (*watch*) stretto(a); (*examination*) attento(a); (*weather*) afoso(a) // *ad* vicino, dappresso; **to ~** *prep* vicino a; **~ by**, **~ at hand** *a, ad* a portata di mano; a **~ friend** un amico intimo; **to have a ~ shave** (*fig*) scamparla bella // *vb and derivatives* [kləuz] *vt* chiudere // *vi* (*shop etc*) chiudere; (*lid, door etc*) chiudersi; (*end*) finire // *n* (*end*) fine *f*; **to ~ down** *vt* chiudere (definitivamente) // *vi* cessare (definitivamente); **~d** *a* chiuso(a); **~d shop** *n* azienda o fabbrica che impiega solo aderenti ai sindacati; **~-knit** *a* (*family, community*) molto unito(a); **~ly** *ad* (*examine, watch*) da vicino.

closet ['klɔzɪt] *n* (*cupboard*) armadio.

close-up ['kləusʌp] *n* primo piano.

closure ['kləuʒə*] *n* chiusura.

clot [klɔt] *n* (*also: blood ~*) coagulo; (*col: idiot*) scemo/a // *vi* coagularsi.

cloth [klɔθ] *n* (*material*) tessuto, stoffa; (*also: tea~*) strofinaccio.

clothe [kləuð] *vt* vestire; **~s** *npl* abiti *mpl*, vestiti *mpl*; **~s brush** *n* spazzola per abiti; **~s line** *n* corda (per stendere il bucato); **~s peg**, (US) **~s pin** n molletta.

clothing ['kləʊðɪŋ] n = **clothes**.

cloud [klaud] n nuvola; **~y** a nuvoloso(a); (liquid) torbido(a).

clout [klaut] vt dare un colpo a.

clove [kləʊv] n chiodo di garofano; ~ of garlic spicchio d'aglio.

clover ['kləʊvə*] n trifoglio.

clown [klaun] n pagliaccio // vi (also: ~ about, ~ around) fare il pagliaccio.

cloying ['klɔɪɪŋ] a (taste, smell) nauseabondo(a).

club [klʌb] n (society) club m inv, circolo; (weapon, GOLF) mazza // vt bastonare // vi: to ~ together associarsi; ~s npl (CARDS) fiori mpl; ~ car n (US RAIL) vagone m ristorante; **~house** n sede f del circolo.

cluck [klʌk] vi chiocciare.

clue [klu:] n indizio; (in crosswords) definizione f; I haven't a ~ non ho la minima idea.

clump [klʌmp] n: ~ of trees folto d'alberi.

clumsy ['klʌmzɪ] a (person) goffo(a), maldestro(a); (object) malfatto(a), mal costruito(a).

clung [klʌŋ] pt, pp of **cling**.

cluster ['klʌstə*] n gruppo // vi raggrupparsi.

clutch [klʌtʃ] n (grip, grasp) presa, stretta; (AUT) frizione f // vt afferrare, stringere forte; to ~ at aggrapparsi a.

clutter ['klʌtə*] vt ingombrare.

CND n abbr = Campaign for Nuclear Disarmament.

Co. abbr = **county; company**.

c/o abbr (= care of) presso.

coach [kəʊtʃ] n (bus) pullman m inv; (horse-drawn, of train) carrozza; (SPORT) allenatore/trice // vt allenare; ~ trip n viaggio in pullman.

coagulate [kəʊ'ægjʊleɪt] vi coagularsi.

coal [kəʊl] n carbone m; ~ **face** n fronte f; **~field** n bacino carbonifero.

coalition [kəʊə'lɪʃən] n coalizione f.

coalman, coal merchant ['kəʊlmən, 'kəʊlmə:tʃənt] n negoziante m di carbone.

coalmine ['kəʊlmaɪn] n miniera di carbone.

coarse [kɔ:s] a (salt, sand etc) grosso(a); (cloth, person) rozzo(a).

coast [kəʊst] n costa // vi (with cycle etc) scendere a ruota libera; **~al** a costiero(a); **~guard** n guardia costiera; **~line** n linea costiera.

coat [kəʊt] n cappotto; (of animal) pelo; (of paint) mano f // vt coprire; ~ of arms n stemma m; **~ hanger** n attaccapanni m inv; **~ing** n rivestimento.

coax [kəʊks] vt indurre (con moine).

cob [kɔb] n see **corn**.

cobbler ['kɔblə*] n calzolaio.

cobbles, cobblestones ['kɔblz, 'kɔblstəʊnz] npl ciottoli mpl.

cobweb ['kɔbweb] n ragnatela.

cocaine [kə'keɪn] n cocaina.

cock [kɔk] n (rooster) gallo; (male bird) maschio // vt (gun) armare; **~erel** n galletto; **~-eyed** a (fig) storto(a); strampalato(a).

cockle ['kɔkl] n cardio.

cockney ['kɔknɪ] n cockney m/f inv (abitante dei quartieri popolari dell'East End di Londra).

cockpit ['kɔkpɪt] n (in aircraft) abitacolo.

cockroach ['kɔkrəʊtʃ] n blatta.

cocktail ['kɔkteɪl] n cocktail m inv; ~ cabinet n mobile m bar inv; ~ party n cocktail m inv.

cocoa ['kəʊkəʊ] n cacao.

coconut ['kəʊkənʌt] n noce f di cocco.

cocoon [kə'ku:n] n bozzolo.

cod [kɔd] n merluzzo.

C.O.D. abbr = **cash on delivery**.

code [kəʊd] n codice m.

cod-liver oil ['kɔdlɪvə*-] n olio di fegato di merluzzo.

coercion [kəʊ'ə:ʃən] n coercizione f.

coffee ['kɔfɪ] n caffè m inv; ~ **bar** n (Brit) caffè m inv; ~ **break** n pausa per il caffè; **~pot** n caffettiera; ~ **table** n tavolino.

coffin ['kɔfɪn] n bara.

cog [kɔg] n dente m.

cogent ['kəʊdʒənt] a convincente.

coherent [kəʊ'hɪərənt] a coerente.

coil [kɔɪl] n rotolo; (one loop) anello; (contraceptive) spirale f // vt avvolgere.

coin [kɔɪn] n moneta // vt (word) coniare; **~age** n sistema m monetario; **~-box** n (Brit) telefono a gettoni.

coincide [kəʊɪn'saɪd] vi coincidere; **~nce** [kəʊ'ɪnsɪdəns] n combinazione f.

coke [kəʊk] n coke m.

colander ['kɔləndə*] n colino.

cold [kəʊld] a freddo(a) // n freddo; (MED) raffreddore m; it's ~ fa freddo; to be ~ aver freddo; to catch ~ prendere freddo; to catch a ~ prendere un raffreddore; in ~ blood a sangue freddo; ~ sore n erpete m.

coleslaw ['kəʊlslɔ:] n insalata di cavolo bianco.

colic ['kɔlɪk] n colica.

collapse [kə'læps] vi crollare // n crollo; (MED) collasso.

collapsible [kə'læpsəbl] a pieghevole.

collar ['kɔlə*] n (of coat, shirt) colletto; **~bone** n clavicola.

collateral [kə'lætərl] n garanzia.

colleague ['kɔli:g] n collega m/f.

collect [kə'lekt] vt (gen) raccogliere; (as a hobby) fare collezione di; (Brit: call and pick up) prendere; (money owed, pension) riscuotere; (donations, subscriptions) fare una colletta di // vi adunarsi, riunirsi; ammucchiarsi; to call ~ (*US TEL*) fare una chiamata a carico del destinatario; **~ion** [kə'lɛkʃən] *n* collezione *f*; raccolta; (*for money*) colletta.

collector [kə'lɛktə*] *n* collezionista *m/f*; (*of taxes*) esattore *m*.

college ['kɔlɪdʒ] *n* (*Brit, US SCOL*) college *m inv*; (*of technology etc*) istituto superiore; (*body*) collegio.

collide [kə'laɪd] *vi*: to ~ (with) scontrarsi (con).

collie ['kɔlɪ] *n* (*dog*) collie *m inv*.

colliery ['kɔlɪərɪ] *n* (*Brit*) miniera di carbone.

collision [kə'lɪʒən] *n* collisione *f*, scontro.

colloquial [kə'ləukwɪəl] *a* familiare.

colon ['kəulən] *n* (*sign*) due punti *mpl*; (*MED*) colon *m inv*.

colonel ['kə:nl] *n* colonnello.

colonial [kə'ləunɪəl] *a* coloniale.

colony, (*US*) **color** ['kɔlənɪ] *n* colonia.

colour, (*US*) **color** ['kʌlə*] *n* colore *m* // *vt* colorare; (*tint, dye*) tingere; (*fig: affect*) influenzare // *vi* (*blush: also: ~ up*) arrossire; **~s** *npl* (*of party, club*) emblemi *mpl*; ~ **bar** *n* discriminazione *f* razziale (*in locali etc*); **~blind** *a* daltonico(a); **~ed** *a* colorato(a); (*photo*) a colori // *n*: **~eds** gente *f* di colore; ~ **film** *n* (*for camera*) pellicola a colori; **~ful** *a* pieno(a) di colore, a vivaci colori; (*personality*) colorato(a); **~ing** *n* colorazione *f*; (*substance*) colorante *m*; (*complexion*) colorito; ~ **scheme** *n* combinazione *f* di colori; ~ **television** *n* televisione *f* a colori.

colt [kəult] *n* puledro.

column ['kɔləm] *n* colonna; **~ist** ['kɔləmnɪst] *n* articolista *m/f*.

coma ['kəumə] *n* coma *m inv*.

comb [kəum] *n* pettine *m* // *vt* (*hair*) pettinare; (*area*) battere a tappeto.

combat ['kɔmbæt] *n* combattimento // *vt* combattere, lottare contro.

combination [kɔmbɪ'neɪʃən] *n* combinazione *f*.

combine *vb* [kəm'baɪn] *vt*: to ~ (with) combinare (con); (*one quality with another*) unire (a) // *vi* unirsi; (*CHEM*) combinarsi // *n* ['kɔmbaɪn] (*ECON*) lega; ~ (**harvester**) *n* mietitrebbia.

come [kʌm], *pt* **came,** *pp* **come** *vi* venire; arrivare; to ~ to (*decision etc*) raggiungere; to ~ **undone** slacciarsi; to ~ **loose** allentarsi; **to ~ about** *vi* succedere; **to ~ across** *vt fus* trovare per caso; **to ~ along** *vi* = **to come on; to ~ away** *vi* venire via; staccarsi; **to ~ back** *vi* ritornare; **to ~ by** *vt fus* (*acquire*) ottenere; procurarsi; **to ~ down** *vi* scendere; (*prices*) calare; (*buildings*) essere demolito(a); **to ~ forward** *vi* farsi avanti;

presentarsi; **to ~ from** *vt fus* venire da; provenire da; **to ~ in** *vi* entrare; **to ~ in for** *vt fus* (*criticism etc*) ricevere; **to ~ into** *vt fus* (*money*) ereditare; **to ~ off** *vi* (*button*) staccarsi; (*stain*) andar via; (*attempt*) riuscire; **to ~ on** *vi* (*pupil, work, project*) fare progressi; (*lights*) accendersi; (*electricity*) entrare in funzione; ~ **on!** avanti!, andiamo!, forza!; **to ~ out** *vi* uscire; (*strike*) entrare in sciopero; **to ~ round** *vi* (*after faint, operation*) riprendere conoscenza, rinvenire; **to ~ to** *vi* rinvenire; **to ~ up** *vi* venire su; **to ~ up against** *vt fus* (*resistance, difficulties*) urtare contro; **to ~ up with** *vt fus*: he came up with an idea venne fuori con un'idea; **to ~ upon** *vt fus* trovare per caso; **~back** *n* (*THEATRE etc*) ritorno.

comedian [kə'mi:dɪən] *n* comico.

comedown ['kʌmdaun] *n* rovescio.

comedy ['kɔmɪdɪ] *n* commedia.

comeuppance [kʌm'ʌpəns] *n*: to get one's ~ ricevere ciò che si merita.

comfort ['kʌmfət] *n* comodità *f inv*, benessere *m*; (*solace*) consolazione *f*, conforto // *vt* consolare, confortare; **~s** *npl* comodità *fpl*; **~able** *a* comodo(a); **~ably** *ad* (*sit etc*) comodamente; (*live*) bene; ~ **station** *n* (*US*) gabinetti *mpl*.

comic ['kɔmɪk] *a* (*also:* **~al**) comico(a) // *n* comico; (*magazine*) giornaletto; ~ **strip** *n* fumetto.

coming ['kʌmɪŋ] *n*-arrivo // *a* (*next*) prossimo(a); (*future*) futuro(a); **~(s) and going(s)** *n(pl)* andirivieni *m inv*.

comma ['kɔmə] *n* virgola.

command [kə'mɑ:nd] *n* ordine *m*, comando; (*MIL: authority*) comando; (*mastery*) padronanza // *vt* comandare; to ~ sb to do ordinare a qn di fare; **~eer** [kɔmən'dɪə*] *vt* requisire; **~er** *n* capo; (*MIL*) comandante *m*.

commando [kə'mɑ:ndəu] *n* commando *m inv*; membro di un commando.

commemorate [kə'mɛmərɪt] *vt* commemorare.

commence [kə'mɛns] *vt, vi* cominciare.

commend [kə'mɛnd] *vt* lodare; raccomandare.

commensurate [kə'mɛnʃərɪt] *a*: ~ with proporzionato(a).

comment ['kɔmɛnt] *n* commento // *vi*: to ~ (on) fare commenti (su); **~ary** ['kɔməntərɪ] *n* commentario; (*SPORT*) radiocronaca; telecronaca; **~ator** ['kɔmənteɪtə*] *n* commentatore/trice; radiocronista *m/f*; telecronista *m/f*.

commerce ['kɔmə:s] *n* commercio.

commercial [kə'mə:ʃəl] *a* commerciale // *n* (*TV: also:* ~ **break**) pubblicità *f inv*.

commiserate [kə'mɪzəreɪt] *vi*: to ~ with condolersi con.

commission [kə'mɪʃən] *n* commissione *f*

// vt (MIL) nominare (al comando); (work of art) commissionare; out of ~ (NAUT) in disarmo; **~aire** [kɔmiʃɔ'nɛə*] n (Brit: at shop, cinema etc) portiere m in livrea; **~er** n commissionario; (POLICE) questore m.

commit [kə'mɪt] vt (act) commettere; (to sb's care) affidare; to ~ o.s. (to do) impegnarsi (a fare); to ~ suicide suicidarsi; **~ment** n impegno; promessa.

committee [kə'mɪtɪ] n comitato.

commodity [kə'mɔdɪtɪ] n prodotto, articolo; (food) derrata.

common ['kɔmən] a comune; (pej) volgare; (usual) normale // n terreno comune; the C~s npl (Brit) la Camera dei Comuni; in ~ in comune; **~er** n cittadino/a (non nobile); ~ **ground** n (fig) terreno comune; ~ **law** n diritto consuetudinario; **~ly** ad comunemente, usualmente; **C~ Market** n Mercato Comune; **~place** a banale, ordinario(a); **~room** n sala di riunione; (SCOL) sala dei professori; ~ **sense** n buon senso; the C~wealth n il Commonwealth.

commotion [kə'məuʃən] n confusione f, tumulto.

communal ['kɔmju:nl] a (life) comunale; (for common use) pubblico(a).

commune n ['kɔmju:n] (group) comune f // a [kə'mju:n]: to ~ with mettersi in comunione con.

communicate [kə'mju:nɪkeɪt] vt comunicare, trasmettere // vi: to ~ (with) comunicare (con).

communication [kəmju:nɪ'keɪʃən] n comunicazione f; ~ **cord** n (Brit) segnale m d'allarme.

communion [kə'mju:nɪən] n (also: Holy C~) comunione f.

communiqué [kə'mju:nɪkeɪ] n comunicato.

communism ['kɔmjunɪzəm] n comunismo; **communist** a, n comunista (m/f).

community [kə'mju:nɪtɪ] n comunità f inv; ~ **centre** n circolo ricreativo; ~ **chest** n (US) fondo di beneficenza.

commutation ticket [kɔmju'teɪʃən-] n (US) biglietto di abbonamento.

commute [kə'mju:t] vi fare il pendolare // vt (LAW) commutare; **~r** n pendolare m/f.

compact a [kəm'pækt] compatto(a) // n ['kɔmpækt] (also: powder ~) portacipria m inv; ~ **disk** n compact disc m inv.

companion [kəm'pænɪən] n compagno/a; **~ship** n compagnia.

company ['kʌmpənɪ] n (also COMM, MIL, THEATRE) compagnia; to keep sb ~ tenere compagnia a qn; ~ **secretary** n (Brit) segretario/a generale.

comparative [kəm'pærətɪv] a

relativo(a); (adjective etc) comparativo(a); **~ly** ad relativamente.

compare [kəm'pɛə*] vt: to ~ sth/sb with/to confrontare qc/qn con/a // vi: to ~ (with) reggere il confronto (con); **comparison** [-'pærɪsn] n confronto.

compartment [kəm'pɑ:tmənt] n compartimento; (RAIL) scompartimento.

compass ['kʌmpəs] n bussola; **~es** npl compasso.

compassion [kəm'pæʃən] n compassione f.

compatible [kəm'pætɪbl] a compatibile.

compel [kəm'pɛl] vt costringere, obbligare; **~ling** a (fig: argument) irresistibile.

compendium [kəm'pɛndɪəm] n compendio.

compensate ['kɔmpənseɪt] vt risarcire // vi: to ~ for compensare; **compensation** [-'seɪʃən] n compensazione f; (money) risarcimento.

compère ['kɔmpɛə*] n presentatore/trice.

compete [kəm'pi:t] vi (take part) concorrere; (vie): to ~ (with) fare concorrenza (a).

competence ['kɔmpɪtəns] n competenza.

competent ['kɔmpɪtənt] a competente.

competition [kɔmpɪ'tɪʃən] n gara; concorso; (ECON) concorrenza.

competitive [kəm'pɛtɪtɪv] a (ECON) concorrenziale; (sport) agonistico(a); (person) che ha spirito di competizione; che ha spirito agonistico; ~ **exam** concorso.

competitor [kəm'pɛtɪtə*] n concorrente m/f.

complacency [kəm'pleɪsnsɪ] n compiacenza di sé.

complain [kəm'pleɪn] vi: to ~ (about) lagnarsi (di); (in shop etc) reclamare (per); **~t** n lamento; reclamo; (MED) malattia.

complement n ['kɔmplɪmənt] complemento; (especially of ship's crew etc) effettivo // vt ['kɔmplɪment] (enhance) accompagnarsi bene a; **~ary** [kɔmplɪ'mentərɪ] a complementare.

complete [kəm'pli:t] a completo(a) // vt completare; (a form) riempire; **~ly** ad completamente; **completion** n completamento.

complex ['kɔmplɛks] a complesso(a) // n (PSYCH, buildings etc) complesso.

complexion [kəm'plɛkʃən] n (of face) carnagione f; (of event etc) aspetto.

compliance [kəm'plaɪəns] n acquiescenza; in ~ with (orders, wishes etc) in conformità con.

complicate ['kɔmplɪkeɪt] vt complicare; **~d** a complicato(a); **complication** [-'keɪʃən] n complicazione f.

compliment n ['kɔmplɪmənt] complimento // vt ['kɔmplɪment] fare un complimento a; **~s** npl complimenti mpl; rispetti *mpl*; **to pay sb a ~** fare un complimento a qn; **~ary** [-'mɛntərɪ] *a* complimentoso(a), elogiativo(a); *(free)* in omaggio; **~ary ticket** *n* biglietto d'omaggio.

comply [kəm'plaɪ] *vi*: **to ~ with** assentire a; conformarsi a.

component [kəm'pəʊnənt] *n* componente *m*.

compose [kəm'pəʊz] *vt* comporre; **to ~ o.s.** ricomporsi; **~d** *a* calmo(a); **~r** *n* (*MUS*) compositore/trice.

composition [kɒmpə'zɪʃən] *n* composizione *f*.

composure [kəm'pəʊʒə*] *n* calma.

compound ['kɒmpaʊnd] *n* (*CHEM*, *LING*) composto; *(enclosure)* recinto // *a* composto(a); **~ fracture** *n* frattura esposta.

comprehend [kɒmprɪ'hɛnd] *vt* comprendere, capire; **comprehension** [-'hɛnʃən] *n* comprensione *f*.

comprehensive [kɒmprɪ'hɛnsɪv] *a* comprensivo(a); **~ policy** *n* (*INSURANCE*) polizza che copre tutti i rischi; **~ (school)** *n* *(Brit)* scuola secondaria aperta a tutti.

compress *vt* [kəm'prɛs] comprimere // *n* ['kɒmprɛs] (*MED*) compressa.

comprise [kəm'praɪz] *vt* (*also*: **be ~d of**) comprendere.

compromise ['kɒmprəmaɪz] *n* compromesso // *vt* compromettere // *vi* venire a un compromesso.

compulsion [kəm'pʌlʃən] *n* costrizione *f*.

compulsive [kəm'pʌlsɪv] *a* (*PSYCH*) incontrollabile.

compulsory [kəm'pʌlsərɪ] *a* obbligatorio(a).

computer [kəm'pju:tə*] *n* computer *m inv*, elaboratore *m* elettronico; **~ize** *vt* computerizzare; **~ programmer** *n* programmatore/trice; **~ programming** *n* programmazione *f* di computer; **~ science, computing** *n* informatica.

comrade ['kɒmrɪd] *n* compagno/a.

con [kɒn] *vt* (*col*) truffare // *n* truffa.

conceal [kən'si:l] *vt* nascondere.

conceit [kən'si:t] *n* presunzione *f*, vanità; **~ed** *a* presuntuoso(a), vanitoso(a).

conceive [kən'si:v] *vt* concepire // *vi* concepire un bambino.

concentrate ['kɒnsəntreɪt] *vi* concentrarsi // *vt* concentrare.

concentration [kɒnsən'treɪʃən] *n* concentrazione *f*; **~ camp** *n* campo di concentramento.

concept ['kɒnsɛpt] *n* concetto.

conception [kən'sɛpʃən] *n* concezione *f*.

concern [kən'sɜ:n] *n* affare *m*; (*COMM*) azienda, ditta; *(anxiety)* preoccupazione *f* // *vt* riguardare; **to be ~ed (about)** preoccuparsi (di); **~ing** *prep* riguardo a, circa.

concert ['kɒnsət] *n* concerto; **~ed**

[kən'sə:tɪd] *a* concertato(a); **~ hall** *n* sala da concerti.

concertina [kɒnsə'ti:nə] *n* piccola fisarmonica // *vi* ridursi come una fisarmonica.

concerto [kən'tʃə:təʊ] *n* concerto.

conclude [kən'klu:d] *vt* concludere; **conclusion** [-'klu:ʒən] *n* conclusione *f*; **conclusive** [-'klu:sɪv] *a* conclusivo(a).

concoct [kən'kɒkt] *vt* inventare; **~ion** [-'kɒkʃən] *n* miscuglio.

concourse ['kɒŋkɔ:s] *n* (*hall*) atrio.

concrete ['kɒŋkri:t] *n* calcestruzzo // *a* concreto(a); di calcestruzzo.

concur [kən'kə:*] *vi* concordare.

concurrently [kən'kʌrntlɪ] *ad* simultaneamente.

concussion [kən'kʌʃən] *n* commozione *f* cerebrale.

condemn [kən'dɛm] *vt* condannare; **~ation** [kɒndɛm'neɪʃən] *n* condanna.

condensation [kɒndɛn'seɪʃən] *n* condensazione *f*.

condense [kən'dɛns] *vi* condensarsi // *vt* condensare; **~d milk** *n* latte *m* condensato.

condition [kən'dɪʃən] *n* condizione *f* // *vt* condizionare, regolare; **on ~ that** a condizione che, a condizione di; **~al** *a* condizionale; **~er** *n* (*for hair*) balsamo.

condolences [kən'dəʊlənsɪz] *npl* condoglianze *fpl*.

condom ['kɒndəm] *n* preservativo.

condominium [kɒndə'mɪnɪəm] *n* (*US*) condominio.

condone [kən'dəʊn] *vt* condonare.

conducive [kən'dju:sɪv] *a*: **~ to** favorevole a.

conduct *n* ['kɒndʌkt] condotta // *vt* [kən'dʌkt] condurre; *(manage)* dirigere; amministrare; (*MUS*) dirigere; **to ~ o.s.** comportarsi; **~ed tour** *n* gita accompagnata; **~or** *n* (*of orchestra*) direttore *m* d'orchestra; (*on bus*) bigliettaio; (*US*: *on train*) controllore *m*; (*ELEC*) conduttore *m*; **~ress** *n* (*on bus*) bigliettaia.

conduit ['kɒndɪt] *n* condotto; tubo.

cone [kəʊn] *n* cono; (*BOT*) pigna.

confectioner [kən'fɛkʃənə*] *n* pasticciere *m*; **~'s (shop)** *n* ≈ pasticceria; **~y** *n* dolciumi *mpl*.

confer [kən'fə:*] *vt*: **to ~ sth on** conferire qc a // *vi* conferire.

conference ['kɒnfərns] *n* congresso.

confess [kən'fɛs] *vt* confessare, ammettere // *vi* confessarsi; **~ion** [-'fɛʃən] *n* confessione *f*.

confetti [kən'fɛtɪ] *n* coriandoli *mpl*.

confide [kən'faɪd] *vi*: **to ~ in** confidarsi con.

confidence ['kɒnfɪdns] *n* confidenza; *(trust)* fiducia; (*also*: **self-~**) sicurezza di sé; **in ~** (*speak*, *write*) in confidenza,

confidenzialmente; ~ **trick** n truffa;
confident a sicuro(a); sicuro(a) di sé;
confidential [kɔnfɪ'dɛnʃəl] a riser-
vato(a).
confine [kən'faɪn] vt limitare; (shut up)
rinchiudere; ~**s** ['kɔnfaɪnz] npl confini
mpl; ~**d** a (space) ristretto(a); ~**ment**
n prigionia; (MIL) consegna; (MED)
parto.
confirm [kən'fə:m] vt confermare; (REL)
cresimare; ~**ation** [kɔnfə'meɪʃən] n
conferma; cresima; ~**ed** a
inveterato(a).
confiscate ['kɔnfɪskeɪt] vt confiscare.
conflict n ['kɔnflɪkt] conflitto // vi
[kən'flɪkt] essere in conflitto; ~**ing** a
contrastante.
conform [kən'fɔ:m] vi: to ~ (to)
conformarsi (a).
confound [kən'faund] vt confondere.
confront [kən'frʌnt] vt confrontare;
(enemy, danger) affrontare; ~**ation**
[kɔnfrən'teɪʃən] n confronto.
confuse [kən'fju:z] vt imbrogliare; (one
thing with another) confondere; ~**d** a
confuso(a); **confusing** a che fa
confondere; **confusion** [-'fju:ʒən] n
confusione f.
congeal [kən'dʒi:l] vi (blood) congelarsi.
congenial [kən'dʒi:nɪəl] a (person)
simpatico(a); (thing) congeniale.
congested [kən'dʒɛstɪd] a conge-
stionato(a).
congestion [kən'dʒɛstʃən] n congestione
f.
congratulate [kən'grætjuleɪt] vt: to ~ sb
(on) congratularsi con qn (per or di);
congratulations [-'leɪʃənz] npl auguri
mpl; (on success) complimenti mpl.
congregate ['kɔŋgrɪgeɪt] vi congregarsi,
riunirsi.
congress ['kɔŋgrɛs] n congresso; ~**man**
n (US) membro del Congresso.
conjecture [kən'dʒɛktʃə*] n congettura.
conjunction [kən'dʒʌŋkʃən] n
congiunzione f.
conjunctivitis [kəndʒʌŋktɪ'vaɪtɪs] n
congiuntivite f.
conjure ['kʌndʒə*] vi fare giochi di prestigio; **to ~ up** vt (ghost, spirit)
evocare; (memories) rievocare; ~**r** n
prestidigitatore/trice, prestigiatore/trice.
conk out [kɔŋk-] vi (col) andare in
panne.
conman ['kɔnmæn] n truffatore m.
connect [kə'nekt] vt connettere,
collegare; (ELEC) collegare; (fig)
associare // vi (train): to ~ with essere
in coincidenza con; to be ~**ed** with
(associated) aver rapporti con; (by
birth, marriage) essere imparentato
con; ~**ion** [-ʃən] n relazione f, rapporto;
(ELEC) connessione f; (TEL)
collegamento; **in** ~**ion with** con
riferimento a.

connive [kə'naɪv] vi: to ~ at essere
connivente in.
connoisseur [kɔnɪ'sə*] n conoscitore/
trice.
conquer ['kɔŋkə*] vt conquistare;
(feelings) vincere.
conquest ['kɔŋkwɛst] n conquista.
cons [kɔnz] npl see **convenience, pro**.
conscience ['kɔnʃəns] n coscienza.
conscientious [kɔnʃɪ'enʃəs] a co-
scienzioso(a).
conscious ['kɔnʃəs] a consapevole;
(MED) conscio(a); ~**ness** n
consapevolezza; coscienza.
conscript ['kɔnskrɪpt] n coscritto.
consent [kən'sɛnt] n consenso // vi: to ~
(to) acconsentire (a).
consequence ['kɔnsɪkwəns] n
conseguenza, risultato; importanza.
consequently ['kɔnsɪkwəntlɪ] ad di
conseguenza, dunque.
conservation [kɔnsə'veɪʃən] n
conservazione f.
conservative [kən'sə:vətɪv] a
conservatore(trice); (cautious) cauto(a); (Brit
POL) C~ a, n conservatore(trice).
conservatory [kən'sə:vətrɪ] n
(greenhouse) serra.
conserve [kən'sə:v] vt conservare // n
conserva.
consider [kən'sɪdə*] vt considerare;
(take into account) tener conto di; to ~
doing sth considerare la possibilità di
fare qc.
considerable [kən'sɪdərəbl] a
considerevole, notevole; **considerably**
ad notevolmente, decisamente.
considerate [kən'sɪdərɪt] a
premuroso(a).
consideration [kənsɪdə'reɪʃən] n
considerazione f; (reward)
rimunerazione f.
considering [kən'sɪdərɪŋ] prep in
considerazione di.
consign [kən'saɪn] vt consegnare; (send
goods) spedire; ~**ment** n consegna;
spedizione f.
consist [kən'sɪst] vi: to ~ of constare di,
essere composto(a) di.
consistency [kən'sɪstənsɪ] n consistenza;
(fig) coerenza.
consistent [kən'sɪstənt] a coerente; (constant) costante; ~ **with** compatibile con.
consolation [kɔnsə'leɪʃən] n consolazione
f.
console vt [kən'səul] consolare // n
['kɔnsəul] quadro di comando.
consonant ['kɔnsənənt] n consonante f.
consortium [kən'sɔ:tɪəm] n consorzio.
conspicuous [kən'spɪkjuəs] a co-
spicuo(a).
conspiracy [kən'spɪrəsɪ] n congiura, cospirazione f.
constable ['kʌnstəbl] n (Brit) ≈
poliziotto, agente m di polizia.

constabulary [kən'stæbjulərɪ] n forze fpl dell'ordine.

constant ['kɔnstənt] a costante; continuo(a); **~ly** ad costantemente; continuamente.

constipated ['kɔnstɪpeɪtɪd] a stitico(a).

constipation [kɔnstɪ'peɪʃən] n stitichezza.

constituency [kən'stɪtjuənsɪ] n collegio elettorale.

constituent [kən'stɪtjuənt] n elettore/trice; (part) elemento componente.

constitution [kɔnstɪ'tjuːʃən] n costituzione f; **~al** a costituzionale.

constraint [kən'streɪnt] n costrizione f.

construct [kən'strʌkt] vt costruire; **~ion** [-ʃən] n costruzione f; **~ive** a costruttivo(a).

construe [kən'struː] vt interpretare.

consul ['kɔnsl] n console m; **~ate** ['kɔnsjulɪt] n consolato.

consult [kən'sʌlt] vt consultare // vi consultarsi; **~ant** n (MED) consulente m medico; (other specialist) consulente; **~ing room** n (Brit) ambulatorio.

consume [kən'sjuːm] vt consumare; **~r** n consumatore/trice; **~r goods** npl beni mpl di consumo; **~r society** n società dei consumi.

consummate ['kɔnsʌmeɪt] vt consumare.

consumption [kən'sʌmpʃən] n consumo; (MED) consunzione f.

cont. abbr = continued.

contact ['kɔntækt] n contatto; (person) conoscenza // vt mettersi in contatto con; **~ lenses** npl lenti fpl a contatto.

contagious [kən'teɪdʒəs] a contagioso(a).

contain [kən'teɪn] vt contenere; to ~ o.s. contenersi; **~er** n recipiente m; (for shipping etc) container m.

contaminate [kən'tæmɪneɪt] vt contaminare.

cont'd abbr = continued.

contemplate ['kɔntəmpleɪt] vt contemplare; (consider) pensare a (or di).

contemporary [kən'tempərərɪ] a contemporaneo(a); (design) moderno(a) // n contemporaneo/a.

contempt [kən'tempt] n disprezzo; ~ of court (LAW) oltraggio alla Corte; **~uous** a sdegnoso(a).

contend [kən'tend] vt: to ~ that sostenere che // vi: to ~ with lottare contro; **~er** n contendente m/f; concorrente m/f.

content [kən'tent] a contento(a), soddisfatto(a) // vt contentare, soddisfare // n ['kɔntent] contenuto; **~s** npl contenuto; (of barrel etc: capacity) capacità f inv; (table of) **~s** indice m; **~ed** a contento(a), soddisfatto(a).

contention [kən'tenʃən] n contesa; (assertion) tesi f inv.

contentment [kən'tentmənt] n contentezza.

contest n ['kɔntest] lotta; (competition) gara, concorso // vt [kən'test] contestare; impugnare; (compete for) contendere; **~ant** [kən'testənt] n concorrente m/f; (in fight) avversario/a.

context ['kɔntekst] n contesto.

continent ['kɔntɪnənt] n continente m; the C~ (Brit) l'Europa continentale; **~al** [-'nentl] a continentale // n abitante m/f dell'Europa continentale; **~al quilt** n (Brit) piumino.

contingency [kən'tɪndʒənsɪ] n eventualità f inv; ~ plan n misura d'emergenza.

continual [kən'tɪnjuəl] a continuo(a).

continuation [kəntɪnju'eɪʃən] n continuazione f; (after interruption) ripresa; (of story) seguito.

continue [kən'tɪnjuː] vi continuare // vt continuare; (start again) riprendere.

continuous [kən'tɪnjuəs] a continuo(a), ininterrotto(a); ~ stationery n carta a moduli continui.

contort [kən'tɔːt] vt contorcere.

contour ['kɔntuə*] n contorno, profilo; (also: ~ line) curva di livello.

contraband ['kɔntrəbænd] n contrabbando.

contraceptive [kɔntrə'septɪv] a contraccettivo(a) // n contraccettivo.

contract n ['kɔntrækt] contratto // vi [kən'trækt] (become smaller) contrarre; (COMM): to ~ to do sth fare un contratto per fare qc; **~ion** [-ʃən] n contrazione f; **~or** n imprenditore m.

contradict [kɔntrə'dɪkt] vt contraddire.

contraption [kən'træpʃən] n (pej) aggeggio.

contrary ['kɔntrərɪ] a contrario(a); (unfavourable) avverso(a), contrario(a); [kən'treərɪ] (perverse) bisbetico(a) // n contrario; on the ~ al contrario; unless you hear to the ~ a meno che non si disdica.

contrast n ['kɔntrɑːst] contrasto // vt [kən'trɑːst] mettere in contrasto.

contribute [kən'trɪbjuːt] vi contribuire // vt: to ~ £10/an article to dare · 10 sterline/un articolo a; to ~ to contribuire a; (newspaper) scrivere per; **contribution** [kɔntrɪ'bjuːʃən] n contribuzione f; **contributor** n (to newspaper) collaboratore/trice.

contrivance [kən'traɪvəns] n congegno; espediente m.

contrive [kən'traɪv] vt inventare; escogitare // vi: to ~ to do fare in modo di fare.

control [kən'trəul] vt dominare; (firm, operation etc) dirigere; (check) controllare // n controllo; **~s** npl comandi mpl; under ~ sotto controllo; to be in ~ of aver autorità su; essere responsabile di; controllare; **to go out of** ~ (*car*) non rispondere ai comandi; (*situation*) sfuggire di mano; ~ **panel** *n* quadro dei comandi; ~ **room** *n* (*NAUT*, *MIL*) sala di comando; (*RADIO*, *TV*) sala di regia; ~ **tower** *n* (*AVIAT*) torre *f* di controllo.

controversial [kɔntrə'və:ʃl] *a* controverso(a), polemico(a).

controversy ['kɔntrəvə:sɪ] *n* controversia, polemica.

convalesce [kɔnvə'lɛs] *vi* rimettersi in salute.

convene [kən'vi:n] *vt* convocare // *vi* convenire, adunarsi.

convenience [kən'vi:nɪəns] *n* comodità *f* inv; **at your** ~ a suo comodo; **all modern** ~**s**, (*Brit*) all mod cons tutte le comodità moderne.

convenient [kən'vi:nɪənt] *a* conveniente, comodo(a).

convent ['kɔnvənt] *n* convento.

convention [kən'vɛnʃən] *n* convenzione *f*; (*meeting*) convegno; ~**al** *a* convenzionale.

conversant [kən'və:snt] *a*: **to be** ~ **with** essere al corrente di; essere pratico(a) di.

conversation [kɔnvə'seɪʃən] *n* conversazione *f*; ~**al** *a* non formale.

converse *n* ['kɔnvə:s] contrario, opposto // *vi* [kən'və:s] conversare; ~**ly** [-'və:slɪ] *ad* al contrario, per contro.

convert *vt* [kən'və:t] (*REL*, *COMM*) convertire; (*alter*) trasformare *n* ['kɔnvə:t] convertito/a; ~**ible** *a* (*currency*) convertibile // *n* macchina decappottabile.

convex ['kɔnvɛks] *a* convesso(a).

convey [kən'veɪ] *vt* trasportare; (*thanks*) comunicare; (*idea*) dare; ~**or belt** *n* nastro trasportatore.

convict *vt* [kən'vɪkt] dichiarare colpevole // *n* ['kɔnvɪkt] carcerato/a; ~**ion** [-ʃən] *n* condanna; (*belief*) convinzione *f*.

convince [kən'vɪns] *vt* convincere, persuadere; **convincing** *a* convincente.

convivial [kən'vɪvɪəl] *a* allegro(a).

convoluted [kɔnvə'lu:tɪd] *a* (*argument etc*) involuto(a).

convoy ['kɔnvɔɪ] *n* convoglio.

convulse [kən'vʌls] *vt* sconvolgere; **to be** ~**d with laughter** contorcersi dalle risa.

coo [ku:] *vi* tubare.

cook [kuk] *vt* cucinare, cuocere // *vi* cuocere; (*person*) cucinare // *n* cuoco/a; ~**book** *n* libro di cucina; ~**er** *n* fornello, cucina; ~**ery** *n* cucina; ~**ery book** *n* (*Brit*) = ~**book**; ~**ie** *n* (*US*) biscotto; ~**ing** *n* cucina.

cool [ku:l] *a* fresco(a); (*not afraid*) calmo(a); (*unfriendly*) freddo(a); (*impertinent*) sfacciato(a) // *vt* raffreddare, rinfrescare // *vi* raffreddarsi, rinfrescarsi.

coop [ku:p] *n* stia // *vt*: **to** ~ **up** (*fig*) rin-

chiudere.

cooperate [kəu'ɔpəreɪt] *vi* cooperare, collaborare; **cooperation** [-'reɪʃən] *n* cooperazione *f*, collaborazione *f*.

cooperative [kəu'ɔpərətɪv] *a* cooperativo(a) // *n* cooperativa.

coordinate *vt* [kəu'ɔ:dɪneɪt] coordinare // *n* [kəu'ɔ:dɪnət] (*MATH*) coordinata; ~**s** *npl* (*clothes*) coordinati *mpl*.

cop [kɔp] *n* (*col*) sbirro.

cope [kəup] *vi* farcela; **to** ~ **with** (*problems*) far fronte a.

copper ['kɔpə*] *n* rame *m*; (*col: policeman*) sbirro; ~**s** *npl* spiccioli *mpl*.

coppice ['kɔpɪs] *n*, **copse** [kɔps] *n* bosco ceduo.

copulate ['kɔpjuleɪt] *vi* accoppiarsi.

copy ['kɔpɪ] *n* copia; (*book etc*) esemplare *m* // *vt* copiare; ~**right** *n* diritto d'autore.

coral ['kɔrəl] *n* corallo.

cord [kɔ:d] *n* corda; (*fabric*) velluto a coste.

cordial ['kɔ:dɪəl] *a*, *n* cordiale (*m*).

cordon ['kɔ:dn] *n* cordone *m*; **to** ~ **off** *vt* fare cordone a.

corduroy ['kɔ:dərɔɪ] *n* fustagno.

core [kɔ:*] *n* (*of fruit*) torsolo; (*TECH*) centro // *vt* estrarre il torsolo da.

cork [kɔ:k] *n* sughero; (*of bottle*) tappo; ~**screw** *n* cavatappi *m inv*.

corn [kɔ:n] *n* (*Brit: wheat*) grano; (*US: maize*) granturco; (*on foot*) callo; ~ **on the cob** (*CULIN*) pannocchia cotta.

corned beef ['kɔ:nd-] *n* carne *f* di manzo in scatola.

corner ['kɔ:nə*] *n* angolo; (*AUT*) curva // *vt* intrappolare; mettere con le spalle al muro; (*COMM: market*) accaparrare // *vi* prendere una curva; ~**stone** *n* pietra angolare.

cornet ['kɔ:nɪt] *n* (*MUS*) cornetta; (*Brit: of ice-cream*) cono.

cornflakes ['kɔ:nfleɪks] *npl* fiocchi *mpl* di granturco.

cornflour ['kɔ:nflauə*] *n* (*Brit*) farina finissima di granturco.

cornstarch ['kɔ:nstɑ:tʃ] *n* (*US*) = **cornflour**.

Cornwall ['kɔ:nwəl] *n* Cornovaglia.

corny ['kɔ:nɪ] *a* (*col*) trito(a).

coronary ['kɔrənərɪ] *n*: ~ (**thrombosis**) trombosi *f* coronaria.

coronation [kɔrə'neɪʃən] *n* incoronazione *f*.

coroner ['kɔrənə*] *n* magistrato incaricato di indagare la causa di morte in circostanze sospette.

coronet ['kɔrənɪt] *n* diadema *m*.

corporal ['kɔ:pərl] *n* caporalmaggiore *m* // *a*: ~ **punishment** pena corporale.

corporate ['kɔ:pərɪt] *a* costituito(a) (in corporazione); comune.

corporation [kɔ:pə'reɪʃən] *n* (*of town*) consiglio comunale; (*COMM*) ente *m*.

corps [kɔː*], pl **corps** [kɔːz] n corpo.

corpse [kɔːps] n cadavere m.

corral [kə'rɑːl] n recinto.

correct [kə'rɛkt] a (accurate) corretto(a), esatto(a); (proper) corretto(a) // vt correggere; **~ion** [-ʃən] n correzione f.

correspond [kɔrɪs'pɔnd] vi corrispondere; **~ence** n corrispondenza; **~ence course** n corso per corrispondenza; **~ent** n corrispondente m/f.

corridor ['kɔrɪdɔː*] n corridoio.

corrode [kə'rəud] vt corrodere // vi corrodersi.

corrugated ['kɔrəgeɪtɪd] a increspato(a); ondulato(a); ~ **iron** n lamiera di ferro ondulata.

corrupt [kə'rʌpt] a corrotto(a) // vt corrompere; **~ion** [-ʃən] n corruzione f.

corset ['kɔːsɪt] n busto.

cortège [kɔː'teɪʒ] n corteo.

cosh [kɔʃ] n (Brit) randello (corto).

cosmetic [kɔz'mɛtɪk] n cosmetico.

cosset ['kɔsɪt] vt vezzeggiare.

cost [kɔst] n costo // vb (pt, pp **cost**) vi costare // vt stabilire il prezzo di; **~s** npl (LAW) spese fpl; **it ~s £5/too much** costa 5 sterline/troppo; **at all ~s** a ogni costo.

co-star ['kəustɑː*] n attore/trice della stessa importanza del protagonista.

cost-effective [kɔstɪ'fɛktɪv] a conveniente.

costly ['kɔstlɪ] a costoso(a), caro(a).

cost-of-living [kɔstəv'lɪvɪŋ] a: ~ **allowance** indennità f inv di contingenza; ~ **index** indice n della scala mobile.

cost price n (Brit) prezzo all'ingrosso.

costume ['kɔstjuːm] n costume m; (lady's suit) tailleur m inv; (Brit: also: **swimming ~**) costume da bagno; ~ **jewellery** n bigiotteria.

cosy, (US) **cozy** ['kəuzɪ] a intimo(a).

cot [kɔt] n (Brit: child's) lettino; (US: campbed) brandina.

cottage ['kɔtɪdʒ] n cottage m inv; ~ **cheese** n fiocchi mpl di latte magro; ~ **industry** n industria artigianale basata sul lavoro a cottimo; ~ **pie** n piatto a base di carne macinata in sugo e purè di patate.

cotton ['kɔtn] n cotone m; **to ~ on to** vt fus (col) afferrare; ~ **candy** n (US) zucchero filato; ~ **wool** n (Brit) cotone idrofilo.

couch [kautʃ] n sofà m inv // vt esprimere.

couchette [kuː'ʃɛt] n (on train, boat) cuccetta.

cough [kɔf] vi tossire // n tosse f; ~ **drop** n pasticca per la tosse.

could [kud] pt of **can**; **~n't** = **could not**.

council ['kaunsl] n consiglio; **city** or **town ~** consiglio comunale; ~ **estate** n (Brit) quartiere m di case popolari; ~

house n (Brit) casa popolare; **~lor** n consigliere/a.

counsel ['kaunsl] n avvocato; consultazione f; **~lor** n consigliere/a.

count [kaunt] vt, vi contare // n conto; (nobleman) conte m; **to ~ on** vt fus contare su; **~down** n conto alla rovescia.

countenance ['kauntɪnəns] n volto, aspetto // vt approvare.

counter ['kauntə*] n banco // vt opporsi a; (blow) parare // ad: ~ **to** contro; in opposizione a; **~act** vt agire in opposizione a; (poison etc) annullare gli effetti di; **~-espionage** n controspionaggio.

counterfeit ['kauntəfɪt] n contraffazione f, falso // vt contraffare, falsificare // a falso(a).

counterfoil ['kauntəfɔɪl] n matrice f.

countermand [kauntə'mɑːnd] vt annullare.

counterpart ['kauntəpɑːt] n (of document etc) copia; (of person) corrispondente m/f.

counter-productive [kauntəprə'dʌktɪv] a controproducente.

countersign ['kauntəsaɪn] vt controfirmare.

countess ['kauntɪs] n contessa.

countless ['kauntlɪs] a innumerevole.

country ['kʌntrɪ] n paese m; (native land) patria; (as opposed to town) campagna; (region) regione f; ~ **dancing** n (Brit) danza popolare; ~ **house** n villa in campagna; **~man** n (national) compatriota m; (rural) contadino; **~side** n campagna.

county ['kauntɪ] n contea.

coup, **~s** [kuː, -z] n colpo; (also: ~ d'état) colpo di Stato.

couple ['kʌpl] n coppia // vt (carriages) agganciare; (TECH) accoppiare; (ideas, names) associare; **a ~ of** un paio di.

coupon ['kuːpɔn] n buono; (COMM) coupon m inv.

courage ['kʌrɪdʒ] n coraggio.

courgette [kuə'ʒɛt] n (Brit) zucchina.

courier ['kurɪə*] n corriere m; (for tourists) guida.

course [kɔːs] n corso; (of ship) rotta; (for golf) campo; (part of meal) piatto; **first ~** primo piatto; **of ~** ad senz'altro, naturalmente; **~ of action** modo d'agire; **~ of lectures** corso di lezioni; **a ~ of treatment** (MED) una cura.

court [kɔːt] n corte f; (TENNIS) campo // vt (woman) fare la corte a; **to take to ~** citare in tribunale.

courteous ['kɔːtɪəs] a cortese.

courtesan [kɔːtɪ'zɛn] n cortigiana.

courtesy ['kɔːtəsɪ] n cortesia; **by ~ of** per gentile concessione di.

court-house ['kɔːthaus] n (US) palazzo di giustizia.

courtier ['kɔ:tɪə*] n cortigiano/a.

court-martial, pl **courts-martial** ['kɔ:t'mɑ:ʃəl] n corte f marziale.

courtroom ['kɔ:trum] n tribunale m.

courtyard ['kɔ:tjɑ:d] n cortile m.

cousin ['kʌzn] n cugino/a; **first** ~ cugino di primo grado.

cove [kəuv] n piccola baia.

covenant ['kʌvənənt] n accordo.

cover ['kʌvə*] vt coprire // n (of pan) coperchio; (over furniture) fodera; (of book) copertina; (shelter) riparo; (COMM, INSURANCE) copertura; **to take** ~ (shelter) ripararsi; **under** ~ al riparo; **under** ~ **of darkness** protetto dall'oscurità; **under separate** ~ (COMM) a parte, in plico separato; to ~ **up for sb** coprire qn; ~**age** n (PRESS, TV, RADIO): **to give full** ~**age to sth** fare un ampio servizio su qc; ~**ing** n copertura; ~**ing letter,** (US) ~ **letter** n lettera d'accompagnamento; ~ **note** n (INSURANCE) polizza (di assicurazione) provvisoria.

covert ['kʌvət] a (hidden) nascosto(a); (glance) furtivo(a).

cover-up ['kʌvərʌp] n occultamento (di informazioni).

covet ['kʌvɪt] vt bramare.

cow [kau] n vacca // vt (person) intimidire.

coward ['kauəd] n vigliacco/a; ~**ice** [-ɪs] n vigliaccheria; ~**ly** a vigliacco(a).

cowboy ['kaubɔɪ] n cow-boy m inv.

cower ['kauə*] vi acquattarsi.

coxswain ['kɔksn] n (abbr: cox) timoniere m.

coy [kɔɪ] a falsamente timido(a).

cozy ['kəuzɪ] a (US) = **cosy.**

CPA n abbr (US) = **certified public accountant.**

crab [kræb] n granchio; ~ **apple** n mela selvatica.

crack [kræk] n fessura, crepa; incrinatura; (noise) schiocco; (: of gun) scoppio; (joke) battuta; (col: attempt): **to have a** ~ **at sth** tentare qc // vt spaccare; incrinare; (whip) schioccare; (nut) schiacciare // a (troops) fuori classe; **to** ~ **down on** vt fus porre freno a; **to** ~ **up** vi crollare; ~**er** n cracker m inv; petardo.

crackle ['krækl] vi crepitare.

cradle ['kreɪdl] n culla.

craft [krɑ:ft] n mestiere m; (cunning) astuzia; (boat) naviglio; ~**sman** n artigiano; ~**smanship** n abilità; ~**y** a furbo(a), astuto(a).

crag [kræg] n roccia.

cram [kræm] vt (fill): **to** ~ **sth with** riempire qc di; (put): **to** ~ **sth into** stipare qc in // vi (for exams) prepararsi (in gran fretta).

cramp [kræmp] n crampo; ~**ed** a ristretto(a).

crampon ['kræmpən] n (CLIMBING) rampone m.

cranberry ['krænbərɪ] n mirtillo.

crane [kreɪn] n gru f inv.

crank [kræŋk] n manovella; (person) persona stramba; ~**shaft** n albero a gomiti.

cranny ['krænɪ] n see **nook.**

crash [kræʃ] n fragore m; (of car) incidente m; (of plane) caduta // vt fracassare // vi (plane) fracassarsi; (car) avere un incidente; (two cars) scontrarsi; (fig) fallire, andare in rovina; **to** ~ **into** scontrarsi con; ~ **course** n corso intensivo; ~ **helmet** n casco; ~ **landing** n atterraggio di fortuna.

crate [kreɪt] n gabbia.

cravat(e) [krə'væt] n fazzoletto da collo.

crave [kreɪv] vt, vi: **to** ~ **(for)** desiderare ardentemente.

crawl [krɔ:l] vi strisciare carponi; (vehicle) avanzare lentamente // n (SWIMMING) crawl m.

crayfish ['kreɪfɪʃ] n (pl inv) (freshwater) gambero (d'acqua dolce); (saltwater) gambero.

crayon ['kreɪən] n matita colorata.

craze [kreɪz] n mania.

crazy ['kreɪzɪ] a matto(a); ~ **paving** n lastricato a mosaico irregolare.

creak [kri:k] vi cigolare, scricchiolare.

cream [kri:m] n crema; (fresh) panna // a (colour) color crema inv; ~ **cake** n torta alla panna; ~ **cheese** n formaggio fresco; ~**y** a cremoso(a).

crease [kri:s] n grinza; (deliberate) piega // vt sgualcire.

create [kri:'eɪt] vt creare; **creation** [-ʃən] n creazione f; **creative** a creativo(a).

creature ['kri:tʃə*] n creatura.

crèche, creche [krɛʃ] n asilo infantile.

credence ['kri:dns] n: **to lend** or **give** ~ **to** prestare fede a.

credentials [krɪ'denʃlz] npl (papers) credenziali fpl.

credit ['kredɪt] n credito; onore m // vt (COMM) accreditare; (believe: also: **give** ~ **to**) credere, prestar fede a; ~**s** npl (CINEMA) titoli mpl; **to** ~ **sb with** (fig) attribuire a qn; **to be in** ~ (person) essere creditore(trice); (bank account) essere coperto(a); ~ **card** n carta di credito; ~**or** n creditore/trice.

creed [kri:d] n credo; dottrina.

creek [kri:k] n insenatura; (US) piccolo fiume m.

creep [kri:p], pt, pp **crept** vi avanzare furtivamente (or pian piano); (plant) arrampicarsi; ~**er** n pianta rampicante; ~**y** a (frightening) che fa accapponare la pelle.

cremate [krɪ'meɪt] vt cremare.

crematorium, pl **crematoria**

[kremə'tɔːrɪəm, -'tɔːrɪə] n forno crematorio.

crêpe [kreɪp] n crespo; ~ **bandage** n (Brit) fascia elastica.

crept [krept] pt, pp of **creep**.

crescent ['kresnt] n (shape) mezzaluna; (street) strada semicircolare.

cress [kres] n crescione m.

crest [krest] n cresta; (of helmet) pennacchiera; (of coat of arms) cimiero; ~**fallen** a mortificato(a).

crevasse [krɪ'væs] n crepaccio.

crevice ['krevɪs] n fessura, crepa.

crew [kruː] n equipaggio; to have a ~-cut avere i capelli a spazzola; ~-neck n girocollo.

crib [krɪb] n culla; (REL) presepio // vt (col) copiare.

crick [krɪk] n crampo.

cricket ['krɪkɪt] n (insect) grillo; (game) cricket m.

crime [kraɪm] n crimine m; **criminal** ['krɪmɪnl] a, n criminale (m/f).

crimson ['krɪmzn] a color cremisi inv.

cringe [krɪndʒ] vi acquattarsi; (fig) essere servile.

crinkle ['krɪŋkl] vt arricciare, increspare.

cripple ['krɪpl] n zoppo/a // vt azzoppare.

crisis, pl **crises** ['kraɪsɪs, -siːz] n crisi f inv.

crisp [krɪsp] a croccante; (fig) frizzante; vivace; deciso(a); ~**s** npl (Brit) patatine fpl.

criss-cross ['krɪskrɔs] a incrociato(a).

criterion, pl **criteria** [kraɪ'tɪərɪən, -'tɪərɪə] n criterio.

critic ['krɪtɪk] n critico; ~**al** a critico(a); ~**ally** ad (speak etc) criticamente; ~**ally** ill gravemente malato; ~**ism** ['krɪtɪsɪzm] n critica; ~**ize** ['krɪtɪsaɪz] vt criticare.

croak [krəuk] vi gracchiare; (frog) gracidare.

crochet ['krəuʃeɪ] n lavoro all'uncinetto.

crockery ['krɒkərɪ] n vasellame m.

crocodile ['krɒkədaɪl] n coccodrillo.

crocus ['krəukəs] n croco.

croft [krɒft] n (Brit) piccolo podere m.

crony ['krəunɪ] n (col) amicone/a.

crook [kruk] n truffatore m; (of shepherd) bastone m; ~**ed** ['krukɪd] a curvo(a), storto(a); (action) disonesto(a).

crop [krɒp] n (produce) coltivazione f; (amount produced) raccolto; (riding ~) frustino; to ~ up vi presentarsi.

croquette [krə'kɛt] n crocchetta.

cross [krɔs] n croce f; (BIOL) incrocio // vt (street etc) attraversare; (arms, legs, BIOL) incrociare; (cheque) sbarrare // a di cattivo umore; to ~ o.s. fare il segno della croce, segnarsi; to ~ out vt cancellare; to ~ over vi attraversare; ~**bar** n traversa; ~**country (race)** n cross-country m inv; ~**examine** vt

(LAW) interrogare in contraddittorio; ~-**eyed** a strabico(a); ~**fire** n fuoco incrociato; ~**ing** n incrocio; (sea passage) traversata; (also: pedestrian ~ing) passaggio pedonale; ~**ing guard** n (US) dipendente comunale che aiuta i bambini ad attraversare la strada; ~ **purposes** npl: to be at ~ purposes non parlare della stessa cosa; ~**reference** n rinvio, rimando; ~**roads** n incrocio; ~ **section** n (BIOL) sezione f trasversale; (in population) settore m rappresentativo; ~**walk** n (US) strisce fpl pedonali, passaggio pedonale; ~**wind** n vento di traverso; ~**wise** ad di traverso; ~**word** n cruciverba m inv.

crotch [krɒtʃ] n (of garment) pattina.

crotchety ['krɒtʃɪtɪ] a (person) burbero(a).

crouch [krautʃ] vi acquattarsi; rannicchiarsi.

crouton ['kruːtɒn] n crostino.

crow [krəu] n (bird) cornacchia; (of cock) canto del gallo // vi (cock) cantare; (fig) vantarsi; cantar vittoria.

crowbar ['krəubɑː*] n piede m di porco.

crowd [kraud] n folla // vt affollare, stipare // vi affollarsi; ~**ed** a affollato(a); ~**ed with** stipato(a) di.

crown [kraun] n corona; (of head) calotta cranica; (of hat) cocuzzolo; (of hill) cima // vt incoronare; ~ **jewels** npl gioielli mpl della Corona; ~ **prince** n principe m ereditario.

crow's feet npl zampe fpl di gallina.

crucial ['kruːʃl] a cruciale, decisivo(a).

crucifix ['kruːsɪfɪks] n crocifisso; ~**ion** [-'fɪkʃən] n crocifissione f.

crude [kruːd] a (materials) greggio(a); non raffinato(a); (fig: basic) crudo(a), primitivo(a); (: vulgar) rozzo(a), grossolano(a); ~ **(oil)** n (petrolio) greggio.

cruel ['kruəl] a crudele; ~**ty** n crudeltà f inv.

cruet ['kruːɪt] n ampolla.

cruise [kruːz] n crociera // vi andare a velocità di crociera; (taxi) circolare; ~**r** n incrociatore m.

crumb [krʌm] n briciola.

crumble ['krʌmbl] vt sbriciolare // vi sbriciolarsi; (plaster etc) sgretolarsi; (land, earth) franare; (building, fig) crollare; **crumbly** a friabile.

crumpet ['krʌmpɪt] n specie di frittella.

crumple ['krʌmpl] vt raggrinzare, spiegazzare.

crunch [krʌntʃ] vt sgranocchiare; (underfoot) scricchiolare // n (fig) punto or momento cruciale; ~**y** a croccante.

crusade [kruː'seɪd] n crociata.

crush [krʌʃ] n folla // vt schiacciare; (crumple) sgualcire.

crust [krʌst] n crosta.

crutch [krʌtʃ] n gruccia.

crux [krʌks] n nodo.
cry [kraɪ] vi piangere; (shout: also: ~ out) urlare // n urlo, grido; **to ~ off** vi ritirarsi.
cryptic ['krɪptɪk] a ermetico(a).
crystal ['krɪstl] n cristallo; **~-clear** a cristallino(a).
cub [kʌb] n cucciolo; (also: ~ scout) lupetto.
Cuba ['kjuːbə] n Cuba.
cubbyhole ['kʌbɪhəul] n angolino.
cube [kjuːb] n cubo // vt (MATH) elevare al cubo; **cubic** a cubico(a); (metre, foot) cubo(a); **cubic capacity** n cilindrata.
cubicle ['kjuːbɪkl] n scompartimento separato; cabina.
cuckoo ['kuku:] n cucù m inv; ~ **clock** n orologio a cucù.
cucumber ['kjuːkʌmbə*] n cetriolo.
cuddle ['kʌdl] vt abbracciare, coccolare // vi abbracciarsi.
cue [kju:] n (snooker ~) stecca; (THEATRE etc) segnale m.
cuff [kʌf] n (Brit: of shirt, coat etc) polsino; (US: of trousers) risvolto; **off the ~** ad improvvisando; **~link** n gemello.
cuisine [kwɪ'ziːn] n cucina.
cul-de-sac ['kʌldəsæk] n vicolo cieco.
culminate ['kʌlmɪneɪt] vi: **to ~ in** culminare con; **culmination** [-'neɪʃən] n culmine m.
culottes [kjuː'lɔts] npl gonna f pantalone inv.
culpable ['kʌlpəbl] a colpevole.
culprit ['kʌlprɪt] n colpevole m/f.
cult [kʌlt] n culto.
cultivate ['kʌltɪveɪt] vt (also fig) coltivare; **cultivation** [-'veɪʃən] n coltivazione f.
cultural ['kʌltʃərəl] a culturale.
culture ['kʌltʃə*] n (also fig) cultura; **~d** a colto(a).
cumbersome ['kʌmbəsəm] a ingombrante.
cunning ['kʌnɪŋ] n astuzia, furberia // a astuto(a), furbo(a).
cup [kʌp] n tazza; (prize) coppa.
cupboard ['kʌbəd] n armadio.
cup-tie ['kʌptaɪ] n (Brit) partita di coppa.
curate ['kjuərɪt] n cappellano.
curator [kjuə'reɪtə*] n direttore m (di museo etc).
curb [kɜːb] vt tenere a freno // n freno; (US) = **kerb**.
curdle ['kɜːdl] vi cagliare.
cure [kjuə*] vt guarire; (CULIN) trattare; affumicare; essicare // n rimedio.
curfew ['kɜːfju:] n coprifuoco.
curio ['kjuərɪəu] n curiosità f inv.
curiosity [kjuərɪ'ɔsɪtɪ] n curiosità.
curious ['kjuərɪəs] a curioso(a).
curl [kɜːl] n riccio // vt ondulare; (tightly)

arricciare // vi arricciarsi; **to ~ up** vi avvolgersi a spirale; rannicchiarsi; **~er** n bigodino.
curly ['kɜːlɪ] a ricciuto(a).
currant ['kʌrnt] n uva passa.
currency ['kʌrnsɪ] n moneta; **to gain ~** (fig) acquistare larga diffusione.
current ['kʌrnt] a, n corrente (f); ~ **account** n (Brit) conto corrente; ~ **affairs** npl attualità fpl; **~ly** ad attualmente.
curriculum, pl **~s** or **curricula** [kə'rɪkjuləm, -lə] n curriculum m inv; ~ **vitae (CV)** n curriculum vitae m inv.
curry ['kʌrɪ] n curry m inv // vt: **to ~ favour with** cercare di attirarsi i favori di.
curse [kɜːs] vt maledire // vi bestemmiare // n maledizione f; bestemmia.
cursor ['kɜːsə*] n (COMPUT) cursore m.
cursory ['kɜːsərɪ] a superficiale.
curt [kɜːt] a secco(a).
curtail [kɜː'teɪl] vt (visit etc) accorciare; (expenses etc) ridurre, decurtare.
curtain ['kɜːtn] n tenda.
curts(e)y ['kɜːtsɪ] n inchino, riverenza // vi fare un inchino or una riverenza.
curve [kɜːv] n curva // vi curvarsi.
cushion ['kuʃən] n cuscino // vt (shock) fare da cuscinetto a.
custard ['kʌstəd] n (for pouring) crema.
custodian [kʌs'təudɪən] n custode m/f.
custody ['kʌstədɪ] n (of child) tutela; (for offenders) arresto.
custom ['kʌstəm] n costume m, usanza; (LAW) consuetudine f; (COMM) clientela; **~ary** a consueto(a).
customer ['kʌstəmə*] n cliente m/f.
customized ['kʌstəmaɪzd] a (car etc) fuoriserie inv.
custom-made ['kʌstəm'meɪd] a (clothes) fatto(a) su misura; (other goods) fatto(a) su ordinazione.
customs ['kʌstəmz] npl dogana; ~ **officer** n doganiere m.
cut [kʌt] vb (pt, pp **cut**) vt tagliare; (shape, make) intagliare; (reduce) ridurre // vi tagliare; (intersect) tagliarsi // n taglio; (in salary etc) riduzione f; **to ~ a tooth** mettere un dente; **to ~ down** vt (tree etc) abbattere // vt fus (also: ~ **down on**) ridurre; **to ~ off** vt tagliare; (fig) isolare; **to ~ out** vt tagliare fuori; eliminare; ritagliare; **to ~ up** vt (paper, meat) tagliare a pezzi; **~back** n riduzione f.
cute [kjuːt] a grazioso(a); (clever) astuto(a).
cuticle ['kjuːtɪkl] n (on nail) pellicina, cuticola.
cutlery ['kʌtlərɪ] n posate fpl.
cutlet ['kʌtlɪt] n costoletta.
cut: **~out** n interruttore m; (cardboard

~) ritaglio; **~-price**, (*US*) **~-rate** *a* a prezzo ridotto; **~throat** *n* assassino // *a* (*razor*) da barbiere; (*competition*) spietato(a).

cutting ['kʌtɪŋ] *a* tagliente; (*fig*) pungente // *n* (*Brit: from newspaper*) ritaglio (di giornale).

CV *n abbr* = **curriculum vitae**.

cwt *abbr* = **hundredweight(s)**.

cyanide ['saɪənaɪd] *n* cianuro.

cycle ['saɪkl] *n* ciclo; (*bicycle*) bicicletta // *vi* andare in bicicletta.

cycling ['saɪklɪŋ] *n* ciclismo.

cyclist ['saɪklɪst] *n* ciclista *m/f*.

cygnet ['sɪgnɪt] *n* cigno giovane.

cylinder ['sɪlɪndə*] *n* cilindro; **~-head gasket** *n* guarnizione *f* della testata del cilindro.

cymbals ['sɪmblz] *npl* cembali *mpl*.

cynic ['sɪnɪk] *n* cinico/a; **~al** *a* cinico(a); **~ism** ['sɪnɪsɪzəm] *n* cinismo.

Cypriot ['sɪprɪət] *a*, *n* cipriota (*m/f*).

Cyprus ['saɪprəs] *n* Cipro.

cyst [sɪst] *n* cisti *f inv*.

cystitis [sɪs'taɪtɪs] *n* cistite *f*.

czar [zɑ:*] *n* zar *m inv*.

Czech [tʃɛk] *a* ceco(a) // *n* ceco/a; (*LING*) ceco.

Czechoslovakia [tʃɛkəslə'vækɪə] *n* Cecoslovacchia; **~n** *a*, *n* cecoslovacco(a).

D

D [di:] *n* (*MUS*) re *m*.

dab [dæb] *vt* (*eyes*, *wound*) tamponare; (*paint*, *cream*) applicare (con leggeri colpetti).

dabble ['dæbl] *vi*: to **~** in occuparsi (da dilettante) di.

dad, daddy [dæd, 'dædɪ] *n* babbo, papà *m inv*.

daffodil ['dæfədɪl] *n* trombone *m*, giunchiglia.

daft [dɑ:ft] *a* sciocco(a).

dagger ['dægə*] *n* pugnale *m*.

daily ['deɪlɪ] *a* quotidiano(a), giornaliero(a) // *n* quotidiano // *ad* tutti i giorni.

dainty ['deɪntɪ] *a* delicato(a), grazioso(a).

dairy ['dɛərɪ] *n* (*shop*) latteria; (*on farm*) caseificio // *a* caseario(a); **~ produce** *n* latticini *mpl*.

dais ['deɪɪs] *n* pedana, palco.

daisy ['deɪzɪ] *n* margherita; **~ wheel** *n* (*on printer*) margherita.

dale [deɪl] *n* valle *f*.

dam [dæm] *n* diga // *vt* sbarrare; costruire dighe su.

damage ['dæmɪdʒ] *n* danno, danni *mpl*; (*fig*) danno // *vt* danneggiare; (*fig*) recar danno a; **~s** *npl* (*LAW*) danni.

damn [dæm] *vt* condannare; (*curse*) maledire // *n* (*col*): I don't give a **~** non

me ne importa un fico // *a* (*col: also*: **~ed**): this **~** ... questo maledetto ...; **~** (it)! accidenti!

damp [dæmp] *a* umido(a) // *n* umidità, umido // *vt* (*also*: **~en**: *cloth*, *rag*) inumidire, bagnare; (*enthusiasm etc*) spegnere.

damson ['dæmzən] *n* susina damaschina.

dance [dɑ:ns] *n* danza, ballo; (*ball*) ballo // *vi* ballare; **~ hall** *n* dancing *m inv*, sala da ballo; **~r** *n* danzatore/trice; (*professional*) ballerino/a.

dancing ['dɑ:nsɪŋ] *n* danza, ballo.

dandelion ['dændɪlaɪən] *n* dente *m* di leone.

dandruff ['dændrəf] *n* forfora.

Dane [deɪn] *n* danese *m/f*.

danger ['deɪndʒə*] *n* pericolo; there is a **~** of fire c'è pericolo di incendio; **in ~** in pericolo; he was in **~** of falling rischiava di cadere; **~ous** *a* pericoloso(a).

dangle ['dæŋgl] *vt* dondolare; (*fig*) far balenare // *vi* pendolare.

Danish ['deɪnɪʃ] *a* danese // *n* (*LING*) danese *m*.

dapper ['dæpə*] *a* lindo(a).

dare [dɛə*] *vt*: to **~** sb to do sfidare qn a fare // *vi*: to **~** (to) do sth osare fare qc; I **~** say (*I suppose*) immagino (che); **~devil** *n* scavezzacollo *m/f*; **daring** *a* audace, ardito(a) // *n* audacia.

dark [dɑ:k] *a* (*night*, *room*) buio(a), scuro(a); (*colour*, *complexion*) scuro(a); (*fig*) cupo(a), tetro(a), nero(a) // *n*: in the **~** al buio; in the **~** about (*fig*) all'oscuro di; after **~** a notte fatta; **~en** *vt* (*room*) oscurare; (*photo*, *painting*) far scuro(a) // *vi* oscurarsi; imbrunirsi; **~ glasses** *npl* occhiali *mpl* scuri; **~ness** *n* oscurità, buio; **~ room** *n* camera oscura.

darling ['dɑ:lɪŋ] *a* caro(a) // *n* tesoro.

darn [dɑ:n] *vt* rammendare.

dart [dɑ:t] *n* freccetta // *vi*: to **~** towards precipitarsi verso; to **~** away guizzare via; **~s** *n* tiro al bersaglio (con freccette); **~board** *n* bersaglio (per freccette).

dash [dæʃ] *n* (*sign*) lineetta; (*small quantity*) punta // *vt* (*missile*) gettare; (*hopes*) infrangere // *vi*: to **~** towards precipitarsi verso; to **~** away *or* off *vi* scappare via.

dashboard ['dæʃbɔ:d] *n* (*AUT*) cruscotto.

dashing ['dæʃɪŋ] *a* ardito(a).

data ['deɪtə] *npl* dati *mpl*; **~base** *n* base *f* di dati, data base *m inv*; **~ processing** *n* elaborazione *f* (elettronica) dei dati.

date [deɪt] *n* data; appuntamento; (*fruit*) dattero // *vt* datare; **~ of birth** data di nascita; to **~** *ad* fino a oggi; out of **~** scaduto(a); (*old-fashioned*) passato(a) di moda; **~d** *a* passato(a) di moda.

daub [dɔ:b] *vt* imbrattare.

daughter ['dɔ:tə*] n figlia; **~-in-law** n nuora.

daunt [dɔ:nt] vt intimidire; **~ing** a non invidiabile.

dawdle ['dɔ:dl] vi bighellonare.

dawn [dɔ:n] n alba // vi (day) spuntare; (fig) venire in mente; it ~ed on him that ... gli è venuto in mente che ...

day [deɪ] n giorno; (as duration) giornata; (period of time, age) tempo, epoca; the ~ before il giorno avanti or prima; the ~ after, the following ~ il giorno dopo or seguente; the ~ after tomorrow dopodomani; the ~ before yesterday l'altroieri; by ~ di giorno; **~break** n spuntar m del giorno; **~dream** vi sognare a occhi aperti; **~light** n luce f del giorno; ~ return n (Brit) biglietto giornaliero di andata e ritorno; **~time** n giorno; **~-to-~** a (life, organization) quotidiano(a).

daze [deɪz] vt (subject: drug) inebetire; (: blow) stordire // n: in a ~ inebetito(a); stordito(a).

dazzle ['dæzl] vt abbagliare.

DC abbr (= direct current) c.c.

deacon ['di:kən] n diacono.

dead [ded] a morto(a); (numb) intirizzito(a) // ad assolutamente, perfettamente; he was shot ~ fu colpito a morte; ~ on time in perfetto orario; ~ tired stanco(a) morto(a); to stop ~ fermarsi in tronco; the ~ i morti; **~en** vt (blow, sound) ammortire; (make numb) intirizzire; ~ end n vicolo cieco; ~ heat n (SPORT): to finish in a ~ heat finire alla pari; **~line** n scadenza; **~lock** n punto morto; ~ loss n: to be a ~ loss (col: person, thing) non valere niente; **~ly** a mortale; (weapon, poison) micidiale; **~pan** a a faccia impassibile.

deaf [def] a sordo(a); **~en** vt assordare; **~-mute** n sordomuto/a; **~ness** n sordità.

deal [di:l] n accordo; (business ~) affare m // vt (pt, pp dealt [delt]) (blow, cards) dare; a great ~ (of) molto(a); to ~ in vt fus occuparsi di; to ~ with vt fus (COMM) fare affari con, trattare con; (handle) occuparsi di; (be about: book etc) trattare di; **~er** n commerciante m/f; **~ings** npl (COMM) relazioni fpl; (relations) rapporti mpl.

dean [di:n] n (REL) decano; (SCOL) preside m di facoltà (or di collegio).

dear [dɪə*] a caro(a) // n: my ~ caro mio/cara mia; ~ me! Dio mio!; D~ Sir/ Madam (in letter) Egregio Signore/ Egregia Signora; D~ Mr/Mrs X Gentile Signor/Signora X; **~ly** ad (love) moltissimo; (pay) a caro prezzo.

death [deθ] n morte f; (ADMIN) decesso; ~ certificate n atto di decesso; ~ duties npl (Brit) imposta or tassa di successione; **~ly** a di morte; ~ penalty

n pena di morte; ~ rate n indice m di mortalità.

debacle [dɪ'bækl] n fiasco.

debar [dɪ'ba:*] vt: to ~ sb from doing impedire a qn di fare.

debase [dɪ'beɪs] vt (currency) adulterare; (person) degradare.

debatable [dɪ'beɪtəbl] a discutibile.

debate [dɪ'beɪt] n dibattito // vt dibattere; discutere.

debauchery [dɪ'bɔ:tʃərɪ] n dissolutezza.

debit ['debɪt] n debito // vt: to ~ a sum to sb or to sb's account addebitare una somma a qn.

debris ['debri:] n detriti mpl.

debt [det] n debito; to be in ~ essere indebitato(a); **~or** n debitore/trice.

debunk [di:'bʌŋk] vt (theory, claim) smentire.

début ['deɪbju:] n debutto.

decade ['dekeɪd] n decennio.

decadence ['dekədəns] n decadenza.

decaffeinated [dɪ'kæfɪneɪtɪd] a decaffeinato(a).

decanter [dɪ'kæntə*] n caraffa.

decay [dɪ'keɪ] n decadimento; imputridimento; (fig) rovina; (also: tooth ~) carie f // vi (rot) imputridire; (fig) andare in rovina.

deceased [dɪ'si:st] n defunto/a.

deceit [dɪ'si:t] n inganno; **~ful** a ingannevole, perfido(a).

deceive [dɪ'si:v] vt ingannare.

December [dɪ'sembə*] n dicembre m.

decent ['di:sənt] a decente; they were very ~ about it si sono comportati da signori riguardo a ciò.

deception [dɪ'sepʃən] n inganno.

deceptive [dɪ'septɪv] a ingannevole.

decide [dɪ'saɪd] vt (person) far prendere una decisione a; (question, argument) risolvere, decidere // vi decidere, decidersi; to ~ to do/that decidere di fare/che; to ~ on decidere per; **~d** a (resolute) deciso(a); (clear, definite) netto(a), chiaro(a); **~dly** [-dɪdlɪ] ad indubbiamente; decisamente.

decimal ['desɪməl] a, n decimale (m); ~ point n ≈ virgola.

decipher [dɪ'saɪfə*] vt decifrare.

decision [dɪ'sɪʒən] n decisione f.

decisive [dɪ'saɪsɪv] a decisivo(a).

deck [dek] n (NAUT) ponte m; (of bus): top ~ imperiale m; (of cards) mazzo; **~chair** n sedia a sdraio.

declaration [deklə'reɪʃən] n dichiarazione f.

declare [dɪ'klɛə*] vt dichiarare.

decline [dɪ'klaɪn] n (decay) declino; (lessening) ribasso // vt declinare; rifiutare // vi declinare; diminuire.

decode [di:'kəud] vt decifrare.

decompose [di:kəm'pəuz] vi decomporre.

décor ['deɪkɔ:*] n decorazione f.

decorate ['dɛkəreɪt] vt (adorn, give a medal to) decorare; (paint and paper) tinteggiare e tappezzare; **decoration** [-'reɪʃən] n (medal etc, adornment) decorazione f; **decorator** n decoratore m.

decorum [dɪ'kɔːrəm] n decoro.

decoy ['diːkɔɪ] n zimbello.

decrease n ['diːkriːs] diminuzione f // vt, vi [diː'kriːs] diminuire.

decree [dɪ'kriː] n decreto; ~ **nisi** [-'naɪsaɪ] n sentenza provvisoria di divorzio.

dedicate ['dɛdɪkeɪt] vt consacrare; (book etc) dedicare.

dedication [dɛdɪ'keɪʃən] n (devotion) dedizione f.

deduce [dɪ'djuːs] vt dedurre.

deduct [dɪ'dʌkt] vt: to ~ sth (from) dedurre qc (da); (from wage etc) trattenere qc (da); ~**ion** [dɪ'dʌkʃən] n (deducting) deduzione f; (from wage etc) trattenuta; (deducing) deduzione f, conclusione f.

deed [diːd] n azione f, atto; (LAW) atto.

deep [diːp] a profondo(a); 4 metres ~ profondo(a) 4 metri // ad: **spectators stood 20 ~** c'erano 20 file di spettatori; ~**en** vt (hole) approfondire // vi approfondirsi; (darkness) farsi più buio; ~**-freeze** n congelatore m // vt congelare; ~**-fry** vt friggere in olio abbondante; ~**ly** ad profondamente; ~**sea diving** n immersione f in alto mare.

deer [dɪə*] n (pl inv): the ~ i cervidi; (red) ~ cervo; (fallow) ~ daino; (roe) ~ capriolo.

deface [dɪ'feɪs] vt imbrattare.

default [dɪ'fɔːlt] vi (LAW) essere contumace; (gen) essere inadempiente // n (COMPUT: also: ~ **value**) default m inv; **by ~** (LAW) in contumacia; (SPORT) per abbandono.

defeat [dɪ'fiːt] n sconfitta // vt (team, opponents) sconfiggere; (fig: plans, efforts) frustrare; ~**ist** a, n disfattista (m/f).

defect n ['diːfɛkt] difetto // vi [dɪ'fɛkt]: to ~ **to the enemy** passare al nemico; ~**ive** [dɪ'fɛktɪv] a difettoso(a).

defence, (US) defense [dɪ'fɛns] n difesa; **in ~ of** in difesa di; ~**less** a senza difesa.

defend [dɪ'fɛnd] vt difendere; ~**ant** n imputato/a; ~**er** n difensore/a.

defense [dɪ'fɛns] n (US) = **defence**.

defer [dɪ'fɜː*] vt (postpone) differire, rinviare // vi: to ~ **to** rimettersi a.

defiance [dɪ'faɪəns] n sfida; **in ~ of** a dispetto di.

defiant [dɪ'faɪənt] a (attitude) di sfida; (person) ribelle.

deficiency [dɪ'fɪʃənsɪ] n deficienza; carenza.

deficit ['dɛfɪsɪt] n disavanzo.

defile vb [dɪ'faɪl] vt contaminare // vi sfilare // n ['diːfaɪl] gola, stretta.

define [dɪ'faɪn] vt definire.

definite ['dɛfɪnɪt] a (fixed) definito(a), preciso(a); (clear, obvious) ben definito(a), esatto(a); (LING) determinativo(a); **he was ~ about it** ne era sicuro; ~**ly** ad indubbiamente.

definition [dɛfɪ'nɪʃən] n definizione f.

deflate [diː'fleɪt] vt sgonfiare.

deflect [dɪ'flɛkt] vt deflettere, deviare.

deformed [dɪ'fɔːmd] a deforme.

defraud [dɪ'frɔːd] vt defraudare.

defray [dɪ'freɪ] vt: to ~ **sb's expenses** sostenere le spese di qn.

defrost [diː'frɔst] vt (fridge) disgelare; ~**er** n (US: demister) sbrinatore m.

deft [dɛft] a svelto(a), destro(a).

defunct [dɪ'fʌŋkt] a defunto(a).

defuse [diː'fjuːz] vt disinnescare.

defy [dɪ'faɪ] vt sfidare; (efforts etc) resistere a.

degenerate vi [dɪ'dʒɛnəreɪt] degenerare // a [dɪ'dʒɛnərɪt] degenere.

degree [dɪ'griː] n grado; (SCOL) laurea (universitaria); **a (first) ~ in maths** una laurea in matematica; **by ~s** (gradually) gradualmente, a poco a poco; **to some ~** fino a un certo punto, in certa misura.

dehydrated [diːhaɪ'dreɪtɪd] a disidratato(a); (milk, eggs) in polvere.

de-ice [diː'aɪs] vt (windscreen) disgelare.

deign [deɪn] vi: to ~ **to do** degnarsi di fare.

deity ['diːɪtɪ] n divinità f inv.

dejected [dɪ'dʒɛktɪd] a abbattuto(a), avvilito(a).

delay [dɪ'leɪ] vt (journey, operation) ritardare, rinviare; (travellers, trains) ritardare // vi: to ~ (in doing sth) ritardare (a fare qc) // n ritardo.

delectable [dɪ'lɛktəbl] a (person, food) delizioso(a).

delegate n ['dɛlɪgɪt] delegato/a // vt ['dɛlɪgeɪt] delegare.

delete [dɪ'liːt] vt cancellare.

deliberate a [dɪ'lɪbərɪt] (intentional) intenzionale; (slow) misurato(a) // vi [dɪ'lɪbəreɪt] deliberare, riflettere; ~**ly** ad (on purpose) deliberatamente.

delicacy ['dɛlɪkəsɪ] n delicatezza.

delicate ['dɛlɪkɪt] a delicato(a).

delicatessen [dɛlɪkə'tɛsn] n ≈ salumeria.

delicious [dɪ'lɪʃəs] a delizioso(a), squisito(a).

delight [dɪ'laɪt] n delizia, gran piacere m // vt dilettare; ~**ed** a: ~**ed (at or with)** contentissimo(a), felice (di); ~**ed to do** felice di fare; ~**ful** a delizioso(a); incantevole.

delinquent [dɪ'lɪŋkwənt] a, n delinquente (m/f).

delirious [dɪ'lɪrɪəs] a: to be ~ delirare.

deliver [dɪ'lɪvə*] vt (mail) distribuire;

(*goods*) consegnare; (*speech*) pronunciare; (*free*) liberare; (*MED*) far partorire; **~y** n distribuzione f; consegna; (*of speaker*) dizione f; (*MED*) parto.

delude [dɪ'lu:d] vt deludere, illudere.

deluge ['delju:dʒ] n diluvio.

delusion [dɪ'lu:ʒən] n illusione f.

delve [delv] vi: **to ~ into** frugare in; (*subject*) far ricerche in.

demand [dɪ'mɑːnd] vt richiedere // n domanda; (*ECON, claim*) richiesta; **in ~** ricercato(a), richiesto(a); **on ~** a richiesta; **~ing** a (*boss*) esigente; (*work*) impegnativo(a).

demean [dɪ'miːn] vt: **to ~ o.s.** umiliarsi.

demeanour, (*US*) **demeanor** [dɪ'miːnə*] n comportamento; contegno.

demented [dɪ'mentɪd] a demente, impazzito(a).

demise [dɪ'maɪz] n decesso.

demister [di:'mɪstə*] n (*AUT*) sbrinatore m.

demo ['deməu] n abbr (col: = *demonstration*) manifestazione f.

demobilize [di:'məubɪlaɪz] vt smobilitare.

democracy [dɪ'mɔkrəsɪ] n democrazia.

democrat ['deməkræt] n democratico/a; **~ic** [demə'krætɪk] a democratico(a).

demolish [dɪ'mɔlɪʃ] vt demolire.

demonstrate ['demənstreɪt] vt dimostrare, provare // vi: **to ~ (for/against)** dimostrare (per/contro), manifestare (per/contro); **demonstration** [-'streɪʃən] n dimostrazione f; (*POL*) manifestazione f, dimostrazione; **demonstrator** n (*POL*) dimostrante m/f.

demote [dɪ'məut] vt far retrocedere.

demure [dɪ'mjuə*] a contegnoso(a).

den [den] n tana, covo.

denatured alcohol [di:'neɪtʃəd-] n (*US*) alcool m inv denaturato.

denial [dɪ'naɪəl] n diniego; rifiuto.

denim ['denɪm] n tessuto di cotone ritorto; **~s** npl blue jeans mpl.

Denmark ['denmɑːk] n Danimarca.

denomination [dɪnɔmɪ'neɪʃən] n (*money*) valore m; (*REL*) confessione f.

denounce [dɪ'nauns] vt denunciare.

dense [dens] a fitto(a); (*stupid*) ottuso(a), duro(a).

density ['densɪtɪ] n densità f inv.

dent [dent] n ammaccatura // vt (*also:* make a **~ in**) ammaccare.

dental ['dentl] a dentale; **~ surgeon** n medico/a dentista.

dentist ['dentɪst] n dentista m/f; **~ry** n odontoiatria.

denture(s) ['dentʃə(z)] n(pl) dentiera.

deny [dɪ'naɪ] vt negare; (*refuse*) rifiutare.

deodorant [di:'əudərənt] n deodorante m.

depart [dɪ'pɑːt] vi partire; **to ~ from**

(*fig*) deviare da.

department [dɪ'pɑːtmənt] n (*COMM*) reparto; (*SCOL*) sezione f, dipartimento; (*POL*) ministero; **~ store** n grande magazzino.

departure [dɪ'pɑːtʃə*] n partenza; (*fig*): **~ from** deviazione f da; a new **~** una svolta (decisiva); **~ lounge** n (*at airport*) sala d'attesa.

depend [dɪ'pend] vi: **to ~ on** dipendere da; (*rely on*) contare su; **it ~s** dipende; **~ing on the result ...** a seconda del risultato ...; **~able** a fidato(a); (*car etc*) affidabile; **~ant** n persona a carico; **~ent** a: **to be ~ent on** dipendere da; (*child, relative*) essere a carico di // n = **~ant**.

depict [dɪ'pɪkt] vt (*in picture*) dipingere; (*in words*) descrivere.

depleted [dɪ'pli:tɪd] a diminuito(a).

deploy [dɪ'plɔɪ] vt dispiegare.

depopulation ['di:pɔpju'leɪʃən] n spopolamento.

deport [dɪ'pɔːt] vt deportare; espellere.

deportment [dɪ'pɔːtmənt] n portamento.

depose [dɪ'pəuz] vt deporre.

deposit [dɪ'pɔzɪt] n (*COMM, GEO*) deposito; (*of ore, oil*) giacimento; (*CHEM*) sedimento; (*part payment*) acconto; (*for hired goods etc*) cauzione f // vt depositare; dare in acconto; mettere or lasciare in deposito; **~ account** n conto vincolato.

depot ['depəu] n deposito.

depreciate [dɪ'pri:ʃɪeɪt] vt svalutare // vi svalutarsi.

depress [dɪ'pres] vt deprimere; (*press down*) premere; **~ed** a (*person*) depresso(a), abbattuto(a); (*area*) depresso(a); **~ing** a deprimente; **~ion** [dɪ'preʃən] n depressione f.

deprivation [deprɪ'veɪʃən] n privazione f; (*loss*) perdita.

deprive [dɪ'praɪv] vt: **to ~ sb of** privare qn di; **~d** a disgraziato(a).

depth [depθ] n profondità f inv; **in the ~s of** nel profondo di; nel cuore di; **in the ~s of** winter in pieno inverno.

deputize ['depjutaɪz] vi: **to ~ for** svolgere le funzioni di.

deputy ['depjutɪ] a: **~ head** (*SCOL*) vicepreside m/f // n (*replacement*) supplente m/f; (*second in command*) vice m/f.

derail [dɪ'reɪl] vt far deragliare; **to be ~ed** deragliare.

deranged [dɪ'reɪndʒd] a: **to be ~ (mentally)** essere pazzo(a).

derby ['dɔːbɪ] n (*US: bowler hat*) bombetta.

derelict ['derɪlɪkt] a abbandonato(a).

deride [dɪ'raɪd] vt deridere.

derisory [dɪ'raɪsərɪ] a (*sum*) irrisorio(a); (*laughter, person*) beffardo(a).

derive [dɪ'raɪv] vt: **to ~ sth from** derivare qc da; trarre qc da // vi: **to ~**

from derivare da.

derogatory [dɪ'rɔgətərɪ] *a* denigratorio(a).

derrick ['dɛrɪk] *n* gru *f inv*; *(for oil)* derrick *m inv*.

derv [dɘːv] *n (Brit)* gasolio.

descend [dɪ'sɛnd] *vt, vi* discendere, scendere; **to ~ from** discendere da; **~ant** *n* discendente *m/f*.

descent [dɪ'sɛnt] *n* discesa; *(origin)* discendenza, famiglia.

describe [dɪs'kraɪb] *vt* descrivere; **description** [-'krɪpʃən] *n* descrizione *f*; *(sort)* genere *m*, specie *f*.

desecrate ['dɛsɪkreɪt] *vt* profanare.

desert *n* ['dɛzət] deserto // *vb* [dɪ'zɘːt] *vt* lasciare, abbandonare // *vi (MIL)* disertare; **~er** *n* disertore *m*; **~ island** *n* isola deserta; **~s** [dɪ'zɘːts] *npl*: **to get one's just ~s** avere ciò che si merita.

deserve [dɪ'zɘːv] *vt* meritare; **deserving** *a (person)* meritevole, degno(a); *(cause)* meritorio(a).

design [dɪ'zaɪn] *n (sketch)* disegno; *(layout, shape)* linea; *(pattern)* fantasia; *(COMM)* disegno tecnico; *(intention)* intenzione *f* // *vt* disegnare; progettare; **to have ~s on** aver mire su.

designer [dɪ'zaɪnə*] *n (ART, TECH)* disegnatore/trice; *(of fashion)* modellista *m/f*.

desire [dɪ'zaɪə*] *n* desiderio, voglia // *vt* desiderare, volere.

desk [dɛsk] *n (in office)* scrivania; *(for pupil)* banco; *(Brit: in shop, restaurant)* cassa; *(in hotel)* ricevimento; *(at airport)* accettazione *f*.

desolate ['dɛsəlɪt] *a* desolato(a).

despair [dɪs'pɛə*] *n* disperazione *f* // *vi*: **to ~ of** disperare di.

despatch [dɪs'pætʃ] *n, vt* = dispatch.

desperate ['dɛspərɪt] *a* disperato(a); *(fugitive)* capace di tutto; **~ly** *ad* disperatamente; *(very)* terribilmente, estremamente.

desperation [dɛspə'reɪʃən] *n* disperazione *f*.

despicable [dɪs'pɪkəbl] *a* disprezzabile.

despise [dɪs'paɪz] *vt* disprezzare, sdegnare.

despite [dɪs'paɪt] *prep* malgrado, a dispetto di, nonostante.

despondent [dɪs'pɔndənt] *a* abbattuto(a), scoraggiato(a).

dessert [dɪ'zɘːt] *n* dolce *m*; frutta; **~spoon** *n* cucchiaio da dolci.

destination [dɛstɪ'neɪʃən] *n* destinazione *f*.

destiny ['dɛstɪnɪ] *n* destino.

destitute ['dɛstɪtjuːt] *a* indigente, bisognoso(a).

destroy [dɪs'trɔɪ] *vt* distruggere; **~er** *n (NAUT)* cacciatorpediniere *m*.

destruction [dɪs'trʌkʃən] *n* distruzione *f*.

detach [dɪ'tætʃ] *vt* staccare, distaccare;

~ed *a (attitude)* distante; **~ed house** *n* villa; **~ment** *n (MIL)* distaccamento; *(fig)* distacco.

detail ['diːteɪl] *n* particolare *m*, dettaglio // *vt* dettagliare, particolareggiare; **in ~** nei particolari; **~ed** *a* particolareggiato(a).

detain [dɪ'teɪn] *vt* trattenere; *(in captivity)* detenere.

detect [dɪ'tɛkt] *vt* scoprire, scorgere; *(MED, POLICE, RADAR etc)* individuare; **~ion** [dɪ'tɛkʃən] *n* scoperta; individuazione *f*; **~ive** *n* investigatore/trice; **private ~ive** investigatore *m* privato; **~ive story** *n* giallo.

detention [dɪ'tɛnʃən] *n* detenzione *f*; *(SCOL)* permanenza forzata per punizione.

deter [dɪ'tɘː*] *vt* dissuadere.

detergent [dɪ'tɘːdʒənt] *n* detersivo.

deteriorate [dɪ'tɪərɪəreɪt] *vi* deteriorarsi.

determine [dɪ'tɘːmɪn] *vt* determinare; **to ~ to do** decidere di fare; **~d** *a (person)* risoluto(a), deciso(a).

detour ['diːtuə*] *n* deviazione *f* // *vt (US: traffic)* deviare.

detract [dɪ'trækt] *vt*: **to ~ from** detrarre da.

detriment ['dɛtrɪmənt] *n*: **to the ~ of** a detrimento di; **~al** [dɛtrɪ'mɛntl] *a*: **~al to** dannoso(a) a, nocivo(a) a.

devaluation [dɪvælju'eɪʃən] *n* svalutazione *f*.

devastating ['dɛvəsteɪtɪŋ] *a* devastatore(trice).

develop [dɪ'vɛləp] *vt* sviluppare; *(habit)* prendere (gradualmente) // *vi* svilupparsi; *(facts, symptoms: appear)* manifestarsi, rivelarsi; **~ing country** paese *m* in via di sviluppo; **~ment** *n* sviluppo.

device [dɪ'vaɪs] *n (apparatus)* congegno.

devil ['dɛvl] *n* diavolo; demonio.

devious ['diːvɪəs] *a (means)* indiretto(a), tortuoso(a); *(person)* subdolo(a).

devise [dɪ'vaɪz] *vt* escogitare, concepire.

devoid [dɪ'vɔɪd] *a*: **~ of** privo(a) di.

devolution [diːvə'luːʃən] *n (POL)* decentramento.

devote [dɪ'vəut] *vt*: **to ~ sth to** dedicare qc a; **~d** *a* devoto(a); **to be ~d to** essere molto affezionato(a) a; **~e** [dɛvəu'tiː] *n (MUS, SPORT)* appassionato/a.

devotion [dɪ'vəuʃən] *n* devozione *f*, attaccamento; *(REL)* atto di devozione, preghiera.

devour [dɪ'vauə*] *vt* divorare.

devout [dɪ'vaut] *a* pio(a), devoto(a).

dew [djuː] *n* rugiada.

dexterity [dɛks'tɛrɪtɪ] *n* destrezza.

DHSS *n abbr* (= Department of Health and Social Security) ≈ ministero della Sanità e della Previdenza sociale.

diabetes [daɪə'biːtiːz] *n* diabete *m*; **dia-**

betic [-'bɛtɪk] a, n diabetico(a).

diabolical [daɪə'bɔlɪkl] a (col: weather, behaviour) orribile.

diagnosis, pl **diagnoses** [daɪəg'nəʊsɪs, -siːz] n diagnosi f inv.

diagonal [daɪ'ægənl] a, n diagonale (f).

diagram ['daɪəgræm] n diagramma m.

dial ['daɪəl] n quadrante m; (on telephone) disco combinatore // vt (number) fare.

dialect ['daɪəlɛkt] n dialetto.

dialling ['daɪəlɪŋ]: ~ **code**, (US) **dial code** n prefisso; ~ **tone**, (US) **dial tone** n segnale m di linea libera.

dialogue ['daɪəlɔg] n dialogo.

diameter [daɪ'æmɪtə*] n diametro.

diamond ['daɪəmənd] n diamante m; (shape) rombo; ~s npl (CARDS) quadri mpl.

diaper ['daɪəpə*] n (US) pannolino.

diaphragm ['daɪəfræm] n diaframma m.

diarrhoea, (US) **diarrhea** [daɪə'riːə] n diarrea.

diary ['daɪərɪ] n (daily account) diario; (book) agenda.

dice [daɪs] n (pl inv) dado // vt (CULIN) tagliare a dadini.

Dictaphone ['dɪktəfəʊn] n ® dittafono ®.

dictate vt [dɪk'teɪt] dettare // n ['dɪkteɪt] dettame m.

dictation [dɪk'teɪʃən] n dettato.

dictator [dɪk'teɪtə*] n dittatore m; ~**ship** n dittatura.

dictionary ['dɪkʃənrɪ] n dizionario.

did [dɪd] pt of **do**.

didn't = did not.

die [daɪ] n (pl **dies**) conio; matrice f; stampo // vi morire; **to be dying for sth/ to do sth** morire dalla voglia di qc/di fare qc; **to ~ away** vi spegnersi a poco a poco; **to ~ down** vi abbassarsi; **to ~ out** vi estinguersi.

diehard ['daɪhɑːd] n reazionario/a.

Diesel ['diːzəl]: ~ **engine** n motore m diesel inv; ~ **(oil)** n gasolio (per motori diesel).

diet ['daɪət] n alimentazione f; (restricted food) dieta // vi (also: be on a ~) stare a dieta.

differ ['dɪfə*] vi: **to ~ from sth** differire da qc; essere diverso(a) da qc; **to ~ from sb over sth** essere in disaccordo con qn su qc; ~**ence** n differenza; (quarrel) screzio; ~**ent** a diverso(a); ~**entiate** [-'rɛnʃɪeɪt] vi differenziarsi; **to** ~**entiate between** discriminare or fare differenza fra.

difficult ['dɪfɪkəlt] a difficile; ~**y** n difficoltà f inv.

diffident ['dɪfɪdənt] a sfiduciato(a).

dig [dɪg] vt (pt, pp **dug**) (hole) scavare; (garden) vangare // n (prod) gomitata; (fig) frecciata; **to ~ in** vi (MIL: also: ~ o.s. in) trincerarsi; (col: eat) attaccare

a mangiare; **to ~ into** vt fus (snow, soil) scavare; **to ~ one's nails into** conficcare le unghie in; **to ~ up** vt scavare; (tree etc) sradicare.

digest [daɪ'dʒɛst] vt digerire; ~**ion** [dɪ'dʒɛstʃən] n digestione f; ~**ive** a (juices, system) digerente.

digit ['dɪdʒɪt] n cifra; (finger) dito; ~**al** a digitale.

dignified ['dɪgnɪfaɪd] a dignitoso(a).

dignity ['dɪgnɪtɪ] n dignità.

digress [daɪ'grɛs] vi: **to ~ from** divagare da.

digs [dɪgz] npl (Brit col) camera ammobiliata.

dilapidated [dɪ'læpɪdeɪtɪd] a cadente.

dilemma [daɪ'lɛmə] n dilemma m.

diligent ['dɪlɪdʒənt] a diligente.

dilute [daɪ'luːt] vt diluire; (with water) annacquare.

dim [dɪm] a (light, eyesight) debole; (memory, outline) vago(a); (stupid) lento(a) d'ingegno // vt (light) abbassare.

dime [daɪm] n (US) = 10 cents.

dimension [daɪ'mɛnʃən] n dimensione f.

diminish [dɪ'mɪnɪʃ] vt, vi diminuire.

diminutive [dɪ'mɪnjutɪv] a minuscolo(a) // n (LING) diminutivo.

dimmers ['dɪməz] npl (US AUT) anabbaglianti mpl; luci fpl di posizione.

dimple ['dɪmpl] n fossetta.

din [dɪn] n chiasso, fracasso.

dine [daɪn] vi pranzare.

dinghy ['dɪŋgɪ] n battello pneumatico; (also: rubber ~) gommone m; (also: sailing ~) dinghy m inv.

dingy ['dɪndʒɪ] a grigio(a).

dining ['daɪnɪŋ] cpd: ~ **car** n (Brit) vagone m ristorante; ~ **room** n sala da pranzo.

dinner ['dɪnə*] n (lunch) pranzo; (evening meal) cena; (public) banchetto; ~'**s ready!** a tavola!; ~ **jacket** n smoking m inv; ~ **party** n cena; ~ **time** n ora di pranzo (or cena).

dint [dɪnt] n: **by ~ of** a forza di.

dip [dɪp] n discesa; (in sea) bagno // vt immergere; bagnare; (Brit AUT: lights) abbassare // vi abbassarsi.

diphthong ['dɪfθɔŋ] n dittongo.

diploma [dɪ'pləʊmə] n diploma m.

diplomacy [dɪ'pləʊməsɪ] n diplomazia.

diplomat ['dɪpləmæt] n diplomatico; ~**ic** [dɪplə'mætɪk] a diplomatico(a).

dipstick ['dɪpstɪk] n (AUT) indicatore m di livello dell'olio.

dire [daɪə*] a terribile; estremo(a).

direct [daɪ'rɛkt] a diretto(a) // vt dirigere; **can you ~ me to ...?** mi può indicare la strada per ...?

direction [dɪ'rɛkʃən] n direzione f; **sense of ~** senso dell'orientamento; ~**s** npl (advice) chiarimenti mpl; ~**s for use** istruzioni fpl.

directly [dɪ'rɛktlɪ] ad (in straight line) direttamente; (at once) subito.

director [dɪ'rɛktə*] n direttore/trice; amministratore/trice; (THEATRE, CINEMA) regista m/f.

directory [dɪ'rɛktərɪ] n elenco.

dirt [də:t] n sporcizia; immondizia; ~-**cheap** a da due soldi; ~**y** a sporco(a) // vt sporcare; ~**y trick** n brutto scherzo.

disability [dɪsə'bɪlɪtɪ] n invalidità f inv; (LAW) incapacità f inv.

disabled [dɪs'eɪbld] a invalido(a); (maimed) mutilato(a); (through illness, old age) inabile.

disadvantage [dɪsəd'vɑːntɪdʒ] n svantaggio.

disagree [dɪsə'griː] vi (differ) discordare; (be against, think otherwise): to ~ (with) essere in disaccordo (con), dissentire (da); ~**able** a sgradevole; (person) antipatico(a); ~**ment** n disaccordo.

disappear [dɪsə'pɪə*] vi scomparire; ~**ance** n scomparsa.

disappoint [dɪsə'pɔɪnt] vt deludere; ~**ed** a deluso(a); ~**ing** a deludente; ~**ment** n delusione f.

disapproval [dɪsə'pruːvəl] n disapprovazione f.

disapprove [dɪsə'pruːv] vi: to ~ of disapprovare.

disarm [dɪs'ɑːm] vt disarmare; ~**ament** n disarmo.

disarray [dɪsə'reɪ] n: in ~ (army) in rotta; (organization) in uno stato di confusione; (clothes, hair) in disordine.

disaster [dɪ'zɑːstə*] n disastro.

disband [dɪs'bænd] vt sbandare; (MIL) congedare // vi sciogliersi.

disbelief [dɪsbə'liːf] n incredulità.

disc [dɪsk] n disco; (COMPUT) = **disk**.

discard [dɪs'kɑːd] vt (old things) scartare; (fig) abbandonare.

discern [dɪ'səːn] vt discernere, distinguere; ~**ing** a perspicace.

discharge vt [dɪs'tʃɑːdʒ] (duties) compiere; (ELEC, waste etc) scaricare; (MED) emettere; (patient) dimettere; (employee) licenziare; (soldier) congedare; (defendant) liberare // n [dɪs'tʃɑːdʒ] (ELEC) scarica; (MED) emissione f; (dismissal) licenziamento; congedo; liberazione f.

disciple [dɪ'saɪpl] n discepolo.

discipline ['dɪsɪplɪn] n disciplina // vt disciplinare; (punish) punire.

disc jockey n disc jockey m inv.

disclaim [dɪs'kleɪm] vt negare, smentire.

disclose [dɪs'kləuz] vt rivelare, svelare; **disclosure** [-'kləuʒə*] n rivelazione f.

disco ['dɪskəu] n abbr = **discothèque**.

discoloured, (US) **discolored** [dɪs'kʌləd] a scolorito(a); ingiallito(a).

discomfort [dɪs'kʌmfət] n disagio; (lack of comfort) scomodità f inv.

disconcert [dɪskən'səːt] vt sconcertare.

disconnect [dɪskə'nɛkt] vt sconnettere, staccare; (ELEC, RADIO) staccare; (gas, water) chiudere.

disconsolate [dɪs'kɔnsəlɪt] a sconsolato(a).

discontent [dɪskən'tɛnt] n scontentezza; ~**ed** a scontento(a).

discontinue [dɪskən'tɪnjuː] vt smettere, cessare.

discord ['dɪskɔːd] n disaccordo; (MUS) dissonanza.

discothèque ['dɪskəutɛk] n discoteca.

discount n ['dɪskaunt] sconto // vt [dɪs'kaunt] scontare.

discourage [dɪs'kʌrɪdʒ] vt scoraggiare.

discourteous [dɪs'kəːtɪəs] a scortese.

discover [dɪs'kʌvə*] vt scoprire; ~**y** n scoperta.

discredit [dɪs'krɛdɪt] vt screditare; mettere in dubbio.

discreet [dɪ'skriːt] a discreto(a).

discrepancy [dɪ'skrɛpənsɪ] n discrepanza.

discriminate [dɪ'skrɪmɪneɪt] vi: to ~ between distinguere tra; to ~ against discriminare contro; **discriminating** a fine, giudizioso(a); **discrimination** [-'neɪʃən] n discriminazione f; (judgment) discernimento.

discuss [dɪ'skʌs] vt discutere; (debate) dibattere; ~**ion** [dɪ'skʌʃən] n discussione f.

disdain [dɪs'deɪn] n disdegno.

disease [dɪ'ziːz] n malattia.

disembark [dɪsɪm'bɑːk] vt, vi sbarcare.

disengage [dɪsɪn'geɪdʒ] vt disimpegnare; (TECH) distaccare; (AUT: clutch) disinnestare.

disfigure [dɪs'fɪgə*] vt sfigurare.

disgrace [dɪs'greɪs] n vergogna; (disfavour) disgrazia // vt disonorare, far cadere in disgrazia; ~**ful** a scandaloso(a), vergognoso(a).

disgruntled [dɪs'grʌntld] a scontento(a), di cattivo umore.

disguise [dɪs'gaɪz] n travestimento // vt travestire; in ~ travestito(a).

disgust [dɪs'gʌst] n disgusto, nausea // vt disgustare, far schifo a; ~**ing** a disgustoso(a); ripugnante.

dish [dɪʃ] n piatto; to do o wash the ~es fare i piatti; to ~ up vt servire; (facts, statistics) presentare; ~**cloth** n strofinaccio.

dishearten [dɪs'hɑːtn] vt scoraggiare.

dishevelled [dɪ'ʃɛvəld] a arruffato(a); scapigliato(a).

dishonest [dɪs'ɔnɪst] a disonesto(a).

dishonour, (US) **dishonor** [dɪs'ɔnə*] n disonore m; ~**able** a disonorevole.

dish towel n (US) strofinaccio dei piatti.

dishwasher ['dɪʃwɔʃə*] n lavastoviglie f inv; (person) sguattero/a.

disillusion [dısı'lu:ʒən] *vt* disilludere, disingannare // *n* disillusione *f*.

disincentive [dısın'sentıv] *n*: to be a ~ essere demotivante; to be a ~ to sb demotivare qn.

disinfect [dısın'fekt] *vt* disinfettare; ~**ant** *n* disinfettante *m*.

disintegrate [dıs'ıntıgreıt] *vi* disintegrarsi.

disinterested [dıs'ıntrəstıd] *a* disinteressato(a).

disjointed [dıs'dʒɔıntıd] *a* sconnesso(a).

disk [dısk] *n* (COMPUT) disco; **single-/double-sided** ~ disco a facciata singola/doppia; ~ **drive** *n* lettore *m*; ~**ette** *n* (US) = **disk**.

dislike [dıs'laık] *n* antipatia, avversione *f* // *vt*: he ~s it non gli piace.

dislocate ['dısləkeıt] *vt* slogare; disorganizzare.

dislodge [dıs'lɔdʒ] *vt* rimuovere, staccare; (*enemy*) sloggiare.

disloyal [dıs'lɔıəl] *a* sleale.

dismal ['dızml] *a* triste, cupo(a).

dismantle [dıs'mæntl] *vt* smantellare, smontare; (*fort, warship*) disarmare.

dismay [dıs'meı] *n* costernazione *f* // *vt* sgomentare.

dismiss [dıs'mıs] *vt* congedare; (*employee*) licenziare; (*idea*) scacciare; (*LAW*) respingere; ~**al** *n* congedo; licenziamento.

dismount [dıs'maunt] *vi* scendere.

disobedience [dısə'bi:dıəns] *n* disubbidienza.

disobedient [dısə'bi:dıənt] *a* disubbidiente.

disobey [dısə'beı] *vt* disubbidire.

disorder [dıs'ɔ:də*] *n* disordine *m*; (*rioting*) tumulto; (*MED*) disturbo; ~**ly** *a* disordinato(a); tumultuoso(a).

disorientated [dıs'ɔ:rıenteıtıd] *a* disorientato(a).

disown [dıs'əun] *vt* ripudiare.

disparaging [dıs'pærıdʒıŋ] *a* spregiativo(a), sprezzante.

dispassionate [dıs'pæʃənət] *a* calmo(a), freddo(a); imparziale.

dispatch [dıs'pætʃ] *vt* spedire, inviare // *n* spedizione *f*, invio; (*MIL, PRESS*) dispaccio.

dispel [dıs'pel] *vt* dissipare, scacciare.

dispensary [dıs'pensərı] *n* farmacia; (*in chemist's*) dispensario.

dispense [dıs'pens] *vt* distribuire, amministrare; to ~ **with** *vt fus* fare a meno di; ~**r** *n* (*container*) distributore *m*; **dispensing chemist** *n* (*Brit*) farmacista *m/f*.

disperse [dıs'pə:s] *vt* disperdere; (*knowledge*) disseminare // *vi* disperdersi.

dispirited [dıs'pırıtıd] *a* scoraggiato(a), abbattuto(a).

displace [dıs'pleıs] *vt* spostare; ~**d**

person *n* (*POL*) profugo/a.

display [dıs'pleı] *n* mostra; esposizione *f*; (*of feeling etc*) manifestazione *f*; (*screen*) schermo; (*pej*) ostentazione *f* // *vt* mostrare; (*goods*) esporre; (*results*) affiggere; (*departure times*) indicare.

displease [dıs'pli:z] *vt* dispiacere a, scontentare; ~**d with** scontento di; **displeasure** [-'pleʒə*] *n* dispiacere *m*.

disposable [dıs'pəuzəbl] *a* (*pack etc*) a perdere; (*income*) disponibile; ~ **nappy** *n* pannolino di carta.

disposal [dıs'pəuzl] *n* (*of rubbish*) evacuazione *f*; distruzione *f*; at one's ~ alla sua disposizione.

dispose [dıs'pəuz] *vt* disporre; to ~ **of** *vt* (*time, money*) disporre di; (*unwanted goods*) sbarazzarsi di; (*problem*) eliminare; ~**d** *a*: ~**d to do** disposto(a) a fare; **disposition** [-'zıʃən] *n* disposizione *f*; (*temperament*) carattere *m*.

disproportionate [dısprə'pɔ:ʃənət] *a* sproporzionato(a).

disprove [dıs'pru:v] *vt* confutare.

dispute [dıs'pju:t] *n* disputa; (*also*: **industrial** ~) controversia (sindacale) // *vt* contestare; (*matter*) discutere; (*victory*) disputare.

disqualify [dıs'kwɔlıfaı] *vt* (*SPORT*) squalificare; to ~ **sb from sth/from doing** rendere qn incapace a qc/a fare; squalificare qn da qc/da fare; to ~ **sb from driving** ritirare la patente a qn.

disquiet [dıs'kwaıət] *n* inquietudine *f*.

disregard [dısrı'gɑ:d] *vt* non far caso a, non badare a.

disrepair [dısrı'peə*] *n* cattivo stato; to **fall into** ~ (*building*) andare in rovina; (*street*) deteriorarsi.

disreputable [dıs'repjutəbl] *a* (*person*) di cattiva fama.

disrupt [dıs'rʌpt] *vt* mettere in disordine.

dissatisfaction [dıssætıs'fækʃən] *n* scontentezza, insoddisfazione *f*.

dissect [dı'sekt] *vt* sezionare.

dissent [dı'sent] *n* dissenso.

dissertation [dısə'teıʃən] *n* tesi *f inv*, dissertazione *f*.

disservice [dıs'sə:vıs] *n*: to **do sb a** ~ fare un cattivo servizio a qn.

dissimilar [dı'sımılə*] *a*: ~ (**to**) dissimile *or* diverso(a) (da).

dissipate ['dısıpeıt] *vt* dissipare; ~**d** *a* dissipato(a).

dissolute ['dısəlu:t] *a* dissoluto(a), licenzioso(a).

dissolution [dısə'lu:ʃən] *n* (*of organization, marriage, POL*) scioglimento.

dissolve [dı'zɔlv] *vt* dissolvere, sciogliere; (*POL, marriage etc*) sciogliere // *vi* dissolversi, sciogliersi; (*fig*) svanire.

distance ['dıstns] *n* distanza; **in the** ~ in lontananza.

distant ['dıstnt] *a* lontano(a), distante;

(*manner*) riservato(a), freddo(a).
distaste [dɪs'teɪst] *n* ripugnanza; **~ful** *a* ripugnante, sgradevole.
distended [dɪs'tɛndɪd] *a* (*stomach*) dilatato(a).
distil [dɪs'tɪl] *vt* distillare; **~lery** *n* distilleria.
distinct [dɪs'tɪŋkt] *a* distinto(a); (*preference, progress*) definito(a); **as ~ from** a differenza di; **~ion** [dɪs'tɪŋkʃən] *n* distinzione *f*; (*in exam*) lode *f*; **~ive** *a* distintivo(a).
distinguish [dɪs'tɪŋgwɪʃ] *vt* distinguere; discernere; **~ed** *a* (*eminent*) eminente; **~ing** *a* (*feature*) distinto(a), caratteristico(a).
distort [dɪs'tɔːt] *vt* distorcere; (*TECH*) deformare.
distract [dɪs'trækt] *vt* distrarre; **~ed** *a* distratto(a); **~ion** [dɪs'trækʃən] *n* distrazione *f*.
distraught [dɪs'trɔːt] *a* stravolto(a).
distress [dɪs'trɛs] *n* angoscia; (*pain*) dolore *m* // *vt* affliggere; **~ing** *a* doloroso(a).
distribute [dɪs'trɪbjuːt] *vt* distribuire; **distribution** [-'bjuːʃən] *n* distribuzione *f*; **distributor** *n* distributore *m*.
district ['dɪstrɪkt] *n* (*of country*) regione *f*; (*of town*) quartiere *m*; (*ADMIN*) distretto; **~ attorney** *n* (*US*) ≈ sostituto procuratore *m* della Repubblica; **~ nurse** *n* (*Brit*) infermiera di quartiere.
distrust [dɪs'trʌst] *n* diffidenza, sfiducia // *vt* non aver fiducia in.
disturb [dɪs'tɜːb] *vt* disturbare; (*inconvenience*) scomodare; **~ance** *n* disturbo; (*political etc*) tumulto; (*by drunks etc*) disordini *mpl*; **~ed** *a* (*worried, upset*) turbato(a); **emotionally ~ed** con turbe emotive; **~ing** *a* sconvolgente.
disuse [dɪs'juːs] *n*: **to fall into ~** cadere in disuso.
disused [dɪs'juːzd] *a* abbandonato(a).
ditch [dɪtʃ] *n* fossa // *vt* (*col*) piantare in asso.
dither ['dɪðə*] *vi* vacillare.
ditto ['dɪtəu] *ad* idem.
dive [daɪv] *n* tuffo; (*of submarine*) immersione *f*; (*AVIAT*) picchiata; (*pej*) buco // *vi* tuffarsi; **~r** *n* tuffatore/trice; palombaro.
diverse [daɪ'vɜːs] *a* vario(a).
diversion [daɪ'vɜːʃən] *n* (*Brit AUT*) deviazione *f*; (*distraction*) divertimento.
divert [daɪ'vɜːt] *vt* deviare; (*amuse*) divertire.
divide [dɪ'vaɪd] *vt* dividere; (*separate*) separare // *vi* dividersi; **~d highway** *n* (*US*) strada a doppia carreggiata.
dividend ['dɪvɪdɛnd] *n* dividendo.
divine [dɪ'vaɪn] *a* divino(a).
diving ['daɪvɪŋ] *n* tuffo; **~ board** *n* trampolino.

divinity [dɪ'vɪnɪtɪ] *n* divinità *f inv*; teologia.
division [dɪ'vɪʒən] *n* divisione *f*; separazione *f*.
divorce [dɪ'vɔːs] *n* divorzio // *vt* divorziare da; **~d** *a* divorziato(a); **~e** [-'siː] *n* divorziato/a.
D.I.Y. *n abbr* (*Brit*) = **do-it-yourself**.
dizzy ['dɪzɪ] *a* (*height*) vertiginoso(a); **to feel ~** avere il capogiro; **to make sb ~** far venire il capogiro a qn.
DJ *n abbr* = **disc jockey**.
do [duː] ◆ *n* (*col: party etc*) festa; **it was rather a grand ~** è stato un ricevimento piuttosto importante
◆ *vb* (*pt* **did**, *pp* **done**) **1** (*in negative constructions*) *non tradotto*; **I don't understand** non capisco
2 (*to form questions*) *non tradotto*; **didn't you know?** non lo sapevi?; **why didn't you come?** perché non sei venuto?
3 (*for emphasis, in polite expressions*): **she does seem rather late** sembra essere piuttosto in ritardo; **~ sit down** si accomodi la prego, prego si sieda; **~ take care!** mi raccomando, sta attento!
4 (*used to avoid repeating vb*): **she swims better than I ~** lei nuota meglio di me; **~ you agree?** — **yes, I ~/no, I don't** sei d'accordo? — sì/no; **she lives in Glasgow** — **so ~ I** lei vive a Glasgow — anch'io; **he asked me to help him and I did** mi ha chiesto di aiutarlo ed io l'ho fatto
5 (*in question tags*): **you like him, don't you?** ti piace, vero?; **I don't know him, ~ I?** non lo conosco, vero?
◆ *vt* (*gen, carry out, perform etc*) fare; **what are you ~ing tonight?** che fa stasera?; **to ~ the cooking** cucinare; **to ~ the washing-up** fare i piatti; **to ~ one's teeth** lavarsi i denti; **to ~ one's hair/nails** farsi i capelli/le unghie; **the car was ~ing 100** la macchina faceva i 100 all'ora
◆ *vi* **1** (*act, behave*) fare; **~ as I ~** faccia come me, faccia come faccio io
2 (*get on, fare*) andare; **he's ~ing well/badly at school** va bene/male a scuola; **how ~ you ~?** piacere!
3 (*suit*) andare bene; **this room will ~** questa stanza va bene
4 (*be sufficient*) bastare; **will £10 ~?** basteranno 10 sterline?; **that'll ~** basta così; **that'll ~!** (*in annoyance*) ora basta!; **to make ~ (with)** arrangiarsi (con)
to do away with *vt fus* (*kill*) far fuori; (*abolish*) abolire
to do up *vt* (*laces*) allacciare; (*dress, buttons*) abbottonare; (*renovate: room, house*) rimettere a nuovo, rifare
to do with *vt fus* (*need*) aver bisogno di; (*be connected*): **what has it got to ~ with you?** e tu che c'entri?; **I won't have anything to ~ with it** non voglio avere

niente a che farci; **it has to ~ with money** si tratta di soldi
to do without *vi* fare senza ♦ *vt fus* fare a meno di.

dock [dɔk] *n* bacino; (*LAW*) banco degli imputati // *vi* entrare in bacino; **~er** *n* scaricatore *m*; **~yard** *n* cantiere *m* (navale).

doctor ['dɔktə*] *n* medico/a; (*Ph.D. etc*) dottore/essa // *vt* (*fig*) alterare, manipolare; (*drink etc*) adulterare; **D~ of Philosophy (Ph.D.)** *n* dottorato di ricerca; (*person*) titolare *m/f* di un dottorato di ricerca.

doctrine ['dɔktrın] *n* dottrina.

document ['dɔkjumənt] *n* documento; **~ary** [-'mɛntərı] *a* documentario(a); (*evidence*) documentato(a) // *a* documentario.

dodge [dɔdʒ] *n* trucco; schivata // *vt* schivare, eludere.

doe [dəu] *n* (*deer*) femmina di daino; (*rabbit*) coniglia.

does [dʌz] *vb see* **do**; **doesn't** = **does not**.

dog [dɔg] *n* cane *m* // *vt* (*follow closely*) pedinare; (*fig*: *memory etc*) perseguitare; **~ collar** *n* collare *m* di cane; (*fig*) collarino; **~-eared** *a* (*book*) con orecchie.

dogged ['dɔgıd] *a* ostinato(a), tenace.

dogsbody ['dɔgzbɔdı] *n* factotum *m inv*.

doings ['duınz] *npl* attività *fpl*.

do-it-yourself [du:ɪtjɔː'sɛlf] *n* il far da sé.

doldrums ['dɔldrəmz] *npl* (*fig*): **to be in the ~** essere giù.

dole [dəul] *n* (*Brit*) sussidio di disoccupazione; **to be on the ~** vivere del sussidio; **to ~ out** *vt* distribuire.

doleful ['dəulful] *a* triste, doloroso(a).

doll [dɔl] *n* bambola; **to ~ o.s. up** farsi bello(a).

dollar ['dɔlə*] *n* dollaro.

dolphin ['dɔlfın] *n* delfino.

domain [də'meın] *n* dominio.

dome [dəum] *n* cupola.

domestic [də'mɛstık] *a* (*duty, happiness, animal*) domestico(a); (*policy, affairs, flights*) nazionale; **~ated** *a* addomesticato(a).

dominate ['dɔmıneıt] *vt* dominare.

domineering [dɔmı'nıərıŋ] *a* dispotico(a), autoritario(a).

dominion [də'mınıən] *n* dominio; sovranità; dominion *m inv*.

domino, ~es ['dɔmınəu] *n* domino; **~es** *n* (*game*) gioco del domino.

don [dɔn] *n* (*Brit*) docente *m/f* universitario(a).

donate [də'neıt] *vt* donare.

done [dʌn] *pp of* **do**.

donkey ['dɔŋkı] *n* asino.

donor ['dəunə*] *n* donatore/trice.

don't [dəunt] *vb* = **do not**.

doodle ['du:dl] *vi* scarabocchiare.

doom [du:m] *n* destino; rovina // *vt*: **to be ~ed** (**to failure**) essere predestinato(a) (a fallire); **~sday** *n* il giorno del Giudizio.

door [dɔː*] *n* porta; **~bell** *n* campanello; **~man** *n* (*in hotel*) portiere *m* in livrea; (*in block of flats*) portinaio; **~mat** *n* stuoia della porta; **~step** *n* gradino della porta; **~way** *n* porta.

dope [dəup] *n* (*col: drugs*) roba // *vt* (*horse etc*) drogare.

dopey ['dəupı] *a* (*col*) inebetito(a).

dormant ['dɔːmənt] *a* inattivo(a); (*fig*) latente.

dormitory ['dɔːmıtrı] *n* dormitorio.

dose [dəus] *n* dose *f*; (*bout*) attacco.

doss house ['dɔs-] *n* (*Brit*) asilo notturno.

dot [dɔt] *n* punto; macchiolina; **~ted with** punteggiato(a) di; **on the ~** in punto.

dote [dəut]: **to ~ on** *vt fus* essere infatuato(a) di.

dot-matrix printer [dɔt'meıtrıks-] *n* stampante *f* a matrice a punti.

dotted line ['dɔtıd-] *n* linea punteggiata.

double ['dʌbl] *a* doppio(a) // *ad* (*fold*) in due, doppio; (*twice*): **to cost ~** (**sth**) costare il doppio (di qc) // *n* sosia *m inv*; (*CINEMA*) controfigura // *vt* raddoppiare; (*fold*) piegare doppio *or* in due // *vi* raddoppiarsi; **on the ~**, (*Brit*) **at the ~** a passo di corsa; **~s** *n* (*TENNIS*) doppio; **~ bass** *n* contrabbasso; **~ bed** *n* letto matrimoniale; **~-breasted** *a* a doppio petto; **~cross** *vt* fare il doppio gioco con; **~decker** *n* autobus *m inv* a due piani; **~ glazing** *n* (*Brit*) doppi vetri *mpl*; **~ room** *n* camera per due; **doubly** *ad* doppiamente.

doubt [daut] *n* dubbio // *vt* dubitare di; **to ~ that** dubitare che + *sub*; **~ful** *a* dubbioso(a), incerto(a); (*person*) equivoco(a); **~less** *ad* indubbiamente.

dough [dəu] *n* pasta, impasto; **~nut** *n* bombolone *m*.

douse [dauz] *vt* (*drench*) inzuppare; (*extinguish*) spegnere.

dove [dʌv] *n* colombo/a.

dovetail ['dʌvteıl] *vi* (*fig*) combaciare.

dowdy ['daudı] *a* trasandato(a); malvestito(a).

down [daun] *n* (*fluff*) piumino // *ad* giù, di sotto // *prep* giù per // *vt* (*col: drink*) scolarsi; **~ with X!** abbasso X!; **~-and-out** *n* barbone *m*; **~-at-heel** *a* scalcagnato(a); (*fig*) trasandato(a); **~cast** *a* abbattuto(a); **~fall** *n* caduta; rovina; **~hearted** *a* scoraggiato(a); **~hill** *ad*: **to go ~hill** andare in discesa // *n* (*SKI: also*: **~hill race**) discesa libera; **~ payment** *n* acconto; **~pour** *n* scroscio di pioggia; **~right** *a* franco(a); (*refusal*) assoluto(a); **~stairs** *ad* di sotto; al piano inferiore; **~stream** *ad* a valle; **~-to-earth** a pratico(a); **~town** ad in città; **~ under** ad (Australia etc) agli antipodi; **~ward** ['daunwəd] a, ad, **~wards** ['daunwədz] ad in giù, in discesa.

dowry ['dauri] n dote f.

doz. abbr = **dozen**.

doze [dəuz] vi sonnecchiare; **to ~ off** vi appisolarsi.

dozen ['dʌzn] n dozzina; **a ~ books** una dozzina di libri; **~s of** decine fpl di.

Dr. abbr = **doctor**; **drive** (n).

drab [dræb] a tetro(a), grigio(a).

draft [drɑːft] n abbozzo; (COMM) tratta; (US MIL) contingente m; (: call-up) leva // vt abbozzare; see also **draught**.

draftsman ['drɑːftsmən] n (US) = **draughtsman**.

drag [dræg] vt trascinare; (river) dragare // vi trascinarsi // n (col) noioso/a; noia, fatica; (women's clothing): **in ~** travestito (da donna); **to ~ on** vi tirar avanti lentamente.

dragon ['drægən] n drago.

dragonfly ['drægənflai] n libellula.

drain [drein] n canale m di scolo; (for sewage) fogna; (on resources) salasso // vt (land, marshes) prosciugare; (vegetables) scolare; (reservoir etc) vuotare // vi (water) defluire (via); **~age** n prosciugamento; fognatura; **~ing board**, (US) **~board** n piano del lavello; **~pipe** n tubo di scarico.

dram [dræm] n bicchierino.

drama ['drɑːmə] n (art) dramma m, teatro; (play) commedia; (event) dramma; **~tic** [drə'mætik] a drammatico(a); **~tist** ['dræmətist] n drammaturgo/a; **~tize** vt (events) drammatizzare; (adapt: for TV/cinema) ridurre or adattare per la televisione/lo schermo.

drank [dræŋk] pt of **drink**.

drape [dreip] vt drappeggiare; **~s** npl (US) tende fpl; **~r** n (Brit) negoziante m/f di stoffe.

drastic ['dræstik] a drastico(a).

draught, (US) **draft** [drɑːft] n corrente f d'aria; (NAUT) pescaggio; **~s** n (Brit) (gioco della) dama; **on ~** (beer) alla spina; **~board** n (Brit) scacchiera.

draughtsman, (US) **draftsman** ['drɑːftsmən] n disegnatore m.

draw [drɔː] vb (pt **drew**, pp **drawn**) vt tirare; (attract) attirare; (picture) disegnare; (line, circle) tracciare; (money) ritirare // vi (SPORT) pareggiare // n pareggio; (in lottery) estrazione f; (attraction) attrazione f; **to ~ near** vi avvicinarsi; **to ~ out** vi (lengthen) allungarsi // vt (money) ritirare; **to ~ up** vi (stop) arrestarsi, fermarsi // vt (document) compilare; **~back** n svantaggio, inconveniente m; **~bridge** n ponte m levatoio.

drawer [drɔː*] n cassetto; ['drɔː:ə*] (of

cheque) traente m/f.

drawing ['drɔːiŋ] n disegno; **~ board** n tavola da disegno; **~ pin** n (Brit) puntina da disegno; **~ room** n salotto.

drawl [drɔːl] n pronuncia strascicata.

drawn [drɔːn] pp of **draw**.

dread [drɛd] n terrore m // vt tremare all'idea di; **~ful** a terribile.

dream [driːm] n sogno // vt, vi (pt, pp **dreamed** or **dreamt** [drɛmt]) sognare; **~y** a sognante.

dreary ['driəri] a tetro(a); monotono(a).

dredge [drɛdʒ] vt dragare.

dregs [drɛgz] npl feccia.

drench [drɛntʃ] vt inzuppare.

dress [drɛs] n vestito; (clothing) abbigliamento // vt vestire; (wound) fasciare; (food) condire; preparare // vi vestirsi; **to get ~ed** vestirsi; **to ~ up** vi vestirsi a festa; (in fancy dress) vestirsi in costume; **~ circle** n (Brit) prima galleria; **~er** n (THEATRE) assistente m/f del camerino; (furniture) credenza; **~ing** n (MED) benda; (CULIN) condimento; **~ing gown** n (Brit) vestaglia; **~ing room** n (THEATRE) camerino; (SPORT) spogliatoio; **~ing table** n toilette f inv; **~maker** n sarta; **~ rehearsal** n prova generale; **~y** a (col) elegante.

drew [druː] pt of **draw**.

dribble ['dribl] vi gocciolare; (baby) sbavare; (FOOTBALL) dribblare.

dried [draid] a (fruit, beans) secco(a); (eggs, milk) in polvere.

drier ['draiə*] n = **dryer**.

drift [drift] n (of current etc) direzione f; forza; (of sand etc) turbine m; (of snow) cumulo; turbine; (general meaning) senso // vi (boat) essere trasportato/a dalla corrente; (sand, snow) ammucchiarsi; **~wood** n resti mpl della mareggiata.

drill [dril] n trapano; (MIL) esercitazione f // vt trapanare // vi (for oil) fare trivellazioni.

drink [driŋk] n bevanda, bibita // vt, vi (pt **drank**, pp **drunk**) bere; **to have a ~** bere qualcosa; **a ~ of water** un po' d'acqua; **~er** n bevitore/trice; **~ing water** n acqua potabile.

drip [drip] n goccia; gocciolamento; (MED) fleboclisi f inv // vi gocciolare; (washing) sgocciolare; (wall) trasudare; **~-dry** a (shirt) che non si stira; **~ping** n grasso d'arrosto.

drive [draiv] n passeggiata or giro in macchina; (also: **~way**) viale m d'accesso; (energy) energia; (PSYCH) impulso; bisogno; (push) sforzo eccezionale; campagna; (SPORT) drive m inv; (TECH) trasmissione f; propulsione f; presa; (also: **disk ~**) lettore m // vb (pt **drove**, pp **driven**) vt guidare; (nail) piantare; (push) cacciare, spingere; (*TECH: motor*) azionare; far funzionare // vi (*AUT: at controls*) guidare; (*: travel*) andare in macchina; **left-/right-hand ~** guida a sinistra/destra; **to ~ sb mad** far impazzire qn.

drivel ['drɪvl] n idiozie *fpl*.

driven ['drɪvn] *pp of* **drive**.

driver ['draɪvə*] n conducente *m/f*; (*of taxi*) tassista m; (*of bus*) autista m; **~'s license** n (*US*) patente f di guida.

driveway ['draɪvweɪ] n viale m d'accesso.

driving ['draɪvɪŋ] a: **~ rain** pioggia sferzante ~ n guida; **~ instructor** n istruttore/trice di scuola guida; **~ lesson** n lezione f di guida; **~ licence** n (*Brit*) patente f di guida; **~ mirror** n specchietto retrovisore; **~ school** n scuola f guida *inv*; **~ test** n esame m di guida.

drizzle ['drɪzl] n pioggerella.

droll [drəʊl] a buffo(a).

drone [drəʊn] n ronzio; (*male bee*) fuco.

drool [dru:l] vi sbavare.

droop [dru:p] vi abbassarsi; languire.

drop [drɒp] n goccia; (*fall*) caduta; (*also*: **~ parachute ~**) lancio; (*steep incline*) salto // vt lasciare cadere; (*voice, eyes, price*) abbassare; (*set down from car*) far scendere // vi cascare; **~s** npl (*MED*) gocce *fpl*; **to ~ off** vi (*sleep*) addormentarsi; **to ~ out** vi (*withdraw*) ritirarsi; (*student etc*) smettere di studiare; **~-out** n (*from society/from university*) chi ha abbandonato (la società/gli studi); **~pings** npl sterco.

drought [draut] n siccità f inv.

drove [drəʊv] pt of **drive**.

drown [draun] vt affogare // vi affogarsi.

drowsy ['drauzɪ] a sonnolento(a), assonnato(a).

drudgery ['drʌdʒərɪ] n lavoro faticoso.

drug [drʌg] n farmaco; (*narcotic*) droga // vt drogare; **~ addict** n tossicomane *m/f*; **~gist** n (*US*) persona che gestisce un drugstore; **~store** n (*US*) drugstore m inv.

drum [drʌm] n tamburo; (*for oil, petrol*) fusto // vi tamburellare; **~s** npl batteria; **~mer** n batterista *m/f*.

drunk [drʌŋk] pp of **drink** // a ubriaco(a); ebbro(a) // n (*also*: **~ard**) ubriacone/a; **~en** a ubriaco(a); da ubriaco.

dry [draɪ] a secco(a); (*day, clothes*) asciutto(a) // vt seccare; (*clothes, hair, hands*) asciugare // vi asciugarsi; **to ~ up** vi seccarsi; **~-cleaner's** n lavasecco m inv; **~er** n (*for hair*) föhn m inv, asciugacapelli m inv; (*for clothes*) asciugabiancheria; (*US: spin-dryer*) centrifuga; **~ goods store** n (*US*) negozio di stoffe; **~ rot** n fungo del legno.

dual ['djuəl] a doppio(a); **~ carriage-**

way n (*Brit*) strada a doppia carreggiata.

dubbed [dʌbd] a (*CINEMA*) doppiato(a); (*nicknamed*) soprannominato(a).

dubious ['dju:bɪəs] a dubbio(a).

Dublin ['dʌblɪn] n Dublino f.

duchess ['dʌtʃɪs] n duchessa.

duck [dʌk] n anatra // vi abbassare la testa; **~ling** n anatroccolo.

duct [dʌkt] n condotto; (*ANAT*) canale m.

dud [dʌd] n (*shell*) proiettile m che fa cilecca; (*object, tool*): **it's a ~** è inutile, non funziona // a (*Brit: cheque*) a vuoto; (*: note, coin*) falso(a).

due [dju:] a dovuto(a); (*expected*) atteso(a); (*fitting*) giusto(a) // n dovuto // ad: **~ north** diritto verso nord; **~s** npl (*for club, union*) quota; (*in harbour*) diritti mpl di porto; **in ~ course** a tempo debito; **finalmente**; **~ to** dovuto a; a causa di; **to be ~ to do** dover fare.

duet [dju:'ɛt] n duetto.

duffel [dʌfl] a: **~ bag** sacca da viaggio di tela; **~ coat** montgomery m inv.

dug [dʌg] pt, pp of **dig**.

duke [dju:k] n duca m.

dull [dʌl] a (*boring*) noioso(a); (*slow-witted*) ottuso(a); (*sound, pain*) sordo(a); (*weather, day*) fosco(a), scuro(a); (*blade*) smussato(a) // vt (*pain, grief*) attutire; (*mind, senses*) intorpidire.

duly ['dju:lɪ] ad (*on time*) a tempo debito; (*as expected*) debitamente.

dumb [dʌm] a muto(a); (*stupid*) stupido(a); **dumbfounded** [dʌm-'faundɪd] a stupito(a), stordito(a).

dummy ['dʌmɪ] n (*tailor's model*) manichino; (*SPORT*) finto; (*Brit: for baby*) tettarella // a falso(a), finto(a).

dump [dʌmp] n mucchio di rifiuti; (*place*) luogo di scarico; (*MIL*) deposito // vt (*put down*) scaricare; mettere giù; (*get rid of*) buttar via; **~ing** n (*ECON*) dumping m; (*of rubbish*): **"no ~ing"** "vietato lo scarico".

dumpling ['dʌmplɪŋ] n specie di gnocco.

dumpy ['dʌmpɪ] a tracagnotto(a).

dung [dʌŋ] n concime m.

dungarees [dʌŋgə'ri:z] npl tuta.

dungeon ['dʌndʒən] n prigione f sotterranea.

dupe [dju:p] vt gabbare, ingannare.

duplex ['dju:plɛks] n (*US: house*) casa con muro divisorio in comune con un'altra; (*: apartment*) appartamento su due piani.

duplicate n ['dju:plɪkət] doppio // vt ['dju:plɪkeɪt] raddoppiare; (*on machine*) ciclostilare.

durable ['djuərəbl] a durevole; (*clothes, metal*) resistente.

duration [djuə'reɪʃən] n durata.

duress [djuə'rɛs] n: **under ~** sotto costrizione.

during ['djuəriŋ] *prep* durante, nel corso di.

dusk [dʌsk] *n* crepuscolo.

dust [dʌst] *n* polvere *f* // *vt* (*furniture*) spolverare; (*cake etc*): **to ~ with** cospargere con; **~bin** *n* (*Brit*) pattumiera; **~er** *n* straccio per la polvere; **~ jacket** *n* sopraccoperta; **~man** *n* (*Brit*) netturbino; **~y** *a* polveroso(a).

Dutch [dʌtʃ] *a* olandese // *n* (*LING*) olandese *m*; **the ~** *npl* gli Olandesi; **to go ~** fare alla romana; **~man/woman** *n* olandese *m/f.*

dutiful ['dju:tiful] *a* (*child*) rispettoso(a).

duty ['dju:ti] *n* dovere *m*; (*tax*) dazio, tassa; **duties** *npl* mansioni *fpl*; **on ~** di servizio; **off ~** libero(a), fuori servizio; **~-free** *a* esente da dazio.

duvet ['du:vei] *n* (*Brit*) piumino, piumone *m.*

dwarf [dwɔ:f] *n* nano/a // *vt* far apparire piccolo.

dwell, *pt*, *pp* **dwelt** [dwɛl, dwɛlt] *vi* dimorare; **to ~ on** *vt fus* indugiare su; **~ing** *n* dimora.

dwindle ['dwindl] *vi* diminuire, decrescere.

dye [dai] *n* tinta // *vt* tingere.

dying ['daiiŋ] *a* morente, moribondo(a).

dyke [daik] *n* (*Brit*) diga.

dynamic [dai'næmik] *a* dinamico(a).

dynamite ['dainəmait] *n* dinamite *f.*

dynamo ['dainəməu] *n* dinamo *f inv.*

dysentery ['disintri] *n* dissenteria.

dyslexia [dis'lɛksiə] *n* dislessia.

E

E [i:] *n* (*MUS*) mi *m.*

each [i:tʃ] *a* ogni, ciascuno(a) // *pronoun* ciascuno(a), ognuno(a); **~ one** ognuno(a); **~ other** si (*or* ci *etc*); **they hate ~ other** si odiano (l'un l'altro); **you are jealous of ~ other** siete gelosi l'uno dell'altro; **they have 2 books ~** hanno 2 libri ciascuno.

eager ['i:gə*] *a* impaziente; desideroso(a); ardente; **to be ~ for** essere desideroso di, aver gran voglia di.

eagle ['i:gl] *n* aquila.

ear [iə*] *n* orecchio; (*of corn*) pannocchia; **~ache** *n* mal *m* d'orecchi; **~drum** *n* timpano.

earl [ə:l] *n* conte *m.*

earlier ['ə:liə*] *a* precedente // *ad* prima.

early ['ə:li] *ad* presto, di buon'ora; (*ahead of time*) in anticipo // *a* precoce; anticipato(a); che si fa vedere di buon'ora; **to have an ~ night** andare a letto presto; **in the ~ or ~ in the spring/19th century** all'inizio della primavera/dell'Ottocento; **~ retirement** *n* ritiro anticipato.

earmark ['iəma:k] *vt*: **to ~ sth for** destinare qc a.

earn [ə:n] *vt* guadagnare; (*rest, reward*) meritare.

earnest ['ə:nist] *a* serio(a); **in ~** *ad* sul serio.

earnings ['ə:niŋz] *npl* guadagni *mpl*; (*salary*) stipendio.

earphones ['iəfəunz] *npl* cuffia.

earring ['iəriŋ] *n* orecchino.

earshot ['iəʃɔt] *n*: **out of/within ~** fuori portata/a portata d'orecchio.

earth [ə:θ] *n* (*gen, also Brit ELEC*) terra; (*of fox etc*) tana // *vt* (*Brit ELEC*) mettere a terra; **~enware** *n* terracotta; stoviglie *fpl* di terracotta // *a* di terracotta; **~quake** *n* terremoto; **~y** *a* (*fig*) grossolano(a).

ease [i:z] *n* agio, comodo // *vt* (*soothe*) calmare; (*loosen*) allentare; **to ~ sth out/in** tirare fuori/infilare qc con delicatezza; facilitare l'uscita/l'entrata di qc; **at ~** a proprio agio; (*MIL*) a riposo; **to ~ off** *or* **up** *vi* diminuire; (*slow down*) rallentarsi; (*fig*) rilassarsi.

easel ['i:zl] *n* cavalletto.

east [i:st] *n* est *m* // *a* dell'est // *ad* a oriente; **the E~** l'Oriente *m.*

Easter ['i:stə*] *n* Pasqua; **~ egg** *n* uovo di Pasqua.

easterly ['i:stəli] *a* dall'est, d'oriente.

eastern ['i:stən] *a* orientale, d'oriente.

East Germany *n* Germania dell'Est.

eastward(s) ['i:stwəd(z)] *ad* verso est, verso levante.

easy ['i:zi] *a* facile; (*manner*) disinvolto(a) // *ad*: **to take it or things ~** prendersela con calma; **~ chair** *n* poltrona; **~-going** *a* accomodante.

eat, *pt* **ate**, *pp* **eaten** [i:t, eit, 'i:tn] *vt*, *vi* mangiare; **to ~ into, to ~ away at** *vt fus* rodere.

eaves [i:vz] *npl* gronda.

eavesdrop ['i:vzdrɔp] *vi*: **to ~ (on a conversation)** origliare (una conversazione).

ebb [ɛb] *n* riflusso // *vi* rifluire; (*fig: also*: **~ away**) declinare.

ebony ['ɛbəni] *n* ebano.

eccentric [ik'sɛntrik] *a*, *n* eccentrico(a).

echo, **~es** ['ɛkəu] *n* eco *m or f* // *vt* ripetere; fare eco a // *vi* echeggiare; dare un eco.

eclipse [i'klips] *n* eclissi *f inv* // *vt* eclissare.

ecology [i'kɔlədʒi] *n* ecologia.

economic [i:kə'nɔmik] *a* economico(a); **~al** *a* economico(a); (*person*) economo(a); **~s** *n* economia.

economize [i'kɔnəmaiz] *vi* risparmiare, fare economia.

economy [i'kɔnəmi] *n* economia.

ecstasy ['ɛkstəsi] *n* estasi *f inv.*

eczema ['ɛksimə] *n* eczema *m.*

edge [ɛdʒ] *n* margine *m*; (*of table, plate,*

cup) orlo; (*of knife etc*) taglio // *vt* bordare; **on ~** (*fig*) = **edgy; to ~ away from** sgattaiolare da; **~ways** *ad* di fianco; **he couldn't get a word in ~ways** non riuscì a dire una parola.

edgy ['ɛdʒı] *a* nervoso(a).

edible ['ɛdıbl] *a* commestibile; (*meal*) mangiabile.

edict ['iːdıkt] *n* editto.

Edinburgh ['ɛdınbərə] *n* Edimburgo *f*.

edit ['ɛdıt] *vt* curare; **~ion** [ı'dıʃən] *n* edizione *f*; **~or** *n* (*in newspaper*) redattore/trice; redattore/trice capo; (*of sb's work*) curatore/trice; **~orial** [-'tɔːrıəl] *a* redazionale, editoriale // *n* editoriale *m*.

educate ['ɛdjukeıt] *vt* istruire; educare.

education [ɛdju'keıʃən] *n* educazione *f*; (*schooling*) istruzione *f*; **~al** *a* pedagogico(a); scolastico(a); istruttivo(a).

EEC *n abbr* (= *European Economic Community*) C.E.E. *f* (= *Comunità Economica Europea*).

eel [iːl] *n* anguilla.

eerie ['ıərı] *a* che fa accapponare la pelle.

effect [ı'fɛkt] *n* effetto // *vt* effettuare; **~s** *npl* (*THEATRE*) effetti *mpl* scenici; **to take ~** (*law*) entrare in vigore; (*drug*) fare effetto; **in ~** effettivamente; **~ive** *a* efficace; **~ively** *ad* efficacemente; (*in reality*) effettivamente; **~iveness** *n* efficacia.

effeminate [ı'fɛmınıt] *a* effeminato(a).

efficiency [ı'fıʃənsı] *n* efficienza; rendimento effettivo.

efficient [ı'fıʃənt] *a* efficiente.

effort ['ɛfət] *n* sforzo.

effrontery [ı'frʌntərı] *n* sfrontatezza.

effusive [ı'fjuːsıv] *a* (*person*) espansivo(a); (*welcome, letter*) caloroso(a); (*thanks, apologies*) interminabile.

e.g. *ad abbr* (= *exempli gratia*) per esempio, p.es.

egg [ɛg] *n* uovo; **to ~ on** *vt* incitare; **~cup** *n* portauovo *m inv*; **~plant** *n* (*especially US*) melanzana; **~shell** *n* guscio d'uovo.

ego ['iːgəu] *n* ego *m inv*.

egotism ['ɛgəutızəm] *n* egotismo.

egotist ['ɛgəutıst] *n* egotista *m/f*.

Egypt ['iːdʒıpt] *n* Egitto; **~ian** [ı'dʒıpʃən] *a, n* egiziano(a).

eiderdown ['aıdədaun] *n* piumino.

eight [eıt] *num* otto; **~een** *num* diciotto; **eighth** [eıtθ] *num* ottavo(a); **~y** *num* ottanta.

Eire ['ɛərə] *n* Repubblica d'Irlanda.

either ['aıðə*] *a* l'uno(a) o l'altro(a); (*both, each*) ciascuno(a); **on ~ side** su ciascun lato // *pronoun*: **~ (of them)** (o) l'uno(a) o l'altro(a); **I don't like ~** non mi piace né l'uno né l'altro // *ad* neanche; **no, I don't ~** no, neanch'io // *cj*: **~ good or bad** o buono o cattivo.

eject [ı'dʒɛkt] *vt* espellere; lanciare.

eke [iːk]: **to ~ out** *vt* far durare; aumentare.

elaborate *a* [ı'læbərıt] elaborato(a), minuzioso(a) // *vb* [ı'læbəreıt] *vt* elaborare // *vi* fornire i particolari.

elapse [ı'læps] *vi* trascorrere, passare.

elastic [ı'læstık] *a* elastico(a) // *n* elastico; **~ band** *n* (*Brit*) elastico.

elated [ı'leıtıd] *a* pieno(a) di gioia.

elbow ['ɛlbəu] *n* gomito.

elder ['ɛldə*] *a* maggiore, più vecchio(a) // *n* (*tree*) sambuco; **one's ~s** i più anziani; **~ly** *a* anziano(a) // *npl*: **the ~ly** gli anziani.

eldest ['ɛldıst] *a, n*: **the ~** (*child*) il(la) maggiore (dei bambini).

elect [ı'lɛkt] *vt* eleggere; **to ~ to do** decidere di fare // *a*: **the president ~** il presidente designato; **~ion** [ı'lɛkʃən] *n* elezione *f*; **~ioneering** [ılɛkʃə'nıərıŋ] *n* propaganda elettorale; **~or** *n* elettore/trice; **~orate** *n* elettorato.

electric [ı'lɛktrık] *a* elettrico(a); **~al** *a* elettrico(a); **~ blanket** *n* coperta elettrica; **~ fire** *n* stufa elettrica.

electrician [ılɛk'trıʃən] *n* elettricista *m*.

electricity [ılɛk'trısıtı] *n* elettricità.

electrify [ı'lɛktrıfaı] *vt* (*RAIL*) elettrificare; (*audience*) elettrizzare.

electrocute [ı'lɛktrəukjuːt] *vt* fulminare.

electronic [ılɛk'trɒnık] *a* elettronico(a); **~ mail** *n* posta elettronica; **~s** *n* elettronica.

elegant ['ɛlıgənt] *a* elegante.

element ['ɛlımənt] *n* elemento; (*of heater, kettle etc*) resistenza; **~ary** [-'mɛntərı] *a* elementare.

elephant ['ɛlıfənt] *n* elefante/essa.

elevate ['ɛlıveıt] *vt* elevare.

elevator ['ɛlıveıtə*] *n* elevatore *m*; (*US*: *lift*) ascensore *m*.

eleven [ı'lɛvn] *num* undici; **~ses** *npl* (*Brit*) caffè *m* a metà mattina; **~th** *a* undicesimo(a).

elicit [ı'lısıt] *vt*: **to ~ (from)** trarre (da), cavare fuori (da).

eligible ['ɛlıdʒəbl] *a* eleggibile; (*for membership*) che ha i requisiti.

ellipse [ı'lıps] *n* ellisse *f*.

elm [ɛlm] *n* olmo.

elongated ['iːlɒŋgeıtıd] *a* allungato(a).

elope [ı'ləup] *vi* (*lovers*) scappare.

eloquent ['ɛləkwənt] *a* eloquente.

else [ɛls] *ad* altro; **something ~** qualcos'altro; **somewhere ~** altrove; **everywhere ~** in qualsiasi altro luogo; **nobody ~** nessun altro; **where ~?** in quale altro luogo?; **little ~** poco altro; **~where** *ad* altrove.

elucidate [ı'luːsıdeıt] *vt* delucidare.

elude [ı'luːd] *vt* eludere.

elusive [ı'luːsıv] *a* elusivo(a).

emaciated [ɪ'meɪsɪeɪtɪd] *a* emaciato(a).
emancipate [ɪ'mænsɪpeɪt] *vt* emancipare.
embankment [ɪm'bæŋkmənt] *n* (of road, railway) terrapieno; (riverside) argine *m*; (dyke) diga.
embark [ɪm'bɑ:k] *vi*: to ~ (on) imbarcarsi (su) // *vt* imbarcare; to ~ on (fig) imbarcarsi in; ~ation [embɑ:'keɪʃən] *n* imbarco.
embarrass [ɪm'bærəs] *vt* imbarazzare; ~ed *a* imbarazzato(a); ~ing *a* imbarazzante; ~ment *n* imbarazzo.
embassy ['embəsɪ] *n* ambasciata.
embed [ɪm'bed] *vt* conficcare, incastrare.
embellish [ɪm'belɪʃ] *vt* abbellire.
embers ['embəz] *npl* braci *fpl*.
embezzle [ɪm'bezl] *vt* appropriarsi indebitamente di.
embitter [ɪm'bɪtə*] *vt* amareggiare; inasprire.
embody [ɪm'bɔdɪ] *vt* (features) racchiudere, comprendere; (ideas) dar forma concreta a, esprimere.
embossed [ɪm'bɔst] *a* in rilievo; goffrato(a).
embrace [ɪm'breɪs] *vt* abbracciare // *vi* abbracciarsi // *n* abbraccio.
embroider [ɪm'brɔɪdə*] *vt* ricamare; (fig: story) abbellire; ~y *n* ricamo.
embryo ['embrɪəu] *n* (also fig) embrione *m*.
emerald ['emərəld] *n* smeraldo.
emerge [ɪ'mə:dʒ] *vi* apparire, sorgere.
emergence [ɪ'mə:dʒəns] *n* apparizione *f*.
emergency [ɪ'mə:dʒənsɪ] *n* emergenza; in an ~ in caso di emergenza; ~ cord *n* (US) segnale *m* d'allarme; ~ exit *n* uscita di sicurezza; ~ landing *n* atterraggio forzato; the ~ services *npl* (fire, police, ambulance) servizi *mpl* di pronto intervento.
emery board ['eməri-] *n* limetta di carta smerigliata.
emigrate ['emigreit] *vi* emigrare.
eminent ['emɪnənt] *a* eminente.
emit [ɪ'mɪt] *vt* emettere.
emotion [ɪ'məuʃən] *n* emozione *f*; ~al *a* (person) emotivo(a); (scene) commovente; (tone, speech) carico(a) d'emozione.
emperor ['empərə*] *n* imperatore *m*.
emphasis, pl -ases ['emfəsɪs, -si:z] *n* enfasi *f inv*; importanza.
emphasize ['emfəsaiz] *vt* (word, point) sottolineare; (feature) mettere in evidenza.
emphatic [em'fætɪk] *a* (strong) vigoroso(a); (unambiguous, clear) netto(a); ~ally *ad* vigorosamente; nettamente.
empire ['empaɪə*] *n* impero.
employ [ɪm'plɔɪ] *vt* impiegare; ~ee [-'i:] *n* impiegato/a; ~er *n* principale *m/f*, datore *m* di lavoro; ~ment *n* impiego;

~ment agency *n* agenzia di collocamento.
empower [ɪm'pauə*] *vt*: to ~ sb to do concedere autorità a qn di fare.
empress ['emprɪs] *n* imperatrice *f*.
emptiness ['emptɪnɪs] *n* vuoto.
empty ['emptɪ] *a* vuoto(a); (threat, promise) vano(a) // *vt* vuotare // *vi* vuotarsi; (liquid) scaricarsi // *n* (bottle) vuoto; ~-handed *a* a mani vuote.
emulate ['emjuleɪt] *vt* emulare.
emulsion [ɪ'mʌlʃən] *n* emulsione *f*; ~ (paint) *n* colore *m* a tempera.
enable [ɪ'neɪbl] *vt*: to ~ sb to do permettere a qn di fare.
enact [ɪn'ækt] *vt* (law) emanare; (play, scene) rappresentare.
enamel [ɪ'næməl] *n* smalto.
encased [ɪn'keɪst] *a*: ~ in racchiuso(a) in; rivestito(a) di.
enchant [ɪn'tʃɑ:nt] *vt* incantare; (subj: magic spell) catturare; ~ing *a* incantevole, affascinante.
encircle [ɪn'sə:kl] *vt* accerchiare.
encl. *abbr* (= enclosed) all.
enclave ['enkleɪv] *n* enclave *f*.
enclose [ɪn'kləuz] *vt* (land) circondare, recingere; (letter etc): to ~ (with) allegare (con); please find ~d trovi qui accluso.
enclosure [ɪn'kləuʒə*] *n* recinto; (COMM) allegato.
encompass [ɪn'kʌmpəs] *vt* comprendere.
encore [ɔŋ'kɔ:*] *excl*, *n* bis (*m inv*).
encounter [ɪn'kauntə*] *n* incontro // *vt* incontrare.
encourage [ɪn'kʌrɪdʒ] *vt* incoraggiare; ~ment *n* incoraggiamento.
encroach [ɪn'krəutʃ] *vi*: to ~ (up)on (rights) usurpare; (time) abusare di; (land) oltrepassare i limiti di.
encyclop(a)edia [ensaɪkləu'pi:dɪə] *n* enciclopedia.
end [end] *n* fine *f*; (aim) fine *m*; (of table) bordo estremo // *vt* finire; (also: bring to an ~, put an ~ to) mettere fine a // *vi* finire; in the ~ alla fine; on ~ (object) ritto(a); to stand on ~ (hair) rizzarsi; for 5 hours on ~ per 5 ore di fila; to ~ up *vi*: to ~ up in finire in.
endanger [ɪn'deɪndʒə*] *vt* mettere in pericolo.
endearing [ɪn'dɪərɪŋ] *a* accattivante.
endeavour, (US) **endeavor** [ɪn'devə*] *n* sforzo, tentativo // *vi*: to ~ to do cercare *or* sforzarsi di fare.
ending ['endɪŋ] *n* fine *f*, conclusione *f*; (LING) desinenza.
endive ['endaɪv] *n* (curly) indivia (riccia); (smooth, flat) indivia belga.
endless ['endlɪs] *a* senza fine; (patience, resources) infinito(a).
endorse [ɪn'dɔ:s] *vt* (cheque) girare; (approve) approvare, appoggiare; ~ment *n* (on driving licence) con-

travvenzione registrata sulla patente.

endow [ɪn'dau] *vt* (*provide with money*) devolvere denaro a; (*equip*): **to ~ with** fornire di, dotare di.

endurance [ɪn'djuərəns] *n* resistenza; pazienza.

endure [ɪn'djuə•] *vt* sopportare, resistere a // *vi* durare.

enemy ['enəmɪ] *a, n* nemico(a).

energetic [enə'dʒɛtɪk] *a* energico(a); attivo(a).

energy ['enədʒɪ] *n* energia.

enforce [ɪn'fɔ:s] *vt* (*LAW*) applicare, far osservare; **~d** a forzato(a).

engage [ɪn'geɪdʒ] *vt* (*hire*) assumere; (*lawyer*) incaricare; (*attention, interest*) assorbire; (*MIL*) attaccare; (*TECH*): **to ~ gear/the clutch** innestare la marcia/la frizione // *vi* (*TECH*) ingranare; **to ~ in** impegnarsi in; **~d** a (*Brit: busy, in use*) occupato(a); (*betrothed*) fidanzato(a); **to get ~d** fidanzarsi; **~d tone** *n* (*Brit TEL*) segnale *m* di occupato; **~ment** *n* impegno, obbligo; appuntamento; (*to marry*) fidanzamento; (*MIL*) combattimento; **~ment ring** *n* anello di fidanzamento.

engaging [ɪn'geɪdʒɪŋ] *a* attraente.

engender [ɪn'dʒɛndə•] *vt* produrre, causare.

engine ['endʒɪn] *n* (*AUT*) motore *m*; (*RAIL*) locomotiva; **~ driver** *n* (*of train*) macchinista *m*.

engineer [endʒɪ'nɪə•] *n* ingegnere *m*; (*US RAIL*) macchinista *m*; **~ing** *n* ingegneria.

England ['ɪŋglənd] *n* Inghilterra.

English ['ɪŋglɪʃ] *a* inglese // *n* (*LING*) inglese *m*; **the ~** *npl* gli Inglesi; **the ~ Channel** la Manica; **~man/woman** *n* inglese *m/f*.

engraving [ɪn'greɪvɪŋ] *n* incisione *f*.

engrossed [ɪn'grəust] *a*: **~ in** assorbito(a) da, preso(a) da.

engulf [ɪn'gʌlf] *vt* inghiottire.

enhance [ɪn'hɑ:ns] *vt* accrescere.

enjoy [ɪn'dʒɔɪ] *vt* godere; (*have: success, fortune*) avere; **to ~ o.s.** godersela, divertirsi; **~able** a piacevole; **~ment** *n* piacere *m*, godimento.

enlarge [ɪn'lɑ:dʒ] *vt* ingrandire // *vi*: **to ~ on** (*subject*) dilungarsi su.

enlighten [ɪn'laɪtn] *vt* illuminare; dare schiarimenti a; **~ed** a illuminato(a); **~ment** *n*: **the E~ment** (*HISTORY*) l'Illuminismo.

enlist [ɪn'lɪst] *vt* arruolare; (*support*) procurare // *vi* arruolarsi.

enmity ['enmɪtɪ] *n* inimicizia.

enormous [ɪ'nɔ:məs] *a* enorme.

enough [ɪ'nʌf] *a, n*: **~ time/books** assai tempo/libri; **have you got ~?** ne ha abbastanza or a sufficienza? // *ad*: **big ~** abbastanza grande; **he has not worked ~** non ha lavorato abbastanza; **~!** basta!; **that's ~, thanks** basta così, grazie; **I've**

had ~ of him ne ho abbastanza di lui; ... **which, funnily ~** ... che, strano a dirsi.

enquire [ɪn'kwaɪə•] *vt, vi* = **inquire**.

enrage [ɪn'reɪdʒ] *vt* fare arrabbiare.

enrich [ɪn'rɪtʃ] *vt* arricchire.

enrol [ɪn'rəul] *vt* iscrivere // *vi* iscriversi; **~ment** *n* iscrizione *f*.

ensign *n* (*NAUT*) ['ensən] bandiera; (*MIL*) ['ensaɪn] portabandiera *m inv*.

ensue [ɪn'sju:] *vi* seguire, risultare.

ensure [ɪn'fuə•] *vt* assicurare; garantire; **to ~ that** assicurarsi che.

entail [ɪn'teɪl] *vt* comportare.

entangle [ɪn'tæŋgl] *vt* impigliare.

enter ['entə•] *vt* (*room*) entrare in; (*club*) associarsi a; (*army*) arruolarsi in; (*competition*) partecipare a; (*sb for a competition*) iscrivere; (*write down*) registrare; (*COMPUT*) inserire // *vi* entrare; **to ~ for** *vt fus* iscriversi a; **to ~ into** *vt fus* (*explanation*) cominciare a dare; (*debate*) partecipare a; (*agreement*) concludere; **to ~ (up)on** *vt fus* cominciare.

enterprise ['entəpraɪz] *n* (*undertaking, company*) impresa; (*spirit*) iniziativa; **free ~** liberalismo economico; **private ~** iniziativa privata.

enterprising ['entəpraɪzɪŋ] *a* intra-prendente.

entertain [entə'teɪn] *vt* divertire; (*invite*) ricevere; (*idea, plan*) nutrire; **~er** *n* comico/a; **~ing** a divertente; **~ment** *n* (*amusement*) divertimento; (*show*) spettacolo.

enthralled [ɪn'θrɔ:ld] *a* affascinato(a).

enthusiasm [ɪn'θu:zɪæzəm] *n* entusiasmo.

enthusiast [ɪn'θu:zɪæst] *n* entusiasta *m/f*; **~ic** [-'æstɪk] *a* entusiasta, entusia-stico(a); **to be ~ic about sth/sb** essere appassionato di qc/entusiasta di qn.

entice [ɪn'taɪs] *vt* allettare, sedurre.

entire [ɪn'taɪə•] *a* intero(a); **~ly** *ad* completamente, interamente; **~ty** [ɪn'taɪərətɪ] *n*: **in its ~ty** nel suo complesso.

entitle [ɪn'taɪtl] *vt* (*give right*): **to ~ sb to sth/to do** dare diritto a qn a qc/a fare; **~d** a (*book*) che si intitola; **to be ~d to do** avere il diritto di fare.

entrails ['entreɪlz] *npl* interiora *fpl*.

entrance *n* ['entrns] entrata, ingresso; (*of person*) entrata // *vt* [ɪn'trɑ:ns] incantare, rapire; **to gain ~ to** (*university etc*) essere ammesso a; **~ examination** *n* esame *m* di ammissione; **~ fee** *n* tassa d'iscrizione; (*to museum etc*) prezzo d'ingresso; **~ ramp** *n* (*US AUT*) rampa di accesso.

entrant ['entrnt] *n* partecipante *m/f*; concorrente *m/f*.

entreat [en'tri:t] *vt* supplicare.

entrenched [en'trentʃt] *a* radicato(a).

entrepreneur [ɔntrəprə'nə:•] *n* imprenditore *m*.

entrust [ɪnˈtrʌst] *vt*: **to ~ sth to** affidare qc a.

entry [ˈɛntrɪ] *n* entrata; *(way in)* entrata, ingresso; *(item: on list)* iscrizione *f*; *(in dictionary)* voce *f*; **no ~** vietato l'ingresso; *(AUT)* divieto di accesso; **~ form** *n* modulo d'iscrizione; **~ phone** *n* citofono.

envelop [ɪnˈvɛləp] *vt* avvolgere, avviluppare.

envelope [ˈɛnvələup] *n* busta.

envious [ˈɛnvɪəs] *a* invidioso(a).

environment [ɪnˈvaɪərnmənt] *n* ambiente *m*; **~al** [-ˈmɛntl] *a* ecologico(a); ambientale.

envisage [ɪnˈvɪzɪdʒ] *vt* immaginare; prevedere.

envoy [ˈɛnvɔɪ] *n* inviato/a.

envy [ˈɛnvɪ] *n* invidia // *vt* invidiare; **to ~ sb sth** invidiare qn per qc.

epic [ˈɛpɪk] *n* poema *m* epico // *a* epico(a).

epidemic [ɛpɪˈdɛmɪk] *n* epidemia.

epilepsy [ˈɛpɪlɛpsɪ] *n* epilessia.

episode [ˈɛpɪsəud] *n* episodio.

epistle [ɪˈpɪsl] *n* epistola.

epitome [ɪˈpɪtəmɪ] *n* epitome *f*; quintessenza; **epitomize** *vt* *(fig)* incarnare.

equable [ˈɛkwəbl] *a* uniforme; equilibrato(a).

equal [ˈiːkwl] *a, n* uguale *(m/f)* // *vt* uguagliare; **~ to** *(task)* all'altezza di; **~ity** [iːˈkwɔlɪtɪ] *n* uguaglianza; **~ize** *vt, vi* pareggiare; **~izer** *n* pareggio; **~ly** *ad* ugualmente.

equanimity [ɛkwəˈnɪmɪtɪ] *n* serenità.

equate [ɪˈkweɪt] *vt*: **to ~ sth with** considerare qc uguale a; *(compare)* paragonare qc con; **equation** [ɪˈkweɪʃən] *n* *(MATH)* equazione *f*.

equator [ɪˈkweɪtə*] *n* equatore *m*.

equilibrium [iːkwɪˈlɪbrɪəm] *n* equilibrio.

equip [ɪˈkwɪp] *vt* equipaggiare, attrezzare; **to ~ sb/sth with** fornire qn/qc di; **to be well ~ped** *(office etc)* essere ben attrezzato(a); **he is well ~ped for the job** ha i requisiti necessari per quel lavoro; **~ment** *n* attrezzatura; *(electrical etc)* apparecchiatura.

equitable [ˈɛkwɪtəbl] *a* equo(a), giusto(a).

equities [ˈɛkwɪtɪz] *npl* *(Brit COMM)* azioni *fpl* ordinarie.

equivalent [ɪˈkwɪvəlnt] *a, n* equivalente *(m)*; **to be ~ to** equivalere a.

equivocal [ɪˈkwɪvəkl] *a* equivoco(a); *(open to suspicion)* dubbio(a).

era [ˈɪərə] *n* era, età *f inv*.

eradicate [ɪˈrædɪkeɪt] *vt* sradicare.

erase [ɪˈreɪz] *vt* cancellare; **~r** *n* gomma.

erect [ɪˈrɛkt] *a* eretto(a) // *vt* costruire; *(monument, tent)* alzare; **~ion**

[ɪˈrɛkʃən] *n* erezione *f*.

ermine [ˈəːmɪn] *n* ermellino.

erode [ɪˈrəud] *vt* erodere; *(metal)* corrodere.

erotic [ɪˈrɔtɪk] *a* erotico(a).

err [əː*] *vi* errare; *(REL)* peccare.

errand [ˈɛrnd] *n* commissione *f*.

erratic [ɪˈrætɪk] *a* imprevedibile; *(person, mood)* incostante.

error [ˈɛrə*] *n* errore *m*.

erupt [ɪˈrʌpt] *vi* erompere; *(volcano)* mettersi *(or* essere) in eruzione; **~ion** [ɪˈrʌpʃən] *n* eruzione *f*.

escalate [ˈɛskəleɪt] *vi* intensificarsi.

escalator [ˈɛskəleɪtə*] *n* scala mobile.

escapade [ɛskəˈpeɪd] *n* scappatella; avventura.

escape [ɪˈskeɪp] *n* evasione *f*; fuga; *(of gas etc)* fuga, fuoriuscita // *vi* fuggire; *(from jail)* evadere, scappare; *(fig)* sfuggire; *(leak)* uscire // *vt* sfuggire a; **to ~ from sb** sfuggire a qn; **escapism** *n* evasione *f* (dalla realtà).

escort *n* [ˈɛskɔːt] scorta; *(male companion)* cavaliere *m* // *vt* [ɪˈskɔːt] scortare; accompagnare.

Eskimo [ˈɛskɪməu] *n* eschimese *m/f*.

especially [ɪˈspɛʃlɪ] *ad* specialmente; soprattutto; espressamente.

espionage [ˈɛspɪənɑːʒ] *n* spionaggio.

Esquire [ɪˈskwaɪə*] *n (abbr Esq.)*: J. Brown, ~ Signor J. Brown.

essay [ˈɛseɪ] *n (SCOL)* composizione *f*; *(LITERATURE)* saggio.

essence [ˈɛsns] *n* essenza.

essential [ɪˈsɛnʃl] *a* essenziale; *(basic)* fondamentale // *n* elemento essenziale; **~ly** *ad* essenzialmente.

establish [ɪˈstæblɪʃ] *vt* stabilire; *(business)* mettere su; *(one's power etc)* confermare; **~ment** *n* stabilimento; **the E~ment** la classe dirigente, l'establishment *m*.

estate [ɪˈsteɪt] *n* proprietà *f inv*; beni *mpl*, patrimonio; **~ agent** *n (Brit)* agente *m* immobiliare; **~ car** *n (Brit)* giardiniera.

esteem [ɪˈstiːm] *n* stima // *vt* *(think highly of)* stimare; *(consider)* considerare.

esthetic [ɪsˈθɛtɪk] *a (US)* = **aesthetic**.

estimate *n* [ˈɛstɪmət] stima; *(COMM)* preventivo // *vt* [ˈɛstɪmeɪt] stimare, valutare; **estimation** [-ˈmeɪʃən] *n* stima; opinione *f*.

estranged [ɪˈstreɪndʒd] *a* separato(a).

etc *abbr* (= *et cetera*) etc, ecc.

etching [ˈɛtʃɪŋ] *n* acquaforte *f*.

eternal [ɪˈtəːnl] *a* eterno(a).

eternity [ɪˈtəːnɪtɪ] *n* eternità.

ether [ˈiːθə*] *n* etere *m*.

ethical [ˈɛθɪkl] *a* etico(a), morale.

ethics [ˈɛθɪks] *n* etica // *npl* morale *f*.

Ethiopia [iːθɪˈəupɪə] *n* Etiopia.

ethnic [ˈɛθnɪk] *a* etnico(a).

ethos [ˈiːθɔs] *n* norma di vita.

etiquette ['etɪkɛt] *n* etichetta.
Eurocheque ['juərəutʃɛk] *n* eurochèque *m inv*.
Europe ['juərəp] *n* Europa; **~an** [-'pi:ən] *a*, *n* europeo(a).
evacuate [ɪ'vækjueɪt] *vt* evacuare.
evade [ɪ'veɪd] *vt* eludere; *(duties etc)* sottrarsi a.
evaluate [ɪ'væljueɪt] *vt* valutare.
evaporate [ɪ'væpəreɪt] *vi* evaporare // *vt* far evaporare; **~d milk** *n* latte *m* concentrato.
evasion [ɪ'veɪʒən] *n* evasione *f*.
evasive [ɪ'veɪsɪv] *a* evasivo(a).
eve [i:v] *n*: **on the ~ of** alla vigilia di.
even ['i:vn] *a* regolare; *(number)* pari *inv* // *ad* anche, perfino; **~ if**, **~ though** anche se; **~ more** ancora di più; **~ so** ciò nonostante; **not ~** nemmeno; **to get ~ with sb** dare la pari a qn; **to ~ out** *vi* pareggiare.
evening ['i:vnɪŋ] *n* sera; *(as duration, event)* serata; **in the ~** la sera; **~ class** *n* corso serale; **~ dress** *n* *(woman's)* abito da sera; **in ~ dress** *(man)* in abito scuro; *(woman)* in abito lungo.
event [ɪ'vent] *n* avvenimento; *(SPORT)* gara; **in the ~ of** in caso di; **~ful** *a* denso(a) di eventi.
eventual [ɪ'ventʃuəl] *a* finale; **~ity** [-'ælɪti] *n* possibilità *f inv*, eventualità *f inv*; **~ly** *ad* finalmente.
ever ['evə*] *ad* mai; *(at all times)* sempre; **the best ~** il migliore che ci sia mai stato; **have you ~ seen it?** l'ha mai visto?; **~ since** *ad* da allora // *cj* sin da quando; **~ so pretty** così bello(a); **~green** *n* sempreverde *m*; **~lasting** *a* eterno(a).
every ['evrɪ] *a* ogni; **~ day** tutti i giorni, ogni giorno; **~ other/third day** ogni due/tre giorni; **~ other car** una macchina su due; **~ now and then** ogni tanto, di quando in quando; **~body** *pronoun* ognuno, tutti *pl*; **~day** *a* quotidiano(a); di ogni giorno; **~one** = **~body**; **~thing** *pronoun* tutto, ogni cosa; **~where** *ad* *(gen)* dappertutto; *(wherever)* ovunque.
evict [ɪ'vɪkt] *vt* sfrattare.
evidence ['evɪdns] *n* *(proof)* prova; *(of witness)* testimonianza; *(sign)*: **to show ~ of** dare segni di; **to give ~** deporre.
evident ['evɪdnt] *a* evidente; **~ly** *ad* evidentemente.
evil ['i:vl] *a* cattivo(a), maligno(a) // *n* male *m*.
evoke [ɪ'vəuk] *vt* evocare.
evolution [i:və'lu:ʃən] *n* evoluzione *f*.
evolve [ɪ'vɔlv] *vt* elaborare // *vi* svilupparsi, evolversi.
ewe [ju:] *n* pecora.
ex- [ɛks] *prefix* ex.
exacerbate [ɛks'æsəbeɪt] *vt* aggravare.
exact [ɪg'zækt] *a* esatto(a) // *vt*: **to ~ sth**

(from) estorcere qc (da); esigere qc (da); **~ing** *a* esigente; *(work)* faticoso(a); **~itude** *n* esattezza, precisione *f*; **~ly** *ad* esattamente.
exaggerate [ɪg'zædʒəreɪt] *vt*, *vi* esagerare; **exaggeration** [-'reɪʃən] *n* esagerazione *f*.
exalted [ɪg'zɔ:ltɪd] *a* esaltato(a); elevato(a).
exam [ɪg'zæm] *n abbr* *(SCOL)* = **examination**.
examination [ɪgzæmɪ'neɪʃən] *n* *(SCOL)* esame *m*; *(MED)* controllo.
examine [ɪg'zæmɪn] *vt* esaminare; *(LAW: person)* interrogare; **~r** *n* esaminatore/trice.
example [ɪg'zɑ:mpl] *n* esempio; **for ~** ad or per esempio.
exasperate [ɪg'zɑ:spəreɪt] *vt* esasperare; **exasperating** *a* esasperante; **exasperation** [-'reɪʃən] *n* esasperazione *f*.
excavate ['ekskəveɪt] *vt* scavare.
exceed [ɪk'si:d] *vt* superare; *(one's powers, time limit)* oltrepassare; **~ingly** *ad* eccessivamente.
excellent ['eksələnt] *a* eccellente.
except [ɪk'sept] *prep* *(also:* **~ for**, **~ing)** salvo, all'infuori di, eccetto // *vt* escludere; **~ if/when** salvo se/quando; **~ that** salvo che; **~ion** [ɪk'sepʃən] *n* eccezione *f*; **to take ~ion to** trovare a ridire su; **~ional** [ɪk'sepʃənl] *a* eccezionale.
excerpt ['eksə:pt] *n* estratto.
excess [ɪk'ses] *n* eccesso; **~ baggage** *n* bagaglio in eccedenza; **~ fare** *n* supplemento; **~ive** *a* eccessivo(a).
exchange [ɪks'tʃeɪndʒ] *n* scambio; *(also: telephone ~)* centralino // *vt*: **to ~ (for)** scambiare (con); **~ rate** *n* tasso di cambio.
Exchequer [ɪks'tʃekə*] *n*: **the ~** *(Brit)* lo Scacchiere, ≈ il ministero delle Finanze.
excise ['eksaɪz] *n* imposta, dazio.
excite [ɪk'saɪt] *vt* eccitare; **to get ~d** eccitarsi; **~ment** *n* eccitazione *f*; agitazione *f*; **exciting** *a* avventuroso(a); *(film, book)* appassionante.
exclaim [ɪk'skleɪm] *vi* esclamare; **exclamation** [eksklə'meɪʃən] *n* esclamazione *f*; **exclamation mark** *n* punto esclamativo.
exclude [ɪk'sklu:d] *vt* escludere.
exclusive [ɪk'sklu:sɪv] *a* esclusivo(a); *(club)* selettivo(a); *(district)* snob *inv*; **~ of VAT** I.V.A. esclusa.
excommunicate [ekskə'mju:nɪkeɪt] *vt* scomunicare.
excruciating [ɪk'skru:ʃieɪtɪŋ] *a* straziante, atroce.
excursion [ɪk'skə:ʃən] *n* escursione *f*, gita.
excuse *n* [ɪk'skju:s] scusa // *vt* [ɪk'skju:z] scusare; **to ~ sb from** *(activity)* dispensare qn da; **~ me!** mi scusi!; **now,**

if you will ~ me ... ora, mi scusi ma ...

ex-directory [ˈɛksdɪˈrɛktərɪ] *a* (*Brit TEL*): to be ~ non essere sull'elenco.

execute [ˈɛksɪkjuːt] *vt* (*prisoner*) giustiziare; (*plan etc*) eseguire.

execution [ɛksɪˈkjuːʃən] *n* esecuzione *f*; ~**er** *n* boia *m inv*.

executive [ɪgˈzɛkjutɪv] *n* (*COMM*) dirigente *m*; (*POL*) esecutivo // *a* esecutivo(a).

exemplify [ɪgˈzɛmplɪfaɪ] *vt* esemplificare.

exempt [ɪgˈzɛmpt] *a* esentato(a) // *vt*: to ~ **sb** from esentare qn da; ~**ion** [ɪgˈzɛmpʃən] *n* esenzione *f*.

exercise [ˈɛksəsaɪz] *n* esercizio // *vt* esercitare; (*dog*) portar fuori // *vi* fare del movimento *or* moto; ~ **book** *n* quaderno.

exert [ɪgˈzəːt] *vt* esercitare; to ~ o.s. sforzarsi; ~**ion** [-ʃən] *n* sforzo.

exhaust [ɪgˈzɔːst] *n* (*also:* ~ fumes) scappamento; (*also:* ~ pipe) tubo di scappamento // *vt* esaurire; ~**ed** *a* esaurito(a); ~**ion** [ɪgˈzɔːstʃən] *n* esaurimento; **nervous** ~**ion** sovraffaticamento mentale; ~**ive** *a* esauriente.

exhibit [ɪgˈzɪbɪt] *n* (*ART*) oggetto esposto; (*LAW*) documento *or* oggetto esibito // *vt* esporre; (*courage, skill*) dimostrare; ~**ion** [ɛksɪˈbɪʃən] *n* mostra, esposizione *f*.

exhilarating [ɪgˈzɪləreɪtɪŋ] *a* esilarante; stimolante.

exhort [ɪgˈzɔːt] *vt* esortare.

exile [ˈɛksaɪl] *n* esilio; (*person*) esiliato/a // *vt* esiliare.

exist [ɪgˈzɪst] *vi* esistere; ~**ence** *n* esistenza; to be in ~**ence** esistere; ~**ing** *a* esistente.

exit [ˈɛksɪt] *n* uscita // *vi* (*THEATRE, COMPUT*) uscire; ~ **ramp** *n* (*US AUT*) rampa di uscita.

exodus [ˈɛksədəs] *n* esodo.

exonerate [ɪgˈzɔnəreɪt] *vt*: to ~ from discolpare da.

exotic [ɪgˈzɔtɪk] *a* esotico(a).

expand [ɪkˈspænd] *vt* espandere; estendere; allargare // *vi* (*trade etc*) svilupparsi, ampliarsi; espandersi; (*gas*) espandersi; (*metal*) dilatarsi.

expanse [ɪkˈspæns] *n* distesa, estensione *f*.

expansion [ɪkˈspænʃən] *n* (*gen*) espansione *f*; (*of town, economy*) sviluppo; (*of metal*) dilatazione *f*.

expect [ɪkˈspɛkt] *vt* (*anticipate*) prevedere, aspettarsi, prevedere *or* aspettarsi che + *sub*; (*count on*) contare su; (*hope for*) sperare; (*require*) richiedere, esigere; (*suppose*) supporre; (*await, also baby*) aspettare // *vi*: to be ~**ing** essere in stato interessante; to ~ **sb** to do aspettarsi che qn faccia; ~**ancy** *n* (*anticipation*) attesa; **life** ~**ancy**

probabilità *fpl* di vita; ~**ant mother** *n* gestante *f*; ~**ation** [ɛkspɛkˈteɪʃən] *n* aspettativa; speranza.

expedience, expediency [ɪkˈspiːdɪəns, ɪkˈspiːdɪənsɪ] *n* convenienza.

expedient [ɪkˈspiːdɪənt] *a* conveniente; vantaggioso(a) // *n* espediente *m*.

expedite [ˈɛkspədaɪt] *vt* sbrigare; facilitare.

expedition [ɛkspəˈdɪʃən] *n* spedizione *f*.

expel [ɪkˈspɛl] *vt* espellere.

expend [ɪkˈspɛnd] *vt* spendere; (*use up*) consumare; ~**able** *a* sacrificabile; ~**iture** [ɪkˈspɛndɪtʃə*] *n* spesa.

expense [ɪkˈspɛns] *n* spesa; (*high cost*) costo; ~**s** *npl* (*COMM*) spese *fpl*, indennità *fpl*; at the ~ of a spese di; ~ **account** *n* conto *m* spese *inv*.

expensive [ɪkˈspɛnsɪv] *a* caro(a), costoso(a).

experience [ɪkˈspɪərɪəns] *n* esperienza // *vt* (*pleasure*) provare; (*hardship*) soffrire; ~**d** *a* esperto(a).

experiment [ɪkˈspɛrɪmənt] *n* esperimento, esperienza // *vi* [ɪkˈspɛrɪment] fare esperimenti; to ~ with sperimentare.

expert [ˈɛkspəːt] *a, n* esperto(a); ~**ise** [-ˈtiːz] *n* competenza.

expire [ɪkˈspaɪə*] *vi* (*period of time, licence*) scadere; **expiry** *n* scadenza.

explain [ɪkˈspleɪn] *vt* spiegare; **explanation** [ɛkspləˈneɪʃən] *n* spiegazione *f*; **explanatory** [ɪkˈsplænətrɪ] *a* esplicativo(a).

explicit [ɪkˈsplɪsɪt] *a* esplicito(a); (*definite*) netto(a).

explode [ɪkˈspləud] *vi* esplodere.

exploit *n* [ˈɛksplɔɪt] impresa // *vt* [ɪkˈsplɔɪt] sfruttare; ~**ation** [-ˈteɪʃən] *n* sfruttamento.

exploratory [ɪkˈsplɔrətrɪ] *a* (*fig: talks*) esplorativo(a).

explore [ɪkˈsplɔː*] *vt* esplorare; (*possibilities*) esaminare; ~**r** *n* esploratore/trice.

explosion [ɪkˈspləuʒən] *n* esplosione *f*.

explosive [ɪkˈspləusɪv] *a* esplosivo(a) // *n* esplosivo.

exponent [ɪkˈspəunənt] *n* esponente *m/f*.

export *vt* [ɛkˈspɔːt] esportare // *n* [ˈɛkspɔːt] esportazione *f*; articolo di esportazione // *cpd* d'esportazione; ~**er** *n* esportatore *m*.

expose [ɪkˈspəuz] *vt* esporre; (*unmask*) smascherare; ~**d** *a* (*position*) esposto(a).

exposure [ɪkˈspəuʒə*] *n* esposizione *f*; (*PHOT*) posa; (*MED*) assideramento; ~ **meter** *n* esposimetro.

expound [ɪkˈspaund] *vt* esporre.

express [ɪkˈsprɛs] *a* (*definite*) chiaro(a), espresso(a); (*Brit: letter etc*) espresso *inv* // *n* (*train*) espresso // *ad* (*send*) espresso // *vt* esprimere; ~**ion**

[ık'sprɛʃən] n espressione f; ~ive a espressivo(a); ~ly ad espressamente; ~way n (US: urban motorway) autostrada che attraversa la città.

exquisite [ɛk'skwızıt] a squisito(a).

extend [ık'stɛnd] vt (visit) protrarre; (road, deadline) prolungare; (building) ampliare; (offer) offrire, porgere // vi (land) estendersi.

extension [ık'stɛnʃən] n (of road, term) prolungamento; (of contract, deadline) proroga; (building) annesso; (to wire, table) prolunga; (telephone) interno; (: in private house) apparecchio supplementare.

extensive [ık'stɛnsıv] a esteso(a), ampio(a); (damage) su larga scala; (alterations) notevole; (inquiries) esauriente; (use) grande; ~ly ad: he's travelled ~ly ha viaggiato molto.

extent [ık'stɛnt] n estensione f; to some ~ fino a un certo punto; to what ~? fino a che punto?; to the ~ of ... fino al punto di ...

extenuating [ıks'tɛnjueıtıŋ] a: ~ circumstances attenuanti fpl.

exterior [ɛk'stıərıə*] a esteriore, esterno(a) // n esteriore m, esterno; aspetto (esteriore).

exterminate [ık'stə:mıneıt] vt sterminare.

external [ɛk'stə:nl] a esterno(a), esteriore.

extinct [ık'stıŋkt] a estinto(a).

extinguish [ık'stıŋgwıʃ] vt estinguere; ~er n estintore m.

extort [ık'stɔ:t] vt: to ~ sth (from) estorcere qc (da); ~ionate [ık'stɔ:ʃnət] a esorbitante.

extra ['ɛkstrə] a extra inv, supplementare // ad (in addition) di più // n supplemento; (THEATRE) comparso.

extra... ['ɛkstrə] prefix extra... .

extract vt [ık'strækt] estrarre; (money, promise) strappare // n ['ɛkstrækt] estratto; (passage) brano.

extracurricular ['ɛkstrəkə'rıkjulə*] a parascolastico(a).

extradite ['ɛkstrədaıt] vt estradare.

extramarital [ɛkstrə'mærıtl] a extraconiugale.

extramural [ɛkstrə'mjuərl] a fuori dell'università.

extraordinary [ık'strɔ:dnrı] a straordinario(a).

extravagance [ık'strævəgəns] n sperpero; stravaganza.

extravagant [ık'strævəgənt] a stravagante; (in spending) dispendioso(a).

extreme [ık'stri:m] a estremo(a) // n estremo; ~ly ad estremamente.

extricate ['ɛkstrıkeıt] vt: to ~ sth (from) districare qc (da).

extrovert ['ɛkstrəvə:t] n estroverso/a.

exude [ıg'zju:d] vt trasudare; (fig) emanare.

eye [aı] n occhio; (of needle) cruna // vt osservare; to keep an ~ on tenere d'occhio; ~ball n globo dell'occhio; ~bath n occhino; ~brow n sopracciglio; ~brow pencil n matita per le sopracciglia; ~drops npl gocce fpl oculari, collirio; ~lash n ciglio; ~lid n palpebra; ~ liner n eye-liner m inv; ~opener n rivelazione f; ~shadow n ombretto; ~sight n vista; ~sore n pugno nell'occhio; ~ witness n testimone m/f oculare.

F

F [ɛf] n (MUS) fa m.

fable ['feıbl] n favola.

fabric ['fæbrık] n stoffa, tessuto.

fabrication [fæbrı'keıʃən] n fabbricazione f; falsificazione f.

fabulous ['fæbjuləs] a favoloso(a); (col: super) favoloso(a), fantastico(a).

façade [fə'sɑ:d] n facciata.

face [feıs] n faccia, viso, volto; (expression) faccia; (grimace) smorfia; (of clock) quadrante m; (of building) facciata; (side, surface) faccia // vt essere di fronte a; (fig) affrontare; ~ down a faccia in giù; to make or pull a ~ fare una smorfia; in the ~ of (difficulties etc) di fronte a; on the ~ of it a prima vista; ~ to ~ faccia a faccia; to ~ up to vt fus affrontare, far fronte a; ~ cloth n (Brit) guanto di spugna; ~ cream n crema per il viso; ~ lift n lifting m inv; (of façade etc) ripulita.

facet ['fæsıt] n faccetta, sfaccettatura; (fig) sfaccettatura.

facetious [fə'si:ʃəs] a faceto(a).

face value n (of coin) valore m facciale or nominale; to take sth at ~ (fig) giudicare qc dalle apparenze.

facilities [fə'sılıtız] npl attrezzature fpl; credit ~ facilitazioni fpl di credito.

facing ['feısıŋ] prep di fronte a // n (of wall etc) rivestimento; (SEWING) paramontura.

facsimile [fæk'sımılı] n facsimile m inv; ~ machine n telecopiatrice f.

fact [fækt] n fatto; in ~ infatti.

factor ['fæktə*] n fattore m.

factory ['fæktərı] n fabbrica, stabilimento.

factual ['fæktjuəl] a che si attiene ai fatti.

faculty ['fækəltı] n facoltà f inv.

fad [fæd] n mania; capriccio.

fade [feıd] vi sbiadire, sbiadirsi; (light, sound, hope) attenuarsi, affievolirsi; (flower) appassire.

fag [fæg] n (col: cigarette) cicca.

fail [feıl] vt (exam) non superare; (candidate) bocciare; (subj: courage, *memory*) mancare a // *vi* fallire; (*student*) essere respinto(a); (*supplies*) mancare; (*eyesight, health, light*) venire a mancare; **to ~ to do sth** (*neglect*) mancare di fare qc; (*be unable*) non riuscire a fare qc:, **without ~** senza fallo; certamente; **~ing** *n* difetto // *prep* in mancanza di; **~ure** ['feɪljə*] *n* fallimento; (*person*) fallito/a; (*mechanical etc*) guasto.

faint [feɪnt] *a* debole; (*recollection*) vago(a); (*mark*) indistinto(a) // *vi* svenire; **to feel ~** sentirsi svenire.

fair [fɛə*] *a* (*person, decision*) giusto(a), equo(a); (*hair etc*) biondo(a); (*skin, complexion*) bianco(a); (*weather*) bello(a), clemente; (*good enough*) assai buono(a); (*sizeable*) bello(a) // *ad* (*play*) lealmente // *n* fiera; (*Brit: funfair*) luna park *m inv*; **~ly** *ad* equamente; (*quite*) abbastanza; **~ness** *n* equità, giustizia; **~ play** *n* correttezza.

fairy ['fɛərɪ] *n* fata; **~ tale** *n* fiaba.

faith [feɪθ] *n* fede *f*; (*trust*) fiducia; (*sect*) religione *f*, fede *f*; **~ful** *a* fedele; **~fully** *ad* fedelmente; **yours ~fully** (*Brit: in letters*) distinti saluti.

fake [feɪk] *n* imitazione *f*; (*picture*) falso; (*person*) impostore/a // *a* falso(a) // *vt* (*accounts*) falsificare; (*illness*) fingere; (*painting*) contraffare.

falcon ['fɔ:lkən] *n* falco, falcone *m*.

fall [fɔ:l] *n* caduta; (*in temperature*) abbassamento; (*in price*) ribasso; (*US: autumn*) autunno // *vi* (*pt* **fell**, *pp* **fallen**) cadere; (*temperature, price*) abbassare; **~s** *npl* (*waterfall*) cascate *fpl*; **to ~ flat** *vi* (*on one's face*) cadere bocconi; (*joke*) fare cilecca; (*plan*) fallire; **to ~ back** *vi* (*retreat*) indietreggiare; (*MIL*) ritirarsi; **to ~ back on** *vt fus* (*remedy etc*) ripiegare su; **to ~ behind** *vi* rimanere indietro; **to ~ down** *vi* (*person*) cadere; (*building*) crollare; **to ~ for** *vt fus* (*person*) prendere una cotta per; **to ~ for a trick** (*or a story etc*) cascarci; **to ~ in** *vi* crollare; (*MIL*) mettersi in riga; **to ~ off** *vi* cadere; (*diminish*) diminuire, abbassarsi; **to ~ out** *vi* (*friends etc*) litigare; **to ~ through** *vi* (*plan, project*) fallire.

fallacy ['fæləsɪ] *n* errore *m*.

fallen ['fɔ:lən] *pp* of **fall**.

fallout ['fɔ:laut] *n* fall-out *m*; **~ shelter** *n* rifugio antiatomico.

fallow ['fæləu] *a* incolto(a), a maggese.

false [fɔ:ls] *a* falso(a); **under ~ pretences** con l'inganno; **~ teeth** *npl* (*Brit*) denti *mpl* finti.

falter ['fɔ:ltə*] *vi* esitare, vacillare.

fame [feɪm] *n* fama, celebrità.

familiar [fə'mɪlɪə*] *a* familiare; (*common*) comune; (*close*) intimo(a); **to be ~ with** (*subject*) conoscere; **~ity** [fəmɪlɪ'ærɪtɪ] *n* familiarità; intimità;

~ize [fə'mɪlɪəraɪz] *vt*: **to ~ize sb with sth** far conoscere qc a qn.

family ['fæmɪlɪ] *n* famiglia.

famine ['fæmɪn] *n* carestia.

famished ['fæmɪʃt] *a* affamato(a).

famous ['feɪməs] *a* famoso(a); **~ly** *ad* (*get on*) a meraviglia.

fan [fæn] *n* (*folding*) ventaglio; (*ELEC*) ventilatore *m*; (*person*) ammiratore/trice; tifoso/a // *vt* far vento a; (*fire, quarrel*) alimentare; **to ~ out** *vi* spargersi (a ventaglio).

fanatic [fə'nætɪk] *n* fanatico/a.

fan belt *n* cinghia del ventilatore.

fanciful ['fænsɪful] *a* fantasioso(a); (*object*) di fantasia.

fancy ['fænsɪ] *n* immaginazione *f*, fantasia; (*whim*) capriccio // *a* (di) fantasia *inv* // *vt* (*feel like, want*) aver voglia di; **to take a ~ to** incapricciarsi di; **~ dress** *n* costume *m* (per maschera); **~-dress ball** *n* ballo in maschera.

fang [fæŋ] *n* zanna; (*of snake*) dente *m*.

fantastic [fæn'tæstɪk] *a* fantastico(a).

fantasy ['fæntəsɪ] *n* fantasia, immaginazione *f*; fantasticheria; chimera.

far [fɑ:*] *a*: **the ~ side/end** l'altra parte/ l'altro capo // *ad* lontano; **~ away, ~ off** lontano, distante; **~ better** assai migliore; **~ from** lontano da; **by ~** di gran lunga; **go as ~ as the farm** vada fino alla fattoria; **as ~ as I know** per quel che so; **~away** *a* lontano(a).

farce [fɑ:s] *n* farsa.

farcical ['fɑ:sɪkəl] *a* farsesco(a).

fare [fɛə*] *n* (*on trains, buses*) tariffa; (*in taxi*) prezzo della corsa; (*food*) vitto, cibo // *vi* passarsela; **half ~** metà tariffa; **full ~** tariffa intera.

Far East *n*: **the ~** l'Estremo Oriente *m*.

farewell [fɛə'wel] *excl, n* addio.

farm [fɑ:m] *n* fattoria, podere *m* // *vt* coltivare; **~er** *n* coltivatore/trice; agricoltore/trice; **~hand** *n* bracciante *m* agricolo; **~house** *n* fattoria; **~ing** *n* agricoltura; **~ worker** *n* = **~hand**; **~yard** *n* aia.

far-reaching ['fɑ:'ri:tʃɪŋ] *a* di vasta portata.

fart [fɑ:t] (*col!*) *n* scoreggia(!) // *vi* scoreggiare (!).

farther ['fɑ:ðə*] *ad* più lontano // *a* più lontano(a).

farthest ['fɑ:ðɪst] *superlative of* **far**.

fascinate ['fæsɪneɪt] *vt* affascinare; **fascinating** *a* affascinante; **fascination** [-'neɪʃən] *n* fascino.

fascism ['fæʃɪzəm] *n* fascismo.

fascist ['fæʃɪst] *a, n* fascista (*m/f*).

fashion ['fæʃən] *n* moda; (*manner*) maniera, modo // *vt* foggiare, formare; **in ~** alla moda; **out of ~** passato(a) di moda; **~able** *a* alla moda, di moda; **~**

show n sfilata di moda.

fast [fɑ:st] a rapido(a), svelto(a), veloce; (clock): to be ~ andare avanti; (dye, colour) solido(a) // ad rapidamente; (stuck, held) saldamente // n digiuno // vi digiunare; ~ **asleep** profondamente addormentato.

fasten ['fɑ:sn] vt chiudere, fissare; (coat) abbottonare, allacciare // vi chiudersi, fissarsi; ~**er**, ~**ing** n fermaglio, chiusura.

fast food n fast food m.

fastidious [fæs'tɪdɪəs] a esigente, difficile.

fat [fæt] a grasso(a) // n grasso.

fatal ['feɪtl] a fatale; mortale; disastroso(a); ~**ity** [fə'tælɪtɪ] n (road death etc) morto(a, vittima; ~**ly** ad a morte.

fate [feɪt] n destino; (of person) sorte f; ~**ful** a fatidico(a).

father ['fɑ:ðə*] n padre m; ~-**in-law** n suocero; ~**ly** a paterno(a).

fathom ['fæðəm] n braccio (= 1828 mm) // vt (mystery) penetrare, sondare.

fatigue [fə'ti:g] n stanchezza; (MIL) corvé f.

fatten ['fætn] vt, vi ingrassare.

fatty ['fætɪ] a (food) grasso(a) // n (col) ciccione/a.

fatuous ['fætjuəs] a fatuo(a).

faucet ['fɔ:sɪt] n (US) rubinetto.

fault [fɔ:lt] n colpa; (TENNIS) fallo; (defect) difetto; (GEO) faglia // vt criticare; it's my ~ è colpa mia; to **find** ~ **with** trovare da ridire su; at ~ in fallo; to a ~ eccessivamente; ~**less** a perfetto(a); senza difetto, impeccabile; ~**y** a difettoso(a).

fauna ['fɔ:nə] n fauna.

faux pas ['fəu'pɑ:] n gaffe f inv.

favour, (US) **favor** ['feɪvə*] n favore m, cortesia, piacere m // vt (proposition) favorire, essere favorevole a; (pupil etc) favorire; (team, horse) dare per vincente; to do sb a ~ fare un favore or una cortesia a qn; to **find** ~ **with** (subj: person) entrare nelle buone grazie di; (: suggestion) avere l'approvazione di, in ~ of in favore di; ~**able** a favorevole; ~**ite** [-rɪt] a, n favorito(a).

fawn [fɔ:n] n daino // a (also: ~-coloured) marrone chiaro inv // vi: to ~ (up)on adulare servilmente.

fax [fæks] n (document) facsimile m inv, telecopia; (machine) telecopiatrice f.

FBI n abbr (US: = Federal Bureau of Investigation) F.B.I. f.

fear [fɪə*] n paura, timore m // vt aver paura di, temere; for ~ of per paura di; ~**ful** a pauroso(a); (sight, noise) terribile, spaventoso(a).

feasibility [fi:zə'bɪlɪtɪ] n praticabilità.

feasible ['fi:zəbl] a possibile, realizzabile.

feast [fi:st] n festa, banchetto; (REL: also: ~ **day**) festa // vi banchettare.

feat [fi:t] n impresa, fatto insigne.

feather ['fɛðə*] n penna.

feature ['fi:tʃə*] n caratteristica; (article) articolo // vt (subj: film) avere come protagonista // vi figurare; ~**s** npl (of face) fisionomia; ~ **film** n film m inv principale.

February ['fɛbruərɪ] n febbraio.

fed [fɛd] pt, pp of **feed**.

federal ['fɛdərəl] a federale.

fed-up [fɛd'ʌp] a: to be ~ essere stufo(a).

fee [fi:] n pagamento; (of doctor, lawyer) onorario; (for examination) tassa d'esame; **school** ~**s** tasse fpl scolastiche.

feeble ['fi:bl] a debole.

feed [fi:d] n (of baby) pappa; (of animal) mangime m; (on printer) meccanismo di alimentazione // vt (pt, pp **fed**) nutrire; (Brit: baby) allattare; (horse etc) dare da mangiare a; (fire, machine) alimentare; to ~ **material into** introdurre materiale in; to ~ **data/information into** inserire dati/informazioni in; to ~ **on** vt fus nutrirsi di; ~**back** n feed-back m; ~**ing bottle** n (Brit) biberon m inv.

feel [fi:l] n (sense of touch) tatto; (of substance) consistenza // vt (pt, pp **felt**) toccare; palpare; tastare; (cold, pain, anger) sentire; (grief) provare; (think, believe): to ~ (that) pensare che; to ~ **hungry/cold** aver fame/freddo; to ~ **lonely/better** sentirsi solo/meglio; I **don't** ~ **well** non mi sento bene; to ~ **like** (want) aver voglia di; to ~ **about** or **around for** cercare a tastoni; ~**er** n (of insect) antenna; to **put out** ~**ers** (fig) fare un sondaggio; ~**ing** n sensazione f; sentimento.

feet [fi:t] npl of **foot**.

feign [feɪn] vt fingere, simulare.

fell [fɛl] pt of **fall** // vt (tree) abbattere.

fellow ['fɛləu] n individuo, tipo; compagno; (of learned society) membro // cpd: ~ **countryman** n compatriota m; ~**men** npl simili mpl; ~**ship** n associazione f; compagnia; specie di borsa di studio universitaria.

felony ['fɛlənɪ] n reato, crimine m.

felt [fɛlt] pt, pp of **feel** // n feltro; ~-**tip pen** n pennarello.

female ['fi:meɪl] n (ZOOL) femmina; (pej: woman) donna, femmina // a femminile; (BIOL, ELEC) femmina inv; (sex, character) femminile; (vote etc) di donne.

feminine ['fɛmɪnɪn] a, n femminile (m).

feminist ['fɛmɪnɪst] n femminista m/f.

fence [fɛns] n recinto; (col: person) ricettatore/trice // vt (also: ~ **in**) recingere // vi schermire; **fencing** n (SPORT) scherma.

fend [fɛnd] vi: to ~ **for o.s.** arrangiarsi; to ~ **off** vt (attack, attacker) respingere, difendersi da; (questions) eludere.

fender ['fɛndə*] n parafuoco; (US) parafango; paraurti m inv.

ferment vi [fə'mɛnt] fermentare // n ['fə:mɛnt] agitazione f, eccitazione f.

fern [fə:n] n felce f.

ferocious [fə'rəuʃəs] a feroce.

ferret ['fɛrɪt] n furetto.

ferry ['fɛrɪ] n (small) traghetto; (large: also: ~boat) nave f traghetto inv // vt traghettare.

fertile ['fə:taɪl] a fertile; (BIOL) fecondo(a); **fertilizer** ['fə:tɪlaɪzə*] n fertilizzante m.

fester ['fɛstə*] vi suppurare.

festival ['fɛstɪvəl] n (REL) festa; (ART, MUS) festival m inv.

festive ['fɛstɪv] a di festa; the ~ season (Brit: Christmas) il periodo delle feste.

festivities [fɛs'tɪvɪtɪz] npl festeggiamenti mpl.

festoon [fɛs'tu:n] vt: to ~ with ornare di.

fetch [fɛtʃ] vt andare a prendere; (sell for) essere venduto(a) per.

fetching ['fɛtʃɪŋ] a attraente.

fête [feɪt] n festa.

fetish ['fɛtɪʃ] n feticcio.

fetus ['fi:təs] n (US) = **foetus.**

feud [fju:d] n contesa, lotta // vi essere in lotta.

feudal ['fju:dl] a feudale.

fever ['fi:və*] n febbre f; ~ish a febbrile.

few [fju:] a pochi(e); they were ~ erano pochi; a ~ a qualche inv // pronoun alcuni(e); ~er a meno inv; meno numerosi(e); ~est a il minor numero di.

fiancé [fɪ'ā:ŋseɪ] n fidanzato; ~e n fidanzata.

fib [fɪb] n piccola bugia.

fibre, (US) fiber ['faɪbə*] n fibra; ~glass n fibra di vetro.

fickle ['fɪkl] a incostante, capriccioso(a).

fiction ['fɪkʃən] n narrativa, romanzi mpl; (sth made up) finzione f; ~al a immaginario(a).

fictitious [fɪk'tɪʃəs] a fittizio(a).

fiddle ['fɪdl] n (MUS) violino; (cheating) imbroglio; truffa // vt (Brit: accounts) falsificare, falsare; to ~ with vt fus gingillarsi con.

fidelity [fɪ'dɛlɪtɪ] n fedeltà; (accuracy) esattezza.

fidget ['fɪdʒɪt] vi agitarsi.

field [fi:ld] n campo; ~ marshal n feldmaresciallo; ~work n ricerche fpl esterne.

fiend [fi:nd] n demonio.

fierce [fɪəs] a (look, fighting) fiero(a); (wind) furioso(a); (attack) feroce; (enemy) acerrimo(a).

fiery ['faɪərɪ] a ardente; infocato(a).

fifteen [fɪf'ti:n] num quindici.

fifth [fɪfθ] num quinto(a).

fifty ['fɪftɪ] num cinquanta; ~-~ a: a ~-

~ **chance** una possibilità su due // ad fifty-fifty, metà per ciascuno.

fig [fɪg] n fico.

fight [faɪt] n zuffa, rissa; (MIL) battaglia, combattimento; (against cancer etc) lotta // vb (pt, pp **fought**) vt picchiare; combattere; (cancer, alcoholism) lottare contro, combattere // vi battersi, combattere; ~er n combattente m; (plane) aeroplano da caccia; ~ing n combattimento.

figment ['fɪgmənt] n: a ~ of the imagination un parto della fantasia.

figurative ['fɪgjurətɪv] a figurato(a).

figure ['fɪgə*] n (DRAWING, GEOM) figura; (number, cipher) cifra; (body, outline) forma // vi (appear) figurare; (US: make sense) spiegarsi; to ~ out vt riuscire a capire; calcolare; ~head n (NAUT) polena; (pej) prestanome m/f inv; ~ of speech n figura retorica.

file [faɪl] n (tool) lima; (dossier) incartamento; (folder) cartellina; (for loose leaf) raccoglitore m; (COMPUT) archivio; (row) fila // vt (nails, wood) limare; (papers) archiviare; (LAW: claim) presentare; passare agli atti; to ~ in/out vt entrare/uscire in fila; to ~ past vt fus marciare in fila davanti a.

filing ['faɪlɪŋ] n archiviare m; ~ cabinet n casellario.

fill [fɪl] vt riempire; (tooth) otturare; (job) coprire // n: to eat one's ~ mangiare a sazietà; to ~ in vt (hole) riempire; (form) compilare; to ~ up vt riempire // vi (AUT) fare il pieno; ~ it up, please (AUT) mi faccia il pieno, per piacere.

fillet ['fɪlɪt] n filetto; ~ **steak** n bistecca di filetto.

filling ['fɪlɪŋ] n (CULIN) impasto, ripieno; (for tooth) otturazione f; ~ **station** n stazione f di rifornimento.

film [fɪlm] n (CINEMA) film m inv; (PHOT) pellicola; (thin layer) velo // vt (scene) filmare; ~ **star** n divo/a dello schermo; ~ **strip** n filmina.

filter ['fɪltə*] n filtro // vt filtrare; ~ **lane** n (Brit AUT) corsia di svincolo; ~-**tipped** a con filtro.

filth [fɪlθ] n sporcizia; (fig) oscenità; ~**y** a lordo(a), sozzo(a); (language) osceno(a).

fin [fɪn] n (of fish) pinna.

final ['faɪnl] a finale, ultimo(a); definitivo(a) // n (SPORT) finale f; ~s npl (SCOL) esami mpl finali; ~e [fɪ'nɑ:lɪ] n finale m; ~ize vt mettere a punto; ~ly ad (lastly) alla fine; (eventually) finalmente.

finance [faɪ'næns] n finanza // vt finanziare; ~s npl finanze fpl.

financial [faɪ'nænʃəl] a finanziario(a).

financier [faɪ'nænsɪə*] n finanziatore m.

find [faɪnd] vt (pt, pp **found**) trovare;

(*lost object*) ritrovare // *n* trovata, scoperta; **to ~ sb guilty** (*LAW*) giudicare qn colpevole; **to ~ out** *vt* informarsi di; (*truth, secret*) scoprire; (*person*) cogliere in fallo; **to ~ out about** informarsi di; (*by chance*) scoprire; **~ings** *npl* (*LAW*) sentenza, conclusioni *fpl*; (*of report*) conclusioni.

fine [faɪn] *a* bello(a); ottimo(a); (*thin, subtle*) fine // *ad* (*well*) molto bene; (*small*) finemente // *n* (*LAW*) multa // *vt* (*LAW*) multare; **to be ~** (*weather*) far bello; **~ arts** *npl* belle arti *fpl*.

finery ['faɪnərɪ] *n* abiti *mpl* eleganti.

finger ['fɪŋgə*] *n* dito // *vt* toccare, tastare; **little/index ~** mignolo/(dito) indice *m*; **~nail** *n* unghia; **~print** *n* impronta digitale; **~tip** *n* punta del dito.

finicky ['fɪnɪkɪ] *a* esigente, pignolo(a); minuzioso(a).

finish ['fɪnɪʃ] *n* fine *f*; (*polish etc*) finitura // *vt* finire; (*use up*) esaurire // *vi* finire; (*session*) terminare; **to ~ doing sth** finire di fare qc; **to ~ third** arrivare terzo(a); **to ~ off** *vt* compiere; (*kill*) uccidere; **to ~ up** *vi, vt* finire; **~ing line** *n* linea d'arrivo; **~ing school** *n* scuola privata di perfezionamento (*per signorine*).

finite ['faɪnaɪt] *a* limitato(a); (*verb*) finito(a).

Finland ['fɪnlənd] *n* Finlandia.

Finn [fɪn] *n* finlandese *m/f*; **~ish** *a* finlandese // *n* (*LING*) finlandese *m*.

fir [fə:*] *n* abete *m*.

fire [faɪə*] *n* fuoco; incendio // *vt* (*discharge*): **to ~ a gun** scaricare un fucile; (*fig*) infiammare; (*dismiss*) licenziare // *vi* sparare, far fuoco; **on ~** in fiamme; **~ alarm** *n* allarme *m* d'incendio; **~arm** *n* arma da fuoco; **~ brigade**, (*US*) **~ department** *n* (corpo dei) pompieri *mpl*; **~ engine** *n* autopompa; **~ escape** *n* scala di sicurezza; **~ extinguisher** *n* estintore *m*; **~man** *n* pompiere *m*; **~place** *n* focolare *m*; **~side** *n* angolo del focolare; **~ station** *n* caserma dei pompieri; **~wood** *n* legna; **~work** *n* fuoco d'artificio; **~works display** *n* spettacolo pirotecnico.

firing ['faɪərɪŋ] *n* (*MIL*) spari *mpl*, tiro; **~ squad** *n* plotone *m* d'esecuzione.

firm [fə:m] *a* fermo(a) // *n* ditta, azienda; **~ly** *ad* fermamente.

first [fə:st] *a* primo(a) // *ad* (*before others*) il primo, la prima; (*before other things*) per primo; (*when listing reasons etc*) per prima cosa // *n* (*person: in race*) primo(a); (*SCOL*) laurea con lode; (*AUT*) prima; **at ~** dapprima, all'inizio; **~ of all** prima di tutto; **~ aid** *n* pronto soccorso; **~-aid kit** *n* cassetta pronto soccorso; **~-class** *a* di prima classe; **~-hand** *a* di prima mano; **~ lady** *n* (*US*) moglie *f* del presidente; **~ly** *ad* in

primo luogo; **~ name** *n* prenome *m*; **~-rate** *a* di prima qualità, ottimo(a).

fish [fɪʃ] *n* (*pl inv*) pesce *m* // *vi* pescare; **to go ~ing** andare a pesca; **~erman** *n* pescatore *m*; **~ farm** *n* vivaio; **~ fingers** *npl* (*Brit*) bastoncini *mpl* di pesce (surgelati); **~ing boat** *n* barca da pesca; **~ing line** *n* lenza; **~ing rod** *n* canna da pesca; **~monger** *n* pescivendolo; **~monger's (shop)** *n* pescheria; **~ sticks** *npl* (*US*) = **~ fingers**; **~y** *a* (*fig*) sospetto(a).

fist [fɪst] *n* pugno.

fit [fɪt] *a* (*MED, SPORT*) in forma; (*proper*) adatto(a), appropriato(a); conveniente // *vt* (*subj: clothes*) stare bene a; (*adjust*) aggiustare; (*put in, attach*) mettere; installare; (*equip*) fornire, equipaggiare // *vi* (*clothes*) stare bene; (*parts*) andare bene, adattarsi; (*in space, gap*) entrare // *n* (*MED*) accesso, attacco; **~ to** in grado di; **~ for** adatto(a) a; degno(a) di; **a ~ of anger** un accesso d'ira; **this dress is a tight/good ~** questo vestito è stretto/sta bene; **by ~s and starts** a sbalzi; **to ~ in** *vi* accordarsi; adattarsi; **to ~ out** *vt* (*Brit: also: ~ up*) equipaggiare; **~ful** *a* saltuario(a); **~ment** *n* componibile *m*; **~ness** *n* (*MED*) forma fisica; (*of remark*) appropriatezza; **~ted carpet** *n* moquette *f*; **~ted kitchen** *n* cucina componibile; **~ter** *n* aggiustatore *m or* montatore *m* meccanico; (*DRESS-MAKING*) sarto/a; **~ting** *a* appropriato(a) // *n* (*of dress*) prova; (*of piece of equipment*) montaggio, aggiustaggio; **~ting room** *n* camerino; **~tings** *npl* impianti *mpl*.

five [faɪv] *num* cinque; **~r** *n* (*col: Brit*) biglietto da cinque sterline; (: *US*) biglietto da cinque dollari.

fix [fɪks] *vt* fissare; mettere in ordine; (*mend*) riparare // *n*: **to be in a ~** essere nei guai; **to ~ up** *vt* (*meeting*) fissare; **to ~ sb up with sth** procurare qc a qn; **~ation** *n* fissazione *f*; **~ed** [fɪkst] *a* (*prices etc*) fisso(a); **~ture** ['fɪkstʃə*] *n* impianto (fisso); (*SPORT*) incontro del calendario sportivo.

fizz [fɪz] *vi* frizzare.

fizzle ['fɪzl] *vi* frizzare; **to ~ out** *vi* finire in nulla.

fizzy ['fɪzɪ] *a* frizzante; gassato(a).

flabbergasted ['flæbəga:stɪd] *a* sbalordito(a).

flabby ['flæbɪ] *a* flaccido(a).

flag [flæg] *n* bandiera; (*also:* **~stone**) pietra da lastricare // *vi* stancarsi; affievolirsi; **to ~ down** *vt* fare segno (di fermarsi) a.

flagpole ['flægpəʊl] *n* albero.

flair [flɛə*] *n* (*for business etc*) fiuto; (*for languages etc*) facilità.

flak [flæk] *n* (*MIL*) fuoco d'artiglieria;

(col: criticism) critiche fpl.

flake [fleɪk] n (of rust, paint) scaglia; (of snow, soap powder) fiocco // vi (also: ~ off) sfaldarsi.

flamboyant [flæm'bɔɪənt] a sgargiante.

flame [fleɪm] n fiamma.

flamingo [flə'mɪŋgəu] n fenicottero, fiammingo.

flammable ['flæməbl] a infiammabile.

flan [flæn] n (Brit) flan m inv.

flank [flæŋk] n fianco.

flannel ['flænl] n (Brit: also: face ~) guanto di spugna; (fabric) flanella; ~s npl pantaloni mpl di flanella.

flap [flæp] n (of pocket) patta; (of envelope) lembo // vt (wings) battere // vi (sail, flag) sbattere; (col: also: be in a ~) essere in agitazione.

flare [flɛə*] n razzo; (in skirt etc) svasatura; **to ~ up** vi andare in fiamme; (fig: person) infiammarsi di rabbia; (: revolt) scoppiare.

flash [flæʃ] n vampata; (also: news ~) notizia f lampo inv; (PHOT) flash m inv // vt accendere e spegnere; (send: message) trasmettere // vi brillare; (light on ambulance, eyes etc) lampeggiare; in a ~ in un lampo; to ~ one's headlights lampeggiare; he ~ed by or past ci passò davanti come un lampo; ~bulb n cubo m flash inv; ~cube n flash m inv; ~light n lampadina tascabile.

flashy ['flæʃɪ] a (pej) vistoso(a).

flask [flɑːsk] n fiasco; (CHEM) beuta; (also: vacuum ~) thermos m inv ®.

flat [flæt] a piatto(a), a terra; (tyre) sgonfio(a), a terra; (denial) netto(a); (MUS) bemolle inv; (: voice) stonato(a) // n (Brit: rooms) appartamento; (AUT) pneumatico sgonfio; (MUS) bemolle m; to work ~ out lavorare a più non posso; ~ly ad categoricamente; ~ten vt (also: ~ten out) appiattire.

flatter ['flætə*] vt lusingare; ~ing a lusinghiero(a); ~y n adulazione f.

flaunt [flɔːnt] vt fare mostra di.

flavour, (US) **flavor** ['fleɪvə*] n gusto, sapore m // vt insaporire, aggiungere sapore a; **vanilla-~ed** al gusto di vaniglia; ~ing n essenza (artificiale).

flaw [flɔː] n difetto.

flax [flæks] n lino; ~en a biondo(a).

flea [fliː] n pulce f.

fleck [flɛk] n (mark) macchiolina; (pattern) screziatura.

flee, pt, pp **fled** [fliː, flɛd] vt fuggire da // vi fuggire, scappare.

fleece [fliːs] n vello // vt (col) pelare.

fleet [fliːt] n flotta; (of lorries etc) convoglio; parco.

fleeting ['fliːtɪŋ] a fugace, fuggitivo(a); (visit) volante.

Flemish ['flɛmɪʃ] a fiammingo(a) // n (LING) fiammingo.

flesh [flɛʃ] n carne f; (of fruit) polpa; ~ **wound** n ferita superficiale.

flew [fluː] pt of **fly**.

flex [flɛks] n filo (flessibile) // vt flettere; (muscles) contrarre; ~**ible** a flessibile.

flick [flɪk] n colpetto; scarto; **to ~ through** vt fus sfogliare.

flicker ['flɪkə*] vi tremolare // n tremolio.

flier ['flaɪə*] n aviatore m.

flight [flaɪt] n volo; (escape) fuga; (also: ~ of steps) scalinata; ~ **attendant** n (US) steward m inv, hostess f inv; ~ **deck** n (AVIAT) cabina di controllo; (NAUT) ponte m di comando.

flimsy ['flɪmzɪ] a (fabric) inconsistente; (excuse) meschino(a).

flinch [flɪntʃ] vi ritirarsi; **to ~ from** tirarsi indietro di fronte a.

fling [flɪŋ], pt, pp **flung** vt lanciare, gettare.

flint [flɪnt] n selce f; (in lighter) pietrina.

flip [flɪp] n colpetto.

flippant ['flɪpənt] a senza rispetto, irriverente.

flipper ['flɪpə*] n pinna.

flirt [fləːt] vi flirtare // n civetta.

flit [flɪt] vi svolazzare.

float [fləut] n galleggiante m; (in procession) carro; (money) somma // vi galleggiare // vt far galleggiare; (loan, business) lanciare.

flock [flɔk] n gregge m; (of people) folla.

flog [flɔg] vt flagellare.

flood [flʌd] n alluvione m; (of words, tears etc) diluvio // vt allagare; ~**ing** n inondazione f; ~**light** n riflettore m // vt illuminare a giorno.

floor [flɔː*] n pavimento; (storey) piano; (fig: at meeting): **the ~** il pubblico // vt pavimentare; (knock down) atterrare; **on the ~** per terra; **ground ~**, (US) **first ~** pianterreno; **first ~**, (US) **second ~** primo piano; ~**board** n tavellone m di legno; ~ **show** n spettacolo di varietà.

flop [flɔp] n fiasco.

floppy ['flɔpɪ] a floscio(a), molle; ~ **(disk)** n (COMPUT) floppy disk m inv.

flora ['flɔːrə] n flora.

Florence ['flɔrəns] n Firenze f; **Florentine** ['flɔrəntaɪn] a fiorentino(a).

florid ['flɔrɪd] a (complexion) florido(a); (style) fiorito(a).

florist ['flɔrɪst] n fioraio/a.

flounce [flauns] n balzo.

flounder ['flaundə*] vi annaspare // n (ZOOL) passera di mare.

flour ['flauə*] n farina.

flourish ['flʌrɪʃ] vi fiorire // vt brandire // n abbellimento; svolazzo; (of trumpets) fanfara.

flout [flaut] vt (order) contravvenire a; (convention) sfidare.

flow [fləu] n flusso; circolazione f // vi fluire; (traffic, blood in veins) circolare; (hair) scendere; ~ **chart** n schema m di flusso.

flower ['flauə*] n fiore m // vi fiorire; ~ **bed** n aiuola; ~**pot** n vaso da fiori; ~**y** a fiorito(a).

flown [fləun] pp of **fly**.

flu [flu:] n influenza.

fluctuate ['flʌktjueit] vi fluttuare, oscillare.

fluency ['flu:ənsi] n facilità, scioltezza; **his ~ in English** la sua scioltezza nel parlare l'inglese.

fluent ['flu:ənt] a (speech) facile, sciolto(a); corrente; **he speaks ~ Italian** parla l'italiano correntemente.

fluff [flʌf] n lanugine f; ~**y** a lanuginoso(a); (toy) di peluche.

fluid ['flu:id] a fluido(a) // n fluido.

fluke [flu:k] n (col) colpo di fortuna.

flung [flʌŋ] pt, pp of **fling**.

fluoride ['fluəraid] n fluoruro.

flurry ['flʌri] n (of snow) tempesta; a ~ **of activity/excitement** una febbre di attività/improvvisa agitazione.

flush [flʌʃ] n rossore m; (fig) ebbrezza; (: of youth, beauty etc) rigoglio, pieno vigore // vt ripulire con un getto d'acqua // vi arrossire // a: ~ **with** a livello di, pari a; **to ~ the toilet** tirare l'acqua; **to ~ out** vt (birds) far alzare in volo; (animals, fig) stanare; ~**ed** a tutto(a) rosso(a).

flustered ['flʌstəd] a sconvolto(a).

flute [flu:t] n flauto.

flutter ['flʌtə*] n agitazione f; (of wings) frullio // vi (bird) battere le ali.

flux [flʌks] n: **in a state of ~** in continuo mutamento.

fly [flai] n (insect) mosca; (on trousers: also: **flies**) bracchetta // vb (pt **flew**, pp **flown**) vt pilotare; (passengers, cargo) trasportare (in aereo); (distances) percorrere // vi volare; (passengers) andare in aereo; (escape) fuggire; (flag) sventolare; **to ~ away** or **off** vi volare via; ~**ing** n (activity) aviazione f; (action) volo // a: ~**ing visit** visita volante; **with ~ing colours** con risultati brillanti; ~**ing saucer** n disco volante; ~**ing start** n: **to get off to a ~ing start** partire come un razzo; ~**over** n (Brit: bridge) cavalcavia m inv; ~**sheet** n (for tent) soprantetto.

foal [fəul] n puledro.

foam [fəum] n schiuma // vi schiumare; ~ **rubber** n gommapiuma ®.

fob [fɔb] vt: **to ~ sb off with** appioppare qn con; sbarazzarsi di qn con.

focus ['fəukəs] n (pl ~**es**) fuoco; (of interest) centro // vt (field glasses etc) mettere a fuoco // vi: **to ~ on** (with camera) mettere a fuoco; (person) fissare lo sguardo su; **in ~** a fuoco; **out of ~** sfocato(a).

fodder ['fɔdə*] n foraggio.

foe [fəu] n nemico.

foetus, (US) **fetus** ['fi:təs] n feto.

fog [fɔg] n nebbia; ~**gy** a nebbioso(a); **it's ~gy** c'è nebbia; ~ **lamp** n (AUT) faro m antinebbia inv.

foil [fɔil] vt confondere, frustrare // n lamina di metallo; (kitchen ~) foglio di alluminio; (FENCING) fioretto.

fold [fəuld] n (bend, crease) piega; (AGR) ovile m; (fig) gregge m // vt piegare; **to ~ up** vi (business) crollare // vt (map etc) piegare, ripiegare; ~**er** n (for papers) cartella; cartellina; (brochure) dépliant m inv; ~**ing** a (chair, bed) pieghevole.

foliage ['fəuliidʒ] n fogliame m.

folk [fəuk] npl gente f // a popolare; ~**s** npl famiglia; ~**lore** ['fəuklɔ:*] n folclore m; ~ **song** n canto popolare.

follow ['fɔləu] vt seguire // vi seguire; (result) conseguire, risultare; **he ~ed suit** lui ha fatto lo stesso; **to ~ up** vt (victory) sfruttare; (letter, offer) fare seguito a; (case) seguire; ~**er** n seguace m/f, discepolo/a; ~**ing** a seguente, successivo(a) // n seguito, discepoli mpl.

folly ['fɔli] n pazzia, follia.

fond [fɔnd] a (memory, look) tenero(a), affettuoso(a); **to be ~ of** volere bene a.

fondle ['fɔndl] vt accarezzare.

food [fu:d] n cibo; ~ **mixer** n frullatore m; ~ **poisoning** n intossicazione f; ~ **processor** n tritatutto m inv elettrico; ~**stuffs** npl generi fpl alimentari.

fool [fu:l] n sciocco/a; (HISTORY: of king) buffone m; (CULIN) frullato // vt ingannare // vi (gen: ~ **around**) fare lo sciocco; ~**hardy** a avventato(a); ~**ish** a scemo(a), stupido(a); imprudente; ~**proof** a (plan etc) sicurissimo(a).

foot [fut] n (pl **feet**) piede m; (measure) piede (= 304 mm; 12 inches); (of animal) zampa // vt (bill) pagare; **on ~** a piedi; ~**age** n (CINEMA: length) ≈ metraggio; (: material) sequenza; ~**ball** n pallone m; (sport: Brit) calcio; (: US) football m americano; ~**baller** n (Brit) = ~**ball player**; ~**ball ground** n campo di calcio; ~**ball player** n (Brit) calciatore m; (US) giocatore m di football americano; ~**brake** n freno a pedale; ~**bridge** n passerella; ~**hills** npl contrafforti fpl; ~**hold** n punto d'appoggio; ~**ing** n (fig) posizione f; **to lose one's ~ing** mettere un piede in fallo; ~**lights** npl luci fpl della ribalta; ~**man** n lacchè m inv; ~**note** n nota (a piè di pagina); ~**path** n sentiero; (in street) marciapiede m; ~**print** n orma, impronta; ~**step** n passo; ~**wear** n calzatura.

for [fɔ:*] ◆ prep 1 (indicating destination, intention, purpose) per; **the train ~ London** il treno per Londra; **he went ~ the paper** è andato a prendere il giornale; it's time ~ lunch è ora di pranzo; what's it ~? a che serve?; what ~? (why) perché?

2 (on behalf of, representing) per; to work ~ sb/sth lavorare per qn/qc; I'll ask him ~ you glielo chiederò a nome tuo; G ~ George G come George

3 (because of) per, a causa di; ~ this reason per questo motivo

4 (with regard to) per; it's cold ~ July è freddo per luglio; ~ everyone who voted yes, 50 voted no per ogni voto a favore ce n'erano 50 contro

5 (in exchange for) per; I sold it ~ £5 l'ho venduto per 5 sterline

6 (in favour of) per, a favore di; are you ~ or against us? è con noi o contro di noi?; I'm all ~ it sono completamente a favore

7 (referring to distance, time) per; there are roadworks ~ 5 km ci sono lavori in corso per 5 km; he was away ~ 2 years è stato via per 2 anni; she will be away ~ a month starà via un mese; it hasn't rained ~ 3 weeks non piove da 3 settimane; can you do it ~ tomorrow? può farlo per domani?

8 (with infinitive clauses): it is not ~ me to decide non sta a me decidere; it would be best ~ you to leave sarebbe meglio che lei se ne andasse; there is still time ~ you to do it ha ancora tempo per farlo; ~ this to be possible ... perché ciò sia possibile ...

9 (in spite of) nonostante; ~ all his complaints, he's very fond of her nonostante tutte le sue lamentele, le vuole molto bene

◆ cj (since, as: rather formal) dal momento che, poiché.

forage ['fɒrɪdʒ] vi foraggiare.

foray ['fɒreɪ] n incursione f.

forbid, pt **forbad(e)**, pp **forbidden** [fə'bɪd, -'bæd, -'bɪdn] vt vietare, interdire; to ~ sb to do sth proibire a qn di fare qc; ~**den** a vietato(a); ~**ding** a arcigno(a), d'aspetto minaccioso.

force [fɔːs] n forza // vt forzare; the F~s npl (Brit) le forze armate; to ~ o.s. to do costringersi a fare; in ~ (in large numbers) in gran numero; (law) in vigore; to come into ~ entrare in vigore; ~**feed** vt (animal, prisoner) sottoporre ad alimentazione forzata; ~**ful** a forte, vigoroso(a).

forceps ['fɔːseps] npl forcipe m.

forcibly ['fɔːsəblɪ] ad con la forza; (vigorously) vigorosamente.

ford [fɔːd] n guado // vt guadare.

fore [fɔː*] n: to the ~ in prima linea; to come to the ~ mettersi in evidenza.

forearm ['fɔːrɑːm] n avambraccio.

foreboding [fɔː'bəʊdɪŋ] n presagio di male.

forecast ['fɔːkɑːst] n previsione f // vt

(irg: like cast) prevedere.

forecourt ['fɔːkɔːt] n (of garage) corte f esterna.

forefathers ['fɔːfɑːðəz] npl antenati mpl, avi mpl.

forefinger ['fɔːfɪŋgə*] n (dito) indice m.

forefront ['fɔːfrʌnt] n: in the ~ of all'avanguardia in.

forego [fɔː'gəʊ] vt = **forgo**.

foregone ['fɔːgɒn] a: it's a ~ conclusion è una conclusione scontata.

foreground ['fɔːgraʊnd] n primo piano.

forehead ['fɔrɪd] n fronte f.

foreign ['fɒrɪn] a straniero(a); (trade) estero(a); ~ **body** n corpo estraneo; ~**er** n straniero/a; F~ **Office** n (Brit) Ministero degli Esteri; ~ **secretary** n (Brit) ministro degli Affari esteri.

foreleg ['fɔːlɛg] n zampa anteriore.

foreman ['fɔːmən] n caposquadra m.

foremost ['fɔːməʊst] a principale; più in vista // ad: first and ~ innanzitutto.

forensic [fə'rɛnsɪk] a: ~ **medicine** medicina legale.

forerunner ['fɔːrʌnə*] n precursore m.

foresee [fɔː'siː], pt **foresaw**, pp **foreseen** [fɔː'siː, -'sɔː, -'siːn] vt prevedere; ~**able** a prevedibile.

foreshadow [fɔː'ʃædəʊ] vt presagire, far prevedere.

foresight ['fɔːsaɪt] n previdenza.

forest ['fɒrɪst] n foresta.

forestall [fɔː'stɔːl] vt prevenire.

forestry ['fɒrɪstrɪ] n silvicoltura.

foretaste ['fɔːteɪst] n pregustazione f.

foretell, pt, pp **foretold** [fɔː'tɛl, -'təʊld] vt predire.

forever [fə'rɛvə*] ad per sempre; (fig) sempre, di continuo.

foreword ['fɔːwɜːd] n prefazione f.

forfeit ['fɔːfɪt] n ammenda, pena // vt perdere; (one's happiness, health) giocarsi.

forgave [fə'geɪv] pt of **forgive**.

forge [fɔːdʒ] n fucina // vt (signature, Brit: money) contraffare, falsificare; (wrought iron) fucinare, foggiare; to ~ **ahead** vi tirare avanti; ~**r** n contraffattore m; ~**ry** n falso; (activity) contraffazione f.

forget [fə'gɛt], pt **forgot**, pp **forgotten** vt, vi dimenticare; ~**ful** a di corta memoria; ~**ful** of dimentico(a) di; ~**me-not** n nontiscordardimé m inv.

forgive [fə'gɪv], pt **forgave**, pp **forgiven** vt perdonare; to ~ sb for sth perdonare qc a qn; ~**ness** n perdono.

forgo [fɔː'gəʊ], pt **forwent**, pp **forgone** vt rinunciare a.

forgot [fə'gɒt] pt of **forget**.

forgotten [fə'gɒtn] pp of **forget**.

fork [fɔːk] n (for eating) forchetta; (for gardening) forca; (of roads) bivio; (of railways) inforcazione f // vi (road) biforcarsi; to ~ **out** (col: pay) vt sborsare // *vi* pagare; ~**-lift truck** *n* carrello elevatore.

forlorn [fə'lɔ:n] *a* (*person*) sconsolato(a); (*place*) abbandonato(a); (*attempt*) disperato(a); (*hope*) vano(a).

form [fɔ:m] *n* forma; (*SCOL*) classe *f*; (*questionnaire*) scheda // *vt* formare; **in top ~** in gran forma.

formal ['fɔ:məl] *a* (*offer, receipt*) vero(a) e proprio(a); (*person*) cerimonioso(a); (*occasion, dinner*) formale, ufficiale; (*ART, PHILOSOPHY*) formale; ~**ly** *ad* ufficialmente; formalmente; cerimoniosamente.

format ['fɔ:mæt] *n* formato // *vt* (*COMPUT*) formattare.

formation [fɔ:'meɪʃən] *n* formazione *f*.

formative ['fɔ:mətɪv] *a*: ~ **years** anni *mpl* formativi.

former ['fɔ:mə*] *a* vecchio(a) (*before n*), ex *inv* (*before n*); **the ~** ... **the latter** quello ... questo; ~**ly** *ad* in passato.

formula ['fɔ:mjulə] *n* formula.

forsake, *pt* **forsook**, *pp* **forsaken** [fə'seɪk, -'suk, -'seɪkən] *vt* abbandonare.

fort [fɔ:t] *n* forte *m*.

forth [fɔ:θ] *ad* in avanti; **to go back and ~** andare avanti e indietro; **and so ~** e così via; ~**coming** *a* prossimo(a); (*character*) aperto(a), comunicativo(a); ~**right** *a* franco(a), schietto(a); ~**with** *ad* immediatamente, subito.

fortify ['fɔ:tɪfaɪ] *vt* fortificare; **fortified wine** *n* vino ad alta gradazione alcolica.

fortnight ['fɔ:tnaɪt] *n* quindici giorni *mpl*, due settimane *fpl*; ~**ly** *a* bimensile // *ad* ogni quindici giorni.

fortress ['fɔ:trɪs] *n* fortezza, rocca.

fortunate ['fɔ:tʃənɪt] *a* fortunato(a); **it is ~ that** è una fortuna che; ~**ly** *ad* fortunatamente.

fortune ['fɔ:tʃən] *n* fortuna; ~**teller** *n* indovino/a.

forty ['fɔ:tɪ] *num* quaranta.

forum ['fɔ:rəm] *n* foro.

forward ['fɔ:wəd] *a* (*ahead of schedule*) in anticipo; (*movement, position*) in avanti; (*not shy*) aperto(a), diretto(a); sfacciato(a) // *n* (*SPORT*) avanti *m inv* // *vt* (*letter*) inoltrare; (*parcel, goods*) spedire; (*fig*) promuovere, appoggiare; **to move ~** avanzare; ~(**s**) *ad* avanti.

forwent [fɔ:'went] *pt of* **forgo**.

fossil ['fɔsl] *a, n* fossile (*m*).

foster ['fɔstə*] *vt* incoraggiare, nutrire; (*child*) avere in affidamento; ~ **child** *n* bambino/a preso(a) in affidamento; ~ **mother** *n* madre *f* affidataria.

fought [fɔ:t] *pt, pp of* **fight**.

foul [faul] *a* (*smell, food*) cattivo(a); (*weather*) brutto(a); (*language*) osceno(a); (*deed*) infame // *n* (*FOOTBALL*) fallo // *vt* sporcare; (*football player*) commettere un fallo su.

found [faund] *pt, pp of* **find** // *vt* (*es-*

tablish) fondare; ~**ation** [-'deɪʃən] *n* (*act*) fondazione *f*; (*base*) base *f*; (*also:* ~**ation cream**) fondo tinta; ~**ations** *npl* (*of building*) fondamenta *fpl*.

founder ['faundə*] *n* fondatore/trice // *vi* affondare.

foundry ['faundrɪ] *n* fonderia.

fount [faunt] *n* fonte *f*.

fountain ['fauntɪn] *n* fontana; ~ **pen** *n* penna stilografica.

four [fɔ:*] *num* quattro; **on all ~s** a carponi; ~**-poster** *n* (*also:* ~**-poster bed**) letto a quattro colonne; ~**some** ['fɔ:səm] *n* partita a quattro; uscita in quattro; ~**teen** *num* quattordici; ~**th** *num* quarto(a).

fowl [faul] *n* pollame *m*; volatile *m*.

fox [fɔks] *n* volpe *f* // *vt* confondere.

foyer ['fɔɪeɪ] *n* atrio; (*THEATRE*) ridotto.

fraction ['frækʃən] *n* frazione *f*.

fracture ['fræktʃə*] *n* frattura.

fragile ['frædʒaɪl] *a* fragile.

fragment ['frægmənt] *n* frammento.

fragrant ['freɪgrənt] *a* fragrante, profumato(a).

frail [freɪl] *a* debole, delicato(a).

frame [freɪm] *n* (*of building*) armatura; (*of human, animal*) ossatura, corpo; (*of picture*) cornice *f*; (*of door, window*) telaio; (*of spectacles: also:* ~**s**) montatura; ~ **of mind** *n* stato d'animo; ~**work** *n* struttura.

France [frɑ:ns] *n* Francia.

franchise ['fræntʃaɪz] *n* (*POL*) diritto di voto; (*COMM*) concessione *f*.

frank [fræŋk] *a* franco(a), aperto(a) // *vt* (*letter*) affrancare; ~**ly** *ad* francamente, sinceramente.

frantic ['fræntɪk] *a* frenetico(a).

fraternity [frə'tə:nɪtɪ] *n* (*club*) associazione *f*; (*spirit*) fratellanza.

fraud [frɔ:d] *n* truffa; (*LAW*) frode *f*; (*person*) impostore/a.

fraught [frɔ:t] *a*: ~ **with** pieno(a) di, intriso(a) da.

fray [freɪ] *n* baruffa // *vt* logorare // *vi* logorarsi; **her nerves were ~ed** aveva i nervi a pezzi.

freak [fri:k] *n* fenomeno, mostro // *cpd* fenomenale.

freckle ['frekl] *n* lentiggine *f*.

free [fri:] *a* libero(a); (*gratis*) gratuito(a); (*liberal*) generoso(a) // *vt* (*prisoner, jammed person*) liberare; (*jammed object*) districare; ~ (**of charge**), **for ~** *ad* gratuitamente; ~**dom** ['fri:dəm] *n* libertà; ~**-for-all** *n* parapiglia *m* generale; ~ **gift** *n* regalo, omaggio; ~**hold** *n* proprietà assoluta; ~ **kick** *n* calcio libero; ~**lance** *a* indipendente; ~**ly** *ad* liberamente; (*liberally*) liberalmente; ~**mason** *n* massone *m*; ~**post** *n* affrancatura a carico del destinatario; ~**-range** *a* (*hen*) ruspante; (*eggs*) di gallina ruspante; ~ **trade** n libero scambio; ~**way** n (US) superstrada; ~**wheel** vi andare a ruota libera; ~ **will** n libero arbitrio; **of one's own** ~ **will** di spontanea volontà.

freeze [fri:z] vb (pt **froze**, pp **frozen**) vi gelare // vt gelare; (food) congelare; (prices, salaries) bloccare // n gelo; blocco; ~**-dried** a liofilizzato(a); ~**r** n congelatore m.

freezing ['fri:zɪŋ] a: **I'm** ~ mi sto congelando // n (also: ~ **point**) punto di congelamento; **3 degrees below** ~ 3 gradi sotto zero.

freight [freɪt] n (goods) merce f, merci fpl; (money charged) spese fpl di trasporto; ~ **train** n (US) treno m merci inv.

French [frɛntʃ] a francese // n (LING) francese m; **the** ~ npl i Francesi; ~ **bean** n fagiolino; ~ **fried potatoes**, (US) ~ **fries** npl patate fpl fritte; ~**man** n francese m; ~ **window** n portafinestra; ~**woman** n francese f.

frenzy ['frɛnzɪ] n frenesia.

frequent a ['fri:kwənt] frequente // vt [fri'kwɛnt] frequentare; ~**ly** ad frequentemente, spesso.

fresco ['frɛskəu] n affresco.

fresh [frɛʃ] a fresco(a); (new) nuovo(a); (cheeky) sfacciato(a); ~**en** vi (wind, air) rinfrescare; **to** ~**en up** vi rinfrescarsi; ~**er** n (Brit SCOL: col) matricola; ~**ly** ad di recente, di fresco; ~**man** n (US) = ~**er**; ~**ness** n freschezza; ~**water** a (fish) d'acqua dolce.

fret [frɛt] vi agitarsi, affliggersi.

friar ['fraɪə*] n frate m.

friction ['frɪkʃən] n frizione f, attrito.

Friday ['fraɪdɪ] n venerdì m inv.

fridge [frɪdʒ] n (Brit) frigo, frigorifero.

fried [fraɪd] pt, pp of **fry** // a fritto(a).

friend [frɛnd] n amico/a; ~**ly** a amichevole; ~**ship** n amicizia.

frieze [fri:z] n fregio.

fright [fraɪt] n paura, spavento; **to take** ~ spaventarsi; ~**en** vt spaventare, far paura a; ~**ened** a spaventato(a); ~**ening** a spaventoso(a), pauroso(a); ~**ful** a orribile.

frigid ['frɪdʒɪd] a (woman) frigido(a).

frill [frɪl] n balza.

fringe [frɪndʒ] n (Brit: of hair) frangia; (edge: of forest etc) margine m; (fig): **on the** ~ al margine; ~ **benefits** npl vantaggi mpl.

frisk [frɪsk] vt perquisire.

frisky ['frɪskɪ] a vivace, vispo(a).

fritter ['frɪtə*] n frittella; **to** ~ **away** vt sprecare.

frivolity [frɪ'vɔlɪtɪ] n frivolezza.

frivolous ['frɪvələs] a frivolo(a).

frizzy ['frɪzɪ] a crespo(a).

fro [frəu] ad: **to and** ~ avanti e indietro.

frock [frɔk] n vestito.

frog [frɔg] n rana; ~**man** n uomo m rana inv.

frolic ['frɔlɪk] vi sgambettare.

from [frɔm] prep **1** (indicating starting place, origin etc) da; **where do you come** ~?, **where are you** ~? di dove viene?, di dov'è?; ~ **London to Glasgow** da Londra a Glasgow; **a letter** ~ **my sister** una lettera da mia sorella; **tell him** ~ **me that ...** gli dica da parte mia che ...

2 (indicating time) da; ~ **one o'clock to** or **until** or **till two dall'una alle due**; ~ **January (on)** da gennaio, a partire da gennaio

3 (indicating distance) da; **the hotel is 1 km** ~ **the beach** l'albergo è a 1 km dalla spiaggia

4 (indicating price, number etc) da; **prices range** ~ **£10 to £50** i prezzi vanno dalle 10 alle 50 sterline

5 (indicating difference) da; **he can't tell red** ~ **green** non sa distinguere il rosso dal verde

6 (because of, on the basis of): ~ **what he says** da quanto dice lui; **weak** ~ **hunger** debole per la fame.

front [frʌnt] n (of house, dress) davanti m inv; (of train) testa; (of book) copertina; (promenade: also: **sea** ~) lungomare m; (MIL, POL, METEOR) fronte m; (fig: appearances) fronte f // a primo(a); anteriore, davanti inv; **in** ~ of davanti a; ~ **door** n porta d'entrata; (of car) sportello anteriore; ~**ier** ['frʌntɪə*] n frontiera; ~ **page** n prima pagina; ~ **room** n (Brit) salotto; ~**wheel drive** n trasmissione f anteriore.

frost [frɔst] n gelo; (also: **hoar**~) brina; ~**bite** n congelamento; ~**ed** a (glass) smerigliato(a); ~**y** a (window) coperto(a) di ghiaccio; (welcome) gelido(a).

froth ['frɔθ] n spuma; schiuma.

frown [fraun] n cipiglio // vi acciglíarsi.

froze [frəuz] pt of **freeze**; ~**n** pp of **freeze** // a (food) congelato(a).

fruit [fru:t] n (pl inv) frutto; (collectively) frutta; ~**erer** n fruttivendolo; ~**erer's (shop)** n: **at the** ~**erer's (shop)** dal fruttivendolo; ~**ful** a fruttuoso(a); (plant) fruttifero(a); (soil) fertile; ~**ion** [fru:'ɪʃən] n: **to come to** ~**ion** realizzarsi; ~ **juice** n succo di frutta; ~ **machine** n (Brit) macchina f mangiasoldi inv; ~ **salad** n macedonia.

frustrate [frʌs'treɪt] vt frustrare; ~**d** a frustrato(a).

fry [fraɪ], pt, pp **fried** vt friggere; **the small** ~ i pesci piccoli; ~**ing pan** n padella.

ft. abbr = **foot, feet**.

fuddy-duddy ['fʌdɪdʌdɪ] n matusa.

fudge [fʌdʒ] n (CULIN) specie di caramella a base di latte, burro e zucchero.

fuel [fjuəl] n (for heating) combustibile

m; (for propelling) carburante m; ~ **tank** n deposito m nafta inv; (on vehicle) serbatoio (della benzina).

fugitive ['fju:dʒɪtɪv] n fuggitivo/a, profugo/a.

fulfil [ful'fɪl] vt (function) compiere; (order) eseguire; (wish, desire) soddisfare, appagare; ~**ment** n (of wishes) soddisfazione f, appagamento.

full [ful] a pieno(a); (details, skirt) ampio(a) // ad: to know ~ well that sapere benissimo che; I'm ~ (up) sono pieno; ~ **employment** piena occupazione; a ~ **two hours** due ore intere; at ~ **speed** a tutta velocità; in ~ per intero; to pay in ~ pagare tutto; ~ **moon** n luna piena; ~**scale** a (attack, war) su larga scala; (model) in grandezza naturale; ~ **stop** n punto; ~**time** a, ad (work) a tempo pieno // n (SPORT) fine f partita; ~**y** ad interamente, pienamente, completamente; ~**y-fledged** a (teacher, member etc) a tutti gli effetti.

fulsome ['fulsəm] a (pej: praise, gratitude) esagerato(a).

fumble ['fʌmbl] vi brancolare, andare a tentoni; to ~ **with** vt fus trafficare.

fume [fju:m] vi essere furioso(a); ~**s** npl esalazioni fpl, vapori mpl.

fumigate ['fju:mɪgeɪt] vt suffumicare.

fun [fʌn] n divertimento, spasso; to have ~ divertirsi; for ~ per scherzo; to make ~ of vt fus prendersi gioco di.

function ['fʌŋkʃən] n funzione f; cerimonia, ricevimento // vi funzionare; ~**al** a funzionale.

fund [fʌnd] n fondo, cassa; (source) fondo; (store) riserva; ~**s** npl (money) fondi mpl.

fundamental [fʌndə'mentl] a fondamentale.

funeral ['fju:nərəl] n funerale m; ~ **parlour** n impresa di pompe funebri; ~ **service** n ufficio funebre.

fun fair n (Brit) luna park m inv.

fungus, pl **fungi** ['fʌŋgəs, -gaɪ] n fungo; (mould) muffa.

funnel ['fʌnl] n imbuto; (of ship) ciminiera.

funny ['fʌnɪ] a divertente, buffo(a); (strange) strano(a), bizzarro(a).

fur [fə:*] n pelo; pelliccia; (Brit: in kettle etc) deposito calcare; ~ **coat** n pelliccia.

furious ['fjuərɪəs] a furioso(a); (effort) accanito(a).

furlong ['fə:lɔŋ] n = 201.17 m (termine ippico).

furlough ['fə:ləu] n congedo, permesso.

furnace ['fə:nɪs] n fornace f.

furnish ['fə:nɪʃ] vt ammobiliare; (supply) fornire; ~**ings** npl mobili mpl, mobilia.

furniture ['fə:nɪtʃə*] n mobili mpl; piece of ~ mobile m.

furrow ['fʌrəu] n solco.

furry ['fə:rɪ] a (animal) peloso(a).

further ['fə:ðə*] a supplementare, altro(a); nuovo(a); più lontano(a) // ad più lontano; (more) di più; (moreover) inoltre // vt favorire, promuovere; **college of ~ education** n istituto statale con corsi specializzati (di formazione professionale, aggiornamento professionale etc); ~**more** [fə:ðə'mɔ:*] ad inoltre, per di più.

furthest ['fə:ðɪst] superlative of **far**.

fury ['fjuərɪ] n furore m.

fuse [fju:z] n fusibile m; (for bomb etc) miccia, spoletta // vt fondere; (Brit ELEC): to ~ **the lights** far saltare i fusibili // vi fondersi; ~ **box** n cassetta dei fusibili.

fuselage ['fju:zəlɑ:ʒ] n fusoliera.

fuss [fʌs] n chiasso, trambusto, confusione f; (complaining) storie fpl; to **make a** ~ fare delle storie; ~**y** a (person) puntiglioso(a), esigente; che fa le storie; (dress) carico(a) di fronzoli; (style) elaborato(a).

future ['fju:tʃə*] a futuro(a) // n futuro, avvenire m; (LING) futuro; in ~ in futuro.

fuze [fju:z] (US) = **fuse**.

fuzzy ['fʌzɪ] a (PHOT) indistinto(a), sfocato(a); (hair) crespo(a).

G

G [dʒi:] n (MUS) sol m.

gabble ['gæbl] vi borbottare; farfugliare.

gable ['geɪbl] n frontone m.

gadget ['gædʒɪt] n aggeggio.

Gaelic ['geɪlɪk] a gaelico(a) // n (LING) gaelico.

gag [gæg] n bavaglio; (joke) facezia, scherzo // vt imbavagliare.

gaiety ['geɪtɪ] n gaiezza.

gaily ['geɪlɪ] ad allegramente.

gain [geɪn] n guadagno, profitto // vt guadagnare // vi (watch) andare avanti; to ~ **in/by** aumentare di/con; to ~ **3lbs** (in weight) aumentare di 3 libbre.

gait [geɪt] n andatura.

gal. abbr = **gallon**.

galaxy ['gæləksɪ] n galassia.

gale [geɪl] n vento forte; burrasca.

gallant ['gælənt] a valoroso(a); (towards ladies) galante, cortese.

gall bladder ['gɔ:l-] n cistifellea.

gallery ['gælərɪ] n galleria.

galley ['gælɪ] n (ship's kitchen) cambusa; (ship) galea.

gallon ['gælən] n gallone m (= 8 pints; Brit = 4.543l; US = 3.785l).

gallop ['gæləp] n galoppo // vi galoppare.

gallows ['gæləuz] n forca.

gallstone ['gɔ:lstəun] n calcolo biliare.

galore [gə'lɔ:*] ad a iosa, a profusione.

galvanize ['gælvənaız] vt galvanizzare.
gambit ['gæmbıt] n (fig): (opening) ~ prima mossa.
gamble ['gæmbl] n azzardo, rischio calcolato // vt, vi giocare; to ~ on (fig) giocare su; ~r n giocatore/trice d'azzardo; **gambling** n gioco d'azzardo.
game [geım] n gioco; (event) partita; (HUNTING) selvaggina // a coraggioso(a); (ready): to be ~ (for sth/to do) essere pronto(a) (a qc/a fare); **big** ~ n selvaggina grossa; ~**keeper** n guardacaccia m inv.
gammon ['gæmən] n (bacon) quarto di maiale; (ham) prosciutto affumicato.
gamut ['gæmət] n gamma.
gang [gæŋ] n banda, squadra // vi: to ~ up on sb far combutta contro qn.
gangrene ['gæŋgri:n] n cancrena.
gangster ['gæŋstə*] n gangster m inv.
gangway ['gæŋweı] n passerella; (Brit: of bus) corridoio.
gaol [dʒeıl] n, vt (Brit) = **jail**.
gap [gæp] n buco; (in time) intervallo; (fig) lacuna; vuoto.
gape [geıp] vi restare a bocca aperta; **gaping** a (hole) squarciato(a).
garage ['gæra:ʒ] n garage m inv.
garbage ['ga:bıdʒ] n immondizie fpl, rifiuti mpl; ~ **can** n (US) bidone m della spazzatura.
garbled ['ga:bld] a deformato(a); ingarbugliato(a).
garden ['ga:dn] n giardino // vi lavorare nel giardino; ~**er** n giardiniere/a; ~**ing** n giardinaggio.
gargle ['ga:gl] vi fare gargarismi // n gargarismo.
gargoyle ['ga:gɔıl] n gargouille f inv.
garish ['gɛərıʃ] a vistoso(a).
garland ['ga:lənd] n ghirlanda; corona.
garlic ['ga:lık] n aglio.
garment ['ga:mənt] n indumento.
garrison ['gærısn] n guarnigione f.
garrulous ['gærjuləs] a ciarliero(a), loquace.
garter ['ga:tə*] n giarrettiera.
gas [gæs] n gas m inv; (US: gasoline) benzina // vt asfissiare con il gas; (MIL) gasare; ~ **cooker** n (Brit) cucina a gas; ~ **cylinder** n bombola del gas; ~ **fire** n radiatore m a gas.
gash [gæʃ] n sfregio // vt sfregiare.
gasket ['gæskıt] n (AUT) guarnizione f.
gas mask n maschera f antigas inv.
gas meter n contatore m del gas.
gasoline ['gæsəli:n] n (US) benzina.
gasp [ga:sp] vi ansare, boccheggiare; (in surprise) restare senza fiato; to ~ out vt dire affannosamente.
gas ring n fornello a gas.
gassy ['gæsı] a gassoso(a).
gas tap n rubinetto del gas.
gate [geıt] n cancello; ~**crash** vt (Brit) partecipare senza invito a; ~**way** n

porta.
gather ['gæðə*] vt (flowers, fruit) cogliere; (pick up) raccogliere; (assemble) radunare; raccogliere; (understand) capire // vi (assemble) radunarsi; to ~ speed acquistare velocità; ~**ing** n adunanza.
gauche [gəuʃ] a goffo(a), maldestro(a).
gaudy ['gɔ:dı] a vistoso(a).
gauge [geıdʒ] n (standard measure) calibro; (RAIL) scartamento; (instrument) indicatore m // vt misurare.
gaunt [gɔ:nt] a scarno(a); (grim, desolate) desolato(a).
gauntlet ['gɔ:ntlıt] n (fig): to run the ~ through an angry crowd passare sotto il fuoco di una folla ostile; to throw down the ~ gettare il guanto.
gauze [gɔ:z] n garza.
gave [geıv] pt of give.
gay [geı] a (person) gaio(a), allegro(a); (colour) vivace, vivo(a); (col) omosessuale.
gaze [geız] n sguardo fisso // vi: to ~ at guardare fisso.
GB abbr = **Great Britain**.
GCE n abbr (Brit: = General Certificate of Education) ≈ maturità.
GCSE n abbr (Brit) = General Certificate of Secondary Education.
gear [gıə*] n attrezzi mpl, equipaggiamento; (belongings) roba; (TECH) ingranaggio; (AUT) marcia // vt (fig: adapt): to ~ sth to adattare qc a; in top or (US) high/low/bottom ~ in quarta (or quinta)/seconda/prima; in ~ in marcia; to be in ~ essere in marcia; ~ **box** n scatola del cambio; ~ **lever**, (US) ~ **shift** n leva del cambio.
geese [gi:s] npl of **goose**.
gel [dʒel] n gel m inv.
gelignite ['dʒelıgnaıt] n nitroglicerina.
gem [dʒem] n gemma.
Gemini ['dʒemınaı] n Gemelli mpl.
gender ['dʒendə*] n genere m.
general ['dʒenərl] n generale m // a generale; in ~ in genere; ~ **delivery** n (US) fermo posta m; ~ **election** n elezioni fpl generali; ~**ize** vi generalizzare; ~**ly** ad generalmente; ~ **practitioner** n medico generico.
generate ['dʒenəreıt] vt generare.
generation [dʒenə'reıʃən] n generazione f.
generator ['dʒenəreıtə*] n generatore m.
generosity [dʒenə'rɔsıtı] n generosità.
generous ['dʒenərəs] a generoso(a); (copious) abbondante.
genetic [dʒı'netık] a genetico(a).
Geneva [dʒı'ni:və] n Ginevra.
genial ['dʒi:nıəl] a geniale, cordiale.
genitals ['dʒenıtlz] npl genitali mpl.
genius ['dʒi:nıəs] n genio.
Genoa ['dʒenəuə] n Genova.
gent [dʒent] n abbr = **gentleman**.

genteel [dʒɛn'tiːl] *a* raffinato(a), distinto(a).

gentle ['dʒɛntl] *a* delicato(a); (*persona*) dolce.

gentleman ['dʒɛntlmən] *n* signore *m*; (*well-bred man*) gentiluomo.

gently ['dʒɛntlɪ] *ad* delicatamente.

gentry ['dʒɛntrɪ] *n* nobiltà minore.

gents [dʒɛnts] *n* W.C. *m* (per signori).

genuine ['dʒɛnjuɪn] *a* autentico(a); sincero(a).

geography [dʒɪ'ɔgrəfɪ] *n* geografia.

geology [dʒɪ'ɔlədʒɪ] *n* geologia.

geometric(al) [dʒɪə'mɛtrɪk(l)] *a* geometrico(a).

geometry [dʒɪ'ɔmətrɪ] *n* geometria.

geranium [dʒɪ'reɪnjəm] *n* geranio.

geriatric [dʒɛrɪ'ætrɪk] *a* geriatrico(a).

germ [dʒɜːm] *n* (*MED*) microbo; (*BIOL, fig*) germe *m*.

German ['dʒɜːmən] *a* tedesco(a) // *n* tedesco/a; (*LING*) tedesco; ~ **measles** *n* rosolia.

Germany ['dʒɜːmənɪ] *n* Germania.

gesture ['dʒɛstjə*] *n* gesto.

get [gɛt], *pt, pp* **got**, *pp* **gotten** (*US*) ◆ *vi* **1** (*become, be*) diventare, farsi; to ~ old invecchiare; to ~ tired stancarsi; to ~ drunk ubriacarsi; to ~ killed venire *or* rimanere ucciso(a); when do I ~ paid? quando mi pagate?; it's ~ting late si sta facendo tardi

2 (*go*): to ~ to/from andare a/da; to ~ home arrivare *or* tornare a casa; how did you ~ here? come sei venuto?

3 (*begin*) mettersi a, cominciare a; to ~ to know sb incominciare a conoscere qn; let's ~ going *or* started muoviamoci

4 (*modal auxiliary vb*): you've got to do it devi farlo

◆ *vt* **1**: to ~ sth done (*do*) fare qc; (*have done*) far fare qc; to ~ one's hair cut farsi tagliare i capelli; to ~ sb to do sth far fare qc a qn

2 (*obtain: money, permission, results*) ottenere; (*find: job, flat*) trovare; (*fetch: person, doctor*) chiamare; (: *object*) prendere; to ~ sth for sb prendere *or* procurare qc a qn; ~ me Mr Jones, please (*TEL*) mi passi il signor Jones, per favore; can I ~ you a drink? le posso offrire da bere?

3 (*receive: present, letter, prize*) ricevere; (*acquire: reputation*) farsi; how much did you ~ for the painting? quanto le hanno dato per il quadro?

4 (*catch*) prendere; (*hit: target etc*) colpire; to ~ sb by the arm/throat afferrare qn per un braccio/alla gola; ~ him! prendetelo!

5 (*take, move*) portare; to ~ sth to sb far avere qc a qn; do you think we'll ~ it through the door? pensi che riusciremo a farlo passare per la porta?

6 (*catch, take: plane, bus etc*) prendere

7 (*understand*) afferrare; (*hear*) sentire; I've got it! ci sono arrivato!, ci sono!; I'm sorry, I didn't ~ your name scusi, non ho capito (*or* sentito) il suo nome

8 (*have, possess*): to have got avere; how many have you got? quanti ne ha?

to **get about** *vi* muoversi; (*news*) diffondersi

to **get along** *vi* (*agree*) andare d'accordo; (*depart*) andarsene; (*manage*) = to **get by**

to **get at** *vt fus* (*attack*) prendersela con; (*reach*) raggiungere, arrivare a

to **get away** *vi* partire, andarsene; (*escape*) scappare

to **get away with** *vt fus* cavarsela, farla franca

to **get back** *vi* (*return*) ritornare, tornare ◆ *vt* riottenere, riavere

to **get by** *vi* (*pass*) passare; (*manage*) farcela

to **get down** *vi, vt fus* scendere ◆ *vt* far scendere; (*depress*) buttare giù

to **get down to** *vt fus* (*work*) mettersi a (fare)

to **get in** *vi* entrare; (*train*) arrivare; (*arrive home*) tornare, rientrare

to **get into** *vt fus* entrare in; to ~ into a rage incavolarsi

to **get off** *vi* (*from train etc*) scendere; (*depart: person, car*) andare via; (*escape*) cavarsela ◆ *vt* (*remove: clothes, stain*) levare ◆ *vt fus* (*train, bus*) scendere da

to **get on** *vi* (*at exam etc*) andare; (*agree*): to ~ on (*with*) andare d'accordo (con) ◆ *vt fus* montare in; (*horse*) montare su

to **get out** *vi* uscire; (*of vehicle*) scendere ◆ *vt* tirar fuori, far uscire

to **get out of** *vt fus* uscire da; (*duty etc*) evitare

to **get over** *vt fus* (*illness*) riversi da

to **get round** *vt fus* aggirare; (*fig: person*) rigirare

to **get through** *vi* (*TEL*) avere la linea

to **get through to** *vt fus* (*TEL*) parlare a

to **get together** *vi* riunirsi ◆ *vt* raccogliere; (*people*) adunare

to **get up** *vi* (*rise*) alzarsi ◆ *vt fus* salire su per

to **get up to** *vt fus* (*reach*) raggiungere; (*prank etc*) fare.

getaway ['gɛtəweɪ] *n* fuga.

geyser ['giːzə*] *n* scaldabagno; (*GEO*) geyser *m* inv.

Ghana ['gɑːnə] *n* Ghana *m*.

ghastly ['gɑːstlɪ] *a* orribile, orrendo(a).

gherkin ['gɜːkɪn] *n* cetriolino.

ghost [gəust] *n* fantasma *m*, spettro.

giant ['dʒaɪənt] *n* gigante/essa // *a* gigante, enorme.

gibberish ['dʒɪbərɪʃ] *n* parole *fpl* senza

senso.

gibe [dʒaɪb] n frecciata.

giblets ['dʒɪblɪts] npl frattaglie fpl.

Gibraltar [dʒɪ'brɔːltə*] n Gibilterra.

giddy ['gɪdɪ] a (dizzy): to be ~ aver le vertigini; (height) vertiginoso(a).

gift [gɪft] n regalo; (donation, ability) dono; ~ed a dotato(a); ~ token or voucher n buono m omaggio inv.

gigantic [dʒaɪ'gæntɪk] a gigantesco(a).

giggle ['gɪgl] vi ridere scioccamente.

gill [dʒɪl] n (measure) = 0.25 pints (Brit = 0.148l, US = 0.118l).

gills [gɪlz] npl (of fish) branchie fpl.

gilt [gɪlt] n doratura // a dorato(a); ~-edged a (COMM) della massima sicurezza.

gimmick ['gɪmɪk] n trucco.

gin [dʒɪn] n (liquor) gin m inv.

ginger ['dʒɪndʒə*] n zenzero; ~ ale, ~ beer n bibita gassosa allo zenzero; ~bread n pan m di zenzero.

gingerly ['dʒɪndʒəlɪ] ad cautamente.

gipsy ['dʒɪpsɪ] n zingaro/a.

giraffe [dʒɪ'rɑːf] n giraffa.

girder ['gɜːdə*] n trave f.

girdle ['gɜːdl] n (corset) guaina.

girl [gɜːl] n ragazza; (young unmarried woman) signorina; (daughter) figlia, figliola; ~friend n (of girl) amica; (of boy) ragazza; ~ish a da ragazza.

giro ['dʒaɪrəu] n (bank ~) versamento bancario; (post office ~) postagiro.

girth [gɜːθ] n circonferenza; (of horse) cinghia.

gist [dʒɪst] n succo.

give [gɪv] n (pt gave, pp given) vt dare // vi cedere; to ~ sb sth, ~ sth to sb dare qc a qn; to ~ a cry/sigh emettere un grido/sospiro; to ~ away vt dare via; (give free) fare dono di; (betray) tradire; (disclose) rivelare; (bride) condurre all'altare; to ~ back vt rendere; to ~ in vi cedere // vt consegnare; to ~ off vt emettere; to ~ out vt distribuire; annunciare; to ~ up vt rinunciare // vt rinunciare a; to ~ up smoking smettere di fumare; to ~ o.s. up arrendersi; to ~ way vi cedere; (Brit AUT) dare la precedenza.

glacier ['glæsɪə*] n ghiacciaio.

glad [glæd] a lieto(a), contento(a).

gladly ['glædlɪ] ad volentieri.

glamorous ['glæmərəs] a affascinante, seducente.

glamour ['glæmə*] n fascino.

glance [glɑːns] n occhiata, sguardo // vi: to ~ at dare un'occhiata a; to ~ off (bullet) rimbalzare su; **glancing** a (blow) che colpisce di striscio.

gland [glænd] n ghiandola.

glare [glɛə*] n riverbero, luce f abbagliante; (look) sguardo furioso // vi abbagliare; to ~ at guardare male; **glaring** a (mistake) madornale.

glass [glɑːs] n (substance) vetro; (tumbler) bicchiere m; (also: looking ~) specchio; ~es npl (spectacles) occhiali mpl; ~ware n vetrame m; ~y a (eyes) vitreo(a).

glaze [gleɪz] vt (door) fornire di vetri; (pottery) smaltare // n smalto.

glazier ['gleɪzɪə*] n vetraio.

gleam [gliːm] n barlume m; raggio // vi luccicare; ~ing a lucente.

glean [gliːn] vt (information) racimolare.

glee [gliː] n allegrezza, gioia.

glen [glɛn] n valletta.

glib [glɪb] a dalla parola facile; facile.

glide [glaɪd] vi scivolare; (AVIAT, birds) planare; ~r n (AVIAT) aliante m; **gliding** n (AVIAT) volo a vela.

glimmer ['glɪmə*] vi luccicare // n barlume m.

glimpse [glɪmps] n impressione f fugace // vt vedere al volo.

glint [glɪnt] n luccichio // vi luccicare.

glisten ['glɪsn] vi luccicare.

glitter ['glɪtə*] vi scintillare // n scintillio.

gloat [gləut] vi: to ~ (over) gongolare di piacere (per).

global ['gləubl] a globale.

globe [gləub] n globo, sfera.

gloom [gluːm] n oscurità, buio; (sadness) tristezza, malinconia; ~y a fosco(a), triste.

glorious ['glɔːrɪəs] a glorioso(a); magnifico(a).

glory ['glɔːrɪ] n gloria; splendore m // vi: to ~ in gloriarsi di or in.

gloss [glɔs] n (shine) lucentezza; to ~ over vt fus scivolare su.

glossary ['glɔsərɪ] n glossario.

glossy ['glɔsɪ] a lucente.

glove [glʌv] n guanto; ~ compartment n (AUT) vano portaoggetti.

glow [gləu] vi ardere; (face) essere luminoso(a) // n bagliore m; (of face) colorito acceso.

glower ['glauə*] vi: to ~ (at sb) guardare (qn) in cagnesco.

glue [gluː] n colla // vt incollare.

glum [glʌm] a abbattuto(a).

glut [glʌt] n eccesso // vt saziare; (market) saturare.

glutton ['glʌtn] n ghiottone/a; a ~ for work un(a) patito(a) del lavoro.

gnarled [nɑːld] a nodoso(a).

gnat [næt] n moscerino.

gnaw [nɔː] vt rodere.

go [gəu] vb (pt went, pp gone) vi andare; (depart) partire, andarsene; (work) funzionare; (break etc) cedere; (be sold): to ~ for £10 essere venduto per 10 sterline; (fit, suit): to ~ with andare bene con; (become): to ~ pale diventare pallido(a); to ~ mouldy ammuffire // n (pl ~es): to have a ~ (at) provare; to be on the ~ essere in moto; whose ~ is it? a chi tocca?; he's going to do sta per fare; to ~ for a walk andare a fare una passeggiata; to ~ dancing/shopping andare a ballare/fare la spesa; how did it ~? com'è andato?; to ~ round the back/by the shop passare da dietro/davanti al negozio; to ~ about vi (*rumour*) correre, circolare // vt fus: how do I ~ about this? qual'è la prassi per questo?; to ~ ahead vi andare avanti; ~ ahead! faccia pure!; to ~ along vi andare, avanzare // vt fus percorrere; to ~ away vi partire, andarsene; to ~ back vi tornare, ritornare; (*go again*) andare di nuovo; to ~ back on vt fus (*promise*) non mantenere; to ~ by vi (*years, time*) scorrere // vt fus attenersi a, seguire (alla lettera); prestar fede a; to ~ down vi scendere; (*ship*) affondare; (*sun*) tramontare // vt fus scendere; to ~ for vt fus (*fetch*) andare a prendere; (*col: like*) andar matto(a) per; (*attack*) attaccare; saltare addosso a; to ~ in vi entrare; to ~ in for vt fus (*competition*) iscriversi a; (*be interested in*) interessarsi di; to ~ into vt fus entrare in; (*investigate*) indagare, esaminare; (*embark on*) lanciarsi in; to ~ off vi partire, andar via; (*food*) guastarsi; (*explode*) esplodere, scoppiare; (*event*) passare // vt fus: I've gone off chocolate la cioccolata non mi piace più; the gun went off il fucile si scaricò; to ~ on vi continuare; (*happen*) succedere; to ~ on doing continuare a fare; to ~ out vi uscire; (*fire, light*) spegnersi; to ~ over vi (*ship*) ribaltarsi // vt fus (*check*) esaminare; to ~ through vt fus (*town etc*) attraversare; to ~ up vi salire // vt fus salire su per; to ~ without vt fus fare a meno di.

goad [gəud] vt spronare.

go-ahead ['gəuəhɛd] a intraprendente // n via m.

goal [gəul] n (*SPORT*) gol m, rete f; (: *place*) porta; (*fig: aim*) fine m, scopo; ~keeper n portiere m; ~-post n palo (della porta).

goat [gəut] n capra.

gobble ['gɔbl] vt (*also: ~ down, ~ up*) ingoiare.

goblet ['gɔblɪt] n calice m, coppa.

god [gɔd] n dio; G~ n Dio; ~child n figlioccio/a; ~daughter n figlioccia; ~dess n dea; ~father n padrino; ~forsaken a desolato(a), sperduto(a); ~mother n madrina; ~send n dono del cielo; ~son n figlioccio.

goggles ['gɔglz] npl occhiali mpl (di protezione).

going ['gəuɪŋ] n (*conditions*) andare m, stato del terreno // a: the ~ rate la tariffa in vigore.

gold [gəuld] n oro // a d'oro; ~en a

(*made of gold*) d'oro; (*gold in colour*) dorato(a); ~fish n pesce m dorato or rosso; ~-plated a placcato(a) oro inv; ~smith n orefice m, orafo.

golf [gɔlf] n golf m; ~ ball n (*for game*) pallina da golf; (*on typewriter*) pallina; ~ club n circolo di golf; (*stick*) bastone m or mazza da golf; ~ course n campo di golf; ~er n giocatore/trice di golf.

gondola ['gɔndələ] n gondola.

gone [gɔn] pp of go // a partito(a).

gong [gɔŋ] n gong m inv.

good [gud] a buono(a); (*kind*) buono(a), gentile; (*child*) buono(a); ~s npl (*COMM etc*) beni mpl; merci fpl; ~! bene!, ottimo!; to be ~ at essere bravo(a) in; to be ~ for andare bene per; it's ~ for you fa bene; would you be ~ enough to ...? avrebbe la gentilezza di ...?; a ~ deal (of) molto(a), una buona quantità (di); a ~ many molti(e); to make ~ vi (*succeed*) aver successo // vt (*deficit*) colmare; (*losses*) compensare; it's no ~ complaining brontolare non serve a niente; for ~ per sempre, definitivamente; ~ morning! buon giorno!; ~ afternoon/evening! buona sera!; ~ night! buona notte!; ~bye excl arrivederci!; G~ Friday n Venerdì Santo; ~-looking a bello(a); ~natured a affabile; (*discussion*) amichevole, cordiale; ~ness n (*of person*) bontà; for ~ness sake! per amor di Dio!; ~ness gracious! santo cielo!, mamma mia!; ~s train n (*Brit*) treno m merci inv; ~will n amicizia, benevolenza; (*COMM*) avviamento.

goose [gu:s], pl **geese** n oca.

gooseberry ['guzbərɪ] n uva spina; to play ~ tenere la candela.

gooseflesh ['gu:sflɛʃ] n, **goose pimples** npl pelle f d'oca.

gore [gɔ:*] vt incornare // n sangue m (coagulato).

gorge [gɔ:dʒ] n gola // vt: to ~ o.s. (on) ingozzarsi (di).

gorgeous ['gɔ:dʒəs] a magnifico(a).

gorilla [gə'rɪlə] n gorilla m inv.

gorse [gɔ:s] n ginestrone m.

gory ['gɔ:rɪ] a sanguinoso(a).

go-slow ['gəu'sləu] n (*Brit*) rallentamento dei lavori (*per agitazione sindacale*).

gospel ['gɔspl] n vangelo.

gossip ['gɔsɪp] n chiacchiere fpl; pettegolezzi mpl; (*person*) pettegolo/a // vi chiacchierare; (*maliciously*) pettegolare.

got [gɔt] pt, pp of get; ~ten (*US*) pp of get.

gout [gaut] n gotta.

govern ['gʌvən] vt governare; (*LING*) reggere.

governess ['gʌvənɪs] n governante f.

government ['gʌvnmənt] n governo.

governor ['gʌvənə*] n (of state, bank) governatore m; (of school, hospital) amministratore m.

gown [gaun] n vestito lungo; (of teacher, Brit: of judge) toga.

G.P. n abbr = **general practitioner.**

grab [græb] vt afferrare, arraffare; (property, power) impadronirsi di.

grace [greɪs] n grazia // vt onorare; 5 'days' ~ dilazione f di 5 giorni; to say ~ dire il benedicite; ~**ful** a elegante, aggraziato(a); **gracious** ['greɪʃəs] a grazioso(a); misericordioso(a).

grade [greɪd] n (COMM) qualità f inv; classe f; categoria; (in hierarchy) grado; (US: SCOL) voto; classe // vt classificare; ordinare; graduare; ~ **crossing** n (US) passaggio a livello; ~ **school** n (US) scuola elementare.

gradient ['greɪdɪənt] n pendenza, inclinazione f.

gradual ['grædjuəl] a graduale; ~**ly** ad man mano, a poco a poco.

graduate n ['grædjuɪt] laureato/a // vi ['grædjueɪt] laurearsi; **graduation** [-'eɪʃən] n cerimonia del conferimento della laurea.

graffiti [grə'fi:tɪ] npl graffiti mpl.

graft [grɑ:ft] n (AGR, MED) innesto // vt innestare; **hard** ~ n (col): by sheer hard ~ lavorando da matti.

grain [greɪn] n grano; (of sand) granello; (of wood) venatura.

gram [græm] n grammo.

grammar ['græmə*] n grammatica; ~ **school** n (Brit) ≈ liceo.

grammatical [grə'mætɪkl] a grammaticale.

gramme [græm] n = **gram.**

grand [grænd] a grande, magnifico(a); grandioso(a); ~**children** npl nipoti mpl; ~**dad** n (col) nonno; ~**daughter** n nipote f; ~**father** n nonno; ~**ma** n (col) nonna; ~**mother** n nonna; ~**pa** n (col) = ~**dad**; ~**parents** npl nonni mpl; ~ **piano** n pianoforte m a coda; ~**son** n nipote m; ~**stand** n (SPORT) tribuna.

granite ['grænɪt] n granito.

granny ['grænɪ] n (col) nonna.

grant [grɑ:nt] vt accordare; (a request) accogliere; (admit) ammettere, concedere // n (SCOL) borsa; (ADMIN) sussidio, sovvenzione f; to take sth for ~ed dare qc per scontato.

granulated ['grænjuleɪtɪd] a: ~ **sugar** zucchero cristallizzato.

grape [greɪp] n chicco d'uva, acino.

grapefruit ['greɪpfru:t] n pompelmo.

graph [grɑ:f] n grafico; ~**ic** a grafico(a); (vivid) vivido(a); ~**ics** n grafica // npl illustrazioni fpl.

grapple ['græpl] vi: to ~ with essere alle prese con.

grasp [grɑ:sp] vt afferrare // n (grip) presa; (fig) potere m; comprensione f;

~**ing** a avido(a).

grass [grɑ:s] n erba; ~**hopper** n cavalletta; ~-**roots** a di base; ~ **snake** n natrice f.

grate [greɪt] n graticola (del focolare) // vi cigolare, stridere // vt (CULIN) grattugiare.

grateful ['greɪtful] a grato(a), riconoscente; ~**ly** ad con gratitudine.

grater ['greɪtə*] n grattugia.

gratify ['grætɪfaɪ] vt appagare; (whim) soddisfare.

grating ['greɪtɪŋ] n (iron bars) grata // a (noise) stridente, stridulo(a).

gratitude ['grætɪtju:d] n gratitudine f.

gratuity [grə'tju:ɪtɪ] n mancia.

grave [greɪv] n tomba // a grave, serio(a).

gravel ['grævl] n ghiaia.

gravestone ['greɪvstəun] n pietra tombale.

graveyard ['greɪvjɑ:d] n cimitero.

gravity ['grævɪtɪ] n (PHYSICS) gravità; pesantezza; (seriousness) gravità, serietà.

gravy ['greɪvɪ] n intingolo della carne; salsa.

gray [greɪ] a = **grey.**

graze [greɪz] vi pascolare, pascere // vt (touch lightly) sfiorare; (scrape) escoriare // n (MED) escoriazione f.

grease [gri:s] n (fat) grasso; (lubricant) lubrificante m // vt ingrassare; lubrificare; ~-**proof paper** n (Brit) carta oleata; **greasy** a grasso(a), untuoso(a).

great [greɪt] a grande; (col) magnifico(a), meraviglioso(a); **G~ Britain** n Gran Bretagna; ~-**grandfather** n bisnonno; ~-**grandmother** n bisnonna; ~**ly** ad molto; ~**ness** n grandezza.

Greece [gri:s] n Grecia.

greed [gri:d] n (also: ~**iness**) avarizia; (for food) golosità, ghiottoneria; ~**y** a avido(a); goloso(a), ghiotto(a).

Greek [gri:k] a greco(a) // n greco/a; (LING) greco.

green [gri:n] a verde; (inexperienced) inesperto(a), ingenuo(a) // n verde m; (stretch of grass) prato; (also: village ~) ≈ piazza del paese; ~**s** npl (vegetables) verdura; ~ **belt** n (round town) cintura di verde; ~ **card** n (AUT) carta verde; ~**ery** n verde m; ~**gage** n susina Regina Claudia; ~**grocer** n (Brit) fruttivendolo/a, erbivendolo/a; ~**house** n serra.

Greenland ['gri:nlənd] n Groenlandia.

greet [gri:t] vt salutare; ~**ing** n saluto; ~**ing(s) card** n cartolina d'auguri.

grenade [grə'neɪd] n granata.

grew [gru:] pt of **grow.**

grey [greɪ] a grigio(a); ~**hound** n levriere m.

grid [grɪd] n grata; (ELEC) rete f.

grief [gri:f] n dolore m.

grievance ['gri:vəns] n doglianza, lagnanza.

grieve [gri:v] vi addolorarsi; rattristarsi // vt addolorare; **to ~ for sb** (dead person) piangere qn.

grievous ['gri:vəs] a: ~ **bodily harm** (LAW) aggressione f.

grill [grɪl] n (on cooker) griglia // vt (Brit) cuocere ai ferri; (question) interrogare senza sosta.

grille [grɪl] n grata; (AUT) griglia.

grim [grɪm] a sinistro(a), brutto(a).

grimace [grɪ'meɪs] n smorfia // vi fare smorfie; fare boccacce.

grime [graɪm] n sudiciume m.

grimy ['graɪmɪ] a sudicio(a).

grin [grɪn] n sorriso smagliante // vi fare un gran sorriso.

grind [graɪnd] vt (pt, pp **ground**) macinare; (make sharp) arrotare // n (work) sgobbata; **to ~ one's teeth** digrignare i denti.

grip [grɪp] n impugnatura; presa; (holdall) borsa da viaggio // vt impugnare; afferrare; **to come to ~s with** affrontare; cercare di risolvere.

gripping ['grɪpɪŋ] a avvincente.

grisly ['grɪzlɪ] a macabro(a), orrido(a).

gristle ['grɪsl] n cartilagine f.

grit [grɪt] n ghiaia; (courage) fegato // vt (road) coprire di sabbia; **to ~ one's teeth** stringere i denti.

groan [grəun] n gemito // vi gemere.

grocer ['grəusə*] n negoziante m di generi alimentari; **~ies** npl provviste fpl.

groggy ['grɔgɪ] a barcollante.

groin [grɔɪn] n inguine m.

groom [gru:m] n palafreniere m; (also: **bride~**) sposo // vt (horse) strigliare; (fig): **to ~ sb for** avviare qn a.

groove [gru:v] n scanalatura, solco.

grope [grəup] vi andare a tentoni; **to ~ for** vt fus cercare a tastoni.

gross [grəus] a grossolano(a); (COMM) lordo(a) // n (pl inv) (twelve dozen) grossa; **~ly** ad (greatly) molto.

grotesque [grəu'tɛsk] a grottesco(a).

grotto ['grɔtəu] n grotta.

ground [graund] pt, pp of **grind** // n suolo, terra; (land) terreno; (SPORT) campo; (reason: gen pl) ragione f; (US: also: ~ **wire**) terra // vt (plane) tenere a terra // vi (ship) arenarsi; **~s** npl (of coffee etc) fondi mpl; (gardens etc) terreno, giardini mpl; **on/to the ~** per/a terra; **to gain/lose ~** guadagnare/perdere terreno; ~ **cloth** n (US) = **~sheet**; **~ing** n (in education) basi fpl; **~less** a infondato(a); **~sheet** n (Brit) telone m impermeabile; ~ **staff** n personale m di terra; ~ **swell** n maremoto; (fig) movimento d'opinione; **~work** n preparazione f.

group [gru:p] n gruppo // vt (also: ~

together) raggruppare // vi (also: ~ **together**) raggrupparsi.

grouse [graus] n (pl inv) (bird) tetraone m // vi (complain) brontolare.

grove [grəuv] n boschetto.

grovel ['grɔvl] vi (fig): **to ~ (before)** strisciare (di fronte a).

grow [grəu], pt **grew**, pp **grown** vi crescere; (increase) aumentare; (become): **to ~ rich/weak** arricchirsi/indebolirsi // vt coltivare, far crescere; **to ~ up** vi farsi grande, crescere; **~er** n coltivatore/trice; **~ing** a (fear, amount) crescente.

growl [graul] vi ringhiare.

grown [grəun] pp of **grow** // a adulto(a), maturo(a); **~-up** n adulto/a, grande m/f.

growth [grəuθ] n crescita, sviluppo; (what has grown) crescita; (MED) escrescenza, tumore m.

grub [grʌb] n larva; (col: food) roba (da mangiare).

grubby ['grʌbɪ] a sporco(a).

grudge [grʌdʒ] n rancore m // vt: **to ~ sb sth** dare qc a qn di malavoglia; invidiare qc a qn; **to bear sb a ~ (for)** serbar rancore a qn (per).

gruelling ['gruəlɪŋ] a estenuante.

gruesome ['gru:səm] a orribile.

gruff [grʌf] a rozzo(a).

grumble ['grʌmbl] vi brontolare, lagnarsi.

grumpy ['grʌmpɪ] a stizzito(a).

grunt [grʌnt] vi grugnire // n grugnito.

G-string ['dʒi:strɪŋ] n tanga m inv.

guarantee [gærən'ti:] n garanzia // vt garantire.

guard [gɑ:d] n guardia; (BOXING) difesa; (one man) guardia, sentinella; (Brit RAIL) capotreno // vt fare la guardia a; **~ed** a (fig) cauto(a), guardingo(a); **~ian** n custode m; (of minor) tutore/trice; **~'s van** n (Brit RAIL) vagone m di servizio.

guerrilla [gə'rɪlə] n guerrigliero; ~ **warfare** n guerriglia.

guess [gɛs] vi indovinare // vt indovinare; (US) credere, pensare // n congettura; **~work** n: I got the answer by **~work** ho azzeccato la risposta.

guest [gɛst] n ospite m/f; (in hotel) cliente m/f; **~-house** n pensione f; ~ **room** n camera degli ospiti.

guffaw [gʌ'fɔ:] vi scoppiare in una risata sonora.

guidance ['gaɪdəns] n guida, direzione f.

guide [gaɪd] n (person, book etc) guida; (also: **girl ~**) giovane esploratrice f // vt guidare; **~book** n guida; ~ **dog** n cane m guida inv; **~lines** npl (fig) indicazioni fpl, linee fpl direttive.

guild [gɪld] n arte f, corporazione f; associazione f.

guile [gaɪl] n astuzia.

guillotine ['gɪləti:n] n ghigliottina.

guilt [gɪlt] n colpevolezza; **~y** a

colpevole.

guinea pig ['gɪnɪ-] n cavia.

guise [gaɪz] n maschera.

guitar [gɪ'tɑ:*] n chitarra.

gulf [gʌlf] n golfo; (*abyss*) abisso.

gull [gʌl] n gabbiano.

gullet ['gʌlɪt] n gola.

gullible ['gʌlɪbl] a credulo(a).

gully ['gʌlɪ] n burrone m; gola; canale m.

gulp [gʌlp] vi deglutire; (*from emotion*) avere il nodo in gola // vt (*also*: ~ **down**) tracannare, inghiottire.

gum [gʌm] n (ANAT) gengiva; (*glue*) colla; (*sweet*) gelatina di frutta; (*also*: **chewing-~**) chewing-gum m // vt incollare; ~**boots** npl (*Brit*) stivali mpl di gomma.

gun [gʌn] n fucile m; (*small*) pistola, rivoltella; (*rifle*) carabina; (*shotgun*) fucile da caccia; (*cannon*) cannone m; ~**boat** n cannoniera; ~**fire** n spari mpl; ~**man** n bandito armato; ~**ner** n artigliere m; ~**point** n: at ~**point** sotto minaccia di fucile; ~**powder** n polvere f da sparo; ~**shot** n sparo; ~**smith** n armaiolo.

gurgle ['gə:gl] vi gorgogliare.

guru ['guru:] n guru m inv.

gush [gʌʃ] vi sgorgare; (*fig*) abbandonarsi ad effusioni.

gusset ['gʌsɪt] n gherone m.

gust [gʌst] n (*of wind*) raffica; (*of smoke*) buffata.

gusto ['gʌstəu] n entusiasmo.

gut [gʌt] n intestino, budello; (MUS etc) minugia; ~s npl (*courage*) fegato.

gutter ['gʌtə*] n (*of roof*) grondaia; (*in street*) cunetta.

guy [gaɪ] n (*also*: ~**rope**) cavo or corda di fissaggio; (*col: man*) tipo, elemento; (*figure*) effigie di Guy Fawkes.

guzzle ['gʌzl] vi gozzovigliare // vt tranguiare.

gym [dʒɪm] n (*also*: **gymnasium**) palestra; (*also*: **gymnastics**) ginnastica.

gymnast ['dʒɪmnæst] n ginnasta m/f; ~**ics** [-'næstɪks] n, npl ginnastica.

gym shoes npl scarpe fpl da ginnastica.

gym slip n (*Brit*) grembiule m da scuola (*per ragazze*).

gynaecologist, (US) **gynecologist** [gaɪnɪ'kɔlədʒɪst] n ginecologo/a.

gypsy ['dʒɪpsɪ] n = **gipsy**.

gyrate [dʒaɪ'reɪt] vi girare.

H

haberdashery ['hæbə'dæʃərɪ] n (*Brit*) merceria.

habit ['hæbɪt] n abitudine f; (*costume*) abito; (REL) tonaca.

habitation [hæbɪ'teɪʃən] n abitazione f.

habitual [hə'bɪtjuəl] a abituale; (*drinker*, liar) inveterato(a); ~**ly** ad abitualmente, di solito.

hack [hæk] vt tagliare, fare a pezzi // n (*cut*) taglio; (*blow*) colpo; (*pej: writer*) negro.

hackneyed ['hæknɪd] a comune, trito(a).

had [hæd] pt, pp of **have**.

haddock, pl ~ or ~**s** ['hædək] n eglefino.

hadn't ['hædnt] = **had not**.

haemorrhage, (US) **hemorrhage** ['hemərɪdʒ] n emorragia.

haemorrhoids, (US) **hemorrhoids** ['hemərɔɪdz] npl emorroidi fpl.

haggard ['hægəd] a smunto(a).

haggle ['hægl] vi mercanteggiare.

Hague [heɪg] n: The ~ L'Aia.

hail [heɪl] n grandine f // vt (*call*) chiamare; (*greet*) salutare // vi grandinare; ~**stone** n chicco di grandine.

hair [heə*] n capelli mpl; (*single hair: on head*) capello; (: *on body*) pelo; to do one's ~ pettinarsi; ~**brush** n spazzola per capelli; ~**cut** n taglio di capelli; ~**do** ['heədu:] n acconciatura, pettinatura; ~**dresser** n parrucchiere/a; ~**dryer** n asciugacapelli m inv; ~ **grip** n forcina; ~**pin** n forcina; ~**pin bend**, (US) ~**pin curve** n tornante m; ~**raising** a orripilante; ~ **remover** n crema depilatoria; ~ **spray** n lacca per capelli; ~**style** n pettinatura, acconciatura; ~**y** a irsuto(a); peloso(a); (*col: frightening*) spaventoso(a).

hake, pl ~ or ~**s** [heɪk] n nasello.

half [hɑ:f] n (pl **halves**) mezzo, metà f inv // a mezzo(a) // ad a mezzo, a metà; ~ **an hour** mezz'ora; ~ **a dozen** mezza dozzina; ~ **a pound** mezza libbra; **two and a ~** due e mezzo; **a week and a ~** una settimana e mezza; ~ (**of**) la metà; ~ (**of**) la metà di; **to cut sth in ~** tagliare qc in due; ~ **asleep** mezzo(a) addormentato(a); ~**back** n (SPORT) mediano; ~**breed**, ~**caste** n meticcio/a; ~**hearted** a tiepido(a); ~**hour** n mezz'ora; ~**mast** n: at ~**mast** (*flag*) a mezz'asta; ~**penny** ['heɪpnɪ] n (*Brit*) mezzo penny m inv; ~**price** a, ad a metà prezzo; ~ **term** n (*Brit SCOL*) vacanza a or di metà trimestre; ~**time** n (SPORT) intervallo; ~**way** ad a metà strada.

halibut ['hælɪbət] n (pl inv) ippoglosso.

hall [hɔ:l] n sala, salone m; (*entrance way*) entrata; (*corridor*) corridoio; (*mansion*) grande villa, maniero; ~ **of residence** n (*Brit*) casa dello studente.

hallmark ['hɔ:lmɑ:k] n marchio di garanzia; (*fig*) caratteristica.

hallo [hə'ləu] excl = **hello**.

Hallowe'en [hæləu'i:n] n vigilia d'Ognissanti.

hallucination [həlu:sɪ'neɪʃən] n

allucinazione f.

hallway ['hɔːlweɪ] n corridoio; (entrance) ingresso.

halo ['heɪləʊ] n (of saint etc) aureola; (of sun) alone m.

halt [hɔːlt] n fermata // vt fermare // vi fermarsi.

halve [hɑːv] vt (apple etc) dividere a metà; (expense) ridurre di metà.

halves [hɑːvz] npl of **half**.

ham [hæm] n prosciutto.

hamburger ['hæmbɜːgəʳ] n hamburger m inv.

hamlet ['hæmlɪt] n paesetto.

hammer ['hæməʳ] n martello // vt martellare; (fig) sconfiggere duramente // vi: to ~ on or at the door picchiare alla porta.

hammock ['hæmək] n amaca.

hamper ['hæmpəʳ] vt impedire // n cesta.

hamster ['hæmstəʳ] n criceto.

hand [hænd] n mano f; (of clock) lancetta; (handwriting) scrittura; (at cards) mano; (: game) partita; (worker) operaio/a // vt dare, passare; to give sb a ~ dare una mano a qn; at ~ a portata di mano; in ~ a disposizione; (work) in corso; on ~ (person) disponibile; (services) pronto(a) a intervenire; to ~ (information etc) a portata di mano; on the one ~ ..., on the other ~ da un lato ..., dall'altro; to ~ in vt consegnare; to ~ out vt distribuire; to ~ over vt passare; cedere; ~**bag** n borsetta; ~**book** n manuale m; ~**brake** n freno a mano; ~**cuffs** npl manette fpl; ~**ful** n manciata, pugno.

handicap ['hændɪkæp] n handicap m inv // vt handicappare; to be physically ~**ped** essere handicappato(a); to be mentally ~**ped** essere un(a) handicappato(a) mentale.

handicraft ['hændɪkrɑːft] n lavoro d'artigiano.

handiwork ['hændɪwɜːk] n opera.

handkerchief ['hæŋkətʃɪf] n fazzoletto.

handle ['hændl] n (of door etc) maniglia; (of cup etc) ansa; (of knife etc) impugnatura; (of saucepan) manico; (for winding) manovella // vt toccare, maneggiare; (deal with) occuparsi di; (treat: people) trattare; "~ with care" "fragile"; to fly off the ~ (fig) perdere le staffe, uscire dai gangheri; ~**bar(s)** n(pl) manubrio.

hand: ~ **luggage** n bagagli mpl a mano; ~**made** a fatto(a) a mano; ~**out** n (leaflet) volantino; (at lecture) prospetto; ~**rail** n corrimano; ~**shake** n stretta di mano.

handsome ['hænsəm] a bello(a); (reward) generoso(a); (profit, fortune) considerevole.

handwriting ['hændraɪtɪŋ] n scrittura.

handy ['hændɪ] a (person) bravo(a);

(close at hand) a portata di mano; (convenient) comodo(a); ~**man** n tuttofare m inv.

hang [hæŋ], pt, pp **hung** vt appendere; (criminal: pt, pp **hanged**) impiccare // vi pendere; (hair) scendere; (drapery) cadere; to get the ~ of sth (col) capire come qc funziona; to ~ about vi bighellonare, ciondolare; to ~ on vi (wait) aspettare; to ~ up vi (TEL) riattaccare // vt appendere.

hangar ['hæŋəʳ] n hangar m inv.

hanger ['hæŋəʳ] n gruccia.

hanger-on [hæŋər'ɔn] n parassita m.

hang-gliding ['hæŋglaɪdɪŋ] n volo col deltaplano.

hangover ['hæŋəʊvəʳ] n (after drinking) postumi mpl di sbornia.

hang-up ['hæŋʌp] n complesso.

hanker ['hæŋkəʳ] vi: to ~ after bramare.

hankie, hanky ['hæŋkɪ] n abbr = **handkerchief**.

haphazard [hæp'hæzəd] a a casaccio, alla carlona.

happen ['hæpən] vi accadere, succedere; as it ~s guarda caso; ~**ing** n avvenimento.

happily ['hæpɪlɪ] ad felicemente; fortunatamente.

happiness ['hæpɪnɪs] n felicità, contentezza.

happy ['hæpɪ] a felice, contento(a); ~ with (arrangements etc) soddisfatto(a) di; ~ birthday! buon compleanno!; ~-go-lucky a spensierato(a).

harangue [hə'ræŋ] vt arringare.

harass ['hærəs] vt molestare; ~**ment** n molestia.

harbour, (US) **harbor** ['hɑːbəʳ] n porto // vt dare rifugio a.

hard [hɑːd] a duro(a) // ad (work) sodo; (think, try) bene; to look ~ at guardare fissamente; esaminare attentamente; no ~ feelings! senza rancore!; to be ~ of hearing essere duro(a) d'orecchio; to be ~ done by essere trattato(a) ingiustamente; ~**back** n libro rilegato; ~**cash** n denaro in contanti; ~ **disk** n (COMPUT) disco rigido; ~**en** vt, vi indurire; ~-**headed** a pratico(a); ~ **labour** n lavori forzati mpl.

hardly ['hɑːdlɪ] ad (scarcely) appena; it's ~ the case non è proprio il caso; that can ~ be true non può essere vero; ~ anyone/anywhere quasi nessuno/da nessuna parte; ~ ever quasi mai.

hardship ['hɑːdʃɪp] n avversità f inv; privazioni fpl.

hard-up [hɑːd'ʌp] a (col) al verde.

hardware ['hɑːdwɛəʳ] n ferramenta fpl; (COMPUT) hardware m; ~ **shop** n (negozio di) ferramenta fpl.

hard-wearing [hɑːd'wɛərɪŋ] a resistente; (shoes) robusto(a).

hard-working [hɑːd'wɜːkɪŋ] a

lavoratore(trice).

hardy ['hɑ:dɪ] a robusto(a); (plant) resistente al gelo.

hare [hɛə*] n lepre f; **~-brained** a folle; scervellato(a).

harm [hɑ:m] n male m; (wrong) danno // vt (person) fare male a; (thing) danneggiare; out of ~'s way al sicuro; **~ful** a dannoso(a); **~less** a innocuo(a); inoffensivo(a).

harmonica [hɑ:'mɔnɪkə] n armonica.

harmonious [hɑ:'məunɪəs] a armonioso(a).

harmony ['hɑ:mənɪ] n armonia.

harness ['hɑ:nɪs] n bardatura, finimenti mpl // vt (horse) bardare; (resources) sfruttare.

harp [hɑ:p] n arpa // vi: to ~ on about insistere tediosamente su.

harpoon [hɑ:'pu:n] n arpione m.

harrowing ['hærəuɪŋ] a straziante.

harsh [hɑ:ʃ] a (hard) duro(a); (severe) severo(a); (unpleasant: sound) rauco(a); (: colour) chiassoso(a); violento(a); **~ly** ad duramente; severamente.

harvest ['hɑ:vɪst] n raccolto; (of grapes) vendemmia // vt fare il raccolto di, raccogliere; vendemmiare.

has [hæz] vb see **have**.

hash [hæʃ] n (CULIN) specie di spezzatino fatto con carne già cotta; (fig: mess) pasticcio.

hashish ['hæʃɪʃ] n hascisc m.

hasn't ['hæznt] = **has not**.

hassle ['hæsl] n (col) sacco di problemi.

haste [heɪst] n fretta; precipitazione f; **~n** ['heɪsn] vt affrettare // vi affrettarsi; **hastily** ad in fretta; precipitosamente; **hasty** a affrettato(a); precipitoso(a).

hat [hæt] n cappello.

hatch [hætʃ] n (NAUT: also: **~way**) boccaporto; (also: **service ~**) portello di servizio // vi schiudersi // vt covare.

hatchback ['hætʃbæk] n (AUT) tre (or cinque) porte f inv.

hatchet ['hætʃɪt] n accetta.

hate [heɪt] vt odiare, detestare // n odio; **~ful** a odioso(a), detestabile.

hatred ['heɪtrɪd] n odio.

hat trick n: to get a ~ segnare tre punti consecutivi (or vincere per tre volte consecutive).

haughty ['hɔ:tɪ] a altero(a), arrogante.

haul [hɔ:l] vt trascinare, tirare // n (of fish) pescata; (of stolen goods etc) bottino; **~age** n trasporto; autotrasporto; **~ier**, (US) **~er** n trasportatore m.

haunch [hɔ:ntʃ] n anca.

haunt [hɔ:nt] vt (subj: fear) pervadere; (: person) frequentare // n rifugio; a ghost ~s this house questa casa è abitata da un fantasma.

have [hæv], pt, pp **had** ◆ auxiliary vb **1** (gen) avere; essere; to ~ arrived/gone essere arrivato(a)/andato(a); to ~ eaten/slept avere mangiato/dormito; he has been kind/promoted è stato gentile/promosso; having finished or when he had finished, he left dopo aver finito, se n'è andato

2 (in tag questions): you've done it, ~n't you? l'ha fatto, (non è) vero?; he hasn't done it, has he? non l'ha fatto, vero?

3 (in short answers and questions): you've made a mistake — no I ~n't/so I ~ ha fatto un errore — ma no, niente affatto/sì, è vero; we ~n't paid — yes we ~! non abbiamo pagato — ma sì che abbiamo pagato!; I've been there before, ~ you? ci sono già stato, e lei?

◆ modal auxiliary vb (be obliged): to ~ (got) to do sth dover fare qc; I ~n't got or I don't ~ to wear glasses non ho bisogno di portare gli occhiali

◆ vt **1** (possess, obtain) avere; he has (got) blue eyes/dark hair ha gli occhi azzurri/i capelli scuri; do you ~ or ~ you got a car/phone? ha la macchina/il telefono?; may I ~ your address? potrebbe darmi il suo indirizzo?; you can ~ it for £5 te lo lascio per 5 sterline

2 (+ noun: take, keep etc): to ~ breakfast/a swim/a bath fare colazione/una nuotata/un bagno; to ~ lunch pranzare; to ~ dinner cenare; to ~ a drink bere qualcosa; to ~ a cigarette fumare una sigaretta

3: to ~ sth done far fare qc; to ~ one's hair cut farsi tagliare i capelli; to ~ sb do sth far fare qc a qn

4 (experience, suffer) avere; to ~ a cold/flu avere il raffreddore/l'influenza; she had her bag stolen le hanno rubato la borsa

5 (col: dupe): you've been had! ci sei cascato!

to have out vt: to ~ it out with sb (settle a problem etc) mettere le cose in chiaro con qn.

haven ['heɪvn] n porto; (fig) rifugio.

haven't ['hævnt] = **have not**.

haversack ['hævəsæk] n zaino.

havoc ['hævək] n caos m.

hawk [hɔ:k] n falco.

hay [heɪ] n fieno; **~ fever** n febbre f da fieno; **~stack** n pagliaio.

haywire ['heɪwaɪə*] a (col): to go ~ perdere la testa; impazzire.

hazard ['hæzəd] n azzardo, ventura; pericolo, rischio; to ~ (warning) lights npl (AUT) luci fpl di emergenza.

haze [heɪz] n foschia.

hazelnut ['heɪzlnʌt] n nocciola.

hazy ['heɪzɪ] a fosco(a); (idea) vago(a); (photograph) indistinto(a).

he [hi:] pronoun lui, egli; it is ~ who ... è lui che ....

head [hɛd] n testa, capo; (leader) capo //

vt (*list*) essere in testa a; (*group*) essere a capo di; **~s** (*or* **tails**) testa (o croce), pari (o dispari); **~ first** a capofitto, di testa; **~ over heels in love** pazzamente innamorato(a); **to ~ the ball** dare di testa alla palla; **to ~ for** *vt fus* dirigersi verso; **~ache** *n* mal *m* di testa; **~dress** *n* (*of Indian etc*) copricapo; (*of bride*) acconciatura; **~ing** *n* titolo; intestazione *f*; **~lamp** *n* (*Brit*) = **~light**; **~land** *n* promontorio; **~light** *n* fanale *m*; **~line** *n* titolo; **~long** *ad* (*fall*) a capofitto; (*rush*) precipitosamente; **~master** *n* preside *m*; **~mistress** *n* preside *f*; **~ office** *n* sede *f* (centrale); **~on** *a* (*collision*) frontale; **~phones** *npl* cuffia; **~quarters** (**HQ**) *npl* ufficio centrale; (*MIL*) quartiere *m* generale; **~rest** *n* poggiacapo; **~room** *n* (*in car*) altezza dell'abitacolo; (*under bridge*) altezza limite; **~scarf** *n* foulard *m inv*; **~strong** *a* testardo(a); **~ waiter** *n* capocameriere *m*; **~way** *n*: **to make ~way** fare progressi; **~wind** *n* controvento; **~y** *a* (*experience, period*) inebriante.

heal [hi:l] *vt, vi* guarire.

health [hɛlθ] *n* salute *f*; **~ food(s)** *n*(*pl*) alimenti *mpl* integrali; **the H~ Service** *n* (*Brit*) ≈ il Servizio Sanitario Statale; **~y** *a* (*person*) in buona salute; (*climate*) salubre; (*food*) salutare; (*attitude etc*) sano(a).

heap [hi:p] *n* mucchio // *vt* ammucchiare.

hear, *pt, pp* **heard** [hɪə*, hə:d] *vt* sentire; (*news*) ascoltare; (*lecture*) assistere a // *vi* sentire; **to ~ about** avere notizie di; sentire parlare di; **to ~ from sb** ricevere notizie da qn; **~ing** *n* (*sense*) udito; (*of witnesses*) audizione *f*; (*of a case*) udienza; **~ing aid** *n* apparecchio acustico; **~say** *n* dicerie *fpl*, chiacchiere *fpl*.

hearse [hə:s] *n* carro funebre.

heart [hɑ:t] *n* cuore *m*; **~s** *npl* (*CARDS*) cuori *mpl*; **at ~** in fondo; **by ~** (*learn, know*) a memoria; **~ attack** *n* attacco di cuore; **~beat** *n* battito del cuore; **~broken** *a*: **to be ~broken** avere il cuore spezzato; **~burn** *n* bruciore *m* di stomaco; **~ failure** *n* arresto cardiaco; **~felt** *a* sincero(a).

hearth [hɑ:θ] *n* focolare *m*.

heartily ['hɑ:tɪlɪ] *ad* (*laugh*) di cuore; (*eat*) di buon appetito; (*agree*) in pieno, completamente.

hearty ['hɑ:tɪ] *a* caloroso(a); robusto(a), sano(a); vigoroso(a).

heat [hi:t] *n* calore *m*; (*fig*) ardore *m*; fuoco; (*SPORT: also*: qualifying **~**) prova eliminatoria // *vt* scaldare; **to ~ up** *vi* (*liquids*) scaldarsi; (*room*) riscaldarsi // *vt* riscaldare; **~ed** *a* riscaldato(a); (*fig*) appassionato(a); acceso(a), eccitato(a); **~er** *n* stufa; radiatore *m*.

heath [hi:θ] *n* (*Brit*) landa.

heathen ['hi:ðn] *a, n* pagano(a).

heather ['hɛðə*] *n* erica.

heating ['hi:tɪŋ] *n* riscaldamento.

heatstroke ['hi:tstrəuk] *n* colpo di sole.

heatwave ['hi:tweɪv] *n* ondata di caldo.

heave [hi:v] *vt* sollevare (con forza) // *vi* sollevarsi; (*retch*) aver conati di vomito // *n* (*push*) grande spinta.

heaven ['hɛvn] *n* paradiso, cielo; **~ly** *a* divino(a), celeste.

heavily ['hɛvɪlɪ] *ad* pesantemente; (*drink, smoke*) molto.

heavy ['hɛvɪ] *a* pesante; (*sea*) grosso(a); (*rain*) forte; (*drinker, smoker*) gran (*before noun*); **~ goods vehicle** (**HGV**) *n* veicolo per trasporti pesanti; **~weight** *n* (*SPORT*) peso massimo.

Hebrew ['hi:bru:] *a* ebreo(a) // *n* (*LING*) ebraico.

Hebrides ['hɛbrɪdi:z] *npl*: **the ~** le Ebridi.

heckle ['hɛkl] *vt* interpellare e dare noia a (*un oratore*).

hectic ['hɛktɪk] *a* movimentato(a).

he'd [hi:d] = **he would, he had**.

hedge [hɛdʒ] *n* siepe *f* // *vi* essere elusivo(a); **to ~ one's bets** (*fig*) coprirsi dai rischi.

hedgehog ['hɛdʒhɔg] *n* riccio.

heed [hi:d] *vt* (*also*: **take ~ of**) badare a, far conto di; **~less** *a* sbadato(a).

heel [hi:l] *n* (*ANAT*) calcagno; (*of shoe*) tacco // *vt* (*shoe*) rifare i tacchi a.

hefty ['hɛftɪ] *a* (*person*) solido(a); (*parcel*) pesante; (*piece, price*) grosso(a).

heifer ['hɛfə*] *n* giovenca.

height [haɪt] *n* altezza; (*high ground*) altura; (*fig: of glory*) apice *m*; (: *of stupidity*) colmo; **~en** *vt* innalzare; (*fig*) accrescere.

heir [ɛə*] *n* erede *m*; **~ess** *n* erede *f*; **~loom** *n* mobile *m* (*or* gioiello *or* quadro) di famiglia.

held [hɛld] *pt, pp of* **hold**.

helicopter ['hɛlɪkɔptə*] *n* elicottero.

heliport ['hɛlɪpɔ:t] *n* eliporto.

helium ['hi:lɪəm] *n* elio.

hell [hɛl] *n* inferno; **~!** (*col*) porca miseria!, accidenti!

he'll [hi:l] = **he will, he shall**.

hellish ['hɛlɪʃ] *a* infernale.

hello [hə'ləu] *excl* buon giorno!; ciao! (*to sb one addresses as "tu"*); (*surprise*) ma guarda!

helm [hɛlm] *n* (*NAUT*) timone *m*.

helmet ['hɛlmɪt] *n* casco.

help [hɛlp] *n* aiuto; (*charwoman*) donna di servizio; (*assistant etc*) impiegato/a // *vt* aiutare; **~!** aiuto!; **~ yourself** (*to bread*) si serva (del pane); **he can't ~ it** non ci può far niente; **~er** *n* aiutante *m/f*, assistente *m/f*; **~ful** *a* di grande aiuto; (*useful*) utile; **~ing** *n* porzione *f*;

~less *a* impotente; debole.

hem [hɛm] *n* orlo // *vt* fare l'orlo a; **to ~ in** *vt* cingere.

he-man ['hi:mæn] *n* fusto.

hemisphere ['hɛmɪsfɪə*] *n* emisfero.

hemorrhage ['hɛmərɪdʒ] *n* (*US*) = **haemorrhage**.

hemorrhoids ['hɛmərɔɪdz] *npl* (*US*) = **haemorrhoids**.

hen [hɛn] *n* gallina.

hence [hɛns] *ad* (*therefore*) dunque; 2 **years ~** di qui a 2 anni; **~forth** *ad* d'ora in poi.

henchman ['hɛntʃmən] *n* (*pej*) caudatario.

henpecked ['hɛnpɛkt] *a* dominato dalla moglie.

hepatitis [hɛpə'taɪtɪs] *n* epatite *f*.

her [hə:*] *pronoun* (*direct*) la, l' + *vowel*; (*indirect*) le; (*stressed, after prep*) lei; *see note at* **she** // *a* il(la) suo(a), i(le) suoi(sue); *see also* **me, my**.

herald ['hɛrəld] *n* araldo // *vt* annunciare.

heraldry ['hɛrəldrɪ] *n* araldica.

herb [hə:b] *n* erba.

herd [hə:d] *n* mandria.

here [hɪə*] *ad* qui, qua // *excl* ehi!; **~!** (*at roll call*) presente!; **~ is/are** ecco; **~'s my sister** ecco mia sorella; **~ he is** eccolo/eccola; **~ she comes** eccola che viene; **~after** *ad* in futuro; dopo questo // *n:* **the ~after** l'al di là *m*; **~by** *ad* (*in letter*) con la presente.

hereditary [hɪ'rɛdɪtrɪ] *a* ereditario(a).

heresy ['hɛrəsɪ] *n* eresia.

heretic ['hɛrətɪk] *n* eretico/a.

heritage ['hɛrɪtɪdʒ] *n* eredità; (*fig*) retaggio.

hermetically [hə:'mɛtɪklɪ] *ad:* **~ sealed** ermeticamente chiuso(a).

hermit ['hə:mɪt] *n* eremita *m*.

hernia ['hə:nɪə] *n* ernia.

hero, ~es ['hɪərəu] *n* eroe *m*.

heroin ['hɛrəuɪn] *n* eroina.

heroine ['hɛrəuɪn] *n* eroina.

heron ['hɛrən] *n* airone *m*.

herring ['hɛrɪŋ] *n* aringa.

hers [hə:z] *pronoun* il(la) suo(a), i(le) suoi(sue); *see also* **mine**.

herself [hə:'sɛlf] *pronoun* (*reflexive*) si; (*emphatic*) lei stessa; (*after prep*) se stessa, sé; *see also* **oneself**.

he's [hi:z] = **he is, he has**.

hesitant ['hɛzɪtənt] *a* esitante, indeciso(a).

hesitate ['hɛzɪteɪt] *vi:* **to ~** (*about/to do*) esitare (su/a fare); **hesitation** [-'teɪʃən] *n* esitazione *f*.

heterosexual ['hɛtərəu'sɛksjuəl] *a, n* eterosessuale (*m/f*).

hexagon ['hɛksəgən] *n* esagono.

heyday ['heɪdeɪ] *n:* **the ~ of** i bei giorni di, l'età d'oro di.

HGV *n abbr* = **heavy goods vehicle**.

hi [haɪ] *excl* ciao!

hiatus [haɪ'eɪtəs] *n* vuoto; (*LING*) iato.

hibernate ['haɪbəneɪt] *vi* ibernare.

hiccough, hiccup ['hɪkʌp] *vi* singhiozzare // *n* singhiozzo.

hide [haɪd] *n* (*skin*) pelle *f* // *vb* (*pt* **hid**, *pp* **hidden** ['hɪd, 'hɪdn]) *vt:* **to ~ sth (from sb)** nascondere qc (a qn) // *vi:* **to ~ (from sb)** nascondersi (da qn); **~-and-seek** *n* rimpiattino; **~away** *n* nascondiglio.

hideous ['hɪdɪəs] *a* laido(a); orribile.

hiding ['haɪdɪŋ] *n* (*beating*) bastonata; **to be in ~** (*concealed*) tenersi nascosto(a).

hierarchy ['haɪərɑ:kɪ] *n* gerarchia.

hi-fi ['haɪfaɪ] *n* stereo // *a* ad alta fedeltà, hi-fi *inv*.

high [haɪ] *a* alto(a); (*speed, respect, number*) grande; (*wind*) forte // *ad* alto, in alto; **20m ~** alto(a) 20m; **~boy** *n* (*US: tallboy*) cassettone *m*; **~brow** *a, n* intellettuale (*m/f*); **~chair** *n* seggiolone *m*; **~er education** *n* studi *mpl* superiori; **~-handed** *a* prepotente; **~jack** *vt* = **hijack**; **~ jump** *n* (*SPORT*) salto in alto; **the H~lands** *npl* le Highlands scozzesi; **~light** *n* (*fig: of event*) momento culminante // *vt* mettere in evidenza; **~ly** *ad* molto; **~ly strung** *a* teso(a) di nervi, eccitabile; **~ness** *n* altezza; **Her H~ness** Sua Altezza; **~-pitched** *a* acuto(a); **~-rise block** *n* palazzone *m*; **~ school** *n* scuola secondaria; (*US*) istituto superiore d'istruzione; **~ season** *n* (*Brit*) alta stagione; **~ street** *n* (*Brit*) strada principale.

highway ['haɪweɪ] *n* strada maestra; **H~ Code** *n* (*Brit*) codice *m* della strada.

hijack ['haɪdʒæk] *vt* dirottare; **~er** *n* dirottatore/trice.

hike [haɪk] *vi* fare un'escursione a piedi // *n* escursione *f* a piedi; (*in prices*) aumento; **~r** *n* escursionista *m/f*.

hilarious [hɪ'lɛərɪəs] *a* (*behaviour, event*) che fa schiantare dal ridere.

hilarity [hɪ'lærɪtɪ] *n* ilarità.

hill [hɪl] *n* collina, colle *m*; (*fairly high*) montagna; (*on road*) salita; **~side** *n* fianco della collina; **~y** *a* collinoso(a); montagnoso(a).

hilt [hɪlt] *n* (*of sword*) elsa; **to the ~** (*fig: support*) fino in fondo.

him [hɪm] *pronoun* (*direct*) lo, l' + *vowel*; (*indirect*) gli; (*stressed, after prep*) lui; *see also* **me**; **~self** *pronoun* (*reflexive*) si; (*emphatic*) lui stesso; (*after prep*) se stesso, sé; *see also* **oneself**.

hind [haɪnd] *a* posteriore // *n* cerva.

hinder ['hɪndə*] *vt* ostacolare; (*delay*) tardare; (*prevent*): **to ~ sb from doing** impedire a qn di fare; **hindrance** ['hɪndrəns] *n* ostacolo, impedimento.

hindsight ['haɪndsaɪt] *n:* **with ~** con il

senno di poi.

Hindu ['hindu:] *n* indù *m/f inv*.

hinge [hɪndʒ] *n* cardine *m* // *vi* (*fig*): **to ~ on** dipendere da.

hint [hɪnt] *n* accenno, allusione *f*; (*advice*) consiglio // *vt*: **to ~ that** lasciar capire che // *vi*: **to ~ at** accennare a.

hip [hɪp] *n* anca, fianco.

hippopotamus, *pl* **~es** *or* **hippopotami** [hɪpə'pɔtəməs, -'pɔtəmai] *n* ippopotamo.

hire ['haɪə*] *vt* (*Brit*: *car*, *equipment*) noleggiare; (*worker*) assumere, dare lavoro a // *n* nolo, noleggio; **for ~** da nolo; (*taxi*) libero(a); **~ purchase (H.P.)** *n* (*Brit*) acquisto (*or* vendita) rateale.

his [hɪz] *a*, *pronoun* il(la) suo(sua), i(le) suoi(sue); *see also* **my**, **mine**.

hiss [hɪs] *vi* fischiare; (*cat*, *snake*) sibilare // *n* fischio; sibilo.

historic(al) [hɪ'stɔrɪk(l)] *a* storico(a).

history ['hɪstərɪ] *n* storia.

hit [hɪt] *vt* (*pt*, *pp* **hit**) colpire, picchiare; (*knock against*) battere; (*reach*: *target*) raggiungere; (*collide with*: *car*) urtare contro; (*fig*: *affect*) colpire; (*find*: *problem etc*) incontrare // *n* colpo; (*success*, *song*) successo; **to ~ it off with sb** andare molto d'accordo con qn; **~-and-run driver** *n* pirata *m* della strada.

hitch [hɪtʃ] *vt* (*fasten*) attaccare; (*also*: **~ up**) tirare su // *n* (*difficulty*) intoppo, difficoltà *f inv*; **to ~ a lift** fare l'autostop.

hitch-hike ['hɪtʃhaɪk] *vi* fare l'autostop; **~r** *n* autostoppista *m/f*.

hi-tech ['haɪ'tɛk] *a* di alta tecnologia // *n* alta tecnologia.

hitherto [hɪðə'tu:] *ad* in precedenza.

hive [haɪv] *n* alveare *m*; **to ~ off** *vt* separare.

H.M.S. *abbr* = *His* (*Her*) *Majesty's Ship*.

hoard [hɔ:d] *n* (*of food*) provviste *fpl*; (*of money*) gruzzolo // *vt* ammassare.

hoarding ['hɔ:dɪŋ] *n* (*Brit*: *for posters*) tabellone *m* per affissioni.

hoarfrost ['hɔ:frɔst] *n* brina.

hoarse [hɔ:s] *a* rauco(a).

hoax [həuks] *n* scherzo; falso allarme.

hob [hɔb] *n* piastra (con fornelli).

hobble ['hɔbl] *vi* zoppicare.

hobby ['hɔbɪ] *n* hobby *m inv*, passatempo; **~-horse** *n* (*fig*) chiodo fisso.

hobo ['həubəu] *n* (*US*) vagabondo.

hockey ['hɔkɪ] *n* hockey *m*.

hoe [həu] *n* zappa.

hog [hɔg] *n* maiale *m* // *vt* (*fig*) arraffare; **to go the whole ~** farlo fino in fondo.

hoist [hɔɪst] *n* paranco // *vt* issare.

hold [həuld] *vb* (*pt*, *pp* **held**) *vt* tenere; (*contain*) contenere; (*keep back*) trattenere; (*believe*) mantenere;

considerare; (*possess*) avere, possedere; detenere // *vi* (*withstand pressure*) tenere; (*be valid*) essere valido(a) // *n* presa; (*fig*) potere *m*; (*NAUT*) stiva; **~ the line!** (*TEL*) resti in linea!; **to ~ one's own** (*fig*) difendersi bene; **to catch** *or* **get** (a) **~ of** afferrare; **to get ~ of** (*fig*) trovare; **to ~ back** *vt* trattenere; (*secret*) tenere celato(a); **to ~ down** *vt* (*person*) tenere a terra; (*job*) tenere; **to ~ off** *vt* tener lontano; **to ~ on** *vi* tener fermo; (*wait*) aspettare; **~ on!** (*TEL*) resti in linea!; **to ~ on to** *vt fus* tenersi stretto(a) a; (*keep*) conservare; **to ~ out** *vt* offrire // *vi* (*resist*) resistere; **to ~ up** *vt* (*raise*) alzare; (*support*) sostenere; (*delay*) ritardare; **~all** *n* (*Brit*) borsone *m*; **~er** *n* (*of ticket*, *title*) possessore/posseditrice; (*of office etc*) incaricato/a; (*of record*) detentore/trice; **~ing** *n* (*share*) azioni *fpl*, titoli *mpl*; (*farm*) podere *m*, tenuta; **~up** *n* (*robbery*) rapina a mano armata; (*delay*) ritardo; (*Brit*: *in traffic*) blocco.

hole [həul] *n* buco, buca // *vt* bucare.

holiday ['hɔlədɪ] *n* vacanza; (*day off*) giorno di vacanza; (*public*) giorno festivo; **on ~** in vacanza; **~ camp** *n* (*for children*) colonia (di villeggiatura); (*also*: **~ centre**) *n* villaggio (di vacanze); **~-maker** *n* (*Brit*) villeggiante *m/f*; **~ resort** *n* luogo di villeggiatura.

holiness ['həulɪnɪs] *n* santità.

Holland ['hɔlənd] *n* Olanda.

hollow ['hɔləu] *a* cavo(a), vuoto(a); (*fig*) falso(a); vano(a) // *n* cavità *f inv*; (*in land*) valletta, depressione *f* // *vt*: **to ~ out** scavare.

holly ['hɔlɪ] *n* agrifoglio.

holocaust ['hɔləkɔ:st] *n* olocausto.

holster ['həulstə*] *n* fondina (di pistola).

holy ['həulɪ] *a* santo(a); (*bread*) benedetto(a), consacrato(a); (*ground*) consacrato(a); **H~ Ghost** *or* **Spirit** *n* Spirito Santo; **~ orders** *npl* ordini *mpl* (sacri).

homage ['hɔmɪdʒ] *n* omaggio; **to pay ~ to** rendere omaggio a.

home [həum] *n* casa; (*country*) patria; (*institution*) casa, ricovero // *a* familiare; (*cooking etc*) casalingo(a); (*ECON*, *POL*) nazionale, interno(a) // *ad* a casa; in patria; (*right in*: *nail etc*) fino in fondo; **at ~** a casa; **to go** (*or* **come**) **~** tornare a casa (*or* in patria); **make yourself at ~** si metta a suo agio; **~ address** *n* indirizzo di casa; **~ computer** *n* home computer *m inv*; **~land** *n* patria; **~less** *a* senza tetto; spatriato(a); **~ly** *a* semplice, alla buona; accogliente; **~-made** *a* casalingo(a); **H~ Office** *n* (*Brit*) ministero degli Interni; **~ rule** *n* autogoverno; **H~ Secretary** n (*Brit*) ministro degli Interni; **~sick** a: to be **~sick** avere la nostalgia; **~ town** n città f inv natale; **~ward** ['həumwəd] a (*journey*) di ritorno; **~work** n compiti mpl (per casa).

homicide ['hɔmɪsaɪd] n (*US*) omicidio.

homoeopathy [həumɪ'ɔpəθi] n omeopatia.

homogeneous [hɔməu'dʒi:nɪəs] a omogeneo(a).

homosexual [hɔməu'sɛksjuəl] a, n omosessuale (*m/f*).

honest ['ɔnɪst] a onesto(a); sincero(a); **~ly** ad onestamente; sinceramente; **~y** n onestà.

honey ['hʌnɪ] n miele m; **~comb** n favo; **~moon** n luna di miele, viaggio di nozze; **~suckle** n (*BOT*) caprifoglio.

honk [hɔŋk] vi suonare il clacson.

honorary ['ɔnərərɪ] a onorario(a); (*duty, title*) onorifico(a).

honour, (*US* **honor**) ['ɔnə*] vt onorare // n onore m; **~able** a onorevole; **~s degree** n (*SCOL*) laurea specializzata.

hood [hud] n cappuccio; (*Brit AUT*) capote f; (*US AUT*) cofano.

hoodlum ['hu:dləm] n teppista m/f.

hoodwink ['hudwɪŋk] vt infinocchiare.

hoof [hu:f], pl **~s** or **hooves** n zoccolo.

hook [huk] n gancio; (*for fishing*) amo // vt uncinare; (*dress*) agganciare.

hooligan ['hu:lɪgən] n giovinastro, teppista m.

hoop [hu:p] n cerchio.

hoot [hu:t] vi (*AUT*) suonare il clacson; **~er** n (*Brit AUT*) clacson m inv; (*NAUT*) sirena.

hoover ['hu:və*] ® (*Brit*) n aspirapolvere m inv // vt pulire con l'aspirapolvere.

hooves [hu:vz] npl of **hoof**.

hop [hɔp] vi saltellare, saltare; (*on one foot*) saltare su una gamba // n salto.

hope [həup] vt, vi sperare // n speranza; I **~ so/not** spero di sì/no; **~ful** a (*person*) pieno(a) di speranza; (*situation*) promettente; **~fully** ad con speranza; **~fully he will recover** speriamo che si riprenda; **~less** a senza speranza, disperato(a); (*useless*) inutile.

hops [hɔps] npl luppoli mpl.

horde [hɔ:d] n orda.

horizon [hə'raɪzn] n orizzonte m; **~tal** [hɔrɪ'zɔntl] a orizzontale.

hormone ['hɔ:məun] n ormone m.

horn [hɔ:n] n (*ZOOL, MUS*) corno; (*AUT*) clacson m inv.

hornet ['hɔ:nɪt] n calabrone m.

horny ['hɔ:nɪ] a corneo(a); (*hands*) calloso(a); (*col*) arrapato(a).

horoscope ['hɔrəskəup] n oroscopo.

horrendous [hə'rɛndəs] a orrendo(a).

horrible ['hɔrɪbl] a orribile, tremendo(a).

horrid ['hɔrɪd] a orrido(a); (*person*)

antipatico(a).

horrify ['hɔrɪfaɪ] vt scandalizzare.

horror ['hɔrə*] n orrore m; **~ film** n film m inv dell'orrore.

hors d'œuvre [ɔ:'də:vrə] n antipasto.

horse [hɔ:s] n cavallo; **~ back** a: on **~back** a cavallo; **~ chestnut** n ippocastano; **~man** n cavaliere m; **~power** (**h.p.**) n cavallo (vapore); **~racing** n ippica; **~radish** n rafano; **~shoe** n ferro di cavallo; **~woman** n amazzone f.

horticulture ['hɔ:tɪkʌltʃə*] n orticoltura.

hose [həuz] n (*also*: **~pipe**) tubo; (*also*: **garden ~**) tubo per annaffiare.

hospice ['hɔspɪs] n ricovero, ospizio.

hospitable [hɔs'pɪtəbl] a ospitale.

hospital ['hɔspɪtl] n ospedale m.

hospitality [hɔspɪ'tælɪtɪ] n ospitalità.

host [həust] n ospite m; (*REL*) ostia; (*large number*): a **~ of** una schiera di.

hostage ['hɔstɪdʒ] n ostaggio/a.

hostel ['hɔstl] n ostello; (*also*: **youth ~**) ostello della gioventù.

hostess ['həustɪs] n ospite f; (*Brit*: **air ~**) hostess f inv; (*in nightclub*) entraîneuse f inv.

hostile ['hɔstaɪl] a ostile.

hostility [hɔ'stɪlɪtɪ] n ostilità f inv.

hot [hɔt] a caldo(a); (*as opposed to only warm*) molto caldo(a); (*spicy*) piccante; (*fig*) accanito(a); ardente; violento(a), focoso(a); to be **~** (*person*) aver caldo; (*object*) essere caldo(a); (*weather*) far caldo; **~bed** n (*fig*) focolaio; **~ dog** n hot dog m inv.

hotel [həu'tɛl] n albergo; **~ier** n albergatore/trice.

hot: **~headed** a focoso(a), eccitabile; **~house** n serra; **~ line** n (*POL*) telefono rosso; **~ly** ad violentemente; **~plate** n (*on cooker*) piastra riscaldante; **~water bottle** n borsa dell'acqua calda.

hound [haund] vt perseguitare // n segugio.

hour ['auə*] n ora; **~ly** a all'ora // ad ogni ora; **~ly paid** a pagato(a) a ore.

house n [haus] (pl **~s** ['hauzɪz]) (*also*: *firm*) casa; (*POL*) camera; (*THEATRE*) sala; pubblico; spettacolo // vt [hauz] (*person*) ospitare, alloggiare; **on the ~** (*fig*) offerto(a) dalla casa; **~boat** n house boat f inv; **~breaking** n furto con scasso; **~coat** n vestaglia; **~hold** n famiglia; casa; **~keeper** n governante f; **~keeping** n (*work*) governo della casa; **~keeping** (*money*) soldi mpl per le spese di casa; **~warming party** n festa per inaugurare la casa nuova; **~wife** n massaia, casalinga; **~work** n faccende fpl domestiche.

housing ['hauzɪŋ] n alloggio; **~ development**, (*Brit*) **~ estate** n zona residenziale con case popolari e/o *private.*

hovel ['hɔvl] *n* casupola.

hover ['hɔvə*] *vi* (*bird*) librarsi; (*helicopter*) volare a punto fisso; **~craft** *n* hovercraft *m inv.*

how [hau] *ad* come; **~ are you?** come sta?; **~ do you do?** piacere!; **~ far is it to the river?** quanto è lontano il fiume?; **~ long have you been here?** da quando è qui?; **~ lovely!/awful!** che bello!/orrore!; **~ many?** quanti(e)?; **~ much?** quanto(a)?; **~ much milk?** quanto latte?; **~ many people?** quante persone?; **~ old are you?** quanti anni ha?; **~ever** *ad* in qualsiasi modo *or* maniera che; (+ *adjective*) per quanto + *sub*; (*in questions*) come // *cj* comunque, però.

howl [haul] *n* ululato // *vi* ululare.

h.p., H.P. *abbr* = **hire purchase, horsepower.**

HQ *n abbr* = **headquarters.**

hub [hʌb] *n* (*of wheel*) mozzo; (*fig*) fulcro.

hubbub ['hʌbʌb] *n* baccano.

hub cap *n* coprimozzo.

huddle ['hʌdl] *vi:* **to ~ together** rannicchiarsi l'uno contro l'altro.

hue [hju:] *n* tinta; **~ and cry** *n* clamore *m.*

huff [hʌf] *n*: **in a ~** stizzito(a).

hug [hʌg] *vt* abbracciare; (*shore, kerb*) stringere // *n* abbraccio, stretta.

huge [hju:dʒ] *a* enorme, immenso(a).

hulk [hʌlk] *n* (*ship*) nave *f* in disarmo; (*building, car*) carcassa; (*person*) mastodonte *m.*

hull [hʌl] *n* (*of ship*) scafo.

hullo [hə'ləu] *excl* = **hello.**

hum [hʌm] *vt* (*tune*) canticchiare // *vi* canticchiare; (*insect, plane, tool*) ronzare.

human ['hju:mən] *a* umano(a) // *n* essere *m* umano.

humane [hju:'meɪn] *a* umanitario(a).

humanitarian [hju:mænɪ'teərɪən] *a* umanitario(a).

humanity [hju:'mænɪtɪ] *n* umanità.

humble ['hʌmbl] *a* umile, modesto(a) // *vt* umiliare.

humbug ['hʌmbʌg] *n* inganno; sciocchezze *fpl.*

humdrum ['hʌmdrʌm] *a* monotono(a), tedioso(a).

humid ['hju:mɪd] *a* umido(a).

humiliate [hju:'mɪlɪeɪt] *vt* umiliare; **humiliation** [-'eɪʃən] *n* umiliazione *f.*

humility [hju:'mɪlɪtɪ] *n* umiltà.

humorous ['hju:mərəs] *a* umoristico(a); (*person*) buffo(a).

humour, (*US*) **humor** ['hju:mə*] *n* umore *m* // *vt* (*person*) compiacere; (*sb's whims*) assecondare.

hump [hʌmp] *n* gobba.

hunch [hʌntʃ] *n* gobba; (*premonition*)

intuizione *f*; **~back** *n* gobbo/a; **~ed** *a* incurvato(a).

hundred ['hʌndrəd] *num* cento; **~s of** centinaia *fpl* di; **~weight** *n* (*Brit*) = 50.8 kg; 112 lb; (*US*) = 45.3 kg; 100 lb.

hung [hʌŋ] *pt, pp of* **hang.**

Hungary ['hʌŋgərɪ] *n* Ungheria.

hunger ['hʌŋgə*] *n* fame *f* // *vi*: **to ~ for** desiderare ardentemente.

hungry ['hʌŋgrɪ] *a* affamato(a); **to be ~** aver fame.

hunk [hʌŋk] *n* (*of bread etc*) bel pezzo.

hunt [hʌnt] *vt* (*seek*) cercare; (*SPORT*) cacciare // *vi* andare a caccia // *n* caccia; **~er** *n* cacciatore *m*; **~ing** *n* caccia.

hurdle ['hə:dl] *n* (*SPORT, fig*) ostacolo.

hurl [hə:l] *vt* lanciare con violenza.

hurrah, hurray [hu'rɑ:, hu'reɪ] *excl* urra!, evviva!

hurricane ['hʌrɪkən] *n* uragano.

hurried ['hʌrɪd] *a* affrettato(a); (*work*) fatto(a) in fretta; **~ly** *ad* in fretta.

hurry ['hʌrɪ] *n* fretta // *vb* (*also:* **~ up**) *vi* affrettarsi // *vt* (*person*) affrettare; (*work*) far in fretta; **to be in a ~** aver fretta; **to do sth in a ~** fare qc in fretta; **to ~ in/out** entrare/uscire in fretta.

hurt [hə:t] *vb* (*pt, pp* **hurt**) *vt* (*cause pain to*) far male a; (*injure, fig*) ferire // *vi* far male // *a* ferito(a); **~ful** *a* (*remark*) che ferisce.

hurtle ['hə:tl] *vt* scagliare // *vi*: **to ~ past/down** passare/scendere a razzo.

husband ['hʌzbənd] *n* marito.

hush [hʌʃ] *n* silenzio, calma // *vt* zittire; **~!** zitto(a)!

husk [hʌsk] *n* (*of wheat*) cartoccio; (*of rice, maize*) buccia.

husky ['hʌskɪ] *a* roco(a) // *n* cane *m* eschimese.

hustle ['hʌsl] *vt* spingere, incalzare // *n* pigia pigia *m inv*; **~ and bustle** *n* trambusto.

hut [hʌt] *n* rifugio; (*shed*) ripostiglio.

hutch [hʌtʃ] *n* gabbia.

hyacinth ['haɪəsɪnθ] *n* giacinto.

hybrid ['haɪbrɪd] *a* ibrido(a) // *n* ibrido.

hydrant ['haɪdrənt] *n* (*also:* **fire ~**) idrante *m.*

hydraulic [haɪ'drɔ:lɪk] *a* idraulico(a).

hydroelectric [haɪdrəu'lektrɪk] *a* idroelettrico(a).

hydrofoil ['haɪdrəufɔɪl] *n* aliscafo.

hydrogen ['haɪdrədʒən] *n* idrogeno.

hyena [haɪ'i:nə] *n* iena.

hygiene ['haɪdʒi:n] *n* igiene *f.*

hymn [hɪm] *n* inno; cantica.

hype [haɪp] *n* (*col*) campagna pubblicitaria.

hypermarket ['haɪpəmɑ:kɪt] *n* ipermercato.

hyphen ['haɪfn] *n* trattino.

hypnotism ['hɪpnətɪzm] *n* ipnotismo.

hypnotize ['hɪpnətaɪz] *vt* ipnotizzare.

hypocrisy [hɪˈpɔkrɪsɪ] *n* ipocrisia.

hypocrite [ˈhɪpəkrɪt] *n* ipocrita *m/f*; **hypocritical** [-ˈkrɪtɪkl] *a* ipocrita.

hypothermia [haɪpəʊˈθɜːmɪə] *n* ipotermia.

hypothesis, *pl* **hypotheses** [haɪˈpɔθɪsɪs, -siːz] *n* ipotesi *f inv*.

hypothetical [haɪpəʊˈθɛtɪkl] *a* ipotetico(a).

hysterical [hɪˈstɛrɪkl] *a* isterico(a).

hysterics [hɪˈstɛrɪks] *npl* accesso di isteria; (*laughter*) attacco di riso.

I

I [aɪ] *pronoun* io.

ice [aɪs] *n* ghiaccio; (*on road*) gelo // *vt* (*cake*) glassare; (*drink*) mettere in fresco // *vi* (*also:* ~ **over**) ghiacciare; (*also:* ~ **up**) gelare; ~ **axe** *n* piccozza da ghiaccio; ~**berg** *n* iceberg *m inv*; ~**box** *n* (*US*) frigorifero; (*Brit*) reparto ghiaccio; (*insulated box*) frigo portatile; ~ **cream** *n* gelato; ~ **hockey** *n* hockey *m* su ghiaccio.

Iceland [ˈaɪslənd] *n* Islanda.

ice: ~ **lolly** *n* (*Brit*) ghiacciolo; ~ **rink** *n* pista di pattinaggio; ~ **skating** *n* pattinaggio sul ghiaccio.

icicle [ˈaɪsɪkl] *n* ghiacciolo.

icing [ˈaɪsɪŋ] *n* (*AVIAT etc*) patina di ghiaccio; (*CULIN*) glassa; ~ **sugar** *n* (*Brit*) zucchero a velo.

icy [ˈaɪsɪ] *a* ghiacciato(a); (*weather, temperature*) gelido(a).

I'd [aɪd] = **I would, I had**.

idea [aɪˈdɪə] *n* idea.

ideal [aɪˈdɪəl] *a, n* ideale (*m*).

identical [aɪˈdɛntɪkl] *a* identico(a).

identification [aɪdɛntɪfɪˈkeɪʃən] *n* identificazione *f*; **means of** ~ carta d'identità.

identify [aɪˈdɛntɪfaɪ] *vt* identificare.

identikit picture [aɪˈdɛntɪkɪt-] *n* identikit *m inv*.

identity [aɪˈdɛntɪtɪ] *n* identità *f inv*; ~ **card** *n* carta d'identità.

idiom [ˈɪdɪəm] *n* idioma *m*; (*phrase*) espressione *f* idiomatica.

idiot [ˈɪdɪət] *n* idiota *m/f*; ~**ic** [-ˈɔtɪk] *a* idiota.

idle [ˈaɪdl] *a* inattivo(a); (*lazy*) pigro(a), ozioso(a); (*unemployed*) disoccupato(a); (*question, pleasures*) ozioso(a); **to lie** ~ stare fermo, non funzionare; **to** ~ **away** *vt* (*time*) sprecare, buttar via.

idol [ˈaɪdl] *n* idolo; ~**ize** *vt* idoleggiare.

i.e. *ad abbr* (= *that is*) cioè.

if [ɪf] *cj* se; ~ **I were you** ... se fossi in te ..., io al tuo posto ...; ~ **so** se è così; ~ **not** se no; ~ **only** se solo *or* soltanto.

ignite [ɪgˈnaɪt] *vt* accendere // *vi* accendersi.

ignition [ɪgˈnɪʃən] *n* (*AUT*) accensione *f*;

---

to switch on/off the ~ accendere/ spegnere il motore; ~ **key** *n* (*AUT*) chiave *f* dell'accensione.

ignorant [ˈɪgnərənt] *a* ignorante; **to be** ~ **of** (*subject*) essere ignorante in; (*events*) essere ignaro(a) di.

ignore [ɪgˈnɔː*] *vt* non tener conto di; (*person, fact*) ignorare.

I'll [aɪl] = **I will, I shall**.

ill [ɪl] *a* (*sick*) malato(a); (*bad*) cattivo(a) // *n* male *m* // *ad:* **to speak etc** ~ **of sb** parlare *etc* male di qn; **to take** *or* **be taken** ~ ammalarsi; ~-**advised** *a* (*decision*) poco giudizioso(a); (*person*) mal consigliato(a); ~-**at-ease** *a* a disagio.

illegal [ɪˈliːgl] *a* illegale.

illegible [ɪˈlɛdʒɪbl] *a* illeggibile.

illegitimate [ɪlɪˈdʒɪtɪmət] *a* illegittimo(a).

ill-fated [ɪlˈfeɪtɪd] *a* nefasto(a).

ill feeling *n* rancore *m*.

illiterate [ɪˈlɪtərət] *a* analfabeta, illetterato(a); (*letter*) scorretto(a).

illness [ˈɪlnɪs] *n* malattia.

ill-treat [ɪlˈtriːt] *vt* maltrattare.

illuminate [ɪˈluːmɪneɪt] *vt* illuminare; **illumination** [-ˈneɪʃən] *n* illuminazione *f*.

illusion [ɪˈluːʒən] *n* illusione *f*; **to be under the** ~ **that** avere l'impressione che.

illustrate [ˈɪləstreɪt] *vt* illustrare; **illustration** [-ˈstreɪʃən] *n* illustrazione *f*.

ill will *n* cattiva volontà.

I'm [aɪm] = **I am**.

image [ˈɪmɪdʒ] *n* immagine *f*; (*public face*) immagine (pubblica); ~**ry** *n* immagini *fpl*.

imaginary [ɪˈmædʒɪnərɪ] *a* immaginario(a).

imagination [ɪmædʒɪˈneɪʃən] *n* immaginazione *f*, fantasia.

imaginative [ɪˈmædʒɪnətɪv] *a* immaginoso(a).

imagine [ɪˈmædʒɪn] *vt* immaginare.

imbalance [ɪmˈbæləns] *n* squilibrio.

imitate [ˈɪmɪteɪt] *vt* imitare; **imitation** [-ˈteɪʃən] *n* imitazione *f*.

immaculate [ɪˈmækjulət] *a* immacolato(a); (*dress, appearance*) impeccabile.

immaterial [ɪməˈtɪərɪəl] *a* immateriale, indifferente.

immature [ɪməˈtjuə*] *a* immaturo(a).

immediate [ɪˈmiːdɪət] *a* immediato(a); ~**ly** *ad* (*at once*) subito, immediatamente; ~**ly next to** proprio accanto a.

immense [ɪˈmɛns] *a* immenso(a); enorme.

immerse [ɪˈmɜːs] *vt* immergere.

immersion heater [ɪˈmɜːʃən-] *n* (*Brit*) scaldacqua *m inv* a immersione.

immigrant [ˈɪmɪgrənt] *n* immigrante *m/ f*; immigrato/a.

immigration [ˌɪmɪ'greɪʃən] *n* immigrazione *f*.
imminent ['ɪmɪnənt] *a* imminente.
immoral [ɪ'mɒrl] *a* immorale.
immortal [ɪ'mɔːtl] *a*, *n* immortale (*m/f*).
immune [ɪ'mjuːn] *a*: ~ (**to**) immune (da).
immunity [ɪ'mjuːnɪtɪ] *n* immunità.
imp [ɪmp] *n* folletto, diavoletto; (*child*) diavoletto.
impact ['ɪmpækt] *n* impatto.
impair [ɪm'pɛə*] *vt* danneggiare.
impart [ɪm'pɑːt] *vt* (*make known*) comunicare; (*bestow*) impartire.
impartial [ɪm'pɑːʃl] *a* imparziale.
impassable [ɪm'pɑːsəbl] *a* insuperabile; (*road*) impraticabile.
impassive [ɪm'pæsɪv] *a* impassibile.
impatience [ɪm'peɪʃəns] *n* impazienza.
impatient [ɪm'peɪʃənt] *a* impaziente; **to get** *or* **grow** ~ perdere la pazienza.
impeccable [ɪm'pɛkəbl] *a* impeccabile.
impede [ɪm'piːd] *vt* impedire.
impediment [ɪm'pedɪmənt] *n* impedimento; (*also*: **speech** ~) difetto di pronuncia.
impending [ɪm'pendɪŋ] *a* imminente.
imperative [ɪm'pɛrətɪv] *a* imperativo(a); necessario(a), urgente; (*voice*) imperioso(a) // *n* (*LING*) imperativo.
imperfect [ɪm'pɜːfɪkt] *a* imperfetto(a); (*goods etc*) difettoso(a).
imperial [ɪm'pɪərɪəl] *a* imperiale; (*measure*) legale.
impersonal [ɪm'pɜːsənl] *a* impersonale.
impersonate [ɪm'pɜːsəneɪt] *vt* impersonare; (*THEATRE*) fare la mimica di.
impertinent [ɪm'pɜːtɪnənt] *a* insolente, impertinente.
impervious [ɪm'pɜːvɪəs] *a* impermeabile; (*fig*): ~ **to** insensibile a; impassibile di fronte a.
impetuous [ɪm'petjuəs] *a* impetuoso(a), precipitoso(a).
impetus ['ɪmpətəs] *n* impeto.
impinge [ɪm'pɪndʒ]: **to** ~ **on** *vt fus* (*person*) colpire; (*rights*) ledere.
implement *n* ['ɪmplɪmənt] attrezzo; (*for cooking*) utensile *m* // *vt* ['ɪmplɪmənt] effettuare.
implicit [ɪm'plɪsɪt] *a* implicito(a); (*complete*) completo(a).
imply [ɪm'plaɪ] *vt* insinuare; suggerire.
impolite [ɪmpə'laɪt] *a* scortese.
import *vt* [ɪm'pɔːt] importare // *n* ['ɪmpɔːt] (*COMM*) importazione *f*; (*meaning*) significato, senso.
importance [ɪm'pɔːtns] *n* importanza.
important [ɪm'pɔːtnt] *a* importante; **it's not** ~ non ha importanza.
importer [ɪm'pɔːtə*] *n* importatore/trice.
impose [ɪm'pəuz] *vt* imporre // *vi*: **to** ~ **on sb** sfruttare la bontà di qn.
imposing [ɪm'pəuzɪŋ] *a* imponente.

imposition [ɪmpə'zɪʃən] *n* (*of tax etc*) imposizione *f*; **to be an** ~ **on** (*person*) abusare della gentilezza di.
impossibility [ɪmpɒsə'bɪlɪtɪ] *n* impossibilità.
impossible [ɪm'pɒsɪbl] *a* impossibile.
impotent ['ɪmpətnt] *a* impotente.
impound [ɪm'paund] *vt* confiscare.
impoverished [ɪm'pɒvərɪʃt] *a* impoverito(a).
impractical [ɪm'præktɪkl] *a* non pratico(a).
impregnable [ɪm'pregnəbl] *a* (*fortress*) inespugnabile; (*fig*) inoppugnabile; irrefutabile.
impress [ɪm'pres] *vt* impressionare; (*mark*) imprimere, stampare; **to** ~ **sth on sb** far capire qc a qn.
impression [ɪm'preʃən] *n* impressione *f*; **to be under the** ~ **that** avere l'impressione che.
impressive [ɪm'presɪv] *a* impressionante.
imprint ['ɪmprɪnt] *n* (*PUBLISHING*) sigla editoriale.
imprison [ɪm'prɪzn] *vt* imprigionare; ~**ment** *n* imprigionamento.
improbable [ɪm'prɒbəbl] *a* improbabile; (*excuse*) inverosimile.
impromptu [ɪm'prɒmptjuː] *a* improvvisato(a).
improper [ɪm'prɒpə*] *a* scorretto(a); (*unsuitable*) inadatto(a), improprio(a); sconveniente, indecente.
improve [ɪm'pruːv] *vt* migliorare // *vi* migliorare; (*pupil etc*) fare progressi; ~**ment** *n* miglioramento; progresso.
improvise ['ɪmprəvaɪz] *vt*, *vi* improvvisare.
impudent ['ɪmpjudnt] *a* impudente, sfacciato(a).
impulse ['ɪmpʌls] *n* impulso; **on** ~ d'impulso, impulsivamente.
impulsive [ɪm'pʌlsɪv] *a* impulsivo(a).
in [ɪn] ◆ *prep* **1** (*indicating place, position*) in; ~ **the house/garden** in casa/giardino; ~ **the box** nella scatola; ~ **the fridge** nel frigorifero; **I have it** ~ **my hand** ce l'ho in mano; ~ **town/the country** in città/campagna; ~ **school** a scuola; ~ **here/there** qui/lì dentro
2 (*with place names: of town, region, country*): ~ **London** a Londra; ~ **England** in Inghilterra; ~ **the United States** negli Stati Uniti; ~ **Yorkshire** nello Yorkshire
3 (*indicating time: during, in the space of*) in; ~ **spring/summer** in primavera/estate; ~ **1988** nel 1988; ~ **May** in *or* a maggio; **I'll see you** ~ **July** ci vediamo a luglio; ~ **the afternoon** nel pomeriggio; **at 4 o'clock** ~ **the afternoon** alle 4 del pomeriggio; **I did it** ~ **3 hours/days** l'ho fatto in 3 ore/giorni; **I'll see you** ~ **2 weeks** *or* ~ **2 weeks' time** ci vediamo tra 2 settimane

4 (*indicating manner etc*) a; ~ **a loud/ soft voice** a voce alta/bassa; ~ **pencil** a matita; ~ **English/French** in inglese/ francese; **the boy** ~ **the blue shirt** il ragazzo con la camicia blu
5 (*indicating circumstances*): ~ **the sun** al sole; ~ **the shade** all'ombra; ~ **the rain** sotto la pioggia; **a rise** ~ **prices** un aumento dei prezzi
6 (*indicating mood, state*): ~ **tears** in lacrime; ~ **anger** per la rabbia; ~ **despair** disperato(a); ~ **good condition** in buono stato, in buone condizioni; **to live** ~ **luxury** vivere nel lusso
7 (*with ratios, numbers*): **1** ~ **10** 1 su 10; **20 pence** ~ **the pound** 20 pence per sterlina; **they lined up** ~ **twos** si misero in fila a due a due
8 (*referring to people, works*) in; **the disease is common** ~ **children** la malattia è comune nei bambini; ~ (**the works of**) **Dickens** in Dickens
9 (*indicating profession etc*) in; **to be** ~ **teaching** fare l'insegnante, insegnare; **to be** ~ **publishing** essere nell'editoria
10 (*after superlative*) di; **the best** ~ **the class** il migliore della classe
11 (*with present participle*): ~ **saying this** dicendo questo, nel dire questo
◆ *ad*: **to be** ~ (*person: at home, work*) esserci; (*train, ship, plane*) essere arrivato(a); (*in fashion*) essere di moda; **to ask sb** ~ invitare qn ad entrare; **to run/limp** *etc* ~ entrare di corsa/zoppicando *etc*
◆ *n*: **the ~s and outs of the problem** tutti i particolari del problema.

in., ins *abbr* = **inch(es)**.

inability [ɪnə'bɪlɪtɪ] *n* inabilità, incapacità.

inaccurate [ɪn'ækjurət] *a* inesatto(a), impreciso(a).

inadequate [ɪn'ædɪkwət] *a* insufficiente.

inadvertently [ɪnəd'vəːtntlɪ] *ad* senza volerlo.

inane [ɪ'neɪn] *a* vacuo(a), stupido(a).

inanimate [ɪn'ænɪmət] *a* inanimato(a).

inappropriate [ɪnə'prəuprɪət] *a* disadatto(a); (*word, expression*) improprio(a).

inarticulate [ɪnɑː'tɪkjulət] *a* (*person*) che si esprime male; (*speech*) inarticolato(a).

inasmuch as [ɪnəz'mʌtʃæz] *ad* in quanto che; (*seeing that*) poiché.

inaudible [ɪn'ɔːdɪbl] *a* che non si riesce a sentire.

inauguration [ɪnɔːgju'reɪʃən] *n* inaugurazione *f*; insediamento in carica.

in-between [ɪnbɪ'twiːn] *a* fra i (*or* le) due.

inborn [ɪn'bɔːn] *a* (*feeling*) innato(a); (*defect*) congenito(a).

inbred [ɪn'bred] *a* innato(a); (*family*) connaturato(a).

Inc. *abbr* = **incorporated**.

incapable [ɪn'keɪpəbl] *a* incapace.

incapacitate [ɪnkə'pæsɪteɪt] *vt*: **to ~ sb from doing** rendere qn incapace di fare.

incense *n* ['ɪnsens] incenso // *vt* [ɪn'sens] (*anger*) infuriare.

incentive [ɪn'sentɪv] *n* incentivo.

incessant [ɪn'sesnt] *a* incessante; **~ly** *ad* di continuo, senza sosta.

inch [ɪntʃ] *n* pollice *m* (= *25 mm*; *12 in a foot*); **within an** ~ **of** a un pelo da; **he didn't give an** ~ non ha ceduto di un millimetro; **to** ~ **forward** *vi* avanzare pian piano.

incidence ['ɪnsɪdns] *n* (*of crime, disease*) incidenza.

incident ['ɪnsɪdnt] *n* incidente *m*; (*in book*) episodio.

incidental [ɪnsɪ'dentl] *a* accessorio(a), d'accompagnamento; (*unplanned*) incidentale; ~ **to** marginale a; **~ly** [-'dentəlɪ] *ad* (*by the way*) a proposito.

inclination [ɪnklɪ'neɪʃən] *n* inclinazione *f*.

incline *n* ['ɪnklaɪn] pendenza, pendio // *vb* [ɪn'klaɪn] *vt* inclinare // *vi*: **to** ~ **to** tendere a; **to be ~d** to do tendere a fare; essere propenso(a) a fare.

include [ɪn'kluːd] *vt* includere, comprendere; **including** *prep* compreso(a), incluso(a).

inclusive [ɪn'kluːsɪv] *a* incluso(a), compreso(a) // *ad*: ~ **of** tax *etc* tasse *etc* comprese.

incoherent [ɪnkəu'hɪərənt] *a* incoerente.

income ['ɪnkʌm] *n* reddito; ~ **tax** *n* imposta sul reddito.

incompetent [ɪn'kɔmpɪtnt] *a* incompetente, incapace.

incomplete [ɪnkəm'pliːt] *a* incompleto(a).

incongruous [ɪn'kɔŋgruəs] *a* poco appropriato(a); (*remark, act*) incongruo(a).

inconsiderate [ɪnkən'sɪdərət] *a* sconsiderato(a).

inconsistency [ɪnkən'sɪstənsɪ] *n* (*of actions, statement*) incoerenza; (*of work*) irregolarità.

inconspicuous [ɪnkən'spɪkjuəs] *a* incospicuo(a); (*colour*) poco appariscente; (*dress*) dimesso(a).

inconvenience [ɪnkən'viːnjəns] *n* inconveniente *m*; (*trouble*) disturbo // *vt* disturbare.

inconvenient [ɪnkən'viːnjənt] *a* scomodo(a).

incorporate [ɪn'kɔːpəreɪt] *vt* incorporare; (*contain*) contenere; **~d** *a*: **~d company** (*US: abbr* Inc.) società *f* *inv* anonima (S.A.).

incorrect [ɪnkə'rekt] *a* scorretto(a); (*statement*) impreciso(a).

increase *n* ['ɪnkriːs] aumento // *vi, vt* [ɪn'kriːs] aumentare.

increasing [ɪn'kriːsɪŋ] *a* (*number*) crescente; **~ly** *ad* sempre più.

incredible [ɪnˈkrɛdɪbl] a incredibile.
incredulous [ɪnˈkrɛdjuləs] a incredulo(a).
increment [ˈɪnkrɪmənt] n aumento, incremento.
incriminate [ɪnˈkrɪmɪneɪt] vt compromettere.
incubator [ˈɪnkjubeɪtə*] n incubatrice f.
incumbent [ɪnˈkʌmbənt] n titolare m/f // a: to be ~ on sb spettare a qn.
incur [ɪnˈkə:*] vt (expenses) incorrere; (anger, risk) esporsi a; (debt) contrarre; (loss) subire.
indebted [ɪnˈdɛtɪd] a: to be ~ to sb (for) essere obbligato(a) verso qn (per).
indecent [ɪnˈdi:snt] a indecente; ~ **assault** n (Brit) aggressione f a scopo di violenza sessuale; ~ **exposure** n atti mpl osceni in luogo pubblico.
indecisive [ɪndɪˈsaɪsɪv] a indeciso(a); (discussion) non decisivo(a).
indeed [ɪnˈdi:d] ad infatti; veramente; yes ~! certamente!
indefinite [ɪnˈdɛfɪnɪt] a indefinito(a); (answer) vago(a); (period, number) indeterminato(a); ~**ly** ad (wait) indefinitamente.
indemnity [ɪnˈdɛmnɪtɪ] n (insurance) assicurazione f; (compensation) indennità, indennizzo.
independence [ɪndɪˈpɛndns] n indipendenza.
independent [ɪndɪˈpɛndnt] a indipendente.
index [ˈɪndɛks] n (pl ~**es**: in book) indice m; (: in library etc) catalogo; (pl **indices**: ratio, sign) indice m; ~ **card** n scheda; ~ **finger** n (dito) indice m; ~-**linked**, (US) ~**ed** a legato(a) al costo della vita.
India [ˈɪndɪə] n India; ~**n** a, n indiano(a); Red ~ n pellerossa m/f.
indicate [ˈɪndɪkeɪt] vt indicare; **indication** [-ˈkeɪʃən] n indicazione f, segno.
indicative [ɪnˈdɪkətɪv] a: ~ **of** indicativo(a) di // n (LING) indicativo.
indicator [ˈɪndɪkeɪtə*] n indicatore m.
indices [ˈɪndɪsi:z] npl of **index**.
indictment [ɪnˈdaɪtmənt] n accusa.
indifference [ɪnˈdɪfrəns] n indifferenza.
indifferent [ɪnˈdɪfrənt] a indifferente; (poor) mediocre.
indigenous [ɪnˈdɪdʒɪnəs] a indigeno(a).
indigestible [ɪndɪˈdʒɛstɪbl] a indigeribile.
indigestion [ɪndɪˈdʒɛstʃən] n indigestione f.
indignant [ɪnˈdɪgnənt] a: ~ (at sth/with sb) indignato(a) (per qc/contro qn).
indignity [ɪnˈdɪgnɪtɪ] n umiliazione f.
indirect [ɪndɪˈrɛkt] a indiretto(a).
indiscreet [ɪndɪˈskri:t] a indiscreto(a); (rash) imprudente.
indiscriminate [ɪndɪˈskrɪmɪnət] a (person) che non sa discernere; (admiration) cieco(a); (killings) indiscriminato(a).

indisputable [ɪndɪˈspju:təbl] a incontestabile, indiscutibile.
individual [ɪndɪˈvɪdjuəl] n individuo // a individuale; (characteristic) particolare, originale; ~**ist** n individualista m/f; ~**ity** [-ˈælɪtɪ] n individualità.
indoctrination [ɪndɔktrɪˈneɪʃən] n indottrinamento.
Indonesia [ɪndəˈni:zɪə] n Indonesia.
indoor [ˈɪndɔ:*] a da interno; (plant) d'appartamento; (swimming pool) coperto(a); (sport, games) fatto(a) al coperto; ~**s** [ɪnˈdɔ:z] ad all'interno; (at home) in casa.
induce [ɪnˈdju:s] vt persuadere; (bring about) provocare; ~**ment** n incitamento; (incentive) stimolo, incentivo.
induction [ɪnˈdʌkʃən] n (MED: of birth) parto indotto; ~ **course** n (Brit) corso di avviamento.
indulge [ɪnˈdʌldʒ] vt (whim) compiacere, soddisfare; (child) viziare // vi: to ~ in sth concedersi qc; abbandonarsi a qc; ~**nce** n lusso (che uno si permette); (leniency) indulgenza; ~**nt** a indulgente.
industrial [ɪnˈdʌstrɪəl] a industriale; (injury) sul lavoro; (dispute) di lavoro; ~ **action** n azione f rivendicativa; ~ **estate** n (Brit) zona industriale; ~**ist** n industriale m; ~ **park** n (US) = ~ **estate**.
industrious [ɪnˈdʌstrɪəs] a industrioso(a), assiduo(a).
industry [ˈɪndəstrɪ] n industria; (diligence) operosità.
inebriated [ɪˈni:brɪeɪtɪd] a ubriaco(a).
inedible [ɪnˈɛdɪbl] a immangiabile.
ineffective [ɪnɪˈfɛktɪv], **ineffectual** [ɪnɪˈfɛktʃuəl] a inefficace; incompetente.
inefficiency [ɪnɪˈfɪʃənsɪ] n inefficienza.
inefficient [ɪnɪˈfɪʃənt] a inefficiente.
inept [ɪˈnɛpt] a inetto(a).
inequality [ɪnɪˈkwɔlɪtɪ] n ineguaglianza.
inescapable [ɪnɪˈskeɪpəbl] a inevitabile.
inevitable [ɪnˈɛvɪtəbl] a inevitabile; **inevitably** ad inevitabilmente.
inexact [ɪnɪgˈzækt] a inesatto(a).
inexpensive [ɪnɪkˈspɛnsɪv] a poco costoso(a).
inexperienced [ɪnɪksˈpɪərɪənst] a inesperto(a), senza esperienza.
infallible [ɪnˈfælɪbl] a infallibile.
infamous [ˈɪnfəməs] a infame.
infancy [ˈɪnfənsɪ] n infanzia.
infant [ˈɪnfənt] n bambino/a; ~ **school** n (Brit) scuola elementare (per bambini dall'età di 5 a 7 anni).
infantry [ˈɪnfəntrɪ] n fanteria.
infatuated [ɪnˈfætjueɪtɪd] a: ~ **with** infatuato(a) di.
infatuation [ɪnfætjuˈeɪʃən] n infatuazione f.
infect [ɪnˈfɛkt] vt infettare; ~**ion** ·

[ɪn'fɛkʃən] *n* infezione *f*; ~**ious**
[ɪn'fɛkʃəs] *a* (*disease*) infettivo(a),
contagioso(a); (*person*, *laughter*)
contagioso(a).

infer [ɪn'fə:*] *vt* inferire, dedurre.

inferior [ɪn'fɪərɪə*] *a* inferiore; (*goods*)
di qualità scadente // *n* inferiore *m/f*; (*in
rank*) subalterno/a; ~**ity** [ɪnfɪərɪ'ɔrətɪ] *n*
inferiorità; ~**ity complex** *n* complesso
di inferiorità.

infertile [ɪn'fə:taɪl] *a* sterile.

in-fighting ['ɪnfaɪtɪŋ] *n* lotte *fpl* intestine.

infinite ['ɪnfɪnɪt] *a* infinito(a).

infinitive [ɪn'fɪnɪtɪv] *n* infinito.

infinity [ɪn'fɪnɪtɪ] *n* infinità; (*also MATH*)
infinito.

infirmary [ɪn'fə:mərɪ] *n* ospedale *m*; (*in
school*, *factory*) infermeria.

infirmity [ɪn'fə:mɪtɪ] *n* infermità *f inv*.

inflamed [ɪn'fleɪmd] *a* infiammato(a).

inflammable [ɪn'flæməbl] *a* (*Brit*)
infiammabile.

inflammation [ɪnflə'meɪʃən] *n*
infiammazione *f*.

inflatable [ɪn'fleɪtəbl] *a* gonfiabile.

inflate [ɪn'fleɪt] *vt* (*tyre*, *balloon*)
gonfiare; (*fig*) esagerare; gonfiare; **inflation** [ɪn'fleɪʃən] *n* (*ECON*) inflazione *f*;
inflationary [ɪn'fleɪʃnərɪ] *a* inflazioni-
stico(a).

inflict [ɪn'flɪkt] *vt*: to ~ **on** infliggere a.

influence ['ɪnfluəns] *n* influenza // *vt*
influenzare; **under the** ~ **of** sotto
l'influenza di.

influential [ɪnflu'enʃl] *a* influente.

influenza [ɪnflu'enzə] *n* (*MED*) influenza.

influx ['ɪnflʌks] *n* afflusso.

inform [ɪn'fɔ:m] *vt*: to ~ **sb** (**of**)
informare qn (di) // *vi*: to ~ **on sb**
denunciare qn; to ~ **sb about** mettere qn
al corrente di.

informal [ɪn'fɔ:ml] *a* (*person*, *manner*)
alla buona, semplice; (*visit*, *discussion*)
informale; (*announcement*, *invitation*)
non ufficiale; ~**ity** [-'mælɪtɪ] *n* semplicità, informalità; carattere *m* non
ufficiale.

informant [ɪn'fɔ:mənt] *n* informatore/
trice.

information [ɪnfə'meɪʃən] *n* informazioni
fpl; particolari *mpl*; **a piece of** ~
un'informazione; ~ **office** *n* ufficio *m*
informazioni *inv*.

informative [ɪn'fɔ:mətɪv] *a* istruttivo(a).

informer [ɪn'fɔ:mə*] *n* informatore/trice;
to turn ~ (*POLICE*) denunciare i com-
plici.

infringe [ɪn'frɪndʒ] *vt* infrangere // *vi*: to
~ **on** calpestare; ~**ment** *n*: ~**ment** (**of**)
infrazione *f* (di).

infuriating [ɪn'fjʊərɪeɪtɪŋ] *a* molto
irritante.

ingenious [ɪn'dʒi:njəs] *a* ingegnoso(a).

ingenuity [ɪndʒɪ'nju:ɪtɪ] *n* ingegnosità.

ingenuous [ɪn'dʒɛnjuəs] *a* ingenuo(a).

ingot ['ɪŋgət] *n* lingotto.

ingrained [ɪn'greɪnd] *a* radicato(a).

ingratiate [ɪn'greɪʃɪeɪt] *vt*: to ~ **o.s. with
sb** ingraziarsi qn.

ingredient [ɪn'gri:dɪənt] *n* ingrediente *m*;
elemento.

inhabit [ɪn'hæbɪt] *vt* abitare.

inhabitant [ɪn'hæbɪtnt] *n* abitante *m/f*.

inhale [ɪn'heɪl] *vt* inalare // *vi* (*in
smoking*) aspirare.

inherent [ɪn'hɪərənt] *a*: ~ (**in** *or* **to**)
inerente (a).

inherit [ɪn'herɪt] *vt* ereditare; ~**ance** *n*
eredità.

inhibit [ɪn'hɪbɪt] *vt* (*PSYCH*) inibire; to ~
sb from doing impedire a qn di fare;
~**ion** [-'bɪʃən] *n* inibizione *f*.

inhospitable [ɪnhɔs'pɪtəbl] *a* inospitale.

inhuman [ɪn'hju:mən] *a* inumano(a).

initial [ɪ'nɪʃl] *a* iniziale // *n* iniziale *f* // *vt*
siglare; ~**s** *npl* iniziali *fpl*; (*as signature*) sigla; ~**ly** *ad* inizialmente,
all'inizio.

initiate [ɪ'nɪʃɪeɪt] *vt* (*start*) avviare; intraprendere; iniziare; (*person*) iniziare.

initiative [ɪ'nɪʃɪtɪv] *n* iniziativa.

inject [ɪn'dʒɛkt] *vt* (*liquid*) iniettare;
(*person*) fare una puntura a; ~**ion**
[ɪn'dʒɛkʃən] *n* iniezione *f*, puntura.

injure ['ɪndʒə*] *vt* ferire; (*wrong*) fare
male *or* torto a; (*damage*: *reputation
etc*) nuocere a; ~**d** *a* (*person*, *arm*)
ferito(a).

injury ['ɪndʒərɪ] *n* ferita; (*wrong*) torto;
~ **time** *n* (*SPORT*) tempo di ricupero.

injustice [ɪn'dʒʌstɪs] *n* ingiustizia.

ink [ɪŋk] *n* inchiostro.

inkling ['ɪŋklɪŋ] *n* sentore *m*, vaga idea.

inlaid ['ɪnleɪd] *a* incrostato(a); (*table
etc*) intarsiato(a).

inland *a* ['ɪnlənd] interno(a) // *ad*
[ɪn'lænd] all'interno; **I~ Revenue** *n*
(*Brit*) Fisco.

in-laws ['ɪnlɔ:z] *npl* suoceri *mpl*; famiglia del marito (*or* della moglie).

inlet ['ɪnlɛt] *n* (*GEO*) insenatura, baia.

inmate ['ɪnmeɪt] *n* (*in prison*) carcerato/
a; (*in asylum*) ricoverato/a.

inn [ɪn] *n* locanda.

innate [ɪ'neɪt] *a* innato(a).

inner ['ɪnə*] *a* interno(a), interiore; ~
city *n* centro di una zona urbana; ~
tube *n* camera d'aria.

innings ['ɪnɪŋz] *n* (*CRICKET*) turno di
battuta.

innocence ['ɪnəsns] *n* innocenza.

innocent ['ɪnəsnt] *a* innocente.

innocuous [ɪ'nɔkjuəs] *a* innocuo(a).

innuendo, ~**es** [ɪnju'ɛndəʊ] *n*
insinuazione *f*.

innumerable [ɪ'nju:mrəbl] *a*
innumerevole.

inordinately [ɪ'nɔ:dɪnətlɪ] *ad*
smoderatamente.

in-patient ['ɪnpeɪʃənt] *n* ricoverato/a.

input ['input] n (ELEC) energia, potenza; (of machine) alimentazione f; (of computer) input m.

inquest ['ɪnkwest] n inchiesta.

inquire [ɪn'kwaɪə*] vi informarsi // vt domandare, informarsi su; **to ~ about** vt fus informarsi di or su; **to ~ into** vt fus fare indagini su; **inquiry** n domanda; (LAW) indagine f, investigazione f; **inquiry office** n (Brit) ufficio m informazioni inv.

inquisitive [ɪn'kwɪzɪtɪv] a curioso(a).

inroad ['ɪnrəud] n incursione f.

insane [ɪn'seɪn] a matto(a), pazzo(a); (MED) alienato(a).

insanity [ɪn'sænɪtɪ] n follia; (MED) alienazione f mentale.

inscription [ɪn'skrɪpʃən] n iscrizione f; dedica.

inscrutable [ɪn'skruːtəbl] a imperscrutabile.

insect ['ɪnsekt] n insetto; **~icide** [ɪn'sektɪsaɪd] n insetticida m.

insecure [ɪnsɪ'kjuə*] a malsicuro(a); (person) insicuro(a)

insemination [ɪnsemɪ'neɪʃən] n: **artificial ~** fecondazione f artificiale.

insensible [ɪn'sensɪbl] a insensibile; (unconscious) privo(a) di sensi.

insensitive [ɪn'sensɪtɪv] a insensibile.

insert vt [ɪn'səːt] inserire, introdurre // n ['ɪnsəːt] inserto; **~ion** [ɪn'səːʃən] n inserzione f.

in-service [ɪn'səːvɪs] a (training, course) durante l'orario di lavoro.

inshore [ɪn'ʃɔː*] a costiero(a) // ad presso la riva; verso la riva.

inside ['ɪnsaɪd] n interno, parte f interiore // a interno(a), interiore // ad dentro, all'interno // prep dentro, all'interno di; (of time): **~ 10 minutes** entro 10 minuti; **~s** npl (col) ventre m; **~ forward** n (SPORT) mezzala, interno; **~ lane** n (AUT) corsia di marcia; **~ out** ad (turn) a rovescio; (know) in fondo; **to turn sth ~ out** rivoltare qc.

insight ['ɪnsaɪt] n acume m, perspicacia; (glimpse, idea) percezione f.

insignia [ɪn'sɪgnɪə] npl insegne fpl.

insignificant [ɪnsɪg'nɪfɪknt] a insignificante.

insincere [ɪnsɪn'sɪə*] a insincero(a).

insinuate [ɪn'sɪnjueɪt] vt insinuare.

insist [ɪn'sɪst] vi insistere; **to ~ on doing** insistere per fare; **to ~ that** insistere perché + sub; (claim) sostenere che; **~ent** a insistente.

insole ['ɪnsəul] n soletta.

insolent ['ɪnsələnt] a insolente.

insomnia [ɪn'sɔmnɪə] n insonnia.

inspect [ɪn'spekt] vt ispezionare; (ticket) controllare; **~ion** [ɪn'spekʃən] n ispezione f; controllo; **~or** n ispettore/trice; (Brit: on buses, trains) controllore m.

inspire [ɪn'spaɪə*] vt ispirare.

install [ɪn'stɔːl] vt installare; **~ation** [ɪnstə'leɪʃən] n installazione f.

instalment, (US) **installment** [ɪn'stɔːlmənt] n rata; (of TV serial etc) puntata; **in ~s** (pay) a rate; (receive) una parte per volta; (: publication) a fascicoli.

instance ['ɪnstəns] n esempio, caso; **for ~** per or ad esempio; **in many ~s** in molti casi; **in the first ~** in primo luogo.

instant ['ɪnstənt] n istante m, attimo // a immediato(a); urgente; (coffee, food) in polvere; **~ly** ad immediatamente, subito.

instead [ɪn'sted] ad invece; **~ of** invece di; **~ of sb** al posto di qn.

instep ['ɪnstep] n collo del piede; (of shoe) collo della scarpa.

instil [ɪn'stɪl] vt: **to ~ (into)** inculcare (in).

instinct ['ɪnstɪŋkt] n istinto.

institute ['ɪnstɪtjuːt] n istituto // vt istituire, stabilire; (inquiry) avviare; (proceedings) iniziare.

institution [ɪnstɪ'tjuːʃən] n istituzione f; istituto (d'istruzione); istituto (psichiatrico).

instruct [ɪn'strʌkt] vt istruire; **to ~ sb in sth** insegnare qc a qn; **to ~ sb to do** dare ordini a qn di fare; **~ion** [ɪn'strʌkʃən] n istruzione f; **~ions (for use)** istruzioni per l'uso; **~or** n istruttore/trice; (for skiing) maestro/a.

instrument ['ɪnstrəmənt] n strumento; **~al** [-'mentl] a (MUS) strumentale; **to be ~al in** essere d'aiuto in; **~ panel** n quadro m portastrumenti inv.

insufficient [ɪnsə'fɪʃənt] a insufficiente.

insular ['ɪnsjulə*] a insulare; (person) di mente ristretta.

insulate ['ɪnsjuleɪt] vt isolare; **insulating tape** n nastro isolante; **insulation** [-'leɪʃən] n isolamento.

insulin ['ɪnsjulɪn] n insulina.

insult n ['ɪnsʌlt] insulto, affronto // vt [ɪn'sʌlt] insultare; **~ing** a offensivo(a), ingiurioso(a).

insuperable [ɪn'sjuːprəbl] a insormontabile, insuperabile.

insurance [ɪn'ʃuərəns] n assicurazione f; **fire/life ~** assicurazione contro gli incendi/sulla vita; **~ policy** n polizza d'assicurazione.

insure [ɪn'ʃuə*] vt assicurare.

intact [ɪn'tækt] a intatto(a).

intake ['ɪnteɪk] n (TECH) immissione f; (of food) consumo; (Brit: of pupils etc) afflusso.

integral ['ɪntɪgrəl] a integrale; (part) integrante.

integrate ['ɪntɪgreɪt] vt integrare.

integrity [ɪn'tegrɪtɪ] n integrità.

intellect ['ɪntəlekt] n intelletto; **~ual** [-'lektjuəl] a, n intellettuale (m/f).

intelligence [ɪn'tɛlɪdʒəns] *n* intelligenza; (*MIL etc*) informazioni *fpl*.

intelligent [ɪn'tɛlɪdʒənt] *a* intelligente.

intend [ɪn'tɛnd] *vt* (*gift etc*): to ~ sth for destinare qc a; to ~ to do aver l'intenzione di fare; **~ed** *a* (*effect*) voluto(a).

intense [ɪn'tɛns] *a* intenso(a); (*person*) di forti sentimenti; **~ly** *ad* intensamente; profondamente.

intensive [ɪn'tɛnsɪv] *a* intensivo(a); ~ **care unit** *n* reparto terapia intensiva.

intent [ɪn'tɛnt] *n* intenzione *f* // *a*: ~ (on) intento(a), immerso(a) (in); to all ~s and purposes a tutti gli effetti; to be ~ on doing sth essere deciso a fare qc.

intention [ɪn'tɛnʃən] *n* intenzione *f*; **~al** *a* intenzionale, deliberato(a); **~ally** *ad* apposta.

intently [ɪn'tɛntlɪ] *ad* attentamente.

inter [ɪn'tə:*] *vt* sotterrare.

interact [ɪntər'ækt] *vi* agire reciprocamente, interagire.

interchange *n* ['ɪntətʃeɪndʒ] (*exchange*) scambio; (*on motorway*) incrocio pluridirezionale // *vt* [ɪntə'tʃeɪndʒ] scambiare; sostituire l'uno(a) per l'altro(a); **~able** *a* intercambiabile.

intercom ['ɪntəkɔm] *n* interfono.

intercourse ['ɪntəkɔ:s] *n* rapporti *mpl*.

interest ['ɪntrɪst] *n* interesse *m*; (*COMM: stake, share*) interessi *mpl* // *vt* interessare; **~ed** *a* interessato(a); to be **~ed** in interessarsi di; **~ing** *a* interessante; ~ **rate** *n* tasso di interesse.

interface ['ɪntəfeɪs] *n* (*COMPUT*) interfaccia.

interfere [ɪntə'fɪə*] *vi*: to ~ in (*quarrel, other people's business*) immischiarsi in; to ~ with (*object*) toccare; (*plans*) ostacolare; (*duty*) interferire con.

interference [ɪntə'fɪərəns] *n* interferenza.

interim ['ɪntərɪm] *a* provvisorio(a) // *n*: in the ~ nel frattempo.

interior [ɪn'tɪərɪə*] *n* interno; (*of country*) entroterra // *a* interiore, interno(a); ~ **designer** *n* arredatore/trice.

interlock [ɪntə'lɔk] *vi* ingranarsi // *vt* ingranare.

interloper ['ɪntələupə*] *n* intruso/a.

interlude ['ɪntəlu:d] *n* intervallo; (*THEATRE*) intermezzo.

intermediate [ɪntə'mi:dɪət] *a* intermedio(a); (*SCOL: course, level*) medio(a).

intermission [ɪntə'mɪʃən] *n* pausa; (*THEATRE, CINEMA*) intermissione *f*, intervallo.

intern *vt* [ɪn'tə:n] internare // *n* ['ɪntə:n] (*US*) medico interno.

internal [ɪn'tə:nl] *a* interno(a); **~ly** *ad* all'interno; "not to be taken **~ly**" "per uso esterno"; **I~ Revenue Service (IRS)** *n* (*US*) Fisco.

international [ɪntə'næʃənl] *a* internazionale.

interplay ['ɪntəpleɪ] *n* azione e reazione *f*.

interpret [ɪn'tə:prɪt] *vt* interpretare // *vi* fare da interprete; **~er** *n* interprete *m/f*.

interrelated [ɪntərɪ'leɪtɪd] *a* correlato(a).

interrogate [ɪn'tɛrəugeɪt] *vt* interrogare; **interrogation** [-'geɪʃən] *n* interrogazione *f*; (*of suspect etc*) interrogatorio; **interrogative** [ɪntə'rɔgətɪv] *a* interrogativo(a).

interrupt [ɪntə'rʌpt] *vt* interrompere; **~ion** [-'rʌpʃən] *n* interruzione *f*.

intersect [ɪntə'sɛkt] *vt* intersecare // *vi* (*roads*) intersecarsi; **~ion** [-'sɛkʃən] *n* intersezione *f*; (*of roads*) incrocio.

intersperse [ɪntə'spə:s] *vt*: to ~ with costellare di.

intertwine [ɪntə'twaɪn] *vt* intrecciare // *vi* intrecciarsi.

interval ['ɪntəvl] *n* intervallo; at ~s a intervalli.

intervene [ɪntə'vi:n] *vi* (*time*) intercorrere; (*event, person*) intervenire; **intervention** [-'vɛnʃən] *n* intervento.

interview ['ɪntəvju:] *n* (*RADIO, TV etc*) intervista; (*for job*) colloquio // *vt* intervistare; avere un colloquio con; **~er** *n* intervistatore/trice.

intestine [ɪn'tɛstɪn] *n* intestino.

intimacy ['ɪntɪməsɪ] *n* intimità.

intimate *a* ['ɪntɪmət] intimo(a); (*knowledge*) profondo(a) // *vt* ['ɪntɪmeɪt] lasciar capire.

into ['ɪntu:] *prep* dentro, in; come ~ the house vieni dentro la casa; ~ Italian in italiano.

intolerable [ɪn'tɔlərəbl] *a* intollerabile.

intolerance [ɪn'tɔlərns] *n* intolleranza.

intolerant [ɪn'tɔlərnt] *a*: ~ of intollerante di.

intoxicate [ɪn'tɔksɪkeɪt] *vt* inebriare; **~d** *a* inebriato(a); **intoxication** [-'keɪʃən] *n* ebbrezza.

intractable [ɪn'træktəbl] *a* intrattabile.

intransitive [ɪn'trænsɪtɪv] *a* intransitivo(a).

intravenous [ɪntrə'vi:nəs] *a* endovenoso(a).

in-tray ['ɪntreɪ] *n* contenitore *m* per la corrispondenza in arrivo.

intricate ['ɪntrɪkət] *a* intricato(a), complicato(a).

intrigue [ɪn'tri:g] *n* intrigo // *vt* affascinare // *vi* complottare, tramare; **intriguing** *a* affascinante.

intrinsic [ɪn'trɪnsɪk] *a* intrinseco(a).

introduce [ɪntrə'dju:s] *vt* introdurre; to ~ sb (to sb) presentare qn (a qn); to ~ sb to (*pastime, technique*) iniziare qn a; **introduction** [-'dʌkʃən] *n* introduzione *f*; (*of person*) presentazione *f*; **introductory** *a* introduttivo(a).

intrude [ɪn'tru:d] *vi* (*person*): to ~ (on)

intromettersi (in); **am I intruding?** disturbo?; **~r** n intruso/a.
intuition [ɪntju:'ɪʃən] n intuizione f.
inundate [ɪn'ʌndeɪt] vt: **to ~ with** inondare di.
invade [ɪn'veɪd] vt invadere.
invalid n ['ɪnvəlɪd] malato/a; (with disability) invalido/a // a [ɪn'vælɪd] (not valid) invalido(a), non valido(a).
invaluable [ɪn'væljuəbl] a prezioso(a); inestimabile.
invariably [ɪn'vɛərɪəblɪ] ad invariabilmente; sempre.
invasion [ɪn'veɪʒən] n invasione f.
invent [ɪn'vent] vt inventare; **~ion** [ɪn'venʃən] n invenzione f; **~ive** a inventivo(a); **~or** n inventore m.
inventory ['ɪnvəntrɪ] n inventario.
invert [ɪn'vɜ:t] vt invertire; (cup, object) rovesciare; **~ed commas** npl (Brit) virgolette fpl.
invest [ɪn'vest] vt investire // vi fare investimenti.
investigate [ɪn'vestɪgeɪt] vt investigare, indagare; (crime) fare indagini su; **investigation** [-'geɪʃən] n investigazione f; (of crime) indagine f.
investment [ɪn'vestmənt] n investimento.
investor [ɪn'vestə*] n investitore/trice; azionista m/f.
invidious [ɪn'vɪdɪəs] a odioso(a); (task) spiacevole.
invigilate [ɪn'vɪdʒɪleɪt] vt, vi (in exam) sorvegliare.
invigorating [ɪn'vɪgəreɪtɪŋ] a stimolante; vivificante.
invisible [ɪn'vɪzɪbl] a invisibile; **~ ink** n inchiostro simpatico.
invitation [ɪnvɪ'teɪʃən] n invito.
invite [ɪn'vaɪt] vt invitare; (opinions etc) sollecitare; (trouble) provocare; **inviting** a invitante, attraente.
invoice ['ɪnvɔɪs] n fattura.
involuntary [ɪn'vɒləntrɪ] a involontario(a).
involve [ɪn'vɒlv] vt (entail) richiedere, comportare; (associate): **to ~ sb (in)** implicare qn (in); coinvolgere qn (in); **~d** a involuto(a), complesso(a); **to feel ~d** sentirsi coinvolto(a); **~ment** n implicazione f; coinvolgimento; **~ment (in)** impegno (in); partecipazione f (in).
inward ['ɪnwəd] a (movement) verso l'interno; (thought, feeling) interiore, intimo(a); **~(s)** ad verso l'interno.
I/O abbr (COMPUT: = input/output) I/O.
iodine ['aɪəʊdi:n] n iodio.
iota [aɪ'əʊtə] n (fig) briciolo.
IOU n abbr (= I owe you) pagherò m inv.
IQ n abbr (= intelligence quotient) quoziente m d'intelligenza.
IRA n abbr (= Irish Republican Army) IRA f.
Iran [ɪ'rɑ:n] n Iran m.

Iraq [ɪ'rɑ:k] n Iraq m.
Ireland ['aɪələnd] n Irlanda.
iris, **~es** ['aɪrɪs, -ɪz] n iride f; (BOT) giaggiolo, iride.
Irish ['aɪrɪʃ] a irlandese // npl: **the ~** gli Irlandesi; **~man** n irlandese m; **~ Sea** n Mar m d'Irlanda; **~woman** n irlandese f.
irksome ['ə:ksəm] a seccante.
iron ['aɪən] n ferro; (for clothes) ferro da stiro // a di or in ferro // vt (clothes) stirare; **to ~ out** vt (crease) appianare; (fig) spianare; far sparire; **the I~ Curtain** n la cortina di ferro.
ironic(al) [aɪ'rɒnɪk(l)] a ironico(a).
ironing ['aɪənɪŋ] n (act) stirare m; (clothes) roba da stirare; **~ board** n asse f da stiro.
ironmonger ['aɪənmʌŋgə*] n (Brit) negoziante m in ferramenta; **~'s** (shop) n negozio di ferramenta.
ironworks ['aɪənwə:ks] n ferriera.
irony ['aɪrənɪ] n ironia.
irrational [ɪ'ræʃənl] a irrazionale; irragionevole; illogico(a).
irregular [ɪ'regjʊlə*] a irregolare.
irrelevant [ɪ'reləvənt] a non pertinente.
irreplaceable [ɪrɪ'pleɪsəbl] a insostituibile.
irrepressible [ɪrɪ'presəbl] a irrefrenabile.
irresistible [ɪrɪ'zɪstɪbl] a irresistibile.
irrespective [ɪrɪ'spektɪv]: **~ of** prep senza riguardo a.
irresponsible [ɪrɪ'spɒnsɪbl] a irresponsabile.
irrigate ['ɪrɪgeɪt] vt irrigare; **irrigation** [-'geɪʃən] n irrigazione f.
irritable ['ɪrɪtəbl] a irritabile.
irritate ['ɪrɪteɪt] vt irritare; **irritating** a (person, sound etc) irritante; **irritation** [-'teɪʃən] n irritazione f.
IRS n abbr = **Internal Revenue Service**.
is [ɪz] vb see **be**.
Islam ['ɪzlɑ:m] n Islam m.
island ['aɪlənd] n isola; (also: traffic ~) salvagente m; **~er** n isolano/a.
isle [aɪl] n isola.
isn't ['ɪznt] = **is not**.
isolate ['aɪsəleɪt] vt isolare; **~d** a isolato(a); **isolation** [-'leɪʃən] n isolamento.
Israel ['ɪzreɪl] n Israele m; **~i** [ɪz'reɪlɪ] a, n israeliano(a).
issue ['ɪʃju:] n questione f, problema m; (outcome) esito, risultato; (of banknotes etc) emissione f; (of newspaper etc) numero; (offspring) discendenza // vt (rations, equipment) distribuire; (orders) dare; (book) pubblicare; (banknotes, cheques, stamps) emettere; **at ~** in gioco, in discussione; **to take ~ with sb (over sth)** prendere posizione contro qn (riguardo a qc).
isthmus ['ɪsməs] n istmo.

it [ɪt] *pronoun* **1** (*specific: subject*) esso(a); (: *direct object*) lo(la), l'; (: *indirect object*) gli(le); **where's my book?** — **~'s on the table** dov'è il mio libro? — è sulla tavola; **I can't find ~** non lo (*or* la) trovo; **give ~ to me** dammelo (*or* dammela); **about/from/of ~** ne; **I spoke to him about ~** gliene ho parlato; **what did you learn from ~?** quale insegnamento ne hai tratto?; **I'm proud of ~** ne sono fiero; **did you go to ~?** ci sei andato?; **put the book in ~** mettici il libro **2** (*impersonal*): **~'s raining** piove; **~'s Friday tomorrow** domani è venerdì; **~'s 6 o'clock** sono le 6; **who is ~?** — **~'s me** chi è? — sono io.

Italian [ɪ'tæljən] *a* italiano(a) // *n* italiano/a; (*LING*) italiano; **the ~s** gli Italiani.

italic [ɪ'tælɪk] *a* corsivo(a); **~s** *npl* corsivo.

Italy ['ɪtəlɪ] *n* Italia.

itch [ɪtʃ] *n* prurito // *vi* (*person*) avere il prurito; (*part of body*) prudere; **to be ~ing to do sth** aver una gran voglia di fare qc; **~y** *a* che prude; **to be ~y = to ~**.

it'd ['ɪtd] = **it would**; **it had**.

item ['aɪtəm] *n* articolo; (*on agenda*) punto; (*in programme*) numero; (*also*: **news ~**) notizia; **~ize** *vt* specificare, dettagliare.

itinerant [ɪ'tɪnərənt] *a* ambulante.

itinerary [aɪ'tɪnərərɪ] *n* itinerario.

it'll ['ɪtl] = **it will**, **it shall**.

its [ɪts] *a* il(la) suo(a), i(le) suoi(sue).

it's [ɪts] = **it is**; **it has**.

itself [ɪt'sɛlf] *pronoun* (*emphatic*) esso(a) stesso(a); (*reflexive*) si.

ITV *n abbr* (*Brit*: = *Independent Television*) *rete televisiva in concorrenza con la BBC*.

I.U.D. *n abbr* (= *intra-uterine device*) spirale *f*.

I've [aɪv] = **I have**.

ivory ['aɪvərɪ] *n* avorio.

ivy ['aɪvɪ] *n* edera.

J

jab [dʒæb] *vt*: **to ~ sth into** affondare *or* piantare qc dentro // *n* colpo; (*MED*: *col*) puntura.

jack [dʒæk] *n* (*AUT*) cricco; (*CARDS*) fante *m*; **to ~ up** *vt* sollevare sul cricco.

jackal ['dʒækl] *n* sciacallo.

jackdaw ['dʒækdɔ:] *n* taccola.

jacket ['dʒækɪt] *n* giacca; (*of book*) copertura.

jack-knife ['dʒæknaɪf] *vi*: **the lorry ~d** l'autotreno si è piegato su se stesso.

jack plug *n* (*ELEC*) jack *m inv*.

jackpot ['dʒækpɔt] *n* primo premio (in denaro).

jade [dʒeɪd] *n* (*stone*) giada.

jaded ['dʒeɪdɪd] *a* sfinito(a), spossato(a).

jagged ['dʒægɪd] *a* sbocconcellato(a); (*cliffs etc*) frastagliato(a).

jail [dʒeɪl] *n* prigione *f* // *vt* mandare in prigione; **~er** *n* custode *m* del carcere.

jam [dʒæm] *n* marmellata; (*of shoppers etc*) ressa; (*also*: **traffic ~**) ingorgo // *vt* (*passage etc*) ingombrare, ostacolare; (*mechanism, drawer etc*) bloccare; (*RADIO*) disturbare con interferenze // *vi* (*mechanism, sliding part*) incepparsi, bloccarsi; (*gun*) incepparsi; **to ~ sth into** forzare qc dentro; infilare qc a forza dentro.

Jamaica [dʒə'meɪkə] *n* Giamaica.

jangle ['dʒæŋgl] *vi* risuonare; (*bracelet*) tintinnare.

janitor ['dʒænɪtə*] *n* (*caretaker*) portiere *m*; (: *SCOL*) bidello.

January ['dʒænjuərɪ] *n* gennaio.

Japan [dʒə'pæn] *n* Giappone *m*; **~ese** [dʒæpə'ni:z] *a* giapponese // *n* (*pl inv*) giapponese *m/f*; (*LING*) giapponese *m*.

jar [dʒɑ:*] *n* (*glass*) barattolo, vasetto // *vi* (*sound*) stridere; (*colours etc*) stonare.

jargon ['dʒɑ:gən] *n* gergo.

jasmin(e) ['dʒæzmɪn] *n* gelsomino.

jaundice ['dʒɔ:ndɪs] *n* itterizia; **~d** *a* (*fig*) invidioso(a) e critico(a).

jaunt [dʒɔ:nt] *n* gita; **~y** *a* vivace; disinvolto(a).

javelin ['dʒævlɪn] *n* giavellotto.

jaw [dʒɔ:] *n* mascella.

jay [dʒeɪ] *n* ghiandaia.

jaywalker ['dʒeɪwɔ:kə*] *n* pedone(a) indisciplinato(a).

jazz [dʒæz] *n* jazz *m*; **to ~ up** *vt* rendere vivace.

jealous ['dʒɛləs] *a* geloso(a); **~y** *n* gelosia.

jeans [dʒi:nz] *npl* (blue-)jeans *mpl*.

jeer [dʒɪə*] *vi*: **to ~ (at)** fischiare, beffeggiare.

jelly ['dʒɛlɪ] *n* gelatina; **~fish** *n* medusa.

jeopardy ['dʒɛpədɪ] *n*: **in ~** in pericolo.

jerk [dʒə:k] *n* sobbalzo, scossa; sussulto // *vt* dare una scossa a // *vi* (*vehicles*) sobbalzare.

jerkin ['dʒə:kɪn] *n* giubbotto.

jersey ['dʒə:zɪ] *n* maglia.

jest [dʒɛst] *n* scherzo.

Jesus ['dʒi:zəs] *n* Gesù *m*.

jet [dʒɛt] *n* (*of gas, liquid*) getto; (*AVIAT*) aviogetto; **~-black** *a* nero(a) come l'ebano, corvino(a); **~ engine** *n* motore *m* a reazione; **~ lag** *n* (problemi *mpl* dovuti allo) sbalzo dei fusi orari.

jettison ['dʒɛtɪsn] *vt* gettare in mare.

jetty ['dʒɛtɪ] *n* molo.

Jew [dʒu:] *n* ebreo.

jewel ['dʒu:əl] *n* gioiello; **~ler** *n* orefice

m, gioielliere/a; **~ler's (shop)** *n* oreficeria, gioielleria; **~lery** *n* gioielli *mpl*.

Jewess ['dʒu:ɪs] *n* ebrea.

Jewish ['dʒu:ɪʃ] *a* ebreo(a), ebraico(a).

jib [dʒɪb] *n* (NAUT) fiocco; (of crane) braccio.

jibe [dʒaɪb] *n* beffa.

jiffy ['dʒɪfɪ] *n* (col): **in a ~** in un batter d'occhio.

jig [dʒɪg] *n* giga.

jigsaw ['dʒɪgsɔ:] *n* (also: **~ puzzle**) puzzle *m inv.*

jilt [dʒɪlt] *vt* piantare in asso.

jingle ['dʒɪŋgl] *n* (advert) sigla pubblicitaria // *vi* tintinnare, scampanellare.

jinx [dʒɪŋks] *n* (col) iettatura; (person) iettatore/trice.

jitters ['dʒɪtəz] *npl* (col): **to get the ~** aver fifa.

job [dʒɔb] *n* lavoro; (employment) impiego, posto; **it's a good ~ that ...** meno male che ...; **just the ~!** proprio quello che ci vuole; **~ centre** *n* (Brit) ufficio di collocamento; **~less** *a* senza lavoro, disoccupato(a).

jockey ['dʒɔkɪ] *n* fantino, jockey *m inv* // *vi*: **to ~ for position** manovrare per una posizione di vantaggio.

jocular ['dʒɔkjulə*] *a* gioviale; scherzoso(a).

jog [dʒɔg] *vt* urtare // *vi* (SPORT) fare footing, fare jogging; **to ~ along** trottare; (fig) andare avanti piano piano; **~ging** *n* footing *m*, jogging *m*.

join [dʒɔɪn] *vt* unire, congiungere; (become member of) iscriversi a; (meet) raggiungere; riunirsi a // *vi* (roads, rivers) confluire // *n* giuntura; **to ~ in** *vi* partecipare // *vt fus* unirsi a; **to ~ up** *vi* arruolarsi.

joiner ['dʒɔɪnə*] *n* falegname *m*; **~y** *n* falegnameria.

joint [dʒɔɪnt] *n* (TECH) giuntura; giunto; (ANAT) articolazione *f*, giuntura; (Brit CULIN) arrosto; (col: place) locale *m* // *a* comune; **~ account** *n* (at bank etc) conto in partecipazione, conto comune; **~ly** *ad* in comune, insieme.

joist [dʒɔɪst] *n* trave *f*.

joke [dʒəuk] *n* scherzo; (funny story) barzelletta; (also: **practical ~**) beffa // *vi* scherzare; **to play a ~ on sb** fare uno scherzo a qn; **~r** *n* buffone/a, burlone/a; (CARDS) matta, jolly *m inv.*

jolly ['dʒɔlɪ] *a* allegro(a), gioioso(a) // *ad* (col) veramente, proprio.

jolt [dʒəult] *n* scossa, sobbalzo // *vt* urtare.

Jordan ['dʒɔ:dən] *n* (country) Giordania; (river) Giordano.

jostle ['dʒɔsl] *vt* spingere coi gomiti // *vi* farsi spazio coi gomiti.

jot [dʒɔt] *n*: **not one ~** nemmeno un po'; **to ~ down** *vt* annotare in fretta,

buttare giù; **~ter** *n* (Brit) blocco.

journal ['dʒə:nl] *n* giornale *m*; rivista; diario; **~ism** *n* giornalismo; **~ist** *n* giornalista *m/f*.

journey ['dʒə:nɪ] *n* viaggio; (distance covered) tragitto // *vi* viaggiare.

joy [dʒɔɪ] *n* gioia; **~ful**, **~ous** *a* gioioso(a), allegro(a); **~ ride** *n* gita in automobile (specialmente rubata); **~stick** *n* (AVIAT) barra di comando; (COMPUT) joystick *m inv.*

J.P. *n abbr* = **Justice of the Peace.**

Jr, Jun., Junr *abbr* = **junior.**

jubilant ['dʒu:bɪlnt] *a* giubilante; trionfante.

jubilee ['dʒu:bɪli:] *n* giubileo; **silver ~** venticinquesimo anniversario.

judge [dʒʌdʒ] *n* giudice *m/f* // *vt* giudicare; **judg(e)ment** *n* giudizio; (punishment) punizione *f*.

judicial [dʒu:'dɪʃl] *a* giudiziale, giudiziario(a).

judiciary [dʒu:'dɪʃɪərɪ] *n* magistratura.

judo ['dʒu:dəu] *n* judo.

jug [dʒʌg] *n* brocca, bricco.

juggernaut ['dʒʌgənɔ:t] *n* (Brit: huge truck) bestione *m*.

juggle ['dʒʌgl] *vi* fare giochi di destrezza; **~r** *n* giocoliere/a.

Jugoslav ['ju:gəuslɑ:v] *etc* = **Yugoslav** *etc.*

juice [dʒu:s] *n* succo.

juicy ['dʒu:sɪ] *a* succoso(a).

jukebox ['dʒu:kbɔks] *n* juke-box *m inv.*

July [dʒu:'laɪ] *n* luglio.

jumble ['dʒʌmbl] *n* miscuglio // *vt* (also: **~ up**) mischiare; **~ sale** *n* (Brit) vendita di oggetti per beneficenza.

jumbo (jet) ['dʒʌmbəu-] *n* jumbo-jet *m inv.*

jump [dʒʌmp] *vi* saltare, balzare; (start) sobbalzare; (increase) rincarare // *vt* saltare // *n* salto, balzo; sobbalzo.

jumper ['dʒʌmpə*] *n* (Brit: pullover) maglione *m*, pullover *m inv*; (US: dress) scamiciato; **~ cables** *npl* (US) = **jump leads.**

jump leads *npl* (Brit) cavi *mpl* per batteria.

jumpy ['dʒʌmpɪ] *a* nervoso(a), agitato(a).

junction ['dʒʌŋkʃən] *n* (Brit: of roads) incrocio; (of rails) nodo ferroviario.

juncture ['dʒʌŋktʃə*] *n*: **at this ~** in questa congiuntura.

June [dʒu:n] *n* giugno.

jungle ['dʒʌŋgl] *n* giungla.

junior ['dʒu:nɪə*] *a*, *n*: **he's ~ to me (by 2 years)**, **he's my ~ (by 2 years)** è più giovane di me (di 2 anni); **he's ~ to me** (seniority) è al di sotto di me, ho più anzianità di lui; **~ school** *n* (Brit) scuola elementare (da 8 a 11 anni).

junk [dʒʌŋk] *n* (rubbish) chincaglia; (ship) giunca; **~ food** *n* porcherie *fpl*;

~ **shop** n chincaglieria.

juror ['dʒʊərə*] n giurato/a.

jury ['dʒʊərɪ] n giuria.

just [dʒʌst] a giusto(a) // ad: he's ~ done it/left lo ha appena fatto/è appena partito; ~ as I expected proprio come me lo aspettavo; ~ right proprio giusto; ~ 2 o'clock le 2 precise; she's ~ as clever as you è in gamba proprio quanto te; it's ~ as well that ... meno male che ...; ~ as I arrived proprio mentre arrivavo; it was ~ before/enough/here era poco prima/appena assai/proprio qui; it's ~ me sono solo io; it's ~ a mistake non è che uno sbaglio; ~ missed/caught appena perso/preso; ~ listen to this! senta un po' questo!

justice ['dʒʌstɪs] n giustizia; J~ of the Peace (J.P.) n giudice m conciliatore.

justify ['dʒʌstɪfaɪ] vt giustificare.

jut [dʒʌt] vt (also: ~ out) sporgersi.

juvenile ['dʒuːvənaɪl] a giovane, giovanile; (court) dei minorenni; (books) per ragazzi // n giovane m/f, minorenne m/f.

juxtapose ['dʒʌkstəpəʊz] vt giustapporre.

K

K abbr (= one thousand) mille; (= kilobyte) K.

kangaroo [kæŋgə'ruː] n canguro.

karate [kə'rɑːtɪ] n karatè m.

kebab [kə'bæb] n spiedino.

keel [kiːl] n chiglia; on an even ~ (fig) in uno stato normale.

keen [kiːn] a (interest, desire) vivo(a); (eye, intelligence) acuto(a); (competition) serrato(a); (edge) affilato(a); (eager) entusiasta; to be ~ to do or on doing sth avere una gran voglia di fare qc; to be ~ on sth essere appassionato(a) di qc; to be ~ on sb avere un debole per qn.

keep [kiːp] vb (pt, pp kept) vt tenere; (hold back) trattenere; (feed: one's family etc) mantenere, sostentare; (a promise) mantenere; (chickens, bees, pigs etc) allevare // vi (food) mantenersi; (remain: in a certain state or place) restare // n (of castle) maschio; (food etc): enough for his ~ abbastanza per vitto e alloggio; (col): for ~s per sempre; to ~ doing sth continuare a fare qc; (repeat) fare qc di continuo; to ~ sb from doing/sth from happening impedire a qn di fare/che qc succeda; to ~ sb busy/a place tidy tenere qn occupato(a)/ un luogo in ordine; to ~ sth to o.s. tenere qc per sé; to ~ sth (back) from celare qc a qn; to ~ time (clock) andar bene; to ~ on vi continuare; to ~ on doing continuare a fare; to ~ out vt

~ **out** "vietato l'accesso";
to ~ **up** vi mantenersi // vt continuare, mantenere; to ~ **up with** tener dietro a, andare di pari passo con; (work etc) farcela a seguire; ~**er** n custode m/f, guardiano/a; ~**-fit** n ginnastica; ~**ing** n (care) custodia; in ~**ing with** in armonia con; in accordo con; ~**sake** n ricordo.

keg [keg] n barilotto.

kennel ['kɛnl] n canile m.

kept [kɛpt] pt, pp of **keep**.

kerb [kəːb] n (Brit) orlo del marciapiede.

kernel ['kəːnl] n nocciolo.

kettle ['kɛtl] n bollitore m.

kettle drums npl timpano.

key [kiː] n (gen, MUS) chiave f; (of piano, typewriter) tasto // vt (also: ~ in) digitare; ~**board** n tastiera; ~**ed up** a (person) agitato(a); ~**hole** n buco della serratura; ~**note** n (MUS) tonica; (fig) nota dominante; ~ **ring** n portachiavi m inv.

khaki ['kɑːkɪ] a, n cachì (m).

kick [kɪk] vt calciare, dare calci a // vi (horse) tirar calci // n calcio; (of rifle) contraccolpo; (thrill): he does it for ~s lo fa giusto per il piacere di farlo; to ~ **off** vi (SPORT) dare il primo calcio.

kid [kɪd] n (col: child) ragazzino/a; (animal, leather) capretto // vi (col) scherzare // vt (col) prendere in giro.

kidnap ['kɪdnæp] vt rapire, sequestrare; ~**per** n rapitore/trice; ~**ping** n sequestro (di persona).

kidney ['kɪdnɪ] n (ANAT) rene m; (CULIN) rognone m.

kill [kɪl] vt uccidere, ammazzare; (fig) sopprimere; sopraffare; ammazzare // n uccisione f; ~**er** n uccisore m, killer m inv; assassino/a; ~**ing** n assassinio; (massacre) strage f; ~**joy** n guastafeste m/f inv.

kiln [kɪln] n forno.

kilo ['kiːləʊ] n chilo; ~**byte** n (COMPUT) kilobyte m inv; ~**gram(me)** ['kɪləʊgræm] n chilogrammo; ~**metre**, (US) ~**meter** ['kɪləmiːtə*] n chilometro; ~**watt** ['kɪləʊwɒt] n chilowatt m inv.

kilt [kɪlt] n gonnellino scozzese.

kin [kɪn] n see **next**, **kith**.

kind [kaɪnd] a gentile, buono(a) // n sorta, specie f; (species) genere m; to be two of a ~ essere molto simili; in ~ (COMM) in natura.

kindergarten ['kɪndəgaːtn] n giardino d'infanzia.

kind-hearted [kaɪnd'haːtɪd] a di buon cuore.

kindle ['kɪndl] vt accendere, infiammare.

kindly ['kaɪndlɪ] a pieno(a) di bontà, benevolo(a) // ad con bontà, gentilmente; will you ~ ... vuole ... per favore.

kindness ['kaɪndnɪs] n bontà, gentilezza.

kindred ['kɪndrɪd] a imparentato(a); ~ **spirit** n spirito affine.

king [kɪŋ] *n* re *m inv*; ~**dom** *n* regno, reame *m*; ~**fisher** *n* martin *m inv* pescatore; ~-**size** *a* super *inv*; gigante.

kinky ['kɪŋkɪ] *a* (*fig*) eccentrico(a); dai gusti particolari.

kiosk ['kiːɔsk] *n* edicola, chiosco; (*Brit TEL*) cabina (telefonica).

kipper ['kɪpə*] *n* aringa affumicata.

kiss [kɪs] *n* bacio // *vt* baciare; to ~ (**each other**) baciarsi.

kit [kɪt] *n* equipaggiamento, corredo; (*set of tools etc*) attrezzi *mpl*; (*for assembly*) scatola di montaggio.

kitchen ['kɪtʃɪn] *n* cucina; ~ **sink** *n* acquaio.

kite [kaɪt] *n* (*toy*) aquilone *m*; (*ZOOL*) nibbio.

kith [kɪθ] *n*: ~ **and kin** amici e parenti *mpl*.

kitten ['kɪtn] *n* gattino/a, micino/a.

kitty ['kɪtɪ] *n* (*money*) fondo comune.

knack [næk] *n*: to have the ~ of avere l'abilità di; there's a ~ to doing this c'è un trucco per fare questo.

knapsack ['næpsæk] *n* zaino, sacco da montagna.

knead [niːd] *vt* impastare.

knee [niː] *n* ginocchio; ~**cap** *n* rotula.

kneel, *pt*, *pp* **knelt** [niːl, nɛlt] *vi* (*also:* ~ **down**) inginocchiarsi.

knell [nɛl] *n* rintocco.

knew [njuː] *pt of* **know**.

knickers ['nɪkəz] *npl* (*Brit*) mutandine *fpl*.

knife [naɪf] *n* (*pl* **knives**) coltello // *vt* accoltellare, dare una coltellata a.

knight [naɪt] *n* cavaliere *m*; (*CHESS*) cavallo; ~**hood** *n* (*title*): to get a ~**hood** essere fatto cavaliere.

knit [nɪt] *vt* fare a maglia; (*fig*): to ~ **together** unire // *vi* lavorare a maglia; (*broken bones*) saldarsi; ~**ting** *n* lavoro a maglia; ~**ting needle** *n* ferro (da calza); ~**wear** *n* maglieria.

knives [naɪvz] *npl of* **knife**.

knob [nɔb] *n* bottone *m*; manopola.

knock [nɔk] *vt* colpire; urtare; (*fig*: *col*) criticare // *vi* (*engine*) battere; (*at door etc*): to ~ **at**/**on** bussare a // *n* bussata; colpo, botta; to ~ **down** *vt* abbattere; to ~ **off** *vi* (*col*: *finish*) smettere (di lavorare); to ~ **out** *vt* stendere; (*BOXING*) mettere K.O.; to ~ **over** *vt* (*person*) investire; (*object*) far cadere; ~**er** *n* (*on door*) battente *m*; ~-**kneed** *a* che ha le gambe ad x; ~**out** *n* (*BOXING*) knock out *m inv*.

knot [nɔt] *n* nodo // *vt* annodare; ~**ty** *a* (*fig*) spinoso(a).

know [nəu] *vt* (*pt* **knew**, *pp* **known**) sapere; (*person*, *author*, *place*) conoscere; to ~ **how to** sapere fare; to ~ **about** *or of* sth/sb conoscere qc/qn; ~-**all** *n* sapientone/a; ~-**how** *n* tecnica; pratica; ~**ing** *a* (*look etc*) d'intesa; ~**ingly** *ad* (*purposely*) consapevolmente; (*smile*, *look*) con aria d'intesa.

knowledge ['nɔlɪdʒ] *n* consapevolezza; (*learning*) conoscenza, sapere *m*; ~**able** *a* ben informato(a).

known [nəun] *pp of* **know**.

knuckle ['nʌkl] *n* nocca.

Koran [kɔ'rɑːn] *n* Corano.

Korea [kə'rɪə] *n* Corea.

kosher ['kəuʃə*] *a* kasher *inv*.

L

lab [læb] *n abbr* (= *laboratory*) laboratorio.

label ['leɪbl] *n* etichetta, cartellino; (*brand*: *of record*) casa // *vt* etichettare.

laboratory [lə'bɔrətərɪ] *n* laboratorio.

labour, (*US*) **labor** ['leɪbə*] *n* (*task*) lavoro; (*workmen*) manodopera; (*MED*) travaglio del parto, doglie *fpl* // *vi*: to ~ (**at**) lavorare duro (a); **in** ~ (*MED*) il travaglio; ~, the L~ **party** (*Brit*) il partito laburista, i laburisti; ~**ed** *a* (*breathing*) affannoso(a); (*style*) pesante; ~**er** *n* manovale *m*; (*on farm*) lavoratore *m* agricolo.

lace [leɪs] *n* merletto, pizzo; (*of shoe etc*) laccio // *vt* (*shoe*) allacciare.

lack [læk] *n* mancanza // *vt* mancare di; **through** *or* **for** ~ **of** per mancanza di; to be ~**ing** mancare; to be ~**ing in** mancare di.

lackadaisical [lækə'deɪzɪkl] *a* disinteressato(a), noncurante.

lacquer ['lækə*] *n* lacca.

lad [læd] *n* ragazzo, giovanotto.

ladder ['lædə*] *n* scala; (*Brit*: *in tights*) smagliatura // *vt* smagliare // *vi* smagliarsi.

laden ['leɪdn] *a*:~ (**with**) carico(a) *or* caricato(a) (di).

ladle ['leɪdl] *n* mestolo.

lady ['leɪdɪ] *n* signora; dama; L~ **Smith** lady Smith; the **ladies'** (**room**) i gabinetti per signore; ~**bird**, (*US*) ~**bug** *n* coccinella; ~-**in-waiting** *n* dama di compagnia; ~**like** *a* da signora, distinto(a); ~**ship** *n*: your ~**ship** signora contessa (*or* baronessa *etc*).

lag [læg] *vi* (*also:* ~ **behind**) trascinarsi // *vt* (*pipes*) rivestire di materiale isolante.

lager ['lɑːgə*] *n* lager *m inv*.

lagoon [lə'guːn] *n* laguna.

laid [leɪd] *pt*, *pp of* **lay**; ~ **back** *a* (*col*) rilassato(a), tranquillo(a).

lain [leɪn] *pp of* **lie**.

lair [lɛə*] *n* covo, tana.

laity ['leɪətɪ] *n* laici *mpl*.

lake [leɪk] *n* lago.

lamb [læm] *n* agnello.

lame [leɪm] *a* zoppo(a).

lament [lə'mɛnt] *n* lamento // *vt*

lamentare, piangere.
laminated ['læmɪneɪtɪd] *a* laminato(a).
lamp [læmp] *n* lampada.
lampoon [læm'pu:n] *n* satira.
lamp: ~**post** *n* (*Brit*) lampione *m*; ~**shade** *n* paralume *m*.
lance [lɑ:ns] *n* lancia // *vt* (*MED*) incidere; ~ **corporal** *n* (*Brit*) caporale *m*.
land [lænd] *n* (*as opposed to sea*) terra (ferma); (*country*) paese *m*; (*soil*) terreno; suolo; (*estate*) terreni *mpl*, terre *fpl* // *vi* (*from ship*) sbarcare; (*AVIAT*) atterrare; (*fig: fall*) cadere // *vt* (*obtain*) acchiappare; (*passengers*) sbarcare; (*goods*) scaricare; **to ~ up** *vi* andare a finire; ~**ing** *n* sbarco; atterraggio; (*of staircase*) pianerottolo; ~**ing stage** *n* (*Brit*) pontile *m* da sbarco; ~**lady** *n* padrona *or* proprietaria di casa; ~**lord** *n* padrone *m or* proprietario di casa; (*of pub etc*) oste *m*; ~**mark** *n* punto di riferimento; (*fig*) pietra miliare; ~**owner** *n* proprietario(a) terriero(a).
landscape ['lænskeɪp] *n* paesaggio.
landslide ['lændslaɪd] *n* (*GEO*) frana; (*fig: POL*) valanga.
lane [leɪn] *n* (*in country*) viottolo; (*in town*) stradetta; (*AUT, in race*) corsia.
language ['læŋgwɪdʒ] *n* lingua; (*way one speaks*) linguaggio; **bad ~** linguaggio volgare; ~ **laboratory** *n* laboratorio linguistico.
languid ['læŋgwɪd] *a* languente; languido(a).
lank [læŋk] *a* (*hair*) liscio(a) e opaco(a).
lanky ['læŋkɪ] *a* allampanato(a).
lantern ['læntn] *n* lanterna.
lap [læp] *n* (*of track*) giro; (*of body*): **in** *or* **on one's ~** in grembo // *vt* (*also:* ~ **up**) papparsi, leccare // *vi* (*waves*) sciabordare.
lapel [lə'pɛl] *n* risvolto.
Lapland ['læplænd] *n* Lapponia.
lapse [læps] *n* lapsus *m inv*; (*longer*) caduta // *vi* (*law, act*) cadere; (*ticket, passport*) scadere; **to ~ into bad habits** pigliare cattive abitudini; ~ **of time** spazio di tempo.
larceny ['lɑ:sənɪ] *n* furto.
lard [lɑ:d] *n* lardo.
larder ['lɑ:də*] *n* dispensa.
large [lɑ:dʒ] *a* grande; (*person, animal*) grosso(a); **at ~** (*free*) in libertà; (*generally*) in generale; nell'insieme; ~**ly** *ad* in gran parte.
largesse [lɑ:'ʒes] *n* generosità.
lark [lɑ:k] *n* (*bird*) allodola; (*joke*) scherzo, gioco; **to ~ about** *vi* fare lo stupido.
laryngitis [lærɪn'dʒaɪtɪs] *n* laringite *f*.
laser ['leɪzə*] *n* laser *m*; ~ **printer** *n* stampante *f* laser *inv*.
lash [læʃ] *n* frustata; (*also:* eye~) ciglio

// *vt* frustare; (*tie*) assicurare con una corda; **to ~ out** *vi*: **to ~ out** (**at** *or* **against sb/sth**) attaccare violentemente (qn/qc); **to ~ out** (**on sth**) (*col: spend*) spendere un sacco di soldi (per qc).
lass [læs] *n* ragazza.
lasso [læ'su:] *n* laccio.
last [lɑ:st] *a* ultimo(a); (*week, month, year*) scorso(a), passato(a) // *ad* per ultimo // *vi* durare; ~ **week** la settimana scorsa; ~ **night** ieri sera, la notte scorsa; **at ~** finalmente, alla fine; ~ **but one** penultimo(a); ~**ditch** *a* (*attempt*) estremo(a); ~**ing** *a* durevole; ~**ly** *ad* infine, per finire; ~**minute** *a* fatto(a) (*or* preso(a) *etc*) all'ultimo momento.
latch [lætʃ] *n* serratura a scatto.
late [leɪt] *a* (*not on time*) in ritardo; (*far on in day etc*) tardi *inv*; tardo(a); (*recent*) recente, ultimo(a); (*former*) ex; (*dead*) defunto(a) // *ad* tardi; (*behind time, schedule*) in ritardo; **of ~** di recente; **in the ~ afternoon** nel tardo pomeriggio; **in ~ May** verso la fine di maggio; ~**comer** *n* ritardatario/a; ~**ly** *ad* recentemente.
later ['leɪtə*] *a* (*date etc*) posteriore; (*version etc*) successivo(a) // *ad* più tardi; ~ **on** più avanti.
lateral ['lætərl] *a* laterale.
latest ['leɪtɪst] *a* ultimo(a), più recente; **at the ~** al più tardi.
lathe [leɪð] *n* tornio.
lather ['lɑ:ðə*] *n* schiuma di sapone // *vt* insaponare.
Latin ['lætɪn] *n* latino // *a* latino(a); ~ **America** *n* America Latina; ~**American** *a* sudamericano(a).
latitude ['lætɪtju:d] *n* latitudine *f*.
latter ['lætə*] *a* secondo(a); più recente // *n*: **the ~** quest'ultimo, il secondo; ~**ly** *ad* recentemente, negli ultimi tempi.
lattice ['lætɪs] *n* traliccio; graticolato.
laudable ['lɔ:dəbl] *a* lodevole.
laugh [lɑ:f] *n* risata // *vi* ridere; **to ~ at** *vt fus* (*misfortune etc*) ridere di; **to ~ off** *vt* prendere alla leggera; ~**able** *a* ridicolo(a); ~**ing stock** *n*: **the ~ing stock of** lo zimbello di; ~**ter** *n* riso; risate *fpl*.
launch [lɔ:ntʃ] *n* (*of rocket etc*) lancio; (*of new ship*) varo; (*boat*) scialuppa; (*also:* **motor ~**) lancia // *vt* (*rocket*) lanciare; (*ship, plan*) varare; ~(**ing**) **pad** *n* rampa di lancio.
launder ['lɔ:ndə*] *vt* lavare e stirare.
launderette [lɔ:n'drɛt], (*US*) **laundromat** ['lɔ:ndrəmæt] *n* lavanderia (automatica).
laundry ['lɔ:ndrɪ] *n* lavanderia; (*clothes*) biancheria.
laureate ['lɔ:rɪət] *a see* **poet**.
laurel ['lɔrl] *n* lauro.
lava ['lɑ:və] *n* lava.
lavatory ['lævətərɪ] *n* gabinetto.

lavender ['lævəndə*] n lavanda.
lavish ['lævɪʃ] a copioso(a); abbondante; (giving freely): ~ **with** prodigo(a) di, largo(a) in // vt: to ~ **on sb/sth** (care) profondere a qn/qc.
law [lɔ:] n legge f; civil/criminal ~ diritto civile/penale; ~-**abiding** a ubbidiente alla legge; ~ **and order** n l'ordine m pubblico; ~ **court** n tribunale m, corte f di giustizia; ~**ful** a legale; lecito(a).
lawn [lɔ:n] n tappeto erboso; ~**mower** n tosaerba m or f inv; ~ **tennis** n tennis m su prato.
law school n facoltà f inv di legge.
lawsuit ['lɔ:su:t] n processo, causa.
lawyer ['lɔ:jə*] n (consultant, with company) giurista m/f; (for sales, wills etc) ≈ notaio; (partner, in court) ≈ avvocato/essa.
lax [læks] a rilassato(a); negligente.
laxative ['læksətɪv] n lassativo.
laxity ['læksɪtɪ] n rilassatezza; negligenza.
lay [leɪ] pt of **lie** // a laico(a); secolare // vt (pt, pp **laid**) posare, mettere; (eggs) fare; (trap) tendere; (plans) fare, elaborare; to ~ **the table** apparecchiare la tavola; to ~ **aside** or **by** vt mettere da parte; to ~ **down** vt mettere giù; to ~ **down the law** dettar legge; to ~ **off** vt (workers) licenziare; to ~ **on** vt (water, gas) installare, mettere; (provide) fornire; (paint) applicare; to ~ **out** vt (design) progettare; (display) presentare; (spend) sborsare; to ~ **up** vt (to store) accumulare; (ship) mettere in disarmo; (subj: illness) costringere a letto; ~**about** n sfaccendato/a, fannullone/a; ~-**by** n (Brit) piazzola (di sosta).
layer ['leɪə*] n strato.
layman ['leɪmən] n laico; profano.
layout ['leɪaʊt] n lay-out m inv, disposizione f; (PRESS) impaginazione f.
laze [leɪz] vi oziare.
lazy ['leɪzɪ] a pigro(a).
lb. abbr = **pound** (weight).
lead [li:d] n (front position) posizione f di testa; (distance, time ahead) vantaggio; (clue) indizio; (ELEC) filo (elettrico); (for dog) guinzaglio; (THEATRE) parte f principale; [lɛd] (metal) piombo; (in pencil) mina // vb (pt, pp **led**) vt menare, guidare, condurre; (induce) indurre; (be leader of) essere a capo di; (SPORT) essere in testa a // vi condurre, essere in testa; to ~ **astray** vt sviare; to ~ **away** vt condurre via; to ~ **back** vt: to ~ **back to** ricondurre a; to ~ **on** vt (tease) tenere sulla corda; to ~ **on to** (induce) portare a; to ~ **to** vt fus condurre a; portare a; to ~ **up to** vt fus portare a.
leaden ['lɛdn] a (sky, sea) plumbeo(a); (heavy: footsteps) pesante.

leader ['li:də*] n capo; leader m inv; (in newspaper) articolo di fondo; ~**ship** n direzione f; capacità f di comando.
leading ['li:dɪŋ] a primo(a); principale; ~ **man/lady** n (THEATRE) primo attore/prima attrice; ~ **light** n (person) personaggio di primo piano.
leaf [li:f] n (pl **leaves**) foglia; (of table) ribalta // ti: to ~ **through** sth sfogliare qc; to **turn over a new** ~ cambiar vita.
leaflet ['li:flɪt] n dépliant m inv; (POL, REL) volantino.
league [li:g] n lega; (FOOTBALL) campionato; to be in ~ **with** essere in lega con.
leak [li:k] n (out, also fig) fuga; (in) infiltrazione f // vi (roof, bucket) perdere; (liquid) uscire; (shoes) lasciar passare l'acqua // vt (liquid) spandere; (information) divulgare; to ~ **out** vi uscire; (information) trapelare.
lean [li:n] a magro(a) // vb (pt, pp **leaned** or **leant** [lɛnt]) vt: to ~ sth **on** sth appoggiare qc su qc // vi (slope) pendere; (rest): to ~ **against** appoggiarsi contro; essere appoggiato(a) a; to ~ **on** appoggiarsi a; to ~ **back/forward** vi sporgersi in avanti/indietro; to ~ **out** vi sporgersi; to ~ **over** vi inclinarsi; ~**ing** n: ~**ing (towards)** propensione f (per); ~-**to** n (roof) tettoia; (shed) capanno con tetto a una falda.
leap [li:p] n salto, balzo // vi (pt, pp **leaped** or **leapt** [lɛpt]) saltare, balzare; ~**frog** n gioco della cavallina; ~ **year** n anno bisestile.
learn, pt, pp **learned** or **learnt** [lə:n, -t] vt, vi imparare; to ~ **how to do** sth imparare a fare qc; ~**ed** ['lə:nɪd] a erudito(a), dotto(a); ~**er** n principiante m/f; apprendista m/f; (Brit: also: ~**er driver**) guidatore/trice principiante; ~**ing** n erudizione f, sapienza.
lease [li:s] n contratto d'affitto // vt affittare.
leash [li:ʃ] n guinzaglio.
least [li:st] a: the ~ + noun il(la) più piccolo(a), il(la) minimo(a); (smallest amount of) il(la) meno; the ~ + adjective: the ~ **beautiful girl** la ragazza meno bella; the ~ **expensive** il(la) meno caro(a); I **have the** ~ **money** ho meno denaro di tutti; at ~ almeno; not in the ~ affatto, per nulla.
leather ['lɛðə*] n cuoio // cpd di cuoio.
leave [li:v] vb (pt, pp **left**) vt lasciare; (go away from) partire da // vi partire, andarsene // n (time off) congedo; (MIL, also: consent) licenza; to **be left** rimanere; there's some **milk left over** c'è rimasto del latte; on ~ in congedo; to ~ **behind** vt (person, object) lasciare indietro; (: forget) dimenticare; to ~ **out** vt omettere, tralasciare; ~ **of absence** n congedo.

leaves [li:vz] *npl of* leaf.

Lebanon ['lɛbənən] *n* Libano.

lecherous ['lɛtʃərəs] *a* lascivo(a), lubrico(a).

lecture ['lɛktʃə*] *n* conferenza; (*SCOL*) lezione // *vi* fare conferenze; fare lezioni // *vt* (*scold*) rimproverare, fare una ramanzina a; **to ~ on** fare una conferenza su; **to give a ~ on** tenere una conferenza su.

lecturer ['lɛktʃərə*] *n* (*speaker*) conferenziere/a; (*Brit: at university*) professore/essa, docente *m/f*.

led [lɛd] *pt, pp of* lead.

ledge [lɛdʒ] *n* (*of window*) davanzale *m*; (*on wall etc*) sporgenza; (*of mountain*) cornice *f*, cengia.

ledger ['lɛdʒə*] *n* libro maestro, registro.

lee [li:] *n* lato sottovento.

leech [li:tʃ] *n* sanguisuga.

leek [li:k] *n* porro.

leer [liə*] *vi*: **to ~ at sb** gettare uno sguardo voglioso (*or* maligno) su qn.

leeway ['li:wei] *n* (*fig*): **to have some ~** avere una certa libertà di agire.

left [lɛft] *pt, pp of* leave // *a* sinistro(a) // *ad* a sinistra // *n* sinistra; **on the ~,** to **the ~** a sinistra; **the L~** (*POL*) la sinistra; **~-handed** a mancino(a); **~-hand side** *n* lato *or* fianco sinistro; **~ luggage (office)** *n* (*Brit*) deposito *m* bagagli *inv*; **~-overs** *npl* avanzi *mpl*, resti *mpl*; **~-wing** *a* (*POL*) di sinistra.

leg [lɛg] *n* gamba; (*of animal*) zampa; (*of furniture*) piede *m*; (*CULIN: of chicken*) coscia; (*of journey*) tappa; 1st/2nd ~ (*SPORT*) partita di andata/ritorno.

legacy ['lɛgəsɪ] *n* eredità *f inv*.

legal ['li:gl] *a* legale; **~ holiday** *n* (*US*) giorno festivo, festa nazionale; **~ tender** *n* moneta legale.

legend ['lɛdʒənd] *n* leggenda.

legible ['lɛdʒəbl] *a* leggibile.

legislation [lɛdʒɪs'leɪʃən] *n* legislazione *f*; **legislature** ['lɛdʒɪslətʃə*] *n* corpo legislativo.

legitimate [lɪ'dʒɪtɪmət] *a* legittimo(a).

leg-room ['lɛgru:m] *n* spazio per le gambe.

leisure ['lɛʒə*] *n* agio, tempo libero; ricreazioni *fpl*; **at ~** all'agio; a proprio comodo; **~ centre** *n* centro di ricreazione; **~ly** *a* tranquillo(a); fatto(a) con comodo *or* senza fretta.

lemon ['lɛmən] *n* limone *m*; **~ade** [-'neɪd] *n* limonata; **~ tea** *n* tè *m inv* al limone.

lend [lɛnd], *pt, pp* **lent** *vt*: **to ~ sth (to sb)** prestare qc (a sb).

length [lɛŋθ] *n* lunghezza; (*section: of road, pipe etc*) pezzo, tratto; **at ~** (*at last*) finalmente, alla fine; (*lengthily*) a lungo; **~en** *vt* allungare, prolungare // *vi* allungarsi; **~ways** *ad* per il lungo; **~y** *a* molto lungo(a).

lenient ['li:nɪənt] *a* indulgente, clemente.

lens [lɛnz] *n* lente *f*; (*of camera*) obiettivo.

Lent [lɛnt] *n* Quaresima.

lent [lɛnt] *pt, pp of* lend.

lentil ['lɛntl] *n* lenticchia.

Leo ['li:əu] *n* Leone *m*.

leotard ['li:əta:d] *n* calzamaglia.

leper ['lɛpə*] *n* lebbroso/a.

leprosy ['lɛprəsɪ] *n* lebbra.

lesbian ['lɛzbɪən] *n* lesbica.

less [lɛs] *a, pronoun, ad* meno; **~ than you/ever** meno di lei/che mai; **~ than half** meno della metà; **~ and ~** sempre meno; **the ~ he works ...** meno lavora ... .

lessen ['lɛsn] *vi* diminuire, attenuarsi // *vt* diminuire, ridurre.

lesser ['lɛsə*] *a* minore, più piccolo(a); **to a ~ extent** in grado *or* misura minore.

lesson ['lɛsn] *n* lezione *f*.

lest [lɛst] *cj* per paura di + *infinitive*, per paura che + *sub*.

let, *pt, pp* **let** [lɛt] *vt* lasciare; (*Brit: lease*) dare in affitto; **to ~ sb do sth** lasciar fare qc a qn, lasciare che qn faccia qc; **to ~ sb know sth** far sapere qc a qn; **he ~ me go** mi ha lasciato andare; **~'s go** andiamo; **~ him come** lo lasci venire; "**to ~**" "affittasi"; **to ~ down** *vt* (*lower*) abbassare; (*dress*) allungare; (*hair*) sciogliere; (*disappoint*) deludere; **to ~ go** *vt, vi* mollare; **to ~ in** *vt* lasciare entrare; (*visitor etc*) far entrare; **to ~ off** *vt* (*allow to go*) lasciare andare; (*firework etc*) far partire; (*smell etc*) emettere; **to ~ on** *vi* (*col*) dire; **to ~ out** *vt* lasciare uscire; (*dress*) allargare; (*scream*) emettere; **to ~ up** *vi* diminuire.

lethal ['li:θl] *a* letale, mortale.

lethargy ['lɛθədʒɪ] *n* letargia.

letter ['lɛtə*] *n* lettera; **~ bomb** *n* lettera esplosiva; **~box** *n* (*Brit*) buca delle lettere; **~ing** *n* iscrizione *f*; caratteri *mpl*.

lettuce ['lɛtɪs] *n* lattuga, insalata.

leukaemia, (*US*) **leukemia** [lu:'ki:mɪə] *n* leucemia.

level ['lɛvl] *a* piatto(a), piano(a); orizzontale // *n* livello; (*also:* **spirit ~**) livella (a bolla d'aria) // *vt* livellare, spianare; **to be ~ with** essere alla pari di; **A ~s** *npl* (*Brit*) ≈ esami *mpl* di maturità; **O ~s** *npl* (*Brit*) *esami fatti in Inghilterra all'età di 16 anni*; **on the ~** piatto(a); (*fig*) onesto(a); **to ~ off** *or* **out** *vi* (*prices etc*) stabilizzarsi; **~ crossing** *n* (*Brit*) passaggio a livello; **~-headed** *a* equilibrato(a).

lever ['li:və*] *n* leva // *vt*: **to ~ up/out** sollevare/estrarre con una leva; **~age** *n*: **~age (on** *or* **with)** ascendente *m* (su).

levy ['lɛvɪ] *n* tassa, imposta // *vt* imporre.

lewd [lu:d] *a* osceno(a), lascivo(a).

liability [laɪə'bɪlətɪ] n responsabilità f inv; (handicap) peso; **liabilities** npl debiti mpl; (on balance sheet) passivo.

liable ['laɪəbl] a (subject): ~ to soggetto(a) a; passibile di; (responsible): ~ (for) responsabile (di); (likely): ~ to do propenso(a) a fare.

liaison [liː'eɪzɔn] n relazione f; (MIL) collegamento.

liar ['laɪə*] n bugiardo/a.

libel ['laɪbl] n libello, diffamazione f // vt diffamare.

liberal ['lɪbərl] a liberale; (generous): to be ~ with distribuire liberalmente.

liberty ['lɪbətɪ] n libertà f inv; at ~ to do libero(a) di fare.

Libra ['liːbrə] n Bilancia.

librarian [laɪ'brɛərɪən] n bibliotecario/a.

library ['laɪbrərɪ] n biblioteca.

Libya ['lɪbɪə] n Libia.

lice [laɪs] npl of **louse**.

licence, (US) **license** ['laɪsns] n autorizzazione f, permesso; (COMM) licenza; (RADIO, TV) canone m, abbonamento; (also: driving ~, (US) driver's ~) patente f di guida; (excessive freedom) licenza; ~ **number** n numero di targa; ~ **plate** n targa.

license ['laɪsns] n = **licence** // vt dare una licenza a; **~d** a (for alcohol) che ha la licenza di vendere bibite alcoliche.

lick [lɪk] vt leccare.

licorice ['lɪkərɪs] n = **liquorice**.

lid [lɪd] n coperchio.

lie [laɪ] n bugia, menzogna // vi mentire, dire bugie; (pt **lay**, pp **lain**) (rest) giacere, star disteso(a); (in grave) giacere, riposare; (of object: be situated) trovarsi, essere; to ~ **low** (fig) latitare; **to** ~ **about** vi (things) essere in giro; (person) bighellonare; **~-down** n (Brit): to have a ~-down sdraiarsi, riposarsi; **~-in** n (Brit): to have a ~-in rimanere a letto.

lieutenant [lɛf'tɛnənt, (US) luː'tɛnənt] n tenente m.

life [laɪf] n (pl **lives**) vita // cpd di vita; della vita; a vita; ~ **assurance** n (Brit) assicurazione f sulla vita; **~belt** n (Brit) salvagente m; **~boat** n scialuppa di salvataggio; **~guard** n bagnino; ~ **insurance** n = ~ **assurance**; ~ **jacket** n giubbotto di salvataggio; **~less** a senza vita; **~like** a verosimile; rassomigliante; **~long** a per tutta la vita; ~ **preserver** n (US) salvagente m; giubbotto di salvataggio; **~-saver** n bagnino; ~ **sentence** n ergastolo; **~-sized** a a grandezza naturale; ~ **span** n (durata della) vita; **~style** n stile m di vita; ~ **support system** n respiratore m automatico; **~time** n: in his ~time durante la sua vita; once in a ~time una volta nella vita.

lift [lɪft] vt sollevare, levare; (steal) prendere, rubare // vi (fog) alzarsi // n (Brit: elevator) ascensore m; to give sb a ~ (Brit) dare un passaggio a qn; **~-off** n decollo.

light [laɪt] n luce f, lume m; (daylight) luce f, giorno; (lamp) lampada; (AUT: rear ~) luce f di posizione; (: headlamp) fanale m; (for cigarette etc): have you got a ~? ha da accendere? // vt (pt, pp **lighted** or **lit**) (candle, cigarette, fire) accendere; (room) illuminare // a (room, colour) chiaro(a); (not heavy, also fig) leggero(a); **~s** npl (AUT: traffic ~s) semaforo; **to come to** ~ venire alla luce, emergere; **to** ~ **up** vi illuminarsi // vt illuminare; ~ **bulb** n lampadina; **~en** vi schiarirsi // vt (give light to) illuminare; (make lighter) schiarire; (make less heavy) alleggerire; **~er** n (also: cigarette **~er**) accendino; (boat) chiatta; **~-headed** a stordito(a); **~-hearted** a gioioso(a), gaio(a); **~house** n faro; **~ing** n illuminazione f; **~ly** ad leggermente; **to get off** ~ly cavarsela a buon mercato; **~ness** n chiarezza; (in weight) leggerezza.

lightning ['laɪtnɪŋ] n lampo, fulmine m; ~ **conductor**, (US) ~ **rod** n parafulmine m.

light pen n penna ottica.

lightweight ['laɪtweɪt] a (suit) leggero(a); (boxer) peso leggero inv // n (BOXING) peso leggero.

like [laɪk] vt (person) volere bene a; (activity, object, food): I ~ **swimming/ that book/chocolate** mi piace nuotare/ quel libro/il cioccolato // prep come // a simile, uguale // n: the ~ uno(a) uguale; his **~s and dislikes** i suoi gusti; I would ~, I'd ~ mi piacerebbe, vorrei; **would you** ~ **a coffee?** gradirebbe un caffè?; to be/look ~ sb/sth somigliare a qn/qc; that's just ~ him è proprio da lui; do it ~ this fallo così; it is nothing ~ ... non è affatto come ...; **~able** a simpatico(a).

likelihood ['laɪklɪhud] n probabilità.

likely ['laɪklɪ] a probabile; plausibile; he's ~ to leave probabilmente partirà, è probabile che parta; not ~! neanche per sogno!

likeness ['laɪknɪs] n somiglianza.

likewise ['laɪkwaɪz] ad similmente, nello stesso modo.

liking ['laɪkɪŋ] n: ~ (for) debole m (per).

lilac ['laɪlək] n lilla m inv // a lilla inv.

lily ['lɪlɪ] n giglio; ~ **of the valley** n mughetto.

limb [lɪm] n membro.

limber ['lɪmbə*]: **to** ~ **up** vi riscaldarsi i muscoli.

limbo ['lɪmbəu] n: to be in ~ (fig) essere lasciato(a) nel dimenticatoio.

lime [laɪm] n (tree) tiglio; (fruit) limetta; (GEO) calce f.

limelight ['laɪmlaɪt] *n*: **in the ~** (*fig*) alla ribalta, in vista.

limerick ['lɪmərɪk] *n poesiola umoristica di 5 versi.*

limestone ['laɪmstəun] *n* pietra calcarea; (*GEO*) calcare *m*.

limit ['lɪmɪt] *n* limite *m* // *vt* limitare; **~ed** *a* limitato(a), ristretto(a); **to be ~ed to** limitarsi a; **~ed (liability) company (Ltd)** *n* (*Brit*) ≈ società *f inv* a responsabilità limitata (S.r.l.).

limp [lɪmp] *n*: **to have a ~** zoppicare // *vi* zoppicare // *a* floscio(a), flaccido(a).

limpet ['lɪmpɪt] *n* patella.

line [laɪn] *n* linea; (*rope*) corda; (*wire*) filo; (*of poem*) verso; (*row, series*) fila, riga; coda // *vt* (*clothes*): **to ~ (with)** foderare (di); (*box*): **to ~ (with)** rivestire *or* foderare (di); (*subj*: *trees, crowd*) fiancheggiare; **~ of business** settore *m or* ramo d'attività; **in ~ with** in linea con; **to ~ up** *vi* allinearsi, mettersi in fila // *vt* mettere in fila.

lined [laɪnd] *a* (*face*) rugoso(a); (*paper*) a righe, rigato(a).

linen ['lɪnɪn] *n* biancheria, panni *mpl*; (*cloth*) tela di lino.

liner ['laɪnə*] *n* nave *f* di linea.

linesman ['laɪnzmən] *n* guardalinee *m inv.*

line-up ['laɪnʌp] *n* allineamento, fila; (*SPORT*) formazione *f* di gioco.

linger ['lɪŋgə*] *vi* attardarsi; indugiare; (*smell, tradition*) persistere.

lingo, ~es ['lɪŋgəu] *n* (*pej*) gergo.

linguistics [lɪŋ'gwɪstɪks] *n* linguistica.

lining ['laɪnɪŋ] *n* fodera.

link [lɪŋk] *n* (*of a chain*) anello; (*connection*) legame *m*, collegamento // *vt* collegare, unire, congiungere; **~s** *npl* (*GOLF*) pista *or* terreno da golf; **to ~ up** *vt* collegare, unire // *vi* riunirsi; associarsi.

lino ['laɪnəu], **linoleum** [lɪ'nəulɪəm] *n* linoleum *m inv.*

lion ['laɪən] *n* leone *m*; **~ess** *n* leonessa.

lip [lɪp] *n* labbro; (*of cup etc*) orlo; (*insolence*) sfacciataggine *f*; **~read** *vi* leggere sulle labbra; **~ salve** *n* burro di cacao; **~ service** *n*: **to pay ~ service to sth** essere favorevole a qc solo a parole; **~stick** *n* rossetto.

liqueur [lɪ'kjuə*] *n* liquore *m*.

liquid ['lɪkwɪd] *n* liquido // *a* liquido(a).

liquidize ['lɪkwɪdaɪz] *vt* (*CULIN*) passare al frullatore; **~r** *n* frullatore *m* (a brocca).

liquor ['lɪkə*] *n* alcool *m*.

liquorice ['lɪkərɪs] *n* liquirizia.

liquor store *n* (*US*) negozio di liquori.

lisp [lɪsp] *n* difetto nel pronunciare le sibilanti.

list [lɪst] *n* lista, elenco; (*of ship*) sbandamento // *vt* (*write down*) mettere in lista; fare una lista di; (*enumerate*)

elencare // *vi* (*ship*) sbandare.

listen ['lɪsn] *vi* ascoltare; **to ~ to** ascoltare; **~er** *n* ascoltatore/trice.

listless ['lɪstlɪs] *a* apatico(a).

lit [lɪt] *pt, pp of* **light**.

liter ['li:tə*] *n* (*US*) = **litre**.

literacy ['lɪtərəsɪ] *n* il sapere leggere e scrivere.

literal ['lɪtərl] *a* letterale.

literary ['lɪtərərɪ] *a* letterario(a).

literate ['lɪtərət] *a* che sa leggere e scrivere.

literature ['lɪtərɪtʃə*] *n* letteratura; (*brochures etc*) materiale *m*.

lithe [laɪð] *a* agile, snello(a).

litigation [lɪtɪ'geɪʃən] *n* causa.

litre, (US**) liter** ['li:tə*] *n* litro.

litter ['lɪtə*] *n* (*rubbish*) rifiuti *mpl*; (*young animals*) figliata // *vt* sparpagliare; lasciare rifiuti in; **~ bin** *n* (*Brit*) cestino per rifiuti; **~ed** *a*: **~ed with** coperto(a) di.

little ['lɪtl] *a* (*small*) piccolo(a); (*not much*) poco(a) // *ad* poco; **a ~** un po' (di); **a ~ milk** un po' di latte; **~ by ~** a poco a poco.

live *vi* [lɪv] vivere; (*reside*) vivere, abitare // *a* [laɪv] (*animal*) vivo(a); (*wire*) sotto tensione; (*broadcast*) diretto(a); **to ~ down** *vt* far dimenticare (alla gente); **to ~ on** *vt fus* (*food*) vivere di // *vi* sopravvivere, continuare a vivere; **to ~ together** *vi* vivere insieme, convivere; **to ~ up to** *vt fus* tener fede a, non venir meno a.

livelihood ['laɪvlɪhud] *n* mezzi *mpl* di sostentamento.

lively ['laɪvlɪ] *a* vivace, vivo(a).

liven up ['laɪvn'ʌp] *vt* (*discussion, evening*) animare.

liver ['lɪvə*] *n* fegato.

livery ['lɪvərɪ] *n* livrea.

lives [laɪvz] *npl of* **life**.

livestock ['laɪvstɔk] *n* bestiame *m*.

livid ['lɪvɪd] *a* livido(a); (*furious*) livido(a) di rabbia, furibondo(a).

living ['lɪvɪŋ] *a* vivo(a), vivente // *n*: **to earn** *or* **make a ~** guadagnarsi la vita; **~ conditions** *npl* condizioni *fpl* di vita; **~ room** *n* soggiorno; **~ wage** *n* salario sufficiente per vivere.

lizard ['lɪzəd] *n* lucertola.

load [ləud] *n* (*weight*) peso; (*ELEC, TECH, thing carried*) carico // *vt* (*also*: **~ up**): **to ~ (with)** (*lorry, ship*) caricare (di); (*gun, camera, COMPUT*) caricare (con); **a ~ of, ~s of** (*fig*) un sacco di; **~ed** *a* (*dice*) falsato(a); (*question*) capzioso(a); (*col*: *rich*) carico(a); di soldi; (*: drunk*) ubriaco(a); **~ing bay** *n* piazzola di carico.

loaf [ləuf] *n* (*pl* **loaves**) *n* pane *m*, pagnotta // *vi* (*also*: **~ about, ~ around**) bighellonare.

loan [ləun] *n* prestito // *vt* dare in prestito; **on ~** in prestito.

loath [ləʊθ] *a*: **to be ~ to do** essere restio(a) a fare.

loathe [ləʊð] *vt* detestare, aborrire.

loaves [ˈləʊvz] *npl of* **loaf**.

lobby [ˈlɔbɪ] *n* atrio, vestibolo; (*POL: pressure group*) gruppo di pressione // *vt* fare pressione su.

lobster [ˈlɔbstə*] *n* aragosta.

local [ˈləʊkl] *a* locale // *n* (*Brit: pub*) ≈ bar *m inv* all'angolo; **the ~s** *npl* la gente della zona; **~ call** *n* (*TEL*) telefonata urbana; **~ government** *n* amministrazione *f* locale.

locality [ləʊˈkælɪtɪ] *n* località *f inv*; (*position*) posto, luogo.

locally [ˈləʊkəlɪ] *ad* da queste parti; nel vicinato.

locate [ləʊˈkeɪt] *vt* (*find*) trovare; (*situate*) collocare.

location [ləʊˈkeɪʃən] *n* posizione *f*; **on ~** (*CINEMA*) all'esterno.

loch [lɔx] *n* lago.

lock [lɔk] *n* (*of door, box*) serratura; (*of canal*) chiusa; (*of hair*) ciocca, riccio // *vt* (*with key*) chiudere a chiave; (*immobilize*) bloccare // *vi* (*door etc*) chiudersi; (*wheels*) bloccarsi, incepparsi.

locker [ˈlɔkə*] *n* armadietto.

locket [ˈlɔkɪt] *n* medaglione *m*.

locksmith [ˈlɔksmɪθ] *n* magnano.

lock-up [ˈlɔkʌp] *n* (*garage*) box *m inv*.

locomotive [ləʊkəˈməʊtɪv] *n* locomotiva.

locum [ˈləʊkəm] *n* (*MED*) medico sostituto.

locust [ˈləʊkəst] *n* locusta.

lodge [lɔdʒ] *n* casetta, portineria // *vi* (*person*): **to ~ (with)** essere a pensione (presso *or* da) // *vt* (*appeal etc*) presentare, fare; **to ~ a complaint** presentare un reclamo; **~r** *n* affittuario/a; (*with room and meals*) pensionante *m/f*.

lodgings [ˈlɔdʒɪŋz] *npl* camera d'affitto; camera ammobiliata.

loft [lɔft] *n* solaio, soffitta; (*AGR*) granaio.

lofty [ˈlɔftɪ] *a* alto(a); (*haughty*) altezzoso(a).

log [lɔg] *n* (*of wood*) ceppo; (*book*) = **logbook**.

logbook [ˈlɔgbuk] *n* (*NAUT, AVIAT*) diario di bordo; (*AUT*) libretto di circolazione; (*of lorry driver*) registro di viaggio; (*of events, movement of goods etc*) registro.

loggerheads [ˈlɔgəhɛdz] *npl*: **at ~ (with)** ai ferri corti (con).

logic [ˈlɔdʒɪk] *n* logica; **~al** *a* logico(a).

loin [lɔɪn] *n* (*CULIN*) lombata.

loiter [ˈlɔɪtə*] *vi* attardarsi; **to ~ (about)** indugiare, bighellonare.

loll [lɔl] *vi* (*also*: **~ about**) essere stravaccato(a).

lollipop [ˈlɔlɪpɔp] *n* lecca lecca *m inv*; **~ man/lady** *n* (*Brit*) impiegato/a che aiuta i bambini ad attraversare la strada in vicinanza di scuole.

London [ˈlʌndən] *n* Londra; **~er** *n* londinese *m/f*.

lone [ləʊn] *a* solitario(a).

loneliness [ˈləʊnlɪnɪs] *n* solitudine *f*, isolamento.

lonely [ˈləʊnlɪ] *a* solo(a); solitario(a), isolato(a).

long [lɔŋ] *a* lungo(a) // *ad* a lungo, per molto tempo // *vi*: **to ~ for sth/to do** desiderare ardentemente qc/di fare; non veder l'ora di aver qc/di fare; **so or as ~ as** (*while*) finché; (*provided that*) sempre che + *sub*; **don't be ~!** fai presto!; **how ~ is this river/course?** quanto è lungo questo fiume/corso?; **6 metres ~** lungo 6 metri; **6 months ~** che dura 6 mesi, di 6 mesi; **all night ~** tutta la notte; **he no ~er comes** non viene più; **~ before** molto tempo prima; **before ~** (+ *future*) fra poco, (+ *past*) poco tempo dopo; **at ~ last** finalmente; **~-distance** *a* (*race*) di fondo; (*call*) interurbano(a); **~hand** *n* scrittura normale; **~ing** *n* desiderio, voglia, brama // *a* di desiderio; pieno(a) di nostalgia.

longitude [ˈlɔŋgɪtjuːd] *n* longitudine *f*.

long: **~ jump** *n* salto in lungo; **~-playing record (L.P.)** *n* (disco) 33 giri *m inv*; **~-range** *a* a lunga portata; **~-sighted** *a* presbite; (*fig*) lungimirante; **~-standing** *a* di vecchia data; **~-suffering** *a* estremamente paziente; infinitamente tollerante; **~-term** *a* a lungo termine; **~ wave** *n* onde *fpl* lunghe; **~-winded** *a* prolisso(a), interminabile.

loo [luː] *n* (*Brit col*) W.C. *m inv*, cesso.

look [luk] *vi* guardare; (*seem*) sembrare, parere; (*building etc*): **to ~ south/on to the sea** dare a sud/sul mare // *n* sguardo; (*appearance*) aspetto, aria; **~s** *npl* aspetto; bellezza; **to ~ after** *vt fus* occuparsi di, prendere cura di; (*keep an eye on*) guardare, badare a; **to ~ at** *vt fus* guardare; **to ~ back** *vi*: **to ~ back at** voltarsi a guardare; **to ~ back on** (*event etc*) ripensare a; **to ~ down on** *vt fus* (*fig*) guardare dall'alto, disprezzare; **to ~ for** *vt fus* cercare; **to ~ forward to** *vt fus* non veder l'ora di; (*in letters*): **we ~ forward to hearing from you** in attesa di una vostra gentile risposta; **to ~ into** *vt fus* esaminare; **to ~ on** *vi* fare da spettatore; **to ~ out** *vi* (*beware*): **to ~ out (for)** stare in guardia (per); **to ~ out for** *vt fus* cercare; (*watch for*): **to ~ out for sb/sth** guardare se arriva qn/qc; **to ~ round** *vi* (*turn*) girarsi, voltarsi; (*in shop*) dare un'occhiata; **to ~ to** *vt fus* stare attento(a) a; (*rely on*) contare su; **to ~**

up *vi* alzare gli occhi; *(improve)* migliorare // *vt (word)* cercare; *(friend)* andare a trovare; **to ~ up to** *vt fus* avere rispetto per; **~-out** *n* posto d'osservazione; guardia; **to be on the ~-out (for)** stare in guardia (per).

loom [lu:m] *n* telaio // *vi* sorgere; *(fig)* minacciare.

loony ['lu:nɪ] *n (col)* pazzo/a.

loop [lu:p] *n* cappio; **~hole** *n* via d'uscita; scappatoia.

loose [lu:s] *a (knot)* sciolto(a); *(screw)* allentato(a); *(stone)* cadente; *(clothes)* ampio(a), largo(a); *(animal)* in libertà, scappato(a); *(life, morals)* dissoluto(a); *(discipline)* allentato(a); *(thinking)* poco rigoroso(a), vago(a); **~ change** *n* spiccioli *mpl*, moneta; **~ chippings** *npl (on road)* ghiaino; **~ end** *n*: **to be at a ~ end** *or (US)* **at ~ ends** non saper che fare; **~ly** *ad* lentamente; approssimativamente; **~n** *vt* sciogliere.

loot [lu:t] *n* bottino // *vt* saccheggiare.

lop [lɔp] *vt (also: ~ off)* tagliare via, recidere.

lop-sided ['lɔp'saɪdɪd] *a* non equilibrato(a), asimmetrico(a).

lord [lɔ:d] *n* signore *m*; **L~ Smith** lord Smith; **the L~** il Signore; **the (House of) L~s** *(Brit)* la Camera dei Lord; **~ship** *n*: **your L~ship** Sua Eccellenza.

lore [lɔ:*] *n* tradizioni *fpl*.

lorry ['lɔrɪ] *n (Brit)* camion *m inv*; **~ driver** *n (Brit)* camionista *m*.

lose [lu:z], *pt, pp* **lost** *vt* perdere; *(pursuers)* distanziare // *vi* perdere; **to ~ (time) (clock)** ritardare; **to get lost** *vi* perdersi, smarrirsi; **~r** *n* perdente *m/f*.

loss [lɔs] *n* perdita; **to be at a ~** essere perplesso(a).

lost [lɔst] *pt, pp of* **lose** // *a* perduto(a); **~ property**, *(US)* **~ and found** *n* oggetti *mpl* smarriti.

lot [lɔt] *n (at auctions)* lotto; *(destiny)* destino, sorte *f*; **the ~** tutto(a) quanto(a); tutti(e) quanti(e); **a ~** molto(a); **a ~ of** una gran quantità di, un sacco di; **~s of** molto(a); **to draw ~s (for sth)** tirare a sorte (per qc).

lotion ['ləuʃən] *n* lozione *f*.

lottery ['lɔtərɪ] *n* lotteria.

loud [laud] *a* forte, alto(a); *(gaudy)* vistoso(a), sgargiante // *ad (speak etc)* forte; **~hailer** *n (Brit)* portavoce *m inv*; **~ly** *ad* fortemente, ad alta voce; **~speaker** *n* altoparlante *m*.

lounge [laundʒ] *n* salotto, soggiorno // *vi* oziare; starsene colle mani in mano; **~ suit** *n (Brit)* completo da uomo.

louse [laus], *pl* **lice** *n* pidocchio.

lousy ['lauzɪ] *a (fig)* orrendo(a), schifoso(a).

lout [laut] *n* zoticone *m*.

louvre, *(US)* **louver** ['lu:və*] *a (door, window)* con apertura a gelosia.

lovable ['lʌvəbl] *a* simpatico(a), carino(a); amabile.

love [lʌv] *n* amore *m* // *vt* amare; voler bene a; **to ~ to do**: **I ~ to do** mi piace fare; **to be in ~ with** essere innamorato(a) di; **to make ~** fare l'amore; **"15 ~"** *(TENNIS)* "15 a zero"; **~ affair** *n* relazione *f*; **~ life** *n* vita sentimentale.

lovely ['lʌvlɪ] *a* bello(a); *(delicious: smell, meal)* buono(a).

lover ['lʌvə*] *n* amante *m/f*; *(amateur)*: **a ~ of** un(un')amante di; un(un')appassionato(a) di.

loving ['lʌvɪŋ] *a* affettuoso(a), amoroso(a), tenero(a).

low [ləu] *a* basso(a) // *ad* in basso // *n (METEOR)* depressione *f* // *vi (cow)* muggire; **to feel ~** sentirsi giù; **to turn (down) ~** *vt* abbassare; **~ a (dress)** scollato(a); **~er** *vt* calare; *(reduce)* abbassare; **~-fat** *a* magro(a); **~lands** *npl (GEO)* pianura; **~ly** *a* umile, modesto(a); **~-lying** *a* a basso livello.

loyal ['lɔɪəl] *a* fedele, leale; **~ty** *n* fedeltà, lealtà.

lozenge ['lɔzɪndʒ] *n (MED)* pastiglia; *(GEOM)* losanga.

L.P. *n abbr* = **long-playing record.**

L-plates ['ɛlpleɪts] *npl (Brit)* cartelli sui veicoli dei guidatori principianti.

Ltd *abbr* = **limited.**

lubricant ['lu:brɪkənt] *n* lubrificante *m*.

lubricate ['lu:brɪkeɪt] *vt* lubrificare.

luck [lʌk] *n* fortuna, sorte *f*; **bad ~** sfortuna, mala sorte; **good ~!** buona fortuna!; **~ily** *ad* fortunatamente, per fortuna; **~y** *a* fortunato(a); *(number etc)* che porta fortuna.

ludicrous ['lu:dɪkrəs] *a* ridicolo(a), assurdo(a).

lug [lʌg] *vt* trascinare.

luggage ['lʌgɪdʒ] *n* bagagli *mpl*; **~ rack** *n* portabagagli *m inv*.

lukewarm ['lu:kwɔ:m] *a* tiepido(a).

lull [lʌl] *n* intervallo di calma // *vt (child)* cullare; *(person, fear)* acquietare, calmare.

lullaby ['lʌləbaɪ] *n* ninnananna.

lumbago [lʌm'beɪgəu] *n* lombaggine *f*.

lumber ['lʌmbə*] *n* roba vecchia; **~jack** *n* boscaiolo.

luminous ['lu:mɪnəs] *a* luminoso(a).

lump [lʌmp] *n* pezzo; *(in sauce)* grumo; *(swelling)* gonfiore *m* // *vt (also: ~ together)* riunire, mettere insieme; **a ~ sum** una somma globale.

lunacy ['lu:nəsɪ] *n* demenza, follia, pazzia.

lunar ['lu:nə*] *a* lunare.

lunatic ['lu:nətɪk] *a, n* pazzo(a), matto(a).

lunch [lʌntʃ] *n* pranzo, colazione *f*.

luncheon ['lʌntʃən] *n* pranzo; **~ meat** *n*

≈ mortadella; ~ **voucher** n buono m
pasto inv.

lung [lʌŋ] n polmone m.

lunge [lʌndʒ] vi (also: ~ **forward**) fare
un balzo in avanti; **to ~ at** balzare su.

lurch [ləːtʃ] vi vacillare, barcollare // n
scatto improvviso; **to leave sb in the ~**
piantare in asso qn.

lure [luə*] n richiamo; lusinga // vt
attirare (con l'inganno).

lurid ['luərɪd] a sgargiante; (details etc)
impressionante.

lurk [ləːk] vi stare in agguato.

luscious ['lʌʃəs] a succulento(a);
delizioso(a).

lush [lʌʃ] a lussureggiante.

lust [lʌst] n lussuria; cupidigia;
desiderio; (fig): ~ **for** sete f di; **to ~**
after vt fus bramare, desiderare.

lusty ['lʌstɪ] a vigoroso(a), robusto(a).

Luxembourg ['lʌksəmbəːg] n (state)
Lussemburgo m; (city) Lussemburgo f.

luxuriant [lʌg'zjuəriənt] a lussureggiante.

luxurious [lʌg'zjuəriəs] a sontuoso(a), di
lusso.

luxury ['lʌkʃərɪ] n lusso // cpd di lusso.

lying ['laɪɪŋ] n bugie fpl, menzogne fpl.

lynch [lɪntʃ] vt linciare.

lynx [lɪŋks] n lince f.

lyric ['lɪrɪk] a lirico(a); ~**s** npl (of song)
parole fpl; ~**al** a lirico(a).

M

m. abbr = **metre, mile, million.**

M.A. abbr = **Master of Arts.**

mac [mæk] n (Brit) impermeabile m.

macaroni [mækə'rəunɪ] n maccheroni
mpl.

mace [meɪs] n mazza; (spice) macis m
or f.

machine [mə'ʃiːn] n macchina // vt
(dress etc) cucire a macchina; ~ **gun** n
mitragliatrice f; ~**ry** n macchinario,
macchine fpl; (fig) macchina.

mackerel ['mækrl] n (pl inv) sgombro.

mackintosh ['mækɪntɔʃ] n (Brit)
impermeabile m.

mad [mæd] a matto(a), pazzo(a);
(foolish) sciocco(a); (angry) furioso(a).

madam ['mædəm] n signora.

madden ['mædn] vt fare infuriare.

made [meɪd] pt, pp of **make.**

Madeira [mə'dɪərə] n (GEO) Madera;
(wine) madera.

made-to-measure ['meɪdtə'meʒə*] a
(Brit) fatto(a) su misura.

madly ['mædlɪ] ad follemente; (love) alla
follia.

madman ['mædmən] n pazzo, alienato.

madness ['mædnɪs] n pazzia.

magazine [mægə'ziːn] n (PRESS) rivista;
(MIL: store) magazzino, deposito; (of
firearm) caricatore m.

maggot ['mægət] n baco, verme m.

magic ['mædʒɪk] n magia // a magico(a);
~**al** a magico(a); ~**ian** [mə'dʒɪʃən] n
mago/a.

magistrate ['mædʒɪstreɪt] n magistrato;
giudice m/f.

magnet ['mægnɪt] n magnete m,
calamita; ~**ic** [-'netɪk] a magnetico(a).

magnificent [mæg'nɪfɪsnt] a ma-
gnifico(a).

magnify ['mægnɪfaɪ] vt ingrandire; ~**ing**
glass n lente f d'ingrandimento.

magnitude ['mægnɪtjuːd] n grandezza;
importanza.

magpie ['mægpaɪ] n gazza.

mahogany [mə'hɔgənɪ] n mogano // cpd
di or in mogano.

maid [meɪd] n domestica; (in hotel)
cameriera; **old ~** (pej) vecchia zitella.

maiden ['meɪdn] n fanciulla // a (aunt
etc) nubile; (speech, voyage)
inaugurale; ~ **name** n nome m nubile
or da ragazza.

mail [meɪl] n posta // vt spedire (per posta); ~**box** n (US) cassetta delle
lettere; ~**ing list** n elenco d'indirizzi;
~**-order** n vendita (or acquisto) per
corrispondenza.

maim [meɪm] vt mutilare.

main [meɪn] a principale // n (pipe)
conduttura principale; **the ~s** (ELEC) la
linea principale; **in the ~** nel complesso,
nell'insieme; ~**frame** n (COMPUT)
mainframe m inv; ~**land** n continente
m; ~**ly** ad principalmente, soprattutto;
~ **road** n strada principale; ~**stay** n
(fig) sostegno principale; ~**stream** n
(fig) corrente f principale.

maintain [meɪn'teɪn] vt mantenere;
(affirm) sostenere; **maintenance**
['meɪntənəns] n manutenzione f;
(alimony) alimenti mpl.

maize [meɪz] n granturco, mais m.

majestic [mə'dʒestɪk] a maestoso(a).

majesty ['mædʒɪstɪ] n maestà f inv.

major ['meɪdʒə*] n (MIL) maggiore m //
a (greater, MUS) maggiore; (in
importance) principale, importante.

Majorca [mə'jɔːkə] n Maiorca.

majority [mə'dʒɔrɪtɪ] n maggioranza.

make [meɪk] vt (pt, pp **made**) fare;
(manufacture) fare, fabbricare; (cause
to be): **to ~ sb sad** etc rendere qn triste
etc; (force): **to ~ sb do sth** costringere
qn a fare qc, far fare qc a qn; (equal): **2**
and 2 ~ 4 2 più 2 fa 4 // n fabbricazione
f; (brand) marca; **to ~ a fool of sb** far
fare a qn la figura dello scemo; **to ~ a**
profit realizzare un profitto; **to ~ a loss**
subire una perdita; **to ~ it** (arrive)
arrivare; (achieve sth) farcela; **what**
time do you ~ it? che ora fai?; **to ~ do**
with arrangiarsi con; **to ~ for** vt fus
(place) avviarsi verso; **to ~ out** vt
(write out) scrivere; (: cheque)

emettere; (*understand*) capire; (*see*) distinguere; (: *numbers*) decifrare; **to ~ up** vt (*invent*) inventare; (*parcel*) fare // vi conciliarsi; (*with cosmetics*) truccarsi; **to ~ up for** vt fus compensare; ricuperare; **~-believe** n: a world of ~-believe un mondo di favole; it's just ~-believe è tutta un'invenzione; **~r** n fabbricante m; creatore/trice, autore/trice; **~shift** a improvvisato(a); **~-up** n trucco; **~-up remover** n struccatore m.

making ['meɪkɪŋ] n (*fig*): **in the ~** in formazione; **to have the ~s of** (*actor, athlete etc*) avere la stoffa di.

maladjusted [mælə'dʒʌstɪd] a disadattato(a).

malaria [mə'lɛərɪə] n malaria.

Malaya [mə'leɪə] n Malesia.

male [meɪl] n (BIOL, ELEC) maschio // a maschile; maschio(a).

malevolent [mə'levələnt] a malevolo(a).

malfunction [mæl'fʌŋkʃən] n funzione f difettosa.

malice ['mælɪs] n malevolenza; **malicious** [mə'lɪʃəs] a malevolo(a); (LAW) doloso(a).

malign [mə'laɪn] vt malignare su; calunniare.

malignant [mə'lɪgnənt] a (MED) maligno(a).

mall [mɔːl] n (*also*: **shopping ~**) centro commerciale.

mallet ['mælɪt] n maglio.

malnutrition [mælnjuː'trɪʃən] n denutrizione f.

malpractice [mæl'præktɪs] n prevaricazione f; negligenza.

malt [mɔːlt] n malto.

Malta ['mɔːltə] n Malta.

mammal ['mæml] n mammifero.

mammoth ['mæməθ] n mammut m inv // a enorme, gigantesco(a).

man [mæn] n (pl **men**) uomo; (CHESS) pezzo; (DRAUGHTS) pedina // vt fornire d'uomini; stare a; essere di servizio a; **an old ~** un vecchio; **~ and wife** marito e moglie.

manage ['mænɪdʒ] vi farcela // vt (be in charge of) occuparsi di; gestire; **to ~ to do sth** riuscire a far qc; **~able** a maneggevole; fattibile; **~ment** n amministrazione f, direzione f; **~r** n direttore m; (of shop, restaurant) gerente m; (of artist) manager m inv; **~ress** [-ə'rɛs] n direttrice f; gerente f; **~rial** [-ə'dʒɪərɪəl] a dirigenziale; **managing** a: **managing director** amministratore m delegato.

mandarin ['mændərɪn] n (person, fruit) mandarino.

mandatory ['mændətərɪ] a obbligatorio(a); ingiuntivo(a).

mane [meɪn] n criniera.

maneuver [mə'nuːvə*] etc (US) =

manoeuvre etc.

manfully ['mænfəlɪ] ad valorosamente.

mangle ['mæŋgl] vt straziare; mutilare // n strizzatoio.

mango, **~es** ['mæŋgəu] n mango.

mangy ['meɪndʒɪ] a rognoso(a).

manhandle ['mænhændl] vt malmenare.

manhole ['mænhəul] n botola stradale.

manhood ['mænhud] n età virile; virilità.

man-hour ['mæn'auə*] n ora di lavoro.

manhunt ['mænhʌnt] n caccia all'uomo.

mania ['meɪnɪə] n mania; **~c** ['meɪnɪæk] n maniaco/a.

manic ['mænɪk] a (behaviour, activity) maniacale.

manicure ['mænɪkjuə*] n manicure f inv; **~ set** n trousse f inv della manicure.

manifest ['mænɪfest] vt manifestare // a manifesto(a), palese.

manifesto [mænɪ'festəu] n manifesto.

manipulate [mə'nɪpjuleɪt] vt manipolare.

mankind [mæn'kaɪnd] n umanità, genere m umano.

manly ['mænlɪ] a virile; coraggioso(a).

man-made ['mæn'meɪd] a sintetico(a); artificiale.

manner ['mænə*] n maniera, modo; **~s** npl maniere fpl; **~ism** n vezzo, tic m inv.

manoeuvre, (US) **maneuver** [mə'nuːvə*] vt manovrare // vi far manovre // n manovra.

manor ['mænə*] n (also: **~ house**) maniero.

manpower ['mænpauə*] n manodopera.

mansion ['mænʃən] n casa signorile.

manslaughter ['mænslɔːtə*] n omicidio preterintenzionale.

mantelpiece ['mæntlpiːs] n mensola del caminetto.

Mantua ['mæntjuə] n Mantova.

manual ['mænjuəl] a manuale // n manuale m.

manufacture [mænju'fæktʃə*] vt fabbricare // n fabbricazione f, manifattura; **~r** n fabbricante m.

manure [mə'njuə*] n concime m.

manuscript ['mænjuskrɪpt] n manoscritto.

many ['menɪ] a molti(e) // pronoun molti(e), un gran numero; **a great ~** moltissimi(e), un gran numero (di); **~ a ...** molti(e) ..., più di un(a) ... .

map [mæp] n carta (geografica) // vt fare una carta di; **to ~ out** vt tracciare un piano di.

maple ['meɪpl] n acero.

mar [mɑː*] vt sciupare.

marathon ['mærəθən] n maratona.

marauder [mə'rɔːdə*] n saccheggiatore m; predatore m.

marble ['mɑːbl] n marmo; (toy) pallina, bilia; **~s** n (game) palline, bilie.

March [mɑːtʃ] n marzo.

march [ma:tʃ] *vi* marciare; sfilare // *n* marcia; (*demonstration*) dimostrazione *f*.

mare [mɛə*] *n* giumenta.

margarine [ma:dʒə'ri:n] *n* margarina.

margin [ma:dʒɪn] *n* margine *m*; ~**al** (**seat**) *n* (POL) seggio elettorale ottenuto con una stretta maggioranza.

marigold ['mærɪgəuld] *n* calendola.

marijuana [mærɪ'wa:nə] *n* marijuana.

marine [mə'ri:n] *a* (*animal, plant*) marino(a); (*forces, engineering*) marittimo(a) // *n* fante *m* di marina; (US) marine *m inv*.

marital ['mærɪtl] *a* maritale, coniugale; ~ **status** stato coniugale.

mark [ma:k] *n* segno; (*stain*) macchia; (*of skid etc*) traccia; (*Brit SCOL*) voto; (*SPORT*) bersaglio; (*currency*) marco // *vt* segnare; (*stain*) macchiare; (*Brit SCOL*) dare un voto a; correggere; to ~ **time** segnare il passo; **to ~ out** *vt* delimitare; ~**ed** *a* spiccato(a), chiaro(a); ~**er** *n* (*sign*) segno; (*bookmark*) segnalibro.

market ['ma:kɪt] *n* mercato // *vt* (COMM) mettere in vendita; ~ **garden** *n* (*Brit*) orto industriale; ~**ing** *n* marketing *m*; ~ **place** *n* piazza del mercato; (COMM) piazza, mercato; ~ **research** *n* indagine *f* or ricerca di mercato; ~ **value** *n* valore *m* di mercato.

marksman ['ma:ksmən] *n* tiratore *m* scelto.

marmalade ['ma:mələɪd] *n* marmellata d'arance.

maroon [mə'ru:n] *vt* (*fig*): to be ~ed (in or at) essere abbandonato(a) (in) // *a* bordeaux *inv*.

marquee [ma:'ki:] *n* padiglione *m*.

marquess, marquis ['ma:kwɪs] *n* marchese *m*.

marriage ['mærɪdʒ] *n* matrimonio; ~ **bureau** *n* agenzia matrimoniale; ~ **certificate** *n* certificato di matrimonio.

married ['mærɪd] *a* sposato(a); (*life, love*) coniugale, matrimoniale.

marrow ['mærəu] *n* midollo; (*vegetable*) zucca.

marry ['mærɪ] *vt* sposare, sposarsi con; (*subj: father, priest etc*) dare in matrimonio // *vi* (*also*: **get married**) sposarsi.

Mars [ma:z] *n* (*planet*) Marte *m*.

marsh [ma:ʃ] *n* palude *f*.

marshal ['ma:ʃl] *n* maresciallo; (US: *fire*) capo; (: *police*) capitano // *vt* adunare.

martyr ['ma:tə*] *n* martire *m/f* // *vt* martirizzare; ~**dom** *n* martirio.

marvel ['ma:vl] *n* meraviglia // *vi*: to ~ (**at**) meravigliarsi (di); ~**lous**, (US) ~**ous** *a* meraviglioso(a).

Marxist ['ma:ksɪst] *a, n* marxista (*m/f*).

marzipan ['ma:zɪpæn] *n* marzapane *m*.

mascara [mæs'ka:rə] *n* mascara *m*.

masculine ['mæskjulɪn] *a* maschile // *n* genere *m* maschile.

mashed [mæʃt] *a*: ~ **potatoes** purè *m* di patate.

mask [ma:sk] *n* maschera // *vt* mascherare.

mason ['meɪsn] *n* (*also*: **stone~**) scalpellino; (*also*: **free~**) massone *m*; ~**ry** *n* muratura.

masquerade [mæskə'reɪd] *n* ballo in maschera; (*fig*) mascherata // *vi*: **to ~ as** farsi passare per.

mass [mæs] *n* moltitudine *f*, massa; (PHYSICS) massa; (REL) messa // *vi* ammassarsi; **the ~es** le masse.

massacre ['mæsəkə*] *n* massacro.

massage ['mæsa:ʒ] *n* massaggio.

masseur [mæ'sə:*] *n* massaggiatore *m*; **masseuse** [-'sə:z] *n* massaggiatrice *f*.

massive ['mæsɪv] *a* enorme, massiccio(a).

mass media *npl* mass media *mpl*.

mass-produce ['mæsprə'dju:s] *vt* produrre in serie.

mast [ma:st] *n* albero.

master ['ma:stə*] *n* padrone *m*; (ART *etc, teacher: in primary school*) maestro; (: *in secondary school*) professore *m*; (*title for boys*): **M~ X** Signorino X // *vt* domare; (*learn*) imparare a fondo; (*understand*) conoscere a fondo; ~ **key** *n* chiave *f* maestra; ~**ly** *a* magistrale; ~**mind** *n* mente *f* superiore // *vt* essere il cervello di; **M~ of Arts/Science (M.A./M.Sc.)** *n* Master *m inv* in lettere/ scienze; ~**piece** *n* capolavoro; ~**y** *n* dominio; padronanza.

mat [mæt] *n* stuoia; (*also*: **door~**) stoino, zerbino // *a* = **matt**.

match [mætʃ] *n* fiammifero; (*game*) partita, incontro; (*fig*) uguale *m/f*; matrimonio; partito // *vt* intonare; (*go well with*) andare benissimo con; (*equal*) uguagliare // *vi* combaciare; **to be a good** ~ andare bene; ~**box** *n* scatola per fiammiferi; ~**ing** *a* ben assortito(a).

mate [meɪt] *n* compagno/a di lavoro; (*col: friend*) amico/a; (*animal*) compagno/a; (*in merchant navy*) secondo // *vi* accoppiarsi // *vt* accoppiare.

material [mə'tɪərɪəl] *n* (*substance*) materiale *m*, materia; (*cloth*) stoffa // *a* materiale; (*important*) essenziale; ~**s** *npl* materiali *mpl*.

maternal [mə'tə:nl] *a* materno(a).

maternity [mə'tə:nɪtɪ] *n* maternità; ~ **dress** *n* vestito *m* pre-maman *inv*; ~ **hospital** *n* ≈ clinica ostetrica.

math [mæθ] *n* (US) = **maths**.

mathematical [mæθə'mætɪkl] *a* matematico(a).

mathematics [mæθə'mætɪks] *n* matematica.

maths [mæθs], *(US)* **math** [mæθ] *n* matematica.

matinée ['mætɪneɪ] *n* matinée *f inv*.

mating ['meɪtɪŋ] *n* accoppiamento.

matriculation [mətrɪkju'leɪʃən] *n* immatricolazione *f*.

matrimonial [mætrɪ'məunɪəl] *a* matrimoniale, coniugale.

matrimony ['mætrɪmənɪ] *n* matrimonio.

matron ['meɪtrən] *n* (*in hospital*) capoinfermiera; (*in school*) infermiera; ~**ly** *a* da matrona.

mat(t) [mæt] *a* opaco(a).

matted ['mætɪd] *a* ingarbugliato(a).

matter ['mætə*] *n* questione *f*; (*PHYSICS*) materia, sostanza; (*content*) contenuto; (*MED: pus*) pus *m* // *vi* importare; it doesn't ~ non importa; (*I don't mind*) non fa niente; what's the ~? che cosa c'è?; no ~ what qualsiasi cosa accada; as a ~ of course come cosa naturale; as a ~ of fact in verità; ~**-of-fact** *a* prosaico(a).

mattress ['mætrɪs] *n* materasso.

mature [mə'tjuə*] *a* maturo(a); (*cheese*) stagionato(a) // *vi* maturare; stagionare; (*COMM*) scadere.

maul [mɔːl] *vt* lacerare.

mauve [məuv] *a* malva *inv*.

maxim ['mæksɪm] *n* massima.

maximum ['mæksɪməm] *a* massimo(a) // *n* (*pl* **maxima** ['mæksɪmə]) massimo.

May [meɪ] *n* maggio.

may [meɪ] *vi* (*conditional*: **might**) (*indicating possibility*): he ~ come può darsi che venga; (*be allowed to*): ~ I smoke? posso fumare?; (*wishes*): ~ God bless you! Dio la benedica!

maybe ['meɪbiː] *ad* forse, può darsi; ~ he'll ... può darsi che lui ... +*sub*, forse lui ....

May Day *n* il primo maggio.

mayhem ['meɪhem] *n* cagnara.

mayonnaise [meɪə'neɪz] *n* maionese *f*.

mayor [mɛə*] *n* sindaco; ~**ess** *n* sindaco (*donna*); moglie *f* del sindaco.

maze [meɪz] *n* labirinto, dedalo.

M.D. *abbr* = Doctor of Medicine.

me [miː] *pronoun* mi, m' + *vowel or silent 'h'*; (*stressed, after prep*) me; he heard ~ mi ha o m'ha sentito; give ~ a book dammi (*or* mi dia) un libro; it's ~ sono io; with ~ con me; without ~ senza di me.

meadow ['mɛdəu] *n* prato.

meagre, *(US)* meager ['miːgə*] *a* magro(a).

meal [miːl] *n* pasto; (*flour*) farina; ~**time** *n* l'ora di mangiare.

mean [miːn] *a* (*with money*) avaro(a), gretto(a); (*unkind*) meschino(a); maligno(a); (*average*) medio(a) // *vt* (*pt, pp* **meant**) (*signify*) significare, voler dire; (*intend*): to ~ to do aver l'intenzione di fare // *n* mezzo; (*MATH*) media; ~**s** *npl*

mezzi *mpl*; by ~**s** of per mezzo di; (*person*) a mezzo di; by all ~**s** ma certo, prego; to be meant for essere destinato(a) a; do you ~ it? dice sul serio?; what do you ~? che cosa vuol dire?

meander [mɪ'ændə*] *vi* far meandri; (*fig*) divagare.

meaning ['miːnɪŋ] *n* significato, senso; ~**ful** *a* significativo(a); ~**less** *a* senza senso.

meant [ment] *pt, pp of* **mean**.

meantime ['miːntaɪm] *ad*, **meanwhile** ['miːnwaɪl] *ad* (*also*: **in the ~**) nel frattempo.

measles ['miːzlz] *n* morbillo.

measly ['miːzlɪ] *a* (*col*) miserabile.

measure ['mɛʒə*] *vt, vi* misurare // *n* misura; (*ruler*) metro; ~**ments** *npl* misure *fpl*; chest/hip ~**ment** giro petto/ fianchi.

meat [miːt] *n* carne *f*; ~**ball** *n* polpetta di carne; ~**y** *a* che sa di carne; (*fig*) sostanzioso(a).

Mecca ['mɛkə] *n* Mecca.

mechanic [mɪ'kænɪk] *n* meccanico; ~**al** *a* meccanico(a); ~**s** *n* meccanica // *npl* meccanismo.

mechanism ['mɛkənɪzəm] *n* meccanismo.

medal ['mɛdl] *n* medaglia; ~**lion** [mɪ'dælɪən] *n* medaglione *m*.

meddle ['mɛdl] *vi*: to ~ in immischiarsi in, mettere le mani in; to ~ with toccare.

media ['miːdɪə] *npl* media *mpl*.

mediaeval [mɛdɪ'iːvl] *a* = **medieval**.

median ['miːdɪən] *n* mediana; (*US: also*: ~ strip) banchina *f* spartitraffico.

mediate ['miːdɪeɪt] *vi* interporsi; fare da mediatore/trice.

Medicaid ['mɛdɪkeɪd] *n* (*US*) assistenza medica ai poveri.

medical ['mɛdɪkl] *a* medico(a).

Medicare ['mɛdɪkɛə*] *n* (*US*) assistenza medica agli anziani.

medication [mɛdɪ'keɪʃən] *n* medicinali *mpl*, farmaci *mpl*.

medicine ['mɛdsɪn] *n* medicina.

medieval [mɛdɪ'iːvl] *a* medievale.

mediocre [miːdɪ'əukə*] *a* mediocre.

meditate ['mɛdɪteɪt] *vi*: to ~ (on) meditare (su).

Mediterranean [mɛdɪtə'reɪnɪən] *a* mediterraneo(a); the ~ (Sea) il (mare) Mediterraneo.

medium ['miːdɪəm] *a* medio(a) // *n* (*pl* **media**: *means*) mezzo; (*pl* **mediums**: *person*) medium *m inv*; the happy ~ una giusta via di mezzo; ~ **wave** *n* onde *fpl* medie.

medley ['mɛdlɪ] *n* selezione *f*.

meek [miːk] *a* dolce, umile.

meet [miːt], *pt, pp* **met** *vt* incontrare; (*for the first time*) fare la conoscenza di;

(*fig*) affrontare; soddisfare; raggiungere // *vi* incontrarsi; (*in session*) riunirsi; (*join: objects*) unirsi; **I'll ~ you at the station** verrò a prenderla alla stazione; **to ~ with** *vt fus* incontrare; **~ing** *n* incontro; (*session: of club etc*) riunione *f*; (*interview*) intervista; **she's at a ~ing** (*COMM*) è in riunione.

megabyte ['mɛgəbaɪt] *n* (*COMPUT*) megabyte *m inv*.

megaphone ['mɛgəfəun] *n* megafono.

melancholy ['mɛlənkəlɪ] *n* malinconia // *a* malinconico(a).

mellow ['mɛləu] *a* (*wine, sound*) ricco(a); (*person, light*) dolce; (*colour*) caldo(a); (*fruit*) maturo(a) // *vi* (*person*) addolcirsi.

melody ['mɛlədɪ] *n* melodia.

melon ['mɛlən] *n* melone *m*.

melt [mɛlt] *vi* (*gen*) sciogliersi, struggersi; (*metals*) fondersi; (*fig*) intenerirsi // *vt* sciogliere, struggere; fondere; (*person*) commuovere; **to ~ away** *vi* sciogliersi completamente; **to ~ down** *vt* fondere; **~down** *n* (*in nuclear reactor*) fusione *f* (dovuta a surriscaldamento); **~ing pot** *n* (*fig*) crogiolo.

member ['mɛmbə*] *n* membro; **M~ of the European Parliament (MEP)** *n* (*Brit*) eurodeputato; **M~ of Parliament (MP)** *n* (*Brit*) deputato; **~ship** *n* iscrizione *f*; (*numero d'*)iscritti *mpl*; membri *mpl*; **~ship card** *n* tessera (di iscrizione).

memento [mə'mɛntəu] *n* ricordo, souvenir *m inv*.

memo ['mɛməu] *n* appunto; (*COMM etc*) comunicazione *f* di servizio.

memoirs ['mɛmwɑːz] *npl* memorie *fpl*, ricordi *mpl*.

memorandum [mɛmə'rændəm, -də] *pl* **memoranda** *n* appunto; (*COMM etc*) comunicazione *f* di servizio; (*DIPLOMACY*) memorandum *m inv*.

memorial [mɪ'mɔːrɪəl] *n* monumento commemorativo // *a* commemorativo(a).

memorize ['mɛməraɪz] *vt* imparare a memoria.

memory ['mɛmərɪ] *n* (*also COMPUT*) memoria; (*recollection*) ricordo.

men [mɛn] *npl of* **man**.

menace ['mɛnəs] *n* minaccia // *vt* minacciare.

menagerie [mɪ'nædʒərɪ] *n* serraglio.

mend [mɛnd] *vt* aggiustare, riparare; (*darn*) rammendare // *n* rammendo; **on the ~** in via di guarigione.

menial ['miːnɪəl] *a* da servo, domestico(a); umile.

meningitis [mɛnɪn'dʒaɪtɪs] *n* meningite *f*.

menopause ['mɛnəupɔːz] *n* menopausa.

menstruation [mɛnstru'eɪʃən] *n* mestruazione *f*.

mental ['mɛntl] *a* mentale.

mentality [mɛn'tælɪtɪ] *n* mentalità *f inv*.

menthol ['mɛnθəl] *n* mentolo.

mention ['mɛnʃən] *n* menzione *f* // *vt* menzionare, far menzione di; **don't ~ it!** non c'è di che!, prego!

menu ['mɛnjuː] *n* (*set ~, COMPUT*) menù *m inv*; (*printed*) carta.

MEP *n abbr* = **Member of the European Parliament.**

mercenary ['mɜːsɪnərɪ] *a* venale // *n* mercenario.

merchandise ['mɜːtʃəndaɪz] *n* merci *fpl*.

merchant ['mɜːtʃənt] *n* mercante *m*, commerciante *m*; **~ bank** *n* (*Brit*) banca d'affari; **~ navy**, (*US*) **~ marine** *n* marina mercantile.

merciful ['mɜːsɪful] *a* pietoso(a), clemente.

merciless ['mɜːsɪlɪs] *a* spietato(a).

mercury ['mɜːkjurɪ] *n* mercurio.

mercy ['mɜːsɪ] *n* pietà; (*REL*) misericordia; **at the ~ of** alla mercè di.

mere [mɪə*] *a* semplice; **by a ~ chance** per mero caso; **~ly** *ad* semplicemente, non ... che.

merge [mɜːdʒ] *vt* unire // *vi* fondersi, unirsi; (*COMM*) fondersi; **~r** *n* (*COMM*) fusione *f*.

meringue [mə'ræŋ] *n* meringa.

merit ['mɛrɪt] *n* merito, valore *m* // *vt* meritare.

mermaid ['mɜːmeɪd] *n* sirena.

merry ['mɛrɪ] *a* gaio(a), allegro(a); **M~ Christmas!** Buon Natale!; **~-go-round** *n* carosello.

mesh [mɛʃ] *n* maglia; rete *f*.

mesmerize ['mɛzməraɪz] *vt* ipnotizzare; affascinare.

mess [mɛs] *n* confusione *f*, disordine *m*; (*fig*) pasticcio; (*MIL*) mensa; **to ~ about** *or* **around** *vi* (*col*) trastullarsi; **to ~ about** *or* **around with** *vt fus* (*col*) gingillarsi con; (: *plans*) fare un pasticcio di; **to ~ up** *vt* sporcare; fare un pasticcio di; rovinare.

message ['mɛsɪdʒ] *n* messaggio.

messenger ['mɛsɪndʒə*] *n* messaggero/a.

Messrs ['mɛsəz] *abbr* (*on letters*) Spett.

messy ['mɛsɪ] *a* sporco(a); disordinato(a).

met [mɛt] *pt, pp of* **meet**.

metal ['mɛtl] *n* metallo; **~lic** [-'tælɪk] *a* metallico(a).

metaphor ['mɛtəfə*] *n* metafora.

mete [miːt]: **to ~ out** *vt fus* infliggere.

meteorology [miːtɪə'rɔlədʒɪ] *n* meteorologia.

meter ['miːtə*] *n* (*instrument*) contatore *m*; (*US: unit*) = **metre**.

method ['mɛθəd] *n* metodo; **~ical** [mɪ'θɔdɪkl] *a* metodico(a).

Methodist ['mɛθədɪst] *a, n* metodista (*m/f*).

methylated spirit ['mɛθɪleɪtɪd-] *n* (*Brit*:

also: meths) alcool *m* denaturato.

metre, (*US*) **meter** ['mi:tə*] *n* metro.

metric ['mɛtrɪk] *a* metrico(a).

metropolitan [mɛtrə'pɔlɪtən] *a* metropolitano(a); **the M~ Police** *n* (*Brit*) la polizia di Londra.

mettle ['mɛtl] *n* coraggio.

mew [mju:z] *vi* (*cat*) miagolare.

mews [mju:z] *n*: ~ **cottage** (*Brit*) villetta ricavata da un'antica scuderia.

Mexico ['mɛksɪkəu] *n* Messico.

miaow [mi:'au] *vi* miagolare.

mice [maɪs] *npl of* **mouse.**

micro ['maɪkrəu] *n* (*also*: ~-**computer**) microcomputer *m inv.*

microchip ['maɪkrəutʃɪp] *n* microcircuito integrato.

microfilm ['maɪkrəufɪlm] *n* microfilm *m inv* // *vt* microfilmare.

microphone ['maɪkrəfəun] *n* microfono.

microscope ['maɪkrəskəup] *n* microscopio.

microwave ['maɪkrəuweɪv] *n* (*also*: ~ **oven**) forno a microonde.

mid [mɪd] *a*: ~ **May** metà maggio; ~ **afternoon** metà pomeriggio; **in** ~ **air** a mezz'aria; ~**day** *n* mezzogiorno.

middle ['mɪdl] *n* mezzo, centro; (*waist*) vita // *a* di mezzo; **in the** ~ **of the night** nel bel mezzo della notte; ~**-aged** *a* di mezza età; **the M~ Ages** *npl* il Medioevo; ~**-class** *a* ≈ borghese; **the** ~ **class(es)** *n(pl)* ≈ la borghesia; **M~ East** *n* Medio Oriente *m*; ~**man** *n* intermediario; agente *m* rivenditore; ~**name** *n* secondo nome *m*; ~**weight** *n* (*BOXING*) peso medio.

middling ['mɪdlɪŋ] *a* medio(a).

midge [mɪdʒ] *n* moscerino.

midget ['mɪdʒɪt] *n* nano/a.

Midlands ['mɪdləndz] *npl* contee del centro dell'Inghilterra.

midnight ['mɪdnaɪt] *n* mezzanotte *f.*

midriff ['mɪdrɪf] *n* diaframma *m.*

midst [mɪdst] *n*: **in the** ~ **of** in mezzo a.

midsummer [mɪd'sʌmə*] *n* mezza *or* piena estate *f.*

midway [mɪd'weɪ] *a, ad*: ~ (**between**) a mezza strada (fra).

midweek [mɪd'wi:k] *a, ad* a metà settimana.

midwife, *pl* **midwives** ['mɪdwaɪf, -vz] *n* levatrice *f*; ~**ry** [-wɪfərɪ] *n* ostetrica.

might [maɪt] *vb see* **may** // *n* potere *m*, forza; ~**y** *a* forte, potente.

migraine ['mi:greɪn] *n* emicrania.

migrant ['maɪgrənt] *a* (*bird*) migratore(trice); (*person*) nomade; (*worker*) emigrato(a).

migrate [maɪ'greɪt] *vi* migrare.

mike [maɪk] *n abbr* (= **microphone**) microfono.

Milan [mɪ'læn] *n* Milano *f.*

mild [maɪld] *a* mite; (*person, voice*) dolce; (*flavour*) delicato(a); (*illness*)

leggero(a) // *n* birra leggera.

mildew ['mɪldju:] *n* muffa.

mildly ['maɪldlɪ] *ad* mitemente; dolcemente; delicatamente; leggermente; **to put it** ~ a dire poco.

mile [maɪl] *n* miglio; ~**age** *n* distanza in miglia, ≈ chilometraggio; ~**stone** *n* pietra miliare.

milieu ['mi:ljə:] *n* ambiente *m.*

militant ['mɪlɪtnt] *a, n* militante (*m/f*).

military ['mɪlɪtərɪ] *a* militare.

militate ['mɪlɪteɪt] *vi*: **to** ~ **against** essere d'ostacolo a.

milk [mɪlk] *n* latte *m* // *vt* (*cow*) mungere; (*fig*) sfruttare; ~ **chocolate** *n* cioccolato al latte; ~**man** *n* lattaio; ~ **shake** *n* frappé *m inv*; ~**y** *a* lattiginoso(a); (*colour*) latteo(a); **M~y Way** *n* Via Lattea.

mill [mɪl] *n* mulino; (*small: for coffee, pepper etc*) macinino; (*factory*) fabbrica; (*spinning* ~) filatura // *vt* macinare // *vi* (*also*: ~ **about**) formicolare.

millennium, *pl* ~**s** *or* **millennia** [mɪ'lɛnɪəm, -'lɛnɪə] *n* millennio.

miller ['mɪlə*] *n* mugnaio.

millet ['mɪlɪt] *n* miglio.

milli... ['mɪlɪ] *prefix*: ~**gram(me)** *n* milligrammo; ~**metre,** (*US*) ~**meter** *n* millimetro.

millinery ['mɪlɪnərɪ] *n* modisteria.

million ['mɪljən] *n* milione *m*; ~**aire** *n* milionario; ≈ miliardario.

millstone ['mɪlstəun] *n* macina.

milometer [maɪ'lɔmɪtə*] *n* ≈ contachilometri *m inv.*

mime [maɪm] *n* mimo // *vt, vi* mimare.

mimic ['mɪmɪk] *n* imitatore/trice // *vt* fare la mimica di; ~**ry** *n* mimica; (*ZOOL*) mimetismo.

min. *abbr* = **minute(s), minimum.**

mince [mɪns] *vt* tritare, macinare // *vi* (*in walking*) camminare a passettini // *n* (*Brit CULIN*) carne *f* tritata *or* macinata; ~**meat** *n* frutta secca tritata per uso in pasticceria; ~ **pie** *n* specie di torta con frutta secca; ~**r** *n* tritacarne *m inv.*

mind [maɪnd] *n* mente *f* // *vt* (*attend to, look after*) badare a, occuparsi di; (*be careful*) fare attenzione a, stare attento(a) a; (*object to*): **I don't** ~ **the noise** il rumore non mi dà alcun fastidio; **I don't** ~ non m'importa; **it is on my** ~ mi preoccupa; **to my** ~ secondo me, a mio parere; **to be out of one's** ~ essere uscito(a) di mente; **to keep** *or* **bear sth in** ~ non dimenticare qc; **to make up one's** ~ decidersi; ~ **you,** ... sì, però va detto che ...; **never** ~ non importa, non fa niente; "~ **the step**" "attenzione allo scalino"; ~**er** *n* (*child* ~**er**) bambinaia; (*bodyguard*) guardia del corpo; ~**ful** *a*: ~**ful of** attento(a) a; memore di; ~**less**

a idiota.

mine [main] *pronoun* il(la) mio(a), *pl* i(le) miei(mie); **that book is ~** quel libro è mio; **yours is red, ~ is green** il tuo è rosso, il mio è verde; **a friend of ~** un mio amico // *n* miniera; *(explosive)* mina // *vt (coal)* estrarre; *(ship, beach)* minare.

miner ['maɪnə*] *n* minatore *m*.

mineral ['mɪnərəl] *a* minerale // *n* minerale *m*; **~s** *npl (Brit: soft drinks)* bevande *fpl* gasate; **~ water** *n* acqua minerale.

minesweeper ['maɪnswiːpə*] *n* dragamine *m inv*.

mingle ['mɪŋgl] *vi*: **to ~ with** mescolarsi a, mischiarsi con.

miniature ['mɪnətʃə*] *a* in miniatura // *n* miniatura.

minibus ['mɪnɪbʌs] *n* minibus *m inv*.

minim ['mɪnɪm] *n (MUS)* minima.

minimum ['mɪnɪməm] *n (pl* **minima** ['mɪnɪmə]) minimo // *a* minimo(a).

mining ['maɪnɪŋ] *n* industria mineraria // *a* minerario(a); di minatori.

miniskirt ['mɪnɪskəːt] *n* minigonna.

minister ['mɪnɪstə*] *n (Brit POL)* ministro; *(REL)* pastore *m* // *vi*: **to ~ to sb** assistere qn; **to ~ to sb's needs** provvedere ai bisogni di qn; **~ial** [-'tɪərɪəl] *a (Brit POL)* ministeriale.

ministry ['mɪnɪstrɪ] *n (Brit POL)* ministero; *(REL)*: **to go into the ~** diventare pastore.

mink [mɪŋk] *n* visone *m*.

minnow ['mɪnəu] *n* pesciolino d'acqua dolce.

minor ['maɪnə*] *a* minore, di poca importanza; *(MUS)* minore // *n (LAW)* minorenne *m/f*.

minority [maɪ'nɔrɪtɪ] *n* minoranza.

mint [mɪnt] *n (plant)* menta; *(sweet)* pasticca di menta // *vt (coins)* battere; **the (Royal) M~**, *(US)* **the (US) M~** la Zecca; **in ~ condition** come nuovo(a) di zecca.

minus ['maɪnəs] *n (also: ~ sign)* segno meno // *prep* meno.

minute *a* [maɪ'njuːt] minuscolo(a); *(detail)* minuzioso(a) // *n* ['mɪnɪt] minuto; *(official record)* processo verbale, resoconto sommario; **~s** *npl* verbale *m*, verbali *mpl*.

miracle ['mɪrəkl] *n* miracolo.

mirage ['mɪrɑːʒ] *n* miraggio.

mire ['maɪə*] *n* pantano, melma.

mirror ['mɪrə*] *n* specchio // *vt* rispecchiare, riflettere.

mirth [məːθ] *n* gaiezza.

misadventure [mɪsəd'ventʃə*] *n* disavventura; **death by ~** morte *f* accidentale.

misapprehension ['mɪsæprɪ'henʃən] *n* malinteso.

misbehave [mɪsbɪ'heɪv] *vi* comportarsi

male.

miscarriage ['mɪskærɪdʒ] *n (MED)* aborto spontaneo; **~ of justice** errore *m* giudiziario.

miscellaneous [mɪsɪ'leɪnɪəs] *a (items)* vario(a); *(selection)* misto(a).

mischief ['mɪstʃɪf] *n (naughtiness)* birichineria; *(harm)* male *m*, danno; *(maliciousness)* malizia; **mischievous** *a (naughty)* birichino(a); *(harmful)* dannoso(a).

misconception ['mɪskən'sɛpʃən] *n* idea sbagliata.

misconduct [mɪs'kɔndʌkt] *n* cattiva condotta; **professional ~** reato professionale.

misconstrue [mɪskən'struː] *vt* interpretare male.

misdeed [mɪs'diːd] *n* misfatto.

misdemeanour, *(US)* **misdemeanor** [mɪsdɪ'miːnə*] *n* misfatto; infrazione *f*.

miser ['maɪzə*] *n* avaro.

miserable ['mɪzərəbl] *a* infelice; *(wretched)* miserabile.

miserly ['maɪzəlɪ] *a* avaro(a).

misery ['mɪzərɪ] *n (unhappiness)* tristezza; *(pain)* sofferenza; *(wretchedness)* miseria.

misfire [mɪs'faɪə*] *vi* far cilecca; *(car engine)* perdere colpi.

misfit ['mɪsfɪt] *n (person)* spostato/a.

misfortune [mɪs'fɔːtʃən] *n* sfortuna.

misgiving(s) [mɪs'gɪvɪŋ(z)] *n(pl)* dubbi *mpl*, sospetti *mpl*.

misguided [mɪs'gaɪdɪd] *a* sbagliato(a); poco giudizioso(a).

mishandle [mɪs'hændl] *vt (treat roughly)* maltrattare; *(mismanage)* trattare male.

mishap ['mɪshæp] *n* disgrazia.

misinterpret [mɪsɪn'təːprɪt] *vt* interpretare male.

misjudge [mɪs'dʒʌdʒ] *vt* giudicare male.

mislay [mɪs'leɪ] *vt irg* smarrire.

mislead [mɪs'liːd] *vt irg* sviare; **~ing** *a* ingannevole.

misnomer [mɪs'nəumə*] *n* termine *m* sbagliato or improprio.

misplace [mɪs'pleɪs] *vt* smarrire; collocare fuori posto.

misprint ['mɪsprɪnt] *n* errore *m* di stampa.

Miss [mɪs] *n* Signorina.

miss [mɪs] *vt (fail to get)* perdere; *(regret the absence of)*: **I ~ him/it** sento la sua mancanza, lui/esso mi manca // *vi* mancare // *n (shot)* colpo mancato; **to ~ out** *vt (Brit)* omettere.

misshapen [mɪs'ʃeɪpən] *a* deforme.

missile ['mɪsaɪl] *n (AVIAT)* missile *m*; *(object thrown)* proiettile *m*.

missing ['mɪsɪŋ] *a* perso(a), smarrito(a); *(person)* scomparso(a); (: *after disaster, MIL)* disperso(a); **to be ~** mancare.

mission ['mɪʃən] n missione f; ~**ary** n missionario/a.

misspent ['mɪs'spɛnt] a: his ~ youth la sua gioventù sciupata.

mist [mɪst] n nebbia, foschia // vi (also: ~ **over**, ~ **up**) annebbiarsi; (: Brit: windows) appannarsi.

mistake [mɪs'teɪk] n sbaglio, errore m // vt (irg: like **take**) sbagliarsi di; fraintendere; **to make a** ~ fare uno sbaglio, sbagliare; **by** ~ per sbaglio; **to** ~ **for** prendere per; ~ **n a** (idea etc) sbagliato(a); **to be** ~**n** sbagliarsi.

mister ['mɪstə*] n (col) signore m; see **Mr**.

mistletoe ['mɪsltəu] n vischio.

mistook [mɪs'tuk] pt of **mistake**.

mistress ['mɪstrɪs] n padrona; (lover) amante f; (Brit SCOL) insegnante f; see **Mrs**.

mistrust [mɪs'trʌst] vt diffidare di.

misty ['mɪstɪ] a nebbioso(a), brumoso(a).

misunderstand [mɪsʌndə'stænd] vt, vi irg capire male, fraintendere; ~**ing** n malinteso, equivoco.

misuse n [mɪs'ju:s] cattivo uso; (of power) abuso // vt [mɪs'ju:z] far cattivo uso di; abusare di.

mitigate ['mɪtɪgeɪt] vt mitigare.

mitt(en) ['mɪt(n)] n mezzo guanto; manopola.

mix [mɪks] vt mescolare // vi mescolarsi // n mescolanza; preparato; **to** ~ **up** vt mescolare; (confuse) confondere; ~**ed a** misto(a); ~**ed grill** n misto alla griglia; ~**ed-up a** (confused) confuso(a); ~**er** n (for food: electric) frullatore m; (: hand) frullino; (person): **he is a good** ~**er** è molto socievole; ~**ture** n mescolanza; (blend: of tobacco etc) miscela; (MED) sciroppo; ~-**up** n confusione f.

moan [məun] n gemito // vi gemere; (col: complain): **to** ~ (**about**) lamentarsi (di); ~**ing** n gemiti mpl.

moat [məut] n fossato.

mob [mɔb] n folla; (disorderly) calca; (pej): **the** ~ la plebaglia // vt accalcarsi intorno a.

mobile ['məubaɪl] a mobile; ~ **home** n grande roulotte f inv (utilizzata come domicilio).

mock [mɔk] vt deridere, burlarsi di // a falso(a); ~**ery** n derisione f.

mod [mɔd] a see **convenience**.

mode [məud] n modo.

model ['mɔdl] n modello; (person: for fashion) indossatore/trice; (: for artist) modello/a // vt modellare // vi fare l'indossatore (or l'indossatrice) // a (small-scale: railway etc) in miniatura; (child, factory) modello inv; **to** ~ **clothes** presentare degli abiti.

modem ['məudɛm] n modem m inv.

moderate a, n ['mɔdərət] moderato(a) //

vb ['mɔdəreɪt] vi moderarsi, placarsi // vt moderare.

modern ['mɔdən] a moderno(a); ~**ize** vt modernizzare.

modest ['mɔdɪst] a modesto(a); ~**y** n modestia.

modicum ['mɔdɪkəm] n: a ~ **of** un minimo di.

modify ['mɔdɪfaɪ] vt modificare.

mogul ['məugl] n (fig) magnate m, pezzo grosso.

mohair ['məuhɛə*] n mohair m.

moist [mɔɪst] a umido(a); ~**en** ['mɔɪsn] vt inumidire; ~**ure** ['mɔɪstʃə*] n umidità; (on glass) goccioline fpl di vapore; ~**urizer** ['mɔɪstʃəraɪzə*] n idratante f.

molar ['məulə*] n molare m.

molasses [məu'læsɪz] n molassa.

mold [məuld] n, vt (US) = **mould**.

mole [məul] n (animal) talpa; (spot) neo.

molest [məu'lɛst] vt molestare.

mollycoddle ['mɔlɪkɔdl] vt coccolare, vezzeggiare.

molt [məult] vi (US) = **moult**.

molten ['məultən] a fuso(a).

mom [mɔm] n (US) = **mum**.

moment ['məumənt] n momento, istante m; importanza; **at the** ~ al momento, in questo momento; ~**ary** a momentaneo(a), passeggero(a); ~**ous** [-'mɛntəs] a di grande importanza.

momentum [məu'mɛntəm] n velocità acquisita, slancio; (PHYSICS) momento; **to gather** ~ aumentare di velocità.

mommy ['mɔmɪ] n (US) = **mummy**.

Monaco ['mɔnəkəu] n Principato di Monaco.

monarch ['mɔnək] n monarca m; ~**y** n monarchia.

monastery ['mɔnəstərɪ] n monastero.

monastic [mə'næstɪk] a monastico(a).

Monday ['mʌndɪ] n lunedì m inv.

monetary ['mʌnɪtərɪ] a monetario(a).

money ['mʌnɪ] n denaro, soldi mpl; ~**lender** n prestatore m di denaro; ~ **order** n vaglia m inv; ~-**spinner** n (col) miniera d'oro (fig).

mongol ['mɔngəl] a, n (MED) mongoloide (m/f).

mongrel ['mʌngrəl] n (dog) cane m bastardo.

monitor ['mɔnɪtə*] n (SCOL) capoclasse m/f; (TV, COMPUT) monitor m inv // vt controllare.

monk [mʌŋk] n monaco.

monkey ['mʌŋkɪ] n scimmia; ~ **nut** n (Brit) nocciolina americana; ~ **wrench** n chiave f a rullino.

mono... ['mɔnəu] prefix: ~**chrome** a monocromo(a).

monopoly [mə'nɔpəlɪ] n monopolio.

monotone ['mɔnətəun] n pronunzia (or voce f) monotona.

monotonous [mə'nɔtənəs] a monotono(a).

monsoon [mɔn'suːn] n monsone m.

monster ['mɔnstə*] n mostro.

monstrous ['mɔnstrəs] a monstruoso(a).

montage [mɔn'tɑːʒ] n montaggio.

month [mʌnθ] n mese m; **~ly** a mensile // ad al mese; ogni mese // n (magazine) rivista mensile.

monument ['mɔnjumənt] n monumento.

moo [muː] vi muggire, mugghiare.

mood [muːd] n umore m; to be in a good/bad ~ essere di buon/cattivo umore; **~y** a (variable) capriccioso(a), lunatico(a); (sullen) imbronciato(a).

moon [muːn] n luna; **~light** n chiaro di luna; **~lighting** n lavoro nero; **~lit** a: a **~lit** night una notte rischiarata dalla luna.

moor [muə*] n brughiera // vt (ship) ormeggiare // vi ormeggiarsi.

moorland ['muələnd] n brughiera.

moose [muːs] n (pl inv) alce m.

mop [mɔp] n lavapavimenti m inv; (also: ~ of hair) zazzera // vt lavare con lo straccio; **to ~ up** vt asciugare con uno straccio.

mope [məup] vi fare il broncio.

moped ['məuped] n ciclomotore m.

moral ['mɔrl] a morale // n morale f; **~s** npl moralità.

morale [mɔ'rɑːl] n morale m.

morality [mɔ'rælɪtɪ] n moralità.

morass [mə'ræs] n palude f, pantano.

morbid ['mɔːbɪd] a morboso(a).

more [mɔː*] ♦ a 1 (greater in number etc) più; ~ people/letters than we expected più persone/lettere di quante ne aspettavamo; I have ~ wine/money than you ho più vino/soldi di te; I have ~ wine than beer ho più vino che birra
2 (additional) altro(a), ancora; do you want (some) ~ tea? vuole dell'altro tè?, vuole ancora del tè?; I have no or I don't have any ~ money non ho più soldi
♦ pronoun 1 (greater amount) più; ~ than 10 più di 10; it cost ~ than we expected è costato più di quanto ci aspettavamo
2 (further or additional amount) ancora; is there any ~? ce n'è ancora?; there's no ~ non ce n'è più; a little ~ ancora un po'; many/much ~ molti(e)/molto(a) di più
♦ ad: ~ dangerous/easily (than) più pericoloso/facilmente (di); ~ and ~ sempre di più; ~ and ~ difficult sempre più difficile; ~ or less più o meno; ~ than ever più che mai.

moreover [mɔː'rəuvə*] ad inoltre, di più.

morgue [mɔːg] n obitorio.

morning ['mɔːnɪŋ] n mattina, mattino; (duration) mattinata; in the ~ la mattina; 7 o'clock in the ~ le 7 di or della mattina.

Morocco [mə'rɔkəu] n Marocco.

moron ['mɔːrɔn] n deficiente m/f.

morose [mə'rəus] a cupo(a), tetro(a).

Morse [mɔːs] n (also: ~ code) alfabeto Morse.

morsel ['mɔːsl] n boccone m.

mortal ['mɔːtl] a, n mortale (m); **~ity** [-'tælɪtɪ] n mortalità.

mortar ['mɔːtə*] n (CONSTR) malta; (dish) mortaio.

mortgage ['mɔːgɪdʒ] n ipoteca; (loan) prestito ipotecario // vt ipotecare; ~ company n (US) società f inv di credito immobiliare.

mortified ['mɔːtɪfaɪd] a umiliato(a).

mortuary ['mɔːtjuərɪ] n camera mortuaria; obitorio.

mosaic [məu'zeɪk] n mosaico.

Moscow ['mɔskəu] n Mosca.

Moslem ['mɔzləm] a, n = **Muslim**.

mosque [mɔsk] n moschea.

mosquito, ~es [mɔs'kiːtəu] n zanzara.

moss [mɔs] n muschio.

most [məust] a la maggior parte di; il più di // pronoun la maggior parte // ad più; (work, sleep etc) di più; (very) molto, estremamente; the ~ (also: + adjective) il(la) più; ~ of la maggior parte di; ~ of them quasi tutti; I saw (the) ~ ho visto più io; at the (very) ~ al massimo; to make the ~ of trarre il massimo vantaggio da; a ~ interesting book un libro estremamente interessante; **~ly** ad per lo più.

MOT n abbr (Brit: = Ministry of Transport): the ~ (test) revisione annuale obbligatoria degli autoveicoli.

motel [məu'tel] n motel m inv.

moth [mɔθ] n farfalla notturna; tarma; **~ball** n pallina di naftalina.

mother ['mʌðə*] n madre f // vt (care for) fare da madre a; **~hood** n maternità; **~-in-law** n suocera; **~ly** a materno(a); **~-of-pearl** n madreperla; **~-to-be** n futura mamma; ~ **tongue** n madrelingua.

motion ['məuʃən] n movimento, moto; (gesture) gesto; (at meeting) mozione f // vt, vi: to ~ (to) sb to do fare cenno a qn di fare; **~less** a immobile; ~ **picture** n film m inv.

motivated ['məutɪveɪtɪd] a motivato(a).

motive ['məutɪv] n motivo.

motley ['mɔtlɪ] a eterogeneo(a), molto vario(a).

motor ['məutə*] n motore m; (Brit col: vehicle) macchina // a motore(trice); **~bike** n moto f inv; **~boat** n motoscafo; **~car** n (Brit) automobile f; **~cycle** n motocicletta; **~cyclist** n motociclista m/f; **~ing** n (Brit) turismo automobilistico; **~ist** n automobilista m/f; ~ **racing** n (Brit) corse fpl automobilistiche; **~way** n (Brit) autostrada.

mottled ['mɔtld] *a* chiazzato(a), marezzato(a).

motto, ~es ['mɔtəu] *n* motto.

mould, (*US*) **mold** [məuld] *n* forma, stampo; (*mildew*) muffa // *vt* formare; (*fig*) foggiare; **~er** *vi* (*decay*) ammuffire; **~y** *a* ammuffito(a).

moult, (*US*) **molt** [məult] *vi* far la muta.

mound [maund] *n* rialzo, collinetta.

mount [maunt] *n* monte *m*, montagna; (*horse*) cavalcatura; (*for jewel etc*) montatura // *vt* montare; (*horse*) montare a // *vi* salire, montare; (*also:* ~ **up**) aumentare.

mountain ['mauntın] *n* montagna // *cpd* di montagna; **~eer** [-'nıə*] *n* alpinista *m/f*; **~eering** [-'nıərıŋ] *n* alpinismo; **~ous** *a* montagnoso(a); **~side** *n* fianco della montagna.

mourn [mɔːn] *vt* piangere, lamentare // *vi:* **to ~ (for sb)** piangere (la morte di qn); **~er** *n* parente *m/f* or amico/a del defunto; persona venuta a rendere omaggio al defunto; **~ful** *a* triste, lugubre; **~ing** *n* lutto // *cpd* (*dress*) da lutto; **in ~ing** in lutto.

mouse [maus], *pl* **mice** *n* topo; (*COMPUT*) mouse *m* inv; **~trap** *n* trappola per i topi.

mousse [muːs] *n* mousse *f* inv.

moustache [məs'tɑːʃ] *n* baffi *mpl*.

mousy ['mausı] *a* (*person*) timido(a); (*hair*) né chiaro(a) né scuro(a).

mouth [mauθ], **~s** [mauð, -ðz] *n* bocca; (*of river*) bocca, foce *f*; (*opening*) orifizio; **~ful** *n* boccata; **~ organ** *n* armonica; **~piece** *n* (*of musical instrument*) imboccatura, bocchino; (*spokesman*) portavoce *m/f* inv; **~wash** *n* collutorio; **~-watering** *a* che fa venire l'acquolina in bocca.

movable ['muːvəbl] *a* mobile.

move [muːv] *n* (*movement*) movimento; (*in game*) mossa; (*: turn to play*) turno; (*change of house*) trasloco // *vt* muovere, spostare; (*emotionally*) commuovere; (*POL: resolution etc*) proporre // *vi* (*gen*) muoversi, spostarsi; (*traffic*) circolare; (*also:* ~ **house**) cambiar casa, traslocare; **to ~** towards andare verso; **to ~ sb to do sth** indurre or spingere qn a fare qc; **to get a ~ on** affrettarsi, sbrigarsi; **to ~ about** or **around** *vi* (*fidget*) agitarsi; (*travel*) viaggiare; **to ~ along** *vi* muoversi avanti; **to ~ away** *vi* allontanarsi, andarsene; **to ~ back** *vi* indietreggiare; (*return*) ritornare; **to ~ forward** *vi* avanzare // *vt* avanzare, spostare in avanti; (*people*) far avanzare; **to ~ in** *vi* (*to a house*) entrare (in una nuova casa); **to ~ on** *vi* riprendere la strada // *vt* (*onlookers*) far circolare; **to ~ out** *vi* (*of house*) sgombrare; **to ~ over** *vi* spostarsi; **to ~ up** *vi* avanzare.

movement ['muːvmənt] *n* (*gen*) movimento; (*gesture*) gesto; (*of stars, water, physical*) moto.

movie ['muːvı] *n* film *m* inv; **the ~s** il cinema; **~ camera** *n* cinepresa.

moving ['muːvıŋ] *a* mobile; (*causing emotion*) commovente.

mow, *pt* **mowed,** *pp* **mowed** or **mown** [məu, -n] *vt* falciare; (*lawn*) mietere; **to ~ down** *vt* falciare; **~er** *n* (*also:* lawnmower) tagliaerba *m* inv.

MP *n abbr* = **Member of Parliament**.

m.p.h. *abbr* = *miles per hour* (*60 m.p.h. = 96 km/h*).

Mr, Mr. ['mıstə*] *n:* ~ **X** Signor X, Sig. X.

Mrs, Mrs. ['mısız] *n:* ~ **X** Signora X, Sig.ra X.

Ms, Ms. [mız] *n* (= *Miss or Mrs*): ~ **X** ≈ Signora X, Sig.ra X.

M.Sc. *abbr* = **Master of Science**.

much [mʌtʃ] *a* molto(a) // *ad, n* or *pronoun* molto; **how ~ is it?** quanto costa?; **too ~** troppo.

muck [mʌk] *n* (*mud*) fango; (*dirt*) sporcizia; **to ~ about** or **around** *vi* (*col*) fare lo stupido; (*: waste time*) gingillarsi; **to ~ up** *vt* (*col: ruin*) rovinare.

mud [mʌd] *n* fango.

muddle ['mʌdl] *n* confusione *f*, disordine *m*; pasticcio // *vt* (*also:* ~ **up**) impasticciare; **to be in a ~** (*person*) non riuscire a raccapezzarsi; **to ~ through** *vi* cavarsela alla meno peggio.

muddy ['mʌdı] *a* fangoso(a).

mudguard ['mʌdgɑːd] *n* parafango.

mudslinging ['mʌdslıŋıŋ] *n* (*fig*) denigrazione *f*.

muff [mʌf] *n* manicotto // *vt* (*shot, catch etc*) mancare, sbagliare.

muffin ['mʌfın] *n* specie di pasticcino soffice da tè.

muffle ['mʌfl] *vt* (*sound*) smorzare, attutire; (*against cold*) imbacuccare.

muffler ['mʌflə*] *n* (*US AUT*) marmitta; (*: on motorbike*) silenziatore *m*.

mug [mʌg] *n* (*cup*) tazzone *m*; (*for beer*) boccale *m*; (*col: face*) muso; (*: fool*) scemo/a // *vt* (*assault*) assalire; **~ging** *n* assalto.

muggy ['mʌgı] *a* afoso(a).

mule [mjuːl] *n* mulo.

mull [mʌl]: **to ~ over** *vt* rimuginare.

mulled [mʌld] *a:* ~ **wine** vino caldo.

multi-level ['mʌltılevl] *a* (*US*) = **multistorey.**

multiple ['mʌltıpl] *a* multiplo(a); molteplice // *n* multiplo; ~ **sclerosis** *n* sclerosi *f* a placche.

multiplication [mʌltıplı'keıʃən] *n* moltiplicazione *f*.

multiply ['mʌltıplaı] *vt* moltiplicare // *vi* moltiplicarsi.

multistorey ['mʌltı'stɔːrı] *a* (*Brit:*

building, car park) a più piani.
mum [mʌm] *n* (*Brit*) mamma // *a*: **to keep** ~ non aprire bocca.
mumble [ˈmʌmbl] *vt, vi* borbottare.
mummy [ˈmʌmɪ] *n* (*Brit: mother*) mamma; (*embalmed*) mummia.
mumps [mʌmps] *n* orecchioni *mpl*.
munch [mʌntʃ] *vt, vi* sgranocchiare.
mundane [mʌnˈdeɪn] *a* terra a terra *inv.*
municipal [mjuːˈnɪsɪpl] *a* municipale; ~ity [-ˈpælɪtɪ] *n* municipio.
mural [ˈmjuərl] *n* dipinto murale.
murder [ˈmɜːdə*] *n* assassinio, omicidio // *vt* assassinare; ~er *vt* omicida *m*, assassino; ~ous *a* micidiale.
murky [ˈmɜːkɪ] *a* tenebroso(a), buio(a).
murmur [ˈmɜːmə*] *n* mormorio // *vt, vi* mormorare.
muscle [ˈmʌsl] *n* muscolo; **to** ~ **in** *vi* immischiarsi.
muscular [ˈmʌskjulə*] *a* muscolare; (*person, arm*) muscoloso(a).
muse [mjuːz] *vi* meditare, sognare // *n* musa.
museum [mjuːˈzɪəm] *n* museo.
mushroom [ˈmʌʃrum] *n* fungo.
music [ˈmjuːzɪk] *n* musica; ~al *a* musicale // *n* (*show*) commedia musicale; ~al box *n* carillon *m inv*; ~al instrument *n* strumento musicale; ~ hall *n* teatro di varietà; ~ian [-ˈzɪʃən] *n* musicista *m/f*.
musk [mʌsk] *n* muschio.
Muslim [ˈmʌzlɪm] *a, n* musulmano(a).
muslin [ˈmʌzlɪn] *n* mussola.
mussel [ˈmʌsl] *n* cozza.
must [mʌst] *auxiliary vb* (*obligation*): I ~ **do it** devo farlo; (*probability*): **he** ~ **be there by now** dovrebbe essere arrivato ormai; **I** ~ **have made a mistake** devo essermi sbagliato // *n* cosa da non mancare; cosa d'obbligo.
mustard [ˈmʌstəd] *n* senape *f*, mostarda.
muster [ˈmʌstə*] *vt* radunare.
mustn't [ˈmʌsnt] = **must not**.
musty [ˈmʌstɪ] *a* che sa di muffa *or* di rinchiuso.
mutation [mjuːˈteɪʃən] *n* mutazione *f*.
mute [mjuːt] *a, n* muto(a).
muted [ˈmjuːtɪd] *a* (*noise*) attutito(a), smorzato(a); (*criticism*) attenuato(a).
mutiny [ˈmjuːtɪnɪ] *n* ammutinamento.
mutter [ˈmʌtə*] *vt, vi* borbottare, brontolare.
mutton [ˈmʌtn] *n* carne *f* di montone.
mutual [ˈmjuːtʃuəl] *a* mutuo(a), reciproco(a).
muzzle [ˈmʌzl] *n* muso; (*protective device*) museruola; (*of gun*) bocca // *vt* mettere la museruola a.
my [maɪ] *a* il(la) mio(a), *pl* i(le) miei(mie); ~ **house** la mia casa; ~ **books** i miei libri; ~ **brother** mio fratello; **I've washed** ~ **hair/cut** ~ **finger** mi sono lavato i capelli/tagliato il dito.

myself [maɪˈsɛlf] *pronoun* (*reflexive*) mi; (*emphatic*) io stesso(a); (*after prep*) me; *see also* **oneself.**
mysterious [mɪsˈtɪərɪəs] *a* misterioso(a).
mystery [ˈmɪstərɪ] *n* mistero.
mystify [ˈmɪstɪfaɪ] *vt* mistificare; (*puzzle*) confondere.
mystique [mɪsˈtiːk] *n* fascino.
myth [mɪθ] *n* mito; ~ology [mɪˈθɔlədʒɪ] *n* mitologia.

N

n/a *abbr* = **not applicable.**
nab [næb] *vt* (*col*) beccare, acchiappare.
nag [næg] *n* (*pej: horse*) ronzino; (: *person*) brontolone/a // *vt* tormentare // *vi* brontolare in continuazione; ~ging *a* (*doubt, pain*) persistente.
nail [neɪl] *n* (*human*) unghia; (*metal*) chiodo // *vt* inchiodare; **to** ~ **sb down to a date/price** costringere qn a un appuntamento/ad accettare un prezzo; ~brush *n* spazzolino da *or* per unghie; ~file *n* lima da *or* per unghie; ~ **polish** *n* smalto da *or* per unghie; ~ **polish remover** *n* acetone *m*, solvente *m*; ~ **scissors** *npl* forbici *fpl* da *or* per unghie; ~ **varnish** *n* (*Brit*) = ~ **polish.**
naïve [naɪˈiːv] *a* ingenuo(a).
naked [ˈneɪkɪd] *a* nudo(a).
name [neɪm] *n* nome *m*; (*reputation*) nome, reputazione *f* // *vt* (*baby etc*) chiamare; (*plant, illness*) nominare; (*person, object*) identificare; (*price, date*) fissare; **by** ~ di nome; **she knows them all by** ~ li conosce tutti per nome; ~less *a* senza nome; ~ly *ad* cioè; ~sake *n* omonimo.
nanny [ˈnænɪ] *n* bambinaia.
nap [næp] *n* (*sleep*) pisolino; (*of cloth*) peluria; **to be caught** ~ping essere preso alla sprovvista.
nape [neɪp] *n*: ~ **of the neck** nuca.
napkin [ˈnæpkɪn] *n* (*also:* **table** ~) tovagliolo.
nappy [ˈnæpɪ] *n* (*Brit*) pannolino; ~ **rash** *n* arrossamento (causato dal pannolino).
narcissus, *pl* **narcissi** [naːˈsɪsəs, -saɪ] *n* narciso.
narcotic [naːˈkɔtɪk] *n* narcotico // *a* narcotico(a).
narrative [ˈnærətɪv] *n* narrativa // *a* narrativo(a).
narrow [ˈnærəu] *a* stretto(a); (*fig*) limitato(a), ristretto(a) // *vi* restringersi; **to have a** ~ **escape** farcela per un pelo; **to** ~ **sth down to** ridurre qc a; ~ly *ad* per un pelo; (*time*) per poco; ~-**minded** *a* meschino(a).
nasty [ˈnaːstɪ] *a* (*person, remark*) cattivo(a); (*smell, wound, situation*) brutto(a).

nation ['neɪʃən] n nazione f.

national ['næʃənl] a nazionale // n cittadino/a; ~ **dress** n costume m nazionale; **N~ Health Service (NHS)** n (Brit) servizio nazionale di assistenza sanitaria; ≈ S.A.U.B. f; **N~ Insurance** n (Brit) ≈ Previdenza Sociale; ~**ism** n nazionalismo; ~**ity** [-'nælɪtɪ] n nazionalità f inv; ~**ize** vt nazionalizzare; ~**ly** ad a livello nazionale.

nation-wide ['neɪʃənwaɪd] a diffuso(a) in tutto il paese // ad in tutto il paese.

native ['neɪtɪv] n abitante m/f del paese; (in colonies) indigeno/a // a indigeno(a); (country) natio(a); (ability) innato(a); a ~ **of** Russia un nativo della Russia; a ~ **speaker of French** una persona di madrelingua francese; ~ **language** n madrelingua.

NATO ['neɪtəu] n abbr (= North Atlantic Treaty Organization) N.A.T.O. f.

natural ['nætʃrəl] a naturale; (ability) innato(a); (manner) semplice; ~ **gas** n gas m metano; ~**ize** vt naturalizzare; to become ~**ized** (person) naturalizzarsi; ~**ly** ad naturalmente; (by nature: gifted) di natura.

nature ['neɪtʃə*] n natura; (character) natura, indole f; by ~ di natura.

naught [nɔːt] n = **nought**.

naughty ['nɔːtɪ] a (child) birichino(a), cattivello(a); (story, film) spinto(a).

nausea ['nɔːsɪə] n (MED) nausea; (fig: disgust) schifo; ~**te** ['nɔːsɪeɪt] vt nauseare; far schifo a.

nautical ['nɔːtɪkl] a nautico(a).

naval ['neɪvl] a navale; ~ **officer** n ufficiale m di marina.

nave [neɪv] n navata centrale.

navel ['neɪvl] n ombelico.

navigate ['nævɪgeɪt] vt percorrere navigando // vi navigare; (AUT) fare da navigatore; **navigation** [-'geɪʃən] n navigazione f; **navigator** n (NAUT, AVIAT) ufficiale m di rotta; (explorer) navigatore m; (AUT) copilota m/f.

navvy ['nævɪ] n (Brit) manovale m.

navy ['neɪvɪ] n marina; ~**(-blue)** a blu scuro inv.

Nazi ['nɑːtsɪ] n nazista m/f.

NB abbr (= nota bene) N.B.

near [nɪə*] a vicino(a); (relation) prossimo(a) // ad vicino // prep (also: ~ **to**) vicino a, presso; (: time) verso // vt avvicinarsi a; ~**by** [nɪə'baɪ] a vicino(a) // ad vicino; ~**ly** ad quasi; I ~**ly** fell per poco non sono caduto; ~ **miss** n: that was a ~ **miss** c'è mancato poco; ~**side** n (AUT: in Britain) lato sinistro; (: in Italy etc) lato destro; ~**-sighted** a miope.

neat [niːt] a (person, room) ordinato(a); (work) pulito(a); (solution, plan) ben indovinato(a), azzeccato(a); (spirits) li-

scio(a); ~**ly** ad con ordine; (skilfully) abilmente.

necessarily ['nesɪsrɪlɪ] ad necessariamente.

necessary ['nesɪsrɪ] a necessario(a).

necessity [nɪ'sesɪtɪ] n necessità f inv.

neck [nek] n collo; (of garment) colletto // vi (col) pomiciare, sbaciucchiarsi; ~ **and** ~ testa a testa.

necklace ['neklɪs] n collana.

neckline ['neklaɪn] n scollatura.

necktie ['nektaɪ] n cravatta.

née [neɪ] a: ~ **Scott** nata Scott.

need [niːd] n bisogno // vt aver bisogno di; to ~ **to do** dover fare; aver bisogno di fare; **you don't** ~ **to go** non devi andare, non c'è bisogno che tu vada.

needle ['niːdl] n ago // vt punzecchiare.

needless ['niːdlɪs] a inutile.

needlework ['niːdlwəːk] n cucito.

needn't ['niːdnt] = **need not**.

needy ['niːdɪ] a bisognoso(a).

negative ['negətɪv] n (answer) risposta negativa; (LING) negazione f; (PHOT) negativo // a negativo(a).

neglect [nɪ'glekt] vt trascurare // n (of person, duty) negligenza; **state of** ~ stato di abbandono.

negligee ['neglɪʒeɪ] n négligé m inv.

negligence ['neglɪdʒəns] n negligenza.

negligible ['neglɪdʒɪbl] a insignificante, trascurabile.

negotiate [nɪ'gəuʃɪeɪt] vi: to ~ **(with)** negoziare (con) // vt (COMM) negoziare; (obstacle) superare; **negotiation** [-'eɪʃən] n negoziato, trattativa.

Negro ['nɪːgrəu] a, n (pl ~**es**) negro(a).

neigh [neɪ] vi nitrire.

neighbour, (US) **neighbor** ['neɪbə*] n vicino/a; ~**hood** n vicinato; ~**ing** a vicino(a); ~**ly** a: he is a ~**ly** person è un buon vicino.

neither ['naɪðə*] a, pronoun né l'uno(a) né l'altro(a), nessuno(a) dei(delle) due // cj neanche, nemmeno, neppure // ad: ~ **good nor bad** né buono né cattivo; I **didn't move and** ~ **did Claude** io non mi mossi e nemmeno Claude; ..., ~ **did I re-fuse** ..., ma non ho nemmeno rifiutato.

neon ['niːɔn] n neon m; ~ **light** n luce f al neon.

nephew ['nevjuː] n nipote m.

nerve [nəːv] n nervo; (fig) coraggio; (impudence) faccia tosta; a **fit of** ~s una crisi di nervi; ~**-racking** a che spezza i nervi.

nervous ['nəːvəs] a nervoso(a); (anxious) agitato(a), in apprensione; ~ **breakdown** n esaurimento nervoso.

nest [nest] n nido // vi fare il nido, nidificare; ~ **egg** n (fig) gruzzolo.

nestle ['nesl] vi accoccolarsi.

net [net] n rete f // a netto(a) // vt (fish etc) prendere con la rete; (profit) ricavare un utile netto di; ~**ball** n *specie di pallacanestro*; ~ **curtains** *npl* tende *fpl* di tulle.

Netherlands ['nɛðələndz] *npl*: the ~ i Paesi Bassi.

nett [nɛt] *a* = **net**.

netting ['nɛtɪŋ] *n* (*for fence etc*) reticolato.

nettle ['nɛtl] *n* ortica.

network ['nɛtwə:k] *n* rete *f*.

neurotic [njuə'rɔtɪk] *a*, *n* nevrotico(a).

neuter ['nju:tə*] *a* neutro // *n* neutro // *vt* (*cat etc*) castrare.

neutral ['nju:trəl] *a* neutro(a); (*person, nation*) neutrale // *n* (*AUT*): in ~ in folle; ~**ize** *vt* neutralizzare.

never ['nɛvə*] *ad* (non...) mai; ~ again mai più; I'll ~ go there again non ci vado più; ~ in my life mai in vita mia; *see also* **mind**; ~**-ending** *a* interminabile; ~**theless** [nɛvəðə'lɛs] *ad* tuttavia, ciò nonostante, ciò nondimeno.

new [nju:] *a* nuovo(a); (*brand new*) nuovo(a) di zecca; ~**born** *a* neonato(a); ~**comer** ['nju:kʌmə*] *n* nuovo(a) venuto(a); ~**fangled** ['nju:fæŋgld] *a* (*pej*) stramoderno(a); ~**found** *a* nuovo(a); ~**ly** *ad* di recente; ~**ly-weds** *npl* sposini *mpl*, sposi *mpl* novelli.

news [nju:z] *n* notizie *fpl*; (*RADIO*) giornale *m* radio; (*TV*) telegiornale *m*; a piece of ~ una notizia; ~ **agency** *n* agenzia di stampa; ~**agent** *n* (*Brit*) giornalaio; ~**caster** *n* (*RADIO*, *TV*) annunciatore/trice; ~**dealer** *n* (*US*) = ~**agent**; ~ **flash** *n* notizia *f* lampo *inv*; ~**letter** *n* bollettino; ~**paper** *n* giornale *m*; ~**print** *n* carta da giornale; ~**reader** *n* = ~**caster**; ~**reel** *n* cinegiornale *m*; ~ **stand** *n* edicola.

newt [nju:t] *n* tritone *m*.

New Year *n* Anno Nuovo; ~**'s Day** *n* il Capodanno; ~**'s Eve** *n* la vigilia di Capodanno.

New Zealand [-'zi:lənd] *n* Nuova Zelanda; ~**er** *n* neozelandese *m/f*.

next [nɛkst] *a* prossimo(a) // *ad* accanto; (*in time*) dopo; the ~ day il giorno dopo, l'indomani; ~ year l'anno prossimo; when do we meet ~? quando ci rincontriamo?; ~ door *ad* accanto; ~**-of-kin** *n* parente *m/f* prossimo(a); ~ **to** *prep* accanto a; ~ **to nothing** quasi niente.

NHS *n abbr* = **National Health Service.**

nib [nɪb] *n* (*of pen*) pennino.

nibble ['nɪbl] *vt* mordicchiare.

Nicaragua [nɪkə'ræɡjuə] *n* Nicaragua *m*.

nice [naɪs] *a* (*holiday, trip*) piacevole; (*flat, picture*) bello(a); (*person*) simpatico(a), gentile; (*distinction, point*) sottile; ~**looking** *a* bello(a); ~**ly** *ad* bene.

niceties ['naɪsɪtɪz] *npl* finezze *fpl*.

niche [ni:ʃ] *n* nicchia; (*fig*): **to find a ~ for o.s.** trovare la propria strada.

nick [nɪk] *n* tacca // *vt* (*col*) rubare; **in the ~ of time** appena in tempo.

nickel ['nɪkl] *n* nichel *m*; (*US*) moneta da cinque centesimi di dollaro.

nickname ['nɪkneɪm] *n* soprannome *m* // *vt* soprannominare.

niece [ni:s] *n* nipote *f*.

Nigeria [naɪ'dʒɪərɪə] *n* Nigeria.

nigger ['nɪɡə*] *n* (*col!: highly offensive*) negro/a.

niggling ['nɪɡlɪŋ] *a* pignolo(a).

night [naɪt] *n* notte *f*; (*evening*) sera; at ~ la sera; by ~ di notte; the ~ before last l'altro ieri notte (*or* sera); ~**cap** *n* bicchierino prima di andare a letto; ~ **club** *n* locale *m* notturno; ~**dress** *n* camicia da notte; ~**fall** *n* crepuscolo; ~**gown** *n*, ~**ie** ['naɪtɪ] *n* camicia da notte.

nightingale ['naɪtɪŋɡeɪl] *n* usignolo.

night life *n* vita notturna.

nightly ['naɪtlɪ] *a* di ogni notte *or* sera; (*by night*) notturno(a) // *ad* ogni notte *or* sera.

nightmare ['naɪtmɛə*] *n* incubo.

night: ~ **porter** *n* portiere *m* di notte; ~ **school** *n* scuola serale; ~ **shift** *n* turno di notte; ~**time** *n* notte *f*.

nil [nɪl] *n* nulla *m*; (*Brit SPORT*) zero.

Nile [naɪl] *n*: the ~ il Nilo.

nimble ['nɪmbl] *a* agile.

nine [naɪn] *num* nove; ~**teen** *num* diciannove; ~**ty** *num* novanta.

ninth [naɪnθ] *a* nono(a).

nip [nɪp] *vt* pizzicare.

nipple ['nɪpl] *n* (*ANAT*) capezzolo.

nitrogen ['naɪtrədʒən] *n* azoto.

no [nəu] ◆ *ad* (*opposite of "yes"*) no; **are you coming? — — (I'm not)** viene? — no (non vengo); **would you like some more? — — thank you** ne vuole ancora un po'? — no, grazie
◆ *a* (*not any*) nessuno(a); **I have ~ money/time/books** non ho soldi/tempo/libri; ~ **student would have done it** nessuno studente lo avrebbe fatto; "~ **parking**" "divieto di sosta"; "~ **smoking**" "vietato fumare"
◆ *n* (*pl* ~**es**) no *m inv*.

nobility [nəu'bɪlɪtɪ] *n* nobiltà.

noble ['nəubl] *a*, *n* nobile (*m*).

nobody ['nəubədɪ] *pronoun* nessuno.

nod [nɔd] *vi* accennare col capo, fare un cenno; (*sleep*) sonnecchiare // *vt*: **to ~ one's head** fare di sì col capo // *n* cenno; **to ~ off** *vi* assopirsi.

noise [nɔɪz] *n* rumore *m*; (*din, racket*) chiasso; **noisy** *a* (*street, car*) rumoroso(a); (*child*) chiassoso(a).

no man's land ['nəumænzlænd] *n* terra di nessuno.

nominal ['nɔmɪnl] *a* nominale.

nominate ['nɔmɪneɪt] *vt* (*propose*) proporre come candidato; (*elect*) nominare.

nominee [nɔmɪˈniː] *n* persona nominata; candidato/a.

non... [nɔn] *prefix* non...; **~-alcoholic** *a* analcolico(a); **~-committal** [ˈnɔnkə-ˈmɪtl] *a* evasivo(a).

nondescript [ˈnɔndɪskrɪpt] *a* qualunque *inv*.

none [nʌn] *pronoun* (*not one thing*) niente; (*not one person*) nessuno(a); **~ of you** nessuno(a) di voi; **I've ~ left** non ne ho più; **he's ~ the worse for it** non ne ha risentito.

nonentity [nɔˈnɛntɪtɪ] *n* persona insignificante.

nonetheless [nʌnðəˈlɛs] *ad* nondimeno.

non-: ~-existent *a* inesistente; **~-fiction** *n* saggistica.

nonplussed [nɔnˈplʌst] *a* sconcertato(a).

nonsense [ˈnɔnsəns] *n* sciocchezze *fpl*.

non-: ~-smoker *n* non-fumatore/trice; **~-stick** *a* antiaderente, antiadesivo(a); **~-stop** *a* continuo(a); (*train, bus*) direttissimo(a) // *ad* senza sosta.

noodles [ˈnuːdlz] *npl* taglierini *mpl*.

nook [nuk] *n*: **~s and crannies** angoli *mpl*.

noon [nuːn] *n* mezzogiorno.

no one [ˈnəuwʌn] *pronoun* = **nobody**.

noose [nuːs] *n* nodo scorsoio; (*hangman's*) cappio.

nor [nɔːʳ] *cj* = **neither** // *ad see* **neither**.

norm [nɔːm] *n* norma.

normal [ˈnɔːml] *a* normale; **~ly** *ad* normalmente.

north [nɔːθ] *n* nord *m*, settentrione *m* // *a* nord *inv*, del nord, settentrionale // *ad* verso nord; **N~ America** *n* America del Nord; **~-east** *n* nord-est *m*; **~erly** [ˈnɔːðəlɪ] *a* (*point, direction*) verso nord; **~ern** [ˈnɔːðən] *a* del nord, settentrionale; **N~ern Ireland** *n* Irlanda del Nord; **N~ Pole** *n* Polo Nord; **N~ Sea** *n* Mare *m* del Nord; **~ward(s)** [ˈnɔːθwəd(z)] *ad* verso nord; **~-west** *n* nord-ovest *m*.

Norway [ˈnɔːweɪ] *n* Norvegia.

Norwegian [nɔːˈwiːdʒən] *a* norvegese // *n* norvegese *m/f*; (*LING*) norvegese *m*.

nose [nəuz] *n* naso; (*of animal*) muso // *vi*: **to ~ about** aggirarsi; **~bleed** *n* emorragia nasale; **~-dive** *n* picchiata; **~y** *a* = **nosy**.

nostalgia [nɔsˈtældʒɪə] *n* nostalgia.

nostril [ˈnɔstrɪl] *n* narice *f*; (*of horse*) frogia.

nosy [ˈnəuzɪ] *a* curioso(a).

not [nɔt] *ad* non; **he is ~ or isn't here** non è qui, non c'è; **you must ~ or you mustn't do that** non devi fare quello; **it's too late, isn't it** *or* **is it ~?** è troppo tardi, vero?; **~ that I don't like him** non che (lui) non mi piaccia; **~ yet/now** non ancora/ora; *see also* **all, only**.

notably [ˈnəutəblɪ] *ad* (*markedly*)

notevolmente; (*particularly*) in particolare.

notary [ˈnəutərɪ] *n* (*also*: **~ public**) notaio.

notch [nɔtʃ] *n* tacca.

note [nəut] *n* nota; (*letter, banknote*) biglietto // *vt* (*also*: **~ down**) prendere nota di; **to take ~s** prendere appunti; **~book** *n* taccuino; **~d** [ˈnəutɪd] *a* celebre; **~pad** *n* bloc-notes *m inv*; **~paper** *n* carta da lettere.

nothing [ˈnʌθɪŋ] *n* nulla *m*, niente *m*; (*zero*) zero; **he does ~** non fa niente; **~ new** niente di nuovo; **for ~** per niente.

notice [ˈnəutɪs] *n* avviso; (*of leaving*) preavviso // *vt* notare, accorgersi di; **to take ~ of** fare attenzione a; **to bring sth to sb's ~** far notare qc a qn; **at short ~** con un breve preavviso; **until further ~** fino a nuovo avviso; **to hand in one's ~** licenziarsi; **~able** *a* evidente; **~ board** *n* (*Brit*) tabellone *m* per affissi.

notify [ˈnəutɪfaɪ] *vt*: **to ~ sth to sb** far sapere qc a qn; **to ~ sb of sth** avvisare qn di qc.

notion [ˈnəuʃən] *n* idea; (*concept*) nozione *f*.

notorious [nəuˈtɔːrɪəs] *a* famigerato(a).

notwithstanding [nɔtwɪθˈstændɪŋ] *ad* nondimeno // *prep* nonostante, malgrado.

nougat [ˈnuːgaː] *n* torrone *m*.

nought [nɔːt] *n* zero.

noun [naun] *n* nome *m*, sostantivo.

nourish [ˈnʌrɪʃ] *vt* nutrire; **~ing** *a* nutriente; **~ment** *n* nutrimento.

novel [ˈnɔvl] *n* romanzo // *a* nuovo(a); **~ist** *n* romanziere/a; **~ty** *n* novità *f inv*.

November [nəuˈvɛmbəʳ] *n* novembre *m*.

novice [ˈnɔvɪs] *n* principiante *m/f*; (*REL*) novizio/a.

now [nau] *ad* ora, adesso // *cj*: **~ (that)** adesso che, ora che; **by ~** ormai; **just ~** proprio ora; **right ~** subito, immediatamente; **~ and then, ~ and again** ogni tanto; **from ~ on** da ora in poi; **~adays** [ˈnauədeɪz] *ad* oggidì.

nowhere [ˈnəuwɛəʳ] *ad* in nessun luogo, da nessuna parte.

nozzle [ˈnɔzl] *n* (*of hose etc*) boccaglio; (*of fire extinguisher*) lancia.

nuance [njuːˈɑːns] *n* sfumatura.

nuclear [ˈnjuːklɪəʳ] *a* nucleare.

nucleus, *pl* **nuclei** [ˈnjuːklɪəs, ˈnjuːklɪaɪ] *n* nucleo.

nude [njuːd] *a* nudo(a) // *n* (*ART*) nudo; **in the ~** tutto(a) nudo(a).

nudge [nʌdʒ] *vt* dare una gomitata a.

nudist [ˈnjuːdɪst] *n* nudista *m/f*.

nuisance [ˈnjuːsns] *n*: **it's a ~** è una seccatura; **he's a ~** è uno scocciatore; **what a ~!** che seccatura!

null [nʌl] *a*: **~ and void** nullo(a).

numb [nʌm] *a* intorpidito(a); **~ with cold** intirizzito(a) (dal freddo).

number [ˈnʌmbəʳ] *n* numero // *vt*

numerare; (include) contare; **a ~ of** un certo numero di; **to be ~ed among** venire annoverato(a) tra; **they were 10 in ~** erano in tutto 10; **~ plate** n (Brit AUT) targa.

numeral ['nju:mərəl] n numero, cifra.

numerate ['nju:mərɪt] a: **to be ~** avere nozioni di aritmetica.

numerical [nju:'mɛrɪkl] a numerico(a).

numerous ['nju:mərəs] a numeroso(a).

nun [nʌn] n suora, monaca.

nurse [nə:s] n infermiere/a // vt (patient, cold) curare; (baby: Brit) cullare; (: US) allattare, dare il latte a; (hope) nutrire.

nursery ['nə:sərɪ] n (room) camera dei bambini; (institution) asilo; (for plants) vivaio; **~ rhyme** n filastrocca; **~ school** n scuola materna; **~ slope** n (Brit SKI) pista per principianti.

nursing ['nə:sɪŋ] n (profession) professione f di infermiere (or di infermiera); **~ home** n casa di cura.

nurture ['nə:tʃə*] vt allevare; nutrire.

nut [nʌt] n (of metal) dado; (fruit) noce f; **he's ~s** (col) è matto; **~crackers** npl schiaccianoci m inv.

nutmeg ['nʌtmɛg] n noce f moscata.

nutritious [nju:'trɪʃəs] a nutriente.

nutshell ['nʌtʃɛl] n guscio di noce; **in a ~** in poche parole.

nylon ['naɪlɔn] n nailon m // a di nailon.

nymph [nɪmf] n ninfa.

O

oak [əuk] n quercia // a di quercia.

O.A.P. abbr = **old age pensioner**.

oar [ɔ:*] n remo.

oasis, pl **oases** [əu'eɪsɪs] n oasi f inv.

oath [əuθ] n giuramento; (swear word) bestemmia.

oatmeal ['əutmi:l] n farina d'avena.

oats [əuts] npl avena.

obedience [ə'bi:dɪəns] n ubbidienza.

obedient [ə'bi:dɪənt] a ubbidiente.

obey [ə'beɪ] vt ubbidire a; (instructions, regulations) osservare // vi ubbidire.

obituary [ə'bɪtjuərɪ] n necrologia.

object n ['ɔbdʒɪkt] oggetto; (purpose) scopo, intento; (LING) complemento oggetto // vi [əb'dʒɛkt]: **to ~ to** (attitude) disapprovare; (proposal) protestare contro, sollevare delle obiezioni contro; **expense is no ~** non si bada a spese; **I ~! mi oppongo!; **he ~ed that ...** obiettò che ...; **~ion** [əb'dʒɛkʃən] n obiezione f; (drawback) inconveniente m; **~ionable** [əb'dʒɛkʃənəbl] a antipatico(a); (smell) sgradevole; (language) scostumato(a); **~ive** n obiettivo // a obiettivo(a).

obligation [ɔblɪ'geɪʃən] n obbligo, dovere m; (debt) obbligo (di riconoscenza); **without ~** senza impegno.

oblige [ə'blaɪdʒ] vt (force): **to ~ sb to do** costringere qn a fare; (do a favour) fare una cortesia a; **to be ~d to sb for sth** essere grato a qn per qc; **obliging** a servizievole, compiacente.

oblique [ə'bli:k] a obliquo(a); (allusion) indiretto(a).

obliterate [ə'blɪtəreɪt] vt cancellare.

oblivion [ə'blɪvɪən] n oblio.

oblivious [ə'blɪvɪəs] a: **~ of** incurante di; inconscio(a) di.

oblong ['ɔblɔŋ] a oblungo(a) // n rettangolo.

obnoxious [əb'nɔkʃəs] a odioso(a); (smell) disgustoso(a), ripugnante.

oboe ['əubəu] n oboe m.

obscene [əb'si:n] a osceno(a).

obscure [əb'skjuə*] a oscuro(a) // vt oscurare; (hide: sun) nascondere.

observant [əb'zə:vnt] a attento(a).

observation [ɔbzə'veɪʃən] n osservazione f; (by police etc) sorveglianza.

observatory [əb'zə:vətrɪ] n osservatorio.

observe [əb'zə:v] vt osservare; (remark) fare osservare; **~r** n osservatore/trice.

obsess [əb'sɛs] vt ossessionare; **~ive** a ossessivo(a).

obsolescence [ɔbsə'lɛsns] n obsolescenza.

obsolete ['ɔbsəli:t] a obsoleto(a); (word) desueto(a).

obstacle ['ɔbstəkl] n ostacolo.

obstinate ['ɔbstɪnɪt] a ostinato(a).

obstruct [əb'strʌkt] vt (block) ostruire, ostacolare; (halt) fermare; (hinder) impedire.

obtain [əb'teɪn] vt ottenere // vi essere in uso; **~able** a ottenibile.

obtrusive [əb'tru:sɪv] a (person) importuno(a); (smell) invadente; (building etc) imponente e invadente.

obtuse [əb'tju:s] a ottuso(a).

obvious ['ɔbvɪəs] a ovvio(a), evidente; **~ly** ad ovviamente; certo.

occasion [ə'keɪʒən] n occasione f; (event) avvenimento // vt cagionare; **~al** a occasionale; **~ally** ad ogni tanto.

occupation [ɔkju'peɪʃən] n occupazione f; (job) mestiere m, professione f; **~al hazard** n rischio del mestiere.

occupier ['ɔkjupaɪə*] n occupante m/f.

occupy ['ɔkjupaɪ] vt occupare; **to ~ o.s. with** or **by doing** occuparsi a fare.

occur [ə'kə:*] vi accadere; (difficulty, opportunity) capitare; (phenomenon, error) trovarsi; **to ~ to sb** venire in mente a qn; **~rence** n caso, fatto; presenza.

ocean ['əuʃən] n oceano; **~-going** a d'alto mare.

o'clock [ə'klɔk] ad: **it is 5 ~** sono le 5.

OCR n abbr = **optical character recognition/reader**.

octave ['ɔktɪv] n ottavo.

October [ɔk'təubə*] n ottobre m.

octopus ['ɔktəpəs] n polpo, piovra.

odd [ɔd] a (strange) strano(a), bizzarro(a); (number) dispari inv; (left over) in più; (not of a set) spaiato(a); 60-~ 60 e oltre; at ~ times di tanto in tanto; the ~ one out l'eccezione f; ~s and ends npl avanzi mpl; ~ity n bizzarria; (person) originale m; ~ jobs npl lavori mpl occasionali; ~ly ad stranamente; ~ments npl (COMM) rimanenze fpl; ~s npl (in betting) quota; it makes no ~s non importa; at ~s in contesa.

odometer ['ɔdɔmɪtə*] n odometro.

odour, (US) **odor** ['əudə*] n odore m.

of [ɔv, əv] prep 1 (gen) di; a boy ~ 10 un ragazzo di 10 anni; a friend ~ ours un nostro amico; that was kind ~ you è stato molto gentile da parte sua 2 (expressing quantity, amount, dates etc) di; a kilo ~ flour un chilo di farina; how much ~ this do you need? quanto gliene serve?; there were 3 ~ them (people) erano in 3; (objects) ce n'erano 3; 3 ~ us went 3 di noi sono andati; the 5th ~ July il 5 luglio 3 (from, out of) di, in; made ~ wood (fatto) di or in legno.

off [ɔf] a, ad (engine) spento(a); (tap) chiuso(a); (Brit: food: bad) andato(a) a male; (absent) assente; (cancelled) sospeso(a) // prep da; a poca distanza di; to be ~ (to leave) partire, andarsene; to be ~ sick essere assente per malattia; a day ~ un giorno di vacanza; to have an ~ day non essere in forma; he had his coat ~ si era tolto il cappotto; 10% ~ (COMM) con uno sconto di 10%; ~ the coast al largo della costa; I'm ~ meat la carne non mi va più; (no longer eat it) non mangio più la carne; on the ~ chance a caso.

offal ['ɔfl] n (CULIN) frattaglie fpl.

offbeat ['ɔfbiːt] a eccentrico(a).

off-colour ['ɔf'kʌlə*] a (Brit: ill) malato(a), indisposto(a).

offence, (US) **offense** [ə'fɛns] n (LAW) contravvenzione f; (: more serious) reato; to take ~ at offendersi per.

offend [ə'fɛnd] vt (person) offendere; ~er n delinquente m/f; (against regulations) contravventore/trice.

offensive [ə'fɛnsɪv] a offensivo(a); (smell etc) sgradevole, ripugnante // n (MIL) offensiva.

offer ['ɔfə*] n offerta, proposta // vt offrire; "on ~" (COMM) "in offerta speciale"; ~ing n offerta.

offhand [ɔf'hænd] a disinvolto(a), noncurante // ad all'impronto.

office ['ɔfɪs] n (place) ufficio; (position) carica; doctor's ~ (US) studio; to take ~ entrare in carica; ~ automation n automazione f d'ufficio; burotica; ~ block, (US) ~ building n complesso di uffici; ~ hours npl orario d'ufficio; (US MED) orario di visite.

officer ['ɔfɪsə*] n (MIL etc) ufficiale m; (of organization) funzionario; (also: police ~) agente m di polizia.

office worker n impiegato/a d'ufficio.

official [ə'fɪʃl] a (authorized) ufficiale // n ufficiale m; (civil servant) impiegato/a statale; funzionario; ~dom n burocrazia.

officiate [ə'fɪʃɪeɪt] vi presenziare; to ~ at a marriage celebrare un matrimonio.

officious [ə'fɪʃəs] a invadente.

offing ['ɔfɪŋ] n: in the ~ (fig) in vista.

off: ~-licence n (Brit: shop) spaccio di bevande alcoliche; ~-line a, ad (COMPUT) off-line inv, fuori linea; (: switched off) spento(a); ~-peak a (ticket etc) a tariffa ridotta; (time) non di punta; ~-putting a (Brit) sgradevole, antipatico(a); ~-season a, ad fuori stagione.

offset ['ɔfsɛt] vt irg (counteract) controbilanciare, compensare.

offshoot ['ɔfʃuːt] n (fig) diramazione f.

offshore [ɔf'ʃɔː*] a (breeze) di terra; (island) vicino alla costa; (fishing) costiero(a).

offside ['ɔf'saɪd] a (SPORT) fuori gioco; (AUT: in Britain) destro(a); (: in Italy etc) sinistro(a) // n (AUT) lato destro; lato sinistro.

offspring ['ɔfsprɪŋ] n prole f, discendenza.

off: ~stage ad dietro le quinte; ~-the-peg, (US) ~-the-rack ad prêt-à-porter; ~-white a bianco sporco inv.

often ['ɔfn] ad spesso; how ~ do you go? quanto spesso ci vai?

ogle ['əugl] vt occhieggiare.

oh [əu] excl oh!

oil [ɔɪl] n olio; (petroleum) petrolio; (for central heating) nafta // vt (machine) lubrificare; ~can n oliatore m a mano; (for storing) latta da olio; ~field n giacimento petrolifero; ~ filter n (AUT) filtro dell'olio; ~ fired a a nafta; ~ level n livello dell'olio; ~ painting n quadro a olio; ~ refinery n raffineria di petrolio; ~ rig n derrick m inv; (at sea) piattaforma per trivellazioni subacquee; ~skins npl indumenti mpl di tela cerata; ~ tanker n petroliera; ~ well n pozzo petrolifero; ~y a unto(a), oleoso(a); (food) untuoso(a).

ointment ['ɔɪntmənt] n unguento.

O.K., okay ['əu'keɪ] excl d'accordo! // vt approvare; is it ~?, are you ~? tutto bene?

old [əuld] a vecchio(a); (ancient) antico(a), vecchio(a); (person) vecchio(a), anziano(a); how ~ are you? quanti anni ha?; he's 10 years ~ ha 10 anni; ~er brother/sister fratello/sorella maggiore; ~ age n vecchiaia; ~ age

pensioner (O.A.P.) n (Brit) pensionato/a; **~-fashioned** a antiquato(a), fuori moda; (person) all'antica.

olive ['ɔliv] n (fruit) oliva; (tree) olivo // a (also: **~-green**) verde oliva inv; **~ oil** n olio d'oliva.

Olympic [əu'limpik] a olimpico(a); the **~ Games**, the **~s** i giochi olimpici, le Olimpiadi.

omelet(te) ['ɔmlit] n omelette f inv.

omen ['əumən] n presagio, augurio.

ominous ['ɔminəs] a minaccioso(a); (event) di malaugurio.

omit [əu'mit] vt omettere.

on [ɔn] ♦ prep 1 (indicating position) su; **~ the wall** sulla parete; **~ the left** a or sulla sinistra

2 (indicating means, method, condition etc): **~ foot** a piedi; **~ the train/plane** in treno/aereo; **~ the telephone** al telefono; **~ the radio/television** alla radio/televisione; **to be ~ drugs** drogarsi; **~ holiday** in vacanza

3 (referring to time): **~ Friday** venerdì; **~ Fridays** il or di venerdì; **~ June 20th** il 20 giugno; **~ Friday, June 20th** venerdì, 20 giugno; **a week ~ Friday** venerdì a otto; **~ his arrival** al suo arrivo; **~ seeing this** vedendo ciò

4 (about, concerning) su, di; **information ~ train services** informazioni sui collegamenti ferroviari; **a book ~ Goldoni/physics** un libro su Goldoni/di or sulla fisica

♦ ad 1 (referring to dress, covering): **to have one's coat ~** avere indosso il cappotto; **to put one's coat ~** mettersi il cappotto; **what's she got ~?** cosa indossa?; **she put her boots/gloves/hat ~** si mise gli stivali/i guanti/il cappello; **screw the lid ~ tightly** avvita bene il coperchio

2 (further, continuously): **to walk ~, go ~** etc continuare, proseguire etc; **to read ~** continuare a leggere; **~ and off** ogni tanto

♦ a 1 (in operation: machine, TV, light) acceso(a); (: tap) aperto(a); (: brake) inserito(a); **is the meeting still ~?** (in progress) la riunione è ancora in corso?; (not cancelled) è confermato l'incontro?; **there's a good film ~ at the cinema** danno un buon film al cinema

2 (col): **that's not ~!** (not acceptable) non si fa così!; (not possible) non se ne parla neanche!

once [wʌns] ad una volta // cj non appena, quando; **~ he had left/it was done** dopo che se n'era andato/fu fatto; **at ~** subito; (simultaneously) a un tempo; **~ more** ancora una volta; **~ and for all** una volta per sempre; **~ upon a time** c'era una volta.

oncoming ['ɔnkʌmiŋ] a (traffic) che viene in senso opposto.

one [wʌn] ♦ num uno(a); **~ hundred and fifty** centocinquanta; **~ day** un giorno

♦ a 1 (sole) unico(a); **the ~ book which** l'unico libro che; **the ~ man who** l'unico che

2 (same) stesso(a); **they came in the ~ car** sono venuti nella stessa macchina

♦ pronoun 1: **this ~** questo/a; **that ~** quello/a; **I've already got ~/a red ~** ne ho già uno/uno rosso; **~ by ~** uno per uno

2: **~ another** l'un l'altro; **to look at ~ another** guardarsi

3 (impersonal) si; **~ never knows** non si sa mai; **to cut ~'s finger** tagliarsi un dito; **~ needs to eat** bisogna mangiare.

one-: ~-armed bandit n slot-machine f inv; **~-day excursion** n (US) biglietto giornaliero di andata e ritorno; **~-man** a (business) diretto(a) etc da un solo uomo; **~-man band** n suonatore ambulante con vari strumenti; **~-off** n (Brit col) fatto eccezionale.

oneself [wʌn'sɛlf] pronoun (reflexive) si; (after prep) se stesso(a), sé; **to do sth (by) ~** fare qc da sé; **to hurt ~** farsi male; **to keep sth for ~** tenere qc per sé; **to talk to ~** parlare da solo.

one: ~-sided a (argument) unilaterale; **~-to-~** a (relationship) univoco(a); **~-upmanship** [-'ʌpmənʃip] n l'arte di fare sempre meglio degli altri; **~-way** a (street, traffic) a senso unico.

ongoing ['ɔngəuiŋ] a in corso; in attuazione.

onion ['ʌnjən] n cipolla.

on-line ['ɔnlain] a, ad (COMPUT) on-line inv.

onlooker ['ɔnlukə*] n spettatore/trice.

only ['əunli] ad solo, soltanto // a solo(a), unico(a) // cj solo che, ma; **an ~ child** un figlio unico; **not ~ ... but also** non solo ... ma anche; **I ~ took one** ne ho preso soltanto uno, non ne ho preso che uno.

onset ['ɔnsɛt] n inizio; (of winter, old age) approssimarsi m.

onshore ['ɔnʃɔ:*] a (wind) di mare.

onslaught ['ɔnslɔ:t] n attacco, assalto.

onto ['ɔntu] prep su, sopra.

onus ['əunəs] n onere m, peso.

onward(s) ['ɔnwəd(z)] ad (move) in avanti.

onyx ['ɔniks] n onice f.

ooze [u:z] vi stillare.

opaque [əu'peik] a opaco(a).

OPEC ['əupɛk] n abbr (= Organization of Petroleum-Exporting Countries) O.P.E.C. f.

open ['əupn] a aperto(a); (road) libero(a); (meeting) pubblico(a); (admiration) evidente, franco(a); (question) insoluto(a); (enemy) dichiarato(a) // vt aprire // vi (eyes, door, debate) aprirsi; (flower) sbocciare; (shop, bank, museum) aprire; (book etc:

commence) cominciare; **in the ~ (air)** all'aperto; **to ~ on to** *vt fus* (*subj: room, door*) dare su; **to ~ up** *vt* aprire; (*blocked road*) sgombrare // *vi* aprirsi; **~ing** *n* apertura; (*opportunity*) occasione *f*, opportunità *f inv*; sbocco; (*job*) posto vacante; **~ly** *ad* apertamente; **~-minded** *a* che ha la mente aperta; **~-plan** *a* senza pareti divisorie.

opera ['ɔpərə] *n* opera; **~ house** *n* opera.

operate ['ɔpəreɪt] *vt* (*machine*) azionare, far funzionare; (*system*) usare // *vi* funzionare; (*drug*) essere efficace; **to ~ on sb (for)** (*MED*) operare qn (di).

operatic [ɔpə'rætɪk] *a* dell'opera, lirico(a).

operating ['ɔpəreɪtɪŋ] *a*: **~ table** tavolo operatorio; **~ theatre** sala operatoria.

operation [ɔpə'reɪʃən] *n* operazione *f*; **to be in ~** (*machine*) essere in azione *or* funzionamento; (*system*) essere in vigore; **to have an ~** (*MED*) subire un'operazione; **~al** *a* in funzione; d'esercizio.

operative ['ɔpərətɪv] *a* (*measure*) operativo(a).

operator ['ɔpəreɪtə*] *n* (*of machine*) operatore/trice; (*TEL*) centralinista *m/f*.

opinion [ə'pɪnɪən] *n* opinione *f*, parere *m*; **in my ~** secondo me, a mio avviso; **~ated** *a* dogmatico(a); **~ poll** *n* sondaggio di opinioni.

opium ['əupɪəm] *n* oppio.

opponent [ə'pəunənt] *n* avversario/a.

opportunist [ɔpə'tjuːnɪst] *n* opportunista *m/f*.

opportunity [ɔpə'tjuːnɪtɪ] *n* opportunità *f inv*, occasione *f*; **to take the ~ of doing** cogliere l'occasione per fare.

oppose [ə'pəuz] *vt* opporsi a; **~d to** *a* contrario a; **as ~d to** in contrasto con; **opposing** *a* opposto(a); (*team*) avversario(a).

opposite ['ɔpəzɪt] *a* opposto(a); (*house etc*) di fronte // *ad* di fronte, dirimpetto // *prep* di fronte a // *n* opposto, contrario; (*of word*) contrario.

opposition [ɔpə'zɪʃən] *n* opposizione *f*.

oppress [ə'prɛs] *vt* opprimere.

opt [ɔpt] *vi*: **to ~ for** optare per; **to ~ to do** scegliere di fare; **to ~ out of** ritirarsi da.

optical ['ɔptɪkl] *a* ottico(a); **~ character recognition (OCR)** *n* lettura ottica; **~ character reader (OCR)** *n* lettore ottico.

optician [ɔp'tɪʃən] *n* ottico.

optimist ['ɔptɪmɪst] *n* ottimista *m/f*; **~ic** [-'mɪstɪk] *a* ottimistico(a).

optimum ['ɔptɪməm] *a* ottimale.

option ['ɔpʃən] *n* scelta; (*SCOL*) materia facoltativa; (*COMM*) opzione *f*; **~al** *a* facoltativo(a); (*COMM*) a scelta.

or [ɔ:*] *cj* o, oppure; (*with negative*): **he hasn't seen ~ heard anything** non ha visto né sentito niente; **~ else** se no, altrimenti; oppure.

oral ['ɔːrəl] *a* orale // *n* esame *m* orale.

orange ['ɔrɪndʒ] *n* (*fruit*) arancia // *a* arancione.

orator ['ɔrətə*] *n* oratore/trice.

orbit ['ɔ:bɪt] *n* orbita.

orchard ['ɔ:tʃəd] *n* frutteto.

orchestra ['ɔ:kɪstrə] *n* orchestra; (*US: seating*) platea; **~l** [-'kɛstrəl] *a* orchestrale; (*concert*) sinfonico(a).

orchid ['ɔ:kɪd] *n* orchidea.

ordain [ɔ:'deɪn] *vt* (*REL*) ordinare; (*decide*) decretare.

ordeal [ɔ:'diːl] *n* prova, travaglio.

order ['ɔ:də*] *n* ordine *m*; (*COMM*) ordinazione *f* // *vt* ordinare; **in ~** in ordine; (*of document*) in regola; **in (working) ~** funzionante; **in ~ of size** in ordine di grandezza; **in ~ to do** per fare; **in ~ that** affinché +*sub*; **on ~** (*COMM*) in ordinazione; **to ~ sb to do** ordinare a qn di fare; **the lower ~s** (*pej*) i ceti inferiori; **~ form** *n* modulo d'ordinazione; **~ly** *n* (*MIL*) attendente *m* // *a* (*room*) in ordine; (*mind*) metodico(a); (*person*) ordinato(a), metodico(a).

ordinary ['ɔ:dnrɪ] *a* normale, comune; (*pej*) mediocre; **out of the ~** diverso dal solito, fuori dell'ordinario.

ore [ɔ:*] *n* minerale *m* grezzo.

organ ['ɔ:gən] *n* organo; **~ic** [ɔ:'gænɪk] *a* organico(a).

organization [ɔ:gənaɪ'zeɪʃən] *n* organizzazione *f*.

organize ['ɔ:gənaɪz] *vt* organizzare; **~r** *n* organizzatore/trice.

orgasm ['ɔ:gæzəm] *n* orgasmo.

orgy ['ɔ:dʒɪ] *n* orgia.

Orient ['ɔ:rɪənt] *n*: **the ~** l'Oriente *m*; **oriental** [-'ɛntl] *a*, *n* orientale (*m/f*).

origin ['ɔrɪdʒɪn] *n* origine *f*.

original [ə'rɪdʒɪnl] *a* originale; (*earliest*) originario(a) // *n* originale *m*; **~ly** *ad* (*at first*) all'inizio.

originate [ə'rɪdʒɪneɪt] *vi*: **to ~ from** essere originario(a) da; (*suggestion*) provenire da; **to ~ in** avere origine in.

Orkneys ['ɔ:knɪz] *npl*: **the ~** (*also:* **the Orkney Islands**) le Orcadi.

ornament ['ɔ:nəmənt] *n* ornamento; (*trinket*) ninnolo; **~al** [-'mɛntl] *a* ornamentale.

ornate [ɔ:'neɪt] *a* molto ornato(a).

orphan ['ɔ:fn] *n* orfano/a // *vt*: **to be ~ed** diventare orfano; **~age** *n* orfanotrofio.

orthodox ['ɔ:θədɔks] *a* ortodosso(a).

orthopaedic, (*US*) **orthopedic** [ɔ:θə'piːdɪk] *a* ortopedico(a).

ostensibly [ɔs'tɛnsɪblɪ] *ad* all'apparenza.

ostentatious [ɔstɛn'teɪʃəs] *a* pretenzioso(a); ostentato(a).

ostrich ['ɔstritʃ] *n* struzzo.

other ['ʌðə*] *a* altro(a) // *pronoun*: the ~ (one) l'altro(a); ~s (~ *people*) altri *mpl*; ~ **than** altro che; a parte; ~**wise** *ad*, *cj* altrimenti.

otter ['ɔtə*] *n* lontra.

ouch [autʃ] *excl* ohi!, ahi!

ought, *pt* ought [ɔ:t] *auxiliary vb*: I ~ to do it dovrei farlo; this ~ to have been corrected questo avrebbe dovuto essere corretto; he ~ to win dovrebbe vincere.

ounce [auns] *n* oncia (= 28.35 *g*; 16 in a *pound*).

our ['auə*] *a* il(la) nostro(a), *pl* i(le) nostri(e); *see also* **my**; ~**s** *pronoun* il(la) nostro(a), *pl* i(le) nostri(e); *see also* **mine**; ~**selves** *pronoun pl (reflexive)* ci; *(after preposition)* noi; *(emphatic)* noi stessi(e); *see also* **oneself**.

oust [aust] *vt* cacciare, espellere.

out [aut] *ad* fuori; *(published, not at home etc)* uscito(a); *(light, fire)* spento(a); ~ **here** qui fuori; ~ **there** là fuori; he's ~ è uscito; *(unconscious)* ha perso conoscenza; **to be** ~ **in one's calculations** essersi sbagliato nei calcoli; **to run/back** *etc* ~ uscire di corsa/a marcia indietro *etc*; ~ **loud** *ad* ad alta voce; ~ **of** *(outside)* fuori di; *(because of: anger etc)* per; *(from among)*: ~ **of** 10 su 10; *(without)*: ~ **of petrol** senza benzina, a corto di benzina; ~ **of order** *(machine etc)* guasto(a); ~**-and-**~ *a (liar, thief etc)* vero(a) e proprio(a).

outback ['autbæk] *n (in Australia)* interno, entroterra.

outboard ['autbɔ:d] *n*: ~ *(motor)* (motore *m*) fuoribordo.

outbreak ['autbreik] *n* scoppio; epidemia.

outburst ['autbə:st] *n* scoppio.

outcast ['autkɑ:st] *n* esule *m/f*; *(socially)* paria *m inv*.

outcome ['autkʌm] *n* esito, risultato.

outcrop ['autkrɔp] *n (of rock)* affioramento.

outcry ['autkrai] *n* protesta, clamore *m*.

outdated [aut'deitid] *a (custom, clothes)* fuori moda; *(idea)* sorpassato(a).

outdo [aut'du:] *vt irg* sorpassare.

outdoor [aut'dɔ:*] *a* all'aperto; ~**s** *ad* fuori; all'aria aperta.

outer ['autə*] *a* esteriore; ~ **space** *n* spazio cosmico.

outfit ['autfit] *n* equipaggiamento; *(clothes)* abito; "~**ter's**" *(Brit)* "confezioni da uomo".

outgoing ['autgəuiŋ] *a (character)* socievole; ~**s** *npl (Brit: expenses)* spese *fpl*, uscite *fpl*.

outgrow [aut'grəu] *vt irg (clothes)* diventare troppo grande per.

outhouse ['authaus] *n* costruzione *f* annessa.

outing ['autiŋ] *n* gita; escursione *f*.

outlandish [aut'lændiʃ] *a* strano(a).

outlaw ['autlɔ:] *n* fuorilegge *m/f*.

outlay ['autlei] *n* spese *fpl*; *(investment)* sborsa, spesa.

outlet ['autlet] *n (for liquid etc)* sbocco, scarico; *(US ELEC)* presa di corrente; *(for emotion)* sfogo; *(for goods)* sbocco; *(also:* retail ~*)* punto di vendita.

outline ['autlain] *n* contorno, profilo; *(summary)* abbozzo, grandi linee *fpl*.

outlive [aut'liv] *vt* sopravvivere a.

outlook ['autluk] *n* prospettiva, vista.

outlying ['autlaiiŋ] *a* periferico(a).

outmoded [aut'məudid] *a* passato(a) di moda; antiquato(a).

outnumber [aut'nʌmbə*] *vt* superare in numero.

out-of-date [autəv'deit] *a (passport)* scaduto(a); *(clothes)* fuori moda *inv*.

out-of-the-way ['autəvðə'wei] *a (place)* fuori mano *inv*.

outpatient ['autpeiʃənt] *n* paziente *m/f* esterno/a.

outpost ['autpəust] *n* avamposto.

output ['autput] *n* produzione *f*; *(COMPUT)* output *m inv*.

outrage ['autreidʒ] *n* oltraggio; scandalo // *vt* oltraggiare; ~**ous** [-'reidʒəs] *a* oltraggioso(a); scandaloso(a).

outright *ad* [aut'rait] completamente; schiettamente; apertamente; sul colpo // *a* ['autrait] completo(a); schietto(a) e netto(a).

outset ['autset] *n* inizio.

outside [aut'said] *n* esterno, esteriore *m* // *a* esterno(a), esteriore // *ad* fuori, all'esterno // *prep* fuori di, all'esterno di; **at the** ~ *(fig)* al massimo; ~ **lane** *n (AUT)* corsia di sorpasso; ~**-left/-right** *n (FOOTBALL)* ala sinistra/destra; ~ **line** *n (TEL)* linea esterna; ~**r** *n (in race etc)* outsider *m inv*; *(stranger)* straniero/a.

outsize ['autsaiz] *a* enorme; *(clothes)* per taglie forti.

outskirts ['autskə:ts] *npl* sobborghi *mpl*.

outspoken [aut'spəukən] *a* molto franco(a).

outstanding [aut'stændiŋ] *a* eccezionale, di rilievo; *(unfinished)* non completo(a); non evaso(a); non regolato(a).

outstay [aut'stei] *vt*: **to** ~ **one's welcome** diventare un ospite sgradito.

outstretched [aut'stretʃt] *a (hand)* teso(a); *(body)* disteso(a).

outstrip [aut'strip] *vt (competitors, demand)* superare.

out-tray ['auttrei] *n* contenitore *m* per la corrispondenza in partenza.

outward ['autwəd] *a (sign, appearances)* esteriore; *(journey)* d'andata; ~**ly** *ad* esteriormente; in apparenza.

outweigh [aut'wei] *vt* avere maggior peso di.

outwit [aut'wit] *vt* superare in astuzia.

oval ['əuvl] *a, n* ovale (*m*).

ovary ['əuvəri] *n* ovaia.

oven ['ʌvn] *n* forno; **~proof** *a* da forno.

over ['əuvə*] *ad* al di sopra // *a* (*or ad*) (*finished*) finito(a), terminato(a); (*too*) troppo; (*remaining*) che avanza // *prep* su; sopra; (*above*) al di sopra di; (*on the other side of*) di là di; (*more than*) più di; (*during*) durante; **~ here** qui; **~ there** là; **all ~** (*everywhere*) dappertutto; (*finished*) tutto(a) finito(a); **~ and ~** (*again*) più e più volte; **~ and above** oltre (a); **to ask sb ~** invitare qn (a passare).

overall *a, n* ['əuvərɔ:l] *a* totale // *n* (*Brit*) grembiule *m* // *ad* [əuvər'ɔ:l] nell'insieme, complessivamente; **~s** *npl* tuta (da lavoro).

overawe [əuvər'ɔ:] *vt* intimidire.

overbalance [əuvə'bæləns] *vi* perdere l'equilibrio.

overbearing [əuvə'bɛəriŋ] *a* imperioso(a), prepotente.

overboard ['əuvəbɔ:d] *ad* (*NAUT*) fuori bordo, in mare.

overbook [əuvə'buk] *vt*: **the hotel was ~ed** le prenotazioni all'albergo superavano i posti disponibili.

overcast ['əuvəkɑ:st] *a* coperto(a).

overcharge [əuvə'tʃɑ:dʒ] *vt*: **to ~ sb for sth** far pagare troppo caro a qn per qc.

overcoat ['əuvəkəut] *n* soprabito, cappotto.

overcome [əuvə'kʌm] *vt irg* superare; sopraffare.

overcrowded [əuvə'kraudid] *a* sovraffollato(a).

overdo [əuvə'du:] *vt irg* esagerare; (*overcook*) cuocere troppo.

overdose ['əuvədəus] *n* dose *f* eccessiva.

overdraft ['əuvədrɑ:ft] *n* scoperto (di conto).

overdrawn [əuvə'drɔ:n] *a* (*account*) scoperto(a).

overdue [əuvə'dju:] *a* in ritardo; (*recognition*) tardivo(a).

overestimate [əuvər'estimeit] *vt* sopravvalutare.

overflow *vi* [əuvə'fləu] traboccare // *n* ['əuvəfləu] troppopieno.

overgrown [əuvə'grəun] *a* (*garden*) ricoperto(a) di vegetazione.

overhaul *vt* [əuvə'hɔ:l] revisionare // *n* ['əuvəhɔ:l] revisione *f*.

overhead *ad* [əuvə'hɛd] di sopra // *a* ['əuvəhɛd] aereo(a); (*lighting*) verticale; **~s** *npl*, (*US*) **~** *n* spese *fpl* generali.

overhear [əuvə'hiə*] *vt irg* sentire (per caso).

overheat [əuvə'hi:t] *vi* (*engine*) surriscaldare.

overjoyed [əuvə'dʒɔid] *a* pazzo(a) di gioia.

overkill ['əuvəkil] *n* (*fig*) eccessi *mpl*.

overlap [əuvə'læp] *vi* sovrapporsi.

overleaf [əuvə'li:f] *ad* a tergo.

overload [əuvə'ləud] *vt* sovraccaricare.

overlook [əuvə'luk] *vt* (*have view of*) dare su; (*miss*) trascurare; (*forgive*) passare sopra a.

overnight [əuvə'nait] *ad* (*happen*) durante la notte; (*fig*) tutto ad un tratto // *a* di notte; fulmineo(a); **he stayed there ~** ci ha passato la notte.

overpower [əuvə'pauə*] *vt* sopraffare; **~ing** *a* irresistibile; (*heat, stench*) soffocante.

overrate [əuvə'reit] *vt* sopravvalutare.

override [əuvə'raid] *vt* (*irg*: *like* ride) (*order, objection*) passar sopra a; (*decision*) annullare; **overriding** *a* preponderante.

overrule [əuvə'ru:l] *vt* (*decision*) annullare; (*claim*) respingere.

overrun [əuvə'rʌn] *vt* (*irg*: *like* run) (*country*) invadere; (*time limit*) superare.

overseas [əuvə'si:z] *ad* oltremare; (*abroad*) all'estero // *a* (*trade*) estero(a); (*visitor*) straniero(a).

overseer ['əuvəsiə*] *n* (*in factory*) caposquadra *m*.

overshadow [əuvə'ʃædəu] *vt* (*fig*) eclissare.

overshoot [əuvə'ʃu:t] *vt irg* superare.

oversight ['əuvəsait] *n* omissione *f*, svista.

oversleep [əuvə'sli:p] *vi irg* dormire troppo a lungo.

overstep [əuvə'stɛp] *vt*: **to ~ the mark** superare ogni limite.

overt [əu'və:t] *a* palese.

overtake [əuvə'teik] *vt irg* sorpassare.

overthrow [əuvə'θrəu] *vt irg* (*government*) rovesciare.

overtime ['əuvətaim] *n* (*lavoro*) straordinario.

overtone ['əuvətəun] *n* (*also*: **~s**) sfumatura.

overture ['əuvətʃuə*] *n* (*MUS*) ouverture *f inv*; (*fig*) approccio.

overturn [əuvə'tə:n] *vt* rovesciare // *vi* rovesciarsi.

overweight [əuvə'weit] *a* (*person*) troppo grasso(a); (*luggage*) troppo pesante.

overwhelm [əuvə'wɛlm] *vt* sopraffare; sommergere; schiacciare; **~ing** *a* (*victory, defeat*) schiacciante; (*desire*) irresistibile.

overwork [əuvə'wə:k] *vt* far lavorare troppo // *vi* lavorare troppo, strapazzarsi.

overwrought [əuvə'rɔ:t] *a* molto agitato(a).

owe [əu] *vt* dovere; **to ~ sb sth, to ~ sth to sb** dovere qc a qn.

owing to ['əuiŋtu:] *prep* a causa di.

owl [aul] *n* gufo.

own [əun] *vt* possedere // *a* proprio(a); **a room of my ~** la mia propria camera; **to**

get one's ~ **back** vendicarsi; on one's ~ tutto(a) solo(a); **to ~ up** vi confessare; ~**er** n proprietario/a; ~**ership** n possesso.

ox, pl **oxen** [ɔks, 'ɔksn] n bue m.

oxtail ['ɔksteɪl] n: ~ **soup** minestra di coda di bue.

oxygen ['ɔksɪdʒən] n ossigeno; ~ **mask** n maschera ad ossigeno.

oyster ['ɔɪstə*] n ostrica.

oz. abbr = **ounce(s)**.

ozone ['əuzəun] n ozono.

P

p [piː] abbr = **penny**, **pence**.

pa [paː] n (col) papà m inv, babbo.

P.A. n abbr = **personal assistant**, **public address system**.

p.a. abbr = **per annum**.

pace [peɪs] n passo; (speed) passo; velocità // vi: to ~ **up and down** camminare su e giù; **to keep ~ with** camminare di pari passo a; (events) tenersi al corrente di; ~**maker** n (MED) segnapasso.

pacific [pə'sɪfɪk] n: **the P~** (Ocean) il Pacifico, l'Oceano Pacifico.

pack [pæk] n pacco; balla; (of hounds) muta; (of thieves etc) banda; (of cards) mazzo // vt (goods) impaccare, imballare; (in suitcase etc) mettere; (box) riempire; (cram) stipare, pigiare; (press down) tamponare, turare; **to ~** (one's bags) fare la valigia; **to ~ off** vt (person) spedire.

package ['pækɪdʒ] n pacco; balla; (also: ~ **deal**) pacchetto; forfait m inv; ~ **tour** n viaggio organizzato.

packed lunch n pranzo al sacco.

packet ['pækɪt] n pacchetto.

packing ['pækɪŋ] n imballaggio; ~ **case** n cassa da imballaggio.

pact [pækt] n patto, accordo; trattato.

pad [pæd] n blocco; (for inking) tampone m; (col: flat) appartamentino // vt imbottire; ~**ding** n imbottitura; (fig) riempitivo.

paddle ['pædl] n (oar) pagaia; (US: for table tennis) racchetta da ping-pong // vi sguazzare // vt: **to ~ a canoe** etc vogare con la pagaia; ~ **steamer** n battello a ruote; **paddling pool** n (Brit) piscina per bambini.

paddy field ['pædɪ-] n risaia.

padlock ['pædlɔk] n lucchetto.

paediatrics, (US) **pediatrics** [piːdɪ'ætrɪks] n pediatria.

pagan ['peɪgən] a, n pagano(a).

page [peɪdʒ] n pagina; (also: ~ **boy**) fattorino; (at wedding) paggio // vt (in hotel etc) (far) chiamare.

pageant ['pædʒənt] n spettacolo storico; grande cerimonia; ~**ry** n pompa.

paid [peɪd] pt, pp of **pay** // a (work, official) rimunerato(a); **to put ~ to** (Brit) mettere fine a.

pail [peɪl] n secchio.

pain [peɪn] n dolore m; **to be in ~** soffrire, aver male; **to take ~s to do** mettercela tutta per fare; ~**ed** a addolorato(a), afflitto(a); ~**ful** a doloroso(a), che fa male; difficile, penoso(a); ~**fully** ad (fig: very) fin troppo; ~**killer** n antalgico, antidolorifico; ~**less** a indolore.

painstaking ['peɪnzteɪkɪŋ] a (person) sollecito(a); (work) accurato(a).

paint [peɪnt] n vernice f, colore m // vt dipingere; (walls, door etc) verniciare; **to ~ the door blue** verniciare la porta di azzurro; ~**brush** n pennello; ~**er** n (artist) pittore m; (decorator) imbianchino; ~**ing** n pittura; verniciatura; (picture) dipinto, quadro; ~**work** n tinta; (of car) vernice f.

pair [pɛə*] n (of shoes, gloves etc) paio; (of people) coppia; duo m inv; **a ~ of scissors/trousers** un paio di forbici/pantaloni.

pajamas [pɪ'dʒaːməz] npl (US) pigiama m.

Pakistan [paːkɪ'staːn] n Pakistan m; ~**i** a, n pakistano(a).

pal [pæl] n (col) amico/a, compagno/a.

palace ['pæləs] n palazzo.

palatable ['pælɪtəbl] a gustoso(a).

palate ['pælɪt] n palato.

palatial [pə'leɪʃəl] a sontuoso(a), sfarzoso(a).

palaver [pə'laːvə*] n chiacchiere fpl; storie fpl.

pale [peɪl] a pallido(a) // n: **to be beyond the ~** aver oltrepassato ogni limite; **to grow ~** diventare pallido, impallidire.

Palestine ['pælɪstaɪn] n Palestina; **Palestinian** [-'tɪnɪən] a, n palestinese (m/f).

palette ['pælɪt] n tavolozza.

paling ['peɪlɪŋ] n (stake) palo; (fence) palizzata.

pall [pɔːl] n (of smoke) cappa // vi: **to ~** (on) diventare noioso(a) (a).

pallet ['pælɪt] n (for goods) paletta.

pallid ['pælɪd] a pallido(a), smorto(a).

pallor ['pælə*] n pallore m.

palm [paːm] n (ANAT) palma, palmo; (also: ~ **tree**) palma // vt: **to ~ sth off on sb** (col) rifilare qc a qn; **P~ Sunday** n Domenica delle Palme.

palpable ['pælpəbl] a palpabile.

paltry ['pɔːltrɪ] a derisorio(a); insignificante.

pamper ['pæmpə*] vt viziare, accarezzare.

pamphlet ['pæmflət] n dépliant m inv.

pan [pæn] n (also: **sauce~**) casseruola; (also: **frying ~**) padella // vi (CINEMA) fare una panoramica.

panache [pə'næʃ] n stile m.

pancake ['pænkeɪk] n frittella.

pancreas ['pæŋkrɪəs] n pancreas m inv.

panda ['pændə] n panda m inv; ~ **car** n (Brit) auto f della polizia.

pandemonium [pændɪ'məunɪəm] n pandemonio.

pander ['pændə*] vi: to ~ to lusingare; concedere tutto a.

pane [peɪn] n vetro.

panel ['pænl] n (of wood, cloth etc) pannello; (RADIO, TV) giuria; ~**ling**, (US) ~**ing** n rivestimento a pannelli.

pang [pæŋ] n: ~s of hunger spasimi mpl della fame; ~s of conscience morsi mpl di coscienza.

panic ['pænɪk] n panico // vi perdere il sangue freddo; ~**ky** a (person) pauroso(a); ~-**stricken** a (person) preso(a) dal panico, in preda al panico, (look) terrorizzato(a).

pansy ['pænzɪ] n (BOT) viola del pensiero, pensée f inv; (col) femminuccia.

pant [pænt] vi ansare.

panther ['pænθə*] n pantera.

panties ['pæntɪz] npl slip m, mutandine fpl.

pantihose ['pæntɪhəuz] n (US) collant m inv.

pantomime ['pæntəmaɪm] n (Brit) pantomima.

pantry ['pæntrɪ] n dispensa.

pants [pænts] npl mutande fpl, slip m; (US: trousers) pantaloni mpl.

papal ['peɪpəl] a papale, pontificio(a).

paper ['peɪpə*] n carta; (also: wall~) carta da parati, tappezzeria; (also: news~) giornale m; (study, article) saggio; (exam) prova scritta // a di carta // vt tappezzare; ~s npl (also: identity ~s) carte fpl, documenti mpl; ~**back** n tascabile m; edizione f economica; ~ **clip** n graffetta, clip f inv; ~ **hankie** n fazzolettino di carta; ~**mill** n cartiera; ~**weight** n fermacarte m inv; ~**work** n lavoro amministrativo.

papier-mâché ['pæpɪeɪ'mæʃeɪ] n cartapesta.

par [pɑː*] n parità, pari f; (GOLF) norma; on a ~ **with** alla pari con.

parable ['pærəbl] n parabola.

parachute ['pærəʃuːt] n paracadute m inv.

parade [pə'reɪd] n parata; (inspection) rivista, rassegna // vt (fig) fare sfoggio di // vi sfilare in parata.

paradise ['pærədaɪs] n paradiso.

paradox ['pærədɔks] n paradosso; ~**ically** [-'dɔksɪklɪ] ad paradossalmente.

paraffin ['pærəfɪn] n (Brit): ~ (**oil**) paraffina.

paragon ['pærəgən] n modello di perfezione or di virtù.

paragraph ['pærəgrɑːf] n paragrafo.

parallel ['pærəlɛl] a parallelo(a); (fig) analogo(a) // n (line) parallela; (fig, GEO) parallelo.

paralysis [pə'rælɪsɪs] n paralisi f inv.

paralyze ['pærəlaɪz] vt paralizzare.

paramount ['pærəmaunt] a: of ~ **importance** di capitale importanza.

paranoid ['pærənɔɪd] a paranoico(a).

paraphernalia [pærəfə'neɪlɪə] n attrezzi mpl, roba.

parasol ['pærəsɔl] n parasole m.

paratrooper ['pærətruːpə*] n paracadutista m (soldato).

parcel ['pɑːsl] n pacco, pacchetto // vt (also: ~ **up**) impaccare.

parch [pɑːtʃ] vt riardere; ~**ed** a (person) assetato(a).

parchment ['pɑːtʃmənt] n pergamena.

pardon ['pɑːdn] n perdono; grazia // vt perdonare; (LAW) graziare; ~ **me**! mi scusi!; **I beg your** ~! scusi!; **I beg your** ~?, (US) ~ **me**? prego?

parent ['pɛərənt] n genitore m; ~s npl genitori mpl; ~**al** [pə'rɛntl] a dei genitori.

parenthesis, pl **parentheses** [pə'rɛnθɪsɪs, -sɪːz] n parentesi f inv.

Paris ['pærɪs] n Parigi f.

parish ['pærɪʃ] n parrocchia; (civil) ≈ municipio // a parrocchiale.

park [pɑːk] n parco // vt, vi parcheggiare.

parka ['pɑːkə] n eskimo.

parking ['pɑːkɪŋ] n parcheggio; "no ~" "sosta vietata"; ~ **lot** n (US) posteggio, parcheggio; ~ **meter** n parchimetro; ~ **ticket** n multa per sosta vietata.

parlance ['pɑːləns] n gergo.

parliament ['pɑːləmənt] n parlamento; ~**ary** [-'mɛntərɪ] a parlamentare.

parlour, (US) **parlor** ['pɑːlə*] n salotto.

parochial [pə'rəukɪəl] a parrocchiale; (pej) provinciale.

parody ['pærədɪ] n parodia.

parole [pə'rəul] n: on ~ in libertà per buona condotta.

parrot ['pærət] n pappagallo.

parry ['pærɪ] vt parare.

parsley ['pɑːslɪ] n prezzemolo.

parsnip ['pɑːsnɪp] n pastinaca.

parson ['pɑːsn] n prete m; (Church of England) parroco.

part [pɑːt] n parte f; (of machine) pezzo; (MUS) voce f; parte; (US: in hair) scriminatura // a in parte // ad ~**partly** // vt separare // vi (people) separarsi; (roads) dividersi; to take ~ in prendere parte a; for my ~ per parte mia; to take sth in good ~ prendere bene qc; to take sb's ~ parteggiare per or prendere le parti di qn; for the most ~ in generale; nella maggior parte dei casi; to ~ **with** vt fus separarsi da; rinunciare a; ~ **exchange** n (Brit): in ~ exchange in pagamento parziale.

partial ['pɑːʃl] a parziale; to be ~ to

avere un debole per.

participate [pɑ:'tɪsɪpeɪt] *vi*: to ~ (in) prendere parte (a), partecipare (a); **participation** [-'peɪʃən] *n* partecipazione *f*.

participle ['pɑ:tɪsɪpl] *n* participio.

particle ['pɑ:tɪkl] *n* particella.

particular [pə'tɪkjulə*] *a* particolare; speciale; (*fussy*) difficile; meticoloso(a); ~**s** *npl* particolari *mpl*, dettagli *mpl*; (*information*) informazioni *fpl*; in ~ in particolare, particolarmente; ~**ly** *ad* particolarmente; in particolare.

parting ['pɑ:tɪŋ] *n* separazione *f*; (*Brit*: *in hair*) scriminatura // *a* d'addio.

partisan [pɑ:tɪ'zæn] *n* partigiano/a // *a* partigiano(a); di parte.

partition [pɑ:'tɪʃən] *n* (*POL*) partizione *f*; (*wall*) tramezzo.

partly ['pɑ:tlɪ] *ad* parzialmente; in parte.

partner ['pɑ:tnə*] *n* (*COMM*) socio/a; (*SPORT*) compagno/a; (*at dance*) cavaliere/dama; ~**ship** *n* associazione *f*; (*COMM*) società *f inv*.

partridge ['pɑ:trɪdʒ] *n* pernice *f*.

part-time ['pɑ:t'taɪm] *a*, *ad* a orario ridotto.

party ['pɑ:tɪ] *n* (*POL*) partito; (*team*) squadra; gruppo; (*LAW*) parte *f*; (*celebration*) ricevimento; serata; festa // *cpd* (*POL*) del partito, di partito; (*dress*, *finery*) della festa; ~ **line** *n* (*TEL*) duplex *m inv*.

pass [pɑ:s] *vt* (*gen*) passare; (*place*) passare davanti a; (*exam*) passare, superare; (*candidate*) promuovere; (*overtake*, *surpass*) sorpassare, superare; (*approve*) approvare // *vi* passare // *n* (*permit*) lasciapassare *m inv*; permesso; (*in mountains*) passo, gola; (*SPORT*) passaggio; (*SCOL*: *also*: ~ **mark**): to **get a ~** prendere la sufficienza; to ~ **sth through a hole** *etc* far passare qc attraverso un buco *etc*; to **make a ~ at sb** (*col*) fare delle proposte *or* delle avances a qn; to ~ **away** *vi* morire; to ~ **by** *vi* passare // *vt* trascurare; to ~ **on** *vt* passare; to ~ **out** *vi* svenire; to ~ **up** *vt* (*opportunity*) lasciarsi sfuggire, perdere; ~**able** *a* (*road*) praticabile; (*work*) accettabile.

passage ['pæsɪdʒ] *n* (*gen*) passaggio; (*also*: ~**way**) corridoio; (*in book*) brano, passo; (*by boat*) traversata.

passbook ['pɑ:sbuk] *n* libretto di risparmio.

passenger ['pæsɪndʒə*] *n* passeggero/a.

passer-by [pɑ:sə'baɪ] *n* passante *m/f*.

passing ['pɑ:sɪŋ] *a* (*fig*) fuggevole; to **mention sth in ~** accennare a qc di sfuggita; ~ **place** *n* (*AUT*) piazzola di sosta.

passion ['pæʃən] *n* passione *f*; amore *m*; ~**ate** *a* appassionato(a).

passive ['pæsɪv] *a* (*also* LING)

passivo(a).

Passover ['pɑ:səuvə*] *n* Pasqua ebraica.

passport ['pɑ:spɔ:t] *n* passaporto; ~ **control** *n* controllo *m* passaporti *inv*.

password ['pɑ:swɔ:d] *n* parola d'ordine.

past [pɑ:st] *prep* (*further than*) oltre, di là di; dopo; (*later than*) dopo // *a* passato(a); (*president etc*) ex *inv* // *n* passato; he's ~ **forty** ha più di quarant'anni; **for the ~ few days** da qualche giorno; in questi ultimi giorni; to **run ~** passare di corsa.

pasta ['pæstə] *n* pasta.

paste [peɪst] *n* (*glue*) colla; (*CULIN*) pâté *m inv*; pasta // *vt* collare.

pastel ['pæstl] *a* pastello *inv*.

pasteurized ['pæstəraɪzd] *a* pastorizzato(a).

pastille ['pæstl] *n* pastiglia.

pastime ['pɑ:staɪm] *n* passatempo.

pastor ['pɑ:stə*] *n* pastore *m*.

pastry ['peɪstrɪ] *n* pasta.

pasture ['pɑ:stʃə*] *n* pascolo.

pasty *n* ['pæstɪ] pasticcio di carne // *a* ['peɪstɪ] pastoso(a); (*complexion*) pallido(a).

pat [pæt] *vt* accarezzare, dare un colpetto (affettuoso) a.

patch [pætʃ] *n* (*of material*) toppa; (*spot*) macchia; (*of land*) pezzo // *vt* (*clothes*) rattoppare; (**to go through**) **a bad ~** (attraversare) un brutto periodo; to ~ **up** *vt* rappezzare; ~**y** *a* irregolare.

pâté ['pæteɪ] *n* pâté *m inv*.

patent ['peɪtnt] *n* brevetto // *vt* brevettare // *a* patente, manifesto(a); ~ **leather** *n* cuoio verniciato.

paternal [pə'tə:nl] *a* paterno(a).

path [pɑ:θ] *n* sentiero, viottolo; viale *m*; (*fig*) via, strada; (*of planet*, *missile*) traiettoria.

pathetic [pə'θetɪk] *a* (*pitiful*) patetico(a); (*very bad*) penoso(a).

pathological [pæθə'lɔdʒɪkl] *a* patologico(a).

patience ['peɪʃns] *n* pazienza; (*Brit CARDS*) solitario.

patient ['peɪʃnt] *n* paziente *m/f*; malato/a // *a* paziente.

patio ['pætɪəu] *n* terrazza.

patriot ['peɪtrɪət] *n* patriota *m/f*; ~**ic** [pætrɪ'ɔtɪk] *a* patriottico(a); ~**ism** *n* patriottismo.

patrol [pə'trəul] *n* pattuglia // *vt* pattugliare; ~ **car** *n* autoradio *f inv* (della polizia); ~**man** *n* (*US*) poliziotto.

patron ['peɪtrən] *n* (*in shop*) cliente *m/f*; (*of charity*) benefattore/trice; ~ **of the arts** mecenate *m/f*; ~**ize** ['pætrənaɪz] *vt* essere cliente abituale di; (*fig*) trattare con condiscendenza.

patter ['pætə*] *n* picchiettio; (*sales talk*) propaganda di vendita.

pattern ['pætən] *n* modello; (*design*)

disegno, motivo; (*sample*) campione *m*.
paunch [pɔ:ntʃ] *n* pancione *m*.
pauper ['pɔ:pə*] *n* indigente *m/f*.
pause [pɔ:z] *n* pausa // *vi* fare una pausa,
arrestarsi.
pave [peɪv] *vt* pavimentare; **to ~ the way
for** aprire la via a.
pavement ['peɪvmənt] *n* (*Brit*)
marciapiede *m*.
pavilion [pə'vɪlɪən] *n* padiglione *m*;
tendone *m*.
paving ['peɪvɪŋ] *n* pavimentazione *f*; ~
stone *n* lastra di pietra.
paw [pɔ:] *n* zampa // *vt* dare una
zampata a; (*subj: person: pej*) palpare.
pawn [pɔ:n] *n* pegno; (*CHESS*) pedone *m*;
(*fig*) pedina // *vt* dare in pegno;
~**broker** *n* prestatore *m* su pegno;
~**shop** *n* monte di pietà.
pay [peɪ] *n* stipendio; paga // *vb* (*pt, pp
paid*) *vt* pagare // *vi* pagare; (*be profitable*) rendere; **to ~ attention (to)** fare
attenzione (a); **to ~ back** *vt*
rimborsare; **to ~ for** *vt fus* pagare; **to
~ in** *vt* versare; **to ~ off** *vt* (*debt*)
saldare; (*person*) pagare; (*employee*)
pagare e licenziare // *vi* (*scheme,
decision*) dare dei frutti; **to ~ up** *vt*
saldare; ~**able** *a* pagabile; ~**ee** *n*
beneficiario/a; **~ envelope** *n* (*US*) =
packet; ~**ment** *n* pagamento;
versamento; saldamento; **advance
~ment** (*part sum*) anticipo, acconto;
(*total sum*) pagamento anticipato; **~
packet** *n* (*Brit*) busta *f* paga *inv*; **~
phone** *n* cabina telefonica; ~**roll** *n*
ruolo (organico); **~ slip** *n* foglio *m* paga
inv.
PC *n abbr* = **personal computer**.
p.c. *abbr* = **per cent**.
pea [pi:] *n* pisello.
peace [pi:s] *n* pace *f*; (*calm*) calma,
tranquillità; ~**able** *a* pacifico(a); ~**ful**
a pacifico(a), calmo(a).
peach [pi:tʃ] *n* pesca.
peacock ['pi:kɔk] *n* pavone *m*.
peak [pi:k] *n* (*of mountain*) cima, vetta;
(*mountain itself*) picco; (*fig*) massimo
(: *of career*) acme *f*; **~ hours** *npl* ore
fpl di punta.
peal [pi:l] *n* (*of bells*) scampanio, carillon
m inv; **~s of laughter** scoppi *mpl* di risa.
peanut ['pi:nʌt] *n* arachide *f*, nocciolina
americana.
pear [pɛə*] *n* pera.
pearl [pə:l] *n* perla.
peasant ['pɛznt] *n* contadino/a.
peat [pi:t] *n* torba.
pebble ['pɛbl] *n* ciottolo.
peck [pɛk] *vt* (*also*: ~ **at**) beccare;
(*food*) mangiucchiare // *n* colpo di becco;
(*kiss*) bacetto; ~**ing order** *n* ordine *m*
gerarchico; ~**ish** *a* (*Brit col*): I feel
~**ish** ho un languorino.
peculiar [pɪ'kju:lɪə*] *a* strano(a),

bizzarro(a); peculiare; ~ **to** peculiare di.
pedal ['pɛdl] *n* pedale *m* // *vi* pedalare.
pedantic [pɪ'dæntɪk] *a* pedantesco(a).
peddler ['pɛdlə*] *n* (*US*) = **pedlar**.
pedestal ['pɛdəstl] *n* piedestallo.
pedestrian [pɪ'dɛstrɪən] *n* pedone/a // *a*
pedonale; (*fig*) prosaico(a), pedestre; ~
crossing *n* (*Brit*) passaggio pedonale.
pediatrics [pi:dɪ'ætrɪks] *n* (*US*) =
paediatrics.
pedigree ['pɛdɪgri:] *n* stirpe *f*; (*of
animal*) pedigree *m inv* // *cpd* (*animal*)
di razza.
pedlar ['pɛdlə*] *n* venditore *m*
ambulante.
pee [pi:] *vi* (*col*) pisciare.
peek [pi:k] *vi* guardare furtivamente.
peel [pi:l] *n* buccia; (*of orange, lemon*)
scorza // *vt* sbucciare // *vi* (*paint etc*)
staccarsi.
peep [pi:p] *n* (*Brit*: *look*) sguardo
furtivo, sbirciata; (*sound*) pigolio // *vi*
(*Brit*) guardare furtivamente; **to ~ out**
vi mostrarsi furtivamente; ~**hole** *n*
spioncino.
peer [pɪə*] *vi*: **to ~ at** scrutare // *n* (*noble*) pari *m inv*; (*equal*) pari *m/f inv*,
uguale *m/f*; ~**age** *n* dignità di pari; pari
mpl.
peeved [pi:vd] *a* stizzito(a).
peevish ['pi:vɪʃ] *a* stizzoso(a).
peg [pɛg] *n* caviglia; (*for coat etc*)
attaccapanni *m inv*; (*Brit: also*: **clothes
~**) molletta // *vt* (*prices*) fissare,
stabilizzare.
Peking [pi:'kɪŋ] *n* Pechino *f*.
pelican ['pɛlɪkən] *n* pellicano; **~ crossing** *n* (*Brit AUT*) attraversamento
pedonale con semaforo a controllo
manuale.
pellet ['pɛlɪt] *n* pallottola, pallina.
pelmet ['pɛlmɪt] *n* mantovana;
cassonetto.
pelt [pɛlt] *vt*: **to ~ sb (with)** bombardare
qn (con) // *vi* (*rain*) piovere a dirotto //
n pelle *f*.
pelvis ['pɛlvɪs] *n* pelvi *f inv*, bacino.
pen [pɛn] *n* penna; (*for sheep*) recinto.
penal ['pi:nl] *a* penale; ~**ize** *vt* punire;
(*SPORT*) penalizzare; (*fig*) svantaggiare.
penalty ['pɛnltɪ] *n* penalità *f inv*;
sanzione *f* penale; (*fine*) ammenda;
(*SPORT*) penalizzazione *f*; **~ (kick)** *n*
(*FOOTBALL*) calcio di rigore.
penance ['pɛnəns] *n* penitenza.
pence [pɛns] *npl of* **penny**.
pencil ['pɛnsl] *n* matita; **~ case** *n*
astuccio per matite; **~ sharpener** *n*
temperamatite *m*.
pendant ['pɛndnt] *n* pendaglio.
pending ['pɛndɪŋ] *prep* in attesa di // *a*
in sospeso.
pendulum ['pɛndjuləm] *n* pendolo.
penetrate ['pɛnɪtreɪt] *vt* penetrare.
penfriend ['pɛnfrɛnd] *n* (*Brit*) corri-

spondente m/f.

penguin ['pengwin] n pinguino.
penicillin [peni'silin] n penicillina.
peninsula [pə'ninsjulə] n penisola.
penis ['pi:nis] n pene m.
penitent ['penitnt] a penitente.
penitentiary [peni'tenʃəri] n (US) carcere m.
penknife ['pennaif] n temperino.
pen name n pseudonimo.
penniless ['peniləs] a senza un soldo.
penny, pl **pennies** or (Brit) **pence** ['peni, 'peniz, pens] n penny m (pl pence); (US) centesimo.
penpal ['penpæl] n corrispondente m/f.
pension ['penʃən] n pensione f; ~**er** n (Brit) pensionato/a.
pensive ['pensiv] a pensoso(a).
penthouse ['penthaus] n appartamento (di lusso) nell'attico.
pent-up ['pentʌp] a (feelings) represso(a).
people ['pi:pl] npl gente f; persone fpl; (citizens) popolo // n (nation, race) popolo // vt popolare; **4/several ~ came** 4/parecchie persone sono venute; **the room was full of ~** la stanza era piena di gente.
pep [pep] n (col) dinamismo; **to ~ up** vt vivacizzare; (food) rendere più gustoso(a).
pepper ['pepə*] n pepe m; (vegetable) peperone m // vt pepare; ~**mint** n (plant) menta peperita; (sweet) pasticca di menta.
peptalk ['peptɔ:k] n (col) discorso di incoraggiamento.
per [pə:*] prep per; a; ~ **hour** all'ora; ~ **kilo** etc il chilo etc; ~ **day** al giorno; ~ **annum** ad all'anno; ~ **capita** a pro capite inv.
perceive [pə'si:v] vt percepire; (notice) accorgersi di.
per cent [pə:'sent] ad per cento.
percentage [pə'sentidʒ] n percentuale f.
perception [pə'sepʃən] n percezione f; sensibilità; perspicacia.
perceptive [pə'septiv] a percettivo(a); perspicace.
perch [pə:tʃ] n (fish) pesce m persico; (for bird) sostegno, ramo // vi appollaiarsi.
percolator ['pə:kəleitə*] n caffettiera a pressione; caffettiera elettrica.
percussion [pə'kʌʃən] n percussione f; (MUS) strumenti mpl a percussione.
peremptory [pə'remptəri] a perentorio(a).
perennial [pə'reniəl] a perenne // n pianta perenne.
perfect a, n ['pə:fikt] a perfetto(a) // n (also: ~ **tense**) perfetto, passato prossimo // vt [pə'fekt] perfezionare; mettere a punto; ~**ly** ad perfettamente, alla perfezione.

perforate ['pə:fəreit] vt perforare; **perforation** [-'reiʃən] n perforazione f; (line of holes) dentellatura.
perform [pə'fɔ:m] vt (carry out) eseguire, fare; (symphony etc) suonare; (play, ballet) dare; (opera) fare // vi suonare; recitare; ~**ance** n esecuzione f; (at theatre etc) rappresentazione f, spettacolo; (of an artist) interpretazione f; (of player etc) performance f; (of car, engine) prestazione f; ~**er** n artista m/f; ~**ing** a (animal) ammaestrato(a).
perfume ['pə:fju:m] n profumo.
perfunctory [pə'fʌŋktəri] a superficiale, per la forma.
perhaps [pə'hæps] ad forse.
peril ['peril] n pericolo.
perimeter [pə'rimitə*] n perimetro; ~ **wall** n muro di cinta.
period ['piəriəd] n periodo; (HISTORY) epoca; (SCOL) lezione f; (full stop) punto; (MED) mestruazioni fpl // a (costume, furniture) d'epoca; ~**ic** [-'ɔdik] a periodico(a); ~**ical** [-'ɔdikl] a periodico(a) // n periodico.
peripheral [pə'rifərəl] a periferico(a) // n (COMPUT) unità f inv periferica.
perish ['periʃ] vi perire, morire; (decay) deteriorarsi; ~**able** a deperibile.
perjury ['pə:dʒəri] n spergiuro.
perk [pə:k] n vantaggio; **to ~ up** vi (cheer up) rianimarsi; ~**y** a (cheerful) vivace, allegro(a).
perm [pə:m] n (for hair) permanente f.
permanent ['pə:mənənt] a permanente.
permeate ['pə:mieit] vi penetrare // vt permeare.
permissible [pə'misibl] a permissibile, ammissibile.
permission [pə'miʃən] n permesso.
permissive [pə'misiv] a tollerante; **the ~ society** la società permissiva.
permit n ['pə:mit] permesso // vt [pə'mit] permettere; **to ~ sb to do** permettere a qn di fare, dare il permesso a qn di fare.
perpendicular [pə:pən'dikjulə*] a, n perpendicolare (f).
perplex [pə'pleks] vt lasciare perplesso(a).
persecute ['pə:sikju:t] vt perseguitare.
persevere [pə:si'viə*] vi perseverare.
Persian ['pə:ʃən] a persiano(a) // n (LING) persiano; **the (~) Gulf** n il Golfo Persico.
persist [pə'sist] vi: **to ~ (in doing)** persistere (nel fare); ostinarsi (a fare); ~**ent** a persistente; ostinato(a).
person ['pə:sn] n persona; **in ~** di or in persona, personalmente; ~**able** a di bell'aspetto; ~**al** a personale; individuale; ~**al assistant (P.A.)** n segretaria personale; ~ **computer (PC)** n personal computer m inv; ~**ality** [-'næliti] n personalità f inv; ~**ally** ad personalmente.

personnel [pɔ:sə'nɛl] *n* personale *m*.
perspective [pə'spɛktɪv] *n* prospettiva.
perspiration [pə:spɪ'reɪʃən] *n* traspirazione *f*, sudore *m*.
persuade [pə'sweɪd] *vt*: to ~ sb to do sth persuadere qn a fare qc.
pert [pə:t] *a* (*bold*) sfacciato(a), impertinente.
pertaining [pə:'teɪnɪŋ]: ~ to *prep* che riguarda.
perturb [pə'tə:b] *vt* turbare.
peruse [pə'ru:z] *vt* leggere.
pervade [pə'veɪd] *vt* pervadere.
perverse [pə'və:s] *a* perverso(a).
pervert *n* ['pə:və:t] pervertito/a // *vt* [pə'və:t] pervertire.
pessimism ['pɛsɪmɪzəm] *n* pessimismo.
pessimist ['pɛsɪmɪst] *n* pessimista *m/f*; ~ic [-'mɪstɪk] *a* pessimistico(a).
pest [pɛst] *n* animale *m* (*or* insetto) pestifero; (*fig*) peste *f*.
pester ['pɛstə*] *vt* tormentare, molestare.
pet [pɛt] *n* animale *m* domestico; (*favourite*) favorito/a // *vt* accarezzare // *vi* (*col*) fare il petting.
petal ['pɛtl] *n* petalo.
peter ['pi:tə*]: to ~ out *vi* esaurirsi; estinguersi.
petite [pə'ti:t] *a* piccolo(a) e aggraziato(a).
petition [pə'tɪʃən] *n* petizione *f*.
petrified ['pɛtrɪfaɪd] *a* (*fig*) morto(a) di paura.
petrol ['pɛtrəl] *n* (*Brit*) benzina; two/four-star ~ ≈ benzina normale/super; ~ can *n* tanica per benzina.
petroleum [pə'trəulɪəm] *n* petrolio.
petrol: ~ **pump** *n* (*Brit*: *in car, at garage*) pompa di benzina; ~ **station** *n* (*Brit*) stazione *f* di rifornimento; ~ **tank** *n* (*Brit*) serbatoio della benzina.
petticoat ['pɛtɪkəut] *n* sottana.
petty ['pɛtɪ] *a* (*mean*) meschino(a); (*unimportant*) insignificante; ~ **cash** *n* piccola cassa; ~ **officer** *n* sottufficiale *m* di marina.
petulant ['pɛtjulənt] *a* irritabile.
pew [pju:] *n* panca (di chiesa).
pewter ['pju:tə*] *n* peltro.
phallic ['fælɪk] *a* fallico(a).
phantom ['fæntəm] *n* fantasma *m*.
pharmaceutical [fɑ:mə'sju:tɪkl] *a* farmaceutico(a).
pharmacy ['fɑ:məsɪ] *n* farmacia.
phase [feɪz] *n* fase *f*, periodo // *vt*: to ~ sth in/out introdurre/eliminare qc progressivamente.
Ph.D. *n abbr* = **Doctor of Philosophy**.
pheasant ['fɛznt] *n* fagiano.
phenomenon, *pl* **phenomena** [fə'nɔmɪnən, -nə] *n* fenomeno.
philanthropist [fɪ'lænθrəpɪst] *n* filantropo.
philately [fɪ'lætəlɪ] *n* filatelia.

philosophical [fɪlə'sɔfɪkl] *a* filosofico(a).
philosophy [fɪ'lɔsəfɪ] *n* filosofia.
phlegmatic [flɛg'mætɪk] *a* flemmatico(a).
phobia ['fəubjə] *n* fobia.
phone [fəun] *n* telefono // *vt* telefonare; to be on the ~ avere il telefono; (*be calling*) essere al telefono; to ~ **back** *vt, vi* richiamare; to ~ **up** *vt* telefonare a // *vi* telefonare; ~ **book** *n* guida del telefono, elenco telefonico; ~ **box** *or* **booth** *n* cabina telefonica; ~ **call** *n* telefonata; ~**-in** *n* (*Brit RADIO, TV*) trasmissione *f* a filo diretto con gli ascoltatori.
phonetics [fə'nɛtɪks] *n* fonetica.
phoney ['fəunɪ] *a* falso(a), fasullo(a) // *n* (*person*) ciarlatano.
phonograph ['fəunəgrɑ:f] *n* (*US*) giradischi *m inv*.
phony ['fəunɪ] *a* = **phoney.**
phosphate ['fɔsfeɪt] *n* fosfato.
phosphorus ['fɔsfərəs] *n* fosforo.
photo ['fəutəu] *n* foto *f inv*.
photo... ['fəutəu] *prefix*: ~**copier** *n* fotocopiatrice *f*; ~**copy** *n* fotocopia // *vt* fotocopiare; ~**graph** *n* fotografia // *vt* fotografare; ~**grapher** [fə'tɔgrəfə*] *n* fotografo; ~**graphy** [fə'tɔgrəfɪ] *n* fotografia.
phrase [freɪz] *n* espressione *f*; (*LING*) locuzione *f*; (*MUS*) frase *f* // *vt* esprimere; ~ **book** *n* vocabolarietto.
physical ['fɪzɪkl] *a* fisico(a); ~ **education** *n* educazione *f* fisica; ~**ly** *ad* fisicamente.
physician [fɪ'zɪʃən] *n* medico.
physicist ['fɪzɪsɪst] *n* fisico.
physics ['fɪzɪks] *n* fisica.
physiology [fɪzɪ'ɔlədʒɪ] *n* fisiologia.
physique [fɪ'zi:k] *n* fisico; costituzione *f*.
pianist ['pi:ənɪst] *n* pianista *m/f*.
piano [pɪ'ænəu] *n* pianoforte *m*.
piccolo ['pɪkələu] *n* ottavino.
pick [pɪk] *n* (*tool*: *also*: ~**-axe**) piccone *m* // *vt* scegliere; (*gather*) cogliere; take your ~ scelga; the ~ of il fior fiore di; to ~ **off** *vt* (*kill*) abbattere (uno dopo l'altro); to ~ **on** *vt fus* (*person*) avercela con; to ~ **out** *vt* scegliere; (*distinguish*) distinguere; to ~ **up** *vi* (*improve*) migliorarsi // *vt* raccogliere; (*collect*) passare a prendere; (*AUT*: *give lift to*) far salire; (*learn*) imparare; to ~ up speed acquistare velocità; to ~ o.s. up rialzarsi.
picket ['pɪkɪt] *n* (*in strike*) scioperante *m/f* che fa parte di un picchetto; picchetto // *vt* picchettare.
pickle ['pɪkl] *n* (*also*: ~**s**: *as condiment*) sottaceti *mpl* // *vt* mettere sottaceto; mettere in salamoia.
pickpocket ['pɪkpɔkɪt] *n* borsaiolo.
pickup ['pɪkʌp] *n* (*Brit*: *on record player*) pick-up *m inv*; (*small truck*)

camioncino.

picnic ['pɪknɪk] n picnic m inv.

pictorial [pɪk'tɔːrɪəl] a illustrato(a).

picture ['pɪktʃə*] n quadro; (painting) pittura; (photograph) foto(grafia); (drawing) disegno; (film) film m inv // vt raffigurarsi; the ~s (Brit) il cinema; ~ **book** n libro illustrato.

picturesque [pɪktʃə'resk] a pittoresco(a).

pidgin English ['pɪdʒɪn-] n inglese semplificato misto ad elementi indigeni.

pie [paɪ] n torta; (of meat) pasticcio.

piece [piːs] n pezzo; (of land) appezzamento; (item): a ~ of furniture/advice un mobile/consiglio // vt: to ~ together mettere insieme; to take to ~s smontare; ~meal ad pezzo a pezzo, a spizzico; ~work n (lavoro a) cottimo.

pie chart n grafico a torta.

pier [pɪə*] n molo; (of bridge etc) pila.

pierce [pɪəs] vt forare; (with arrow etc) trafiggere.

piercing ['pɪəsɪŋ] a (cry) acuto(a).

pig [pɪg] n maiale m, porco.

pigeon ['pɪdʒən] n piccione m; ~hole n casella.

piggy bank ['pɪgɪ-] n salvadanaro.

pigheaded ['pɪg'hedɪd] a caparbio(a), cocciuto(a).

piglet ['pɪglɪt] n porcellino.

pigskin ['pɪgskɪn] n cinghiale m.

pigsty ['pɪgstaɪ] n porcile m.

pigtail ['pɪgteɪl] n treccina.

pike [paɪk] n (spear) picca; (fish) luccio.

pilchard ['pɪltʃəd] n specie di sardina.

pile [paɪl] n (pillar, of books) pila; (heap) mucchio; (of carpet) pelo // vb (also: ~ up) vt ammucchiare // vi ammucchiarsi; to ~ into (car) stiparsi or ammucchiarsi in.

piles [paɪlz] npl emorroidi fpl.

pileup ['paɪlʌp] n (AUT) tamponamento a catena.

pilfering ['pɪlfərɪŋ] n rubacchiare m.

pilgrim ['pɪlgrɪm] n pellegrino/a; ~age n pellegrinaggio.

pill [pɪl] n pillola; the ~ la pillola.

pillage ['pɪlɪdʒ] vt saccheggiare.

pillar ['pɪlə*] n colonna; ~ box n (Brit) cassetta postale.

pillion ['pɪljən] n (of motor cycle) sellino posteriore.

pillory ['pɪlərɪ] vt mettere alla berlina.

pillow ['pɪləu] n guanciale m; ~case n federa.

pilot ['paɪlət] n pilota m/f // cpd (scheme etc) pilota inv // vt pilotare; ~ light n fiamma pilota.

pimp [pɪmp] n mezzano.

pimple ['pɪmpl] n foruncolo.

pin [pɪn] n spillo; (TECH) perno // vt attaccare con uno spillo; ~s and needles formicolio; to ~ sb down (fig) obbligare qn a pronunziarsi; to ~ sth on sb (fig)

addossare la colpa di qc a qn.

pinafore ['pɪnəfɔː*] n grembiule m (senza maniche).

pinball ['pɪnbɔːl] n (also: ~ machine) flipper m inv.

pincers ['pɪnsəz] npl pinzette fpl.

pinch [pɪntʃ] n pizzicotto, pizzico // vt pizzicare; (col: steal) grattare // vi (shoe) stringere; at a ~ in caso di bisogno.

pincushion ['pɪnkuʃən] n puntaspilli m inv.

pine [paɪn] n (also: ~ tree) pino // vi: to ~ for struggersi dal desiderio di; to ~ away vi languire.

pineapple ['paɪnæpl] n ananas m inv.

ping [pɪŋ] n (noise) tintinnio; ~-pong ® ping-pong m ®.

pink [pɪŋk] a rosa inv // n (colour) rosa m inv; (BOT) garofano.

pinpoint ['pɪnpɔɪnt] vt indicare con precisione.

pint [paɪnt] n pinta (Brit = 0.57l; US = 0.47l); (Brit col) ≈ birra da mezzo.

pioneer [paɪə'nɪə*] n pioniere/a.

pious ['paɪəs] a pio(a).

pip [pɪp] n (seed) seme m; (Brit: time signal on radio) segnale m orario.

pipe [paɪp] n tubo; (for smoking) pipa; (MUS) piffero // vt portare per mezzo di tubazione; ~s npl (also: bag~s) cornamusa (scozzese); to ~ down vi (col) calmarsi; ~ cleaner n scovolino; ~ dream n vana speranza; ~line n conduttura; (for oil) oleodotto; ~r n piffero; suonatore/trice di cornamusa.

piping ['paɪpɪŋ] ad: ~ hot caldo bollente.

pique [piːk] n picca.

pirate ['paɪərət] n pirata m.

Pisces ['paɪsiːz] n Pesci mpl.

piss [pɪs] vi (col) pisciare; ~ed a (col: drunk) ubriaco(a) fradicio(a).

pistol ['pɪstl] n pistola.

piston ['pɪstən] n pistone m.

pit [pɪt] n buca, fossa; (also: coal ~) miniera; (also: orchestra ~) orchestra // vt: to ~ sb against sb opporre qn a qn; ~s npl (AUT) box m.

pitch [pɪtʃ] n (throw) lancia; (MUS) tono; (of voice) altezza; (Brit SPORT) campo; (NAUT) beccheggio; (tar) pece f // vt (throw) lanciare // vi (fall) cascare; (NAUT) beccheggiare; to ~ a tent piantare una tenda; ~ed battle n battaglia campale.

pitcher ['pɪtʃə*] n brocca.

pitchfork ['pɪtʃfɔːk] n forcone m.

piteous ['pɪtɪəs] a pietoso(a).

pitfall ['pɪtfɔːl] n trappola.

pith [pɪθ] n (of plant) midollo; (of orange) parte f interna della scorza; (fig) essenza, succo; vigore m.

pithy ['pɪθɪ] a conciso(a); vigoroso(a).

pitiful ['pɪtɪful] a (touching) pietoso(a); (contemptible) miserabile.

pitiless ['pɪtɪlɪs] *a* spietato(a).

pittance ['pɪtns] *n* miseria, magro salario.

pity ['pɪtɪ] *n* pietà // *vt* aver pietà di; **what a ~!** che peccato!

pivot ['pɪvət] *n* perno.

pizza ['piːtsə] *n* pizza.

placard ['plækɑːd] *n* affisso.

placate [plə'keɪt] *vt* placare, calmare.

place [pleɪs] *n* posto, luogo; (*proper position, rank, seat*) posto; (*house*) casa, alloggio; (*home*): **at/to his ~** a casa sua // *vt* (*object*) posare, mettere; (*identify*) riconoscere; individuare; **to take ~** aver luogo; succedere; **to change ~s with sb** scambiare il posto con qn; **out of ~** (*not suitable*) inopportuno(a); **in the first ~** in primo luogo; **to ~ an order** dare un'ordinazione.

placid ['plæsɪd] *a* placido(a), calmo(a).

plagiarism ['pleɪdʒjərɪzm] *n* plagio.

plague [pleɪg] *n* peste *f* // *vt* tormentare.

plaice [pleɪs] *n* (*pl inv*) pianuzza.

plaid [plæd] *n* plaid *m inv*.

plain [pleɪn] *a* (*clear*) chiaro(a), palese; (*simple*) semplice; (*frank*) franco(a), aperto(a); (*not handsome*) bruttino(a); (*without seasoning etc*) scondito(a), naturale; (*in one colour*) tinta unita *inv* // *ad* francamente, chiaramente // *n* pianura; **~ chocolate** *n* cioccolato fondente; **~ clothes** *npl*: **in ~ clothes** (*police*) in borghese; **~ly** *ad* chiaramente; (*frankly*) francamente.

plaintiff ['pleɪntɪf] *n* attore/trice.

plaintive ['pleɪntɪv] *a* (*cry, voice*) dolente, lamentoso(a).

plait [plæt] *n* treccia.

plan [plæn] *n* piano; (*scheme*) progetto, piano // *vt* (*think in advance*) progettare; (*prepare*) organizzare // *vi* far piani *or* progetti.

plane [pleɪn] *n* (AVIAT) aereo; (*tree*) platano; (*tool*) pialla; (ART, MATH *etc*) piano // *a* piano(a), piatto(a) // *vt* (*with tool*) piallare.

planet ['plænɪt] *n* pianeta *m*.

plank [plæŋk] *n* tavola, asse *f*.

planner ['plænə*] *n* pianificatore/trice.

planning ['plænɪŋ] *n* progettazione *f*; **family ~** pianificazione *f* delle nascite; **~ permission** *n* permesso di costruzione.

plant [plɑːnt] *n* pianta; (*machinery*) impianto; (*factory*) fabbrica // *vt* piantare; (*bomb*) mettere.

plantation [plæn'teɪʃən] *n* piantagione *f*.

plaque [plæk] *n* placca.

plaster ['plɑːstə*] *n* intonaco; (*also: ~ of Paris*) gesso; (*Brit: also: sticking ~*) cerotto // *vt* intonacare; ingessare; (*cover*): **to ~ with** coprire di; **in ~** (*leg etc*) ingessato(a); **~ed** *a* (*col*) ubriaco(a) fradicio(a).

plastic ['plæstɪk] *n* plastica // *a* (*made of plastic*) di *or* in plastica; (*flexible*) pla-

stico(a), malleabile; (*art*) plastico(a); **~ bag** *n* sacchetto di plastica.

plasticine ['plæstɪsiːn] *n* ® plastilina ®.

plastic surgery *n* chirurgia plastica.

plate [pleɪt] *n* (*dish*) piatto; (*sheet of metal*) lamiera; (PHOT) lastra; (*in book*) tavola.

plateau, **~s** *or* **~x** ['plætəu, -z] *n* altipiano.

plate glass *n* vetro piano.

platform ['plætfɔːm] *n* (*stage, at meeting*) palco; (RAIL) marciapiede *m*; (*Brit: of bus*) piattaforma; **~ ticket** *n* (*Brit*) biglietto d'ingresso ai binari.

platinum ['plætɪnəm] *n* platino.

platitude ['plætɪtjuːd] *n* luogo comune.

platoon [plə'tuːn] *n* plotone *m*.

platter ['plætə*] *n* piatto.

plausible ['plɔːzɪbl] *a* plausibile, credibile; (*person*) convincente.

play [pleɪ] *n* gioco; (THEATRE) commedia // *vt* (*game*) giocare a; (*team, opponent*) giocare contro; (*instrument, piece of music*) suonare; (*play, part*) interpretare // *vi* giocare; suonare; recitare; **to ~ safe** giocare sul sicuro; **to ~ down** *vt* minimizzare; **to ~ up** *vi* (*cause trouble*) fare i capricci; **~boy** *n* playboy *m inv*; **~er** *n* giocatore/trice; (THEATRE) attore/trice; (MUS) musicista *m/f*; **~ful** *a* giocoso(a); **~ground** *n* (*in school*) cortile *m* per la ricreazione; (*in park*) parco *m* giochi *inv*; **~group** *n* giardino d'infanzia; **~ing card** *n* carta da gioco; **~ing field** *n* campo sportivo; **~mate** *n* compagno/a di gioco; **~-off** *n* (SPORT) bella; **~pen** *n* box *m inv*; **~school** *n* = **~group**; **~thing** *n* giocattolo; **~wright** *n* drammaturgo/a.

plc *abbr* (= *public limited company*) società per azioni a responsabilità limitata quotata in borsa.

plea [pliː] *n* (*request*) preghiera, domanda; (*excuse*) scusa; (LAW) (*argomento di*) difesa.

plead [pliːd] *vt* patrocinare; (*give as excuse*) addurre a pretesto // *vi* (LAW) perorare la causa; (*beg*): **to ~ with sb** implorare qn.

pleasant ['pleznt] *a* piacevole, gradevole; **~ries** *npl* (*polite remarks*): **to exchange ~ries** scambiarsi i convenevoli.

please [pliːz] *vt* piacere a // *vi* (*think fit*): **do as you ~** faccia come le pare; **~!** per piacere!; **~ yourself!** come ti (*or* le) pare!; **~d** *a*: **~d** (*with*) contento(a) (di); **~d to meet you!** piacere!; **pleasing** *a* piacevole, che fa piacere.

pleasure ['pleʒə*] *n* piacere *m*; "**it's a ~**" "prego".

pleat [pliːt] *n* piega.

plectrum ['plɛktrəm] *n* plettro.

pledge [pledʒ] *n* pegno; (*promise*) promessa // *vt* impegnare; promettere.

plentiful [ˈplɛntiful] a abbondante, copioso(a).

plenty [ˈplɛntɪ] n abbondanza; ~ **of** tanto(a), molto(a); un'abbondanza di.

pleurisy [ˈpluərɪsɪ] n pleurite f.

pliable [ˈplaɪəbl] a flessibile; (person) malleabile.

pliers [ˈplaɪəz] npl pinza.

plight [plaɪt] n situazione f critica.

plimsolls [ˈplɪmsəlz] npl (Brit) scarpe fpl da tennis.

plinth [plɪnθ] n plinto; piedistallo.

plod [plɒd] vi camminare a stento; (fig) sgobbare; ~**der** n sgobbone m.

plonk [plɒŋk] (col) n (Brit: wine) vino da poco // vt: **to** ~ **sth down** buttare giù qc bruscamente.

plot [plɒt] n congiura, cospirazione f; (of story, play) trama; (of land) lotto // vt (mark out) fare la pianta di; rilevare; (: diagram etc) tracciare; (conspire) congiurare, cospirare // vi congiurare; ~**ter** n (instrument) plotter m inv.

plough, (US) **plow** [plau] n aratro // vt (earth) arare; **to** ~ **back** vt (COMM) reinvestire; **to** ~ **through** vt fus (snow etc) procedere a fatica in.

ploy [plɔɪ] n stratagemma m.

pluck [plʌk] vt (fruit) cogliere; (musical instrument) pizzicare; (bird) spennare // n coraggio, fegato; **to** ~ **up courage** farsi coraggio; ~**y** a coraggioso(a).

plug [plʌg] n tappo; (ELEC) spina; (AUT: also: **spark(ing)** ~) candela // vt (hole) tappare; (col: advertise) spingere; **to** ~ **in** vt (ELEC) attaccare a una presa.

plum [plʌm] n (fruit) susina // cpd: ~ **job** (col) impiego ottimo or favoloso.

plumb [plʌm] a verticale // n piombo // ad (exactly) esattamente // vt sondare.

plumber [ˈplʌmə*] n idraulico.

plumbing [ˈplʌmɪŋ] n (trade) lavoro di idraulico; (piping) tubature fpl.

plume [pluːm] n piuma, penna; (decorative) pennacchio.

plummet [ˈplʌmɪt] vi cadere a piombo.

plump [plʌmp] a grassoccio(a) // vt: **to** ~ **sth (down)** on lasciar cadere qc di peso su; **to** ~ **for** vt fus (col: choose) decidersi per.

plunder [ˈplʌndə*] n saccheggio // vt saccheggiare.

plunge [plʌndʒ] n tuffo // vt immergere // vi (fall) cadere, precipitare; **to take the** ~ saltare il fosso; ~**r** n sturalavandini m inv; **plunging** a (neckline) profondo(a).

pluperfect [pluːˈpəːfɪkt] n piuccheperfetto.

plural [ˈpluərl] a, n plurale (m).

plus [plʌs] n (also: ~ **sign**) segno più // prep più; **ten/twenty** ~ più di dieci/venti.

plush [plʌʃ] a lussuoso(a).

ply [plaɪ] n (of wool) capo; (of wood) strato // vt (tool) maneggiare; (a trade) esercitare // vi (ship) fare il servizio; **to** ~ **sb with drink** dare di bere continuamente a qn; ~**wood** n legno compensato.

P.M. n abbr = **prime minister**.

p.m. ad abbr (= post meridiem) del pomeriggio.

pneumatic drill [njuːˈmætɪk-] n martello pneumatico.

pneumonia [njuːˈməunɪə] n polmonite f.

poach [pəutʃ] vt (cook) affogare; (steal) cacciare (or pescare) di frodo // vi fare il bracconiere; ~**er** n bracconiere m.

P.O. Box n abbr = **Post Office Box**.

pocket [ˈpɒkɪt] n tasca // vt intascare; **to be out of** ~ (Brit) rimetterci; ~**book** n (wallet) portafoglio; (notebook) taccuino; ~ **knife** n temperino; ~ **money** n paghetta, settimana.

pod [pɒd] n guscio // vt sgusciare.

podgy [ˈpɒdʒɪ] a grassoccio(a).

podiatrist [pɒˈdiːətrɪst] n (US) callista m/f, pedicure m/f.

poem [ˈpəuɪm] n poesia.

poet [ˈpəuɪt] n poeta/essa; ~**ic** [-ˈɛtɪk] a poetico(a); ~ **laureate** n poeta m laureato (nominato dalla Corte Reale); ~**ry** n poesia.

poignant [ˈpɔɪnjənt] a struggente.

point [pɔɪnt] n (gen) punto; (tip: of needle etc) punta; (in time) punto, momento; (SCOL) voto; (main idea, important part) nocciolo; (also: **decimal** ~): 2 ~ 3 (2.3) 2 virgola 3 (2,3) // vt (show) indicare; (gun etc): **to** ~ **sth at** puntare qc contro // vi mostrare a dito; ~**s** npl (AUT) puntine fpl; (RAIL) scambio; **to be on the** ~ **of doing sth** essere sul punto di or stare per fare qc; **to make a** ~ fare un'osservazione; **to get the** ~ capire; **to come to the** ~ venire al fatto; **there's no** ~ (**in doing**) è inutile (fare); **to** ~ **out** vt far notare; **to** ~ **to** vt fus indicare; (fig) dimostrare; ~**blank** ad (also: **at** ~**blank range**) a bruciapelo; (fig) categoricamente; ~**ed** a (shape) aguzzo(a), appuntito(a); (remark) specifico(a), in maniera inequivocabile; ~**er** n (stick) bacchetta; (needle) lancetta; (dog) pointer m, cane m da punta; ~**less** a inutile, vano(a); ~ **of view** n punto di vista.

poise [pɔɪz] n (balance) equilibrio; (of head, body) portamento; (calmness) calma // vt tenere in equilibrio.

poison [ˈpɔɪzn] n veleno // vt avvelenare; ~**ing** n avvelenamento; ~**ous** a velenoso(a).

poke [pəuk] vt (fire) attizzare; (jab with finger, stick etc) punzecchiare; (put): **to** ~ **sth in(to)** spingere qc dentro; **to** ~ **about** vi frugare.

poker [ˈpəukə*] n attizzatoio; (CARDS) poker m; ~**-faced** a dal viso impassibile.

poky ['pəʊkɪ] a piccolo(a) e stretto(a).

Poland ['pəʊlənd] n Polonia.

polar ['pəʊlə*] a polare; **~ bear** n orso bianco.

Pole [pəʊl] n polacco/a.

pole [pəʊl] n (of wood) palo; (ELEC, GEO) polo; **~ bean** n (US: runner bean) fagiolino; **~ vault** n salto con l'asta.

police [pə'li:s] n polizia // vt mantenere l'ordine in; (car) macchina della polizia; **~man** n poliziotto, agente m di polizia; **~ station** n posto di polizia; **~woman** n donna f poliziotto inv.

policy ['pɒlɪsɪ] n politica; (also: insurance **~**) polizza (d'assicurazione).

polio ['pəʊlɪəʊ] n polio f.

Polish ['pəʊlɪʃ] a polacco(a) // n (LING) polacco.

polish ['pɒlɪʃ] n (for shoes) lucido; (for floor) cera; (for nails) smalto; (shine) lucentezza, lustro; (fig: refinement) raffinatezza // vt lucidare; (fig: improve) raffinare; **to ~ off** vt (work) sbrigare; (food) mangiarsi; **~ed** a (fig) raffinato(a).

polite [pə'laɪt] a cortese; **~ness** n cortesia.

politic ['pɒlɪtɪk] a diplomatico(a); **~al** [pə'lɪtɪkl] a politico(a); **~ally** ad politicamente; **~ian** [-'tɪʃən] n politico; **~s** npl politica.

polka ['pɒlkə] n polca; **~ dot** n pois m inv.

poll [pəʊl] n scrutinio; (votes cast) voti mpl; (also: opinion **~**) sondaggio (d'opinioni) // vt ottenere.

pollen ['pɒlən] n polline m.

pollination [pɒlɪ'neɪʃən] n impollinazione f.

polling ['pəʊlɪŋ] (Brit): **~ booth** n cabina elettorale; **~ day** n giorno delle elezioni; **~ station** n sezione f elettorale.

pollute [pə'lu:t] vt inquinare.

pollution [pə'lu:ʃən] n inquinamento.

polo ['pəʊləʊ] n polo; **~-neck** a a collo alto risvoltato.

polyester [pɒlɪ'estə*] n poliestere m.

polystyrene [pɒlɪ'staɪri:n] n polistirolo.

polytechnic [pɒlɪ'teknɪk] n (college) istituto superiore ad indirizzo tecnologico.

polythene ['pɒlɪθi:n] n politene m; **~ bag** n sacco di plastica.

pomegranate ['pɒmɪgrænɪt] n melagrana.

pomp [pɒmp] n pompa, fasto.

pompom ['pɒmpɔm], **pompon** ['pɒmpɔn] n pompon m inv.

pompous ['pɒmpəs] a pomposo(a).

pond [pɒnd] n pozza; stagno.

ponder ['pɒndə*] vt ponderare, riflettere su; **~ous** a ponderoso(a), pesante.

pong [pɔŋ] n (Brit col) puzzo.

pontiff ['pɒntɪf] n pontefice m.

pony ['pəʊnɪ] n pony m inv; **~tail** n coda di cavallo; **~ trekking** n (Brit) escursione f a cavallo.

poodle ['pu:dl] n barboncino, barbone m.

pool [pu:l] n (of rain) pozza; (pond) stagno; (artificial) vasca; (also: swimming **~**) piscina; (sth shared) fondo comune; (billiards) specie di biliardo a buca // vt mettere in comune; **typing ~** servizio comune di dattilografia; (football) **~s** ≈ totocalcio.

poor [puə*] a povero(a); (mediocre) mediocre, cattivo(a) // npl: **the ~** i poveri; **~ly** ad poveramente; a indisposto(a), malato(a).

pop [pɒp] n (noise) schiocco; (MUS) musica pop; (US col: father) babbo // vt (put) mettere (in fretta) // vi scoppiare; (cork) schioccare; **to ~ in** vi passare; **to ~ out** vi fare un salto fuori; **to ~ up** vi apparire, sorgere; **~ concert** n concerto m pop inv; **~corn** n pop-corn m.

pope [pəʊp] n papa m.

poplar ['pɒplə*] n pioppo.

poppy ['pɒpɪ] n papavero.

popsicle ['pɒpsɪkl] n (US: ice lolly) ghiacciolo.

popular ['pɒpjʊlə*] a popolare; (fashionable) in voga; **~ity** [-'lærɪtɪ] n popolarità; **~ize** vt divulgare; (science) volgarizzare.

population [pɒpjʊ'leɪʃən] n popolazione f.

porcelain ['pɔ:slɪn] n porcellana.

porch [pɔ:tʃ] n veranda.

porcupine ['pɔ:kjʊpaɪn] n porcospino.

pore [pɔ:*] n poro // vi: **to ~ over** essere immerso(a) in.

pork [pɔ:k] n carne f di maiale.

pornographic [pɔ:nə'græfɪk] a pornografico(a).

pornography [pɔ:'nɒgrəfɪ] n pornografia.

porpoise ['pɔ:pəs] n focena.

porridge ['pɒrɪdʒ] n porridge m.

port [pɔ:t] n porto; (opening in ship) portello; (NAUT: left side) babordo; (wine) porto; **~ of call** (porto di) scalo.

portable ['pɔ:təbl] a portatile.

portent ['pɔ:tent] n presagio.

porter ['pɔ:tə*] n (for luggage) facchino, portabagagli m inv; (doorkeeper) portiere m, portinaio.

portfolio [pɔ:t'fəʊlɪəʊ] n (case) cartella; (POL, FINANCE) portafoglio; (of artist) raccolta dei propri lavori.

porthole ['pɔ:thəʊl] n oblò m inv.

portion ['pɔ:ʃən] n porzione f.

portly ['pɔ:tlɪ] a corpulento(a).

portrait ['pɔ:treɪt] n ritratto.

portray [pɔ:'treɪ] vt fare il ritratto di; (character on stage) rappresentare; (in writing) ritrarre.

Portugal ['pɔ:tjugl] n Portogallo.
Portuguese [pɔ:tjuˈgiːz] a portoghese // n (pl inv) portoghese m/f; (LING) portoghese m.
pose [pəuz] n posa // vi posare; (pretend): **to ~ as** atteggiarsi a, posare a // vt porre.
posh [pɔʃ] a (col) elegante; (family) per bene.
position [pəˈzɪʃən] n posizione f; (job) posto.
positive ['pɔzɪtɪv] a positivo(a); (certain) sicuro(a), certo(a); (definite) preciso(a); definitivo(a).
posse ['pɔsɪ] n (US) drappello.
possess [pəˈzɛs] vt possedere; **~ion** [pəˈzɛʃən] n possesso; (object) bene m; **~ive** a possessivo(a).
possibility [pɔsɪˈbɪlɪtɪ] n possibilità f inv.
possible ['pɔsɪbl] a possibile; **as big as ~** il più grande possibile.
possibly ['pɔsɪblɪ] ad (perhaps) forse; **if you ~ can** se le è possibile; **I cannot ~ come** proprio non posso venire.
post [pəust] n (Brit) posta; (: collection) levata; (job, situation) posto; (pole) palo // vt (Brit: send by post) impostare; (MIL) appostare; (notice) affiggere; (Brit: appoint): **to ~ to** assegnare a; **~age** n affrancatura; **~al order** n vaglia m inv postale; **~box** n (Brit) cassetta postale; **~card** n cartolina; **~ code** n (Brit) codice m (di avviamento) postale.
poster ['pəustə*] n manifesto, affisso.
poste restante [pəustˈrɛstɑ̃:nt] n (Brit) fermo posta m.
postgraduate ['pəustˈgrædjuət] n laureato/a che continua gli studi.
posthumous ['pɔstjuməs] a postumo(a).
postman ['pəustmən] n postino.
postmark ['pəustmɑ:k] n bollo or timbro postale.
postmaster ['pəustmɑ:stə*] n direttore m d'un ufficio postale.
post-mortem [pəustˈmɔ:təm] n autopsia.
post office n (building) ufficio postale; (organization): **the Post Office** ≈ le Poste e Telecomunicazioni; **Post Office Box (P.O. Box)** n casella postale (C.P.).
postpone [pəsˈpəun] vt rinviare.
postscript ['pəustskrɪpt] n poscritto.
posture ['pɔstʃə*] n portamento; (pose) posa, atteggiamento // vi posare.
postwar ['pəustˈwɔ:*] a del dopoguerra.
posy ['pəuzɪ] n mazzetto di fiori.
pot [pɔt] n (for cooking) pentola; casseruola; (for plants, jam) vaso; (col: marijuana) erba // vt (plant) piantare in vaso; **to go to ~** (col: work, performance) andare in malora.
potato, ~es [pəˈteɪtəu] n patata; **~ peeler** n sbucciapatate m inv.
potent ['pəutnt] a potente, forte.

potential [pəˈtɛnʃl] a potenziale // n possibilità fpl; **~ly** ad potenzialmente.
pothole ['pɔthəul] n (in road) buca; (Brit: underground) caverna; **potholing** n (Brit): **to go potholing** fare la speleologia.
potluck [pɔtˈlʌk] n: **to take ~** tentare la sorte.
potshot ['pɔtʃɔt] n: **to take ~s or a ~ at** tirare a vanvera contro.
potted ['pɔtɪd] a (food) in conserva; (plant) in vaso.
potter ['pɔtə*] n vasaio // vi: **to ~ around, ~ about** lavoracchiare; **~y** n ceramica fpl.
potty ['pɔtɪ] a (col: mad) tocco(a) // n (child's) vasino.
pouch [pautʃ] n borsa; (ZOOL) marsupio.
poultry ['pəultrɪ] n pollame m.
pounce [pauns] vi: **to ~ (on)** balzare addosso a, piombare su // n balzo.
pound [paund] n (weight) libbra; (money) (lira) sterlina; (for dogs) canile m municipale // vt (beat) battere; (crush) pestare, polverizzare // vi (beat) battere, martellare.
pour [pɔ:*] vt versare // vi riversarsi; (rain) piovere a dirotto; **to ~ away or off** vt vuotare; **to ~ in** vi (people) entrare a fiotti; **to ~ out** vt vuotare; versare; (serve: a drink) mescere; **~ing** a: **~ing rain** pioggia torrenziale.
pout [paut] vi sporgere le labbra; fare il broncio.
poverty ['pɔvətɪ] n povertà, miseria; **~-stricken** a molto povero(a), misero(a).
powder ['paudə*] n polvere f // vt spolverizzare; (face) incipriare; **to ~ one's nose** incipriarsi il naso; **~ compact** n portacipria m inv; **~ed milk** n latte m in polvere; **~ puff** n piumino della cipria; **~ room** n toilette f inv (per signore).
power ['pauə*] n (strength) potenza, forza; (ability, POL: of party, leader) potere m; (MATH) potenza; (ELEC) corrente f // vt fornire di energia; **to be in ~** (POL etc) essere al potere; **~ cut** n (Brit) interruzione f or mancanza di corrente; **~ failure** n interruzione f della corrente elettrica; **~ful** a potente, forte; **~less** a impotente, senza potere; **~ point** n (Brit) presa di corrente; **~ station** n centrale f elettrica.
p.p. abbr (= per procurationem): **~ J. Smith** per J. Smith.
PR abbr = **public relations**.
practicable ['præktɪkəbl] a (scheme) praticabile.
practical ['præktɪkl] a pratico(a); **~ity** [-ˈkælɪtɪ] n (no pl) (of situation etc) lato pratico; **~ joke** n beffa; **~ly** ad (almost) quasi.
practice ['præktɪs] n pratica; (of

profession) esercizio; (*at football etc*) allenamento; (*business*) gabinetto; clientela // *vt, vi* (*US*) = **practise**; in ~ (*in reality*) in pratica; out of ~ fuori esercizio.

practise, (*US*) **practice** ['præktɪs] *vt* (*work at: piano, one's backhand etc*) esercitarsi a; (*train for: skiing, running etc*) allenarsi a; (*a sport, religion*) praticare; (*method*) usare; (*profession*) esercitare // *vi* esercitarsi; (*train*) allenarsi; **practising** *a* (*Christian etc*) praticante; (*lawyer*) che esercita la professione.

practitioner [præk'tɪʃənə*] *n* professionista *m/f.*

pragmatic [præg'mætɪk] *a* prammatico(a).

prairie ['prɛərɪ] *n* prateria.

praise [preɪz] *n* elogio, lode *f* // *vt* elogiare, lodare; **~worthy** *a* lodevole.

pram [præm] *n* (*Brit*) carrozzina.

prance [prɑ:ns] *vi* (*horse*) impennarsi.

prank [præŋk] *n* burla.

prawn [prɔ:n] *n* gamberetto.

pray [preɪ] *vi* pregare.

prayer [prɛə*] *n* preghiera.

preach [pri:tʃ] *vt, vi* predicare.

precarious [prɪ'kɛərɪəs] *a* precario(a).

precaution [prɪ'kɔ:ʃən] *n* precauzione *f.*

precede [prɪ'si:d] *vt, vi* precedere.

precedence ['prɛsɪdəns] *n* precedenza.

precedent ['prɛsɪdənt] *n* precedente *m.*

precept ['pri:sept] *n* precetto.

precinct ['pri:sɪŋkt] *n* (*round cathedral*) recinto; **~s** *npl* (*neighbourhood*) dintorni *mpl*, vicinanze *fpl*; **pedestrian** ~ (*Brit*) zona pedonale.

precious ['prɛʃəs] *a* prezioso(a).

precipitate [prɪ'sɪpɪtɪt] *a* (*hasty*) precipitoso(a).

précis, *pl* **précis** ['preɪsi:, -z] *n* riassunto.

precise [prɪ'saɪs] *a* preciso(a); **~ly** *ad* precisamente.

preclude [prɪ'klu:d] *vt* precludere, impedire.

precocious [prɪ'kəuʃəs] *a* precoce.

precondition [pri:kən'dɪʃən] *n* condizione *f* necessaria.

predecessor ['pri:dɪsɛsə*] *n* predecessore/a.

predicament [prɪ'dɪkəmənt] *n* situazione *f* difficile.

predict [prɪ'dɪkt] *vt* predire; **~able** *a* prevedibile.

predominantly [prɪ'dɔmɪnəntlɪ] *ad* in maggior parte; soprattutto.

predominate [prɪ'dɔmɪneɪt] *vi* predominare.

preen [pri:n] *vt*: to ~ itself (*bird*) lisciarsi le penne; to ~ o.s. agghindarsi.

prefab ['pri:fæb] *n* casa prefabbricata.

preface ['prɛfəs] *n* prefazione *f.*

prefect ['pri:fɛkt] *n* (*Brit: in school*) studente/essa con funzioni disciplinari;

(*in Italy*) prefetto.

prefer [prɪ'fə:*] *vt* preferire; **~ably** ['prɛfrəblɪ] *ad* preferibilmente; **~ence** ['prɛfrəns] *n* preferenza; **~ential** [prɛfə'rɛnʃəl] *a* preferenziale.

prefix ['pri:fɪks] *n* prefisso.

pregnancy ['prɛgnənsɪ] *n* gravidanza.

pregnant ['prɛgnənt] *a* incinta *af.*

prehistoric ['pri:hɪs'tɔrɪk] *a* preistorico(a).

prejudice ['prɛdʒudɪs] *n* pregiudizio; (*harm*) torto, danno // *vt* pregiudicare, ledere; **~d** *a* (*person*) pieno(a) di pregiudizi; (*view*) prevenuto(a).

preliminary [prɪ'lɪmɪnərɪ] *a* preliminare; **preliminaries** *npl* preliminari *mpl.*

premarital ['pri:'mærɪtl] *a* prematrimoniale.

premature ['prɛmətʃuə*] *a* prematuro(a).

premier ['prɛmɪə*] *a* primo(a) // *n* (*POL*) primo ministro.

première ['prɛmɪɛə*] *n* prima.

premise ['prɛmɪs] *n* premessa; **~s** *npl* locale *m*; on the **~s** sul posto.

premium ['pri:mɪəm] *n* premio; to be at a ~ essere ricercatissimo; ~ **bond** *n* (*Brit*) obbligazione *f* a premio.

premonition [prɛmə'nɪʃən] *n* premonizione *f.*

preoccupied [pri:'ɔkjupaɪd] *a* preoccupato(a).

prep [prɛp] *n* (*SCOL: study*) studio; ~ **school** *n* = preparatory school.

prepaid [pri:'peɪd] *a* pagato(a) in anticipo.

preparation [prɛpə'reɪʃən] *n* preparazione *f*; **~s** *npl* (*for trip, war*) preparativi *mpl.*

preparatory [prɪ'pærətərɪ] *a* preparatorio(a); ~ **school** *n* scuola elementare privata.

prepare [prɪ'pɛə*] *vt* preparare // *vi*: to ~ for prepararsi a; **~d to** pronto(a) a.

preposition [prɛpə'zɪʃən] *n* preposizione *f.*

preposterous [prɪ'pɔstərəs] *a* assurdo(a).

prerequisite [pri:'rɛkwɪzɪt] *n* requisito indispensabile.

prescribe [prɪ'skraɪb] *vt* prescrivere; (*MED*) ordinare.

prescription [prɪ'skrɪpʃən] *n* prescrizione *f*; (*MED*) ricetta.

presence ['prɛzns] *n* presenza; ~ of mind presenza di spirito.

present ['prɛznt] *a* presente; (*wife, residence, job*) attuale // *n* regalo; (*also:* ~ **tense**) tempo presente // *vt* [prɪ'zɛnt] presentare; (*give*): to ~ sb with sth offrire qc a qn; to give sb a ~ fare un regalo a qn; at ~ al momento; **~ation** [-'teɪʃən] *n* presentazione *f*; (*gift*) regalo, dono; (*ceremony*) consegna ufficiale; **~-day** *a* attuale, d'oggigiorno; **~er** *n*

(*RADIO*, *TV*) presentatore/trice; **~ly** *ad* (*soon*) fra poco, presto; (*at present*) al momento.

preservative [prɪ'zəːvətɪv] *n* conservante *m*.

preserve [prɪ'zəːv] *vt* (*keep safe*) preservare, proteggere; (*maintain*) conservare; (*food*) mettere in conserva // *n* (*for game, fish*) riserva; (*often pl: jam*) marmellata; (: *fruit*) frutta sciroppata.

preside [prɪ'zaɪd] *vi* presiedere.

president ['prezɪdənt] *n* presidente *m*; **~ial** [-'denʃl] *a* presidenziale.

press [pres] *n* (*tool, machine*) pressa; (*for wine*) torchio; (*newspapers*) stampa; (*crowd*) folla // *vt* (*push*) premere, pigiare; (*squeeze*) spremere; (: *hand*) stringere; (*clothes: iron*) stirare; (*pursue*) incalzare; (*insist*): to ~ sth on sb far accettare qc da qn // *vi* premere; accalcare; we are ~ed for time ci manca il tempo; to ~ for sth insistere per avere qc; **to ~ on** *vi* continuare; ~ **conference** *n* conferenza stampa; **~ing** *a* urgente // *n* stiratura; ~ **stud** *n* (*Brit*) bottone *m* a pressione; **~-up** *n* (*Brit*) flessione *f* sulle braccia.

pressure ['preʃə*] *n* pressione *f*; ~ **cooker** *n* pentola a pressione; ~ **gauge** *n* manometro; ~ **group** *n* gruppo di pressione.

prestige [pres'tiːʒ] *n* prestigio.

presumably [prɪ'zjuːməblɪ] *ad* presumibilmente.

presume [prɪ'zjuːm] *vt* supporre; to ~ to do (*dare*) permettersi di fare.

presumption [prɪ'zʌmpʃən] *n* presunzione *f*; (*boldness*) audacia.

presumptuous [prɪ'zʌmpʃəs] *a* presuntuoso(a).

pretence, (*US*) pretense [prɪ'tens] *n* (*claim*) pretesa; to make a ~ of doing far finta di fare.

pretend [prɪ'tend] *vt* (*feign*) fingere // *vi* (*feign*) far finta; (*claim*): to ~ to sth pretendere a qc; to ~ to do far finta di fare.

pretense [prɪ'tens] *n* (*US*) = **pretence**.

pretension [prɪ'tenʃən] *n* (*claim*) pretesa.

pretentious [prɪ'tenʃəs] *a* pretenzioso(a).

pretext ['priːtekst] *n* pretesto.

pretty ['prɪtɪ] *a* grazioso(a), carino(a) // *ad* abbastanza, assai.

prevail [prɪ'veɪl] *vi* (*win, be usual*) prevalere; (*persuade*): to ~ (up)on sb to do persuadere qn a fare; **~ing** *a* dominante.

prevalent ['prevələnt] *a* (*belief*) predominante; (*customs*) diffuso(a); (*fashion*) corrente; (*disease*) comune.

prevent [prɪ'vent] *vt* prevenire; to ~ sb from doing impedire a qn di fare; **~ion**

[-'venʃən] *n* prevenzione *f*; **~ive** *a* preventivo(a).

preview ['priːvjuː] *n* (*of film*) anteprima.

previous ['priːvɪəs] *a* precedente; anteriore; **~ly** *ad* prima.

prewar ['priː'wɔː*] *a* anteguerra *inv*.

prey [preɪ]. *n* preda // *vi*: to ~ on far preda di.

price [praɪs] *n* prezzo // *vt* (*goods*) fissare il prezzo di; valutare; **~less** *a* inapprezzabile; ~ **list** *n* listino (dei) prezzi.

prick [prɪk] *n* puntura // *vt* pungere; to ~ up one's ears drizzare gli orecchi.

prickle ['prɪkl] *n* (*of plant*) spina; (*sensation*) pizzicore *m*.

prickly ['prɪklɪ] *a* spinoso(a); (*fig: person*) permaloso(a); ~ **heat** *n* sudamina.

pride [praɪd] *n* orgoglio; superbia // *vt*: to ~ o.s. on essere orgoglioso(a) di; vantarsi di.

priest [priːst] *n* prete *m*, sacerdote *m*; **~hood** *n* sacerdozio.

prig [prɪg] *n*: he's a ~ è compiaciuto di se stesso.

prim [prɪm] *a* pudico(a); contegnoso(a).

primarily ['praɪmərɪlɪ] *ad* principalmente, essenzialmente.

primary ['praɪmərɪ] *a* primario(a); (*first in importance*) primo(a); ~ **school** *n* (*Brit*) scuola elementare.

prime [praɪm] *a* primario(a), fondamentale; (*excellent*) di prima qualità // *vt* (*gun*) innescare; (*pump*) adescare; (*fig*) mettere al corrente; in the ~ of life nel fiore della vita; **P~ Minister (P.M.)** *n* primo ministro.

primer ['praɪmə*] *n* (*book*) testo elementare.

primeval [praɪ'miːvl] *a* primitivo(a).

primitive ['prɪmɪtɪv] *a* primitivo(a).

primrose ['prɪmrəuz] *n* primavera.

primus (stove) ['praɪməs(stəuv)] *n* ® (*Brit*) fornello a petrolio.

prince [prɪns] *n* principe *m*.

princess [prɪn'ses] *n* principessa.

principal ['prɪnsɪpl] *a* principale // *n* (*headmaster*) preside *m*.

principle ['prɪnsɪpl] *n* principio; **in** ~ in linea di principio; **on** ~ per principio.

print [prɪnt] *n* (*mark*) impronta; (*letters*) caratteri *mpl*; (*fabric*) tessuto stampato; (*ART, PHOT*) stampa // *vt* imprimere; (*publish*) stampare, pubblicare; (*write in capitals*) scrivere in stampatello; out of ~ esaurito(a); **~ed matter** *n* stampe *fpl*; **~er** *n* tipografo; (*machine*) stampante *f*; **~ing** *n* stampa; **~-out** *n* (*COMPUT*) tabulato.

prior ['praɪə*] *a* precedente // *n* priore *m*; ~ **to doing** prima di fare.

priority [praɪ'ɔrɪtɪ] *n* priorità *f inv*; precedenza.

priory ['praɪərɪ] *n* monastero.

prise [praɪz] *vt*: to ~ open forzare.

prison ['prɪzn] n prigione f // cpd (system) carcerario(a); (conditions, food) nelle or delle prigioni; **~er** n prigioniero/a.

pristine ['prɪstiːn] a immacolato(a).

privacy ['prɪvəsɪ] n solitudine f, intimità.

private ['praɪvɪt] a privato(a); personale // n soldato semplice; "~" (on envelope) "riservata"; **in ~** in privato; **~ enterprise** n iniziativa privata; **~ eye** n investigatore m privato; **~ly** ad in privato; (within oneself) dentro di sé; **~ property** n proprietà privata; **privatize** vt privatizzare.

privet ['prɪvɪt] n ligustro.

privilege ['prɪvɪlɪdʒ] n privilegio.

privy ['prɪvɪ] a: **to be ~** to essere al corrente di; **~ council** n Consiglio della Corona.

prize [praɪz] n premio // a (example, idiot) perfetto(a); (bull, novel) premiato(a) // vt apprezzare, pregiare; **~ giving** n premiazione f; **~winner** n premiato/a.

pro [prəʊ] n (SPORT) professionista m/f; **the ~s and cons** il pro e il contro.

probability [prɔbə'bɪlɪtɪ] n probabilità f inv.

probable ['prɔbəbl] a probabile; **probably** ad probabilmente.

probation [prə'beɪʃən] n (in employment) periodo di prova; (LAW) libertà vigilata; **on ~** (employee) in prova; (LAW) in libertà vigilata.

probe [prəʊb] n (MED, SPACE) sonda; (enquiry) indagine f, investigazione f // vt sondare, esplorare; indagare.

problem ['prɔbləm] n problema m.

procedure [prə'siːdʒə*] n (ADMIN, LAW) procedura; (method) metodo, procedimento.

proceed [prə'siːd] vi (go forward) avanzare, andare avanti; (go about it) procedere; (continue): **to ~ (with)** continuare; **to ~** to andare a; passare a; **to ~** to do mettersi a fare; **~ings** npl misure fpl; (LAW) procedimento; (meeting) riunione f; (records) rendiconti mpl; atti mpl; **~s** ['prəʊsiːdz] npl profitto, incasso.

process ['prəʊses] n processo; (method) metodo, sistema m // vt trattare; (information) elaborare; **~ing** n trattamento; elaborazione f.

procession [prə'seʃən] n processione f, corteo; **funeral ~** corteo funebre.

proclaim [prə'kleɪm] vt proclamare, dichiarare.

procrastinate [prəʊ'kræstɪneɪt] vi procrastinare.

prod [prɔd] vt dare un colpetto a; pungolare.

prodigal ['prɔdɪgl] a prodigo(a).

prodigy ['prɔdɪdʒɪ] n prodigio.

produce n ['prɔdjuːs] (AGR) prodotto, prodotti mpl // vt [prə'djuːs] produrre; (to show) esibire, mostrare; (cause) cagionare, causare; (THEATRE) mettere in scena; **~r** n (THEATRE) direttore/trice; (AGR, CINEMA) produttore m.

product ['prɔdʌkt] n prodotto.

production [prə'dʌkʃən] n produzione f; (THEATRE) messa in scena; **~ line** n catena di lavorazione.

productivity [prɔdʌk'tɪvɪtɪ] n produttività.

profane [prə'feɪn] a profano(a); (language) empio(a).

profession [prə'feʃən] n professione f; **~al** (SPORT) professionista m/f // a professionale; (work) da professionista; **~alism** n professionismo.

professor [prə'fesə*] n professore m (titolare di una cattedra).

proficiency [prə'fɪʃənsɪ] n competenza, abilità.

profile ['prəʊfaɪl] n profilo.

profit ['prɔfɪt] n profitto; beneficio // vi: **to ~** (by or from) approfittare (di); **~ability** [-'bɪlɪtɪ] n redditività; **~able** a redditizio(a).

profiteering [prɔfɪ'tɪərɪŋ] n (pej) affarismo.

profound [prə'faʊnd] a profondo(a).

profusely [prə'fjuːslɪ] ad con grande effusione.

progeny ['prɔdʒɪnɪ] n progenie f; discendenti mpl.

programme, (US) **program** ['prəʊgræm] n programma m // vt programmare; **~r**, (US) **programer** n programmatore/trice.

progress n ['prəʊgres] progresso // vi [prə'gres] avanzare, procedere; **in ~** in corso; **to make ~** far progressi; **~ive** [-'gresɪv] a progressivo(a); (person) progressista m/f.

prohibit [prə'hɪbɪt] vt proibire, vietare; **~ion** [prəʊɪ'bɪʃən] n (US) proibizionismo, **~ive** a (price etc) proibitivo(a).

project n ['prɔdʒekt] (plan) piano; (venture) progetto; (SCOL) studio // vb [prə'dʒekt] vt proiettare // vi (stick out) sporgere.

projectile [prə'dʒektaɪl] n proiettile m.

projector [prə'dʒektə*] n proiettore m.

prolong [prə'lɔŋ] vt prolungare.

prom [prɔm] n abbr = **promenade**; (US: ball) ballo studentesco.

promenade [prɔmə'nɑːd] n (by sea) lungomare m; **~ concert** n concerto di musica classica.

prominent ['prɔmɪnənt] a (standing out) prominente; (important) importante.

promiscuous [prə'mɪskjuəs] a (sexually) di facili costumi.

promise ['prɔmɪs] n promessa // vt, vi promettere; **promising** a promettente.

promote [prə'məʊt] vt promuovere; (venture, event) organizzare; **~r** n (of

sporting event) organizzatore/trice;
promotion [-'məʊʃən] *n* promozione *f*.

prompt [prɔmpt] *a* rapido(a), svelto(a);
puntuale; (*reply*) sollecito(a) // *ad*
(*punctually*) in punto // *n* (*COMPUT*)
prompt *m* // *vt* incitare; provocare;
(*THEATRE*) suggerire a; **~ly** *ad*
prontamente; puntualmente; **~ness** *n*
prontezza; puntualità.

prone [prəʊn] *a* (*lying*) prono(a); **~ to**
propenso(a) a, incline a.

prong [prɔŋ] *n* rebbio, punta.

pronoun ['prəʊnaʊn] *n* pronome *m*.

pronounce [prə'naʊns] *vt* pronunziare //
vi: to **~ (up)on** pronunziare su.

pronunciation [prənʌnsɪ'eɪʃən] *n*
pronunzia.

proof [pru:f] *n* prova; (*of book*) bozza;
(*PHOT*) provino; (*of alcohol*) grado // *a*:
~ against a prova di.

prop [prɔp] *n* sostegno, appoggio // *vt*
(*also*: **~ up**) sostenere, appoggiare;
(*lean*): to **~ sth against** appoggiare qc
contro *or* a.

propaganda [prɔpə'gændə] *n*
propaganda.

propel [prə'pɛl] *vt* spingere (in avanti),
muovere; **~ler** *n* elica; **~ling pencil** *n*
(*Brit*) matita a mina.

propensity [prə'pɛnsɪtɪ] *n* tendenza.

proper ['prɔpə*] *a* (*suited, right*)
adatto(a), appropriato(a); (*seemly*)
decente; (*authentic*) vero(a); (*col: real*)
noun + vero(a) e proprio(a); **~ly** *ad*
(*eat, study*) bene; (*behave*) come si
deve; **~ noun** *n* nome *m* proprio.

property ['prɔpətɪ] *n* (*things owned*) beni
mpl; (*land, building*) proprietà *f inv*;
(*CHEM etc: quality*) proprietà; **~
owner** *n* proprietario/a.

prophecy ['prɔfɪsɪ] *n* profezia.

prophesy ['prɔfɪsaɪ] *vt* predire.

prophet ['prɔfɪt] *n* profeta *m*.

proportion [prə'pɔːʃən] *n* proporzione *f*;
(*share*) parte *f* // *vt* proporzionare,
commisurare; **~al** *a* proporzionale;
~ate *a* proporzionato(a).

proposal [prə'pəʊzl] *n* proposta; (*plan*)
progetto; (*of marriage*) proposta di matrimonio.

propose [prə'pəʊz] *vt* proporre,
suggerire // *vi* fare una proposta di matrimonio; to **~ to do** proporsi di fare,
aver l'intenzione di fare.

proposition [prɔpə'zɪʃən] *n* proposizione
f.

proprietor [prə'praɪətə*] *n* proprietario/
a.

propriety [prə'praɪətɪ] *n* (*seemliness*)
decoro, rispetto delle convenienze sociali.

prose [prəʊz] *n* prosa; (*SCOL: translation*) traduzione *f* dalla madrelingua.

prosecute ['prɔsɪkjuːt] *vt* processare;
prosecution [-'kjuːʃən] *n* processo;
(*accusing side*) accusa; **prosecutor** *n*

(*also*: **public prosecutor**) ≈ procuratore
m della Repubblica.

prospect *n* ['prɔspɛkt] prospettiva;
(*hope*) speranza // *vb* [prə'spɛkt] *vt* fare
assaggi in // *vi* fare assaggi; **~s** *npl* (*for
work etc*) prospettive *fpl*; **prospective**
[-'spɛktɪv] *a* possibile; futuro(a).

prospectus [prə'spɛktəs] *n* prospetto,
programma *m*.

prosperity [prɔ'spɛrɪtɪ] *n* prosperità.

prostitute ['prɔstɪtjuːt] *n* prostituta.

protect [prə'tɛkt] *vt* proteggere,
salvaguardare; **~ion** *n* protezione *f*;
~ive *a* protettivo(a).

protégé ['prəʊtəʒeɪ] *n* protetto; **~e** *n*
protetta.

protein ['prəʊtiːn] *n* proteina.

protest *n* ['prəʊtɛst] protesta // *vt*, *vi*
[prə'tɛst] protestare.

Protestant ['prɔtɪstənt] *a*, *n* protestante
(*m/f*).

protester [prə'tɛstə*] *n* dimostrante *m/f*.

prototype ['prəʊtətaɪp] *n* prototipo.

protracted [prə'træktɪd] *a* tirato(a) per
le lunghe.

protrude [prə'truːd] *vi* sporgere.

protuberance [prə'tjuːbərəns] *n*
sporgenza.

proud [praʊd] *a* fiero(a), orgoglioso(a);
(*pej*) superbo(a).

prove [pruːv] *vt* provare, dimostrare //
vi: to **~ correct** *etc* risultare vero(a)
etc; to **~ o.s.** mostrare le proprie
capacità.

proverb ['prɔvəːb] *n* proverbio.

provide [prə'vaɪd] *vt* fornire,
provvedere; to **~ sb with sth** fornire *or*
provvedere qn di qc; to **~ for** *vt fus*
provvedere a; **~d (that)** *cj* purché +
sub, a condizione che + *sub*.

providing [prə'vaɪdɪŋ] *cj* purché + *sub*, a
condizione che + *sub*.

province ['prɔvɪns] *n* provincia;
provincial [prə'vɪnʃəl] *a* provinciale.

provision [prə'vɪʒən] *n* (*supply*) riserva;
(*supplying*) provvista; rifornimento;
(*stipulation*) condizione *f*; **~s** *npl* (*food*)
provviste *fpl*; **~al** *a* provvisorio(a).

proviso [prə'vaɪzəʊ] *n* condizione *f*.

provocative [prə'vɔkətɪv] *a* (*aggressive*)
provocatorio(a); (*thought-provoking*)
stimolante; (*seductive*) provocante.

provoke [prə'vəʊk] *vt* provocare;
incitare.

prow [praʊ] *n* prua.

prowess ['praʊɪs] *n* prodezza.

prowl [praʊl] *vi* (*also*: **~ about**, **~
around**) aggirarsi; **~er** *n* tipo sospetto
(*che s'aggira con l'intenzione di rubare,
aggredire etc*).

proximity [prɔk'sɪmɪtɪ] *n* prossimità.

proxy ['prɔksɪ] *n* procura.

prudent ['pruːdnt] *a* prudente.

prudish ['pruːdɪʃ] *a* puritano(a).

prune [pruːn] *n* prugna secca // *vt* potare.

pry [praɪ] *vi*: to ~ into ficcare il naso in.
PS *abbr* (= *postscript*) P.S.
psalm [sɑːm] *n* salmo.
pseudo- ['sjuːdəu] *prefix* pseudo...
pseudonym ['sjuːdənɪm] *n* pseudonimo.
psyche ['saɪkɪ] *n* psiche *f*.
psychiatric [saɪkɪ'ætrɪk] *a* psichiatrico(a).
psychiatrist [saɪ'kaɪətrɪst] *n* psichiatra *m/f*.
psychic ['saɪkɪk] *a* (*also*: ~al) psichico(a); (*person*) dotato(a) di qualità telepatiche.
psychoanalyst [saɪkəu'ænəlɪst] *n* psicanalista *m/f*.
psychological [saɪkə'lɔdʒɪkl] *a* psicologico(a).
psychologist [saɪ'kɔlədʒɪst] *n* psicologo/a.
psychology [saɪ'kɔlədʒɪ] *n* psicologia.
psychopath ['saɪkəupæθ] *n* psicopatico/a.
P.T.O. *abbr* (= *please turn over*) v.r.
pub [pʌb] *n abbr* (= *public house*) pub *m inv*.
pubic ['pjuːbɪk] *a* pubico(a), del pube.
public ['pʌblɪk] *a* pubblico(a) // *n* pubblico; **in** ~ in pubblico; ~ **address system (P.A.)** *n* impianto di amplificazione.
publican ['pʌblɪkən] *n* proprietario di un pub.
publication [pʌblɪ'keɪʃən] *n* pubblicazione *f*.
public: ~ **company** *n* società *f inv* per azioni (*costituita tramite pubblica sottoscrizione*); ~ **convenience** *n* (*Brit*) gabinetti *mpl*; ~ **holiday** *n* giorno festivo, festa nazionale; ~ **house** *n* (*Brit*) pub *m inv*.
publicity [pʌb'lɪsɪtɪ] *n* pubblicità.
publicize ['pʌblɪsaɪz] *vt* rendere pubblico(a).
publicly ['pʌblɪklɪ] *ad* pubblicamente.
public: ~ **opinion** *n* opinione *f* pubblica; ~ **relations (PR)** *n* pubbliche relazioni *fpl*; ~ **school** *n* (*Brit*) scuola privata; (*US*) scuola statale; ~-**spirited** *a* che ha senso civico; ~ **transport** *n* mezzi *mpl* pubblici.
publish ['pʌblɪʃ] *vt* pubblicare; ~**er** *n* editore *m*; ~**ing** *n* (*industry*) editoria; (*of a book*) pubblicazione *f*.
puck [pʌk] *n* (*ICE HOCKEY*) disco.
pucker ['pʌkə*] *vt* corrugare.
pudding ['pudɪŋ] *n* budino; (*Brit: dessert*) dolce *m*; **black** ~ sanguinaccio.
puddle ['pʌdl] *n* pozza, pozzanghera.
puff [pʌf] *n* sbuffo // *vt*: to ~ one's pipe tirare sboccate di fumo // *vi* uscire a sbuffi; (*pant*) ansare; to ~ out smoke mandar fuori sbuffi di fumo; ~**ed** *a* (*col: out of breath*) senza fiato; ~ **pastry** *n* pasta sfoglia; ~**y** *a* gonfio(a).
pull [pul] *n* (*tug*): to give sth a ~ tirare su qc; (*fig*) influenza // *vt* tirare; (*mus*-

cle) strappare // *vi* tirare; to ~ to pieces fare a pezzi; to ~ one's punches (*BOXING*) risparmiare l'avversario; to ~ one's weight dare il proprio contributo; to ~ o.s. together ricomporsi, riprendersi; to ~ sb's leg prendere in giro qn; to ~ apart *vt* (*break*) fare a pezzi; to ~ down *vt* (*house*) demolire; (*tree*) abbattere; to ~ in *vi* (*AUT: at the kerb*) accostarsi; (*RAIL*) entrare in stazione; to ~ off *vt* (*deal etc*) portare a compimento; to ~ out *vi* partire; (*AUT: come out of line*) spostarsi sulla mezzeria // *vt* staccare; far uscire; (*withdraw*) ritirare; to ~ over *vi* (*AUT*) accostare; to ~ through *vi* farcela; to ~ up *vi* (*stop*) fermarsi // *vt* (*uproot*) sradicare; (*stop*) fermare.
pulley ['pulɪ] *n* puleggia, carrucola.
pullover ['pulouvə*] *n* pullover *m inv*.
pulp [pʌlp] *n* (*of fruit*) polpa; (*for paper*) pasta per carta.
pulpit ['pulpɪt] *n* pulpito.
pulsate [pʌl'seɪt] *vi* battere, palpitare.
pulse [pʌls] *n* polso.
pummel ['pʌml] *vt* dare pugni a.
pump [pʌmp] *n* pompa; (*shoe*) scarpetta // *vt* pompare; (*fig: col*) far parlare; to ~ up *vt* gonfiare.
pumpkin ['pʌmpkɪn] *n* zucca.
pun [pʌn] *n* gioco di parole.
punch [pʌntʃ] *n* (*blow*) pugno; (*fig: force*) forza; (*tool*) punzone *m*; (*drink*) ponce *m* // *vt* (*hit*): to ~ sb/sth dare un pugno a qn/qc; to ~ a hole (in) fare un buco (in); ~ line *n* (*of joke*) battuta finale; ~-up *n* (*Brit col*) rissa.
punctual ['pʌŋktjuəl] *a* puntuale; ~**ity** [-'ælɪtɪ] *n* puntualità.
punctuation [pʌŋktju'eɪʃən] *n* interpunzione *f*, punteggiatura.
puncture ['pʌŋktʃə*] *n* foratura // *vt* forare.
pundit ['pʌndɪt] *n* sapientone/a.
pungent ['pʌndʒənt] *a* piccante; (*fig*) mordace, caustico(a).
punish ['pʌnɪʃ] *vt* punire; ~**ment** *n* punizione *f*.
punk [pʌŋk] *n* (*also*: ~ rocker) punk *m/f inv*; (*also*: ~ rock) musica punk, punk rock *m*; (*US col: hoodlum*) teppista *m*.
punt [pʌnt] *n* (*boat*) barchino; (*FOOTBALL*) colpo a volo.
punter ['pʌntə*] *n* (*Brit: gambler*) scommettitore/trice.
puny ['pjuːnɪ] *a* gracile.
pup [pʌp] *n* cucciolo/a.
pupil ['pjuːpl] *n* allievo/a; (*ANAT*) pupilla.
puppet ['pʌpɪt] *n* burattino.
puppy ['pʌpɪ] *n* cucciolo/a, cagnolino/a.
purchase ['pəːtʃɪs] *n* acquisto, compera // *vt* comprare; ~**r** *n* compratore/trice.
pure [pjuə*] *a* puro(a).
purely ['pjuəlɪ] *ad* puramente.
purge [pəːdʒ] *n* (*MED*) purga; (*POL*)

epurazione f // vt purgare; (fig) epurare.

puritan ['pjuərɪtən] a, n puritano(a).

purl [pə:l] n punto rovescio.

purple ['pə:pl] a di porpora; viola inv.

purport [pə:'pɔ:t] vi: to ~ to be/do pretendere di essere/fare.

purpose ['pə:pəs] n intenzione f, scopo; on ~ apposta; ~ful a deciso(a), risoluto(a).

purr [pə:*] vi fare le fusa.

purse [pə:s] n borsellino // vt contrarre.

purser ['pə:sə*] n (NAUT) commissario di bordo.

pursue [pə'sju:] vt inseguire.

pursuit [pə'sju:t] n inseguimento; (occupation) occupazione f, attività f inv.

purveyor [pə'veɪə*] n fornitore/trice.

push [puʃ] n spinta; (effort) grande sforzo; (drive) energia // vt spingere; (button) premere; (thrust): to ~ sth (into) ficcare qc (in); (fig) fare pubblicità a // vi spingere; premere; to ~ aside vt scostare; to ~ off vi (col) filare; to ~ on vi (continue) continuare; to ~ through vt (measure) far approvare; to ~ up vt (total, prices) far salire; ~chair n (Brit) passeggino; ~er n (drug ~er) spacciatore/trice; ~over n (col): it's a ~over è un lavoro da bambini; ~-up n (US: press-up) flessione f sulle braccia; ~y a (pej) opportunista.

puss, pussy(-cat) [pus, 'pusɪ(kæt)] n micio.

put, pt, pp put [put] vt mettere, porre; (say) dire, esprimere; (a question) fare; (estimate) stimare; to ~ about vi (NAUT) virare di bordo // vt (rumour) diffondere; to ~ across vt (ideas etc) comunicare; far capire; to ~ away vt (return) mettere a posto; to ~ back vt (replace) rimettere (a posto); (postpone) rinviare; (delay) ritardare; to ~ by vt (money) mettere da parte; to ~ down vt (parcel etc) posare, mettere giù; (pay) versare; (in writing) mettere per iscritto; (suppress: revolt etc) reprimere, sopprimere; (attribute) attribuire; to ~ forward vt (ideas) avanzare, proporre; (date) anticipare; to ~ in vt (application, complaint) presentare; to ~ off vt (postpone) rimandare, rinviare; (discourage) dissuadere; to ~ on vt (clothes, lipstick etc) mettere; (light etc) accendere; (play etc) mettere in scena; (food, meal) servire; (brake) mettere; to ~ on weight ingrassare; to ~ on airs darsi delle arie; to ~ out vt mettere fuori; (one's hand) porgere; (light etc) spegnere; (person: inconvenience) scomodare; to ~ up vt (raise) sollevare, alzare; (pin up) affiggere; (hang) appendere; (build) costruire, erigere; (increase) aumentare;

(accommodate) alloggiare; to ~ up with vt fus sopportare.

putt [pʌt] vt (ball) colpire leggermente // n colpo leggero; ~ing green n green m inv; campo da putting.

putty ['pʌtɪ] n stucco.

puzzle ['pʌzl] n enigma m, mistero; (jigsaw) puzzle m; (also: crossword ~) parole fpl incrociate, cruciverba m inv // vt confondere, rendere perplesso(a) // vi scervellarsi.

pyjamas [pɪ'dʒɑ:məz] npl (Brit) pigiama m.

pylon ['paɪlən] n pilone m.

pyramid ['pɪrəmɪd] n piramide f.

Pyrenees [pɪrɪ'ni:z] npl: the ~ i Pirenei.

Q

quack [kwæk] n (of duck) qua qua m inv; (pej: doctor) dottoruccio/a.

quad [kwɔd] n abbr = **quadrangle**, **quadruplet**.

quadrangle ['kwɔdræŋgl] n (MATH) quadrilatero; (courtyard) cortile m.

quadruple [kwɔ'drupl] vt quadruplicare // vi quadruplicarsi.

quadruplet [kwɔ'dru:plɪt] n uno/a di quattro gemelli.

quagmire ['kwægmaɪə*] n pantano.

quail [kweɪl] n (ZOOL) quaglia // vi (person) perdersi d'animo.

quaint [kweɪnt] a bizzarro(a); (old-fashioned) antiquato(a); grazioso(a), pittoresco(a).

quake [kweɪk] vi tremare // n abbr = **earthquake**.

Quaker ['kweɪkə*] n quacchero/a.

qualification [kwɔlɪfɪ'keɪʃən] n (degree etc) qualifica, titolo; (ability) competenza, qualificazione f; (limitation) riserva, restrizione f.

qualified ['kwɔlɪfaɪd] a qualificato(a); (able) competente, qualificato(a); (limited) condizionato(a).

qualify ['kwɔlɪfaɪ] vt abilitare; (limit: statement) modificare, precisare // vi: to ~ (as) qualificarsi (come); to ~ (for) acquistare i requisiti necessari (per); (SPORT) qualificarsi (per or a).

quality ['kwɔlɪtɪ] n qualità f inv.

qualm [kwɑ:m] n dubbio; scrupolo.

quandary ['kwɔndrɪ] n: in a ~ in un dilemma.

quantity ['kwɔntɪtɪ] n quantità f inv; ~ surveyor n geometra m (specializzato nel calcolare la quantità e il costo del materiale da costruzione).

quarantine ['kwɔrnti:n] n quarantena.

quarrel ['kwɔrl] n lite f, disputa // vi litigare; ~some a litigioso(a).

quarry ['kwɔrɪ] n (for stone) cava; (animal) preda // vt (marble etc) estrarre.

quart [kwɔ:t] n ≈ litro.
quarter ['kwɔ:tə*] n quarto; (of year) trimestre m; (district) quartiere m // vt dividere in quattro; (MIL) alloggiare; ~s npl alloggio; (MIL) alloggi mpl, quadrato; a ~ of an hour un quarto d'ora; ~ **final** n quarto di finale; ~**ly** a trimestrale // ad trimestralmente // ~**master** n (MIL) furiere m.
quartet(te) [kwɔ:'tɛt] n quartetto.
quartz [kwɔ:ts] n quarzo; ~ **watch** n orologio al quarzo.
quash [kwɔʃ] vt (verdict) annullare.
quaver ['kweɪvə*] n (Brit MUS) croma // vi tremolare.
quay [ki:] n (also: ~side) banchina.
queasy ['kwi:zɪ] a (stomach) delicato(a); to feel ~ aver la nausea.
queen [kwi:n] n (gen) regina; (CARDS etc) regina, donna; ~ **mother** n regina madre.
queer [kwɪə*] a strano(a), curioso(a); (suspicious) dubbio(a), sospetto(a); (sick): I feel ~ mi sento poco bene // n (col) finocchio.
quell [kwɛl] vt domare.
quench [kwɛntʃ] vt (flames) spegnere; to ~ one's thirst dissetarsi.
querulous ['kwɛrʊləs] a querulo(a).
query ['kwɪərɪ] n domanda, questione f; (doubt) dubbio // vt mettere in questione.
quest [kwɛst] n cerca, ricerca.
question ['kwɛstʃən] n domanda, questione f // vt (person) interrogare; (plan, idea) mettere in questione or in dubbio; it's a ~ of doing si tratta di fare; beyond ~ fuori di dubbio; out of the ~ fuori discussione, impossibile; ~**able** a discutibile; ~ **mark** n punto interrogativo.
questionnaire [kwɛstʃə'nɛə*] n questionario.
queue [kju:] n (Brit) coda, fila // vi fare la coda.
quibble ['kwɪbl] vi cavillare.
quick [kwɪk] a rapido(a), veloce; (reply) pronto(a); (mind) pronto(a), acuto(a) // ad rapidamente, presto // n: cut to the ~ (fig) toccato(a) sul vivo; be ~! fa presto!; ~**en** vt accelerare, affrettare; (rouse) animare, stimolare // vi accelerare, affrettarsi; ~**ly** ad rapidamente, velocemente; ~**sand** n sabbie fpl mobili; ~-**witted** a pronto(a) d'ingegno.
quid [kwɪd] n (pl inv) (Brit col) sterlina.
quiet ['kwaɪət] a tranquillo(a), quieto(a); (ceremony) semplice; (colour) discreto(a) // n tranquillità, calma // vt, vi (US) = ~**en**; keep ~! sta zitto!; ~**en** (also: ~**en down**) vi calmarsi, chetarsi // vt calmare, chetare; ~**ly** ad tranquillamente, calmamente; sommessamente; discretamente.
quilt [kwɪlt] n trapunta; (continental ~) piumino.

quin [kwɪn] n abbr = **quintuplet**.
quinine [kwɪ'ni:n] n chinino.
quintuplet [kwɪn'tju:plɪt] n uno/a di cinque gemelli.
quip [kwɪp] n frizzo.
quirk [kwə:k] n ghiribizzo.
quit, pt, pp **quit** or **quitted** [kwɪt] vt lasciare, partire da // vi (give up) mollare; (resign) dimettersi; **notice to** ~ preavviso (dato all'inquilino).
quite [kwaɪt] ad (rather) assai; (entirely) completamente, del tutto; I understand capisco perfettamente; ~ a few of them non pochi di loro; ~ (so)! esatto!
quits [kwɪts] a: ~ (with) pari (con); let's call it ~ adesso siamo pari.
quiver ['kwɪvə*] vi tremare, fremere // n (for arrows) faretra.
quiz [kwɪz] n (game) quiz m inv; indovinello // vt interrogare; ~**zical** a enigmatico(a).
quota ['kwəʊtə] n quota.
quotation [kwəʊ'teɪʃən] n citazione f; (of shares etc) quotazione f; (estimate) preventivo; ~ **marks** npl virgolette fpl.
quote [kwəʊt] n citazione f // vt (sentence) citare; (price) dare, fissare; (shares) quotare // vi: to ~ from citare.

R

rabbi ['ræbaɪ] n rabbino.
rabbit ['ræbɪt] n coniglio; ~ **hutch** n conigliera.
rabble ['ræbl] n (pej) canaglia, plebaglia.
rabies ['reɪbi:z] n rabbia.
RAC n abbr (Brit) = Royal Automobile Club.
race [reɪs] n razza; (competition, rush) corsa // vt (person) gareggiare (in corsa) con; (horse) far correre; (engine) imballare // vi correre; ~ **car** n (US) = **racing car**; ~ **car driver** n (US) = **racing driver**; ~**course** n campo di corse, ippodromo; ~**horse** n cavallo da corsa; ~ **relations** npl rapporti mpl razziali; ~**track** n pista.
racial ['reɪʃl] a razziale; ~**ist** a, n razzista (m/f).
racing ['reɪsɪŋ] n corsa; ~ **car** n (Brit) macchina da corsa; ~ **driver** n (Brit) corridore m automobilista.
racism ['reɪsɪzəm] n razzismo; **racist** a, n razzista (m/f).
rack [ræk] n rastrelliera; (also: luggage ~) rete f, portabagagli m inv; (also: roof ~) portabagagli // vt torturare, tormentare; **to** ~ **one's brains** scervellarsi.
racket ['rækɪt] n (for tennis) racchetta; (noise) fracasso; baccano; (swindle) imbroglio, truffa; (organized crime) racket m inv.

racquet ['rækɪt] *n* racchetta.
racy ['reɪsɪ] *a* brioso(a); piccante.
radar ['reɪdɑ:*] *n* radar *m* // *cpd* radar *inv.*
radial5.5 ['reɪdɪəl] *a* (*also:* ~-ply) radiale.
radiant ['reɪdɪənt] *a* raggiante; (*PHYSICS*) radiante.
radiate ['reɪdɪeɪt] *vt* (*heat*) irraggiare, irradiare // *vi* (*lines*) irradiarsi.
radiation [reɪdɪ'eɪʃən] *n* irradiamento; (*radioactive*) radiazione *f.*
radiator ['reɪdɪeɪtə*] *n* radiatore *m.*
radical ['rædɪkl] *a* radicale.
radii ['reɪdɪaɪ] *npl of* **radius.**
radio ['reɪdɪəu] *n* radio *f inv;* on the ~ alla radio.
radioactive [reɪdɪəu'æktɪv] *a* radioattivo(a).
radio station *n* stazione *f* radio *inv.*
radish ['rædɪʃ] *n* ravanello.
radium ['reɪdɪəm] *n* radio.
radius ['reɪdɪəs], *pl* **radii** *n* raggio; (*ANAT*) radio.
RAF *n abbr* = **Royal Air Force.**
raffle ['ræfl] *n* lotteria.
raft [rɑ:ft] *n* zattera; (*also:* life ~) zattera di salvataggio.
rafter ['rɑ:ftə*] *n* trave *f.*
rag [ræg] *n* straccio, cencio; (*pej: newspaper*) giornalaccio, bandiera; (*for charity*) iniziativa studentesca a scopo benefico // *vt* (*Brit*) prendere in giro; ~**s** *npl* stracci *mpl*, brandelli *mpl*; ~-**and-bone man** *n* (*Brit*) = **ragman;** ~ **doll** *n* bambola di pezza.
rage [reɪdʒ] *n* (*fury*) collera, furia // *vi* (*person*) andare su tutte le furie; (*storm*) infuriare; it's all the ~ fa furore.
ragged ['rægɪd] *a* (*edge*) irregolare; (*cuff*) logoro(a); (*appearance*) pezzente.
ragman ['rægmæn] *n* straccivendolo.
raid [reɪd] *n* (*MIL*) incursione *f;* (*criminal*) rapina; (*by police*) irruzione *f* // *vt* fare un'incursione in; rapinare; fare irruzione in.
rail [reɪl] *n* (*on stair*) ringhiera; (*on bridge, balcony*) parapetto; (*of ship*) battagliola; (*for train*) rotaia; ~**s** *npl* binario, rotaie *fpl;* by ~ per ferrovia; ~**ing(s)** *n(pl)* ringhiere *fpl;* ~**road** *n* (*US*) = ~**way;** ~**way** *n* (*Brit*) ferrovia; ~**way line** *n* (*Brit*) linea ferroviaria; ~**wayman** *n* (*Brit*) ferroviere *m;* ~**way station** *n* (*Brit*) stazione *f* ferroviaria.
rain [reɪn] *n* pioggia // *vi* piovere; in the ~ sotto la pioggia; it's ~**ing** piove; ~**bow** *n* arcobaleno; ~**coat** *n* impermeabile *m;* ~**drop** *n* goccia di pioggia; ~**fall** *n* pioggia; (*measurement*) piovosità; ~**y** *a* piovoso(a).
raise [reɪz] *n* aumento // *vt* (*lift*) alzare; sollevare; (*build*) erigere; (*increase*)

aumentare; (*a protest, doubt, question*) sollevare; (*cattle, family*) allevare; (*crop*) coltivare; (*army, funds*) raccogliere; (*loan*) ottenere; to ~ one's voice alzare la voce.
raisin ['reɪzn] *n* uva secca.
rajah ['rɑ:dʒə] *n* ragià *m inv.*
rake [reɪk] *n* (*tool*) rastrello; (*person*) libertino // *vt* (*garden*) rastrellare; (*with machine gun*) spazzare.
rally ['rælɪ] *n* (*POL etc*) riunione *f;* (*AUT*) rally *m inv;* (*TENNIS*) scambio // *vt* riunire, radunare // *vi* raccogliersi, radunarsi; (*sick person, Stock Exchange*) riprendersi; to ~ **round** *vt fus* raggrupparsi intorno a; venire in aiuto di.
RAM [ræm] *n abbr* (= *random access memory*) memoria ad accesso casuale.
ram [ræm] *n* montone *m,* ariete *m;* (*device*) ariete // *vt* conficcare; (*crash into*) cozzare, sbattere contro; percuotere; speronare.
ramble ['ræmbl] *n* escursione *f* // *vi* (*pej: also:* ~ **on**) divagare; ~**r** *n* escursionista *m/f;* (*BOT*) rosa rampicante; **rambling** *a* (*speech*) sconnesso(a); (*BOT*) rampicante.
ramp [ræmp] *n* rampa; **on/off** ~ (*US AUT*) raccordo di entrata/uscita.
rampage [ræm'peɪdʒ] *n:* to go on the ~ scatenarsi in modo violento.
rampant ['ræmpənt] *a* (*disease etc*) che infierisce.
rampart ['ræmpɑ:t] *n* bastione *m.*
ramshackle ['ræmʃækl] *a* (*house*) cadente; (*car etc*) sgangherato(a).
ran [ræn] *pt of* **run.**
ranch [rɑ:ntʃ] *n* ranch *m inv;* ~**er** *n* proprietario di un ranch; cowboy *m inv.*
rancid ['rænsɪd] *a* rancido(a).
rancour, (*US*) **rancor** ['ræŋkə*] *n* rancore *m.*
random ['rændəm] *a* fatto(a) *or* detto(a) per caso // *n:* at ~ a casaccio; ~ **access** *n* (*COMPUT*) accesso casuale.
randy ['rændɪ] *a* (*Brit col*) arrapato(a); lascivo(a).
rang [ræŋ] *pt of* **ring.**
range [reɪndʒ] *n* (*of mountains*) catena; (*of missile, voice*) portata; (*of products*) gamma; (*MIL: also:* **shooting** ~) campo di tiro; (*also:* **kitchen** ~) fornello, cucina economica // *vi:* to ~ **over** coprire; to ~ **from ... to** andare da ... a ...
ranger ['reɪndʒə*] *n* guardia forestale.
rank [ræŋk] *n* fila; (*MIL*) grado; (*Brit: also:* **taxi** ~) posteggio di taxi // *vi:* to ~ **among** essere nel numero di // *a* puzzolente; vero(a) e proprio(a); **the** ~**s** (*MIL*) la truppa; **the** ~ **and file** (*fig*) la gran massa.
rankle ['ræŋkl] *vi* bruciare.
ransack ['rænsæk] *vt* rovistare; (*plunder*) saccheggiare.

ransom ['rænsəm] n riscatto; **to hold sb to ~** (fig) esercitare pressione su qn.

rant [rænt] vi vociare.

rap [ræp] vt bussare a; picchiare su.

rape [reɪp] n violenza carnale, stupro; (BOT) ravizzone m // vt violentare; **~(seed) oil** n olio di ravizzone.

rapid ['ræpɪd] a rapido(a); **~s** npl (GEO) rapida; **~ly** ad rapidamente.

rapist ['reɪpɪst] n violentatore m.

rapport [ræ'pɔ:*] n rapporto.

rapture ['ræptʃə*] n estasi f inv.

rare [rɛə*] a raro(a); (CULIN: steak) al sangue.

rarefied ['rɛərɪfaɪd] a (air, atmosphere) rarefatto(a).

rarely ['rɛəlɪ] ad raramente.

raring ['rɛərɪŋ] a: **to be ~ to go** (col) non veder l'ora di cominciare.

rascal ['rɑːskl] n mascalzone m.

rash [ræʃ] a imprudente, sconsiderato(a) // n (MED) eruzione f.

rasher ['ræʃə*] n fetta sottile (di lardo or prosciutto).

raspberry ['rɑːzbərɪ] n lampone m.

rasping ['rɑːspɪŋ] a stridulo(a).

rat [ræt] n ratto.

rate [reɪt] n (proportion) tasso, percentuale f; (speed) velocità f inv; (price) tariffa // vt giudicare; stimare; **to ~ sb/sth as** valutare qn/qc come; **~s** npl (Brit) imposte fpl comunali; (fees) tariffe fpl; **~able value** n (Brit) valore m imponibile or locativo (di una proprietà); **~payer** n (Brit) contribuente m/f (che paga le imposte comunali).

rather ['rɑːðə*] ad piuttosto; **it's ~ expensive** è piuttosto caro; (too much) è un po' caro; **there's ~ a lot** ce n'è parecchio; **I would** or **I'd ~ go** preferirei andare.

ratify ['rætɪfaɪ] vt ratificare.

rating ['reɪtɪŋ] n classificazione f; punteggio di merito; (NAUT: category) classe f; (: Brit: sailor) marinaio semplice.

ratio ['reɪʃɪəu] n proporzione f.

ration ['ræʃən] n (gen pl) razioni fpl // vt razionare.

rational ['ræʃənl] a razionale, ragionevole; (solution, reasoning) logico(a); **~e** [-'nɑːl] n fondamento logico; giustificazione f; **~ize** vt razionalizzare.

rat race n carrierismo, corsa al successo.

rattle ['rætl] n tintinnio; (louder) strepito; (object: of baby) sonaglino; (: of sports fan) raganella // vi risuonare, tintinnare; fare un rumore di ferraglia // vt scuotere (con strepito); **~snake** n serpente m a sonagli.

raucous ['rɔːkəs] a rauco(a).

ravage ['rævɪdʒ] vt devastare; **~s** npl danni mpl.

rave [reɪv] vi (in anger) infuriarsi; (with enthusiasm) andare in estasi; (MED) delirare.

raven ['reɪvən] n corvo.

ravenous ['rævənəs] a affamato(a).

ravine [rə'viːn] n burrone m.

raving ['reɪvɪŋ] a: **~ lunatic** pazzo(a) furioso(a).

ravioli [rævɪ'əulɪ] n ravioli mpl.

ravishing ['rævɪʃɪŋ] a incantevole.

raw [rɔː] a (uncooked) crudo(a); (not processed) greggio(a); (sore) vivo(a); (inexperienced) inesperto(a); **~ deal** (col) bidonata; **~ material** n materia prima.

ray [reɪ] n raggio; **a ~ of hope** un barlume di speranza.

rayon ['reɪɔn] n raion m.

raze [reɪz] vt radere, distruggere.

razor ['reɪzə*] n rasoio; **~ blade** n lama di rasoio.

Rd abbr = **road**.

re [riː] prep con riferimento a.

reach [riːtʃ] n portata; (of river etc) tratto // vt raggiungere; arrivare a // vi stendersi; out of/within ~ fuori/a portata di mano; **to ~ out** vi: **to ~ out for** stendere la mano per prendere.

react [riː'ækt] vi reagire; **~ion** [-'ækʃən] n reazione f.

reactor [riː'æktə*] n reattore m.

read, pt, pp **read** [riːd, rɛd] vi leggere // vt leggere; (understand) intendere, interpretare; (study) studiare // vi (writing) leggibile; (book etc) che si legge volentieri; **~er** n lettore/trice; (book) libro di lettura; (Brit: at university) professore con funzioni preminenti di ricerca; **~ership** n (of paper etc) numero di lettori.

readily ['rɛdɪlɪ] ad volentieri; (easily) facilmente.

readiness ['rɛdɪnɪs] n prontezza; **in ~** (prepared) pronto(a).

reading ['riːdɪŋ] n lettura; (understanding) interpretazione f; (on instrument) indicazione f.

ready ['rɛdɪ] a pronto(a); (willing) pronto(a), disposto(a); (quick) rapido(a); (available) disponibile // ad: **~-cooked** già cotto(a) // n: **at the ~** (MIL) pronto a sparare; (fig) tutto(a) pronto(a); **to get ~** vi prepararsi // vt preparare; **~-made** a prefabbricato(a); (clothes) confezionato(a); **~ money** n denaro contante, contanti mpl; **~ reckoner** n prontuario di calcolo; **~-to-wear** a prêt-à-porter inv.

real [rɪəl] a reale; vero(a); **in ~ terms** in realtà; **~ estate** n beni mpl immobili; **~ism** n (also ART) realismo; **~ist** n realista m/f; **~istic** [-'lɪstɪk] a realistico(a).

reality [riː'ælɪtɪ] n realtà f inv.

realization [rɪəlaɪ'zeɪʃən] n presa di coscienza; realizzazione f.

realize ['rɪəlaɪz] vt (understand) rendersi conto di; (a project, COMM: asset) realizzare.

really ['rɪəlɪ] ad veramente, davvero.

realm [rɛlm] n reame m, regno.

realtor ['rɪəltɔ:*] n (US) agente m immobiliare.

reap [ri:p] vt mietere; (fig) raccogliere.

reappear [ri:ə'pɪə*] vi ricomparire, riapparire.

rear [rɪə*] a di dietro; (AUT: wheel etc) posteriore // n didietro, parte f posteriore // vt (cattle, family) allevare // vi (also: ~ up: animal) impennarsi.

rearmament [ri:'ɑ:məmənt] n riarmo.

rearrange [ri:ə'reɪndʒ] vt riordinare.

rear-view mirror ['rɪəvju:-] n (AUT) specchio retrovisore.

reason ['ri:zn] n ragione f; (cause, motive) ragione, motivo // vi: to ~ with sb far ragionare qn; to have ~ to think avere motivi per pensare; it stands to ~ that è ovvio che; ~able a ragionevole; (not bad) accettabile; ~ably ad ragionevolmente; ~ing n ragionamento.

reassurance [ri:ə'ʃuərəns] n rassicurazione f.

reassure [ri:ə'ʃuə*] vt rassicurare; to ~ sb of rassicurare qn di or su.

rebate ['ri:beɪt] n (on product) ribasso; (on tax etc) sgravio; (repayment) rimborso.

rebel n ['rɛbl] ribelle m/f // vi [rɪ'bɛl] ribellarsi; ~lion n ribellione f; ~lious a ribelle.

rebound vi [rɪ'baund] (ball) rimbalzare // n ['ri:baund] rimbalzo.

rebuff [rɪ'bʌf] n secco rifiuto.

rebuke [rɪ'bju:k] vt rimproverare.

rebut [rɪ'bʌt] vt rifiutare.

recall [rɪ'kɔ:l] vt richiamare; (remember) ricordare, richiamare alla mente // n richiamo.

recant [rɪ'kænt] vi ritrattarsi; (REL) fare abiura.

recap ['ri:kæp] vt ricapitolare // vi riassumere.

recapitulate [ri:kə'pɪtjuleɪt] vt, vi = recap.

rec'd abbr = received.

recede [rɪ'si:d] vi allontanarsi; ritirarsi; calare; **receding** a (forehead, chin) sfuggente; he's got a receding hairline sta stempiando.

receipt [rɪ'si:t] n (document) ricevuta; (act of receiving) ricevimento; ~s npl (COMM) introiti mpl.

receive [rɪ'si:v] vt ricevere; (guest) ricevere, accogliere.

receiver [rɪ'si:və*] n (TEL) ricevitore m; (of stolen goods) ricettatore/trice; (LAW) curatore m fallimentare.

recent ['ri:snt] a recente; ~ly ad recentemente.

receptacle [rɪ'sɛptɪkl] n recipiente m.

reception [rɪ'sɛpʃən] n ricevimento; (welcome) accoglienza; (TV etc) ricezione f; ~ **desk** n (in hotel) reception f inv; (in hospital, at doctor's) accettazione f; (in offices etc) portineria; ~ist n receptionist m/f inv.

receptive [rɪ'sɛptɪv] a ricettivo(a).

recess [rɪ'sɛs] n (in room) alcova; (POL etc: holiday) vacanze fpl; ~ion [-'sɛʃən] n recessione f.

recharge [ri:'tʃɑ:dʒ] vt (battery) ricaricare.

recipe ['rɛsɪpɪ] n ricetta.

recipient [rɪ'sɪpɪənt] n beneficiario/a; (of letter) destinatario/a.

recital [rɪ'saɪtl] n recital m inv.

recite [rɪ'saɪt] vt (poem) recitare.

reckless ['rɛkləs] a (driver etc) spericolato(a).

reckon ['rɛkən] vt (count) calcolare; (consider) considerare, stimare; (think): I ~ that ... penso che ...; to ~ on vt fus contare su; ~ing n conto; stima.

reclaim [rɪ'kleɪm] vt (land) bonificare; (demand back) richiedere, reclamare.

recline [rɪ'klaɪn] vi stare sdraiato(a); **reclining** a (seat) ribaltabile.

recluse [rɪ'klu:s] n eremita m, appartato/a.

recognition [rɛkəg'nɪʃən] n riconoscimento; to gain ~ essere riconosciuto(a); transformed beyond ~ irriconoscibile.

recognize ['rɛkəgnaɪz] vt: to ~ (by/as) riconoscere (a or da/come).

recoil [rɪ'kɔɪl] vi (person): to ~ (from) indietreggiare (davanti a) // n (of gun) rinculo.

recollect [rɛkə'lɛkt] vt ricordare; ~ion [-'lɛkʃən] n ricordo.

recommend [rɛkə'mɛnd] vt raccomandare; (advise) consigliare.

reconcile ['rɛkənsaɪl] vt (two people) riconciliare; (two facts) conciliare, quadrare; to ~ o.s. to rassegnarsi a.

recondition [ri:kən'dɪʃən] vt rimettere a nuovo.

reconnaissance [rɪ'kɔnɪsns] n (MIL) ricognizione f.

reconnoitre, (US) **reconnoiter** [rɛkə'nɔɪtə*] (MIL) vt fare una ricognizione di // vi fare una ricognizione.

reconstruct [ri:kən'strʌkt] vt ricostruire.

record n ['rɛkɔ:d] ricordo, documento; (of meeting etc) nota, verbale m; (register) registro; (file) pratica, dossier m inv; (also: police ~) fedina penale sporca; (MUS: disc) disco; (SPORT) record m inv, primato // vt [rɪ'kɔ:d] (set down) prendere nota di, registrare; (relate) raccontare; (MUS: song etc) registrare; in ~ time a tempo di record; to keep a ~ of tener nota di; off the ~ a ufficioso(a) // ad ufficiosamente; ~ **card** n (in file) scheda; ~**ed delivery** n (Brit POST): ~**ed delivery letter** etc lettera etc raccomandata; ~**er** n (LAW) avvocato che funge da giudice; (MUS) flauto diritto; ~ **holder** n (SPORT) primatista m/f; ~**ing** n (MUS) registrazione f; ~ **player** n giradischi m inv.

recount [rɪˈkaunt] vt raccontare, narrare.

re-count n [ˈriːkaunt] (POL: of votes) nuovo computo // vt [riːˈkaunt] ricontare.

recoup [rɪˈkuːp] vt ricuperare.

recourse [rɪˈkɔːs] n ricorso; rimedio.

recover [rɪˈkʌvə*] vt ricuperare // vi (from illness) rimettersi (in salute), ristabilirsi; (country, person: from shock) riprendersi.

recovery [rɪˈkʌvərɪ] n ricupero; ristabilimento; ripresa.

recreation [rɛkrɪˈeɪʃən] n ricreazione f; svago; ~**al** a ricreativo(a).

recrimination [rɪkrɪmɪˈneɪʃən] n recriminazione f.

recruit [rɪˈkruːt] n recluta // vt reclutare.

rectangle [ˈrɛktæŋgl] n rettangolo; **rectangular** [-ˈtæŋgjulə*] a rettangolare.

rectify [ˈrɛktɪfaɪ] vt (error) rettificare; (omission) riparare.

rector [ˈrɛktə*] n (REL) parroco (anglicano); **rectory** n presbiterio.

recuperate [rɪˈkjuːpəreɪt] vi ristabilirsi.

recur [rɪˈkəː*] vi riaccadere; (idea, opportunity) riapparire; (symptoms) ripresentarsi; ~**rent** a ricorrente, periodico(a).

red [rɛd] n rosso; (POL: pej) rosso/a // a rosso(a); **in the ~** (account) scoperto; (business) in deficit; ~ **carpet treatment** n cerimonia col gran pavese; **R~ Cross** n Croce f Rossa; ~**currant** n ribes m inv; ~**den** vt arrossare // vi arrossire; ~**dish** a rossiccio(a).

redeem [rɪˈdiːm] vt (debt) riscattare; (sth in pawn) ritirare; (fig, also REL) redimere; ~**ing** a (feature) che salva.

redeploy [riːdɪˈplɔɪ] vt (resources) riorganizzare.

red-haired [rɛdˈhɛəd] a dai capelli rossi.

red-handed [rɛdˈhændɪd] a: **to be caught ~** essere preso(a) in flagrante or con le mani nel sacco.

redhead [ˈrɛdhɛd] n rosso/a.

red herring n (fig) falsa pista.

red-hot [rɛdˈhɔt] a arroventato(a).

redirect [riːdaɪˈrɛkt] vt (mail) far seguire.

redistribute [riːdɪˈstrɪbjuːt] vt ridistribuire.

red light n: **to go through a ~** (AUT) passare col rosso; **red-light district** n quartiere m luce rossa inv.

redo [riːˈduː] vt irg rifare.

redolent [ˈrɛdələnt] a: ~ **of** che sa di; (fig) che ricorda.

redouble [riːˈdʌbl] vt: **to ~ one's efforts** raddoppiare gli sforzi.

redress [rɪˈdrɛs] n riparazione f // vt riparare.

Red Sea n: **the ~** il Mar Rosso.

redskin [ˈrɛdskɪn] n pellerossa m/f.

red tape n (fig) burocrazia.

reduce [rɪˈdjuːs] vt ridurre; (lower) ridurre, abbassare; "**~ speed now**" (AUT) "rallentare"; **reduction** [rɪˈdʌkʃən] n riduzione f; (of price) ribasso; (discount) sconto.

redundancy [rɪˈdʌndənsɪ] n licenziamento.

redundant [rɪˈdʌndnt] a (worker) licenziato(a); (detail, object) superfluo(a); **to be made ~** essere licenziato (per eccesso di personale).

reed [riːd] n (BOT) canna; (MUS: of clarinet etc) ancia.

reef [riːf] n (at sea) scogliera.

reek [riːk] vi: **to ~ (of)** puzzare (di).

reel [riːl] n bobina, rocchetto; (TECH) aspo; (FISHING) mulinello; (CINEMA) rotolo // vt (TECH) annaspare; (also: ~ up) avvolgere // vi (sway) barcollare.

ref [rɛf] n abbr (col: = referee) arbitro.

refectory [rɪˈfɛktərɪ] n refettorio.

refer [rɪˈfəː*] vt: **to ~ sth to** (dispute, decision) deferire qc a; **to ~ sb to** (inquirer: for information) indirizzare qn a; (reader: to text) rimandare qn a; **to ~ to** vt fus (allude to) accennare a; (apply to) riferire a; (consult) rivolgersi a.

referee [rɛfəˈriː] n arbitro; (Brit: for job application) referenza // vt arbitrare.

reference [ˈrɛfrəns] n riferimento; (mention) menzione f, allusione f; (for job application: letter) referenza; (: person) referenza; **with ~ to** riguardo a; (COMM: in letter) in or con riferimento a; ~ **book** n libro di consultazione; ~ **number** n numero di riferimento.

referendum, pl **referenda** [rɛfəˈrɛndəm, -də] n referendum m inv.

refill vt [riːˈfɪl] riempire di nuovo; (pen, lighter etc) ricaricare // n [ˈriːfɪl] (for pen etc) ricambio.

refine [rɪˈfaɪn] vt raffinare; ~**d** a (person, taste) raffinato(a).

reflect [rɪˈflɛkt] vt (light, image) riflettere; (fig) rispecchiare // vi (think) riflettere, considerare; **to ~ on** vt fus (discredit) rispecchiarsi su; ~**ion** [-ˈflɛkʃən] n riflessione f; (image) riflesso; (criticism): ~**ion on** giudizio su; attacco a; **on ~ion** pensandoci sopra.

reflex [ˈriːflɛks] a riflesso(a) // n riflesso; ~**ive** [rɪˈflɛksɪv] a (LING) riflessivo(a).

reform [rɪˈfɔːm] n riforma // vt riformare; **the R~ation** [rɛfəˈmeɪʃən] n la Riforma; ~**atory** n (US) riformatorio.

refrain [rɪˈfreɪn] *vi*: to ~ from doing trattenersi dal fare // *n* ritornello.
refresh [rɪˈfreʃ] *vt* rinfrescare; (*subj: food, sleep*) ristorare; ~**er course** *n* (*Brit*) corso di aggiornamento; ~**ing** *a* (*drink*) rinfrescante; (*sleep*) riposante, ristoratore(trice); ~**ments** *npl* rinfreschi *mpl*.
refrigerator [rɪˈfrɪdʒəreɪtə*] *n* frigorifero.
refuel [riːˈfjuəl] *vi* far rifornimento (di carburante).
refuge [ˈrefjuːdʒ] *n* rifugio; to take ~ in rifugiarsi in.
refugee [refjuˈdʒiː] *n* rifugiato/a, profugo/a.
refund *n* [ˈriːfʌnd] rimborso // *vt* [rɪˈfʌnd] rimborsare.
refurbish [riːˈfəːbɪʃ] *vt* rimettere a nuovo.
refusal [rɪˈfjuːzəl] *n* rifiuto; to have first ~ on avere il diritto d'opzione su.
refuse *n* [ˈrefjuːs] rifiuti *mpl* // *vt, vi* [rɪˈfjuːz] rifiutare; to ~ to do rifiutare di fare; ~ **collection** *n* raccolta di rifiuti.
refute [rɪˈfjuːt] *vt* confutare.
regain [rɪˈɡeɪn] *vt* riguadagnare; riacquistare, recuperare.
regal [ˈriːɡl] *a* regio(a); ~**ia** [rɪˈɡeɪlɪə] *n* insegne *fpl* regie.
regard [rɪˈɡɑːd] *n* riguardo, stima // *vt* considerare, stimare; to give one's ~s to porgere i suoi saluti a; "with kindest ~s" "cordiali saluti"; ~**ing**, as ~s, with ~ to riguardo a; ~**less** *ad* lo stesso; ~less of a dispetto di, nonostante.
regenerate [rɪˈdʒenəreɪt] *vt* rigenerare.
régime [reɪˈʒiːm] *n* regime *m*.
regiment *n* [ˈredʒɪmənt] reggimento // *vt* [ˈredʒɪment] irreggimentare; ~**al** [-ˈmentl] *a* reggimentale.
region [ˈriːdʒən] *n* regione *f*; in the ~ of (*fig*) all'incirca di; ~**al** *a* regionale.
register [ˈredʒɪstə*] *n* registro; (*also: electoral* ~) lista elettorale // *vt* registrare; (*vehicle*) immatricolare; (*luggage*) spedire assicurato(a); (*letter*) assicurare; (*subj: instrument*) segnare // *vi* iscriversi; (*at hotel*) firmare il registro; (*make impression*) entrare in testa; ~**ed** *a* (*design*) depositato(a); (*Brit: letter*) assicurato(a); ~**ed trademark** *n* marchio depositato.
registrar [ˈredʒɪstrɑː*] *n* ufficiale *m* di stato civile; segretario.
registration [redʒɪsˈtreɪʃən] *n* (*act*) registrazione *f*; iscrizione *f*; (*AUT: also:* ~ **number**) numero di targa.
registry [ˈredʒɪstrɪ] *n* ufficio del registro; ~ **office** *n* (*Brit*) anagrafe *f*; to get married in a ~ **office** ≈ sposarsi in municipio.
regret [rɪˈɡret] *n* rimpianto, rincrescimento // *vt* rimpiangere; ~**fully** *ad* con rincrescimento; ~**table** *a* de-

plorevole.
regular [ˈreɡjulə*] *a* regolare; (*usual*) abituale, normale; (*soldier*) dell'esercito regolare; (*COMM: size*) normale // *n* (*client etc*) cliente *m/f* abituale; ~**ly** *ad* regolarmente.
regulate [ˈreɡjuleɪt] *vt* regolare; **regulation** [-ˈleɪʃən] *n* (*rule*) regola, regolamento; (*adjustment*) regolazione *f*.
rehabilitation [ˈriːhəbɪlɪˈteɪʃən] *n* (*of offender*) riabilitazione *f*; (*of disabled*) riadattamento.
rehearsal [rɪˈhəːsəl] *n* prova.
rehearse [rɪˈhəːs] *vt* provare.
reign [reɪn] *n* regno // *vi* regnare.
reimburse [riːɪmˈbəːs] *vt* rimborsare.
rein [reɪn] *n* (*for horse*) briglia.
reindeer [ˈreɪndɪə*] *n* (*pl inv*) renna.
reinforce [riːɪnˈfɔːs] *vt* rinforzare; ~**d concrete** *n* cemento armato; ~**ments** *npl* (*MIL*) rinforzi *mpl*.
reinstate [riːɪnˈsteɪt] *vt* reintegrare.
reiterate [riːˈɪtəreɪt] *vt* reiterare, ripetere.
reject *n* [ˈriːdʒekt] (*COMM*) scarto // *vt* [rɪˈdʒekt] rifiutare, respingere; (*COMM: goods*) scartare; ~**ion** [rɪˈdʒekʃən] *n* rifiuto.
rejoice [rɪˈdʒɔɪs] *vi*: to ~ (at *or* over) provare diletto in.
rejuvenate [rɪˈdʒuːvəneɪt] *vt* ringiovanire.
relapse [rɪˈlæps] *n* (*MED*) ricaduta.
relate [rɪˈleɪt] *vt* (*tell*) raccontare; (*connect*) collegare // *vi*: to ~ to (*connect*) riferirsi a; (*get on with*) stabilire un rapporto con; ~**d** *a* imparentato(a); collegato(a), connesso(a); **relating to** *prep* che riguarda, rispetto a.
relation [rɪˈleɪʃən] *n* (*person*) parente *m/f*; (*link*) rapporto, relazione *f*; ~**ship** *n* rapporto; (*personal ties*) rapporti *mpl*, relazioni *fpl*; (*also:* **family** ~**ship**) legami *mpl* di parentela.
relative [ˈrelətɪv] *n* parente *m/f* // *a* relativo(a); (*respective*) rispettivo(a).
relax [rɪˈlæks] *vi* rilasciarsi; (*person: unwind*) rilassarsi // *vt* rilasciare; (*mind, person*) rilassare; ~**ation** [riːlækˈseɪʃən] *n* rilasciamento; rilassamento; (*entertainment*) ricreazione *f*, svago; ~**ed** *a* rilasciato(a); rilassato(a); ~**ing** *a* rilassante.
relay [ˈriːleɪ] *n* (*SPORT*) corsa a staffetta // *vt* (*message*) trasmettere.
release [rɪˈliːs] *n* (*from prison*) rilascio; (*from obligation*) liberazione *f*; (*of gas etc*) emissione *f*; (*of film etc*) distribuzione *f*; (*record*) disco; (*device*) disinnesto // *vt* (*prisoner*) rilasciare; (*from obligation, wreckage etc*) liberare; (*book, film*) fare uscire; (*news*) rendere pubblico(a); (*gas etc*) emettere; (*TECH: catch, spring etc*) disinnestare; (*let go*)

rilasciare; lasciar andare; sciogliere.

relegate ['rɛləgeɪt] vt relegare; (SPORT): to be ~d essere retrocesso(a).

relent [rɪ'lɛnt] vi cedere; ~less a implacabile.

relevant ['rɛlɪvənt] a pertinente; (chapter) in questione; ~ to pertinente a.

reliability [rɪlaɪə'bɪlɪtɪ] n (of person) serietà; (of machine) affidabilità.

reliable [rɪ'laɪəbl] a (person, firm) fidato(a), che dà affidamento; (method) sicuro(a); (machine) affidabile; **reliably** ad: to be reliably informed sapere da fonti sicure.

reliance [rɪ'laɪəns] n: ~ (on) fiducia (in); bisogno (di).

relic ['rɛlɪk] n (REL) reliquia; (of the past) resto.

relief [rɪ'liːf] n (from pain, anxiety) sollievo; (help, supplies) soccorsi mpl; (of guard) cambio; (ART, GEO) rilievo.

relieve [rɪ'liːv] vt (pain, patient) sollevare; (bring help) soccorrere; (take over from: gen) sostituire; (: guard) rilevare; to ~ sb of sth (load) alleggerire qn di qc; to ~ o.s. fare i propri bisogni.

religion [rɪ'lɪdʒən] n religione f; **religious** a religioso(a).

relinquish [rɪ'lɪŋkwɪʃ] vt abbandonare; (plan, habit) rinunziare a.

relish ['rɛlɪʃ] n (CULIN) condimento; (enjoyment) gran piacere m // vt (food etc) godere; to ~ doing adorare fare.

relocate ['riːləʊ'keɪt] vt trasferire // vi trasferirsi.

reluctance [rɪ'lʌktəns] n riluttanza.

reluctant [rɪ'lʌktənt] a riluttante, mal disposto(a); ~ly ad di mala voglia, a malincuore.

rely [rɪ'laɪ]: to ~ on vt fus contare su; (be dependent) dipendere da.

remain [rɪ'meɪn] vi restare, rimanere; ~der n resto; (COMM) rimanenza; ~ing a che rimane; ~s npl resti mpl.

remand [rɪ'mɑːnd] n: on ~ in detenzione preventiva // vt: to be in ~ custody rinviare in carcere; trattenere a disposizione della legge; ~ home n (Brit) riformatorio, casa di correzione.

remark [rɪ'mɑːk] n osservazione f // vt osservare, dire; (notice) notare; ~able a notevole; eccezionale.

remedial [rɪ'miːdɪəl] a (tuition, classes) di riparazione.

remedy ['rɛmədɪ] n: ~ (for) rimedio (per) // vt rimediare a.

remember [rɪ'mɛmbə*] vt ricordare, ricordarsi di; **remembrance** n memoria; ricordo.

remind [rɪ'maɪnd] vt: to ~ sb of sth ricordare qc a qn; to ~ sb to do ricordare a qn di fare; ~er n richiamo; (note etc) promemoria m inv.

reminisce [rɛmɪ'nɪs] vi: to ~ (about) abbandonarsi ai ricordi (di).

reminiscent [rɛmɪ'nɪsnt] a: ~ of che fa pensare a, che richiama.

remiss [rɪ'mɪs] a negligente.

remission [rɪ'mɪʃən] n remissione f; (of fee) esonero.

remit [rɪ'mɪt] vt (send: money) rimettere; ~tance n rimessa.

remnant ['rɛmnənt] n resto, avanzo; ~s npl (COMM) scampoli mpl; fine f serie.

remorse [rɪ'mɔːs] n rimorso; ~ful a pieno(a) di rimorsi; ~less a (fig) spietato(a).

remote [rɪ'məʊt] a remoto(a), lontano(a); (person) distaccato(a); ~ control n telecomando; ~ly ad remotamente; (slightly) vagamente.

remould ['riːməʊld] n (Brit: tyre) gomma rivestita.

removable [rɪ'muːvəbl] a (detachable) staccabile.

removal [rɪ'muːvəl] n (taking away) rimozione f; soppressione f; (Brit: from house) trasloco; (from office: dismissal) destituzione f; (MED) ablazione f; ~ van n (Brit) furgone m per traslochi.

remove [rɪ'muːv] vt togliere, rimuovere; (employee) destituire; (stain) far sparire; (doubt, abuse) sopprimere, eliminare; ~rs npl (Brit: company) ditta or impresa di traslochi.

Renaissance [rɪ'neɪsɑːns] n: the ~ il Rinascimento.

render ['rɛndə*] vt rendere; (CULIN: fat) struggere; ~ing n (MUS etc) interpretazione f.

rendez-vous ['rɔndɪvuː] n appuntamento; (place) luogo d'incontro; (meeting) incontro.

renegade ['rɛnɪgeɪd] n rinnegato/a.

renew [rɪ'njuː] vt rinnovare; (negotiations) riprendere; ~al n rinnovamento; ripresa.

renounce [rɪ'naʊns] vt rinunziare a; (disown) ripudiare.

renovate ['rɛnəveɪt] vt rinnovare; (art work) restaurare; **renovation** [-'veɪʃən] n rinnovamento; restauro.

renown [rɪ'naʊn] n rinomanza; ~ed a rinomato(a).

rent [rɛnt] n affitto // vt (take for rent) prendere in affitto; (also: ~ out) dare in affitto; ~al n (for television, car) fitto.

renunciation [rɪnʌnsɪ'eɪʃən] n rinnegamento; (self-denial) rinunzia.

rep [rɛp] n abbr (COMM: = representative) rappresentante m/f; (THEATRE: = repertory) teatro di repertorio.

repair [rɪ'pɛə*] n riparazione f // vt riparare; in good/bad ~ in buona/cattiva condizione; ~ kit n corredo per riparazioni; ~ shop n (AUT etc) officina.

repartee [rɛpɑː'tiː] n risposta pronta.

repatriate [riː'pætrieit] *vt* rimpatriare.

repay [riː'pei] *vt irg* (*money, creditor*) rimborsare, ripagare; (*sb's efforts*) ricompensare; **~ment** *n* rimborsamento; ricompensa.

repeal [riː'piːl] *n* (*of law*) abrogazione *f*; (*of sentence*) annullamento // *vt* abrogare; annullare.

repeat [riː'piːt] *n* (*RADIO, TV*) replica // *vt* ripetere; (*pattern*) riprodurre; (*promise, attack, also COMM: order*) rinnovare // *vi* ripetere; **~edly** *ad* ripetutamente, spesso.

repel [ri'pel] *vt* respingere; **~lent** *a* repellente // *n*: insect **~lent** prodotto *m* anti-insetti *inv*.

repent [ri'pent] *vi*: to **~** (of) pentirsi (di); **~ance** *n* pentimento.

repertoire ['repətwɑ:*] *n* repertorio.

repertory ['repətəri] *n* (*also*: **~ theatre**) teatro di repertorio.

repetition [repɪ'tɪʃən] *n* ripetizione *f*; (*COMM: of order etc*) rinnovo.

repetitive [ri'petitiv] *a* (*movement*) che si ripete; (*work*) monotono(a); (*speech*) pieno(a) di ripetizioni.

replace [ri'pleis] *vt* (*put back*) rimettere a posto; (*take the place of*) sostituire; **~ment** *n* rimessa; sostituzione *f*; (*person*) sostituto/a.

replay ['riːplei] *n* (*of match*) partita ripetuta; (*of tape, film*) replay *m inv*.

replenish [ri'plenɪʃ] *vt* (*glass*) riempire; (*stock etc*) rifornire.

replete [ri'pliːt] *a* ripieno(a); (*well-fed*) sazio(a).

replica ['replikə] *n* replica, copia.

reply [ri'plai] *n* risposta // *vi* rispondere; **~ coupon** *n* buono di risposta.

report [ri'pɔːt] *n* rapporto; (*PRESS etc*) cronaca; (*Brit: also*: **school ~**) pagella // *vt* riportare; (*PRESS etc*) fare una cronaca su; (*bring to notice: occurrence*) segnalare; (: *person*) denunciare // *vi* (*make a report*) fare un rapporto (*or* una cronaca); (*present o.s.*): to **~** (to sb) presentarsi (a qn); **~ card** *n* (*US, Scottish*) pagella; **~edly** *ad* stando a quanto si dice; he **~edly** told them to ... avrebbe detto loro di ...; **~er** *n* reporter *m inv*.

repose [ri'pəuz] *n*: in **~** (*face, mouth*) in riposo.

reprehensible [repri'hensɪbl] *a* riprensibile.

represent [repri'zent] *vt* rappresentare; **~ation** [-'teiʃən] *n* rappresentazione *f*; **~ations** *npl* (*protest*) protesta; **~ative** *n* rappresentativo/a; (*US POL*) deputato/a // *a* rappresentativo(a), caratteristico(a).

repress [ri'pres] *vt* reprimere; **~ion** [-'preʃən] *n* repressione *f*.

reprieve [ri'priːv] *n* (*LAW*) sospensione *f* dell'esecuzione della condanna; (*fig*) dilazione *f*.

reprimand ['reprimɑːnd] *n* rimprovero // *vt* rimproverare.

reprisal [ri'praizl] *n* rappresaglia.

reproach [ri'prəutʃ] *n* rimprovero // *vt*: to **~** sb with sth rimproverare qn di qc; **~ful** *a* di rimprovero.

reproduce [riːprə'djuːs] *vt* riprodurre // *vi* riprodursi; **reproduction** [-'dʌkʃən] *n* riproduzione *f*.

reproof [ri'pruːf] *n* riprovazione *f*.

reprove [ri'pruːv] *vt* (*action*) disapprovare; (*person*): to **~** (for) biasimare (per).

reptile ['reptail] *n* rettile *m*.

republic [ri'pʌblɪk] *n* repubblica; **~an** *a, n* repubblicano(a).

repulse [ri'pʌls] *vt* respingere.

repulsive [ri'pʌlsiv] *a* ripugnante, ripulsivo(a).

reputable ['repjutəbl] *a* di buona reputazione; (*occupation*) rispettabile.

reputation [repju'teiʃən] *n* reputazione *f*.

repute [ri'pjuːt] *n* reputazione *f*; **~d** *a* reputato(a); **~dly** *ad* secondo quanto si dice.

request [ri'kwest] *n* domanda; (*formal*) richiesta // *vt*: to **~** (of *or* from sb) chiedere (a qn); **~ stop** *n* (*Brit: for bus*) fermata facoltativa *or* a richiesta.

require [ri'kwaiə*] *vt* (*need: subj: person*) aver bisogno di; (: *thing, situation*) richiedere; (*want*) volere; esigere; (*order*) obbligare; **~ment** *n* esigenza; bisogno; requisito.

requisite ['rekwizit] *n* cosa necessaria // *a* necessario(a).

requisition [rekwi'ziʃən] *n*: **~** (for) richiesta (di) // *vt* (*MIL*) requisire.

rescue ['reskjuː] *n* salvataggio; (*help*) soccorso // *vt* salvare; **~ party** *n* squadra di salvataggio; **~r** *n* salvatore/trice.

research [ri'səːtʃ] *n* ricerca, ricerche *fpl* // *vt* fare ricerche su.

resemblance [ri'zembləns] *n* somiglianza.

resemble [ri'zembl] *vt* assomigliare a.

resent [ri'zent] *vt* risentirsi di; **~ful** *a* pieno(a) di risentimento; **~ment** *n* risentimento.

reservation [rezə'veiʃən] *n* (*booking*) prenotazione *f*; (*doubt*) dubbio; (*protected area*) riserva; (*Brit: on road: also*: **central ~**) spartitraffico *m inv*; to make a **~** (*in an hotel/a restaurant/on a plane*) prenotare (una camera/una tavola/un posto).

reserve [ri'zəːv] *n* riserva // *vt* (*seats etc*) prenotare; **~s** *npl* (*MIL*) riserve *fpl*; in **~** in serbo; **~d** *a* (*shy*) riservato(a); (*seat*) prenotato(a).

reservoir ['rezəvwɑː*] *n* serbatoio.

reshuffle [riː'ʃʌfl] *n*: **Cabinet ~** (*POL*) rimpasto governativo.

reside [ri'zaid] *vi* risiedere.

residence ['rezidəns] *n* residenza; **~**

permit n (Brit) permesso di soggiorno.
resident ['rezidənt] n residente m/f; (in hotel) cliente m/f fisso(a) // a residente; ~**ial** [-'denʃəl] a di residenza; (area) residenziale.
residue ['rezidju:] n resto; (CHEM. PHYSICS) residuo.
resign [ri'zain] vt (one's post) dimettersi da // vi dimettersi; **to** ~ **o.s. to** rassegnarsi a; ~**ation** [rezig'neiʃən] n dimissioni fpl; rassegnazione f; ~**ed** a rassegnato(a).
resilience [ri'ziliəns] n (of material) elasticità, resilienza; (of person) capacità di recupero.
resilient [ri'ziliənt] a (person) che si riprende facilmente.
resin ['rezin] n resina.
resist [ri'zist] vt resistere a; ~**ance** n resistenza.
resolution [rezə'lu:ʃən] n risoluzione f.
resolve [ri'zolv] n risoluzione f // vi (decide): **to** ~ **to do** decidere di fare // vt (problem) risolvere.
resort [ri'zo:t] n (town) stazione f; (recourse) ricorso // vi: **to** ~ **to** aver ricorso a; **as a last** ~ come ultimo ricorso.
resounding [ri'zaundiŋ] a risonante; (fig) clamoroso(a).
resource [ri'so:s] n risorsa; ~**s** npl risorse fpl; ~**ful** a pieno(a) di risorse, intraprendente.
respect [ris'pekt] n rispetto // vt rispettare; ~**s** npl ossequi mpl; **with** ~ **to** rispetto a, riguardo a; **in this** ~ per questo riguardo; ~**able** a rispettabile; ~**ful** a rispettoso(a).
respective [ris'pektiv] a rispettivo(a).
respite ['respait] n respiro, tregua.
resplendent [ris'plendənt] a risplendente.
respond [ris'pond] vi rispondere.
response [ris'pons] n risposta.
responsibility [risponsi'biliti] n responsabilità f inv.
responsible [ris'ponsibl] a (trustworthy) fidato(a); (job) di (grande) responsabilità; (liable): ~ (for) responsabile (di); **responsibly** ad responsabilmente.
responsive [ris'ponsiv] a che reagisce.
rest [rest] n riposo; (stop) sosta, pausa; (MUS) pausa; (support) appoggio, sostegno; (remainder) resto, avanzi mpl // vi riposarsi; (remain) rimanere, restare; (be supported): **to** ~ **on** appoggiarsi su // vt (lean): **to** ~ **sth on/against** appoggiare qc su/contro; **the** ~ **of them** gli altri; **it** ~**s with him to decide** sta a lui decidere.
restaurant ['restərɔŋ] n ristorante m; ~ **car** n (Brit) vagone m ristorante.
restful ['restful] a riposante.
rest home n casa di riposo.
restitution [resti'tju:ʃən] n (act) re-

stituzione f; (reparation) riparazione f.
restive ['restiv] a agitato(a), impaziente; (horse) restio(a).
restless ['restlis] a agitato(a), irrequieto(a).
restoration [restə'reiʃən] n restauro; restituzione f.
restore [ri'sto:*] vt (building) restaurare; (sth stolen) restituire; (peace, health) ristorare.
restrain [ris'trein] vt (feeling) contenere, frenare; (person): **to** ~ (**from doing**) trattenere (dal fare); ~**ed** a (style) contenuto(a), sobrio(a); (manner) riservato(a); ~**t** n (restriction) limitazione f; (moderation) ritegno.
restrict [ris'trikt] vt restringere, limitare; ~**ion** [-kʃən] n restrizione f, limitazione f.
rest room n (US) toletta.
restructure [ri:'strʌktʃə*] vt ristrutturare.
result [ri'zʌlt] n risultato // vi: **to** ~ **in** avere per risultato; **as a** ~ **of** in or di conseguenza a, in seguito a.
resume [ri'zju:m] vt, vi (work, journey) riprendere.
résumé ['reizjumei] n riassunto.
resumption [ri'zʌmpʃən] n ripresa.
resurgence [ri'sə:dʒəns] n rinascita.
resurrection [rezə'rekʃən] n risurrezione f.
resuscitate [ri'sʌsiteit] vt (MED) risuscitare; **resuscitation** [-'teiʃən] n rianimazione f.
retail ['ri:teil] n (vendita al) minuto // cpd al minuto // vt vendere al minuto; ~**er** n commerciante m/f al minuto, dettagliante m/f; ~ **price** n prezzo al minuto.
retain [ri'tein] vt (keep) tenere, serbare; ~**er** n (servant) servitore m; (fee) onorario.
retaliate [ri'tælieit] vi: **to** ~ (**against**) vendicarsi (di); **retaliation** [-'eiʃən] n rappresaglie fpl.
retarded [ri'tɑ:did] a ritardato(a); (also: **mentally** ~) tardo(a) (di mente).
retch [retʃ] vi aver conati di vomito.
retire [ri'taiə*] vi (give up work) andare in pensione; (withdraw) ritirarsi, andarsene; (go to bed) andare a letto, ritirarsi; ~**d** a (person) pensionato(a); ~**ment** n pensione f; **retiring** a (person) riservato(a).
retort [ri'tɔ:t] n (reply) rimbecco; (container) storta // vi rimbeccare.
retrace [ri:'treis] vt ricostruire; **to** ~ **one's steps** tornare sui passi.
retract [ri'trækt] vt (statement) ritrattare; (claws, undercarriage, aerial) ritrarre, ritirare // vi ritrarsi.
retrain [ri:'trein] vt (worker) riaddestrare.
retread ['ri:tred] n (tyre) gomma rigenerata.

retreat [rɪ'tri:t] *n* ritirata; *(place)* rifugio // *vi* battere in ritirata; *(flood)* ritirarsi.

retribution [retrɪ'bju:ʃən] *n* castigo.

retrieval [rɪ'tri:vəl] *n* *(see vb)* ricupero; riparazione *f*.

retrieve [rɪ'tri:v] *vt* *(sth lost)* ricuperare, ritrovare; *(situation, honour)* salvare; *(error, loss)* riparare; *(COMPUT)* ricuperare; ~**r** *n* cane *m* da riporto.

retrospect ['retrəspekt] *n*: in ~ guardando indietro; ~**ive** [-'spektɪv] *a* retrospettivo(a); *(law)* retroattivo(a).

return [rɪ'tə:n] *n* *(going or coming back)* ritorno; *(of sth stolen etc)* restituzione *f*; *(recompense)* ricompensa; *(FINANCE: from land, shares)* profitto, reddito; *(report)* rapporto // *cpd* *(journey, match)* di ritorno; *(Brit: ticket)* di andata e ritorno // *vi* tornare, ritornare // *vt* rendere, restituire; *(bring back)* riportare; *(send back)* mandare indietro; *(put back)* rimettere; *(POL: candidate)* eleggere; ~**s** *npl* *(COMM)* incassi *mpl*; profitti *mpl*; in ~ *(for)* in cambio *(di)*; by ~ of post a stretto giro di posta; many happy ~**s** *(of the day)*! auguri!, buon compleanno!

reunion [ri:'ju:nɪən] *n* riunione *f*.

reunite [ri:ju:'naɪt] *vt* riunire.

rev [rev] *n abbr* (= *revolution*: *AUT*) giro // *vb* *(also:* ~ up) *vt* imballare // *vi* imballarsi.

revamp ['ri:'væmp] *vt* *(house)* rinnovare; *(firm)* riorganizzare.

reveal [rɪ'vi:l] *vt* *(make known)* rivelare, svelare; *(display)* rivelare, mostrare; ~**ing** *a* rivelatore(trice); *(dress)* scollato(a).

reveille [rɪ'vælɪ] *n* *(MIL)* sveglia.

revel ['revl] *vi*: to ~ in sth/in doing dilettarsi di qc/a fare.

revelation [revə'leɪʃən] *n* rivelazione *f*.

revelry ['revlrɪ] *n* baldoria.

revenge [rɪ'vendʒ] *n* vendetta; *(in game etc)* rivincita // *vt* vendicare; to take ~ vendicarsi.

revenue ['revənju:] *n* reddito.

reverberate [rɪ'və:bəreɪt] *vi* *(sound)* rimbombare; *(light)* riverberarsi.

reverence ['revərəns] *n* venerazione *f*, riverenza.

Reverend ['revərənd] *a* *(in titles)* reverendo(a).

reverie ['revərɪ] *n* fantasticheria.

reversal [rɪ'və:sl] *n* capovolgimento.

reverse [rɪ'və:s] *n* contrario, opposto; *(back)* rovescio; *(AUT: also:* ~ gear) marcia indietro // *a* *(order, direction)* contrario(a), opposto(a) // *vt* *(turn)* invertire, rivoltare; *(change)* capovolgere, rovesciare; *(LAW: judgment)* cassare // *vi* *(Brit AUT)* fare marcia indietro; ~**d charge call** *n* *(Brit TEL)* telefonata con addebito al ricevente; **reversing lights** *npl* *(Brit AUT)* luci *fpl* per la retromarcia.

revert [rɪ'və:t] *vi*: to ~ to tornare a.

review [rɪ'vju:] *n* rivista; *(of book, film)* recensione *f* // *vt* passare in rivista; fare la recensione di; ~**er** *n* recensore/a.

revile [rɪ'vaɪl] *vt* insultare.

revise [rɪ'vaɪz] *vt* *(manuscript)* rivedere, correggere; *(opinion)* emendare, modificare; *(study: subject, notes)* ripassare; **revision** [rɪ'vɪʒən] *n* revisione *f*; ripasso.

revitalize [ri:'vaɪtəlaɪz] *vt* ravvivare.

revival [rɪ'vaɪvəl] *n* ripresa; ristabilimento; *(of faith)* risveglio.

revive [rɪ'vaɪv] *vt* *(person)* rianimare; *(custom)* far rivivere; *(hope, courage)* ravvivare; *(play, fashion)* riesumare // *vi* *(person)* rianimarsi; *(hope)* ravvivarsi; *(activity)* riprendersi.

revolt [rɪ'vəult] *n* rivolta, ribellione *f* // *vi* rivoltarsi, ribellarsi // *vt* *(far)* rivoltare; ~**ing** *a* ripugnante.

revolution [revə'lu:ʃən] *n* rivoluzione *f*; *(of wheel etc)* rivoluzione, giro; ~**ary** *a*, *n* rivoluzionario(a).

revolve [rɪ'vɔlv] *vi* girare.

revolver [rɪ'vɔlvə*] *n* rivoltella.

revolving [rɪ'vɔlvɪŋ] *a* girevole.

revue [rɪ'vju:] *n* *(THEATRE)* rivista.

revulsion [rɪ'vʌlʃən] *n* ripugnanza.

reward [rɪ'wɔ:d] *n* ricompensa, premio // *vt*: to ~ *(for)* ricompensare *(per)*; ~**ing** *a* *(fig)* soddisfacente.

rewind [ri:'waɪnd] *vt* *irg* *(watch)* ricaricare; *(ribbon etc)* riavvolgere.

rewire [ri:'waɪə*] *vt* *(house)* rifare l'impianto elettrico di.

reword [ri:'wə:d] *vt* formulare *or* esprimere con altre parole.

rheumatism ['ru:mətɪzəm] *n* reumatismo.

Rhine [raɪn] *n*: the ~ il Reno.

rhinoceros [raɪ'nɔsərəs] *n* rinoceronte *m*.

rhododendron [rəudə'dendrən] *n* rododendro.

Rhone [rəun] *n*: the ~ il Rodano.

rhubarb ['ru:bɑ:b] *n* rabarbaro.

rhyme [raɪm] *n* rima; *(verse)* poesia.

rhythm ['rɪðm] *n* ritmo.

rib [rɪb] *n* *(ANAT)* costola // *vt* *(tease)* punzecchiare.

ribald ['rɪbəld] *a* licenzioso(a), volgare.

ribbon ['rɪbən] *n* nastro; in ~**s** *(torn)* a brandelli.

rice [raɪs] *n* riso.

rich [rɪtʃ] *a* ricco(a); *(clothes)* sontuoso(a); the ~ *npl* i ricchi; ~**es** *npl* ricchezze *fpl*; ~**ly** *ad* riccamente; *(dressed)* sontuosamente; *(deserved)* pienamente; ~**ness** *n* ricchezza.

rickets ['rɪkɪts] *n* rachitismo.

rickety ['rɪkɪtɪ] *a* zoppicante.

rickshaw ['rɪkʃɔ:] *n* risciò *m inv*.

ricochet ['rɪkəʃeɪ] *n* rimbalzo // *vi* rimbalzare.

rid, *pt*, *pp* **rid** [rɪd] *vt*: **to ~ sb of** sbarazzare *or* liberare qn di; **to get ~ of** sbarazzarsi di.

ridden ['rɪdn] *pp of* **ride**.

riddle ['rɪdl] *n* (*puzzle*) indovinello // *vt*: **to be ~d with** essere crivellato(a) di.

ride [raɪd] *n* (*on horse*) cavalcata; (*outing*) passeggiata; (*distance covered*) cavalcata; corsa // *vb* (*pt* **rode**, *pp* **ridden**) *vi* (*as sport*) cavalcare; (*go somewhere: on horse, bicycle*) andare (a cavallo *or* in bicicletta *etc*); (*journey: on bicycle, motorcycle, bus*) andare, viaggiare // *vt* (*a horse*) montare, cavalcare; **to ~ a horse/bicycle/camel** montare a cavallo/in bicicletta/in groppa a un cammello; **to ~ at anchor** (*NAUT*) essere alla fonda; **to take sb for a ~** (*fig*) prendere in giro qn; fregare qn; **~r** *n* cavalcatore/trice; (*in race*) fantino; (*on bicycle*) ciclista *m/f*; (*on motorcycle*) motociclista *m/f*; (*in document*) clausola addizionale, aggiunta.

ridge [rɪdʒ] *n* (*of hill*) cresta; (*of roof*) colmo; (*of mountain*) giogo; (*on object*) riga (in rilievo).

ridicule ['rɪdɪkjuːl] *n* ridicolo; scherno // *vt* mettere in ridicolo.

ridiculous [rɪ'dɪkjuləs] *a* ridicolo(a).

riding ['raɪdɪŋ] *n* equitazione *f*; **~ school** *n* scuola d'equitazione.

rife [raɪf] *a* diffuso(a); **to be ~ with** abbondare di.

riffraff ['rɪfræf] *n* canaglia.

rifle ['raɪfl] *n* carabina // *vt* vuotare; **~ range** *n* campo di tiro; (*at fair*) tiro a segno.

rift [rɪft] *n* fessura, crepatura; (*fig: disagreement*) incrinatura, disaccordo.

rig [rɪg] *n* (*also: oil ~: on land*) derrick *m inv*; (*: at sea*) piattaforma di trivellazione // *vt* (*election etc*) truccare; **to ~ out** (*Brit*) attrezzare; (*pej*) abbigliare, agghindare; **to ~ up** *vt* allestire; **~ging** *n* (*NAUT*) attrezzatura.

right [raɪt] *a* giusto(a); (*suitable*) appropriato(a); (*not left*) destro(a) // *n* (*title, claim*) diritto; (*not left*) destra // *ad* (*answer*) correttamente; (*not on the left*) a destra // *vt* raddrizzare; (*fig*) riparare // *excl* bene!; **to be ~** (*person*) aver ragione; (*answer*) essere giusto(a) *or* corretto(a); **by ~s** di diritto; **on the ~** a destra; **to be in the ~** aver ragione, essere nel giusto; **~ now** proprio adesso; subito; **~ against the wall** proprio contro il muro; **~ ahead** sempre diritto; proprio davanti; **~ in the middle** proprio nel mezzo; **~ away** subito; **~ angle** *n* angolo retto; **~eous** ['raɪtʃəs] *a* retto(a), virtuoso(a); (*anger*) giusto(a), giustificato(a); **~ful** *a* (*heir*) legittimo(a); **~-handed** *a* (*person*) che adopera la mano destra; **~-hand man** *n* braccio destro; **~-hand side** *n* lato destro; **~ly**

ad bene, correttamente; (*with reason*) a ragione; **~ of way** *n* diritto di passaggio; (*AUT*) precedenza; **~-wing** *a* (*POL*) di destra.

rigid ['rɪdʒɪd] *a* rigido(a); (*principle*) rigoroso(a).

rigmarole ['rɪgmərəul] *n* tiritera; commedia.

rigorous ['rɪgərəs] *a* rigoroso(a).

rile [raɪl] *vt* irritare, seccare.

rim [rɪm] *n* orlo; (*of spectacles*) montatura; (*of wheel*) cerchione *m*.

rind [raɪnd] *n* (*of bacon*) cotenna; (*of lemon etc*) scorza.

ring [rɪŋ] *n* anello; (*also: wedding ~*) fede *f*; (*of people, objects*) cerchio; (*of spies*) giro; (*of smoke etc*) spirale *m*; (*arena*) pista, arena; (*for boxing*) ring *m inv*; (*sound of bell*) scampanio; (*telephone call*) colpo di telefono // *vb* (*pt* **rang**, *pp* **rung**) *vi* (*person, bell, telephone*) suonare; (*also: ~ out: voice, words*) risuonare; (*TEL*) telefonare // *vt* (*Brit TEL: also: ~ up*) telefonare a; **to ~ the bell** suonare; **to ~ back** *vt*, *vi* (*TEL*) richiamare; **to ~ off** *vi* (*Brit TEL*) mettere giù, riattaccare; **~ing** *n* (*of bell*) scampanio; (*of telephone*) squillo; (*in ears*) ronzio; **~ing tone** *n* (*Brit TEL*) segnale *m* di libero; **~leader** *n* (*of gang*) capobanda *m*.

ringlets ['rɪŋlɪts] *npl* boccoli *mpl*.

ring road *n* (*Brit*) raccordo anulare.

rink [rɪŋk] *n* (*also: ice ~*) pista di pattinaggio.

rinse [rɪns] *n* risciacquatura; (*hair tint*) cachet *m inv* // *vt* sciacquare.

riot ['raɪət] *n* sommossa, tumulto // *vi* tumultuare; **to run ~** creare disordine; **~ous** *a* tumultuoso(a); che fa crepare dal ridere.

rip [rɪp] *n* strappo // *vt* strappare // *vi* strapparsi; **~cord** *n* cavo di sfilamento.

ripe [raɪp] *a* (*fruit*) maturo(a); (*cheese*) stagionato(a); **~n** *vt* maturare // *vi* maturarsi; stagionarsi.

rip-off ['rɪpɔf] *n* (*col*): it's a ~! è un furto!

ripple ['rɪpl] *n* increspamento, ondulazione *f*; mormorio // *vi* incresparsi.

rise [raɪz] *n* (*slope*) salita, pendio; (*hill*) altura; (*increase: in wages: Brit*) aumento; (*: in prices, temperature*) rialzo, aumento; (*fig: to power etc*) ascesa // *vi* (*pt* **rose**, *pp* **risen** [rəuz, 'rɪzn]) alzarsi, levarsi; (*prices*) aumentare; (*waters, river*) crescere; (*sun, wind, person: from chair, bed*) levarsi; (*also: ~ up: rebel*) insorgere; ribellarsi; **to give ~ to** provocare, dare origine a; **to ~ to the occasion** essere all'altezza; **rising** *a* (*increasing: number*) sempre crescente; (*: prices*) in aumento; (*tide*) montante; (*sun, moon*) nascente, che sorge // n (*uprising*) sommossa.

risk [rɪsk] n rischio; pericolo // vt rischiare; **to take** or **run the ~ of doing** correre il rischio di fare; **at ~** in pericolo; **at one's own ~** a proprio rischio e pericolo; **~y** a rischioso(a).

risqué ['riːskeɪ] a (*joke*) spinto(a).

rissole ['rɪsəul] n crocchetta.

rite [raɪt] n rito; **last ~s** l'estrema unzione.

ritual ['rɪtjuəl] a, n rituale (m).

rival ['raɪvl] n rivale m/f; (*in business*) concorrente m/f // a rivale; che fa concorrenza // vt essere in concorrenza con; **to ~ sb/sth in** competere con qn/qc in; **~ry** n rivalità; concorrenza.

river ['rɪvə*] n fiume m // cpd (*port, traffic*) fluviale; **up/down ~** a monte/valle; **~bank** n argine m.

rivet ['rɪvɪt] n ribattino, rivetto // vt ribadire; (*fig*) concentrare, fissare.

Riviera [rɪvɪ'eərə] n: **the** (French) **~** la Costa Azzurra; **the Italian ~** la Riviera.

road [rəud] n strada; (*small*) cammino; (*in town*) via; **major/minor ~** strada con/senza diritto di precedenza; **~block** n blocco stradale; **~hog** n guidatore m egoista e spericolato; **~ map** n carta stradale; **~ safety** n sicurezza sulle strade; **~side** n margine m della strada; **~sign** n cartello stradale; **~way** n carreggiata; **~works** npl lavori mpl stradali; **~worthy** a in buono stato di marcia.

roam [rəum] vi errare, vagabondare // vt vagare per.

roar [rɔː*] n ruggito; (*of crowd*) tumulto; (*of thunder, storm*) muggito // vi ruggire; tumultuare; muggire; **to ~ with laughter** scoppiare dalle risa; **to do a ~ing trade** fare affari d'oro.

roast [rəust] n arrosto // vt (*meat*) arrostire; **~ beef** n arrosto di manzo.

rob [rɔb] vt (*person*) rubare; (*bank*) svaligiare; **to ~ sb of sth** derubare qn di qc; (*fig: deprive*) privare qn di qc; **~ber** n ladro; (*armed*) rapinatore m; **~bery** n furto; rapina.

robe [rəub] n (*for ceremony etc*) abito; (*also:* **bath ~**) accappatoio; (*US: cover*) coperta // vt vestire.

robin ['rɔbɪn] n pettirosso.

robot ['rəubɔt] n robot m inv.

robust [rəu'bʌst] a robusto(a); (*material*) solido(a).

rock [rɔk] n (*substance*) roccia; (*boulder*) masso; roccia; (*in sea*) scoglio; (*Brit: sweet*) zucchero candito // vt (*swing gently: cradle*) dondolare; (: *child*) cullare; (*shake*) scrollare, far tremare // vi dondolarsi; scrollarsi, tremare; **on the ~s** (*drink*) col ghiaccio; (*ship*) sugli scogli; (*marriage etc*) in crisi; **~ and roll** n rock and roll m; **~-**

bottom n (*fig*) stremo // a bassissimo(a); **~ery** n giardino roccioso.

rocket ['rɔkɪt] n razzo; (*MIL*) razzo, missile m.

rock fall n caduta di massi.

rocking ['rɔkɪŋ]: **~ chair** n sedia a dondolo; **~ horse** n cavallo a dondolo.

rocky ['rɔkɪ] a (*hill*) roccioso(a); (*path*) sassoso(a); (*unsteady: table*) traballante.

rod [rɔd] n (*metallic, TECH*) asta; (*wooden*) bacchetta; (*also:* **fishing ~**) canna da pesca.

rode [rəud] pt of **ride.**

rodent ['rəudnt] n roditore m.

rodeo ['rəudɪəu] n rodeo.

roe [rəu] n (*species: also:* **~ deer**) capriolo; (*of fish, also:* **hard ~**) uova fpl di pesce; **soft ~** latte m di pesce.

rogue [rəug] n mascalzone m.

role [rəul] n ruolo.

roll [rəul] n rotolo; (*of banknotes*) mazzo; (*also:* **bread ~**) panino; (*register*) lista; (*sound: of drums etc*) rullo; (*movement: of ship*) rullio // vt rotolare; (*also:* **~ up: string**) aggomitolare; (*also:* **~ out: pastry**) stendere // vi rotolare; (*wheel*) girare; **to ~ about** or **around** vi rotolare qua e là; (*person*) rotolarsi; **to ~ by** vi (*time*) passare; **to ~ in** vi (*mail, cash*) arrivare a bizzeffe; **to ~ over** vi rivoltarsi; **to ~ up** vi (*col: arrive*) arrivare // vt (*carpet*) arrotolare; **~ call** n appello; **~er** n rullo; (*wheel*) rotella; **~er coaster** n montagne fpl russe; **~er skates** npl pattini mpl a rotelle.

rolling ['rəulɪŋ] a (*landscape*) ondulato(a); **~ pin** n matterello; **~ stock** n (*RAIL*) materiale m rotabile.

ROM [rɔm] n abbr (= *read only memory*) memoria di sola lettura.

Roman ['rəumən] a, n romano(a); **~ Catholic** a, n cattolico(a).

romance [rə'mæns] n storia (*or avventura or film m inv*) romantico(a); (*charm*) poesia; (*love affair*) idillio.

Romania [rəu'meɪnɪə] n = **Rumania.**

Roman numeral n numero romano.

romantic [rə'mæntɪk] a romantico(a); sentimentale.

romanticism [rə'mæntɪsɪzəm] n romanticismo.

Rome [rəum] n Roma.

romp [rɔmp] n gioco rumoroso // vi (*also:* **~ about**) far chiasso, giocare in un modo rumoroso.

rompers ['rɔmpəz] npl pagliaccetto.

roof, pl **~s** [ruːf] n tetto; (*of tunnel, cave*) volta // vt coprire (con un tetto); **~ of the mouth** palato; **~ing** n materiale m per copertura; **~ rack** n (*AUT*) portabagagli m inv.

rook [ruk] n (*bird*) corvo nero; (*CHESS*)

torre f.

room [ruːm] n (in house) stanza; (also: bed~) camera; (in school etc) sala; (space) posto, spazio; ~s npl (lodging) alloggio; "~s to let", (US) "~s for rent" "si affittano camere"; ~**ing house** n (US) casa in cui si affittano camere o appartamentini ammobiliati; ~**mate** n compagno/a di stanza; ~ **service** n servizio da camera; ~**y** a spazioso(a); (garment) ampio(a).

roost [ruːst] n appollaiato // vi appollaiarsi.

rooster ['ruːstə*] n gallo.

root [ruːt] n radice f // vt (plant, belief) far radicare; **to ~ about** vi (fig) frugare; **to ~ for** vt fus fare il tifo per; **to ~ out** vt estirpare.

rope [rəup] n corda, fune f; (NAUT) cavo // vt (box) legare; (climbers) legare in cordata; **to ~ sb in** (fig) coinvolgere qn; **to know the ~s** (fig) conoscere i trucchi del mestiere.

rosary ['rəuzərı] n rosario; roseto.

rose [rəuz] pt of **rise** // n rosa; (also: ~ bush) rosaio; (on watering can) rosetta // a rosa inv.

rosé ['rəuzeı] n vino rosato.

rose: ~**bud** n bocciolo di rosa; ~**bush** n rosaio.

rosemary ['rəuzmərı] n rosmarino.

rosette [rəu'zɛt] n coccarda.

roster ['rɔstə*] n: **duty ~** ruolino di servizio.

rostrum ['rɔstrəm] n tribuna.

rosy ['rəuzı] a roseo(a).

rot [rɔt] n (decay) putrefazione f; (col: nonsense) stupidaggini fpl // vt, vi imputridire, marcire.

rota ['rəutə] n tabella dei turni; **on a ~ basis** a turno.

rotary ['rəutərı] a rotante.

rotate [rəu'teıt] vt (revolve) far girare; (change round: crops) avvicendare; (: jobs) fare a turno // vi (revolve) girare; **rotating** a (movement) rotante.

rote [rəut] n: **by ~** (by heart) a memoria; (mechanically) meccanicamente.

rotten ['rɔtn] a (decayed) putrido(a), marcio(a); (dishonest) corrotto(a); (col: bad) brutto(a); (: action) vigliacco(a); **to feel ~** (ill) sentirsi proprio male.

rouge [ruːʒ] n belletto.

rough [rʌf] a aspro(a); (person, manner: coarse) rozzo(a), aspro(a); (: violent) brutale; (district) malfamato(a); (weather) cattivo(a); (plan) abbozzato(a); (guess) approssimativo(a) // n (GOLF) macchia; **to ~ it** far vita dura; **to sleep ~** (Brit) dormire all'addiaccio; **to feel ~** sentirsi male; ~**age** n alimenti mpl ricchi in cellulosa; ~**-and-ready** a rudimentale; ~**cast** n intonaco grezzo; ~ **copy**, ~ **draft** n

brutta copia; ~**ly** ad (handle) rudemente, brutalmente; (make) grossolanamente; (approximately) approssimativamente.

roulette [ruː'lɛt] n roulette f.

Roumania [ruː'meınıə] n = **Rumania**.

round [raund] a rotondo(a) // n tondo, cerchio; (Brit: of toast) fetta; (duty: of policeman, milkman etc) giro; (: of doctor) visite fpl; (game: of cards, in competition) partita; (BOXING) round m inv; (of talks) serie f inv // vt (corner) girare; (bend) prendere; (cape) doppiare // prep intorno a // ad: **all ~** tutt'attorno; **to go the long way ~** fare il giro più lungo; **all the year ~** tutto l'anno; **it's just ~ the corner** (also fig) è dietro; l'angolo; ~ **the clock** ad ininterrottamente; **to go ~** fare il giro; **to go ~ to sb's house** andare da qn; **to go ~ the back** passi dietro; **to go ~ a house** visitare una casa; **enough to go ~** abbastanza per tutti; **to go the ~s** (story) circolare; ~ **of ammunition** n cartuccia; ~ **of applause** n applausi mpl; ~ **of drinks** n giro di bibite; ~ **of sandwiches** n sandwich m inv; **to ~ off** vt (speech etc) finire; **to ~ up** vt radunare; (criminals) fare una retata di; (prices) arrotondare; ~**about** n (Brit AUT) rotatoria; (: at fair) giostra // a (route, means) indiretto(a); ~**ers** npl (game) gioco simile al baseball; ~**ly** ad (fig) chiaro e tondo; ~**-shouldered** a dalle spalle tonde; ~ **trip** n (viaggio di) andata e ritorno; ~**up** n raduno; (of criminals) retata.

rouse [rauz] vt (wake up) svegliare; (stir up) destare; provocare; risvegliare; **rousing** a (speech, applause) entusiastico(a).

rout [raut] n (MIL) rotta.

route [ruːt] n itinerario; (of bus) percorso; (of trade, shipping) rotta; ~ **map** n (Brit: for journey) cartina di itinerario.

routine [ruː'tiːn] a (work) corrente, abituale; (procedure) solito(a) // n (pej) routine f, tran tran m; (THEATRE) numero; **daily ~** orario quotidiano.

roving ['rəuvıŋ] a (life) itinerante.

row [rəu] n (line) riga, fila; (KNITTING) ferro; (behind one another: of cars, people) fila; [rau] (noise) baccano, chiasso; (dispute) lite f // vi (in boat) remare; (as sport) vogare; [rau] litigare // vt (boat) manovrare a remi; **in a ~** (fig) di fila; ~**boat** n (US) barca a remi.

rowdy ['raudı] a chiassoso(a); turbolento(a) // n teppista m/f.

rowing ['rəuıŋ] n canottaggio; ~ **boat** n (Brit) barca a remi.

royal ['rɔıəl] a reale; **R~ Air Force (RAF)** n aeronautica militare britannica.

royalty ['rɔıəltı] n (royal persons) (membri *mpl* della) famiglia reale; *(payment: to author)* diritti *mpl* d'autore; (: *to inventor)* diritti di brevetto.

r.p.m. *abbr* (= *revolutions per minute)* giri/min.

R.S.V.P. *abbr* (= *répondez s'il vous plaît)* R.S.V.P.

Rt Hon. *abbr (Brit:* = *Right Honourable)* ≈ Onorevole.

rub [rʌb] *n (with cloth)* fregata, strofinata; *(on person)* frizione *f*, massaggio // *vt* fregare, strofinare; frizionare; to ~ sb up *or (US)* ~ sb the wrong way lisciare qn contro pelo; to ~ off *vi* andare via; to ~ off on *vt fus* lasciare una traccia su; to ~ out *vt* cancellare.

rubber ['rʌbə*] *n* gomma; ~ band *n* elastico; ~ plant *n* ficus *m inv*.

rubbish ['rʌbɪʃ] *n (from household)* immondizie *fpl*, rifiuti *mpl*; *(fig: pej)* cose *fpl* senza valore; robaccia; sciocchezze *fpl*; ~ bin *n (Brit)* pattumiera; ~ dump *n (in town)* immondezzaio.

rubble ['rʌbl] *n* macerie *fpl*; *(smaller)* pietrisco.

ruby ['ru:bɪ] *n* rubino.

rucksack ['rʌksæk] *n* zaino.

ructions ['rʌkʃənz] *npl* putiferio, finimondo.

rudder ['rʌdə*] *n* timone *m*.

ruddy ['rʌdɪ] *a (face)* fresco(a); *(col: damned)* maledetto(a).

rude [ru:d] *a (impolite: person)* scortese, rozzo(a); (: *word, manners)* grossolano(a), rozzo(a); *(shocking)* indecente; ~ness *n* scortesia; grossolanità.

rueful ['ru:ful] *a* mesto(a), triste.

ruffian ['rʌfɪən] *n* briccone *m*, furfante *m*.

ruffle ['rʌfl] *vt (hair)* scompigliare; *(clothes, water)* increspare; *(fig: person)* turbare.

rug [rʌg] *n* tappeto; *(Brit: for knees)* coperta.

rugby ['rʌgbɪ] *n (also:* ~ football) rugby *m*.

rugged ['rʌgɪd] *a (landscape)* aspro(a); *(features, determination)* duro(a); *(character)* brusco(a).

rugger ['rʌgə*] *n (Brit col)* rugby *m*.

ruin ['ru:ɪn] *n* rovina // *vt* rovinare; *(spoil: clothes)* sciupare; ~s *npl* rovine *fpl*, ruderi *mpl*; ~ous *a* rovinoso(a); *(expenditure)* inverosimile.

rule [ru:l] *n* regola; *(regulation)* regolamento, regola; *(government)* governo // *vt (country)* governare; *(person)* dominare; *(decide)* decidere // *vi* regnare; decidere; *(LAW)* dichiarare; as a ~ normalmente; to ~ out *vt* escludere; ~d *a (paper)* vergato(a); ~r *n (sovereign)* sovrano/a; *(leader)* capo (dello Stato); *(for measuring)*

regolo, riga; **ruling** *a (party)* al potere; *(class)* dirigente // *n (LAW)* decisione *f*.

rum [rʌm] *n* rum *m* // *a (col)* strano(a).

Rumania [ru:'meɪnɪə] *n* Romania.

rumble ['rʌmbl] *n* rimbombo; brontolio // *vi* rimbombare; *(stomach, pipe)* brontolare.

rummage ['rʌmɪdʒ] *vi* frugare.

rumour, *(US)* **rumor** ['ru:mə*] *n* voce *f* // *vt*: it is ~ed that corre voce che.

rump [rʌmp] *n (of animal)* groppa; ~ steak *n* bistecca di girello.

rumpus ['rʌmpəs] *n (col)* baccano; (: *quarrel)* rissa.

run [rʌn] *n* corsa; *(outing)* gita (in macchina); *(distance travelled)* percorso, tragitto; *(series)* serie *f*; *(THEATRE)* periodo di rappresentazione; *(SKI)* pista; *(in tights, stockings)* smagliatura // *vb (pt ran, pp run) vt (operate: business)* gestire, dirigere; (: *competition, course)* organizzare; (: *hotel)* gestire; (: *house)* governare; *(COMPUT)* eseguire; *(water, bath)* far scorrere; *(force through: rope, pipe)*: to ~ sth through far passare qc attraverso; *(to pass: hand, finger)*: to ~ sth over passare qc su // *vi* correre; *(pass: road etc)* passare; *(work: machine, factory)* funzionare, andare; *(bus, train: operate)* far servizio; (: *travel)* circolare; *(continue: play, contract)* durare; *(slide: drawer; flow: river, bath)* scorrere; *(colours, washing)* stemperarsi; *(in election)* presentarsi candidato; there was a ~ on ... c'era una corsa a ...; in the long ~ a lungo andare; on the ~ in fuga; I'll ~ you to the station la porto alla stazione; to ~ a risk correre un rischio; to ~ about *or* around *vi (children)* correre qua e là; to ~ across *vt fus (find)* trovare per caso; to ~ away *vi* fuggire; to ~ down *vi (clock)* scaricarsi // *vt (production)* ridurre gradualmente; *(factory)* rallentare l'attività di; *(AUT)* investire; *(criticize)* criticare; to be ~ down *(person: tired)* essere esausto(a); to ~ in *vt (Brit: car)* rodare, fare il rodaggio di; to ~ into *vt fus (meet: person)* incontrare per caso; (: *trouble)* incontrare, trovare; *(collide with)* andare a sbattere contro; to ~ off *vi* fuggire // *vt (copies)* fare; to ~ out *vi (person)* uscire di corsa; *(liquid)* colare; *(lease)* scadere; *(money)* esaurirsi; to ~ out of *vt fus* rimanere a corto di; to ~ over *vt (AUT)* investire, mettere sotto // *vt fus (revise)* rivedere; to ~ through *vt fus (instructions)* dare una scorsa a; to ~ up *vt (debt)* lasciar accumulare; to ~ up against *(difficulties)* incontrare; ~away *a (person)* fuggiasco(a); *(horse)* in libertà; *(truck)* fuori controllo; *(inflation)* galoppante.

rung [rʌŋ] *pp of* **ring** // *n* (*of ladder*) piolo.

runner ['rʌnə*] *n* (*in race*) corridore *m*; (*on sledge*) pattino; (*for drawer etc, carpet: in hall etc*) guida; ~ **bean** *n* (*Brit*) fagiolo rampicante; ~**-up** *n* secondo(a) arrivato(a).

running ['rʌnɪŋ] *n* corsa; direzione *f*; organizzazione *f*; funzionamento // *a* (*water*) corrente; (*commentary*) simultaneo(a); to be in/out of the ~ for sth essere/non essere più in lizza per qc; 6 days ~ 6 giorni di seguito.

runny ['rʌnɪ] *a* che cola.

run-of-the-mill ['rʌnəvðə'mɪl] *a* solito(a), banale.

runt [rʌnt] *n* (*also pej*) omuncolo; (*ZOOL*) animale *m* più piccolo del normale.

run-through ['rʌnθruː] *n* prova.

run-up ['rʌnʌp] *n*: ~ to (*election etc*) periodo che precede.

runway ['rʌnweɪ] *n* (*AVIAT*) pista (di decollo).

rupee [ruː'piː] *n* rupia.

rupture ['rʌptʃə*] *n* (*MED*) ernia.

rural ['ruərl] *a* rurale.

ruse [ruːz] *n* trucco.

rush [rʌʃ] *n* corsa precipitosa; (*of crowd*) afflusso; (*hurry*) furia, fretta; (*current*) flusso // *vt* mandare *or* spedire velocemente; (*attack: town etc*) prendere d'assalto // *vi* precipitarsi; ~**es** *npl* (*BOT*) giunchi *mpl*; ~ **hour** *n* ora di punta.

rusk [rʌsk] *n* biscotto.

Russia ['rʌʃə] *n* Russia; ~**n** *a* russo(a) // *n* russo/a; (*LING*) russo.

rust [rʌst] *n* ruggine *f* // *vi* arrugginirsi.

rustic ['rʌstɪk] *a* rustico(a).

rustle ['rʌsl] *vi* frusciare // *vt* (*paper*) far frusciare; (*US: cattle*) rubare.

rustproof ['rʌstpruːf] *a* inossidabile.

rusty ['rʌstɪ] *a* arrugginito(a).

rut [rʌt] *n* solco; (*ZOOL*) fregola; to get into a ~ (*fig*) adagiarsi troppo.

ruthless ['ruːθlɪs] *a* spietato(a).

rye [raɪ] *n* segale *f*; ~ **bread** *n* pane *m* di segale.

S

Sabbath ['sæbəθ] *n* (*Jewish*) sabato; (*Christian*) domenica.

sabotage ['sæbətɑːʒ] *n* sabotaggio // *vt* sabotare.

saccharin(e) ['sækərɪn] *n* saccarina.

sachet ['sæʃeɪ] *n* bustina.

sack [sæk] *n* (*bag*) sacco // *vt* (*dismiss*) licenziare, mandare a spasso; (*plunder*) saccheggiare; to get the ~ essere mandato a spasso; ~**ing** *n* tela di sacco; (*dismissal*) licenziamento.

sacrament ['sækrəmənt] *n* sacramento.

sacred ['seɪkrɪd] *a* sacro(a).

sacrifice ['sækrɪfaɪs] *n* sacrificio // *vt* sacrificare.

sad [sæd] *a* triste.

saddle ['sædl] *n* sella // *vt* (*horse*) sellare; to be ~d with sth (*col*) avere qc sulle spalle; ~**bag** *n* bisaccia; (*on bicycle*) borsa.

sadistic [sə'dɪstɪk] *a* sadico(a).

sadness ['sædnɪs] *n* tristezza.

s.a.e. *n abbr* = stamped addressed envelope.

safe [seɪf] *a* sicuro(a); (*out of danger*) salvo(a), al sicuro; (*cautious*) prudente // *n* cassaforte *f*; ~ from al sicuro da; ~ and sound sano(a) e salvo(a); (just) to be on the ~ side per non correre rischi; ~**-conduct** *n* salvacondotto; ~**-deposit** *n* (*vault*) caveau *m inv*; (*box*) cassetta di sicurezza; ~**guard** *n* salvaguardia // *vt* salvaguardare; ~**keeping** *n* custodia; ~**ly** *ad* sicuramente; sano(a) e salvo(a); prudentemente.

safety ['seɪftɪ] *n* sicurezza; ~ **belt** *n* cintura di sicurezza; ~ **pin** *n* spilla di sicurezza; ~ **valve** *n* valvola di sicurezza.

saffron ['sæfrən] *n* zafferano.

sag [sæg] *vi* incurvarsi; afflosciarsi.

sage [seɪdʒ] *n* (*herb*) salvia; (*man*) saggio.

Sagittarius [sædʒɪ'tɛərɪəs] *n* Sagittario.

Sahara [sə'hɑːrə] *n*: the ~ (Desert) il (deserto del) Sahara.

said [sed] *pt, pp of* **say**.

sail [seɪl] *n* (*on boat*) vela; (*trip*): to go for a ~ fare un giro in barca a vela // *vt* (*boat*) condurre, governare // *vi* (*travel: ship*) navigare; (: *passenger*) viaggiare per mare; (*set off*) salpare; (*sport*) fare della vela; they ~ed into Genoa entrarono nel porto di Genova; to ~ through (*fig*) *vt fus* superare senza difficoltà // *vi* farcela senza difficoltà; ~**boat** *n* (*US*) barca a vela; ~**ing** *n* (*sport*) vela; to go ~ing fare della vela; ~**ing boat** *n* barca a vela; ~**ing ship** *n* veliero; ~**or** *n* marinaio.

saint [seɪnt] *n* santo/a.

sake [seɪk] *n*: for the ~ of per, per amore di.

salad ['sæləd] *n* insalata; ~ **bowl** *n* insalatiera; ~ **cream** *n* (*Brit*) (tipo di) maionese *f*; ~ **dressing** *n* condimento per insalata.

salary ['sælərɪ] *n* stipendio.

sale [seɪl] *n* vendita; (*at reduced prices*) svendita, liquidazione *f*; "for ~" "in vendita"; on ~ in vendita; on ~ or return da vendere o rimandare; ~**room** *n* sala delle aste; ~**s assistant**, (*US*) ~**s clerk** *n* commesso/a; (*representative*) ~**sman** *n* rappresentante *m*; ~**swoman** *n* commessa.

salient ['seɪlɪənt] *a* saliente.

sallow ['sæləu] a giallastro(a).
salmon ['sæmən] n (pl inv) salmone m.
saloon [sə'lu:n] n (US) saloon m inv, bar m inv; (Brit AUT) berlina; (ship's lounge) salone m.
salt [sɔlt] n sale m // vt salare // cpd di sale; (CULIN) salato(a); **to ~ away** vt (col: money) mettere via; **~ cellar** n saliera; **~-water** a di mare; **~y** a salato(a).
salute [sə'lu:t] n saluto // vt salutare.
salvage ['sælvɪdʒ] n (saving) salvataggio; (things saved) beni mpl salvati or recuperati // vt salvare, mettere in salvo.
salvation [sæl'veɪʃən] n salvezza; **S~ Army** n Esercito della Salvezza.
same [seɪm] a stesso(a), medesimo(a) // pronoun: **the ~** lo(la) stesso(a), gli(le) stessi(e); **the ~ book** as lo stesso libro di (o che); **at the ~ time** allo stesso tempo; **all** or **just the ~** tuttavia; **to do the ~** fare la stessa cosa; **to do the ~** as sb fare come qn; **the ~ to you!** altrettanto a te!
sample ['sɑ:mpl] n campione m // vt (food) assaggiare; (wine) degustare.
sanctimonious [sæŋktɪ'məunɪəs] a bigotto(a), bacchettone(a).
sanction ['sæŋkʃən] n sanzione f // vt sancire, sanzionare.
sanctity ['sæŋktɪtɪ] n santità.
sanctuary ['sæŋktjuərɪ] n (holy place) santuario; (refuge) rifugio; (for wildlife) riserva.
sand [sænd] n sabbia // vt cospargere di sabbia.
sandal ['sændl] n sandalo.
sandbox ['sændbɔks] n (US) = **sandpit.**
sandcastle ['sændkɑ:sl] n castello di sabbia.
sandpaper ['sændpeɪpə*] n carta vetrata.
sandpit ['sændpɪt] n (for children) buca di sabbia.
sandstone ['sændstəun] n arenaria.
sandwich ['sændwɪtʃ] n tramezzino, panino, sandwich m inv // vt (also: ~ in) infilare; **~ed between** incastrato(a) fra; **cheese/ham ~** sandwich al formaggio/prosciutto; **~ course** n (Brit) corso di formazione professionale; **~ man** n uomo m sandwich inv.
sandy ['sændɪ] a sabbioso(a); (colour) color sabbia inv, biondo(a) rossiccio(a).
sane [seɪn] a (person) sano(a) di mente; (outlook) sensato(a).
sang [sæŋ] pt of **sing.**
sanitary ['sænɪtərɪ] a (system, arrangements) sanitario(a); (clean) igienico(a); **~ towel,** (US) **~ napkin** n assorbente m (igienico).
sanitation [sænɪ'teɪʃən] n (in house) impianti mpl sanitari; (in town) fognature fpl; **~ department** n (US)

nettezza urbana.
sanity ['sænɪtɪ] n sanità mentale; (common sense) buon senso.
sank [sæŋk] pt of **sink.**
Santa Claus [sæntə'klɔ:z] n Babbo Natale.
sap [sæp] n (of plants) linfa // vt (strength) fiaccare.
sapling ['sæplɪŋ] n alberello.
sapphire ['sæfaɪə*] n zaffiro.
sarcasm ['sɑ:kæzm] n sarcasmo.
sardine [sɑ:'di:n] n sardina.
Sardinia [sɑ:'dɪnɪə] n Sardegna.
sash [sæʃ] n fascia; **~ window** n finestra a ghigliottina.
sat [sæt] pt, pp of **sit.**
Satan ['seɪtən] n Satana m.
satchel ['sætʃl] n cartella.
sated ['seɪtɪd] a (appetite) soddisfatto(a); (person): **~ (with)** sazio(a) (di).
satellite ['sætəlaɪt] a, n satellite (m).
satin ['sætɪn] n raso // a di raso.
satire ['sætaɪə*] n satira.
satisfaction [sætɪs'fækʃən] n soddisfazione f.
satisfactory [sætɪs'fæktərɪ] a soddisfacente.
satisfy ['sætɪsfaɪ] vt soddisfare; (convince) convincere; **~ing** a soddisfacente.
Saturday ['sætədɪ] n sabato.
sauce [sɔ:s] n salsa; (containing meat, fish) sugo; **~pan** n casseruola.
saucer ['sɔ:sə*] n sottocoppa m, piattino.
saucy ['sɔ:sɪ] a impertinente.
Saudi ['saudɪ]: **~ Arabia** n Arabia Saudita; **~ (Arabian)** a, n arabo(a) saudita.
sauna ['sɔ:nə] n sauna.
saunter ['sɔ:ntə*] vi andare a zonzo, bighellonare.
sausage ['sɔsɪdʒ] n salsiccia; **~ roll** n rotolo di pasta sfoglia ripieno di salsiccia.
savage ['sævɪdʒ] a (cruel, fierce) selvaggio(a), feroce; (primitive) primitivo(a) // n selvaggio/a // vt attaccare selvaggiamente.
save [seɪv] vt (person, belongings, COMPUT) salvare; (money) risparmiare, mettere da parte; (time) risparmiare; (food) conservare; (avoid: trouble) evitare // vi (also: ~ up) economizzare // n (SPORT) parata // prep salvo, a eccezione di.
saving ['seɪvɪŋ] n risparmio // a: **the ~ grace of** l'unica cosa buona di; **~s** npl risparmi mpl; **~s bank** n cassa di risparmio.
saviour, (US) **savior** ['seɪvjə*] n salvatore m.
savour, (US) **savor** ['seɪvə*] n sapore m, gusto // vt gustare; **~y** a saporito(a); (dish: not sweet) salato(a).

saw [sɔ:] *pt of* **see** // *n* (*tool*) sega // *vt* (*pt* **sawed**, *pp* **sawed** *or* **sawn** [sɔ:n]) segare; **~dust** *n* segatura; **~mill** *n* segheria; **~n-off shotgun** *n* fucile *m* a canne mozze.

saxophone ['sæksəfəun] *n* sassofono.

say [seɪ] *n*: **to have one's ~** fare sentire il proprio parere; **to have a** *or* **some ~** avere voce in capitolo // *vt* (*pt, pp* **said**) dire; **could you ~ that again?** potrebbe ripeterlo?; **that goes without ~ing** va da sé; **~ing** *n* proverbio, detto.

scab [skæb] *n* crosta; (*pej*) crumiro/a.

scaffold ['skæfəuld] *n* impalcatura; (*gallows*) patibolo; **~ing** *n* impalcatura.

scald [skɔ:ld] *n* scottatura // *vt* scottare.

scale [skeɪl] *n* scala; (*of fish*) squama // *vt* (*mountain*) scalare; **~s** *npl* bilancia; **on a large ~** su vasta scala; **~ of charges** tariffa; **to ~ down** *vt* ridurre (proporzionalmente); **~ model** *n* modello in scala.

scallop ['skɔləp] *n* pettine *m*.

scalp [skælp] *n* cuoio capelluto // *vt* scotennare.

scalpel ['skælpl] *n* bisturi *m inv*.

scamper ['skæmpə*] *vi*: **to ~ away**, **~ off** darsela a gambe.

scampi ['skæmpɪ] *npl* scampi *mpl*.

scan [skæn] *vt* scrutare; (*glance at quickly*) scorrere, dare un'occhiata a; (*poetry*) scandire; (*TV*) analizzare; (*RADAR*) esplorare // *n* (*MED*) ecografia.

scandal ['skændl] *n* scandalo; (*gossip*) pettegolezzi *mpl*.

Scandinavia [skændɪ'neɪvɪə] *n* Scandinavia; **~n** *a, n* scandinavo(a).

scant [skænt] *a* scarso(a); **~y** *a* insufficiente; (*swimsuit*) ridotto(a).

scapegoat ['skeɪpgəut] *n* capro espiatorio.

scar [ska:] *n* cicatrice *f* // *vt* sfregiare.

scarce [skeəs] *a* scarso(a); (*copy, edition*) raro(a); **~ly** *ad* appena; **scarcity** *n* scarsità, mancanza.

scare [skeə*] *n* spavento; panico // *vt* spaventare, atterrire; **there was a bomb ~ at the bank** hanno evacuato la banca per paura di un attentato dinamitardo; **to ~ sb stiff** spaventare a morte qn; **~crow** *n* spaventapasseri *m inv*; **~d** *a*: **to be ~d** aver paura.

scarf, pl scarves [ska:f, ska:vz] *n* (*long*) sciarpa; (*square*) fazzoletto da testa, foulard *m inv*.

scarlet ['ska:lɪt] *a* scarlatto(a).

scathing ['skeɪðɪŋ] *a* aspro(a).

scatter ['skætə*] *vt* spargere; (*crowd*) disperdere // *vi* disperdersi; **~brained** *a* scervellato(a), sbadato(a).

scavenger ['skævəndʒə*] *n* spazzino.

scenario [sɪ'nɑ:rɪəu] *n* (*THEATRE, CINEMA*) copione *m*; (*fig*) situazione *f*.

scene [si:n] *n* (*THEATRE, fig etc*) scena; (*of crime, accident*) scena, luogo; (*sight,*

view) vista, veduta; **~ry** *n* (*THEATRE*) scenario; (*landscape*) panorama *m*; **scenic** *a* scenico(a); panoramico(a).

scent [sent] *n* odore *m*, profumo; (*sense of smell*) olfatto, odorato; (*fig: track*) pista.

sceptical, (*US*) **skeptical** ['skeptɪkəl] *a* scettico(a).

sceptre, (*US*) **scepter** ['septə*] *n* scettro.

schedule ['ʃedju:l, (*US*) 'skedju:l] *n* programma *m*, piano; (*of trains*) orario; (*of prices etc*) lista, tabella // *vt* fissare; **on ~** in orario; **to be ahead of/behind ~** essere in anticipo/ritardo sul previsto; **~d flight** *n* volo di linea.

scheme [ski:m] *n* piano, progetto; (*method*) sistema *m*; (*dishonest plan, plot*) intrigo, trama; (*arrangement*) disposizione *f*, sistemazione *f*; (*pension etc*) programma *m* // *vi* fare progetti; (*intrigue*) complottare; **scheming** *a* intrigante // *n* intrighi *mpl*, macchinazioni *fpl*.

schism ['skɪzəm] *n* scisma *m*.

scholar ['skɔlə*] *n* erudito/a; **~ly** *a* dotto(a), erudito(a); **~ship** *n* erudizione *f*; (*grant*) borsa di studio.

school [sku:l] *n* scuola; (*in university*) scuola, facoltà *f inv* // *cpd* scolare, scolastico(a) // *vt* (*animal*) addestrare; **~book** *n* libro scolastico; **~boy** *n* scolaro; **~children** *npl* scolari *mpl*; **~days** *npl* giorni *mpl* di scuola; **~girl** *n* scolara; **~ing** *n* istruzione *f*; **~master** *n* (*primary*) maestro; (*secondary*) insegnante *m*; **~mistress** *n* maestra; insegnante *f*; **~teacher** *n* insegnante *m/f*, docente *m/f*; (*primary*) maestro/a.

sciatica [saɪ'ætɪkə] *n* sciatica.

science ['saɪəns] *n* scienza; **~ fiction** *n* fantascienza; **scientific** [-'tɪfɪk] *a* scientifico(a); **scientist** *n* scienziato/a.

scissors ['sɪzəz] *npl* forbici *fpl*.

scoff [skɔf] *vt* (*Brit col: eat*) tranguiare, ingozzare // *vi*: **to ~ (at)** (*mock*) farsi beffe (di).

scold [skəuld] *vt* rimproverare.

scone [skɔn] *n* focaccina da tè.

scoop [sku:p] *n* mestolo; (*for ice cream*) cucchiaio dosatore; (*PRESS*) colpo giornalistico, notizia (in) esclusiva; **to ~ out** *vt* scavare; **to ~ up** *vt* tirare su, sollevare.

scooter ['sku:tə*] *n* (*motor cycle*) motoretta, scooter *m inv*; (*toy*) monopattino.

scope [skəup] *n* (*capacity: of plan, undertaking*) portata; (*: of person*) capacità *fpl*; (*opportunity*) possibilità *fpl*; **within the ~ of** nei limiti di.

scorch [skɔ:tʃ] *vt* (*clothes*) strinare, bruciacchiare; (*earth, grass*) seccare, bruciare.

score [skɔ:*] *n* punti *mpl*, punteggio;

(MUS) partitura, spartito; (twenty) venti // vt (goal, point) segnare, fare; (success) ottenere // vi segnare; (FOOTBALL) fare un goal; (keep score) segnare i punti; **on that ~** a questo riguardo; **to ~ 6 out of 10** prendere 6 su 10; **to ~ out** vt cancellare con un segno; **~board** n tabellone m segnapunti.

scorn [skɔːn] n disprezzo // vt disprezzare.

Scorpio ['skɔːpɪəu] n Scorpione m.

scorpion ['skɔːpɪən] n scorpione m.

Scot [skɔt] n scozzese m/f.

scotch [skɔtʃ] vt (rumour etc) soffocare; **S~** n whisky m scozzese, scotch m.

scot-free ['skɔt'friː] ad: **to get off ~** farla franca.

Scotland ['skɔtlənd] n Scozia.

Scots [skɔts] a scozzese; **~man/woman** n scozzese m/f.

Scottish ['skɔtɪʃ] a scozzese.

scoundrel ['skaundrl] n farabutto/a; (child) furfantello/a.

scour ['skauə*] vt (clean) pulire strofinando; raschiare via; ripulire; (search) battere, perlustrare.

scourge [skəːdʒ] n flagello.

scout [skaut] n (MIL) esploratore m; (also: **boy ~**) giovane esploratore, scout m inv; **to ~ around** vi cercare in giro.

scowl [skaul] vi accigliarsi, aggrottare le sopracciglia; **to ~ at** guardare torvo.

scrabble ['skræbl] vi (claw): **to ~ (at)** graffiare, grattare; (also: **~ around:** search) cercare a tentoni // n: **S~** ® Scarabeo ®.

scraggy ['skrægɪ] a scarno(a), molto magro(a).

scram [skræm] vi (col) filare via.

scramble ['skræmbl] n arrampicata // vi inerpicarsi; **to ~ out** etc uscire etc in fretta; **to ~ for** azzuffarsi per; **~d eggs** npl uova fpl strapazzate.

scrap [skræp] n pezzo, pezzetto; (fight) zuffa; (also: **~ iron**) rottami mpl di ferro, ferraglia // vt demolire; (fig) scartare // vi: **to ~ (with sb)** fare a botte (con qn); **~s** npl (waste) scarti mpl; **~book** n album m inv di ritagli; **~ dealer** n commerciante m di ferraglia.

scrape [skreɪp] vt, vi raschiare, grattare // n: **to get into a ~** cacciarsi in un guaio; **to ~ through** vi farcela per un pelo; **~r** n raschietto.

scrap: **~ heap** n mucchio di rottami; **~ merchant** n (Brit) commerciante m di ferraglia; **~ paper** n cartaccia.

scratch [skrætʃ] n graffio // cpd: **~ team** squadra raccogliticcia // vt graffiare, rigare // vi grattare, graffiare; **to start from ~** cominciare or partire da zero; **to be up to ~** essere all'altezza.

scrawl [skrɔːl] n scarabocchio // vi scarabocchiare.

scrawny ['skrɔːnɪ] a scarno(a), pelle e

ossa inv.

scream [skriːm] n grido, urlo // vi urlare, gridare.

scree [skriː] n ghiaione m.

screech [skriːtʃ] n strido; (of tyres, brakes) stridore m // vi stridere.

screen [skriːn] n schermo; (fig) muro, cortina, velo // vt schermare, fare schermo a; (from the wind etc) riparare; (film) proiettare; (book) adattare per lo schermo; (candidates etc) selezionare; **~ing** n (MED) dépistage m inv; **~play** n sceneggiatura.

screw [skruː] n vite f; (propeller) elica // vt avvitare; **to ~ up** vt (paper etc) spiegazzare; (col: ruin) rovinare; **to ~ up one's eyes** strizzare gli occhi; **~driver** n cacciavite m.

scribble ['skrɪbl] n scarabocchio // vt scribacchiare in fretta // vi scarabocchiare.

script [skrɪpt] n (CINEMA etc) copione m; (in exam) elaborato or compito d'esame.

Scripture ['skrɪptʃə*] n sacre Scritture fpl.

scroll [skrəul] n rotolo di carta.

scrounge [skraundʒ] vt (col): **to ~ sth (off or from sb)** scroccare qc (a qn) // vi: **to ~ on sb** vivere alle spalle di qn.

scrub [skrʌb] n (clean) strofinata; (land) boscaglia // vt pulire strofinando; (reject) annullare.

scruff [skrʌf] n: **by the ~ of the neck** per la collottola.

scruffy ['skrʌfɪ] a sciatto(a).

scrum(mage) ['skrʌm(ɪdʒ)] n mischia.

scruple ['skruːpl] n scrupolo.

scrutiny ['skruːtɪnɪ] n esame m accurato.

scuff [skʌf] vt (shoes) consumare strascicando.

scuffle ['skʌfl] n baruffa, tafferuglio.

scullery ['skʌlərɪ] n retrocucina m or f.

sculptor ['skʌlptə*] n scultore m.

sculpture ['skʌlptʃə*] n scultura.

scum [skʌm] n schiuma; (pej: people) feccia.

scupper ['skʌpə*] vt (NAUT) autoaffondare; (fig) far naufragare.

scurrilous ['skʌrɪləs] a scurrile, volgare.

scurry ['skʌrɪ] vi sgambare, affrettarsi; **to ~ off** andarsene a tutta velocità.

scuttle ['skʌtl] n (NAUT) portellino; (also: **coal ~**) secchio del carbone // vt (ship) autoaffondare // vi (scamper): **to ~ away, ~ off** darsela a gambe, scappare.

scythe [saɪð] n falce f.

SDP n abbr (Brit) = Social Democratic Party.

sea [siː] n mare m // cpd marino(a), del mare; (ship, sailor, port) marittimo(a), di mare; (travel) per mare; **on the ~** (boat) in mare; (town) di mare; **to be all at ~** (fig) non sapere che pesci pigliare; **out to ~** al largo; (out) **at ~** in mare; **~board** n costa; **~food** n frutti mpl di mare; **~ front** n lungomare m; **~gull** n gabbiano.

seal [si:l] n (animal) foca; (stamp) sigillo; (impression) impronta del sigillo // vt sigillare; **to ~ off** vt (close) sigillare; (forbid entry to) bloccare l'accesso a.

sea level n livello del mare.

seam [si:m] n cucitura; (of coal) filone m.

seaman ['si:mən] n marinaio.

seamy ['si:mɪ] a orribile.

seance ['seɪɔns] n seduta spiritica.

seaplane ['si:pleɪn] n idrovolante m.

search [sɔ:tʃ] n (for person, thing) ricerca; (of drawer, pockets) esame m accurato; (LAW: at sb's home) perquisizione f // vt perlustrare, frugare; (examine) esaminare minuziosamente // vi: **to ~ for** ricercare; **in ~ of** alla ricerca di; **to ~ through** vt fus frugare; **~ing** a minuzioso(a); penetrante; **~light** n proiettore m; **~ party** n squadra di soccorso; **~ warrant** n mandato di perquisizione.

seashore ['si:ʃɔ:*] n spiaggia.

seasick ['si:sɪk] a che soffre il mal di mare.

seaside ['si:saɪd] n spiaggia; **~ resort** n stazione f balneare.

season ['si:zn] n stagione f // vt condire, insaporire; **~al** a stagionale; **~ed** a (fig) con esperienza; **~ing** n condimento; **~ ticket** n abbonamento.

seat [si:t] n sedile m; (in bus, train: place) posto; (PARLIAMENT) seggio; (buttocks) didietro; (of trousers) fondo // vt far sedere; (have room for) avere or essere fornito(a) di posti a sedere per; **~ belt** n cintura di sicurezza.

sea water n acqua di mare.

seaweed ['si:wi:d] n alghe fpl.

seaworthy ['si:wə:ðɪ] a atto(a) alla navigazione.

sec. abbr = **second(s)**.

secluded [sɪ'klu:dɪd] a isolato(a), appartato(a).

seclusion [sɪ'klu:ʒən] n isolamento.

second ['sɛkənd] num secondo(a) // ad (in race etc) al secondo posto; (RAIL) in seconda // n (unit of time) secondo; (in series, position) secondo/a; (AUT: also: **~ gear**) seconda; (COMM: imperfect) scarto; (Brit SCOL: degree) laurea con punteggio discreto // vt (motion) appoggiare; **~ary** a secondario(a); **~ary school** n scuola secondaria; **~class** a di seconda classe; **~er** n sostenitore/trice; **~hand** a di seconda mano, usato(a); **~ hand** n (on clock) lancetta dei secondi; **~ in secondo luogo**; **~ment** [sɪ'kɔndmənt] n (Brit) distaccamento; **~-rate** a scadente; **~ thoughts** npl ripensamenti mpl; **on ~**

thoughts or (US) thought ripensandoci bene.

secrecy ['si:krəsɪ] n segretezza.

secret ['si:krɪt] a segreto(a) // n segreto; **in ~** in segreto.

secretariat [sɛkrɪ'tɛərɪət] n segretariato.

secretary ['sɛkrətərɪ] n segretario/a; S~ **of State (for)** (Brit POL) ministro (di).

secretive ['si:krətɪv] a riservato(a).

sect [sɛkt] n setta; **~arian** [-'tɛərɪən] a settario(a).

section ['sɛkʃən] n sezione f.

sector ['sɛktə*] n settore m.

secure [sɪ'kjuə*] a (free from anxiety) sicuro(a); (firmly fixed) assicurato(a), ben fermato(a); (in safe place) al sicuro // vt (fix) fissare, assicurare; (get) ottenere, assicurarsi.

security [sɪ'kjuərɪtɪ] n sicurezza; (for loan) garanzia.

sedan [sɪ'dæn] n (US AUT) berlina.

sedate [sɪ'deɪt] a posato(a); calmo(a) // vt calmare.

sedation [sɪ'deɪʃən] n (MED) l'effetto dei sedativi.

sedative ['sɛdɪtɪv] n sedativo, calmante m.

seduce [sɪ'dju:s] vt sedurre; **seduction** [-'dʌkʃən] n seduzione f; **seductive** [-'dʌktɪv] a seducente.

see [si:] vb (pt **saw**, pp **seen**) vt vedere; (accompany): **to ~ sb to the door** accompagnare qn alla porta // vi vedere; (understand) capire // in sede f vescovile; **to ~ that** (ensure) badare che + sub, fare in modo che + sub; **~ you soon!** a presto!; **to ~ about** vt fus occuparsi di; **to ~ off** vt salutare alla partenza; **to ~ through** vt portare a termine // vt fus non lasciarsi ingannare da; **to ~ to** vt fus occuparsi di.

seed [si:d] n seme m; (fig) germe m; (TENNIS) testa di serie; **to go to ~** fare seme; (fig) scadere; **~ling** n piantina di semenzaio; **~y** a (shabby: person) sciatto(a); (: place) cadente.

seeing ['si:ɪŋ] cj: **~ (that)** visto che.

seek [si:k], pt, pp **sought** vt cercare.

seem [si:m] vi sembrare, parere; **there ~s to be ...** sembra che ci sia ...; **~ingly** ad apparentemente.

seen [si:n] pp of **see**.

seep [si:p] vi filtrare, trapelare.

seesaw ['si:sɔ:] n altalena a bilico.

seethe [si:ð] vi ribollire; **to ~ with anger** fremere di rabbia.

see-through ['si:θru:] a trasparente.

segregate ['sɛgrɪgeɪt] vt segregare, isolare.

seize [si:z] vt (grasp) afferrare; (take possession of) impadronirsi di; (LAW) sequestrare; **to ~ (up)on** vt fus ricorrere a; **to ~ up** vi (TECH) grippare.

seizure ['si:ʒə*] n (MED) attacco; (LAW)

confisca, sequestro.

seldom ['sɛldəm] *ad* raramente.

select [sɪ'lɛkt] *a* scelto(a) // *vt* scegliere, selezionare; **~ion** [-'lɛkʃən] *n* selezione *f*, scelta.

self [sɛlf] *n* (*pl* **selves** [sɛlvz]): **the ~** l'io *m* // *prefix* auto...; **~-catering** *a* (*Brit*) in cui ci si cucina da sé; **~-centred**, (*US*) **~-centered** *a* egocentrico(a); **~coloured**, (*US*) **~-colored** *a* monocolore; **~-confidence** *n* sicurezza di sé; **~-conscious** *a* timido(a); **~contained** *a* (*Brit*: *flat*) indipendente; **~-control** *n* autocontrollo; **~-defence**, (*US*) **~-defense** *n* autodifesa; (*LAW*) legittima difesa; **~-discipline** *n* autodisciplina; **~-employed** *a* che lavora in proprio; **~-evident** *a* evidente; **~governing** *a* autonomo(a); **~indulgent** *a* indulgente verso se stesso(a); **~-interest** *n* interesse *m* personale; **~-ish** *a* egoista; **~ishness** *n* egoismo; **~less** *a* dimentico(a) di sé, altruista; **~-pity** *n* autocommiserazione *f*; **~-portrait** *n* autoritratto; **~-possessed** *a* controllato(a); **~-preservation** *n* istinto di conservazione; **~-respect** *n* rispetto di sé, amor proprio; **~-righteous** *a* soddisfatto(a) di sé; **~-sacrifice** *n* abnegazione *f*; **~-satisfied** *a* compiaciuto(a) di sé; **~-service** *n* autoservizio, self-service *m*; **~sufficient** *a* autosufficiente; **~-taught** *a* autodidatta.

sell [sɛl], *pt, pp* **sold** *vt* vendere // *vi* vendersi; **to ~ at** *or* **for 1000 lire** essere in vendita a 1000 lire; **to ~ off** *vt* svendere, liquidare; **to ~ out** *vi*: **to ~ out** (**to sb/sth**) (*COMM*) vendere (tutto) (a qn/qc) // *vt* esaurire; **the tickets are all sold out** i biglietti sono esauriti; **~-by date** *n* data di scadenza; **~er** *n* venditore/trice; **~ing price** *n* prezzo di vendita.

sellotape ['sɛləteɪp] *n* ® (*Brit*) nastro adesivo, scotch *m* ®.

sellout ['sɛlaut] *n* tradimento; (*of tickets*): **it was a ~** registrò un tutto esaurito.

selves [sɛlvz] *npl of* **self**.

semblance ['sɛmbləns] *n* parvenza, apparenza.

semen ['si:mən] *n* sperma *m*.

semester [sɪ'mɛstə*] *n* (*US*) semestre *m*.

semi... ['sɛmɪ] *prefix* semi...; **~circle** *n* semicerchio; **~colon** *n* punto e virgola; **~detached (house)** *n* (*Brit*) casa gemella; **~final** *n* semifinale *f*.

seminar ['sɛmɪnɑ:*] *n* seminario.

seminary ['sɛmɪnərɪ] *n* (*REL*) seminario.

semiquaver ['sɛmɪkweɪvə*] *n* semicroma.

semiskilled ['sɛmɪ'skɪld] *a* (*worker*) parzialmente qualificato(a); (*work*) che richiede una qualificazione parziale.

senate ['sɛnɪt] *n* senato; **senator** *n* senatore/trice.

send [sɛnd], *pt, pp* **sent** *vt* mandare; **to ~ away** *vt* (*letter, goods*) spedire; (*person*) mandare via; **to ~ away for** *vt fus* richiedere per posta, farsi spedire; **to ~ back** *vt* rimandare; **to ~ for** *vt fus* mandare a chiamare, far venire; **to ~ off** *vt* (*goods*) spedire; (*Brit SPORT: player*) espellere; **to ~ out** *vt* (*invitation*) diramare; **to ~ up** *vt* (*person, price*) far salire; (*Brit: parody*) mettere in ridicolo; **~er** *n* mittente *m/f*; **~-off** *n*: **to give sb a good ~-off** festeggiare la partenza di qn.

senior ['si:nɪə*] *a* (*older*) più vecchio(a); (*of higher rank*) di grado più elevato // *n* persona più anziana; (*in service*) persona con maggiore anzianità; **~ citizen** *n* persona anziana; **~ity** [-'ɔrɪtɪ] *n* anzianità.

sensation [sɛn'seɪʃən] *n* sensazione *f*; **to create a ~** fare scalpore; **~al** *a* sensazionale; (*marvellous*) eccezionale.

sense [sɛns] *n* senso; (*feeling*) sensazione *f*, senso; (*meaning*) senso, significato; (*wisdom*) buonsenso // *vt* sentire, percepire; **~s** *npl* (*sanity*) ragione *f*; **it makes ~** ha senso; **~less** *a* sciocco(a); (*unconscious*) privo(a) di sensi.

sensibility [sɛnsɪ'bɪlɪtɪ] *n* sensibilità; **sensibilities** *npl* sensibilità *sg*.

sensible ['sɛnsɪbl] *a* sensato(a), ragionevole.

sensitive ['sɛnsɪtɪv] *a*: **~ (to)** sensibile (a).

sensual ['sɛnsjuəl] *a* sensuale.

sensuous ['sɛnsjuəs] *a* sensuale.

sent [sɛnt] *pt, pp of* **send**.

sentence ['sɛntns] *n* (*LING*) frase *f*; (*LAW: judgment*) sentenza; (: *punishment*) condanna // *vt*: **to ~ sb to death/to 5 years** condannare qn a morte/ a 5 anni.

sentiment ['sɛntɪmənt] *n* sentimento; (*opinion*) opinione *f*; **~al** [-'mɛntl] *a* sentimentale.

sentry ['sɛntrɪ] *n* sentinella.

separate *a* ['sɛprɪt] separato(a) // *vb* ['sɛpəreɪt] *vt* separare // *vi* separarsi; **~s** *npl* (*clothes*) coordinati *mpl*; **~ly** *ad* separatamente; **separation** [-'reɪʃən] *n* separazione *f*.

September [sɛp'tɛmbə*] *n* settembre *m*.

septic ['sɛptɪk] *a* settico(a); (*wound*) infettato(a); **~ tank** *n* fossa settica.

sequel ['si:kwl] *n* conseguenza; (*of story*) seguito.

sequence ['si:kwəns] *n* (*series*) serie *f*; (*order*) ordine *m*.

sequin ['si:kwɪn] *n* lustrino, paillette *f inv*.

serene [sə'ri:n] *a* sereno(a), calmo(a).

sergeant ['sɑ:dʒənt] *n* sergente *m*; (*POLICE*) brigadiere *m*.

serial ['sɪərɪəl] *n* (*PRESS*) romanzo a puntate; (*RADIO*, *TV*) trasmissione *f* a puntate // *a* (*number*) di serie; ~ **number** *n* numero di serie.

series ['sɪəri:z] *n* (*pl inv*) serie *f inv*; (*PUBLISHING*) collana.

serious ['sɪərɪəs] *a* serio(a), grave; ~**ly** *ad* seriamente.

sermon ['sə:mən] *n* sermone *m*.

serrated [sɪ'reɪtɪd] *a* seghettato(a).

serum ['sɪərəm] *n* siero.

servant ['sə:vənt] *n* domestico/a.

serve [sə:v] *vt* (*employer etc*) servire, essere a servizio di; (*purpose*) servire a; (*customer*, *food*, *meal*) servire; (*apprenticeship*) fare; (*prison term*) scontare // *vi* (*also TENNIS*) servire; (*be useful*): **to** ~ **as/for/to do** servire da/per/per fare // *n* (*TENNIS*) servizio; **it** ~**s him right** ben gli sta, se l'è meritata; **to** ~ **out**, ~ **up** *vt* (*food*) servire.

service ['sə:vɪs] *n* servizio; (*AUT*: *maintenance*) assistenza, revisione *f* // *vt* (*car*, *washing machine*) revisionare; **the** S~**s** le forze armate; **to be of** ~ **to sb** essere d'aiuto a qn; **dinner** ~ servizio da tavola; ~**able** *a* pratico(a), utile; ~ **charge** *n* (*Brit*) servizio; ~**man** *n* militare *m*; ~ **station** *n* stazione *f* di servizio.

serviette [sə:vɪ'et] *n* (*Brit*) tovagliolo.

session ['sɛʃən] *n* (*sitting*) seduta, sessione *f*; (*SCOL*) anno scolastico (*or* accademico).

set [sɛt] *n* serie *f inv*; (*RADIO*, *TV*) apparecchio; (*TENNIS*) set *m inv*; (*group of people*) mondo, ambiente *m*; (*CINEMA*) scenario; (*THEATRE*: *stage*) scene *fpl*; (: *scenery*) scenario; (*MATH*) insieme *m*; (*HAIRDRESSING*) messa in piega // *a* (*fixed*) stabilito(a), determinato(a); (*ready*) pronto(a) // *vb* (*pt*, *pp* **set**) (*place*) posare, mettere; (*fix*) fissare; (*adjust*) regolare; (*decide*: *rules etc*) stabilire, fissare; (*TYP*) comporre // *vi* (*sun*) tramontare; (*jam*, *jelly*) rapprendersi; (*concrete*) fare presa; **to be** ~ **on doing** essere deciso a fare; **to** ~ **to music** mettere in musica; **to** ~ **on fire** dare fuoco a; **to** ~ **free** liberare; **to** ~ **sth going** mettere in moto qc; **to** ~ **sail** prendere il mare; **to** ~ **about** *vt fus* (*task*) intraprendere, mettersi a; **to** ~ **aside** *vt* mettere da parte; **to** ~ **back** *vt* (*in time*): **to** ~ **back** (**by**) mettere indietro (di); **to** ~ **off** *vi* partire // *vt* (*bomb*) far scoppiare; (*cause to start*) mettere in moto; (*show up well*) dare risalto a; **to** ~ **out** *vi* partire; (*aim*): **to** ~ **out to do** proporsi di fare // *vt* (*arrange*) disporre; (*state*) esporre, presentare; **to** ~ **up** *vt* (*organization*) fondare, costituire; (*monument*) innalzare; ~**back** *n* (*hitch*) contrattempo, inconveniente *m*; ~

menu *n* menù *m inv* fisso.

settee [sɛ'ti:] *n* divano, sofà *m inv*.

setting ['sɛtɪŋ] *n* ambiente *m*; (*of jewel*) montatura.

settle ['sɛtl] *vt* (*argument*, *matter*) appianare; (*problem*) risolvere; (*MED*: *calm*) calmare // *vi* (*bird*, *dust etc*) posarsi; (*sediment*) depositarsi; (*also*: ~ **down**) sistemarsi, stabilirsi; calmarsi; **to** ~ **for sth** accontentarsi di qc; **to** ~ **on sth** decidersi per qc; **to** ~ **in** *vi* sistemarsi; **to** ~ **up** *vi*: **to** ~ **up with sb** regolare i conti con qn; ~**ment** *n* (*payment*) pagamento, saldo; (*agreement*) accordo; (*colony*) colonia; (*village etc*) villaggio, comunità *f inv*; ~**r** *n* colonizzatore/trice.

setup ['sɛtʌp] *n* (*arrangement*) sistemazione *f*; (*situation*) situazione *f*.

seven ['sɛvn] *num* sette; ~**teen** *num* diciassette; ~**th** *num* settimo(a); ~**ty** *num* settanta.

sever ['sɛvə*] *vt* recidere, tagliare; (*relations*) troncare.

several ['sɛvərl] *a*, *pronoun* alcuni(e), diversi(e); ~ **of us** alcuni di noi.

severance ['sɛvərəns] *n* (*of relations*) rottura; ~ **pay** *n* indennità di licenziamento.

severe [sɪ'vɪə*] *a* severo(a); (*serious*) serio(a), grave; (*hard*) duro(a); (*plain*) semplice, sobrio(a); **severity** [sɪ'vɛrɪtɪ] *n* severità; gravità; (*of weather*) rigore *m*.

sew [səu], *pt* **sewed**, *pp* **sewn** *vt*, *vi* cucire; **to** ~ **up** *vt* ricucire.

sewage ['su:ɪdʒ] *n* acque *fpl* di scolo.

sewer ['su:ə*] *n* fogna.

sewing ['səuɪŋ] *n* cucitura; cucito; ~ **machine** *n* macchina da cucire.

sewn [səun] *pp of* **sew**.

sex [sɛks] *n* sesso; **to have** ~ **with** avere rapporti sessuali con; ~**ist** *a*, *n* sessista (*m/f*).

sexual ['sɛksjuəl] *a* sessuale.

sexy ['sɛksɪ] *a* provocante, sexy *inv*.

shabby ['ʃæbɪ] *a* malandato(a); (*behaviour*) vergognoso(a).

shack [ʃæk] *n* baracca, capanna.

shackles ['ʃæklz] *npl* ferri *mpl*, catene *fpl*.

shade [ʃeɪd] *n* ombra; (*for lamp*) paralume *m*; (*of colour*) tonalità *f inv*; (*small quantity*): **a** ~ **of** un po' or un'ombra di // *vt* ombreggiare, fare ombra a; **in the** ~ all'ombra; **a** ~ **smaller** un tantino più piccolo.

shadow ['ʃædəu] *n* ombra // *vt* (*follow*) pedinare; ~ **cabinet** *n* (*Brit POL*) governo *m* ombra *inv*; ~**y** *a* ombreggiato(a), ombroso(a); (*dim*) vago(a), indistinto(a).

shady ['ʃeɪdɪ] *a* ombroso(a); (*fig*: *dishonest*) losco(a), equivoco(a).

shaft [ʃɑ:ft] *n* (*of arrow*, *spear*) asta; (*AUT*, *TECH*) albero; (*of mine*) pozzo; (*of lift*) tromba; (*of light*) raggio.

shaggy [ˈʃægɪ] a ispido(a).

shake [ʃeɪk] vb (pt **shook**, pp **shaken** [ʃuk, ˈʃeɪkn]) vt scuotere; (bottle, cocktail) agitare // vi tremare // n scossa; to ~ one's head (in refusal, dismay) scuotere la testa; to ~ hands with sb stringere or dare la mano a qn; to ~ off vt scrollare (via); (fig) sbarazzarsi di; to ~ up vt scuotere; **shaky** a (hand, voice) tremante; (building) traballante.

shale [ʃeɪl] n roccia scistosa.

shall [ʃæl] auxiliary vb: I ~ go andrò; ~ I open the door? apro io la porta?; I'll get some, ~ I? ne prendo un po', va bene?

shallow [ˈʃæləʊ] a poco profondo(a); (fig) superficiale.

sham [ʃæm] n finzione f, messinscena; (jewellery, furniture) imitazione f.

shambles [ˈʃæmblz] n confusione f, baraonda, scompiglio.

shame [ʃeɪm] n vergogna // vt far vergognare; it is a ~ (that/to do) è un peccato (che + sub/fare); what a ~! che peccato!; ~**faced** a vergognoso(a); ~**ful** a vergognoso(a); ~**less** a sfrontato(a); (immodest) spudorato(a).

shampoo [ʃæmˈpuː] n shampoo m inv // vt fare lo shampoo a; ~ **and set** n shampoo e messa in piega.

shamrock [ˈʃæmrɒk] n trifoglio (simbolo nazionale dell'Irlanda).

shandy [ˈʃændɪ] n birra con gassosa.

shan't [ʃɑːnt] = shall not.

shanty town [ˈʃæntɪ-] n bidonville f inv.

shape [ʃeɪp] n forma // vt formare; (statement) formulare; (sb's ideas) condizionare // vi (also: ~ up) (events) andare, mettersi; (person) cavarsela; to take ~ prendere forma; -**shaped** suffix: heart-shaped a forma di cuore; ~**less** a senza forma, informe; ~**ly** a ben proporzionato(a).

share [ʃɛə*] n (thing received, contribution) parte f; (COMM) azione f // vt dividere; (have in common) condividere, avere in comune; to ~ out (among or between) dividere (tra); ~**holder** n azionista m/f.

shark [ʃɑːk] n squalo, pescecane m.

sharp [ʃɑːp] a (razor, knife) affilato(a); (point) acuto(a), acuminato(a); (nose, chin) aguzzo(a); (outline) netto(a); (cold, pain) pungente; (voice) stridulo(a); (person: quick-witted) sveglio(a); (: unscrupulous) disonesto(a); (MUS): C ~ do diesis // n (MUS) diesis m inv // ad: at 2 o'clock ~ alle due in punto; ~**en** vt affilare; (pencil) fare la punta a; (fig) aguzzare; ~**ener** n (also: pencil ~ener) temperamatite m inv; ~**eyed** a dalla vista acuta; ~**ly** ad (turn, stop) bruscamente; (criticize, retort) duramen-

te, aspramente.

shatter [ˈʃætə*] vt mandare in frantumi, frantumare; (fig: upset) distruggere; (: ruin) rovinare // vi frantumarsi, andare in pezzi.

shave [ʃeɪv] vt radere, rasare // vi radersi, farsi la barba // n: to have a ~ farsi la barba; ~**r** n (also: electric ~r) rasoio elettrico.

shaving [ˈʃeɪvɪŋ] n (action) rasatura; ~**s** npl (of wood etc) trucioli mpl; ~ **brush** n pennello da barba; ~ **cream** n crema da barba.

shawl [ʃɔːl] n scialle m.

she [ʃiː] pronoun ella, lei; ~**-cat** n gatta; ~**-elephant** n elefantessa; NB: for ships, countries follow the gender of your translation.

sheaf [ʃiːf], pl **sheaves** n covone m.

shear [ʃɪə*] vt (pt ~**ed**, pp ~**ed** or **shorn**) (sheep) tosare; to ~ **off** vi spezzarsi; ~**s** npl (for hedge) cesoie fpl.

sheath [ʃiːθ] n fodero, guaina; (contraceptive) preservativo.

sheaves [ʃiːvz] npl of sheaf.

shed [ʃɛd] n capannone m // vt (pt, pp **shed**) (leaves, fur etc) perdere; (tears) versare.

she'd [ʃiːd] = she had, she would.

sheen [ʃiːn] n lucentezza.

sheep [ʃiːp] n (pl inv) pecora; ~**dog** n cane m da pastore; ~**ish** a vergognoso(a), timido(a); ~**skin** n pelle f di pecora.

sheer [ʃɪə*] a (utter) vero(a) (e proprio(a)); (steep) a picco, perpendicolare; (almost transparent) sottile // ad a picco.

sheet [ʃiːt] n (on bed) lenzuolo; (of paper) foglio; (of glass) lastra; (of metal) foglio, lamina; ~ **lightning** n lampo diffuso.

sheik(h) [ʃeɪk] n sceicco.

shelf [ʃɛlf], pl **shelves** n scaffale m, mensola.

shell [ʃɛl] n (on beach) conchiglia; (of egg, nut etc) guscio; (explosive) granata; (of building) scheletro // vt (peas) sgranare; (MIL) bombardare, cannoneggiare.

she'll [ʃiːl] = she will, she shall.

shellfish [ˈʃɛlfɪʃ] n (pl inv) (crab etc) crostaceo; (scallop etc) mollusco; (pl: as food) crostacei; molluschi.

shelter [ˈʃɛltə*] n riparo, rifugio // vt riparare, proteggere; (give lodging to) dare rifugio or asilo a // vi ripararsi, mettersi al riparo.

shelve [ʃɛlv] vt (fig) accantonare, rimandare; ~**s** npl of shelf.

shepherd [ˈʃɛpəd] n pastore m // vt (guide) guidare; ~'**s pie** n timballo di carne macinata e purè di patate.

sheriff [ˈʃɛrɪf] n sceriffo.

sherry [ˈʃɛrɪ] n sherry m inv.

Shetland ['ʃɛtlənd] n (also: the ~s, the ~ Isles) le isole Shetland, le Shetland.

shield [ʃiːld] n scudo // vt: to ~ (from) riparare (da), proteggere (da or contro).

shift [ʃɪft] n (change) cambiamento; (of workers) turno // vt spostare, muovere; (remove) rimuovere // vi spostarsi, muoversi; ~**less** a: a ~less person un(a) fannullone(a); ~ **work** n lavoro a squadre; ~**y** a ambiguo(a); (eyes) sfuggente.

shilling ['ʃɪlɪŋ] n (Brit) scellino (= 12 old pence; 20 in a pound).

shilly-shally ['ʃɪlɪʃælɪ] vi tentennare, esitare.

shimmer ['ʃɪmə*] vi brillare, luccicare.

shin [ʃɪn] n tibia.

shine [ʃaɪn] n splendore m, lucentezza // vb (pt, pp **shone**) vi (ri)splendere, brillare // vt far brillare, far risplendere; (torch): to ~ sth on puntare qc verso.

shingle ['ʃɪŋgl] n (on beach) ciottoli mpl; (on roof) assicella di copertura; ~**s** n (MED) herpes zoster m.

shiny ['ʃaɪnɪ] a lucente, lucido(a).

ship [ʃɪp] n nave f // vt trasportare (via mare); (send) spedire (via mare); (load) imbarcare, caricare; ~**building** n costruzione f navale; ~**ment** n carico; ~**ping** n (ships) naviglio; (traffic) navigazione f; ~**shape** a in perfetto ordine; ~**wreck** n relitto; (event) naufragio // vt: to be ~wrecked naufragare, fare naufragio; ~**yard** n cantiere m navale.

shire ['ʃaɪə*] n (Brit) contea.

shirk [ʃəːk] vt sottrarsi a, evitare.

shirt [ʃəːt] n (man's) camicia; in ~ sleeves in maniche di camicia.

shit [ʃɪt] excl (col!) merda (!).

shiver ['ʃɪvə*] n brivido // vi rabbrividire, tremare.

shoal [ʃəul] n (of fish) banco.

shock [ʃɔk] n (impact) urto, colpo; (ELEC) scossa; (emotional) colpo, shock m inv; (MED) shock // vt colpire, scioccare; scandalizzare; ~ **absorber** n ammortizzatore m; ~**ing** a scioccante, traumatizzante; scandaloso(a).

shod [ʃɔd] pt, pp of **shoe**.

shoddy ['ʃɔdɪ] a scadente.

shoe [ʃuː] n scarpa; (also: horse~) ferro di cavallo // vt (pt, pp **shod**) (horse) ferrare; ~**horn** n calzante m; ~**lace** n stringa; ~ **polish** n lucido per scarpe; ~**shop** n calzoleria; ~**string** n (fig): on a ~string con quattro soldi.

shone [ʃɔn] pt, pp of **shine**.

shoo [ʃuː] excl sciò!, via!

shook [ʃuk] pt of **shake**.

shoot [ʃuːt] n (on branch, seedling) germoglio // vb (pt, pp **shot**) vt (game) cacciare, andare a caccia di; (person) sparare a; (execute) fucilare; (film) girare // vi (with gun): to ~ (at) sparare

(a), fare fuoco (su); (with bow): to ~ (at) tirare (su); (FOOTBALL) sparare, tirare (forte); **to ~ in/out** vi entrare/uscire come una freccia; **to ~ up** vi (fig) salire alle stelle; ~**ing** n (shots) sparatoria; (HUNTING) caccia; ~**ing star** n stella cadente.

shop [ʃɔp] n negozio; (workshop) officina // vi (also: go ~ping) fare spese; ~ **assistant** n (Brit) commesso/a; ~ **floor** n officina; (Brit fig) operai mpl, maestranze fpl; ~**keeper** n negoziante m/f, bottegaio/a; ~**lifting** n taccheggio; ~**per** n compratore/trice; ~**ping** n (goods) spesa, acquisti mpl; ~**ping bag** n borsa per la spesa; ~**ping centre**, (US) ~**ping center** n centro commerciale; ~-**soiled** a sciupato(a) a forza di stare in vetrina; ~ **steward** n (Brit INDUSTRY) rappresentante m sindacale; ~ **window** n vetrina.

shore [ʃɔː*] n (of sea) riva, spiaggia; (of lake) riva // vt: to ~ (up) puntellare.

shorn [ʃɔːn] pp of **shear**.

short [ʃɔːt] a (not long) corto(a); (soon finished) breve; (person) basso(a); (curt) brusco(a), secco(a); (insufficient) insufficiente // n (also: ~ film) cortometraggio; (a pair of) ~s (i) calzoncini; to be ~ of sth essere a corto di or mancare di qc; in ~ in breve; ~ of doing a meno che non si faccia; everything ~ of tutto fuorché; it is ~ for è l'abbreviazione or il diminutivo di; to cut ~ (speech, visit) accorciare, abbreviare; (person) interrompere; to fall ~ of venir meno a; non soddisfare; to stop ~ fermarsi di colpo; to stop ~ of non arrivare fino a; ~**age** n scarsezza, carenza; ~**bread** n biscotto di pasta frolla; ~-**change** vt: to ~-**change** sb imbrogliare qn sul resto; ~-**circuit** n cortocircuito // vt cortocircuitare // vi fare cortocircuito; ~-**coming** n difetto; ~(**crust**) **pastry** n (Brit) pasta frolla; ~-**cut** n scorciatoia; ~**en** vt accorciare, ridurre; ~**fall** n deficit m; ~**hand** n (Brit) stenografia; ~**hand typist** n (Brit) stenodattilografo/a; ~ **list** n (Brit: for job) rosa dei candidati; ~**ly** ad fra poco; ~-**sighted** a (Brit) miope; ~-**staffed** a a corto di personale; ~ **story** n racconto, novella; ~-**tempered** a irascibile; ~-**term** a (effect) di or a breve durata; ~**wave** n (RADIO) onde fpl corte.

shot [ʃɔt] pt, pp of **shoot** // n sparo, colpo; (person) tiratore m; (try) prova; (injection) iniezione f; (PHOT) foto f inv; like a ~ come un razzo; (very readily) immediatamente; ~**gun** n fucile m da caccia.

should [ʃud] auxiliary vb: I ~ go now dovrei andare ora; he ~ be there now dovrebbe essere arrivato ora; I ~ go if I were you se fossi in te andrei; I ~ like to mi piacerebbe.

shoulder ['∫əuldə*] n spalla; (Brit: of road): **hard** ~ banchina // vt (fig) addossarsi, prendere sulle proprie spalle; ~ **bag** n borsa a tracolla; ~ **blade** n scapola; ~ **strap** n bretella, spallina.

shouldn't ['∫udnt] = **should not**.

shout [∫aut] n urlo, grido // vt gridare // vi urlare, gridare; **to** ~ **down** vt zittire gridando; ~**ing** n urli mpl.

shove [∫ʌv] vt spingere; (col: put): **to** ~ **sth in** ficcare qc in; **to** ~ **off** vi (NAUT) scostarsi.

shovel ['∫ʌvl] n pala // vt spalare.

show [∫əu] n (of emotion) dimostrazione f, manifestazione f; (semblance) apparenza; (exhibition) mostra, esposizione f; (THEATRE, CINEMA) spettacolo // vb (pt ~**ed**, pp **shown**) vt far vedere, mostrare; (courage etc) dimostrare, dar prova di; (exhibit) esporre // vi vedersi, essere visibile; on ~ (exhibits etc) esposto(a); **to** ~ **in** vt (person) far entrare; **to** ~ **off** vi (pej) esibirsi, mettersi in mostra // vt (display) mettere in risalto; (pej) mettere in mostra; **to** ~ **out** vt (person) accompagnare alla porta; **to** ~ **up** vi (stand out) essere ben visibile; (col: turn up) farsi vedere // vt mettere in risalto; (unmask) smascherare; ~ **business** n industria dello spettacolo; ~**down** n prova di forza.

shower ['∫auə*] n (rain) acquazzone m; (of stones etc) pioggia; (also: ~**bath**) doccia // vi fare la doccia // vt: **to** ~ **sb with** (gifts, abuse etc) coprire qn di; (missiles) lanciare contro qn una pioggia di; ~**proof** a impermeabile.

showing ['∫əuiŋ] n (of film) proiezione f.

show jumping n concorso ippico (di salto ad ostacoli).

shown [∫əun] pp of **show**.

show-off ['∫əuɔf] n (col: person) esibizionista m/f.

showroom ['∫əurum] n sala d'esposizione.

shrank [∫ræŋk] pt of **shrink**.

shrapnel ['∫ræpnl] n shrapnel m.

shred [∫red] n (gen pl) brandello // vt fare a brandelli; (CULIN) sminuzzare, tagliuzzare; ~**der** n (vegetable ~**der**) grattugia; (document ~**der**) distruttore m di documenti.

shrewd [∫ru:d] a astuto(a), scaltro(a).

shriek [∫ri:k] n strillo // vt, vi strillare.

shrill [∫ril] a acuto(a), stridulo(a), stridente.

shrimp [∫rimp] n gamberetto.

shrine [∫rain] n reliquario; (place) santuario.

shrink [∫riŋk] vb (pt **shrank**, pp

shrunk) vi restringersi; (fig) ridursi // vt (wool) far restringere // n (col: pej) psicanalista m/f; **to** ~ **from doing sth** rifuggire dal fare qc; ~**age** n restringimento; ~**wrap** vt confezionare con pellicola di plastica.

shrivel ['∫rivl] (also: ~ **up**) vt raggrinzare, avvizzire // vi raggrinzirsi, avvizzire.

shroud [∫raud] n sudario // vt: ~**ed in mystery** avvolto(a) nel mistero.

Shrove Tuesday ['∫rəuv-] n martedì m grasso.

shrub [∫rʌb] n arbusto; ~**bery** n arbusti mpl.

shrug [∫rʌg] n scrollata di spalle // vt, vi: **to** ~ (**one's shoulders**) alzare le spalle, fare spallucce; **to** ~ **off** vt passare sopra a.

shrunk [∫rʌŋk] pp of **shrink**.

shudder ['∫ʌdə*] n brivido // vi rabbrividire.

shuffle ['∫ʌfl] vt (cards) mescolare; **to** ~ (**one's feet**) strascicare i piedi.

shun [∫ʌn] vt fuggire, evitare.

shunt [∫ʌnt] vt (RAIL: direct) smistare; (: divert) deviare.

shut, pt, pp **shut** [∫ʌt] vt chiudere // vi chiudersi, chiudere; **to** ~ **down** vt, vi chiudere definitivamente; **to** ~ **off** vt fermare, bloccare; **to** ~ **up** vi (col: keep quiet) stare zitto(a), fare silenzio // vt (close) chiudere; (silence) far tacere; ~**ter** n imposta; (PHOT) otturatore m.

shuttle ['∫ʌtl] n spola, navetta; (also: ~ **service**) servizio m navetta inv.

shuttlecock ['∫ʌtlkɔk] n volano.

shy [∫ai] a timido(a).

sibling ['sibliŋ] n fratello/sorella.

Sicily ['sisili] n Sicilia.

sick [sik] a (ill) malato(a); (vomiting): **to be** ~ vomitare; (humour) macabro(a); **to feel** ~ avere la nausea; **to be** ~ **of** (fig) averne abbastanza di; ~ **bay** n infermeria; ~**en** vt nauseare // vi: **to be** ~**ening for sth** (cold etc) cavare qc.

sickle ['sikl] n falcetto.

sick: ~ **leave** n congedo per malattia; ~**ly** a malaticcio(a); (causing nausea) nauseante; ~**ness** n malattia; (vomiting) vomito; ~ **pay** n sussidio per malattia.

side [said] n lato; (of lake) riva // cpd (door, entrance) laterale // vi: **to** ~ **with sb** parteggiare per qn, prendere le parti di qn; **by the** ~ **of** a fianco di; (road) sul ciglio di; ~ **by** ~ fianco a fianco; **to take** ~**s** (**with**) schierarsi (con); ~**board** n credenza; ~**boards** (Brit), ~**burns** npl (whiskers) basette fpl; ~ **effect** n (MED) effetto collaterale; ~**light** n (AUT) luce f di posizione; ~**line** n (SPORT) linea laterale; (fig) attività secondaria; ~**long** a obliquo(a); ~**saddle** ad all'amazzone; ~ **show** n attrazione f; ~**step** vt (question) eludere; (problem) scavalcare; ~ **street** n traversa; ~**track** vt (fig) distrarre; ~**walk** n (US) marciapiede m; ~**ways** ad (move) di lato, di fianco; (look) con la coda dell'occhio.

siding ['saɪdɪŋ] n (RAIL) binario di raccordo.

sidle ['saɪdl] vi: to ~ up (to) avvicinarsi furtivamente (a).

siege [si:dʒ] n assedio.

sieve [sɪv] n setaccio // vt setacciare.

sift [sɪft] vt passare al crivello; (fig) vagliare.

sigh [saɪ] n sospiro // vi sospirare.

sight [saɪt] n (faculty) vista; (spectacle) spettacolo; (on gun) mira // vt avvistare; in ~ in vista; out of ~ non visibile; ~**seeing** n giro turistico; to go ~**seeing** visitare una località.

sign [saɪn] n segno; (with hand etc) segno, gesto; (notice) insegna, cartello // vt firmare; **to** ~ **on** vi (MIL) arruolarsi; (as unemployed) iscriversi sulla lista (dell'ufficio di collocamento) // vt (MIL) arruolare; (employee) assumere; **to** ~ **over** vt: to ~ sth over to sb cedere qc con scrittura legale a qn; **to** ~ **up** (MIL) vt arruolare // vi arruolarsi.

signal ['sɪgnl] n segnale m // vi (AUT) segnalare, mettere la freccia // vt (person) fare segno a; (message) comunicare per mezzo di segnali; ~**man** n (RAIL) deviatore m.

signature ['sɪgnətʃəʳ] n firma; ~ **tune** n sigla musicale.

signet ring ['sɪgnət-] n anello con sigillo.

significance [sɪg'nɪfɪkəns] n significato; importanza.

significant [sɪg'nɪfɪkənt] a significativo(a).

signpost ['saɪnpəust] n cartello indicatore.

silence ['saɪləns] n silenzio // vt far tacere, ridurre al silenzio; ~**r** n (on gun, Brit AUT) silenziatore m.

silent ['saɪlnt] a silenzioso(a); (film) muto(a); to **remain** ~ tacere, stare zitto; ~ **partner** n (COMM) socio inattivo.

silhouette [sɪlu:'ɛt] n silhouette f inv.

silicon chip ['sɪlɪkən-] n piastrina di silicio.

silk [sɪlk] n seta // cpd di seta; ~**y** a di seta.

silly ['sɪlɪ] a stupido(a), sciocco(a).

silt [sɪlt] n limo.

silver ['sɪlvəʳ] n argento; (money) monete da 5, 10 or 50 pence; (also: ~**ware**) argenteria // cpd d'argento; ~ **paper** n (Brit) carta argentata, (carta) stagnola; ~-**plated** a argentato(a); ~**smith** n argentiere m; ~**y** a (colour) argenteo(a); (sound) argentino(a).

similar ['sɪmɪləʳ] a: ~ (to) simile (a); ~**ly** ad allo stesso modo; così pure.

simile ['sɪmɪlɪ] n similitudine f.

simmer ['sɪməʳ] vi cuocere a fuoco lento.

simpering ['sɪmpərɪŋ] a lezioso(a), smorfioso(a).

simple ['sɪmpl] a semplice; **simplicity** [-'plɪsɪtɪ] n semplicità.

simultaneous [sɪməl'teɪnɪəs] a simultaneo(a).

sin [sɪn] n peccato // vi peccare.

since [sɪns] ad da allora // prep da // cj (time) da quando; (because) poiché, dato che; ~ **then** da allora.

sincere [sɪn'sɪəʳ] a sincero(a); ~**ly** ad: yours ~**ly** (in letters) distinti saluti; **sincerity** [-'sɛrɪtɪ] n sincerità.

sinew ['sɪnju:] n tendine m; ~s npl (muscles) muscoli mpl.

sinful ['sɪnful] a peccaminoso(a).

sing [sɪŋ], pt **sang**, pp **sung** vt, vi cantare.

singe [sɪndʒ] vt bruciacchiare.

singer ['sɪŋəʳ] n cantante m/f.

singing ['sɪŋɪŋ] n canto.

single ['sɪŋgl] a solo(a), unico(a); (unmarried: man) celibe; (: woman) nubile; (not double) semplice // n (Brit: also: ~ **ticket**) biglietto di (sola) andata; (record) 45 giri m; ~s npl (TENNIS) singolo; **to** ~ **out** vt scegliere; (distinguish) distinguere; ~ **bed** n letto a una piazza; ~-**breasted** a a un petto; ~ **file** n: in ~ **file** in fila indiana; ~-**handed** ad senza aiuto, da solo(a); ~-**minded** a tenace, risoluto(a); ~ **room** n camera singola.

singlet ['sɪŋglɪt] n canottiera.

singly ['sɪŋglɪ] ad separatamente.

singular ['sɪŋgjuləʳ] a (exceptional, LING) singolare; (unusual) strano(a) // n (LING) singolare m.

sinister ['sɪnɪstəʳ] a sinistro(a).

sink [sɪŋk] n lavandino, acquaio // vb (pt **sank**, pp **sunk**) vt (ship) (fare) affondare, colare a picco; (foundations) scavare; (piles etc): to ~ sth into conficcare qc in // vi affondare, andare a fondo; (ground etc) cedere, avvallarsi; **to** ~ **in** vi penetrare.

sinner ['sɪnəʳ] n peccatore/trice.

sinus ['saɪnəs] n (ANAT) seno.

sip [sɪp] n sorso // vt sorseggiare.

siphon ['saɪfən] n sifone m; **to** ~ **off** vt travasare (con un sifone).

sir [səʳ] n signore m; S~ **John Smith** Sir John Smith; yes ~ sì, signore.

siren ['saɪərn] n sirena.

sirloin ['sə:lɔɪn] n controfiletto.

sissy ['sɪsɪ] n (col) femminuccia.

sister ['sɪstəʳ] n sorella; (nun) suora; (Brit: nurse) infermiera f caposala inv; ~-**in-law** n cognata.

sit [sɪt], pt, pp **sat** vi sedere, sedersi; (assembly) essere in seduta // vt (exam) sostenere, dare; **to** ~ **down** vi sedersi; **to** ~ **in on** vt fus assistere a; **to** ~ **up**

vi tirarsi su a sedere; (*not go to bed*) stare alzato(a) fino a tardi.

sitcom ['sɪtkɔm] *n abbr* (= *situation comedy*) commedia di situazione.

site [saɪt] *n* posto; (*also: building ~*) cantiere *m* // *vt* situare.

sit-in ['sɪtɪn] *n* (*demonstration*) sit-in *m inv*.

sitting ['sɪtɪŋ] *n* (*of assembly etc*) seduta; (*in canteen*) turno; **~ room** *n* soggiorno.

situated ['sɪtjueɪtɪd] *a* situato(a).

situation [sɪtju'eɪʃən] *n* situazione *f*; "**~s vacant**" (*Brit*) "offerte *fpl* di impiego".

six [sɪks] *num* sei; **~teen** *num* sedici; **~th** *num* sesto(a); **~ty** *num* sessanta.

size [saɪz] *n* dimensioni *fpl*; (*of clothing*) taglia, misura; (*of shoes*) numero; (*glue*) colla; **to ~ up** *vt* giudicare, farsi un'idea di; **~able** *a* considerevole.

sizzle ['sɪzl] *vi* sfrigolare.

skate [skeɪt] *n* pattino; (*fish: pl inv*) razza // *vi* pattinare; **~board** *n* skateboard *m inv*; **~r** *n* pattinatore/ trice; **skating** *n* pattinaggio; **skating rink** *n* pista di pattinaggio.

skeleton ['skelɪtn] *n* scheletro; **~ key** *n* passe-partout *m inv*; **~ staff** *n* personale *m* ridotto.

skeptical ['skeptɪkl] *a* (*US*) = **sceptical**.

sketch [sketʃ] *n* (*drawing*) schizzo, abbozzo; (*THEATRE*) scenetta comica, sketch *m inv* // *vt* abbozzare, schizzare; **~ book** *n* album *m inv* per schizzi; **~y** *a* incompleto(a), lacunoso(a).

skewer ['skju:ə*] *n* spiedo.

ski [ski:] *n* sci *m inv* // *vi* sciare; **~ boot** *n* scarpone *m* da sci.

skid [skɪd] *n* slittamento // *vi* slittare.

skier ['ski:ə*] *n* sciatore/trice.

skiing ['ski:ɪŋ] *n* sci *m*.

ski jump *n* (*ramp*) trampolino; (*event*) salto con gli sci.

skilful ['skɪlful] *a* abile.

ski lift ['ski:lɪft] *n* sciovia.

skill [skɪl] *n* abilità *f inv*, capacità *f inv*; **~ed** *a* esperto(a); (*worker*) qualificato(a), specializzato(a).

skim [skɪm] *vt* (*milk*) scremare; (*soup*) schiumare; (*glide over*) sfiorare // *vi*: **to ~ through** (*fig*) scorrere, dare una scorsa a; **~med milk** *n* latte *m* scremato.

skimp [skɪmp] *vt* (*work*) fare alla carlona; (*cloth etc*) lesinare; **~y** *a* misero(a); striminzito(a); frugale.

skin [skɪn] *n* pelle *f* // *vt* (*fruit etc*) sbucciare; (*animal*) scuoiare, spellare; **~-deep** *a* superficiale; **~ diving** *n* nuoto subacqueo; **~ny** *a* molto magro(a), pelle e ossa *inv*; **~tight** *a* (*dress etc*) aderente.

skip [skɪp] *n* saltello, balzo; (*container*) benna // *vi* saltare; (*with rope*) saltare la corda // *vt* (*pass over*) saltare.

ski: ~ pants *npl* pantaloni *mpl* da sci; **~ pole** *n* racchetta (da sci).

skipper ['skɪpə*] *n* (*NAUT*, *SPORT*) capitano.

skipping rope ['skɪpɪŋ-] *n* (*Brit*) corda per saltare.

skirmish ['skə:mɪʃ] *n* scaramuccia.

skirt [skə:t] *n* gonna, sottana // *vt* fiancheggiare, costeggiare; **~ing board** *n* (*Brit*) zoccolo.

ski suit *n* tuta da sci.

skit [skɪt] *n* parodia; scenetta satirica.

skittle ['skɪtl] *n* birillo; **~s** *n* (*game*) (gioco dei) birilli *mpl*.

skive [skaɪv] *vi* (*Brit col*) fare il lavativo.

skulk [skʌlk] *vi* muoversi furtivamente.

skull [skʌl] *n* cranio, teschio.

skunk [skʌŋk] *n* moffetta.

sky [skaɪ] *n* cielo; **~light** *n* lucernario; **~scraper** *n* grattacielo.

slab [slæb] *n* lastra.

slack [slæk] *a* (*loose*) allentato(a); (*slow*) lento(a); (*careless*) negligente // *n* (*in rope etc*) parte *f* non tesa; **~s** *npl* pantaloni *mpl*; **~en** (*also: ~en off*) *vi* rallentare, diminuire // *vt* allentare.

slag [slæg] *n* scorie *fpl*; **~ heap** *n* ammasso di scorie.

slain [sleɪn] *pp of* **slay**.

slam [slæm] *vt* (*door*) sbattere; (*throw*) scaraventare; (*criticize*) stroncare // *vi* sbattere.

slander ['slɑ:ndə*] *n* calunnia; diffamazione *f* // *vt* calunniare; diffamare.

slang [slæŋ] *n* gergo, slang *m*.

slant [slɑ:nt] *n* pendenza, inclinazione *f*; (*fig*) angolazione *f*, punto di vista; **~ed** *a* tendenzioso(a); **~ing** *a* in pendenza, inclinato(a).

slap [slæp] *n* manata, pacca; (*on face*) schiaffo // *vt* dare una manata a; schiaffeggiare // *ad* (*directly*) in pieno; **~dash** *a* abborracciato(a); **~stick** *n* (*comedy*) farsa grossolana; **~-up** *a*: a **~-up meal** (*Brit*) un pranzo (*or* una cena) coi fiocchi.

slash [slæʃ] *vt* squarciare; (*face*) sfregiare; (*fig: prices*) ridurre drasticamente, tagliare.

slat [slæt] *n* (*of wood*) stecca; (*of plastic*) lamina.

slate [sleɪt] *n* ardesia // *vt* (*fig: criticize*) stroncare, distruggere.

slaughter ['slɔ:tə*] *n* strage *f*, massacro // *vt* (*animal*) macellare; (*people*) trucidare, massacrare.

slave [sleɪv] *n* schiavo/a // *vi* (*also: ~ away*) lavorare come uno schiavo; **~ry** *n* schiavitù *f*.

slay [sleɪ], *pt* **slew**, *pp* **slain** *vt* (*formal*) uccidere.

SLD *n abbr* (*Brit*) = *Social and Liberal Democrats*.

sleazy ['sli:zɪ] *a* trasandato(a).

sledge [slɛdʒ] n slitta; **~hammer** n mazza, martello da fabbro.

sleek [sli:k] a (hair, fur) lucido(a), lucente; (car, boat) slanciato(a), affusolato(a).

sleep [sli:p] n sonno // vi (pt, pp **slept**) dormire; **to go to ~** addormentarsi; **to ~ in** vi (lie late) alzarsi tardi; (oversleep) dormire fino a tardi; **~er** n (person) dormiente m/f; (Brit RAIL: on track) traversina; (: train) treno di vagoni letto; **~ing bag** n sacco a pelo; **~ing car** n vagone m letto inv, carrozza f letto inv; **~ing pill** n sonnifero; **~less** a: **a ~less night** una notte in bianco; **~walker** n sonnambulo/a; **~y** a assonnato(a), sonnolento(a); (fig) addormentato(a).

sleet [sli:t] n nevischio.

sleeve [sli:v] n manica.

sleigh [sleɪ] n slitta.

sleight [slaɪt] n: **~ of hand** gioco di destrezza.

slender ['slɛndə*] a snello(a), sottile; (not enough) scarso(a), esiguo(a).

slept [slɛpt] pt, pp of **sleep**.

slew [slu:] vi girare // pt of **slay**.

slice [slaɪs] n fetta // vt affettare, tagliare a fette.

slick [slɪk] a (clever) brillante; (insincere) untuoso(a), falso(a) // n (also: oil **~**) chiazza di petrolio.

slide [slaɪd] n (in playground) scivolo; (PHOT) diapositiva; (Brit: also: hair **~**) fermaglio (per capelli); (in prices) caduta // vb (pt, pp **slid** [slɪd]) vt far scivolare // vi scivolare; **~ rule** n regolo calcolatore; **sliding** a (door) scorrevole; **sliding scale** n scala mobile.

slight [slaɪt] a (slim) snello(a), sottile; (frail) delicato(a), fragile; (trivial) insignificante; (small) piccolo(a) // n offesa, affronto // vt (offend) offendere, fare un affronto a; **not in the ~est** affatto, neppure per sogno; **~ly** ad lievemente, un po'.

slim [slɪm] a magro(a), snello(a) // vi dimagrire; fare (or seguire) una dieta dimagrante.

slime [slaɪm] n limo, melma; viscidume m.

slimming ['slɪmɪŋ] n (diet) dimagrante; (food) ipocalorico(a).

sling [slɪŋ] n (MED) benda al collo // vt (pt, pp **slung**) lanciare, tirare.

slip [slɪp] n scivolata, scivolone m; (mistake) errore m, sbaglio; (underskirt) sottoveste f; (of paper) striscia di carta; tagliando, scontrino // vt (slide) far scivolare // vi (slide) scivolare; (move smoothly): **to ~ into/out of** scivolare in/via da; (decline) declinare; **to ~ sth on/off** infilarsi/togliersi qc; **to give sb the ~** sfuggire qn; **a ~ of the tongue** un lapsus linguae; **to ~ away** vi

svignarsela; **~ped disc** n spostamento delle vertebre.

slipper ['slɪpə*] n pantofola.

slippery ['slɪpərɪ] a scivoloso(a).

slip road n (Brit: to motorway) rampa di accesso.

slipshod ['slɪpʃɔd] a sciatto(a), trasandato(a).

slip-up ['slɪpʌp] n granchio (fig).

slipway ['slɪpweɪ] n scalo di costruzione.

slit [slɪt] n fessura, fenditura; (cut) taglio; (tear) squarcio; strappo // vt (pt, pp **slit**) tagliare; (make a slit) squarciare; strappare.

slither ['slɪðə*] vi scivolare, sdrucciolare.

sliver ['slɪvə*] n (of glass, wood) scheggia; (of cheese) fettina.

slob [slɔb] n (col) sciattone/a.

slog [slɔg] (Brit) n faticata // vi lavorare con accanimento, sgobbare.

slogan ['sləʊgən] n motto, slogan m inv.

slop [slɔp] vi (also: **~ over**) traboccare; versarsi // vt spandere; versare.

slope [sləʊp] n pendio; (side of mountain) versante m; (of roof) pendenza; (of floor) inclinazione // vi: **to ~ down** declinare; **to ~ up** essere in salita.

sloppy ['slɔpɪ] a (work) tirato(a) via; (appearance) sciatto(a); (film etc) sdolcinato(a).

slot [slɔt] n fessura // vt: **to ~ sth into** infilare qc in // vi: **to ~ into** inserirsi in.

sloth [sləʊθ] n (laziness) pigrizia, accidia.

slot machine n (Brit: vending machine) distributore m automatico; (for gambling) slot-machine f inv.

slouch [slautʃ] vi (when walking) camminare dinoccolato(a); **she was ~ing in a chair** era sprofondata in una poltrona; **to ~ about** vi (laze) oziare.

slovenly ['slʌvənlɪ] a sciatto(a), trasandato(a).

slow [sləʊ] a lento(a); (watch): **to be ~** essere indietro // ad lentamente // vt, vi (also: **~ down**, **~ up**) rallentare; "**~**" (road sign) "rallentare"; **~ly** ad lentamente; **~ motion** n: **in ~ motion** al rallentatore.

sludge [slʌdʒ] n fanghiglia.

slug [slʌg] n lumaca; (bullet) pallottola; **~gish** a lento(a).

sluice [slu:s] n chiusa.

slum [slʌm] n catapecchia.

slumber ['slʌmbə*] n sonno.

slump [slʌmp] n crollo, caduta; (economic) depressione f, crisi f inv // vi crollare.

slung [slʌŋ] pt, pp of **sling**.

slur [slə:*] n pronuncia indistinta; (stigma) diffamazione f, calunnia; (smear): **~ (on)** macchia (su); (MUS) legatura // vt pronunciare in modo indistinto.

slush [slʌʃ] *n* neve *f* mista a fango; ~ **fund** *n* fondi *mpl* neri.

slut [slʌt] *n* donna trasandata, sciattona.

sly [slaɪ] *a* furbo(a), scaltro(a).

smack [smæk] *n* (*slap*) pacca; (*on face*) schiaffo // *vt* schiaffeggiare; (*child*) picchiare // *vi*: **to ~ of** puzzare di.

small [smɔ:l] *a* piccolo(a); ~ **ads** *npl* (*Brit*) piccola pubblicità; ~ **change** *n* moneta, spiccioli *mpl*; ~**holder** *n* piccolo proprietario; ~ **hours** *npl*: **in the ~ hours** alle ore piccole; ~**pox** *n* vaiolo; ~ **talk** *n* chiacchiere *fpl*.

smart [smɑ:t] *a* elegante; (*clever*) intelligente; (*quick*) sveglio(a) // *vi* bruciare; **to ~en up** *vi* farsi bello(a) // *vt* (*people*) fare bello(a); (*things*) abbellire.

smash [smæʃ] *n* (*also:* ~-up) scontro, collisione *f* // *vt* frantumare, fracassare; (*opponent*) annientare, schiacciare; (*hopes*) distruggere; (*SPORT: record*) battere // *vi* frantumarsi, andare in pezzi; ~**ing** *a* (*col*) favoloso(a), formidabile.

smattering [ˈsmætərɪŋ] *n*: **a ~ of** un'infarinatura di.

smear [smɪə*] *n* macchia; (*MED*) striscio // *vt* ungere; (*fig*) denigrare, diffamare.

smell [smɛl] *n* odore *m*; (*sense*) olfatto, odorato // *vb* (*pt, pp* **smelt** *or* **smelled** [smɛlt, smɛld]) *vt* sentire (l') odore di // *vi* (*food etc*): **to ~ (of)** avere odore (di); (*pej*) puzzare, avere un cattivo odore; it ~s **good** ha un buon odore; ~**y** *a* puzzolente.

smile [smaɪl] *n* sorriso // *vi* sorridere.

smirk [smɜ:k] *n* sorriso furbo; sorriso compiaciuto.

smith [smɪθ] *n* fabbro; ~**y** *n* fucina.

smock [smɒk] *n* grembiule *m*, camice *m*.

smog [smɒg] *n* smog *m*.

smoke [sməuk] *n* fumo // *vt, vi* fumare; ~**d** *a* (*bacon, glass*) affumicato(a); ~**r** *n* (*person*) fumatore/trice; (*RAIL*) carrozza per fumatori; ~ **screen** *n* (*MIL*) cortina fumogena *or* di fumo; (*fig*) copertura; **smoking** *n* fumo; "no smoking" (*sign*) "vietato fumare"; **smoky** *a* fumoso(a); (*surface*) affumicato(a).

smolder [ˈsməuldə*] *vi* (*US*) = **smoulder**.

smooth [smu:ð] *a* liscio(a); (*sauce*) omogeneo(a); (*flavour, whisky*) amabile; (*movement*) regolare; (*person*) mellifluo(a) // *vt* lisciare, spianare; (*also*: ~ **out**: *difficulties*) appianare.

smother [ˈsmʌðə*] *vt* soffocare.

smoulder [ˈsməuldə*] *vi* covare sotto la cenere.

smudge [smʌdʒ] *n* macchia; sbavatura // *vt* imbrattare, sporcare.

smug [smʌg] *a* soddisfatto(a), compiaciuto(a).

smuggle [ˈsmʌgl] *vt* contrabbandare; ~**r** *n* contrabbandiere/a; **smuggling** *n* contrabbando.

smutty [ˈsmʌtɪ] *a* (*fig*) osceno(a), indecente.

snack [snæk] *n* spuntino; ~ **bar** *n* tavola calda, snack bar *m inv*.

snag [snæg] *n* intoppo, ostacolo imprevisto.

snail [sneɪl] *n* chiocciola.

snake [sneɪk] *n* serpente *m*.

snap [snæp] *n* (*sound*) schianto, colpo secco; (*photograph*) istantanea; (*game*) rubamazzo // *a* improvviso(a) // *vt* (far) schioccare; (*break*) spezzare di netto; (*photograph*) scattare un'istantanea di // *vi* spezzarsi con un rumore secco; **to ~ open/shut** aprirsi/chiudersi di scatto; **to ~ at** *vt fus* (*subj: dog*) cercare di mordere; **to ~ off** *vt* (*break*) schiantare; **to ~ up** *vt* afferrare; ~**py** *a* (*col: answer, slogan*) d'effetto; **make it ~py!** (*hurry up*) sbrigati!, svelto!; ~**shot** *n* istantanea.

snare [snɛə*] *n* trappola.

snarl [snɑ:l] *vi* ringhiare.

snatch [snætʃ] *n* (*fig*) furto con strappo, scippo; (*small amount*): ~**es of** frammenti *mpl* di // *vt* strappare (con violenza); (*steal*) rubare.

sneak [sni:k] *vi*: **to ~ in/out** entrare/uscire di nascosto; ~**ers** *npl* scarpe *fpl* da ginnastica; ~**y** *a* falso(a), disonesto(a).

sneer [snɪə*] *vi* ghignare, sogghignare.

sneeze [sni:z] *vi* starnutire.

sniff [snɪf] *n* fiutata, annusata // *vi* fiutare, annusare; tirare su col naso; (*in contempt*) arricciare il naso // *vt* fiutare, annusare.

snigger [ˈsnɪgə*] *n* riso represso // *vi* ridacchiare, ridere sotto i baffi.

snip [snɪp] *n* pezzetto; (*bargain*) (buon) affare *m*, occasione *f* // *vt* tagliare.

sniper [ˈsnaɪpə*] *n* (*marksman*) franco tiratore *m*, cecchino.

snippet [ˈsnɪpɪt] *n* frammento.

snivelling [ˈsnɪvlɪŋ] *a* (*whimpering*) piagnucoloso(a).

snob [snɒb] *n* snob *m/f inv*; ~**bish** *a* snob *inv*.

snooker [ˈsnu:kə*] *n* tipo di gioco del biliardo.

snoop [snu:p] *vi*: **to ~ on sb** spiare qn; **to ~ about** curiosare.

snooty [ˈsnu:tɪ] *a* borioso(a), snob *inv*.

snooze [snu:z] *n* sonnellino, pisolino // *vi* fare un sonnellino.

snore [snɔ:*] *vi* russare.

snorkel [ˈsnɔ:kl] *n* (*of swimmer*) respiratore *m* a tubo.

snort [snɔ:t] *n* sbuffo // *vi* sbuffare.

snotty [ˈsnɒtɪ] *a* moccioso(a).

snout [snaut] *n* muso.

snow [snəu] *n* neve *f* // *vi* nevicare; ~**ball** *n* palla di neve; ~**bound** *a* bloccato(a) dalla neve; ~**drift** n cumulo di neve (ammucchiato dal vento); ~**drop** n bucaneve m inv; ~**fall** n nevicata; ~**flake** n fiocco di neve; ~**man** n pupazzo di neve; ~**plough**, (US) ~**plow** n spazzaneve m inv; ~**shoe** n racchetta da neve; ~**storm** n tormenta.

snub [snʌb] vt snobbare // n offesa, affronto; ~**-nosed** a dal naso camuso.

snuff [snʌf] n tabacco da fiuto.

snug [snʌg] a comodo(a); (room, house) accogliente, comodo(a).

snuggle ['snʌgl] vi: to ~ up to sb stringersi a qn.

so [səu] ♦ ad 1 (thus, likewise) così; if ~ se è così, quand'è così; I didn't do it — you did ~! non l'ho fatto io — sì che l'hai fatto!; ~ do I, ~ am I etc anch'io; it's 5 o'clock — ~ it is! sono le 5 — davvero!; I hope ~ lo spero; I think ~ penso di sì; ~ far finora, fin qui; (in past) fino ad allora

2 (in comparisons etc: to such a degree) così; ~ **big** (that) così grande (che); she's not ~ **clever** as her brother lei non è (così) intelligente come suo fratello

3: ~ **much** a tanto(a) ♦ ad tanto; I've got ~ much work/money ho tanto lavoro/ tanti soldi; I love you ~ much ti amo tanto; ~ **many** tanti(e)

4 (phrases): 10 or ~ circa 10; ~ **long!** (col: goodbye) ciao!, ci vediamo!

♦ cj 1 (expressing purpose): ~ as to do in modo or così da fare; we hurried ~ as not to be late ci affrettammo per non fare tardi; ~ (that) affinché + sub, perché + sub

2 (expressing result): he didn't arrive ~ I left non è venuto così me ne sono andata; ~ you see, I could have gone vedi, sarei potuto andare.

soak [səuk] vt inzuppare; (clothes) mettere a mollo // vi inzupparsi; (clothes) essere a mollo; to ~ **in** vi penetrare; to ~ **up** vt assorbire.

so-and-so ['səuəndsəu] n (somebody) un tale.

soap [səup] n sapone m; ~**flakes** npl sapone m in scaglie; ~ **opera** n soap opera f inv; ~ **powder** n detersivo; ~**y** a insaponato(a).

soar [sɔː*] vi volare in alto.

sob [sɔb] n singhiozzo // vi singhiozzare.

sober ['səubə*] a non ubriaco(a); (sedate) serio(a); (moderate) moderato(a); (colour, style) sobrio(a); to ~ **up** vt far passare la sbornia a // vi farsi passare la sbornia.

so-called ['səu'kɔːld] a cosiddetto(a).

soccer ['sɔkə*] n calcio.

sociable ['səuʃəbl] a socievole.

social ['səuʃl] a sociale // n festa, serata; ~ **club** n club m inv sociale; ~**ism** n socialismo; ~**ist** a, n socialista (m/f);

~**ize** vi: to ~ize (with) socializzare (con); ~ **security** n previdenza sociale; ~ **work** n servizio sociale; ~ **worker** n assistente m/f sociale.

society [sə'saiəti] n società f inv; (club) società, associazione f; (also: high ~) alta società.

sociology [səusi'ɔlədʒi] n sociologia.

sock [sɔk] n calzino // vt (hit) dare un pugno a.

socket ['sɔkit] n cavità f inv; (of eye) orbita; (Brit ELEC: also: wall ~) presa di corrente; (: for light bulb) portalampada m inv.

sod [sɔd] n (of earth) zolla erbosa; (Brit col!) bastardo/a (!).

soda ['səudə] n (CHEM) soda; (also: ~ water) acqua di seltz; (US: also: ~ pop) gassosa.

sodden ['sɔdn] a fradicio(a).

sodium ['səudiəm] n sodio.

sofa ['səufə] n sofà m inv.

soft [sɔft] a (not rough) morbido(a); (not hard) soffice; (not loud) sommesso(a); (kind) gentile; (weak) debole; (stupid) stupido(a); ~ **drink** n analcolico; ~**en** ['sɔfn] vt ammorbidire; addolcire; attenuare // vi ammorbidirsi; addolcirsi; attenuarsi; ~**ly** ad dolcemente; morbidamente; ~**ness** n dolcezza; morbidezza.

software ['sɔftwɛə*] n (COMPUT) software m.

soggy ['sɔgi] a inzuppato(a).

soil [sɔil] n (earth) terreno, suolo // vt sporcare; (fig) macchiare.

solace ['sɔlis] n consolazione f.

solar ['səulə*] a solare.

sold [səuld] pt, pp of **sell**; ~ **out** a (COMM) esaurito(a).

solder ['səuldə*] vt saldare // n saldatura.

soldier ['səuldʒə*] n soldato, militare m.

sole [səul] n (of foot) pianta (del piede); (of shoe) suola; (fish: pl inv) sogliola // a solo(a), unico(a).

solemn ['sɔləm] a solenne; grave; serio(a).

sole trader n (COMM) commerciante m in proprio.

solicit [sə'lisit] vt (request) richiedere, sollecitare // vi (prostitute) adescare i passanti.

solicitor [sə'lisitə*] n (Brit: for wills etc) ≈ notaio; (: in court) ≈ avvocato.

solid ['sɔlid] a (not hollow) pieno(a); (strong, sound, reliable, not liquid) solido(a); (meal) sostanzioso(a) // n solido.

solidarity [sɔli'dæriti] n solidarietà.

solitaire [sɔli'tɛə*] n (games, gem) solitario.

solitary ['sɔlitəri] a solitario(a); ~ **confinement** n (LAW): in ~ confinement in cella d'isolamento.

solo ['səuləu] n assolo; ~**ist** n solista m/f.

soluble ['sɔljubl] a solubile.

solution [sə'lu:ʃən] n soluzione f.

solve [sɔlv] vt risolvere.

solvent ['sɔlvənt] a (COMM) solvibile // n (CHEM) solvente m.

sombre, (US) **somber** ['sɔmbə*] a scuro(a); (mood, person) triste.

some [sʌm] ♦ a 1 (a certain amount or number of): ~ **tea/water/cream** del tè/dell'acqua/della panna; ~ **children/apples** dei bambini/delle mele
2 (certain: in contrasts) certo(a); ~ **people say that ...** alcuni dicono che ..., certa gente dice che ...
3 (unspecified) un(a) certo(a), qualche; ~ **woman was asking for you** una tale chiedeva di lei; ~ **day** un giorno; ~ **day next week** un giorno della prossima settimana
♦ pronoun **1** (a certain number) alcuni(e), certi(e); **I've got** ~ (books etc) ne ho alcuni; ~ **(of them) have been sold** alcuni sono stati venduti
2 (a certain amount) un po'; **I've got** ~ (money, milk) ne ho un po'; **I've read** ~ **of the book** ho letto parte del libro
♦ ad: ~ **10 people** circa 10 persone.

somebody ['sʌmbədɪ] pronoun = **someone**.

somehow ['sʌmhau] ad in un modo o nell'altro, in qualche modo; (for some reason) per qualche ragione.

someone ['sʌmwʌn] pronoun qualcuno.

someplace ['sʌmpleɪs] ad (US) = **somewhere**.

somersault ['sʌməsɔ:lt] n capriola; salto mortale // vi fare una capriola (or un salto mortale); (car) cappottare.

something ['sʌmθɪŋ] pronoun qualcosa, qualche cosa; ~ **nice** qualcosa di bello; ~ **to do** qualcosa da fare.

sometime ['sʌmtaɪm] ad (in future) una volta o l'altra; (in past): ~ **last month** durante il mese scorso.

sometimes ['sʌmtaɪmz] ad qualche volta.

somewhat ['sʌmwɔt] ad piuttosto.

somewhere ['sʌmwɛə*] ad in or da qualche parte.

son [sʌn] n figlio.

song [sɔŋ] n canzone f.

sonic ['sɔnɪk] a (boom) sonico(a).

son-in-law ['sʌnɪnlɔ:] n genero.

sonnet ['sɔnɪt] n sonetto.

sonny ['sʌnɪ] n (col) ragazzo mio.

soon [su:n] ad presto, fra poco; (early) presto; ~ **afterwards** poco dopo; **as** ~ **as possible** prima possibile; **I'll do it as** ~ **as I can** lo farò appena posso; ~**er** ad (time) prima; (preference): **I would** ~**er do** preferirei fare; ~**er or later** prima o poi.

soot [sut] n fuliggine f.

soothe [su:ð] vt calmare.

sophisticated [sə'fɪstɪkeɪtɪd] a sofisticato(a); raffinato(a); complesso(a).

sophomore ['sɔfəmɔ:*] n (US) studente/essa del secondo anno.

sopping ['sɔpɪŋ] a (also: ~ **wet**) bagnato(a) fradicio(a).

soppy ['sɔpɪ] a (pej) sentimentale.

soprano [sə'prɑ:nəu] n (voice) soprano m; (singer) soprano m/f.

sorcerer ['sɔ:sərə*] n stregone m, mago.

sore [sɔ:*] a (painful) dolorante; (col: offended) offeso(a) // n piaga; ~**ly** ad (tempted) fortemente.

sorrow ['sɔrəu] n dolore m.

sorry ['sɔrɪ] a spiacente; (condition, excuse) misero(a); ~**!** scusa! (or scusi! or scusate!); **to feel** ~ **for sb** rincrescersi per qn.

sort [sɔ:t] n specie f, genere m // vt (also: ~ **out**: papers) classificare; ordinare; (: letters etc) smistare; (: problems) risolvere; ~**ing office** n ufficio m smistamento inv.

SOS n abbr (= save our souls) S.O.S. m inv.

so-so ['səusəu] ad così così.

sought [sɔ:t] pt, pp of **seek**.

soul [səul] n anima; ~**-destroying** a demoralizzante; ~**ful** a pieno(a) di sentimento.

sound [saund] a (healthy) sano(a); (safe, not damaged) solido(a), in buono stato; (reliable, not superficial) solido(a); (sensible) giudizioso(a), di buon senso // ad: ~ **asleep** profondamente addormentato // n (noise) suono; rumore m; (GEO) stretto // vt (alarm) suonare; (also: ~ **out**: opinions) sondare // vi suonare; (fig: seem) sembrare; **to** ~ **like** rassomigliare a; ~ **barrier** n muro del suono; ~ **effects** npl effetti sonori; ~**ly** ad (sleep) profondamente; (beat) duramente; ~**proof** vt insonorizzare, isolare acusticamente // a insonorizzato(a), isolato(a) acusticamente; ~**track** n (of film) colonna sonora.

soup [su:p] n minestra; brodo; zuppa; **in the** ~ (fig) nei guai; ~ **plate** n piatto fondo; ~**spoon** n cucchiaio da minestra.

sour ['sauə*] a aspro(a); (fruit) acerbo(a); (milk) acido(a), fermentato(a); (fig) arcigno(a); acido(a); **it's** ~ **grapes** è soltanto invidia.

source [sɔ:s] n fonte f, sorgente f; (fig) fonte.

south [sauθ] n sud m, meridione m, mezzogiorno // a del sud, sud inv, meridionale // ad verso sud; **S~ Africa** n Sudafrica m; **S~ African** a, n sudafricano(a); **S~ America** n Sudamerica m, America del sud; **S~ American** a, n sudamericano(a); ~**-east** n sud-est m; ~**erly** ['sʌðəlɪ] a del sud; ~**ern** ['sʌðən**

a del sud, meridionale; esposto(a) a sud; **S~ Pole** *n* Polo Sud; **~ward(s)** *ad* verso sud; **~-west** *n* sud-ovest *m*.

souvenir [su:və'nɪə*] *n* ricordo, souvenir *m inv*.

sovereign ['sɔvrɪn] *a*, *n* sovrano(a).

soviet ['səuvɪət] *a* sovietico(a); **the S~ Union** l'Unione *f* Sovietica.

sow *n* [sau] scrofa // *vt* [səu] (*pt* **~ed**, *pp* **sown** [səun]) seminare.

soya ['sɔɪə], (*US*) **soy** [sɔɪ] *n*: **~ bean** *n* seme *m* di soia; **~ sauce** *n* salsa di soia.

spa [spa:] *n* (*resort*) stazione *f* termale; (*US: also*: **health ~**) centro di cure estetiche.

space [speɪs] *n* spazio; (*room*) posto; spazio; (*length of time*) intervallo // *cpd* spaziale // *vt* (*also*: **~ out**) distanziare; **~craft** *n* (*pl inv*) veicolo spaziale; **~man/woman** *n* astronauta *m/f*, cosmonauta *m/f*; **~ship** *n* = **~craft**; **spacing** *n* spaziatura.

spacious ['speɪʃəs] *a* spazioso(a), ampio(a).

spade [speɪd] *n* (*tool*) vanga; pala; (*child's*) paletta; **~s** *npl* (*CARDS*) picche *fpl*.

Spain [speɪn] *n* Spagna.

span [spæn] *pt of* **spin** // *n* (*of bird, plane*) apertura alare; (*of arch*) campata; (*in time*) periodo; durata // *vt* attraversare; (*fig*) abbracciare.

Spaniard ['spænjəd] *n* spagnolo/a.

spaniel ['spænjəl] *n* spaniel *m inv*.

Spanish ['spænɪʃ] *a* spagnolo(a) // *n* (*LING*) spagnolo; **the ~** *npl* gli Spagnoli.

spank [spæŋk] *vt* sculacciare.

spanner ['spænə*] *n* (*Brit*) chiave *f* inglese.

spar [spa:*] *n* asta, palo // *vi* (*BOXING*) allenarsi.

spare [spɛə*] *a* di riserva, di scorta; (*surplus*) in più, d'avanzo // *n* (*part*) pezzo di ricambio // *vt* (*do without*) fare a meno di; (*afford to give*) concedere; (*refrain from hurting, using*) risparmiare; **to ~** (*surplus*) d'avanzo; **~ part** *n* pezzo di ricambio; **~ time** *n* tempo libero; **~ wheel** *n* (*AUT*) ruota di scorta.

sparing ['spɛərɪŋ] *a*: **to be ~ with sth** risparmiare qc; **~ly** *ad* moderatamente.

spark [spa:k] *n* scintilla // **~(ing) plug** *n* candela.

sparkle ['spa:kl] *n* scintillio, sfavillio // *vi* scintillare, sfavillare; (*bubble*) spumeggiare, frizzare; **sparkling** *a* scintillante, sfavillante; (*wine*) spumante.

sparrow ['spærəu] *n* passero.

sparse [spa:s] *a* sparso(a), rado(a).

spartan ['spa:tən] *a* (*fig*) spartano(a).

spasm ['spæzəm] *n* (*MED*) spasmo; (*fig*) accesso, attacco; **~odic** [spæz'mɔdɪk] *a*

spasmodico(a); (*fig*) intermittente.

spastic ['spæstɪk] *n* spastico/a.

spat [spæt] *pt*, *pp of* **spit**.

spate [speɪt] *n* (*fig*): **~ of** diluvio *or* fiume *m* di; **in ~** (*river*) in piena.

spatter ['spætə*] *vt*, *vi* schizzare.

spawn [spɔ:n] *vt* deporre // *vi* deporre le uova // *n* uova *fpl*.

speak [spi:k], *pt* **spoke**, *pp* **spoken** *vt* (*language*) parlare; (*truth*) dire // *vi* parlare; **to ~ to sb/of** *or* **about sth** parlare a qn/di qc; (*truth*) parla più forte!; **~ up!** parla più forte!; **~er** *n* (*in public*) oratore/trice; (*also*: **loud~er**) altoparlante *m*; (*POL*): **the S~er** il presidente della Camera dei Comuni (*Brit*) *or* dei Rappresentanti (*US*).

spear [spɪə*] *n* lancia; **~head** *vt* (*attack etc*) condurre.

spec [spɛk] *n* (*col*): **on ~** sperando bene.

special ['spɛʃl] *a* speciale; **~ist** *n* specialista *m/f*; **~ity** [spɛʃɪ'ælɪtɪ] *n* specialità *f inv*; **~ize** *vi*: **to ~ize (in)** specializzarsi (in); **~ly** *ad* specialmente, particolarmente.

species ['spi:ʃi:z] *n* (*pl inv*) specie *f inv*.

specific [spə'sɪfɪk] *a* specifico(a); preciso(a); **~ally** *ad* esplicitamente; (*especially*) appositamente.

specimen ['spɛsɪmən] *n* esemplare *m*, modello; (*MED*) campione *m*.

speck [spɛk] *n* puntino, macchiolina; (*particle*) granello.

speckled ['spɛkld] *a* macchiettato(a).

specs [spɛks] *npl* (*col*) occhiali *mpl*.

spectacle ['spɛktəkl] *n* spettacolo; **~s** *npl* (*glasses*) occhiali *mpl*; **spectacular** [-'tækjulə*] *a* spettacolare // *n* (*CINEMA etc*) film *m inv etc* spettacolare.

spectator [spɛk'teɪtə*] *n* spettatore *m*.

spectre, (*US*) **specter** ['spɛktə*] *n* spettro.

spectrum, *pl* **spectra** ['spɛktrəm, -rə] *n* spettro; (*fig*) gamma.

speculation [spɛkju'leɪʃən] *n* speculazione *f*; congetture *fpl*.

speech [spi:tʃ] *n* (*faculty*) parola; (*talk*) discorso; (*manner of speaking*) parlata; (*enunciation*) elocuzione *f*; **~less** *a* ammutolito(a), muto(a).

speed [spi:d] *n* velocità *f inv*; (*promptness*) prontezza; **at full** *or* **top ~** a tutta velocità; **to ~ up** *vi*, *vt* accelerare; **~boat** *n* motoscafo; **~ily** *ad* velocemente; prontamente; **~ing** *n* (*AUT*) eccesso di velocità; **~ limit** *n* limite *m* di velocità; **~ometer** [spɪ'dɔmɪtə*] *n* tachimetro; **~way** *n* (*SPORT*) pista per motociclismo; (*also*: **~way racing**) corsa motociclistica (su pista); **~y** *a* veloce, rapido(a); pronto(a).

spell [spɛl] *n* (*also*: **magic ~**) incantesimo; (*period of time*) (*breve*) periodo // *vt* (*pt*, *pp* **spelt** (*Brit*) *or* **~ed**

[spɛlt, speld]) (*in writing*) scrivere (lettera per lettera); (*aloud*) dire lettera per lettera; (*fig*) significare; **to cast a ~ on sb** fare un incantesimo a qn; **he can't ~** fa errori di ortografia; **~bound** *a* incantato(a); affascinato(a); **~ing** *n* ortografia.

spend, *pt*, *pp* **spent** [spɛnd, spɛnt] *vt* (*money*) spendere; (*time, life*) passare; **~thrift** *n* spendaccione/a.

sperm [spə:m] *n* sperma *m*.

spew [spju:] *vt* vomitare.

sphere [sfɪə*] *n* sfera.

spice [spaɪs] *n* spezia // *vt* aromatizzare.

spick-and-span [ˈspɪkənˈspæn] *a* impeccabile.

spicy [ˈspaɪsɪ] *a* piccante.

spider [ˈspaɪdə*] *n* ragno.

spike [spaɪk] *n* punta.

spill, *pt*, *pp* **spilt** *or* **~ed** [spɪl, -t, -d] *vt* versare, rovesciare // *vi* versarsi, rovesciarsi; **to ~ over** *vi* (*liquid*) versarsi; (*crowd*) riversarsi.

spin [spɪn] *n* (*revolution of wheel*) rotazione *f*; (*AVIAT*) avvitamento; (*trip in car*) giretto // *vb* (*pt* **spun, span**, *pp* **spun**) *vt* (*wool etc*) filare; (*wheel*) far girare // *vi* girare; **to ~ out** *vt* far durare.

spinach [ˈspɪnɪtʃ] *n* spinacio; (*as food*) spinaci *mpl*.

spinal [ˈspaɪnl] *a* spinale; **~ cord** *n* midollo spinale.

spindly [ˈspɪndlɪ] *a* lungo(a) e sottile, filiforme.

spin-dryer [spɪnˈdraɪə*] *n* (*Brit*) centrifuga.

spine [spaɪn] *n* spina dorsale; (*thorn*) spina.

spinning [ˈspɪnɪŋ] *n* filatura; **~ top** *n* trottola; **~ wheel** *n* filatoio.

spin-off [ˈspɪnɔf] *n* applicazione *f* secondaria; (*product*) prodotto secondario.

spinster [ˈspɪnstə*] *n* nubile *f*; zitella.

spiral [ˈspaɪərl] *n* spirale *f* // *a* a spirale // *vi* (*fig*) salire a spirale; **~ staircase** *n* scala a chiocciola.

spire [ˈspaɪə*] *n* guglia.

spirit [ˈspɪrɪt] *n* (*soul*) spirito, anima; (*ghost*) spirito, fantasma *m*; (*mood*) stato d'animo, umore *m*; (*courage*) coraggio; **~s** *npl* (*drink*) alcolici *mpl*; **in good ~s** di buon umore; **~ed** *a* vivace, vigoroso(a); (*horse*) focoso(a); **~ level** *n* livella a bolla (d'aria).

spiritual [ˈspɪrɪtjuəl] *a* spirituale.

spit [spɪt] *n* (*for roasting*) spiedo // *vi* (*pt*, *pp* **spat**) sputare; (*fire, fat*) scoppiettare.

spite [spaɪt] *n* dispetto // *vt* contrariare, far dispetto a; **in ~ of** nonostante, malgrado; **~ful** *a* dispettoso(a).

spittle [ˈspɪtl] *n* saliva; sputo.

splash [splæʃ] *n* spruzzo; (*sound*) ciac *m*

inv; (*of colour*) schizzo // *vt* spruzzare // *vi* (*also*: **~ about**) sguazzare.

spleen [spli:n] *n* (*ANAT*) milza.

splendid [ˈsplɛndɪd] *a* splendido(a), magnifico(a).

splint [splɪnt] *n* (*MED*) stecca.

splinter [ˈsplɪntə*] *n* scheggia // *vi* scheggiarsi.

split [splɪt] *n* spaccatura; (*fig: division, quarrel*) scissione *f* // *vb* (*pt*, *pp* **split**) *vt* spaccare; (*party*) dividere; (*work, profits*) spartire, ripartire // *vi* (*divide*) dividersi; **to ~ up** *vi* (*couple*) separarsi, rompere; (*meeting*) sciogliersi.

splutter [ˈsplʌtə*] *vi* farfugliare; sputacchiare.

spoil, *pt*, *pp* **spoilt** *or* **~ed** [spɔɪl, -t, -d] *vt* (*damage*) rovinare, guastare; (*mar*) sciupare; (*child*) viziare; **~s** *npl* bottino; **~sport** *n* guastafeste *m/f inv*.

spoke [spəuk] *pt of* **speak** // *n* raggio.

spoken [ˈspəukn] *pp of* **speak**.

spokesman [ˈspəuksmən], **spokeswoman** [-wumən] *n* portavoce *m/f inv*.

sponge [spʌndʒ] *n* spugna // *vt* spugnare, pulire con una spugna // *vi*: **to ~ off** *or* **on** scroccare a; **~ bag** *n* (*Brit*) necessaire *m inv*; **~ (cake)** *n* pan *m* di Spagna.

sponsor [ˈspɒnsə*] *n* (*RADIO, TV, SPORT etc*) finanziatore/trice (a scopo pubblicitario) // *vt* sostenere; patrocinare; **~ship** *n* finanziamento (a scopo pubblicitario); patrocinio.

spontaneous [spɒnˈteɪnɪəs] *a* spontaneo(a).

spooky [ˈspu:kɪ] *a* che fa accapponare la pelle.

spool [spu:l] *n* bobina.

spoon [spu:n] *n* cucchiaio; **~-feed** *vt* nutrire con il cucchiaio; (*fig*) imboccare; **~ful** *n* cucchiaiata.

sport [spɔ:t] *n* sport *m inv*; (*person*) persona di spirito // *vt* sfoggiare; **~ing** *a* sportivo(a); **to give sb a ~ing chance** dare a qn una possibilità (di vincere); **~ jacket** *n* (*US*) = **~s jacket**; **~s car** *n* automobile *f* sportiva; **~s jacket** *n* giacca sportiva; **~sman** *n* sportivo; **~smanship** *n* spirito sportivo; **~swear** *n* abiti *mpl* sportivi; **~swoman** *n* sportiva; **~y** *a* sportivo(a).

spot [spɔt] *n* punto; (*mark*) macchia; (*dot: on pattern*) pallino; (*pimple*) foruncolo; (*place*) posto; (*small amount*): **a ~** di un po' di // *vt* (*notice*) individuare, distinguere; **on the ~** sul posto; su due piedi; **~ check** *n* controllo senza preavviso; **~less** *a* immacolato(a); **~light** *n* proiettore *m*; (*AUT*) faro ausiliario; **~ted** *a* macchiato(a); a puntini, a pallini; **~ty** *a* (*face*) foruncoloso(a).

spouse [spauz] *n* sposo/a.

spout [spaut] n (of jug) beccuccio; (of liquid) zampillo, getto // vi zampillare.

sprain [sprein] n storta, distorsione f // vt: **to ~ one's ankle** storcersi una caviglia.

sprang [spræŋ] pt of **spring**.

sprawl [sprɔ:l] vi sdraiarsi (in modo scomposto).

spray [sprei] n spruzzo; (container) nebulizzatore m, spray m inv; (of flowers) mazzetto // vt spruzzare; (crops) irrorare.

spread [spred] n diffusione f; (distribution) distribuzione f; (CULIN) pasta (da spalmare) // vb (pt, pp **spread**) vt (cloth) stendere, distendere; (butter etc) spalmare; (disease, knowledge) propagare, diffondere // vi stendersi, distendersi; spalmarsi; propagarsi, diffondersi; **~-eagled** ['spredi:gld] a a gambe e braccia aperte; **~sheet** n (COMPUT) foglio elettronico ad espansione.

spree [spri:] n: **to go on a ~** fare baldoria.

sprightly ['spraitli] a vivace.

spring [spriŋ] n (leap) salto, balzo; (coiled metal) molla; (season) primavera; (of water) sorgente f // vi (pt **sprang**, pp **sprung**) saltare, balzare; **to ~ from** provenire da; **to ~ up** vi (problem) presentarsi; **~board** n trampolino; **~-clean** n (also: **~-cleaning**) grandi pulizie fpl di primavera; **~time** n primavera; **~y** a elastico(a).

sprinkle ['spriŋkl] vt spruzzare; spargere; **to ~ water etc on, ~ with water etc** spruzzare dell'acqua etc su; **to ~ sugar etc on, ~ with sugar etc** spolverizzare di zucchero etc; **~r** n (for lawn) irrigatore m; (to put out fire) sprinkler m inv.

sprint [sprint] n scatto // vi scattare; **~er** n (SPORT) velocista m/f.

sprout [spraut] vi germogliare; **~s** npl (also: **Brussels ~s**) cavolini mpl di Bruxelles.

spruce [spru:s] n abete m rosso // a lindo(a); azzimato(a).

sprung [sprʌŋ] pp of **spring**.

spry [sprai] a arzillo(a), sveglio(a).

spun [spʌn] pt, pp of **spin**.

spur [spə:*] n sperone m; (fig) sprone m, incentivo // vt (also: **~ on**) spronare; **on the ~ of the moment** lì per lì.

spurious ['spjuəriəs] a falso(a).

spurn [spə:n] vt rifiutare con disprezzo, sdegnare.

spurt [spə:t] vi sgorgare; zampillare.

spy [spai] n spia // vi: **to ~ on** spiare // vt (see) scorgere; **~ing** n spionaggio.

Sq. abbr (in address) = **square**.

sq. abbr (MATH) = **square**.

squabble ['skwɔbl] vi bisticciare.

squad [skwɔd] n (MIL) plotone m; (POLICE) squadra.

squadron ['skwɔdrn] n (MIL) squadrone m; (AVIAT, NAUT) squadriglia.

squalid ['skwɔlid] a sordido(a).

squall [skwɔ:l] n raffica; burrasca.

squalor ['skwɔlə*] n squallore m.

squander ['skwɔndə*] vt dissipare.

square [skwɛə*] n quadrato; (in town) piazza; (instrument) squadra // a quadrato(a); (honest) onesto(a); (col: ideas, person) di vecchio stampo // vt (arrange) regolare; (MATH) elevare al quadrato // vi (agree) quadrare; **all ~** pari; **a ~ meal** un pasto abbondante; **2 metres ~** di 2 metri per 2; **1 ~ metre** 1 metro quadrato; **~ly** ad diritto; fermamente.

squash [skwɔʃ] n (SPORT) squash m; (Brit: drink): **lemon/orange ~** sciroppo di limone/arancia // vt schiacciare.

squat [skwɔt] a tarchiato(a), tozzo(a) // vi accovacciarsi; **~ter** n occupante m/f abusivo(a).

squawk [skwɔ:k] vi emettere strida rauche.

squeak [skwi:k] vi squittire.

squeal [skwi:l] vi strillare.

squeamish ['skwi:miʃ] a schizzinoso(a); disgustato(a).

squeeze [skwi:z] n pressione f; (also ECON) stretta // vt premere; (hand, arm) stringere; **to ~ out** vt spremere.

squelch [skweltʃ] vi fare ciac; sguazzare.

squib [skwib] n petardo.

squid [skwid] n calamaro.

squiggle ['skwigl] n ghirigoro.

squint [skwint] vi essere strabico(a) // n: **he has a ~** è strabico; **to ~ at** sth guardare qc di traverso; (quickly) dare un'occhiata a qc.

squire ['skwaiə*] n (Brit) proprietario terriero.

squirm [skwə:m] vi contorcersi.

squirrel ['skwirəl] n scoiattolo.

squirt [skwə:t] vi schizzare; zampillare.

Sr abbr = **senior**.

St abbr = **saint**, **street**.

stab [stæb] n (with knife etc) pugnalata; (col: try): **to have a ~ at (doing) sth** provare a fare qc // vt pugnalare.

stable ['steibl] n (for horses) scuderia; (for cattle) stalla // a stabile.

stack [stæk] n catasta, pila // vt accatastare, ammucchiare.

stadium ['steidiəm] n stadio.

staff [stɑ:f] n (work force: gen) personale m; (: Brit SCOL) personale insegnante; (: servants) personale di servizio; (MIL) stato maggiore; (stick) bastone m // vt fornire di personale.

stag [stæg] n cervo.

stage [steidʒ] n palcoscenico; (profession): **the ~** il teatro, la scena;

(*point*) punto; (*platform*) palco // *vt* (*play*) allestire, mettere in scena; (*demonstration*) organizzare; (*fig: perform: recovery etc*) effettuare; **in ~s** per gradi; a tappe; **~coach** *n* diligenza; **~ door** *n* ingresso degli artisti; **~ manager** *n* direttore *m* di scena.

stagger ['stægə*] *vi* barcollare // *vt* (*person*) sbalordire; (*hours, holidays*) scaglionare.

stagnate [stæg'neɪt] *vi* stagnare.

stag party *n* festa di addio al celibato.

staid [steɪd] *a* posato(a), serio(a).

stain [steɪn] *n* macchia; (*colouring*) colorante *m* // *vt* macchiare; (*wood*) tingere; **~ed glass window** *n* vetrata; **~less** *a* (*steel*) inossidabile; **~ remover** *n* smacchiatore *m*.

stair [steə*] *n* (*step*) gradino; **~s** *npl* (*flight of ~s*) scale *fpl*, scala; **on the ~s** sulle scale; **~case, ~way** *n* scale *fpl*, scala.

stake [steɪk] *n* palo, piolo; (*BETTING*) puntata, scommessa // *vt* (*bet*) scommettere; (*risk*) rischiare; **to be at ~** essere in gioco.

stale [steɪl] *a* (*bread*) raffermo(a), stantio(a); (*beer*) svaporato(a); (*smell*) di chiuso.

stalemate ['steɪlmeɪt] *n* stallo; (*fig*) punto morto.

stalk [stɔ:k] *n* gambo, stelo // *vt* inseguire // *vi* camminare con sussiego.

stall [stɔ:l] *n* bancarella; (*in stable*) box *m inv* di stalla // *vt* (*AUT*) far spegnere // *vi* (*AUT*) spegnersi, fermarsi; (*fig*) temporeggiare; **~s** *npl* (*Brit: in cinema, theatre*) platea.

stallion ['stælɪən] *n* stallone *m*.

stalwart ['stɔ:lwət] *n* membro fidato.

stamina ['stæmɪnə] *n* vigore *m*, resistenza.

stammer ['stæmə*] *n* balbuzie *f* // *vi* balbettare.

stamp [stæmp] *n* (*postage ~*) francobollo; (*implement*) timbro; (*mark, also fig*) marchio, impronta; (*on document*) bollo; timbro // *vi* (*also: ~ one's foot*) battere il piede // *vt* battere; (*letter*) affrancare; (*mark with a ~*) timbrare; **~ album** *n* album *m inv* per francobolli; **~ collecting** *n* filatelia.

stampede [stæm'pi:d] *n* fuggi fuggi *m inv*.

stance [stæns] *n* posizione *f*.

stand [stænd] *n* (*position*) posizione *f*; (*MIL*) resistenza; (*structure*) supporto, sostegno; (*at exhibition*) stand *m inv*; (*in shop*) banco; (*at market*) bancarella; (*booth*) chiosco; (*SPORT*) tribuna // *vb* (*pt, pp* **stood**) *vi* stare in piedi; (*rise*) alzarsi in piedi; (*be placed*) trovarsi // *vt* (*place*) mettere, porre; (*tolerate, withstand*) resistere, sopportare; **to make a ~** prendere

posizione; **to ~ for parliament** (*Brit*) presentarsi come candidato (per il parlamento); **to ~ by** *vi* (*be ready*) tenersi pronto(a) // *vt fus* (*opinion*) sostenere; **to ~ down** *vi* (*withdraw*) ritirarsi; **to ~ for** *vt fus* (*signify*) rappresentare, significare; (*tolerate*) sopportare, tollerare; **to ~ in for** *vt fus* sostituire; **to ~ out** *vi* (*be prominent*) spiccare; **to ~ up** *vi* (*rise*) alzarsi in piedi; **to ~ up for** *vt fus* difendere; **to ~ up to** *vt fus* tener testa a, resistere a.

standard ['stændəd] *n* modello, standard *m inv*; (*level*) livello; (*flag*) stendardo // *a* (*size etc*) normale, standard *inv*; **~s** *npl* (*morals*) principi *mpl*, valori *mpl*; **~ lamp** *n* (*Brit*) lampada a stelo; **~ of living** *n* livello di vita.

stand-by ['stændbaɪ] *n* riserva, sostituto; **to be on ~** (*gen*) tenersi pronto(a); (*doctor*) essere di guardia; **~ ticket** *n* (*AVIAT*) biglietto senza garanzia.

stand-in ['stændɪn] *n* sostituto/a; (*CINEMA*) controfigura.

standing ['stændɪŋ] *a* diritto(a), in piedi // *n* rango, condizione *f*, posizione *f*; **of many years' ~** che esiste da molti anni; **~ order** *n* (*Brit: at bank*) ordine *m* di pagamento (permanente); **~ orders** *npl* (*MIL*) regolamento; **~ room** *n* posto all'impiedi.

standoffish [stænd'ɔfɪʃ] *a* scostante, freddo(a).

standpoint ['stændpɔɪnt] *n* punto di vista.

standstill ['stændstɪl] *n*: **at a ~** fermo(a); (*fig*) a un punto morto; **to come to a ~** fermarsi; giungere a un punto morto.

stank [stæŋk] *pt of* **stink**.

staple ['steɪpl] *n* (*for papers*) graffetta // *a* (*food etc*) di base // *vt* cucire; **~r** *n* cucitrice *f*.

star [stɑ:*] *n* stella; (*celebrity*) divo/a; (*principal actor*) vedette *f inv* // *vi*: **to ~ (in)** essere il (*or* la) protagonista (di) // *vt* (*CINEMA*) essere interpretato(a) da.

starboard ['stɑ:bəd] *n* dritta.

starch [stɑ:tʃ] *n* amido.

stardom ['stɑ:dəm] *n* celebrità.

stare [steə*] *n* sguardo fisso // *vi*: **to ~ at** fissare.

starfish ['stɑ:fɪʃ] *n* stella di mare.

stark [stɑ:k] *a* (*bleak*) desolato(a) // *ad*: **~ naked** completamente nudo(a).

starling ['stɑ:lɪŋ] *n* storno.

starry ['stɑ:rɪ] *a* stellato(a); **~-eyed** *a* (*innocent*) ingenuo(a).

start [stɑ:t] *n* inizio; (*of race*) partenza; (*sudden movement*) sobbalzo // *vt* cominciare, iniziare // *vi* cominciare; (*on journey*) partire, mettersi in viaggio; (*jump*) sobbalzare; **to ~ doing** *or* **to do sth** (in)cominciare a fare qc; **to ~ off**

vi cominciare; (*leave*) partire; **to ~ up** *vi* cominciare; (*car*) avviarsi // *vt* iniziare; (*car*) avviare; **~er** *n* (*AUT*) motorino d'avviamento; (*SPORT*) *official*) starter *m inv*; (: *runner, horse*) partente *m/f*; (*Brit CULIN*) primo piatto; **~ing point** *n* punto di partenza.

startle ['stɑːtl] *vt* far trasalire.

starvation [stɑːˈveɪʃən] *n* fame *f*, inedia.

starve [stɑːv] *vi* morire di fame; soffrire la fame // *vt* far morire di fame, affamare.

state [steɪt] *n* stato // *vt* dichiarare, affermare; annunciare; **the S~s** (*USA*) gli Stati Uniti; **to be in a ~** essere agitato(a); **~ly** *a* maestoso(a); imponente; **~ment** *n* dichiarazione *f*; (*LAW*) deposizione *f*; **~sman** *n* statista *m*.

static ['stætɪk] *n* (*RADIO*) scariche *fpl* // *a* statico(a).

station ['steɪʃən] *n* stazione *f*; (*rank*) rango, condizione *f* // *vt* collocare, disporre.

stationary ['steɪʃənərɪ] *a* fermo(a), immobile.

stationer ['steɪʃənə*] *n* cartolaio/a; **~'s (shop)** *n* cartoleria; **~y** *n* articoli *mpl* di cancelleria.

station master *n* (*RAIL*) capostazione *m*.

station wagon *n* (*US*) giardinetta.

statistic [stəˈtɪstɪk] *n* statistica; **~s** *n* (*science*) statistica.

statue ['stætjuː] *n* statua.

status ['steɪtəs] *n* posizione *f*, condizione *f* sociale; prestigio; stato; **~ symbol** *n* simbolo di prestigio.

statute ['stætjuːt] *n* legge *f*; **~s** *npl* (*of club etc*) statuto; **statutory** *a* stabilito(a) dalla legge, statutario(a).

staunch [stɔːntʃ] *a* fidato(a), leale.

stave [steɪv] *n* (*MUS*) rigo // *vt*: **to ~ off** (*attack*) respingere; (*threat*) evitare.

stay [steɪ] *n* (*period of time*) soggiorno, permanenza // *vi* rimanere; (*reside*) alloggiare, stare; (*spend some time*) trattenersi, soggiornare; **to ~ put** non muoversi; **to ~ with friends** stare presso amici; **to ~ the night** passare la notte; **to ~ behind** *vi* restare indietro; **to ~ in** *vi* (*at home*) stare in casa; **to ~ on** *vi* restare, rimanere; **to ~ out** *vi* (*of house*) rimanere fuori (di casa); **to ~ up** *vi* (*at night*) rimanere alzato(a); **~ing power** *n* capacità di resistenza.

stead [stɛd] *n*: **in sb's ~** al posto di qn; **to stand sb in good ~** essere utile a qn.

steadfast ['stɛdfɑːst] *a* fermo(a), risoluto(a).

steadily ['stɛdɪlɪ] *ad* continuamente; (*walk*) con passo sicuro.

steady ['stɛdɪ] *a* stabile, solido(a), fermo(a); (*regular*) costante; (*person*) calmo(a), tranquillo(a) // *vt* stabilizzare;

calmare; **to ~ oneself** ritrovare l'equilibrio.

steak [steɪk] *n* (*meat*) bistecca; (*fish*) trancia.

steal [stiːl], *pt* **stole**, *pp* **stolen** *vt*, *vi* rubare.

stealth [stɛlθ] *n*: **by ~** furtivamente; **~y** *a* furtivo(a).

steam [stiːm] *n* vapore *m* // *vt* trattare con vapore; (*CULIN*) cuocere a vapore // *vi* fumare; (*ship*): **to ~ along** filare; **~ engine** *n* macchina a vapore; (*RAIL*) locomotiva a vapore; **~er** *n* piroscafo, vapore *m*; **~roller** *n* rullo compressore; **~ship** *n* = **~er**; **~y** *a* (*room*) pieno(a) di vapore; (*window*) appannato(a).

steel [stiːl] *n* acciaio // *cpd* di acciaio; **~works** *n* acciaieria.

steep [stiːp] *a* ripido(a), scosceso(a); (*price*) eccessivo(a) // *vt* inzuppare; (*washing*) mettere a mollo.

steeple ['stiːpl] *n* campanile *m*.

steer [stɪə*] *n* manzo // *vt* (*ship*) governare; (*car*) guidare // *vi* (*NAUT: person*) governare; (: *ship*) rispondere al timone; (*car*) guidarsi; **~ing** *n* (*AUT*) sterzo; **~ing wheel** *n* volante *m*.

stem [stɛm] *n* (*of flower, plant*) stelo; (*of tree*) fusto; (*of glass*) gambo; (*of fruit, leaf*) picciolo // *vt* contenere, arginare; **to ~ from** *vt fus* provenire da, derivare da.

stench [stɛntʃ] *n* puzzo, fetore *m*.

stencil ['stɛnsl] *n* (*of metal, cardboard*) stampino, mascherina; (*in typing*) matrice *f*.

stenographer [stɛˈnɔgrəfə*] *n* (*US*) stenografo/a.

step [stɛp] *n* passo; (*stair*) gradino, scalino; (*action*) mossa, azione *f* // *vi*: **to ~ forward** fare un passo avanti; **~s** *npl* (*Brit*) = **stepladder**; **to be in/out of ~ (with)** stare/non stare al passo (con); **to ~ down** *vi* (*fig*) ritirarsi; **to ~ off** *vt fus* scendere da; **to ~ up** *vt* aumentare; intensificare; **~brother** *n* fratellastro; **~daughter** *n* figliastra; **~father** *n* patrigno; **~ladder** *n* scala a libretto; **~mother** *n* matrigna; **~ping stone** *n* pietra di un guado; (*fig*) trampolino; **~sister** *n* sorellastra; **~son** *n* figliastro.

stereo ['stɛrɪəu] *n* (*system*) sistema *m* stereofonico; (*record player*) stereo *m inv* // *a* (*also*: **~phonic**) stereofonico(a).

sterile ['stɛraɪl] *a* sterile; **sterilize** ['stɛrɪlaɪz] *vt* sterilizzare.

sterling ['stɜːlɪŋ] *a* (*gold, silver*) di buona lega; (*fig*) autentico(a), genuino(a) // *n* (*ECON*) (lira) sterlina; a **pound ~** una lira sterlina.

stern [stɜːn] *a* severo(a) // *n* (*NAUT*) poppa.

stew [stjuː] *n* stufato // *vt*, *vi* cuocere in

umido.

steward ['stju:əd] n (AVIAT, NAUT, RAIL) steward m inv; (in club etc) dispensiere m; ~**ess** n assistente f di volo, hostess f inv.

stick [stik] n bastone m; (of rhubarb, celery) gambo // vb (pt, pp **stuck**) vt (glue) attaccare; (thrust): **to ~ sth into** conficcare or piantare or infiggere qc in; (col: put) ficcare; (col: tolerate) sopportare // vi conficcarsi; tenere; (remain) restare, rimanere; **to ~ out**, **to ~ up** vi sporgere, spuntare; **to ~ up for** vt fus difendere; ~**er** n cartellino adesivo; ~**ing plaster** n cerotto adesivo.

stickler ['stiklə*] n: **to be a ~ for** essere pignolo(a) su, tenere molto a.

stick-up ['stikʌp] n rapina a mano armata.

sticky ['stiki] a attaccaticcio(a), vischioso(a); (label) adesivo(a).

stiff [stif] a rigido(a), duro(a); (muscle) legato(a), indolenzito(a); (difficult) difficile, arduo(a); (cold) freddo(a), formale; (strong) forte; (high: price) molto alto(a); ~**en** vt irrigidire; rinforzare // vi irrigidirsi; indurirsi; ~ **neck** n torcicollo.

stifle ['staifl] vt soffocare.

stigma ['stigmə] n (BOT, fig) stigma m; ~**ta** [stig'mɑ:tə] npl (REL) stigmate fpl.

stile [stail] n cavalcasiepe m; cavalcasteccato.

stiletto [sti'letəu] n (Brit: also: ~ **heel**) tacco a spillo.

still [stil] a fermo(a); silenzioso(a) // ad (up to this time, even) ancora; (nonetheless) tuttavia, ciò nonostante; ~**born** a nato(a) morto(a); ~ **life** n natura morta.

stilt [stilt] n trampolo; (pile) palo.

stilted ['stiltid] a freddo(a), formale; artificiale.

stimulate ['stimjuleit] vt stimolare.

stimulus, pl **stimuli** ['stimjuləs, 'stimjulai] n stimolo.

sting [stiŋ] n puntura; (organ) pungiglione m // vt (pt, pp **stung**) pungere.

stingy ['stindʒi] a spilorcio(a), tirchio(a).

stink [stiŋk] n fetore m, puzzo // vi (pt **stank**, pp **stunk**) puzzare; ~**ing** a (fig: col): a ~**ing** ... uno schifo di ..., un(a) maledetto(a) ... .

stint [stint] n lavoro, compito // vi: **to ~ on** lesinare su.

stir [stə:*] n agitazione f, clamore m // vt rimescolare; (move) smuovere, agitare // vi muoversi; **to ~ up** vt provocare, suscitare.

stirrup ['stirəp] n staffa.

stitch [stitʃ] n (SEWING) punto; (KNITTING) maglia; (MED) punto (di sutura); (pain) fitta // vt cucire, attaccare; suturare.

stoat [stəut] n ermellino.

stock [stɔk] n riserva, provvista; (COMM) giacenza, stock m inv; (AGR) bestiame m; (CULIN) brodo; (FINANCE) titoli mpl, azioni fpl // a (fig: reply etc) consueto(a); classico(a) // vt (have in stock) avere, vendere; **well-~ed** ben fornito(a); **in ~** in magazzino; **out of ~** esaurito(a); **to take ~ of** (fig) fare il punto di; ~**s and shares** valori mpl di borsa; **to ~ up** vi: **to ~ up (with)** fare provvista (di).

stockbroker ['stɔkbrəukə*] n agente m di cambio.

stock cube n (Brit) dado.

stock exchange n Borsa (valori).

stocking ['stɔkiŋ] n calza.

stockist ['stɔkist] n (Brit) fornitore m.

stock: ~ **market** n Borsa, mercato finanziario; ~ **phrase** n cliché m inv; ~**pile** n riserva // vt accumulare riserve di; ~**taking** n (Brit COMM) inventario.

stocky ['stɔki] a tarchiato(a), tozzo(a).

stodgy ['stɔdʒi] a pesante, indigesto(a).

stoke [stəuk] vt alimentare.

stole [stəul] pt of **steal** // n stola.

stolen ['stəuln] pp of **steal**.

stolid ['stɔlid] a impassibile.

stomach ['stʌmək] n stomaco; (abdomen) ventre m // vt sopportare, digerire; ~**ache** n mal m di stomaco.

stone [stəun] n pietra; (pebble) sasso, ciottolo; (in fruit) nocciolo; (MED) calcolo; (Brit: weight) = 6.348 kg.; 14 libbre // cpd di pietra // vt lapidare; ~-**cold** a gelido(a); ~-**deaf** a sordo(a) come una campana; ~**work** n muratura.

stood [stud] pt, pp of **stand**.

stool [stu:l] n sgabello.

stoop [stu:p] vi (also: **have a ~**) avere una curvatura; (bend) chinarsi, curvarsi.

stop [stɔp] n arresto; (stopping place) fermata; (in punctuation) punto // vt arrestare, fermare; (break off) interrompere; (also: **put a ~ to**) porre fine a // vi fermarsi; (rain, noise etc) cessare, finire; **to ~ doing sth** cessare or finire di fare qc; **to ~ dead** fermarsi di colpo; **to ~ off** vi sostare brevemente; **to ~ up** vt (hole) chiudere, turare; ~**gap** n (person) tappabuchi m/f inv; (measure) ripiego; ~**lights** npl (AUT) stop mpl; ~**over** n breve sosta; (AVIAT) scalo.

stoppage ['stɔpidʒ] n arresto, fermata; (of pay) trattenuta; (strike) interruzione f del lavoro.

stopper ['stɔpə*] n tappo.

stop press n ultimissime fpl.

stopwatch ['stɔpwɔtʃ] n cronometro.

storage ['stɔ:ridʒ] n immagazzinamento; (COMPUT) memoria; ~ **heater** n radiatore m elettrico che accumula calore.

store [stɔ:*] *n* provvista, riserva; (*depot*) deposito; (*Brit: department ~*) grande magazzino; (*US: shop*) negozio // *vt* immagazzinare; **~s** *npl* (*provisions*) rifornimenti *mpl*, scorte *fpl*; **to ~ up** *vt* mettere in serbo, conservare; **~room** *n* dispensa.

storey, (*US*) **story** ['stɔ:rɪ] *n* piano.

stork [stɔ:k] *n* cicogna.

storm [stɔ:m] *n* tempesta, temporale *m*, burrasca; uragano // *vi* (*fig*) infuriarsi // *vt* prendere d'assalto; **~y** *a* tempestoso(a), burrascoso(a).

story ['stɔ:rɪ] *n* storia; favola; racconto; (*US*) = **storey**; **~book** *n* libro di racconti.

stout [staut] *a* solido(a), robusto(a); (*brave*) coraggioso(a); (*fat*) corpulento(a), grasso(a) // *n* birra scura.

stove [stəuv] *n* (*for cooking*) fornello; (: *small*) fornelletto; (*for heating*) stufa.

stow [stəu] *vt* mettere via; **~away** *n* passeggero(a) clandestino(a).

straddle ['strædl] *vt* stare a cavalcioni di.

straggle ['strægl] *vi* crescere (*or* estendersi) disordinatamente; trascinarsi; rimanere indietro; **~r** *n* sbandato/a.

straight [streɪt] *a* dritto(a); (*frank*) onesto(a), franco(a) // *ad* diritto; (*drink*) liscio // *n*: **the ~** la linea retta; (*RAIL*) il rettilineo; (*SPORT*) la dirittura d'arrivo; **to put** *or* **get ~** mettere in ordine, mettere ordine in; **~ away, ~ off** (*at once*) immediatamente; **~en** *vt* (*also*: **~en out**) raddrizzare; **~-faced** *a* impassibile, imperturbabile; **~forward** *a* semplice; onesto(a), franco(a).

strain [streɪn] *n* (*TECH*) sollecitazione *f*; (*physical*) sforzo; (*mental*) tensione *f*; (*MED*) strappo; distorsione *f*; (*streak, trace*) tendenza; elemento // *vt* tendere; (*muscle*) sforzare; (*ankle*) storcere; (*friendship, marriage*) mettere a dura prova; (*filter*) colare, filtrare // *vi* sforzarsi; **~s** *npl* (*MUS*) note *fpl*; **~ed** *a* (*laugh etc*) forzato(a); (*relations*) teso(a); **~er** *n* passino, colino.

strait [streɪt] *n* (*GEO*) stretto; **~jacket** *n* camicia di forza; **~-laced** *a* bacchettone(a).

strand [strænd] *n* (*of thread*) filo; **~ed** *a* nei guai; senza mezzi di trasporto.

strange [streɪndʒ] *a* (*not known*) sconosciuto(a); (*odd*) strano(a), bizzarro(a); **~r** *n* sconosciuto/a; estraneo/a.

strangle ['stræŋgl] *vt* strangolare; **~hold** *n* (*fig*) stretta (mortale).

strap [stræp] *n* cinghia; (*of slip, dress*) spallina, bretella // *vt* legare con una cinghia; (*child etc*) punire (con una cinghia).

strategic [strə'ti:dʒɪk] *a* strategico(a).

strategy ['strætɪdʒɪ] *n* strategia.

straw [strɔ:] *n* paglia; (*drinking ~*) cannuccia; **that's the last ~!** è la goccia che fa traboccare il vaso!

strawberry ['strɔ:bərɪ] *n* fragola.

stray [streɪ] *a* (*animal*) randagio(a) // *vi* perdersi; **~ bullet** *n* proiettile *m* vagante.

streak [stri:k] *n* striscia; (*fig: of madness etc*): **a ~ of** una vena di // *vt* striare, screziare // *vi*: **to ~ past** passare come un fulmine.

stream [stri:m] *n* ruscello; corrente *f*; (*of people*) fiume *m* // *vt* (*SCOL*) dividere in livelli di rendimento // *vi* scorrere; **to ~ in/out** entrare/uscire a fiotti.

streamer ['stri:mə*] *n* (*of paper*) stella filante.

streamlined ['stri:mlaɪnd] *a* aerodinamico(a), affusolato(a); (*fig*) razionalizzato(a).

street [stri:t] *n* strada, via // *cpd* stradale, di strada; **~car** *n* (*US*) tram *m inv*; **~ lamp** *n* lampione *m*; **~ plan** *n* pianta (di una città); **~wise** *a* (*col*) esperto(a) dei bassifondi.

strength [streŋθ] *n* forza; (*of girder, knot etc*) resistenza, solidità; **~en** *vt* rinforzare; fortificare; consolidare.

strenuous ['strenjuəs] *a* vigoroso(a), energico(a); (*tiring*) duro(a), pesante.

stress [stres] *n* (*force, pressure*) pressione *f*; (*mental strain*) tensione *f*; (*accent*) accento // *vt* insistere su, sottolineare.

stretch [stretʃ] *n* (*of sand etc*) distesa // *vi* stirarsi; (*extend*): **to ~ to** *or* **as far as** estendersi fino a // *vt* tendere, allungare; (*spread*) distendere; (*fig*) spingere (al massimo); **to ~ out** *vi* allungarsi, estendersi // *vt* (*arm etc*) allungare, tendere; (*to spread*) distendere.

stretcher ['stretʃə*] *n* barella, lettiga.

strewn [stru:n] *a*: **~ with** cosparso(a) di.

stricken ['strɪkən] *a* (*person*) provato(a); (*city, industry etc*) colpito(a); **~ with** (*disease etc*) colpito(a) da.

strict [strɪkt] *a* (*severe*) rigido(a), severo(a); (*precise*) preciso(a), stretto(a).

stride [straɪd] *n* passo lungo // *vi* (*pt* **strode**, *pp* **stridden** ['strɔud, 'strɪdn]) camminare a grandi passi.

strife [straɪf] *n* conflitto; litigi *mpl*.

strike [straɪk] *n* sciopero; (*of oil etc*) scoperta; (*attack*) attacco // *vb* (*pt, pp* **struck**) *vt* colpire; (*oil etc*) scoprire, trovare // *vi* far sciopero, scioperare; (*attack*) attaccare; (*clock*) suonare; **on ~** (*workers*) in sciopero; **to ~ a match** accendere un fiammifero; **to ~ down** *vt* (*fig*) atterrare; **to ~ out** *vt* depennare; **to ~ up** *vt* (*MUS*) attaccare; **to ~ up a friendship with** fare amicizia con; **~r** *n* scioperante *m/f*; (*SPORT*) attaccante *m*; **striking** *a* che colpisce.

string [striŋ] n spago; (row) fila; sequenza; catena; (MUS) corda // vt (pt, pp **strung**): to ~ out disporre di fianco; to ~ **together** (words, ideas) mettere insieme; the ~s npl (MUS) gli archi; to pull ~s for sb (fig) raccomandare qn; ~ **bean** n fagiolino; ~(**ed**) **instrument** n (MUS) strumento a corda.

stringent ['strindʒənt] a rigoroso(a); (reasons, arguments) stringente, impellente.

strip [strip] n striscia // vt spogliare; (also: ~ **down**: machine) smontare // vi spogliarsi; ~ **cartoon** n fumetto.

stripe [straip] n striscia, riga; ~**d** a a strisce or righe.

strip lighting n illuminazione f al neon.

stripper ['stripə*] n spogliarellista.

striptease ['striptiːz] n spogliarello.

strive, pt **strove**, pp **striven** [straiv, strəuv, 'strivn] vi: to ~ to do sforzarsi di fare.

strode [strəud] pt of **stride**.

stroke [strəuk] n colpo; (MED) colpo apoplettico; (caress) carezza // vt accarezzare; at a ~ in un attimo.

stroll [strəul] n giretto, passeggiatina // vi andare a spasso; ~**er** n (US) passeggino.

strong [strɔŋ] a (gen) forte; (sturdy: table, fabric etc) solido(a); they are 50 ~ sono in 50; ~**box** n cassaforte f; ~**hold** n fortezza, roccaforte f; ~**ly** ad fortemente, con forza; energicamente; vivamente; ~**room** n camera di sicurezza.

strove [strəuv] pt of **strive**.

struck [strʌk] pt, pp of **strike**.

structural ['strʌktʃərəl] a strutturale; (CONSTR) di costruzione; di struttura.

structure ['strʌktʃə*] n struttura; (building) costruzione f, fabbricato.

struggle ['strʌgl] n lotta // vi lottare.

strum [strʌm] vt (guitar) strimpellare.

strung [strʌŋ] pt, pp of **string**.

strut [strʌt] n sostegno, supporto // vi pavoneggiarsi.

stub [stʌb] n mozzicone m; (of ticket etc) matrice f, talloncino // vt: to ~ one's toe urtare or sbattere il dito del piede; to ~ **out** vt schiacciare.

stubble ['stʌbl] n stoppia; (on chin) barba ispida.

stubborn ['stʌbən] a testardo(a), ostinato(a).

stuck [stʌk] pt, pp of **stick** // a (jammed) bloccato(a); ~-**up** a presuntuoso(a).

stud [stʌd] n bottoncino; borchia; (of horses) scuderia, allevamento di cavalli; (also: ~ **horse**) stallone m // vt (fig): ~**ded** **with** tempestato(a).

student ['stjuːdənt] n studente/essa // cpd studentesco(a); universitario(a); degli studenti; ~ **driver** n (US) conducente

m/f principiante.

studio ['stjuːdɪəu] n studio; ~ **flat**, (US) ~ **apartment** n appartamento monolocale.

studious ['stjuːdɪəs] a studioso(a); (studied) studiato(a), voluto(a); ~**ly** ad (carefully) deliberatamente, di proposito.

study ['stʌdɪ] n studio // vt studiare; esaminare // vi studiare.

stuff [stʌf] n cosa, roba; (belongings) cose fpl, roba; (substance) sostanza, materiale m // vt imbottire; (CULIN) farcire; ~**ing** n imbottitura; (CULIN) ripieno; ~**y** a (room) mal ventilato(a), senz'aria; (ideas) antiquato(a).

stumble ['stʌmbl] vi inciampare; to ~ **across** (fig) imbattersi in; **stumbling block** n ostacolo, scoglio.

stump [stʌmp] n ceppo; (of limb) moncone m // vt sconcertare, lasciare perplesso(a).

stun [stʌn] vt stordire; (amaze) sbalordire.

stung [stʌŋ] pt, pp of **sting**.

stunk [stʌŋk] pp of **stink**.

stunt [stʌnt] n bravata; trucco pubblicitario; (AVIAT) acrobazia // vt arrestare; ~**ed** a stentato(a), rachitico(a); ~**man** n cascatore m.

stupefy ['stjuːpɪfaɪ] vt stordire; intontire; (fig) stupire.

stupendous [stjuː'pɛndəs] a stupendo(a), meraviglioso(a).

stupid ['stjuːpɪd] a stupido(a); ~**ity** [-'pɪdɪtɪ] n stupidità f inv, stupidaggine f.

stupor ['stjuːpə*] n torpore m.

sturdy ['stɜːdɪ] a robusto(a), vigoroso(a); solido(a).

sturgeon ['stɜːdʒən] n storione m.

stutter ['stʌtə*] n balbuzie f // vi balbettare.

sty [staɪ] n (of pigs) porcile m.

stye [staɪ] n (MED) orzaiolo.

style [staɪl] n stile m; (distinction) eleganza, classe f; **stylish** a elegante; **stylist** n (hair stylist) parrucchiere/a.

stylus ['staɪləs] n (of record player) puntina.

suave [swɑːv] a untuoso(a).

sub... [sʌb] prefix sub..., sotto...; ~**conscious** a n subcosciente (m); ~**contract** vt subappaltare.

subdue [səb'djuː] vt sottomettere, soggiogare; ~**d** a pacato(a); (light) attenuato(a); (person) poco esuberante.

subject n ['sʌbdʒɪkt] soggetto; (citizen etc) cittadino/a; (SCOL) materia // vt [səb'dʒɛkt]: to ~ to sottomettere a; esporre a; to be ~ to (law) essere sottomesso a; (disease) essere soggetto(a) a; ~**ive** [-'dʒɛktɪv] a soggettivo(a); ~ **matter** n argomento; contenuto.

subjunctive [səb'dʒʌŋktɪv] a

congiuntivo(a) // n congiuntivo.
sublet [sʌb'let] vt subaffittare.
submachine gun ['sʌbmə'ʃiːn-] n mitra m inv.
submarine [sʌbmə'riːn] n sommergibile m.
submerge [səb'məːdʒ] vt sommergere; immergere // vi immergersi.
submission [səb'mɪʃən] n sottomissione f.
submissive [səb'mɪsɪv] a remissivo(a).
submit [səb'mɪt] vt sottomettere // vi sottomettersi.
subnormal [sʌb'nɔːməl] a subnormale.
subordinate [sə'bɔːdɪnət] a, n subordinato(a).
subpoena [səb'piːnə] n (LAW) citazione f, mandato di comparizione.
subscribe [səb'skraɪb] vi contribuire; to ~ to (opinion) approvare, condividere; (fund) sottoscrivere; (newspaper) abbonarsi a; essere abbonato(a) a; ~r n (to periodical, telephone) abbonato/a.
subscription [səb'skrɪpʃən] n sottoscrizione f; abbonamento.
subsequent ['sʌbsɪkwənt] a successivo(a), seguente; conseguente; ~ly ad in seguito, successivamente.
subside [səb'saɪd] vi cedere, abbassarsi; (flood) decrescere; (wind) calmarsi; ~nce [-'saɪdns] n cedimento, abbassamento.
subsidiary [səb'sɪdɪərɪ] a sussidiario(a); accessorio(a) // n filiale f.
subsidize ['sʌbsɪdaɪz] vt sovvenzionare.
subsidy ['sʌbsɪdɪ] n sovvenzione f.
subsistence [səb'sɪstəns] n esistenza; mezzi mpl di sostentamento.
substance ['sʌbstəns] n sostanza; (fig) essenza.
substantial [səb'stænʃl] a solido(a); (amount, progress etc) notevole; (meal) sostanzioso(a).
substantiate [səb'stænʃɪeɪt] vt comprovare.
substitute ['sʌbstɪtjuːt] n (person) sostituto/a; (thing) succedaneo, surrogato // vt: to ~ sth/sb for sostituire qc/qn a.
subterfuge ['sʌbtəfjuːdʒ] n sotterfugio.
subterranean [sʌbtə'reɪnɪən] a sotterraneo(a).
subtitle ['sʌbtaɪtl] n (CINEMA) sottotitolo.
subtle ['sʌtl] a sottile.
subtotal [sʌb'təʊtl] n somma parziale.
subtract [səb'trækt] vt sottrarre; ~ion [-'trækʃən] n sottrazione f.
suburb ['sʌbəːb] n sobborgo; the ~s la periferia; ~an [sə'bəːbən] a suburbano(a); ~ia n periferia, sobborghi mpl.
subversive [səb'vəːsɪv] a sovversivo(a).
subway ['sʌbweɪ] n (US: underground) metropolitana; (Brit: underpass) sottopassaggio.

succeed [sək'siːd] vi riuscire; avere successo // vt succedere a; to ~ in doing riuscire a fare; ~ing a (following) successivo(a).
success [sək'ses] n successo; ~ful a (venture) coronato(a) da successo, riuscito(a); to be ~ful (in doing) riuscire (a fare); ~fully ad con successo.
succession [sək'seʃən] n successione f.
successive [sək'sesɪv] a successivo(a); consecutivo(a).
succumb [sə'kʌm] vi soccombere.
such [sʌtʃ] a tale; (of that kind): ~ a book un tale libro, un libro del genere; ~ books tali libri, libri del genere; (so much): ~ courage tanto coraggio // ad talmente, così; ~ a long trip un viaggio così lungo; ~ good books libri così buoni; ~ a lot of talmente or così tanto(a); ~ as (like) come; a noise ~ as to un rumore tale da; as ~ ad come or in quanto tale; ~-and-~ a tale (after noun).
suck [sʌk] vt succhiare; (breast, bottle) poppare; ~er n (ZOOL, TECH) ventosa; (BOT) pollone m; (col) gonzo/a, babbeo/a.
suction ['sʌkʃən] n succhiamento; (TECH) aspirazione f.
sudden ['sʌdn] a improvviso(a); all of a ~ improvvisamente, all'improvviso; ~ly ad bruscamente, improvvisamente, di colpo.
suds [sʌdz] npl schiuma (di sapone).
sue [suː] vt citare in giudizio.
suede [sweɪd] n pelle f scamosciata // cpd scamosciato(a).
suet ['suɪt] n grasso di rognone.
suffer ['sʌfə*] vt soffrire, patire; (bear) sopportare, tollerare // vi soffrire; ~er n malato/a; ~ing n sofferenza.
suffice [sə'faɪs] vi essere sufficiente, bastare.
sufficient [sə'fɪʃənt] a sufficiente; ~ money abbastanza soldi; ~ly ad sufficientemente, abbastanza.
suffocate ['sʌfəkeɪt] vi (have difficulty breathing) soffocare; (die through lack of air) asfissiare.
suffused [sə'fjuːzd] a: ~ with (colour) tinto(a) di; the room was ~ with light nella stanza c'era una luce soffusa.
sugar ['ʃʊgə*] n zucchero // vt zuccherare; ~ beet n barbabietola da zucchero; ~ cane n canna da zucchero; ~y a zuccherino(a), dolce; (fig) sdolcinato(a).
suggest [sə'dʒest] vt proporre, suggerire; indicare; ~ion [-'dʒestʃən] n suggerimento, proposta.
suicide ['suɪsaɪd] n (person) suicida m/f; (act) suicidio.
suit [suːt] n (man's) vestito; (woman's) completo, tailleur m inv; (CARDS) seme m, colore m // vt andar bene a or per;

essere adatto(a) a *or* per; (*adapt*): to ~ sth to adattare qc a; ~**able** a adatto(a); appropriato(a); ~**ably** ad (*dress*) in modo adatto; (*thank*) adeguatamente.

suitcase ['su:tkeıs] n valigia.

suite [swi:t] n (*of rooms*) appartamento; (*MUS*) suite f inv; (*furniture*): bedroom/dining room ~ arredo *or* mobilia per la camera da letto/sala da pranzo.

suitor ['su:tə*] n corteggiatore m, spasimante m.

sulfur ['sʌlfə*] n (*US*) = **sulphur**.

sulk [sʌlk] vi fare il broncio; ~**y** a imbronciato(a).

sullen ['sʌlən] a scontroso(a); cupo(a).

sulphur, (*US*) **sulfur** ['sʌlfə*] n zolfo.

sultana [sʌl'tɑ:nə] n (*fruit*) uva (secca) sultanina.

sultry ['sʌltrı] a afoso(a).

sum [sʌm] n somma; (*SCOL etc*) addizione f; to ~ up vt, vi riassumere.

summarize ['sʌmərаız] vt riassumere, riepilogare.

summary ['sʌmərı] n riassunto // a (*justice*) sommario(a).

summer ['sʌmə*] n estate f // cpd d'estate, estivo(a); ~**house** n (*in garden*) padiglione m; ~**time** n (*season*) estate f; ~ **time** n (*by clock*) ora legale (estiva).

summit ['sʌmıt] n cima, sommità; (*POL*) vertice m.

summon ['sʌmən] vt chiamare, convocare; to ~ up vt raccogliere, fare appello a; ~**s** n ordine m di comparizione // vt citare.

sump [sʌmp] n (*Brit AUT*) coppa dell'olio.

sumptuous ['sʌmptjuəs] a sontuoso(a).

sun [sʌn] n sole m; in the ~ al sole; ~**bathe** vi prendere un bagno di sole; ~**burn** n abbronzatura; (*painful*) scottatura; ~ **cream** n crema solare.

Sunday ['sʌndı] n domenica; ~ **school** n ≈ scuola di catechismo.

sundial ['sʌndaıəl] n meridiana.

sundown ['sʌndaun] n tramonto.

sundry ['sʌndrı] a vari(e), diversi(e); all and ~ tutti quanti; **sundries** npl articoli diversi, cose diverse.

sunflower ['sʌnflauə*] n girasole m.

sung [sʌŋ] pp of **sing**.

sunglasses ['sʌnglɑ:sız] npl occhiali mpl da sole.

sunk [sʌŋk] pp of **sink**.

sun: ~**light** n (luce f del) sole m; ~**ny** a assolato(a), soleggiato(a); (*fig*) allegro(a), felice; ~**rise** n levata del sole, alba; ~ **roof** n (*AUT*) tetto apribile; ~**set** n tramonto; ~**shade** n parasole m; ~**shine** n (luce f del) sole m; ~**stroke** n insolazione f, colpo di sole; ~**tan** n abbronzatura; ~**tan oil** n olio solare.

super ['su:pə*] a (*col*) fantastico(a).

superannuation [su:pərænju'eıʃən] n contributi mpl pensionistici; pensione f.

superb [su:'pə:b] a magnifico(a).

supercilious [su:pə'sılıəs] a sprezzante, sdegnoso(a).

superficial [su:pə'fıʃəl] a superficiale.

superhuman [su:pə'hju:mən] a sovrumano(a).

superimpose ['su:pərım'pəuz] vt sovrapporre.

superintendent [su:pərın'tɛndənt] n direttore/trice; (*POLICE*) ≈ commissario (capo).

superior [su'pıərıə*] a, n superiore (m/f); ~**ity** [-'ɔrıtı] n superiorità.

superlative [su'pə:lətıv] a superlativo(a), supremo(a) // n (*LING*) superlativo.

superman ['su:pəmæn] n superuomo.

supermarket ['su:pəmɑ:kıt] n supermercato.

supernatural [su:pə'nætʃərəl] a soprannaturale.

superpower ['su:pəpauə*] n (*POL*) superpotenza.

supersede [su:pə'si:d] vt sostituire, soppiantare.

superstitious [su:pə'stıʃəs] a superstizioso(a).

supervise ['su:pəvаız] vt (*person etc*) sorvegliare; (*organization*) soprintendere a; **supervision** [-'vıʒən] n sorveglianza; supervisione f; **supervisor** n sorvegliante m/f; soprintendente m/f; (*in shop*) capocommesso/a.

supine ['su:paın] a supino(a).

supper ['sʌpə*] n cena.

supplant [sə'plɑ:nt] vt (*person, thing*) soppiantare.

supple ['sʌpl] a flessibile; agile.

supplement n ['sʌplımənt] supplemento // vt [sʌplı'mɛnt] completare, integrare; ~**ary** [-'mɛntərı] a supplementare.

supplier [sə'plaıə*] n fornitore m.

supply [sə'plaı] vt (*provide*) fornire; (*equip*): to ~ (with) approvvigionare (di); attrezzare (con) // n riserva, provvista; (*supplying*) approvvigionamento; (*TECH*) alimentazione f; **supplies** npl (*food*) viveri mpl; (*MIL*) sussistenza; ~ **teacher** n (*Brit*) supplente m/f.

support [sə'pɔ:t] n (moral, financial etc) sostegno, appoggio; (*TECH*) supporto // vt sostenere; (*financially*) mantenere; (*uphold*) sostenere, difendere; ~**er** n (*POL etc*) sostenitore/trice, fautore/trice; (*SPORT*) tifoso/a.

suppose [sə'pəuz] vt, vi supporre; immaginare; to be ~**d** to do essere tenuto(a) a fare; ~**dly** [sə'pəuzıdlı] ad presumibilmente; (*seemingly*) apparentemente; **supposing** cj se, ammesso che + sub.

suppress [sə'prɛs] vt reprimere; sop-

primere; tenere segreto(a).
supreme [su'pri:m] a supremo(a).
surcharge ['sə:tʃɑ:dʒ] n supplemento;
(extra tax) soprattassa.
sure [ʃuə*] a sicuro(a); (definite,
convinced) sicuro(a), certo(a); ~! (of
course) senz'altro!, certo!; ~ **enough**
infatti; **to make ~ of sth/that** assicurarsi
di qc/che; ~**ly** ad sicuramente;
certamente.
surety ['ʃuərətɪ] n garanzia.
surf [sə:f] n (waves) cavalloni mpl;
(foam) spuma.
surface ['sə:fɪs] n superficie f // vt (road)
asfaltare // vi risalire alla superficie;
(fig: person) venire a galla, farsi
vivo(a); ~ **mail** n posta ordinaria.
surfboard ['sə:fbɔ:d] n tavola per
surfing.
surfeit ['sə:fɪt] n: a ~ of un eccesso di;
un'indigestione di.
surfing ['sə:fɪŋ] n surfing m.
surge [sə:dʒ] n (strong movement)
ondata; (of feeling) impeto // vi (waves)
gonfiarsi; (ELEC: power) aumentare improvvisamente; (people) riversarsi.
surgeon ['sə:dʒən] n chirurgo.
surgery ['sə:dʒərɪ] n chirurgia; (Brit:
room) studio or gabinetto medico,
ambulatorio; **to undergo ~** subire un
intervento chirurgico; ~ **hours** npl
(Brit) orario delle visite or di
consultazione.
surgical ['sə:dʒɪkl] a chirurgico(a); ~
spirit n (Brit) alcool m denaturato.
surly ['sə:lɪ] a scontroso(a), burbero(a).
surname ['sə:neɪm] n cognome m.
surpass [sə:'pɑ:s] vt superare.
surplus ['sə:pləs] n eccedenza; (ECON)
surplus m inv // a eccedente, d'avanzo.
surprise [sə'praɪz] n sorpresa;
(astonishment) stupore m // vt sorprendere; stupire; **surprising** a sorprendente, stupefacente; **surprisingly**
ad (easy, helpful) sorprendentemente.
surrender [sə'rendə*] n resa,
capitolazione f // vi arrendersi.
surreptitious [sʌrəp'tɪʃəs] a furtivo(a).
surrogate ['sʌrəgɪt] n surrogato; ~
mother n madre f sostitutiva.
surround [sə'raund] vt circondare; (MIL
etc) accerchiare; ~**ing** a circostante;
~**ings** npl dintorni mpl; (fig) ambiente
m.
surveillance [sə:'veɪləns] n sorveglianza,
controllo.
survey n ['sə:veɪ] quadro generale;
(study) esame m; (in housebuying etc)
perizia; (of land) rilevamento, rilievo
topografico // vt [sə:'veɪ] osservare;
esaminare; valutare; rilevare; ~**or** n
perito; geometra m; (of land)
agrimensore m.
survival [sə'vaɪvl] n sopravvivenza;
(relic) reliquia, vestigio.

survive [sə'vaɪv] vi sopravvivere // vt sopravvivere a; **survivor** n superstite m/f,
sopravvissuto/a.
susceptible [sə'septəbl] a: ~ **(to)**
sensibile (a); (disease) predisposto(a)
(a).
suspect a, n ['sʌspekt] a sospetto(a) // n
persona sospetta // vt [səs'pekt] so-
spettare; (think likely) supporre;
(doubt) dubitare.
suspend [səs'pend] vt sospendere; ~**ed**
sentence n condanna con la
condizionale; ~**er belt** n reggicalze m
inv; ~**ers** npl (Brit) giarrettiere fpl;
(US) bretelle fpl.
suspense [səs'pens] n apprensione f; (in
film etc) suspense m.
suspension [səs'penʃən] n (gen AUT) sospensione f; (of driving licence) ritiro
temporaneo; ~ **bridge** n ponte m sospeso.
suspicion [səs'pɪʃən] n sospetto.
suspicious [səs'pɪʃəs] a (suspecting) so-
spettoso(a); (causing suspicion) so-
spetto(a).
sustain [səs'teɪn] vt sostenere;
sopportare; (LAW: charge) confermare;
(suffer) subire; ~**ed** a (effort)
prolungato(a).
sustenance ['sʌstɪnəns] n nutrimento;
mezzi mpl di sostentamento.
swab [swɔb] n (MED) tampone m.
swagger ['swægə*] vi pavoneggiarsi.
swallow ['swɔləu] n (bird) rondine f //
vt inghiottire; (fig: story) bere; **to ~**
up vt inghiottire.
swam [swæm] pt of swim.
swamp [swɔmp] n palude f // vt
sommergere.
swan [swɔn] n cigno.
swap [swɔp] vt: **to ~ (for)** scambiare
(con).
swarm [swɔ:m] n sciame m // vi
formicolare; (bees) sciamare.
swarthy ['swɔ:ðɪ] a di carnagione scura.
swastika ['swɔstɪkə] n croce f uncinata,
svastica.
swat [swɔt] vt schiacciare.
sway [sweɪ] vi (building) oscillare; (tree)
ondeggiare; (person) barcollare // vt
(influence) influenzare, dominare.
swear [sweə*], pt swore, pp sworn vi
(witness etc) giurare; (curse) bestemmiare, imprecare; **to ~ to sth**
giurare qc; ~**word** n parolaccia.
sweat [swet] n sudore m, traspirazione f
// vi sudare.
sweater ['swetə*] n maglione m.
sweatshirt ['swetʃə:t] n felpa.
sweaty ['swetɪ] a sudato(a); bagnato(a)
di sudore.
Swede [swi:d] n svedese m/f.
swede [swi:d] n (Brit) rapa svedese.
Sweden ['swi:dn] n Svezia.
Swedish ['swi:dɪʃ] a svedese // n (LING)

svedese *m*.

sweep [swi:p] *n* spazzata; (*curve*) curva; (*expanse*) distesa; (*range*) portata; (*also:* **chimney ~**) spazzacamino // *vb* (*pt, pp* **swept**) *vt* spazzare, scopare // *vi* camminare maestosamente; precipitarsi, lanciarsi; (e)stendersi; **to ~ away** *vt* spazzare via; trascinare via; **to ~ past** *vi* sfrecciare accanto; passare accanto maestosamente; **to ~ up** *vt, vi* spazzare; **~ing** *a* (*gesture*) largo(a); circolare; **a ~ing statement** un'affermazione generica.

sweet [swi:t] *n* (*Brit: pudding*) dolce *m*; (*candy*) caramella // *a* dolce; (*fresh*) fresco(a); (*fig*) piacevole; delicato(a), grazioso(a); gentile; **~corn** *n* granturco dolce; **~en** *vt* addolcire; zuccherare; **~heart** *n* innamorato/a; **~ness** *n* sapore *m* dolce; dolcezza; **~ pea** *n* pisello odoroso.

swell [swɛl] *n* (*of sea*) mare *m* lungo // *a* (*col: excellent*) favoloso(a) // *vb* (*pt* **~ed**, *pp* **swollen**, **~ed**) *vt* gonfiare, ingrossare; aumentare // *vi* gonfiarsi, ingrossarsi; (*sound*) crescere; (*MED*) gonfiarsi; **~ing** *n* (*MED*) tumefazione *f*, gonfiore *m*.

sweltering ['swɛltərɪŋ] *a* soffocante.

swept [swɛpt] *pt, pp* of **sweep**.

swerve [swə:v] *vi* deviare; (*driver*) sterzare; (*boxer*) scartare.

swift [swɪft] *n* (*bird*) rondone *m* // *a* rapido(a), veloce.

swig [swɪg] *n* (*col: drink*) sorsata.

swill [swɪl] *n* broda // *vt* (*also:* **~ out**, **~ down**) risciacquare.

swim [swɪm] *n*: **to go for a ~** andare a fare una nuotata // *vb* (*pt* **swam**, *pp* **swum**) *vi* nuotare; (*SPORT*) fare del nuoto; (*head, room*) girare // *vt* (*river, channel*) attraversare *or* percorrere a nuoto; (*length*) nuotare; **~mer** *n* nuotatore/trice; **~ming** *n* nuoto; **~ming cap** *n* cuffia; **~ming costume** *n* (*Brit*) costume *m* da bagno; **~ming pool** *n* piscina; **~suit** *n* costume *m* da bagno.

swindle ['swɪndl] *n* truffa // *vt* truffare.

swine [swaɪn] *n* (*pl inv*) maiale *m*, porco; (*col!*) porco(!).

swing [swɪŋ] *n* altalena; (*movement*) oscillazione *f*; (*MUS*) ritmo; swing *m* // *vb* (*pt, pp* **swung**) *vt* dondolare, far oscillare; (*also:* **~ round**) far girare // *vi* oscillare, dondolare; (*also:* **~ round**: *object*) roteare; (*: person*) girarsi, voltarsi; **to be in full ~** (*activity*) essere in piena attività; (*party etc*) essere nel pieno; **~ door**, (*US*) **~ing door** *n* porta battente.

swingeing ['swɪndʒɪŋ] *a* (*Brit: defeat*) violento(a); (*: price increase*) enorme.

swipe [swaɪp] *vt* (*hit*) colpire con forza; dare uno schiaffo a; (*col: steal*) sgraffignare.

swirl [swə:l] *vi* turbinare, far mulinello.

swish [swɪʃ] *a* (*col: smart*) all'ultimo grido, alla moda // *vi* sibilare.

Swiss [swɪs] *a, n* (*pl inv*) svizzero(a).

switch [swɪtʃ] *n* (*for light, radio etc*) interruttore *m*; (*change*) cambiamento // *vt* (*change*) cambiare; scambiare; **to ~ off** *vt* spegnere; **to ~ on** *vt* accendere; (*engine, machine*) mettere in moto, avviare; **~board** *n* (*TEL*) centralino.

Switzerland ['swɪtsələnd] *n* Svizzera.

swivel ['swɪvl] *vi* (*also:* **~ round**) girare.

swollen ['swəulən] *pp of* **swell**.

swoon [swu:n] *vi* svenire.

swoop [swu:p] *vi* (*also:* **~ down**) scendere in picchiata, piombare.

swop [swɔp] *n, vt* = **swap**.

sword [sɔ:d] *n* spada; **~fish** *n* pesce *m* spada *inv*.

swore [swɔ:*] *pt of* **swear**.

sworn [swɔ:n] *pp of* **swear**.

swot [swɔt] *vt* sgobbare su // *vi* sgobbare.

swum [swʌm] *pp of* **swim**.

swung [swʌŋ] *pt, pp of* **swing**.

syllable ['sɪləbl] *n* sillaba.

syllabus ['sɪləbəs] *n* programma *m*.

symbol ['sɪmbl] *n* simbolo.

symmetry ['sɪmɪtrɪ] *n* simmetria.

sympathetic [sɪmpə'θɛtɪk] *a* (*showing pity*) compassionevole; (*kind*) comprensivo(a); **~ towards** sb disposto(a) verso.

sympathize ['sɪmpəθaɪz] *vi*: **to ~ with** sb compatire qn; partecipare al dolore di qn; **~r** *n* (*POL*) simpatizzante *m/f*.

sympathy ['sɪmpəθɪ] *n* compassione *f*; **in ~ with** d'accordo con; (*strike*) per solidarietà con; **with our deepest ~** con le nostre più sincere condoglianze.

symphony ['sɪmfənɪ] *n* sinfonia.

symptom ['sɪmptəm] *n* sintomo; indizio.

synagogue ['sɪnəgɔg] *n* sinagoga.

syndicate ['sɪndɪkɪt] *n* sindacato.

synonym ['sɪnənɪm] *n* sinonimo.

synopsis, *pl* **synopses** [sɪ'nɔpsɪs, -si:z] *n* sommario, sinossi *f inv*.

syntax ['sɪntæks] *n* sintassi *f inv*.

synthesis, *pl* **syntheses** ['sɪnθəsɪs, -si:z] *n* sintesi *f inv*.

synthetic [sɪn'θɛtɪk] *a* sintetico(a).

syphilis ['sɪfɪlɪs] *n* sifilide *f*.

syphon ['saɪfən] *n, vb* = **siphon**.

Syria ['sɪrɪə] *n* Siria.

syringe [sɪ'rɪndʒ] *n* siringa.

syrup ['sɪrəp] *n* sciroppo; (*also:* **golden ~**) melassa raffinata.

system ['sɪstəm] *n* sistema *m*; (*order*) metodo; (*ANAT*) organismo; **~atic** [-'mætɪk] *a* sistematico(a); metodico(a); **~ disk** *n* (*COMPUT*) disco del sistema; **~s analyst** *n* analista *m* programmatore.

T

ta [tɑ:] *excl* (*Brit col*) grazie!

tab [tæb] *n* (*loop on coat etc*) laccetto; (*label*) etichetta; **to keep ~s on** (*fig*) tenere d'occhio.

tabby ['tæbɪ] *n* (*also: ~ cat*) (gatto) soriano, gatto tigrato.

table ['teɪbl] *n* tavolo, tavola // *vt* (*Brit: motion etc*) presentare; **to lay** *or* **set the ~** apparecchiare *or* preparare la tavola; **~cloth** *n* tovaglia; **~ of contents** *n* indice *m*; **~ d'hôte** [tɑ:bl'dəut] *a* (*meal*) a prezzo fisso; **~ lamp** *n* lampada da tavolo; **~mat** *n* sottopiatto; **~spoon** *n* cucchiaio da tavola; (*also: ~spoonful: as measurement*) cucchiaiata.

tablet ['tæblɪt] *n* (*MED*) compressa; (: *for sucking*) pastiglia; (*for writing*) blocco; (*of stone*) targa.

table: ~ tennis *n* tennis *m* da tavolo, ping-pong *m* ®; **~ wine** *n* vino da tavola.

tabulate ['tæbjuleɪt] *vt* (*data, figures*) tabulare, disporre in tabelle.

tacit ['tæsɪt] *a* tacito(a).

tack [tæk] *n* (*nail*) bulletta; (*stitch*) punto d'imbastitura; (*NAUT*) bordo, bordata // *vt* imbullettare; imbastire // *vi* bordeggiare.

tackle ['tækl] *n* attrezzatura, equipaggiamento; (*for lifting*) paranco; (*RUGBY*) placcaggio // *vt* (*difficulty*) affrontare; (*RUGBY*) placcare.

tacky ['tækɪ] *a* colloso(a), appiccicaticcio(a); ancora bagnato(a).

tact [tækt] *n* tatto; **~ful** *a* delicato(a), discreto(a).

tactical ['tæktɪkl] *a* tattico(a).

tactics ['tæktɪks] *n, npl* tattica.

tactless ['tæktlɪs] *a* che manca di tatto.

tadpole ['tædpəul] *n* girino.

taffy ['tæfɪ] *n* (*US*) caramella *f* mou *inv*.

tag [tæg] *n* etichetta; **to ~ along** *vi* seguire.

tail [teɪl] *n* coda; (*of shirt*) falda // *vt* (*follow*) seguire, pedinare; **to ~ away, ~ off** *vi* (*in size, quality etc*) diminuire gradatamente; **~back** *n* (*Brit AUT*) ingorgo; **~ coat** *n* marsina; **~ end** *n* (*of train, procession etc*) coda; (*of meeting etc*) fine *f*; **~gate** *n* (*AUT*) portellone *m* posteriore.

tailor ['teɪlə*] *n* sarto; **~ing** *n* (*cut*) stile *m*; **~-made** *a* (*also fig*) fatto(a) su misura.

tailwind ['teɪlwɪnd] *n* vento di coda.

tainted ['teɪntɪd] *a* (*food*) guasto(a); (*water, air*) infetto(a); (*fig*) corrotto(a).

take [teɪk], *pt* **took**, *pp* **taken** [teɪk, tuk, 'teɪkn] *vt* prendere; (*gain: prize*) ottenere, vincere; (*require: effort, courage*) occorrere, volerci; (*tolerate*) accettare, sopportare; (*hold: passengers etc*) contenere; (*accompany*) accompagnare; (*bring, carry*) portare; (*exam*) sostenere, presentarsi a; **I ~ it that** suppongo che; **to ~ for a walk** (*child, dog*) portare a fare una passeggiata; **to ~ after** *vt fus* assomigliare a; **to ~ apart** *vt* smontare; **to ~ away** *vt* portare via; togliere; **to ~ back** *vt* (*return*) restituire; riportare; (*one's words*) ritirare; **to ~ down** *vt* (*building*) demolire; (*letter etc*) scrivere; **to ~ in** *vt* (*deceive*) imbrogliare, abbindolare; (*understand*) capire; (*include*) comprendere, includere; (*lodger*) prendere, ospitare; **to ~ off** *vi* (*AVIAT*) decollare // *vt* (*remove*) togliere; (*imitate*) imitare; **to ~ on** *vt* (*work*) accettare, intraprendere; (*employee*) assumere; (*opponent*) sfidare, affrontare; **to ~ out** *vt* portare fuori; (*remove*) togliere; (*licence*) prendere, ottenere; **to ~ sth out of sth** (*drawer, pocket etc*) tirare qc fuori da qc; estrarre qc da qc; **to ~ over** *vt* (*business*) rilevare // *vi*: **to ~ over from sb** prendere le consegne *or* il controllo da qn; **to ~ to** *vt fus* (*person*) prendere in simpatia; (*activity*) prendere gusto a; **to ~ up** *vt* (*one's story*) riprendere; (*dress*) accorciare; (*occupy: time, space*) occupare; (*engage in: hobby etc*) mettersi a; **~away** *a* (*food*) da portar via; **~-home pay** *n* stipendio netto; **~off** *n* (*AVIAT*) decollo; **~out** *a* (*US*) = **~away**; **~over** *n* (*COMM*) assorbimento.

takings ['teɪkɪŋz] *npl* (*COMM*) incasso.

talc [tælk] *n* (*also: ~um powder*) talco.

tale [teɪl] *n* racconto, storia; (*pej*) fandonia; **to tell ~s** (*fig: to teacher, parent etc*) fare la spia.

talent ['tælnt] *n* talento; **~ed** *a* di talento.

talk [tɔ:k] *n* discorso; (*gossip*) chiacchiere *fpl*; (*conversation*) conversazione *f*; (*interview*) discussione *f* // *vi* (*chatter*) chiacchierare; **~s** *npl* (*POL etc*) colloqui *mpl*; **to ~** *vt* parlare di; (*converse*) discorrere *or* conversare su; **to ~ sb out of/into doing** dissuadere qn da/convincere qn a fare; **to ~ shop** parlare del lavoro *or* degli affari; **to ~ over** *vt* discutere; **~ative** *a* loquace, ciarliero(a); **~ show** *n* conversazione *f* televisiva, talk show *m inv*.

tall [tɔ:l] *a* alto(a); **to be 6 feet ~** essere alto 1 metro e 80; **~boy** *n* (*Brit*) cassettone *m* alto; **~ story** *n* panzana, frottola.

tally ['tælɪ] *n* conto, conteggio // *vi*: **to ~ (with)** corrispondere (a).

talon ['tælən] *n* artiglio.

tambourine [tæmbə'ri:n] *n* tamburello.

tame [teɪm] *a* addomesticato(a); (*fig:*

story, style) insipido(a), scialbo(a).

tamper ['tæmpə*] *vi*: to ~ with manomettere.

tampon ['tæmpɔn] *n* tampone *m*.

tan [tæn] *n* (*also*: sun~) abbronzatura // *vt* abbronzare // *vi* abbronzarsi // *a* (*colour*) marrone rossiccio *inv*.

tang [tæŋ] *n* odore *m* penetrante; sapore *m* piccante.

tangent ['tændʒənt] *n* (MATH) tangente *f*; to go off at a ~ (*fig*) partire per la tangente.

tangerine [tændʒə'ri:n] *n* mandarino.

tangle ['tæŋgl] *n* groviglio // *vt* aggrovigliare.

tank [tæŋk] *n* serbatoio; (*for processing*) vasca; (*for fish*) acquario; (MIL) carro armato.

tanker ['tæŋkə*] *n* (*ship*) nave *f* cisterna *inv*; (*truck*) autobotte *f*, autocisterna.

tantalizing ['tæntəlaızıŋ] *a* allettante.

tantamount ['tæntəmaunt] *a*: ~ to equivalente a.

tantrum ['tæntrəm] *n* accesso di collera.

tap [tæp] *n* (*on sink etc*) rubinetto; (*gentle blow*) colpetto // *vt* dare un colpetto a; (*resources*) sfruttare, utilizzare; (*telephone*) mettere sotto controllo; **on** ~ (*fig*: *resources*) a disposizione; ~ **dancing** *n* tip tap *m*.

tape [teıp] *n* nastro; (*also*: **magnetic** ~) nastro (magnetico) // *vt* (*record*) registrare (su nastro); ~ **measure** *n* metro a nastro.

taper ['teıpə*] *n* candelina // *vi* assottigliarsi.

tape recorder *n* registratore *m* (a nastro).

tapestry ['tæpıstrı] *n* arazzo; tappezzeria.

tar [tɑ:*] *n* catrame *m*.

target ['tɑ:gıt] *n* bersaglio; (*fig*: *objective*) obiettivo.

tariff ['tærıf] *n* (COMM) tariffa; (*taxes*) tariffe *fpl* doganali.

tarmac ['tɑ:mæk] *n* (Brit: on road) macadam *m* al catrame; (AVIAT) pista di decollo.

tarnish ['tɑ:nıʃ] *vt* offuscare, annerire; (*fig*) macchiare.

tarpaulin [tɑ:'pɔ:lın] *n* tela incatramata.

tarragon ['tærəgən] *n* dragoncello.

tart [tɑ:t] *n* (CULIN) crostata; (Brit col: *pej*: *woman*) sgualdrina // *a* (*flavour*) aspro(a), agro(a); **to** ~ **up** *vt* (*col*): to ~ o.s. up farsi bello(a); (*pej*) agghindarsi.

tartan ['tɑ:tn] *n* tartan *m inv*.

tartar ['tɑ:tə*] *n* (*on teeth*) tartaro; ~ **sauce** *n* salsa tartara.

task [tɑ:sk] *n* compito; to take to ~ rimproverare; ~ **force** *n* (MIL. POLICE) unità operativa.

tassel ['tæsl] *n* fiocco.

taste [teıst] *n* gusto; (*flavour*) sapore *m*, gusto; (*fig*: *glimpse, idea*) idea // *vt* gu-

stare; (*sample*) assaggiare // *vi*: to ~ of (*fish etc*) sapere *or* avere sapore di; it ~s like fish sa di pesce; can I have a ~ of this wine? posso assaggiare un po' di questo vino?; to have a ~ for sth avere un'inclinazione per qc; in good/bad ~ di buon/cattivo gusto; ~**ful** *a* di buon gusto; ~**less** *a* (*food*) insipido(a); (*remark*) di cattivo gusto; **tasty** *a* saporito(a), gustoso(a).

tatters ['tætəz] *npl*: in ~ (*also*: tattered) a brandelli, sbrindellato(a).

tattoo [tə'tu:] *n* tatuaggio; (*spectacle*) parata militare // *vt* tatuare.

taught [tɔ:t] *pt, pp* of **teach**.

taunt [tɔ:nt] *n* scherno // *vt* schernire.

Taurus ['tɔ:rəs] *n* Toro.

taut [tɔ:t] *a* teso(a).

tawdry ['tɔ:drı] *a* pacchiano(a).

tax [tæks] *n* (*on goods*) imposta; (*on services*) tassa; (*on income*) imposte *fpl*, tasse *fpl* // *vt* tassare; (*fig*: *strain*: *patience etc*) mettere alla prova; ~**able** *a* (*income*) imponibile; ~**ation** [-'seıʃən] *n* tassazione *f*; tasse *fpl*, imposte *fpl*; ~ **avoidance** *n* l'evitare legalmente il pagamento di imposte; ~ **collector** *n* esattore *m* delle imposte; ~ **disc** *n* (Brit AUT) ≈ bollo; ~ **evasion** *n* evasione *f* fiscale; ~**free** *a* esente da imposte.

taxi ['tæksı] *n* taxi *m inv* // *vi* (AVIAT) rullare; ~ **driver** *n* tassista *m/f*; ~ **rank** (Brit), ~ **stand** *n* posteggio dei taxi.

tax: ~ **payer** *n* contribuente *m/f*; ~ **relief** *n* agevolazioni *fpl* fiscali; ~ **return** *n* dichiarazione *f* dei redditi.

TB *n abbr* = **tuberculosis**.

tea [ti:] *n* tè *m inv*; (Brit: *snack: for children*) merenda; **high** ~ (Brit) cena leggera (*presa nel tardo pomeriggio*); ~ **bag** *n* bustina di tè; ~ **break** *n* (Brit) intervallo per il tè.

teach [ti:tʃ], *pt, pp* **taught** *vt*: to ~ sb sth, ~ sth to sb insegnare qc a qn // *vi* insegnare; ~**er** *n* insegnante *m/f*; (*in secondary school*) professore/essa; (*in primary school*) maestro/a; ~**ing** *n* insegnamento.

tea cosy *n* copriteiera *m inv*.

teacup ['ti:kʌp] *n* tazza da tè.

teak [ti:k] *n* teak *m*.

team [ti:m] *n* squadra; (*of animals*) tiro; ~**work** *n* lavoro di squadra.

teapot ['ti:pɔt] *n* teiera.

tear *n* [teə*] strappo; [tıə*] lacrima // *vb* [tɛə*] (*pt* **tore**, *pp* **torn**) *vt* strappare // *vi* strapparsi; in ~s in lacrime; to ~ along *vi* (*rush*) correre all'impazzata; to ~ up *vt* (*sheet of paper etc*) strappare; ~**ful** *a* piangente, lacrimoso(a); ~ **gas** *n* gas *m* lacrimogeno.

tearoom ['ti:ru:m] *n* sala da tè.

tease [ti:z] *vt* canzonare; (*unkindly*)

tormentare.

tea set n servizio da tè.

teaspoon ['ti:spu:n] n cucchiaino da tè; (also: ~ful: as measurement) cucchiaino.

teat [ti:t] n capezzolo.

teatime ['ti:taɪm] n ora del tè.

tea towel n (Brit) strofinaccio (per i piatti).

technical ['tɛknɪkl] a tecnico(a); ~ity [-'kælɪtɪ] n tecnicità; (detail) dettaglio tecnico.

technician [tɛk'nɪʃən] n tecnico/a.

technique [tɛk'ni:k] n tecnica.

technological [tɛknə'lɔdʒɪkl] a tecnologico(a).

technology [tɛk'nɔlədʒɪ] n tecnologia.

teddy (bear) ['tɛdɪ-] n orsacchiotto.

tedious ['ti:dɪəs] a noioso(a), tedioso(a).

tee [ti:] n (GOLF) tee m inv.

teem [ti:m] vi abbondare, brulicare; to ~ with brulicare di; it is ~ing (with rain) piove a dirotto.

teenage ['ti:neɪdʒ] a (fashions etc) per giovani, per adolescenti; ~r n adolescente m/f.

teens [ti:nz] npl: to be in one's ~ essere adolescente.

tee-shirt ['ti:ʃə:t] n = T-shirt.

teeter ['ti:tə*] vi barcollare, vacillare.

teeth [ti:θ] npl of **tooth**.

teethe [ti:ð] vi mettere i denti.

teething ['ti:ðɪŋ]: ~ ring n dentaruolo; ~ troubles npl (fig) difficoltà fpl iniziali.

teetotal ['ti:'təutl] a astemio(a).

telegram ['tɛlɪgræm] n telegramma m.

telegraph ['tɛlɪgrɑ:f] n telegrafo.

telepathy [tə'lɛpəθɪ] n telepatia.

telephone ['tɛlɪfəun] n telefono // vt (person) telefonare a; (message) telefonare; ~ booth, (Brit) ~ box n cabina telefonica; ~ call n telefonata; ~ directory n elenco telefonico; ~ number n numero di telefono; telephonist [tə'lɛfənɪst] n (Brit) telefonista m/f.

telephoto ['tɛlɪ'fəutəu] a: ~ lens teleobiettivo.

telescope ['tɛlɪskəup] n telescopio // vt incastrare a cannocchiale.

televise ['tɛlɪvaɪz] vt teletrasmettere.

television ['tɛlɪvɪʒən] n televisione f; ~ set n televisore m.

telex ['tɛlɛks] n telex m inv // vt, vi trasmettere per telex; to ~ sb contattare qn via telex.

tell [tɛl], pt, pp **told** vt dire; (relate: story) raccontare; (distinguish): to ~ sth from distinguere qc da // vi (talk): to ~ (of) parlare (di); (have effect) farsi sentire, avere effetto; to ~ sb to do dire a qn di fare; to ~ off vt rimproverare, sgridare; ~er n (in bank) cassiere/a; ~ing a (remark, detail)

rivelatore(trice); ~tale a (sign) rivelatore(trice).

telly ['tɛlɪ] n abbr (Brit col: = television) tivù f inv.

temerity [tə'mɛrɪtɪ] n temerarietà.

temp [tɛmp] n abbr (= temporary) segretaria temporanea.

temper ['tɛmpə*] n (nature) carattere m; (mood) umore m; (fit of anger) collera // vt (moderate) temperare, moderare; to be in a ~ essere in collera; to lose one's ~ andare in collera.

temperament ['tɛmprəmənt] n (nature) temperamento m; ~al [-'mɛntl] a capriccioso(a).

temperate ['tɛmprət] a moderato(a); (climate) temperato(a).

temperature ['tɛmprətʃə*] n temperatura; to have or run a ~ avere la febbre.

tempest ['tɛmpɪst] n tempesta.

template ['tɛmplɪt] n sagoma.

temple ['tɛmpl] n (building) tempio; (ANAT) tempia.

temporary ['tɛmpərərɪ] a temporaneo(a); (job, worker) avventizio(a), temporaneo(a); ~ secretary n segretaria temporanea.

tempt [tɛmpt] vt tentare; to ~ sb into doing indurre qn a fare; ~ation [-'teɪʃən] n tentazione f.

ten [tɛn] num dieci.

tenable ['tɛnəbl] a sostenibile.

tenacity [tə'næsɪtɪ] n tenacia.

tenancy ['tɛnənsɪ] n affitto; condizione f di inquilino.

tenant ['tɛnənt] n inquilino/a.

tend [tɛnd] vt badare a, occuparsi di // vi: to ~ to do tendere a fare.

tendency ['tɛndənsɪ] n tendenza.

tender ['tɛndə*] a (delicate) tenero(a); (delicate) fragile; (sore) dolorante; (affectionate) affettuoso(a) // n (COMM: offer) offerta // vt offrire.

tendon ['tɛndən] n tendine m.

tenement ['tɛnəmənt] n casamento.

tenet ['tɛnət] n principio.

tennis ['tɛnɪs] n tennis m; ~ ball n palla da tennis; ~ court n campo da tennis; ~ player n tennista m/f; ~ racket n racchetta da tennis; ~ shoes npl scarpe fpl da tennis.

tenor ['tɛnə*] n (MUS, of speech etc) tenore m.

tense [tɛns] a teso(a) // n (LING) tempo.

tension ['tɛnʃən] n tensione f.

tent [tɛnt] n tenda.

tentative ['tɛntətɪv] a esitante, incerto(a); (conclusion) provvisorio(a).

tenterhooks ['tɛntəhuks] npl: on ~ sulle spine.

tenth [tɛnθ] num decimo(a).

tent: ~ peg n picchetto da tenda; ~ pole n palo della tenda, montante m.

tenuous ['tɛnjuəs] a tenue.

tenure [ˈtɛnjuəˢ] n (of property) possesso; (of job) permanenza; titolarità.

tepid [ˈtɛpɪd] a tiepido(a).

term [təːm] n (limit) termine m; (word) vocabolo, termine; (SCOL) trimestre m; (LAW) sessione f // vt chiamare, definire; ~s npl (conditions) condizioni fpl; (COMM) prezzi mpl, tariffe fpl; ~ of imprisonment periodo di prigionia; in the short/long ~ a breve/lunga scadenza; to come to ~s with (problem) affrontare.

terminal [ˈtəːmɪnl] a finale, terminale; (disease) nella fase terminale // n (ELEC) morsetto; (COMPUT) terminale m; (AVIAT, for oil, ore etc) terminal m inv; (Brit: also: coach ~) capolinea m.

terminate [ˈtəːmɪneɪt] vt mettere fine a // vi: to ~ in finire in or con.

terminus, pl **termini** [ˈtəːmɪnəs, ˈtəːmɪnaɪ] n (for buses) capolinea m; (for trains) stazione f terminale.

terrace [ˈtɛrəs] n terrazza; (Brit: row of houses) fila di case a schiera; the ~s npl (Brit SPORT) le gradinate; ~d a (garden) a terrazze.

terracotta [ˈtɛrəˈkɔtə] n terracotta.

terrain [tɛˈreɪn] n terreno.

terrible [ˈtɛrɪbl] a terribile; (weather) bruttissimo(a); (work) orribile; **terribly** ad terribilmente; (very badly) malissimo.

terrier [ˈtɛrɪəˢ] n terrier m inv.

terrific [təˈrɪfɪk] a incredibile, fantastico(a); (wonderful) formidabile, eccezionale.

terrify [ˈtɛrɪfaɪ] vt terrorizzare.

territory [ˈtɛrɪtərɪ] n territorio.

terror [ˈtɛrəˢ] n terrore m; ~ism n terrorismo; ~ist n terrorista m/f.

terse [təːs] a (style) conciso(a); (reply) laconico(a).

Terylene [ˈtɛrəliːn] n ® terital m ®, terilene m ®.

test [tɛst] n (trial, check, of courage etc) prova; (: of goods in factory) controllo, collaudo; (MED) esame m; (CHEM) analisi f inv; (exam: of intelligence etc) test m inv; (: in school) compito in classe; (also: driving ~) esame m di guida // vt provare; controllare, collaudare; esaminare; analizzare; sottoporre ad esame; to ~ sb in history esaminare qn in storia.

testament [ˈtɛstəmənt] n testamento; the Old/New T~ il Vecchio/Nuovo testamento.

testicle [ˈtɛstɪkl] n testicolo.

testify [ˈtɛstɪfaɪ] vi (LAW) testimoniare, deporre; to ~ to sth (LAW) testimoniare qc; (gen) comprovare or dimostrare qc; (: be sign of) essere una prova di qc.

testimony [ˈtɛstɪmənɪ] n (LAW) testimonianza, deposizione f.

test: ~ **match** n (CRICKET, RUGBY) partita internazionale; ~ **pilot** n pilota m collaudatore; ~ **tube** n provetta.

tetanus [ˈtɛtənəs] n tetano.

tether [ˈtɛðəˢ] vt legare // n: at the end of one's ~ al limite (della pazienza).

text [tɛkst] n testo; ~**book** n libro di testo.

textile [ˈtɛkstaɪl] n tessile m.

texture [ˈtɛkstʃəˢ] n tessitura; (of skin, paper etc) struttura.

Thames [tɛmz] n: the ~ il Tamigi.

than [ðæn, ðən] cj (in comparisons) che; (with numerals, pronouns, proper names) di; more ~ 10/once più di 10/una volta; I have more/less ~ you ne ho più/meno di te; I have more pens ~ pencils ho più penne che matite; she is older ~ you think è più vecchia di quanto tu (non) pensi.

thank [θæŋk] vt ringraziare; ~ you (very much) grazie (tante); ~s npl ringraziamenti mpl, grazie fpl // excl grazie!; ~s to prep grazie a; ~ful a: ~ful (for) riconoscente (per); ~less a ingrato(a); T~sgiving (Day) n giorno del ringraziamento.

that [ðæt] ♦ a (demonstrative: pl those) quel(quell', quello) m; quella(quell') f; ~ man/woman/book quell'uomo/quella donna/quel libro; (not "this") quell'uomo/quella donna/quel libro là; ~ one quello(a) là
♦ pronoun 1 (demonstrative: pl those) ciò; (not "this one") quello(a); who's ~? chi è?; what's ~? cos'è quello?; is ~ you? sei tu?; I prefer this to ~ preferisco questo a quello; ~'s what he said questo è ciò che ha detto; what happened after ~? che è successo dopo?; ~ is (to say) cioè
2 (relative: direct) che; (: indirect) cui; the book (~) I read il libro che ho letto; the box (~) I put it in la scatola in cui l'ho messo; the people (~) I spoke to le persone con cui or con le quali ho parlato
3 (relative: of time) in cui; the day (~) he came il giorno in cui è venuto
♦ cj che; he thought ~ I was ill pensava che io fossi malato
♦ ad (demonstrative) così; I can't work ~ much non posso lavorare (così) tanto; ~ high così alto; the wall's about ~ high and ~ thick il muro è alto circa così e spesso circa così.

thatched [θætʃt] a (roof) di paglia; ~ **cottage** n cottage m inv col tetto di paglia.

thaw [θɔː] n disgelo // vi (ice) sciogliersi; (food) scongelarsi // vt (food) (fare) scongelare; it's ~ing (weather) sta sgelando.

the [ðiː, ðə] definite article 1 (gen) il(lo, l') m; la(l') f; i(gli) mpl; le fpl; ~ boy/girl/ink il ragazzo/la ragazza/l'inchiostro;

~ books/pencils i libri/le matite; ~ history of ~ world la storia del mondo; give it to ~ postman dallo al postino; I haven't ~ time/money non ho tempo/soldi; ~ rich and ~ poor i ricchi e i poveri

2 (*in titles*): Elizabeth ~ First Elisabetta prima; Peter ~ Great Pietro il grande

3 (*in comparisons*): ~ more he works, ~ more he earns più lavora più guadagna.

theatre, (*US*) **theater** ['θɪətə*] *n* teatro; ~**-goer** *n* frequentatore/trice di teatri.

theatrical [θɪ'ætrɪkl] *a* teatrale.

theft [θɛft] *n* furto.

their [ðɛə*] *a* il(la) loro, *pl* i(le) loro; ~**s** *pronoun* il(la) loro, *pl* i(le) loro; *see also* **my, mine.**

them [ðɛm, ðəm] *pronoun* (*direct*) li(le); (*indirect*) gli, loro (*after vb*); (*stressed, after prep: people*) loro; (: *people, things*) essi(e); *see also* **me.**

theme [θi:m] *n* tema *m*; ~ **song** *n* tema musicale.

themselves [ðəm'sɛlvz] *pl pronoun* (*reflexive*) si; (*emphatic*) loro stessi(e); (*after prep*) se stessi(e); **between** ~ tra (di) loro; *see also* **oneself.**

then [ðɛn] *ad* (*at that time*) allora; (*next*) poi, dopo; (*and also*) e poi // *cj* (*therefore*) perciò, dunque, quindi // *a*: **the** ~ **president** il presidente di allora; **by** ~ allora; **from** ~ **on** da allora in poi.

theologian [θɪə'ləudʒən] *n* teologo/a.

theology [θɪ'ɔlədʒɪ] *n* teologia.

theorem ['θɪərəm] *n* teorema *m*.

theoretical [θɪə'rɛtɪkl] *a* teorico(a).

theory ['θɪərɪ] *n* teoria.

therapeutic(al) [θɛrə'pju:tɪk(l)] *a* terapeutico(a).

therapy ['θɛrəpɪ] *n* terapia.

there [ðɛə*] *ad* **1**: ~ **is,** ~ **are** c'è, ci sono; ~ **are 3 of them** (*people*) sono in 3; (*things*) ce ne sono 3; ~ **is no-one here** non c'è nessuno qui; ~ **has been an accident** c'è stato un incidente

2 (*referring to place*) là, lì; **up/in/down** ~ lassù/là dentro/laggiù; **he went** ~ **on Friday** ci è andato venerdì; **I want that book** ~ voglio quel libro là *or* lì; ~ **he is!** eccolo!

3: ~, ~, (*esp to child*) su, su.

thereabouts [ðɛərə'bauts] *ad* (*place*) nei pressi, da quelle parti; (*amount*) giù di lì, all'incirca.

thereafter [ðɛər'ɑ:ftə*] *ad* da allora in poi.

thereby [ðɛə'baɪ] *ad* con ciò.

therefore ['ðɛəfɔ:*] *ad* perciò, quindi.

there's [ðɛəz] = **there is, there has.**

thermal ['θə:ml] *a* termico(a).

thermometer [θə'mɔmɪtə*] *n* termometro.

thermonuclear ['θə:məu'nju:klɪə*] *a* termonucleare.

Thermos ['θə:məs] *n* ® (*also:* ~ **flask**) thermos *m inv* ®.

thermostat ['θə:məstæt] *n* termostato.

thesaurus [θɪ'sɔ:rəs] *n* dizionario dei sinonimi.

these [ði:z] *pl pronoun, a* questi(e).

thesis, *pl* **theses** ['θi:sɪs, 'θi:si:z] *n* tesi *f inv.*

they [ðeɪ] *pl pronoun* essi(esse); (*people only*) loro; ~ **say that ...** (*it is said that*) si dice che ...; ~**'d = they had, they would;** ~**'ll = they shall, they will;** ~**'re = they are;** ~**'ve = they have.**

thick [θɪk] *a* spesso(a); (*crowd*) compatto(a); (*stupid*) ottuso(a), lento(a) // *n*: **in the** ~ **of** nel folto di; **it's 20 cm** ~ ha uno spessore di 20 cm; ~**en** *vi* ispessire // *vt* (*sauce etc*) ispessire, rendere più denso(a); ~**ly** *ad* (*spread*) a strati spessi; (*cut*) a fette grosse; (*populated*) densamente; ~**ness** *n* spessore *m*; ~**set** *a* tarchiato(a), tozzo(a); ~**skinned** *a* (*fig*) insensibile.

thief, *pl* **thieves** [θi:f, θi:vz] *n* ladro/a.

thigh [θaɪ] *n* coscia.

thimble ['θɪmbl] *n* ditale *m*.

thin [θɪn] *a* sottile; (*person*) magro(a); (*soup*) poco denso(a); (*hair, crowd*) rado(a); (*fog*) leggero(a) // *vt* (*hair*) sfoltire; ~ (**down**) (*sauce, paint*) diluire.

thing [θɪŋ] *n* cosa; (*object*) oggetto; (*contraption*) aggeggio; ~**s** *npl* (*belongings*) cose *fpl*; **for one** ~ tanto per cominciare; **the best** ~ **would be to** la cosa migliore sarebbe di; **how are** ~**s?** come va?

think [θɪŋk], *pt, pp* **thought** *vi* pensare, riflettere // *vt* pensare, credere; (*imagine*) immaginare; **to** ~ **of** pensare a; **what did you** ~ **of them?** cosa ne ha pensato?; **to** ~ **about sth/sb** pensare a qc/qn; **I'll** ~ **about it** ci penserò; **to** ~ **of doing** pensare di fare; **I** ~ **so/not** penso di sì/no; **to** ~ **well of** avere una buona opinione di; **to** ~ **out** *vt* (*plan*) elaborare; (*solution*) trovare; **to** ~ **over** *vt* riflettere su; **to** ~ **through** *vt* riflettere a fondo su; **to** ~ **up** *vt* ideare; ~ **tank** *n* commissione *f* di esperti.

third [θə:d] *num* terzo(a) // *n* terzo/a; (*fraction*) terzo, terza parte *f*; (*Brit SCOL: degree*) laurea col minimo dei voti; ~**ly** *ad* in terzo luogo; ~ **party insurance** *n* (*Brit*) assicurazione *f* contro terzi; ~**-rate** *a* di qualità scadente; **the T~ World** *n* il Terzo Mondo.

thirst [θə:st] *n* sete *f*; ~**y** *a* (*person*) assetato(a), che ha sete.

thirteen [θə:'ti:n] *num* tredici.

thirty ['θə:tɪ] *num* trenta.

this [ðɪs] ♦ *a* (*demonstrative:* *pl* **these**) questo(a); ~ **man/woman/book** quest'uomo/questa donna/questo libro; (*not "that"*) quest'uomo/questa donna/

questo libro qui; ~ **one** questo(a) qui
◆ *pronoun* (*demonstrative*: *pl* **these**)
questo(a); (*not "that one"*) questo(a)
qui; **who/what** is ~? chi è/che cos'è questo?; I **prefer** ~ **to** that preferisco questo
a quello; ~ **is where** I live io abito qui;
~ **is what** he said questo è ciò che ha
detto; ~ **is** Mr Brown (*in introductions,
photo*) questo è il signor Brown; (*on
telephone*) sono il signor Brown
◆ *ad* (*demonstrative*): ~ **high/long** *etc*
alto/lungo *etc* così; I **didn't know things
were** ~ **bad** non sapevo andasse così
male.

thistle [ˈθɪsl] *n* cardo.

thong [θɔŋ] *n* cinghia.

thorn [θɔːn] *n* spina.

thorough [ˈθʌrə] *a* (*search*)
minuzioso(a); (*knowledge, research*) approfondito(a), profondo(a); co-
scienzioso(a); (*cleaning*) a fondo;
~**bred** *n* (*horse*) purosangue *m/f inv*;
~**fare** *n* strada transitabile; "no ~**fare**"
"divieto di transito"; ~**ly** *ad*
minuziosamente; in profondità; a fondo;
he ~**ly** agreed fu completamente
d'accordo.

those [ðəʊz] *pl pronoun* quelli(e) // *pl a*
quei(quegli) *mpl*; quelle *fpl*.

though [ðəʊ] *cj* benché, sebbene // *ad*
comunque.

thought [θɔːt] *pt, pp of* **think** // *n*
pensiero; (*opinion*) opinione *f*;
(*intention*) intenzione *f*; ~**ful** *a*
pensieroso(a), pensoso(a); (*considerate*)
premuroso(a); ~**less** *a* sconsiderato(a);
(*behaviour*) scortese.

thousand [ˈθaʊzənd] *num* mille; **one** ~
mille; ~**s of** migliaia di; ~**th** *num*
millesimo(a).

thrash [θræʃ] *vt* picchiare; bastonare;
(*defeat*) battere; **to** ~ **about** *vi*
dibattersi; **to** ~ **out** *vt* dibattere.

thread [θrɛd] *n* filo; (*of screw*) filetto //
vt (*needle*) infilare; ~**bare** *a* consumato(a), logoro(a).

threat [θrɛt] *n* minaccia; ~**en** *vi* (*storm*)
minacciare // *vt*: **to** ~**en sb with** sth/**to do**
minacciare qn con qc/di fare.

three [θriː] *num* tre; ~-**dimensional** *a*
tridimensionale; (*film*) stereoscopico(a);
~-**piece suit** *n* completo (con gilè); ~-
piece suite *n* salotto comprendente un
divano e due poltrone; ~-**ply** *a* (*wood*) a
tre strati; (*wool*) a tre fili.

thresh [θrɛʃ] *vt* (*AGR*) trebbiare.

threshold [ˈθrɛʃhəʊld] *n* soglia.

threw [θruː] *pt of* **throw**.

thrifty [ˈθrɪftɪ] *a* economico(a).

thrill [θrɪl] *n* brivido // *vi* eccitarsi,
tremare // *vt* (*audience*) elettrizzare; **to
be** ~**ed** (*with gift etc*) essere
commosso(a); ~**er** *n* film *m inv* (*or
dramma m or libro*) del brivido; ~**ing** *a*
(*book*) pieno(a) di suspense; (*news,*

discovery) entusiasmante.

thrive, *pt* **thrived, throve**, *pp* **thrived,
thriven** [θraɪv, θrəʊv, ˈθrɪvn] *vi* crescere
or svilupparsi bene; (*business*) prosperare; he ~**s** on it gli fa bene, ne
gode; **thriving** *a* fiorente.

throat [θrəʊt] *n* gola; **to have a sore** ~
avere (un *or* il) mal di gola.

throb [θrɔb] *vi* (*heart*) palpitare;
(*engine*) vibrare; (*with pain*) pulsare.

throes [θrəʊz] *npl*: **in the** ~ **of** alle prese
con; in preda a.

thrombosis [θrɔmˈbəʊsɪs] *n* trombosi *f*.

throne [θrəʊn] *n* trono.

throng [θrɔŋ] *n* moltitudine *f* // *vt*
affollare.

throttle [ˈθrɔtl] *n* (*AUT*) valvola a
farfalla // *vt* strangolare.

through [θruː] *prep* attraverso; (*time*)
per, durante; (*by means of*) per mezzo
di; (*owing to*) a causa di // *a* (*ticket,
train, passage*) diretto(a) // *ad* attraverso; **to put sb** ~ **to sb** (*TEL*)
passare qn a qn; **to be** ~ (*TEL*) ottenere
la comunicazione; (*have finished*) avere
finito; "**no** ~ **way**" (*Brit*) "strada senza
sbocco"; ~**out** *prep* (*place*) dappertutto
in; (*time*) per *or* durante tutto(a) // *ad*
dappertutto; sempre.

throve [θrəʊv] *pt of* **thrive**.

throw [θrəʊ] *n* tiro, getto; (*SPORT*) lancio
// *vt* (*pt* **threw**, *pp* **thrown** [θruː,
θrəʊn]) tirare, gettare; (*SPORT*)
lanciare; (*rider*) disarcionare; (*fig*)
confondere; (*pottery*) formare al tornio;
to ~ **a party** dare una festa; **to** ~ **away**
vt gettare *or* buttare via; **to** ~ **off** *vt*
sbarazzarsi di; **to** ~ **out** *vt* buttare
fuori; (*reject*) respingere; **to** ~ **up** *vi*
vomitare; ~**away** *a* da buttare; ~-**in** *n*
(*SPORT*) rimessa in gioco.

thru [θruː] *prep, a, ad* (*US*) = **through**.

thrush [θrʌʃ] *n* tordo.

thrust [θrʌst] *n* (*TECH*) spinta // *vt* (*pt,
pp* **thrust**) spingere con forza; (*push in*)
conficcare.

thud [θʌd] *n* tonfo.

thug [θʌg] *n* delinquente *m*.

thumb [θʌm] *n* (*ANAT*) pollice *m* // *vt*
(*book*) sfogliare; **to** ~ **a lift** fare l'autostop; ~**tack** *n* (*US*) puntina da disegno.

thump [θʌmp] *n* colpo forte; (*sound*)
tonfo // *vt* battere su // *vi* picchiare,
battere.

thunder [ˈθʌndə*] *n* tuono // *vi* tuonare;
(*train etc*): **to** ~ **past** passare con un
rombo; ~**bolt** *n* fulmine *m*; ~**clap** *n*
rombo di tuono; ~**ous** [ˈθʌndrəs] *a*
fragoroso(a); ~**storm** *n* temporale *m*;
~**y** *a* temporalesco(a).

Thursday [ˈθəːzdɪ] *n* giovedì *m inv*.

thus [ðʌs] *ad* così.

thwart [θwɔːt] *vt* contrastare.

thyme [taɪm] *n* timo.

thyroid [ˈθaɪrɔɪd] *n* tiroide *f*.

tiara [tɪˈɑːrə] *n* (*woman's*) diadema *m*.

Tiber [ˈtaɪbə•] *n*: the ~ il Tevere.

tick [tɪk] *n* (*sound: of clock*) tic tac *m inv*; (*mark*) segno; spunta; (*ZOOL*) zecca; (*Brit col*): **in a** ~ in un attimo // *vi* fare tic tac // *vt* spuntare; **to** ~ **off** *vt* spuntare; (*person*) sgridare; **to** ~ **over** *vi* (*engine*) andare al minimo; (*fig*) andare avanti come al solito.

ticket [ˈtɪkɪt] *n* biglietto; (*in shop: on goods*) etichetta; (: *from cash register*) scontrino; (*for library*) scheda; ~ **collector** *n* bigliettaio; ~ **office** *n* biglietteria.

tickle [ˈtɪkl] *n* solletico // *vt* fare il solletico a, solleticare; (*fig*) stuzzicare; piacere a; far ridere.

tidal [ˈtaɪdl] *a* di marea; ~ **wave** *n* onda anomala.

tidbit [ˈtɪdbɪt] *n* (*US*) = **titbit**.

tiddlywinks [ˈtɪdlɪwɪŋks] *n* gioco della pulce.

tide [taɪd] *n* marea; (*fig: of events*) corso; **to** ~ **sb over** dare una mano a qn; **high/low** ~ alta/bassa marea.

tidy [ˈtaɪdɪ] *a* (*room*) ordinato(a), lindo(a); (*dress, work*) curato(a), in ordine; (*person*) ordinato(a) // *vt* (*also*: ~ **up**) riordinare, mettere in ordine; **to** ~ **o.s. up** rassettarsi.

tie [taɪ] *n* (*string etc*) legaccio; (*Brit: also*: **neck**~) cravatta; (*fig: link*) legame *m*; (*SPORT: draw*) pareggio // *vt* (*parcel*) legare; (*ribbon*) annodare // *vi* (*SPORT*) pareggiare; **to** ~ **sth in a bow** annodare qc; **to** ~ **a knot in sth** fare un nodo a qc; **to** ~ **down** *vt* fissare con una corda; (*fig*): **to** ~ **sb down to** costringere qn a accettare; **to** ~ **up** *vt* (*parcel, dog*) legare; (*boat*) ormeggiare; (*arrangements*) concludere; **to be** ~**d up** (*busy*) essere occupato *or* preso.

tier [tɪə•] *n* fila; (*of cake*) piano, strato.

tiff [tɪf] *n* battibecco.

tiger [ˈtaɪgə•] *n* tigre *f*.

tight [taɪt] *a* (*rope*) teso(a), tirato(a); (*clothes*) stretto(a); (*budget, programme, bend*) stretto(a); (*control*) severo(a), fermo(a); (*col: drunk*) sbronzo(a) // *ad* (*squeeze*) fortemente, (*shut*) ermeticamente; ~**s** *npl* (*Brit*) collant *m inv*; ~**en** *vt* (*rope*) tendere; (*screw*) stringere; (*control*) rinforzare // *vi* tendersi; stringersi; ~**-fisted** *a* avaro(a); ~**ly** *ad* (*grasp*) bene, saldamente; ~**rope** *n* corda (da acrobata).

tile [taɪl] *n* (*on roof*) tegola; (*on wall or floor*) piastrella, mattonella.

till [tɪl] *n* registratore *m* di cassa // *vt* (*land*) coltivare // *prep, cj* = **until**.

tiller [ˈtɪlə•] *n* (*NAUT*) barra del timone.

tilt [tɪlt] *vt* inclinare, far pendere // *vi* inclinarsi, pendere.

timber [ˈtɪmbə•] *n* (*material*) legname *m*; (*trees*) alberi *mpl* da legname.

time [taɪm] *n* tempo; (*epoch: often pl*) epoca, tempo; (*by clock*) ora; (*moment*) momento; (*occasion, also MATH*) volta; (*MUS*) tempo // *vt* (*race*) cronometrare; (*programme*) calcolare la durata di; (*remark etc*) dire (*or* fare) al momento giusto; **a long** ~ molto tempo; **for the** ~ **being** per il momento; **4 at a** ~ **4** per *or* alla volta; **from** ~ **to** ~ ogni tanto; **in** ~ (*soon enough*) in tempo; (*after some time*) col tempo; (*MUS*) a tempo; **in a week's** ~ fra una settimana; **in no** ~ in un attimo; **any** ~ in qualsiasi momento; **on** ~ puntualmente; **5** ~**s 5** 5 volte 5, 5 per 5; **what** ~ **is it?** che ora è?, che ore sono?; **to have a good** ~ divertirsi; ~**'s up!** è (l')ora!; ~ **bomb** *n* bomba a orologeria; ~ **lag** *n* intervallo, ritardo; (*in travel*) differenza di fuso orario; ~**less** *a* eterno(a); ~**ly** *a* opportuno(a); ~ **off** *n* tempo libero; ~**r** *n* (~ **switch**) temporizzatore *m*; (*in kitchen*) contaminuti *m inv*; ~ **scale** *n* periodo; ~ **switch** *n* (*Brit*) temporizzatore *m*; ~**table** *n* orario; ~ **zone** *n* fuso orario.

timid [ˈtɪmɪd] *a* timido(a); (*easily scared*) pauroso(a).

timing [ˈtaɪmɪŋ] *n* sincronizzazione *f*; (*fig*) scelta del momento opportuno, tempismo; (*SPORT*) cronometraggio.

timpani [ˈtɪmpənɪ] *npl* timpani *mpl*.

tin [tɪn] *n* stagno; (*also*: ~ **plate**) latta; (*Brit: can*) barattolo (di latta), lattina, scatola; (*for baking*) teglia; ~**foil** *n* stagnola.

tinge [tɪndʒ] *n* sfumatura // *vt*: ~**d with** tinto(a) di.

tingle [ˈtɪŋgl] *vi* pizzicare.

tinker [ˈtɪŋkə•] *n* stagnino ambulante; (*gipsy*) zingaro/a; **to** ~ **with** *vt fus* armeggiare intorno a; cercare di riparare.

tinkle [ˈtɪŋkl] *vi* tintinnare.

tinned [tɪnd] *a* (*Brit: food*) in scatola.

tin opener [ˈ-əupnə•] *n* (*Brit*) apriscatole *m inv*.

tinsel [ˈtɪnsl] *n* decorazioni *fpl* natalizie (*argentate*).

tint [tɪnt] *n* tinta; ~**ed** *a* (*hair*) tinto(a); (*spectacles, glass*) colorato(a).

tiny [ˈtaɪnɪ] *a* minuscolo(a).

tip [tɪp] *n* (*end*) punta; (*protective: on umbrella etc*) puntale *m*; (*gratuity*) mancia; (*for coal*) discarica; (*Brit: for rubbish*) immondezzaio; (*advice*) suggerimento // *vt* (*waiter*) dare la mancia a; (*tilt*) inclinare; (*overturn: also*: ~ **over**) capovolgere; (*empty: also*: ~ **out**) scaricare; ~**-off** *n* (*hint*) soffiata; ~**ped** *a* (*Brit: cigarette*) col filtro.

Tipp-Ex [ˈtɪpeks] *n* ® correttore *m*.

tipsy [ˈtɪpsɪ] *a* brillo(a).

tiptoe [ˈtɪptəu] *n*: **on** ~ in punta di piedi.

tiptop ['tɪp'tɔp] a: in ~ **condition** in ottime condizioni.

tire ['taɪə*] n (US) = **tyre** // vt stancare // vi stancarsi; ~**d** a stanco(a); **to be** ~**d of** essere stanco or stufo di; ~**some** a noioso(a); **tiring** a faticoso(a).

tissue ['tɪʃuː] n tessuto; (paper handkerchief) fazzoletto di carta; ~ **paper** n carta velina.

tit [tɪt] n (bird) cinciallegra; **to give** ~ **for tat** rendere pan per focaccia.

titbit ['tɪtbɪt], (US) **tidbit** ['tɪdbɪt] n (food) leccornia; (news) notizia ghiotta.

titivate ['tɪtɪveɪt] vt agghindare.

title ['taɪtl] n titolo; ~ **deed** n (LAW) titolo di proprietà; ~ **role** n ruolo or parte f principale.

titter ['tɪtə*] vi ridere scioccamente.

TM abbr = **trademark**.

to [tuː, tə] ♦ prep 1 (direction) a; **to go** ~ **France/London/school** andare in Francia/a Londra/a scuola; **to go** ~ **Paul's/the doctor's** andare da Paul/dal dottore; **the road** ~ **Edinburgh** la strada per Edimburgo; ~ **the left/right** a sinistra/destra
2 (as far as) (fino) a; **from here** ~ **London** da qui a Londra; **to count** ~ **10** contare fino a 10; **from 40** ~ **50 people** da 40 a 50 persone
3 (with expressions of time): **a quarter** ~ **5** le 5 meno un quarto; **it's twenty** ~ **3** sono le 3 meno venti
4 (for, of): **the key** ~ **the front door** la chiave della porta d'ingresso; **a letter** ~ **his wife** una lettera per la moglie
5 (expressing indirect object) a; **to give sth** ~ **sb** dare qc a qn; **to talk** ~ **sb** parlare a qn; **to be a danger** ~ **sb/sth** rappresentare un pericolo per qn/qc
6 (in relation to): **3 goals** ~ **2** 3 goal a 2; **30 miles** ~ **the gallon** ≈ 11 chilometri con un litro
7 (purpose, result): **to come** ~ **sb's aid** venire in aiuto a qn; **to sentence sb** ~ **death** condannare a morte qn; ~ **my surprise** con mia sorpresa
♦ with vb 1 (simple infinitive): ~ **go/eat etc** andare/mangiare etc
2 (following another vb): **to want/try/start** ~ **do** volere/cercare di/cominciare a fare
3 (with vb omitted): **I don't want** ~ non voglio (farlo); **you ought** ~ devi (farlo)
4 (purpose, result) per; **I did it** ~ **help you** l'ho fatto per aiutarti
5 (equivalent to relative clause): **I have things** ~ **do** ho da fare; **the main thing is** ~ **try** la cosa più importante è provare
6 (after adjective etc): **ready** ~ **go** pronto a partire; **too old/young** ~ ... troppo vecchio/giovane per ...
♦ ad: **to push the door** ~ accostare la porta.

toad [təud] n rospo; ~**stool** n fungo (velenoso).

toast [təust] n (CULIN) toast m, pane m abbrustolito; (drink, speech) brindisi m inv // vt (CULIN) abbrustolire; (drink to) brindare a; **a piece or slice of** ~ una fetta di pane abbrustolito; ~**er** n tostapane m inv.

tobacco [tə'bækəu] n tabacco; ~**nist** n tabaccaio/a; ~**nist's (shop)** n tabaccheria.

toboggan [tə'bɔgən] n toboga m inv; (child's) slitta.

today [tə'deɪ] ad, n (also fig) oggi (m).

toddler ['tɔdlə*] n bambino/a che impara a camminare.

toddy ['tɔdɪ] n grog m inv.

to-do [tə'duː] n (fuss) storie fpl.

toe [təu] n dito del piede; (of shoe) punta; **to** ~ **the line** (fig) stare in riga, conformarsi.

toffee ['tɔfɪ] n caramella.

toga ['təugə] n toga.

together [tə'gɛðə*] ad insieme; (at same time) allo stesso tempo; ~ **with** insieme a.

toil [tɔɪl] n travaglio, fatica // vi affannarsi; sgobbare.

toilet ['tɔɪlət] n (Brit: lavatory) gabinetto // cpd (bag, soap etc) da toletta; ~ **bowl** n vaso or tazza del gabinetto; ~ **paper** n carta igienica; ~**ries** npl articoli mpl da toletta; ~ **roll** n rotolo di carta igienica; ~ **water** n acqua di colonia.

token ['təukən] n (sign) segno; (voucher) buono; **book/record** ~ (Brit) buono-libro/disco.

told [təuld] pt, pp of **tell**.

tolerable ['tɔlərəbl] a (bearable) tollerabile; (fairly good) passabile.

tolerant ['tɔlərnt] a: ~ (of) tollerante (nei confronti di).

tolerate ['tɔləreɪt] vt sopportare; (MED, TECH) tollerare.

toll [təul] n (tax, charge) pedaggio // vi (bell) suonare; **the accident** ~ **on the roads** il numero delle vittime della strada.

tomato, ~**es** [tə'mɑːtəu] n pomodoro.

tomb [tuːm] n tomba.

tomboy ['tɔmbɔɪ] n maschiaccio.

tombstone ['tuːmstəun] n pietra tombale.

tomcat ['tɔmkæt] n gatto.

tomorrow [tə'mɔrəu] ad, n (also fig) domani (m inv); **the day after** ~ dopodomani; **a week** ~ domani a otto; ~ **morning** domani mattina.

ton [tʌn] n tonnellata (Brit = 1016 kg; US = 907 kg; metric = 1000 kg); (NAUT: also: **register** ~) tonnellata di stazza (= 2.83 cu.m); ~**s of** (col) un mucchio or sacco di.

tone [təun] n tono // vi intonarsi; **to** ~ **down** vt (colour, criticism, sound) attenuare; **to ~ up** vt (muscles) tonificare; **~-deaf** a che non ha orecchio (musicale).

tongs [tɔŋz] npl tenaglie fpl; (for coal) molle fpl; (for hair) arricciacapelli m inv.

tongue [tʌŋ] n lingua; **~ in cheek** ad ironicamente; **~-tied** a (fig) muto(a); **~-twister** n scioglilingua m inv.

tonic ['tɔnɪk] n (MED) tonico; (MUS) nota tonica; (also: **~ water**) acqua tonica.

tonight [tə'naɪt] ad stanotte; (this evening) stasera // n questa notte; questa sera.

tonnage ['tʌnɪdʒ] n (NAUT) tonnellaggio, stazza.

tonne [tʌn] n (metric ton) tonnellata.

tonsil ['tɔnsl] n tonsilla; **~litis** [-'laɪtɪs] n tonsillite f.

too [tu:] ad (excessively) troppo; (also) anche; **~ much** ad troppo // a troppo(a); **~ many** a troppi(e); **~ bad!** tanto peggio!, peggio così!

took [tuk] pt of **take**.

tool [tu:l] n utensile m, attrezzo // vt lavorare con un attrezzo; **~ box/kit** n cassetta f portautensili/attrezzi inv.

toot [tu:t] vi suonare; (with car horn) suonare il clacson.

tooth [tu:θ], pl **teeth** n (ANAT, TECH) dente m; **~ache** n mal m di denti; **~brush** n spazzolino da denti; **~paste** n dentifricio; **~pick** n stuzzicadenti m inv.

top [tɔp] n (of mountain, page, ladder) cima; (of box, cupboard, table) sopra m inv, parte f superiore; (lid: of box, jar) coperchio; (: of bottle) tappo; (toy) trottola // a più alto(a); (in rank) primo(a); (best) migliore // vt (exceed) superare; (be first in) essere in testa a; **on ~ of** sopra, in cima a; (in addition to) oltre a; **from ~ to bottom** da cima a fondo; **to ~ up**, (US) **~ off** vt riempire; **~ floor** n ultimo piano; **~ hat** n cilindro; **~-heavy** a (object) con la parte superiore troppo pesante.

topic ['tɔpɪk] n argomento; **~al** a d'attualità.

top: **~less** a (bather etc) col seno scoperto; **~-level** a (talks) ad alto livello; **~most** a il(la) più alto(a).

topple ['tɔpl] vt rovesciare, far cadere // vi cadere; traballare.

top-secret ['tɔp'si:krɪt] a segretissimo(a).

topsy-turvy ['tɔpsɪ'tə:vɪ] a, ad sottosopra (inv).

torch [tɔ:tʃ] n torcia; (Brit: electric) lampadina tascabile.

tore [tɔ:*] pt of **tear**.

torment n ['tɔ:mɛnt] tormento // vt [tɔ:'mɛnt] tormentare; (fig: annoy) infastidire.

torn [tɔ:n] pp of **tear**.

tornado, **~es** [tɔ:'neɪdəu] n tornado.

torpedo, **~es** [tɔ:'pi:dəu] n siluro.

torrent ['tɔrnt] n torrente m.

tortoise ['tɔ:təs] n tartaruga; **~shell** ['tɔ:təʃel] a di tartaruga.

torture ['tɔ:tʃə*] n tortura // vt torturare.

Tory ['tɔ:rɪ] (Brit POL) a dei tories, conservatore(trice) // n tory m/f inv, conservatore/trice.

toss [tɔs] vt gettare, lanciare; (pancake) far saltare; (head) scuotere; **to ~ a coin** fare a testa o croce; **to ~ up for sth** fare a testa o croce per qc; **to ~ and turn** (in bed) girarsi e rigirarsi.

tot [tɔt] n (Brit: drink) bicchierino; (child) bimbo/a.

total ['təutl] a totale // n totale m // vt (add up) sommare; (amount to) ammontare a.

totally ['təutəlɪ] ad completamente.

totter ['tɔtə*] vi barcollare.

touch [tʌtʃ] n tocco, (sense) tatto; (contact) contatto, (FOOTBALL) fuori gioco m // vt toccare; **a ~ of** (fig) un tocco di; un pizzico di; **in ~ with** in contatto con; **to get in ~ with** mettersi in contatto con; **to lose ~** (friends) perdersi di vista; **to ~ on** vt fus (topic) sfiorare, accennare a; **to ~ up** vt (paint) ritoccare; **~-and-go** a incerto(a); **~down** n atterraggio; (on sea) ammaraggio; (US FOOTBALL) meta; **~ed** a commosso(a); (col) tocco(a), toccato(a); **~ing** a commovente; **~line** n (SPORT) linea laterale; **~y** a (person) suscettibile.

tough [tʌf] a duro(a); (resistant) resistente; (meat) duro(a), tiglioso(a).

toupee ['tu:peɪ] n parrucchino.

tour ['tuə*] n viaggio; (also: **package ~**) viaggio organizzato or tutto compreso; (of town, museum) visita; (by artist) tournée f inv // vt visitare; **~ing** n turismo.

tourism ['tuərɪzəm] n turismo.

tourist ['tuərɪst] n turista m/f // ad (travel) in classe turistica // cpd turistico(a); **~ office** n pro loco f inv.

tournament ['tuənəmənt] n torneo.

tousled ['tauzld] a (hair) arruffato(a).

tout [taut] vi: **to ~ for** procacciare, raccogliere; cercare clienti per // n (also: **ticket ~**) bagarino.

tow [təu] vt rimorchiare; "**on or** (US) **in ~**" (AUT) "veicolo rimorchiato".

toward(s) [tə'wɔ:d(z)] prep verso; (of attitude) nei confronti di; (of purpose) per.

towel ['tauəl] n asciugamano; (also: **tea ~**) strofinaccio; **~ling** n (fabric) spugna; **~ rail**, (US) **~ rack** n portasciugamano.

tower ['tauə*] n torre f; **~ block** n (Brit) palazzone m; **~ing** a altissimo(a), imponente.

town [taun] n città f inv; **to go to** ~ andare in città; (fig) mettercela tutta; ~ **centre** n centro (città); ~ **clerk** n segretario comunale; ~ **council** n consiglio comunale; ~ **hall** n ≈ municipio; ~ **plan** n pianta della città; ~ **planning** n urbanistica.

towrope ['təurəup] n (cavo da) rimorchio.

tow truck n (US) carro m attrezzi inv.

toxic ['tɔksɪk] a tossico(a).

toy [tɔɪ] n giocattolo; **to** ~ **with** vt fus giocare con; (idea) accarezzare, trastullarsi con.

trace [treɪs] n traccia // vt (draw) tracciare; (follow) seguire; (locate) rintracciare; **tracing paper** n carta da ricalco.

track [træk] n (of person, animal) traccia; (on tape, SPORT, path: gen) pista; (: of bullet etc) traiettoria; (: of suspect, animal) pista, tracce fpl; (RAIL) binario, rotaie fpl // vt seguire le tracce di; **to keep** ~ **of** seguire; **to** ~ **down** vt (prey) scovare; snidare; (sth lost) rintracciare; ~**suit** n tuta sportiva.

tract [trækt] n (GEO) tratto, estensione f; (pamphlet) opuscolo, libretto.

tractor ['træktə*] n trattore m.

trade [treɪd] n commercio; (skill, job) mestiere m // vi commerciare; **to** ~ **with/in** commerciare con/in; **to** ~ **in** vt (old car etc) dare come pagamento parziale; ~ **fair** n fiera commerciale; ~**-in price** n prezzo di permuta; ~**mark** n marchio di fabbrica; ~ **name** n marca, nome m depositato; ~**r** n commerciante m/f; ~**sman** n fornitore m; (shopkeeper) negoziante m; ~ **union** n sindacato; ~ **unionist** n sindacalista m/f; **trading** n commercio; **trading estate** n (Brit) zona industriale.

tradition [trə'dɪʃən] n tradizione f; ~**al** a tradizionale.

traffic ['træfɪk] n traffico // vi: **to** ~ **in** (pej: liquor, drugs) trafficare in; ~ **circle** n (US) isola rotatoria; ~ **jam** n ingorgo (del traffico); ~ **lights** npl semaforo; ~ **warden** n addetto/a al controllo del traffico e del parcheggio.

tragedy ['trædʒədɪ] n tragedia.

tragic ['trædʒɪk] a tragico(a).

trail [treɪl] n (tracks) tracce fpl, pista; (path) sentiero; (of smoke etc) scia // vt trascinare, strascicare; (follow) seguire // vi essere al traino; (dress etc) strusciare; (plant) arrampicarsi; strisciare; **to** ~ **behind** vi essere al traino; ~**er** n (AUT) rimorchio; (US) roulotte f inv; (CINEMA) prossimamente m inv; ~**er truck** n (US: articulated lorry) autoarticolato.

train [treɪn] n treno; (of dress) coda, strascico // vt (apprentice, doctor etc)

formare; (sportsman) allenare; (dog) addestrare; (memory) esercitare; (point: gun etc): **to** ~ **on** puntare qc contro // vi formarsi; allenarsi; **one's** ~ **of thought** il filo dei propri pensieri; ~**ed** a qualificato(a); allenato(a); addestrato(a); ~**ee** [treɪ'niː] n allievo/a; (in trade) apprendista m/f; ~**er** n (SPORT) allenatore/trice; (of dogs etc) addestratore/trice; ~**ing** n formazione f; allenamento; addestramento; **in** ~**ing** (SPORT) in allenamento; (fit) in forma; ~**ing college** n istituto professionale; (for teachers) ≈ istituto magistrale; ~**ing shoes** npl scarpe fpl da ginnastica.

traipse [treɪps] vi girovagare, andare a zonzo.

trait [treɪt] n tratto.

traitor ['treɪtə*] n traditore m.

trajectory [trə'dʒektərɪ] n traiettoria.

tram [træm] n (Brit: also: ~**car**) tram m inv.

tramp [træmp] n (person) vagabondo/a; (col: pej: woman) sgualdrina // vi camminare con passo pesante // vt (walk through: town, streets) percorrere a piedi.

trample ['træmpl] vt: **to** ~ **(underfoot)** calpestare.

trampoline ['træmpəliːn] n trampolino.

tranquil ['træŋkwɪl] a tranquillo(a); ~**lizer** n (MED) tranquillante m.

transact [træn'zækt] vt (business) trattare; ~**ion** [-'zækʃən] n transazione f; ~**ions** npl (minutes) atti mpl.

transatlantic ['trænzət'læntɪk] a transatlantico(a).

transcript ['trænskrɪpt] n trascrizione f.

transfer n ['trænsfə*] (gen, also SPORT) trasferimento; (POL: of power) passaggio; (picture, design) decalcomania; (: stick-on) autoadesivo // vt [træns'fə:*] trasferire; passare; decalcare.

transform [træns'fɔ:m] vt trasformare.

transfusion [træns'fju:ʒən] n trasfusione f.

transient ['trænzɪənt] a transitorio(a), fugace.

transistor [træn'zɪstə*] n (ELEC) transistor m inv; (also: ~ **radio**) radio f inv a transistor.

transit ['trænzɪt] n: **in** ~ in transito.

transitive ['trænzɪtɪv] a (LING) transitivo(a).

translate [trænz'leɪt] vt tradurre; **translation** [-'leɪʃən] n traduzione f; (SCOL: as opposed to prose) versione f; **translator** n traduttore/trice.

transmission [trænz'mɪʃən] n trasmissione f.

transmit [trænz'mɪt] vt trasmettere; ~**ter** n trasmettitore m.

transparency [træns'pɛərnsɪ] n (Brit:

PHOT) diapositiva.

transparent [træns'pærnt] *a* trasparente.

transpire [træn'spaɪə*] *vi* (*happen*) succedere; (*turn out*): it ~d that si venne a sapere che.

transplant *vt* [træns'plɑ:nt] trapiantare // *n* ['trænsplɑ:nt] (*MED*) trapianto.

transport *n* ['trænspɔ:t] trasporto // *vt* [træns'pɔ:t] trasportare; **~ation** [-'teɪʃən] *n* (*mezzo di*) trasporto; (*of prisoners*) deportazione *f*; ~ **café** *n* (*Brit*) trattoria per camionisti.

trap [træp] *n* (*snare, trick*) trappola; (*carriage*) calesse *m* // *vt* prendere in trappola, intrappolare; (*immobilize*) bloccare; (*jam*) chiudere, schiacciare; ~ **door** *n* botola.

trapeze [trə'pi:z] *n* trapezio.

trapper ['træpə*] *n* cacciatore *m* di animali da pelliccia.

trappings ['træpɪŋz] *npl* ornamenti *mpl*; indoratura, sfarzo.

trash [træʃ] *n* (*pej: goods*) ciarpame *m*; (: *nonsense*) sciocchezze *fpl*; ~ **can** *n* (*US*) secchio della spazzatura.

trauma ['trɔ:mə] *n* trauma *m*; **~tic** [-'mætɪk] *a* traumatico(a).

travel ['trævl] *n* viaggio; viaggi *mpl* // *vi* viaggiare; (*move*) andare, spostarsi // *vt* (*distance*) percorrere; ~ **agency** *n* agenzia (di) viaggi; ~ **agent** *n* agente *m* di viaggio; ~**ler**, (*US*) ~**er** *n* viaggiatore/trice; ~**ler's cheque** *n* assegno turistico; ~**ling**, (*US*) ~**ing** *n* viaggi *mpl* // *cpd* (*bag, clock*) da viaggio; (*expenses*) di viaggio; ~ **sickness** *n* mal *m* d'auto (*or* di mare *or* d'aria).

travesty ['trævəstɪ] *n* parodia.

trawler ['trɔ:lə*] *n* peschereccio (a strascico).

tray [treɪ] *n* (*for carrying*) vassoio; (*on desk*) vaschetta.

treachery ['tretʃərɪ] *n* tradimento.

treacle ['tri:kl] *n* melassa.

tread [tred] *n* passo; (*sound*) rumore *m* di passi; (*of tyre*) battistrada *m inv* // *vi* (*pt* **trod**, *pp* **trodden**) camminare; **to ~ on** *vt fus* calpestare.

treason ['tri:zn] *n* tradimento.

treasure ['treʒə*] *n* tesoro // *vt* (*value*) tenere in gran conto, apprezzare molto; (*store*) custodire gelosamente.

treasurer ['treʒərə*] *n* tesoriere/a.

treasury ['treʒərɪ] *n* tesoreria; **the T~**, (*US*) **the T~ Department** il ministero del Tesoro.

treat [tri:t] *n* regalo // *vt* trattare; (*MED*) curare; **to ~ sb to sth** offrire qc a qn.

treatise ['tri:tɪz] *n* trattato.

treatment ['tri:tmənt] *n* trattamento.

treaty ['tri:tɪ] *n* patto, trattato.

treble ['trebl] *a* triplo(a), triplice // *vt* triplicare // *vi* triplicarsi; ~ **clef** *n* chiave *f* di violino.

tree [tri:] *n* albero.

trek [trek] *n* viaggio; camminata; (*tiring walk*) tirata a piedi // *vi* (*as holiday*) fare dell'escursionismo.

trellis ['trelɪs] *n* graticcio.

tremble ['trembl] *vi* tremare; (*machine*) vibrare.

tremendous [trɪ'mendəs] *a* (*enormous*) enorme; (*excellent*) meraviglioso(a), formidabile.

tremor ['tremə*] *n* tremore *m*, tremito; (*also: earth ~*) scossa sismica.

trench [trentʃ] *n* trincea.

trend [trend] *n* (*tendency*) tendenza; (*of events*) corso; (*fashion*) moda; **~y** *a* (*idea*) di moda; (*clothes*) all'ultima moda.

trepidation [trepɪ'deɪʃən] *n* trepidazione *f*, agitazione *f*.

trespass ['trespəs] *vi*: **to ~ on** entrare abusivamente in; (*fig*) abusare di; "**no ~ing**" "proprietà privata", "vietato l'accesso".

trestle ['tresl] *n* cavalletto; ~ **table** *n* tavolo su cavalletti.

trial ['traɪəl] *n* (*LAW*) processo; (*test: of machine etc*) collaudo; (*hardship*) prova, difficoltà *f inv*; (*worry*) cruccio; **by ~ and error** a tentoni.

triangle ['traɪæŋgl] *n* (*MATH, MUS*) triangolo.

tribe [traɪb] *n* tribù *f inv*.

tribunal [traɪ'bju:nl] *n* tribunale *m*.

tributary ['trɪbjutərɪ] *n* (*river*) tributario, affluente *m*.

tribute ['trɪbju:t] *n* tributo, omaggio; **to pay ~ to** rendere omaggio a.

trice [traɪs] *n*: **in a ~** in un attimo.

trick [trɪk] *n* trucco; (*joke*) tiro; (*CARDS*) presa // *vt* imbrogliare, ingannare; **to play a ~ on sb** giocare un tiro a qn; **that should do the ~** vedrai che funziona; **~ery** *n* inganno.

trickle ['trɪkl] *n* (*of water etc*) rivolo; gocciolio // *vi* gocciolare.

tricky ['trɪkɪ] *a* difficile, delicato(a).

tricycle ['traɪsɪkl] *n* triciclo.

trifle ['traɪfl] *n* sciocchezza; (*Brit CULIN*) ≈ zuppa inglese // *ad*: **a ~ long** un po' lungo; **trifling** *a* insignificante.

trigger ['trɪgə*] *n* (*of gun*) grilletto; **to ~ off** *vt* dare l'avvio a.

trim [trɪm] *a* ordinato(a); (*house, garden*) ben tenuto(a); (*figure*) snello(a) // *n* (*haircut etc*) spuntata, regolata; (*embellishment*) finiture *fpl*; (*on car*) guarnizioni *fpl* // *vt* spuntare; (*decorate*): **to ~ (with)** decorare (con); (*NAUT: a sail*) orientare; **~mings** *npl* decorazioni *fpl*; (*extras: gen CULIN*) guarnizione *f*.

trinket ['trɪŋkɪt] *n* gingillo; (*piece of jewellery*) ciondolo.

trip [trɪp] *n* viaggio; (*excursion*) gita, escursione *f*; (*stumble*) passo falso // *vi* inciampare; *(go lightly)* camminare con passo leggero; **on a ~** in viaggio; **to ~ up** *vi* inciampare // *vt* fare lo sgambetto a.

tripe |traɪp| *n (CULIN)* trippa; *(pej: rubbish)* sciocchezze *fpl*, fesserie *fpl*.

triple |'trɪpl| *a* triplo(a).

triplets |'trɪplɪts| *npl* bambini(e) trigemini(e).

tripod |'traɪpɔd| *n* treppiede *m*.

trite |traɪt| *a* banale, trito(a).

triumph |'traɪʌmf| *n* trionfo // *vi*: **to ~ (over)** trionfare (su).

trivia |'trɪvɪə| *npl* banalità *fpl*.

trivial |'trɪvɪəl| *a* insignificante; *(commonplace)* banale.

trod |trɔd| *pt of* **tread**; **~den** *pp of* **tread**.

trolley |'trɔlɪ| *n* carrello; **~ bus** *n* filobus *m inv*.

trombone |trɔm'bəun| *n* trombone *m*.

troop |tru:p| *n* gruppo; *(MIL)* squadrone *m*; **~s** *npl (MIL)* truppe *fpl*; **to ~ in/out** *vi* entrare/uscire a frotte; **~er** *n (MIL)* soldato di cavalleria; **~ing the colour** *n (ceremony)* sfilata della bandiera.

trophy |'trəufɪ| *n* trofeo.

tropic |'trɔpɪk| *n* tropico; **~al** *a* tropicale.

trot |trɔt| *n* trotto // *vi* trottare; **on the ~** *(Brit: fig)* di fila, uno(a) dopo l'altro(a).

trouble |'trʌbl| *n* difficoltà *f inv*, problema *m*; difficoltà *fpl*, problemi; *(worry)* preoccupazione *f*; *(bother, effort)* sforzo; *(POL)* conflitti *mpl*, disordine *m*; *(MED)*: **stomach** *etc* **~** disturbi *mpl* gastrici *etc* // *vt* disturbare; *(worry)* preoccupare // *vi*: **to ~ to do** disturbarsi a fare; **~s** *npl (POL etc)* disordini *mpl*; **to be in ~** avere dei problemi; **it's no ~!** di niente!; **what's the ~?** cosa c'è che non va?; **~d** *a (person)* preoccupato(a), inquieto(a); *(epoch, life)* agitato(a), difficile; **~maker** *n* elemento disturbatore, agitatore/trice; **~shooter** *n (in conflict)* conciliatore *m*; **~some** *a* fastidioso(a), seccante.

trough |trɔf| *n (also:* **drinking ~)** abbeveratoio; *(also:* **feeding ~)** trogolo, mangiatoia; *(channel)* canale *m*.

trousers |'trauzəz| *npl* pantaloni *mpl*, calzoni *mpl*; **short ~** calzoncini *mpl*.

trousseau, *pl* **~x** *or* **~s** |'tru:səu, -z| *n* corredo da sposa.

trout |traut| *n (pl inv)* trota.

trowel |'trauəl| *n* cazzuola.

truant |'truənt| *n*: **to play ~** *(Brit)* marinare la scuola.

truce |tru:s| *n* tregua.

truck |trʌk| *n* autocarro, camion *m inv*; *(RAIL)* carro merci aperto; *(for luggage)* carrello *m* portabagagli *inv*; **~ driver** *n* camionista *m/f*; **~ farm** *n (US)* orto industriale.

truculent |'trʌkjulənt| *a* aggressivo(a), brutale.

trudge |trʌdʒ| *vi* trascinarsi pesantemente.

true |tru:| *a* vero(a); *(accurate)* accurato(a), esatto(a); *(genuine)* reale; *(faithful)* fedele.

truffle |'trʌfl| *n* tartufo.

truly |'tru:lɪ| *ad* veramente; *(truthfully)* sinceramente; *(faithfully)* fedelmente.

trump |trʌmp| *n* atout *m inv*; **~ed-up** *a* inventato(a).

trumpet |'trʌmpɪt| *n* tromba.

truncheon |'trʌntʃən| *n* sfollagente *m inv*.

trundle |'trʌndl| *vt, vi*: **to ~ along** rotolare rumorosamente.

trunk |trʌŋk| *n (of tree, person)* tronco; *(of elephant)* proboscide *f*; *(case)* baule *m*; *(US AUT)* bagagliaio; **~s** *npl (also:* **swimming ~s)** calzoncini *mpl* da bagno.

truss |trʌs| *n (MED)* cinto erniario; **to ~ (up)** *vt (CULIN)* legare.

trust |trʌst| *n* fiducia; *(LAW)* amministrazione *f* fiduciaria; *(COMM)* trust *m inv* // *vt (rely on)* contare su; *(entrust)*: **to ~ sth to sb** affidare qc a qn; **~ed** *a* fidato(a); **~ee** |trʌs'ti:| *n (LAW)* amministratore(trice) fiduciario(a); *(of school etc)* amministratore/trice; **~ful, ~ing** *a* fiducioso(a); **~worthy** *a* fidato(a), degno(a) di fiducia.

truth, ~s |tru:θ, tru:ðz| *n* verità *f inv*; **~ful** *a (person)* sincero(a); *(description)* veritiero(a), esatto(a).

try |traɪ| *n* prova, tentativo; *(RUGBY)* meta // *vt (LAW)* giudicare; *(test: sth new)* provare; *(strain)* mettere alla prova // *vi* provare; **to ~ to do** provare a fare; *(seek)* cercare di fare; **to ~ on** *vt (clothes)* provare; **to ~ out** *vt* provare, mettere alla prova; **~ing** *a (day, experience)* logorante, pesante; *(child)* difficile, insopportabile.

tsar |zɑ:*| *n* zar *m inv*.

T-shirt |'ti:fə:t| *n* maglietta.

T-square |'ti:skweə*| *n* riga a T.

tub |tʌb| *n* tinozza; mastello; *(bath)* bagno.

tuba |'tju:bə| *n* tuba.

tubby |'tʌbɪ| *a* grassoccio(a).

tube |tju:b| *n* tubo; *(Brit: underground)* metropolitana, metrò *m inv*; *(for tyre)* camera d'aria.

tubing |'tju:bɪŋ| *n* tubazione *f*; **a piece of ~** un tubo.

tubular |'tju:bjulə*| *a* tubolare.

TUC *n abbr (Brit:* = *Trades Union Congress)* confederazione *f* dei sindacati britannici.

tuck |tʌk| *n (SEWING)* piega // *vt (put)* mettere; **to ~ away** *vt* riporre; **to ~ in** *vt* mettere dentro; *(child)* rimboccare // *vi (eat)* mangiare di buon appetito; abbuffarsi; **to ~ up** *vt (child)* rimboccare; **~ shop** n negozio di pasticceria (in una scuola).

Tuesday ['tju:zdı] n martedì m inv.

tuft [tʌft] n ciuffo.

tug [tʌg] n (ship) rimorchiatore m // vt tirare con forza; **~-of-war** n tiro alla fune.

tuition [tju:'ıʃən] n (Brit) lezioni fpl; (: private ~) lezioni fpl private; (US: school fees) tasse fpl scolastiche.

tulip ['tju:lıp] n tulipano.

tumble ['tʌmbl] n (fall) capitombolo // vi capitombolare, ruzzolare; (somersault) fare capriole; **to ~ to sth** (col) realizzare qc; **~down** a cadente, diroccato(a); **~ dryer** n (Brit) asciugatrice f.

tumbler ['tʌmblə*] n bicchiere m (senza stelo); acrobata m/f.

tummy ['tʌmı] n (col) pancia.

tumour, (US) **tumor** ['tju:mə*] n tumore m.

tuna ['tju:nə] n (pl inv) (also: ~ fish) tonno.

tune [tju:n] n (melody) melodia, aria // vt (MUS) accordare; (RADIO, TV, AUT) regolare, mettere a punto; **to be in/out of ~** (instrument) essere accordato(a)/scordato(a); (singer) essere intonato(a)/stonato(a); **to ~ in** vi: **to ~ in (to)** (RADIO, TV) sintonizzarsi (su); **to ~ up** vi (musician) accordare lo strumento; **~ful** a melodioso(a).

tunic ['tju:nık] n tunica.

tuning ['tju:nıŋ] n messa a punto; **~ fork** n diapason m inv.

Tunisia [tju:'nızıə] n Tunisia.

tunnel ['tʌnl] n galleria // vi scavare una galleria.

turban ['tə:bən] n turbante m.

turbot ['tə:bət] n (pl inv) rombo gigante.

turbulence ['tə:bjuləns] n (AVIAT) turbolenza.

tureen [tə'ri:n] n zuppiera.

turf [tə:f] n terreno erboso; (clod) zolla // vt coprire di zolle erbose; **to ~ out** vt (col) buttar fuori.

turgid ['tə:dʒıd] a (speech) ampolloso(a), pomposo(a).

Turin [tju'rın] n Torino f.

Turk [tə:k] n turco/a.

Turkey ['tə:kı] n Turchia.

turkey ['tə:kı] n tacchino.

Turkish ['tə:kıʃ] a turco(a) // n (LING) turco.

turmoil ['tə:mɔıl] n confusione f, tumulto.

turn [tə:n] n giro; (in road) curva; (tendency: of mind, events) tendenza; (performance) numero; (MED) crisi f inv, attacco // vt girare, voltare; (milk) far andare a male; (change): **to ~ sth into** trasformare qc in // vi girare; (person: look back) girarsi, voltarsi; (reverse direction) girarsi indietro; (change) cambiare; (become) diventare; **to ~ into** trasformarsi in; a

good **~** un buon servizio; **it gave me quite a ~** mi ha fatto prendere un bello spavento; **"no left ~"** (AUT) "divieto di svolta a sinistra"; **it's your ~** tocca a lei; **in ~** a sua volta; a turno; **to take ~s** (at sth) fare (qc) a turno; **to ~ away** vi girarsi (dall'altra parte); **to ~ back** vi ritornare, tornare indietro; **to ~ down** vt (refuse) rifiutare; (reduce) abbassare; (fold) ripiegare; **to ~ in** vi (col: go to bed) andare a letto // vt (fold) voltare in dentro; **to ~ off** vi (from road) girare, voltare // vt (light, radio, engine etc) spegnere; **to ~ on** vt (light, radio etc) accendere; (engine) avviare; **to ~ out** vt (light, gas) chiudere, spegnere // vi: **to ~ out to be ...** rivelarsi ..., risultare ...; **to ~ over** vi (person) girarsi // vt girare; **to ~ round** vi girare; (person) girarsi; **to ~ up** vi (person) arrivare, presentarsi; (lost object) saltar fuori // vt (collar, sound) alzare; **~ing** n (in road) curva; **~ing point** n (fig) svolta decisiva.

turnip ['tə:nıp] n rapa.

turnout ['tə:naut] n presenza, affluenza.

turnover ['tə:nəuvə*] n (COMM) giro di affari.

turnpike ['tə:npaık] n (US) autostrada a pedaggio.

turnstile ['tə:nstaıl] n tornella.

turntable ['tə:nteıbl] n (on record player) piatto.

turn-up ['tə:nʌp] n (Brit: on trousers) risvolto.

turpentine ['tə:pəntaın] n (also: turps) acqua ragia.

turquoise ['tə:kwɔız] n (stone) turchese m // a color turchese; di turchese.

turret ['tʌrıt] n torretta.

turtle ['tə:tl] n testuggine f; **~neck (sweater)** n maglione m con il collo alto.

tusk [tʌsk] n zanna.

tussle ['tʌsl] n baruffa, mischia.

tutor ['tju:tə*] n (in college) docente m/f (responsabile di un gruppo di studenti); (private teacher) precettore m; **~ial** [-'tə:rıəl] n (SCOL) lezione f con discussione (a un gruppo limitato).

tuxedo [tʌk'si:dəu] n (US) smoking m inv.

TV [ti:'vi:] n abbr (= television) tivù f inv.

twang [twæŋ] n (of instrument) suono vibrante; (of voice) accento nasale.

tweed [twi:d] n tweed m inv.

tweezers ['twi:zəz] npl pinzette fpl.

twelfth [twelfθ] num dodicesimo(a).

twelve [twelv] num dodici; **at ~ (o'clock)** alle dodici, a mezzogiorno; (midnight) a mezzanotte.

twentieth ['twentııθ] num ventesimo(a).

twenty ['twentı] num venti.

twice [twaıs] ad due volte; **~ as much**

due volte tanto.

twiddle ['twɪdl] *vt, vi*: to ~ (with) sth giocherellare con qc; to ~ one's thumbs (*fig*) girarsi i pollici.

twig [twɪg] *n* ramoscello // *vt, vi* (*col*) capire.

twilight ['twaɪlaɪt] *n* crepuscolo.

twin [twɪn] *a, n* gemello(a) // *vt*: to ~ one town with another fare il gemellaggio di una città con un'altra; ~-bedded room *n* stanza con letti gemelli.

twine [twaɪn] *n* spago, cordicella // *vi* attorcigliarsi.

twinge [twɪndʒ] *n* (*of pain*) fitta; a ~ of conscience/regret un rimorso/rimpianto.

twinkle ['twɪŋkl] *n* scintillio // *vi* scintillare; (*eyes*) brillare.

twirl [twə:l] *n* piroetta // *vt* far roteare // *vi* roteare.

twist [twɪst] *n* torsione *f*; (*in wire, flex*) storta; (*in story*) colpo di scena // *vt* attorcigliare; (*weave*) intrecciare; (*roll around*) arrotolare; (*fig*) deformare // *vi* attorcigliarsi; arrotolarsi; (*road*) serpeggiare.

twit [twɪt] *n* (*col*) minchione/a.

twitch [twɪtʃ] *n* tiratina; (*nervous*) tic *m inv* // *vi* contrarsi; avere un tic.

two [tu:] *num* due; to put ~ and ~ together (*fig*) trarre le conclusioni; ~-door *a* (*AUT*) a due porte; ~-faced *a* (*pej: person*) falso(a); ~fold *ad*: to increase ~fold aumentare del doppio; ~-piece (suit) *n* due pezzi *m inv*; ~-piece (swimsuit) *n* (costume *m* da bagno a) due pezzi *m inv*; ~-seater *n* (*plane*) biposto; (*car*) macchina a due posti; ~some *n* (*people*) coppia; ~-way *a* (*traffic*) a due sensi.

tycoon [taɪ'ku:n] *n*: (*business*) ~ magnate *m*.

type [taɪp] *n* (*category*) genere *m*; (*model*) modello; (*example*) tipo; (*TYP*) tipo, carattere *m* // *vt* (*letter etc*) battere (a macchina), dattilografare; ~-cast *a* (*actor*) a ruolo fisso; ~face *n* carattere *m* tipografico; ~script *n* dattiloscritto; ~writer *n* macchina da scrivere; ~written *a* dattiloscritto(a), battuto(a) a macchina.

typhoid ['taɪfɔɪd] *n* tifoidea.

typhoon [taɪ'fu:n] *n* tifone *m*.

typhus ['taɪfəs] *n* tifo.

typical ['tɪpɪkl] *a* tipico(a).

typing ['taɪpɪŋ] *n* dattilografia.

typist ['taɪpɪst] *n* dattilografo/a.

tyrant ['taɪərnt] *n* tiranno.

tyre, (*US*) **tire** ['taɪə*] *n* pneumatico, gomma; ~ **pressure** *n* pressione *f* (delle gomme).

tzar [zɑ:*] *n* = **tsar**.

U

U-bend ['ju:'bɛnd] *n* (*in pipe*) sifone *m*.

udder ['ʌdə*] *n* mammella.

UFO ['ju:fəu] *n abbr* (= *unidentified flying object*) UFO *m inv*.

ugh [ə:h] *excl* puah!

ugly ['ʌglɪ] *a* brutto(a).

UK *n abbr* = **United Kingdom**.

ulcer ['ʌlsə*] *n* ulcera; (*also*: mouth ~) afta.

Ulster ['ʌlstə*] *n* Ulster *m*.

ulterior [ʌl'tɪərɪə*] *a* ulteriore; ~ motive *n* secondo fine *m*.

ultimate ['ʌltɪmət] *a* ultimo(a), finale; (*authority*) massimo(a), supremo(a); ~ly *ad* alla fine; in definitiva, in fin dei conti.

ultrasound [ʌltrə'saund] *n* (*MED*) ultrasuono.

umbilical cord [ʌmbɪ'laɪkl-] *n* cordone *m* ombelicale.

umbrage ['ʌmbrɪdʒ] *n*: to take ~ offendersi, impermalirsi.

umbrella [ʌm'brɛlə] *n* ombrello.

umpire ['ʌmpaɪə*] *n* arbitro.

umpteen [ʌmp'ti:n] *a* non so quanti(e); for the ~th time per l'ennesima volta.

UN, UNO *n abbr* = **United Nations (Organization)**.

unable [ʌn'eɪbl] *a*: to be ~ to non potere, essere nell'impossibilità di; essere incapace di.

unaccompanied [ʌnə'kʌmpənɪd] *a* (*child, lady*) non accompagnato(a).

unaccountably [ʌnə'kauntəblɪ] *ad* inesplicabilmente.

unaccustomed [ʌnə'kʌstəmd] *a* insolito(a); to be ~ to sth non essere abituato a qc.

unanimous [ju:'nænɪməs] *a* unanime; ~ly *ad* all'unanimità.

unarmed [ʌn'ɑ:md] *a* (*without a weapon*) disarmato(a); (*combat*) senz'armi.

unassuming [ʌnə'sju:mɪŋ] *a* modesto(a), senza pretese.

unattached [ʌnə'tætʃt] *a* senza legami, libero(a).

unattended [ʌnə'tɛndɪd] *a* (*car, child, luggage*) incustodito(a).

unauthorized [ʌn'ɔ:θəraɪzd] *a* non autorizzato(a).

unavoidable [ʌnə'vɔɪdəbl] *a* inevitabile.

unaware [ʌnə'wɛə*] *a*: to be ~ of non sapere, ignorare; ~s *ad* di sorpresa, alla sprovvista.

unbalanced [ʌn'bælənst] *a* squilibrato(a).

unbearable [ʌn'bɛərəbl] *a* insopportabile.

unbeknown(st) [ʌnbɪ'nəun(st)] *ad*: ~ to all'insaputa di.

unbelievable [ʌnbɪ'liːvəbl] a incredibile.

unbend [ʌn'bɛnd] vb (irg) vi distendersi // vt (wire) raddrizzare.

unbias(s)ed [ʌn'baɪəst] a (person, report) obiettivo(a), imparziale.

unborn [ʌn'bɔːn] a non ancora nato(a).

unbreakable [ʌn'breɪkəbl] a infrangibile.

unbroken [ʌn'brəukən] a intero(a); continuo(a).

unbutton [ʌn'bʌtn] vt sbottonare.

uncalled-for [ʌn'kɔːldfɔː*] a (remark) fuori luogo inv; (action) ingiustificato(a).

uncanny [ʌn'kænɪ] a misterioso(a), strano(a).

unceasing [ʌn'siːsɪŋ] a incessante.

unceremonious ['ʌnsɛrɪ'məunɪəs] a (abrupt, rude) senza tante cerimonie.

uncertain [ʌn'sɜːtn] a incerto(a); dubbio(a); ~ty n incertezza.

unchecked [ʌn'tʃɛkt] a incontrollato(a).

uncivilized [ʌn'sɪvɪlaɪzd] a (gen) selvaggio(a); (fig) incivile, barbaro(a).

uncle ['ʌŋkl] n zio.

uncomfortable [ʌn'kʌmfətəbl] a scomodo(a); (uneasy) a disagio, agitato(a); fastidioso(a).

uncommon [ʌn'kɔmən] a raro(a), insolito(a), non comune.

uncompromising [ʌn'kɔmprəmaɪzɪŋ] a intransigente, inflessibile.

unconcerned [ʌnkən'sɜːnd] a: to be ~ (about) non preoccuparsi (di or per).

unconditional [ʌnkən'dɪʃənl] a incondizionato(a), senza condizioni.

unconscious [ʌn'kɔnʃəs] a privo(a) di sensi, svenuto(a); (unaware) inconsapevole, inconscio(a) // n: the ~ l'inconscio; ~ly ad inconsciamente.

uncontrollable [ʌnkən'trəuləbl] a incontrollabile; indisciplinato(a).

unconventional [ʌnkən'vɛnʃənl] a poco convenzionale.

uncouth [ʌn'kuːθ] a maleducato(a), grossolano(a).

uncover [ʌn'kʌvə*] vt scoprire.

undecided [ʌndɪ'saɪdɪd] a indeciso(a).

under ['ʌndə*] prep sotto; (less than) meno di; al disotto di; (according to) secondo, in conformità a // ad (al) disotto; from ~ sth da sotto a or dal disotto di qc; ~ there là sotto; ~ repair in riparazione.

under... ['ʌndə*] prefix sotto..., sub...; ~ age a minorenne; ~**carriage** n (Brit) carrello (d'atterraggio); ~**charge** vt far pagare di meno a; ~**coat** n (paint) mano f di fondo; ~**cover** a segreto(a), clandestino(a); ~**current** n corrente f sottomarina; ~**cut** vt irg vendere a prezzo minore di; ~**developed** a sottosviluppato(a); ~**dog** n oppresso(a); ~**done** a (CULIN) al sangue; (pej) poco cotto(a); ~**estimate** vt sottovalutare; ~**fed** a

denutrito(a); ~**foot** ad sotto i piedi; ~**go** vt irg subire; (treatment) sottoporsi a; ~**graduate** n studente(essa) universitario(a); ~**ground** n (Brit: railway) metropolitana; (POL) movimento clandestino // a sotterraneo(a); (fig) clandestino(a); ~**growth** n sottobosco; ~**hand(ed)** a (fig) furtivo(a), subdolo(a); ~**lie** vt irg essere alla base di; ~**line** vt sottolineare; ~**ling** ['ʌndəlɪŋ] n (pej) subalterno/a, tirapiedi m/f inv; ~**mine** vt minare; ~**neath** [ʌndə'niːθ] ad sotto, disotto // prep sotto, al di sotto di; ~**paid** a mal pagato(a); ~**pants** npl mutande fpl, slip m inv; ~**pass** n (Brit) sottopassaggio; ~**privileged** a non abbiente; meno favorito(a); ~**rate** vt sottovalutare; ~**shirt** n (US) maglietta; ~**shorts** npl (US) mutande fpl, slip m inv; ~**side** n disotto; ~**skirt** n (Brit) sottoveste f.

understand [ʌndə'stænd] vb (irg: like stand) vt, vi capire, comprendere; I ~ that ... sento che ...; credo di capire che ...; ~**able** a comprensibile; ~**ing** a comprensivo(a) // n comprensione f; (agreement) accordo.

understatement [ʌndə'steɪtmənt] n: that's an ~! a dire poco!

understood [ʌndə'stud] pt, pp of **understand** // a inteso(a); (implied) sottinteso(a).

understudy ['ʌndəstʌdɪ] n sostituto/a, attore/trice supplente.

undertake [ʌndə'teɪk] vt irg intraprendere; to ~ to do sth impegnarsi a fare qc.

undertaker ['ʌndəteɪkə*] n impresario di pompe funebri.

undertaking [ʌndə'teɪkɪŋ] n impresa; (promise) promessa.

undertone ['ʌndətəun] n: in an ~ a mezza voce, a voce bassa.

underwater [ʌndə'wɔːtə*] ad sott'acqua // a subacqueo(a).

underwear ['ʌndəwɛə*] n biancheria (intima).

underworld ['ʌndəwɜːld] n (of crime) malavita.

underwriter ['ʌndəraɪtə*] n (INSURANCE) sottoscrittore/trice.

undies ['ʌndɪz] npl (col) robina, biancheria intima da donna.

undo [ʌn'duː] vt irg disfare; ~**ing** n rovina, perdita.

undoubted [ʌn'dautɪd] a sicuro(a), certo(a); ~**ly** ad senza alcun dubbio.

undress [ʌn'drɛs] vi spogliarsi.

undue [ʌn'djuː] a eccessivo(a).

undulating ['ʌndjuleɪtɪŋ] a ondeggiante; ondulato(a).

unduly [ʌn'djuːlɪ] ad eccessivamente.

unearth [ʌn'ɜːθ] vt dissotterrare; (fig) scoprire.

unearthly [ʌn'ə:θlɪ] a soprannaturale; (hour) impossibile.

uneasy [ʌn'i:zɪ] a a disagio; (worried) preoccupato(a).

unemployed [ʌnɪm'plɔɪd] a disoccupato(a) // npl: the ~ i disoccupati.

unemployment [ʌnɪm'plɔɪmənt] n disoccupazione f.

unending [ʌn'ɛndɪŋ] a senza fine.

unerring [ʌn'ə:rɪŋ] a infallibile.

uneven [ʌn'i:vn] a ineguale; irregolare.

unexpected [ʌnɪk'spɛktɪd] a inatteso(a), imprevisto(a); ~ly ad inaspettatamente.

unfailing [ʌn'feɪlɪŋ] a (supply, energy) inesauribile; (remedy) infallibile.

unfair [ʌn'fɛə*] a: ~ (to) ingiusto(a) (nei confronti di).

unfaithful [ʌn'feɪθful] a infedele.

unfamiliar [ʌnfə'mɪlɪə*] a sconosciuto(a), strano(a).

unfashionable [ʌn'fæʃnəbl] a (clothes) fuori moda; (district) non alla moda.

unfasten [ʌn'fɑ:sn] vt slacciare; sciogliere.

unfavourable, (US) **unfavorable** [ʌn'feɪvərəbl] a sfavorevole.

unfeeling [ʌn'fi:lɪŋ] a insensibile, duro(a).

unfit [ʌn'fɪt] a inadatto(a); (ill) malato(a), in cattiva salute; (incompetent): ~ (for) incompetente (in); (: work, MIL) inabile (a).

unfold [ʌn'fəuld] vt spiegare; (fig) rivelare // vi (view, countryside) distendersi; (story, plot) svelarsi.

unforeseen ['ʌnfɔ:'si:n] a imprevisto(a).

unforgettable [ʌnfə'gɛtəbl] a indimenticabile.

unfortunate [ʌn'fɔ:tʃnət] a sfortunato(a); (event, remark) infelice; ~ly ad sfortunatamente, purtroppo.

unfounded [ʌn'faundɪd] a infondato(a).

unfriendly [ʌn'frɛndlɪ] a poco amichevole, freddo(a).

ungainly [ʌn'geɪnlɪ] a goffo(a), impacciato(a).

ungodly [ʌn'gɔdlɪ] a empio(a); at an ~ hour a un'ora impossibile.

ungrateful [ʌn'greɪtful] a ingrato(a).

unhappiness [ʌn'hæpɪnɪs] n infelicità.

unhappy [ʌn'hæpɪ] a infelice; ~ with (arrangements etc) insoddisfatto(a) di.

unharmed [ʌn'hɑ:md] a incolume, sano(a) e salvo(a).

unhealthy [ʌn'hɛlθɪ] a (gen) malsano(a); (person) malaticcio(a).

unheard-of [ʌn'hə:dɔv] a inaudito(a), senza precedenti.

uniform ['ju:nɪfɔ:m] n uniforme f, divisa // a uniforme.

uninhabited [ʌnɪn'hæbɪtɪd] a disabitato(a).

union ['ju:njən] n unione f; (also: trade ~) sindacato // cpd sindacale, dei sindacati; **U~ Jack** n bandiera nazionale britannica.

unique [ju:'ni:k] a unico(a).

unit ['ju:nɪt] n unità f inv; (section: of furniture etc) elemento; (team, squad) reparto, squadra.

unite [ju:'naɪt] vt unire // vi unirsi; ~d a unito(a); unificato(a); (efforts) congiunto(a); **U~d Kingdom (UK)** n Regno Unito; **U~d Nations (Organization) (UN, UNO)** n (Organizzazione f delle) Nazioni Unite (O.N.U.); **U~d States (of America) (US, USA)** n Stati mpl Uniti (d'America) (USA).

unit trust n (Brit) fondo d'investimento.

unity ['ju:nɪtɪ] n unità.

universal [ju:nɪ'və:sl] a universale.

universe ['ju:nɪvə:s] n universo.

university [ju:nɪ'və:sɪtɪ] n università f inv.

unjust [ʌn'dʒʌst] a ingiusto(a).

unkempt [ʌn'kɛmpt] a trasandato(a); spettinato(a).

unkind [ʌn'kaɪnd] a scortese; crudele.

unknown [ʌn'nəun] a sconosciuto(a).

unlawful [ʌn'lɔ:ful] a illecito(a), illegale.

unleash [ʌn'li:ʃ] vt sguinzagliare; (fig) scatenare.

unless [ʌn'lɛs] cj a meno che (non) + sub; ~ otherwise stated salvo indicazione contraria.

unlike [ʌn'laɪk] a diverso(a) // prep a differenza di, contrariamente a.

unlikely [ʌn'laɪklɪ] a improbabile; inverosimile.

unlisted [ʌn'lɪstɪd] a (US TEL): to be ~ non essere sull'elenco.

unload [ʌn'ləud] vt scaricare.

unlock [ʌn'lɔk] vt aprire.

unlucky [ʌn'lʌkɪ] a sfortunato(a); (object, number) che porta sfortuna, di malaugurio; to be ~ essere sfortunato, non avere fortuna.

unmarried [ʌn'mærɪd] a non sposato(a); (man only) scapolo, celibe; (woman only) nubile.

unmistakable [ʌnmɪs'teɪkəbl] a indubbio(a); facilmente riconoscibile.

unmitigated [ʌn'mɪtɪgeɪtɪd] a non mitigato(a), assoluto(a), vero(a) e proprio(a).

unnatural [ʌn'nætʃrəl] a innaturale; contro natura.

unnecessary [ʌn'nɛsəsərɪ] a inutile, superfluo(a).

unnoticed [ʌn'nəutɪst] a: (to go) ~ (passare) inosservato(a).

UNO ['ju:nəu] n abbr = **United Nations Organization**.

unobtainable [ʌnəb'teɪnəbl] a (TEL) non ottenibile.

unobtrusive [ʌnəb'tru:sɪv] a discreto(a).

unofficial [ʌnə'fɪʃl] a non ufficiale; (strike) non dichiarato(a) dal sindacato.

unpack [ʌn'pæk] vi disfare la valigia (or

le valigie).

unpalatable [ʌn'pælətəbl] *a* (*truth*) sgradevole.

unparalleled [ʌn'pærəlɛld] *a* incomparabile, impareggiabile.

unpleasant [ʌn'plɛznt] *a* spiacevole.

unplug [ʌn'plʌg] *vt* staccare.

unpopular [ʌn'pɔpjulə*] *a* impopolare.

unprecedented [ʌn'prɛsɪdəntɪd] *a* senza precedenti.

unpredictable [ʌnprɪ'dɪktəbl] *a* imprevedibile.

unprofessional [ʌnprə'fɛʃənl] *a*: ~ conduct scorrettezza professionale.

unqualified [ʌn'kwɔlɪfaɪd] *a* (*teacher*) non abilitato(a); (*success*) assoluto(a), senza riserve.

unquestionably [ʌn'kwɛstʃənəblɪ] *ad* indiscutibilmente.

unravel [ʌn'rævl] *vt* dipanare, districare.

unreal [ʌn'rɪəl] *a* irreale.

unrealistic [ʌnrɪə'lɪstɪk] *a* (*idea*) illusorio(a); (*estimate*) non realistico(a).

unreasonable [ʌn'ri:znəbl] *a* irragionevole.

unrelated [ʌnrɪ'leɪtɪd] *a*: ~ (to) senza rapporto (con); non imparentato(a) (con).

unreliable [ʌnrɪ'laɪəbl] *a* (*person, machine*) che non dà affidamento; (*news, source of information*) inattendibile.

unremitting [ʌnrɪ'mɪtɪŋ] *a* incessante.

unreservedly [ʌnrɪ'zə:vɪdlɪ] *ad* senza riserve.

unrest [ʌn'rɛst] *n* agitazione *f*.

unroll [ʌn'rəul] *vt* srotolare.

unruly [ʌn'ru:lɪ] *a* indisciplinato(a).

unsafe [ʌn'seɪf] *a* pericoloso(a), rischioso(a).

unsaid [ʌn'sɛd] *a*: to leave sth ~ passare qc sotto silenzio.

unsatisfactory ['ʌnsætɪs'fæktərɪ] *a* che lascia a desiderare, insufficiente.

unsavoury, (*US*) **unsavory** [ʌn'seɪvərɪ] *a* (*fig: person*) losco(a); (: *reputation, subject*) disgustoso(a), ripugnante.

unscathed [ʌn'skeɪðd] *a* incolume.

unscrew [ʌn'skru:] *vt* svitare.

unscrupulous [ʌn'skru:pjuləs] *a* senza scrupoli.

unsettled [ʌn'sɛtld] *a* turbato(a); instabile; indeciso(a).

unshaven [ʌn'ʃeɪvn] *a* non rasato(a).

unsightly [ʌn'saɪtlɪ] *a* brutto(a), sgradevole a vedersi.

unskilled [ʌn'skɪld] *a*: ~ worker manovale *m*.

unspeakable [ʌn'spi:kəbl] *a* (*awful*) abominevole.

unstable [ʌn'steɪbl] *a* (*gen*) instabile; (*mentally*) squilibrato(a).

unsteady [ʌn'stɛdɪ] *a* instabile, malsicuro(a).

unstuck [ʌn'stʌk] *a*: to come ~ scollarsi; (*fig*) fare fiasco.

unsuccessful [ʌnsək'sɛsful] *a* (*writer, proposal*) che non ha successo; (*marriage, attempt*) mal riuscito(a), fallito(a); to be ~ (*in attempting sth*) non riuscire; non avere successo; (*application*) non essere considerato(a).

unsuitable [ʌn'su:təbl] *a* inadatto(a); inopportuno(a); sconveniente.

unsure [ʌn'ʃuə*] *a* incerto(a); to be ~ of o.s. essere insicuro(a).

unsympathetic [ʌnsɪmpə'θɛtɪk] *a* (*person*) antipatico(a); (*attitude*) poco incoraggiante.

untapped [ʌn'tæpt] *a* (*resources*) non sfruttato(a).

unthinkable [ʌn'θɪŋkəbl] *a* impensabile, inconcepibile.

untidy [ʌn'taɪdɪ] *a* (*room*) in disordine; (*appearance, work*) trascurato(a); (*person, writing*) disordinato(a).

untie [ʌn'taɪ] *vt* (*knot, parcel*) disfare; (*prisoner, dog*) slegare.

until [ʌn'tɪl] *prep* fino a; (*after negative*) prima di // *cj* finché, fino a quando; (*in past, after negative*) prima che + *sub*, prima di + *infinitive*; ~ now finora; ~ then fino ad allora.

untimely [ʌn'taɪmlɪ] *a* intempestivo(a), inopportuno(a); (*death*) prematuro(a).

untold [ʌn'təuld] *a* incalcolabile; indescrivibile.

untoward [ʌntə'wɔ:d] *a* sfortunato(a), sconveniente.

untranslatable [ʌntrænz'leɪtəbl] *a* intraducibile.

unused [ʌn'ju:zd] *a* nuovo(a).

unusual [ʌn'ju:ʒuəl] *a* insolito(a), eccezionale, raro(a).

unveil [ʌn'veɪl] *vt* scoprire; svelare.

unwavering [ʌn'weɪvərɪŋ] *a* fermo(a), incrollabile.

unwelcome [ʌn'wɛlkəm] *a* non gradito(a).

unwell [ʌn'wɛl] *a* indisposto(a); to feel ~ non sentirsi bene.

unwieldy [ʌn'wi:ldɪ] *a* poco maneggevole.

unwilling [ʌn'wɪlɪŋ] *a*: to be ~ to do non voler fare; ~ly *ad* malvolentieri.

unwind [ʌn'waɪnd] *vb* (*irg*) *vt* svolgere, srotolare // *vi* (*relax*) rilassarsi.

unwise [ʌn'waɪz] *a* poco saggio(a); (*decision*) avventato(a).

unwitting [ʌn'wɪtɪŋ] *a* involontario(a).

unworkable [ʌn'wə:kəbl] *a* (*plan*) inattuabile.

unworthy [ʌn'wə:ðɪ] *a* indegno(a).

unwrap [ʌn'ræp] *vt* disfare; aprire.

unwritten [ʌn'rɪtn] *a* (*agreement*) tacito(a); (*law*) non scritto(a).

up [ʌp] ◆ *prep*: he went ~ the stairs/the hill è salito su per le scale/sulla collina; the cat was ~ a tree il gatto era su un albero; they live further ~ the street vivono un po' più su nella stessa strada

◆ *ad* 1 (*upwards, higher*) su, in alto; ~ in the sky/the mountains su nel cielo/in montagna; ~ there lassù; ~ above su in alto

2: to be ~ (*out of bed*) essere alzato(a); (*prices, level*) essere salito(a)

3: ~ to (*as far as*) fino a; ~ to now finora

4: to be ~ to (*depending on*): it's ~ to you sta a lei, dipende da lei; (*equal to*): he's not ~ to it (*job, task etc*) non ne è all'altezza; (*col: be doing*): what is he ~ to? cosa sta combinando?

◆ *n*: ~s and downs alti e bassi *mpl*.

up-and-coming [ʌpəndˈkʌmɪŋ] *a* pieno(a) di promesse, promettente.

upbringing [ˈʌpbrɪŋɪŋ] *n* educazione *f*.

update [ʌpˈdeɪt] *vt* aggiornare.

upheaval [ʌpˈhiːvl] *n* sconvolgimento; tumulto.

uphill [ʌpˈhɪl] *a* in salita; (*fig: task*) difficile // *ad*: to go ~ andare in salita, salire.

uphold [ʌpˈhəʊld] *vt irg* approvare; sostenere.

upholstery [ʌpˈhəʊlstərɪ] *n* tappezzeria.

upkeep [ˈʌpkiːp] *n* manutenzione *f*.

upon [əˈpɒn] *prep* su.

upper [ˈʌpə*] *a* superiore // *n* (*of shoe*) tomaia; ~-class *a* dell'alta borghesia; ~ hand *n*: to have the ~ hand avere il coltello dalla parte del manico; ~most *a* il(la) più alto(a); predominante.

upright [ˈʌpraɪt] *a* diritto(a); verticale; (*fig*) diritto(a), onesto(a) // *n* montante *m*.

uprising [ˈʌpraɪzɪŋ] *n* insurrezione *f*, rivolta.

uproar [ˈʌprɔː*] *n* tumulto, clamore *m*.

uproot [ʌpˈruːt] *vt* sradicare.

upset *n* [ˈʌpsɛt] turbamento // *vt* [ʌpˈsɛt] (*irg: like* set) (*glass etc*) rovesciare; (*plan, stomach*) scombussolare; (*person: offend*) contrariare; (*: grieve*) addolorare; sconvolgere // *a* [ʌpˈsɛt] contrariato(a); addolorato(a); (*stomach*) scombussolato(a), disturbato(a).

upshot [ˈʌpʃɒt] *n* risultato.

upside-down [ˈʌpsaɪdˈdaʊn] *ad* sottosopra.

upstairs [ʌpˈstɛəz] *ad, a* di sopra, al piano superiore.

upstart [ˈʌpstɑːt] *n* parvenu *m inv*.

upstream [ʌpˈstriːm] *ad* a monte.

uptake [ˈʌpteɪk] *n*: he is quick/slow on the ~ è pronto/lento di comprendonio.

uptight [ʌpˈtaɪt] *a* (*col*) teso(a).

up-to-date [ˈʌptəˈdeɪt] *a* moderno(a); aggiornato(a).

upturn [ˈʌptəːn] *n* (*in luck*) svolta favorevole; (*COMM: in market*) rialzo.

upward [ˈʌpwəd] *a* ascendente; verso l'alto; ~(s) *ad* in su, verso l'alto.

urban [ˈəːbən] *a* urbano(a).

urbane [əːˈbeɪn] *a* civile, urbano(a),

educato(a).

urchin [ˈəːtʃɪn] *n* monello.

urge [əːdʒ] *n* impulso; stimolo; forte desiderio // *vt*: to ~ sb to do esortare qn a fare, spingere qn a fare; raccomandare a qn di fare.

urgency [ˈəːdʒənsɪ] *n* urgenza; (*of tone*) insistenza.

urgent [ˈəːdʒənt] *a* urgente.

urinate [ˈjuərɪneɪt] *vi* orinare.

urine [ˈjuərɪn] *n* orina.

urn [əːn] *n* urna; (*also:* tea ~) bollitore *m* per il tè.

US, USA *n abbr* = United States (of America).

us [ʌs] *pronoun* ci; (*stressed, after prep*) noi; *see also* me.

usage [ˈjuːzɪdʒ] *n* uso.

use *n* [juːs] uso; impiego, utilizzazione *f* // *vt* [juːz] usare, utilizzare, servirsi di; ~d to do it lo faceva (una volta), era solita farlo; in ~ in uso; out of ~ fuori uso; to be of ~ essere utile, servire; it's no ~ non serve, è inutile; to be ~d to avere l'abitudine di; to ~ up *vt* consumare; esaurire; ~d *a* (*car*) d'occasione; ~ful *a* utile; ~fulness *n* utilità; ~less *a* inutile; ~r *n* utente *m/f*; ~r-friendly *a* (*computer*) di facile uso.

usher [ˈʌʃə*] *n* usciere *m*; (*in cinema*) maschera; ~ette [-ˈrɛt] *n* (*in cinema*) maschera.

USSR *n*: the ~ l'URSS *f*.

usual [ˈjuːʒuəl] *a* solito(a); as ~ come al solito, come d'abitudine; ~ly *ad* di solito.

utensil [juːˈtɛnsl] *n* utensile *m*; kitchen ~s utensili da cucina.

uterus [ˈjuːtərəs] *n* utero.

utility [juːˈtɪlɪtɪ] *n* utilità; (*also:* public ~) servizio pubblico; ~ room *n* locale adibito alla stiratura dei panni etc.

utmost [ˈʌtməʊst] *a* estremo(a) // *n*: to do one's ~ fare il possibile *or* di tutto.

utter [ˈʌtə*] *a* assoluto(a), totale // *vt* pronunciare, proferire; emettere; ~ance *n* espressione *f*; parole *fpl*; ~ly *ad* completamente, del tutto.

U-turn [ˈjuːˈtəːn] *n* inversione *f* a U.

V

v. *abbr* = verse, versus, volt; (= *vide*) vedi, vedere.

vacancy [ˈveɪkənsɪ] *n* (*Brit: job*) posto libero; (*room*) stanza libera.

vacant [ˈveɪkənt] *a* (*job, seat etc*) libero(a); (*expression*) assente; ~ lot *n* (*US*) terreno non occupato; (*: for sale*) terreno in vendita.

vacate [vəˈkeɪt] *vt* lasciare libero(a).

vacation [vəˈkeɪʃən] *n* vacanze *fpl*.

vaccinate [ˈvæksɪneɪt] *vt* vaccinare.

vacuum ['vækjum] n vuoto; ~ **bottle** n (US) = ~ **flask**; ~ **cleaner** n aspirapolvere m inv; ~ **flask** n (Brit) thermos m inv ®; ~**-packed** a confezionato(a) sottovuoto.

vagina [və'dʒaɪnə] n vagina.

vagrant ['veɪgrnt] n vagabondo/a.

vague [veɪg] a vago(a); (blurred: photo, memory) sfocato(a); ~**ly** ad vagamente.

vain [veɪn] a (useless) inutile, vano(a); (conceited) vanitoso(a); **in** ~ inutilmente, invano.

valentine ['væləntaɪn] n (also: ~ **card**) cartolina or biglietto di San Valentino.

valet ['væleɪ] n cameriere m personale.

valiant ['væliənt] a valoroso(a), coraggioso(a).

valid ['vælɪd] a valido(a), valevole; (excuse) valido(a).

valley ['vælɪ] n valle f.

valour, (US) **valor** ['vælə*] n valore m.

valuable ['væljuəbl] a (jewel) di (grande) valore; (time) prezioso(a); ~**s** npl oggetti mpl di valore.

valuation [vælju'eɪʃən] n valutazione f, stima.

value ['vælju:] n valore m // vt (fix price) valutare, dare un prezzo a; (cherish) apprezzare, tenere a; ~ **added tax (VAT)** n (Brit) imposta sul valore aggiunto (I.V.A.); ~**d** a (appreciated) stimato(a), apprezzato(a).

valve [vælv] n valvola.

van [væn] n (AUT) furgone m; (Brit RAIL) vagone m.

vandal ['vændl] n vandalo/a; ~**ism** n vandalismo.

vanilla [və'nɪlə] n vaniglia // cpd (ice cream) alla vaniglia.

vanish ['vænɪʃ] vi svanire, scomparire.

vanity ['vænɪtɪ] n vanità; ~ **case** n valigetta per cosmetici.

vantage ['vɑːntɪdʒ] n: ~ **point** posizione f or punto di osservazione; (fig) posizione vantaggiosa.

vapour, (US) **vapor** ['veɪpə*] n vapore m.

variable ['vɛərɪəbl] a variabile; (mood) mutevole.

variance ['vɛərɪəns] n: **to be at** ~ (**with**) essere in disaccordo (con); (facts) essere in contraddizione (con).

varicose ['værɪkəus] a: ~ **veins** varici fpl.

varied ['vɛərɪd] a vario(a), diverso(a).

variety [və'raɪətɪ] n varietà f inv; (quantity) quantità, numero; ~ **show** n varietà m inv.

various ['vɛərɪəs] a vario(a), diverso(a); (several) parecchi(e), molti(e).

varnish ['vɑːnɪʃ] n vernice f // vt verniciare.

vary ['vɛərɪ] vt, vi variare, mutare.

vase [vɑːz] n vaso.

vaseline ['væsɪliːn] n ® vaselina.

vast [vɑːst] a vasto(a); (amount, success) enorme; ~**ly** ad enormemente.

VAT [væt] n abbr = **value added tax**.

vat [væt] n tino.

Vatican ['vætɪkən] n: **the** ~ il Vaticano.

vault [vɔːlt] n (of roof) volta; (tomb) tomba; (in bank) camera blindata; (jump) salto // vt (also: ~ **over**) saltare (d'un balzo).

vaunted ['vɔːntɪd] a: **much-**~ tanto celebrato(a).

VCR n abbr = **video cassette recorder**.

VD n abbr = **venereal disease**.

VDU n abbr = **visual display unit**.

veal [viːl] n vitello.

veer [vɪə*] vi girare; virare.

vegetable ['vedʒtəbl] n verdura, ortaggio // a vegetale.

vegetarian [vedʒɪ'tɛərɪən] a, n vegetariano(a).

vehement ['viːɪmənt] a veemente, violento(a).

vehicle ['viːɪkl] n veicolo.

veil [veɪl] n velo // vt velare.

vein [veɪn] n vena; (on leaf) nervatura; (fig: mood) vena, umore m.

velvet ['velvɪt] n velluto.

vending machine ['vendɪŋ-] n distributore m automatico.

veneer [və'nɪə*] n impiallacciatura; (fig) vernice f.

venereal [vɪ'nɪərɪəl] a: ~ **disease (VD)** malattia venerea.

Venetian [vɪ'niːʃən] a veneziano(a); ~ **blind** n (tenda alla) veneziana.

vengeance ['vendʒəns] n vendetta; **with a** ~ (fig) davvero; furiosamente.

Venice ['venɪs] n Venezia.

venison ['venɪsn] n carne f di cervo.

venom ['venəm] n veleno.

vent [vent] n foro, apertura; (in dress, jacket) spacco // vt (fig: one's feelings) sfogare, dare sfogo a.

ventilate ['ventɪleɪt] vt (room) dare aria a, arieggiare; **ventilator** n ventilatore m.

ventriloquist [ven'trɪləkwɪst] n ventriloquo/a.

venture ['ventʃə*] n impresa (rischiosa) // vt rischiare, azzardare // vi arrischiarsi, azzardarsi.

venue ['venjuː] n luogo di incontro; (SPORT) luogo (designato) per l'incontro.

verb [vəːb] n verbo; ~**al** a verbale; (translation) letterale.

verbatim [vəː'beɪtɪm] a, ad parola per parola.

verdict ['vəːdɪkt] n verdetto.

verge [vəːdʒ] n (Brit) bordo, orlo; **on the** ~ **of doing** sul punto di fare; **to** ~ **on** vt fus rasentare.

verification [verɪfɪ'keɪʃən] n verifica.

veritable ['verɪtəbl] a vero(a).

vermin ['vəːmɪn] npl animali mpl nocivi;

(insects) insetti mpl parassiti.
vermouth ['vɜːməθ] n vermut m inv.
versatile ['vɜːsətail] a (person) versatile; (machine, tool etc) (che si presta) a molti usi.
verse [vɜːs] n versi mpl; (stanza) stanza, strofa; (in bible) versetto.
version ['vɜːʃən] n versione f.
versus ['vɜːsəs] prep contro.
vertical ['vɜːtɪkl] a, n verticale (m); ~ly ad verticalmente.
vertigo ['vɜːtɪgəu] n vertigine f.
verve [vɜːv] n brio; entusiasmo.
very ['vɛrɪ] ad molto // a: the ~ book which proprio il libro che; at the ~ end proprio alla fine; the ~ last proprio l'ultimo; at the ~ least almeno; ~ much moltissimo.
vessel ['vɛsl] n (ANAT) vaso; (NAUT) nave f; (container) recipiente m.
vest [vɛst] n (Brit) maglia; (: sleeveless) canottiera; (US: waistcoat) gilè m inv; ~ed interests npl (COMM) diritti mpl acquisiti.
vestment ['vɛstmənt] n (REL) paramento liturgico.
vestry ['vɛstrɪ] n sagrestia.
vet [vɛt] n abbr (= veterinary surgeon) veterinario // vt esaminare minuziosamente; (text) rivedere.
veteran ['vɛtərn] n veterano; (also: war ~) reduce m.
veterinary ['vɛtrɪnərɪ] a veterinario(a); ~ surgeon, (US) **veterinarian** n veterinario.
veto ['viːtəu] n, pl ~es veto // vt opporre il veto a.
vex [vɛks] vt irritare, contrariare; ~ed a (question) controverso(a), dibattuto(a).
VHF abbr (= very high frequency) VHF, altissima frequenza.
via ['vaɪə] prep (by way of) via; (by means of) tramite.
viable ['vaɪəbl] a attuabile; vitale.
viaduct ['vaɪədʌkt] n viadotto.
vibrate [vaɪ'breɪt] vi: to ~ (with) vibrare (di); (resound) risonare (di).
vicar ['vɪkə*] n pastore m; ~age n presbiterio.
vicarious [vɪ'kɛərɪəs] a indiretto(a).
vice [vaɪs] n (evil) vizio; (TECH) morsa.
vice- [vaɪs] prefix vice....
vice squad n (squadra del) buon costume f.
vice versa ['vaɪsɪ'vɜːsə] ad viceversa.
vicinity [vɪ'sɪnɪtɪ] n vicinanze fpl.
vicious ['vɪʃəs] a (remark) maligno(a), cattivo(a); (blow) violento(a); ~ circle n circolo vizioso.
victim ['vɪktɪm] n vittima.
victor ['vɪktə*] n vincitore m.
Victorian [vɪk'tɔːrɪən] a vittoriano(a).
victory ['vɪktərɪ] n vittoria.
video ['vɪdɪəu] cpd video... // n (~ film) video m inv; (also: ~ cassette)

videocassetta; (also: ~ cassette recorder) videoregistratore m; ~ tape n videotape m inv.
vie [vaɪ] vi: to ~ with competere con, rivaleggiare con.
Vienna [vɪ'ɛnə] n Vienna.
Vietnam [vjɛt'næm] n Vietnam m; ~ese a, n (pl inv) vietnamita (m/f).
view [vjuː] n vista, veduta; (opinion) opinione f // vt (situation) considerare; (house) visitare; on ~ (in museum etc) esposto(a); in full ~ of sotto gli occhi di; in ~ of the fact that considerato che; ~er n (viewfinder) mirino; (small projector) visore m; (TV) telespettatore/trice; ~finder n mirino; ~point n punto di vista.
vigil ['vɪdʒɪl] n veglia.
vigorous ['vɪgərəs] a vigoroso(a).
vile [vaɪl] a (action) vile; (smell) disgustoso(a), nauseante; (temper) pessimo(a).
villa ['vɪlə] n villa.
village ['vɪlɪdʒ] n villaggio; ~r n abitante m/f di villaggio.
villain ['vɪlən] n (scoundrel) canaglia; (criminal) criminale m; (in novel etc) cattivo.
vindicate ['vɪndɪkeɪt] vt comprovare; giustificare.
vindictive [vɪn'dɪktɪv] a vendicativo(a).
vine [vaɪn] n vite f; (climbing plant) rampicante m.
vinegar ['vɪnɪgə*] n aceto.
vineyard ['vɪnjɑːd] n vigna, vigneto.
vintage ['vɪntɪdʒ] n (year) annata, produzione f; ~ wine n vino d'annata.
vinyl ['vaɪnl] n vinile m.
violate ['vaɪəleɪt] vt violare.
violence ['vaɪələns] n violenza; (POL etc) incidenti mpl violenti.
violent ['vaɪələnt] a violento(a).
violet ['vaɪələt] a (colour) viola inv, violetto(a) // n (plant) violetta.
violin [vaɪə'lɪn] n violino; ~ist n violinista m/f.
VIP n abbr (= very important person) V.I.P. m/f inv.
virgin ['vɜːdʒɪn] n vergine f // a vergine inv.
Virgo ['vɜːgəu] n (sign) Vergine f.
virile ['vɪraɪl] a virile.
virtually ['vɜːtjuəlɪ] ad (almost) praticamente.
virtue ['vɜːtjuː] n virtù f inv; (advantage) pregio, vantaggio; by ~ of grazie a.
virtuous ['vɜːtjuəs] a virtuoso(a).
virus ['vaɪərəs] n virus m inv.
visa ['viːzə] n visto.
vis-à-vis [viːzə'viː] prep rispetto a, nei riguardi di.
visibility [vɪzɪ'bɪlɪtɪ] n visibilità.
visible ['vɪzəbl] a visibile.
vision ['vɪʒən] n (sight) vista; (foresight, in dream) visione f.

visit ['vızıt] *n* visita; (*stay*) soggiorno // *vt* (*person*) andare a trovare; (*place*) visitare; **~ing hours** *npl* (*in hospital etc*) orario delle visite; **~or** *n* visitatore/trice; (*guest*) ospite *m/f*; (*in hotel*) cliente *m/f*; **~ors' book** *n* libro d'oro; (*in hotel*) registro.

visor ['vaızə*] *n* visiera.

vista ['vıstə] *n* vista, prospettiva.

visual ['vızjuəl] *a* visivo(a); visuale; ottico(a); **~ aid** *n* sussidio visivo; **~ display unit (VDU)** *n* visualizzatore *m*.

visualize ['vızjuəlaız] *vt* immaginare, figurarsi; (*foresee*) prevedere.

vital ['vaıtl] *a* vitale; **~ly** *ad* estremamente; **~ statistics** *npl* (*fig*) misure *fpl*.

vitamin ['vıtəmın] *n* vitamina.

vivacious [vı'veıʃəs] *a* vivace.

vivid ['vıvıd] *a* vivido(a); **~ly** *ad* (*describe*) vividamente; (*remember*) con precisione.

V-neck ['vi:nɛk] *n* maglione *m* con lo scollo a V.

vocabulary [vəu'kæbjulərı] *n* vocabolario.

vocal ['vəukl] *a* (*MUS*) vocale; (*communication*) verbale; **~ chords** *npl* corde *fpl* vocali.

vocation [vəu'keıʃən] *n* vocazione *f*; **~al** *a* professionale.

vociferous [və'sıfərəs] *a* rumoroso(a).

vodka ['vɔdkə] *n* vodka *f inv*.

vogue [vəug] *n* moda; (*popularity*) popolarità, voga.

voice [vɔıs] *n* voce *f* // *vt* (*opinion*) esprimere.

void [vɔıd] *n* vuoto // *a* (*invalid*) nullo(a); (*empty*) vuoto(a); **~ of** privo(a) di.

volatile ['vɔlətaıl] *a* volatile; (*fig*) volubile.

volcano, ~es [vɔl'keınəu] *n* vulcano.

volition [və'lıʃən] *n*: of one's own **~** di sua volontà.

volley ['vɔlı] *n* (*of gunfire*) salva; (*of stones etc*) raffica, gragnola; (*TENNIS etc*) volata; **~ball** *n* pallavolo *f*.

volt [vəult] *n* volt *m inv*; **~age** *n* tensione *f*, voltaggio.

voluble ['vɔljubl] *a* loquace, ciarliero(a).

volume ['vɔlju:m] *n* volume *m*; **~ control** *a* (*RADIO, TV*) regolatore *m* or manopola del volume.

voluntarily ['vɔləntrılı] *ad* volontariamente; gratuitamente.

voluntary ['vɔləntərı] *a* volontario(a); (*unpaid*) gratuito(a), non retribuito(a).

volunteer [vɔlən'tıə*] *n* volontario/a // *vi* (*MIL*) arruolarsi volontario; to **~** to do offrire (volontariamente) di fare.

voluptuous [və'lʌptjuəs] *a* voluttuoso(a).

vomit ['vɔmıt] *n* vomito // *vt*, *vi* vomitare.

vote [vəut] *n* voto, suffragio; (*cast*) voto; (*franchise*) diritto di voto // *vi* votare; **~** of thanks discorso di ringraziamento; **~** *n* elettore/trice; **voting** *n* scrutinio.

vouch [vautʃ]: to **~** for *vt fus* farsi garante di.

voucher ['vautʃə*] *n* (*for meal, petrol*) buono; (*receipt*) ricevuta.

vow [vau] *n* voto, promessa solenne // *vi* giurare.

vowel ['vauəl] *n* vocale *f*.

voyage ['vɔıdʒ] *n* viaggio per mare, traversata.

vulgar ['vʌlgə*] *a* volgare.

vulnerable ['vʌlnərəbl] *a* vulnerabile.

vulture ['vʌltʃə*] *n* avvoltoio.

W

wad [wɔd] *n* (*of cotton wool, paper*) tampone *m*; (*of banknotes etc*) fascio.

waddle ['wɔdl] *vi* camminare come una papera.

wade [weıd] *vi*: to **~** through camminare a stento in // *vt* guadare.

wafer ['weıfə*] *n* (*CULIN*) cialda; (*REL*) ostia; (*COMPUT*) wafer *m inv*.

waffle ['wɔfl] *n* (*CULIN*) cialda; (*col*) ciance *fpl*; riempitivo // *vi* cianciare; parlare a vuoto.

waft [wɔft] *vt* portare // *vi* diffondersi.

wag [wæg] *vt* agitare, muovere // *vi* agitarsi.

wage [weıdʒ] *n* (*also*: **~s**) salario, paga // *vt*: to **~** war fare la guerra; **~ packet** *n* busta *f* paga *inv*.

wager ['weıdʒə*] *n* scommessa.

waggle ['wægl] *vt* dimenare, agitare // *vi* dimenarsi, agitarsi.

wag(g)on ['wægən] *n* (*horse-drawn*) carro; (*Brit RAIL*) vagone *m* (merci).

wail [weıl] *n* gemito; (*of siren*) urlo // *vi* gemere; urlare.

waist [weıst] *n* vita, cintola; **~coat** *n* (*Brit*) panciotto, gilè *m inv*; **~line** *n* (giro di) vita.

wait [weıt] *n* attesa // *vi* aspettare, attendere; to lie in **~** for stare in agguato a; to **~** for aspettare; I can't **~** to (*fig*) non vedo l'ora di; to **~** behind *vi* rimanere (ad aspettare); to **~** on *vt fus* servire; **~er** *n* cameriere *m*; **~ing** *n*: "no **~ing**" (*Brit AUT*) "divieto di sosta"; **~ing list** *n* lista di attesa; **~ing room** *n* sala d'aspetto *or* d'attesa; **~ress** *n* cameriera.

waive [weıv] *vt* rinunciare a, abbandonare.

wake [weık] *vb* (*pt* **woke, ~d**, *pp* **woken, ~d**) *vt* (*also*: **~ up**) svegliare // *vi* (*also*: **~ up**) svegliarsi // *n* (*for dead person*) veglia funebre; (*NAUT*) scia; **~n** *vt*, *vi* = **wake**.

Wales [weılz] *n* Galles *m*.

walk [wɔ:k] *n* passeggiata; (*short*) giretto; (*gait*) passo, andatura; (*path*) sentiero; (*in park etc*) sentiero, vialetto // *vi* camminare; (*for pleasure, exercise*) passeggiare // *vt* (*distance*) fare *or* percorrere a piedi; (*dog*) accompagnare, portare a passeggiare; **10 minutes' ~ from** 10 minuti di cammino *or* a piedi da; **from all ~s of life** di tutte le condizioni sociali; **to ~ out on** *vt fus* (*col*) piantare in asso; **~er** *n* (*person*) camminatore/trice; **~ie-talkie** ['wɔːkɪ'tɔːkɪ] *n* walkie-talkie *m inv*; **~ing** *n* camminare *m*; **~ing stick** *n* bastone *m* da passeggio; **~out** *n* (*of workers*) sciopero senza preavviso *or* a sorpresa; **~over** *n* (*col*) vittoria facile, gioco da ragazzi; **~way** *n* passaggio pedonale.

wall [wɔːl] *n* muro; (*internal, of tunnel, cave*) parete *f*; **~ed** *a* (*city*) fortificato(a).

wallet ['wɔlɪt] *n* portafoglio.

wallflower ['wɔːlflauə*] *n* violacciocca; **to be a ~** (*fig*) fare da tappezzeria.

wallop ['wɔləp] *vt* (*col*) pestare.

wallow ['wɔləu] *vi* sguazzare, voltolarsi.

wallpaper ['wɔːlpeɪpə*] *n* carta da parati.

wally ['wɔlɪ] *n* (*col*) imbecille *m/f*.

walnut ['wɔːlnʌt] *n* noce *f*; (*tree*) noce *m*.

walrus, *pl* ~ *or* **~es** ['wɔːlrəs] *n* tricheco.

waltz [wɔːls] *n* valzer *m inv* // *vi* ballare il valzer.

wan [wɔn] *a* pallido(a), smorto(a); triste.

wand [wɔnd] *n* (*also*: **magic ~**) bacchetta (magica).

wander ['wɔndə*] *vi* (*person*) girare senza meta, girovagare; (*thoughts*) vagare; (*river*) serpeggiare // *vt* girovagare per.

wane [weɪn] *vi* (*moon*) calare; (*reputation*) declinare.

wangle [wæŋgl] *vt* (*Brit col*): **to ~ sth** procurare qc con l'astuzia.

want [wɔnt] *vt* volere; (*need*) aver bisogno di; (*lack*) mancare di // *n*: **for ~ of** per mancanza di; **~s** *npl* (*needs*) bisogni *mpl*; **to ~ to do** volere fare; **to ~ sb to do** volere che qn faccia; **~ing** *a*: **to be found ~ing** non risultare all'altezza.

wanton ['wɔntn] *a* sfrenato(a); senza motivo.

war [wɔː*] *n* guerra; **to go to ~** entrare in guerra.

ward [wɔːd] *n* (*in hospital: room*) corsia; (: *section*) reparto; (*POL*) circoscrizione *f*; (*LAW: child*) pupillo/a; **to ~ off** *vt* parare, schivare.

warden ['wɔːdn] *n* (*Brit: of institution*) direttore/trice; (*of park, game reserve*) guardiano/a; (*Brit: also*: **traffic ~**) addetto/a al controllo del traffico e del parcheggio.

warder ['wɔːdə*] *n* (*Brit*) guardia carceraria.

wardrobe ['wɔːdrəub] *n* (*cupboard*) guardaroba *m inv*, armadio; (*clothes*) guardaroba; (*THEATRE*) costumi *mpl*.

warehouse ['wɛəhaus] *n* magazzino.

wares [wɛəz] *npl* merci *fpl*.

warfare ['wɔːfɛə*] *n* guerra.

warhead ['wɔːhɛd] *n* (*MIL*) testata.

warily ['wɛərɪlɪ] *ad* cautamente, con prudenza.

warm [wɔːm] *a* caldo(a); (*thanks, welcome, applause*) caloroso(a); **it's ~** fa caldo; **I'm ~** ho caldo; **to ~ up** *vi* scaldarsi, riscaldarsi; (*athlete, discussion*) riscaldarsi // *vt* scaldare, riscaldare; (*engine*) far scaldare; **~-hearted** *a* affettuoso(a); **~ly** *ad* caldamente; calorosamente; vivamente; **~th** *n* calore *m*.

warn [wɔːn] *vt* avvertire, avvisare; **~ing** *n* avvertimento; (*notice*) avviso; **~ing light** *n* spia luminosa; **~ing triangle** *n* (*AUT*) triangolo.

warp [wɔːp] *vi* deformarsi // *vt* deformare; (*fig*) corrompere.

warrant ['wɔrnt] *n* (*LAW: to arrest*) mandato di cattura; (: *to search*) mandato di perquisizione.

warranty ['wɔrəntɪ] *n* garanzia.

warren ['wɔrən] *n* (*of rabbits*) tana.

warrior ['wɔrɪə*] *n* guerriero/a.

Warsaw ['wɔːsɔː] *n* Varsavia.

warship ['wɔːʃɪp] *n* nave *f* da guerra.

wart [wɔːt] *n* verruca.

wartime ['wɔːtaɪm] *n*: **in ~** in tempo di guerra.

wary ['wɛərɪ] *a* prudente.

was [wɔz] *pt* of **be**.

wash [wɔʃ] *vt* lavare // *vi* lavarsi // *n*: **to give sth a ~** lavare qc, dare una lavata a qc; **to have a ~** lavarsi; **to ~ away** *vt* (*stain*) togliere lavando; (*subj: river etc*) trascinare via; **to ~ off** *vi* andare via con il lavaggio; **to ~ up** *vi* (*Brit*) lavare i piatti; (*US*) darsi una lavata; **~able** *a* lavabile; **~basin**, (*US*) **~bowl** *n* lavabo; **~cloth** *n* (*US: face cloth*) pezzuola (per lavarsi); **~er** *n* (*TECH*) rondella; **~ing** *n* (*linen etc*) bucato; **~ing machine** *n* lavatrice *f*; **~ing powder** *n* (*Brit*) detersivo (in polvere); **~ing-up** *n* rigovernatura, lavatura dei piatti; **~ing-up liquid** *n* detersivo liquido (per stoviglie); **~-out** *n* (*col*) disastro; **~room** *n* gabinetto.

wasn't ['wɔznt] = **was not**.

wasp [wɔsp] *n* vespa.

wastage ['weɪstɪdʒ] *n* spreco; (*in manufacturing*) scarti *mpl*; **natural ~** diminuzione *f* di manodopera (*per pensionamento, decesso etc*).

waste [weɪst] *n* spreco; (*of time*) perdita; (*rubbish*) rifiuti *mpl* // *a* (*material*) di scarto; (*food*) avanzato(a)

// vt sprecare; (time, opportunity) perdere; ~s npl distesa desolata; **to lay ~** (destroy) devastare; **to ~ away** vi deperire; ~ **disposal unit** n (Brit) eliminatore m di rifiuti; ~**ful** a sprecone(a); (process) dispendioso(a); ~ **ground** n (Brit) terreno incolto or abbandonato; ~**paper basket** n cestino per la carta straccia; ~**pipe** n tubo di scarico.

watch [wɔtʃ] n orologio; (act of watching) sorveglianza; (guard: MIL, NAUT) guardia; (NAUT: spell of duty) quarto // vt (look at) osservare; (: match, programme) guardare; (spy on, guard) sorvegliare, tenere d'occhio; (be careful of) fare attenzione a // vi osservare, guardare; (keep guard) fare or montare la guardia; **to ~ out** vi fare attenzione; ~**dog** n cane m da guardia; ~**ful** a attento(a), vigile; ~**maker** n orologiaio/a; ~**man** n guardiano; (also: night ~**man**) guardiano notturno; ~ **strap** n cinturino da orologio.

water ['wɔːtə*] n acqua // vt (plant) annaffiare // vi (eyes) lacrimare; **in British ~s** nelle acque territoriali britanniche; **to ~ down** vt (milk) diluire; (fig: story) edulcorare; ~**colour** n acquerello; ~**colours** npl colori mpl per acquarello; ~**cress** n crescione m; ~**fall** n cascata; ~ **heater** n scaldabagno; ~ **lily** n ninfea; ~**line** n (NAUT) linea di galleggiamento; ~**logged** a saturo(a) d'acqua; imbevuto(a) d'acqua; (football pitch etc) allagato(a); ~ **main** n conduttura dell'acqua; ~**mark** n (on paper) filigrana; ~**melon** n anguria, cocomero; ~**proof** a impermeabile; ~**shed** n (GEO, fig) spartiacque m; ~-**skiing** n sci m acquatico; ~**tight** a stagno(a); ~**way** n corso d'acqua navigabile; ~**works** npl impianto idrico; ~**y** a (colour) slavato(a); (coffee) acquoso(a).

watt [wɔt] n watt m inv.

wave [weiv] n onda; (of hand) gesto, segno; (in hair) ondulazione f // vi fare un cenno con la mano; (flag) sventolare // vt (handkerchief) sventolare; (stick) brandire; ~**length** n lunghezza d'onda.

waver ['weivə*] vi vacillare; (voice) tremolare.

wavy ['weivi] a ondulato(a); ondeggiante.

wax [wæks] n cera // vt dare la cera a; (car) lucidare // vi (moon) crescere; ~**works** npl cere fpl; museo delle cere.

way [wei] n via, strada; (path, access) passaggio; (distance) distanza; (direction) parte f, direzione f; (manner) modo, stile m; (habit) abitudine f; (condition) condizione f; **which ~?** — **this ~** da che parte or in quale direzione? — da questa parte or per di qua; **on the ~** (en route) per strada; **to be on one's ~** essere in cammino or sulla strada; **to be in the ~** bloccare il passaggio; (fig) essere tra i piedi or d'impiccio; **to go out of one's ~ to do** (fig) mettercela tutta or fare di tutto per fare; **to lose one's ~** perdere la strada; **in a ~** in un certo senso; **in some ~s** sotto certi aspetti; **by the ~ ...** a proposito ...; "**~ in**" (Brit) "entrata", "ingresso"; "**~ out**" (Brit) "uscita".

waylay [wei'lei] vt irg tendere un agguato a; attendere al passaggio.

wayward ['weiwəd] a capriccioso(a); testardo(a).

W.C. ['dʌblju'siː] n (Brit) W.C. m inv, gabinetto.

we [wiː] pl pronoun noi.

weak [wiːk] a debole; (health) precario(a); (beam etc) fragile; ~**en** vi indebolirsi // vt indebolire; ~**ling** ['wiːklɪŋ] n smidollato/a; debole m/f; ~**ness** n debolezza; (fault) punto debole, difetto.

wealth [welθ] n (money, resources) ricchezza, ricchezze fpl; (of details) abbondanza, profusione f; ~**y** a ricco(a).

wean [wiːn] vt svezzare.

weapon ['wepən] n arma.

wear [weə*] n (use) uso; (deterioration through use) logorio, usura; (clothing): **sports/baby ~** abbigliamento sportivo/per neonati // vb (pt **wore**, pp **worn**) vt (clothes) portare; mettersi; (damage: through use) consumare // vi (last) durare; (rub etc through) consumarsi; **evening ~** abiti mpl or tenuta da sera; **to ~ away** vt consumare; erodere // vi consumarsi; essere eroso(a); **to ~ down** vt consumare; (strength) esaurire; **to ~ off** vi sparire lentamente; **to ~ on** vi passare; **to ~ out** vt consumare; (person, strength) esaurire; ~ **and tear** n usura, consumo.

weary ['wiəri] a stanco(a); (tiring) faticoso(a).

weasel ['wiːzl] n (ZOOL) donnola.

weather ['weðə*] n tempo // vt (wood) stagionare; (storm, crisis) superare; **under the ~** (fig: ill) poco bene; ~-**beaten** a (person) segnato(a) dalle intemperie; (building) logorato(a) dalle intemperie; ~**cock** n banderuola; ~ **forecast** n previsioni fpl del tempo, bollettino meteorologico; ~ **vane** n = ~**cock**.

weave [wiːv], pt **wove**, pp **woven** vt (cloth) tessere; (basket) intrecciare; ~**r** n tessitore/trice; **weaving** n tessitura.

web [web] n (of spider) ragnatela; (on foot) palma; (fabric, also fig) tessuto.

wed [wed] vt (pt, pp **wedded**) sposare // vi sposarsi.

we'd [wiːd] = **we had, we would**.

wedding ['wɛdɪŋ] n matrimonio; **silver/golden ~ anniversary** n nozze fpl d'argento/d'oro; **~ day** n giorno delle nozze or del matrimonio; **~ dress** n abito nuziale; **~ ring** n fede f.

wedge [wɛdʒ] n (of wood etc) cuneo; (under door etc) zeppa; (of cake) spicchio, fetta // vt (fix) fissare con zeppe; (push) incuneare.

wedlock ['wɛdlɔk] n vincolo matrimoniale.

Wednesday ['wɛdnzdɪ] n mercoledì m inv.

wee [wi:] a (Scottish) piccolo(a).

weed [wi:d] n erbaccia // vt diserbare; **~killer** n diserbante m; **~y** a (person) allampanato(a).

week [wi:k] n settimana; **a ~ today/on Friday** oggi/venerdì a otto; **~day** n giorno feriale; (COMM) giornata lavorativa; **~end** n fine settimana m or f inv, weekend m inv; **~ly** ad ogni settimana, settimanalmente // a, n settimanale (m).

weep [wi:p], pt, pp **wept** vi (person) piangere; **~ing willow** n salice m piangente.

weigh [weɪ] vt, vi pesare; **to ~ down** vt (branch) piegare; (fig: with worry) opprimere, caricare; **to ~ up** vt valutare.

weight [weɪt] n peso; **to lose/put on ~** dimagrire/ingrassare; **~ing** n (allowance) indennità; **~ lifter** n pesista m; **~y** a pesante; (fig) importante, grave.

weir [wɪə*] n diga.

weird [wɪəd] a strano(a), bizzarro(a); (eerie) soprannaturale.

welcome ['wɛlkəm] a benvenuto(a) // n accoglienza, benvenuto // vt accogliere cordialmente; (also: bid ~) dare il benvenuto a; (be glad of) rallegrarsi di; **to be ~** essere il(la) benvenuto(a); **thank you — you're ~!** grazie — prego!

weld [wɛld] n saldatura // vt saldare.

welfare ['wɛlfɛə*] n benessere m; **~ state** n stato assistenziale.

well [wɛl] n pozzo // ad bene // a: **to be ~** andare bene; (person) stare bene // excl allora!; ma!; ebbene!; **as ~** anche; **as ~ as** così come; oltre a; **X as ~ as Y** sia X che Y; **he did as ~ as he could** ha fatto come meglio poteva; **~ done!** bravo(a)!; **get ~ soon!** guarisci presto!; **to do ~ in sth** riuscire in qc; **to ~ up** vi sgorgare.

we'll [wi:l] = **we will, we shall**.

well: **~-behaved** a ubbidiente; **~-being** n benessere m; **~-built** a (person) ben fatto(a); **~-dressed** a ben vestito(a), vestito(a) bene; **~-heeled** a (col: wealthy) agiato(a), facoltoso(a).

wellingtons ['wɛlɪŋtənz] npl (also: wellington boots) stivali mpl di gomma.

well: **~-known** a noto(a), famoso(a); **~-mannered** a ben educato(a); **~-meaning** a ben intenzionato(a); **~-off** a benestante, danaroso(a); **~-read** a colto(a); **~-to-do** a abbiente, benestante; **~-wisher** n ammiratore/trice.

Welsh [wɛlʃ] a gallese // n (LING) gallese m; **the ~** npl i Gallesi; **~man/woman** n gallese m/f; **~ rarebit** n crostino al formaggio.

went [wɛnt] pt of **go**.

wept [wɛpt] pt, pp of **weep**.

were [wə:*] pt of **be**.

we're [wɪə*] = **we are**.

weren't [wə:nt] = **were not**.

west [wɛst] n ovest m, occidente m, ponente m // a (a) ovest inv, occidentale // ad verso ovest; **the W~** l'Occidente m; **the W~ Country** n (Brit) il sudovest dell'Inghilterra; **~erly** a (wind) occidentale, da ovest; **~ern** a occidentale, dell'ovest // n (CINEMA) western m inv; **W~ Germany** n Germania Occidentale; **W~ Indian** a delle Indie Occidentali // n abitante m/f delle Indie Occidentali; **W~ Indies** npl Indie fpl Occidentali; **~ward(s)** ad verso ovest.

wet [wɛt] a umido(a), bagnato(a); (soaked) fradicio(a); (rainy) piovoso(a); **to get ~** bagnarsi; "**~ paint**" "vernice fresca"; **~ blanket** n (fig) guastafeste m/f; **~ suit** n tuta da sub.

we've [wi:v] = **we have**.

whack [wæk] vt picchiare, battere.

whale [weɪl] n (ZOOL) balena.

wharf, pl **wharves** [wɔ:f, wɔ:vz] n banchina.

what [wɔt] ◆ ad 1 (in direct/indirect questions) che; quale; **~ size is it?** che taglia è?; **~ colour is it?** di che colore è?; **~ books do you want?** quali or che libri vuole?

2 (in exclamations) che; **~ a mess!** che disordine!

◆ pronoun 1 (interrogative) che cosa, cosa, che; **~ are you doing?** che or (che) cosa fai?; **~ are you talking about?** di che cosa parli?; **~ is it called?** come si chiama?; **~ about me?** e io?; **~ about doing ...?** e se facessimo ...?

2 (relative) ciò che, quello che; **I saw ~ you did/was on the table** ho visto quello che hai fatto/quello che era sul tavolo

3 (indirect use) (che) cosa; **he asked me ~ she had said** mi ha chiesto che cosa avesse detto; **tell me ~ you're thinking about** dimmi a cosa stai pensando

◆ excl (disbelieving) cosa!, come!

whatever [wɔt'ɛvə*] a: **~ book** qualunque or qualsiasi libro + sub // pronoun: **do ~ is necessary/you want** faccia qualunque or qualsiasi cosa sia necessaria/lei voglia; ~ **happens** qualunque cosa accada; **no reason** ~ **or whatsoever** nessuna ragione affatto *or* al mondo; **nothing** ~ proprio niente.

whatsoever [wɔtsəu'ɛvə*] *a see* **whatever**.

wheat [wi:t] *n* grano, frumento.

wheedle ['wi:dl] *vt*: **to** ~ **sb into doing sth** convincere qn a fare qc (con lusinghe); **to** ~ **sth out of sb** ottenere qc da qn (con lusinghe).

wheel [wi:l] *n* ruota; (*AUT*: *also*: steering ~) volante *m*; (*NAUT*: ruota del) timone *m* // *vt* spingere // *vi* (*also*: ~ **round**) girare; **~barrow** *n* carriola; **~chair** *n* sedia a rotelle; ~ **clamp** *n* (*AUT*) morsa che blocca la ruota di una vettura in sosta vietata.

wheeze [wi:z] *vi* ansimare.

when [wɛn] ♦ *ad* quando; ~ **did it happen?** quando è successo?
♦ *cj* **1** (*at, during, after the time that*) quando; **she was reading** ~ **I came in** quando sono entrato lei leggeva; **that was** ~ **I needed you** era allora che avevo bisogno di te
2 (*on, at which*): **on the day** ~ **I met him** il giorno in cui l'ho incontrato; **one day** ~ **it was raining** un giorno che pioveva
3 (*whereas*) quando, mentre; **you said I was wrong** ~ **in fact I was right** mi hai detto che avevo torto, quando in realtà avevo ragione.

whenever [wɛn'ɛvə*] *ad* quando mai // *cj* quando; (*every time that*) ogni volta che.

where [wɛə*] *ad, cj* dove; **this is** ~ è qui che; **~abouts** *ad* dove // *n*: **sb's ~abouts** luogo dove qn si trova; **~as** *cj* mentre; **~by** *pronoun* per cui; **~upon** *cj* al che; **wherever** [-'ɛvə*] *ad* dove mai // *cj* dovunque + *sub*; **~withal** *n* mezzi *mpl*.

whet [wɛt] *vt* (*tool*) affilare; (*appetite etc*) stimolare.

whether ['wɛðə*] *cj* se; **I don't know** ~ **to accept or not** non so se accettare o no; **it's doubtful** ~ è poco probabile che; ~ **you go or not** che lei vada o no.

which [wɪtʃ] ♦ *a* **1** (*interrogative: direct, indirect*) quale; ~ **picture do you want?** quale quadro vuole?; ~ **one?** quale?; ~ **one of you did it?** chi di voi lo ha fatto?
2: **in** ~ **case** nel qual caso
♦ *pronoun* **1** (*interrogative*) quale; ~ (**of these**) **are yours?** quali di questi sono suoi?; ~ **of you are coming?** chi di voi viene?
2 (*relative*) che; (: *indirect*) cui, il(la) quale; **the apple** ~ **you ate/**~ **is on the table** la mela che hai mangiato/che è sul tavolo; **the chair on** ~ **you are sitting** la sedia sulla quale *or* su cui sei seduto; **he**

said he knew, ~ **is true** ha detto che lo sapeva, il che è vero; **after** ~ dopo di che.

whichever [wɪtʃ'ɛvə*] *a*: **take** ~ **book you prefer** prenda qualsiasi libro che preferisce; ~ **book you take** qualsiasi libro prenda.

whiff [wɪf] *n* soffio; sbuffo; odore *m*.

while [waɪl] *n* momento // *cj* mentre; (*as long as*) finché; (*although*) sebbene + *sub*; per quanto + *sub*; **for a** ~ per un po'; **to** ~ **away** *vt* (*time*) far passare.

whim [wɪm] *n* capriccio.

whimper ['wɪmpə*] *n* piagnucolio // *vi* piagnucolare.

whimsical ['wɪmzɪkl] *a* (*person*) capriccioso(a); (*look*) strano(a).

whine [waɪn] *n* gemito // *vi* gemere; uggiolare; piagnucolare.

whip [wɪp] *n* frusta; (*for riding*) frustino; (*POL*: *person*) capogruppo (*che sovrintende alla disciplina dei colleghi di partito*) // *vt* frustare; (*snatch*) sollevare (*or* estrarre) bruscamente; **~ped cream** *n* panna montata; **~-round** *n* (*Brit*) colletta.

whirl [wə:l] *n* turbine *m* // *vt* (far) girare rapidamente; (far) turbinare // *vi* turbinare; **~pool** *n* mulinello; **~wind** *n* turbine *m*.

whirr [wə:*] *vi* ronzare; rombare; frullare.

whisk [wɪsk] *n* (*CULIN*) frusta; frullino // *vt* sbattere, frullare; **to** ~ **sb away** *or* **off** portar via qn a tutta velocità.

whiskers ['wɪskəz] *npl* (*of animal*) baffi *mpl*; (*of man*) favoriti *mpl*.

whisky, (*US, Ireland*) **whiskey** ['wɪskɪ] *n* whisky *m inv*.

whisper ['wɪspə*] *n* sussurro; (*rumour*) voce *f* // *vt, vi* sussurrare.

whistle ['wɪsl] *n* (*sound*) fischio; (*object*) fischietto // *vi* fischiare.

white [waɪt] *a* bianco(a); (*with fear*) pallido(a) // *n* bianco; (*person*) bianco/a; ~ **coffee** *n* (*Brit*) caffellatte *m inv*; ~ **collar worker** *n* impiegato; ~ **elephant** *n* (*fig*) oggetto (*or* progetto) costoso ma inutile; ~ **lie** *n* bugia pietosa; ~ **paper** *n* (*POL*) libro bianco; **~wash** *n* (*paint*) bianco di calce // *vt* imbiancare; (*fig*) coprire.

whiting ['waɪtɪŋ] *n* (*pl inv*) (*fish*) merlango.

Whitsun ['wɪtsn] *n* Pentecoste *f*.

whittle ['wɪtl] *vt*: **to** ~ **away,** ~ **down** ridurre, tagliare.

whizz [wɪz] *vi* sfrecciare; ~ **kid** *n* (*col*) prodigio.

who [hu:] *pronoun* **1** (*interrogative*) chi; ~ **is it?,** ~**'s there?** chi è?
2 (*relative*) che; **the man** ~ **spoke to me** l'uomo che ha parlato con me; **those** ~ **can swim** quelli che sanno nuotare.

whodunit [hu:'dʌnɪt] *n* (*col*) giallo.

whoever [hu:'ɛvə*] pronoun: ~ finds it chiunque lo trovi; ask ~ you like lo chieda a chiunque vuole; ~ she marries chiunque sposerà, non importa chi sposerà; ~ told you that? chi mai gliel'ha detto?

whole [həul] a (complete) tutto(a), completo(a); (not broken) intero(a), intatto(a) // n (total) totale m; (sth not broken) tutto; the ~ of the time tutto il tempo; on the ~, as a ~ nel complesso, nell'insieme; ~hearted a sincero(a); ~meal a (bread, flour) integrale; ~sale n commercio or vendita all'ingrosso // a all'ingrosso; (destruction) totale; ~saler n grossista m/f; ~some a sano(a); salutare; ~wheat a = ~meal; wholly ad completamente, del tutto.

whom [hu:m] pronoun 1 (interrogative) chi; ~ did you see? chi hai visto?; to ~ did you give it? a chi lo hai dato? 2 (relative) che, prep + il (la) quale (check syntax of Italian verb used); the man ~ I saw/to ~ I spoke l'uomo che ho visto/al quale ho parlato.

whooping cough ['hu:pɪŋ-] n pertosse f.

whore [hɔ:*] n (pej) puttana.

whose [hu:z] ♦ a 1 (possessive: interrogative) di chi; ~ book is this?, ~ is this book? di chi è questo libro?; ~ daughter are you? di chi sei figlia? 2 (possessive: relative): the man ~ son you rescued l'uomo il cui figlio hai salvato; the girl ~ sister you were speaking to la ragazza alla cui sorella stavi parlando ♦ pronoun di chi; ~ is this? di chi è questo?; I know ~ it is so di chi è.

why [waɪ] ad, cj perché // excl (surprise) ma guarda un po'!; (remonstrating) ma (via)!; (explaining) ebbene!; ~ not? perché no?; ~ not do it now? perché non farlo adesso?; that's not ~ I'm here non è questo il motivo per cui sono qui; the reason ~ il motivo per cui; ~ever ad perché mai.

wick [wɪk] n lucignolo, stoppino.

wicked ['wɪkɪd] a cattivo(a), malvagio(a); maligno(a); perfido(a); (mischievous) malizioso(a).

wicker ['wɪkə*] n vimine m; (also: ~work) articoli mpl di vimini.

wicket ['wɪkɪt] n (CRICKET) porta; area tra le due porte.

wide [waɪd] a largo(a); (area, knowledge) vasto(a); (choice) ampio(a) // ad: to open ~ spalancare; to shoot ~ tirare a vuoto or fuori bersaglio; ~-angle lens n grandangolare m; ~-awake a completamente sveglio(a); ~ly ad (differing) molto, completamente; (believed) generalmente; ~ly spaced molto distanziati(e); ~n vt allargare, ampliare; ~ open a

spalancato(a); ~spread a (belief etc) molto or assai diffuso(a).

widow ['wɪdəu] n vedova; ~er n vedovo.

width [wɪdθ] n larghezza.

wield [wi:ld] vt (sword) maneggiare; (power) esercitare.

wife [waɪf], pl wives n moglie f.

wig [wɪg] n parrucca.

wiggle ['wɪgl] vt dimenare, agitare.

wild [waɪld] a selvatico(a); selvaggio(a); (sea) tempestoso(a); (idea, life) folle; stravagante; ~s npl regione f selvaggia; ~erness ['wɪldənɪs] n deserto; ~ goose chase n (fig) pista falsa; ~life n natura; ~ly ad (applaud) freneticamente; (hit, guess) a casaccio; (happy) follemente.

wilful ['wɪlful] a (person) testardo(a), ostinato(a); (action) intenzionale; (crime) premeditato(a).

will [wɪl] ♦ auxiliary vb 1 (forming future tense): I ~ finish it tomorrow lo finirò domani; I ~ have finished it by tomorrow lo finirò entro domani; ~ you do it? — yes I ~/no I won't lo farai? — sì (lo farò)/no (non lo farò) 2 (in conjectures, predictions): he ~ or he'll be there by now dovrebbe essere arrivato ora; that ~ be the postman sarà il postino 3 (in commands, requests, offers): ~ you be quiet! vuoi stare zitto?; ~ you come? vieni anche tu?; ~ you help me? mi aiuti?, mi puoi aiutare?; ~ you have a cup of tea? vorrebbe una tazza di tè?; I won't put up with it! non lo accetterò! ♦ vt (pt, pp ~ed): to ~ sb to do volere che qn faccia; he ~ed himself to go on continuò grazie a un grande sforzo di volontà ♦ n volontà; testamento.

willing ['wɪlɪŋ] a volonteroso(a); ~ to do disposto(a) a fare; ~ly ad volontieri; ~ness n buona volontà.

willow ['wɪləu] n salice m.

will power n forza di volontà.

willy-nilly [wɪlɪ'nɪlɪ] ad volente o nolente.

wilt [wɪlt] vi appassire.

wily ['waɪlɪ] a furbo(a).

win [wɪn] n (in sports etc) vittoria // vb (pt, pp won [wʌn]) vt (battle, prize) vincere; (money) guadagnare; (popularity) conquistare // vi vincere; to ~ over, (Brit) ~ round vt convincere.

wince [wɪns] n trasalimento, sussulto // vi trasalire.

winch [wɪntʃ] n verricello, argano.

wind n [wɪnd] vento; (MED) flatulenza // vb [waɪnd] (pt, pp wound [waund]) vt attorcigliare; (wrap) avvolgere; (clock, toy) caricare; (take breath away: [wɪnd]) far restare senza fiato // vi (road, river) serpeggiare; to ~ up vt (clock) caricare; (debate) concludere; ~fall n colpo di fortuna; ~ing ['waɪndɪŋ] a (road) serpeggiante; (staircase) a chiocciola; ~ **instrument** n (MUS) strumento a fiato; ~**mill** n mulino a vento.

window ['wɪndəu] n finestra; (in car, train) finestrino; (in shop etc) vetrina; (also: ~ **pane**) vetro; ~ **box** n cassetta da fiori; ~ **cleaner** n (person) pulitore m di finestre; ~ **ledge** n davanzale m; ~ **pane** n vetro; ~**sill** n davanzale m.

windpipe ['wɪndpaɪp] n trachea.

windscreen, (US) **windshield** ['wɪndskriːn, 'wɪndʃiːld] n parabrezza m inv; ~ **washer** n lavacristallo; ~ **wiper** n tergicristallo.

windswept ['wɪndswept] a spazzato(a) dal vento.

windy ['wɪndɪ] a ventoso(a); it's ~ c'è vento.

wine [waɪn] n vino; ~ **cellar** n cantina; ~ **glass** n bicchiere m da vino; ~ **list** n lista dei vini; ~ **tasting** n degustazione f dei vini; ~ **waiter** n sommelier m inv.

wing [wɪŋ] n ala; ~s npl (THEATRE) quinte fpl; ~er n (SPORT) ala.

wink [wɪŋk] n ammiccamento // vi ammiccare, fare l'occhiolino.

winner ['wɪnə*] n vincitore/trice.

winning ['wɪnɪŋ] a (team) vincente; (goal) decisivo(a); ~s npl vincite fpl; ~ **post** n traguardo.

winter ['wɪntə*] n inverno; ~ **sports** npl sport mpl invernali.

wintry ['wɪntrɪ] a invernale.

wipe [waɪp] n pulita, passata // vt pulire (strofinando); (dishes) asciugare; **to** ~ **off** vt cancellare; (stains) togliere strofinando; **to** ~ **out** vt (debt) pagare, liquidare; (memory) cancellare; (destroy) annientare; **to** ~ **up** vt asciugare.

wire ['waɪə*] n filo; (ELEC) filo elettrico; (TEL) telegramma m // vt (house) fare l'impianto elettrico di; (also: ~ **up**) collegare, allacciare.

wireless ['waɪəlɪs] n (Brit) telegrafia senza fili; (set) (apparecchio m) radio f inv.

wiring ['waɪərɪŋ] n impianto elettrico.

wiry ['waɪərɪ] a magro(a) e nerboruto(a).

wisdom ['wɪzdəm] n saggezza; (of action) prudenza; ~ **tooth** n dente m del giudizio.

wise [waɪz] a saggio(a); prudente; giudizioso(a).

...wise [waɪz] suffix: time~ per quanto riguarda il tempo, in termini di tempo.

wish [wɪʃ] n (desire) desiderio; (specific desire) richiesta // vt desiderare, volere; best ~es (on birthday etc) i migliori auguri; with best ~es (in letter) cordiali saluti, con i migliori saluti; **to** ~ **sb good-bye** dire arrivederci a qn; he ~ed me well mi augurò di riuscire; **to** ~ **to do/sb to do** desiderare o volere fare/che qn faccia; **to** ~ **for** desiderare; it's ~ful

thinking è prendere i desideri per realtà.

wishy-washy [wɪʃɪ'wɒʃɪ] a (col: colour) slavato(a); (: ideas, argument) insulso(a).

wisp [wɪsp] n ciuffo, ciocca; (of smoke, straw) filo.

wistful ['wɪstful] a malinconico(a).

wit [wɪt] n (gen pl) intelligenza; presenza di spirito; (wittiness) spirito, arguzia; (person) bello spirito; to be at one's ~s' end (fig) non sapere più cosa fare; **to** ~ ad cioè.

witch [wɪtʃ] n strega.

with [wɪð, wɪθ] prep 1 (in the company of) con; I was ~ him ero con lui; we stayed ~ friends siamo stati da amici; I'll be ~ you in a minute vengo subito

2 (descriptive) con; a room ~ a view una stanza con vista sul mare (or sulle montagne etc); the man ~ the grey hat/ blue eyes l'uomo con il cappello grigio/ gli occhi blu

3 (indicating manner, means, cause): ~ tears in her eyes con le lacrime agli occhi; red ~ anger rosso dalla rabbia; to shake ~ fear tremare di paura

4: I'm ~ you (I understand) la seguo; to be ~ it (col: up-to-date) essere alla moda; (: alert) essere sveglio(a).

withdraw [wɪθ'drɔː] vb (irg) vt ritirare; (money from bank) ritirare; prelevare // vi ritirarsi; ~**al** n ritiro; prelievo; (of army) ritirata; (MED) stato di privazione; ~n a (person) distaccato(a).

wither ['wɪðə*] vi appassire.

withhold [wɪθ'həuld] vt irg (money) trattenere; (decision) rimettere, rimandare; (permission): **to** ~ (**from**) rifiutare (a); (information): **to** ~ (**from**) nascondere (a).

within [wɪð'ɪn] prep all'interno; (in time, distances) entro // ad all'interno, dentro; ~ sight of in vista di; ~ a mile of entro un miglio da; ~ **the week** prima della fine della settimana.

without [wɪð'aut] prep senza.

withstand [wɪθ'stænd] vt irg resistere a.

witness ['wɪtnɪs] n (person) testimone m/f // vt (event) essere testimone di; (document) attestare l'autenticità di; ~ **box,** (US) ~ **stand** n banco dei testimoni.

witticism ['wɪtɪsɪzm] n spiritosaggine f.

witty ['wɪtɪ] a spiritoso(a).

wives [waɪvz] npl of **wife**.

wizard ['wɪzəd] n mago.

wk abbr = **week**.

wobble ['wɒbl] vi tremare; (chair) traballare.

woe [wəu] n dolore m; disgrazia.

woke [wəuk] pt of **wake**; ~**n** pp of **wake**.

wolf, pl **wolves** [wulf, wulvz] n lupo.

woman ['wumən], pl **women** n donna; ~ **doctor** n dottoressa; **women's lib** n *(col)* movimento femminista.

womb [wu:m] *n* (ANAT) utero.

women ['wımın] *npl of* **woman**.

won [wʌn] *pt, pp of* **win**.

wonder ['wʌndə*] *n* meraviglia // *vi*: to ~ **whether** domandarsi se; to ~ **at** essere sorpreso(a) di; meravigliarsi di; to ~ **about** domandarsi di; pensare a; it's no ~ that c'è poco *or* non c'è da meravigliarsi che + *sub*; ~**ful** *a* meraviglioso(a).

won't [wəunt] = **will not**.

woo [wu:] *vt (woman)* fare la corte a.

wood [wud] *n* legno; *(timber)* legname *m*; *(forest)* bosco; ~ **carving** *n* scultura in legno, intaglio; ~**ed** *a* boschivo(a); boscoso(a); ~**en** *a* di legno; *(fig)* rigido(a); inespressivo(a); ~**pecker** *n* picchio; ~**wind** *npl* (MUS): **the** ~**wind** i legni; ~**work** *n* parti *fpl* in legno; *(craft, subject)* falegnameria; ~**worm** *n* tarlo del legno.

wool [wul] *n* lana; to pull the ~ over sb's eyes *(fig)* imbrogliare qn; ~**len**, *(US)* ~**en** *a* di lana; ~**lens** *npl* indumenti *mpl* di lana; ~**ly**, *(US)* ~**y** *a* lanoso(a); *(fig: ideas)* confuso(a).

word [wə:d] *n* parola; *(news)* notizie *fpl* // *vt* esprimere, formulare; in other ~s in altre parole; to break/keep one's ~ non mantenere/mantenere la propria parola; ~**ing** *n* formulazione *f*; ~ **processing** *n* elaborazione *f* di testi, word processing *m*; ~ **processor** *n* word processor *m inv*; ~**y** *a* verboso(a).

wore [wɔ:*] *pt of* **wear**.

work [wə:k] *n* lavoro; *(ART, LITERATURE)* opera // *vi* lavorare; *(mechanism, plan etc)* funzionare; *(medicine)* essere efficace // *vt (clay, wood etc)* lavorare; *(mine etc)* sfruttare; *(machine)* far funzionare; to be out of ~ essere disoccupato(a); ~s *n* *(Brit: factory)* fabbrica // *npl (of clock, machine)* meccanismo; to ~ **loose** *vi* allentarsi; **to** ~ **on** *vt fus* lavorare a; *(principle)* basarsi su; **to** ~ **out** *vi* *(plans etc)* riuscire, andare bene // *vt* *(problem)* risolvere; *(plan)* elaborare; ~s out at £100 fa 100 sterline; to get ~ed up andare su tutte le furie; eccitarsi; ~**able** *a (solution)* realizzabile; ~**aholic** *n* maniaco/a del lavoro; ~**er** *n* lavoratore/trice, operaio/a; ~**force** *n* forza lavoro; ~**ing class** *n* classe *f* operaia *or* lavoratrice; ~**ing-class** *a* operaio(a); ~**ing man** *n* lavoratore *m*; ~**ing order** *n*: in ~**ing order** funzionante; ~**man** *n* operaio; ~**manship** *n* abilità; lavoro; fattura; ~**sheet** *n* foglio col programma di lavoro; ~**shop** *n* officina; ~ **station** *n* stazione *f* di lavoro; ~**-to-rule** *n (Brit)* sciopero bianco.

world [wə:ld] *n* mondo // *cpd (champion)* del mondo; *(power, war)* mondiale; to think the ~ of sb *(fig)* pensare un gran bene di qn; ~**ly** *a* di questo mondo; ~**wide** *a* universale.

worm [wə:m] *n* verme *m*.

worn [wɔ:n] *pp of* **wear** // *a* usato(a); ~**-out** *a (object)* consumato(a), logoro(a); *(person)* sfinito(a).

worried ['wʌrɪd] *a* preoccupato(a).

worry ['wʌrɪ] *n* preoccupazione *f* // *vt* preoccupare // *vi* preoccuparsi.

worse [wə:s] *a* peggiore // *ad*, *n* peggio; a change for the ~ un peggioramento; ~ **off** *a* in condizioni (economiche) peggiori; ~**n** *vt, vi* peggiorare.

worship ['wə:ʃɪp] *n* culto // *vt (God)* adorare, venerare; *(person)* adorare; Your W~ *(Brit: to mayor)* signor sindaco; (: *to judge)* signor giudice.

worst [wə:st] *a* il(la) peggiore // *ad*, *n* peggio; at ~ al peggio, per male che vada.

worsted ['wustɪd] *n*: **(wool)** ~ lana pettinata.

worth [wə:θ] *n* valore *m* // *a*: to be ~ valere; it's ~ it ne vale la pena; it is ~ one's while (to do) vale la pena (fare); ~**less** *a* di nessun valore; ~**while** *a (activity)* utile; *(cause)* lodevole.

worthy ['wə:ðɪ] *a (person)* degno(a); *(motive)* lodevole; ~ *of* degno di.

would [wud] *auxiliary vb* **1** *(conditional tense)*: if you asked him he ~ do it se glielo chiedesse lo farebbe; if you had asked him he ~ have done it se glielo avesse chiesto lo avrebbe fatto **2** *(in offers, invitations, requests)*: you like a biscuit? vorrebbe *or* vuole un biscotto?; ~ you ask him to come in? lo faccia entrare, per cortesia; ~ you open the window please? apra la finestra, per favore **3** *(in indirect speech)*: I said I ~ do it ho detto che l'avrei fatto **4** *(emphatic)*: it WOULD have to snow today! doveva proprio nevicare oggi! **5** *(insistence)*: she ~n't do it non ha voluto farlo **6** *(conjecture)*: it ~ have been midnight sarà stato mezzanotte; it ~ seem so sembrerebbe proprio **7** *(indicating habit)*: he ~ go there on Mondays andava lì ogni lunedì.

would-be ['wudbi:] *a (pej)* sedicente.

wouldn't ['wudnt] = **would not**.

wound *vb* [waund] *pt, pp of* **wind** // *n, vt* [wu:nd] *n* ferita // *vt* ferire.

wove [wəuv] *pt of* **weave**; ~**n** *pp of* **weave**.

wrangle ['ræŋgl] *n* litigio // *vi* litigare.

wrap [ræp] *n (stole)* scialle *m*; *(cape)* mantellina // *vt (also:* ~ up) avvolgere; *(parcel)* incartare; ~**per** *n (Brit: of book)* copertina; ~**ping paper** *n* carta da pacchi; *(for gift)* carta da regali.

wrath [rɔθ] *n* collera, ira.
wreak [ri:k] *vt* (*havoc*) portare, causare;
to ~ vengeance on vendicarsi su.
wreath, **~s** [ri:θ, ri:ðz] *n* corona.
wreck [rɛk] *n* (*sea disaster*) naufragio;
(*ship*) relitto; (*pej: person*) rottame *m* //
vt demolire; (*ship*) far naufragare; (*fig*)
rovinare; **~age** *n* rottami *mpl*; (*of
building*) macerie *fpl*; (*of ship*) relitti
mpl.
wren [rɛn] *n* (*ZOOL*) scricciolo.
wrench [rɛntʃ] *n* (*TECH*) chiave *f*; (*tug*)
torsione *f* brusca; (*fig*) strazio // *vt*
strappare; storcere; to ~ sth from
strappare qc a or da.
wrestle ['rɛsl] *vi*: to ~ (with sb) lottare
(con qn); to ~ with (*fig*) combattere *or*
lottare contro; **~r** *n* lottatore/trice;
wrestling *n* lotta; (*also*: all-in wrestling) catch *m*, lotta libera.
wretched ['rɛtʃɪd] *a* disgraziato(a);
(*col: weather, holiday*) orrendo(a),
orribile; (: *child, dog*) pestifero(a).
wriggle ['rɪgl] *vi* dimenarsi; (*snake,
worm*) serpeggiare, muoversi
serpeggiando.
wring [rɪŋ], *pt, pp* **wrung** *vt* torcere;
(*wet clothes*) strizzare; (*fig*): to ~ sth
out of strappare qc a.
wrinkle ['rɪŋkl] *n* (*on skin*) ruga; (*on
paper etc*) grinza // *vt* corrugare; rag-
grinzire // *vi* corrugarsi; raggrinzirsi.
wrist [rɪst] *n* polso; **~watch** *n* orologio
da polso.
writ [rɪt] *n* ordine *m*; mandato.
write [raɪt], *pt* **wrote**, *pp* **written** *vt, vi*
scrivere; to ~ down *vt* annotare; (*put
in writing*) mettere per iscritto; to ~
off *vt* (*debt*) cancellare; (*depreciate*)
deprezzare; to ~ out *vt* scrivere;
(*copy*) ricopiare; to ~ up *vt* redigere;
~-off *n* perdita completa; **~r** *n* autore/
trice, scrittore/trice.
writhe [raɪð] *vi* contorcersi.
writing ['raɪtɪŋ] *n* scrittura; (*of author*)
scritto, opera; in ~ per iscritto; ~
paper *n* carta da scrivere.
written ['rɪtn] *pp of* **write**.
wrong [rɔŋ] *a* sbagliato(a); (*not suitable*) inadatto(a); (*wicked*) cattivo(a);
(*unfair*) ingiusto(a) // *ad* in modo sbagliato, erroneamente // *n* (*evil*) male *m*;
(*injustice*) torto // *vt* fare torto a; you
are ~ to do it ha torto a farlo; you are ~
about that, you've got it ~ si sbaglia; to
be in the ~ avere torto; what's ~? cosa
c'è che non va?; to go ~ (*person*) sbagliarsi; (*plan*) fallire, non riuscire; (*machine*) guastarsi; **~ful** *a* illegittimo(a);
ingiusto(a); **~ly** *ad* a torto.
wrote [raut] *pt of* **write**.
wrought [rɔ:t] *a*: ~ **iron** ferro battuto.
wrung [rʌŋ] *pt, pp of* **wring**.
wry [raɪ] *a* storto(a).
wt. *abbr* = **weight**.

X

Xmas ['ɛksməs] *n abbr* = **Christmas**.
X-ray ['ɛks'reɪ] *n* raggio X; (*photograph*)
radiografia // *vt* radiografare.
xylophone ['zaɪləfəun] *n* xilofono.

Y

yacht [jɔt] *n* panfilo, yacht *m inv*; **~ing**
n yachting *m*, sport *m* della vela.
Yank [jæŋk], **Yankee** ['jæŋkɪ] *n* (*pej*)
yankee *m/f inv*.
yap [jæp] *vi* (*dog*) guaire.
yard [jɑ:d] *n* (*of house etc*) cortile *m*;
(*measure*) iarda (= 914 *mm*; 3 *feet*);
~stick *n* (*fig*) misura, criterio.
yarn [jɑ:n] *n* filato; (*tale*) lunga storia.
yawn [jɔ:n] *n* sbadiglio // *vi* sbadigliare;
~ing *a* (*gap*) spalancato(a).
yd. *abbr* = **yard(s)**.
yeah [jɛə] *ad* (*col*) sì.
year [jɪə*] *n* anno; (*referring to harvest,
wine etc*) annata; **he is 8 ~s old** ha 8
anni; **an eight-~-old child** un(a)
bambino(a) di otto anni; **~ly** *a* annuale
// *ad* annualmente.
yearn [jə:n] *vi*: to ~ for sth/to do
desiderare ardentemente qc/di fare;
~ing *n* desiderio intenso.
yeast [ji:st] *n* lievito.
yell [jɛl] *n* urlo // *vi* urlare.
yellow ['jɛləu] *a* giallo(a).
yelp [jɛlp] *vi* guaire, uggiolare.
yeoman ['jəumən] *n*: **Y~ of the Guard**
guardiano della Torre di Londra.
yes [jɛs] *ad, n* sì (*m inv*); to say/answer
~ dire/rispondere di sì.
yesterday ['jɛstədɪ] *ad, n* ieri (*m inv*); ~
morning/evening ieri mattina/sera; **all
day** ~ ieri per tutta la giornata.
yet [jɛt] *ad* ancora; già // *cj* ma, tuttavia;
it is not finished ~ non è ancora finito;
the best ~ finora il migliore; **as** ~ finora.
yew [ju:] *n* tasso (*albero*).
yield [ji:ld] *n* produzione *f*, resa; reddito
// *vt* produrre, rendere; (*surrender*)
cedere // *vi* cedere; (*US AUT*) dare la
precedenza.
YMCA *n abbr* (= *Young Men's Christian
Association*) Y.M.C.A. *m*.
yoga ['jəugə] *n* yoga *m*.
yog(h)ourt, yog(h)urt ['jəugət] *n* iogurt
m inv.
yoke [jəuk] *n* giogo.
yolk [jəuk] *n* tuorlo, rosso d'uovo.
yonder ['jɔndə*] *ad* là.
you [ju:] *pronoun* **1** (*subject*) tu; (: *polite
form*) lei; (: *pl*) voi; (: *very formal*)
loro; ~ **Italians enjoy your food** a voi
Italiani piace mangiare bene; ~ **and I
will go** tu ed io *or* lei ed io andiamo

2 (*object: direct*) ti; la; vi; loro (*after vb*); (: *indirect*) ti; le; vi; loro (*after vb*); **I know** ~ ti *or* la *or* vi conosco; I gave it to ~ te l'ho dato; gliel'ho dato; ve l'ho dato; l'ho dato loro

3 (*stressed, after prep, in comparisons*) te; lei; voi; loro; **I told** YOU **to do it** ho detto a TE (*or* a LEI *etc*) di farlo; **she's younger than** ~ è più giovane di te (*or* lei *etc*)

4 (*impersonal: one*) si; **fresh air does** ~ **good** l'aria fresca fa bene; ~ **never know** non si sa mai.

you'd [ju:d] = **you had, you would**.

you'll [ju:l] = **you will, you shall**.

young [jʌŋ] *a* giovane // *npl* (*of animal*) piccoli *mpl*; (*people*): **the** ~ i giovani, la gioventù; ~**ster** *n* giovanotto, ragazzo; (*child*) bambino/a.

your [jɔ:*] *a* il(la) tuo(a), *pl* i(le) tuoi(tue); il(la) suo(a), *pl* i(le) suoi(sue); il(la) vostro(a), *pl* i(le) vostri(e); il(la) loro, *pl* i(le) loro; *see also* **my**.

you're [juə*] = **you are**.

yours [jɔ:z] *pronoun* il(la) tuo(a), *pl* i(le) tuoi(tue); (*polite form*) il(la) suo(a), *pl* i(le) suoi(sue); (*pl*) il(la) vostro(a), *pl* i(le) vostri(e); (: *very formal*) il(la) loro, *pl* i(le) loro; ~ **sincerely/faithfully** cordiali/distinti saluti; *see also* **mine**.

yourself [jɔ:'sɛlf] *pronoun* (*reflexive*) ti; si; (*after prep*) te; sé; (*emphatic*) tu stesso(a); lei stesso(a); **yourselves** *pl pronoun* (*reflexive*) vi; si; (*after prep*) voi; loro; (*emphatic*) voi stessi(e); loro stessi(e); *see also* **oneself**.

youth [ju:θ] *n* gioventù *f*; (*young man: pl* ~**s** [ju:ðz]) giovane *m*, ragazzo; ~**club** *n* centro giovanile; ~**ful** *a* giovane; da giovane; giovanile; ~ **hostel** *n* ostello della gioventù.

you've [ju:v] = **you have**.

YTS *n abbr* (*Brit*: = *Youth Training Scheme*) *programma di addestramento professionale per giovani.*

Yugoslav ['ju:gəu'slɑ:v] *a, n* jugoslavo(a).

Yugoslavia ['ju:gəu'slɑ:vɪə] *n* Jugoslavia.

yuppie ['jʌpɪ] *n, a* (*col*) yuppie (*m/f inv*).

YWCA *n abbr* (= *Young Women's Christian Association*) Y.W.C.A. *m*.

Z

zany ['zeɪnɪ] *a* un po' pazzo(a).

zap [zæp] *vt* (*COMPUT*) cancellare.

zeal [zi:l] *n* zelo; entusiasmo.

zebra ['zi:brə] *n* zebra; ~ **crossing** *n* (*Brit*) (passaggio pedonale a) strisce *fpl*, zebre *fpl*.

zero ['zɪərəu] *n* zero.

zest [zɛst] *n* gusto; (*CULIN*) buccia.

zigzag ['zɪgzæg] *n* zigzag *m inv* // *vi* zigzagare.

Zimbabwe [zɪm'bɑ:bwɪ] *n* Zimbabwe *m*.

zinc [zɪŋk] *n* zinco.

zip [zɪp] *n* (*also*: ~ **fastener**, (*US*) ~**per**) chiusura *f or* cerniera *f* lampo *inv* // *vt* (*also*: ~ **up**) chiudere con una cerniera lampo; ~ **code** *n* (*US*) codice *m* di avviamento postale.

zodiac ['zəudɪæk] *n* zodiaco.

zombie ['zɔmbɪ] *n* (*fig*): **like a** ~ come un morto che cammina.

zone [zəun] *n* zona; (*subdivision of town*) quartiere *m*.

zoo [zu:] *n* zoo *m inv*.

zoology [zu:'ɔlədʒɪ] *n* zoologia.

zoom [zu:m] *vi*: **to** ~ **past** sfrecciare; ~ **lens** *n* zoom *m inv*, obiettivo a focale variabile.

zucchini [zu:'ki:nɪ] *npl* (*US: courgettes*) zucchine *fpl*.

ITALIAN VERBS

1 Gerundio *2* Participio passato *3* Presente *4* Imperfetto *5* Passato remoto *6* Futuro *7* Condizionale *8* Congiuntivo presente *9* Congiuntivo passato *10* Imperativo

andare *3* vado, vai, va, andiamo, andate, vanno *6* andrò *etc 8* vada *10* va'!, vada!, andate!, vadano!

apparire *2* apparso *3* appaio, appari *o* apparisci, appare *o* apparisce, appaiono *o* appariscono *5* apparvi *o* apparsi, apparisti, apparve *o* apparì *o* apparse, apparvero *o* apparirono *o* apparsero *8* appaia *o* apparisca

aprire *2* aperto *3* apro *5* aprii *o* apersi, apristi *8* apra

AVERE *3* ho, hai, ha, abbiamo, avete, hanno *5* ebbi, avesti, ebbe, avemmo, aveste, ebbero *6* avrò *etc 8* abbia *etc 10* abbi!, abbia!, abbiate!, abbiano!

bere *1* bevendo *2* bevuto *3* bevo *etc 4* bevevo *etc 8* beva *etc 9* bevessi *etc*

cadere *1* caddi, cadesti *6* cadrò *etc*

cogliere *2* colto *3* colgo, colgono *5* colsi, cogliesti *8* colga

correre *5* corso *5* corsi, corresti

cuocere *2* cotto *3* cuocio, cociamo, cuociono *5* cossi, cocesti

dare *3* do, dai, dà, diamo, date, danno *5* diedi *o* detti, desti *6* darò *etc 8* dia *etc 9* dessi *etc 10* da'!, dia!, date!, diano!

dire *1* dicendo *2* detto *3* dico, dici, dice, diciamo, dite, dicono *4* dicevo *etc 5* dissi, dicesti *6* dirò *etc 8* dica, diciamo, diciate, dicano *9* dicessi *etc 10* di'!, dica!, dite!, dicano!

dolere *3* dolgo, duoli, duole, dolgono *5* dolsi, dolesti *6* dorrò *etc 8* dolga

dovere *3* devo *o* debbo, devi, deve, dobbiamo, dovete, devono *o* debbono *6* dovrò *etc 8* debba, dobbiamo, dobbiate, devano *o* debbano

ESSERE *2* stato *3* sono, sei, è, siamo, siete, sono *4* ero, eri, era, eravamo, eravate, erano *5* fui, fosti, fu, fummo, foste, furono *6* sarò *etc 8* sia *etc 9* fossi, fossi, fosse, fossimo, fóste, fossero *10* sii!, sia!, siate!, siano!

fare *1* facendo *2* fatto *3* faccio, fai, fa, facciamo, fate, fanno *4* facevo *etc 5* feci, facesti *6* farò *etc 8* faccia *etc 9* facessi *etc 10* fa'!, faccia!, fate!, facciano!

FINIRE *1* finendo *2* finito *3* finisco, finisci, finisce, finiamo, finite, finiscono *4* finivo, finivi, finiva, finivamo, finivate, finivano *5* finii, finisti, finì, finimmo, finiste, finirono *6* finirai, finirai, finirà, finiremo, finirete, finiranno *7* finirei, finiresti, finirebbe, finiremmo, finireste, finirebbero *8* finisca, finisca, finisca, finiamo, finiate, finiscano *9* finissi, finissi, finisse, finissimo, finiste, finissero *10* finisci!, finisca!, finite!, finiscano!

giungere *2* giunto *5* giunsi, giungesti

leggere *2* letto *5* lessi, leggesti

mettere *2* messo *5* misi, mettesti

morire *2* morto *3* muoio, muori, muore, moriamo, morite, muoiono *6* morirò *o* morrò *etc 8* muoia

muovere *2* mosso *5* mossi, movesti

nascere *2* nato *5* nacqui, nascesti

nuocere *2* nuociuto *3* nuoccio, nuoci, nuoce, nociamo *o* nuociamo, nuocete, nuocciono *4* nuocevo *etc 5* nocqui, nuocesti *6* nuocerò *etc 7* nuoccia

offrire *2* offerto *3* offro *5* offersi *o* offrii, offristi *8* offra

parere *2* parso *3* paio, paiamo, paiono *5* parvi *o* parsi, paresti *6* parrò *etc 8* paia, paiamo, paiate, paiano

PARLARE *1* parlando *2* parlato *3* parlo, parli, parla, parliamo, parlate, parlano *4* parlavo, parlavi, parlava, parlavamo, parlavate, parlavano *5* parlai, parlasti, parlò, parlammo, parlaste, parlarono *6* parlerò, parlerai, parlerà, parleremo, parlerete, parleranno *7* parlerei, parleresti, parlerebbe, parleremmo, parlereste, parlerebbero *8* parli, parli, parli, parliamo, parliate, parlino *9* parlassi, parlassi, parlasse, parlassimo, parlaste, parlassero *10* parla!, parli!, parlate!, parlino!

piacere *2* piaciuto *3* piaccio, piacciamo, piacciono *5* piacqui, piacesti *8* piaccia *etc*

porre *1* ponendo *2* posto *3* pongo, poni, pone, poniamo, ponete, pongono *4* ponevo *etc 5* posi, ponesti *6* porrò *etc 8* ponga, poniamo, poniate, pongano *9* ponessi *etc*

potere *3* posso, puoi, può, possiamo, potete, possono *6* potrò *etc 8* possa, possiamo, possiate, possano

prendere *2* preso *5* presi, prendesti

ridurre *1* riducendo *2* ridotto *3* riduco *etc 4* riducevo *etc 5* ridussi, riducesti *6* ridurrò *etc 8* riduca *etc 9* riducessi *etc*

riempire *1* riempiendo *3* riempio, riempi, riempie, riempiono

rimanere *2* rimasto *3* rimango, rimangono *5* rimasi, rimanesti *6* rimarrò *etc 8* rimanga

rispondere *2* risposto *5* risposi, rispondesti

salire *3* salgo, sali, salgono *8* salga

sapere *3* so, sai, sa, sappiamo, sapete, sanno *5* seppi, sapesti *6* saprò *etc 8* sappia *etc 10* sappi!, sappia!, sappiate!, sappiano!

scrivere *2* scritto *5* scrissi, scrivesti

sedere *3* siedo, siedi, siede, siedono *8* sieda

spegnere *2* spento *3* spengo, spengono *5*

spensi, spegnesti 8 spenga

stare 2 stato 3 sto, stai, sta, stiamo, state, stanno 5 stetti, stesti 6 starò etc 8 stia etc 9 stessi etc 10 sta'!, stia!, state!, stiano!

tacere 2 taciuto 3 taccio, tacciono 5 tacqui, tacesti 8 taccia

tenere 3 tengo, tieni, tiene, tengono 5 tenni, tenesti 6 terrò etc 8 tenga

trarre 1 traendo 2 tratto 3 traggo, trai, trae, traiamo, traete, traggono 4 traevo etc 5 trassi, traesti 6 trarrò etc 8 tragga 9 traessi etc

udire 3 odo, odi, ode, odono 8 oda

uscire 3 esco, esci, esce, escono 8 esca

valere 2 valso 3 valgo, valgono 5 valsi, valesti 6 varrò etc 8 valga

vedere 2 visto o veduto 5 vidi, vedesti 6 vedrò etc

VENDERE 1 vendendo 2 venduto 3 vendo, vendi, vende, vendiamo, vendete, vendono 4 vendevo, vendevi, vendeva, vendevamo, vendevate, vendevano 5 vendei o vendetti, vendesti, vendé o vendette, vendemmo, vendeste, venderono o vendettero 6 venderò, venderai, venderà, venderemo, venderete, venderanno 7 venderei, venderesti, venderebbe, venderemmo, vendereste, venderebbero 8 venda, venda, venda, vendiamo, vendiate, vendano 9 vendessi, vendessi, vendesse, vendessimo, vendeste, vendessero 10 vendi!, venda!, vendete!, vendano!

venire 2 venuto 3 vengo, vieni, viene, vengono 5 venni, venisti 6 verrò etc 8 venga

vivere 2 vissuto 5 vissi, vivesti

volere 3 voglio, vuoi, vuole, vogliamo, volete, vogliono 5 volli, volesti 6 vorrò etc 8 voglia etc 10 vogli!, voglia!, vogliate!, vogliano!

VERBI INGLESI

present	pt	pp
arise	arose	arisen
awake	awoke	awaked
be (am, is, are; being)	was, were	been
bear	bore	born(e)
beat	beat	beaten
become	became	become
begin	began	begun
behold	beheld	beheld
bend	bent	bent
beseech	besought	besought
beset	beset	beset
bet	bet, betted	bet, betted
bid	bid, bade	bid, bidden
bind	bound	bound
bite	bit	bitten
bleed	bled	bled
blow	blew	blown
break	broke	broken
breed	bred	bred
bring	brought	brought
build	built	built
burn	burnt, burned	burnt, burned
burst	burst	burst
buy	bought	bought
can	could	(been able)
cast	cast	cast
catch	caught	caught
choose	chose	chosen
cling	clung	clung
come	came	come
cost	cost	cost
creep	crept	crept
cut	cut	cut
deal	dealt	dealt
dig	dug	dug
do (3rd person; he/she/it does)	did	done
draw	drew	drawn
dream	dreamed, dreamt	dreamed, dreamt
drink	drank	drunk
drive	drove	driven
dwell	dwelt	dwelt
eat	ate	eaten
fall	fell	fallen
feed	fed	fed
feel	felt	felt
fight	fought	fought
find	found	found
flee	fled	fled
fling	flung	flung
fly (flies)	flew	flown
forbid	forbade	forbidden
forecast	forecast	forecast
forego	forewent	foregone
foresee	foresaw	foreseen
foretell	foretold	foretold
forget	forgot	forgotten
forgive	forgave	forgiven
forsake	forsook	forsaken
freeze	froze	frozen
get	got	got, (US) gotten
give	gave	given
go (goes)	went	gone
grind	ground	ground
grow	grew	grown
hang	hung, hanged	hung, hanged
have (has; having)	had	had
hear	heard	heard
hide	hid	hidden
hit	hit	hit
hold	held	held
hurt	hurt	hurt
keep	kept	kept
kneel	knelt, kneeled	knelt, kneeled
know	knew	known
lay	laid	laid
lead	led	led
lean	leant, leaned	leant, leaned
leap	leapt, leaped	leapt, leaped
learn	learnt, learned	learnt, learned
leave	left	left
lend	lent	lent
let	let	let
lie (lying)	lay	lain
light	lit, lighted	lit, lighted
lose	lost	lost
make	made	made
may	might	—
mean	meant	meant
meet	met	met
mistake	mistook	mistaken
mow	mowed	mown, mowed
must	(had to)	(had to)
pay	paid	paid
put	put	put
quit	quit, quitted	quit, quitted
read	read	read
rid	rid	rid
ride	rode	ridden

present	pt	pp	present	pt	pp
ring	rang	rung	spoil	spoiled, spoilt	spoiled, spoilt
rise	rose	risen	spread	spread	spread
run	ran	run	spring	sprang	sprung
saw	sawed	sawn	stand	stood	stood
say	said	said	steal	stole	stolen
see	saw	seen	stick	stuck	stuck
seek	sought	sought	sting	stung	stung
sell	sold	sold	stink	stank	stunk
send	sent	sent	stride	strode	stridden
set	set	set	strike	struck	struck, stricken
shake	shook	shaken			
shall	should	—	strive	strove	striven
shear	sheared	shorn, sheared	swear	swore	sworn
			sweep	swept	swept
shed	shed	shed	swell	swelled	swollen, swelled
shine	shone	shone			
shoot	shot	shot	swim	swam	swum
show	showed	shown	swing	swung	swung
shrink	shrank	shrunk	take	took	taken
shut	shut	shut	teach	taught	taught
sing	sang	sung	tear	tore	torn
sink	sank	sunk	tell	told	told
sit	sat	sat	think	thought	thought
slay	slew	slain	throw	threw	thrown
sleep	slept	slept	thrust	thrust	thrust
slide	slid	slid	tread	trod	trodden
sling	slung	slung	wake	woke, waked	woken, waked
slit	slit	slit	waylay	waylaid	waylaid
smell	smelt, smelled	smelt, smelled	wear	wore	worn
			weave	wove, weaved	woven, weaved
sow	sowed	sown, sowed			
speak	spoke	spoken	wed	wedded, wed	wedded, wed
speed	sped, speeded	sped, speeded	weep	wept	wept
			win	won	won
spell	spelt, spelled	spelt, spelled	wind	wound	wound
			withdraw	withdrew	withdrawn
spend	spent	spent	withhold	withheld	withheld
spill	spilt, spilled	spilt, spilled	withstand	withstood	withstood
spin	spun	spun	wring	wrung	wrung
spit	spat	spat	write	wrote	written
split	split	split			

I NUMERI

NUMBERS

uno(a)	1	one
due	2	two
tre	3	three
quattro	4	four
cinque	5	five
sei	6	six
sette	7	seven
otto	8	eight
nove	9	nine
dieci	10	ten
undici	11	eleven
dodici	12	twelve
tredici	13	thirteen
quattordici	14	fourteen
quindici	15	fifteen
sedici	16	sixteen
diciassette	17	seventeen
diciotto	18	eighteen
diciannove	19	nineteen
venti	20	twenty
ventuno	21	twenty-one
ventidue	22	twenty-two
ventitré	23	twenty-three
ventotto	28	twenty-eight
trenta	30	thirty
quaranta	40	forty
cinquanta	50	fifty
sessanta	60	sixty
settanta	70	seventy
ottanta	80	eighty
novanta	90	ninety
cento	100	a hundred, one hundred
cento uno	101	a hundred and one
duecento	200	two hundred
mille	1 000	a thousand, one thousand
milleduecentodue	1 202	one thousand two hundred and two
cinquemila	5 000	five thousand
un milione	1 000 000	a million, one million

primo(a), 1°	first, 1st
secondo(a), 2°	second, 2nd
terzo(a), 3°	third, 3rd
quarto(a)	fourth, 4th
quinto(a)	fifth, 5th
sesto(a)	sixth, 6th
settimo(a)	seventh
ottavo(a)	eighth
nono(a)	ninth
decimo(a)	tenth
undicesimo(a)	eleventh
dodicesimo(a)	twelfth

I NUMERI

NUMBERS

tredicesimo(a)	thirteenth
quattordicesimo(a)	fourteenth
quindicesimo(a)	fifteenth
sedicesimo(a)	sixteenth
diciassettesimo(a)	seventeenth
diciottesimo(a)	eighteenth
diciannovesimo(a)	nineteenth
ventesimo(a)	twentieth
ventunesimo(a)	twenty-first
ventiduesimo(a)	twenty-second
ventitreesimo(a)	twenty-third
ventottesimo(a)	twenty-eighth
trentesimo(a)	thirtieth
centesimo(a)	hundredth
centunesimo(a)	hundred-and-first
millesimo(a)	thousandth
milionesimo(a)	millionth

Frazioni etc

Fractions etc

mezzo	half
terzo	third
due terzi	two thirds
quarto	quarter
quinto	fifth
zero virgola cinque, 0,5	(nought) point five, 0.5
tre virgola quattro, 3,4	three point four, 3.4
dieci per cento	ten per cent
cento per cento	a hundred per cent

Esempi

Examples

abita al numero dieci	he lives at number 10
si trova nel capitolo sette, a pagina sette	it's in chapter 7, on page 7
abita al terzo piano	he lives on the 3rd floor
arrivò quarto	he came in 4th
scala uno a venticinquemila	scale 1:25,000

L'ORA

che ora è?, che ore sono?

è..., sono...

mezzanotte
l'una (della mattina)
l'una e cinque
l'una e dieci
l'una e un quarto, l'una e quindici
l'una e venticinque
l'una e mezzo o mezza, l'una e trenta
le due meno venticinque, l'una e
  trentacinque
le due meno venti, l'una e quaranta
le due meno un quarto, l'una e
  quarantacinque
le due meno dieci, l'una e cinquanta
mezzogiorno
l'una, le tredici
le sette (di sera), le diciannove

a che ora?

a mezzanotte
all'una, alle tredici

fra venti minuti
venti minuti fa

THE TIME

what time is it?

it is...

midnight, twelve pm
one o'clock (in the morning), one (am)
five past one
ten past one
a quarter past one, one fifteen
twenty-five past one, one twenty-five
half-past one, one thirty
twenty-five to two, one thirty-five

twenty to two, one forty
a quarter to two, one forty-five

ten to two, one fifty
twelve o'clock, midday, noon
one o'clock (in the afternoon), one (pm)
seven o'clock (in the evening), seven
  (pm)

at what time?

at midnight
at one o'clock

in twenty minutes
twenty minutes ago